THE WAY OF THE LORD JESUS

Volume Three

DIFFICULT MORAL QUESTIONS

THE WAY OF THE LORD JESUS

Volume Three

DIFFICULT MORAL QUESTIONS

by

Germain Grisez

The *Flynn* Professor of Christian Ethics
Mount Saint Mary's College   Emmitsburg, Maryland

with the help of

Joseph Boyle, John Finnis, Jeannette Grisez, Russell Shaw, and others

The Way of the Lord Jesus, volume three, *Difficult Moral Questions,* by Germain Grisez, with the help of Joseph Boyle, John Finnis, Jeannette Grisez, Russell Shaw, and others.

Nihil Obstat:
> Rev. Kevin T. McMahon, S.T.D.
> *Censor Deputatus*

Imprimatur:
> His Eminence,
> ✠James Cardinal Hickey
> Archbishop of Washington
> 28 January 1997

The *nihil obstat* and *imprimatur* are official declarations that a book or pamphlet is free of doctrinal or moral error. No implication is contained therein that those who have granted the *nihil obstat* and the *imprimatur* agree with the content, opinions, or statements expressed.

Library of Congress Cataloging-in-Publication Data
Grisez, Germain Gabriel, 1929–
    The Way of the Lord Jesus.
    Vol. 3- published: Quincy, IL: Franciscan Press, Quincy University.
    Contents: v. 1. Christian moral principles—v. 2. Living a Christian life—
        v. 3. Difficult moral questions.
BJ1249.G74   1983
  241'.042   **SEP** 2 2 1998   83-1508
                                      CIP
ISBN 0-8199-0861-4 (v. 1)
ISBN 0-8199-0961-0 (v. 2)
ISBN 0-8199-0981-5 (v. 3)

BJ
124 9
G 74
1983
vol. 3

To help limit the cost of this book, the author set it in Postscript™ Times-Roman using Ventura Publisher™. Athens Enterprises, Ltd., Frederick, MD made the reproduction proofs. The book was printed and bound in the U.S.A.

Vatican Council II, *Gaudium et spes,* 38 (in part) and 39:

Now, the gifts of the Spirit are diverse: he calls some to bear clear witness to the desire for a heavenly home and to keep that desire lively in the human family; he calls others to dedicate themselves to the earthly service of human persons, and by this ministry of theirs to prepare material for the heavenly kingdom. He frees all, however, so that—having set aside self-love and taken up and humanized all earthly forces—they can reach out toward that future when humanity itself will become an offering accepted by God.[14]

As a down payment on this hope and as nourishment for the journey, the Lord left to his own that sacrament of faith in which natural elements worked on by human hands are turned into his glorified body and blood—a supper of familial communion and a foretaste of the heavenly banquet.

39. *The New Earth and New Heaven*

We do not know the time for the consummation of the earth and of humanity,[15] nor do we know how the universe is to be transformed. As deformed by sin, the form of this world is passing away,[16] but we are taught that God is preparing a new home and a new earth where justice abides,[17] one whose happiness will fulfill to overflowing all the desires for peace which mount up in human hearts.[18] Then, with death conquered, the children of God will be raised up in Christ, and what was sown in weakness and corruption will put on incorruptibility;[19] then too, charity and its works staying in place,[20] the whole of the creation[21] which God created for humankind's sake will be freed from slavery to vanity.

We are warned that it profits one nothing if one gain the whole world but lose one's very self.[22] Still, the expectation of a new earth ought not to dampen but rather to enkindle our concern for cultivating this earth, where the body of the new human family grows, that body which already provides a sort of foreshadowing of the new age. So, although earthly progress must be carefully distinguished from the growth of Christ's kingdom, still, insofar as earthly progress can contribute to the better ordering of human society, it is very important to God's kingdom.[23]

For after we have promoted on earth, in the Spirit of the Lord and in accord with his command, the goods of human dignity, familial communion, and freedom— that is to say, all the good fruits of our nature and effort—then we shall find them once more, but cleansed of all dirt, lit up, and transformed, when Christ gives back to the Father an eternal and universal kingdom: "a kingdom of truth and life, a kingdom of holiness and grace, a kingdom of justice, love, and peace."[24] On this earth the kingdom is present in mystery even now; with the Lord's coming, however, it will be consummated.

---

14. See Rom 15.16.   15. See Acts 1.7.
16. See 1 Cor 7.31; St. Irenaeus, *Adversus haereses,* 5.36.1, *PG,* 7:1222.
17. See 2 Cor 5.2; 2 Pt 3.13.   18. See 1 Cor 2.9; Rv 21.4-5.   19. See 1 Cor 15.42, 53.
20. See 1 Cor 13.8; cf. 3.14.   21. See Rom 8.19-21.   22. See Lk 9.25.
23. See Pius XI, *Quadragesimo anno, AAS* 23 (1931) 207.
24. *Roman Missal,* Preface of the Feast of Christ the King.

A Prayer of Longing for Heaven

attributed to St. Thomas Aquinas

O God of every consolation, I call upon you,
who see in me nothing but what you have given me:
May you be pleased to give me, after this life's end, the gift
of knowing the first truth, of rejoicing in your divine majesty.
Most lavish rewarder:
Give, also, to my body
the beauty of spiritual radiance,
the mobility of matter subject to mind,
the responsiveness suited to its perfection, and
the bold assurance of flesh free of all vulnerability.
And please add to these
riches pouring over, delights pouring in, and
goods pouring together: so that
I may rejoice
in your comfort above me,
in your land's loveliness beneath me,
in body and soul's glorification within me, and
in the fellowship of friends and angels delightfully around me.
Most merciful Father, with you let my capacities be fulfilled:
of reasoning, by reaching the light of wisdom,
of desiring, by possessing true goods, and
of striving, by attaining the honor of triumph–
in your presence, where there is
freedom from threats, variety of dwellings, and harmony of wills;
spring's pleasantness, summer's brightness, fall's plenty, and winter's rest.
Lord God, give me
life without death, joy without sorrow;
in your presence, where there is
supreme freedom, freedom from all care, carefree tranquillity,
joyful happiness, happy endlessness, endless blessedness,
the sight and praise of truth, my God.
Amen.

CONTENTS

PREFACE AND USER'S GUIDE

Warning: This book is dangerous! If used improperly, it could cause serious injury to the moral lives of its readers and/or people they mean to help. One often can skip a book's front matter without missing anything essential, but to understand this book and use it properly, one must know what sort of book it is and what it offers. It is a peculiar book offering both somewhat more and somewhat less than one might expect. Students and other readers, teachers considering it as a text or instructional resource, and conscientious critics will do well to read the following explanations of the book's character, purposes, and limitations.

This book is the third in a four-volume effort to contribute to the renewal of Catholic moral theology called for by Vatican Council II. Volume one, *Christian Moral Principles* (which I shall refer to by *CMP*, with page numbers) articulated a general theory of morality and theology of Christian life; volume two, *Living a Christian Life* (*LCL*), treated the moral responsibilities common to most or all Catholic lay people and those common to clerics, religious, and laity. This volume deals with the responsibilities of lay people in various specific occupations and relationships; since the potential subject matter is endless, however, it treats only some difficult questions that are widespread, especially important, or usefully illustrative.

Like the other volumes, this one is intended primarily for use as a seminary text or instructional resource. But unlike the earlier volumes, which mainly present common Catholic teaching and reflect on it theologically, it deals with questions not yet the subject of explicit or clearly applicable Church teachings. Conscientious lay people facing challenging moral questions and those from whom they seek advice will find here guidance not available elsewhere: if not replies to their questions, a model for thinking about questions more or less like those they have. But like many helpful medications, tools, and appliances, the book will be used safely and effectively, as I said, only if its character, purposes, and limitations are borne in mind.

Avoiding legalism without refusing to answer moral questions

Two fundamental misconceptions of moral theology and its application in particular cases could lead to either misuses of the replies I propose here or a refusal to use them—perhaps even a refusal to consider them except as possible targets for scornful criticism. Both misconceptions were manifested in a session at a seminary where I was invited to spend an afternoon discussing two of the questions and my tentative answers.

Two faculty members said talking about how one might reply to the questions I had proposed for discussion would be pointless; they heatedly challenged the very idea of trying to answer people's actual moral questions. Replying to such questions, they said, is telling people what to do and not do, and that inevitably leads to judging and condemning those who do not docilely do as they are told or who fail to seek permission to make exceptions to moral rules. What I planned to do in this book seemed presumptuous to them, and they felt sure that the result, if published, would be pernicious.

One pressed me: "Why are you trying to tell people what to do?" "Because they ask me," I said. "You ought to tell them to follow their own consciences!" she shot back. "Of course I tell people that," I said, "but some people think they need help in forming their consciences." "That does not justify telling them what to do," her colleague maintained. "Moral theology," he held, "can articulate Christian ideals and tell inspiring stories but cannot legitimately say anything about actual problems, every one of which is unique." "What should pastoral workers do when people ask for moral guidance?" I asked. They answered: "Encourage them to talk about their problems and feelings, listen sympathetically, pray with them, assure them God will love them no matter what they decide, and tell them they must follow their consciences."

The two professors had adopted the position that there are no general moral truths in whose light one might argue to a judgment that it would be right (or wrong) to make this or that choice. That position, which would find little support even among theologians who dissent from Church teachings, is at odds with the entire Judeo-Christian tradition, including its sources witnessed in Scripture—for example, St. Paul's application to a unique case of the norm excluding incest (see 1 Cor 5.1–5) and his nuanced answer to a difficult moral question about eating food sacrificed to idols (see 1 Cor 8–10). The position also is at odds with itself and therefore rationally untenable. By maintaining that I should tell people to follow their own consciences and not tell them what to do and not do, the professors applied a norm, which they assumed true in general, to my unique case and told me what I should do and not do—thereby themselves doing what the norm they were assuming excluded. By maintaining that pastoral workers should tell people they must follow their consciences, they applied additional general norms to people with moral problems and to the pastoral workers who wish to help them. And they seemed ready to judge and condemn anyone who might judge and condemn someone.

Nevertheless, their vehement interventions call attention to the grave errors of the legalism against which they were reacting—a caricature of a misconception of moral theology and its pastoral application that was widespread in the Church before Vatican II. While the professors regard moral principles and norms as ideals with no practical implications, legalism regarded them as rules to be imposed. Both views are mistaken. As John Paul II's encyclical *Veritatis splendor (The splendor of truth)* makes clear, sound moral principles and norms are practical truths that safeguard fundamental human goods and help reasonable persons and communities shape their actions and lives toward their own fulfillment and that of others.

Conscience is a person's last and best judgment as to what he or she should, or may, or should not do here and now (see *CMP*, 75–78). As truths about what is good for human persons and communities, sound moral principles and norms usually help a reasonable person arrive at that judgment. When people with moral problems ask for help, it is usually because they do not know what is right and good, and want to find out—in other words, they realize that they do not yet have the conscience they need and wish to form it. It is unhelpful either to give them a rule and tell them to obey it, or to grant them an exception to a rule they find burdensome. Doing either assumes that those asking for help are incapable of thinking and shaping their own lives—that they are like small children whose outward behavior must be managed for their own good and to maintain order—and that one has the duty and right to direct their lives for them. But it is equally unhelpful to tell people with moral problems to follow their own consciences. Moreover, it is likely to be misleading. In the context, "Follow your conscience" will seem to mean: Neither any Catholic teaching nor any reasoning we might carry out together could help you find out what is right and good; so, without further reflection, proceed to choose. That is tantamount to saying: "Do whatever you feel like doing!"—a prescription for subjectivism.

A sound alternative to legalism is to assume that people who ask moral questions are capable of moral reflection and judgment but need and want help in carrying them out. To be helpful, one must begin by trying to understand the problem as they themselves see it, taking into account their purposes, difficulties, prior commitments, and apparent options. One also must realize that moral questions are not so limited as many people think. There is a richness and complexity to moral life, and diverse kinds of questions must be distinguished. They need not concern strict obligations, and they often bear on subjects other than sexual behavior and possible injustices. Indeed, whether to do or not do something always is a moral question, insofar as it calls for an answer in terms of what would be reasonable and good not merely in reference to a particular goal or in some limited respect but ultimately and unqualifiedly.

Some questions are matters for discernment between or among morally acceptable options, and one can help only by making that clear, calling attention to things to be considered, and explaining how discernment is to be carried out. Others are questions of right and wrong that cannot be answered by deductive reasoning, and one helps by providing guidance, which never can be definitive, for making the necessary judgment. Some matters do require that a morally unacceptable option be excluded by deductively applying a negative norm; but, even in such cases, one usually provides adequate help in answering the question only if one also points out a possible way of fulfilling responsibilities with respect to the people and the goods at stake.

If someone asking a moral question seems to be overlooking facts or possibilities, or to be mistaken about them, one calls attention to these as perhaps relevant realities. If a questioner seems to be overlooking or mistaken about some norm or its application, one proposes it with as much explanation and support from faith and/or reason as seems necessary to make clear its truth and how it might help solve the problem. One does not presume to give orders and permissions, even if one occasionally lapses into the imperative form in spelling out details of a proposed plan of action rather than repeatedly saying: "If, as I expect, you judge it right to proceed in the way proposed, you should . . .."

If someone asking a question seems to have done or to be doing or to be about to do something wrong, that usually must be pointed out. In doing so, however, one must not judge and condemn the person: God alone knows whether and how clearly he or she knows that the act is wrong, and whether and how freely he or she chooses to act contrary to that conscience. Likewise, rather than judging and condemning someone who seems to ignore advice offered in response to his or her moral question, one realizes that one's reply may have been unsound or inadequate, communication may have failed, the person may have been unable to appropriate and use the advice, and/or his or her capacity to choose freely may be limited.

Advice for studying each question and reply

The questions dealt with in this book really are difficult. In applying moral principles and norms taught by the Church to matters on which she has never taught at all or not yet taught explicitly, I do not claim that the Church herself would make the same applications, much less endorse any other advice I offer. Undoubtedly, some of my proposed replies contain errors. If any reply should lead in practice to a judgment in conflict with the Church's teaching, I would follow and urge others to follow the Church's teaching. In what I have written here, as in everything I think, I submit gladly and wholeheartedly to the better judgment of the Catholic Church.

Every question dealt with in this volume could be taken up in a systematic treatise on a set of problems wider than the one the question poses. But this volume is not systematic; the replies proposed deliberately avoid broadening the inquiry more than will be practically helpful to questioners. Readers should not draw any conclusions from what is *not said* here about interesting and important matters closely related to those treated—and reasonable critics will not fault the volume for failing to address questions beyond those posed by questioners.

In each case, the initial, one-sentence question is a title, intended only to indicate in a summary way the subject matter of the moral problem articulated in the paragraphs that immediately follow it, down to the section headed "Analysis." The one-sentence title almost always is more general than the problem actually presented. Some of the specific features of the latter always must be taken into account by sound moral reflection and judgment. Thus, the analysis and proposed reply do not address all the morally diverse problems that could be expressed by the initial question; and, if applied without necessary adjustments to a case significantly different from the one actually treated, the analysis and reply will be at best inadequate and at worst unsound and seriously misleading.

Most of the problems are more difficult than it initially might seem. Even able and attentive readers of preliminary drafts rather often overlooked some significant feature of a problem and tried to improve a proposed reply by offering objections or suggestions that were beside the questioner's point. So, anyone who wishes thoroughly to understand a proposed reply—which will be necessary to apply it to another case—should compare the reply with the problem it addresses and note each feature of the problem taken into account in the reply.

Quite often, the proposed reply qualifies or disagrees with something asserted or assumed by the questioner. However, in some cases, though I disagree with or disapprove of something in the question, I do not think criticizing it would be helpful, and so ignore it. Again, in some cases a questioner would not have the problem he or she presents if others had done or would do what they should. But unless I think discussing that fact would help the questioner, I do not mention it. Thus, readers should not take a proposed reply's silence about something in the question as agreement with it or approval of it, or silence about wrongs that contributed to the problem as condoning them.

The section headed "Analysis" might appear to be a summary of the proposed reply. But it has a different function—to set out the thinking a moral adviser should do *before* beginning to formulate a reply. The section identifies the type of moral problem the question presents, points out the tools to be employed in dealing with it, and states how they must be used. Thus, the analysis is meant for students and other readers interested not only in the reply proposed to the particular question but also, and perhaps mainly, in learning how to use moral principles and norms. In pointing out relevant principles and norms, however, the analysis usually must anticipate—and so, in fact, summarize—key elements of the reply. Still, taken as a summary of the reply, the analysis almost always will be inadequate, for it will omit some essential elements of the reply, including subordinate arguments, clarifications of likely misunderstandings, necessary qualifications, possible alternatives, and answers to objections. Anyone treating an analysis section as if it were an adequate reply to the question is likely to be misled and to mislead others, and any critic who supposes the analysis is meant to be an adequate reply will misrepresent my thinking.

Given its function, the analysis section necessarily presupposes a foundation in sound moral theology—which I naturally hope will have been acquired by previous study of *CMP* and *LCL!* Those who wish to use the analysis also should study this book's two appendices, which not only summarize but in some respects amend and expand the earlier volumes' treatments of cooperation and of moral judgments, particularly those about accepting side effects. However, anything in the analysis essential to understanding the proposed reply is repeated there. So, readers mainly interested in the particular question need not read the analysis; and, usually, they also will be able to understand the proposed reply without previous study of moral theology.

The statement introducing the reply to each question, *The reply could be along the following lines,* is meant to remind readers that replies more or less different from the one I propose might be as sound and helpful or even sounder and more helpful. Of course, I am convinced that some elements of each proposed reply are certainly true and think some of those truths would be essential to any acceptable reply. But, as I said before, some of my proposed replies undoubtedly contain errors. Then too, I recognize that even the truths included in the proposed replies always could be articulated differently and usually could be augmented by different and/or additional advice about secondary matters. Besides, one always could provide additional support for the propositions on which a reply is based, explain matters more fully, raise and answer additional objections, point out and clarify further possible misunderstandings.

In each of the proposed replies, I try to supply everything I think the questioner will need to understand it and reasonably accept it. Since each questioner's self-description and statements are the basis for judging what can be taken for granted in replying to him or her, different replies proceed on somewhat different assumptions. But since most questioners are Catholics prepared to accept the Church's clear teachings, in this volume the truth of such teachings almost always is assumed rather than defended.

In each proposed reply, I also try to supply only what I think the questioner needs to make use of the help I think I can offer. But it always is debatable how much is enough, neither too little nor too much. That is especially true with respect to subordinate advice regarding the carrying out of responsibilities. Saying too much ventures beyond moral theology's boundaries—which, as I explained above, are broader than many people think—and risks making mistakes and inviting comparison with newspaper personal-advice columnists who answer questions about everything though they are competent in respect to nothing. However, saying too little risks leaving someone ready to do the appropriate thing puzzled about how to begin doing it. Wishing to help and trusting people to consider my advice discriminatingly, I often prefer to risk saying too much. But such subordinate advice is especially likely to be faulty.

In many replies, it would be appropriate to offer additional spiritual advice—pray to the Holy Spirit for light to guide your judgment and strength to carry it out, examine your conscience and go to confession regularly, thank God for his blessings, and so on. In many cases, it also would be appropriate to recommend that a questioner obtain regular guidance and support from a sound spiritual director or other saintly friend. However, to avoid constant repetition, in this book I usually omit most such spiritual advice, though I would give it in replying to questioners separately.

The footnotes and references within the text of a proposed reply are not meant for the questioner, and in that sense are not part of the reply. But readers who wish to follow my explanations to their starting points, whether only to grasp them fully or authentically to criticize them, will find the notes and references helpful and sometimes indispensable. Still, not every allusion to Scripture and other sources is annotated; references to the first two volumes of *The Way of the Lord Jesus,* where many sources are quoted and cited, often take the place of annotation that would have either increased the size and cost of this book or reduced its fresh content. Moreover, even the references to earlier volumes that are supplied are intended mainly for casual readers. When I began work on this book, I decided to assume that its more studious users would be familiar with both the principles articulated in *CMP* and the parts of *LCL* relevant to questions on which they work. Therefore, matters already dealt with in those volumes are not always explicitly referenced and seldom are treated here with care and in depth.

Advice for using the book in pastoral formation

Though moral theology can be applied rightly in helping people form their consciences, this book could be pernicious if used inappropriately as a seminary textbook or instructional resource. Seminarians need to learn—and priests and other pastoral workers need to put into practice—not only many things no book can teach but some things treated in other books but not in this one. Those using this book to prepare for and carry on pastoral work, or to help others to do so, should take into account its specific value and limitations, use it for what it offers, and find other means of achieving essential aspects of pastoral formation to which it will contribute inadequately if at all.

The questions in this book are theoretically difficult. Most people seeking pastoral guidance have questions that are theoretically easy but sometimes quite difficult in practical terms, in reference to the suffering from which they arise or to which truthful answers will lead, or both. Packaged answers quickly delivered seldom help people with their actual problems. Some of the questions in this book were appropriately asked and answered in writing, but most people in need of pastoral help talk with a priest or pastoral worker, and almost always people should be invited and encouraged to discuss their problems face to face. The person must be understood before his or her problem can be understood and before an adviser can begin effectively to communicate the help that seems appropriate. For understanding someone, developing a personal relationship, and carrying on delicate communication, letters usually are less useful than telephone conversation, which, in turn, almost always is far less adequate than unhurried, face-to-face discussion.

In the previous volume, I briefly treated the responsibilities of moral advisers (see *LCL,* 300–303). But besides awareness of responsibilities and commitment to fulfill them, sound and effective pastoral work also presupposes some knowledge of psychology and counseling technique. A few of this book's questions and proposed replies summarize lengthy discussions. Patient and attentive listening was needed as questioners presented their problems piecemeal, mixed with much seemingly irrelevant information which, nevertheless, often suggested essential considerations that were articulated only in response to questions. Like Socrates' conversations with young interlocutors, such listening and gentle probing sometimes enable conscientious questioners to think their problems through and answer their own questions—and this is the ideal to strive after. If questioners come to see for themselves the principles and norms they need, and use them spontaneously to form their consciences, the counselor not only has thought out and communicated a sound reply, without telling the questioner to do or not do anything, but has encouraged the appropriation of relevant truths and supported the commitment to act on them. When this is achieved, moreover, not only legalism but even its appearance is avoided.

Still, Socrates gained the insights to which he led others by thinking through problems before proposing them for discussion. Similarly, as advisers begin to grasp a moral problem, they must be able to identify the sort of question the person is posing and see how to help him or her deal with it. Moral principles and norms found in Catholic teaching or consonant with it were presented, explained, and defended in the earlier volumes; this one is a book of exercises in applying those principles and norms to many kinds of moral questions arising in different subject matters and involving diverse complicating features.

Those who use the book for such exercises would do well to begin by studying the two appendices. In working on each question, they should first read only the question, then think about it and/or discuss it, and next read and reflect on the analysis. Having accepted or modified the analysis—or perhaps replaced it with their own—they should outline what they think needs to be communicated in an adequate reply before considering the one I propose, so that they can compare it with their own outline.

Though this book should not be regarded as a model for the *process* of pastoral moral guidance, it does exemplify *certain features* which, I believe, the process must have if it is to be sound and effective.

The focus in this book always is on trying to help a questioner form his or her own conscience and make good choices; the train of thought never is derailed into general social and cultural criticism, sketches of how things ought to be, and prescriptions for people other than the questioner. Questioners always are presumed to be both honest and sufficiently self-aware so that they not only mean what they say but understand its significance. Questions are never treated as symptoms of deeper problems the questioner cannot articulate. So, while the psychological and ecclesiological dimensions of moral problems are regularly recognized and addressed, moral questions never are deconstructed—for instance, by reducing them to psychological problems or management problems regarding the relations of the Church as a voluntary association with her uneasy and restless members.

Public opinion polls and the opinions of supposed experts are never treated as morally authoritative. Legalistic minimalism and impracticable idealism are avoided by putting each problem into the wider but concrete context of the questioner's prior commitments and/or personal vocation as a whole. The gospel and the Church's social teaching are brought into play to clarify the requirements not only of justice but of mercy. Legitimate alternative ways of dealing with problems often are suggested. The motive of hope—intending heaven and fearing hell—regularly overarches and undergirds every other motive proposed for living the truth of a well-formed conscience.

Advice for using the book in other ways

This book does not provide a systematic ethics for health care, business, education, legal problems and practice, or any of the other fields on which it touches. However, the greater part of any adequate systematic Christian ethics for a particular field would deal with principles and norms treated in the earlier volumes—for instance, a systematic treatment of health care ethics would summarize many matters dealt with in *CMP* and would include not only most of chapter eight of *LCL* but large parts of several of its other chapters. And, though not developed into systematic treatises, the sets of questions bearing on particular fields in this volume (for example, health care in questions 43 through 92) do deal with the specific principles of responsibilities in that field (for example, the common good of health care providers and those they serve, and the physician-patient relationship), and the questions in each such set are arranged in a sequence to facilitate using them to study the field as a whole.

Among books dealing with the ethics of various fields, some propose admirable ideals and attitudes, and take defensible stands on particular issues, but are short on precise analysis and rational method, so that they provide little help in analyzing difficult moral questions and forming conscience in accord with sound principles. Many other such books presuppose unsound ethical theories and principles, or proceed without any basis at all to propose cases for discussion—thereby implicitly inculcating either erroneous views or a conscience-numbing subjectivism. Together with the earlier volumes, this book can be used to learn and teach how to analyze problems that arise in a particular field and form a conscience in regard to them embodying principles and norms taught by the Church or, at least, rationally defensible and consistent with her teaching. A professional or someone offering moral advice to professionals who has learned how to answer moral questions as they arise is better off than one who only has good answers to some, even many, common and familiar questions. Moreover, when studying and teaching professional ethics by the case method, tendencies toward subjectivism are forestalled and authentic practical reasonableness is promoted when, as in this book, each case is presented by a conscientious person with a real moral problem who wants a reasonable answer to the question: What should (or may) I do?

The ethics of the diverse fields dealt with in this book also is enriched in various ways precisely as a result of the treatment's nonsystematic character. Many matters that pose problems are considered from different points of view—contraception and sterilization, for example, are touched on by questions asked by gynecologists, a pathologist, a medical student, patients, hospital administrators, and a pharmacist. And, in responding to questions asked by people in one profession, treatments of certain problems—for example, those dealing with compassion, burnout, and fees and income—can easily be applied to people in other professions.

The index of subjects and names is designed to help users find scattered treatments not only of topics pertaining to the same or many fields but of principles, norms, and types of problem—the universal destination of goods, the application of the Golden Rule, formal and material cooperation, and so on. To save users' time, not every occurrence of key words is indexed but only those where something significant is said about the topic.

+　+　+

About the questions

Almost everyone who has seen any of this book in manuscript has asked: "Where did you get these questions?" Some were asked of me or of others who gave them to me. Some were drawn from books, mainly ethics case books. A few are entirely fictitious. The origin of a question does not affect its potential utility for the various purposes of the book. Still, to satisfy curiosity, I shall explain a bit more how the questions were developed.

When I began preparations for this volume in 1992, I published a letter or notice in many media sketching out the project and inviting questions, and in other ways spread the same message as widely as I could. I received many questions: some from people seeking help with current problems, others from people asking for my comments on something they did in the past, others from people concerned about problems other people were facing or had faced. Priests asked or told me about cases of conscience that currently confronted them or that they had dealt with in the past. Most questions came in writing; some letters that presented serious, current questions led to telephone conversations or more than one round of correspondence. Some people who wanted help with current problems telephoned, and a few came to see me.

The experience of dealing with these questions shaped the book. But working on the material to make the book sound and useful also required that the questions themselves and my replies to them be reshaped, revised, and built up. People's names and other morally irrelevant details had to be changed to protect privacy and preserve confidentiality. In several instances, two or more similar questions were melded into one. Sometimes, circumstances were introduced to lend moral complexity to questions that initially were too easy; in other cases, legal or other technical problems were dropped out to eliminate complexities that had to be settled by other specialists.

Moral problems in case books in legal ethics and business ethics often are lengthy and rich in ethically irrelevant detail. They usually describe complex, unsavory states of affairs involving many persons. Yet they seldom adopt the perspective of any one conscientious person who wishes to know what to do. Discussion of such cases easily falls into consequentialist speculation about how to improve the state of affairs as a whole, and such discussion also can encourage ethical agnosticism about the responsibilities of individuals caught up in the situation. Still, even when cases for discussion are presented in this way and without any ethical framework, morally serious people who have never studied moral theology or ethics usually easily identify the moral questions a case should raise for each person involved. Therefore, in drawing problems from case books in business ethics and legal ethics, I eliminated the irrelevant detail and created a conscientious person to ask the question.

Some purely fictitious questions were created to deal with issues that nobody raised but that are important to many people—some of them questions widely discussed, some issues of general concern but never or rarely regarded as ethical issues. Other purely fictitious questions were created to illustrate some principle, norm, or element of ethical analysis and moral judgment. However, the manuscript has been revised so much and so often that even questions that began as real and current problems for people contain significant fictional elements.

Readers will notice that the two hundred questioners hardly are a representative sample of the population as a whole or even of practicing Catholics. Many are unusually faithful, unusually conscientious, or unusually generous. Why are they not more representative? To begin with, they are more nearly representative of people conscientious enough to ask moral questions than of people, and contemporary Catholics, in general. Again, to sharpen the difficult issues, I sometimes amended questions so that the questioner expressly excludes a morally unacceptable option, such as lying. But my selection of questions also had a lot to do with the nonrepresentative character of the questioners. Seldom did the legalistic moral theology of times past regard as really difficult any moral question not involving grave matter; so, hardly ever were most other questions seriously dealt with. For the theology of *The Way of the Lord Jesus,* questions involving only light matter or morally acceptable options can be difficult and worthy of careful analysis and reflection. Thinking such questions would enrich the book and make it more interesting and useful to most readers, I especially welcomed them.

Readers also will notice that the priests described by various questioners hardly are representative of contemporary priests. Most priests in this book are not fulfilling their responsibilities. Some make errors in their teaching and counseling, abuse the liturgy, give bad moral advice, and so on; even the better ones may be confused and unhelpful. The main reason why the sample of priests in this book is not representative is that priests who are good and holy, faithful and competent do not create moral problems for people. But, again, my selection of questions was a factor. Priests who create moral problems for people were central in many real moral questions presented by deeply troubled, conscientious Catholics. Neither traditional moral theology nor the contemporary magisterium has addressed or is addressing these questions, which are both new and officially unrecognized. Reflecting on such questions should be profitable for seminarians, and principled answers to them should help many lay Catholics. So, I include several such questions in the book, often melding many similar questions into one.

The project of which this book is a part

As noted above, this volume is the third of a four-volume project. The fourth volume is to treat the special responsibilities of clerics and religious. Originally, the whole project was to be completed by the year 2000, but the fourth volume will not be near completion by then. It will appear, God willing, in 2004.

Readers who have studied and understood the two preceding volumes will notice how tightly this one is integrated with them. Its two hundred proposed replies embody and illustrate the principles and norms set forth and explained in the earlier ones, and concrete examples always help make abstract statements understandable. So, this volume, more concrete and immediately practical than the others, will make their content more accessible. At the same time, it manifests the theory's capacity to deal with all sorts of problems, and so proves its fruitfulness. For anyone who believes that the principles and norms set forth in volume one are true, the evidence of the theory's fruitfulness should argue in its favor.

John Paul II's encyclical *Veritatis splendor* (1993), which deals with fundamental moral theology, does not require any revision of the treatment of principles and criticism of dissenting theology in my volume one, *Christian Moral Principles.* Indeed, the encyclical confirms the soundness and appropriateness of treating the Beatitudes as organizing principles, identifying faith as the fundamental option of Christian life, seeing exceptionless moral norms as protecting fundamental human goods, defining human acts by what is chosen rather than by outward behavior, rejecting proportionalism, and judging certain dissenting positions incompatible with divine revelation.

Franciscan Press, the publisher of this volume, also published volume two and reprinted volume one. It plans to keep all three volumes in print. Its address and telephone number can be found on the title page.

Key to references in the text and notes

Quotations from the Bible (except those within other quotations) are from the New Revised Standard Version. References are made by means of the following abbreviations:

Acts	Acts of the Apostles	Lk	Luke
Col	Colossians	Mk	Mark
1 Cor	1 Corinthians	Mt	Matthew
2 Cor	2 Corinthians	Phil	Philippians
Dn	Daniel	Prv	Proverbs
Dt	Deuteronomy	Ps	Psalms
Eph	Ephesians	1 Pt	1 Peter
Ex	Exodus	2 Pt	2 Peter
Gal	Galatians	Rom	Romans
Gn	Genesis	Rv	Revelation
Heb	Hebrews	Sir	Sirach (Ecclesiasticus)
Is	Isaiah	2 Thes	2 Thessalonians
Jas	James	1 Tm	1 Timothy
Jn	John (Gospel)	Wis	Wisdom
1 Jn	1 John (Epistle)	+	

For quotations from the Vatican II documents, the point of departure was a set of translations provided during the Council by the National Catholic Welfare Conference. Those translations were prepared quickly and were originally distributed as the Council completed its work on each document; later they were published in various forms, among which is a convenient, one-volume edition: *The Sixteen Documents of Vatican II and the Instruction on the Liturgy with Commentaries by the Council Fathers,* compiled by J. L. Gonzalez, S.S.P., and the Daughters of St. Paul (Boston, Mass.: Daughters of St. Paul, 1967). In each instance, the National Catholic Welfare Conference translation has been checked against the official text of the document, and amended or replaced whenever necessary to express more accurately the meaning of the Latin, and also to bring the English into accord with current usage and the editorial style generally followed throughout this volume. References to the Vatican II documents use the abbreviations derived from the initial letters of the Latin text of each document, and then the numbers of the articles into which the documents were divided by the Council itself.

AA   *Apostolicam actuositatem* (Laity)
AG   *Ad gentes* (Missions)
DH   *Dignitatis humanae* (Religious Liberty)
DV   *Dei verbum* (Divine Revelation)
GS   *Gaudium et spes* (Church in the World)
LG   *Lumen gentium* (On the Church)
PC   *Perfectae caritatis* (Religious Life)
PO   *Presbyterorum ordinis* (Priestly Life)
SC   *Sacrosanctum Concilium* (Liturgy)
UR   *Unitatis redintegratio* (Ecumenism)

Users of the Abbott–Gallagher edition should keep in mind that only the footnotes *italicized* in that edition are part of the Council documents. So, in that edition the Council's own notes usually have numbers different from those in the official texts.

AAS refers to *Acta Apostolicae Sedis,* the journal of the Holy See in which are published the official texts of documents issued by the popes and the Holy See's congregations. *AAS* began publication in 1909; its predecessor, from 1865–1908, was *Acta Sanctae Sedis* (*ASS*).

CCC refers to *Catechism of the Catholic Church* (1994). References are to paragraphs, not pages; note that the paragraph numbers are printed in bold type at the beginning of each paragraph.

CIC refers to *Codex iuris canonici,* auctoritate Ioannis Pauli Pp. II promulgatus (Vatican City: Libreria Editrice Vaticana, 1983), which contains the law currently in force in the Latin Church. Quotations from the code, unless otherwise noted, are from *The Code of Canon Law: A Text and Commentary,* ed. James A. Coriden, Thomas J. Green, and Donald E. Heintschel (New York: Paulist Press, 1985).

CMP and *LCL* refer to the earlier volumes of this work: volume one, *Christian Moral Principles,* and volume two, *Living a Christian Life.* References are to page numbers.

DS refers to Henricus Denzinger—Adolfus Schönmetzer, S.J., *Enchiridion Symbolorum Definitionum et Declarationum de Rebus Fidei et Morum,* ed. 36 (Freiburg im Breisgau: Herder, 1976). This volume, as its title indicates, is a collection of "creeds, definitions, and declarations on matters of faith and morals." Texts are in chronological order. Two sequences of numbers appear in the margins; both are indicated in references in the present text. Quotations from this collection, unless otherwise noted, are from *Denzinger: The Sources of Catholic Dogma,* trans. Roy J. Deferrari from the 30th ed. of *Enchiridion Symbolorum* (St. Louis: B. Herder Book Co., 1957). The translation uses the lower sequence of DS numbers.

Flannery, 1, refers to *Vatican Council II: The Conciliar and Post Conciliar Documents,* ed. Austin Flannery, O.P., new rev. ed. (Northport, N.Y.: Costello, 1992). **Flannery, 2,** refers to *Vatican Council II: More Postconciliar Documents,* ed. Austin Flannery, O.P. (Northport, N.Y.: Costello, 1982). The reference includes the relevant page number or numbers.

OR refers to the English-language, weekly edition of the Vatican newspaper, *L'Osservatore Romano.* The reference includes the date of the issue cited and the relevant page number or numbers.

PE refers to *The Papal Encyclicals,* ed. Claudia Carlen, I.H.M., 5 vols. (1981; reprint, Ann Arbor, Mich.: Pierian Press, 1990). Quotations from papal encyclicals published before 1982, unless otherwise noted, are from this edition. In it, the encyclicals are numbered consecutively through the five volumes, and each is divided into numbered sections; in references, the number of the encyclical referred to appears first, followed by a period, and then the number or numbers of the relevant section or sections.

The Rites refers to *The Rites of the Catholic Church as Revised by Decree of the Second Vatican Council and Published by Authority of Pope Paul VI* (New York: Pueblo, 1976). References are to the page numbers in this collected edition.

S.t. refers to the *Summa theologiae* of St. Thomas Aquinas. This work is cited by its five main divisions: 1 (the first part or *prima pars*), 1–2 (the first part of the second part or *prima secundae*), 2–2 (the second part of the second part or *secunda secundae*), 3 (the third part or *tertia pars*), and sup. (the supplement compiled from an earlier work after Thomas's death). These main divisions are subdivided into questions (cited by q. with the question number), the questions into articles (cited by a. with the article number), and the articles into a body (c. for *corpus*) and replies to objections (cited ad 1, ad 2, and so forth). *S.c.g.* refers to St. Thomas's *Summa contra gentiles,* which is divided into four books and these into chapters. This work is cited by book and chapter, separated by a period.

In Sent. refers to St. Thomas Aquinas, *Scriptum super libros Sententiarum magistri Petri Lombardi.* This work is divided into four books (1, 2, 3, or 4), each of which is divided into distinctions (d.), the distinctions into questions (q.), the questions into articles (a.), and the articles (sometimes, but not always) into little questions (qu'la). The ultimate unit is divided into a body (c.) and replies to objections (ad 1, ad 2, and so on).

Acknowledgments

The acknowledgments section of the "User's Guide and Preface" of *CMP* explains the origin and sponsorship of the moral theology project which resulted in that volume, *LCL,* and this one. Dr. Robert J. Wickenheiser, President of Mount Saint Mary's College until mid-1993, Rev. Dr. James N. Loughran, S.J., interim President during 1993–94, and Mr. George R. Houston, Jr., President since mid-1994, continued encouraging the work in every possible way. President Houston also cooperated in working out generous arrangements that will allow work on volume four to proceed toward projected publication in 2004.

This project also continues to depend on the substantial help of many persons.

The librarians at my College regularly provide fine service; Lisa Davis, who handles interlibrary loans, was especially helpful with this volume. The Hesburgh Library at the University of Notre Dame allowed me guest privileges, and its reference librarians gave me all the help I requested. Peter J. Cataldo and Russell E. Smith of The Pope John XXIII Medical-Moral and Research Center shared with me material on many real questions, carefully censoring it to maintain confidentiality.

An irreplaceable contribution was made by the many people who gave me questions. Those who wanted help perhaps helped me more than I helped them. Some responded to my first reply, and some greatly encouraged me. All of them must of course remain unnamed here, but I pray that each one's name is written in the book of life.

My greatest debt is to the four persons whose names appear on the title page. Joseph Boyle and John Finnis helped plan the volume and develop many of the questions; they also thoroughly criticized the entire manuscript. Each devoted about two months, spread over four years, to the book; both contributed greatly to its explanations and arguments. Jeannette Grisez, my wife, served as administrative assistant and secretary, helping with the work on a daily basis. Russell Shaw not only heavily edited the manuscript, but made many valuable criticisms and suggestions for substantive improvement, thus contributing significantly not only to the book's language but to its content.

Gerard V. Bradley examined and criticized in depth the proposed replies dealing with legal matters and the practice of law. Joseph H. Casey, S.J., commented on the entire manuscript, providing many helpful criticisms and suggestions for improvement. Basil Cole, O.P., suggested references to *CCC* and commented on the entire manuscript. Anthony Fisher, O.P., spent a month going over the entire manuscript with me; his excellent work greatly improved not only the book's substance but its rhetorical tone. Kevin L. Flannery, S.J., and Peter F. Ryan, S.J., helped develop some of the questions and commented extensively on many of the proposed replies. Robert G. Kennedy introduced me to the problems of business ethics, supplied valuable resources, and criticized many of the proposed replies. He also checked out references to and quotations from Scripture, and Edward N. Peters did the same for canon law. James J. O'Rourke and Joseph S. Spoerl worked through half the manuscript with me at an early stage, and the latter commented on the first draft of the other half. Nicholas Tonti-Filippini provided research assistance on several matters related to health care and commented in depth on a few questions.

The following helped in lesser but significant ways with the proposed replies to at least some questions:

Scott FitzGibbon, Robert P. George, Thomas W. Hilgers, M.D.,
Robert E. Joyce, Patrick Lee, David G. C. McCann, M.D.,
George E. Maloof, M.D., William E. May, Stephen F. Miletic,
Renée Mirkes, O.S.F., Luana R. C. Moore, M.D., Charles P. Prezzia, M.D.,
D. Alan Shewmon, M.D., Leonie Watson, M.D., Richard A. Watson, M.D.

In April 1994, Judith A. McMorrow, Associate Dean for Academic Affairs at Boston College Law School, invited me to participate in a one-day symposium on legal ethics with about twenty lawyers, including a number of experts in legal ethics and professional discipline. The sessions dealt with four questions I had formulated. In each case, after other participants criticized my formulation and discussed the problem the question posed, I summarized my tentative reply, and participants then commented on it. Besides the help this symposium gave me with the four questions discussed that day, several participants offered constructive advice on the project and/or generously provided published materials.

With that valuable experience as a model, I subsequently engaged in more or less similar sessions with many small groups, in the course of which most of the questions and proposed replies were discussed and criticized.

In January 1995, Joseph Boyle, Principal of University of St. Michael's College, Toronto, arranged sessions at the University with groups of students and elsewhere in that city with groups of health care ethicists, priests and seminarians, and business persons.

In January-February 1995, John Finnis, Professor of Law and Legal Philosophy, organized and initiated a seminar, *Difficult Moral Problems,* in the sub-Faculty of Philosophy and the Faculties of Theology and Law of the University of Oxford, and joined me in leading three sessions of the seminar, during which six questions were discussed. While residing in Oxford, I was invited to conduct similar but less formal sessions at Blackfriars, Campion Hall, Greyfriars, Oriel College, Regents Park College, St. Benet's Hall, Grandpont House of Opus Dei, and the home of Denis and Valerie Riches, leaders of The Gift of Human Life. In London, Luke Gormally, Director of the Linacre Centre for health care ethics, organized and sponsored a one-day symposium, which dealt with four questions.

In May 1995, Robert G. Kennedy, Professor of Management, University of St.Thomas, St. Paul, Minnesota, organized sessions with several groups of business persons, two groups of seminarians, and a group of philosophy faculty.

In May 1996, Joseph G. and Soonie Santamaria, friends deeply interested in the entire project of which this book is a part, kindly and very generously sponsored and hosted a visit by Jeannette and me to Australia. With the help of Anthony Fisher, O.P, and Nicholas Tonti-Filippini in Melbourne, and Robert O'Connell in Sydney, Joseph Santamaria organized twenty-nine sessions during which I obtained useful feedback on fifty-two questions. Many of the groups consisted of people especially competent to criticize the proposed replies to certain questions—barristers, business people, labor leaders, natural family planning teachers, nurses, physicians, priests, provincial legislators, psychiatrists, students, and so on. Some participants had prepared in advance and many participated enthusiastically; discussion was lively and criticism frank, and most participants seemed to enjoy the sessions.

Most parts of the manuscript were used in at least one class at Mount Saint Mary's College and Seminary. Edward J. Filardi, Jacqueline M. Israel, Thomas R. Klein, Meghan M. McArdle, and Mary E. Scarola helped me begin work on the book; Richard W. Champagne, Patrick J. DeMeulemeester, Peter A. Giannamore,

Daniel P. Leary, and An N. Vu read and criticized more than half the manuscript; as the book neared completion, B. Wayne Blanchard, Kathleen E. Caulfield, Megan L. Dove, and Wieslaw Walawender worked with me on selected questions. Each of these students taught me many things, but Wayne Blanchard's comments and criticisms were exceptional in quantity and quality—the work of a mature and able colleague.

I thank all these persons for their help. Each contributed something of value to this book.

Because of the difficulty of the questions, those who helped with the volume often disagreed with one another and with me. Most of those disagreements have been resolved, but not all. Indeed, no one who contributed to the book agrees with *everything* in it. Therefore, those whose help I acknowledge should not be regarded as coauthors, and nothing in the book is to be attributed to any of them as if it were his or her publication. Like me, my collaborators here and in other publications assert only those things to which they attach their names as authors or coauthors.

Mount Saint Mary's College
Emmitsburg, Maryland 21727–7799

2 February 1997
Feast of the Presentation of the Lord

THE QUESTIONS

1: Should a man act on his religious belief and risk damage to family unity?

My wife, our six children, and I were baptized and confirmed in the Greek Orthodox Church, to which all our close relatives also belong. Six years ago, due to a job transfer, we moved to a small, midwestern city where there is no Orthodox congregation; in fact, there is none within over a hundred miles. Near here, however, there are both a Catholic parish and an Episcopal church, which happens to belong to the more conservative wing of the Anglican communion. For the first few years, my family and I worshiped sometimes at the Catholic parish but more often at the Episcopal church, without receiving Communion in either, but neither my wife nor I was satisfied with that.

During my wife's formative years, her family worshiped for a time at an Episcopal church, and she also has some bias, due to the way she was brought up, against the Catholic Church. Finding herself more comfortable with the Episcopalians, she gradually joined fully and regularly in their services. Our girls, who are among the younger children, accompanied her. She wanted me to do so as well, but I could not, because I knew that Orthodoxy and Roman Catholicism have more in common. I began going regularly to the Catholic parish, and the two older boys accompanied me. Eventually I requested the Catholic bishop's permission for us to receive Communion each Sunday, and he granted it. I now accept the Catholic faith without any reservations, so that, even if there were an Orthodox congregation nearby, I could not go back. Instead, I feel a strong desire to become fully Catholic and to bring my wife and all my children into the Catholic fold.

My wife refuses to discuss the matter. We have been blessed with a wonderful, loving, and peaceful marriage, but on this issue we cannot communicate and reach a mutual understanding. I am in a quandary. For some time, I have waited and prayed, regarding the situation as a cross to be accepted. Should I keep doing that? It no longer seems right to delay indefinitely. Should I proceed alone, hoping my wife and children will follow? Except for the older boys, that seems unlikely, and I do not feel it right to go ahead without my wife and the other children, for that will divide the family. Is there some other approach I have overlooked?

Analysis:

This question concerns the religious obligation, flowing from faith itself, to worship God in accord with one's faith. Since the separation of other Christian churches from the Catholic Church is not total, neither is the already-existing religious division between the questioner and his wife. Still, there are essential differences between the Catholic Church and other Christian bodies, and each spouse ought to act on what he or she believes true. The questioner should not delay taking the steps necessary to be received into the Catholic Church, even though that will risk damage to family unity. At the same time, he should not press his wife to act contrary to her conscientious convictions and should assure her that he will respect them. He ought also to take into account their real, though imperfect, religious unity.

The reply could be along the following lines:

In responding, I shall take for granted something of which you already are aware: though other Christian communions, including the Churches of the East, are separated from the Catholic Church, that separation is not total (see UR 13–23). In particular, the Churches of the East have much in common with the Catholic Church, and not all the differences concern essentials (see UR 14–18). Similarly, the religious difference between your wife and you, though important, is not total, and it may seem greater than it really is. Therefore, both in your own thinking and in communicating with your wife, you should avoid exaggerating the problem of family division.

Still, every person bears personal responsibility for seeking religious truth, embracing it when found, and living in accord with it (see DH 2; *CCC,* 2104–9). Though Jesus knew that fulfilling this responsibility sometimes would damage familial unity, he offered no compromise (see Mt 10.34–36, Lk 12.51–53). In this matter, then, you and your wife have distinct responsibilities. I strongly suspect that at least a little, and perhaps most, of the strain you have experienced and/or anticipate has arisen from not distinguishing carefully between your direct responsibility for making the right choices bearing on your own religious life and your indirect responsibility regarding the choices your wife and children ought to make regarding their religious lives.

You say you "accept the Catholic faith without any reservations." That faith includes two beliefs: that only someone invincibly ignorant of the obligation to belong to Christ's Church can be saved outside her (see LG 14, AG 7), and that Christ's Church subsists fully in the Catholic Church, but not fully in the Orthodox churches, although they are, in most respects, truly and richly Christian (see UR 2–3, 13–18; *CCC,* 838). Some might argue that the issues that divide the Orthodox churches from the Catholic Church are not important enough to risk injuring your marriage. But those issues involve truths that, even if not the most central, are essential to the integrity of Catholic faith, so that, having accepted them, you could not concede them without entirely denying your faith (see *LCL,* 40–41).

You are responsible for acting in accord with what you believe. So, you may not remain Orthodox; you should ask to be received into the Catholic Church. Of course, you must try to choose a propitious time to take this step, and you may have some special reason to delay it briefly. However, there is no reason to think that indefinite delay will win your wife over. On the contrary, acting on your conviction will bear witness to her and your children, and so provide them with an incentive to follow your example, though, of course, they may not. Moreover, if you go on delaying, you are not accepting your cross but failing to take it up, for belonging to the worshiping community whose faith one fully shares is not some sort of self-indulgence but one's duty to the Lord (see Mt 10.34–39). Then too, failing to act on your conviction will damage your own integrity, your wife's respect for you, and, therefore, your mutual relationship. Without further delay, then, you should take the steps necessary to be received into the Catholic Church.

At the same time, your wife's refusal to discuss the matter makes it clear she does not wish to be pressed to enter the Catholic Church. You should fully respect her conscience and her religious liberty. Believing as you do, it is right for you to hope she and all your children will come into the Catholic fold. But it would be wrong to wish that good end to be achieved in any other way than by their coming to see their personal obligation to become Catholics and freely choosing to fulfill this duty, despite the very real sacrifices that might entail—sacrifices of ethnic attachments, relationships with relatives, and so forth. Consequently, you should not press your wife or any of your children who do not see the matter as you do to enter the Catholic Church. Rather, you should continue to pray for them, provide good example, explain your Catholic faith when occasion offers, and hope for the best.

Since the differences between you and your wife in religious belief and in conscientious conviction about what it requires of you already exist, and already you usually attend different churches, you need only openly acknowledge your beliefs and act on them. Pray that your good marriage will weather the storm and trust the Lord to hear and answer your prayer. Remember Peter's attempt to walk on the water (see Mt 14.28–31), pray for the faith he lacked, and take the step you hesitate to take. Being blessed in other respects with a loving and peaceful marriage, you have good reason to hope your entry into the Catholic Church will not permanently harm your marital communion.

Of course, decisive action by you probably will cause some temporary difficulty, for it will clarify the existing division. But making special efforts to show your wife how much you love her and putting the matter to her in the right way may avoid even temporary trouble. Since she does not wish to discuss the issue, it probably would be better not to try to discuss what you will do, but simply to inform her, as gently as possible, that you are about to take this step. That might be more easily done in writing, very shortly before you are going to be admitted to the Catholic Church. In any case, make it clear that you respect her conscience and will never ask her to act contrary to it. Then, point out that you too are acting out of conscientious conviction, ask her to respect your conscience, and say you trust she will not insist that you refuse to carry out what you believe is God's will in this matter.

It might or might not help if you can go to Mass Saturday evening or at a time on Sunday that will allow you to accompany your wife to Episcopal services on Sunday. The problem is that you may not receive Communion or participate actively in other elements of Episcopal worship that explicitly or implicitly diverge from Catholic faith (see *LCL,* 158–59), and sometimes it generates more strain to accompany another family member to his or her church without participating fully than it does to stay away. If you do accompany her, be careful not even to appear to go too far, because she and the children will hardly come to see the truth of Catholic faith if you do not bear clear and consistent witness to it by your behavior.

If you can find a suitable opportunity to discuss with your wife her own choice to participate in Episcopal services, point out to her the real and important differences between Orthodoxy and Anglicanism. If your wife, like many other faithful members of Orthodox churches, shares the faith of the Catholic Church in the matters on which Orthodoxy differs from Anglicanism, she should not be satisfied with participation in Episcopal services. Moreover, if she continues to believe that the Eucharist is what the Churches of both East and West always have agreed in believing it to be, and if she wishes to receive Communion in the Catholic Church, she could be allowed to do so even without assenting to other elements of Catholic teaching—for example, regarding papal primacy—if she considers them false (see *CIC,* c. 844, §3).

Since you and your wife agree on many truths of Christian faith and requirements of Christian life, you should continue to cooperate, insofar as possible, in catechizing and forming your children. In doing so, as in everything else, both of you must follow your consciences, while doing your best to avoid conflict with each other. So, while trying to avoid conflict with your wife, you should do what you can to catechize your children, including the younger ones, in the fullness of Catholic teaching. Just as you should try to hand on to your children other things you enjoy that you believe to be true and good, so you should try to hand on to them the fullness of Catholic faith, with which God has blessed you (see *CCC,* 2225–26).

2: What should parents do when a child questions a truth of faith?

Our son, Bob, goes to a Catholic high school, and we keep careful track of what he is getting by way of religious education. The school's program seems sound, and we have been pleased with it. However, our son made friends with a classmate whose dad is an ex-priest, and this man told the boys a story about original sin that Bob enthusiastically reported to us and we are sure is wrong.

The underlying idea is that original sin is not something that was done by the earliest people, a long time ago, but is simply the immaturity everyone suffers from and the impact sinful social structures have on people, especially as they are growing up. Immaturity leads people to give in to their natural impulses, and sinful social structures involve everybody in injustices. Also, according to this story, death is the natural end of bodily life and not really a punishment, but sinfulness makes people afraid of death. In looking forward to another, happier life, their fear of death is overcome so that they no longer mistakenly regard death as bad. Finally, according to this story, the Blessed Virgin's immunity from original sin means only that she was providentially protected by her angelic disposition, good upbringing, and place in society from the irresistible temptations most people experience, and she was entirely free of fear of death.

Bob never before raised objections to what he learned in religion class and what we taught him ourselves. But now we are up against this ex-priest's influence. We tried to explain the doctrine of original sin to Bob, and he did think about it. But he raised some questions we do not know how to answer. How can a sin be inherited? Why wouldn't God have prevented the first man from sinning? Wouldn't it be unfair for God to punish everybody, including babies, for something done by some cave man long ago? Isn't death really natural, since all living things in the world eventually die? And if original sin were part of our hereditary make up, how could God prevent Mary from inheriting it?

We do not know what to tell our son about all these things. Also, we are not sure how important they are, since believing in original sin and the Immaculate Conception is not like believing in the Trinity or the Incarnation. We also wonder whether we should confront Bob's friend's dad about this.

Analysis:

This question concerns both parental responsibility with respect to the religious education of children and every Catholic's responsibility with respect to difficulties about matters of faith. The parents should be encouraged to continue to discuss their son's views with him, and, in doing so, to take a moderate stance, neither treating as acceptable doubts about truths of faith nor pressing him to stifle the questions that trouble him, but striving to help him strengthen his faith and grow in it. The parents' question concerning the importance of the doctrines of original sin and the Immaculate Conception should be answered by clarifying the responsibility to believe all the truths of faith. Whether the parents should talk with the father of their son's friend is a matter for conscientious judgment.

The reply could be along the following lines:

Do not be surprised that your previously docile son is now raising questions about some of the truths of faith. Thoughtful young people often develop a critical attitude around Bob's age, and something else probably would have started him asking questions even if he were not being influenced by his friend's dad. Your son's questions are a good sign insofar as they indicate that he is earnest enough about religious truth to take such matters seriously. Some young people are so religiously indifferent they casually set aside truths of faith or never even think about or discuss such matters. And some would never bring such questions up to parents who are vigilant, as you are, about orthodoxy. That Bob discusses these questions with you is a sign that you have built a sound relationship with him, and that he respects and trusts you.

When young people experience difficulties and crises of faith, their parents have a special opportunity and responsibility to help them resolve their problems and encourage them to reaffirm their faith with a clearer, more self-conscious commitment. You also should realize that being unable to provide satisfactory answers to your son's questions challenges you to clarify and strengthen your own faith. In doing that, you will become able to help Bob. Do not let this matter rest, as if it were acceptable to doubt truths of faith or his questions were unimportant. At the same time, do not assume he is sinning against faith and do not exert any sort of pressure on him.

The teaching of Vatican II with respect to religious liberty applies to young people and their parents. Young people should seek truth in matters religious, embrace what they believe to be the truth, and live by it (see DH 2; *LCL,* 707). But they cannot fulfill these responsibilities unless they are free of pressure from their parents. Therefore, you should talk with Bob much as you would with an adult friend, seeking to clarify the points at issue so that he will see the truth for himself and accept it as his own: "The truth cannot impose itself except by virtue of its own truth, as it makes its entrance into the mind at once quietly and with power" (DH 1). Of course, this teaching presupposes that God makes religious truth available to us and that his grace ensures that a sincere quest for it will not be vain. Thus, with prayer for that grace, patient inquiry, and discussion, you and Bob should work together to preserve and strengthen his faith and yours.

Help your son deal not only with the particular difficulties of faith that currently concern you but with the many others he is sure to encounter. Warn him that even some individuals and programs within the Church either altogether lack Christian faith or are letting it slip away. Having some alternative notion about what will make life worth living, some Catholics fail to appreciate the importance of many truths of faith, and can be expected to challenge them. Since the religious education program at your son's high school seems sound, encourage him to take advantage of it by raising questions in class when appropriate or discussing them after class with his religion teacher. But beyond that, show him how to use sources such as the *Catechism of the Catholic Church* and to look for solutions to difficulties about matters of faith in sacred Scripture, by reading it with readiness to hear what God wishes to tell him.

The story about original sin and the Immaculate Conception that you have summarized includes the claim that people experience irresistible temptations. Whether the idea that some temptations are irresistible came from the father of Bob's friend or somewhere else, do not let it go unchallenged. Since succumbing to something truly irresistible would be guiltless, this claim, especially in the context of the statement that "immaturity leads people to give in to their natural impulses," is bound to be seductive for someone experiencing powerful and not-yet-mastered desires, as your son might well be at his age. The claim also is incoherent. An irresistible impulse simply would not be a temptation, and someone undergoing such an impulse would have an experience, not of giving in to it, but of simply undergoing it, as one experiences falling asleep despite trying in vain to stay awake during a boring class, homily, or entertainment. You ought to explain this point to Bob, and in any case you should be trying to help him understand and deal with his temptations, not least his sexual desires.[1] As part of this effort, assure him that he can resist and master temptation by using all available means, including prayer and the sacraments (see *LCL,* 216–26 and 669–78).

In revealing himself in Jesus, God invites human persons to become his children, whom he wishes to bring up to be adult members of his family, sharing forever in his life and joy. Hoping for heaven, believers accept this invitation. Since the truths of faith articulate God's invitation, they are like truths two people share with each other as they become acquainted with a view to becoming true friends. Such truths are not mere matters of fact or pieces of impersonal practical information; they are sharings of each person with the other. Each such truth is precious, and all of them are to be cherished and pondered. Though understood, such truths can never be exhausted, so that questions will always remain—questions that should draw a person into deeper intimacy. Thus, truths of faith are divinely given elements of a Christian's self-understanding, necessary for enjoying his or her identity as a child of God and living according to it.

As you rightly say, the truths about the Trinity, the redemptive Incarnation, and the calling of human persons to become God's children are more fundamental than those about original sin and Mary's Immaculate Conception, which are subordinate. Still, one should believe all these truths with the same faith, since God has revealed all of them (see UR 11; *LCL,* 3–6, 40–42). Someone who believed only the more fundamental secrets another shared about himself or herself would lack the trust necessary for genuine friendship. As the liver and kidneys are vital organs, though less important than the heart and brain, even these subordinate doctrines are essential to the living body of faith, so that faithful Catholics will believe them along with everything in Scripture or tradition that the Church teaches as belonging to God's revelation (see DS 3011/1792).

Therefore, when one hears a story denying or calling into question what one has received as the Church's faith, one should make sure one knows the authentic Catholic teaching on the matter and should take it for granted that the teaching is true. Relevant, unanswered questions should be regarded as difficulties to be investigated, not as indications that an alternative "story" might be acceptable. Rather, the inquiry should proceed with confidence that all the difficulties can and will be resolved, and the truth of faith vindicated and, perhaps, more fully and accurately understood.

In dealing with your son's questions, take this attitude and try to communicate it to him. You are right that the story his friend's dad gave him about original sin and the Immaculate Conception is mistaken. The Church definitively teaches that, at the beginning of human history, our first parents committed a sin by which they lost God's friendship, that this sin is handed down to their descendants, that both our first parents and we suffer death as a punishment for this sin, that baptism takes away this sin by the merit of Christ's sacrifice, and that, in anticipation of that same

---

1. See Pontifical Council for the Family, *The Truth and Meaning of Human Sexuality: Guidelines for Education within the Family, Origins,* 25:32 (1 Feb. 1996): 529, 531–52; also see *LCL,* 710–12.

merit, Mary enjoyed the special grace of being preserved from this sin from the first moment of her conception.[2]

Since baptism obviously does not overcome immaturity or sinful social structures, the false story implicitly denies that it takes away original sin. Even more important, since baptism is effective through Jesus' redemptive suffering, death, and resurrection, the story implicitly calls into question both the need for God's redemptive work in Christ and its effectiveness (see *CCC*, 389). Then too, while hope of resurrection and everlasting life makes death acceptable to Christians as an unavoidable passage, its fearsome reality as personal dissolution remains—"The last enemy to be destroyed is death" (1 Cor 15.26)—and devout Christians rightly continue to fear it both for themselves and for their loved ones (see q. 43, below). Moreover, the false story makes it impossible to understand how the anticipated merit of Jesus' redemptive act preserved Mary from original sin and why her Immaculate Conception was a singular privilege rather than a fortunate state of affairs that in principle could be shared by others. Accepting this story would seriously disrupt the body of doctrine, much as replacing the liver with a more attractive organ that could not perform the liver's function would lead quickly to death.

Your son has asked several interesting questions bearing on the authentic doctrines of original sin and the Immaculate Conception.

First, how can a sin be inherited? Part of the answer is that the Church does not teach that our first parents' sinful choice is inherited, but only that part of the state of sin resulting from that act is handed on, together with the consequences of that sinful condition (see *CCC*, 404–5; *CMP*, 348–51). God gave the first humans grace—the capacity to live together as his own family—and called them to be the beginning of the community of humankind actually living together in the world as his family. Someone whom we call "Adam" was in a position to determine the course taken by the initial human community, considered as a social body. Had Adam not sinned, each new person procreated in the human community also would have shared in grace. That community also would have been God's human family, undivided in itself and living at peace with God. But, having sinned, Adam and Eve were no longer at peace with God or each other, and so they passed on human nature deprived of grace, and weakened in its natural capacities, to offspring whose conflict was deadly and whose descendants divided into many communities. Even the best of those communities, God's chosen people, was only one small nation, warring constantly with other human communities. Thus, people coming into existence in fallen humankind cannot receive grace along with their human nature

---

    2. See DS 1511–16/788–92, 2803–4/1641; *CCC*, 385–412, 490–93, 1008; *CMP*, 335–36. The tradition regarding original sin is especially manifest in the liturgy, which makes clear the doctrine's inseparability from the doctrine about redemption by and in Christ; see G. M. Lukken, *Original Sin in the Roman Liturgy: Research into the Theology of Original Sin in the Roman Sacramentaria and the Early Baptismal Liturgy* (Leiden: E. J. Brill, 1973), esp. 352–94. On Mary's Immaculate Conception, see Bernard A. McKenna, *The Dogma of the Immaculate Conception: Historical Development and Dogmatic Fulfillment* (Washington, D.C.: The Catholic University of America, 1929), and bibliography, 572–601.

and, considered simply as members of the human race, are not members of God's family. That is why God sent his Son to establish the new covenant, which is the Church, and called all human beings to enter it and form his family on earth. And it also is why babies are not members of the Church merely by being born of Christian parents but only by baptism, in which they are born again by water and the Spirit, so that they no longer are members only of fallen humankind but also of the family of God on earth.

Second, why wouldn't God have prevented the first man from sinning? Though God did not intend that sin and could have prevented it, he allowed it to be committed so that he could draw forth something better, as St. Thomas explains (see *S.t.*, 3, q. 1, a. 3, ad 3; cf. *CCC,* 412). The exultant proclamation sung at the Easter Vigil explains:

> Father, how wonderful your care for us!
> How boundless your merciful love!
> To ransom a slave you gave away your Son.
> O happy fault, O necessary sin of Adam,
> which gained for us so great a Redeemer!

The first man's sin is not called a "happy fault" and a "necessary sin" as if in itself a sin could be either fortunate or inevitable, but because it turned out to be to humankind's advantage: Adam's wrongdoing posed a question to God the Father that evoked his supremely loving answer: his Word made man, given in sacrifice, and raised to glory.[3] Likewise, following Jesus through suffering and struggle to glory—as Mary, the martyrs, and all the saints did—becomes possible only in a world fallen and redeemed. And just as Jesus' wounds remained in him after he rose from the dead (see Lk 24.39–40; Jn 20.20, 27), so he remains the man he became in laying down his life for us, and so his followers will remain the splendid characters they become by playing their own parts in the drama of salvation. For this entire drama, as it takes place in this world, is but the prologue for an unending performance, the heavenly marriage feast, in which every person, having come to be himself or herself, will play his or her unique role.

Third, wouldn't it be unfair for God to punish everybody, including babies, for something done by some cave man long ago? To see why not, one must take into account the difference between human and divine punishments. Human punishments for crimes are chosen from among various possibilities and imposed on criminals, and if one imagines that God similarly chooses and imposes punishments for sins, the punishment of original sin will seem unfair. But God's punishments for sins are their inevitable bad consequences considered insofar as he permits them in dealing appropriately with the sins (see *CCC,* 1472). In the case of original sin, the consequences are indeed horrible, yet, as explained in answer to the second question, God permits them because they make possible great goods—ultimately the goods of salvation and everlasting life through Christ Jesus (see Rom 5.12–21). Still, though these goods might explain why God allows people who did not commit original sin to suffer its consequences, the consequences would not count as a

---

3. See Lukken, op. cit., 291–92, 391–94.

punishment if those suffering them did not somehow share in the sin. But, as explained in answer to the first question, all of us do share in original sin simply by coming to be as members of fallen humankind.

Fourth, isn't death really natural, since all living things in the world eventually die? Death is natural in two senses. In the world as it is, death is naturally inevitable; and human persons, insofar as they are bodily, are in principle susceptible to death. As the destruction of the bodily person, however, death is a great evil and hardly appropriate for persons created in God's image and called to communion with him. So, following indications in sacred Scripture, the Church teaches that humans would have been preserved from bodily death if they had not sinned (see GS 18; *CMP,* 346–48).

Fifth, if original sin is something included in humankind's hereditary makeup, how did God prevent Mary from inheriting it? Original sin is not included in humankind's hereditary makeup as an essential part of human nature. It is not something added—for example, in the genes—that corrupts and replaces human nature as it was in the beginning. If it were, Mary (and, for that matter, Jesus himself) could not have come to be without inheriting original sin along with human nature. But original sin did not change human nature in itself. It only put human nature in a sorry state—a bad condition in which people do not receive grace along with their nature, and are both wounded in their capacities and unable, insofar as their nature is fallen, to reestablish a human community in friendship with God. But God's intention for Mary was that she be the first person to cooperate fully and directly in Jesus' redemptive act, countering what Eve did by cooperating fully and directly in original sin. So, God brought Mary into being full of grace and he predestined her to participate in advance in Jesus' redemptive act, when the angel announced to her that she was to be the mother of the savior (see Lk 1.26–38) and she agreed to the Father's plan: "Let it be with me according to your word" (Lk 1.38). Jesus' redemptive act would overcome original sin by establishing the new covenant into which all human persons are called to form a universal and inclusive community in friendship with God. So, Mary, destined to say "let it be," always belonged to the new covenant community, and her human nature never shared the sorry state of fallen humankind, incapacitated to form a community in friendship with God.

Finally, you wonder whether you should "confront" your son's friend's father. An aggressive approach probably would not be helpful, but whether you should talk with the man is a reasonable question. I cannot give you a definite answer, since there may be good reasons both for and against. Your first responsibility in this situation is to your son. For you to confront this man might get in the way of your son's talking with his friend, interfere with the boys' friendship, and make it more difficult for you to help your son. Still, if you already know the man and talk with him from time to time, you might bring up the matter in a friendly way, hoping to encourage him to reexamine his views. In that case, you are more likely to help him by asking questions than pressing arguments, especially since, having been exposed to some formal theological training, he is unlikely to be receptive to direct criticism of his theological opinions.

3: May twins in conflict over Church teaching stop corresponding?

My twin brother and I are no longer communicating, though we live not far away from each other. The falling-out began a few years ago. Each family member (three brothers, two sisters) used to write a family letter on a regular basis, sending it to all the others. Having a very religious background, we began discussing the Church's teaching, especially in the area of morals. My twin brother and I found ourselves on opposite sides of the contemporary conflict in the Catholic Church. He is quite conservative and I am quite progressive. (Our other brother is progressive, and our sisters also are similarly divided.)

Neither of us could agree with the other's viewpoint. I stated my ideas and reasons, drawing on mainstream theologians such as Charles Curran, whose books I have read and found convincing. My brother refused to read anything I recommended, condemned my ideas, and maintained I was going against the pope and the true Catholic Church. I countered that I believe members of the Church can dissent on particular moral questions and remain good Catholics.

I also argued that people could remain good friends while disagreeing on many topics, including religion, so that there was no need for our differences of opinion to divide us. He said people have to agree about important things to remain friends. He asked me a number of times to quit telling him about my "heretical" ideas but I insisted that our divergent views shouldn't ruin our friendship.

Eventually he stopped writing family letters almost completely. His last letter came about a year ago; he had been writing almost monthly until then. In that last letter, he said that he wished to be left alone. I wrote another letter or two—and also talked with the sister who was on his side—trying to revive the friendship. But with no success.

The moral question is: What do I do to revive and build up friendship with my brother? Christ's law of love says: "Go and be reconciled." But how can I when he doesn't want to communicate any more? I can think of only two solutions:

(1) Continue to write, but avoid any topic that might be controversial. Since I consider religion a very important area of life, I think such a solution would be practically impossible. As my other brother says, it's almost impossible to write without giving some opinion that could be considered controversial.

(2) Quit sending family letters to him. This is the solution I have chosen for now, and it seems to comply with our Lord's advice: "Shake the dust from your sandals and go elsewhere." My brother's statement that he wants to be left alone also seems to point to it as the right solution. Still, the hurt of a lost friendship remains.

What would be your solution?

Analysis:

This question concerns the duty to maintain familial bonds, insofar as possible, despite conflicts. The questioner is perplexed because, having adopted dissenting opinions, he has repeatedly and unreasonably pressed his brother, by words and deeds, to approve or condone what he has done. A sound response to the question cannot support dissent. But one can advise the questioner to take into account that his brother cannot consistently regard dissenting opinions as acceptable, stop pressing for the approval his brother cannot rightly give, reexamine his own position, and try to engage in the communication appropriate between brothers who disagree about important matters.

The reply could be along the following lines:

In your letter, you do not specify the issues about which you and your brother disagree. However, you make it clear that you share the views of theologians such as Charles Curran, while your twin brother rejects such views, regarding them as heresies. Perhaps he goes too far in so characterizing the particular positions that you have drawn from Curran. But the Congregation for the Doctrine of the Faith, with papal endorsement, has deprived Curran of the right to call himself a "Catholic theologian."[4] Moreover, John Paul II, in his encyclical, *Veritatis splendor,* not only asserts but cogently argues that important elements of the outlook of theologians who dissent from the Church's moral teachings are incompatible with divine revelation.[5]

Since the tone of your letter suggests that you are not aware of where I stand on these matters, let me put my cards on the table. In *Christian Moral Principles,* I make the case against theological dissent, including Curran's, especially in chapters one, three, six, sixteen, twenty-three, and thirty-six. In *Living a Christian Life,* I explain in chapter one the responsibilities of Catholics with respect to Church teaching, and provide reasons in other chapters, especially eight and nine, supporting most of the moral norms from which dissent is widespread. So, my advice to you is: Examine your conscience, repent of your dissent, and then go and be reconciled with your brother.

You might say: "I am as sincerely convinced of my progressive views as you and my brother are of your conservative views, and I must follow my own conscience. It is outrageous for you to offer advice from your point of view rather than consider my situation and problem from mine. You are just like my brother in refusing to admit that my view, as genuinely Catholic as yours, is an entirely legitimate option in today's Church."

Such a reply sounds reasonable. Assuming you are sincere, your brother and I must concede that you should follow your own conscience.[6] But consider what else that reply would demand of your brother and me. The precise issue is whether dissenting views are legitimate. If we concede that they are, we abandon what we believe true. Of course, while we can continue to think what we always have believed, we no longer would be able to regard it as the sacred and certain belief and teaching of the Church. Instead, it would be nothing more

4. See Congregation for the Doctrine of the Faith, "Letter to Father Charles Curran," *AAS* 79 (1987) 116–18, *OR,* 25 Aug. 1986, 3.

5. See Germain Grisez, *"Veritatis Splendor:* Revealed Truth vs. Dissent," *Homiletic and Pastoral Review,* 94:6 (Mar. 1994): 8–17.

6. Of course, if conscience errs culpably, following it is not guiltless. See John Paul II, *Veritatis splendor,* 32–34, 62–64, *AAS* 85 (1993) 1159–61, 1182–84, *OR,* 6 Oct. 1993, v–vi, ix–x; *CMP,* 78–80, 86–87.

than one of various "opinions" that Catholics are free to hold, and so would be possibly false. Some of those "opinions" must be false, after all, since they are incompatible with one another.

Of course, friends can disagree about fundamental questions that are very central to their identities. For instance, I have friends who are believing Jews. But there are three obstacles to your carrying on this sort of friendship with your brother.

One of them is nobody's fault. Since your family, like mine, regarded Catholic faith as a divine gift of the greatest importance, it was central to the family's very being; so, conflict about what faith is and what it requires profoundly divides your family. Jesus predicted such division when he said: "Do you think that I have come to bring peace to the earth? No, I tell you, but rather division! From now on five in one household will be divided, three against two and two against three" (Lk 12.51–52). Jesus certainly did not desire such division, but he knew it would result from the fact that the gospel, including the moral truth belonging to it, is transcendently important, and that some would accept the gospel, while others would reject it.

A second obstacle is of your brother's making. Finding his relationship with you unsatisfactory and burdensome, he has simply withdrawn from it. I understand and sympathize with him, and perhaps would do no better myself. Still, I am afraid his preference to be left alone falls short of our Lord's teachings, which call for endless patience and forgiveness (see Mt 18.21–35; cf. 6.12–15).

Your brother's shortcomings, however, do not relieve you of responsibility, and the third obstacle is of your making. Like many dissenters I have known, you feel obliged to thrust the fact of your dissent on others while at the same time demanding that they accept you as a friend, and in this way you subtly demand that they affirm you as dissenting—that is, treat your dissent as an acceptable difference of opinion and so provide you with a sense of being justified. This they are bound in conscience not to do. Love for you as well as for the truth requires others to challenge your dissent as often as you confront them with it.

You might say: "You misrepresent my attitude. You are not Jesus, able to read hearts! Without evidence, you outrageously project unworthy intentions upon me."

I do not presume to read your heart. But there is evidence about your intentions. You write: "He asked me a number of times to quit telling him about my 'heretical' ideas but I insisted that our divergent views shouldn't ruin our friendship." One friend, however, does not persist in professing his or her views to the other after being asked to stop.

Again, you exclude the possibility of continuing to write without including in your letters the matters that have proved controversial. In writing, however, you need not avoid every "opinion that could be considered controversial," as you exaggeratedly suggest in stating your first proposed "solution," for surely your brother would be happy to argue with you about many things.

Finally, and most tellingly, you support your present course by citing our Lord's advice: "Shake the dust from your sandals and go elsewhere." But he gave that advice to disciples as he sent them out to preach the good news of the kingdom; it concerned towns where people simply refused to hear the gospel (see Lk 9.1–5).

The implication: Since your brother is not open to the "gospel" of dissent, you rightly leave him behind as you proceed to spread that message to others more receptive to it.

You might reply: "For heaven's sake, quit begging the question and challenging my motives. Suppose my brothers, sisters, and I belonged to liberal and conservative Protestant groups, both of which you consider to be in error. If a progressive Christian in such a situation asked for your advice, surely you would have something better to offer than what you have given me. What would be your solution?"

As a matter of fact, I consider both liberal and conservative Protestants to be partly right and partly wrong about the issues that divide them. So, I would say something along the following lines to a Protestant belonging to either camp. It seems that at this moment you are firmly convinced of your view, but I implore you to consider the possibility that in some respects you may be mistaken. Have you really examined the arguments against your view? Tell your brothers and sisters that while you still think you are right, you now see that you should carefully reconsider your view. Sincerely ask their help in carrying on that inquiry.

Still, while I would suggest that course of action to separated Christians, I do not think it sufficient for you, insofar as you are separated, not merely from a fellow Christian and erstwhile friend, but from your very own twin brother. Brothers certainly ought to be friends, but even if that is impossible, they remain inseparably joined, of the same flesh and blood, parts of each other. You seem to overlook this familial bond while focusing exclusively on the question of friendship.

Consequently, I urge you: Setting aside your false dilemma between cutting yourself off from your brother and communicating with him only about things entirely noncontroversial, write to him! But stop badgering him with your dissenting opinions, as he repeatedly asked you to do. Instead, begin to communicate again about other things, not least the many things family members still have in common, even when they are divided two against three and three against two.

4: In which cases should nurses baptize babies in danger of death?

Having previously worked in the pediatric department, I have been transferred to the neonatal nursery at this public hospital. Sometimes babies are in danger of death, and the question arises whether to baptize them. The answer, of course, is clear in certain cases. If Catholic parents ask that their baby be baptized, I don't hesitate. On the other hand, if the parents of a possibly dying baby say they are nonbelievers and certainly do not want me to baptize the child, that is the end of the matter. But there are many other cases that are not so clear.

Perhaps you will tell me to avoid the difficulty by leaving it to the chaplain. However, we have no resident chaplain in the hospital and, while I can call a priest from one of the nearby parishes, it usually takes a while to locate one and the priests often take their time coming. Moreover, I've asked them the question I'm asking you—when to baptize a baby in distress—and gotten conflicting and confusing answers. One priest even told me the baptism of babies is no longer necessary and my concern is "preconciliar."

Analysis:

This question concerns the responsibility to baptize babies in danger of death. In general, babies ought to be baptized, and claims to the contrary should not guide action. Ordinarily, the service of an ordinary minister—deacon, priest, or bishop—should be sought for baptizing babies of Catholic parents unless the baby's death is imminent. According to the Church's law, babies in danger of death *may* be baptized even against non-Catholic parents' wishes. However, both prudence and respect for the parents' role argue against baptizing babies contrary to the expressed wishes of parents. If the parents' wishes cannot be ascertained, one should proceed on a reasonable presumption regarding them or, if doubt remains and death is imminent, one should baptize the baby.

The reply could be along the following lines:

Though your question does not concern the babies of Catholic parents who wish them to be baptized, I shall begin with that sort of case. Since bishops, priests, and deacons are the ordinary ministers of baptism (see *CIC*, c. 861, §1), you should not baptize a baby whose parents are Catholic unless the child is in imminent danger of death and an ordinary minister is unavailable. Despite the inconvenience and difficulty you have encountered, try to obtain a cleric's service when such a baby needs to be baptized unless the need is plainly urgent. Moreover, many other pastoral services should be readily available to meet other Catholic patients' spiritual needs. The bishop probably has assigned some priest—or, perhaps, due to scarcity of priests, a nonclerical pastoral worker—primary responsibility for the hospital. Find out who that person is and ask him or her to do three things: see to it that he or she or someone competent to provide the necessary service is always available, provide an efficient way of summoning the person who is needed, and make known throughout the hospital the availability of this Catholic pastoral service. If you cannot identify a person who has been assigned to serve Catholic patients in the hospital or if the assigned person is uncooperative, bring the problem to the bishop's attention.

Similarly, you should find out what pastoral services are available for non-Catholic Christians who make use of the hospital, and, when possible, should encourage and assist those whose babies require baptism to make use of the services of their own church's ministers.

I turn now to your question, which concerns cases that will pose a problem even if and when adequate pastoral services are provided.

You certainly are right to ignore the advice of the priest who told you baptizing of babies is no longer necessary. Based on the words of Jesus himself, the whole Catholic tradition is that baptism is necessary for salvation.[7] This belief implies

---

7. See DS 184/88, 223/102, 780/410, 794/424, 1349/712, 1514/791, 1626/869; *CCC*, 1257). Well before Vatican II, theologians argued for the view, now proposed by the magisterium, that there is reason "to hope that there is a way of salvation for children who have died without Baptism"

that infants ought to be baptized, and almost all Christians have baptized them.[8] In accord with this tradition, the Catholic Church's law still requires infant baptism, normally within the first few weeks after birth, but without delay if a baby is in danger of death (see *CIC,* c. 867). The Congregation for the Doctrine of the Faith has reiterated the traditional doctrine about infant baptism in the face of theological speculation to the contrary.[9] Even those who think that such speculation is plausible should not put it into practice—the baby's eternal welfare may be at stake, and baptizing him or her is very easy. Therefore, to withhold baptism would be inexcusable; it would be like withholding a cheap and readily available drug that surely would cause no harm and might be absolutely essential to prevent death.

Someone might object that since the Church teaches that a person not actually baptized can be saved by baptism of desire (see DS 1524/796), baptizing babies is not essential provided a parent or someone else desires their baptism—a desire at least implicit in a parent's intention to meet a baby's needs, your concern about baptizing babies, and the Church's constant effort to carry out her salvific mission.

This objection is unsound, however, for two reasons. First, while the Church does teach that an individual's desire for baptism can suffice for his or her own salvation, she nowhere teaches that others' desire that a baby be baptized suffices for the baby's salvation. Second, someone who consciously and sincerely desires that a baby be baptized will see to it, if possible, that baptism is administered when the baby is in danger of death. Thus, if you and others did not try to administer baptism when you can to babies in danger of death, there would be no sincere desire that they be baptized.

Focusing exclusively on the preceding considerations, many sound theologians in times past held that every baby in danger of death should be baptized. Moreover, the Church's law states: "The infant of Catholic parents, in fact of non-Catholic parents also, who is in danger of death is licitly baptized even against the will of the parents" (*CIC,* c. 868, §2). However, not all that is licit (that is, in accord with law) is obligatory; and even what is in general obligatory sometimes is rightly omitted in particular cases to avoid bad side effects. Like other aspects of the care of children, their religious care is primarily their parents' responsibility, and parents are likely to resent the unwanted baptism of their child. In our society, such resentment might well lead to hatred—of those immediately responsible, of the Church, and even of the Christian religion as such—and that hatred often would

---

(*CCC,* 1261). But neither those theologians nor the magisterium regards that reason to hope as a justification for neglecting infant baptism; see William A. Van Roo, S.J., "Infants Dying without Baptism: A Survey of Recent Literature and Determination of the State of the Question," *Gregorianum,* 35 (1954): 406–73.

8. Cogent arguments support the position that infant baptism was practiced from apostolic times; see Joachim Jeremias, *Infant Baptism in the First Four Centuries,* trans. David Cairns (Philadelphia: Westminster Press, 1960); *The Origins of Infant Baptism: A Further Study in Reply to Kurt Aland,* trans. Dorothea M. Barton (London: SCM Press, 1963).

9. See *Instruction on Infant Baptism, AAS* 72 (1980) 1137–56, Flannery, 2:103–17.

have further bad effects. Therefore, it seems to me you should try to conform to parents' wishes about the baptism of their infants.[10]

You plainly are assuming and acting on that norm in the clear cases you mention. Of course, parents sometimes misunderstand their responsibility and, for example, might want their baby baptized in the hospital even though there is no significant danger of death. In such a case, you should not comply but, instead, should explain that they ought to arrange their baby's baptism in the usual way as soon as convenient after taking him or her home from the hospital. In other cases, where the child is in serious distress and the parents ask you to baptize, or where you communicate with the parents and obtain approval, you should comply with their wish.

If you cannot communicate with the parents but know they are Catholics or members of another Christian communion that practices infant baptism, proceed on the reasonable presumption that they would desire baptism for their baby in danger of death and baptize him or her. Similarly, if you know that the parents' convictions exclude or are incompatible with infant baptism, proceed on the assumption that they refuse consent and do not baptize the baby.

If you neither can communicate with the parents nor have any ground for a reasonable presumption regarding their wishes, delay acting, unless the infant's death is imminent, and try to ascertain the parents' wishes. But if death is imminent, baptize the baby, on the basis that the parents should desire eternal life for their child and probably would wish him or her to be baptized if they were accurately and fully informed and could express their wishes.

In speaking here of "the parents," I also am referring to a guardian, foster parent, or other person who takes the place of a baby's parents. Moreover, if only one parent is available, you may assume that he or she speaks for both. If the two should disagree, accept as authoritative the judgment of the one who wishes the baby baptized, since that judgment is objectively correct.

What about deliberately aborted babies who certainly are or may be alive but are sure to die soon? They have been abandoned by their parents and left to die. Like other abandoned children, they need and deserve adoption by anyone willing to fulfill, insofar as possible, parental duties toward them. Therefore, you should fulfill the urgent parental duty of providing for their salvation by baptizing them (see *CIC,* cc. 867, §2; 870; 871).

If an aborted baby—or any other baby to be baptized—is still enclosed within tissues, open them so that the baptismal water will flow on the baby's skin as you pronounce the words of baptism. Only a living human individual can be baptized, and sometimes you will be unsure whether that is what you are dealing with. In such cases, baptism should be administered. In doing so, your intention will be conditional: "If this is a living human individual, I baptize you . . .," though the condition need not be expressed in words.

---

10. St. Thomas, *S.t.,* 2–2, q. 10, a. 12; 3, q. 68, a. 10, teaches that the children of Jews and unbelievers should not be baptized against their parents' wishes. He points out that doing so would violate the Church's practice and infringe upon parents' responsibility over their children.

In every case in which you administer baptism, carefully and promptly record as much of the following information as is available: the date, the baby's name, his or her date and place of birth, the parents' names and address or addresses, whether one or both are Catholic, and the name of the parish in which the Catholic parent or parents reside. As soon as convenient, send this information to the pastor of the parish in which the hospital is located (see *CIC,* c. 878). When applicable and different, send it also to the pastor of the parish in which the baby would have resided—or, if the baby survives, will reside—with a Catholic parent or parents. You also should call Catholic parents' attention to the need to arrange with their pastor to supply the rites of baptism. When neither parent is a Catholic, you should encourage the parent or parents to report the baby's baptism to their church, so that its baptism will be recorded.

Since you will not always be on duty when babies need to be baptized, you also should discuss this matter with the physicians and other nurses with whom you work. Perhaps Catholics and some other Christians who practice infant baptism will cooperate with you in meeting this need. If necessary, even a non-Christian can baptize validly, provided he or she both intends (simply as a favor to a Christian) to do what a Christian would do in baptizing and performs the rite correctly—that is, by pouring water on the head of the child while saying: "I baptize you in the name of the Father and of the Son and of the Holy Spirit."

5: May one support charities sponsored by non-Catholic religious bodies?

As a locally well-known professional person active in civic affairs, I often am asked to support various charities, including some sponsored by Protestant and Jewish groups. Usually the request is simply for a donation, an ad in a program, or something of that sort. Sometimes, though, I am asked to lend my name to an appeal or even to participate in directing some charitable undertaking or fund-raising effort.

Before Vatican II, I said yes to such requests only in a very limited way. For example, I made small donations when that seemed warranted to keep or win the good will of clients and potential clients. I had two reasons for this policy. First, although in supporting non-Catholic groups' charities one does not directly support their religious activities, support of the former inevitably helps them carry on the latter, and so spread their beliefs. Second, I thought that as a loyal Catholic I ought to give most of my support to our own charitable activities, particularly those in mission territories, which help spread the faith.

In recent years, however, while continuing to devote the greater part of my charitable donations and efforts to various Catholic charities, I have lent more support than before to those sponsored by non-Catholics. For several years, for instance, I have served on the board of a shelter for homeless people sponsored by a Lutheran church, because this shelter has been meeting an urgent need which no Catholic organization here has addressed. In general, moreover, I have decided whether or not to support non-Catholic charities on the basis of the merit of their cause rather than for the sake of good will.

Still, I sometimes wonder whether I may have become too loose in this matter. Talking it over with various priests and thoughtful lay people, I have not found any clear and helpful guidelines. What do you say?

Analysis:

This question concerns the criteria Catholics should use in selecting organizations to which they donate money. The point of donating is to use one's surplus wealth to benefit others. Some organizations both benefit and harm people. One might consider donating to them for the sake of the good they do, and only materially cooperate with their harmful activities. But such material cooperation always can be avoided by donating to other organizations. So, Catholics should not support non-Catholic activities that involve partly false religious instruction. Other non-Catholic charitable activities bear witness to the faith of those sponsoring them, but materially cooperating with this partially mistaken witness can be justified. Duties of kinship, friendship, and neighborliness can provide the justification; so can the urgent and serious needs of some members of a community for whom help otherwise is unavailable.

The reply could be along the following lines:

Since you speak only of charities with specific religious ties, whether Catholic or not, and make no mention of the many organizations unaffiliated with any religious body, I shall not explicitly deal with a Catholic's responsibilities regarding the latter. Though they do not pose the specific problem you raise about supporting religiously based non-Catholic organizations, they sometimes pose other important problems, as some of my examples will indicate.

Also, your question presupposes a more basic one: How should people use wealth and possessions beyond those required to meet their own and their dependents' genuine needs? The answer: to meet others' genuine needs (see *LCL,* 780–82, 789–92, 800–806, 811–14). That can be done in various ways, including donations to so-called charities. I say "so-called," since for many donors appropriate contributions to such causes are a way of meeting a duty of strict justice. That is so when the alternatives are to amass unneeded wealth and to use one's resources for luxuries. Given your conscientious concern to choose carefully among possible recipients of your donations, however, I assume you are disposing of as much of your wealth as you should.

There are three reasons why a so-called charitable organization should not receive one's support. You probably already take all of them into account, but I shall mention them in case you do not. Sometimes an organization, due to the erroneous beliefs and/or defective values of those who control it, does nothing but harm people rather than meeting any of their genuine needs—Planned Parenthood is an example. Sometimes an organization is fraudulent inasmuch as its activities and resources are not entirely—or, perhaps, not at all—directed toward its purported purpose. Sometimes an organization, even if directed toward a good and honest cause, is so inefficient that it would be wasteful, and so unreasonable, to use it as a channel for meeting others' needs. Since even a Catholic organization can err in one or more of these three ways, one cannot assume that every Catholic charity may be supported.

What about the many honest and efficient organizations that, while meeting some genuine needs, also harm people, not only incidentally to doing their good work, but through putting into practice partially erroneous beliefs and/or false values? (Examples would be a shelter that helps young people in difficulty but also counsels them to practice "safe sex," an association that assists people suffering from birth defects but also counsels abortion if the defect is discovered before the baby is born, a fund that mainly helps the poor but sometimes finances terrorism, or a church sponsored program to feed the hungry that also seeks to evangelize them with a mixture of true and mistaken beliefs.) One might contribute to such organizations intending to support the good they do and only accepting as an unwanted side effect one's contribution to the harm. Still, in my judgment, contributing to the harm is not justified, for there always are ways to put surplus wealth and other resources to work meeting others' genuine needs without contributing to anything one recognizes as bad.

In considering what charities to support, even if one excludes all non-Catholic organizations and any Catholic organization one has any reason to exclude, there remain many worthy potential recipients. One must discern among them. In discerning, one should resist irrelevant emotional factors, such as good feelings aroused by flattery, while taking a number of factors into account. Is the charity tax-exempt? What is the likelihood other people will meet various needs if one does not? Will supporting an organization promote goods to which one already is specially committed? Can one ensure that the contribution will be used well? Will one's involvement in an organization engage and so benefit oneself more than merely writing a check would do? Will involvement somehow build up communion between oneself and those who will benefit by one's contribution? What will be the witness value of one's contribution? In considering all these matters, as in discerning any subordinate element of personal vocation, one should compare the feelings aroused by one's informed awareness of alternatives with one's feelings related to and integrated with faith and one's prior commitments implementing it (see *LCL,* 291–93). Then one should allocate donations in whatever way seems fitting.

Turning to your specific question, I believe it is clear that one should not support non-Catholic charitable activities commingled with partly false religious instruction—for example, a summer camp program for indigent children that will include evangelization and catechesis partly at odds with Catholic faith. Though one might intend only the genuine good the program will do, one's contribution will support the inculcation of error as well as truth and inevitably will suggest that the doctrinal content of the religious instruction is a matter of indifference. This is likely to lead people astray.

Even if an activity sponsored by a non-Catholic religious body involves nothing at all unacceptable in itself, it seems to me that, in sponsoring charities, religious bodies always bear witness to their faith. Thus, insofar as a sponsor falls short of the truth of Catholic faith and/or diverges from it, a Catholic contributing to the charity it sponsors incidentally lends support to its partially false witness. Still, doing that may be justified if you have a special reason to contribute to a non-Catholic charitable activity that involves nothing unacceptable in itself. Your earlier practice of making small donations to non-Catholic charities when necessary to obtain or retain the goodwill of clients and potential clients was for public relations rather than charity, and perhaps was justified by your obligation to build up your professional practice, both for the sake of the service you render and to earn a living. Duties of kinship, friendship, or neighborliness toward persons involved in non-Catholic charitable activities also can require a Catholic to contribute something to them. Similarly, Catholics can owe support to non-Catholic activities that benefit members of the community who need help otherwise unavailable or less adequately provided.

When a worthwhile charitable project sponsored by a non-Catholic religious body involves nothing at odds with Catholicism, Catholics called upon to participate significantly in it might reasonably ask that its official sponsorship be broadened, if possible, since joint non-Catholic and Catholic sponsorship would better reflect the reality of the cooperation to be carried on, promote ecumenism, bear witness to the shared body of truth and values, and perhaps attract broader support for the good cause.

Probably you should take this approach in your collaboration as a director of the shelter for homeless people. Of course, if that project involves anything inconsistent with Catholicism, you should not help direct it. But if every element of the project is acceptable in itself, you rightly support it in meeting a need otherwise unmet in the community. Still, you and any other Catholics who share in the activity also should share in its value as a witness to our faith.

May I offer one final suggestion? Perhaps you already contribute your services in helping to direct some Catholic charitable activities. If so, it seems to me you would do well to contribute heavily to them. But if not, unless you judge you ought to put your time and energy to other uses, consider taking a special interest in some particular Catholic activity, sharing in its direction, and making it a major recipient of your surplus wealth.

6: Should one expect that nobody will go to hell?

We belong to a good parish, and my husband and I generally are pleased with its religious education program. Mrs. Green, who teaches the Confraternity of Christian Doctrine class attended by our daughter, Angela, seems to be a faithful and devout Catholic. But the class last week was on heaven, purgatory, and hell, and Angela told us the teacher said we should suppose that everyone but ourselves will go to heaven. I thought that could not be right, since we learned as children that unrepentant mortal sinners go to hell, and I wondered if Angela had misunderstood. So I went to see Mrs. Green. She showed me the book on which she based the class. It is by Hans Urs von Balthasar, who, she said, "is practically a Doctor of the Church." It seems he was a famous Swiss theologian much admired by Pope John Paul II. Mrs. Green said the Pope named him a cardinal but that he died before receiving his red hat. She pointed out passages in the book that seem to say we should expect that nobody will go to hell, though he also says no individual should take it for granted he or she will not go there.

I do not see how the two things can fit together. More important, it seems to me wrong not to teach our children to fear hell, both for themselves and for others. I said to Mrs. Green that, if we did not worry about our children's and other people's salvation, we would not work to build up their faith or make converts. She said it is selfishness, not real love of God, to want to avoid sin and do what is right out of fear of hell. The really important thing, she said, is to love God just for himself, with no thought of reward and punishment; if people loved God as they should, they would never even think about hell.

I am pulled this way and that. Perhaps I have been teaching my children mistaken ideas. It surely is important to love God unselfishly, and I wonder whether I do that. Yet I feel there is something wrong here. What Mrs. Green says is very different from what we were taught, and I do not see how we could have been taught mistakes about such important things. I need to find out what we ought to think and teach our children—and, above all, how to love God as we should. Since this question is so important, I hope you will not only answer but show that the answer is what the Church teaches us to believe. For I have concluded that we can no longer believe theologians, even those who seem faithful.

Analysis:

Though this question might seem to pertain to dogmatic theology rather than moral theology, at issue here are the true meaning and requirements of Christian hope and love. Having proposed von Balthasar's theological opinion about hell to the CCD class, the teacher then went beyond that opinion in responding to the mother's objection. The excessive authority attributed to the theologian must be denied, and both his opinion and the teacher's further explanation must be criticized and rejected as erroneous on the basis of Scripture and the Church's teaching. Drawing on the same sources, the real requirements of Christian hope and love should be stated.

The reply could be along the following lines:

Since only what the Church believes and hands on as pertaining to God's revelation is worthy of belief in the strict sense, I agree that it is a mistake for the faithful to believe theologians, including me (see *LCL,* 43). Theologians can call attention to truths of faith and provide some insight into their meaning, so that their views often deserve thoughtful consideration. Still, the faithful should evaluate what any theologian says, primarily by the Church's teaching but also by their own cultivated Christian insight and experience (see *LCL,* 55–61), and by other appropriate sources to verify historical statements and other claims about matters of fact.

I agree that we should teach our children to fear hell both for themselves and others. If one does not fear hell, heaven seems a sure thing, so that one simply anticipates it rather than hopes for it. Anticipating heaven no matter what one does, a person cannot intend it as an end, since one can intend something as an end only if one thinks acting for it will make a difference. Not intending heaven as an end, however, a person will organize his or her life in view of some other end or ends. Instead of seeking the kingdom first of all, as Jesus told his disciples to do (see Mt 6.33), we will seek the same things nonbelievers do, and our lives will hardly differ from theirs (see *LCL,* 89–92). Similarly, if one does not fear hell for others but anticipates that they will inherit the kingdom no matter what they do, one will tend to focus on their well-being and happiness in this world, while neglecting catechesis and evangelization.

While John Paul II plainly had a high regard for Hans Urs von Balthasar, Mrs. Green exaggerated this eminent theologian's status in saying he "is practically a Doctor of the Church." Only certain saints have been named "Doctors of the Church." The title is an authoritative commendation of their thought to the faithful (but even this commendation cannot be understood as an unqualified endorsement of everything they held, since sometimes different Church Doctors' views conflict even on essential questions). By contrast, in appointing someone a cardinal, the pope does not authoritatively commend his thought. Besides, John Paul II's thought regarding hell seems incompatible with von Balthasar's view.[11] But even if the Pope did personally agree with von Balthasar on this matter, his expression of a personal opinion would not be a teaching act.

Can everyone be saved? Yes, in the sense that God's saving work in Jesus is meant for everyone and excludes no one: Jesus overcomes original sin by establishing the new covenant (see Rom 5.12–21), calling everyone to enter into it (see Mt 28.19–20, Jn 12.32), and meriting for everyone grace sufficient so that all can answer that call and freely accept God's mercy (see Rom 11.32, 1 Tm 2.4, 2 Pt 3.9).

But will everyone be saved? The answer is in sacred Scripture, which has been interpreted authoritatively by the Church's teaching. For example, Vatican II, basing itself on the New Testament, teaches:

> Indeed, since we know neither the day nor the hour, it is necessary, as the Lord has warned, to keep watch constantly, so that, having completed the one course of our earthly life (see Heb 9.27), we may merit to enter the marriage banquet with him and be counted among the blessed (see Mt 25.31–46) and not be ordered, as bad and lazy servants (see Mt 25.26), to go down into eternal fire (see Mt 25.41), into the exterior darkness where there will be "weeping and gnashing of teeth" (Mt 22.13, 25.30). For, before we reign gloriously with Christ, all of us will appear "before the judgment seat of Christ, so that each may receive recompense for what has been done in the body, whether good or evil" (2 Cor 5.10), and at the end of the world "those who have done good will go to the

---

11. John Paul II, *Crossing the Threshold of Hope,* ed. Vittorio Messori (New York: Alfred A. Knopf, 1994), 185–86, in a carefully written, brief passage responding to the concern of "great thinkers in the Church," including von Balthasar, who have been "disturbed" by the problem of hell, refers to Jesus' "unequivocal" words: "He speaks clearly of those who will go to eternal punishment (cf. Mt 25:46)." Though the Pope makes it clear that the Church's teaching provides no basis for identifying these individuals, he ends his remarks on the subject with four rhetorical questions indicating that some sinners *will* end in hell: "Is not God who is Love also ultimate Justice? Can He tolerate these terrible crimes, can they go unpunished? Isn't final punishment in some way necessary in order to reestablish moral equilibrium in the complex history of humanity? Is not hell in a certain sense the ultimate safeguard of man's moral conscience?"

resurrection of life, and those who have done evil will go to the resurrection of condemnation" (Jn 5.29; cf. Mt 25.46). (LG 48)

When the bishops of Vatican II approved *Lumen gentium,* Jesus' words quoted at the end of this passage had been officially explained to them as meaning that some will be damned—in other words, not all will be saved—so that hell is not a mere possibility that will go unrealized.[12] Moreover, previous definitive conciliar and papal teachings already made it clear that, just as the good *will* enjoy everlasting life with Christ, so unrepentant sinners *will* receive perpetual punishment (see DS 801/429, 1002/531).[13]

In the book to which you refer, Hans Urs von Balthasar claims that, while it cannot be theoretically certain that all will be saved, we ought to hope, and so believe it to be possible, that no human being will ever go to hell.[14] He appears to endorse the view that it is incompatible with hope and unreserved love of others to consider damnation a real possibility for them.[15] Von Balthasar's position seems close to universalism, the view that every human being will be saved. Yet he seems to avoid universalism, because he also maintains that we should believe that damnation is a possibility whose realization one should fear for oneself.[16]

Now, von Balthasar certainly is right in insisting that I ought to fear hell for myself. But, as you point out, taking the attitude toward others that he commends is incompatible with holding that each of us should fear hell for ourselves. Consider two persons, Smith and Jones. Smith thinks Smith can be damned but damnation is not a real possibility for Jones; Jones thinks Jones can be damned but damnation is not a real possibility for Smith. Both persons are thinking as they should, according to von Balthasar. But the thoughts of Smith and Jones about Smith's salvation are contradictory, as are their thoughts about

12. A bishop had suggested that a sentence be added making it clear that some are in fact damned, so as to exclude the view that damnation is a mere possibility. The commission handling proposed amendments set aside the proposal, not as unsound but as unsuited to the context and unnecessary: "What is proposed does not fit in this context. Besides, in n. 48 are cited the words of the gospel in which the Lord himself speaks about the damned in a form that is grammatically future" (*Acta Synodalia Sacrosancti Concilii Oecumenici Vaticani II,* 3:8 [Vatican City: Vatican Polyglot Press, 1976], 144–45); cf. James T. O'Connor, *Land of the Living* (New York: Catholic Book Publishing, 1992), 77–80. Thus, while Vatican II does not explicitly teach that some will be damned, its teaching in the quoted passage should be read in the light of the commission's interpretation of "will go" as excluding the view that damnation is a mere possibility.

13. Cf. DS 76/40, 411/211, 858/464, 1306/693); Congregation for the Doctrine of the Faith, *Letter on Certain Questions Pertaining to Eschatology,"* AAS 71 (1979) 941–42, Flannery, 2:502; see also E. J. Fortman, S.J., *Everlasting Life after Death* (New York: Alba House, 1976), 157–81; esp. 175: "It may be true enough that the New Testament gives no clear-cut witness to any particular person being in hell. But the clear *implication* of the biblical statements is that there is a hell and it is not just an abstract threat, an 'abstract possibility of perdition,' but a concrete reality with actual occupants."

14. *Dare We Hope "That All Men Be Saved"? with a Short Discourse on Hell* (San Francisco: Ignatius Press, 1988), 45, 166–67, 187.

15. See ibid., 78–79.

16. See ibid., 13, 25, 32, 80–81, 85–86, 88, 164, 189–91, 211, 248–50; note, however, 166: "But: if I hope for you, for others, for everyone, then in the end I am also allowed to include myself."

Jones's salvation. So, von Balthasar's view implies that different people can rightly think contradictory propositions true.[17]

Moreover, in calling into question that some will be damned so as to ground hope for universal salvation, von Balthasar offers arguments that prove nothing whatsoever if they fail to show that none will be damned.

He regularly gives a universalist interpretation to those Scripture passages making it clear that God desires and makes possible everyone's salvation.[18] For instance, he repeatedly interprets Jesus' word, "And I, when I am lifted up from the earth, will draw all people to myself" (Jn 12.32), as if this drawing were, not the powerful appeal of incarnate divine love that, nevertheless, can be refused, but an irresistible attraction.[19] At the same time, von Balthasar claims that it is humanly impossible to synthesize such Scripture passages with those that speak about the damned in a form that is grammatically future.[20] However, anybody who accepts both sets of passages as God's word must try to synthesize them, and von Balthasar himself tries—precisely in a universalist sense.

Von Balthasar also regularly refers to scriptural passages about the damnation of unrepentant sinners as "threats."[21] And he asserts that we cannot know "whether these threats by God, who 'reconciles himself in Christ with the world', will be actually realized in the way stated."[22] This claim that the Scripture passages which speak of the future damnation of unrepentant sinners are threats that may not be actually realized in the way stated implies that those making the threats—and, therefore, the Holy Spirit, who asserts whatever the human authors of Scripture assert (see DV 11)—may have been bluffing, that is, may have lied.

Indeed, in suggesting that Jesus' warnings—for example, those quoted by Vatican II—may have been empty threats, von Balthasar implies that Jesus himself may have misrepresented the Father, making him seem other than Jesus knew him to be. But the Holy Spirit cannot have lied, and Jesus cannot have misrepresented the Father. So, von Balthasar's attempt to deal with those Scripture passages is unacceptable. Nor does he help matters by suggesting, as he sometimes does, that such Scripture passages can be understood as warnings that tell us nothing about what will actually happen in the future but are meant only to motivate present repentance and fidelity.[23] For the very notions of threat and warning imply a

---

17. Von Balthasar might not be impressed by this argument, for he sometimes explicitly embraces inconsistency, as when he quotes (ibid., 69) Adrienne von Speyr with approval: "The truth is not simply an either-or: either somebody is in hell or nobody is. Both are partial expressions of the whole truth." Von Balthasar also *seems* to hold (143–47) as certain the reality and eternal damnation of Satan, which is hardly consistent with his position; yet he seems unaware of the problem.

18. See ibid., 23, 35, 39–40, 183–87, 213.

19. See ibid., esp. 184; also 21, 26, 39–40, 113.

20. See ibid., 23, 29, 44, 177.

21. See ibid., 20, 25, 30, 31, 34, 42, 68–69, 80, 84, 123, 142, 166, 183, 186–87, 211, 237.

22. Ibid., 183.

23. See ibid., 165.

reference—truthful or not, accurate or not—to what *will* happen if a certain condition is fulfilled, in this case if one dies in unrepented mortal sin.[24]

Still, ought we not hope for the salvation of everyone else as well as of ourselves? Yes, but this hope does not reduce Scripture's warnings about hell to empty threats.

To see the point, one must distinguish between ordinary human hope and theological hope. Ordinary human hope extends to all sorts of things, including our own future free choices; theological hope bears on God's promises regarding heaven's availability by his gift and help. With theological hope, we ought, indeed, to hope for everyone, including ourselves. But theological hope is in God, not in ourselves. By hope we have absolute assurance that God will keep his promises as we seek his kingdom, which by ourselves we are incapable of attaining. But theological hope for our own salvation does not bear on what we ourselves can and must do, considered precisely insofar as that is our own action; hope does not guarantee that we will be faithful (see DS 1541/806; *LCL*, 84–85). Given God's grace, for which we confidently hope, we do not theologically hope to do his will; rather, we either freely choose to do it or fail to accept grace and commit sin. Likewise, in theologically hoping for others' salvation, we rely on God to do everything he has promised. But at the same time we do not theologically hope they will do what they ought. So, we do what we can to teach, admonish, and help others to choose freely to do God's will. Therefore, theologically hoping for everyone's salvation is entirely compatible with taking Jesus' statement that some human beings will end up in hell to mean just that and believing that some will.

But von Balthasar is not satisfied with such hope; rather, extending hope to our own acts and those of others, he repeatedly suggests, either in his own words or by quoting others, that sinful human free choices may in the end prove ineffectual,[25] perhaps by being reversed after death.[26] This suggestion is incompatible with definitive teachings, already referred to, which are summarized in the *Catechism of the Catholic Church,* 1033: "To die in mortal sin without repenting and accepting God's merciful love means remaining separated from him forever by our own free choice. This state of definitive self-exclusion from communion with God and the blessed is called 'hell.'"

Consequently, I share your misgivings about von Balthasar's view. I also think that, despite his desire to retain the moral impact of the Scripture passages that

24. Like von Balthasar, Karl Rahner, S.J., "Hell," in *Encyclopedia of Theology: The Concise Sacramentum Mundi,* ed. Karl Rahner (New York: Seabury Press, 1975), 602–3, assumes that a threat can be meaningful without referring to future reality: "For a proper understanding of the matter, all the rules for the hermeneutics of eschatological assertions are to be observed, as must also be done in all preaching on hell. This means that what Scripture says about hell is to be interpreted in keeping with its literary character of 'threat-discourse' and hence not to be read as a preview of something which will exist some day." Neither von Balthasar nor Rahner offers any explanation of how eschatological discourse would motivate anyone if people read it as they say it should be read.

25. See Von Balthasar, op. cit., 15, 23–24, 184–85, 248.

26. See ibid., 208–9, 218–19.

speak of hell, we cannot accept the arguments he offers and still regard eternal loss as a real possibility either for ourselves or for anyone else.[27]

In calling it "selfishness, not real love of God, to want to avoid sin and do what is right out of fear of hell," Mrs. Green went beyond anything von Balthasar says. Indeed, in arguing that if one loved God as one should, one would never even think of hell, she contradicted his explicit position: it is "indispensable that every individual Christian be confronted, in the greatest seriousness, with the possibility of his becoming lost."[28] Some seventeenth century theologians did hold that one should not think of reward or punishment, heaven or hell, death or eternity; the Church rejected that view as erroneous and likewise rejected the notion that real love of God excludes concern about one's own perfection and happiness (see DS 2207/1227, 2351–52/1327–28, 2354–56/1330–32). Two propositions closely related to those errors had previously been solemnly condemned by the Council of Trent: "If anyone shall say that the fear of hell, whereby by grieving for sins we flee to the mercy of God or refrain from sinning, is a sin or makes sinners worse: let him be anathema" (DS 1558/818); "If anyone shall say that the one justified sins, when he performs good works with a view to an eternal reward: let him be anathema" (DS 1581/841; cf. DS 1576/836).

In this teaching, the Church is true to the New Testament, which repeatedly encourages Jesus' followers both to love God and hope for happiness with him and to fear separation from him. The Scriptures also make it clear that we should do good works, and repent and avoid sins, both out of love for God and out of concern for ourselves. The two motives are by no means incompatible. In truly loving God one loves whomever he loves, including oneself, and so wills the blessed communion of love—the kingdom of heaven—for which God, generously desiring that there be others to share his happiness, created angels and human persons. So, God does not arbitrarily award heavenly happiness as a prize for living a good life nor withhold it as an arbitrary punishment for dying in sin. Rather, he prepares a unique life of good deeds for each of us to live (see Eph 2.10) so that in living it each may cooperate with him and thus remain his friend.

How, then, do we love God as we should? Love of God is not our work but a gift we receive: "God's love has been poured into our hearts through the Holy Spirit that has been given to us" (Rom 5.5; cf. *CMP*, 592–94, *LCL*, 132–33). Yet this gift of love requires good works. Jesus teaches: "If you keep my commandments, you will abide in my love, just as I have kept my Father's commandments and abide in his love" (Jn 15.10; cf. 1 Jn 2.3–6). In revealing himself, God offers a covenant to a group of people—a form of association between them and himself that, like a blood relationship, is meant to be permanent and very close. Those who accept the covenant, trusting God to keep his word, hope to enjoy the blessings he promises.

---

27. Jan Ambaum, "An Empty Hell? The Restoration of All Things?: Balthasar's Concept of Hope for Salvation," *Communio* (U.S.), 18 (1991): 35–52, briefly puts von Balthasar's view into its historical and theological context; though sympathetic, Ambaum also points out difficulties, particularly with respect to von Balthasar's understanding of hope and his hypothesis of a "fundamental decision" that transcends particular choices.

28. Von Balthasar, op. cit., 85.

For them, in turn, to love God is faithfully to keep the terms of the covenant to which they have committed themselves. In revealing himself in Jesus, God offers all humankind a new and perfect covenantal communion. Those who believe the gospel and enter Jesus' covenantal society, which is the Church, are united with God in a bond intimate and unbreakable, like the one-flesh union of indissoluble marriage.

Just as a good bride and groom hope for a happy marriage, relying on each other to be faithful spouses, so Christians hope for blessed intimacy with God in heaven, relying on his grace. But just as spouses know that their own infidelity could prevent them from enjoying a happy marriage, so Christians know that mortal sin could prevent them from sharing in the unending marriage feast of heaven. As fear of offending his or her spouse and spoiling marital happiness helps a husband or wife resist temptations to be unfaithful, so fear of hell helps a Christian resist temptations. And just as that concern on the part of husbands and wives, far from being merely selfish, is consistent with truly loving their spouses and, indeed, is a result of that love, so fear of losing one's intimacy with God is inseparable from really loving him.

You should speak again with Mrs. Green. Take for granted her desire to be faithful to Jesus' word and the Church's teaching and be gentle. Perhaps you should call her attention to the sources I have pointed out, tell her you do not see how what she said can be reconciled with them, and ask her to reconsider. In this way, you can hope to help her purify her own faith and become an even better catechist, as she no doubt wishes to be.

7: Should a man set out to be both a scholar and a priest?

Being fascinated by the required college courses in philosophy, I majored in it. Then I went on to law school, graduating a year ago last spring near the top of my class. As I studied law, however, I found the prospect of practicing it less and less appealing. Instead of taking the bar examination, I went to work on a master's degree in philosophy, which I will complete in May. While my M.A. program does not allow much specialization, in my thesis I am pursuing my interest in the foundations of morality, law, and politics, and have found your work and that of John Finnis helpful.

I would appreciate your advice about my plans for the future. Early in law school, I was engaged to a former college classmate, and we were planning to be married when I finished. She became pregnant, said nothing to me about it, and had our baby aborted. Soon after, she became interested in an older man, and we broke up. The shock led me to go on a retreat, and I went to confession for the first time since grade school. Becoming more serious than I had been about my faith, I started going to Mass and Communion most days and became friendly with the priest who usually says the weekday Mass I attend. One day, after I had confessed to him and we were talking, he asked me if I had ever considered becoming a priest. I hadn't, but his question started me thinking, and I am more and more drawn to the priesthood. At the same time, I am sure that I have the gifts for scholarly work and teaching in philosophy, and that there is a real need for more Catholics in the area of my interests. Therefore, I am planning to go on for a doctorate, probably in one of the more diversified non-Catholic university departments.

Do you think it would be feasible for me to combine a scholarly career with the priesthood? After looking into the Jesuits, I am not attracted to religious life. But I have talked with the vocation directors of a few dioceses, and found that, while some frown on my idea, others seem more open to it. Do you know which of the larger dioceses would provide the best situation for what I have in mind? Do you have other suggestions?

Analysis:

This questioner must discern his vocation, that is, seek God's plan for his life. To do this, he should identify his gifts and limitations, and consider all existing opportunities to use them in service to others. He also needs to understand more clearly what would be involved in a commitment to diocesan priesthood or religious life. If one makes such a commitment, all other commitments except faith itself must be subordinated to it. So, the questioner must discern whether he is primarily called to scholarly activity, or to diocesan priesthood or religious life. He should not consider priesthood as a means to a scholarly career. The questioner also should discern whether to seek a doctorate and, if so, where to seek it.

The reply could be along the following lines:

I am always happy to offer advice to someone trying to plan rightly for the future, and your question is especially welcome since few young men today are even thinking about the possibility that they are called to priesthood or religious life.[29] You have been on a good path, and I hope what I tell you will help you see where it may be leading.

Suppose I could tell you of a diocese whose vocation director and bishop would welcome your plan to study for the priesthood and also for a doctorate in philosophy, with the prospect of serving on the faculty of the diocesan seminary. Suppose, too, that, after you were ordained, as you completed your doctorate, that bishop died or was transferred to another diocese, and his successor closed the seminary, decided he needed you in the chancery office, and told you to study for a degree in canon law. Would you gladly accept your bishop's plan, dedicate yourself to working for him on civil and canonical legal problems, and be content to do that five days a week and help out in a parish on weekends? Or suppose the diocese had no such use for your special bent toward scholarship, and your bishop decided he could best use you as an assistant in a parish where few people ever read a book? Would you try to persuade him to let you look elsewhere for an academic appointment? Or would you comply with his wishes only reluctantly, feeling your plan of life had been frustrated?

I am not just calling your attention to a grave risk, inherent in your plan, that you should not ignore—though you will be running that risk if you proceed in your

---

29. In volume four I hope to deal with many questions involved in and underlying this reply, and here only sketch out lines of thought that will be developed there and, perhaps, corrected in some respects.

present frame of mind. My point, rather, is to suggest that you take a different approach in thinking about your future.

Your primary focus must not be on your own feelings: you found philosophy fascinating, did not find the practice of law appealing, and are drawn to the priesthood. Such feelings should be taken into account in considering what to do with your life, but your primary focus should be on what God wants. Pray for the Holy Spirit's help so that you can discern and live out God's plan: the unique life of faith and good deeds he has prepared for you (see Eph 2.8–10).

To discover this plan, stir up your faith and hope by earnest prayer, and then in their light look at all your gifts, as well as your limitations, and at all existing opportunities to use your gifts in service to others. You do seem to be doing this to some extent, for you say you have been living more devoutly and are convinced that you have the gifts for scholarly work and teaching in philosophy, and you observe that there is a real need for more Catholics where your interests lie. However, you seem not to be thinking about the priesthood and religious life in the same way. While your tentative plan to pursue a doctorate in philosophy in one of the more diversified non-Catholic university departments might comport well with the prospect of a scholarly career, it seems unrelated, at best, to your interest in the priesthood, and apparently you have not yet considered what is characteristic of religious life as distinct from the diocesan priesthood. Then too, you seem not to have taken into account the gifts evidenced by your success in legal studies—finishing near the top of your class. In considering your gifts and limitations, your feelings should come into play only toward the end of prayerful discernment, after you have gathered facts about various options and carefully examined the pros and cons of each.

Appropriate commitment to the ordained priesthood plainly does not absolutely exclude certain other major commitments, such as a serious commitment to scholarship. Indeed, some priests, including a number of canonized saints, have been outstanding scholars. Moreover, both bishops and the superiors of religious institutes need some scholarly priests to fill certain important roles, especially in seminaries and formation programs. However, a priest is not free to pursue his scholarly career just as he pleases, since the priesthood carries with it a sacred duty of obedience, specified by the promise a diocesan priest makes to obey his bishop or by the vow of the religious to obey superiors (see *CIC,* cc. 273, 601; *CCC,* 1567). Moreover, a man's commitment to the ordained priesthood should be primary and his other commitments not only should be coordinated with it but subordinated to it, since ordination consecrates a man to serve the Church by acting in the person of Christ (see *CCC,* 1548–51). A sign of the primacy the commitment to the ordained priesthood should have in a man's life is that the Church generally forbids the ordination of men who lack the gift for celibacy (see *CCC,* 1579, 1599). Though the Church does not regard the ordination of married men as impossible, she considers priestly celibacy fitting partly because it frees men from the duties of marriage and family life so that they can prefer priestly service to everything else (see PO 16). Consequently, the first thing you should try to discern is whether God is calling you to the ordained priesthood, in which scholarly work might play some subordinate role, or to a primary commitment to scholarship and teaching in philosophy.

While you must discern your vocation for yourself, I venture to point out some things for you to think about.

First, that you have begun to think in vocational terms about a possible career in scholarship but speak only of being "drawn to" the priesthood suggests, though it by no means shows, that you are not called to the priesthood. Are you, perhaps, thinking of the priesthood, at least in part, as a means to a scholarly career—a way of obtaining support for your studies and/or a form of life free of burdens and distractions that might impede your professional work? If so, reconsider the possibility of a priestly vocation without regarding it as instrumental to something else. No major commitment—and certainly not that of the priesthood—should be undertaken as instrumental to anything else. Be confident that if you accurately discern your vocation, make the major commitments God is asking of you, and do your best faithfully to fulfill them, he will supply whatever is necessary. Hence, concerns about means never should be allowed to shape discernment about major commitments.

Second, while any commitment you might make to study and teaching should be subordinated if you are called to the ordained priesthood, you certainly should try to identify a form of priestly ministry and life in which you can make good use of all your gifts. Some communities of religious, rather than the diocesan priesthood, offer clear and substantial prospects of utilizing the gifts of people called to the study and teaching of philosophy. But the profound reality of any form of religious life is to be a particular way of responding to Jesus' challenge to pursue perfect charity by means of vows or other solemn commitments to poverty, chastity, and obedience (see LG 43–44, PC 12–14). So, if you think God wants you to be a priest, you also should try to discern whether he is calling you to be a religious.

If, but only if, that seems to be so, look carefully into many possibilities, including the Dominicans and various Benedictine abbeys. Nor should you rule out of consideration other institutes, including the Jesuits, for though the Society has severe problems, it has not lost its unique charism. No alternative will be entirely free of difficulties, and all need new members who will strive to overcome difficulties in harmony with their founders' visions.

Third, keep in mind that even an institute that joins a commitment to scholarship with priestly life and service requires all its members to subordinate their scholarly careers to its common apostolate and obliges some to set scholarship aside for a time, or even permanently, to serve as superiors or work in other ways for the institute's common purpose. If your central calling is to use your gifts to the fullest in the study and teaching of philosophy, you should not become a priest or religious, or make any other commitment that demands that the commitment to scholarship be subordinate to it rather than coordinated with it. It is worth noting, however, that, while incompatible with the ordained priesthood and religious life, a commitment to scholarship subordinated only to the fundamental commitment of faith itself is compatible with consecrated life in a secular institute whose members are free to make full use of their individual gifts in unique, personal apostolates (see *CCC,* 928–29; *CIC,* cc. 710, 713, 714, 716).

Someone might object that, though the commitment to marriage and parenthood often is as demanding as the priesthood or religious life, a man need only coordinate his roles as husband and father with his profession or other work, not subordinate his career to his family. Unlike marriage and family life, however, the ordained priesthood is a profession, though not merely that; ordination consecrates a man— sets him apart—precisely for priestly service to all who need his ministry. And unlike both marriage and consecrated life in a secular institute, religious life subordinates to an institute's common mission its members' commitments to a profession or other work, which must be carried out cooperatively in obedience to superiors. Marriage and parenthood, by contrast, usually require a man to engage in other work and plainly are compatible with his carrying on a professional career shaped by his own gifts and his work's exigencies; in pursuing their careers, married women, too, enjoy freedom that religious women surrender to their institute's common apostolate (see *LCL,* 623–26).

Fourth, your sense of being drawn to the priesthood may have been generated not only by the salutary effect of the termination of your engagement—namely, that it occasioned your repentance and more devout life—but by its painful emotional consequences, which may be making the thought of marriage unattractive or even repugnant and moving you not to risk another romantic relationship. If such mixed motives may be at work, you perhaps need to deal with the psychological trauma you suffered when your fiancée aborted your baby.[30] Then too, take care to appreciate the dignity of both marriage and celibacy. Marriage is intrinsically good; it is a basic human good (see *LCL,* 555–69). Moreover, though some Christians receive the grace to become good and holy without marrying, marriage is part of the fulfillment natural to human persons. That is why Jesus, even while highly commending celibacy or virginity for the kingdom's sake, compares this condition with that of one who is a eunuch due to castration or a birth defect (see Mt 19.12). Nevertheless, so worthy is it to consecrate one's life to the kingdom in priestly service or vowed religion that the forgoing of fulfillment in marriage incidental to that consecration is reasonable, just as is the martyr's laying down of his or her life in bearing faithful witness to God's truth and love. Only those who see the matter in this way fully appreciate the dignity of celibacy or virginity for the kingdom's sake, and only they can make and live out the necessary commitment without ever denigrating, even subtly, the natural and sacramental dignity of marriage and parenthood.

Fifth, if your central calling is to study and teach philosophy, you should carry out your plan to go on for a doctorate. But whether to pursue it in a non-Catholic university department is a matter for further discernment. Will that be the best way to develop your talents so that you can use them well in effective service? In considering this question, take into account the witness you will be able to give,

---

30. See Vincent M. Rue and Cynthia Tellefsen, "The Effects of Abortion on Men," *Ethics and Medics,* 21:4 (Apr. 1996): 3–4.

not only if you eventually become a scholar and teacher, but even in the course of your studies. Ask yourself, too, whether a Catholic university's department might benefit from your contribution as a student and an alumnus.

Finally, be confident that God will lead you according to his plan, provided you are honest and fully ready to respond to his call. Bear in mind, too, that God's plan for your life will not be unveiled all at once. Suppose, for example, that after much fact gathering, prayer, and reflection it seems clear to you that God is calling you to be a Dominican priest. Then, of course, you should apply for admission into that order. But it could in fact be your calling to spend only some years in studies and formation with the Dominicans. A calling to religious life is verified only when candidates are allowed to make their final vows; a calling to priesthood is verified only when a candidate is invited to receive orders and is ordained.

The same is true of other possible aspects of one's vocation: a calling to scholarship is verified by the granting of a necessary degree and academic appointment; a calling to married life is verified by another's acceptance and mutual consent to marriage; and so on. Faithfully responding to God's calling very often does not bring one to the goal one was aiming at. No matter what you discern and undertake, the Lord may wish you to stretch out your hands and take up an unexpected cross. Always be ready, if that should happen, to follow where you never wished to go. Only then will your feelings about what you might do with your life be shaped by the Christian meekness that merits the blessing of inheriting the earth (see Mt 5.5; *CMP*, 637–39).

8: Should a person distracted in prayer pray less?

I am a college junior who thinks she may have a vocation to become a nursing sister. An appendectomy I had eighteen months ago turned my life around, partly because I was frightened and began thinking a lot about life and death, but more because I became friends with one of the sisters at the hospital. Since then I have gotten my life straightened out and gone to confession regularly. When I came back to school last year, I also began going to daily Mass, saying the rosary with a friend most days after lunch, and making a fifteen-minute visit to the Blessed Sacrament in the evening.

I have been doing these things partly to test whether I really do have a vocation. It obviously would be silly for me to become a sister if I cannot be comfortable with going to Mass and praying every day—if I can't do these things well and find some satisfaction in doing them. The biggest problem I have is being distracted. It's strange, because when I was going to Mass only on Sundays, I seldom had any trouble paying attention. Now, during Mass and whenever I am trying to pray, I keep thinking about whatever is most on my mind: studies, friends' problems, news from home, plans for the weekend, whatever.

Here at school, the only person who ever says anything about prayer is the priest to whom I go to confession. I asked him about my problem with distractions, and he told me that it used to be a big topic in books of spiritual formation for priests and religious, since everybody has the same sort of problem. His advice was simple: Stop praying so much and so long; go for quality instead of quantity.

His advice makes sense and seems to work, but I am worried that I am not carrying out all the regular prayers I had undertaken and wonder whether that shows I do not have a vocation. I am not familiar with the books he referred to and wonder if there is something else I should do.

Analysis:

This question calls for an explanation of what prayer is and how to deal with distractions, and for guidance about how a vocation is discerned. Satisfaction in prayer and ease in avoiding distractions are not criteria of its quality. So, though the quality of prayer is more important than its quantity, one should not try to reduce distractions by praying less. While prayer is essential to discerning one's vocation, the questioner should not be using a program of prayer to test her possible vocation to become a nursing sister. A possible vocation to religious life can only be tested rightly as a candidate progresses through a formation program and arrives at the moment for commitment.

The reply could be along the following lines:

It is good that you are thinking seriously about your vocation and that you have undertaken a more devout Christian life. Plainly, through the sister who became your friend, God is blessing you with some special graces, and you are trying to cooperate with them. I trust you thank God every day for his goodness to you and also are grateful to your friend, the sister, for having been a channel of God's grace. Your gratitude will be an important gift to her, since it will strengthen and encourage her in fulfilling her own vocation.

You ask what to do about distractions in prayer. I agree with your confessor—everyone who prays has the problem.[31] Just as one should try to learn how to do without distractions other things that require concentration, such as studying, so one should try to overcome distractions in prayer. Nevertheless, the most important thing one does in praying is to choose to pray and do one's best to carry out that choice. In making the effort, one remembers God and tries to converse with him, and he, like a mother delighted by her baby's first attempts to talk, understands and helps:

> The Spirit helps us in our weakness; for we do not know how to pray as we ought, but that very Spirit intercedes with sighs too deep for words. And God, who searches the heart, knows what is the mind of the Spirit, because the Spirit intercedes for the saints according to the will of God. (Rom 8.26–27)

Thus, weakness need not limit prayer's fruitfulness. When distractions continue to occur despite one's best efforts, even that has a good aspect—it offers occasions for repeatedly reaffirming one's determination to pray.

Moreover, the appropriate standard for judging the quality of one's prayer is, not whether prayer is satisfying and distractions infrequent, but whether one's hope to live with God forever grows, so that doing his will becomes easier and tempta-

---

31. A brief, contemporary, and helpful summary of Catholic spirituality regarding prayer: Michael Francis Pennock, *The Ways of Prayer: An Introduction* (Notre Dame, Ind.: Ave Maria Press, 1987); on distractions, 28–31.

tions to sin become less frequent. For prayer's perfect fulfillment is in being happy with God forever in heaven, and Jesus teaches: "Not everyone who says to me, 'Lord, Lord,' will enter the kingdom of heaven, but only the one who does the will of my Father in heaven" (Mt 7.21).

But perhaps you are more distracted than you might be. If so, the problem's principal cause may be that, in undertaking your program of prayer as a kind of test—Do I have what it takes to be a religious?—you have made a mistake. By using prayer as a test, you have lost its immediate significance, which is to make your relationship with God the center of your present, daily life.

If we live in God's presence, strive to do his will, and avoid mortal sin, we are in union with him, since we are consciously cooperating with him. All our good works are his before they are ours, and they always remain more his than ours (see DS 1545–50/809–10; *CCC,* 308, 2008). Working closely with God, we must try to understand the general plan of his work—of creation, redemption, and sanctification—and try to discover our own small part in that plan. So, we must listen constantly for God's direction. At the same time, just as in working with anyone else, we should tell God how things are going with us, seek his help in every need, freely express our feelings toward him, apologize to him, and thank him when appropriate. Thought of in this way, prayer is conversation with God, never long interrupted (see *CMP,* 706–7). Like conversations with other friends and loved ones, prayer is not so much a means of seeking the goal of union with God as it is an intrinsic and central aspect of communion with him, which already exists but may never be taken for granted.

Conversation unites friends and loved ones when it is authentic sharing about things close to their hearts. When you talk with a member of your family or a good friend about something you really care about, I am sure you seldom if ever find yourself being distracted. *The Catechism of the Catholic Church* teaches:

> The habitual difficulty in prayer is *distraction.* . . . To set about hunting down distractions would be to fall into their trap, when all that is necessary is to turn back to our heart: for a distraction reveals to us what we are attached to, and this humble awareness before the Lord should awaken our preferential love for him and lead us resolutely to offer him our heart to be purified. Therein lies the battle, the choice of which master to serve (cf. Mt 6:21, 24). (*CCC,* 2729)

You would do well to study the cited passages of Matthew's Gospel, and indeed the whole of chapter six, which contains much of Jesus' own teaching on prayer. The key to dealing with distractions is to put God first in our lives and to organize everything else so that it carries out his plan for us.

Therefore, while I agree with your confessor that the quality of prayer is more important than its quantity, I do not think the quantity of prayer is the principal reason why one is distracted. Most of us probably could reduce the amount of our prayer to the vanishing point and still be distracted. Perhaps, though, your confessor's real point was to warn you against trying to carry out a program of prayer as a test of your possible future vocation, and to encourage you to integrate prayer more closely with other aspects of your present life. Part of that life, of course, is preparing for the future, and your prayer will help you do this, provided it is a genuine conversation in which you listen to God's plan for your life.

If you have stopped going to daily Mass, I think you should begin again. Daily Mass differs from all other prayers, since the Eucharist should be the center of every Catholic's life, and daily participation is appropriate for everyone capable of it (see *LCL*, 150). If you find yourself distracted, ask God to help you with that problem as you would ask his help with any other, try to overcome the distractions you experience, bear with those you fail to overcome, and be patient with God and yourself.

What does *try to overcome distractions* mean in practice? As I already explained, when we talk with someone we love about something we care deeply about, we are rarely distracted. The way to overcome distractions at Mass is to care more about what is going on. In this context, *caring more* primarily means choosing what is good with greater appreciation of its true goodness, and then bringing feelings into line with that choice. Briefly preparing oneself before Mass helps focus the commitment to participate properly. To care more, it also will help to understand the Mass better, not simply as a sort of performance one attends, but as cooperation with Jesus by which we offer our lives to the Father, join in Jesus' sacrifice, receive him bodily, and so are intimately united with him—and in him also with one another.

Probably it will be fairly easy to overcome distractions during the readings and the other parts of the Mass that change day by day. It may help if you obtain a missal and read these in advance. Then, as you listen to them, ask yourself what they mean and what message is there for you, or, perhaps, for passing on to someone else.

Your mind is more likely to wander during the parts of the Mass that do not change day by day, which are more familiar, but whose meaning you may not sufficiently understand. Some people find it helpful to use a missal to follow the Mass. Reading a sound theological explanation of the Mass also will help. Although addressed to priests, John Paul II's letter, *On the Mystery and Worship of the Eucharist*, will reward your careful study; perhaps you could get your confessor and/or some of your friends to work through it together.[32] You also would do well to study the eucharistic prayers, so that you will better understand each of their elements. As you understand the more familiar parts of the Mass more deeply, you can put your imagination to work, picturing yourself doing what you are in fact doing: joining with Jesus at the Last Supper, being with him on Calvary, celebrating his resurrection with him and the whole throng of angels and saints in heaven, and being swept up into their intimate communion with the Father in the Holy Spirit.

As for overcoming distractions in other prayers, I doubt that you should cut back on what you were doing. Indeed, I think you should make one addition to your regular prayer: a reflection, as you prepare for bed, on the various things you have done throughout the day, at the end of which you thank God for all that was good

---

32. John Paul II, *Dominicae cenae, AAS* 72 (1980) 113–48, Flannery, 2:64–92.

in it and ask his forgiveness for any sins. I would not stop saying the rosary, which is wisely designed in view of the tendency to be distracted: one says repeated vocal prayers while purposely distracting oneself by thinking about the mystery assigned for each decade. Thus, properly saying the rosary helps develop a habit of praying while doing other things. To exercise this habit, one can select certain events that occur routinely throughout the day—for example, getting out of bed, beginning to get cleaned up, heading for the cafeteria and for each class—and use these events as reminders that one is living in God's presence. A moment of sharing naturally follows. Such a habit of praying often and briefly tends to make it easier to pray.

When distractions nevertheless occur, the general strategy will be the same as for dealing with distractions during Mass: deepen your concern about what your prayers are about. Finding yourself being distracted in prayer, do not focus on the distraction and try to get rid of it, but either turn back to what you were praying about or begin to pray about what is distracting you. For instance, if you make a visit to the Blessed Sacrament and find yourself worrying about a coming examination instead of concentrating on the prayer of adoration you meant to say, tell Jesus why you are worried, ask him for his help, promise him to do your best to prepare for the examination, and leave the rest in his hands. Then pause for a bit and listen, and be certain that, whether you do badly or well on the examination, there is nothing to worry about. Changes in the time and/or situation of prayer also sometimes help. For example, if you made your visit to the Blessed Sacrament first thing in the morning rather than in the evening, you might find it easier to pray for fifteen minutes without distractions.

Having tried to answer your explicit question, I wish to offer a few suggestions concerning vocation.

You can be absolutely certain you do have a vocation, since God calls each and every one of us to a unique life of good deeds (see Eph 2.10; *LCL,* 113–18). What you cannot be certain about at present is precisely what the content of your vocation will be at various stages in your future life. Right now, God seems to have called you to be a single person living in the world, a college student, a daughter of your parents, a friend of that sister, and so on. God has not yet called you to be a nursing sister, although you are right to consider the possibility that his plan for your life will unfold in that way.

Many people who have a profound spiritual experience such as you had while in the hospital think they must respond by committing themselves to some special form of Christian life, and many good-hearted people who begin to think seriously about their vocations are impatient to know for certain the later stages of God's plan for them. Thus, your attempt to test whether you really do have a vocation to be a nursing sister is not surprising. Nevertheless, I think it mistaken, and your anxiety premature. At present, while rightly considering the possibility that you might be called to be a nursing sister, you simply are not in the appropriate situation to discern whether that really is your vocation. What you could discern now is whether you are called to seek admission to your friend's congregation. Once admitted, you would proceed step by step through the congregation's program of formation. Along the way, those in charge of the formation program might judge that your gifts do not suit you for their form of life and suggest that you leave, or you might come to see for yourself that, while God wanted you to enjoy the benefits of the formation program, he was calling you to a more or less different way of life. If you continue in the program, however, the time for discerning whether you were called to commit yourself to that form of religious life would come as the time for making vows approached. Stop trying to test now whether you are called to be a religious. Do not be anxious; be confident that God, who sees everything ahead of you, will lead you safely step by step.

I am a bit puzzled about your present academic status and plans. You say you are a college junior, but you do not say whether you are in a nursing program. If not, it seems to me you should try to discern whether to transfer into one, and, if so, whether to do that without first discerning whether you also are called to seek admission to a religious congregation.

Also, if you think God may be calling you to religious life, I suggest you carefully investigate not only your friend's congregation but other institutes. Some, such as the Missionaries of Charity, founded by Mother Teresa, have implemented very well Vatican II's directions for renewal, so that they are both up-to-date and excellent realizations of religious life. Some others, unfortunately, have deviated so greatly from the Council's norms that it probably is a mistake for anyone to think she is called to join them.

Finally, you might share this letter with your friend, the sister, and discuss my suggestions with her. She will be able to provide all the information you will need about her own congregation, and she probably will give you additional advice about prayer and its different forms.

9: What are the responsibilities of a professional suffering from burnout?

I was full of enthusiasm when I began my career and really enjoyed the work. My training was good, and I quickly and steadily advanced to my present position, which is about as far as a person can go in this profession. During the past few years, however, I have found my work becoming more and more burdensome. Various things have contributed to my loss of enthusiasm. People used to trust persons in my profession more and were more ready to cooperate, and when professionals gave their best, people were grateful. Today, it is like picking your way through a minefield. The professional gets very little positive feedback when things go well, but when they go badly, there is plenty of negative feedback. Then too, laws, regulations, and budget constraints inhibit one's freedom to do the job as it should be done.

I am not suffering from depression. I still enjoy other activities, especially my marriage and family life—though lately even they have begun to suffer from the wear and tear of the daily grind. I tried psychological counseling. That helped me become more aware of my feelings, but it did not change them. The counselor suggested I make small changes in my daily routine and develop a hobby I could carry on in odd moments during my working hours. I did that, and it helped me get through the day, but it did not make the work itself any more fulfilling. Then he told me I am suffering from burnout and suggested I take several months off. Being self-employed, I was able to arrange it, and my wife and I did a number of things we had been putting off. The time went well. But since getting back into harness four months ago, I have found the drudgery even more oppressive than before.

While I meet my professional responsibilities well enough that nobody can fault me, I seldom provide people with the service I once did. That bothers me, for I would not wish to be in their place. Yet I simply do not know what I should do in this situation. If I could retire early or quit and go into something else, I would. But with my family responsibilities, I cannot get by without the income I now make or something close to it, and, being fifty-one, I am too young to retire and too old to change jobs without giving up at least half of my present after-tax income.[33]

Analysis:

The explicit question is whether the questioner may continue professional practice of reduced quality due to burnout. The answer is yes if, despite emotional obstacles, he continues to do as well as he can under the circumstances and regularly meets at least the minimum standard for competent practitioners of his profession. If the answer is no, the questioner must give up his profession regardless of the consequences. The implicit question is whether the feeling of burnout is in part due to a moral failing. It may well be. So, possible moral failings also should be indicated and ways of dealing with them suggested.

The reply could be along the following lines:

Though the facts you present do indicate that you are not suffering from depression, your state of mind with respect to your professional work is similar to depression inasmuch as it involves strong negative feelings you cannot ignore. That being so, it is good that you are not concerned exclusively with your feelings but also are anxious about the possibility that you are being unfair toward those you serve. This commendable concern is encouraging evidence that, despite everything, your essential professional commitment remains and can serve as a basis for renewing your dedication to your professional work and, perhaps, regaining your lost enthusiasm for it.[34]

Your situation raises both psychological and moral questions. Perhaps the counseling you already received has dealt as fully as possible with the psychological dimension. But perhaps the psychologist you consulted overlooked something—for example, something in your life affecting your work in a way entirely hidden from your conscious awareness. Unless you are confident that possible

33. Because some readers project into this question ideas of their own about the questioner's profession, character, and spirituality, it must be noted that he never says what his profession is, and gives very little information about his character and spirituality.

34. See Jessica Skorupa and Albert A. Agresti, "Ethical Beliefs about Burnout and Continued Professional Practice," *Professional Psychology: Research and Practice,* 24 (1993): 281–85, for references to the psychological literature.

psychological sources of your problem have been adequately investigated, you might do well to seek additional expert help in looking into them.[35]

You explicitly pose one moral question but implicitly raise another. I shall consider first your explicit question and answer it briefly, then deal with your more difficult, implicit question.

The explicit question can be sharpened by rewording: May I continue practicing my profession despite my present inability to provide the service I once did? A negative answer may seem demanded by the Golden Rule, to which you allude in saying you would not wish to be in the place of the people you serve. Yet that would be very difficult for you to accept, given what you say about your responsibilities and your need for income.

Only you can judge whether you may continue. To make that judgment, you must answer two factual questions. First, does your performance regularly meet at least the minimum standard for competent practitioners of your profession? Second, despite emotional obstacles, are you willing to continue to do your work as well as you can under the circumstances? An affirmative answer to the first question seems indicated by your statement that you fulfill your "professional responsibilities well enough that nobody can fault" you. An affirmative answer to the second question is within your own power. But if you cannot or will not answer yes to both questions, you cannot fairly continue to offer your service and must give up your profession, despite the consequences for you and your family. If you can and do honestly say yes to both, however, I see no reason why continuing to practice your profession would necessarily be unfair to those you serve. In that case, you may dismiss your guilt feelings and carry on as well as you can.

Sometimes, of course, clients and colleagues with whom you have dealt previously will expect from you work of a quality you no longer can provide. In such cases, consider the facts of the situation and apply the Golden Rule to judge whether you must warn someone that you are no longer functioning as well as you used to. Special challenges perhaps will arouse your interest and spark the enthusiasm you generally lack, so that they will present no problem. But if you do not expect to be able to do an adequate job in some cases, you should, like any practitioner of limited competence, refer them to someone more competent or obtain a colleague's help to ensure adequate service.

So much for your explicit question. Your implicit question also can be sharpened by rewording: Is my feeling that I am professionally burned out the result of some moral fault? You have tried psychological counseling, a diverting hobby, and time off from work, but none of these has helped; your work remains drudgery. Now you present your problem to me, hoping for helpful advice, and I shall try to provide it, for the problem may well be, at least in part, a moral one.

In the first place, if you continue to practice your profession, you should resist the wish that you could retire early or quit and do something else. That wish is inconsistent with your professional commitment, and imagining appealing alterna-

---

35. A psychological approach to burnout that in some respects complements the moral considerations I shall propose: Ayala Pines and Elliot Aronson, *Career Burnout: Causes and Cures* (New York: Free Press, 1988).

tives arouses emotions contrary to the ones you need. Regard the wish as a bad thought, and do not deliberately entertain it. Moreover, though vacations and hobbies are appropriate parts of most everyone's life, using them as partial escapes from professional responsibilities—as you did in taking several months off and taking up a diversion during working hours—predictably intensifies the wish you should resist and so exacerbates your problem rather than helping to solve it. A more effective tactic would be to intensify your professional involvement—for example, by updating your knowledge, trying out promising new approaches, helping young colleagues just beginning their careers, or working through a professional body to improve your profession's ethical standards.

Second, in serving people, including those who seem uncooperative and ungrateful, you continue to carry out the commitment you made in embarking on your professional career. Though not a vow of fidelity for better or worse until death, that commitment, like consent to marriage, took into account the likelihood that the people involved—those you serve and you yourself—might change in unforeseen and disagreeable ways. Yet you made the commitment, expecting to carry on your profession for many years, probably until the age of retirement. With that in mind, refocus your concern on the true purpose to which you always should direct your work. That is not professional status, which you already have achieved, but something more important, which you cannot achieve once and for all: genuine benefits you can help bring about in those you serve. When you began your career, you obtained emotional gratification from other things: attaining career goals, professional recognition, the gratitude of those you served. Such gratification is not bad in itself, but perhaps you relied too heavily on it, so that, as you reached the summit of your profession and experienced less positive feedback from those you serve, you were deprived of emotional motivation on which you had become dependent.

Refocusing your concern to the true purpose of your profession will help you develop a different attitude toward the changed circumstances of your work. Insofar as the changes make it harder to benefit those you serve, think of the altered circumstances as challenges to your ingenuity and skill, just as you would if you were only now entering the profession. Bear in mind that each person you serve is unique, and providing him or her with the best service you can under the existing conditions is a unique problem. If the people you try to serve today really are less cooperative than those you previously served, try to persuade them to be more cooperative. If that does not work, accept that fact and lower your expectations. You should not expect more of yourself than God does. He never asks you to accomplish the impossible, but only to do what you can under the conditions in which you find yourself.

Third, while all of us need positive emotional motivation to do our work, focusing on our own feelings is self-defeating. People who work well at a craft and make a good product are absorbed in their work until it is completed; then they have the satisfaction of looking at the result and seeing all the skill and effort embodied in it. A professional seldom has quite that satisfaction, since the important results of his or her effort are within a person and, generally, are harder to assess.

Nevertheless, like a skilled craftsperson, a professional can focus on how his or her work measures up to reasonable standards as it progresses, and this focus will bring some well-grounded satisfaction.

Fourth, while you tried psychological counseling, you say nothing about your specifically religious activities and whether you have modified them in any way so as to deal with your problem, which actually may be a God-given challenge to grow in holiness. If you have not already done so, I suggest you find an experienced person as a spiritual director (see *CCC,* 2690). Probably this person should be a priest, to whom you can confess your sins regularly and with whom you also can discuss your life as a whole and your problem with your professional work. In such discussion, you perhaps will find ways to draw greater patience and strength from prayer, to receive the sacraments more devoutly and fruitfully, and, in general, to integrate your work more perfectly with your faith. If you cannot identify someone suitable to serve as your regular spiritual director, you might use some of your next vacation for a retreat, during which you could obtain some guidance. In seeking a spiritual director or retreat master, of course, you should look for someone who is not only entirely faithful to the Church's teaching but a real guide in religious thought and practice, so that you will receive something besides psychological counseling, which you already have tried.

Finally, since Jesus teaches that his followers should not try to dominate others but serve them, Christian professionals should take to heart the New Testament's catechesis for slaves: "Obey your earthly masters in everything, not only while being watched and in order to please them, but wholeheartedly, fearing the Lord. Whatever your task, put yourselves into it, as done for the Lord and not for your masters, since you know that from the Lord you will receive the inheritance as your reward; you serve the Lord Christ" (Col 3.22–24; cf. Eph 6.5–8, 1 Tm 6.1–2, 1 Pt 2.18–21).

Do not expect too much in this life. In the fallen human condition, people often behave badly and are ungrateful to those who serve them well. Accepting this fact as part of the cross the Lord has called you to carry, you will find in it peace and profound joy, for you will anticipate beyond present sufferings the happiness of heaven. Provided you are faithful to the end, you will find again in heaven, too, the good fruits of your effort, healed of their defects and completed (see GS 38–39).

10: Must one participate in questionable Sunday celebrations in the priest's absence?

Where we live there are not many Catholics and even fewer priests. The priest who takes care of our parish also has three others. Usually he is at each of them only every fourth weekend. (On Christmas and Easter, and now and then at other times, he or another priest says Mass at two of the parishes, and then almost everyone makes it to one or the other of them.) Anyway, most weekends we do not have Mass at our parish. Instead, Sister Bernice, who runs both our parish and the one nearest us, does a "Sunday celebration," though it actually is Saturday evening every other weekend, since Sister alternates Sundays at the two parishes.

Everything is exactly the same as Mass through the collection after the prayers of the faithful; then Sister skips to the Our Father, and everything is the same as Mass right to the end. Sister and three women, friends of hers, do everything: lead the hymns, give out hosts Father consecrated the last time he was here to say Mass, and even take up the collection. Sister wears an alb and a stole—though, for some reason, she wears it over one shoulder and tied at the opposite hip—and the other women wear cassocks and surplices, like altar girls. All this is pretty obnoxious to my wife and me, and we also do not care for Sister's sermons, which are awfully long-winded.

We have been told that going to this celebration "fulfills the Sunday obligation." But I do not see how that can be, since I thought the Sunday obligation was to hear Mass, and this celebration is not Mass (as Sister Bernice says every time before the opening hymn). If I am right, I do not see that we need to go to it at all. We could as well watch a Mass on television. I asked the priest about this the last time he was here, but he just said the Sunday obligation isn't eliminated because he isn't here to say Mass and this is the best they can do.

Analysis:

The question is whether Catholics ought to attend Sunday celebrations in the absence of a priest. The Church's law requiring Sunday Mass attendance does not exhaust Catholics' obligation of Sunday worship. When one cannot participate in Sunday Mass, it is appropriate to join in a Sunday celebration, especially one including holy Communion. Sister Bernice apparently leads the Sunday celebration as a deacon would rather than as a layperson should. The questioner should ask her and/or the pastor to correct this abuse, and, if necessary, should petition the bishop to do so.

The reply could be along the following lines:

You say your wife and you find Sister Bernice's Sunday celebrations "obnoxious" and apparently you feel some resentment toward her. In the situation you describe, negative feelings are natural enough. But in trying to deal with the situation, you must guard against acting on resentment or other hostile feelings. Your sole aim should be to try to improve matters, not only for your own family and other parishioners but for your pastor and Sister Bernice. Assume that they mean well. Ask the Holy Spirit for the light and love you will need, and strive to build up and heal their relationship with disaffected parishioners. If your efforts seem fruitless, try to be patient, and, when you can participate in a Mass, offer this and all your sufferings along with Jesus' sacrifice.

I shall attempt to respond to your question, but you also might profit by studying the relevant documents of the Holy See and of the National Conference of Catholic Bishops.[36] Even though your parish's Sunday celebration involves certain abuses,

---

36. Congregation for Divine Worship, *Directory for Sunday Celebrations in the Absence of a Priest,* approved and confirmed by Pope John Paul II (21 May 1988) and issued by the Congregation (2 June 1988), *Origins,* 18:19 (20 Oct. 1988): 301, 303–7; Bishops' Committee on the Liturgy, National Conference of Catholic Bishops, *Gathered in Steadfast Faith: Statement on*

I do not agree that you "could as well watch a Mass on television." I shall try, first, to clarify the Sunday obligation of Catholics whose parishes have a Sunday celebration authorized by the bishop when no priest is available to offer Mass. Then I shall make some suggestions about dealing with the abuses.

To understand the Sunday obligation, one must bear several things in mind. All human beings, as rational creatures, owe God worship. In revealing himself, God established the weekly cycle for work and worship, so that all who accept God's revelation in the Old Testament should set aside one day each week primarily to worship him. At the Last Supper, Jesus commanded his followers to do the Eucharist in memory of him, thus specifying the central act of Christian worship. Since he rose from the dead on Sunday, Christians from the beginning recognized that day, rather than the Jewish Sabbath, as appropriate for their regular celebration of the Eucharist (see *LCL,* 146–47). So, although the Church's law reminds Catholics of their Sunday obligation (see *CIC,* c. 1247), this obligation would exist even if there were no such law regarding it. Therefore, the law should not be read legalistically as if it exhausted the obligation.

When possible, Catholics should gather together on Sunday to celebrate the Eucharist by participating in a complete Mass. The Mass makes Jesus' sacrifice present in order that his disciples may join him in it, and thereby realize and experience their communion with him and one another—a communion that begins in the Church's eucharistic worship but is to be perfected in unending heavenly communion. When no priest is available to say Mass, the Sunday gathering of the parish community to listen to the day's readings from sacred Scripture and receive holy Communion is appropriate for two reasons. First, under these circumstances this fulfills as well as possible the obligation to worship—an obligation incumbent not only on individuals but on the community, whose duty it is to form and actualize a church, that is, a portion of Jesus' body. Second, by worthily receiving holy Communion, one is bodily united with Jesus and shares in his resurrection life.

It is better for Catholics who cannot come to any sort of communal celebration on Sunday to watch a Mass on television than entirely omit worship, since thereby they listen to the day's readings and are helped to lift their minds and hearts to God in personal worship. Still, watching the Mass on television hardly is adequate for those able to participate in a communal celebration, since people watching television do not thereby come together as a church or receive holy Communion. Therefore, although there can be exceptions, Catholics who cannot participate in a Sunday Mass generally should participate in a Sunday celebration authorized by the bishop if one is available.

Sunday Worship in the Absence of a Priest (Washington, D.C.: United States Catholic Conference, 1991); *Sunday Celebrations in the Absence of a Priest: Leader's Edition,* approved for use in the dioceses of the United States of America by the National Conference of Catholic Bishops (New York: Catholic Book Publishing, 1994). There may be additional binding diocesan norms about this matter; you can write or call the office of the diocese and ask whether such regulations exist and, if so, how to obtain a copy. If supplementary norms have been issued, they specify the responsibilities legislated by the universal Church and ought to be taken into account in considering the advice offered in this response.

Do the faithful have a legal obligation to do so? Strictly speaking, no. The relevant provision of the Church's law is:

> If because of lack of a sacred minister or for other grave cause participation in the celebration of the Eucharist is impossible, it is specially recommended that the faithful take part in the liturgy of the word if it is celebrated in the parish church or in another sacred place according to the prescriptions of the diocesan bishop, or engage in prayer for an appropriate amount of time personally or in a family or, as occasion offers, in groups of families. (*CIC*, c. 1248, §2)

Participation in a Sunday celebration is recommended, not required, and another option also is offered: prayer by individuals, families, or groups of families.

At the same time, the Congregation for Divine Worship strongly urges the faithful to adopt the latter option when "a celebration of the word of God along with the giving of holy Communion is *not possible*" and observes that in such circumstances the televising of liturgical services can be helpful.[37] This suggests that in a situation like yours, where a celebration of the word with holy Communion is available, it would be inappropriate to use the option of worshipping in the family or group of families, or to watch a televised Mass instead.

It appears from your description of the arrangement for Christmas, Easter, and some other times that, on at least some Sundays when there is no Mass in your own parish, it would be no great hardship for you to go to another parish where Mass is offered. If so, should you? Certainly, you may, but I do not think you must. By authorizing a Sunday celebration in your parish, the bishop implies that he judges going elsewhere to Mass too difficult for members of your parish considered as a whole. Therefore, as part of the parish community, even those who could go to Mass elsewhere may worship with their fellow parishioners so as to maintain solidarity with them and help sustain the parish as a worshipping body. However, you can fulfill that responsibility to your parish not only by participating in the Sunday celebration when you cannot get to Mass elsewhere but by contributing generously to other parish activities, such as catechetical programs.

At the same time, in many situations the faithful should, in my judgment, be willing to make greater sacrifices to gather for Mass, so that Sunday celebrations without a priest would seldom if ever seem appropriate to a bishop. As the numbers of ordained priests decline, the faithful also should be prepared to accept the combining of parishes and closing of churches. Under persecution, the faithful frequently have taken great risks, even to life itself, to hear Mass and receive holy Communion. So, people in your area should consider traveling the required distance every Sunday, as they do on Christmas and Easter, to obviate or, at least, reduce the need for Sunday celebrations without a priest, and they should consider asking the bishop to reorganize the four parishes into two, at each of which Mass could be offered at least every other Sunday.[38]

---

37. *Directory*, 2, 32 (emphasis added), *Origins*, 306.

38. Archbishop James Keleher of Kansas City and the other bishops of Kansas issued a joint pastoral, "Sunday Eucharist: Do This in Memory of Me"—see "Kansas Bishops: Policy Restricts Sunday Communion without Mass," *Origins*, 25:8 (13 July 1995): 121, 123–24—in which they explained (123) that "holy communion regularly received outside of Mass is a short-term solution

Meanwhile, however, the Sunday celebrations in your parish present a problem. How serious is it and how should you deal with it?

Sister Bernice appropriately makes it clear that the Sunday celebration she conducts is not a Mass, and she rightly skips from the collection after the prayers of the faithful to the Our Father, omitting entirely the central parts of the Mass—the preparation of the gifts, preface, and eucharistic prayer—which can be carried out only by an ordained priest. However, she should not be wearing a stole, which is reserved to those who have been ordained and which, according to your description, she wears as deacons do. Also, if you are correct in saying she does everything through the prayers of the faithful and from the Our Father on, "exactly the same as Mass," she is inappropriately doing other things proper to a deacon or priest, such as using forms of greeting and blessing reserved to them, and using the presidential chair. For Sister Bernice and her three friends to monopolize ministerial roles also is questionable, for it is appropriate that even the ordained who preside invite and encourage other suitable members of the congregation to serve by turns as lectors, altar servers, leaders of song, and ushers. If her sermons are homilies provided by the bishop or pastor for her to read, it is right for her to read them. If she has been delegated by the bishop to preach, she "may give those present a brief explanation of the biblical text, so that they may understand through faith the meaning of the celebration."[39] But if she gives her own homilies, in this respect, too, Sister Bernice is assuming a function reserved to the ordained.[40]

While these abuses do not negate the celebration's essential value as worship, they are serious. What might you do about them?

Since your parish's community already is weakened by not having a full-time pastor, I would be cautious about discussing the abuses with other parishioners lest the parish be divided into factions. Still, by means of discreet conversations with a small number of devout and sensible parishioners on good terms with the pastor, you might try to enlist the cooperation of three or four in an effort to bring about the abuses' correction. Without the support of such a group, your concerns are more likely to be ignored or rejected as the complaints of a persnickety conservative. Accompanied by a few others of the right sort and reinforced by their testimony, you are more likely to obtain a serious hearing and favorable action.

You could begin by gently questioning Sister Bernice about the matters that have concerned you, and you also could provide her with copies of the relevant documents if she does not already have them. If the abuses are not corrected, you could next discuss them with the pastor. If both of them ever are at the parish at the same time, it probably would be best to try to see them together.

---

that has all the makings of becoming a long-term problem" and that it "has implications that are disturbing"; they therefore established a policy restricting Sunday celebrations without a priest, and added: "We recognize that this policy calls some of the faithful to sacrifices and hardships that match those of our ancestors in the faith." James Dallen, *The Dilemma of Priestless Sundays* (Chicago: Liturgy Training Publications, 1994), argues against forgoing the Sunday Eucharist; though I do not agree with everything Dallen says, his main argument seems sound and compelling.

39. *Sunday Celebrations in the Absence of a Priest: Leader's Edition,* 121.

40. See *CIC,* c. 767, §1; Congregation for Divine Worship, *Directory,* 3, 43, *Origins,* 306.

If such efforts do not lead to appropriate changes, you should call the matter to the bishop's attention. You could write to him, carefully describing the way Sister Bernice conducts the Sunday celebration and briefly summarizing your conversation with her and/or the pastor. In speaking with the pastor and writing to the bishop, do not judge and condemn what Sister Bernice has been doing. Instead, question its conformity to relevant Church norms, its suitability to the spiritual needs of parishioners, and the likelihood that it will sustain their solidarity. Moreover, in communicating with your bishop, show the respect you would show to Jesus, in whose person the bishop leads the Church in your region. If he approves some of the things to which you object, accept his judgment in a docile spirit. However, if he does not respond to you within a reasonable time, or seems to tolerate recognized and admitted abuses, or promises action but fails to bring about reforms, you should communicate with him persistently, as children with a serious problem do with a distracted parent whom they expect to respond with faithful love.

If nothing is ever done about the abuses, you probably should put up with them and continue to participate in the Sunday celebration at your parish except when you can go to Mass elsewhere. Even though you could worship within your own household, or with one or more neighboring families, that would both deprive you of holy Communion and further weaken the parish community. Nevertheless, if the Sunday celebrations become intolerable—for example, through the introduction of more serious abuses—never neglect Sunday worship. On those Sundays when you cannot go elsewhere to Mass or a properly conducted celebration, carefully plan and carry out Sunday worship with your own family and, perhaps, some others. Its suitable elements might include the offices of readings and/or morning prayer from the day's Liturgy of the Hours (for some families, the devout recitation of five decades of the rosary with meditation on the glorious mysteries), reading and discussion of the Scripture passages assigned for the day in the lectionary, recitation of the Creed, petitions for various needs, and spiritual communion—that is, an act of faith in Jesus' bodily presence in the Eucharist together with appropriate meditation to elicit the desire actually to receive him.

If your diocese has a program for the permanent diaconate, you might ask the bishop whether he would appoint a deacon to preside at the Sunday celebration if a deacon were available. If he says yes, you might look into the diaconate program and consider whether you might be called to serve the Church in this way. You also should encourage men you know, who might be called to this service even if you are not, to consider the possibility that they have this calling. Finally, if you are not already doing so, you should pray for an increase in vocations to the priesthood, and should encourage and support anyone who seems to have such a vocation in pursuing it.

11: What should the faithful do about a priest's liturgical abuses?

I am writing on behalf of six couples from the same parish. We meet weekly for prayer and once a month share a potluck supper at one another's homes. Last year we got missals so we could take some parts of the Mass and the next Sunday's readings as starting points for our prayer together, which was becoming routine. That helped, and we also found we began to understand the Mass better.

Lately we have been worried about the liturgies in our parish. The new assistant pastor has been making quite a few changes. Not only do these make it hard to follow along in the missal, but, more important, some of them make us wonder whether we really are participating in a Mass. We also are worried about the bad effects on our children and other young people—on their faith, their reverence for the Blessed Sacrament, their respect for rules. And while some parishioners are very happy with what is going on, others are not, and the more vocal people on both sides have had some nasty arguments.

Our pastor always has said some things differently than they are in the missal, but most of these are changes priests often make, and we never worried about them. For instance, at many points he adds the words *here* and *now;* in the prayer after the Our Father he says "protect us from *useless worry*"; before Communion he says, "Happy are *we* who are called to *this* supper"; and when he gives Communion he says, "*Receive* the body of Christ."

The new assistant is doing some little things like that but he also is doing many more drastic things. In the penitential rite and throughout the Mass, he never uses the word *sin.* He sometimes has a layperson, usually a woman, read the Gospel and give the homily. He always skips the Creed. Right after the prayers of the faithful, which take a long time because he asks everyone to join in, he receives the gifts and begins the dialogue before the preface, skipping the offertory. He uses the third eucharistic prayer for children, with some changes, at Sunday Masses in which most participants are adults, and he wants everyone to say the words of consecration with him. The sign of peace takes a long time because he goes around the church making contact with as many people as possible: he encourages everyone to express their feelings by hugging and kissing, and he does a good deal of that himself. Then he has the eucharistic ministers give everyone in the church a host to hold, so that all receive at the same time, and he has the ministers put the cups on the altar rail and urges everyone to help themselves. He says everybody should feel free to receive.

We were hesitant to talk with the assistant, but we prayed about it and decided it was the right thing to do. The other couples elected my wife and me to represent the whole group. We made an appointment with him and discussed the things he does, especially his asking everyone to say the words of consecration and the way he has the ministers handle Communion. He pointed out that most priests make some changes in the liturgy, and said his changes are in line with the fact that the Mass is not a reenactment of the Last Supper, but a memorial meal in which all Jesus' disciples share and everyone should be active.

We replied that, while we do want to participate actively, it does not seem right for lay people to join with the priest, or even replace him, in doing things the priest alone usually does, and that while the Mass is a memorial meal, it also is Christ's sacrifice, and it seems to us that the priest alone should say Jesus' words that change the bread and wine into his body and blood, and that the priest should receive

Communion first. He said all Christians ought to be equal and the idea of the Eucharist as magic was just an excuse for dividing them into castes and denying that Christ can act through everyone, including women.

We asked what he meant by "the idea of the Eucharist as magic." He said he meant the idea that it is something other than the action of both the priest and the people, using bread and wine, in a meal that reminds everyone that Jesus loves them and that all God's People are equal. We said we and the other couples had not felt unequal and did not feel changes were needed. He said he had received a great deal of feedback from the parish and most people like what he is doing.

We expressed our concern about the effects on our children and other young people. At that he became irritated and said he refused to be bound by a straitjacket of liturgical rules and was not going to be told by a little group of laypeople how to preside at the liturgy. My wife made the mistake of asking if that meant we belonged to an inferior caste. Though she immediately apologized for her sarcasm, the priest banged his fist on the table, angrily accused us of being pre–Vatican II and divisive, said talking with us was a waste of time, and showed us to the door.

After that meeting with the assistant, we talked things over with the pastor. We were careful not to say that all the unauthorized changes priests make are wrong, because that would have been criticizing him too. Instead, we mentioned only the more important things the new assistant has been doing and reported our discussion with him, leaving out only the assistant's argument that most priests make some changes. The pastor seemed shocked, said the things we described are serious abuses, and promised to get after the assistant. He also suggested that we avoid going to Mass with the assistant, and said that by noon each Friday he would change the recorded message giving the Mass schedule to indicate which Masses he and the assistant would be saying that weekend.

That was a couple of months ago. Most of the time, all six families have been avoiding the assistant's Masses, but one family took a chance last Saturday evening, and found him still doing things just as he was. Should we do something more? We don't want to get our pastor into trouble. He has been good, and his homilies show he really has faith. He supports the pope's teaching, and he encouraged our prayer group.

Analysis:

This question concerns the responsibilities to admonish those engaged in serious liturgical abuses and to petition authority for their correction. The group on whose behalf the questioner writes has taken appropriate action by communicating with the assistant himself and with the pastor. Another attempt to get the pastor to correct the abuses and bring about reconciliation in the parish seems warranted. Because the pastor apparently does not understand how important it is to abide by liturgical norms, an adequate response to the question must include a statement of the reasons why priests should not make even small unauthorized changes in the liturgy and why the assistant's serious aberrations should not be tolerated. Given the gravity of the latter, if the pastor does not put a stop to them, the bishop should be informed.

The reply could be along the following lines:

You are rightly concerned about the liturgies in your parish, and I think it was appropriate to discuss the problem with the new assistant and your pastor. That was much sounder than engaging in acrimonious debate, as some of your fellow parishioners have been doing, since arguments among parishioners cannot correct abuses by priests and tend to exacerbate the divisions such abuses inevitably generate.

As members of a parish, you have a special responsibility for its well-being. Serious liturgical abuses are not mere rule breaking; the Church has good reasons for her liturgical norms. Since the assistant's abuses continue and a further effort by you might lead to action that would put a stop to them and help restore harmony in the parish, I think you ought to communicate again with your pastor. He has the authority and the duty to deal with the problem, and the conflict it is generating probably will do more harm and be less likely to heal if he fails to act promptly and decisively.

If you have not already done so, I suggest you prepare a memorandum with a description—more detailed than you have given me—of the various things the assistant has been doing and a report of your conversation with him. Give this memorandum to the pastor when you meet with him. That document is likely to help him focus his attention on the problem, and he also may find it useful as a basis for discussion with the assistant and in presenting the problem to the bishop, if he sees fit to do that. Putting the matters that concern you in writing also will dispose you to be careful and precise, and will allow the assistant a fair opportunity to consider what you say about what he is doing and respond.

In reporting your conversation with the assistant, I think you should include his argument that most priests make unauthorized changes in the liturgy. I also think you should give your pastor reasons not only why the changes the assistant is making are intolerable but why it is wrong for priests intentionally to make any unauthorized liturgical changes whatsoever. This seems to me necessary for at least two reasons. First, since your pastor is a good priest, he almost certainly would not continue making unauthorized changes if he understood why he should not, and his amendment in this matter would be both desirable in itself and likely to increase his ability and readiness to deal with the assistant's aberrations. Second, in speaking with the assistant (and perhaps also with the bishop), the pastor needs to be in a position to present as full and effective a case as possible, which necessarily includes the reasons why even less serious unauthorized changes are to be excluded. At the same time, I do not think you need explicitly point out in your memorandum that the pastor himself makes unauthorized changes.

When you meet with the pastor, I suggest you first thank him for changing the recorded telephone message each week, so that people can find out which priest will be saying which Mass. But even though this information helps, you can point out that it does not solve the problem, because avoiding the assistant sometimes is inconvenient and because what he is doing is both serious in itself and a source of conflict among parishioners.

In discussing liturgical changes, it is important to maintain a clear distinction between unauthorized changes and those that have been authorized—for example, in the liturgical books or in the official instructions for their use. Instead of the former uniformity and rigid precision in the celebration of the liturgy, the Church has authorized a good deal of variety and flexibility, precisely to foster a genuinely communal celebration in which the faithful participate actively. Priests who use legitimate options in an effort to help the faithful understand the meaning of the sacred action and share in it should be commended. And most priests who adopt some of the more common and less significant unauthorized changes surely do so in a well-intentioned, though mistaken, effort to pursue more effectively the good purpose of the authorized changes.

It also is important to bear in mind that, in celebrating the liturgy, even the most conscientious priests sometimes become confused, make mistakes, or forget to say or do something. Emergencies and other special situations also can render it morally impossible to do and say everything precisely according to liturgical norms, so that in choosing to celebrate despite obstacles a priest may be compelled to proceed in ways that are not explicitly authorized. In such a case, however, the unauthorized changes are not intended to substitute for the liturgy authorized by the Church but rather to carry it out as well as possible under the circumstances.

Some argue that pastoral considerations can require changes to make the liturgy more spontaneous and friendly, so that the Eucharist really will be a joyful experience of celebration for the assembled community, not merely the cold and formal fulfillment of a duty. In reply, three things can be said. First, though a joyful experience of celebration is desirable, it is not essential to the fruitfulness of the Eucharist; the joy that is essential to it flows from charity—the fellowship of the Holy Spirit. The ritual kiss of peace, for instance, is meant to express the divine love that unites Jesus' disciples who abide in it, and not merely or even primarily to manifest human good will and feelings of affection, appropriate as they too are among fellow Christians. Second, provided those who participate wish to worship God appropriately, a well-planned liturgy can be a joyful experience without any unauthorized changes; important factors leading to a good experience are the reverence and sincerity of the celebrant and other ministers, a good homily, suitable music performed well, and the appropriate use of legitimate options. Third, even minor unauthorized changes distract and irritate many of the faithful, and serious aberrations can be very distressing, so that participation in the liturgy becomes for some a wretched experience.

There are many reasons why it is wrong for priests intentionally to make unauthorized liturgical changes. Two are especially important. First, such changes sometimes embody or imply deviations from Catholic faith; even when they do not, they often omit or obscure something of the liturgy's expression of faith. Thus, the Church teaches:

> The law of prayer is the law of faith: the Church believes as she prays. Liturgy is a constitutive element of the holy and living Tradition (cf. DV 8).
> For this reason no sacramental rite may be modified or manipulated at the will of the minister or the community. Even the supreme authority in the Church may

not change the liturgy arbitrarily, but only in the obedience of faith and with religious respect for the mystery of the liturgy. (*CCC*, 1124–25)

Second, in the Eucharist, a priest acts in the person of Christ, who joins humankind to the Father; but in making unauthorized changes, a priest obscures Jesus' action, focuses attention on himself, and becomes an obstacle to the relationship between God and his People that priests are ordained to serve. Imagine that a family's rich uncle, living abroad, promised them the gift of a new Rolls Royce and directed a local dealer to deliver it, but the dealer decided the family would do better with a Jaguar, and so delivered that instead. The family had no right to the gift of the Rolls, and might even be satisfied with the Jaguar. Still, the dealer has defrauded not only the uncle but the family, who should have received what they had been given. Priests are agents ordained to deliver God's gifts to his People. If they deliver some substitute for what Jesus has entrusted to them, they interpose themselves between—and defraud—both God and his People.

There are five additional reasons why unauthorized changes should not be made in the liturgy. First, the liturgy is the worship of the Church as a body, and those who are ordained act as Church officials in performing liturgical roles. So, insofar as a priest makes unauthorized changes, he misrepresents as the Church's what is in fact only his or some limited group's. Even if this misrepresentation deceives no one and is intended for some good end, it is at odds with the reverence necessary for true worship (see *LCL*, 145). Second, this essential irreverence and the obvious arbitrariness of intentional, unauthorized changes strongly suggest that the Eucharist is not sacred, and this suggestion tends to undermine not only faith in Jesus' bodily presence in the consecrated elements, but faith that the Eucharist is Jesus' sacrifice made present for the faithful to share in. Third, a priest who makes intentional, unauthorized changes acts with deplorable clericalism by imposing his personal preferences on the laity and violating the rights of those who quite reasonably wish only to participate in the Church's worship.[41] Fourth, intentionally making unauthorized changes sets a bad example of serious disobedience to the Church's norms, and this bad example is likely to encourage some people to think and do as they please not only in liturgical and canonical matters but in matters of faith and morals. Fifth, as has happened in your parish, unauthorized liturgical changes often become a needless, divisive issue for the faithful, thus impeding the charity that the Eucharist should express and foster.

Consequently, as the passage quoted from the *Catechism* makes clear, the Church's teaching absolutely excludes intentional, unauthorized changes in the liturgy. The Council of Trent solemnly taught: "If anyone shall say that the received and approved rites of the Catholic Church accustomed to be used in the solemn administration of the sacraments may be disdained or omitted by the minister without sin and at pleasure, or may be changed by any pastor of the churches to other new ones: let him be anathema" (DS 1613/856). Vatican II's teaching is no less clear. While some elements of the liturgy "can and even ought to vary in the course of time" (SC 21), only the pope and, as laws may determine, other bishops

---

41. See *CIC*, c. 214; *LCL*, 145 with n. 31.

and bodies of bishops may make such changes: "Therefore, absolutely no other person, not even a priest, may add, remove, or change anything in the liturgy on his own authority" (SC 22). In conformity with her teaching, the Church's law prescribes: "The liturgical books approved by the competent authority are to be faithfully observed in the celebration of the sacraments; therefore no one on personal authority may add, remove or change anything in them" (*CIC,* c. 846, §1).

Besides the preceding points, which you may wish to include in some form in your memorandum, there are some additional points that it may be helpful to have in mind.

The reasons why priests should not make unauthorized liturgical changes also make it clear, I believe, that a priest's intentionally doing so is of itself matter of grave sin. Of course, many changes are in themselves very minor, and a few perhaps even are real improvements. But though this kind of sin admits parvity, such small changes also are scandalous, not only because they give the faithful a bad example of disobedience but because they contribute to a clerical culture in which liturgical abuse is widely tolerated and sometimes even expected, so that some are encouraged to engage in far graver abuses. Now, even a sin venial in itself becomes grave scandal when one foresees that it is likely to lead others to commit grave sin; thus, the element of scandal makes grave matter of even minor liturgical abuses likely to encourage more serious abuses by other priests. (Due to widespread confusion and negligence of some bishops, many priests undoubtedly lack sufficient reflection regarding this sin.)

Someone might object that, if the preceding argument were sound, every white lie would become grave matter, since a culture in which lying is prevalent encourages perjury and other lying that is gravely wrong. However, individuals who lie in light matter usually have no reason to expect that their venial sin will lead others to commit grave sins of lying. Still, if one has reason in a particular situation to think a small lie is likely to be conducive to another's gravely sinful lie, then the small lie becomes grave matter. For example, parents who lie in light matter, foreseeing that their bad example will provide their children with a rationalization for lying in grave matter, commit grave scandal. Now, priests belong to a closely knit fraternity; and in presiding at the Eucharist they perform their most official and sacred acts, so that intentional, unauthorized changes by any priest—especially one generally faithful to the Church's teaching—are likely to encourage more serious abuses by others. Note that when you talked to the assistant, he defended his aberrations partly on the grounds that most priests make some liturgical changes.

A mere reenactment of a historical event—for example, the signing of an armistice on its anniversary—is a dramatization that imitates the event but lacks real continuity with it. In celebrating Mass, however, we are not merely imitating the words and deeds of Jesus and his companions at the Last Supper; in that sense, the Mass is not a reenactment. Rather, it is, as the assistant says, a memorial meal in which all Jesus' disciples should actively participate. But you were correct in pointing out that this memorial meal is a sacrifice. It is Jesus' unique sacrifice, made present through the ministry of ordained priests, so that Christians of all times and places can join him in offering it and themselves with him, and share in its benefits. Vatican II beautifully teaches:

> At the Last Supper, on the night when he was betrayed, our Savior instituted the eucharistic sacrifice of his body and blood. He did this in order to perpetuate the sacrifice of the cross throughout the centuries until he should come again, and so to entrust to his beloved Bride, the Church, a memorial of his death and resurrection: a sacrament of love, a sign of unity, a bond of charity, a paschal banquet in which Christ is eaten, the mind is filled with grace, and a pledge of future glory is given to us. (SC 47, notes omitted; cf. *CCC,* 1362–72)

Thus, in participating in the Mass, Catholics today share in the unique communion of the new covenant. Those at the Last Supper were the initial participants in it, and all who die in Christ will continue to participate in it forever.

In many ways, the assistant blurs and even implicitly denies the distinction between the ordained priesthood and the priesthood shared by all the baptized: by having a layperson read the gospel and give the homily, by asking the congregation to join in the words of consecration, by arranging the Communion as he does, and by minimizing his proper role, for example, using in a parish Sunday Mass with a majority of adults a very brief eucharistic prayer authorized only for use in Masses where the majority of participants are children.[42] By regularly omitting the Creed and encouraging everyone present to receive Communion, he suggests that faith and a clear conscience are not necessary to share fully in the Eucharist. While he seems to have evaded your question as to what he meant by "the idea of the Eucharist as magic," that phrase and his minimizing the distinction between the ordained priesthood and the priesthood of all the baptized suggest that he may not believe that the consecration, by the Holy Spirit's power, really transforms the bread and wine into Jesus' body and blood.

Given the assistant's attitude and state of mind, as manifested by the changes he makes and what he said to you, one reasonably wonders whether he shares the Catholic Church's faith regarding the Mass. Of course, the priest acts in the sacraments only as the human instrument of Jesus, who is the principal minister. So, even if a priest lacks faith, the Mass he offers is valid if he was validly ordained, says the words of consecration over appropriate matter, and intends to celebrate Mass—"to do what the Church does," as Trent puts it.[43] Probably the assistant does

42. See Sacred Congregation for Divine Worship, Decree *Postquam de Precibus* (1 Nov. 1974); Sacred Congregation for Sacraments and Divine Worship, Letter *Sacrum hoc Dicasterium* (10 Dec. 1977), in International Commission on English in the Liturgy, *Documents on the Liturgy, 1963–1979: Conciliar, Papal, and Curial Texts* (Collegeville, Minn.: Liturgical Press, 1982), 630, 635.

43. See DS 1611/854; cf 1262/672, 1312/695; cf. Bernard Leeming, S.J., *Principles of Sacramental Theology* (Westminster, Md.: Newman Press, 1956), 435–55. The required intention is minimal. For example, if a Catholic woman's newborn baby is in danger of death, a nonbelieving physician or nurse who thinks baptism is simply superstition but means to follow the mother's directions can validly baptize the child (see q. 4, above). A priest would not intend to do what the Church does if he performed the outward behavior while drugged or demented so that he did not know what he was doing, or while only acting the part of someone saying Mass, or while pretending to say Mass but deliberately meaning not to consecrate. But a

intend that, but like many well-meaning priests is deeply confused about both matters of faith and his own responsibilities.

Even if the assistant's grave aberrations do not deprive the faithful of a valid Eucharist, they certainly tend to undermine faith and divide the parish, according to whether individuals accept or reject the ideology presupposed by the aberrations. Even those happy with what he is doing are being injured and cheated. The pastor should not continue tolerating these abuses. If he cannot put a stop to them, he ought to take the matter up with the bishop or the vicar designated to deal with such matters. In talking with the pastor, however, do not threaten to take the matter to the bishop. Simply ask him to consider seeking the bishop's help, if necessary, to solve the problem posed by the assistant for the parish as a whole.

While I do not think you need mention to your pastor the unauthorized changes he himself makes, be prepared if he brings them up. His small changes obscure some important aspects of the reality of the Eucharist. Adding the words *here* and *now* at many points focuses on the visible assembly at the expense of its continuity with the Church in heaven, in purgatory, and spread throughout the world. Replacing "protect us from all anxiety" with "protect us from *useless worry*" obscures the prayer's reference to the Eucharist's fulfillment—for which "we wait in joyful hope," as the prayer goes on to say: a hope in relation to which useful worry is no more possible than are reasonable doubts against faith or justifiable hatred of a neighbor. "Happy are *we* who are called to *this* supper" transforms a beatitude for the communion of saints as a whole into a self-congratulatory exclamation for the present assembly. "*Receive* the body of Christ" does not involve any doctrinal error and probably is a well-intentioned attempt to call attention to Jesus' bodily presence in the consecrated host. But it inappropriately commands the faithful to do what they already wish to do and limits the meaning of "The body of Christ," so that the mind is arrested by the truth of faith rather than being led to hope for the heavenly communion the Eucharist anticipates.

If the pastor is unable or unwilling to put a stop to the assistant's aberrations and does not present the matter to the bishop, I think you ought to communicate directly with the bishop. You might write to him, as you have to me, on behalf of the six couples, and send him a memorandum describing what the assistant does, reporting your conversation with him, briefly reporting your conversations with your pastor, and offering, but not requesting, to come to his office to answer any further questions.

In this communication, avoid characterizing even the assistant's abuses as such; simply describe what he does and ask the bishop to evaluate it and do what he considers appropriate. In reporting your conversations with the pastor, I suggest that you summarize the case against unauthorized liturgical changes in general, but avoid mentioning the small changes the pastor makes and other criticism of him. I also suggest that you carefully describe the division developing in the parish and stress the need for prompt action to limit it and bring about reconciliation. It

---

priest who did not believe in transubstantiation would intend to do what the Church does if he meant to do whatever it is he thinks priests can do and usually do when they celebrate Mass.

probably would be good to ask some faithful and competent person to go over this letter with you before you send it, to identify and correct any mistakes or infelicities in wording that might distract the bishop.

If you write the bishop and he does not answer within a few months, or seems tolerant of the assistant's aberrations, or promises to take action but without effect, communicate with him persistently, and keep copies of the correspondence. If the problem remains unresolved after a year or so, send copies of everything to the Apostolic Nuncio, with a brief note respectfully requesting that the matter be looked into. Still, experience suggests that even doing that may not lead to action that ends the abuses.

While the assistant's aberrations continue, take no part in any liturgy he conducts, in order to avoid injury to yourselves and your children. I do not think you have an obligation publicly to warn others to avoid participation, since that probably would have both bad and good effects. But when occasion offers—for instance, if other parishioners ask—I think you should quietly explain why you avoid the assistant's liturgies.

Do not be hostile toward the assistant or anyone else involved. The young priest probably picked up his strange ideas from others who should have known better; he may well have been badly trained in the seminary. Bear in mind that we cannot read others' inmost hearts, and pray that God will preserve in his grace those who are living in it, move anyone not living in it to repent, and help everyone concerned to recall and faithfully carry out his or her vocation. While avoiding the assistant's liturgies, continue to participate fully in everything sound in your parish and support it.

Be careful not to foster alienation from the Church herself or disrespect for legitimate pastoral authority. Pray regularly for the Church, not least that the authentic liturgical renewal she has authorized will be realized rather than frustrated by resistance and abuses. Remember, too, that priests need the support of lay people through prayer and other means, not least words of gratitude and encouragement. No matter how some priests abuse their role, their ministry is essential. Contrary to the suggestion implicit in the assistant's abuses, ordained priests alone, acting in the person of Christ, can make Jesus' sacrifice available so that all can share in it and be bodily united with him.[44]

---

44. One of the most important documents about abuses in the Mass and in eucharistic worship outside Mass: Congregation for the Sacraments and Divine Worship, *Inaestimabile donum* (3 Apr. 1980), *AAS* 72 (1980) 331–43, Flannery, 2:93–102. For many other Church documents that authorize and limit variations in the liturgy see *Documents on the Liturgy, 1963–1979*. For a clear explanation of how a priest ought to celebrate the Eucharist: Peter J. Elliott, *Ceremonies of the Modern Roman Rite: The Eucharist and the Liturgy of the Hours* (San Francisco: Ignatius Press, 1995). In responding to questions like this one, I avoid discussion of whether all the authorized liturgical changes have been sound and prudently made. Most discussions of that question are, in my judgment, neither theologically sound nor helpful to the faithful. But the question is legitimately discussable, and for those interested I recommend: Aidan Nichols, O.P., *Looking at the Liturgy: A Critical View of Its Contemporary Form* (San Francisco: Ignatius Press, 1996). Though not Nichols's purpose, his book also supports the case made here against unauthorized changes.

12: May a Catholic family whose parish is bad join a Greek Orthodox parish?

My wife and I are what most people call conservative Catholics. Both of us were born in 1961 and grew up in Philadelphia during the years after Vatican II. Our parents and teachers were enthusiastic about the changes that began with the Council, especially the new liturgy. But both her folks and mine always followed the Church's teaching about marriage and the family. They regarded the permissiveness of the 1960s and '70s as a plague to be resisted and tried to bring up their children as if the sexual revolution had never occurred. In short, we are conservative Catholics in the sense that we think what the pope says is right, but not like those people who seem unhappy even with many of the changes the popes have approved.

After we completed our education, we married and moved to this small city. We have three children: Mary Pat, in third grade; George, ready for kindergarten; and Betty, just two. In general, we have done well here and are very happy, but there is one big problem. Our local parish, the only Catholic church here, has gone downhill since we arrived. When the old pastor died five years ago and the new priest came, he began making changes. Right from the start he has done a number of very strange things.

He often substitutes readings from contemporary sources for the epistles and gospels, and his homilies often include ideas at odds with what we know is the Church's teaching. He never hears confessions but occasionally has a penance service at which he gives absolution to everyone at the same time. When Mary Pat was preparing for first Communion and the religious education teacher did nothing to prepare her for confession, we did it ourselves and asked Father to hear her confession. He refused, saying children her age cannot commit sins, and confession is not necessary anyway, because God forgives sins as soon as a person feels sorry. Shortly after he came, he set up a liturgy committee. With its support, he began giving us hosts that seem more like cookies, and made various other changes, including a lot of little things, such as saying "The Lord is with us" instead of "The Lord be with you," but also more important changes. For instance, at the consecration, instead of saying, "this is my body" and "this is the cup of my blood" he sometimes said, "this is the sacrament of my body" and "this is the sacrament of my blood."

When the new pastor set up a pre-Cana program and asked for volunteers, we volunteered and tried to work with him on it. It was difficult. The first few meetings seemed to both my wife and me to be missing a lot about marriage, since he said nothing about its being indissoluble or being a sacrament. But things really went bad when he got to sex. The material he provided described all sorts of ways of trying to make it more enjoyable and then went on to discuss all the methods of contraception, including sterilization, and the pros and cons of each. "Rhythm" was treated along with the rest, as a way of preventing conception by limiting intercourse to infertile periods, but there was no information about how to identify those periods. The pastor said that, while the Church's official teaching frowns on all the other methods, most couples need a more reliable method and find the abstinence required by rhythm too frustrating, so they exercise their right to follow their own consciences and choose some other method. After that class, we had a long talk with Father, which ended in a shouting match between him and me, with my wife standing by and crying.

That was all bad enough but then we had the trouble about Mary Pat's preparation for first Communion, and a number of similar problems with the religious education teacher. Neighbors of ours with children in the higher grades also had problems. Around Easter, the teacher told the children in one class that it did not really matter if Jesus' remains were still in a grave somewhere in Israel. The same teacher's sex education classes upset a good many parents, because she clearly told the children that masturbation, premarital sex, and homosexual behavior "generally are no big deal" (that is, usually should not be regarded as seriously wrong).

We and those other parents have tried to discuss these problems with the pastor and the religious education teacher. We tried not once or a few times, but many times over the past five years. We always have been told something like: "I am the pastor, and it is up to me to decide about these things. I am sorry that I cannot please everybody. You are just too conservative." Or: "I am in charge of religious education, and have a master's degree in it. The program here follows the latest and best approaches. You should not try to interfere by telling your children something different from what I am teaching them." The pastor and teacher always support each other.

As a result of these rebuffs, most people, some more or less willingly and others reluctantly, gave up and went along with the pastor, though a few apparently gave up on the Church altogether. We and a few other couples wrote to the bishop and finally had a meeting with him. On the whole, he did not seem surprised by the things we complained of and did not deny they had been going on, though he did say he found it hard to believe Father was changing the words of the consecration. He would not discuss whether any of the other things was a serious abuse, but only said it was not our place to pass judgment. He talked about the shortage of priests and the difficulty he has in trying to care for so many parishes. He said there are too many divisions among Catholics and the most important thing we need to keep in mind is to be charitable and not divisive. When we kept pressing him, he became irritated and told us it was time to go, but as we were leaving he apologized and promised to talk with the pastor. That was well over a year ago, and, apart from the fact that the pastor no longer changes the words of consecration, nothing has changed for the better. Six months after seeing the bishop, we wrote a letter to the Apostolic Nuncio in Washington, telling him everything that had happened. We got an acknowledgment, but that was all.

If there were another, good Catholic parish nearby, we would go there instead. But the nearest place is thirty miles away, and it seems to share some of the same problems, though the priest uses regular hosts for Communion and also will hear confessions when asked. There is a better parish, a little over fifty miles away. Right here in town, though, there is a small Greek Orthodox parish. Out of curiosity, we went there and found that the liturgy, which they also do in English, is very much like ours, except that it is carried out with great devotion. The people chant much of the Mass and the pastor gives excellent homilies. They also have religious education for their children. We looked into the materials, and they seem very sound. In fact, some are published by Catholic publishers. Talking to the priest about the problems at our church, he told us we would be welcome to come to Mass and Communion there.

We know the Greek Orthodox Church is not yet in full union with the pope. But we were told when we were studying Vatican II that Catholics sometimes may participate in its worship. Would it be all right for us to join the Orthodox parish and send our children there for religious education?

Analysis:

The first question is whether Catholics whose parish no longer provides essential services may join a Greek Orthodox parish. The answer is no. To join that parish would be to separate themselves from the Catholic Church. The next question is: What should these Catholics do? They should either move elsewhere or travel as often as possible to a Catholic parish where the sacraments are both available and celebrated properly, and they should obtain or themselves provide sound religious instruction for their children. Still, under specified conditions, Catholics may participate in the liturgy at an Orthodox church, receive holy Communion at such a liturgy, and receive the sacraments of penance and anointing from an Orthodox priest.

The reply could be along the following lines:

The many abuses you describe gravely violate the rights of the faithful. I sympathize with you for all you have suffered and commend you for the way you have tried to deal with the situation. But even though your motives for wishing to join the Greek Orthodox parish are good, you ought not to do it.

While the Orthodox churches are not completely separated from the Catholic Church and in most ways remain united with her in belief and practice, the bishops of the Orthodox churches are not in communion with the pope and they do not agree with certain essential Catholic teachings. To join the Orthodox parish would be to commit yourself to that church's division from the pope and the bishops in communion with him; it also would be to embrace its distinctive teachings and reject the authority of the ecumenical councils, including Vatican II, in which the Orthodox did not participate. You may not do that. The pope is the principle of union with Jesus and among the members of his body, the Church, because the pope is the successor of Peter, appointed for just this reason. Moreover, as faithful Catholics, you believe what the Catholic Church believes, and not even the least central of her beliefs can be given up without giving up Catholic faith itself (see q. 2, above). When bad conditions in the Church cause problems for faithful Catholics, they must remain faithful, for they cannot abandon communion with the pope or any truth of Catholic faith to solve their problems.

How then should you proceed to fulfill, as best you can, your responsibilities to participate in the life of the Church and to hand on your faith to your children?

Assuming all you have said about your parish is true, I do not think you should participate in it. The sacraments certainly are not being celebrated properly—and perhaps not even validly. Moreover, the so-called religious education is far more likely to hurt your children than help them. As things are, you have no obligation to support the parish. Of course, if a couple wish to marry, they must go to the bishop of the diocese or the pastor of a parish in which one of the parties (or, in a mixed marriage, the Catholic party) lives (see *CIC,* c. 1108, §1). But apart from marriages and a possible duty to help others deal with the problems your parish presents, you and other faithful Catholics in the parish may proceed in your religious activities and the formation of your children much as you would if the parish were not there, unless and until it is straightened out.

You might consider moving to a place where it would be possible for you to fulfill your religious responsibilities fully and easily. That probably would require considerable sacrifices, but you should be ready to sacrifice for this purpose. At the same time, you should take into account that moving where the situation seems more favorable may not permanently solve your problem, since the pastor there could be replaced and that parish could deteriorate just as your present parish has. Moreover, you should not overlook the service you may be able to perform by helping others cope with the bad situation where you are.

If you judge that you cannot or should not move, receiving the sacraments remains very important. Making a sixty-mile or one-hundred-mile round trip at least on Sundays may be a hardship, but many people regularly travel that far for less important purposes and, considering what is at stake, you should make the trip as often as you can. When you cannot, though you must not join the Orthodox church, you may participate in its eucharistic liturgy on Sundays or holydays of obligation so as not to miss Mass (see *LCL,* 157). What about holy Communion and the sacrament of penance? Since the Orthodox priest agrees, you may on occasion receive if you otherwise would be deprived of Communion for what you judge too long a time; if truly necessary, you also may receive the sacraments of penance and anointing from the Orthodox priest (see *CIC,* c. 844, §2). Still, you must be on guard against the temptation to embrace Orthodoxy and be unfaithful to the Catholic Church.

You and others who are aware of the grave problems with your parish should work together to form a Catholic community in your area. Do not organize it in competition with the parish, but simply as a help to the prayer life of the families involved and to the religious formation of their children. Meet regularly to read passages from Scripture and discuss them. Pray together. The rosary and other prayers accessible to children are appropriate for families and groups including young children. Praying the Liturgy of the Hours requires neither a cleric to lead nor the bishop's permission; you should consider doing this when possible, especially as community prayer for adults and older children (see *CMP,* 799–800).

If you sent your children to the Orthodox parish for religious education, they would be formed as Orthodox Christians, and you would be cooperating with the defects as well as with the values of that formation. Therefore, you and other Catholic parents should, if possible, obtain sound religious education for your children at one of the parishes you mention. If necessary, you should set up your own religious education program for your children, making sure it is well organized and dividing the work. Doing this with adequate care may require much time and effort, but you should be ready to make considerable sacrifices for the religious formation of your children, since it is both very important and your primary responsibility. You should be careful to use only sound materials; those doing the teaching should use the *Catechism of the Catholic Church* as a resource for themselves.

When the pastor realizes what you and others are doing, he very likely will accuse the group of being divisive and perhaps even claim it is schismatic. Having taken care to provide no basis for such charges, do not be intimidated by them. You and the others should avoid falling into negativism and bitterness. Do not attack the local pastor or the bishop, and pray for them. Pray, too, for changes for the better in both the parish and the diocese, and be ready to resume normal participation in the parish if that becomes appropriate.

Keep the faith and spread it. Catholic lay people lacking the services of priests have done this before, sometimes over many decades. In 1783, a Korean went to China on business and was baptized a Catholic; he returned home and spread the faith. A Chinese Catholic priest who slipped into Korea in 1794 found four thousand Catholics—and none of them had ever even seen a priest! During its entire first century, the Catholic community in Korea was persecuted severely and had few priests, yet it survived and grew. Though we have not yet experienced the hardships those Catholics suffered, we should pray for the light and strength to imitate them.[45]

13: How should one help a housebound neighbor seemingly neglected by the priest?

We live in a four-unit tenement. The neighbors across the hall, John and Mary, are an elderly couple. Mary is not a Catholic, but John is. He has emphysema and is on oxygen; for over a year he has not been doing well and has hardly been able to venture outside. Mary is strong and capable, and she takes good care of him. My husband and I and the people downstairs have helped out when we can, especially with shopping and getting John to the doctor's office.

The priest at our parish knows about John and has come to see him, but not often. He used to come more frequently, but has not been here now for almost two months. Yesterday, after I helped Mary with their shopping, she and John and I were talking about this. He would like to get to Mass on Sundays, but just cannot do it, and he wants to receive Communion more often. Mary is angry, because she feels the priest is neglecting John because she is not a Catholic and he never contributed much to the Church.

I do not know whether that is why the priest has not been coming. But I do think something should be done about this situation. What is the right thing to do?

45. See *New Catholic Encyclopedia,* 8:254–55. Today, in many nations where the Church has been long established, many Catholic families face problems similar to those described in this question, though usually less serious. Not all the advice offered in this response will apply to them. In many cases, however, they will be justified in looking for and joining a sound Catholic parish, especially when doing so is necessary for the religious formation of their children.

Analysis:

The question is how to help a housebound neighbor obtain needed pastoral service. The questioner should talk with the pastor about the neighbor's need, and also should do what she can to help meet it. If the pastor cannot or will not meet the neighbor's needs, the questioner should ask other priests in the area to do so and, if necessary, inform the bishop of the situation.

The reply could be along the following lines:

You do well to take an interest in John. All of us should be concerned about one another's unmet needs, and Christian love certainly requires special concern about our neighbors' spiritual needs. As a Catholic, John should receive the sacraments regularly, and it is good that you are looking for some way to help him obtain pastoral service.

I think it unlikely that the things Mary mentioned would lead any priest to neglect a parishioner, and there may be a good reason in this case why the priest cannot provide better service. He too may be unwell, or perhaps he has other problems not obvious to you. Also, with the number of priests declining, some simply cannot meet all their parishioners' needs.

The first thing to do is make an appointment to see the priest. When you see him, do not ask why he has not visited John for almost two months. Instead, begin by telling him gently and encouragingly about John's need and desire for more frequent pastoral visits. In explaining the situation, you should mention Mary's suspicions while being careful not to endorse them. You might introduce this element of the story by saying: "You probably should know, too, that John's wife, Mary, who is not a Catholic, is upset about this and imagines that . . .."

You may be able to help the priest meet John's needs and, perhaps, those of one or more other housebound persons living in your neighborhood. A lay person can serve as an extraordinary minister of the Eucharist, and the Church has a ceremony, which you could carry out, for Communion outside Mass.[46] So, unless you have some reason for not doing so, you should tell the priest you are willing to help in this way if he will obtain the necessary authorization and teach you how. If the priest accepts your offer, on Sundays and/or certain weekdays he will give you a consecrated host for John and, perhaps, one or more other housebound persons. I suggest that, before talking with the priest, you have in mind whether and to what extent you will be able to serve others, and how often you will be able to provide this service. Though visiting the sick for a longer time often would be desirable, carefully carrying out the ceremony and visiting briefly will require less than one-half hour per person. If, as appears to be the case, your parish has not organized this ministry to its housebound members, you also might consider offering to help organize it.

If your offer to serve John's need is accepted and you begin to act as a eucharistic minister, prepare well and avoid hurrying through the shortest form of the rite. Instead, provide a richer service for a recipient who welcomes it, and, in any case,

---

46. See *The Rites,* 459–83.

carry out the ceremony each time as devoutly as you can. Our Lord deserves no less, and your effort not only will help dispose those to whom you bring him to receive him well but will benefit you by nurturing your faith, hope, and love. If you have the opportunity, share your faith in the Eucharist with Mary by answering any questions she asks about the ceremony. If she is a Christian, you might invite her to participate by reading a passage from the Bible and joining in the Our Father—and, perhaps, also in an opening and/or closing hymn.

Even if you help in this way, however, John should see a priest from time to time to receive the sacraments of penance and anointing of the sick (see Jas 5.14–15; CCC, 1499–1523). If possible, he also should participate in Mass at least occasionally. Since you and the people downstairs can help get him to the doctor's office when necessary, perhaps you could get him to church now and then, if not on Sunday, then some other day, when the liturgy would not be too long. The priest could hear John's confession, and at suitable intervals, anoint him before or after Mass. Perhaps, too, you could get a priest to stop by occasionally at John's apartment on a weekday to hear his confession and say a Mass in which you and other neighbors could participate.

Even if John always has been derelict in his duty to support the Church, he ought to receive the Church's service. That service is needed as a means of receiving God's saving grace, to which none of us is entitled. So, even if those who shirk their duty are not entitled to the Church's service, we are no more entitled to grace than they are. Like the rest of us, priests desire and receive unmerited grace. Mercy received demands that mercy be given. So, priests, like other Christians, owe others undeserved service when it is needed.[47]

Therefore, I expect the parish priest will appreciate your concern about John, accept your offer of help, and do what he can to meet John's spiritual needs. But what if he is unresponsive or simply cannot provide adequate service? In that event, talk with priests in adjacent parishes or in nearby houses of religious orders, since any Catholic priest able and willing to visit John can provide pastoral care for him. If necessary, write to the bishop of the diocese and explain the problem. Also, if ever a Catholic priest in good standing were unavailable and John were in danger of death, he could be absolved by a Catholic priest who had left the priesthood—even if he did not obtain permission to do so (see CIC, c. 976)—and could receive not only absolution but anointing and Viaticum from a priest of an Orthodox church (see CIC, c. 844, §2).

One final point. Not now, but once John's spiritual needs are being met, perhaps you should speak gently to him about the fact that, as Mary reports, he never contributed much to his Church. He may have had good reasons, either because this family always has been poor or because Mary, not being Catholic, resented such expenditures and put pressure on him to limit his contributions. But if he could have given more yet failed to do his fair share, he owes restitution to any parish and diocese in which he has lived (see LCL, 444–58). Of course, his obligation to

---

47. CIC, c. 843, §1: "The sacred ministers cannot refuse the sacraments to those who ask for them at appropriate times, are properly disposed and are not prohibited by law from receiving them."

make this restitution or any other he might owe would be limited by his present ability. Still, if restitution would be appropriate and he cannot pay, he should pray for those to whom he was unfair and offer his sufferings for them.

14: Must a family participate in a parish tithing program?

Our parish has an elected finance council that advises the pastor about money matters and puts out regular reports, which are included in the Sunday bulletin. With the pastor's approval, the council is now setting up a parish tithing program, to go into effect the first of the year. The first step is for every family to sign a pledge to contribute ten percent of its take-home pay. The idea is that this would replace and supplement all other donations currently being made to the Church and various charities. Half the money paid as tithes will stay in the parish—paying off the debt, supporting the clergy, covering all the other usual parish expenses, subsidizing our grade school, and helping needy people in the parish. The other half will go outside the parish, partly as our contribution to the diocesan Catholic charities campaign and other special collections authorized by the bishop, and partly as donations by the parish to various charities and missionary activities selected by the parish finance council.

The literature the council has distributed in support of the tithing program offers three closely related arguments for signing up. First, it says the Council of Trent taught that "the payment of tithes is due to God" and cited several passages from Scripture to prove it, so that even though the Church's law no longer explicitly requires tithing, it remains obligatory for those who can. Second, the literature quotes the Church's current law (*CIC*, c. 222):

§1. The Christian faithful are obliged to assist with the needs of the Church so that the Church has what is necessary for divine worship, for apostolic works and works of charity and for the decent sustenance of ministers.
§2. They are also obliged to promote social justice and, mindful of the precept of the Lord, to assist the poor from their own resources.

The argument is that tithing best fulfills these obligations. The third argument is that most Catholics who do not tithe fail to donate as much as they should to the Church and to charity. People in Old Testament times and Catholics in times past, many quite poor by our standards, tithed. Many non-Catholics today tithe, and giving by Protestants on the average exceeds Catholic giving.

Must we sign up for the tithing program?

Analysis:

This question concerns the obligation to contribute to the support of the Church and the needs of the poor. The Church's law does not specify how much Catholics should contribute. Thus, though each family should contribute its fair share to the parish in which it participates and the diocese, and also should help the poor in other ways, these obligations must be specified by the family's own conscientious judgments, taking all relevant considerations into account. Therefore, the questioner need not sign up for the tithing program.

The reply could be along the following lines:

Tithe in a narrow sense, in accord with the word's etymology, meant a tax of ten percent, but it came to be used in a broader sense to refer to any legally required payment for the support of the Church. Tithes in Old Testament law—which applied only to the produce of farming and cattle breeding—were a tax on the people of ancient Israel.[48] But, like many other elements of the old law that are not doctrinal or moral truths, the tithing laws were abrogated by Jesus' new law, as St. Thomas points out (*S.t.,* 2–2, q. 87, a. 1). The requirement of tithing was not reinstated by the early Church; but later, when laws were enacted requiring payments to support the Church, those payments were called "tithes." Today, neither the law of the universal Church nor the particular law of the Church in the United States specifies how much is to be paid. The responsibility to support the Church thus must be fulfilled according to the conscientious judgment of the faithful, taking into account all their resources and their other genuine needs.[49]

The "tithing" program your parish finance council has adopted is an attempt to specify for members of your parish, as ten percent of take-home pay, their duty to support the Church and contribute to charity. Since parishioners cannot be compelled to participate, you are being asked to sign a pledge. You rightly ask about your moral responsibility in the matter.

The Council of Trent does say: "the payment of tithes is due to God."[50] But what did the Council mean by *tithes?* The answer is found in the conclusion Trent draws: "The holy council therefore orders all, of whatever rank and condition they may be, who are concerned with the payment of tithes, to pay henceforth those to which they are *bound in law"* (emphasis added); it then backs up this order with the penalty of excommunication. Plainly, Trent was legislating to enforce the Church taxes exacted by law at that time; the Council was not teaching that all the faithful ought to contribute ten percent of their take-home pay.

What about the Scripture passages Trent cites? Inasmuch as such legal requirements of the Old Testament are not binding on Christians, those passages do not show that Christians ought to contribute a specific amount, and the Council of Trent should not be interpreted as having made so unsound an argument. Rather, the Council should be understood as using those passages to show precisely what they can prove that is relevant to the decree's purpose: God has made known to his People that they ought to pay the taxes required by just laws for Church support—something true not only in Old Testament times but forever.

The current law of the Church (*CIC,* c. 222), which the literature quotes, does point out and confirm real obligations, but does not specify how much each family must contribute.

48. See Robert A. Oden, Jr., "Taxation in Biblical Israel," *Journal of Religious Ethics,* 12 (1984): 170–71.

49. See *LCL,* 169–70, 173, 801. On the complex history of Catholic Church financial support, see Robert L. Kealy, *Diocesan Financial Support: Its History and Canonical Status* (Rome: Pontificia Universitas Gregoriana Facultas Iuris Canonici, 1986).

50. Council of Trent, session 25, *Decree on General Reform,* chap. 12, in *Decrees of the Ecumenical Councils,* vol. 2, *Trent to Vatican II,* ed. Norman P. Tanner, S.J., (London and Washington, D.C.: Sheed and Ward, and Georgetown University Press, 1990), 792.

You certainly ought to contribute to the parish in which you participate a fair share of its budget for the items listed in the first section of the canon you quote. The amount contributed should reflect not only the parish's needs and the number of parishioners but your other responsibilities, other donations, and comparative wealth, since it is fair that wealthier parishioners, other things being equal, contribute considerably more than poorer ones, and those with few other responsibilities and few or no other channels of charitable giving, other things being equal, contribute more than others. People who accept a parish's service but contribute nothing or significantly less than their fair share are guilty of grave injustice. Similarly, people should contribute enough to cover their fair share of their diocese's needs.

Some people who fail or refuse to make fair contributions to their parish and/or diocese rationalize their injustice—for example, by alleging that the Church is a patriarchal institution that deserves no support until she reforms herself, or by pointing to various abuses in the Church, tolerated or committed by priests or even by bishops, as if these wrongs justified cheating fellow Catholics who suffer the same abuses.

You also should assist the poor, as the second section of the canon prescribes. However, the canon does not say you should do this by contributing to your diocese and the parish you participate in more than your fair share of their budgets, which also include something for the poor. You might fulfill this further responsibility to the poor by directly meeting the needs of people you know, contributing to various suitable Catholic organizations, and/or in other ways. Your identification of appropriate beneficiaries should take into account your own gifts and prior commitments (see q. 5, above). Insofar as the proposed tithing program would include collecting and disbursing all the funds that most parishioners will use "to assist the poor from their own resources," the parish finance council seems to be trying to usurp parishioners' responsibility to identify appropriate beneficiaries.

Given these clarifications, it is easy to see the unsoundness of the argument that participating in the proposed tithing program will best fulfill the responsibilities indicated by canon law. In the first place, in some cases people ought to use more than ten percent of their take-home pay to meet the canonically specified responsibilities, especially the responsibility to assist the poor. That is true not only of the very wealthy but even of many less affluent people, at stages in their lives when financial resources significantly exceed current and reasonably predictable needs. In the second place, in some cases the demand for ten percent of a family's take-home pay is excessive. Less affluent individuals' and families' fair shares of the parish and diocesan budgets, other things being equal, plainly will not be the same proportion of take-home pay as those of more affluent individuals and families. Then too, the taxes levied by various governments already include a significant transfer of resources to the poor, and many people, at least at some stages in their lives, can afford little or no more. Consequently, the proposed tithing program, especially in being presented as obligatory for everyone, plainly is an imprudent, legalistic attempt to specify a moral responsibility wisely left to the faithful's conscientious judgment by canon law.[51]

The third argument proposed in the literature distributed by the finance council also is unsound. The claim that most Catholics who do not tithe fail to give what they should may be correct, but I do not know how that could be proved. Certainly, giving by Protestants cannot be presumed to be the proper measure of Catholics' duty.[52] More important, even if the claim is granted, the fact that many people who do not tithe fail to fulfill their responsibilities to donate to the Church and assist the poor while most people who tithe do fulfill those responsibilities is not an argument for tithing. Many people who do not tithe probably also fulfill their responsibilities, a few by giving more than ten percent of their after-tax income, many by giving less. Moreover, some people who tithe very likely do not fulfill their responsibilities—some because they should do more, others because part of the money for tithing should be used in fulfilling other, more exigent responsibilities.

In sum, it seems to me that the parish finance council and the pastor are making serious mistakes in setting up the tithing program. The program pressures some to contribute more than they should, and these people are being defrauded in the name of God by being told his law requires them to tithe. At the same time, the program falsely reassures others, who should contribute more than ten percent of take-home pay, that they are doing enough. The tithing program, in reality, is no different from any other inappropriate standard that might be set for meeting a common obligation that ought to be specified by each family's or individual's conscientious judgment.

Despite its essential defect, however, the tithing program would remind parishioners of their financial obligations, too often neglected, toward the Church and the poor. Moreover, it includes features that might well be beneficial, in particular the serious effort to elicit the cooperation of all parishioners and the replacement of other parish collections and fund-raising efforts by one regular payment of a pledged amount. Consequently, I do not suggest you reject everything about the proposed program. Instead, I recommend that you urge your pastor and the parish finance council to amend the proposal by eliminating the claim that donating ten percent of one's income is obligatory and by forgoing any other attempt to specify the proportion of income parishioners should contribute, and instead asking each family or individual to judge conscientiously what percentage of income to pledge.[53]

51. In the early Church, with no law of tithe or taxation, Christians recognized a great moral obligation of sacrificial giving; see Kealy, op. cit., 6–50.

52. See John L. Ronsvalle and Sylvia Ronsvalle, *The State of Church Giving through 1993* (Champaign, Ill.: Empty Tomb, 1995), 59–78, for a discussion of Catholic giving patterns, in the context of a study of giving by members of various Christian denominations in the United States. A complex set of factors must be taken into account in any attempt to explain the differences; see Dean R. Hoge and Fenggang Yang, "Determinants of Religious Giving in American Denominations: Data from Two Nationwide Surveys," *Review of Religious Research,* 36 (1994–95): 123–48.

53. Virginia Ann Hodgkinson and Murray S. Weitzman, *The Charitable Behavior of Americans,* a national survey conducted by Yankelovich, Skelly and White, Inc. (Washington, D.C.: Independent Sector, 1986), 33–34, show that donors to churches and synagogues who pledge a fixed amount give almost twice as much as those who do not, and donors who pledge a percentage of income donate almost three times as much as those who do not pledge at all.

Of course, the pastor and finance council also should make a serious effort to educate all members of the parish about their financial responsibilities toward the Church and the poor, thus helping them to form their consciences rightly in this important matter (see *LCL,* 169–70, 173, 780–82, 789–92, 800–806, 811–14). Moreover, it would be appropriate for the council to gather and make available to all parishioners information that would help each family judge how much to pledge—the parish's budget and amount of diocesan assessments, the number of families in the parish, their approximate average net take-home pay, and so on—and to point out the probable implications of this information for a sound judgment by an average family in the parish.

15: Must a businesswoman do voluntary parish work?

Our parish is trying to set up a day care program, a service some parishioners not only want but badly need since for many the alternatives are unsatisfactory—the better day care programs charge a great deal, while the poorer ones are wretched. Individuals who provide day care in their homes are not monitored, and they sometimes mistreat or neglect the children. Seldom does any day care operation provide the attention and affection children need. A committee set up by the pastor has worked out a plan to offer the best possible care at a reasonable cost by using parish facilities and employing a small, full-time staff of well-qualified people assisted by many volunteers.

The plan's success depends on getting good volunteers from the parish who will do their work just as dependably as if they were being paid. The pool of people free to help out is limited, and, despite the fact that I operate a catering business that takes a good deal of my time, the pastor is pressing me to commit myself to a full day each week. When he talked with me and I demurred, he asked how I managed when my own children, now grown, were younger. I told him I used various kinds of day care over the years, and none was entirely satisfactory. He then asked whether I would not have been glad to use a service like that planned for the parish, and I admitted that I would have been glad if a good program like that had been available. He then said: "Well, you surely can afford to give one day a week, and our Lord taught, 'Do to others as you would have them do to you,' so you ought to volunteer!" I said an obligation to volunteer doesn't make much sense to me, and he replied: "Then consider yourself drafted! Seriously, you do have a real obligation to help with this." I said I would think about it.

As far as the money is concerned, the pastor is right—I could afford to give one day a week. My husband has a good job, we have a beautiful home and no debts, and we could live quite comfortably on his salary alone, now that our children have finished college, without the income I derive from the catering business. Yet I am reluctant to volunteer because it would be burdensome and would interfere with my work.

The business has been very successful. While my work is heaviest on weekends, I normally have some things to do every weekday and seldom take a full day off, except when I close down for vacation. I employ two full-time people and about twenty more on weekends, and we give such good service that we never need to advertise, since we get plenty of business by word-of-mouth referrals and are booked up well in advance. Contributing a day every week to the parish, I would have to cut back somewhat on the jobs we accept while still having to work harder on the other weekdays than I do now. In short, while I could afford the money, I don't feel I can afford the time and energy to volunteer. Besides, I enjoy my work and find it fulfilling. I could do the day care work, but caring for other people's children is outside my field, and I am not enthusiastic about the idea.

Do you think I have an obligation to volunteer? Will I be violating the Golden Rule if I don't?

Analysis:

This question concerns the application of the Golden Rule. The pastor's use of it is not sound. The questioner's capacities for service and existing responsibilities might differ significantly from those of persons who would have appropriately volunteered for the day care program of which she would have wished to take advantage. The questioner does have an obligation as a parish member to make an appropriate contribution to its good projects. But it is for her to discern how to fulfill this obligation. As aids to discernment, the response might well include discussion of considerations for and against volunteering service outside one's field.

The reply could be along the following lines:

If you do not volunteer for the day care program, I doubt that you will be violating the Golden Rule. The fact that you would have been happy to take advantage of a program of day care to which others volunteered their services does not by itself imply that you have an obligation to volunteer your service to the program planned at your parish. The Golden Rule requires only that in our behavior toward others we follow the same sound principles and norms we apply when making claims for ourselves and those near and dear to us. One may not change one's standards or ignore some of them when they happen to be inconvenient. However, in applying the Golden Rule, differences between individuals' capacities to serve and existing responsibilities cannot be ignored.

It follows that, where there is no reason rooted in an intelligible human good to prefer one person to another and we are consulting our feelings regarding various goods and bads, the Golden Rule requires that we set aside the differences in our feelings toward different persons. One may not adjust one's estimate of the magnitude of burdens and benefits according to who happens to be suffering or enjoying them, unless some *reason* distinguishes one person from another, and not merely the fact that *this* person is myself or someone near and dear while *that* person is someone I am indifferent to or dislike. But the Golden Rule does not require us to ignore reasons that affect the significance of a burden or benefit for different persons.

In considering whether to volunteer for the day care program, then, you can legitimately take into account the fact that it would interfere with your work—which benefits not only you but many others—and so perhaps judge it better not to volunteer. And without any inconsistency, you can think at the same time that it would have been appropriate for others, with more energy and free time, to have volunteered for a similar program of which you would have taken advantage. Moreover, even now, you can judge without inconsistency that it would be appropriate for others to volunteer while you do not.

Still, like every other member of the parish, you do have an obligation to help meet its needs insofar as you reasonably can. These needs include all it requires for the success of its legitimate and worthwhile projects. On this basis, perhaps some members of the parish ought, morally speaking, to volunteer their service in the day care program, and you could be among them.[54] However, since the moral responsibility to help meet the parish's needs is limited by each parishioner's resources and other responsibilities, no law or pastoral precept can reasonably determine what this duty requires in each particular case. Each parishioner must conscientiously judge what his or her appropriate contribution is, and this judgment will specify the individual's moral responsibility. Therefore, you need to stir up your sentiments of love for Christ and his Church, and consider the value of the proposed day care program, what will be required for its success, your own limitations and resources, and your other responsibilities, including those pertaining to your business. Having done all this, you must discern what would be a suitable contribution for you to make (see *LCL*, 291–93).

In his eagerness to promote this worthwhile project, your pastor seems to be trying to do your discerning for you. While you certainly should submit to his decisions within his proper sphere of authority, your resistance to his pressure in this matter is understandable. Even so, be open to God's will and fulfill your obligation to discern your appropriate contribution. As an aid, not a substitute, I offer the following considerations and suggestions.

First, though your reluctance to cut back on your business is partly a matter of self-interest, that concern may well be legitimate, for we really fulfill ourselves by using our talents in doing good work (see *LCL*, 755–58). Moreover, assuming you conscientiously manage this successful business for the common good of everyone involved, your work significantly benefits your employees, customers, and suppliers. Therefore, your duties related to your business are moral responsibilities. The commitments underlying them should not be lightly set aside or compromised in favor of other claims on your time and resources.

Second, you make the point that taking care of other people's children is not your field, and you are not enthusiastic about the idea. That certainly is relevant, for in discerning what work to do one generally should strive to use one's talents

---

54. In granting that the project is worthwhile, I am not conceding that it is desirable to place children in day care. Caring for children, especially those under three, is a demanding job that requires the affection, skill, and commitment of strong and psychologically healthy people; Elinor Goldschmied and Sonia Jackson, *People under Three: Young Children in Day Care* (New York: Routledge, 1994), specify what good day care requires and thus provide a standard by which available day care might be judged—and, I expect, often found wanting. Therefore, parents should care for their own children. But sometimes that is not feasible, and day care is a necessary evil; see Marian Blum, *The Day-Care Dilemma: Women and Children First* (Lexington, Mass.: D. C. Heath, 1983), whose research and analysis led her to conclude (115): "There are no easy answers, no quick fixes, no victimless solutions to the problems of child care for working parents."

as appropriately as possible, and lack of enthusiasm often is a sign that a job's requirements and one's talents are more or less poorly matched. Still, members of any community sometimes ought to take on jobs that do not make full use of their talents or accept tasks for which they are not very well qualified. That is so not only when the job must be done and nobody else is available to do it, but also when the mutuality—of love, respect, camaraderie—among a community's members requires the specially talented and better placed to set aside talents and position and share common tasks. In a family, for instance, the husband and father who is a highly paid professional still must be ready to pitch in; he may not evade household jobs and the less enjoyable aspects of parenting as outside his field. Similarly in other communities, setting aside specific roles and pitching in to share in carrying out some common undertaking sometimes is appropriate and doing so in a generous spirit powerfully builds up community. Taking care of other people's children is hardly likely to be the proper field of anyone in the parish free to volunteer for the day care program. Still, pitching in probably is appropriate for some, and you should not rule out the possibility that you might be among them.

Third, even many Christians share the modern idea that people may keep for themselves any money they earn or do with it whatever they please. On the contrary, excess income carries with it a strict duty to use it to meet others' urgent needs (see *LCL,* 780–82, 789–92, 800–806, 811–14). You make it clear that you and your husband could live comfortably on his salary alone and no longer need the income from your business. Perhaps you already are donating your excess income to good causes, but if not, you either are accumulating wealth unjustifiably or spending money on luxuries. In any case, when you consider your own resources in discerning, do not overlook the portion of your income you could contribute to your parish without slighting any other moral responsibility.

Fourth, rather than considering only the two possibilities—agreeing to serve in the day care program as the pastor wishes or refusing to help with it—try to think of alternative ways of contributing to the program and consider making one or more counterproposals. For instance, you could donate money to help finance the project. Then too, just as we are bound to share our excess income with others, so we ought to share any spare capacity to exercise our special gifts. With your experience in organizing and managing, you might be able to help set up the program, train people, manage finances, or deal with licensing and insurance problems. No doubt, snacks and lunches will be provided for the children, and at least in that regard you should be able to put your talents to work very helpfully, even without committing yourself to being present for a certain number of hours every week. Again, you might be able to make it easier for others to volunteer by using your talents and resources to help volunteers provide good dinners for their families on the days they serve in the program.

+   +   +

16: How can an elderly man make up for
many years of fraud?

My eldest brother's wife died three years ago, and he now is in a nursing home, where I visit him every week. He is sixty-seven and dying of lung cancer. As a young man, he went to work in the coal pits. He began at sixteen and worked until he was forty-five, when he was disabled by losing his right arm in what we all thought was an accident. Now he tells me he did it on purpose. He saw more and more of his buddies coming down with lung disease, wanted out, and decided to retire on disability. By claiming that his handicap resulted from a work related accident, he managed to collect disability benefits until he was sixty-five, and over the years he also cashed in on other public and private assistance programs, raising his family and surviving in meager comfort.

My brother has not gone to church since his wife died. His conscience does not seem to bother him about that, but he is troubled about all the money he collected for his disability. He seems to feel he should admit what he did. I told him to talk with the priest who takes care of the nursing home, but he does not want to do that. I think he is afraid the priest would tell him he must repay all the disability money. But he has no money and no way of getting any. He no longer receives disability, but the government pays for the nursing home.

I would like to know what somebody in my brother's position has to do. If I could get him to see what it is and do it, I think it would help him so that he could die with a peaceful conscience.

Analysis:

The explicit question concerns the duty to make restitution. Though the questioner's brother does owe restitution to those he defrauded, nobody has an obligation to do what is truly impossible. Still, the brother can make restitution in spiritual goods to those he injured. The implicit question is how to help him prepare for death. The questioner should identify a suitable priest with whom his or her brother might be willing to talk and cooperate with that priest's effort to provide appropriate pastoral care.

The reply could be along the following lines:

Your regular, weekly visits to your brother show that you love him. Now you wish to help him spiritually, and rightly so. Nothing is more important than that he prepare his soul for death, and you should assume his salvation depends on your help. Of course, only God can read hearts, and we must not judge anyone's internal guilt—and you do not seem inclined to judge your brother. Still, not only can we evaluate others' outward actions by moral standards, but at times we cannot help thinking they probably have been guilty of mortal sins.

Those who have committed mortal sins cannot be saved unless God's grace turns them from sin and creates new hearts in them (see q. 6, above). The most important thing you can do for your brother from now on is to pray for him and ask others to pray for him, so that, if he is not living in God's love, the Holy Spirit will move him to repent, restore him to grace, renew his faith and hope, and sanctify him through the regular and devout reception of the sacraments, and good works. An excellent way for you to begin to fulfill this responsibility would be to have Mass offered for the intention that your brother die in God's love, participate devoutly in that Mass yourself, and invite other relatives and friends to do so. You also could pray to St. Joseph for your brother's happy death, and to the Blessed Mother: "Pray for us sinners, now and at the hour of our death."

The working conditions of miners when your brother labored in the coal pits very likely were the product of pervasive social and economic injustices. Understandably resentful and fearful for his life, he desperately took what probably seemed to him the only way out: deliberately disabling himself. Then he could not survive and support his family except by keeping up the pretense that he had lost his arm by accident. Objectively, however, what he had done was a gravely evil means to his good end. Even if he could have collected disability benefits and other assistance from public and private programs without lying, what he did objectively was grave fraud. And his failure to practice his faith since his wife's death objectively has been grave neglect of his religious duties.

If your brother is in a state of mortal sin, a peaceful conscience may not be enough to save him from hell. People with consciences in culpable error can be at peace due to self-deception, and such peaceful consciences block repentance (see *CMP,* 78–80 and 92–93). It is a good sign that his conscience is bothering him. Of course, he needs confident hope in God's mercy, so that he will wholeheartedly repent any and every mortal sin of which he is guilty. Though perhaps tempted to despair, he also seems ready to repent, for, after all these years, he has told you his secret and seems to feel he should admit what he did. Most important is that he admit it to our Lord and receive his forgiveness.

Therefore, I think you should ask a priest to visit your brother, talk things over with him, and try to get him to make a good confession. Your suggestion that he talk with the priest at the nursing home was appropriate, but he may have some reason for not wishing to talk with that particular priest. Before your next visit to the nursing home, then, try to find another priest, faithful to the Church's teaching and gentle in manner, with whom your brother might be willing to talk. Perhaps you know a good priest he once knew and liked, or else one who is the sort of person he would like. If necessary, contact the diocesan office and seek help in identifying a suitable priest.

Having chosen a priest, tell him not only what you have told me but anything else that might help him understand your brother's situation and his unwillingness to talk with the priest at the nursing home. If he asks you any questions, be very careful to answer them accurately and honestly. Also, tell him that you asked me what your brother has to do by way of restitution, and that I offered the following thoughts for his consideration.

In general, those who cause others to suffer an injustice owe them restitution (see *LCL,* 444–58). Your brother did injustices to those on whom his disabling himself imposed various burdens and hardships. Still, the injustices under which he labored and his desperation certainly mitigated the gravity of the injustices he did. Moreover, though he was responsible for his own disability, his family was not, and surely they, if not he, rightly accepted the assistance they received. Most important, in making restitution, nobody is morally required to do the impossible. So, unless your brother gets some money, he need never repay what he received and should not worry about that. Nevertheless, he can and should make restitution by praying for all those harmed by his wrongdoing, offering his suffering and dying for them, and accepting God's saving grace so that he will be able to intercede in heaven for them. If he comes to see his situation in this light, his concern to make up for what he did is likely to arouse his hope and lead him to desire to receive the sacraments worthily.

Probably it will be best to tell your brother in advance you have asked the priest to come. You might lay some groundwork by telling him you have been thinking over what he told you, and you are sure he can make up for what he did; he need only do what he can, since God never asks anyone to do the impossible. You also might remind him of the good thief, who, admitting his crimes and asking Jesus to remember him, at once received the promise: "Today you will be with me in Paradise" (Lk 23.43). Like every human person who will share in heavenly glory, the thief received as Jesus' free gift the thing of greatest value, which cannot be stolen. Yet one could say jokingly that the thief made his best haul that day and stole Paradise, and you might encourage your brother, who has been cheating people for more than twenty years, to do likewise. Finally, remind him that, if he confesses his sins, the priest will keep his secrets as if he had never heard them, since a priest's duty in hearing confessions is to make available to each penitent Jesus' patient ears, merciful heart, and forgiving words.

These, however, are only my thoughts, considering your brother's situation from a distance. When you have talked with the priest, he will decide how best to proceed. Accept his judgment and cooperate with him. Your brother, very likely, will make a good confession, receive Communion and the sacrament of anointing, and be ready to die devoutly. And if not? The priest may wish to drop in from time to time. If so, keep in touch with him and follow his advice. If not, tell the priest who takes care of the nursing home about your brother's situation, so that he can look for the right moment to try to talk with him. Meanwhile, do not nag your brother, and continue to visit him and listen to what he has to say. By doing what you can for him, you will make it clear that you love him. You should keep on praying for him and also should invite him to pray with you for everything that concerns you, not least his well-being.

If your brother seems to die unrepentant, beg our Lord to be merciful to him, and be consoled that you have done your best for him. And remember that only God knows what is in human hearts.

17: Must a widow leave tainted money to charity?

Four years ago Dad died, leaving everything to Mother. When she went through his papers and sorted things out with the help of the family lawyer, they discovered something none of us had known. While Dad carried on a legitimate business, he also engaged in certain questionable transactions. In some cases, identifiable individuals clearly had been cheated, and, following her lawyer's advice, Mother straightened things out with all of them. In other cases, however, it was impossible to identify those who were cheated, either because the records did not provide enough information or because of the nature of the transactions—for example, some trades on the stock market in which Dad apparently took advantage of inside information. The lawyer and our pastor both told mother not to worry about the money from those transactions—she could consider it her own.

Dad and Mother had trusts, primarily leaving everything to each other, but then providing that in case both died everything would be divided equally among the children: my two brothers, my sister, and me. After Dad's death, Mother changed her trust, skipping us and instead dividing everything equally among our children. She explained that, since the four of us are already well established in life, she preferred to help our children. That was fine with us.

Now, however, Mother has inoperable liver cancer and has only a few months to live. She is putting her affairs in order, and, talking with the pastor, she brought up the matter of Dad's questionable transactions. The pastor took a different position than he had before, telling her the money from those transactions, including all investment earnings, "is tainted and should be left to charity." Specifically, he urged her to leave it to a fund for which the bishop has been trying to raise money. This fund was set up to provide for elderly sisters of two congregations, now dying out, that used to staff many of the schools in this diocese.

Mother wants to do the right thing, but is not sure what that is. We agree with her that if the pastor is right, she should leave the money to charity, though that would mean leaving virtually nothing to our children. The inheritance would pay for their higher education, weddings, and at least something toward their first homes; we can manage without it, but will have to make a good many sacrifices and will not be able to provide the children with such a good start in life.

Since the pastor has changed his view, we wonder whether he is right. I do not want to be cynical, but perhaps his thinking has been influenced by the bishop's interest in raising money for the elderly sisters. Also, even if Mother should leave the money to charity, she wonders whether she ought to leave some of it or all of it to that particular cause. No doubt the elderly sisters deserve help, but so do many other people even worse off.

Since you are in no way involved, we wonder how you would answer this question, and we will be grateful if you will reply as soon as possible.

Analysis:

This question concerns the duty to make restitution. One can determine whether and to what extent restitution is required only by considering all the relevant facts and applying the Golden Rule. The questioner's mother perhaps made restitution that was objectively adequate when his father died. Now, however, she is in a position to make restitution in spiritual goods to the unidentifiable persons who were cheated, by donating to charity on their behalf, and, in my judgment, she should do so. Whether to make some or all of that donation to the fund for the elderly sisters is a matter for her discernment.

The reply could be along the following lines:

Perhaps the pastor was lax four years ago due to reluctance to ask of your mother, at that difficult time, all that justice really required of her, and perhaps he is being rigorous now due to eagerness to obtain money for the fund for the elderly sisters. However, we should not try to judge his motives, which, in any case, are irrelevant to the truth about what your mother should do. Therefore, doubts about the pastor must be set aside, and the question you pose considered on its merits.

Your mother certainly acted rightly four years ago insofar as she straightened things out with all the identifiable individuals your father had cheated. Should she also have done something by way of restitution for his other questionable transactions? There is a case for saying yes. The unidentifiable individuals were no less cheated than the identifiable ones, and St. Thomas, for example, suggests that restitution can be made to entirely unidentifiable individuals, whether dead or alive, by donating the item or money on their behalf as alms, so that they may enjoy the donation's spiritual benefits (see *S.t.,* 2–2, q. 62, a. 5, ad 3).

However, I do not think one can answer questions about restitution by appealing to specific norms. Rather, one must consider all the facts and apply the Golden Rule (see *LCL,* 444–58). Doing that, it hardly seems that fairness required more of your mother than she had already done. She faced a widowhood of unpredictable duration and needed adequate funds to meet her own needs; and giving alms on behalf of those adversely affected by your father's actions would not have undone the actual harm they had suffered, which, as St. Thomas also teaches, is the main point of restitution (see *S.t.,* 2–2, q. 62, a. 6, ad 3).

But your mother's situation has changed greatly. Her widowhood has turned out to be brief, and she has a substantial amount of money left, much of it, according to your account, deriving from your father's questionable activities. If her grandchildren really needed the money—for example, if their not inheriting it meant they would be deprived of an adequate education—perhaps she could fairly leave her trust unchanged. As you indicate, though, the needs of her intended heirs can be met even if she leaves this money to charity. In this situation, it seems to me that, even if there were no question of restitution, it would be appropriate for your mother to leave at least part of her money to those with needs more pressing than her grandchildren's. Therefore, it seems appropriate that she give as alms on behalf of those harmed by your father's questionable activities the entire amount wrongly deriving from them.

Of course, insofar as this conclusion is based on the requirement of justice to make restitution, the amount to be given as alms should be determined by reasonable judgments based on a careful study of the records. If a questionable transaction was not clearly unjust, not the whole amount gained by it but some fair portion is due as restitution. Even if a transaction clearly was wrong—for example, trading based on inside information—not the whole proceeds of the transaction but only the amount resulting from the abuse is due. At the same time, not only the principal amount of each wrongful gain is due but interest at a reasonable rate. To simplify this task and minimize temptation, I suggest you have a capable, disinterested person examine the records and judge how much of the remaining estate originated in the ill-gotten gains and their investment.

Your mother also wonders whether she should leave any of the money, or all of it, to the fund for the elderly sisters, considering that many other people are even worse off than they. In my judgment, both options are morally acceptable, and your mother must discern which is more appropriate for her, all things considered. But I shall offer some thoughts she might find helpful.

Since the extreme need of the very poor argues strongly for preferring them, she surely will do well if she leaves the money to some charitable group that would use it to meet the needs of the poorest of the poor. If she chooses to do this, I suggest you help her ascertain two things: that the organization she selects does not spend too great a part of its receipts for overhead, and that her bequest will not be subject to taxation.

Still, a case can be made for leaving some or all of the money to the fund for the elderly sisters. Assuming the two congregations are similar to others with which I am acquainted, the elderly sisters devoted their lives to serving this local church and were inadequately compensated, and now their congregations are dying out due to various conditions for which they probably bore little or no responsibility. So, the diocese does owe them support, and your mother's bequest not only would help fulfill this duty of justice but could build up communion in several ways. Most important, your mother could communicate with the bishop, the pastor, and the sisters—perhaps even meet with all of them—and obtain their promise to offer Masses and pray regularly for her intentions: for the salvation of those harmed by your father's questionable activities, for her children and grandchildren, for herself, and not least for your father. In this way she could assure that her bequest would benefit everyone concerned.

So, without knowing the persons involved or being nearly as close to the situation as your pastor, I nevertheless am inclined to endorse his advice. Specifically, I think your mother should make fair restitution by donating to charity for the benefit of those who were cheated by your father's questionable transactions. And, while I do not think it would be wrong to leave that portion of the estate to some other suitable charity, it seems to me entirely appropriate that the bequest—or, at least, a substantial part of it—be to the fund for the elderly sisters.

18: Should social workers adhere to rules or compassionately evade them?

I am in the final semester of a program that prepares people to serve as caseworkers for county or city welfare departments. One of my courses is a required seminar, conducted by the case study method, on how to deal with various difficult situations. Often we find ourselves discussing whether the law and regulations should be strictly followed, or bent, stretched, even clearly violated, for the sake of a more compassionate outcome.

The professor and many of the students take the latter view. For example, they argue that a caseworker should ignore the fact that an unmarried mother of two, collecting unemployment benefits, is earning twelve hundred dollars a month providing several other children with day care—which she also is not licensed to do. They think it would be heartless to go by the book, force the woman to choose between the unemployment benefits and her earnings, and deprive her of money she needs.

Other students argue that caseworkers should not allow their feelings to get them personally involved with clients, and should go by the book.

I cannot side completely with either view. I agree that the law and rules can be awfully harsh and more ought to be done for the sort of people who will be our clients. But I do not believe it would be right for us, as public employees, to throw away the rule book and write our own. Yet that is what we will be doing unless we limit exceptions to emergencies. At the same time, most of us are going into social work because we want to help the people who will be our clients, and I believe we ought to be compassionate toward them. In fact, I cannot imagine dealing regularly with peoples' problems and not being emotionally involved.

What do you think?

Analysis:

The question is whether compassion justifies social caseworkers in making exceptions to laws and regulations governing their work. To answer, one must explain what compassion is. The word *compassion* has two meanings; in one sense it refers to an emotion, in the other to a virtue. Actions motivated by the emotion, as by other normal feelings, can be sinful. Actions motivated by the virtue always conform to other moral requirements. Therefore, social caseworkers should shape the behavior to which their feelings of compassion move them by all relevant moral norms, including the usual norms about obedience to the law and lawful regulations that govern their work.

The reply could be along the following lines:

People in various professions other than social work—including some physicians, lawyers, judges, public administrators, teachers, and pastors—share the view that achieving a more "compassionate" outcome sometimes calls for stretching, bending, and violating laws, rules, and even moral norms against lying, killing the innocent, and so on. Since this view often is held and asserted as if it were self-evident, those who find it unacceptable are more likely to be dismissed as cruel and heartless than offered any rational argument. However, like some other, related positions in normative ethics, the seemingly self-evident view that compassion should prevail over other norms is confused and mistaken—though it contains just enough truth to make it plausible and appealing to morally serious, upright people. Consequently, before responding to your specific question, I shall try to clarify this confusion.

Partly it arises from the fact that *compassion* has two meanings. In one sense it refers to an emotion and in another to a virtue: mercy. By definition, mercy, as a virtue, is morally good and disposes one only to do what is right. The emotion is neither morally good nor evil in itself. Nevertheless, many people today unquestioningly act as if the *feeling* of compassion were a moral principle.

As an emotion, compassion is akin to pity. Both are sorts of sympathy. Pity differs from compassion in that it need not incline those experiencing it to do anything to help, while compassion connotes just such an inclination. Sympathy is an emotional response to the perceived condition of others—in principle, to their good or bad condition (one rejoices as well as mourns with others), though nowadays we speak of sympathy only in reference to evils.

Sympathetic persons emotionally react to others' misery and suffering as if it were their own. This response is natural. Human beings are not isolated from one another, as individualists suppose, but are members of a single, extended family, unified by organic bonds, mutually interdependent, and even linked to subhuman animals. Thus, not only family members and friends but strangers often are moved by compassion to sense and spontaneously respond to one another's needs, and many people, especially children, wish to help and save injured and hungry animals.

Though compassion, as a natural emotional response, is neither morally good nor evil in itself, it is morally significant in at least two ways. Lack of compassionate feeling, heartlessness, often is a consequence of moral immaturity or selfishness, and sometimes even of hatred. Yet compassion often inclines imprudent people to act unreasonably—and so immorally, even if blamelessly due to lack of sufficient reflection. The unreasonable response can be of different sorts. Very often, compassionate people fail to fulfill responsibilities, so as not to inflict pain or hardship —for example, softhearted people in positions of authority tolerate wrongdoing they really ought to deal with. Sometimes, though lacking adequate skill or resources, compassionate people try to help others, and the well-intentioned effort only makes matters worse—for example, a passing motorist tries to comfort an accident victim whose back is broken and greatly aggravates the injury. Again, and even more seriously, people moved by compassion for someone whose misery and suffering are manifest sometimes condone or take part in serious injustices toward others. Compassion for the oppressed led some people to support left-wing totalitarianism; compassion for unwillingly pregnant women and suffering patients leads some people to condone killing the innocent; compassion for drug addicts, alcoholics, and sexual compulsives leads some people to tolerate and even facilitate their antisocial and self-destructive behavior; and so on.[55]

This moral ambiguity of compassionate feelings often is overlooked today. Our culture has been influenced by secularism, which always denies original sin and usually regards altruistic sentiments as a sound guide to right and wrong. Popularized versions of utilitarianism are prevalent, so that pain and suffering are widely

---

55. Lawrence A. Blum, *Moral Perception and Particularity* (New York: Cambridge University Press, 1994), 173–82, provides a phenomenology of compassion considered as an emotional attitude, and points out (182): "Compassion can also be misguided, grounded in superficial understanding of a situation. Compassion is not necessarily wise or appropriate. The compassionate person may even end up doing more harm than good." C. Daniel Batson et al., "Immorality from Empathy-Induced Altruism: When Compassion and Justice Conflict," *Journal of Personality and Social Psychology,* 68 (1995): 1042–54, report experiments showing that people stirred to compassionate feelings manifested partiality in allocating resources in a way they themselves admitted to be less fair and less moral than the alternative chosen by the control group.

regarded not only as intrinsically evil but as the worst evils, even the only ones, while pleasure and enjoyment are regarded as intrinsically good and even as the only or the highest goods. Morality is reduced to doing what one can to minimize pain and suffering, and maximize pleasure and enjoyment.

Because utilitarianism locates the ultimate principles of morality in human experience rather than beyond it, people who do not believe in God find it congenial. They also like the way it displaces traditional morality's focus on intelligible goods—the integrity of the bodily and spiritual person, fidelity, human life, marriage itself—and makes way for a permissive new morality regarding sex, marriage, and killing the innocent. Many believers also uncritically accept secularist ideas, fail to distinguish the feeling of compassion from the virtue of mercy, and regard compassion as a virtual moral absolute. Thus, many people would regard the view of your professor and the students who agree with him or her as simple common sense.

In many places in the Old Testament, especially in Psalms and Isaiah, God is said to be compassionate and his people often appeal to his compassion. But even though the words used certainly signify feelings of sympathy, when said of God by analogy they refer not to emotions, which cannot be ascribed to him, but to an aspect of divine perfection: God's mercy, which is the form his goodness, benevolence, graciousness, and faithful love take in forgiving and saving his people.[56] In the New Testament, Jesus' actions often are said to be motivated by compassion, and here the word plainly does refer to his human feelings for the hungry, the sick, and the spiritually lost (see Mt 9.36, 14.14, 15.32, 20.34; Mk 6.34, 8.2; Lk 7.13). However, just as Jesus in the Garden of Gethsemane subordinated his fear of death to his commitment to do the Father's will, so throughout his life he subordinated every feeling, including compassion, to that same overriding purpose. Thus, Jesus' compassion was integrated with and governed by the merciful love by which he laid down his life for us.

Like Jesus, we should not be hardened by selfishness or by antipathy toward anyone. Everyone's misery and suffering should touch us, make us wish to give comfort and help. But we also must be like Jesus in deciding what to do and doing it: dedicated above all to pleasing God, committed to the true good of neighbors afflicted and enslaved by evil, aware that sin is a far greater evil than pain, respectful toward others' rights, ready to sacrifice ourselves and serve others unselfishly. In short, when moved by feelings of compassion, we must conscientiously decide what to do and do it out of love of neighbor, taking the form of mercy (see *LCL*, 360–71). Since love fulfills all the commandments (see Rom 13.8–10), in judging and acting out of love we never will condone others' sins, or ourselves violate any moral requirement. Virtuous compassion will not lead us to violate justice by sacrificing others' legitimate interests and just claims to bring about a seemingly more compassionate outcome for those whose plight moves us. Rather, true compassion will be allied with confident hope in God. Keeping always in mind the

56. See Ceslas Spicq, O.P., *Theological Lexicon of the New Testament,* trans. and ed. James D. Ernest (Peabody, Mass.: Hendrickson, 1994), 1:471–79.

limits of our ability and responsibility to overcome evil and refusing to overstep them, we shall trust God's wisdom and love to protect or achieve the good for whose sake we cannot rightly act.

Very often, the intense emotional component of virtuous compassion energizes creative intelligence. Love becomes the will that finds a way—not a way extending evil by some facile moral compromise, but a way both legitimate and effective. Unless integrated with the virtue of mercy, compassionate feelings cannot bring practical wisdom into play, and all too often lead people to the folly of trying to achieve good by doing evil.[57]

Your assessment of the opposing views of the seminar participants seems to me sound. Though caseworkers must not become too emotionally involved in their clients' problems, lest their own emotional well-being and their job performance both suffer, a cultivated detachment blocking normal feelings of compassion would be incompatible with an authentic commitment to help these needy people. Social work then would become a mere technical handling of cases, without genuine, human care for and service to those in need. Moreover, caseworkers would lack the emotional motivation to do dedicated work and the stimulus for creativity on behalf of the people they serve.

At the same time, social workers, like other citizens, should obey all just and applicable laws and lawful regulations (see *LCL,* 874–78). This duty of civic obedience is reinforced for them, as government employees, by the duty to fulfill the responsibilities of their job. Setting aside applicable laws and rules to follow feelings also will result in different treatment for clients with similar problems and situations, and such unevenness in treatment not only will be unfair to clients but will subvert the sense of security and order that would help them act reasonably despite their problems.

Of course, sometimes a law or regulation is truly inapplicable, in the sense that applying it would be contrary to the reasonable intention of the authority that issued it. This would constitute what you call an "emergency." In an emergency, you should seek a superior's authorization, if possible; you also should note in the record an indication that you made an exception and why you considered it necessary. The possibility that a law or regulation might be unjust presents a more difficult problem. One should begin by assuming that laws and lawful regulations are just, and not judge them unjust without careful inquiry and conscientious reflection. Note, too, that the common good or other responsibilities often require complying even with an unjust law or regulation (see *LCL,* 880–81).

Nevertheless, one must *not* comply if that would mean doing something in itself immoral: "We must obey God rather than any human authority" (Acts 5.29; cf. DH 11). For example, if a regulation required caseworkers to urge pregnant, unmarried women to obtain abortions, one could not comply. One would not be obliged voluntarily to report one's noncompliance, but even in such a case it would be wrong to lie about it. Therefore, social workers must be

---

57. The preceding analysis of compassion draws on, but freely recasts and develops, helpful insights of Edmund D. Pellegrino, "The Moral Status of Compassion in Bioethics: The Sacred and the Secular," *Ethics and Medics,* 20:9 (Sept. 1995): 3–4.

prepared to give up their jobs rather than comply with laws and regulations requiring any sort of wrongdoing by them.

You propose an interesting example: An unmarried mother receives unemployment benefits but earns twelve hundred dollars a month doing day care, for which she also is unlicensed. Should the caseworker ignore this breach of the law or compel the woman to choose between her unemployment benefits and her earnings? Since you are asking this question, I assume dealing with the client's unreported income falls within the responsibility of the caseworker. If so, it cannot be ignored. Nothing suggests that the situation is an emergency or that relevant laws and rules will require the caseworker to do anything in itself immoral. Moreover, condoning an unlicensed day care operation could risk the children's health and safety. So, the caseworker should go by the book, while also seeking legitimate ways of helping the client in order to mitigate the hardship for her and her children.

Someone might argue that the relevant laws and rules are a product of social injustice, either because affluent people use their political power to block tax increases and public programs transferring a fair share of their resources to the needy, or because the whole welfare system is an overly ambitious governmental attempt to save people from themselves and manage their personal and family lives. I think much can be said for both views. But even if so, caseworkers will not rectify the injustices by setting aside relevant laws and rules. Indeed, though public funds may be unfairly limited, the laws and rules may well be distributing the available money fairly, so that ignoring the unreported earnings of someone receiving unemployment benefits might well be unfair to someone in still greater need. And even though governments may have taken more responsibility for people's welfare than they should have, people who depend on the existing system should receive their fair share of its benefits. Therefore, caseworkers who consider either their clients or tax payers or both to be victims of injustice should not ignore the laws and rules governing their work. Rather, they should use other, legitimate means of working for social justice, such as political action and publicity.[58]

19: May a woman tolerate her husband's incest with their daughter?

I dropped out of the seminary just before being ordained deacon, and am now serving as a pastoral worker in a parish. I encounter situations that involve not just

---

58. Barbara Garson, *The Electronic Sweatshop: How Computers Are Transforming the Office of the Future into the Factory of the Past* (New York: Penguin, 1989), 73–114, describes and sharply criticizes one jurisdiction's attempt to transform professional social workers into—or replace them with—clerks who unthinkingly follow a system of rules, some unreasonable in themselves and others unreasonable in many of their applications. Someone might cite her account as evidence that some social workers today cannot serve their clients without evading and breaking rules. But Garson's description makes it clear that evading and breaking unreasonable rules actually contribute to the system's workability and therefore to its persistence. This sort of complicity in an irrational, and therefore unjust, system might be necessary to keep one's job but is hardly required by mercy toward clients.

difficult moral questions but absolutely insoluble dilemmas—situations in which people choose the lesser evil, knowing it is evil, and commit no sin in doing so. Here is one example, and it is only the latest in a whole string.

A woman brought in her fifteen-year-old daughter, the eldest of six children in the family. These people are legal immigrants, and the man makes a steady income working as the head of a crew that installs dry wall. He never has been faithful to his wife, and she has tolerated it. He always has treated the daughter affectionately and, after she started menstruating about a year ago, they began engaging in sex play and now are having intercourse. They are not being discreet about it, and the girl shows no sense of guilt; she also is contemptuous of her mother. The mother told her husband that she was going to the police to put a stop to the incest, but he threatened, as he often has before, to desert the family and return to their country of origin. This is a credible threat, for apparently he could work at his trade there. However, if she tried to follow him, the authorities in that country would do nothing for her and the children. In short, she has no practical alternative to tolerating the incest.

This woman was so desperate that she was nearly incoherent telling me her story. It took more than an hour, repeatedly interrupted by exchanges with her daughter, for her to get it out and for me to identify the two things bothering her that I could do something about. One was that the woman felt guilty, even though the situation is not her fault. I tried to reassure her but could not, so I got the priest and helped her go to confession. (She needed help because she speaks no English and the priest hardly speaks her language.) When we told her God understood and would forgive her, and the priest gave her absolution, she obviously was freed from a crushing load of guilt. The other thing bothering her was that the girl would get pregnant. I solved that by sending them to the Planned Parenthood clinic to get the girl put on the pill. Fortunately, she seemed willing to cooperate, and, no matter what the Church says about it, contraception clearly is appropriate in a case like this.

Analysis:

The central question, overlooked by the questioner, is: Should the woman tolerate her husband's incest with their daughter? In view of the grave injury the incest is doing to the daughter and the family as a whole, the answer is no. The questioner also abused the sacrament of penance by using it to deal with what he regarded as a psychological problem. His attempted justification for violating the moral norm taught by the Church regarding contraception is an instance of consequentialism or proportionalism, rejected by John Paul II and rationally indefensible. An adequate response must indicate how the questioner should have handled this case.

The reply could be along the following lines:

I am appalled by your letter and even more appalled by the way you handled the case you describe.

In the first place, you failed to consider all the facts of the case in the light of relevant moral truths and instead looked only for the things you "could do something about." Thus, you overlooked the moral question at the heart of the situation: May this woman tolerate her husband's ongoing incest with their daughter? She may not. Perhaps she was justified in tolerating her husband's previous infidelity. But incest is intolerable. It is an especially grave sin and very injurious to the whole family (see *CCC*, 2388). Moreover, the father's incest is a crime against his daughter, and the mother has a clear legal duty to report it to the authorities, just as she would have a duty to call the police if her husband were beating one of the children severely enough to draw blood and break bones.

Even though the daughter shows no sense of guilt, she could be sinning mortally. About that, of course, only God knows. But the young woman plainly is being morally corrupted. Even if her responsibility for the incest is mitigated, she acts with contempt for her mother and disregard for the effect of the incest on her siblings. Moreover, the incest hardly is preparing her for a good marriage with a man who will respect her and be faithful to her. Rather, she is learning both to submit to sexual abuse and to abuse her own sexuality, and these lessons are likely to prepare her for a poor marriage, promiscuity, or even a life of prostitution.[59]

Since the incest is being carried on openly, it also gives very bad example to the younger children. If some are sons, they are learning how to exploit women; if some are daughters, they are being taught to submit to abuse. Also, if the mother tolerates her husband's incest with the eldest daughter, her other daughters, if any, are likely to be victimized in turn as they mature.

As mother both to the eldest daughter and the other children, the woman is responsible for their well-being, and their moral character certainly is more important than anything the husband's income can buy. The woman herself, moreover, has been injured by the husband's infidelity and is further injured by the incest and her daughter's contempt. She urgently needs to be freed from her husband's oppression.[60] Moreover, his soul also may well be at stake. If he is living in mortal sin, tolerating the incest hardly will motivate him to repent. Then too, the couple's relationship has been gravely injured by the man's infidelity; indeed, the marriage might well be invalid, particularly if he *never* has been faithful.

You assumed the woman must tolerate the incest, because otherwise her husband threatens to desert and leave the family destitute. Perhaps it is true that the man may flee the country or be sent to jail, either of which would result in the loss of his support for the woman and children. However, either also would end the incest, and time in jail might benefit the man by leading him to repent. Moreover, you should not be so unimaginative as to ignore or foreclose other possible ways of helping this woman. Various forms of public assistance surely can be obtained for her and her children, and, if necessary, it also would be suitable to enlist the help of parishioners and use the Church's resources to help extricate this family from its wretched situation. Many people seek the Church's help, but few have so great

59. Though Elaine Westerlund, *Women's Sexuality after Childhood Incest* (New York: W. W. Norton, 1992), rejects excessive generalizations on these matters by previous researchers, her work bears out this point; see especially the summary, 178–79.

60. Even if the mothers of girls who are victims of incest do not do all they should to oppose it, the mothers themselves often are victims; see Janis Tyler Johnson, *Mothers of Incest Survivors: Another Side of the Story* (Bloomington, Ind.: Indiana University Press, 1992).

a claim on Christian mercy. If the parish's resources are inadequate, you should not hesitate to ask for the diocese's help, since poor parishes need and deserve the help of more affluent ones.

Therefore, you should encourage and help this woman to put an end to the incest. Almost certainly that will require compelling the husband to leave the household, and an appropriate public agency and/or the police should be asked to apply the necessary coercion. Indeed, having learned of the sexual abuse of a minor child, you as a counselor may well have a legal obligation to report the father's wrong-doing to the public authorities. However, to forestall an accusation of parental neglect against the mother, you probably should persuade her to join you in asking the authorities to intervene. Moreover, if their intervention does not at once make it impossible for the man to continue abusing his daughter, you should help the mother find another, safe and decent place for the young woman to live.

In the second place, the sacrament of penance is one thing, psychological therapy another, and you are confusing the two.

The purpose of the sacrament of penance is to free Christians from their sins, not relieve their groundless guilt feelings. But even though you thought that the situation was not the woman's fault, having tried but failed to relieve her sense of guilt by reassuring her, you called in the priest and helped her go to confession. You think you benefited the woman, since "she obviously was freed from a crushing load of guilt." Instead of judging the woman innocent and proceeding as you did, you should have encouraged her to examine her conscience properly and, if necessary, make a good confession. Rather than focusing on guilt feelings, you should have focused on the possibility of real guilt. Objectively, at least, she should not have tolerated the incest so as to retain the man's support. Still, her responsibility for the incest undoubtedly was limited. But, regardless of the degree of her guilt, this woman needed—and perhaps still needs—to repent whatever sins she actually committed.

The daughter, too, needs pastoral help to comprehend not only what her father has done to her but what she has done to herself, her mother, and her siblings. She should be encouraged to repent, to receive the sacrament of penance worthily, to forgive her father, and to treat her mother with respect. Only in this way can this young woman be liberated and recover her integrity and true sense of self-respect.

Though the mother quite naturally resents her daughter's behavior, she should be encouraged not to hate her, but rather to forgive her and try to build a better relationship with her. To this end, both mother and daughter no doubt could also benefit from sound counseling by someone both competent in psychology and faithful to Catholic teaching. Such sound counseling would help them understand what they have suffered, come to terms with their feelings, and develop a better relationship with each other.

In the third place, it was wrong to send the mother and daughter to the Planned Parenthood clinic to have the girl put on the pill. That only facilitated the ongoing incest. Besides, though one might argue that the girl, due to immaturity, is being raped by her father, you and the girl's mother decided to tolerate the rape. So, the effort to prevent the incest from resulting in conception plainly was not meant to oppose it as the culmination of rape but as the beginning of new life, and so was contraceptive. Moreover, since the pill on occasion functions as an abortifacient, you and the mother, by unjustifiably resorting to the pill, also wrongly accepted abortion as a side effect (see *LCL,* 504–5).

In trying to justify exceptions to the norms excluding contraception and other intrinsically evil acts, you assume that one can compare diverse evils and rationally judge which of the options available for choice offers the prospect of a less bad outcome. Apparently, like many people engaged in pastoral ministry, you have been influenced by theological dissent and have adopted a form of consequentialism or proportionalism. However, John Paul II condemned those dissenting views and reaffirmed the exceptionless moral norms that the Church has constantly taught.[61] Moreover, your argument serves to illustrate the error of such views. They sacrifice the genuine goods of the person, which moral absolutes protect, in order to spare people hardships and sufferings that, though painful, are morally acceptable.

In sum, as a pastoral worker, in situations such as this you should speak God's saving word and serve his People's true interests by trying to help everyone involved to save his or her soul. You seem to have proceeded as if you were a social worker devoid of faith and concerned only about dealing with immediate problems. I know you were trying to help, and I assume you did what you thought right in light of your training, which perhaps makes it appear that compassionate pastoral practice consists simply in following feelings. But your way of dealing with this situation fell far short of authentic pastoral care. To make up for this, you should do all you can to assure that each member of this family, including the father, receives the spiritual help she or he needs, not only now but in the future.

People who come to the Church with their problems should find genuine love and the help necessary to escape from sin and deal with the evils they are suffering. They never should be encouraged and supported in living a sinful life or facilitating the sins of others. It never is necessary to choose an evil knowing it to be evil, for at least one morally right option always is available, though choosing it and accepting its bad side effects may be very hard. Thus, a so-called moral dilemma is insoluble only in the sense that none of the options is appealing—a state of affairs not uncommon in our fallen world. True pastoral ministry requires the courage to help each person take up his or her cross rather than take a seemingly easy way out.

20: What should a woman do about the possibility of being raped?

Next fall I will be a resident student on a college campus in a very rough part of the city. I've heard that in recent years a number of women have been raped by strangers around the campus. I also have read that a large percentage of the women residing on nearly any campus are raped at least once during their college years by a fellow student or other acquaintance. As a potential rape

---

61. See John Paul II, *Veritatis splendor,* 71–83, *AAS* 85 (1993) 1190–1200, *OR,* 6 Oct. 1993, xi–xiii; cf. *CMP,* 141–71.

victim, I am wondering what I should do about it. And even though the answer might seem obvious, I am confused.

I have several questions. What should I do to avoid being raped? How can a college woman enjoy a normal social life and intimate friendships with men without taking chances? If someone tries to rape me, should I resist? Some people say no, because a victim who resists is more likely to be seriously injured or even killed. But the Church offers as models Susanna in the Old Testament and Maria Goretti, and both risked their lives by resisting. If I were about to be raped, should I urge the man to use a condom? What could I do to avoid becoming pregnant? Would I be obliged to report being raped to the police? They say rape victims who report it to the police always go through a great deal of unpleasantness, usually for nothing, since rapists seldom are punished.

I read a magazine article about rape, and am not sure what to think about the author's ideas. She says society must stop blaming the victim, as if she somehow shared responsibility for being raped, and start punishing the rapist. She argues that rape always is a crime of violence, not of lust—the rapist is seeking the emotional gratification of dominating his victim rather than sexual pleasure—so that no woman becomes a victim of rape by dressing or acting in a so-called provocative manner. The rapist is no less guilty if the victim was dressed sensually or if she flirted with him and led him on; in fact, even if a woman changes her mind after she has begun to have intercourse with a man, he becomes a rapist if he does not withdraw when she tells him to. This writer also says that unless the woman's consent is totally free, the man's act is rape, not sex. She argues that a woman is not totally free if she is under any pressure at all, and verbal pressure is the same as physical force. So, she says, many women raped by an acquaintance do not even realize they are victims, and mistakenly feel guilty about having given in to the rapist's repeated demands.

Analysis:

This question concerns a woman's responsibilities with regard to rape. To avoid being raped, a woman should take reasonable precautions and avoid unreasonable risks. Under duress, a victim should not consent to sexual intercourse, but consent must be distinguished from choices (1) not to resist being raped and (2) to do various things demanded by the rapist and not wrong in themselves. Depending on her own responsibilities and the anticipated risks, a woman generally should resist being raped but sometimes need not. If conception can be prevented, the victim may try to prevent it, but she should not attempt abortion. Since citizens should report crimes, a woman who has been raped has a duty to report the crime, but this affirmative responsibility admits of exceptions.

The reply could be along the following lines:

I set aside as outside your present concern the rape of young children and others who lack the capacity to consent, homosexual rape, and intercourse forced on a woman by her husband. Still, I wish to include everything that does concern you. To most people, the word *rape* probably suggests a man using physical force to achieve vaginal penetration (the insertion of the penis into the vagina) despite the woman's manifest unwillingness to have intercourse with him. This is too narrow an understanding, however, since anal and oral intercourse also can be rape. Moreover, a woman unable to resist—for example, because she is unconscious or paralyzed—can be raped without any sort of force. Likewise a woman too frightened or otherwise unable to manifest her unwillingness can be the victim of rape. And the rapist can use psychological duress—for example, a threat to kill or injure—rather than physical force. In what follows, *rape* refers to heterosexual, extramarital intercourse, natural or sodomitical, initiated by a man without the woman's consent—and it will be assumed here that the woman has the power to consent to sexual activity, though not that she is able to exercise that power here and now.

Pivotal in this definition is that the woman does not consent. Since the act in question is interpersonal, merely inward consent is not sufficient: a man commits rape if he initiates intercourse without the woman having *communicated* consent. But a woman who willingly engages in intercourse often gives her consent without words, by a gesture or by behavior that initiates or facilitates intercourse. Moreover, since there is a natural progression in the behavior that ends in intercourse, consent can be given by cooperation in mutually arousing activities of increasing intimacy. Still, if a woman cooperating in such activities makes clear her unwillingness to proceed, her earlier cooperation cannot be regarded as consent to the final step.

Even though she might otherwise refuse intercourse, a woman who *chooses* to engage in it when her inhibitions are lowered—for example, by fatigue, the excitement of a celebration, unfamiliar surroundings, alcohol or drugs, other couples' behavior, and/or her own sexual arousal—truly consents provided she remains sufficiently conscious and in control of herself *to be able* to refuse. Even if a man does not rape a woman, however, he gravely wrongs her in seeking to engage in nonmarital intercourse with her, more gravely wrongs her if he does so knowing her usual inhibitions are lowered, and still more gravely wrongs her if he has intentionally done something to lower them. Though rape is worse in that it violates the woman's autonomy, the wrongdoing just described is worse than rape in that it induces the woman to share moral responsibility for the abuse of her own body, and suffering evil is not as bad as cooperating in it.

Even if a woman's choice to engage in intercourse is elicited by prolonged cajoling, a threat to break off a romantic relationship, or a promise of payment or some other benefit, her choice remains a preference of intercourse to the alternative, and so constitutes consent. It is not true that exerting any sort of pressure on a woman to consent to intercourse makes a man a rapist. Here, too, however, a man who presses a woman to engage in nonmarital intercourse gravely wrongs her, and that wrongdoing is in one respect worse—insofar as it involves inducing the woman's wrongful consent—than rape would be. Then too, if men with power (employers, professors, public officials, and so on) use promises and threats to elicit women's consent to nonmarital intercourse, they do additional injustices by abusing their power with respect to the other goods at stake (employment opportunities, job advancement, grades, governmental action, and so on). Moreover, both in taking advantage of a woman's lowered inhibitions and in exerting pressure on her, a man without regard for a woman's autonomy can seek her consent solely to avoid being guilty of the crime of rape. Such a man would rape the woman if he dared, and so is morally guilty of rape (*CMP*, 369–74).

The choice to engage in intercourse must be distinguished from the choice not to resist rape. Typically, a couple's agreement to have intercourse includes the choice of both parties to seek integral, mutual sexual satisfaction. However, a woman's choice to engage in intercourse is at least her choice to do something, if only express consent, so as to help bring about vaginal (or oral or anal) penetration. Considered in itself, a woman's choice not to resist rape is a choice, not to *do* anything, but to *suffer*—that is, passively accept—penetration rather than suffer the rapist's other violence and/or accept the risk of death or injury. A woman being raped also can rightly obey the rapist's orders to do various things not wrong in themselves: undress, lie down, spread her legs, and so on. Though such behavior facilitates penetration, she need not choose it for that end, but can choose it, without consenting to intercourse, to avoid undergoing other evils.

In considering what to do to avoid being raped, begin by rejecting two claims made in the article you summarize: that rape never is a crime of lust and that victims never share responsibility for the injury they suffer.[62]

As to the first claim: Though rape certainly is not a sex crime as much as it is a crime of violence, lust and violence are by no means mutually exclusive. Indeed, they often are intertwined. Undoubtedly, men whose primary motive is to dominate and degrade women in general or a particular woman sometimes use rape as the bad means to their bad end. But some men obtain sexual gratification by acting with violence, and any woman who arouses their lust is likely to be treated violently. And some men's lust, by displacing affection and depersonalizing women, disposes them to do violence to a woman they lust after who resists their advances.

As to the second claim: Though every rapist is guilty and many victims of rape could not have done anything to avoid it, others, especially some raped by acquaintances, would not have been raped had they not misbehaved. They did not intend to be raped—something logically impossible—but they shared responsibility for what they suffered if they willingly cooperated in sexual sins preceding and leading up to the rape, or if they otherwise willingly took unreasonable risks or failed to take reasonable precautions. They are something like fraud victims who never intended to be defrauded but who share responsibility for their loss because greed and carelessness made them vulnerable.

Of course, no man who rapes a woman should be excused (see *CCC*, 2356; *LCL*, 548–49), even if her wrongdoing made her vulnerable. But while such a rapist is guilty, his victim is not entirely innocent. Women who deliberately arouse men's lust and then claim their right to limit the resulting behavior are not only imprudent but unjustly manipulative. A man whose wrongly aroused lust transforms him into an abject suppliant for sexual satisfaction or moves him to criminal misbehavior

---

62. Katherine Anne Roiphe, *The Morning After: Sex, Fear, and Feminism on Campus* (Boston: Little, Brown, 1993), responds at length to such ideas; though not entirely consistent with Christian moral standards, her views are marked by a respect for reality missing in many ideologically driven treatments of the subject.

has been rendered servile. Thus, those who try to justify arousing men's lust apparently want, not true community with men, but domination over them, perhaps in retaliation for some men's abuses of power—whether the latter are identified accurately, exaggerated, or, perhaps, merely imagined. Therefore, to avoid being raped, think of sins you might be tempted to commit that would increase the risk, recognize that this risk is an additional good reason not to commit those sins, and firmly resolve to avoid them.

You ask how a college woman can enjoy a normal social life and intimate friendships with men without taking chances. The question is ambiguous. If *a normal social life* refers to partying that includes using illegal drugs or abusing alcohol, and if *intimate friendships* refers to relationships in which the couple intentionally cause each other's sexual arousal and seek sexual satisfaction, I do not see how a college woman can enjoy these things without risking acquaintance rape. However, there is no place for such enjoyments in a good Christian life. Men and women committed to living such a life do not use illegal drugs or abuse alcohol. Except within marriage, they do not intentionally cause or maintain their own or anyone else's sexual arousal, or seek their own or anyone else's sexual satisfaction. They dress and behave modestly, that is, in ways likely to dispose others to regard them as persons rather than as sex objects. Being considerate of others, they learn what stimuli are likely to trouble someone of the opposite sex who is trying to be chaste and do all they reasonably can to avoid presenting those stimuli.

On some of these matters you perhaps do not accept traditional Christian morality. Even so, you surely recognize some limits to morally acceptable behavior, and you should consider the risks not only of violating those limits but even of approaching them. Many rapes by acquaintances would not occur if women stayed away from or left parties at which people take illegal drugs or drink excessively, and if they abstained from participating in behavior appropriate only to prepare for sexual intercourse.

Sometimes, too, a timely call for help would prevent rape by an acquaintance. Some women fail to call for help because they do not wish to bother those they might summon, or are embarrassed, or are reluctant to report to authorities the threatening behavior of someone they know. Plan never to let such considerations keep you from summoning help if the need arises.

What about the risk of being raped by a stranger? Collect information about situations in which there is a significant risk of that happening, and think about each of them. In most if not all of them, there also is significant risk of being mugged. Thus, like men at the college, you should consider whether you have a good reason to be in those situations, and, if so, whether there are precautions you could take to reduce the risk.

Some muggings and rapes by strangers can be avoided by good planning: doing errands at less dangerous times, going about in groups, using a campus escort service, and so on. Heed any advice or warnings by the city police and/or the campus security office.

Of course, one also should be ready to use elementary means of avoiding and warding off assault: flight and a call for help. A young man or woman in good condition who has the presence of mind to get rid of any encumbrances has a good chance of outrunning many would-be attackers—and the regular exercise required to keep in shape has many other benefits. As for calling for help, be prepared to do it without hesitation at the first clear sign one is likely to be attacked.[63]

Much of the preceding advice will be offensive to some people, who maintain that women have the right to the same freedom as men to do as they please and go where they like, that women also have the right to exercise their feminine sexual appeal by dressing and acting attractively, that society should vindicate these rights by giving women adequate protection and punishing rapists consistently and severely, and that women should not collaborate in maintaining the present unjust state of affairs by accepting all sorts of constraints that compromise their freedom.

Three things must be said in response.

First, as has been explained already, there would be a lot less acquaintance rape if couples abstained from the sexual sins and abuse of drugs and/or alcohol that often occasion it. Since neither men nor women have any right to the freedom to commit such sins, women have no right to equal freedom to behave as wrongly as many men do in those matters.

Second, none of my advice requires women to conceal their femininity or prohibits their dressing and acting attractively. However, to exercise sexual appeal means deliberately arousing others' erotic desire, and doing that, except between spouses, is wrong. Even those who do not accept traditional Christian morality, which limits sexual activity to marriage, should admit that deliberately arousing others' sexual desire without their consent is unjust, since the desire either will cause them frustration or lead them into sexual activity they may prefer to avoid. So, just as a man has no right to initiate sexual contact without a woman's consent, a woman has no right to arouse a man sexually without his consent.

Third, rape is one of the cruelest forms of criminal assault; indeed, it is a wrong comparable in gravity to homicide and, in some cases, even worse (see *LCL*, 548–49). Society often does fail to provide adequate protection against it, and the criminal law and its enforcement doubtless should be improved. Women do suffer an injustice in this matter, and it is unfair that they have to accept some of the constraints they must to reduce the risk of being raped. Moreover, if most ignored the risks, the crime's frequency undoubtedly would increase, and that might lead society to provide women with better protection. However, those who suggest you should ignore risks are trivializing what being raped would mean to you and inviting you to be a victim-martyr for their cause. That probably would not accomplish much, since few other women are likely to do the same. One suspects that even those who issue the invitation do not themselves do as they suggest, either because they prudently avoid risks of being raped or because their lifestyle keeps them out of situations of significant risk.

---

63. Research supports the view that calling for help, fleeing, and perhaps fighting back are more effective than verbal strategies for avoiding rape; see Joyce Levine-MacCombie and Mary P. Koss, "Acquaintance Rape: Effective Avoidance Strategies," *Psychology of Women Quarterly,* 10 (1986): 311–19, which includes references to previous research bearing mainly on rape by strangers.

If a man is about to rape you, should you resist? As explained above, not resisting rape does not constitute consenting to it. Since being raped is a grave injury, however, a victim always has a strong reason to resist. In some cases of incipient acquaintance rape, minimal force is used and the risks involved in resisting are slight, so that nonresistance is likely to be misinterpreted as expressing consent. Especially if her own wrongdoing has helped create the situation, the victim in such cases has a duty to resist, not only to prevent the injury to herself but to save the acquaintance who already is guilty of attempted rape from committing the greater crime.

However, the burdens and risks of resisting, especially if resistance is likely to be futile, can provide a compelling reason not to resist. Assaulted by a stranger and already injured or threatened with a deadly weapon, a woman might well suffer great injury or even death. In that situation, many women would not think of resisting, and only those well prepared to repel such an attack would be likely to succeed. Still, if a woman were ready and able to use force against a would-be rapist, her resistance would be justified even if it were likely to result in the attacker's death, provided she intended only self-defense and chose only the least destructive means that is available and adequate for that purpose (see *LCL,* 483–85). (I am not telling you to obtain training in self-defense or to equip yourself with a repellent or weapon; such tactics might be self-defeating, and only someone with the relevant expertise could provide reliable advice about them.)

The Church does indeed offer Susanna and Maria Goretti as models, but it does not follow that a woman always is morally obliged to resist being raped. Susanna was presented with a choice. The two old men said: "We are burning with desire for you; so give your consent, and lie with us. If you refuse, we will testify against you that a young man was with you, and this was why you sent your maids away."[64] Understanding her predicament in terms of a choice between refusing and consenting, she would have sinned had she consented, and so she rightly refused.[65] Maria Goretti, whose father had died and who kept house while her mother labored in the fields, repeatedly rejected a neighbor's attempts to seduce her, yet did not tell anyone because the young man threatened to kill her if she did. Finally, he menaced her with a dagger, but she refused to yield, saying: "No, God does not wish it. It is a sin. You would go to hell for it." Perhaps it did not occur to Maria that she could choose not to resist, or perhaps her passive compliance would not have satisfied the young man. In any case, the Church proposes her as a model both for her refusal to consent to fornication and for her merciful concern for the soul of her tormentor, whom she also forgave before she died.[66] Both cases illustrate the point that consent to nonmarital intercourse is always wrong, but neither shows it is wrong to suffer rape passively rather than actively resist.

Should you urge a rapist to use a condom? In some situations, that might seem to express consent, and, in any case, such a request should not be an alternative to resisting, if appropriate. Having made clear your unwillingness to engage in

---

64. Dn 13.20–21 (in the *NRSV* Bible, Dn 13 is Susanna, among the apocryphal books).
65. See John Paul II, *Veritatis splendor,* 91, *AAS* 85 (1993) 1205, *OR,* 6 Oct. 1993, xiv.
66. See *New Catholic Encyclopedia,* 6:632.

intercourse, however, your intention in urging a rapist to use a condom presumably would be to lessen the likelihood both of conception and of being infected with HIV and/or other diseases. The latter intention plainly is good, and so is the former insofar as it bears, not on preventing a baby, but on limiting the violent and unwanted union (see *LCL,* 512; q. 54, below). Moreover, inasmuch as the point of the request would be to prevent the fullness of wrongful intercourse, it would not constitute consent to intercourse. So, unless you feared the request would increase the likelihood that the rapist would carry on with the rape or inflict other injury, it would be morally acceptable.

If you were raped, what could you do about the possibility of becoming pregnant? The chance of becoming pregnant would be small, since conception seldom results from a single act of intercourse and is even less likely to result if that single act is rape (see q. 64, below). You might be able to further reduce the chance of conception, and it would help if you were aware of the stage of your menstrual cycle at the time. Fertility awareness also will be useful if you marry. So, you would do well to begin learning about natural family planning so that you will understand and be aware of your cycle, during which there is a stretch of only a few days when conception is possible.[67]

If the rape occurred after the fertile days had already passed, pregnancy would be impossible. If it occurred at the time of ovulation or shortly thereafter, nothing that can be done would reduce the chance of conception. If conception did occur, it certainly would be wrong to destroy the new individual who had come to be. So, it would be wrong to accept the abortifacient medication generally offered victims of rape who go to a hospital emergency room.[68] If it occurred after a menstrual period but before the signs of fertility had appeared, you could go *as soon as possible* to a hospital emergency room or *at once* see a physician. If you knew you could not be pregnant or a pregnancy test were negative, and if additional tests indicated that ovulation was not imminent, you could accept medication to suppress ovulation.[69]

Seeking medical care after rape and reporting the crime to the police are related. In some places, care providers are required by law to report the crime when a rape victim comes to them. Any woman who is raped should seek appropriate help, though that need not always mean medical care. But even if you were not interested in medical care after being raped, you have a serious responsibility as a citizen to report crimes and to help bring criminals to justice. Now, if a rape victim goes to a hospital emergency room as soon as possible, without cleansing herself or

---

67. See, e.g., John F. Kippley and Sheila K. Kippley, *The Art of Natural Family Planning,* 4th ed. (Cincinnati, Ohio.: Couple to Couple League, 1996); Evelyn Billings and Ann Westmore, *The Billings Method: Controlling Fertility without Drugs or Devices* (New York: Ballantine, 1983).

68. See Eugene F. Diamond, "Rape Protocol," *Linacre Quarterly,* 60:3 (Aug. 1993): 8–19, focusing on the use of Ovral; also see q. 64, below.

69. See *LCL,* 512, n. 103. Eugene F. Diamond, "Ovral in Rape Protocols," *Ethics and Medics,* 21:10 (Oct. 1996): 1–2, says (2) that determining the stage of the cycle "will require objective laboratory evidence such as the *Ovutest* to detect the LH surge, urine pregnanediol, and serum progesterone levels."

changing her clothing, the physician often can recover semen and/or other physical evidence useful in prosecuting the rapist; thus, a timely visit to a hospital emergency room probably would be part of your civic responsibility.

Strong negative emotions aroused by a horrible experience might tempt you not to report the crime. But one important reason why few rapists are punished is that many women do not fulfill this responsibility. Putting yourself in the place of others whom the rapist might victimize, you, as a victim of rape, would recognize your civic duty. If raped by a stranger you could not describe or identify, you might suppose reporting the crime would be pointless. But even such reports can alert others to danger and provide helpful information to the police. If raped by an acquaintance, you might suppose that reporting the crime to the police would be pitiless or that the matter should be dealt with by the college's disciplinary process. But prosecution in such a case not only could save other women from becoming the man's victims but could induce his repentance, and no college's disciplinary process is adequate to bring a rapist to justice. Only special circumstances would justify not reporting the crime to the police. Such circumstances could be of two sorts: the police and other law enforcement authorities were so sure to perform poorly that reporting certainly would be a waste of time, or reporting raised the prospect of such great burdens to you that not even the most conscientious citizens would expect you to bear them.[70]

Finally, though you do well to think about your responsibilities—being raped would be horrible and the danger of rape is real—do not be overly concerned about this single threat.[71] Some feminists have exaggerated the frequency of rape.[72] No doubt, acquaintance rape has increased in recent years, but a chaste and temperate woman is not very likely to be in a situation where a man she knows will rape her. And reasonable precautions, which will hardly add to the trouble both men and women must take to avoid being mugged, will greatly reduce the risk of being raped by a stranger.

21: May a man wish that his sister would kill herself?

I happen to be a priest, but my problem could just as well be a layman's. My parents were nearly forty when they married; I was born first and my sister five years later. Our relationship always was difficult; she resented my role as her big brother and felt that our parents favored me, though, in fact, they were too preoccupied with their careers to pay much attention to either of us. She married young, and her marriage lasted fifteen years though it was always miserable. After the divorce, she went through a period of promiscuity and drugs. By that time, our parents had died, and I more or less had to take over trying to help

70. Linda Fairstein, *Sexual Violence: Our War against Rape* (New York: William Morrow, 1993), makes a strong case for reporting rape and other sexual assault, and pressing charges; she admits that victims often used to be mistreated by police and prosecutors, but argues that those who report these crimes are likely to be treated better today.

71. Roiphe, op. cit., 51–71, puts the threat into perspective.

72. See Christina Hoff Sommers, *Who Stole Feminism: How Women Have Betrayed Women* (New York: Simon and Schuster, 1994), 209–26.

her. I did what I could, and she finally got clean when she saw that the alternative was losing her children.

At that point, I thought her other problems would be solved, but they have continued and even grown worse. She has had a succession of jobs, always ending in her being fired or quitting in anger, with intervening periods of unemployment, during which she has needed help from me. She has problems with her children, quarrels with teachers and neighbors, conflict everywhere. She is likely to do just the opposite of whatever I suggest and is never grateful for my help even when she has asked for it and I have done all she asked. She keeps burdening me with her problems, regardless of whether I can do anything about them; she seems to get some satisfaction out of forcing me to share her misery. She is immature, still like a teenager, and I am convinced she needs serious psychological help, but she will not cooperate. Usually she is more or less depressed and sometimes she says she is thinking of solving all her problems by killing herself.

My sister's visits and calls, often at very inconvenient times, have worn me down and interfered with my pastoral work. I feel that no busy professional should have to put up with a sister like mine. I used to be irritated with her occasionally; now I have a permanent feeling of resentment toward her. One form that feeling takes is the wish that she would follow through on her threats of suicide. I am not proud of that, but it is how I feel, and there is no use repressing one's feelings.

For a long time I tried to put that thought out of my mind. But I have come to accept it as a natural reaction. It is not that I want my sister dead, only that I want to be free of the burden she is imposing on me, and I see no end as long as we both live. Besides, I am convinced that people who kill themselves hardly ever are fully responsible, so it would not be a mortal sin if she did kill herself. Still, I sometimes feel guilty about this.

Analysis:

The explicit question concerns the moral acceptability of wishing that someone commit suicide. Whether another's suicide would be a mortal sin for him or her, one is responsible for one's own willing, and should not will that anyone commit suicide. If one merely imagines the suicide and its effect of relieving one's burden, that thought is not sinful in itself, but is an occasion of sin that ought to be avoided. The preceding norms are unlikely to be of practical help unless the questioner uncovers the roots of his resentment and deals with them. An implicit question concerns the integration of pastoral and familial responsibilities. An adequate response must clarify the questioner's responsibilities in each role.

The reply could be along the following lines:

I agree that it does not help to repress one's feelings, but I also think it is wrong to accept and endorse inappropriate feelings such as resentment. Rather than either repressing or accepting such feelings, one must try to uncover their deeper causes, deal appropriately with these, and so reduce inner tensions. Your account of your relationship with your sister suggests its unsatisfactoriness has roots going back to your childhood. Consequently, I think that, in addition to the moral advice I can give, you need the wise guidance and support of a good counselor or spiritual director: someone entirely faithful to Catholic teaching, mature, experienced in advising, and preferably with some formal training in psychology. If you do not know a suitable person, I suggest you confide in your bishop or the appropriate member of his staff, and seek assistance in obtaining help.

With respect to your moral problem, I cannot truthfully offer you reassuring advice to make things easy for you. If you deliberately wish your sister would follow through on her threats of suicide, that wish is a sin in grave matter, and you rightly "feel guilty about this." Whether her suicide would be a mortal sin for her is irrelevant; you are responsible for your own willing and may not will that anyone commit suicide. If you are only imagining that your sister might kill herself and thinking that would simplify your life—which seems to fit your description of your feelings—that thought is not sinful in itself. Still, hostile feelings may lead you from this sort of thinking into deliberate approval of the thought that it would be good if she committed suicide, and so you should try to avoid such thinking as an occasion of sin. You also should try to avoid it so that it will neither lead you to say or do anything that would reinforce your sister's temptation to commit suicide nor give you guilt feelings. These latter probably would have the bad result of inhibiting you from resisting your sister's unreasonable demands, which seem to provide her with an inadequate substitute for the psychological help she needs.

It may be that many people kill themselves without committing a mortal sin, but only God knows each person's heart well enough to judge his or her moral responsibility, and you should not be complacent about the prospect of your sister's suicide (see *CCC,* 2280–83; *LCL,* 477). For all you know, it could result in her eternal damnation. (In case thoughts about suicide ever lead to a temptation to take your own life, that frightful prospect should not be ignored.) Moreover, even if a suicide is not mortally sinful, it is likely to injure survivors gravely. Consider how your sister's suicide might affect her children and you.

While the preceding paragraphs respond to your specific question, I would be remiss if I did not offer you a wider perspective for reflecting on your problem. God calls every person to fulfill his or her personal vocation, which embraces not only a certain state of life and other appropriate upright commitments but conditions beyond one's control, such as sickness, unemployment, and other forms of suffering. For God sometimes allows bad things to happen to us and calls on us to make the most of them for the sake of witness and service to the kingdom (see *CCC,* 309–14). Each of us should discover, accept, and faithfully fulfill all the elements of his or her vocation, weaving them together to form a seamless whole (see *LCL,* 113–29). God has called you to be both a brother for your sister and a priest for the people he entrusts to your care, and you must integrate these two roles with each other. Your statement that you "feel that no busy professional should have to put up with a sister like mine" seems to me to reveal tension between the two roles, arising at least partly from an inadequate understanding of the responsibilities pertaining to each.

Your sister's inner tensions, it seems to me, at least in part interlock with yours. You describe her as "immature, still like a teenager," and the other things you say about her seem to bear out that description. Unlike well-integrated young children or mature adults, many teenagers make demands on parents even while resenting their authority, and are unready for independence even while they are intensely eager for it. Thus, your sister ignores your advice and is ungrateful for your help even when she demands it, because she is ambivalent about your persistent efforts to fulfill a parental role toward her. Indeed, these efforts of yours may be enabling her to persist in her immaturity, and you might well give her more real help by doing less for her. At the same time, desisting from your misplaced efforts is likely to reduce your own burden and the hostile feelings it provokes. Therefore, it seems to me you should stop trying to play a parental role and instead should play only the appropriate roles of pastor and brother.

In calling men to the priesthood, Jesus asks them to leave their families behind in order to serve him and his people (see Mt 4.18–22, 19.27; Lk 5.11, 18.28–29)—a very severe demand in his society, where family responsibilities were taken far more seriously than in ours. So, there are real limits to the time and energy you may rightly spend on family affairs. The limits would be the same, though, even if your sister had no problems and were a source of enjoyable and diverting companionship for you. Moreover, priesthood carries with it no right to immunity from any miseries of the human condition, and many busy professionals must deal with family problems as stressful as yours. Therefore, the unsatisfactoriness to you of the relationship with your sister should not enter into your judgments concerning your responsibilities either as brother or as pastor.

On the other hand, as a priest, you are not merely a busy professional. Your responsibility is not merely to do certain things for certain people during certain hours of the day. It begins with preaching the gospel, administering the sacraments, and leading your flock, but it extends to helping anyone with serious moral and spiritual problems whenever you can. Your sister plainly has had such problems and has them now, and so you owed and owe her now the same pastoral care you would have given and would give her were she not your sister. Pastoral care surely includes directing people who seem to need psychological help to those likely to be able to provide it. But even when someone does not accept such advice, pastoral care also includes listening to his or her problems, whether or not you can do anything about them, and encouraging the person to hope and pray that God will do what you cannot. People do get some satisfaction out of sharing their problems, even with someone who cannot solve them; a sympathetic ear reassures suffering persons that they are respected and loved for themselves. As a pastor you should try to help people, including your sister, by providing such reassurance and then encouraging them to take their troubles to God, with the confidence that he will prove to be a loving and merciful Father.

No doubt you have your sister's true good at heart. Recommit yourself to it with brotherly love. But your sister must live her own life, and you cannot live it for her. Think of her well-being, not as a goal she will attain by following your planning and direction, but rather as her own ongoing fulfillment, which cannot progress except by her own decisions and efforts, guided and sustained by the light and power only the Holy Spirit provides. Make constant prayer for your sister your contribution to this end, offering with it as sacrifice whatever distress she continues to cause you. You should respond calmly and gently to her demands, however, informing her of appropriate sources of help, just as you inform other people in the course of your pastoral work. But rather than pressing such help upon her, with the likelihood that she will refuse, politely reject her emotional demands, perhaps by saying: "I have obtained the kind of help I needed to deal with my problems, and perhaps you should do that too. I always will be here to listen to your problems and to pray with you about them, but I have come to see I cannot help you much in any other way."

Your troubled relationship with your sister may have damaged your pastoral relationship with those you are called to serve. If so, you should also recommit yourself to your responsibilities as pastor toward every member of your flock. Bear in mind that every adult must live his or her own life; avoid taking an inappropriate parental role toward anyone. Though you should strive to be a spiritual father to all, that fatherhood should nurture maturity, not dependency. Remember, too, that, though your service deserves gratitude, ungrateful spiritual children require appropriate service. The ingratitude of God's People did not deter the Good Shepherd, and ingratitude never deters a loving father from taking good care of his children.

Suffering naturally provokes resentment, and so it is not surprising that the suffering your sister causes you has led to your resenting her. But the gospel calls us to accept the suffering that comes our way as a share in Jesus' cross and to respond to provocations with healing love. Very likely, you never will be free of the "endless burden" your sister imposes on you, but if you share it with the suffering Jesus, it will become light and easy for you to bear (see Mt 11.30). As I have said, your suffering will be a suitable sacrifice for you to offer on your sister's behalf, and your willing acceptance of your cross will contribute to the witness your life should give to the truth of the gospel you preach.

Last, not least, transformed by faith and love, your appropriate efforts to help your sister, and your difficult relationship with her, will be suitable material for the heavenly kingdom (see GS 38–39). Though hidden now, the kingdom is not far off. Its reality is present to us every time we receive the body and blood of the Lord, and we need serve him here on earth only briefly before the mystery will be unveiled to us. When every other tear is wiped away, so too will your seemingly endless burden end.

22: Should a parent say: "If you can't be good, be careful"?

I am the father of two teenagers, the elder of whom, a boy, will be going away to college in the fall. I have tried to convey to them the Church's rules about the proper use of sexuality, emphasizing that sexual relations are for married couples and that intercourse always should be a real act of love.

Now my problem. In view of the AIDS epidemic, not to mention the high infection rates of other sexually transmitted diseases, what should I say about the use of condoms? May I say, "Try to stay out of bed, but if you can't, protect yourself"? I'm very reluctant to tell my son that. But I know that if I do not and he contracts AIDS, I will wish I had urged him to take precautions. Then too, if a vaccine were available for AIDS, I am sure I would want him to have it. But for the time being, condoms are the only protection. So, it seems a matter of hygiene to recommend their use.

I realize that the problem has other dimensions—whether even mentioning using condoms implicitly encourages extramarital relations, how effective condoms are, and so on. But I am interested only in the moral question: whether, in today's circumstances, a father may encourage the use of condoms to impede the spread of AIDS, a deadly disease, and other diseases that are nasty enough.

Analysis:

The question is whether parents should advise their children about how to mitigate the bad effects of their possible, future, sexual misbehavior. The questioner should not give such advice. It would suggest to his son that he is unable to avoid sexual immorality—a view incompatible with Catholic faith. Parents not only should communicate the Church's teachings about sexuality, but should explain them, so that these truths about human and Christian fulfillment will be persuasive reasons for living chastely. Since it always is gravely wrong to take unnecessary risks to health, the truth about condoms' limited effectiveness provides the basis for another argument against promoting so-called safe sex.

The reply could be along the following lines:

Without misbehaving in any way, a man or a woman could be infected with HIV. Blood screening is not absolutely perfect, and contact with infected blood could occur in an accident. Men as well as women sometimes are raped, and a careless infected surgeon or dentist might transmit the disease to a patient. With these risks and the deadliness of the disease in view, most conscientious parents surely would have their children vaccinated against HIV if a safe and effective vaccine were available at a reasonable price. Recommending condoms to one's children is an entirely different matter, however, because doing so is pointless unless one assumes they are going to engage in illicit sexual behavior.

You ask: "May I say, 'Try to stay out of bed, but if you can't, protect yourself'?" No. In the first place, your son hardly needs that advice; he surely has heard it many times. More important, "try to" and "if you can't" imply that sexual immorality is unavoidable—a view incompatible with the Church's defined doctrine that every Christian can avoid mortal sin (see DS 1568/828). But a young person who experiences temptation is all too likely to embrace that erroneous view, for, if it were correct, there would be no guilt in giving in to the temptation.

That evasion of guilt, no doubt, along with the lack of experience of God's grace given in answer to sincere and trusting prayer explain why many nonbelievers claim that no normal person can be chaste. But, in fact, some healthy young people entirely avoid sexual intimacy until marriage. Even if they are a minority, they falsify the general thesis that "everyone does it." And falsifying that general position by contrary examples is not simply a logical trick. Even one counterexample shows that the general thesis is erroneous and that the theory of which it is a part requires fundamental changes.

Moreover, among the important things parents need to communicate to their children—in addition to the truth of faith that with God's grace every Christian can avoid evil and become holy—are that the parents are confident this is true of their children and *expect* it of them. Your son is not an animal driven by sexual instinct; though subject to temptation as all of us are, he is a person, rational and free. If you think of him and deal with him as if he were not, you will deprive him of the respect you owe him. That will undermine his self-respect and your relationship with him.

Someone might object: "But shouldn't a mother tell her daughter: 'Stay out of bed, but if you ever do get pregnant, don't get an abortion'?" That advice would not be so bad. It does not imply that sin is inevitable, and it warns against committing a greater sin to deal with the result of a lesser sin, rather than recommending that one sin be committed to try to forestall a feared bad consequence of another. Even so, making the point in that way would communicate a lack of maternal confidence and low expectations of the daughter. The point should be made in a different way, for instance: "Very likely some of your acquaintances will get pregnant and be tempted to get an abortion, and you might not want to get involved in their problem. But a girl is more likely to do the wrong thing if people who know better shy away. So, do listen, sympathize, and encourage anyone who gets pregnant to talk with her parents. If they are like us, they will surely help her, so that she will love her baby and not kill him or her."

You also realize that the problem has other dimensions—"whether even mentioning using condoms implicitly encourages extramarital relations, how effective condoms are, and so on"—but you wish to set them aside. However, I would not be responding adequately to your question if I did so, since that would abstract from relevant facts with important moral implications.

Merely *mentioning* the use of condoms need not encourage extramarital relations. For, as I shall explain in a moment, parents and teachers can mention condoms in order to make it clear that they offer only an illusion of security. However, even implicitly suggesting their use would convey a clear message to your son: "I do not have faith in you, and I do not really expect you to be chaste." Moreover, it might well convey an even more corrupting message: "Chastity may be ideal, but it's not obligatory for red-blooded men like you and me. Welcome to the club, son, where the norm is fornication for the single man and adultery for the married man." Even the less harmful of those messages, especially coming from you as a father, certainly will undermine all the efforts you have rightly made to convey the Church's teachings about sexuality to your children.

Those teachings not only should be conveyed but explained, so that your children will understand them, not as arbitrary and outdated rules meant to spoil their enjoyment and make them feel guilty, but as ever-relevant truths that direct them toward real happiness and away from the burden of real guilt, which is the harm people do to their innermost selves when they follow the lure of their feelings and violate the truth.

The first part of that explanation should be that our bodies are our very selves, not mere things we have and use, and that our genital organs are a divine gift empowering us to enter into the one-flesh communion of faithful marriage and to fulfill that communion by having and raising our own children. Moreover, because the divine Word became flesh and has joined us to himself in faith by means of baptism and in bodily communion by means of the sacrament of the Eucharist, our bodies are sacred: temples of the Holy Spirit called to resurrection and everlasting life in heavenly communion. So, to abuse one's sexuality not only is to degrade oneself but to be unfaithful to Jesus and to make oneself unfit for heaven (see 1 Cor 6.9–20).

Next, you should explain why sexual activity apart from marriage is wrong (see *LCL,* 648–68). Genuine love is communion of persons, a union in which each gives himself or herself to the other, while both become more perfectly themselves, fulfilled as distinct persons. On the one hand, sexual activity apart from marriage very often has nothing whatever to do with genuine love; it is no more than the use of one's own body and that of another person as mere instruments to provide an enjoyable experience. That experience, like a chemical "high," contributes nothing to, but rather displaces, the activities that really fulfill individuals and build up their communion. On the other hand, sometimes a man and a woman who engage in sexual activity apart from marriage wish to share in a one-flesh communion, but their lack of permanent commitment and unreadiness for parenthood make authentic one-flesh communion impossible, so that their intimate experience is only an illusion; they feel as though they are experiencing marital communion but do not really achieve it.

At the same time, young couples who engage in sex without marrying miss out on chaste friendship, which they could have had if they had restrained themselves and cultivated it. Such friendships are an excellent preparation for marriage, in which the spouses must cooperate generously, often selflessly sacrificing immediate satisfaction for each other's good and their children's well-being. Moreover, chastity before marriage allows a newly wed couple to enjoy together all the novelty and wonder of sexual intimacy, and in this way to experience their unique bonding in committed communion. This experience cannot be anticipated by premarital experiments in intimacy; rather, these impede it and perhaps even render it impossible.

You also should make it clear to your son that you fully realize you cannot force him to follow your advice and have no desire to do so. You fully recognize that he must make his own choices, and you realize from your own experience how hard it can be for a young man to be chaste. Still, you believe that, with the help of God's grace, everyone who really wants to be chaste can resist temptation and make consistently good choices, and that the necessary grace always is available to those who seek it through prayer and the devout reception of the sacraments.

Since young people often are influenced by peer pressure, try to ensure that your son goes to a school whose moral environment is, if not salubrious, at least not aggressively corrupting. Point out to your children that self-respect is worth far more than acceptance by the crowd. Of course, not everyone, in even the most decadent schools, engages in premarital sex. Individuals of like character usually can identify one another easily, and you should encourage your son to make friends with people of both sexes who are trying to conform in every respect to the way of the Lord Jesus. Forming a few genuine and close friendships with those who share one's profound beliefs and values overcomes loneliness and provides many other benefits. In no way, moreover, does it preclude friendly association with other members of the college community, whose beliefs and values differ, in mutually enriching dialogue and the pursuit of common interests in cultural activities, sports, and so on.[73]

The preceding considerations constitute an adequate case against advising your son along the lines you are considering. However, since it always is gravely wrong to take unnecessary risks to health, both one's own and others', the facts about currently available condoms point to a secondary moral argument against promoting so-called safe sex.

Used as contraceptives, condoms often fail.[74] Even used perfectly, that is, precisely according to directions and without any exceptions whatsoever, condoms still fail; two women per hundred will experience an unintended pregnancy during the first year of use.[75] The reason for this irreducible failure rate is that condoms sometimes break, tear, leak, or slip off entirely.

Besides, in considering the implications for so-called safe sex of condoms' failure rate as contraceptives, one must bear in mind that women naturally are fertile only part of the time, so that most of the time a condom's failure *cannot* lead to pregnancy. By contrast, anyone engaging in intimate contact is susceptible on every occasion to any sexually transmitted disease his or her partner has.[76] Furthermore, even if people coolly plan to use condoms regularly, hot passion will lead most of them to take a chance now and then—when a condom is not at hand, or when using it seems inconvenient, or when a sexual partner resists this hindrance to intimacy.

True enough, on any single occasion, if a condom is carefully and correctly used, it will reduce somewhat the probability of transmitting various diseases. Perhaps the widespread use of condoms would slow the spread of sexually transmitted diseases. I say *perhaps* because the widespread practice of sexual abstinence outside marriage would be even more effective, and increased use of condoms is counterproductive insofar as, making abstinence seem less necessary, it leads to more frequent illicit intercourse. Still, the net effect might be to reduce the rate at which venereal diseases spread, which is why many public health officials and others less concerned about individual well-being

---

73. Mary Beth Bonacci, *Real Love* (San Francisco: Ignatius Press, 1996), provides sound, clear, and appealing answers to many of the questions asked by young adults. Many parents would find her book helpful; they might use it either as a resource for themselves, a basis for discussion with their children, or a gift for their children to read and share with friends.

74. Susan Harlap, Kathryn Kost, and Jacqueline Darroch Forrest, *Preventing Pregnancy, Protecting Health: A New Look at Birth Control Choices in the United States* (New York: The Alan Guttmacher Institute, 1991), 120, estimate that with average use of condoms, sixteen women per hundred will experience an unintended pregnancy during the first year of use.

75. Ibid.

76. See Susan C. Weller, "A Meta-Analysis of Condom Effectiveness in Reducing Sexually Transmitted HIV," *Social Science and Medicine,* 36 (1993): 1635–44; she concludes (1642): "The public at large may not understand the difference between 'condoms may reduce risk of' and 'condoms will prevent' HIV infection. It is a disservice to encourage the belief that condoms *will prevent* sexual transmission of HIV. Condoms will not eliminate risk of sexual transmission and, in fact, may only lower the risk somewhat."

than about social problems promote "safe sex" or "safer sex" (more accurately called "maybe-not-quite-so-risky sex").

In the long run, however, even regular condom use will not indefinitely protect an individual from contracting a disease. Due to condoms' failure rate, depending on them to prevent the transmission of diseases makes it virtually certain that sooner or later those infected will transmit their infections to their noninfected sex partners. The odds may be better than those facing people who play Russian roulette, but the principle is the same: Even with favorable odds, a gambler who repeatedly risks everything eventually loses everything.

You say: "I know that if I do not [tell my son to protect himself] and he contracts AIDS, I will wish I had urged him to take precautions." If you give your son sound moral advice and he engages in intercourse despite it, he might contract a disease, whether or not he uses condoms.[77] But the preceding explanation makes it clear that in neither case will you have any reason to wish you had advised him to use them. However, if you warn your son to protect himself and, following your advice, he uses condoms and contracts a venereal disease, you will have good reason to wish you had urged him to be chaste and warned him not to be misled by the illusory protection of condoms.

If I were you, I would indeed tell my children about condoms. But I would begin by telling them about umbrellas. I would say: "Umbrellas often keep you from getting soaked when you must go out in a heavy rain. But they don't keep the rain off you entirely, and sometimes the wind blows them around, despite your best efforts to hold them steady, or they tear or turn inside out, and you do get soaked. If your life depended on not getting rained on, I wouldn't tell you: 'Don't go out in the rain without your umbrella!' No, I'd just tell you: 'Never go out in the rain!' Now, when people engage in sexual intercourse and try to protect themselves by using a condom, their lives may well depend on its working perfectly. But condoms are like umbrellas. They sometimes break, tear, leak, or slip off entirely. So, nobody should imagine that condoms make risky sex safe. Any sex outside chaste marriage can give you a miserable disease and might even kill you."

23: May a parent condone a son's homosexual activity?

I find myself the mother of a homosexually active son. The youngest of five children, he now is in his early twenties. In all respects except his sexual orientation, this young man is very normal and masculine in manner; he also is a caring and responsible person. Because he feels that the Church scorns homosexuals and encourages discrimination against them, he is very alienated. I've talked with two priests who encouraged me to soften the Church's official message to him, but despite my attempts to do so, he no longer goes to Mass.

While my first reactions on learning about his homosexual activity were dismay and guilt, the reading I've done has convinced me that homosexuality is a prede-

---

77. I say "a disease" rather than "AIDS," because heterosexual intercourse seldom transmits HIV infection; see Michael B. Flanagan, "A Study of AIDS," *Linacre Quarterly,* 63:1 (Feb. 1996): 61–74.

termined condition. I've been told that the Church did not always distinguish between the homosexual condition and homosexual acts, and all homosexual acts used to be regarded as if they were freely chosen by perverted heterosexuals. Today, many Catholic writers seem to realize that people do not freely choose to be homosexuals, but even they refuse to deal with the realities of a homosexual's life.

As I understand it, the Church's position is that the homosexual condition may be accepted as a given but should never be acted upon—those who find themselves in this condition are required under pain of sin to live totally celibate lives. That would be ideal, I'm sure. But how can I as a mother make my son feel guilty about wanting a normal sex life? How can I tell him his desire for a loving, committed relationship with another man is a sin? Were he to accept a celibate lifestyle voluntarily by becoming a priest or religious, that choice would be his. As it is, he had no choice; causes beyond his control have made him naturally homosexual in orientation, just as they have given him naturally wavy hair.

What position do I take? I would truly like to know how far I may go in supporting my son and where I must draw the line.

Analysis:

This question concerns the responsibilities of parents toward adult children who habitually engage in homosexual behavior. While the questioner should continue to love her son and work to promote his true good, she may not condone his homosexual activity. She should encourage him to live chastely, and should not encourage him to try to establish a so-called committed relationship. An adequate reply must criticize the considerations proposed to rationalize habitual homosexual behavior and to distinguish it from other habits of objectively immoral behavior, such as alcohol abuse.

The reply could be along the following lines:

Your question indeed is difficult, and the anguish you feel, torn between love for your son and conscientious concern to avoid going too far in supporting him, deserves and has my sincere sympathy. If I could truthfully offer reassuring advice to make the problem easy for you, I would. But I cannot, for I believe what the Catholic Church teaches about sexual acts outside marriage, namely, that they are always grave matter.[78] This teaching not only is grounded in divine revelation but understandable, since people who engage in sexual acts outside marriage inevitably bring serious harm upon themselves and others.[79]

---

78. See Congregation for the Doctrine of the Faith, *Persona humana,* 10, *AAS* 68 (1976) 89, Flannery, 2:494; *Letter to Bishops of the Catholic Church on the Pastoral Care of Homosexual Persons,* 2–7, *AAS* 79 (1987) 543–47, *OR,* 10 Nov. 1986, 2. The Congregation's use of Scripture regarding sodomy often is criticized, but there are cogent replies to the exegetical arguments offered in defense of sodomy. Besides the works cited in *LCL,* 654, n. 194, see Thomas E. Schmidt, *Straight and Narrow: Compassion and Clarity in the Homosexual Debate* (Downers Grove, Ill.: InterVarsity Press, 1995), 39–99; Dennis Prager, "Homosexuality, the Bible, and Us: A Jewish Perspective," *Public Interest,* 112 (Summer 1993): 60–83.

79. The wrongness and seriousness of sexual sins outside marriage are treated at length in *LCL,* 648–68; dissenting theological views were examined and answered in *CMP,* 141–71, 381–90, and 831–916. John Paul II, *Veritatis splendor,* 28–83, *AAS* 85 (1993) 1156–1200, *OR,* 6

This teaching should not be softened in any way, but it must be understood in proper perspective. To begin with, the Church's teaching regarding sexual sins does not single out sodomy; it refers as well to all the unchaste acts of heterosexual couples and to masturbation. Moreover, though this moral teaching is part of our faith, it is not so central as the more fundamental truths that God loves each and every person as the unique individual he or she is, that he calls all of us to everlasting happiness in his kingdom, that all of us sin and need the salvation Jesus won for us, that everyone who repents and asks for forgiveness will receive it, and that Christians should love one another, have compassion for one another, and support one another's struggles against temptations to commit any serious sin, whether of pride, avarice, lust, revenge, or any other sort.

It seems that your reading has given you an inadequate view of homosexuality and the Church's teaching about it.[80] Though it is true that theologians until recent times paid little attention to predispositions to homosexual behavior, alcohol abuse, violence toward others, and so on, confessors certainly always realized that not everyone exercises the same freedom in these matters. They recognized that human nature, wounded by original sin, leaves every human being with moral handicaps of one kind or another. But they thought that, just as all of us must struggle to overcome natural tendencies to self-centeredness, so those afflicted with less common moral handicaps may not affirm and yield to them, as if their naturalness made them good.

Still, you are correct in noting that the Church today clearly distinguishes between homosexual acts and the homosexual condition—that is, the stable disposition of an adult toward sexually arousing and gratifying bodily contact with persons of the same sex. The homosexual condition is subject to degree. While most people are exclusively heterosexual, only a very small minority is exclusively homosexual; between the two groups is a spectrum of people. Thus, homosexual acts sometimes are chosen by people with a predominantly heterosexual condition, and some adolescents and young adults who experience homosexual attraction and engage in some homosexual acts later become entirely heterosexual.

Insofar as homosexuality is an inclination arising independently of an individual's choices, the factors disposing to it, while perhaps in part genetic (like those that cause wavy hair) or otherwise biological, also apparently are at least in part psychodynamic, having to do with inadequacies in the person's development in early childhood, before he or she can make free choices.[81] At

---

Oct. 1993, v–xiii, examines dissenting theological views, finds them in some respects incompatible with divine revelation, and reaffirms the exceptionless moral norms contained in the Church's most firm and constant teaching.

80. For a more adequate view, see John F. Harvey, O.S.F.S., *The Homosexual Person: New Thinking in Pastoral Care* (San Francisco: Ignatius Press, 1987); *The Truth about Homosexuality: The Cry of the Faithful* (San Francisco: Ignatius Press, 1996). Harvey, a priest, has devoted many years to helping homosexual persons; his books are both sound and compassionate.

81. While genetic and other biological factors perhaps predispose toward a homosexual condition, it also appears to depend on social experience affecting the individual's development. A sound treatment of this issue: Jeffrey Keefe, O.F.M.Conv., "Key Aspects of Homosexuality," in Harvey, *The Truth about Homosexuality,* 31–67. For a detailed study of the issue with no theological presuppositions: Michael Ruse, *Homosexuality: A Philosophical Inquiry* (New York:

least in some cases, moreover, a young person's sexual tendencies are ambiguous, and the choices he or she makes can develop and confirm either a heterosexual or a homosexual condition.

It also is worth noting that, while about sixty percent of American psychiatrists voted in 1973 no longer to classify homosexuality as a psychological illness in and of itself, many therapists continue to treat it as a psychological problem and report success in helping persons who find themselves homosexual and wish to become heterosexual.[82] If people with an inclination to homosexual behavior can afford to seek such help and could change their inclination by cooperating with it, their condition, even if it existed prior to their free choice, is not absolutely determined, and so lies within the field of their moral responsibility.

Those more or less definitely homosexual in condition enjoy diverse degrees of self-control. Like other sexual behavior—compulsive masturbation, pathological heterosexual promiscuity, and so on—homosexual behavior can be compulsive. And like other forms of compulsive behavior, such as kleptomania, any sort of compulsive sexual behavior is a serious and painful psychological illness that calls for therapy. Those suffering from a psychological compulsion are not morally guilty for each instance of the compulsive behavior, but they do have a grave responsibility to seek help and commit themselves to cooperate with it so as to overcome the compulsion.

Persons who have a homosexual inclination but not a compulsion to act upon it can and should freely commit themselves to living chastely. That may not be as hard for women as for men, but, however that may be, I shall consider only men, since your question concerns your son.

Living chastely surely will not be easy for any young man; indeed, many will experience it as part of the cross they are called to bear. Homosexually inclined men are not the only ones called to bear this cross, nor the only ones given it without their choosing it. Until heterosexual boys and men can marry validly, all of them also are called to perfect continence, and married men are morally required to abstain from sexual activity during illnesses, separations, fertile times when birth

---

Basil Blackwell, 1988), 21–175, esp. 164–65. J. Michael Bailey and Richard C. Pillard, "A Genetic Study of Male Sexual Orientation," *Archives of General Psychiatry,* 48 (1991): 1089–96, studied fifty-six homosexual or bisexual men having identical-twin brothers and found twenty-seven heterosexuals among those twins. Since these pairs of identical twins not only had exactly the same genes but also were affected similarly by many other common conditions before birth and during childhood, this study shows that the homosexual condition is neither straightforwardly inherited (as wavy hair is) nor determined by the many environmental factors common to identical twins. All those factors and the common heredity together only predisposed toward homosexuality in ways that allowed other factors to exclude it from almost half the identical twin brothers. In support of this point, Schmidt, op. cit., 131–53, summarizes additional evidence.

82. See, e.g., Elizabeth Moberly, *Psychogenesis: The Early Development of Gender Identity* (London: Routledge and Kegan Paul, 1983); Gerard J. M. van den Aardweg, *On the Origins and Treatment of Homosexuality: A Psychoanalytic Reinterpretation* (New York: Praeger, 1986); Irving Bieber et al., *Homosexuality: A Psychoanalytic Study* (Northvale, N.J.: Jason Aronson, 1988); Charles W. Socarides, *Homosexuality: Psychoanalytic Therapy* (Northvale, N.J.: Jason Aronson, 1989); Joseph Nicolosi, *Reparative Therapy of Male Homosexuality: A New Clinical Approach* (Northvale, N.J.: Jason Aronson, 1991).

regulation is appropriate, and so on. Indeed, like men whose homosexual condition resists change, probably at least as many men who are heterosexual are morally required to abstain permanently—for example, because they cannot marry or because, though married, they are divorced or permanently separated, or no longer can engage in marital intercourse due to some health problem of their own or their spouse's.

Thus, while the frequent and regular experience of sexual satisfaction may be statistically normal in contemporary post-Christian society, that hardly establishes the moral norm for faithful Christians. Indeed, the assumption that people with a homosexual condition are entitled to "a normal sex life" is both confused and misleading.

It is confused because, while many contemporary nonbelievers suppose that everyone is entitled to regular sexual satisfaction, the Catholic Church firmly holds—and until quite recently all other Christian communities also held—that only married couples are entitled to sexual activity and that even they have only a limited right to it.[83] And while people today often take it for granted that sexual abstinence always leads to virtually unbearable tension, many Christians know by experience that, with God's grace and appropriate support, peaceful self-mastery is attainable.[84]

The notion of a "normal" sex life constituted by homosexual acts is misleading for at least two reasons. First, though human sexuality's meaning and value transcend the biological, sexual behavior fundamentally pertains to a person's reproductive capacity. This basic meaning and value of sex grounds every other aspect of its personal and interpersonal significance, so that humans can fulfill themselves through sexual behavior only in marriage—the stable communion of a man and a woman that is appropriate for having children and raising them (see *LCL*, 553–647).[85] So, like other sexual behavior apart from marriage, homosexual acts cannot express and perfect authentic interpersonal communion; those who

---

83. The belief of Christians—universal until quite recently—that all sexual activities outside marriage gravely violate God's law cannot have been mistaken, for, as Vatican II teaches: "The body of the faithful as a whole, anointed as they are by the Holy One (cf. Jn 2.20, 27), cannot err in matters of belief. Thanks to a supernatural sense of the faith that characterizes the People as a whole, it manifests this unerring quality when, 'from the bishops down to the last member of the laity,' [note omitted] it shows universal agreement in matters of faith and morals" (LG 12).

84. A sound work offering helpful insight and many suggestions for nurturing the virtue of chastity: Benedict J. Groeschel, O.F.M.Cap., *The Courage to Be Chaste* (New York: Paulist Press, 1985).

85. G. Robina Quale, *A History of Marriage Systems,* (New York: Greenwood Press, 1988), 305, summarizes the anthropological data: "Marriage *is* an alliance before it is anything else. It is an alliance between the two who are marrying. It is an alliance between families who become more closely linked . . . .. Marriage is the means by which the larger social system recognizes not only the mother, but also the father of the children whom the mother bears. Marriage acknowledges each as the other's partner in bringing children into the world and raising them. Marriage is also the means by which the larger social system seeks to control the expression of the powerful instincts of sexual attraction." Thus, *homosexual marriage* is a self-contradictory expression; of course, like certain other absurdities, it could be used to name a fiction by which the advantages of the legal status enjoyed by married couples would be extended to certain pairs of persons of the same sex.

engage in them at best achieve only an unsatisfying illusion of intimacy and at worst simply use one another as means to self-satisfaction (see *LCL,* 648–54). Second, the ideal of a "loving, committed relationship" is hard enough for heterosexual couples to realize in Christian marriage; for men who engage in homosexual activity together, its pursuit hardly is realistic. Serious research indicates that, though some such men form couples and share living quarters, few such relationships are lasting, and almost none are faithful, excluding all other partners.[86]

This conclusion by no means implies that your son must live without love. Like all of us, he may and should love and be loved, since love is not reducible to sexual activity and is an essential part of every good human life. Like all of us, he may and should cultivate friendships, truly committed relationships, with people of both sexes. Love and commitment, far from requiring sexual activity, entirely exclude it, not only from relationships among men, but from every form of interpersonal association except marriage.

While considering it necessary to offer you a view of homosexuality more nuanced than the one you seem to have gathered from your reading, I am anxious not to reawaken the guilt you experienced on learning about your son's homosexual condition and activity. Some parents, having been grossly negligent with respect to their duties, no doubt are morally responsible for many of their children's problems. But assuming you have been a dutiful and caring mother, you need not and should not hold yourself responsible for your son's problems, even if you fully accept the view I have summarized.

You surely never intended that your son have this trait, and you never anticipated that anything you might do or fail to do would contribute to its development. Looking back, of course, you realize that you were not a perfect parent; no parent is, and I myself certainly was not. But, while not perfect parents, we cannot bear grave guilt for anything we neither intended nor foresaw, and this remains true whether the problems and misbehavior of our children result partly from our inadequacies in dealing with them and relating to them, or entirely from other factors, such as genetic defects, the post-Christian cultural environment, and their own wrong free choices.

Though some Catholics, including some priests, have had wrong attitudes toward persons who are homosexual and sometimes treated them badly, the

---

86. Alan P. Bell and Martin S. Weinberg, *Homosexualities: A Study of Diversity among Men and Women* (New York: Simon and Schuster, 1978), 81–93, 308–9, studied 574 white male homosexuals, 100% of whom had already had at least three sexual partners, 97% at least ten, 75% at least one hundred, and 28% at least one thousand. David P. McWhirter and Andrew W. Mattison (both homosexual), *The Male Couple: How Relationships Develop* (Englewood Cliffs, N.J.: Prentice Hall, 1984), 252–59, studied 156 male homosexual couples, most of whom once expected to have a sexually exclusive relationship, and found that only seven of these couples—none of whom had been together five years—claimed to have succeeded. Many apologists for the moral acceptability of homosexual behavior blame such promiscuity and failure to maintain stable relationships on society's mistreatment of, and negative attitude toward, people who are homosexual; however, Marshall Kirk and Hunter Madsen (again, both homosexual), *After the Ball: How America Will Conquer Its Fear and Hatred of Gays in the '90s* (New York: Doubleday, 1989), 302–7, 318–32, honestly and clearly explain the psychological causes *within* such people that account for those phenomena.

Catholic Church neither scorns such persons nor encourages unfairness to them (see *CCC*, 2358). Some who claim to defend and promote the rights of people with a homosexual condition spread these calumnies against the Church as part of their effort to coerce her into condoning homosexual behavior and supporting their effort to gain social and legal acceptance for it.

The Church, I repeat, does not scorn people with a homosexual condition, any more than she scorns people afflicted with other psychological deficits that give rise to temptations—a volcanic temper, say, or a tendency toward miserliness. Even those who engage in homosexual acts are no more scorned by the Church than are masturbators or fornicators. Like the loving mother you wish to be to your son, the Church loves all her sinful children, seeking their true good by teaching them what that is, offering them many helps to escape the slavery of sin and grow in holiness, and praying constantly for them.

The Church does not encourage or condone unjust discrimination against persons who are homosexual. She teaches constantly and most firmly that every human being has fundamental rights, flowing from the nature of human persons made in God's image and called to share in divine life (see *CCC*, 1929–35; *LCL*, 382–83). On this basis, she insists that each and every person's intrinsic dignity always should be respected in words, in actions, and by the law, and firmly condemns offenses against that dignity, including assaults on people identified as homosexuals and unjust discrimination against them.

At the same time, to protect other people's rights, the Church holds that in some areas, such as the placement of children for adoption and the employment of teachers, an individual's avowed homosexual condition can be considered, with no unjust discrimination, a disqualifying characteristic. Moreover, the Church rejects the claim that the homosexual condition should be treated as one of those characteristics, like race and sex, on whose basis laws in the U.S. and some other nations mandate special treatment for members of groups so identified, on the theory that this is necessary to overcome disadvantages they have been unjustly subjected to.[87]

The fallacy in this claim is that, unlike race or sex, the homosexual condition is not a neutral or valuable trait but a tendency to engage in morally excluded behavior. If and insofar as homosexuality results from a natural disposition, it is a handicap, similar to other dispositions to morally excluded behavior. As persons, moreover, homosexual individuals in this country and others like it already enjoy the legal rights to which they are entitled, and the law provides adequate remedies for violations of those rights. To accord persons who are homosexual precisely as such any rights or special protections would not be remedying any injustice they have suffered but contributing to the moral and social harms consequent upon homosexual behavior.

As the mother of a homosexually active son, you undoubtedly suffer vicariously due to the strong antipathy that many heterosexual people feel toward homosexual behavior. Understanding the sources of this antipathy might help mitigate that

---

87. See Congregation for the Doctrine of the Faith, "Some Considerations Concerning the Response to Legislative Proposals on the Non-Discrimination of Homosexual Persons," *OR*, 29 July 1992, 5.

suffering. Fear is often said to be the source, since many people, having at one or another time experienced homosexual impulses, are insecure about their own sexual identities. That explanation is plausible but other factors also undoubtedly play a part. For example, the revulsion people feel toward contact with feces extends to the anal intercourse usually practiced by homosexually active men. Then too, some heterosexual boys and men have been harassed by an aggressive man who made unwelcome sexual advances.

In an illuminating book, two men, themselves homosexual, argue that persons who are homosexual are victims of widespread prejudice and propose a public relations strategy for overcoming it. However, the authors frankly admit that a public relations campaign by itself is not enough:

> But we can't hide forever beneath a coat of whitewash; we have to step out from behind the façade eventually, and unless we've made some real changes by the time we do, people will see that we're still the same old queers. Straights hate gays not just for what their myths and lies *say* we are, but also for what we *really* are; all the squeaky-clean media propaganda in the world won't sustain a positive image in the long run unless we start scrubbing to make ourselves a little squeakier and cleaner in reality. And as it happens, our noses (and other parts) are far from clean. In one major respect, America's homohaters have, like the proverbial blind pig, rooted up the truffle of truth: the gay lifestyle—not our sexuality, but our *lifestyle*—is the pits.[88]

These authors go on to describe public misbehavior, which they say is not at all uncommon, that provokes revulsion in nonhomosexuals, and also make it clear that sexually aggressive men frighten some boys and men.[89] People—not least parents who fear that their children might be introduced into the "gay lifestyle"—naturally generalize from such bad experiences while overlooking men who experience homosexual desires but abstain from inappropriate activities. In short, much of people's antagonism toward homosexual persons "in general" is provoked by sexually aggressive men who make themselves obnoxious. But if your son lives chastely, few people are likely to know about his homosexual inclination, and those who do are unlikely to be hostile to him.

While you say nothing in your letter about AIDS, it would be wrong not to mention the vulnerability to this deadly disease of those who, as is typical, engage repeatedly in homosexual acts with diverse partners. The risk of transmitting HIV infection through sodomitical intercourse is not removed by the practice of so-called safe sex (see q. 22, above). The only truly safe sex is complete abstinence outside marriage and perfect fidelity in marriage. True, on any single occasion, a condom carefully and correctly used reduces the probability of transmitting the HIV virus. But condoms sometimes break, tear, leak, or slip off entirely, and regularly using them to prevent the transmission of HIV makes it virtually certain that sooner or later those infected will transmit the virus to their noninfected sex partners. Moreover, in anal intercourse, the demands on condoms are especially

---

88. Kirk and Madsen, op. cit., 275–76; their description (280–356) of the lifestyle common among active homosexual males is both frank and detailed.

89. Ibid., 307–12.

great and the likelihood that a partner will be infected is especially high—and, as has been noted above, most men who engage in sodomy have, not one or a few, but many different partners.[90]

How far may you go in supporting your son, and where should you draw the line? Assure him that God loves him, that Jesus wishes to have a committed relationship with him, and that the Church, like you, wants nothing more than to be a good mother to him. Stir up your own hope for heaven and do your best to share it with him, for without lively hope none of us can remain faithful through life's struggles and sufferings. Encourage him to pray and go to Mass.

You also should encourage him to repent and commit himself to living chastely, and to make a good confession to a priest who believes that every man not only must live chastely but can do so by the Holy Spirit's grace, always available to repentant sinners who seek it in the sacrament of penance. If you can afford it and your son is willing, help him obtain the professional assistance of a therapist who has successfully worked with others who wished to overcome homosexuality. In many places, there now are groups, somewhat similar to those of Alcoholics Anonymous, for persons with a homosexual condition. Among them are Sexaholics Anonymous, Regeneration, and Courage. Unlike the religiously based "Gay" organizations that try to reconcile sinful practices with faith, these groups offer spiritual and moral support for those who wish to live chastely. Try to locate such a group and suggest that your son participate in it.[91]

And if your son spurns such support and persists in homosexual activity? Suppose he were abusing alcohol. Very probably you would look back, recall anything you did or failed to do that you think might have contributed to his problem, wish you had been a perfect parent, and feel guilty; but, as has been explained, that reaction would be neither appropriate nor helpful. You would not know how guilty he was, how deeply he understood the wrong he was doing or how free he was to avoid it. You would leave judgment to God, and pray unceasingly that your son be moved by grace to quit drinking. You would realize that condoning his alcohol abuse or helping him rationalize it would be gravely wrong; and while sympathy might tempt you to those wrongs, you would firmly resist the temptation, not only to avoid incurring real guilt for making your son's problem worse but out of compassion for him, since genuine compassion never is satisfied with anodynes but always seeks true healing.

In short, you would love and support your son in many ways. But you would never supply him with alcohol or do anything else to contribute to his continuing self-destruction. For example, you would not tell lies to cover his alcohol abuse or allow him and his drinking buddies to use your home for their "parties." Probably

---

90. Schmidt, op. cit., 100–130, summarizes available evidence about diseases transmitted by homosexual practices, and concludes (130): "For the vast majority of homosexual men, and for a significant number of homosexual women—even apart from the deadly plague of AIDS—sexual behavior is obsessive, psychopathological and destructive of the body."

91. One may obtain more information about Courage, including suggestions for setting up a group, by writing to: Courage, St. Michael's Rectory, 424 West 34th Street, New York, N.Y. 10001. Schmidt, op. cit., 153–59, cogently defends the potential of therapy and healing against some common criticisms.

you would do well not to nag your son about his drinking, since that would be unlikely to lead him to repent and seek the help he needed. You would be concerned about his missing Mass, but would recognize that omission as a sign of his moral and spiritual deterioration rather than regard it as the result of harshness in the Church's teaching on drunkenness or of defects in her pastoral stance toward alcohol abusers.

As the mother of a son who engages in homosexual activity, your problem is not very different.[92] You certainly should continue to love him. You should pray constantly for him, welcome him to your home, encourage his good aspirations, share his sufferings, and treat him with kindness and motherly affection. But love requires more of you: that you do what you can for your son's true moral and spiritual good. Condoning homosexual activity and supporting attempts to establish and maintain a "committed relationship" that involves such activity will not contribute to his true good. Gently and firmly maintaining the truth of the Church's teaching, without softening it in any way, will not make your son feel guilty, but may help him acknowledge the guilt he appropriately feels, while pointing to the only effective way of dealing with it: sincere repentance and amendment of life. Thus, by genuinely loving your son and avoiding the softheartedness that obscures truth, you will do what you can to help him acknowledge that truth, resist temptation, live chastely, abide in God's love, and arrive at last in heaven, where there will be no more people who are heterosexual or homosexual, but all who have persevered will be one in Jesus.

24: May one lend money to co-workers who need it to commit sins?

As a businessman who travels a good deal, I often have problems dealing with colleagues who behave differently on the road than they would at home. One kind of case that often comes up involves lending money. One evening, for example, one of the boys and I were having a nightcap in a hotel lounge when we were approached by an unusually attractive call girl. I tried to get rid of her, but he was intrigued and chatted with her. She wanted more cash than he happened to have, so he asked me for a loan. This fellow's wife is a very decent and faithful woman, and I felt he was making a big mistake, so I did not hesitate to say no. The girl left, he was angry with me, and our relationship has not been the same since. Now, I wonder whether it would have been wrong to lend him the cash, which I might have done if I did not know his wife or had foreseen how he would take being turned down.

The problem is even worse when it involves my boss. Last month we were walking along an avenue in the best section of a large city, when an oriental bracelet in a shop window caught his eye. We went in, and he decided to buy it after working

---

92. There are some disanalogies between homosexual behavior and alcohol abuse, but they do not undercut the point being made here. That point does not concern the responsibilities of active homosexuals and alcohol abusers; it concerns the appropriate response of parents and others to such persons, given their behavior.

the price down to fifteen hundred dollars. I was surprised when he asked me to charge it on my credit card, even though he has ample credit of his own. The purchase was going to push my balance close to the limit, and, not wanting to do that, I hesitated. He explained that he did not want the item to show up on one of his statements, because his wife would ask about it, and he wanted the bracelet for his "friend" (with whom he has been having an affair for about a year that I've known about). The boss is the boss, so I charged the bracelet. He reimbursed me the day we got back to the office. Of course, I told my wife about it—otherwise, she would have been asking about that fifteen-hundred-dollar item—and she said I should not have helped the boss cheat on his wife. I see her point, but it still seems to me I had little choice.

Analysis:

This question concerns the moral acceptability of cooperating in wrongdoing by lending money needed to engage in it. The cooperation need not be formal, but even material cooperation often occasions the sin of formal cooperation, impedes witness to moral truth, and is unfair to wronged parties. Such cooperation should therefore be refused unless that is likely to result in grave harm to oneself or others. People are less likely to expect one's cooperation in their wrongdoing if one's own conduct has been exemplary and one's relationships with them have been conducted in accord with Christian norms.

The reply could be along the following lines:

Though it usually is good to lend to someone in need, one generally should not lend money in situations like those you describe, where the loan helps the borrower to commit a sin. However, since the money in both cases was only an extrinsic means to the wrongdoing, lending it did not require you in either case to share in the sinner's evil will. Moreover, the loan to your boss did not directly facilitate adultery, but his gift giving in the context of an adulterous relationship. Therefore, provided you did not intend the bad uses to which your loans were or would have been put, your making the one was not wrong in itself, nor would making the other have been.

Not intending the bad uses of the money, one making such loans intends something else: to accommodate a colleague or friend. For that, one may have good and even morally pressing reasons—for example, to forestall retaliation that would impede or prevent one from adequately supporting one's family or meeting some other responsibility.

That, however, is not the end of the matter. For doing such a favor facilitates an instance of sin that cannot be carried out without your help, and your involvement in the execution of the sin may lead others into sin. Moreover, by making the loan you run the risk of being invited and tempted to become personally involved in your co-workers' sinful escapades or, at least, of approving of what they are doing. Then too, doing as you are asked tends to undercut the witness you should give to moral truth; instead of cooperating, you ordinarily should take this kind of request for your help as an opportunity to try to dissuade others from carrying out their sinful choices and encourage them to repent. Whether or not you are acquainted with the spouse, easily avoidable complicity in adultery or an ongoing extramarital relationship is, in my judgment, gravely unfair to her. Therefore, unless your refusal to provide the wherewithal for sinning seems likely to result in grave harm to yourself or others, you should not make the requested loan, even if you foresee that your unwillingness to cooperate will be resented.

By behaving appropriately toward co-workers at other times, you may be able to forestall their pressure to become involved in their sins on out-of-town trips and perhaps can mitigate their resentment if you refuse. Make it a habit to treat others at the office kindly and be as helpful as you can. When they are anxious or sad, be sympathetic; when they are irritable, be gentle; if they wrong you, be patient and ready to forgive. Rather than demanding everything to which you think you have a right and conceding only what you think others have a right to, be as compliant and generous as possible. In short, put into practice Jesus' teaching about how to treat others.

At the same time, even though an office is seldom the place for explicit evangelizing, be open about your faith so that everyone will come to see that it underlies your behavior. As part of this openness, let others know you are committed to traditional Christian sexual morality. One way of doing this is by being modest—avoiding dirty jokes, sexual banter, and so on—and frowning on others' immodesty. Such a pattern of behavior will shape your relationships with co-workers and their expectations of you. If they do not mistake your decency for weakness, they will come to respect you and regard you as an agreeable person despite being rather straitlaced, and, when you are on the road together, they either will not ask you to cooperate in their sinning or will not be surprised when you say no. Moreover, your good example might well render some of your co-workers receptive to your witness and inspire them to amend their own lives.

Even in a situation involving your boss, such as the one you describe, do not take it for granted, as you apparently do, that you must do something that contributes to his wrongdoing just because he is the boss. As with your co-workers, by behaving appropriately toward him at other times, you can try to forestall his pressure and lessen his resentment. Insofar as possible, do your best to please him when what he asks of you is both morally acceptable and an appropriate part of your job. At the same time, make it clear to him that your other commitments—to your faith, your family, and so on—rule out catering to his whims outside the sphere of his managerial authority. Acting this way may well lead him to respect and value you as an employee, and thus make him less likely to make illegitimate demands on you. If he does not respond well, however, that would be a sign of something fundamentally wrong in his attitude toward you. In that case, you face a prospect of continuing mistreatment, and probably should begin looking for other employment.

Nevertheless, I agree with you that the problem is compounded when refusing to have anything to do with another's sinning is likely to result in serious harm to you or others. That may have been so when your boss asked you to charge the bracelet on your credit card, for you may have had good reason to fear he would retaliate in a way you could not accept—for example, by discharging you from the job you need to support your family. What should you have done in that case? It seems to me that, without refusing his request, you first should have taken a minimal risk by making an effort to admonish him gently, perhaps by taking him aside and saying: "Do you really think that is right?" If he persisted in his request, unless the risk seemed excessive, you also should have borne witness to the truth about adultery by making it clear that you did not wish to be involved: "I do not want to have anything to do with this affair; please do not insist." However, if you confronted a realistic prospect of serious harm, you could have blamelessly done what you did, since your own action and intention could have been upright even though it facilitated your boss's carrying out a sinful choice.

25: Should a woman be friends with an acquaintance of poor character?

A woman I'll call Marcia, an acquaintance of mine who was raised a Catholic, recently got married and quit her job as head nurse at an abortion clinic. She has had no obvious conversion experience, and is quite vocal in opposing the Church's teaching on abortion. Both Marcia and her husband, also raised Catholic, were married before. She knew this man had been sterilized, but shortly after they married she began to want a baby. He said he would support whatever she wished to do. A physician who is a friend of hers injected her with frozen semen from a donor she does not know; she became pregnant, and now has a lovely baby girl.

While Marcia makes me uncomfortable, she keeps seeking my friendship. She likes me because, she says, I'm "such a good Catholic, so conservative." I am not sure I want her friendship or that associating with these people would be good for my husband and children. Still, despite everything, she is a sweet person. I have not had the courage either to voice my disapproval of her choices (though, of course, she knows my views) or avoid her altogether.

May I—should I—carry on a friendly relationship with Marcia, hating the sin but loving the sinner? If I do accept her as a friend, how should I deal with the huge gap between what I know is right and the things she has done, and very likely will go on doing?

Analysis:

The question is whether one should befriend a person who appears to be an unrepentant, grave sinner. If one is morally free to befriend such a person, one should do so as a work of mercy. But duties to oneself, others, or both may require that one not befriend such a person. The questioner's duty to bear witness to the wrongness of abortion and maintain solidarity with its victims argues against entering into a real friendship with Marcia, but does not preclude treating her with a friendliness appropriate to the relationship in which they have become acquainted.

The reply could be along the following lines:

As a basis for discussing your question about carrying on a friendly relationship with Marcia, who seems to be living a gravely sinful life, I distinguish between those judgments we cannot and must not make and those we can and ought to make. Only God knows to what extent Marcia is morally guilty—that is, clear about relevant moral norms and freely acting contrary to them. That no doubt is one reason why Jesus warns us against passing judgment on others (see Mt 7.1; *LCL,* 227–28). Still, abstracting from her guilt or innocence, you can judge the objective rightness or wrongness of what she has done and is doing. This judgment is important, because even when subjective factors reduce a person's responsibility for objectively wrongful choices and behavior, they harm both that person and those affected by what he or she does.[93] Moreover, not judging Marcia does not mean judging her innocent. Perhaps she is self-enslaved by sin and, more than anything else, needs help to acknowledge that fact, but instead is seeking some sort of affirmation ("moral support") for continuing to live in sin.

Still, for someone of poor character, friendship with an upright person can be a saving grace. To save us, God befriended us in Jesus while we were still sinners, and we ought to imitate him by reaching out to others, not with arrogance, but with humble awareness that what we have received, by no merit of our own, is not given us solely for our own benefit. Marcia's Catholic upbringing and the small voice of her conscience may be haunting her. In seeking your friendship, Marcia could be attracted by the grace God gave you when he drew you into friendship with himself, and she may be sensing the weight of her sins holding her back from his friendship. Therefore, if no morally compelling reason excludes a friendly relationship with her, you might carry it on in the hope that doing so will provide for her a channel of the grace she needs to repent and amend her life.

However, sometimes one should not carry on a friendly relationship with a person who seems to be living a gravely sinful life. The relationship may be too risky to oneself or someone else (for example, one's children); it may mislead others by suggesting that gravely wrongful behavior is acceptable or of little importance; it may only facilitate the person's wrongdoing and delay conversion; it may be unfair to an individual or group suffering due to the person's wrongdoing, which ought to be opposed by good people. In particular, two things in your question suggest it might well be wrong for you to carry on a friendship with Marcia.

First, it is strange and mysterious for someone who acts as she does, despite having been raised a Catholic, to say she likes you *because* you are "such a good Catholic, so conservative." This remark—especially when considered in conjunction with her vocal opposition to Catholic teaching on abortion and her openness about having been artificially inseminated—perhaps reveals Marcia's very questionable motive for seeking your friendship. She may want it so as to reassure herself that she is not, after all, so bad a Catholic and so sinful a person as she suspects she is.

Second, while there are certain important differences between the present worldwide destruction of unborn children and the Nazis' destruction of millions of Jews and other people before and during World War II, there also are important

---

93. John Paul II, *Veritatis splendor,* 51, *AAS* 85 (1993) 1175, *OR,* 6 Oct. 1993, viii: When "they disregard the law, or even are merely ignorant of it, whether culpably or not, our acts damage the communion of persons, to the detriment of each."

similarities between the two mass murders. Not the least is that both surely call for unambiguous witness to the truth about the right to life of the innocent and the evil of killing them. In such cases, anyone who perceives the injustice should stand up for its victims and avoid doing anything to condone what is being done to them. The other things Marcia has done might not preclude friendship with her, but it is hard to see how you could tolerate her open rejection of the Church's teaching on abortion and ignore her past involvement in it, without undermining the clear witness you ought to give to the sanctity of life of unborn children. Moreover, everyone who regards abortion as the unjust killing of unborn babies—the slaughter of innocent people—should stand firmly in solidarity with its past and future victims. Do you think that, even while clearly perceiving the evil of ongoing Nazi genocide, a faithful and devout Christian could and should have carried on a friendship with someone who not only had participated actively in it but seemed unrepentant and continued to reject the Church's teaching forbidding such killing?

In deciding whether to accept Marcia's friendship, meditate on and imitate Jesus. He showed how to love the sinner while hating the sin. He associated with sinners, but he told them very clearly what he thought about their lives. Then, too, straightforward communication about mutual concerns is absolutely essential for friendship. Marcia wishes to be your friend and you are considering her proposal, but you have yet to talk with her about your profound disapproval of her choices and your consequent hesitation to carry on a friendship with her. So, if you do speak frankly with her about your hesitation to carry on a closer relationship with her, you certainly ought to explore her motivation and make it clear that you cannot in any way affirm her in choices you consider seriously wrong. Failing to talk frankly with Marcia while allowing your relationship with her to develop would be inconsistent both with Jesus' practice and the serious sharing essential to true friendship.

Your acquaintance with Marcia probably is based on some ongoing relationship—for example, as co-workers, neighbors, or parties to business transactions. If so, a decision not to respond to her quest for friendship need not preclude your being friendly toward her in ways appropriate in that relationship. Nor need you try to minimize your contacts with her.

Finally, even if you judge that you should not carry on a friendship with Marcia, you nevertheless should tell her frankly what you think about her opinions and actions, especially with regard to abortion, and make it clear to her that these have led you to decide to keep your distance. This message, conveyed calmly and with regret, could lead her to reflect and repent, probably not immediately but perhaps eventually. For this you ought also to pray, in the hope that one day—in heaven, at least—you will be able to share with her the friendship you forgo for now.

+   +   +

26: What should a woman do to rectify a friend's fraud?

Ten years ago, as a novice of a religious community in a distant city that I'll call Rivertown, I made friends with a fellow novice, whom I'll call Christine. I dropped out before final vows, got a job with the government, and moved to a suburb of the capital. Christine made her profession, and three years ago her superior sent her to Rome to work on a doctorate in theology.

On her way back to Rivertown this summer, she stopped over with me for a day. I had bought a laser printer a few months before, but still had my old dot matrix. Christine needed a good printer for the summer to work on her dissertation, and I reluctantly lent her my new one. Two weeks later, she called and said the printer was not working, and I faxed her instructions for getting it fixed under the warranty. Last week, on her way back to Rome, Christine dropped off what I assumed was my printer. But when I unpacked it, I noticed that my name, which I had engraved in an inconspicuous spot, was missing, and the serial number confirmed that the printer is not mine.

I called Christine, and she told me the same make and model printer as mine had been on sale at a store in Rivertown. Rather than take the trouble of getting mine repaired, she had purchased a replacement with cash, and then got her money back by turning my printer into the store as defective merchandise, pretending it was the one she had purchased. Having used a fictitious name and address, she thought there was no problem. I said I would have to return the one she left with me to the store she got it from and try to get mine back. I explained that I had sent the manufacturer the card that came with my printer and has its serial number on it, and also that the printer has my name engraved on it. But Christine said I should not be so worried about getting into trouble, refused to tell me the name of the dealer, and urged me to forget the whole thing. When I continued to press her, she got angry and hung up.

I checked with the manufacturer to try to get the name of the dealer who sold the printer I now have, saying I suspected it might have been stolen by someone who had left it with me. But they said they give that information only to law enforcement agencies, and if I thought I had stolen property, I should talk to the police about it.

I do not know what I should do. If I do nothing, I am keeping something that is not mine, and I am afraid I might get into trouble. I could contact the police in Rivertown and explain exactly what happened. But telling on Christine would be painful and also might cause trouble for her community, which I am anxious not to hurt. Then too, I am worried about Christine. Her casual attitude about what she did is appalling, and I wish I could think of a way to encourage her toward a real change of heart. But I am afraid our friendship is over and doubt she would listen to anything I could say to her.

Analysis:

This question is complex. First, the questioner is in possession of property that was obtained by fraud and should be returned to its true owner. She also is the victim of theft, and has the right to reclaim her own property. Second, she rightly wishes to do something about Christine's wrongdoing, which seems to manifest serious character flaws. Third, the questioner is reasonably concerned that reporting Christine's wrongdoing to the police in Rivertown will harm her community. Despite the second and third considerations, the questioner should fulfill her responsibility to return the stolen property by reporting the matter, unless she can find an alternative that would both fulfill that responsibility and better serve the other purposes.

The reply could be along the following lines:

By fraudulently obtaining a new printer in exchange for yours and delivering that new printer to you, Christine certainly has wronged both the dealer and you. Since the printer Christine left with you belongs to the dealer from whom she obtained it by her deception, it would be wrong for you to keep it, and, as you say, you might get into trouble. But if you return the new printer and claim back the one Christine stole from you by turning it in to the store, you should get it back provided the store still has it or can recover it. So, if making and obtaining restitution were the only morally significant consideration, contacting the police in Rivertown, as you have thought of doing, would be appropriate.

But you also are concerned, and I think rightly, about Christine's soul and her community's well-being. Moreover, your statement that it would be painful for you to turn Christine in suggests that, though you think your friendship with her is over, you still feel some affection for her and/or wish to be loyal to her, and are reluctant to initiate a process that might eventually lead to her being dealt with as the criminal she apparently is. Although these considerations are weighty, I do not think they can justify inaction on your part. Making appropriate restitution also is important, and, though you probably are not in great danger of getting into trouble with the law for keeping stolen property, such trouble would be so serious for you that even a small risk of it is important. Besides, Christine actually might benefit if she were convicted of her crime and punished, since that might lead her to reflect and change for the better. Therefore, it seems to me that, unless you can think of and carry out an alternative you believe will better meet your responsibilities, including that of returning the printer Christine left with you to its owner, you should communicate with the Rivertown police without delay.

While you may be able to think of other possibilities, I suggest three for your consideration.

First, you might discuss your problem with the police where you live, or, perhaps better, ask a priest to do so on your behalf. Perhaps they would obtain from the manufacturer the name of the store that sold the printer Christine left with you, so that you could contact that store directly and try to resolve the matter, as you had thought of doing. If you manage to work things out in such a way that Christine does not suffer the possible legal consequences of her action, you could tell her afterwards what you had done for her, express your deep concern about her behavior, and exhort her to think and pray about it. Still, if you pursue this course of action, you almost certainly will have to reveal Christine's identity, and the store may well prosecute her.

Second, you might contact the (or a) superior of Christine's community in Rivertown, talk the matter over, and, if that person seems trustworthy and is cooperative, turn the entire problem over to her. Indeed, if you already know and trust such a person there, you might simply write her a letter explaining what happened, send her the letter along with the printer, and ask her to deal with the various aspects of the problem—including, of course, retrieving your own printer for you. Provided you are confident that the superior will see to it that the printer is returned to the store, sending it to her will meet your duty in that respect; at the same time, this approach is most likely to safeguard the community's interests. Above all, if Christine's superior is sound and capable, she is likely to be more able than anyone else to get her to take stock and undergo the change of heart that seems necessary. I say "seems" because, in the circumstances, Christine's behavior is so bizarre that it might be a symptom of psychological stress rather than bad character.

Third, if you lack confidence in Christine's superior or superiors—and especially if you think her behavior might be related to wider problems in the community—you might contact the bishop of Rivertown or, if he has one, his vicar for religious, and perhaps turn the matter over to him.

Finally, considering Christine's behavior toward you, your concern for her and apparent lack of resentment manifest meekness and readiness to forgive. If you persist in that attitude and pray for her, perhaps your friendship will not be over. At least, if you both die in God's friendship, you will be friends again in heaven.

27: Should one intervene when parents mistreat their children?

In public places, especially in supermarkets and other self-service stores, I often see parents mistreating their children, either verbally or physically or, sometimes, both. For example, not long ago I saw a little girl, three or four, being slapped by her angry father; he was holding her firmly by the shoulder with one hand and slapping her with the other, at the same time harshly scolding her. The child, terrified and in pain, was wailing for her mother. I felt I should intervene, but, not knowing what to do, simply stood there watching. The man scooped the child up and headed for the exit, all the while continuing to scold her. I followed them out and saw the man toss the child into the back seat of his car, pick up his wife, by now standing in front of the store, and drive off.

What should you do in a situation like that? Should you intervene, and, if so, how? The parent is likely to take anything you say or do as meddling. That may even provoke the parent into worse abuse and probably will draw his or her wrath upon oneself. But it seems wrong to stand by and do nothing, for, if you were in the child's place, you would want somebody to come to the rescue.

I suppose just about everyone sometimes encounters such situations, but nobody I have talked with knows what to do. It seems to me that the question really is difficult and worth considering.

Analysis:

This question concerns the application of norms regarding admonishing apparent sinners. Intervention is not warranted unless one is confident the adult's behavior is objectively morally wrong. When intervention is warranted, one should try to identify cases in which public authorities probably would intervene. If an adult's treatment of a child certainly is morally unacceptable, yet not such that the authorities would be likely to intervene, one should communicate with the adult. In such communication, anger and self-righteousness must be avoided; one's sole purpose should be to help the parent, the child, and their relationship. If possible, one should do or say something likely to induce the adult not only to moderate his or her present behavior but to reflect on it afterward and, perhaps, amend it.

The reply could be along the following lines:

The parent-child relationship is both important and delicate, and a family is a bit like a circus troupe doing a high-wire act together. Even if there are real inadequacies on the part of one or both parents, outsiders' well-intentioned efforts to help matters risk weakening the relationship and upsetting the family with little real benefit to the children. Therefore, neither public authorities nor concerned individuals outside the family should intervene unless the need is clear. Moreover, if an intervention is essential, every effort should be made to minimize harmful effects on the family, and generally interventions should be limited in scope and directed toward encouraging and helping parents to fulfill their responsibilities.

In some cases, mistreatment of a child is so severe—for example, likely to break bones or do some other serious injury—that reasonable people would agree that anyone who can stop the violence should do so, even using force if necessary. Apart from such cases, though, it would be fruitless to intervene physically to stop mistreatment, since physical force will not alter bad parental attitudes and habits. Moreover, using force might violate the law and render a person intervening vulnerable to a civil lawsuit. In what follows, then, I deal only with less severe cases and assume physical intervention is excluded.

Less extreme instances of real or apparent parental mistreatment of children vary greatly in their seriousness. Cases you encounter in the future will not be exactly like the one you describe, but only more or less similar. Thus, your question really bears on a spectrum of cases, not all of which call for the same kind of response. First are instances so severe that the public authorities probably would intervene if they were aware of what was happening. Second are instances in which parental behavior certainly is unreasonable and unfair to a child, yet not so severe that the public authorities would take action. Third are instances in which you or other observers find a parent's behavior repugnant and think it inappropriate, but it may not be unreasonable and unfair.

Cases of the third sort occur due to two factors, either or both of which can be at work in any given instance. First, sometimes a child misbehaves, a parent observes the misbehavior and punishes it, the child acts as if he or she were suffering far more than is really the case, and bystanders unaware of what prompted the parent's action feel sorry for the frustrated and suffering child. Second, the treatment of children varies considerably in different cultures, including those of different groups living in the same community—some are more permissive, others stricter; some virtually exclude physical discipline, others accept it within limits. So, parental behavior that an observer thinks is inappropriate or even violent may simply be culturally different, without being wrong by objective standards. Consequently, when you notice an instance of what seems like parental mistreatment, give the parent the benefit of any doubt and never intervene unless you are confident that the observed behavior is morally unacceptable.

How can one recognize and deal with cases of the first sort—those in which the public authorities probably would intervene? Since laws and their enforcement vary in different jurisdictions, you will need—unless certain of the policy in the place where you are—to get in touch with the authorities who handle reports of children's mistreatment. They will be able to clarify what sorts of behavior should be called to their attention and offer suggestions about how to proceed. Once you have this information, you will sometimes be able to summon the authorities to deal at once with an ongoing case of mistreatment. If not, you may recognize the abusive parent or be able to learn his or her identity—for instance, from a check or credit card slip if a cashier or store manager is cooperative. In the case you describe, you might have been able to note the automobile license number, which probably would have sufficed for the authorities to identify the misbehaving parent. I wonder, however, whether the authorities in many places would have seen fit to intervene in that case.[94]

Thus, there remain cases of the second sort, about which, no doubt, you are mainly concerned. Parental behavior toward a child certainly is unreasonable and unfair, and may even be violent, yet is not so severe that the public authorities would take action. Since intervention by physical force is excluded, you have only two options: either do nothing or try to communicate in some way with the parent. As you say, an abusive parent is likely to regard any outsider's intervention as meddling. While that could provoke the parent into worse mistreatment, I do not think that is likely. Still, you are probably correct in expecting the abusing parent to become angry with you if you question his or her behavior. But that probably will not lead to any serious harm, and, unlike people who keep their distance from crime victims crying out for help, you should be prepared to accept some risk and other burdens to respond to children's need. Fear of the parent should not keep you from doing what you otherwise would judge appropriate.

Nobody should challenge another's wrongful behavior, however, without first examining his or her own motives. Upright people often feel indignant at seeing the weak unjustly treated, but merely venting one's feelings is likely to do more harm than good, and self-righteousness must be avoided. Your sole purpose should be to help the parent, the child, and their relationship with each other by encouraging the parent to be a better parent. Thus, the point of intervening should be to

---

94. When the mistreatment of a child is not observed but alleged by the child or a third party, one should be cautious about notifying the authorities. Reports of mistreatment sometimes are false, and being investigated by public authorities can gravely disrupt a family and always is a traumatic experience.

move the parent to think about his or her wrongful behavior, see its wrongness, and wish to change it for the better.

But can you communicate in a way likely to help? Perhaps. Much depends on your personality, sensitivity to the different circumstances of each case, quick-wittedness, and various personal attributes (such as your age, sex, and appearance) that could affect the other party's receptivity. No single remark or gesture will be appropriate for every case. Sometimes, simply staring at abusing parents makes them self-conscious, so that they moderate their behavior, and talking about some unrelated matter can distract an angry person. Such tactics, however, are not likely to yield lasting benefits; that requires addressing the underlying attitude. Probably best would be to begin with some very brief remark—for example, one might try to distract the parent and invite conversation by a nonthreatening remark: "It looks as though she (he) is giving you a hard time!" Or one might look intently at the parent until he or she notices, then say something in a calm and gentle tone that might serve as a seed of later reflection.: "Sometimes children get to you, don't they? Still, I'm sure you want your little girl (boy) to love you." A remark of that sort, while appealing immediately to feeling, points to one reason why parents should not mistreat their children: the good of the parent-child relationship. Or, again, one may not be able to do better than to say with a smile: "She (he) will be a teenager before you know it."

Even such attempts to provoke thought are likely to elicit a defensive reaction: "Mind your own business!" Once again, there may be no point in replying. Or, perhaps, a soft answer might help: "Please forgive me. I would rather mind my own business, but I cannot help putting myself in your little girl's (boy's) place."

Public mistreatment of children very likely is only the tip of the iceberg—a small portion of the widespread violent treatment, psychological cruelty, verbal abuse, and gross neglect of children, most of it going on in private. Since you are sensitive to the plight of children suffering mistreatment and wish to do something to help them, you should consider the larger phenomenon and ask yourself whether you have any gifts or resources that you could use to combat this evil. For example, perhaps you might serve as a volunteer with some private or public agency that deals with some of the more serious cases.

You also might take a radical approach to the mistreatment of children by doing whatever you can to support the Church's teaching on the sanctity of life and the moral norms regarding its transmission, and by taking an active part in the prolife movement. Proponents of contraception and abortion long have argued that making them available to everybody would prevent or eliminate unwanted children, so that every child would be wanted and none mistreated. With the wider availability of contraception and abortion, however, mistreatment of children has shown no signs of abating and even seems to have increased.[95]

---

95. Andrea J. Sedlak and Diane D. Broadhurst, *Executive Summary of the Third National Incidence Study of Child Abuse and Neglect,* (Washington, D.C.: U.S. Department of Health and Human Services, National Center on Child Abuse and Neglect, 1996), 3, report that abuse and neglect resulted in demonstrable harm to an estimated 1,553,800 children in the U.S. in 1993, an

While there no doubt are other contributing factors, rejection of traditional Christian values surely is part of the explanation. When children were regarded as a normal part of marriage and family life, a child was likely to be accepted as a gift; now that children often are counted among the various things a couple (or even an individual) might or might not want, a child is likely to be rated, like other possessions, as more or less satisfactory. Parents who take care to have only "wanted children" often soon find themselves inescapably burdened with unsatisfactory children, who also frustrate some of their other desires.

If society rationalized killing children already born as it rationalizes abortion, these previously wanted but now unwanted infants and small children would perhaps be killed. But why should people who can imagine that killing their children would be acceptable scruple at mistreating them? Because everyone should be concerned, as you are, about the mistreatment of children, all of us should do everything we can to support the Church's teaching about the sanctity of human life and its transmission.

28: May an oppressed wife who should avoid pregnancy practice contraception?

Eighteen years ago, I graduated from college and married Dan, who was just beginning to practice his profession. Though he had been raised Catholic, by that time he considered himself an agnostic. I had been only a nominal Catholic. As a child I shared my parents' faith, but I did not make it my own as I grew up. For twelve years, we lived like most other nonreligious couples of our social and economic class, and neither of us went to church.

Six years ago last spring, I was feeling a lot of stress. Not only was I raising our three children and managing the household, but I also was trying to cope with grief over the loss of my mother, who had died that February of brain cancer. My father was too overwhelmed himself to give me any support, and since Dan was, as always, deeply involved in his work and hardly involved in the family, I was getting no support from him. I literally cried that I could not go on alone any longer. Then I found myself doing something I had not done since I was thirteen or fourteen: praying for help. Though time went by and no help came, for some reason I continued praying. One morning after about a month, I awakened before the alarm went off. The rising sun was shining through the window, and all the pressure was gone. I felt greatly strengthened and hopeful, and as I peacefully lay there, I plainly received an answer to my prayer—the Lord would walk with me and take care of me if only I would follow a faith-filled way of life. I promised I would.

I went to confession, began going to Mass and Communion every Sunday, and started looking after the children's neglected religious formation. A month or so later I read the encyclical *Humanae vitae,* which up to then I had ignored. It became clear to me that I had to stop using contraception, and I threw away my diaphragm and jelly. In a book store, I found a used book, *The Rhythm Way to Family*

---

increase of 67% from the 931,000 children harmed by abuse and neglect in 1986 and of 149% from the 625,100 children harmed by abuse and neglect in 1980.

Happiness, which explains how to regulate births by abstaining from intercourse during the days of the cycle when conception is likely; its charts make it easy to identify the "baby days." Since Dan considered our family complete, I wanted to use rhythm as a Church-approved method of family planning.

Though Dan did not want to cooperate, I tried for over two years to avoid intercourse on baby days. He became more and more frustrated and irate, and finally sent me to a psychiatrist, saying that I was a religious fanatic and obviously neurotic. I had several sessions with the psychiatrist, who put me through a series of psychological tests. Then he had Dan and me in, reported that I had no symptoms of mental illness, and recommended that we obtain joint marital counseling. We began going weekly, but Dan did not like the counselor, who was raising questions about communication and cooperation. After the third session, he canceled our next appointment, and we never went again.

Not long after, I found myself pregnant with our fourth child. During that pregnancy, I began having symptoms of what turned out to be a chronic disease. My obstetrician recommended an abortion, but, of course, I did not agree. I was very worried, but with a lot of prayer and good care managed to get through the pregnancy and deliver a healthy baby boy, now two, who is my delight and also the pet of the older children. The specialist who cares for me said my condition is progressive; it will never get better, only gradually worse. He warned me sternly not to get pregnant again. Both he and my obstetrician urged me to be sterilized, but I refused.

At first, I added more days to the baby days, but that left only a few days in each cycle when we could have intercourse, and after three months Dan called my attention to a magazine article about how divorce affects the wife's and children's standard of living and threatened to end our marriage. I thought about leaving him, but, with no experience working outside my home, I felt I could not face trying to raise the children and care for myself without his full financial support and his health coverage. I asked a priest what to do, and he told me to follow my conscience. I reluctantly decided to get a new diaphragm and went back to using it and the jelly during the baby days. I never used contraception during the safe time toward the end of each cycle just before my period. In this way, I felt I still was open to God's gift of life if he really wanted me to become pregnant. And I did not see how I could do better. Yet my conscience has been bothering me, and I doubt I am living the faith-filled life I promised the Lord that sunny morning six years ago.

Though the priest who told me to follow my conscience later said he does not think contraception is seriously wrong for couples who really should not have another baby, I felt that simply following his advice would be cheating and useless. I hunted around and finally found a priest, Father Gibson, who urges couples to follow the Church's teaching. I made my confession to him and told him about my problem. After doing his best to look into it for me, he thinks it might be all right for me to continue with the diaphragm and jelly, reluctantly accepting this means of preventing pregnancy while intending only to have marital intercourse as often as necessary to satisfy Dan. Father said there are two possible ways of seeing what I am doing as "permissible material cooperation."

First, he said you have argued that contraception is wrong because it is the effort to prevent the beginning of a new life. In my case, continuing with the diaphragm and jelly, he said, "would not be contralife," since my intention would be to please Dan while avoiding a pregnancy that would endanger my life.

Second, he said Edward J. Bayer, a moral theologian who is faithful to the Church's teaching, has argued that a married woman may protect herself against rape when she really should not have another baby but her unreasonable husband is compelling her to have intercourse. I seem to meet these conditions, since I really should not have another baby, Dan is unreasonable in demanding intercourse, and I am not in a position to separate from him.

Father Gibson suggested I ask for your comments. If you do not approve of what I am doing but know some other way to solve my problem, I will be grateful for any help you can give me.

Analysis:

This question concerns the possible justification of contraception by a married woman who ought to avoid pregnancy but is being sexually oppressed by her husband. Her use of contraception must be morally evaluated insofar as it is her own act. Because that act carries out a choice to prevent conception, it is contralife, and the sexual intercourse it facilitates is not marital intercourse. Its nonmarital character also follows from the fact that it is imposed on the questioner contrary to her reasonable will. Still, because she reluctantly consents to the imposed intercourse, it is not rape or analogous to rape. Therefore, unless her husband repents and agrees to abstain from intercourse insofar as necessary to avoid pregnancy, the questioner should refuse to cooperate with him in intercourse.

The reply could be along the following lines:

Surely the Lord is pleased with your persistent effort to keep your promise—to walk a faith-filled way of life—despite Dan's refusal to cooperate, his gross disrespect for your conscience and body, and his intimidation. You were courageous in refusing abortion and sterilization, and have been unusually clearheaded and conscientious in seeking a true answer to your moral difficulty rather than accepting and following advice based on opinions that dissent from the Church's teaching. Still, I think you are right in doubting that your use of contraception is consistent with your promise to the Lord.

Since your obstetrician recommended abortion, and both he and the specialist who cares for you recommended sterilization, they clearly do not practice medicine within the framework of traditional Christian morality. Perhaps they have exaggerated the dangers of another pregnancy. Therefore, it seems to me you should obtain a second opinion on that question from competent Catholic physicians entirely faithful to the Church's teachings on abortion, sterilization, and contraception. Even if another pregnancy would not be so dangerous as you have been led to believe, however, I think it likely—and shall assume in what follows— that your marital and health problems constitute a morally compelling reason to avoid pregnancy.

The suggestion that what you are doing might be permissible material cooperation is mistaken. Though using a diaphragm and jelly enables you to satisfy Dan's sexual demands, it must be morally evaluated as your own act rather than as cooperation with anything he does. Considered as your own act and as distinct from the sexual acts it facilitates, it carries out your reluctant choice to prevent conception.

The Church's teaching is that each and every marital act must be open to new life. In reaffirming this constant and most firm teaching about contraception, Paul VI clearly states what the teaching excludes: "any action which is done—either in anticipation of marital intercourse, or during it, or while its natural effects are unfolding—so as to impede procreation, whether that is intended as an end to be obtained or as a means to be employed."[96] Although you intend to prevent conception as a means of safeguarding your health, using a diaphragm and jelly precisely to prevent it is an instance of the contraception the Church's teaching excludes.

You realize that many Catholics, including many priests, do not accept the Church's teaching about contraception and would find nothing wrong with your practice of it. They are mistaken, and the Church's teaching is true. Jesus promised that the Holy Spirit would guide the Church, and that certainly means the whole body of the faithful cannot have been wrong down through the centuries about how they were to live as God's children (see LG 12). But the Church's teaching on contraception and other matters now disputed is nothing new; indeed it was shared by all Christians until this century.[97] So, its truth is guaranteed by the Holy Spirit, who makes no mistakes and tells no lies.

I have argued that one reason why contraception is always wrong is that it is contralife (see *LCL,* 506–19). However, the truth of the Church's teaching that contraception is wrong does not depend on my (or anyone else's) attempt to explain why it is wrong. Even if your use of a diaphragm and jelly were not contralife, it would be wrong insofar as it is an instance of a kind of act excluded by the Church's teaching. Still, in my judgment, even your reluctant choice to use contraception is accurately called "contralife." To use a diaphragm and jelly is to prevent conception, not avoid it, as abstaining from intercourse is. Of course, you are not choosing to prevent conception as an end in itself. Your end in view is different and entirely good: to forestall the seriously bad effects on your health of another pregnancy while at the same time preserving your family. For those reasons, you wish not to be pregnant—that is, not to be nurturing a developing baby in your womb—and that wish, too, is morally acceptable. But in order not to be pregnant, you choose to prevent conception—the coming to be of the baby. Thus, although the end you are willing is in no way against life, your intended means is *contrary* to the coming *to be* of a new person, and for that reason is contralife.

Moreover, within marriage, contraception is wrong for another reason—the intention to use it is incompatible with the intention required for authentic marital

---

96. *Humanae vitae,* 14, *AAS* 60 (1968) 490, *PE,* 277.14 (translation amended); cf. *CCC,* 2370.

97. See Charles D. Provan, *The Bible and Birth Control* (Monongahela, Penn.: Zimmer, 1989), for the witness of the Protestant tradition against contraception.

intercourse (see *LCL,* 633–43). While marital intercourse is far more than a reproductive-type act, it must at least be that if it is to make the couple one flesh and allow them to experience themselves as one (see q. 29, below). Among all sexual performances, only a reproductive-type act is one act of the mated pair. Other sexual acts involving a male and female, even if they involve coupling the genitals, are really two separate and distinct acts, which in reality are not unlike mutual masturbation. Now, regardless of the method used, contracepted intercourse, by the intention it involves, is not a reproductive-type act. By contrast, even when a couple know they are sterile, if they act as they would if they were fertile and hoped to have a baby, they do a reproductive-type act in which they really become one agent (they are one flesh), and so not only feel close to each other but experience a unity that is real. Contracepted "intercourse" really is not marital intercourse at all. It is a mutual (or even a one-sided) use of the other person for sexual satisfaction, perhaps including an illusion of intimate communion. Since a contracepted sexual act cannot be marital intercourse, you cannot use contraception "while intending only to have marital intercourse as often as necessary to satisfy Dan."[98]

Paul VI also teaches: "A conjugal act imposed on one's partner without regard to his or her condition of personal and reasonable wishes in the matter, is no true act of love."[99] Dan's sexual acts with you cannot be true acts of love, for, by threatening to leave, he is psychologically coercing you to provide him with sexual services, disregarding your wish to avoid pregnancy by abstinence—a wish that is reasonable inasmuch as abstinence is the only morally acceptable way to fulfill the duty you both have to avoid a pregnancy that would injure your health. Not being true acts of love, the sexual acts Dan is imposing on you are neither realizations nor expressions of marital communion. On this score, too, they can hardly be authentic marital intercourse.

Inasmuch as they are not and are being imposed on you against your reasonable wishes, you are suffering a grave injustice. You would be justified in refusing absolutely to participate in those acts and, if necessary, resisting forcefully any attempt by Dan to force himself upon you. Therefore, it might seem that you really are being raped and can rightly use the diaphragm and jelly to protect yourself.

Apparently, that would be so according to Edward J. Bayer's view. He distinguishes between (1) *contraception* by someone who engages in a true marital act and at the same time intends to impede procreation, and (2) *prevention of*

---

98. In taking the position that a contracepted sexual act cannot be authentic marital intercourse, I implicitly disagree both with canon lawyers who have held that certain sorts of contracepted acts could consummate a marriage and with those moralists (and the suggestion of the magisterium on which they depend) who think that one spouse can engage in a marital act even when the other is using a method of contraception that does not prevent semen from reaching the vagina (see *LCL,* 646, n. 184). My view implies that a couple who use any sort of contraception from the beginning of their marriage do not consummate it unless and until they engage in authentic marital intercourse—that is, intercourse without contraception and meeting the requirements for marital intercourse in other respects. My view does not imply, however, that such a couple are invalidly married; provided neither entirely excluded children in consenting to marry, the marriage will be valid if it is not otherwise impeded.

99. *Humanae vitae,* 13, *AAS* 60 (1968) 489, *PE,* 277.13.

pregnancy by a wife who justifiably refuses consent to acts that might impregnate her and are unreasonably imposed by her husband.[100] Bayer agrees that the first is always excluded by the Church's teaching, but he maintains that the second can be consistent with it and morally acceptable.[101] Father Gibson is suggesting that your use of diaphragm and jelly falls within (2) rather than (1). In my judgment, however, Bayer's classification is inadequate, and what you are doing falls within neither (1) nor (2).

While agreeing that a wife whose husband insists on intercourse against her reasonable will suffers a grave injustice and that such a sexual act is not true marital intercourse, I think this imposed intercourse is morally different in kind from rape.[102] And although it can be analogous to rape, I do not think the conditions required for the analogy are met in a situation, like yours, in which a wife gives in to her husband's unreasonable demands. Thus, though you are the victim of gravely unjust sexual oppression by your husband, I do not think your situation is similar in the relevant respects to that of a rape victim.

Why is intercourse imposed by a husband on a wife in a situation like yours morally different in kind from rape? Since marriage is an indissoluble covenant and a married couple really are one flesh (see *LCL*, 555–84), sexual violence within marriage, unlike rape, does not merely violate *another's* body. Rather, such violence is a special form of infidelity that in one central respect is worse than rape: A husband owes his wife marital love, and in sexually abusing her, he treats her as a mere sex object. Therefore, when a man sexually abuses his own wife his evil act is different in kind from rape—it is an act against the marriage itself. When forcible intercourse within marriage is called "rape," then, the word is used in an analogous sense.

Moreover, even the analogous use of the word *rape* to refer to intercourse imposed by a husband on his wife is misleading unless the other features and implications of being raped hold true. The victim neither initiates the act nor consents to it, and she does what she can to avoid being raped; she should neither try to satisfy the rapist nor seek her own sexual satisfaction. If the victim can do so without excessive risk, she should resist sexual contact and penetration; even if resistance is impossible or seems too risky, she may not choose to engage in the sexual act, but should remain passive insofar as possible, performing only those outward behaviors demanded by the rapist.

Are all these requirements being fulfilled by wives who are imposed on by their husbands as you are? I do not think so. The wife yields to her husband's unjust pressure and reluctantly consents to more or less regular intercourse; she chooses to engage in unwanted sexual acts, rather than resist them or remain passive, and

100. See Edward J. Bayer, *Rape within Marriage: A Moral Analysis Delayed* (Lanham, Md.: University Press of America, 1985), 4–7.

101. Ibid., 124–41.

102. The fact and gravity of some husbands' sexual violence against their wives has been studied and discussed in many substantial scholarly publications; see, e.g., Diana E. H. Russell, *Rape and Marriage,* rev. ed. (Bloomington, Ind.: Indiana University Press, 1990). But the specific wrong and full seriousness of sexual abuse within marriage is missed, in my judgment, by classifying it as rape.

attempts to satisfy her husband's wrongful sexual demands. Plainly, such sexual acts cannot constitute true marital intercourse. However, neither do they constitute rape within marriage as Bayer defines it, for that involves the withholding of free consent. Moreover, unless a married woman responds to her husband's sexual violence as she would to any rapist's, the other conditions for the analogy with rape are not met.[103]

They apparently are not met in your case. You explicitly state your intention: to have "intercourse as often as necessary to satisfy Dan." That implies the reluctant intention to engage in sexual acts rather than resistance or passivity in response to sexual violence. You are the victim of gravely unjust sexual oppression, but you are not being raped, and so your use of the diaphragm and jelly cannot be protection against rape.

Of course, a rapist need not use physical force to dominate his victim; he can use explicit or implicit threats of force or other forms of psychological coercion. Bayer might argue that, because a wife in your situation is being coerced psychologically, she lacks the freedom of choice necessary for consent, and so really is being raped. But that argument would not be sound. While psychological coercion can cause a woman who never consents to sexual activity to endure being raped, it also can motivate a woman to consent reluctantly to unwanted sexual activity to avoid an alternative she finds even more repugnant. That is true of the typical wife in your situation. She faces a hard choice: between meeting her husband's demands, which are unreasonable inasmuch as the couple has morally compelling reasons for avoiding pregnancy, and accepting or initiating a separation, which would deprive her of at least part of her husband's financial support and perhaps other advantages of maintaining the relationship, bad as it is. In such a case, the man exercising the coercion is no less guilty of gravely unjust sexual oppression than he would be if the woman refused to consent. Yet she is not being raped. Under duress, which no doubt reduces her moral responsibility, she reluctantly chooses to submit to her own victimization, much like the woman who reluctantly chooses prostitution so that she and her children will not starve.

Again, in my judgment, that is your case. You think you must choose between satisfying Dan's sexual demands and separation. Lacking experience working outside your home, you could not face the prospect of trying to raise the children and care for yourself without his full financial support and health coverage. So, you reluctantly have chosen to have intercourse as often as necessary to satisfy him. In my judgment, Dan is not raping you, but he is treating you like a prostitute by not only imposing nonmarital sexual activity on you but using your dependence to extort your submission.

Having considered the two views of your situation—that Dan is raping you and that he is treating you like a prostitute—you should act on the one you believe true. What you should do if you believe you are being raped is clear: never consent,

---

103. Indeed, Bayer, op. cit., 86–96, presents the views of Jan Visser, C.Ss.R, and Marcellino Zalba, S.J., as approximating his own, and both of these authors seem to be concerned, not with an ongoing situation, but with isolated incidents of sexual violence by a husband against his wife, and both make it clear that the wife must act in the same way as any woman being raped.

never initiate sexual activity, never seek pleasure in it, and never do more than perform those outward behaviors Dan demands, while otherwise remaining entirely passive and never trying to satisfy him.

But what should you do if you accept the alternative view I have proposed?

First, after careful preparation—with which Father Gibson probably will help—tell Dan how you see the situation and invite him to repent. Be both gentle and firm, neither judging his inmost heart and condemning him nor softening the truth about what he is doing and excusing it. Make it clear that you will never again use contraception or consent to intercourse that might result in pregnancy. At the same time, offer him your forgiveness, appeal to him to respect your conscience, ask for his cooperation, and promise to respond to it by doing everything you can to help build a better, happier marriage.

In preparing for this important conversation, learn more about natural family planning (NFP). While the rhythm method you tried so hard to use is morally acceptable, it is based on applying statistics about when women whose cycles vary within certain limits are likely to be fertile, not on positive evidence that a particular woman is fertile or not. Today, however, a woman can obtain such evidence about her own fertility, and most couples who practice NFP easily gather it by taking note of certain cyclic changes that occur in a woman's body during every menstrual cycle in which conception could occur.[104] Couples who cooperate in acting consistently on this information almost always can avoid pregnancy not only with greater security than you achieve by using a diaphragm and jelly but with less abstinence than you thought necessary after your last baby was born.

If Dan rejects your view of the situation and refuses to cooperate, do not consent either to any further sexual intercourse with him, since that would not be true marital intercourse, or to any other erotic activity legitimate only for married couples, since the moral acceptability of such activity depends on its relationship to true marital intercourse. That might lead Dan to repent, and you not only should pray that it will but should do everything you can without violating your conscience to encourage him to cooperate. But no longer getting what he wants also might, and perhaps more likely will, lead to the separation you wished to avoid (see q. 30, below). While the shock of separation also might bring him to a change of heart, you and your children no doubt will suffer economic hardship if it does not. However, you surely will be legally entitled to substantial support from Dan and should get the legal advice and help necessary to obtain it.

I realize that it will be very hard for you to take the steps I have outlined. But if you think my view of the situation true, this is the way you must follow to keep your promise to walk with the Lord. Do not think keeping your promise and living according to what you believe true will involve only pointless suffering. Instead,

---

104. On the development of natural family planning (NFP) see Mary Shivanandan, "After Rhythm: The Development of NFP," *Ethics and Medics*, 20:4 (Apr. 1995): 3–4. Sound and useful practical treatments of NFP: John F. Kippley and Sheila K. Kippley, *The Art of Natural Family Planning*, 4th ed. (Cincinnati, Ohio: Couple to Couple League, 1996); Evelyn Billings and Ann Westmore, *The Billings Method: Controlling Fertility without Drugs or Devices* (New York: Ballantine, 1983). On the scientific aspects of NFP, see *Natural Family Planning: Nature's Way–God's Way*, ed. Anthony Zimmerman, S.V.D. (Milwaukee: DeRance, 1980), 81–140.

keep before your mind the short-term and long-term benefits for which you should hope and pray.

As for the short term, in standing up to Dan, you should hope not simply to escape the guilt of contraception, but to change your marriage for the better—not superficially, but in a deep and true way. That would require his repentance, and separating from him might help bring it about. If not, at least it will involve your faithfulness to your vocation as a Christian, wife, and mother, even if you must live in permanent separation from him, rather than submit to him and betray your vocation and promise to the Lord.

Separation will not be bad in every respect. You surely realize that your marriage has been deeply troubled for a very long time, if not from the start. Dan always has been more involved in his work than in your family. Six years ago, you were in great distress because of his failure to provide the domestic help and psychological support you needed. When you struggled to use periodic abstinence, he showed no respect for your belief, conscience, and feelings, but sent you to a psychiatrist. When the psychiatrist found you mentally healthy and recommended marriage counseling, Dan stopped going after only three sessions. When your chronic illness required pregnancy avoidance and you conscientiously judged more extensive abstinence from marital intercourse necessary, he would not accept his share of responsibility in the matter, but threatened to leave you unless you satisfied his sexual demands. Spouses should cooperate, but the record shows Dan has not been doing that. He has succeeded in dominating you, and you have submitted. That is bad not only for you and for your marriage, but for him, since he is missing out on being a good husband, failing to become a good person, and acting as your oppressor. This situation also is bad for your children. A man simply cannot be a good father without being a good husband, and your children need the love, dedicated care, guidance, and example of a good father—or, at least, they need to be freed of the bad example of a father who succeeds in dominating their mother.

As for the long term, while striving and praying and hoping for the best, you must realistically be prepared for much suffering. But even though miserable days and sad years seem so very long, life on earth is short. Quite soon it will be over. To walk with him, Jesus told you, you must take up your cross. But he also showed you where the walk with him that begins on Good Friday leads: to Easter morning's victory and the joy of everlasting life. If you do not miss out on that glory, you will find again in heaven everything good about you and your life and effort here, but cleansed, healed, completed as you always wished (see GS 38–39). Pray you will find your children there, and Dan too.

29: What sexual activity is permissible for elderly married couples?

After teaching natural family planning (NFP) for several years, I recently began working as a nurse practitioner in a Catholic home for the elderly. The staff here has undertaken to improve health care for the residents without increasing costs. We are trying to reduce the rate of hospitalizations and contacts with physicians, especially specialists, by managing residents' care, and at the same time supply some of the services physicians have been providing, promote more effective cooperation by patients, and answer many of the questions a doctor otherwise would answer. I am getting to know our residents personally, and they are beginning to trust me and talk about their problems.

About one-third of our residents are married couples, who occupy spacious double rooms with private bathrooms. Having heard that I had taught NFP, several couples have asked me about difficulties they have with marital intercourse. The men are more or less impotent. The wives are postmenopausal, so that contraception is never an issue, but the couples' attempts to deal with the problem of impotence do raise some moral questions.[105] I hope you will be able to answer them, since we do not have a resident chaplain, and, though the assistant at the parish is here part time, he is not sure about these questions and is too busy to look into them.

(1) In a few cases, where the husbands are completely impotent, the couples no longer attempt intercourse. Instead, they only snuggle and fondle each other's genitals. They experience some sexual arousal and find it satisfying, though neither has an orgasm. Is this permissible? I think it is, but the priest is not sure, since these couples have no prospect of having intercourse.

(2) One husband can obtain an erection, but only if his wife stimulates his penis manually or orally, and she prefers to do it orally. They prepare beforehand by applying a lubricant to the wife's labia and vagina to facilitate intercourse; she stops the stimulation just before he climaxes; they have vaginal intercourse during which he immediately ejaculates; and he then stimulates her manually to orgasm. Is this permissible? The priest, though not sure, thinks the oral-genital contact and the manual stimulation of the wife to orgasm may be wrong.

(3) Another husband's complete impotence greatly frustrated his wife, who has been on estrogen replacement therapy since menopause and wants regular intercourse. The couple are quite determined, and have tried various remedies for impotence. To avoid the disadvantages of other approaches, they are using a vacuum device placed over the penis so that the air pressure surrounding it is lowered, bringing on an erection, which is then sustained by placing an elastic constriction ring around the base of the penis. The vacuum device then is removed, and they engage in satisfying intercourse. However, the constriction ring not only keeps blood in the penis but interferes with ejaculation; when the husband removes the ring after withdrawal, quite a bit of semen flows from his penis. The question is: If no semen reaches the wife's vagina—perhaps a little does but they are not sure—are this couple engaging in sinful, nonmarital acts? I have no idea what to tell them.

(4) In a few other cases where the husband is totally impotent, couples have tried various remedies without finding any satisfactory. Is it permissible for such a couple

---

105. *Impotence* means incapacity for sexual intercourse, usually due to a man's inability to have or maintain an erection adequate for intercourse. Impotence is distinct from infertility—that is, the inability of a couple to have a baby. All postmenopausal women are infertile, but not all elderly men are impotent, let alone infertile.

to stimulate each other to orgasm without any genital contact? I do not think it is. But is it permissible if the couple make genital contact so that the husband ejaculates at the mouth of the vagina, and he then manually stimulates his wife to orgasm?

Analysis:

Several questions are asked about sexual activity within marriage. Questions (1), (2), and the first part of (4) can be answered by applying accepted norms for marital sexual activity. The other questions cannot be answered except by identifying the minimal condition a couple's outward behavior must meet to be the performance of an instance of intercourse as a moral species of action. In my judgment, the minimal condition is that the couple's behavior be the performance required for a reproductive-type act. By that criterion, intercourse with the use of a constriction ring to overcome impotence is true sexual intercourse—and so can be marital intercourse—if any semen whatsoever reaches the vagina, which may be assumed in case of doubt. Similarly, if, but only if, an impotent husband can ejaculate some semen into the vagina, the couple are capable of marital intercourse—which answers the second part of (4). An adequate response to these questions should also include an indication of other requirements for marital intercourse, so that the proposed reply will not be misinterpreted as reducing the marital act to its minimal behavioral conditions.

The reply could be along the following lines:

Your questions are important ones, since the moral issues they raise are by no means trivial, and answers are needed for the peace of conscience and happiness of many elderly people. Moreover, many couples now live longer than formerly, and Catholic moralists have devoted very little attention to these matters.[106] The marital sexual activity and satisfaction of elderly couples remain significant goods, both in themselves and for their contribution to other aspects of their lives. Therefore, I welcome these questions, even though dealing with them will require a rather clinical discussion that may provoke reproach or ridicule from people lacking your training and sympathy for those needing help.

Men usually should consult a physician about impotence. As you undoubtedly know, in many cases it is either a side effect of medication or a symptom of some illness, such as diabetes, that might be discovered by a thorough examination and remedied by suitable treatment. However, given your professional role, I assume you have seen to it that these men are receiving appropriate health care.

Sometimes impotence results from a man doing something he should not, such as drinking too much or obtaining sexual satisfaction apart from intercourse by masturbating. Gently mention such possibilities and encourage the men you deal with to examine their consciences. If their impotence results from some sin, they obviously should deal with the problem by repenting and amending their lives.

---

106. They are dealt with amorally, however, by otherwise sound health care providers and counselors; see, e.g., Edward M. Brecher, *Love, Sex, and Aging: A Consumers Union Report* (Boston: Little, Brown, 1984).

The sexual activities of a married couple cannot be marital unless carried out as acts of marital love.[107] That requires mutual consent; it is impossible for either spouse to compel the other, physically or psychologically, to participate in authentic marital sexual acts. Marital love also requires that, in both intercourse and the sexual activity leading up to it and following it, the couple seek, not pleasure alone, but the wider good of marital communion, in which pleasure, though an important element, is subordinate. Efforts to deal with impotence cannot be morally acceptable unless the behavior of both spouses expresses marital affection, is mutually agreeable, and is at least implicitly intended by both to serve the good of their marriage.

Moreover, sexual acts cannot be acts of marital love unless two conditions are met: (1) during them neither spouse deliberately entertains wishes that he or she were instead having intercourse with someone else, and (2) neither would be willing to engage in these activities if they were not with the spouse but adulterous. This consideration excludes not only individuals but couples from using pornography to try to overcome impotence, for either those doing this conditionally intend adultery or, at least, deliberately arouse themselves by means of the erotic appeal of someone other than their spouses. If that is not adultery in the heart—which I am inclined to think it is—it surely is an occasion of sin that one cannot rightly enter into.

All moralists faithful to the Church's teaching agree that the intentional stimulation of either or both spouses to orgasm entirely apart from genital contact must be excluded as morally unacceptable. By involving orgasm, that behavior constitutes a sexual act complete in itself, yet one that cannot unite the couple in one flesh. A sexual act complete in itself cannot extend previous, or prepare for prospective, marital intercourse; an act that does not unite the couple in one flesh is not intercourse, and so cannot be marital intercourse. In fact, it is masturbation; and if mutual it is mutual masturbation. Thus, your view with regard to the first question in (4) is sound. I shall treat the other questions before returning to the second question in (4).

Many faithful moralists have discussed questions about the morality of a married couple's sexual acts short of intercourse (see *LCL,* 641–42).[108] Provided such activities are acts of marital love, in the sense already explained, and provided neither spouse intends or is likely to have an orgasm apart from intercourse, incomplete sexual acts, which lead to sexual arousal, are morally acceptable expressions of marital affection.[109] For most married couples, such acts both bring

107. The response given here condenses parts of the treatment of the sexual activities of married couples in *LCL,* 633–47.

108. A sound treatment of these matters, including the morality of oral-genital contacts preparatory to intercourse: John C. Ford, S.J., and Gerald Kelly, S.J., *Contemporary Moral Theology,* vol. 2, *Marriage Questions* (Westminster, Md.: Newman Press, 1964), 210–13, 224–34.

109. If marital sexual acts short of intercourse cause a spouse to have an accidental (unintended) orgasm apart from intercourse, that event is not in itself a human act, and so is not a sin. But unless a couple are attempting to engage in intercourse, for either spouse deliberately to take a significant risk of orgasm apart from intercourse is, in my judgment, either conditionally to intend nonmarital satisfaction or an occasion of that sin that should be avoided.

about a continuing experience of one-flesh communion and prepare, at least indirectly and remotely, for eventual marital intercourse. Even for elderly couples who no longer have any prospect of intercourse, such incomplete sexual acts can be appropriate expressions of marital affection inasmuch as they continue to realize, to the extent possible, the one-flesh unity realized in previous acts of marital intercourse and to provide the couple with an experience, though imperfect, of their unity. So, your view with regard to (1) is sound: Even if there is no prospect that a married couple will again have intercourse, they may express their affection by means of mutually agreeable sexual activities that cause some sexual arousal and pleasure, provided neither intends or wrongly risks having an orgasm or seeks satisfaction by subsequent self-stimulation.

In many cases, a wife's oral stimulation of her husband's penis is morally unacceptable. Sometimes, either or both spouses intend this behavior to bring about ejaculation apart from intercourse. In that case, it is sodomy, and, as already explained, is morally excluded. Even when neither spouse has that wrongful intention, this behavior cannot carry out an act of marital love if the wife finds it repugnant, as many do. Nor can the behavior effectively serve as an incomplete act leading to marital intercourse if in fact it impedes intercourse by bringing about ejaculation apart from it, even if unintentionally.

However, sometimes the wife's oral stimulation of the husband's penis is no less natural than other affectionate kisses and touches that prepare for intercourse. That is so when it is intended by both spouses to be an incomplete sexual act leading to marital intercourse, is willingly done by the wife for that purpose, and serves the purpose effectively. And that is so with the couple in (2). Nor is there any moral problem in this husband's manually stimulating his wife to orgasm immediately after intercourse, which is over too quickly to give her complete satisfaction. Unlike the husband's orgasm, the wife's need not occur during intercourse itself, since the time at which she is completely satisfied does not affect intercourse insofar as it is a reproductive function. So, since this stimulation continues that begun in intercourse, it can pertain to the couple's marital act, which realizes their one-flesh communion and provides them with an experience of it.

My reply to question (3), about the constriction ring, is that using it can be morally acceptable. If any semen whatsoever reaches the wife's vagina, the couple's acts are authentic marital intercourse and will be virtuous, provided they are not morally defective in some other way. To see why this is so, it is necessary to understand the minimum requirements for marital intercourse considered as a reproductive-type *human* act.

Marital intercourse, as has been explained, is much more than a reproductive-type act, but it must at least be that if it is to make the couple two in one flesh and thereby allow them to experience themselves as one. For, among all sexual performances, only a reproductive-type act is a single function of a mated pair. Other sexual acts of a male and a female, even if they involve intimate genital contact, are really two separate and distinct sexual performances, and so must be excluded as nonmarital, even when engaged in by a married couple. It follows that marital intercourse must have both the intention and the outward behavior characteristic of a reproductive-type act.

For the act to be reproductive as to intention, the couple need not intend to reproduce. Other animals generally are inclined to mate only at fertile times, but humans' inclination to mate is not so limited; yet, given the appropriate behavior and intention, such an act still is reproductive in kind. Two things are necessary with respect to intention: (1) there must not be an intention to impede conception—irrelevant here, since couples who know they are not fertile cannot have that intention—and (2) there must be the intention to carry out the appropriate behavior. Given the latter intention, the act, morally speaking, will be intercourse (and so, if marital, will be marital intercourse) even if the behavior unintentionally is defective, for example, if the man cannot reach orgasm.

The appropriate outward behavior for a typical reproductive-type human act is the same as in other mammals. The couple adjust their bodies so that the head of the male's penis is inside the female's vagina, and then move in a manner that causes the membrane covering the head of the penis to be stimulated until the male's orgasm occurs, whereupon the penis becomes limp and intercourse naturally ends.

Various conditions prevent or impede subsequent stages of the normal reproductive process. For example, a woman might lack a uterus, either due to a birth defect or (more likely) a hysterectomy; a man who has had prostate surgery may have retrograde ejaculations (rather than being ejaculated normally from the penis, almost all the semen flows into the bladder and is voided when the man next urinates). But such conditions in no way affect the behavior essential to the human act, so knowing they exist does not prevent couples from engaging in human acts of sexual intercourse.[110]

The vacuum device and constriction ring are used to obtain and sustain the erection needed for sexual intercourse. Preventing normal ejaculation is an unintended side effect of the ring, and so its use would be consistent with the intention required for human sexual intercourse even if this couple were potentially fertile. The ring's effect on ejaculation is no more drastic than the effect prostate surgery sometimes has. The behavior directly in the couple's power, which brings about ejaculation, remains possible, and the couple engage in it. So, the act is an act of sexual intercourse. Being uncertain whether some ejaculate reaches the vagina, the couple, in my judgment, may assume that at least some does.

Someone might object that, if a younger couple believed they were fertile and wanted to have children, they would not deal with the husband's impotence by using the constriction ring, which interferes with ejaculation, but would choose some method ensuring that all the ejaculate reached the vagina. So, the objection could conclude, the behavior of this elderly couple is not adequate for a reproductive-type act. The answer is twofold. First, the fertile couple no doubt would use some other method to overcome impotence if they could, but if they could not, they might well deal with it by using the vacuum device and constriction

110. See Thomas J. O'Donnell, S.J., *Medicine and Christian Morality,* 2nd ed. rev. (New York: Alba House, 1991), 231–32, regarding retrograde ejaculation after prostate surgery; he supposes that a small amount of ejaculate probably reaches the vagina.

ring, hoping some semen would be ejaculated into the vagina. Second, even without penetration and ejaculation in the vagina, pregnancy can result if semen is deposited at the entrance to the vagina. So, a fertile couple using the constriction ring could increase the likelihood of conception by positioning themselves so that, when the husband removes the ring, the semen that flows from his penis falls into the entrance to the vagina.

An elderly couple using the device also can do that. Still, since I think the elderly couple who use the constriction ring meet the behavioral requirement for a reproductive-type act in having intercourse and may assume that some ejaculate reaches the vagina, I do not think that, in removing the ring, they need take the further step the fertile couple would take. However, they certainly may do so if that is conducive to their peace of conscience.

The preceding discussion suggests the answer to the second question in (4). If a couple make genital contact in which ejaculation occurs with the tip of the penis just within the entrance of the vagina, they meet the minimal behavioral conditions for a reproductive type act, and so for marital intercourse.[111] As explained in answer to the second question, the husband may then stimulate the wife to orgasm.

30: How should a wife conduct a separation from her violent husband?

Fred and I are both Catholic. He was a college classmate; we married just after graduation two years ago. Now I am twenty-four. We have one child, a boy nine months. I have a decent job, and my mother cares for the baby while I work. Fred settled for a job doing technical support with a computer software company. The work is below his abilities and bores him, but he does not have enough ambition to look for something more challenging. He is very good at certain computer games in which two players compete; every weekend he plays these games with anyone willing to gamble. Even giving a handicap, he usually wins and his average weekend winnings are over a hundred dollars.

Fred does not drink much and never gets drunk, but he does have a terrible temper. I knew that when we married, because during our college days he often got into fights. Yet he has many good qualities, and he never turned his temper on me until after we married. Serious quarreling began while I was pregnant and has gotten steadily worse. During the last six months he has been hitting me; this usually happens on weekends, especially when he has not done well at his computer games. He comes home in a bad mood, has one drink, and gets very nasty. Afterwards, he is remorseful and promises never to do it again.

A deacon at our parish does marriage counseling, and I got Fred to go. But after going twice, he said it was a waste of time and would not continue. Two months

---

111. According to Canon Law, even if the husband is incapable of a normal erection, partial penetration of the vagina is sufficient for intercourse: see The Canon Law Society of Great Britain and Ireland in association with The Canadian Canon Law Society, *The Canon Law: Letter and Spirit: A Practical Guide to the Code of Canon Law* (Collegeville, Minn.: Liturgical Press, 1995), commentary on c. 1084, §§1–2.

ago he beat me severely, and I called the police. They arrested him and locked him up until I bailed him out. The judge ordered him into individual counseling, and he goes, but it does not seem to be helping. He has hit me twice in the past three weeks. Up to now, he has not hit the baby, but sometimes I can tell that he is barely restraining himself. That worries me, since it was like that before he first hit me.

I feel things cannot go on this way, and something must be done. I asked the deacon for advice, but he said he can only counsel couples. A friend of mine who was in one of your classes suggested I get in touch with you.

I could go back to the prosecutor, and the judge would send Fred to jail. But after talking it over with people I trust, I doubt that putting him in jail would do much good and am reluctant to do it. I could try to avoid trouble by taking the baby and going to my mother's or a friend's before Fred comes home from playing his games. Or I could demand that he move out and, if necessary, get a court order to put him out. But if I do, I am not sure whether to allow him to visit. Of course, cutting off marital relations might force Fred to get straightened out. But our sex life always has been good, and I would find it hard to give up that part of marriage. He never has mistreated me during sex; when he is angry, he is not even interested in it. Perhaps I could allow him to visit some weekday evenings but make him stay away entirely on weekends, when he usually loses his temper.

The only thing I am sure about is that I have to find some solution. If nothing else works, I suppose I will have to get a divorce, and I cannot see myself living alone for the rest of my life. What should I do?

Analysis:

The questioner is asking whether to separate and, if so, whether to continue marital relations during the separation; she also seems to desire support in considering divorce and remarriage as an option. The significant risk that the questioner's husband will injure their baby demands that she separate at once. The marriage ought to be presumed valid, and the option of divorce and remarriage should be excluded. Since neither the magisterium nor traditional Catholic theology has addressed the question about continuing marital relations during a separation, the goods at stake must be considered and a suitable norm derived. Engaging in intercourse during the separation, in my opinion, would be inappropriate inasmuch as it would not correspond to the truth of the couple's relationship.

The reply could be along the following lines:

In my judgment, you need more help than I, as a moral theologian, can give you. I think you need the pastoral guidance of a priest who has experience with troubled marriages, faithfully applies the Church's teaching, and is equipped with some knowledge of psychology. He could help you identify your resources and options, so that you will be able to determine what God is calling you to do. He also could help you identify any moral shortcomings and use the sacrament of penance to deal with them. Then, by constant prayer and devout participation in the Eucharist you can obtain the grace you need to deal with your difficult situation, and even to grow spiritually by taking up your cross and following Jesus.

Still, I shall try to clarify the moral responsibilities to which your description of the situation points. Though you may well consider what I shall say unrealistic and more than you can deal with at this time, you might share this letter with the priest from whom you seek help, and discuss its bearing on your situation with him.

Your husband's seriously abusive behavior is inconsistent with genuine marital love. Only God knows the extent to which Fred freely chooses to misbehave in each particular instance, and your account suggests that underlying psychological factors lead to his loss of control. But even with the motivation of the judge's order, he seems to be failing to cooperate with the help he needs, just as he earlier refused to continue in marriage counseling—something he surely could have done. Now you have reason to fear he might injure the baby, and you have a grave obligation to prevent both the physical and the psychological trauma to which your nine-month-old child is vulnerable. Therefore, you have good reasons to separate and, in view of the risk to the child, you ought to do so at once (see *CIC*, c. 1153, §1; *LCL*, 725–29).

Your intention in separating should be to promote the good of your family, not only by protecting your child and yourself, but by obtaining psychological space in which to work out a sounder relationship with your husband, and to encourage his repentance, healing, and growth toward holiness. To achieve these benefits, you should be prepared to make all necessary sacrifices, not for some limited time, but indefinitely. In marrying, you committed yourself to Fred "for better, for worse, . . . in sickness and in health, until death." Remember how lovingly you made that commitment. As you surely know, marriage is indissoluble except by death, and a "remarriage" after divorce is an adulterous relationship. So, with mind and heart set on preserving your love, the only question for you should be what sort of marriage you and Fred will have. To think divorce and remarriage might serve as a last resort not only will undermine your resolve to make the best of your marriage but will violate marital love and be a first step toward infidelity. Put that thought aside, and renew your commitment to your husband even as you separate from him.[112]

Perhaps you should reconsider the possibility of putting Fred in jail. It would be a way of separating from him, and the shock might lead him to genuine repentance. He probably would not remain in jail long, but would be ordered to accept additional help and report regularly to a probation officer. The experience might encourage him to commit himself to do what he must to amend. Still, you need not choose this course. But if you do not, you must separate at least sufficiently to ensure the safety of your baby, and it hardly seems adequate to absent yourself only when Fred usually becomes violent. Therefore, either you should ask—and, if necessary, compel—Fred to move out or you and the baby should do so.

---

112. At present, a moral and pastoral adviser should presume this marriage valid and try to help the couple overcome their difficulties: see *CIC*, cc. 1060; 1063, 4°; 1695. However, if the questioner eventually were civilly divorced, it might be appropriate to suggest to her that she look into the possibility of asking a tribunal to consider the case. Her narrative suggests several possible grounds on which the marriage might be judged null.

You ask about the possibility of one or another form of limited separation together with occasional marital intercourse. Of course, a married couple who separate do not lose their right to engage in intercourse by mutual consent. The question is whether it would be appropriate to separate as much as necessary to forestall abuse while also continuing to engage in intercourse. Since nothing in the Church's teaching points clearly to an answer, I can offer only an opinion, together with reasons for it.

I believe that in separating you should entirely discontinue marital intercourse. Moreover, if you give up marital intercourse, you also should forgo all intimacies short of intercourse that tend to lead to it, since such intimacies will be occasions of sin for both of you—at least, the sin of engaging in the marital intercourse you ought to forgo. Therefore, you should limit expressions of affection to those appropriate for a chaste engaged couple (see *LCL,* 745–46, 749–50).

My main reason for this judgment is that marital intercourse should not be a mere means to pleasure or anything else. Rather, it should express the real unity of spouses and allow them to experience it, and this unity includes their mutual love. But Fred's failure to curb his abusive behavior is gravely inconsistent with marital love, inasmuch as it requires that you no longer live in the same household. Continuing intercourse would provide both of you with an experience divergent from reality, which would be a falsification. Though not mutually deceptive, this falsification might well be self-deceptive, enabling you both to avoid confronting the truth about yourselves and your marital relationship as a whole, which involves far more than your sexual activity. Rather than working together to heal your wounded marriage, you probably would prolong the present bad situation. This abnormal relationship also would be detrimental to your child, since it would deprive him indefinitely of the stable, unified parental principle he needs as a solid basis for his personal development.

Another reason to abstain from marital intercourse during the separation is that having another baby would greatly complicate your problems. Both the pregnancy and caring for the infant would be more difficult without your husband's full help and support; that might lead you to end the separation too soon and accept unreasonable risk of serious abuse to yourself and your children. At the same time, forgoing this part of your marriage will prevent Fred from using sexual activity to play on your emotions and manipulate your behavior, as, I suspect, he has been doing.[113]

Still, you should not proceed in a manipulative spirit, as if discontinuing marital intercourse were a way to "force Fred to get straightened out." Regard it as an expression of the truth—your marriage is so badly crippled that you cannot function as a normal married couple. Since you will find it hard to give up this part of your

---

113. Even when couples live apart for reasons other than marital discord, they are much more likely to divorce than cohabiting couples; see Ronald R. Rindfuss and Elizabeth Hervey Stephen, "Marital Noncohabitation: Separation Does Not Make the Heart Grow Fonder," *Journal of Marriage and the Family,* 52 (1990): 259–70. Thus, I recognize that excluding sexual intercourse during the separation risks alienating the husband and leading to infidelity by both spouses. Still, the reasons given seem to me sufficient to rule out the questioner's proposal to separate from board but not bed.

marriage, your choice to abstain will be a significant sacrifice—an appropriate expression of the fact that your love sincerely seeks, not simply sexual satisfaction and other benefits for yourself, but the true good of your husband and mutual fulfillment in a happy marriage.

You should explain to Fred your intentions in separating; it probably would be best to write him a letter or talk in the presence of a third party who could prevent him from hurting you. First, make it clear why you are taking this difficult step. He does not seem to be making an honest effort to put an end to his abusive behavior, and, while he has never hit the baby, you fear he will. Explain that you are acting, not out of anger, but out of love, in the hope that the separation will provide an opportunity for him to develop the self-control he must have to be a good husband and father, not only for the sakes of your marriage and your child, but for his own sake. I think you also would do well to explain to him that you had considered the possibility of allowing marital intercourse during this necessary separation, and you expect to find it difficult to forgo this part of your marriage, but you have concluded that the sacrifice is necessary to express the truth about your relationship's present condition. Make it clear that you still love him and will never be unfaithful to him. Recall his good qualities, tell him you believe he can change for the better, and express your hope for a happy marriage and good family life after he has done so.

In separating, do not set an arbitrary deadline for solving the problems and coming back together; remarriage being excluded, the only acceptable alternative to a prolonged separation is a change in the circumstances that require it. If the separation continues for a long time and the lack of resolution tries your patience, as it will, recognize that this abnormal condition of marriage may be the best you can achieve. Therefore, in separating you should commit yourself to living apart from your husband but with perfect fidelity to him for the rest of your life, if need be. Eventually a civil divorce might be warranted, but only if there remained no realistic prospect of reconciliation and the divorce was necessary to settle legal rights and responsibilities with respect to custody of your child, property, and so on (see *CIC*, cc. 1672 and 1692).

While separated, you need not, and should not, try to avoid all contact with your husband. Your parental responsibilities will call for continuing cooperation, and, no doubt, Fred will wish to spend some time with the baby. Given your well-grounded fears, however, try to avoid leaving him alone with the child. Try to arrange to do some things as a family, but always either in public or with others, and at times when Fred is least likely to become violent. If the conditions for visitation are not mutually agreed upon but imposed by the court, comply only if that involves no risk for the baby, or Fred insists and the judge leaves you no choice.

Once separated, be on guard against allowing your sexual desire or other need for Fred to generate in you an unreasonable urgency about reconciling. While understandable, such an emotional desire is likely to lead you to end the separation before changes have occurred that warrant doing so. For your own good and Fred's, make a check list of indications of change in him that would provide a reasonable assurance of safety for you and the baby and a well-grounded hope that you can live together in harmony. Remember, too, that no one is perfect, so that, while no defect of yours could justify Fred's abusive behavior, nevertheless you should examine yourself and try to discover anything that needs changing in your attitudes, expectations, habits, and behavior. In thinking about what must change in both of you, it probably will be helpful, as I suggested at the outset, to talk with a pastoral counselor who is faithful to the Church's teaching and has some training in psychology.

Besides the pastoral guidance the priest can give you, he also may be able to introduce you to one or more women who have undergone abuse, separated, faithfully fulfilled their marital and maternal responsibilities, and achieved a more serene life, whether separated or reconciled in a healed marriage. The friendly advice and encouragement of such women, I believe, would help you calm your anxieties, nurture your self-confidence, and gain insight into your relationship with Fred and your life as a whole. Of course, you probably could easily find a support group of battered women, but be on your guard against false ideologies, bitterness, and selfish attitudes at odds with Christian faith and values.

In your self-examination, consider whatever criticisms or accusations Fred may have made against you. Though many no doubt would reflect his bias and be exaggerated, at least some almost certainly would contain important elements of truth. Ask yourself, too, whether your work outside the home is necessary and compatible with fulfilling your responsibilities as mother and homemaker. Also, in leaving your baby in your mother's care, are you imposing unfairly on her? Of course, during the separation, it probably will be necessary for you to continue working and relying on your mother's help in caring for the baby. Then too, if Fred gives up his gambling, he also will forgo that source of income. Still, you should consider all of your responsibilities, and be prepared to meet them as perfectly as possible in cooperation with your husband.

In asking how Fred must change, consider several things. His gambling is morally questionable, since the fact that he regularly wins suggests that he is taking unfair advantage of less skillful opponents, at least some of whom probably are gambling money they ought to be using to meet their responsibilities. It also is questionable for him to spend time on this form of play, especially since it must reduce the time he devotes to you and your baby. Moreover, while his drinking apparently is not in itself excessive, both it and his gambling seem to have been proximate occasions of his gravely abusive behavior, and for that reason he almost certainly should have given up both. His anger when he has not done well at his computer games suggests that winning those games has an undue psychological significance for him. Whatever is behind that might also explain why he stays in a job that bores him instead of seeking more challenging work. Probably he needs insight into the psychological causes of his terrible temper, but it is certain that he needs to organize his life better: in view of his faith, his commitments to marriage and fatherhood, and his talents. He ought to regard his talents as gifts to be used as fully as possible in service to others, as means to support his family, and as opportunities for genuine self-fulfillment in worthwhile work.

Even if the conditions for you to reconcile are met, you will continue to encounter marital difficulties. Both of you should do all you can to overcome them (see *LCL,* 721–25). The regular use of spiritual means—prayer and the reception of the sacraments of penance and the Eucharist—will be essential. And so will be unquestioning determination by both of you faithfully to fulfill your mutual responsibilities, so that you will be good spouses and parents who may hope to live together forever in heaven.

31: May a woman deliberately risk having a baby her husband does not want?

I am in my late thirties, and my husband, Greg, is in his mid-forties. We have three children—a boy nine, and girls seven and four—and all of us are in good health. We are comfortably well off, since my husband has a good job, and I am happy to be a full-time wife, mother, and homemaker. Greg is good with the children, often taking them along on errands and doing things with them, and we also have good times together as a family.

We always have obeyed the Church's teaching on birth regulation and have practiced natural family planning (NFP) since we married, using it to space our children. Greg never has had a very strong sex drive, and since our last baby was born he has insisted that we take no chances. This always requires continuous abstinence of at least two weeks and sometimes as much as three. The result is that during the past four years we have seldom had intercourse more than a few times a cycle, and sometimes not at all, since other things interfere. Greg also has left it to me to make all the observations and judgments about which days are possibly fertile, and so it always has been up to me to tell him yes or no. Ironically, when he is interested, I often must say no, but he always accepts it in good grace.

My problem is this. In about a year, our youngest will be in kindergarten, and I would like to have another baby; I have plenty of energy and still feel young. The children also want a new brother or sister. But Greg says that we have enough children and does not want another. He argues that if I have a baby now, it might be seriously defective, since we did not marry young, and I am nearing forty. I do not believe that risk is very significant and, even if we were to have a child afflicted with Down's syndrome, for example, we have the financial and other resources to handle that.

I also feel sexually deprived by our extensive abstinence, and would like a more intimate marital bond with a more romantic and emotionally satisfying relationship. In some ways, our relationship is excellent; when something must be done, we always work well together. I take good care of myself, and try to please Greg. He appreciates it and always is cordial. But he is never very affectionate, and I sometimes feel we are more like friendly co-workers than a married couple. I think this situation is unfair, but do not press Greg for my "marital rights." I never have been unfaithful, but I often have to pray and struggle to control my imagination and sexual feelings.

I am a devout Catholic; Greg goes to Church, but his faith does not seem to mean very much to him. I feel we should trust God more and be willing to take a chance with another baby; Greg does not take providence very seriously. Though I feel cheated, my faith helps me to compartmentalize this problem and put up with the situation. If necessary, I suppose, I will continue to do that indefinitely.

Lately, however, I have been toying with the idea of cutting corners a bit on NFP. The point would be to facilitate more frequent marital intercourse and, while not trying to become pregnant, to open the door a bit, so as to let God decide. I would be disobeying Greg's wishes, but he would never know. So, I will welcome your prayers and insights.

Analysis:

The questioner asks whether she may intentionally risk having a child without her husband's consent. Vatican II teaches that the decision to have a child or another child belongs to the couple. In my opinion, for the questioner to risk pregnancy in the absence of consensus would be unfair both to her husband and to the child. The questioner should try to persuade her husband to cooperate more closely in the practice of NFP and should communicate with him about her desires. If he remains unwilling to have another baby, she should consider other ways of using her maternal gifts to benefit babies who need care; she also should try to involve her husband in the children's religious formation.

The reply could be along the following lines:

You say taking no chances on having another baby always requires you and Greg to abstain continuously during at least two weeks each cycle and sometimes as much as three. Perhaps you are not making use of all the available ways of identifying the times when you are not fertile. If that is possible, I suggest you look into current information regarding the practice of NFP.[114] However, I shall assume that, even if your technique of NFP might be improved, your problem will remain substantially as stated.

May you cut corners on NFP to facilitate more frequent marital intercourse and make it possible that you will become pregnant? In my judgment, you may not. I have two reasons for this answer.

First, having accepted responsibility for identifying the fertile days and yielded, however reluctantly, to your husband's unwillingness to have another child, you have agreed to take no chances of becoming pregnant. That undertaking was an implicit promise—it makes no difference whether you ever used the words "I promise"—and, like any promise, it may not be broken unfairly. Set aside the fact that you could break it without your husband's knowing, imagine that corner cutting results in pregnancy, apply the Golden Rule, and put yourself in his place. Surely you would feel betrayed in a very serious way. You would think: "She never should have done this unilaterally. At least, she should have talked it over with me first!"

---

114. See John F. Kippley and Sheila K. Kippley, *The Art of Natural Family Planning,* 4th ed. (Cincinnati, Ohio: Couple to Couple League, 1996); Evelyn Billings and Ann Westmore, *The Billings Method: Controlling Fertility without Drugs or Devices* (New York: Ballantine, 1983).

Second, as Vatican II teaches, only the couple may decide about regulating births. This implies that the decision should be by the agreement of both spouses (see GS 50; *LCL,* 681–84). Their consensus is necessary because the new person emerges from his or her parents insofar as they are one, so that the child's procreation presupposes the parents' unity. The complete genesis of the child does not end with conception, however, but ends only when the child has been raised to maturity. Ongoing parental unity is necessary for the child's proper development in every aspect of his or her being as a human person, and this unity should extend to the parents' minds and hearts. Every child therefore needs to be welcomed by both parents and has a right to their wholehearted commitment to love and care for him or her. The possibility of adoptive parenthood shows that this commitment not only is essential to parenthood but is more central to it, in some ways, than biological paternity or maternity. If you cut corners and become pregnant, you will have caused your child to come into being not only without this vital commitment by his or her father but despite his having made it clear that he did not wish to make this commitment. Of course, it would be Greg's duty to accept what had happened and commit himself to being a good father to the child, and perhaps he would. But perhaps he would not, and for you to cut corners and run that risk would be terribly unfair to the child.

Perhaps your husband's reasons for not wishing to have another child are inadequate. Since children are the "supreme gift of marriage" (GS 50), married couples well able to have another child need a serious reason to avoid pregnancy. Greg plainly is a good father who provides well, and you plainly have not only the desire but the capacity to mother at least one more child. Nevertheless, Greg's reasons may be better than they seem from what you have said. I do not mean you are misrepresenting the situation, but he may have failed to articulate everything he has in mind or you may have failed to comprehend some of his concerns. For example, if he became a father to another baby, he would be accepting a responsibility extending into his sixties, and he may be concerned about being able to fulfill it as he grows older. He may be thinking about the costs of the children's education and the need to save for retirement. The chances of your having a seriously defective child may not be great, but your husband may have recognized in himself some weakness that makes it unacceptable for him to take the risk. In any case, the fact that he is a good father to the three children you have suggests that his motives for resisting your wish for another are not merely selfish.

Nevertheless, even if there are sound reasons for avoiding another pregnancy, they may not be so weighty that your desire for more frequent marital intercourse should be excluded from consideration. Since marriage is one-flesh unity, it appropriately regularly includes emotionally satisfying experiences of intimacy. Thus, you may be right in thinking that Greg and you should not be practicing NFP so strictly. If so, it would be appropriate to accept some possibility of having another child. Greg certainly should seriously consider this view of the matter and perhaps should accept it, since in marrying he has conceded to you, as you to him, a real and strict right to marital affection, including intercourse whenever there is no reason to forgo it. However, even if Greg should accept this view, you must bear in mind that your right to marital intercourse is not absolute but limited by various moral responsibilities not to have it. That you might have a child without the necessary consensus always will morally require you not to have intercourse on days that might be fertile. So, unless you can persuade Greg to modify his position, you must continue limiting the exercise of your marital right.

When you speak of possible corner cutting on NFP as opening the door to pregnancy "so as to let God decide," you manifest a mistaken conception of divine providence. Cutting corners will not set the stage for any divine decision. God always decides, but he also calls on us to use our intelligence and capacity to make free choices to shape our own lives, and he will hold us responsible for our failures to do so. His providential plan includes all created reality, everything that is and all that is to be. Included in that plan is the life of good deeds he has prepared for each of us to live. We must discover his plan for our lives, accept it, and faithfully carry it out. As we do so, we are bound to be frustrated at times by other people and situations. Then, we must trust and pray that God will change hearts and solve the problems we cannot. Waiting and praying for a change of heart or God's solution is the way to rely on his providence. Acting instead on a mistaken conception of providence might well lead to disaster. If you betray your husband's trust, cut corners, and become pregnant, he may change for the worse. He might refuse to accept the baby he was unwilling to have, become alienated from you, and/or either withdraw entirely from marital intimacy or demand effective measures to prevent any future pregnancy. God might prevent such disastrous consequences, but you would be irresponsible to count on him to do so.

What I have said thus far has been largely negative with respect to your idea of corner cutting on NFP. I do wish to offer you some positive advice.

First, try very hard to persuade Greg to cooperate in attending to the signs of fertility. This cooperation will make him more aware of your sexuality and will tend of itself to foster intimacy. It also will make Greg aware of when marital intercourse is appropriate within the framework of your mutually agreed objective in practicing NFP, and will lead him to accept the responsibility of regulating his own romantic initiatives. Explain to him that this will help you by lessening the conflict you experience between your own sexual desire and your desire for another child, on the one hand, and, on the other, your desire to respect his wishes. You also might do well to admit to him that you have been tempted to cut corners on NFP, and point out that his sharing responsibility with you for making it work will eliminate that temptation.

My second suggestion is that at least temporarily you set aside your desire to have another baby, but plan and make a serious effort to get Greg to understand and cooperate with your desire for a more satisfying intimate relationship and more frequent marital intercourse, at least within the framework of practicing NFP as you now do, and perhaps within the framework of its somewhat less stringent practice. You might plan a brief vacation or a couples retreat, in order to go somewhere together where you can talk without pressure of time about your concerns. In stating those concerns, be gentle and take care not to make Greg feel threatened, since that could reduce his already weak sex drive. Avoid criticizing him and focus instead on articulating your own feelings, thus inviting him to help you deal with your problems rather than suggesting that he is the cause of shared problems. You say that when you and Greg must do something, you always work well together. I think therefore that in this conversation you should put your points as a proposal of a common project, something for the two of you to do together.

I suggest that you not say everything at once, but try to lead Greg step by step to accept something of your view. The main points I suggest you try to make are as follows. (1) You desire a richer intimate relationship, which will be possible even without more frequent marital intercourse if the two of you cooperate in certain ways. (Be prepared to offer specific suggestions which you think he might accept.) (2) You also would like more frequent marital intercourse. Without altering your present practice of NFP, it will be possible if the two of you cooperate in certain ways so as not to miss out, as you sometimes now do, on the opportunities it affords. (Again, you should be prepared to offer specific suggestions with a chance of being accepted.) (3) By altering your present practice of NFP, still more frequent marital intercourse would be possible with little additional likelihood of pregnancy. (Be prepared to explain precisely what alteration is possible, and to estimate realistically just how great the increased likelihood of pregnancy would be.)

Third, if the preceding effort seems to you successful, I suggest you then try something similar with respect to having another baby. But if the preceding effort seems to you unsuccessful, perhaps you should consider proposing that you and Greg seek joint marital counseling. Given what you say about your relationship, I think it would very likely help provided you find the right counselor. Unfortunately, though, poor counselors abound, and often do more harm than good. You need someone entirely faithful to the Church's teaching, experienced in marriage counseling, and with some training in psychology; probably a Catholic psychologist who supports *Humanae vitae* and has done marriage counseling successfully would be your best choice. A faithful priest or physician might be able to recommend the right person; perhaps you should conduct your own preliminary interview with anyone recommended to you, to make certain he or she has the necessary qualities.

My fourth suggestion is that, if Greg remains unwilling to have another baby and you give up that idea, you should consider other ways of employing your maternal gifts for the benefit of one or more babies who need care. He might be agreeable to providing a temporary home for a series of babies who need foster parenting for brief periods. Or, perhaps, once all your children are in school, you could volunteer to help out in a nonprofit day care center, or even organize one, if your neighborhood has none. In any case, if you discern that the needs of some babies match up well with your gifts, you can assume that God is calling you to serve them, and that he will bless you for loving them tenderly even though you cannot cherish them as your own.

My fifth suggestion is a warning. Exercise care in your relationships with other men. You say you have never been unfaithful but often must pray and struggle to control your imagination and sexual feelings. With some basis, you are dissatisfied with the romantic dimension of your marriage, and such dissatisfaction often is a motive for adultery, with the basis for dissatisfaction serving as an excuse. Moreover, you already are toying with the idea of betraying your husband's confidence in a very important matter, and in this connection you say: "I would be disobeying Greg's wishes, but he would never know." That suggests a spirit of duplicity. So, I think, you are vulnerable and might be seduced, sooner or later, unless you either take care to forestall temptation or your intimate relationship with your husband greatly improves. Of course, I hope that you will take care, it will improve, and this suggestion will prove to have been pointless.

Sixth, encourage Greg to participate as fully as possible in the children's religious formation. Since he is good with them and you work well together when engaged in a project, cooperation in this matter is likely to go well. In trying to nurture the children's faith, he is likely to become more serious about his own, and in working with him to catechize the children, you are likely to communicate something of your own devotion.

You ask for and certainly have my prayers. Among them is the prayer that you will count your blessings. Even though you do have a problem with your marriage, it also has many good features, not least that you are living it in faith, sustained by sacramental grace and prayer. The frustration of your desire for another child and the unsatisfactoriness of your intimate relationship with your husband surely are a serious cross for you, and by no means do I wish to belittle it. But thinking about others' problems may lighten your burden by putting it in perspective. Do you know a couple both of whom must work in order barely to scrape by? Do you know a couple who are of one mind and heart in wishing to have even one child, but are infertile? Do you know a woman who, like you, is committed to living in accord with the Church's teaching, but whose husband insists on having intercourse when they should not and she does not wish to? Do you know a woman whose husband is happy to give her as many children as she wishes but who makes no effort to be a real father to any of them? Do you know a woman whose husband is a great lover, but not only of her—and, perhaps, now only of someone else? Look around and count your blessings!

Finally, I am not sure exactly what you mean when you say that your faith enables you to compartmentalize your problem and that, if necessary, you will continue to do that indefinitely. Perhaps you mean you have been able to resign yourself to the situation, to fulfill your responsibilities as a wife and mother, and to act toward Greg and the children much as you would if your intimate relationship were more satisfying. So far, so good. If you have not gone beyond that, though, I suggest you pray for the light to discover some deeper meaning in this problem and for the strength to use it as a means of perfecting your love and strengthening Greg's faith, so that you, he, and your children will live together in the perfectly joyful intimacy of heaven.

32: May a man continue a friendship with a woman against her husband's wishes?

I am an unmarried man, twenty-six, teaching high school religion. Ann, a colleague who teaches chemistry, is a childless married woman, thirty-five. We have been friendly since I began teaching here two years ago last September, and during the past several months we have been lunching together regularly. Ann's marriage has not been entirely happy, and I have been trying to encourage and support her.

One day last week we wanted to continue talking after school, and she invited me to her place for dinner, expecting that her husband would get home shortly after we arrived. As it happened, he had left a message on the answering machine that he would be delayed, but we had a pleasant dinner and sat talking at the table until he finally arrived around nine. He and I had met before, but do not know each other well. He greeted me coolly; she explained to him what had happened; and I left.

Ann called the next morning and told me that she and her husband had exchanged words about our friendship. He told her it plainly is becoming too warm. Though she insisted that it is no different from her friendships with various other people, to which he does not object, he not only said she should never invite me over again but insisted she quit lunching with me—something he knew about because she had mentioned our lunchtime conversations. She ended by telling me that, when her husband is so domineering, she wishes she had never married him. I refrained from telling her I share that wish, but instead said she must make the best of her marriage. We concluded that we would have to be careful and, except for formal greetings and the like, have not talked since then.

Ann seems miserable, and I find it terribly frustrating to be unable to comfort her. Her husband is being completely unreasonable. Married people surely have the right to be friends with people of both sexes, and we have never done anything unchaste, but always limited ourselves to a friendly squeeze of the hand or a consoling hug. Our conversations have been entirely innocent, mostly just small talk about matters of common interest. The others with whom we could share lunch spend the whole time gossiping and complaining, so that conversing with them is a boring waste of time. Also, breaking off our friendship is unfair to Ann, for she has benefited by my encouragement and support, and still needs my help.

Therefore, I am inclined to suggest to her that we give up other contacts but maintain our friendship by lunching together. Her husband need never know, and, since she is not obliged to obey his arbitrary order, she has no obligation to tell him. Otherwise, I see no alternative but entirely breaking off our friendship, and I hardly can do that without quitting my job. That would be a pity, since my teaching has been going well.

May I suggest to Ann that we resume lunching together, or must I begin looking for another job?

Analysis:

The question is whether this teacher may ask his colleague to resume lunching together despite her husband's insistence that they not do so. The matter calls for conscientious judgment, which must take into account the good of the troubled marriage. A clandestine relationship would involve both an implicit, conditional intention to deceive and serious risks. Certain elements in the statement of the question indicate that the colleagues' relationship has an unacknowledged romantic element, at least for the questioner. So, in my judgment, an attempt by the questioner to continue the relationship is likely to hurt his colleague rather than help her. Therefore, it seems to me, rather than ask her to resume lunching together, he should suggest that she seek appropriate pastoral assistance.

The reply could be along the following lines:

I often wish it were possible to talk in person with the people who write to me, so as to clarify what they have told me about the complex situations giving rise to their moral questions. That is especially so with questions such as yours, which involve subtle nuances of meaning and feeling. While doing my best to respond, I realize that I may miss the mark in some respects. If so, do not be offended, but make what use you can of my response in judging for yourself, as you must, what you ought to do.

If it is possible and prudent for you and Ann to have any further relationship, beyond what you and she have with other colleagues, surely her husband must be fully informed. If he were not, he might well question her, and keeping the secret would then require evasion, deception, and perhaps even outright lying. Implicitly, then, the choice to resume lunching without telling him would include at least a conditional readiness to deceive him. And even if you could be sure he never would question her, he might nevertheless learn of the continuing relationship, think he had been misled, and conclude that Ann was doing something she needed to conceal. Because of the power of rumor and gossip, and the likelihood of accidental disclosures, there would be a substantial risk of that happening. And because their marriage already is troubled, the husband's perception that she is being somehow untrue to him might well spell disaster for them.

But should you and Ann try to continue your friendship even without hiding it from him?

The requirements of marital fidelity, which are identical for husbands and wives, do not preclude either spouse from participating in any genuine human good, including friendship, compatible with fulfilling marital responsibilities. And, in general, married persons can carry on legitimate friendships with persons of the opposite sex. Couples very often are friends with other couples, or both husband and wife enjoy a common friendship with a single person. Even when a friendship is not fully shared, it can be carried on safely under certain conditions. The marital relationship itself must be happy and secure enough that it always will seem to the married party to be his or her best and most valued friendship. The married friend's spouse must always be kept informed, so that nothing is done clandestinely. To avoid conflict with the marital relationship, the friends must forgo doing things that would interfere with fulfilling marital and familial responsibilities; plans for common activities (such as an invitation to dinner) generally should be cleared beforehand with the spouse. Finally, the friends must not allow their relationship to become romantic (see *LCL,* 428–30).

Among the marks of an incipient romantic relationship are a couple's becoming more interested in each other than in any common interest beyond themselves, separating themselves from the surrounding group and wishing to be alone together, feeling deprived when they cannot spend time together, believing themselves uniquely suited to meet each other's needs, being preoccupied with each other, and experiencing even light bodily contact as significant in itself rather than merely symbolic (for example, the typical handshake) or incidental to communication (for example, the friendly pat on the back accompanying words of praise or encouragement). A married person developing an extramarital romantic relationship very often shares marital problems with his or her friend, and, feeling drawn toward intimate union, the two of them wish they were free to marry.

Erotic feelings will arise at times within most heterosexual relationships, and they must be recognized as such (not always easy for those experiencing them!), regarded as inappropriate, and not acted on. Candid spouses confident of each other's understanding do well routinely to share such experiences. Matter-of-fact openness objectifies the feelings, firmly puts them in their place, and prevents them from acquiring undue significance. Such openness also enables the spouses to support each other in maintaining their chastity. Other spouses and single persons can serve the same ends by sharing such experiences with a confessor or other confidant who will take a sound and detached attitude toward them.

You say that you see no alternative to resuming lunching with Ann except entirely breaking off the friendship by quitting your job. I do not accept your view of your alternatives.

Suppose a young man's father punished him with a severe beating for using foul language to his mother. The father says: "Of course, I feel terrible about beating my son, but I had to teach him a lesson, so that he will learn to respect his mother." Outsiders would see clearly that he was ignoring other possible methods of discipline. Moved not only by his stated reason but by unacknowledged hostility, he saw the beating as the only adequate means of discipline. Had he acknowledged his anger and considered the inappropriateness of indulging it, he would have thought of less violent alternatives and chosen a form of punishment more likely to nurture respect. Thus, the father's blindness to an alternative obvious to others is evidence that his practical thinking is vitiated by self-deception regarding his own mixed motives (see *LCL,* 276–77 and 280).

I see no reason why you cannot continue working at the school, share your lunch with others or eat alone, and behave toward Ann as you do toward your other colleagues. That you overlook this alternative suggests you are partly motivated by unacknowledged feelings that make it seem necessary to lunch with her. What are those feelings? Several things in your letter suggest an answer. You say you have been lunching together *regularly* for several months, apart from the others, whose company you disdain. You say that, since her husband told her to stop lunching with you, she seems *miserable,* and you find it terribly *frustrating* to be unable to comfort her—indications of a sense of deprivation. You feel she still *needs* your help, as if your encouragement and support were irreplaceable. You say you always *limited* yourselves to a friendly squeeze of the hand or a consoling hug—a hint that you needed to restrain impulses toward more intimate contact. While you characterize your conversations as "mostly just small talk about matters of common interest," they included Ann's important confidences about her unhappy marriage and your significant efforts to help her. Finally, you say you share her wish that she had never married her husband.

To me, it seems clear that this friendship has developed into romance, at least for you. No doubt, you did not will to become romantically involved with Ann; you meant only to be friends, and to encourage and support her in her unhappy marriage. However, you apparently did not recognize and deal with your erotic feelings, as you would have had to do in order to conduct your friendship appropriately. Unfortunately, moreover, Ann's marriage is troubled. Her wish that she had not married her husband implies that she does not consider her relationship with him her best friendship. She apparently was trying to include her husband in your friendship when she told him about your lunchtime conversations and invited you for dinner, expecting him to share it. But it is not clear she told her husband she was confiding in you about her marital dissatisfactions, as she might have told him that she was seeking help from a counselor. To resume lunching surreptitiously—"Ann's husband need never know"—definitely would be to exclude him from your ongoing relationship.

Plainly you meant well in trying to encourage and support Ann in her troubled marriage, but you underestimated the difficulties. Because lovers often are discreet and romance often blossoms suddenly and unexpectedly, even the most chaste heterosexual friendship, viewed from the outside, appears ambiguous, and friendships marked by signs of romance, no matter how slight and unclear, are likely to cause strain even between trusting spouses in a happy marriage. Apparently, Ann's husband has noticed signs and drawn the same conclusion I have. Even if you think us mistaken, you surely can see that our inference is plausible.

Put yourself in Ann's husband's place, and realize that you must seem a rival for her affection. Given his perception of your friendship with her, trying to continue it is likely to generate more conflict and make matters worse for her, not better. Granted that she needs help, you cannot be the only person in the world who can help her, and, indeed, your emotional involvement prevents you from really doing so. Therefore, it seems to me, you should not try to continue your friendship with her, even without hiding anything from her husband.

What should you do? As I said above, you can lunch with the others or eat alone and treat Ann as you treat your other colleagues. If that seems impossibly difficult, consider it a clear sign of your inappropriate feeling for her. Still, you need quit your job only if you judge that continuing at the school will be an occasion of sin.

Ann and her husband should seek appropriate professional help if they have not done that. Troubled marriages generally improve only if the couple cooperate in examining themselves, identifying factors that have led to the trouble, and dealing with them (see *LCL*, 721–25). If joint marital counseling has been tried unsuccessfully or is not feasible, Ann probably needs pastoral guidance and support. In that case, it seems to me, very likely the greatest kindness you can do her would be to suggest that she seek appropriate help and, perhaps, identify someone from whom she might seek it—an experienced and successful pastoral counselor entirely faithful to the Church's teaching.

If you are not already doing so, I suggest that you also obtain pastoral help to examine yourself, make a good confession, and clarify the steps you must take. Keep in mind that God's plan includes a resolution of your difficulty that you should discover and welcome, and pray earnestly and constantly for the light and strength you will need to do whatever God asks of you.

The will to be married to one's spouse is central to marital love; directly contrary to that will is the wish that one had never married or had not married this person (see *LCL*, 619–20). Regardless of the provocation, Ann's wish that she had not married her husband is a very serious matter. So, it also seems to me that you should suggest to her that she discuss that wish with her pastoral counselor, if she seeks such help, or with her confessor.

To avoid communicating your own feelings about what has happened—which would risk inflaming them and provoking a response from Ann—you probably should make these suggestions in a brief, careful note. Without saying so, make that note your last outward act of friendship toward her. Of course, you may continue your friendship for her by praying that she and her husband grow in mutual love and enjoy a more satisfying marriage.

Finally, you could go on being friendly toward Ann without treating her differently than your other colleagues if you began treating them more affably. You say the others spend the whole lunch hour gossiping and complaining, so that conversing with them is a boring waste of time. Surely, not all of them are that bad. Perhaps the lunchroom conversation does leave much to be desired, but constructive efforts by you and one or two others might well raise its quality. As it is, your colleagues probably sense your disdain, even if they are not fully conscious of it; and, if you stay at the school, you must make a serious effort to improve your relationship with them. On the other hand, if you change jobs, learn from this painful experience to seek better relationships with all your colleagues while taking care to avoid inappropriate emotional involvement with any.

33: Should NFP be taught to a couple whose marital intercourse might transmit HIV?

My husband and I teach natural family planning (NFP) at our parish as part of the pre-Cana program for engaged couples. We like to take the couples in groups, not privately, both to save time and because we believe it works better. Our pastor is asking us to make an exception and take one couple separately. Two years ago, while in Africa working on famine relief, the man, whom I'll call John, received unscreened blood transfusions when he had emergency surgery and he has now tested positive for HIV. Though the woman, whom I'll call Felicity, knows this, she still wishes to marry him. The couple want to try to have a child as soon as they can after they marry, and, in the hope that Felicity and the baby will not become infected, to do this with the fewest possible number of acts of marital intercourse. John and Felicity hope NFP will help them accomplish this. The pastor told me he asked the chancery office about their plan, and the bishop told him to treat them the same as any other couple.

My husband and I have talked this over, and we do not think this couple should be getting married. They are risking Felicity's life and taking a chance on having a child afflicted with AIDS. Moreover, they are risking imposing a huge monetary burden on everyone in their health insurance group and, if their insurance runs out, on the public. We wonder whether we should teach them at all and, if we do, whether we should take them separately as the pastor wishes.

Since the bishop has approved their plan to marry, and the pastor is going to go ahead with the wedding, I realize you might say: "Who are you to argue?" But this is not a question of Church teaching, so we feel we must make our own judgment. To us, it just does not seem right to help John and Felicity do what we think they should not be doing.

Of course, we have talked this over with the pastor. He seems to agree with our view, and, though he did not say so, we have the impression he had hoped the bishop would forbid the marriage. He wants us to do as he asked, but says he will understand if we refuse. That leaves it up to us.

Analysis:

The questioner explicitly asks about her and her husband's teaching responsibilities, but implicitly asks whether John and Felicity should marry. The Church's law does not forbid a man infected with HIV and the woman who wishes to marry him from exercising their natural right to marry. The possible moral permissibility of their taking the risks to themselves and their offspring follows from the inherent goodness of marriage and marital intercourse, the dignity and heavenly calling of any child or children they might have, and the moral acceptability of taking risks in pursuing goods. Yet the couple could have a moral obligation not to exercise their right to marry. But even if the questioner and her husband believe it is wrong for John and Felicity to marry, they may, and I think should, instruct them in NFP with the intention of facilitating their chastity, perhaps leading them to reconsider marrying, and, if they marry, reducing the risks they will be taking.

The reply could be along the following lines:

It would be wrong for you to help John and Felicity unless you come to see either that what they are doing probably is not wrong or that you may help them even if it is. First I shall consider whether they can rightly marry and then whether you may help them even if they should not.

Even though the bishop told the pastor to treat John and Felicity like any other couple, it is possible that, morally speaking, they should not marry.

Consider why the bishop responded as he did. Since marriage is a fundamental human good (see *LCL,* 555–69), people have a natural right to marry, so that couples free to marry and capable of doing so generally should not be impeded by the wider society. Accordingly, the Church's law provides: "All persons who are not prohibited by law can contract marriage" (*CIC,* c. 1058). Church law identifies various impediments to marriage, but nowhere says couples may not marry when afflicted with a deadly, communicable disease and faced with the prospects of John and Felicity. At the same time, Church law provides that a sacrament cannot be denied those who are properly disposed and ask for it at an appropriate time unless the law prohibits its reception (see *CIC*, c. 843, §1), and also specifies that Catholics' marriages ordinarily must be witnessed by the bishop or pastor, or a priest or deacon delegated by either of them (see *CIC*, c. 1108, §1). So, when nothing mentioned in the law would prevent a couple from marrying validly and no other condition specified by the Church's law provides a basis for refusing their request to be married in the Church, the couple have the legal right to the pastoral service required to celebrate their marriage in the Church. That, no doubt, is why the bishop told the pastor to treat John and Felicity like any other couple.

Nevertheless, the marriage of a particular couple, though permitted by Church law, can be imprudent or unfair to others—for example, due to their poor health, poverty, or prior obligations to others, such as aged parents. The Church's law leaves judgment on such matters to the consciences of the couple themselves. So, the moral question about this marriage is not settled by the bishop's directive to the pastor.

Does sacred Scripture, tradition, or the authoritative teaching of the magisterium settle it? I find nothing in those sources to indicate that this couple cannot rightly marry and engage in marital intercourse. It might be thought that the issue had not been addressed until now because infection with HIV has occurred only recently. But Christians throughout history have been afflicted with various deadly, communicable diseases, or have foreseen the likelihood that a woman might die in giving birth, yet some chose to accept the risks of marrying and having children.

Of course, during recent centuries many Catholic moral theologians, in considering spouses' responsibilities with regard to marital intercourse, held that they should abstain from it if necessary to avoid taking serious health risks. These theologians no doubt would have said that John and Felicity should not carry out their plan. But theological opinion by itself does not demand religious assent. Moreover, the theologians' opinion on this matter, in my judgment, should be regarded with suspicion, because they failed to grasp the inherent value of marriage and marital intercourse, which they regarded as merely instrumental goods. Therefore, the question of whether the couple may marry can be dealt with only by rational reflection in the light of relevant moral principles.[115]

One reason why AIDS seems to many people more horrible than other deadly diseases is that HIV infection generally is transmitted irresponsibly, by conduct that is, at least objectively, gravely evil. That thought and the negative feelings it appropriately evokes must be excluded carefully from the following reflection. The issue is whether the couple's plan is morally acceptable. Letting horror related to immorality come into play would prejudice judgment.

Your argument for the view that John and Felicity should not marry is that in doing so they would risk her life, risk having a baby afflicted with AIDS, and risk

---

115. John M. Haas, "HIV and Marriage—I," *Ethics and Medics*, 16:2 (Feb. 1991), 1–3; "HIV and Marriage—II," *Ethics and Medics*, 16:3 (Mar. 1991), 3–4, argues that marital intercourse is morally excluded in cases like that discussed here. But though he appeals to certain teachings of the magisterium, none of them logically require the conclusion he draws. In my judgment, he also overestimates the risks and inadequately appreciates the benefits of marital intercourse in such circumstances.

imposing a huge monetary burden on everyone in their health insurance group and on the public at large.

Heterosexual behavior seldom results in HIV infection.[116] Each act of marital intercourse would involve some risk that John would transmit the infection to Felicity, but she might well escape infection if the couple take care to avoid lacerating her genital tissues, abstain from intercourse if the tissues already are lacerated or sore, and limit the number of times they engage in intercourse, as they are planning to do. Moreover, if she does become infected, she might not die of the disease; something else might cause her death, or a lifesaving treatment for AIDS might become available. So, in marrying, she would accept, not death, but only some risk of it.

If Felicity may accept this risk to her own life and freely chooses to accept it, I see no reason why John will do wrong by joining her in taking the risk. May she? Risks to one's own life and health are accepted rightly or wrongly depending on whether they are accepted for a good reason, that is, as incidental to the pursuit of an intelligible human good by appropriate means. Now, even though John is HIV positive, marriage and its fulfillment in parenthood remain intelligible goods, and the couple can pursue them only by consenting to marriage and engaging in marital intercourse. Thus, if Felicity intends to marry for the good of marriage—and she will intend that good if she validly consents to marry—she need not violate any mode of responsibility in accepting the risk to her own life.

Someone might object that Felicity almost certainly is motivated primarily by feelings of affection and erotic attraction, for she hardly would be prepared to risk her life so heroically on the basis of a calm and cool grasp upon the intelligible goodness of marriage. That may be so, but very few couples today marry unless they have those emotional motives—unless they are "in love." But being in love harmonizes with good reasons to marry, so the emotional motives do not vitiate anyone's consent to marry. Therefore, if Felicity really consents to marriage, she will intend the intelligible goods that can make it reasonable for her to accept the risk to her own life.

Again, someone might argue that, if John does not truly love Felicity, he should not marry her, and if he did truly love her, he would not wish to marry her. I answer: To accept risks to others by cooperating with them in doing something inherently good is entirely compatible with loving them and willing their true human fulfillment. Indeed, just as loving oneself regularly requires that one take various risks in pursuing goods, so loving others regularly requires that one accept various risks to them as well as to oneself in cooperating with them. What is peculiar about the present case is the kind and, perhaps, the magnitude of the risk. But if there is no injustice in taking this risk, John and Felicity themselves must discover whether taking it pertains to their vocations. If they are convinced that they are called to marry and have a child, it would be presumptuous for others to judge that the

116. See Michael B. Flanagan, "A Study of AIDS," *Linacre Quarterly,* 63:1 (Feb. 1996): 61–74.

magnitude of the risk shows their choice to marry to be incompatible with authentic, mutual love.

May John and Felicity risk having a baby who will die of AIDS? This risk, too, should not be exaggerated; it is considerably less than the risk some couples take of passing on a very serious hereditary disease. Unless a woman is infected with HIV, she will not infect her baby, and even if a woman becomes HIV positive before the baby is born, her child may not be infected.[117] Moreover, even if the baby is infected with HIV, he or she may not die of AIDS; something else might be fatal, and more effective treatment for HIV infection might become available.

More important, parenthood and the very being of a new person are goods, and it is not inherently wrong for a couple to accept the risk that a baby will be afflicted with some congenital defect or disease. Indeed, every couple who expect to have children accept some such risk, so one must ask why accepting the risk of HIV infection would be wrong. The plausible answer is that in this case the prospect is worse than it generally is, namely, that the baby will have only a short and sickly life. If a person's fulfillment were in this world only, that prospect might seem to preclude taking such a risk. But the baby's sufferings in this life will be insignificant by comparison with the joy of everlasting life (see Rom 8.18). With that prospect, why should it be sinful for John and Felicity to accept some risk of having a child who will die of AIDS or for other couples to take even greater risks of having a child die of certain genetic diseases?

Someone might object that, while nobody is excluded from the hope of heaven by the circumstances of his or her conception, parents surely can wrong children in the very act of procreating them—for example, people wrong prospective children when they try to have them produced in a laboratory or risk having them outside marriage (see *LCL,* 267–68, 643–44, 655, 684). True, but in these cases the wrong is inherent in the acts of producing babies in a laboratory and of extramarital intercourse. Deliberately conceiving or risking conception in acts wrong in themselves unjustly deprives a baby of something due each new human person: to be received as the God-given fruit of authentic marital love. Since babies are not due good health, however, except insofar as their parents and others can and should protect and promote it, risking having a baby afflicted with some defect or disease does not wrong that child unless it is wrong to take the risk. But since that is the precise point the objection was meant to prove, it begs the question.

Again, someone might object that, just as other couples should regulate births by morally acceptable means so that they will not have more children than they can reasonably expect to raise properly, so John and Felicity should avoid having a

---

117. Edward M. Connor et al., "Reduction of Maternal–Infant Transmission of Human Immunodeficiency Virus Type 1 with Zidovudine Treatment," *New England Journal of Medicine,* 331:18 (1994): 1173–80, report the results of a study of the use of zidovudine (AZT) during pregnancy, delivery, and the first six weeks after birth to impede the transmission to infants of HIV infection from mothers already mildly symptomatic with AIDS. Without AZT, 25.5% (one out of four) infants were HIV infected at eighteen months; using it, only 8.3% (one out of twelve) were. The European Collaborative Study, "Caesarean Section and Risk of Vertical Transmission of HIV–1 Infection," *Lancet,* 343 (11 June 1994): 1164–67, report that in women with advanced AIDs, caesarean delivery reduced transmission by about half.

baby they may not be alive and able to care for. My reply is twofold. First, when a couple already have children, fairness to those children often precludes having more. But the question concerns John and Felicity having their first, and perhaps their only, child. Second, John and Felicity should consider the prospects that their child will not be cared for properly, but only they are in a position to judge whether those prospects make carrying out their plan unreasonable.

May the couple risk imposing a huge monetary burden on everyone in their health insurance group and on the public at large? Whether they marry or not, the man almost certainly will require extensive health care. So, the question is: Will they act unfairly in risking the additional burden on others if the woman and one or more children also are infected with HIV and contract AIDS?

Perhaps they will act unfairly, especially since the burden here is not only monetary, but extends to the difficulties and risks for caregivers and others in dealing with people afflicted with this disease. The couple could argue, however, that many women who learn that they are HIV positive do not alter their sexual activity or make special efforts to avoid pregnancy.[118] Moreover, government officials, the medical profession, and the public at large have been quite tolerant not only of infected women's behavior but of men who persistently engage in sodomy, which is even more likely to transmit HIV infection. If such people are doing others a grave injustice, they might say, why has nothing been done except to urge them to practice so-called safe sex, which by no means eliminates the risk but only reduces it in particular sodomitical acts? Those who engage in sodomy are not punished even for disregarding that advice; those who take such risks are not tested for HIV and isolated from society if they test positive; those who lose their gamble and develop AIDS are not limited to palliative care and denied expensive, life-prolonging treatment. How, then, John and Felicity might ask, can it be a great injustice for them to risk imposing similar burdens on others by entering marriage and engaging in marital intercourse, which are actions good in themselves?

That argument would deserve respect, but it would not be cogent. In a nation that has legalized abortion and that condones and even facilitates sexual irresponsibility despite the huge burdens it unjustly imposes on society, the attitudes of government officials, the medical profession, and the majority of the people cannot be considered a reliable index of the demands of justice.

In sum, it seems to me that, while the case against the couple's marrying is inconclusive, their doing so might well be unfair to others. Perhaps they have not thought about the grave burdens they might impose on others by marrying and having a baby, or have not applied the Golden Rule and put themselves in the place of those others. Surely, they should not marry without considering this aspect of the matter and reaching a confident judgment that doing as they propose will not be unfair to others.

---

118. See Anna Kline, Jennifer Strickler, and Judith Kempf, "Factors Associated with Pregnancy and Pregnancy Resolution in HIV Seropositive Women," *Social Science and Medicine,* 40 (1995): 1539–47.

Besides the moral questions you raised, at least two others ought to be considered by the young couple.

First, John and Felicity plan to try to have a child with the fewest possible acts of marital intercourse. Perhaps they do not realize that they might not be very fertile—they might even be sterile—and so they may not have considered how many acts of marital intercourse might be required to bring about conception or to discover their infertility. Then too, perhaps they have not considered what they will do to express affection apart from those acts of marital intercourse. They may think it will not be wrong to attempt intercourse while using a condom or to engage in sexual acts leading to orgasm apart from intercourse. But "intercourse" with a condom is not truly intercourse, and so cannot be marital intercourse, even if the intention is, not to prevent conception, but to prevent the transmission of disease.[119] Moreover, so-called safe sex, practiced repeatedly, eventually will have the result it is meant to prevent (see q. 22, above). And any sexual stimulation to orgasm apart from marital intercourse is gravely sinful. Perhaps, however, they plan to practice perfect continence apart from the acts of marital intercourse required to have a baby. If that is their plan, they may be tempted to set it aside and either wrongly engage in marital intercourse when they have grave reasons for abstaining or to commit other sexual sins. But unless they are committed to a chaste marriage and can reasonably hope to fulfill that commitment, they should not marry.

Second, though John and Felicity no doubt intend intelligible goods, they may be being moved too much by feelings and too little by insight into how to pursue those goods. Have they thought carefully and in detail about the prospective course of their entire lives and considered all the risks they will be accepting? Loving each other, Felicity should ask how best to serve John, and he should ask whether it is best that he accept the sort of self-sacrifice Felicity is offering. Before long, he may need a healthy, motherly nurse more than a wife. And despite Felicity's present heroism, she eventually may be overwhelmed by the extraordinary responsibilities she will have accepted, especially if, after John dies, she finds herself and her child afflicted with AIDS. Surely, this couple should examine their feelings very carefully. Like every other couple preparing to marry, they should not proceed unless both are convinced that the marriage is, not simply what they want for themselves, but what they want for one another and, even more important, what is God's will, his vocation, for them.

All these things considered, should you and your husband help John and Felicity carry out their plan?

You do not have a strict duty, analogous to the pastor's, to help the couple carry out what you may still regard as a bad plan. Nevertheless, you may cooperate with them in the same way the pastor must, not intending that they marry or do anything they should not. If you do not teach them, they might proceed with even greater risks. So, you can teach them NFP intending nothing other than to provide sound

---

119. See *LCL,* 634–36; cf. William E. May, "AIDS, Marriage and Condoms," *Ethics and Medics,* 13:9 (Sept. 1988): 3–4.

counseling and instruction that will promote their chastity and mitigate the bad consequences of what they are planning to do.

Moreover, it seems to me you not only may but should teach John and Felicity, for in this way you will have the opportunity to raise questions about their plan. In preparing them for marriage, the pastor should and probably will deal with some of these questions, namely, the ones regarding marital chastity. But he may consider it prudent to focus exclusively on matters he must discuss with them, so as not to distract them from the essentials or render them unreceptive by challenging them unnecessarily. You will have greater latitude. Proposed gently and discussed with sympathetic understanding, the various questions sketched out above, and others that may occur to you, might well lead John and Felicity to reconsider and decide not to marry. And if they do marry, you will be in a position to continue to advise and encourage them to fulfill their marital responsibilities in their unusual situation.

In view of this possibility of getting them to reconsider, you probably should make an exception to your usual practice and take them privately, despite the extra work that will involve. If you included them in a group, you could not give them the special attention they need without more or less neglecting the other couples—while that special attention itself probably would cause them embarrassment. I assume they therefore desire to be taught separately, and, by doing them this favor, you probably will render them more receptive to the questions you raise. Finally, having this couple in the group might make the other couples anxious and distract them, which would detract from the effectiveness of your teaching.

Still, while meeting John and Felicity separately insofar as necessary, it might be advantageous to encourage them to meet with the group as well. If they agree, you could consider with them whether and how to share their secret with the other couples—perhaps not at the beginning of the course but near its end. The communication, while perhaps difficult, could benefit both them and the other couples, for it might lead everyone to reflect more deeply on the significance of what they are doing in marrying and the grave responsibilities they are assuming. Moreover, having become acquainted with John and Felicity, the other couples perhaps may keep in touch with them and offer appropriate support.

34: Should parents consent to their underage daughter's marriage?

Our daughter, Grace, is finishing her junior year of high school. For about six months, she has been going with a young man, Larry. She is not yet seventeen; he is twenty. My wife and I approved of Grace's going with Larry, since he is a Catholic and, in general, seems decent enough, and we already knew and liked his sister, who has been Grace's close friend since they met last September. Larry graduated from high school almost two years ago and is in his second year of apprenticeship as an electrician. It is a good trade, and he seems to be doing well with the work. He already makes enough to support himself living on his own.

Two months ago, Grace and Larry began talking about marriage and went to see Father Kane, our pastor. After several sessions with the young couple, he had my wife and me in and asked us to give our consent. We think Grace and Larry are too young to marry. Until she is eighteen, she cannot get married without our consent, and we think they should wait until then. Grace will be out of high school, and Larry will be over twenty-one and almost finished with his apprenticeship, so they will have a bit of a financial head start. Even more important, they will have had time to grow up a little more, get to know each other really well, and think about the responsibilities of marriage. But they do not want to wait, and Father Kane is urging us to let them get married in June, less than two months from now.

Father Kane said that in his judgment Grace and Larry are at least as mature and ready to marry as most young couples these days. He argued that everyone has a natural right to marry, and that making young people wait many years beyond the time when they become physically mature frustrates nature. He also said that, although the law authorizes us as Grace's parents to refuse to let her marry until she is eighteen, we have no moral right to refuse, since a person's decisions about her or his vocation are not subject to parental authority, and marriage is as much a vocation as being a priest or a nun.

While Father Kane spoke to my wife and me apart from the young couple, he apparently also conveyed his point about a natural right to marry to Grace. This afternoon she and Larry told my wife they think they have the right to get married. If we do not consent to their marrying now, more than a year is too long to wait. Grace will move in with Larry this June, and they will start their family at once. When I got home and heard the news, I asked Grace why she wished to take on the responsibilities of parenthood so soon, and she said that she loves Larry so much that she cannot wait to have a baby by him. I then told her again why I think they should wait, and, of course, said that living together before marriage would be wrong. My wife pointed out that having a baby without being married is likely to be hard on the child and is no way to begin being a loving mother. But we got nowhere.

I called Father Kane, told him about the new development, and asked him to try to talk them out of living together before marriage. He refused, insisting they have the right to get married, and went on to say that, if Grace gets pregnant, our grandchild will be illegitimate because we said no to the marriage. That, he said, would violate a right of the child clearly affirmed by Catholic teaching, which he called back a few minutes later and quoted: "The child has the right to be conceived, carried in the womb, brought into the world and brought up within marriage."[120]

My wife and I are not sure what to do. We still don't think the young couple are ready for marriage and remain convinced they should wait. But if what Father Kane says is true, we have no right to refuse, and so I suppose we must give our consent. Even apart from that, Grace is forcing us to choose between consenting to her marrying Larry and standing by while she moves in with him. I almost wish we had nothing to say about the matter. Still, the law does require our consent. What are we to do?

---

120. Congregation for the Doctrine of the Faith, *Donum vitae,* II, A, 1, *AAS* 80 (1988) 87, *OR,* 16 Mar. 1987, 4.

Analysis:

The question is whether the parents ought to consent to the marriage of their daughter, who is not yet seventeen. It is reasonable for law to assign parents the responsibility of judging the appropriateness of marriage for persons below a certain age. The pastor's arguments that the couple have a right to marry are unsound. So, he is mistaken in claiming that the parents have no right to refuse their consent. The parents' judgment that their daughter is not yet mature enough to marry seems reasonable. Given that judgment, they should persist in trying to delay the marriage and in discouraging the young couple from beginning to live together. In my judgment, they should not consent to the marriage even to prevent the young couple from fornicating or to forestall an illegitimate birth.

The reply could be along the following lines:

Perhaps Father Kane will conduct Grace's and Larry's marriage ceremony despite the law's requirement and your refusal to consent. If he does that, though the marriage will not be recognized by civil law, you should presume it valid and sacramental. Your concern about whether to consent would be irrelevant, and your duty would be to do what you could to support the marriage.

Thus far, Father Kane's handling of this matter may be at odds with Church policy in your diocese. Faced with very high rates of marital separation and divorce, most bishops have been trying to strengthen marriages by requiring more extensive preparation, often leading to waiting periods of several months. Also, almost certainly diocesan policy implements relevant provisions of the Church's law: "Except in case of necessity, no one is to assist at the following marriages without the permission of the local ordinary: . . . 2° a marriage which cannot be recognized or celebrated in accord with the norm of civil law; . . . 6° a marriage of a minor child when the parents are unaware of it or are reasonably opposed to it" (*CIC*, c. 1071); and: "Pastors of souls are to take care to prevent youths from celebrating marriage before the age at which marriage is usually contracted in accord with the accepted practice of the region" (*CIC*, c. 1072). The Church's law classes young people under eighteen as minors (see *CIC*, c. 97, §1), and the civil law requirement of parental consent for your daughter to marry under eighteen makes it clear that her marriage without your consent would not be in accord with the accepted practice where you live. Thus, it seems Father Kane should respect your reasonable opposition to Grace's marrying now, and he should have discouraged, rather than supported, her and Larry in their desire to marry two months from now.

Because time is short, I suggest you at once write to the diocesan pastoral office, presenting the facts of the situation as you have in your letter to me, and asking for guidance and help. I would send Father Kane a copy of the letter. Do not suggest in it that he may be acting contrary to the Church's law or diocesan policy—those are matters for the bishop or his delegate to consider. Perhaps the letter will bring action that will resolve your problem or, at least, significantly change it. If the problem or important elements of it remain as they now stand, however, I offer the following reflections, which I hope will clarify matters for you and perhaps be of some help.

I understand why you would rather not have the responsibility, assigned you by the law, of giving or refusing consent to Grace's marrying. However, this provision of the law protects children from rashly assuming responsibilities they do not fully understand and serves an important public interest in encouraging enduring marriages and stable families. The wider society needs them both to constitute it and to help prevent, insofar as possible, the many bad social consequences of dysfunctional families, not least the burden of public aid to the children of parents not united in stable marriages.

It is obvious that almost all adolescents below a certain age (fourteen or sixteen, say) are too young to marry, and that young people who have attained a certain age (eighteen, say) must be regarded as adults and considered old enough. Therefore, legislators entirely exclude marriage until the minimum age is reached and permit marriage without any special age-based condition once a certain age has been attained. Between the two ages, however, different young people are more or less ready to marry, depending both on their personal characteristics and on various circumstances. Therefore, to be fair, legislators permit the marriage of individuals in this age group who seem likely to form a stable union. But someone must make a judgment whether that is the case. Legislators could assign this role to a public official, such as a judge or the clerk who issues marriage licenses, but no public official is likely to know enough about an individual and his or her circumstances, except perhaps after a prolonged and costly investigation. Parents generally have their children's interests at heart and know them and their circumstances better than anyone else does. Moreover, the stability of younger couples' marriages partly depends on how supportive parents are. So, lack of parental consent is likely to indicate that such a marriage will not enjoy the support it needs to last. Consequently, legislators have assigned the necessary judgment to parents, who in giving or refusing consent are not precisely exercising their own parental authority but acting as public officials.

Father Kane is correct in saying that marriage is a natural right.[121] But I think he manifests a misunderstanding of that right in saying that making young people wait beyond the time when they are physically mature frustrates nature. It may frustrate erotic inclination, but that inclination must be frustrated at times in every state of life, including marriage, if people are to fulfill their vocations. The right to marry, in any case, is not grounded only in the value of sexual fulfillment but in the good of marriage as a whole, of which sexual fulfillment is only a part. To participate effectively in the good of marriage demands more than physical maturity; the spouses also need enough psychological and moral maturity to fulfill all the responsibilities of marriage and parenthood. The canonical jurisprudence that has developed in recent years using psychological and moral immaturity as a ground for discovering and declaring nullity also manifests the Church's judgment that physical maturity alone is not an adequate index of readiness for marriage.

Moreover, the exercise of the right to marry is appropriately limited in various ways. Both Church and political society not only recognize some natural limits—

---

121. See *CIC,* c. 1058: "All persons who are not prohibited by law can contract marriage."

for example, certain family members may not marry each other—but establish some limits by law: the observance of certain formalities, a waiting period, and so on. Thus, the right to marry is conditional and may be exercised only if there is no impediment. Though the Church's law does not exclude the marriage of a young woman of Grace's age (see *CIC,* c. 1083, §1), it does forbid the pastor to assist at a marriage without the bishop's approval when civil law establishes an impediment. Civil law makes the absence of parental consent an impediment for a woman of Grace's age, and this impediment is reasonable. Maturity is necessary for marriage, and underage people who want to marry are hardly likely to be good judges of their own maturity, so that, as already explained, the public authorities depute parents to make the necessary judgment. Therefore, the exercise of Grace's right to marry is limited reasonably by the legal requirement of your consent.

Father Kane also is right both in pointing out that marriage is as much a vocation as the priesthood or religious life and in saying parents cannot make vocational decisions for their children. Such decisions require discernment, and, while parents and/or others can help in various ways, one ultimately must discern for oneself. Still, parents do have a responsibility to limit or even prevent a child from doing some things the child believes appropriate to carry out what seems to be God's call. For example, if a fourteen-year-old girl thinks she is called to become a postulant in a religious community that takes candidates at that age, her parents could reasonably judge her insufficiently mature to live apart from them and rightly require her to delay entering the community. On the same basis, deputed by public authority to judge whether Grace is mature enough to marry, you can rightly refuse consent if you judge that she is not sufficiently mature.

Apparently Father Kane is ignoring the question of Grace's maturity, which really is the central issue. His judgment that Grace and Larry are "as mature and ready to marry as most young couples these days" is not reassuring, since the failure rate indicates that most couples attempting marriage at such early ages are not mature enough. No doubt they were in earlier times and simpler cultures, but contemporary culture makes much heavier demands, not only because of the need for more prolonged education and training, but also and especially because of the need for greater virtue. When everything supported a young couple's faithful fulfillment of their marital and parental responsibilities, and relatively few tempting alternatives to persevering in marriage were available, people could safely marry at earlier ages. Now, as I said at the outset, many dioceses require not only young couples but all those marrying in the Church to wait some months while they prepare for marriage. The trend toward such requirements manifests the sense of the Church that some delay is likely to prevent imprudent marriages and promote marital stability. Father Kane is going against the trend in urging that the young couple be allowed to marry very soon. Perhaps you could get them to talk with another, more prudent priest.

Then, too, if you have not already done so, you might discuss the situation with Larry's parents. If they share your concerns, perhaps you could work together to encourage Grace and Larry to wait, if not until Grace is eighteen, at least for six months or so. Those months could be crucial for the couple's more mature reflection, and their preparation for marriage would compel them to face issues they have not yet adequately considered. If they prepare as carefully as they should, you perhaps would have evidence of their maturity so that you could consent in good conscience.

What if Grace and Larry next announce that she already is pregnant or they begin living together and she soon becomes pregnant? I do not think even such a pregnancy would give you a good reason to consent to the marriage. Young couples in this situation generally are better advised to delay marrying until after the baby is born (see *LCL,* 719–20). The right, affirmed by the Church's teaching, that every child come to be and be raised within a stable marriage is not violated when parents refuse consent to a young couple's marriage, but when the couple fornicate; and the child's right is not vindicated by a marriage with poor prospects.

In times past, of course, many upright people felt that young couples free to marry should do so promptly if fornication resulted in pregnancy. But although until quite recently even marriages entered into in these circumstances had a good chance of success and illegitimacy had seriously detrimental legal and social consequences for children, the Church never taught that marriage was obligatory in this situation. Today, most of illegitimacy's bad consequences for the child have been eliminated or greatly mitigated, so that, from the child's point of view, legitimacy's chief value lies in the prospect of parental solidarity and stability as a dependable basis for his or her own development. But when immaturity is the reason for delaying marriage, a child's prospects are improved little if at all by the parents' marrying. Thus, Father Kane's attempt to support his position by appealing to the Church's teaching about the child's right is hardly convincing.

In sum, it is reasonable for you to be concerned that Grace and Larry are not sufficiently mature—that they need "time to grow up a little more, get to know each other really well, and think about the responsibilities of marriage." In my judgment, you have on that basis not only a moral right but a duty to refuse consent.

Of course, without badgering them, you should continue trying to get Grace and Larry to see why you do not accept Father Kane's arguments and are refusing to consent, and why they should not begin living together as if they were a married couple. If they see the reasonableness of your position and accept it, the problem will be solved. If they do not, and begin living together, the thought that Grace is committing the sin of fornication probably will cause you and your wife great distress. However, only God would know the degree of her guilt. It might well be mitigated by her psychological immaturity. Even if it is not, her decision to live in sin would manifest a deeper, moral immaturity—that is, lack of virtuous character—that your consenting to an imprudent marriage would not remedy. Thus, if the young couple do begin living together, that in itself will support your judgment that they are not sufficiently mature to marry. That being so, you should not allow the young couple's threat to influence your judgment.

At the same time, no matter what Grace does, she will remain your daughter. You must not break off your relationship with her, but do your best to continue to help and encourage her to form a sound conscience and act in accord with it. Moreover, you must always stand ready to welcome her visits, to share her sorrows, and to support her morally acceptable efforts—for example, to bear any child she conceives rather than have an abortion.

Finally, pray constantly for Grace and Larry, and entrust them to God's kindness. If you stand fast and the outcome seems to you good, thank God for it. If it seems disastrous, do not blame yourself, but continue to pray and trust in God.

35: Should parents sponsor their born-again daughter's Protestant wedding?

Where we live, Catholics are a small minority; most people are either nonbelievers or evangelical Protestants. During high school, our eldest daughter, Helen, gravitated toward the latter group. We approved, since her friends were decent young people, and there was no practical alternative. When Helen began participating in a Bible study and prayer group with some of her friends, we did not oppose it, though my husband did regularly talk with her about the ideas she was picking up, and we also insisted that she continue to attend the religious education classes at our parish.

Nevertheless, without our realizing it, Helen was being converted by her Protestant friends. Last year, just after her high school graduation, she told us one Saturday evening that she considered herself a born-again Christian and not a Catholic. She said she no longer believed in the Mass and could not go to church with us any more. At first we argued with her, and my husband got her to talk with our former pastor, a very good priest who retired some years ago. But she would not change her mind. Soon she was enrolled in a Protestant church and since then has been a very active member of it.

For several months, Helen has been going with a man, just a few years older, who was baptized and brought up in that church, and also is very active in it. Mark is a fine young man—mature, strong yet gentle, and very respectful and friendly toward us. He also has a good job in his dad's business. So, when Helen and Mark told us recently that they are engaged, we would have been pleased, except that, as we had expected, they plan to get married in the Protestant church.

Helen wants us to finance the wedding and participate in it, as the bride's parents normally do. My husband and I are not sure what we should do. In the first place, our former pastor told us he does not think Helen will really be getting married if the wedding is in the Protestant church, since Catholics normally must be married by a priest. But I talked with our present pastor, and he did not think that would be a problem, because, he said, the rule about being married by a priest no longer applies to people who leave the Church. Not knowing which priest is right, we are not sure whether Helen and Mark really will be getting married, though they certainly will think they are. In the second place, even if that is not a problem, we are not sure how involved we ought to be in this Protestant wedding. (Our worry is about what is right, not about money. The young couple already have told us they do not want a fancy wedding and have said they will pay any bills that would be a problem for us.)

Though I have examined my conscience and cannot see where we went wrong, I feel as if Helen's leaving the Church and becoming a Protestant somehow were our fault. That makes me very anxious not to do anything to make her situation worse. My husband feels we did the best we could by her, but he also is worried about how far we should go in cooperating with the wedding plans, especially if she won't really be getting married.

Analysis:

There are two questions: whether the marriage will be valid, and to what extent the parents should participate in the wedding. According to the present law of the Catholic Church, if Helen has left the Church by a *formal act* and no other impediment exists, she can be married validly in a Protestant ceremony. She probably has left the Church by a formal act, but to ease her parents' concern, she could easily do what would certainly be a formal act of leaving the Catholic Church. Once assured that Helen's marriage will be valid, her parents may finance the wedding and attend it, and may participate in elements of worship consistent with Catholic faith. A full response to the parents' concerns also will offer advice about carrying on the religious dimension of their relationship with the young couple and helping them prepare for marriage.

The reply could be along the following lines:

Your former pastor is right: Catholics normally must be married by a priest—or, more precisely, must make their marital vows in the presence of the bishop or pastor, or a priest or deacon delegated by either of them, who asks for the couple's consent to marriage and receives it in the name of the Church.[122] Under the 1917 Code of Canon Law, which your former pastor no doubt studied and worked with, Helen would have been bound by this requirement, so that her planned marriage in a Protestant church could not have been valid. But your present pastor also is right in saying the rule has changed. It no longer applies to those who, though baptized as Catholics or received into the Church, have "left it by a formal act" (*CIC*, c. 1117). Your former pastor perhaps is not aware of the change in the law (which went into effect only in 1983), or, if he is, does not think Helen has left the Church by a formal act. Your present pastor undoubtedly thinks Helen did that, and so thinks she will be marrying validly in the Protestant church.

Neither priest is simply mistaken. Their disagreement can be resolved by answering the question: Has Helen left the Catholic Church by a formal act? Unfortunately, canon lawyers I have consulted say that nothing in the Church's law precisely defines what counts as leaving *by a formal act*.[123] Still, they do agree that some cases are clear. Merely ceasing to practice the Catholic faith, even if one

---

122. See *CIC*, c. 1108, §1. The requirement admits of certain exceptions, and can be dispensed by the bishop (see *CIC*, cc. 1116 and 1127), but these provisions are not relevant to the present problem.

123. For discussion and references to some studies, see The Canon Law Society of Great Britain and Ireland in association with The Canadian Canon Law Society, *The Canon Law: Letter and Spirit: A Practical Guide to the Code of Canon Law* (Collegeville, Minn.: Liturgical Press, 1995), commentary on c. 1086, §1).

sometimes participates in non-Catholic worship, is not enough. However, not only ceasing to practice the faith but notifying one's bishop or pastor in writing that one has decided to withdraw from the Catholic Church and no longer considers oneself bound by her law would count as leaving by a formal act. So would ceasing to participate in the Catholic Church and being admitted to membership in a non-Catholic religious body by means of a ceremony in which one abjured Catholicism and promised fidelity to that religious body.

The church Helen joined perhaps has no admission ceremony in which she would have had to renounce her Catholicism. However, you say she was enrolled in it, and she clearly expressed her intentions the evening she told you and your husband she could not go to church with you any more; her actions since then have shown she meant what she said and is carrying out a firm decision. That evidence, it seems to me, indicates that Helen would have complied with any formalities the church she joined required of her, and this in turn implies, I believe, that she has indeed left the Catholic Church by a formal act. Otherwise, whether the Catholic Church counts someone as having left would be contingent on differences among other religious bodies' various requirements for admission; and these differences are irrelevant to the relationships to the Catholic Church of people who choose to leave her.

Since Helen no longer considers herself Catholic, she is not likely to be concerned about this problem, but she should be able to see why it concerns you. You could explain to her that, though you hope she eventually will return to the Catholic Church, she would put your mind at rest regarding this possible impediment to her marriage if she would send your pastor a written statement of what she told you last year: that she considers herself a born-again Christian and not a Catholic, and that she does not wish to be counted as a Catholic or bound by the Church's law. She should have no trouble doing that and, if she does, she certainly will have left the Church by a formal act.

You might hesitate to ask Helen to send such a statement to the pastor, feeling that doing so would make her break with the Church irrevocable. But she already has made clear her present position, and her written statement will pose no obstacle to returning to the Church if she comes to see that she should not have left.

The requirement discussed thus far, as you are no doubt aware, is by no means the only one for a valid marriage. Attempted marriages can be invalid for many other reasons—for example, because one or both parties remain validly married to someone else despite having obtained a civil divorce. Before concluding that Helen's marriage to Mark will be valid, consider other possible impediments that would apply to non-Catholics as well as Catholics. Your former or present pastor will be able to give you a check list and, I am sure, will advise you about how to carry out the suggestions I shall make about helping the young couple prepare for marriage.

Having assured yourself that Helen and Mark really are getting married, you and your husband, as the bride's parents, may finance the wedding and attend it. However, though you should assume that Helen has been following her conscience and should not press her to act against it, you should not do anything to suggest that her leaving the Catholic Church was objectively right or that both faiths are equally good ways to follow Christ, for any such suggestion would be at odds with your own faith. To avoid that, you also should leave planning the Protestant ceremony, carrying it out, and paying any stipends connected with it to the young couple themselves and those who share their beliefs. Moreover, though a Catholic attending a Protestant service may join in it insofar as it is compatible with Catholic faith, Catholics should never receive at a Protestant communion service or join in any prayers or hymns at odds with Catholic doctrine.

In planning and limiting your involvement in the wedding, you and your husband should discuss any problems with the young couple, and ask them to respect your consciences as you will respect theirs. Bear in mind that Helen and Mark still share genuine Christian faith with you, and, like other faithful Protestants, are not entirely separated from the Catholic Church (see UR 3–4). Learn about their religious outlook and try to understand it as sympathetically as possible. Encourage Helen to help Mark understand your Catholic convictions and practices. Such communication will help everyone concerned appreciate how much you share in common. Pray together, using mutually acceptable prayers; you also might visit the young couple's church occasionally. At the same time, take care always to make it clear that you firmly hold everything the Catholic Church believes and teaches. In this way, you will practice genuine ecumenism in this difficult family situation.

Since both Helen and Mark are Christians, their marriage, if valid, also will be a sacrament, even if the young couple do not think it is. You should rejoice at the prospect of their marriage and support them in preparing appropriately for it. Encourage them to be chaste during the engagement period, to discuss with each other and resolve questions about how they will handle typical problems such as finances and child spacing, and to prepare to commit themselves unconditionally to an unbreakable union.

In offering them this help in preparing for marriage, you should try not to make issues of matters on which their Protestant beliefs diverge from Catholic teaching—for example, concerning contraception, the sacramentality of marriage, and marriage's indissolubility. Non-Catholics can form valid sacramental marriages despite holding erroneous views on these matters. (A couple's plan sometimes to practice contraception does not invalidate a marriage, though their determination entirely to exclude children would; similarly, a Protestant couple's taking for granted their church's views on divorce does not invalidate their marriage, though limiting their consent to exclude an indissoluble relationship in their own case would.)

Rather than talking about the sacramentality of marriage, you might discuss with the young couple scriptural passages bearing on marriage (you will find a good collection of such passages in the Lectionary of the Mass).[124] If Helen and/or Mark tell you they are planning to practice contraception, you might point out to them

---

124. The relevant passages, together with sound marriage preparation guidance, are in: John F. Kippley, *Marriage Is for Keeps: Foundations for Christian Marriage,* wedding edition with marriage rite and readings (Cincinnati, Ohio: Foundation for the Family, 1994).

that some Protestants regard it as gravely immoral.[125] In any case, give the reasons for practicing natural family planning (NFP) instead and point out the negative aspects of various methods of contraception—for example, that IUDs and contraceptive drugs in any form sometimes prevent births by acting as abortifacients. Likewise, warn them that, once married, they are likely to encounter difficulties that will challenge their love and faithfulness, and tell them that, by self-sacrificing mutual love and individual self-control, they must resist all such temptations, beginning with the temptation to wish they had not married or had chosen someone else—a gravely bad thought that spouses always must put aside firmly (see *LCL,* 619–20).

Like many parents today, you feel guilty that your child has left the Church. But everything you say about your relationship with Helen and your concern about her indicates that your responsibility for what she did was very limited. Your husband probably is right—you did the best you could. No doubt, you were not perfect but made some mistakes and were guilty of some venial sins of commission and omission. Having examined your conscience, however, you are not aware of anything you should have done differently. So, there never was a time when you were aware of some grave duty toward Helen and chose not to fulfill it.

Your heart should be at peace. Pray constantly not only for Helen, as I am sure you are doing, but for Mark too. Thank God that they believe in Jesus—many young people have entirely abandoned faith—and pray that they will faithfully live according to what they believe true. If they do, they will be faithful to Christ, and you can hope with confidence that they will live and die in God's love, so that all of you will be able to love one another as Jesus wills, both in this world and forever in heaven, where all divisions will be overcome.

36: Should the family of someone marrying invalidly participate in the wedding?

I am writing on behalf of my husband and eldest daughter as well as myself. My second daughter, Irene, is about to attempt marriage with a should-be Catholic, Nick, who was married in the Church and then divorced. He thinks he can get an annulment, but he has not yet done anything about it. A college classmate of his who is now a minister will perform the ceremony at a Protestant church. Though Irene has no intention of leaving the Catholic Church, she agreed to this after our pastor told her that she could not marry Nick unless and until his first marriage is annulled.

Irene expects us to fulfill the social and financial responsibilities of the bride's parents, as we would if she were marrying in the Church, and she also has asked her sister to be maid of honor. If Irene were marrying someone free to marry and marrying in the Church, we would have no problem with any of this, especially because Nick, apart from his marital situation, seems to us entirely acceptable. As

---

125. Charles D. Provan, *The Bible and Birth Control* (Monongahela, Penn.: Zimmer, 1989), presents nine scripturally based arguments against contraception and cites many Protestant theologians against it from the Reformation until recently.

it is, though, it does not seem right to act as if there were no problem. But if we do not go along with Irene's plans, we are afraid she will never forgive us.

Should we cooperate? If not, should we even so much as attend the wedding? Whatever we do right now, we also are wondering how we should treat the couple afterwards. In the eyes of the Church, they will not be married. Still, we will want to have some sort of relationship with them.

Analysis:

This question concerns two things: material cooperation by family members with an invalid wedding and norms for relating to the couple afterwards. At all times, family members should maintain familial solidarity with their daughter and sister. But cooperating with the wedding, and even attending it, would have several bad moral effects. So, family members, in my opinion, should not cooperate with the wedding ceremony, attend it, or give the couple a wedding gift. Afterwards, family members should not treat the couple as married, but should treat the man as a close friend of their daughter and sister, and, without nagging, should encourage the couple to fulfill their responsibilities.

The reply could be along the following lines:

Despite Irene's decision to enter a union that will not be a valid marriage, she is and always will remain your daughter and sister. You must continue to honor the reality and value of these relationships, and always treat her with familial affection and concern. No matter what else you do, avoid all harshness and do whatever is both morally permissible and otherwise possible to sustain good parental and sisterly relationships with her.

Nevertheless, in my judgment, you should not help organize, pay for, or participate in the wedding ceremony or any of the celebrations connected with it. I do not think you should give the couple a wedding gift, attend the ceremony, or do anything else that would be inappropriate if they were simply setting up housekeeping together without any pretense of marrying.[126] Why? Because in this situation, as in all others, you should bear witness to the faith, which includes the truth about marriage's indissolubility. To act as if an attempted remarriage after divorce were a real marriage is to belie the truth; to refuse to be involved is necessary to proclaim your faith about this matter, which, though not so basic as the truths that comprise the Creed, is as essential as any other truth of faith. Helping organize, paying for, or participating in the ceremony would imply that you approved, and your approval not only would encourage them but could give encouragement to other couples similarly situated to attempt marriage and so enter into ongoing nonmarital relationships. Even giving the couple a wedding gift or attending the ceremony would suggest that they really are marrying; moreover, you hardly could attend without seeming to approve unless you made your disapproval

---

126. Some able theologians who do not dissent from any Catholic teaching would take a less restrictive position on this matter, particularly with respect to attending the ceremony and giving the couple a gift; see, e.g., William B. Smith, "May One Attend an Invalid Marriage?" *Homiletic and Pastoral Review,* 93:9 (June 1993): 71–72.

clear to everyone concerned, which very likely would be more alienating than simply staying away.

Someone might argue that you could cooperate in Irene's wedding while at the same time making your disapproval clear to the couple. In support of that view, it might be pointed out that, if invited, you probably would attend the wedding celebration of a divorced non-Catholic who was a close friend and certainly would send a gift. In Irene's case, however, you are certain that the attempted marriage will be invalid, while the significance of others' attempts often is unclear. Even more important, toward your daughter and sister you have a responsibility you seldom have toward others: to try to dissuade her from going through with her plan. Your admonition will be undercut if you simultaneously agree to cooperate in carrying the plan out, and you cannot truthfully refuse cooperation while at the same time meaning to cooperate if she goes ahead despite your effort to dissuade her.

Moreover, attending a friend's party and giving a gift manifests solidarity with the person as a friend without expressing a definite view about the occasion of the celebration. By contrast, a son's or daughter's wedding, though the beginning of a new family, is also in some way a completing of the parents' work, so that normally they celebrate this fulfillment of their own marriage as well as the beginning of the young couple's.

Then too, even in our society, parents and elder siblings generally have some influence upon a young person's decision to marry. If therefore you conformed to social conventions about the family's role in weddings, you would manifest approval and joy; whereas conforming to social conventions when one's friends attempt marriage lacks that parental significance. One usually has nothing to do with their decision and is not celebrating one's own fulfillment.

If you refuse to do what Irene wants, what should you do? In my judgment, your best approach probably will be to sit down with her and Nick, tell them you are not going to cooperate with or participate in the wedding, and explain exactly why, namely, because you consider yourselves bound in conscience not to act as if their legal relationship were going to be a genuine marriage. Tell them that you realize your course of action will cause them pain, as it does you, and express your regret about that. You should try to dissuade them from proceeding, but make no threats. Be prepared to remain calm and gentle even if they become angry and abusive. Make it clear you are not cutting them off, as if you expected never to see them again. But do not say how you plan to treat them if they go ahead, since that would presuppose they are going to proceed and so would undercut your effort to dissuade them.

Of course, they probably will proceed, and then you should consider communicating directly with Nick's parents to explain to them why you will not fulfill the usual responsibilities of a bride's parents. If you do communicate with them, tell them that you are not motivated by any antagonism toward Nick or them, and that you regret any pain or inconvenience your noncooperation with the wedding will cause them. Nick's parents may distrust your motives and suggest that you are trying to evade your financial responsibilities. Such an accusation should not trouble you, but if it does, you might counter it by making a charitable donation in their name of money you would have spent on the wedding.

In the aftermath of the wedding, treat Irene with familial affection, keep in touch with her, and welcome her calls and visits. When the couple are together, you should treat them as you would if they were not married and the man were Irene's close friend. Do not invite them to your home to stay overnight as if they were married. You may, however, invite them to family celebrations and may visit their residence. But you should discourage behavior in your presence that would be appropriate only if they were validly married. You may give gifts on occasions such as birthdays and Christmas that would be appropriate even if Irene were living by herself and the man were simply a family friend, but do not remember wedding anniversaries or give anything specifically suited to a married couple.

Irene and Nick still should pray and fulfill their other religious responsibilities, including going to Mass, but they should not receive Communion. When appropriate, encourage them to fulfill these responsibilities. If the couple have children, you should welcome them as your grandchildren and treat them accordingly. Encourage the parents to have their children baptized and to bring them up in the faith.[127]

All this is appropriate to maintain familial solidarity with Irene, to encourage the couple eventually to repent, and, meanwhile, to fulfill other responsibilities and avoid other sins. Therefore, I think you should explain to Irene, shortly after the wedding ceremony, how you plan to act toward her and Nick and your reasons for doing so. Over the long term, it will be hard not to treat the continuing situation as settled and entirely acceptable, especially if they get along reasonably well and have children, for there will be a real family bond between you and your grandchildren. But, without constantly nagging and scolding, you should resist the tendency to endorse the nonmarital relationship. While your rejection of it should be gentle, it should be sufficiently clear so that the couple never will be able to feel it has ceased to be a problem.

37: Should the father of a financially pressed family agree to a costly wedding?

We are a middle-class family with six children, two girls and four boys. We were comfortably well-off until I lost my job two years ago. For six months now I have been back at work, but while I was unemployed we used up our savings and ran up debts. Our house is mortgaged but we have some equity in it, and now that I have settled into my new job we could borrow up to fifteen thousand dollars against the equity and pay off some of the high-interest loans.

Our eldest child, Janet, has been going with a fine young man for some time, and they are planning to marry next spring. Neither has any savings, and his family is even worse off than we are. The problem is that Janet and my wife want to take

---

127. See *CIC,* c. 867, regarding parents' duty to have children baptized; there need only be a well-founded hope that the children will be raised as Catholics (see *CIC,* c. 868, §2); and Catholic parents in irregular unions have a duty to raise their children in the faith—see John Paul II, *Familiaris consortio,* 84, *AAS* 74 (1982) 185, *OR,* 21–28 Dec. 1981, 17.

the practice of our relatives and neighbors as the model for what we will do in putting on the wedding. They originally wanted an affair that would have cost more than twenty thousand dollars, but when I showed them we simply could not spend that much, they reluctantly said the fifteen thousand we could borrow on the house would do. But using that money for the wedding would make it far harder to pay off our other debts, so that austerity measures affecting all of us would be necessary for a long time. Besides, if I am out of work again or we run into other financial problems, we probably will not be able to borrow more and could even lose our house.

My brother has offered to make us an interest-free loan of three thousand, and I think we should take it and not spend more on the wedding, which still could be a respectable party if all of us pitch in and put on the party ourselves at the parish hall. Janet thinks that would be grossly inadequate. Her mother agrees with her. And even the younger children are enthusiastic about the idea of a catered affair at a country club and accuse me of being a tightwad.

If I give in, I will not be taking care of the family finances as I really believe I should, especially in view of the impact on the younger children. But if I refuse to give in, it looks as though Janet is going to be very alienated from me, and my wife also seems likely to resent it for a long time. That will be hard to take, especially because our financial problems during the past couple of years already have caused a lot of stress between us, making our relationship difficult for the first time in our married life.

Should I accept further damage to our difficult financial situation in order to make the rest of the family happy, or accept the damage to our family's relationships in order to take better care of them?

Analysis:

The questioner asks whether he should give in to his wife's and daughter's financial demand. This question presupposes two others. The first is: How much should the family spend for the wedding? In answering, false standards of what is appropriate must be set aside. The second question is: How should the questioner deal with his disagreement with his wife? He should again try to reason with her. If she insists on spending more than he judges appropriate, he could refuse his consent to any borrowing and/or spending that requires it. But perhaps he should give in. To decide that, he must consider the reasons both for giving in and for refusing his consent, and judge which set of reasons makes the better case.

The reply could be along the following lines:

The first step is the one you are taking in asking the question: Set aside the emotional pressures being exerted on you and ask yourself what you should do. Rather than treat money as if it were a human value in itself, people should regard it as far inferior to good human relationships. But money is necessary for many human goods, and the issue here does not pit money against relationships, but relationships against other human goods for which the money also happens to be needed. To be specific, if you provide weddings costing fifteen thousand rather than three thousand dollars for each of your two daughters (assuming that Janet's sister will want a wedding comparable to hers and that there will not have been much inflation in the meantime), that will be twenty-four thousand dollars less available for the needs of the family as a whole.

Marriage is a great human good, but a costly wedding is not especially likely to contribute to a good marriage, and everything essential for a wedding that begins a good marriage can be supplied at minimal cost. The standards for weddings in many cultures impose great hardship on families, but unless such societies' practices promote true human goods their unreasonable standards should be recognized as sinful social structures. Family celebrations can be real instances of familial communion, and so can be good in themselves, but their value is almost entirely in the spirit that participants bring to them, rather than in their material magnitude. Celebrating a marriage is appropriately one of the biggest, if not the biggest, of family celebrations, since it concerns the whole family, the parents' fulfillment of their role in bringing a child to maturity, and the family's continuation into the future. But it does not follow that your family's wedding celebrations should meet the material standards set by families financially better off than yours or whose sense of values may be distorted—much less, as is common in our consumerist society, the standards proposed by businesses that profit from weddings. Rather, it follows that, in keeping with your financial condition, you should do more for your daughters' weddings than you would for a christening, a birthday, a graduation, or an anniversary. Applying these criteria to your situation as you describe it, I think you will be doing enough, and perhaps more than enough, if you accept your brother's offer and celebrate the wedding within that budget.[128]

Having clarified the matter for yourself, talk about it again with your wife. Major expenditures affect the good of the family as a whole, for which you bear primary responsibility. But your daughter and wife seem to have made up their minds without even consulting you. Point out, gently but firmly, that you have reasons, which your wife should consider, for your position. In making your case, the central and most obvious points to emphasize are the unfairness to the younger children of contracting more debt and the riskiness of extending the family's credit to the limit. Therefore, you should argue that what Janet and others involved stand to gain from a costly celebration cannot justify giving up and risking what the family as a whole stands to lose or may lose. The argument is a straightforward application of the Golden Rule. Your wife may point out that in fact the younger children are on her side. While conceding that, you can reply that the younger children are in no position to be good judges of their own true interests.

If your wife remains unconvinced, you might suggest that, even though she does not see the matter as you do, she should go along with your decision as head of the family (see *LCL,* 629–33). Put this gently, not truculently, making

---

128. Denise and Alan Fields, *Bridal Bargains: Secrets to Throwing a Fantastic Wedding on a Realistic Budget,* 3rd ed. (Boulder, Colo.: Windsor Peak Press, 1996), 5, report that the average cost of a formal U.S. wedding (based on industry estimates for 200 people) is $15,425, not including wedding rings and honeymoon; their book provides many suggestions for reducing costs.

it clear that you are trying to serve the family's interests, not just impose your will. If the family's financial problems perhaps are in some respects your fault, admit your failings and ask for forgiveness, but point out that the problems' causes are irrelevant to the question of how to deal with them. If your wife generally accepts your authority, she may accept your judgment.

And if she does not? Very likely she has previously taken the position that the two of you should not proceed in any important matter without consensus. If so, without compromising the point about your role as head of the family, you can remind her that she has insisted on consensus in the past, and that, to be consistent, she should not make a unilateral demand now. In the absence of consensus to spend more than three thousand dollars on the wedding, she should not insist on borrowing and/or spending more; in particular, she should not insist on taking out a home equity loan to pay for the wedding.

But suppose your wife continues to demand what she and Janet want. I presume taking out a home equity loan would require your consent. If so, you can refuse and so unilaterally either limit the budget for the wedding to three thousand dollars or agree to spend somewhat more, but less than fifteen thousand. Should you use that power? Using it can be justified in principle, since you have that authority and would be exercising it in the family's best interest. Of course, that will mean your wife will be forced against her will to accept the outcome; but your giving in will mean you are forced to act against your better judgment. The question is: Will the likely long-term effects—on your marital relationship and your relationships with Janet and your other children—be so bad that it would be better to accept the bad effects of giving in? To answer this question, you must consider the reasons for and against giving in and judge which set of reasons makes the stronger case. If you conclude that, considering your wife's attitude, it is more reasonable to give in, that too will be a proper exercise of your authority.

Whether your wife accepts your decision, or you and she finally compromise, or you refuse entirely to give in to her, the tensions in your marital relationship generated by the family's financial problems need to be addressed. The conflicts you have been experiencing, for the first time in your married life, may point to deeper trouble. In any case, you should work together to overcome them (see *LCL*, 721–25).

Finally, be grateful that Janet's fiancé is a fine young man. Encourage the couple not only to do carefully what your diocese requires by way of marriage preparation but to look beyond their honeymoon and do everything they can to prepare themselves for marriage. They should think through their vocation's responsibilities, try to settle issues that might lead to serious disagreement, and prepare spiritually—for instance, by helping each other remain chaste, praying for each other and praying together, reading the liturgy for marriage including the Scripture readings and discussing these materials' implications for their marriage, and worthily receiving the sacraments.

And just as the young couple should not be distracted by the wedding from their marriage preparation, you and your wife should not be impeded by your disagreement from working together to support Janet and her fiancé in setting out to live a good and holy life together.[129]

38: Should a separated Catholic get a divorce to seek an annulment?

My wife, who also was a Catholic, and I married in the Church the day after graduating from college, ten years ago. She was three months pregnant, and her parents put the pressure on. Five years later, when I went through a detoxification program and quit drinking, I realized I already was an alcoholic when we married. Also, we never got along well, even at the start.

By the time I quit drinking, we had two children, and the next year we had our third. I thought our marriage would improve, but soon after the last baby my wife took a real estate course in the evenings, got her agent's license, put the children in day care, and went to work. She is very good at it; beginning in her second year, she has made more money than I do. As her income grew, she became increasingly independent. Six months ago, I found out she was having an affair with the broker. We had a fight about that; she moved out and left me with the children. We now have arranged a legal separation, and I am managing okay.

She does not care whether we get divorced; she says she does not believe in marriage anyway. The pastor at my parish told me there are good reasons to think we never really were married, and a Church tribunal would declare the marriage null. But he also said the tribunal will not consider the case unless we get divorced. Now, if I am not married, I would like to know it and be free to marry. However, if I am married, I do not want to get a divorce. I believe in marriage and think divorce, even without remarriage, violates the sacrament. Besides, many women regard a divorced man as available, and, knowing my own weakness, I think I would be more likely to get mixed up with someone if I were divorced.

Should I get a divorce so that I can seek an annulment? Or should I go on as I am and give up the possibility of marrying and having a happy family life?

Analysis:

The questioner may be able to resolve his dilemma. Though tribunals usually will not consider any marriage case prior to a final decree of civil divorce, that practice is not required by Church law. and the questioner has good reasons for wishing to seek an annulment without first obtaining a divorce. So, it would be appropriate for him to ask for an exception to the tribunal's usual policy. If this request is not granted, he could ask a canon lawyer experienced in dealing with marriage cases how likely it is that the marriage would be found null. If the likelihood is great, the reasons against getting a civil divorce probably do not apply, and, in any case, those reasons do not absolutely exclude doing so. With good

---

129. Other family disagreements can be handled in the way outlined here. Still, I wish to emphasize that my answer should not be mistaken as license for any husband and father to reject other family members' claims on family resources so as to monopolize them in serving his personal interests as distinct from those of the family as a whole.

reasons both for and against obtaining a civil divorce, the questioner must judge which of the two morally acceptable options to prefer.

The reply could be along the following lines:

A civil divorce sometimes is necessary to forestall legal problems or vindicate legal rights. Competent legal advice regarding the possibility that a divorce would be appropriate for that reason might render your question moot. I shall assume, however, that you already have obtained such advice or that after obtaining it you will remain reluctant to get a divorce.

Civil divorce cannot dissolve the bond of marriage or, if the marriage is sacramental, affect the sacrament's fruitfulness for a spouse who remains faithful despite his or her partner's unfaithfulness. Still, by your fidelity in the face of your wife's betrayal, you have sustained and even enhanced the effectiveness of your marriage, assuming it is valid, as a sign of Jesus' irrevocable fidelity to his Church, whereas a civil divorce would obscure that sign, besides opening you to grave temptations, as you realistically acknowledge. So, your reasons for not wanting a civil divorce if in fact you are validly married certainly are sound. Your reason for wishing to know whether your marriage is valid also is sound, for, if it is not valid, you could be free to marry and would wish to do so, hoping for a happy family life for both yourself and your children.

Nevertheless, as you may know, according to the law of the Catholic Church, you must presume that your marriage is valid until the opposite has been proved and a decree of nullity issued by a Church tribunal (see *CIC,* cc. 1060, 1671). Until the tribunal makes its judgment, you will not be free to marry; and you cannot be certain that a decree of nullity will be issued until it is. Therefore, until then, you cannot enter in good conscience into any romantic relationship whatsoever. But the tribunal will accept your case only if you first obtain a civil divorce.[130] Hence, you have a problem that seems not merely difficult but insoluble.

No doubt, there are reasons for the practice of Church tribunals in refusing to consider a case for annulment until after a civil divorce has been obtained. Canon lawyers whom I have consulted mention two. First, the Church does not wish to encourage people who think their marriages might be invalid to separate; rather, she prefers that they work out their problems and put to rest any doubts about validity by renewing their marital consent. Second, proceeding on the petition of one party toward the annulment of an existing, civilly valid marriage might provoke the other party into legal action against the diocese and/or its tribunal personnel.[131]

The practice of tribunals in this matter plainly is not based on divine law or on any exceptionless moral norm; indeed, it is not even mandated by the Code of

130. Ronald T. Smith, *Annulment: A Step-by-Step Guide for Divorced Catholics* (Chicago: Acta Publications, 1995), 19, states the requirement for divorce: "Since an annulment is a judgment solely of the Catholic Church, it is solely a spiritual matter. It has no civil effects on the children or the parties involved. This is one of the reasons a person must have obtained a civil divorce before the Catholic diocesan marriage tribunal will consider the case. The Catholic Church cannot annul a marriage that is still recognized as valid by a civil jurisdiction."

131. In some jurisdictions, the Church and/or her tribunal personnel might be legally vulnerable if tribunals declared the nullity of marriages that are valid according to civil law.

Canon Law.[132] While there probably are very few cases in which this practice has serious bad consequences, it seems to me that in your case the practice is imposing a grave burden, which you should not have to accept. Therefore, I think that, for the sake of justice, the tribunal can and should make an exception in your case, and my first suggestion is that you appeal to the bishop of your diocese (or of any other diocese whose tribunal would have jurisdiction) to direct the tribunal to consider your case without requiring you first to obtain a civil divorce. (If and when the tribunal decided that your marriage is null, perhaps it could tell you informally that you would be free to marry but delay issuing the decree of nullity until after you obtained a civil divorce.)

Your request is more likely to be granted, I think, if you can obtain from your wife a written statement saying she does not object to the tribunal dealing with your case before you seek a divorce. As a practical matter, you probably should seek a canon lawyer's help in preparing your request to the bishop and drawing up the statement you will ask your wife to sign.

If your request is granted, the problem you pose is solved. What if it is rejected? You could appeal to the Holy See, but that probably would be time consuming, and I doubt it would be effective. The Holy See seldom overrules a bishop's administrative decisions unless they are plainly and grossly wrong, which would not be so in your case.

Therefore, if your request is rejected, you will have to reconsider your good reasons against getting a civil divorce. The more likely it is that your marriage will be found to be null, the less likely it is that those reasons apply. Like the priest you consulted, I think there are good reasons for doubting the validity of the marriage, but neither he nor I is an expert in this matter. Consult a canon lawyer experienced in dealing with marriage cases and candidly tell him or her all the facts about your marriage, which your question summarizes. Studying those facts, the canonist can give you a well-informed opinion as to the chances a tribunal would judge your marriage invalid.

No matter how that inquiry turns out, your good reasons for not getting a civil divorce do not absolutely morally exclude it. If your marriage in reality is invalid, your interest in the possibility of marrying provides you with a good reason for wanting to test its validity in a tribunal; and, if that cannot be done without first obtaining a civil divorce, that interest gives you a good reason for doing so. Morally speaking, you could act on the good reasons on either side, and you need only judge which alternative is more reasonable for you to take, all things considered. Of course, if you get a civil divorce yet fail to obtain an annulment, you should strive to minimize temptations to commit adultery and to cause scandal, especially to your children (see *LCL*, 216–26, 232–35, 669–78).

Finally, in thinking about your future, I encourage you to be realistic, rather than overly optimistic, about the prospects of a happy family life. No earthly marriage is perfect, so that even the happiest marriages involve some hardships and suffering. The sacramentality of Christian marriage ensures graces that strengthen spouses to

---

132. In fact, the practice is arguably incompatible with *CIC*, c. 1505, §2.

overcome difficulties, perhaps mitigate suffering, and certainly consecrate it as the couple's share in Jesus' cross. Only by accepting this cross with loving faithfulness can couples hope to take part in the only perfect marriage—the heavenly one that will begin with the wedding feast of the Lamb (see Rv 19.6–9).

39: May a gangster's sister accept his money for her college expenses?

There are no Catholic schools where we live, but our parish director of religious education, Mrs. Lindsey, has been taking my class through the *Catechism of the Catholic Church* during the past two years. She has been telling us how much better it is than the teaching that is common in most Catholic colleges and schools. The Catholic university where Mrs. Lindsey got her master's degree is one of the few, she says, where Church teachings are treated with the respect they deserve. I want to go there to college after I finish high school this year. I think the Lord may be calling me to try to do for other teenagers what Mrs. Lindsey has been doing for me.

Money is the problem. I am the fourth child, and the first girl, in a family of eight. My parents never finished high school, and we are not well off. Everyone works who is at home and old enough, but we just get by. We have no savings, and my parents will not be able to help me with college. My high school record and test scores are very good, but the university has few full scholarships. The financial aid office has put together a package for me, but even with the grants and loans, a partial scholarship, and the maximum I can earn under the work-study program, it still falls almost five thousand dollars short of what I need for the first year.

Paul, my eldest brother, belongs to some sort of criminal organization. The police have arrested him many times but never held him long. We do not know exactly what he does. In high school he worked part time at a trucking company, and soon after he graduated he said the company's owner had given him a much better job. Suddenly Paul had plenty of money—a thick stack of hundred dollar bills that never seemed to get thinner. Dad and Mom were happy at first, but they soon began to worry about how he could be earning so much. They caught on when some men demanded that Mom's sister pay protection money for her pizza shop; Paul told her he'd take care of it, and the men didn't come back. Mom asked him if he had become a racketeer; he always had trouble lying to her, and didn't deny it. Dad tried to talk him into quitting and looking for an honest job, but he refused and moved out. Since then, Mom and Dad have not accepted or let us accept anything from him except the small presents we've always exchanged for birthdays and at Christmas.

Still, Paul keeps in touch, and I often chat with him when he calls. He is proud of how well I've been doing in school, and he asked me about my plans for college. I probably should not have told him about my money problem, but he had more or less figured it out. When I said I would need almost five thousand dollars for the first year alone, he said he would give me six, so that I would have some spending money.

Dad and Mom don't want me to take any of it, and I would not disobey them. But I talked with Mrs. Lindsey, and she came over and talked with the three of us. She thinks the question for me is not obedience but conscience—I must judge for myself whether it would be right to take Paul's money. Since Dad and Mom respect Mrs. Lindsey and think she is a good person, they accepted what she said about obedience. But while Mrs. Lindsey is not sure what I ought to do, Dad and Mom are still sure none of us should take Paul's money.

If it would not be wrong for me to take it, I think I should. But would it be wrong? Also, if I should not take it as a gift, could I accept it as a loan that I would pay back when I could? Mrs. Lindsey advised me to pray and seek advice, and she mentioned two people, one of them you. I have been praying. Can you help me figure out what to do?

Analysis:

This questioner's problem is similar to a problem about cooperation, though accepting her brother's money would not involve cooperating with his wrong-doing. Not knowing exactly what her brother does, the questioner might be justified in taking money from him if she were in dire need. But she is not. Despite having a genuine need for the money offered by her brother, the prospective bad moral side effects strongly argue against accepting it. The bad effects would be somewhat mitigated if she ruled out future gifts and accepted only the money her brother now offers. If she does accept money from him, she probably should not treat it as either a loan or a simple gift, but as money for her to use temporarily but eventually to donate to charity.

The reply could be along the following lines:

If you knew Paul was offering you stolen or extorted money, you could not accept it to keep or spend, but only to return to those from whom it was wrongly taken. Not knowing exactly what your brother does, though, you cannot know that the money he has belongs to others, and you could not return it if it does. Still, you know it comes from immoral and illegal activities, perhaps including homicide, traffic in drugs, stealing, prostitution, smuggling goods and persons, and illicit gambling. You know he ought not to have the money and should stop doing whatever he does to get it.

Even so, it would not be wrong to accept money from Paul under certain circumstances. The evil he does to get it has been done. He will do something with the money, and he could use it in more wrongdoing, which would be worse than giving it to you. If you were in dire need—for example, if your very life depended on it—you would have a compelling reason to accept his tainted money and might well do so blamelessly.

You certainly have a good reason for wishing to go to college at the university you have selected—doing that would be an appropriate response to what you think is your vocation. You have a genuine need for the five thousand dollars, and I agree that, if you may accept Paul's offer, you should. But since your need for the money is not overwhelming, your question really is difficult.

Why not take the money you need from Paul? For his sake, your own sake, your other brothers' sake, and your parents' sake.

You ought to be encouraging Paul to repent—not necessarily by harping on repentance, but by making it clear that, while you will always love him as your big brother, you disapprove of his life of crime and hope he will give it up. But how can you do that if you accept his money? You would be helping him rationalize: "What I do is helping my sister get an education, and I certainly could not do that, and other good things I shall do eventually, if I gave up my present source of income. Besides, by helping my sister prepare to serve the Church, I am paying the taxes I owe God on my ill-gotten income." Now he will have a sense of righteous purpose to confirm him in his wrongdoing, and he will be less likely to heed, or even experience, the salutary pangs of conscience that might move him to repent.

Taking his money also would be dangerous for you. You should hope his crimes and those of his associates will be detected, proved, and punished, since that at least would limit the injuries they do to many individuals and society at large. And you should wish Paul to repent and be ready to do what you can to encourage that. But how could you hope for these things if you accept his money? The danger to you would be especially great if you accepted it not once but repeatedly, since looking to him to meet your ongoing need for money would motivate you to will that he could do it—to will that he continue committing whatever crimes he is being paid to commit. That would not make you his legal accomplice, but in your heart you would be his moral partner. Besides, those involved in organized crime seldom give anyone something for nothing. Eventually, Paul or his associates might well demand that you become an accomplice in some wrongful activity.

Taking his money would be bad for your other brothers. It would make Paul's way of life seem less bad and more attractive. It would blur the alternative you should offer them: a life of perfect integrity, rooted in faith and confidence in God, who takes care of those who seek first his kingdom and righteousness.

These reasons for not taking the money are, no doubt, similar to or part of your parents' reasons for refusing to accept, or allow you and the other children to accept, anything from Paul except small presents. By their silent admonition, which speaks loudly because of the family's need, they have powerfully expressed their horror at Paul's wrongdoing, and done their best to move him to repent. They have kept themselves clear of that wrongdoing, maintained their own integrity, and protected you and your brothers from the lure of evil. They are convinced you should not take Paul's money. While I agree that you do not owe them a child's obedience in this matter—you no longer are a child and you would use the money for your education as an adult—you do owe your parents a family member's support (see *LCL,* 714–16). But how supportive will you be if you depart from their policy?

I think the four preceding considerations, taken together, will convince you it would be wrong to plan to get—or wish to receive—money from Paul, year after year, until you complete your education. But what about accepting his offer just this once? Firmly excluding ongoing aid would mitigate the bad consequences of taking his tainted money, but not eliminate them. Nor would it be likely to solve your problem; unless you find some other source of support, you still would not have enough to continue your education beyond the first year. Then too, you very likely would be tempted to go back on your resolution and accept Paul's money again and again.

If you nevertheless come to the contrary conclusion—that you may (and so should) accept Paul's money just this once—it seems to me you should not take more than the five thousand dollars you need, and should not accept even that as either a simple gift or a loan. True, accepting it as a loan would mitigate some of the bad consequences of accepting it as a simple gift. But repaying Paul probably would not help him unless his criminal activity had ceased. Rather, if you accept anything from him, I think it would be preferable to tell him, and firmly commit yourself to it, that you will not regard the money as your own but will pass it on, as soon as you reasonably can, to some appropriate charity. In this way, the bad consequences of taking his money would be mitigated still more, while the money would thus become alms, which you could offer with prayers for Paul's repentance and the well-being of those injured by his crimes.

If you conclude, as I am inclined to think you should, that you must not even once accept from Paul the money you need, try to get it elsewhere. The president of the university or dean of the college you wish to attend probably has some fund that could be used to meet your need. I suggest you meet with them or at least write to them, and ask them for the five thousand dollars. Give them the reasons to respond favorably: your motives for wishing to come to their school and your money problem. Again, you could approach your pastor or someone else who might have the money or know how to get it. The request for help would not be unreasonable, particularly since you hope to be a catechist—that is, to exercise the ministry of religious education, which is vital to the Church.

If you fail to get the money despite your best efforts, do not give up on continuing your education. Perhaps you could begin your college work, at least on a part-time basis, at a local community college or nearby campus of the state university. And perhaps Mrs. Lindsey could provide you with reading lists and other helps to continue your Catholic intellectual formation. Or perhaps you could find full-time work for a while, and even work more than one job, so that you could contribute to your family and save enough to go to college eventually.

No matter what, continue to pray, and do not suppose you cannot fulfill your vocation. God never asks the impossible, and he always can make possible what he wants of us. If you do your best but moral considerations prevent you from doing what you thought God wanted, be sure he did not want it and your vocation lies elsewhere. Humbly seek it, meekly accept it, faithfully live it. That will bring you to heaven, where the poor will enjoy well-gotten wealth.

40: Must a graduate student risk his academic career to support his illegitimate son?

I am twenty-four years old and working on a doctorate in mathematics, which will take about another two years to finish. I have a teaching assistantship, which pays me barely enough to survive on. I met Louise, a woman my own age, at the

Catholic students' club on campus when we began our graduate work two years ago last September; she meant to get a master's in education. Before long we considered ourselves engaged and were spending a lot of time together. We never quite had intercourse, but we would lie naked together fondling each other until we were both satisfied. We didn't think what we were doing could result in pregnancy, and we got away with it for a long time, but Louise became pregnant eleven months ago.[133]

Though some of her friends and the doctor she went to urged her to get an abortion, neither of us even considered it. Louise wanted to get married as soon as possible. But I realized that my feelings for her had been changing even before she got pregnant, and that I should have broken off the relationship. However, though she had not gone on with her graduate work after the first year, she had remained here and gotten a job in order to be near me. I did not have the heart to break up and, frankly, was not really thinking clearly about it, because I still enjoyed sex with her. Confronted with her desire to get married, though, I felt sure it would be a mistake. Naturally, she was hurt and angry. We had been sharing a little apartment. She made me leave, and friends took me in.

Louise's family lives three hundred miles away and is not well off. She cannot expect anything from them. Fortunately, her health insurance from the place where she works covered most of the cost of having the baby, and my parents loaned me some money to help out. I wanted Louise to give the baby up for adoption, and she said she would, but when he was born, she delayed going through with it. Now he is seven weeks old, and she says she cannot part with him.

I realize I have some responsibility to help Louise care for the baby. But how far do I have to go? When she did not put the baby up for adoption, my dad told me not to give her any more money. He said I should demand paternity tests and offered to cover legal expenses "to limit the damage as much as possible." But I am sure the baby is mine, I want to do the right thing, and I do not want to waste money on lawyers. Louise will be putting the baby in day care and going back to work soon, and she will need at least four hundred a month more than her take-home pay to make ends meet. If I do not follow my dad's advice, however, he will not lend me any more money. Thus, I have no way of coming up with what Louise needs unless I give up my teaching assistantship and get a full-time job. But my department chair has warned me that in that case my chances of completing my degree will be slim.

Analysis:

The questioner should be affirmed in his present will "to do the right thing." If he has not already done so, he should be encouraged to repent his grave sins of unchastity and injustice, and to make restitution for the latter sin. The woman's refusal to give up the baby for adoption does not negate or even limit the questioner's paternal responsibility. He should embrace this responsibility whole-heartedly, and, if necessary, give up his graduate study and plans for the future. But

---

133. Sexual behavior short of intercourse can lead to pregnancy if any of the man's semen is deposited within the woman's labia.

he also should look for a more appealing, morally acceptable alternative. Even if he must give up his assistantship, he should try to complete his degree if he can.

The reply could be along the following lines:

In refraining from actually having intercourse, you and Louise no doubt meant to limit your misbehavior. But what you did was both foolishly risky and gravely sinful. You committed sins not only of unchastity but of injustice toward Louise. You continued to take advantage of her belief that you were committed to her when you no longer were prepared to marry her. I trust you have repented and confessed those and all your other sins.

Even if you have, the injustice you did to Louise, like any injustice that results in injury and alienation, requires you to make appropriate restitution: to do whatever you rightly can to make up to her for what you did to her, win her forgiveness, and so make peace with her (see *LCL*, 444–58). I suggest that, if you have not already done so, you frankly acknowledge to her that you wronged her, beg her forgiveness, especially for using her and continuing to lead her into sin even after your feelings for her had changed, and humbly ask her what you might rightly do, whether now or later, to mitigate and make up for the injury and suffering you inflicted on her.

If you have repented, done what you can to make peace with Louise, and otherwise amended your life, you once again have good reason to hope to be among those who one day will hear our Lord say: "Come, you that are blessed by my Father, inherit the kingdom prepared for you from the foundation of the world" (Mt 25.34). What one does to vulnerable members of Jesus' family—which surely includes the unborn—one does to Jesus himself (see Mt 25.40). In refusing to consider abortion, though Louise's friends and doctor urged it, she and you both recognized that the human embryo or fetus should be regarded as a person, and fulfilled your first responsibility toward your son: You allowed him to live and be born. So, though in other respects Louise acted very differently from the Virgin Mary, she truly echoed Mary's fiat. Moreover, though you, unlike Joseph, had been unchaste and unjust, you now are ready to accept the baby as your son, and desire to do the right thing by him. In this way, you mirror Joseph's willingness to meet his responsibilities toward Jesus.

By contrast, in proposing that you seek "to limit the damage as much as possible," your father seems to be advocating that irresponsibility toward children all too common among men who exploit women. It also is discouraging that he conditioned any further help on your following his bad advice. Nevertheless, for the good of Louise, your son, yourself, and your father, I think you should try to get him to change his mind. To that end, I suggest that you try to get Louise's cooperation in acting on part of his advice: to obtain tests to confirm your paternity. For while you are sure you are the father and while babies sometimes are conceived without intercourse, your father's reaction probably partly resulted from understandable skepticism. If so, meeting him part way and confirming your paternity might help persuade him to reconsider and provide the help you need.

What if the tests confirm your paternity, as you are sure they will, and your father still refuses to change his position?

You may feel frustrated and even resent the baby, but you must keep in mind that he is completely innocent and is your son. Though different in important ways, a man's failure to support his child and a woman's killing hers are alike in at least one crucial respect: Fathers no more have a right to abandon children by nonsupport than mothers have a right to get rid of them by abortion. Moreover, since your actual relationship to your son, grounded in your own free choice, is the source of your responsibility to support him, Louise's abandonment of the plan to give him up for adoption in no way nullifies or even reduces your obligation to him.

Still, if you really believe that adoption would be best for your son—as I think it probably would—you should try once more to persuade Louise to give him up. Assure her that, whatever she decides, you will fulfill your responsibilities toward him. Admit that neither you nor anyone else can know for certain that adoption would be in his best interests. But point out that he is likely to be well cared for and properly educated by a married couple who would adopt him and cherish him as their own and that she perhaps can have no greater love for him than to surrender him, painful as that would be, to such a couple. By now, too, she probably has experienced some of the hardships of caring for a small baby. If so, you might gently remind her of them and point out that children make even greater demands as they grow up, especially during adolescence.

If Louise continues to reject adoption, do not try to evade your duty to meet your son's needs, and you should recognize that this duty extends beyond paying the money that you could be legally compelled to pay. More than that may be needed; and you also must do what you can to give him a father's love, guidance, and personal help.[134] Indeed, insofar as you can, you must see to it that the child is brought up well in every respect. Consequently, if necessary, you must give up your graduate studies and plans for the future, and seek permanent, full-time employment. In doing that, you perhaps can take advantage of the graduate work you already have completed—for example, by teaching mathematics in high school.

Before giving up your graduate studies, however, you should try to find a better alternative. Perhaps Louise and you could solve the immediate problem by cooperating in caring for your baby. You might be able to study and care for him simultaneously—at her apartment or elsewhere—during much of the time he otherwise would be in day care as well as some time on weekends, and your friends and hers might help out when neither of you can care for him. This arrangement not only would save money and allow you to keep your assistantship but, very likely, would assure better care than paid providers would give. For a baby needs the personal love and tender care that hired hands are unlikely to give, since, even if they take on the work with an upright attitude, their attention and affection

---

134. A good summary of a father's responsibilities: Clayton C. Barbeau, *Father of the Family: A Christian Perspective,* rev. by Mitch Finley (Huntington, Ind.: Our Sunday Visitor, 1990). A cogent psychological argument showing the need for fathers to fulfill their responsibilities: David Popenoe, *Life without Father* (New York: The Free Press, 1996).

generally are dispersed, and they naturally try to avoid becoming fully attached to a child from whom they expect to part.

No doubt, cooperation would be difficult at first, but two things seem to point to the likelihood of success: Louise and you have shown some good character traits, and you both loved your baby enough to let him be born. Moreover, while it was right for you not to marry Louise when you felt sure marriage would be a mistake and you should not marry her now merely to assuage your guilt feelings or to solve the problem of caring for the baby, the experience of cooperating in caring for your son might well lead to a renewal of your relationship in a chaste and more mature form, and eventually this might lead both of you to discern that, after all, you are called to marry each other. You ought to be open-minded about this possibility, for if you and Louise became convinced that marriage to each other is your vocation and fully committed yourselves to it, you could reasonably hope for a good and happy marriage.

If you and she cannot cooperate in caring for your baby, perhaps you can borrow the necessary money from someone other than your father, finish your degree, get a job, repay the loan, and eventually provide Louise and your son with the more adequate help they will need. Or, perhaps, you might both keep your assistantship and get another part-time job, earning enough to meet all your responsibilties.

Finally, even if you must give up your assistantship and get a full-time job, you should not let the department chair's warning discourage you from doing your best to complete your degree. His advice, probably influenced by the department's interest in having you continue in your assistantship, may well be too pessimistic. Of course, many entry-level, full-time, teaching positions and other jobs that take far more than forty hours per week of one's time are likely to be incompatible with completing a doctoral degree. However, you might be able to find less time-consuming employment which, nevertheless, would put your education to use and pay enough to balance your budget. In that case, you will have a good chance of completing your degree—perhaps not in two years but in three or four—if you focus your time and energy on that objective. Though you must fulfill other duties, including those toward yourself, you can cut out optional activities, such as most entertainment and social life, and discipline yourself to avoid idleness, resist distractions, and use every minute as fully as possible. For example, give up unnecessary reading; seldom or never watch television; use the time while you are getting cleaned up or walking from here to there to pray and plan your work; study while you eat, during breaks at work, while riding public transportation, and so on.

While such sacrifices and self-discipline will be hard, you will be capable of them if you keep your purposes in mind and pray for the grace you need. Besides, following an austere lifestyle for a few years will be good for your character and will serve as appropriate, ongoing penance for the sins that led to your present problem (see *CCC,* 2015; *LCL,* 190–96, 217–18).

+   +   +

41: May a woman who was adopted try to contact her natural parents?

My parents had been married six years and thought they could have no children when they adopted me, but then they had my three brothers. Dad and Mom told me when I was very young that I was adopted, so it seems I always have known. They have been good to me, treating us all the same. Or so it seems to me. The boys think I have been treated better, but Mom always says: "Not better, but differently, because she's a girl and older than you!"

Lately I have been wondering about my natural parents. Last year I had a very thorough physical when it was suspected I might have a serious health problem, and the doctors would have liked information about my family medical history. We could not provide it, since my adoption was through an agency that allowed no contact between natural and adoptive parents. The problem turned out not to be serious, but now I am a senior in college and, though not yet engaged, am thinking about getting married, and it might be good to know something about my hereditary background. Mainly, though, I am just curious about how I came to be. Also, I imagine it must have been hard for my natural mother to give me up, and, assuming she is still alive, she might be happy to learn how well things have gone for me.

I have looked into it just enough to know that, if I want to, I can find out who my natural parents are and probably can locate them. I have talked with various people about it, starting with Dad and Mom. They are not enthusiastic, mainly because they feel it is unnecessary and might lead to problems. Still, they always are supportive when I do something that, without agreeing with it, they do not consider wrong, and I am sure that will be so in this case. Dad summed it up, "I'd be inclined to let sleeping dogs lie, but if you decide to wake this one up, we'll just hope he won't be nasty." I also asked the college chaplain whether he thought it would be wrong for me to get in touch with my natural parents. He told me he did not see anything wrong with it, but did not know for sure, and suggested I ask you.

Analysis:

This question calls for a judgment about communication with natural parents. The questioner's reasons for doing so are sound but not compelling. Communicating with her natural parents could have various harmful results, especially for her natural mother. So, in my judgment, fairness to others, especially her natural mother, and reasonable self-interest require the questioner to forgo communicating directly with her natural parents. However, she could try to learn what she can about them without communicating with them in any way. She also might try to communicate by means of a carefully chosen intermediary.

The reply could be along the following lines:

Some adopted children have cogent reasons for identifying and communicating with their natural parents. For instance, for their children's very survival or other vital interests, some parents in poor and/or war ravaged nations have been compelled to give them up for adoption by families in better circumstances; if the children prosper, they have a reason, and perhaps even a duty, to locate their natural parents and help them if possible.

Other people have questionable motives for wishing to find their natural parents. Some have psychological problems that they unreasonably hope will be solved in this way; for them, the quest can become an obsession. Rebellious adolescents sometimes hope to fulfill their fantasies of having "perfect" parents by replacing those who raised them with their "real" parents. My advice to a person with such a project would be short and definite: Accept those who adopted you as your real parents, for they are that in every respect except the biological, which is not as essential to parenthood as the unconditional commitment to accept a child as one's own and fulfill one's parental responsibilities toward him or her.

By contrast, your motives, though not extraordinary, seem healthy and mature: a practical concern to obtain information that might be relevant to your future health care and marriage, a kindly wish to let your natural mother know that her giving you up for adoption benefited you, and curiosity about your origin. The last motive might be questioned by some, but it is good to wish to know oneself, and one's biological origins and ancestry are an essential part of one's personal reality. So, though not every adopted person wonders about these matters and some are more interested in them than others, they do fall within the range of natural curiosity about oneself. Moreover, you have shown maturity and prudence by not rushing into this project, but first discussing it with your parents and then seeking advice from the college chaplain. Therefore, as posed by you, your question really is difficult.

While I endorse your motives for wishing to communicate with your natural parents, in my judgment you also should think seriously about the possible harmful results.[135] These, it seems to me, are of three sorts.

First, your natural mother very likely could have aborted you had she willed, but she loved you enough to bear you and give you up for adoption. As you say, that probably was hard for her. She almost certainly did it with the intention and hope that you would be loved and brought up well, as, indeed, you have been. So, you are right to feel toward her the gratitude you manifest in wishing to console her by letting her know you have been cherished and have done well. She might be delighted to hear from you, and perhaps the two of you would develop a mutually enriching relationship. However, making contact with her might injure rather than benefit her, and the injury could be very grave, due to at least two things: first, the painful recalling of the past, including the circumstances of your birth, and, perhaps, the intimate relationship that led to your conception; and second, the possible revelation of that past to others from whom it has been kept secret, and the disturbing effects that might have on her present life.

Second, you also cannot predict the trouble initiating some sort of relationship with your natural parents might cause yourself and your adoptive parents. While

---

135. Karen March, *The Stranger Who Bore Me: Adoptee-Birth Mother Relationships* (Toronto: University of Toronto Press, 1995), studied sixty reunited adoptees. Though favoring the undertaking by adoptees, she found that the majority failed to establish a satisfying, continuing relationship with their birth mothers (97–117).

everything might go well, in speaking of "sleeping dogs" your Dad actually understates the potential emotional problems and other serious, practical burdens that might arise. In retrospect—to change the metaphor—you might well regret having opened a Pandora's box.

Third, if people like you identify and communicate with their natural parents, the example will encourage immature and less well-motivated individuals to do the same, to their own and others' detriment. Indeed, widespread breaching of the confidentiality that has surrounded adoptions like yours will tend to undermine the practice of handling adoptions as yours was handled. Yet entirely excluding contact between the children and their natural parents can offer significant advantages to all parties.[136] The natural parents are relieved of further parental responsibilities, protected to a great extent from ongoing emotional suffering, and freed to go on with their lives, putting the past behind them and, perhaps, even hiding it. These benefits are especially important today for the encouragement they give women who otherwise might abort their babies to regard adoption as an appealing alternative. The adoptive parents are relieved of competition for filial affection, possible interference with their parenting, the burden of conducting additional quasi-familial relationships, and a possible source of temptation to be tentative in their parental commitment or to renege on it. The adopted child also benefits by having a single, unified, unambiguous parental principle, which is conducive to secure self-confidence and a sense of personal identity.

In view of these considerations, identifying and communicating directly with your natural parents would, it seems to me, be both unfair to others, especially your natural mother, and an unreasonable risk to yourself. Still, to accomplish at least some of your good purposes, you might consider two alternatives: (1) trying to learn what you can about your natural parents without communicating with them in any way; and (2) employing a suitable intermediary to find them and communicate with them within certain fixed limits.

Unless you decide simply to let the matter rest, I think you should begin with the first alternative. An initial cautious inquiry might well yield information that would give you additional reasons for proceeding or not proceeding with the second. Then, if you decide to undertake indirect communication, the intermediary would have to be someone trustworthy, discreet, and prudent, who would proceed very cautiously so as to minimize the risk of baring secrets or causing other serious injuries. Again, to minimize risks, your instructions to the intermediary should be only to obtain information that may be of use in your health care and plans regarding marriage, and to convey your consoling message to your natural mother. In this way, the intermediary could pursue those good purposes without initiating an interpersonal relationship or even establishing a channel of ongoing communication.

---

136. Many researchers favor open adoption—see Harriet E. Gross, "Open Adoption: A Research-Based Literature Review and New Data," *Child Welfare*, 72 (1993): 269–84—but seem to me to discount disadvantages and bad outcomes, and to focus on the majority of cases, in which the adults involved judge the experience satisfactory.

If you do employ an intermediary, I suggest you instruct him or her to communicate first with your natural mother, who probably is more vulnerable. Only with her consent and if necessary to achieve your purpose, it seems to me, would it be fair to her to risk communicating in a similar indirect way with your natural father.

Of course, proceeding this way, you will not fully satisfy your curiosity about your roots and will forgo a possibly worthwhile relationship with your natural parents. But many adopted people have lived good lives without these things, and you have done well up to now without them. Forgoing such things out of consideration for others and reasonable self-concern need not mean being deprived of them forever. Our lives in this world are brief. You can pray for your natural parents, and hope to meet them in heaven and there enjoy perfect and unending communion with them, as well as with your Dad and Mom, and everyone else who has contributed to your life in this world.

42: Should a man stop his elderly mother from driving?

My mother is eighty and in fairly good physical and mental condition for her age. She shops for herself, does household chores well, and visits regularly with friends and relatives. She has been a widow for more than ten years, and has adjusted well.

However, there are problems. She no longer can remember which day of the week it is, and often is confused about where she is in her day's routine. She is not up to dealing with problems as they arise—for example, we do not feel we can leave her in charge of our two-year-old child, even for two or three hours. Having lost a great deal of her short-term memory, she repeats the same questions over a period of days or even several times in an hour. She is not irritable, and in all other respects, given her age, is quite healthy. Her vision (with glasses) and hearing remain good for her age.

Due mostly to Mother's forgetfulness, we have moved her to an apartment only about half a mile from our house. The move has placed her within easy reach. Our older children are encouraged to visit her regularly and they do, both to keep an eye on her and give her a hand with things. In addition, she has given me a power of attorney and her checkbook, and I handle all her financial affairs. This arrangement has been satisfactory, although she does feel some resentment about her loss of independence—for example, not being able to cash a check when buying groceries.

Due to various impairments, elderly people sometimes cause serious accidents. I recently read a report of an accident in which a man of eighty-three, trying to round a corner in a large parking area, lost control of his car for no apparent reason, ran over the curb, and plowed into a group of small children, killing three and injuring several others. My wife and I also have read about elderly people with poor memories driving off intending to go to the grocery store and being found hours or days later hundreds of miles away, alive and well but confused. As time passes, my sister and I worry more that something like this could happen with Mother.

However, we have reservations about simply taking her car away. She will be tied down (we live in a suburban area without mass transit), and the burden on my wife and me will be great (we have eight children under sixteen). Further, does Mother have a property right to her car, or more precisely, to its benefits in terms of mobility and convenience? I know I would be justified, even obliged, to take the car away if she had a serious accident or wandered off. But must I act before that occurs? Finally, if I do take the car away and her mental health deteriorates as a result, would I not be responsible? I expect I would feel: "I shouldn't have taken this from you, too."

This question may not be a moral one; it may fall more within the province of psychological evaluation. But even a competent psychologist cannot evaluate Mother's condition precisely enough to say, for example, "Six months from now, she will not be able to exercise control of her driving."

Analysis:

Whether a person with diminishing capacities should continue driving is a question of fairness, and whether a family member should prevent such a person from driving also is a question of fairness. The questioner may be too inclined to restrict his mother's autonomy. Still, if she continues driving despite increasing risks, he eventually will have to judge whether to exercise his power to limit or stop her driving. That judgment mainly concerns the fairness of accepting the risks posed to others by her driving; in making it, the questioner should also take into account the burdens to everyone concerned of her no longer driving. If he judges that the risks to others can be accepted fairly, he should allow his mother to accept any risk to herself. But if he judges that he cannot fairly accept the risks to others, he should do what he can to minimize the negative impact on his mother of restricting or stopping her driving.

The reply could be along the following lines:

Taking for granted that your mother possesses her car legitimately and fairly, she certainly has a property right to it, and so she has a prima facie right to use it for the benefits of mobility and convenience. But that does not settle anything, since such rights are not absolute and, in any case, your mother has given you a power of attorney, which you could use to sell her car. Nor does it make any difference whether anyone can predict that at some future date she will be unable to "exercise control of her driving." Rather, the crucial question concerns the risks your mother's driving imposes on others right now.

What you say in stating your question seems to indicate, on the one hand, that she still is mentally competent and acting responsibly, and, on the other, that you feel impelled to make many decisions for her. While her short-term memory is declining and she may not be able to keep pace with your two-year-old child (I no longer could do that myself!), her motor skills may still be adequate to drive (you say she does her household chores well). Your reference to the possibility that your mother might have a serious accident suggests she has not yet had one, and I assume she has been a good driver, does not drive after drinking, and has not been convicted of an above-average number of traffic law violations. So, especially if she avoids expressways and downtown traffic and drives only under favorable weather conditions to familiar destinations, the risk of a serious accident probably is not excessive.[137]

Since in many ways persons can fulfill themselves only by shaping their own lives, many risks are warranted to allow children, persons who are retarded, and the declining elderly to make their own decisions. Perhaps your sincere concerns about safety, together with a tendency to be somewhat too cautious, are leading you to take too much responsibility for your mother. If so, the straightforward way to deal with your anxieties would be to discuss them frankly with her, while respecting her judgment in the matter. Treating her as a responsible person is likely to encourage her to act responsibly. Conversely, treating her as less responsible than she is might well diminish her self-respect and lead her to act imprudently.[138]

In some communities, the American Automobile Association, the American Association of Retired Persons, or some other organization offers a driving refresher course for senior citizens. If such a course is available and you can get your mother to take it, she might either improve her driving so that it is acceptably safe or come to see she should quit. Perhaps, however, you already have tried such approaches, and she has insisted on continuing driving. In some places, the public authorities periodically retest all drivers or those over a certain age, identify drivers whose limitations impose excessive risks on others, and either restrict their driving or withdraw their licenses. If such a system is in effect where you live, that may solve the problem for you. Perhaps, on the other hand, the law does not provide any solution, in which case the answer will be that only you can restrict your mother's driving or take her car away, and unless you do, she will go on driving, with increasing risks. In that case, your question actually is how to judge whether her decision is so unreasonable that you must exercise your power to prevent her from running risks she really should avoid.

Why should this be your responsibility? Because you have accepted the role you describe. Morally, even if not legally, this role is something like that of a parent of a not fully competent, though not infantile, child. Someone filling such a role must compensate for any failure of the child—or the declining parent—to recognize his or her responsibilities, and must act to safeguard others' rights.

137. Substantial research supports the judgment that an eighty-year-old woman with normal sight and hearing who has been a good driver, has not had an excessive number of convictions for traffic offenses, has avoided serious accidents, does not drive after drinking, and drives only to familiar destinations under favorable weather conditions is not at excessive risk; see P. J. Cooper, "Different Ages, Different Risks: The Realm of Accident Statistics," in J. Peter Rothe, *The Safety of Elderly Drivers: Yesterday's Young in Today's Traffic* (New Brunswick, N.J.: Transaction Publishers, 1990), 85–133.

138. Diane Persson, "The Elderly Driver: Deciding When to Stop," *The Gerontologist,* 33 (1993): 88–91, in discussing her study, concludes (90): "The findings indicate that older drivers believe *they* should make the decision to stop driving. Following that, they prefer that physicians recommend driving be discontinued and, as a final recourse, that family should discuss their concerns."

Everyone's driving imposes some risks on others. The risks are greater with some groups of people than others, and insurance companies to some extent adjust rates accordingly. But even the driving of most less competent drivers does not impose unfair risks on others, provided those drivers are licensed and insured, and they drive as carefully as they can. Still, some people simply should not be on the road. The question therefore is whether your mother's driving already imposes unfair risks on others.

To answer that, the Golden Rule must be applied. Eventually, you will be elderly and declining. At what stage do you think your children should take away your car? Again, your mother's driving does involve risks to others. How do you feel about the risks imposed on you and your children by the driving of other people about as competent as your mother? In attempting to answer the latter question, you might find a good indicator in the views of sensible, sympathetic people, less emotionally involved than you, who have ridden with your mother or observed her driving—say, her friends or neighbors and your teenaged children.

In applying the Golden Rule in cases of this sort, it is necessary to consider the urgency of a legitimate need to engage in the risky behavior and the burdens on everyone involved if the risky behavior were given up. So, take into account a realistic expectation of both the inconvenience for you and your wife and the hardship for your mother if you take her car away. But one also must take into account the natural tendency to overestimate burdens to oneself and those near and dear while underestimating risks to strangers. So, ask yourself how good an excuse the expected hardship to your mother and the inconvenience to you would seem to impartial observers if she continues driving and causes an accident that does grave harm to others.

If you conscientiously judge it more likely than not that her continuing to drive imposes no unfair risks on others, you should not prevent her from driving. Most accidents she might be in would be as likely to harm others as herself; and so, if her driving does not unfairly impose risks on others, it does not unreasonably involve risks for her. If she ends up hundreds of miles away, that would only be an inconvenience—and might be the occasion to persuade her to give up the car, though I doubt it would justify taking it away. But if you consider it more likely that her driving does impose unfair risks on others, I think you should restrict her driving or even take the car away, both in their interests and in hers. And that should not wait until she has a serious accident, since the injustice already is present in accepting the risk.

The effects on your mother of taking her car away also would partly depend on how you did it and how she saw it. Perhaps her primary care physician or someone else friendly with her could propose the idea and get her to accept it. Perhaps she would better accept it from you if you explained to her precisely how you reached your conscientious judgment. Maybe neither approach would be appropriate, but you must do your best to think of the most suitable way. If you do what you can to soften the blow, I doubt it will have any profound psychological effect on her, though it probably will grieve her for a time.

Also, your mother probably would find the loss of her car more acceptable if you could make other provisions for her mobility, say, by setting up an account for her with a local taxi company.[139] You would be freed of concerns about her driving, and she would remain free to go and come as she pleases. Considering the savings from her no longer owning and operating a car, such an arrangement might well prove economical.

Having done your best to make the right judgment, do not blame yourself for acting on it even if the results are bad. That works both ways. If you think it more likely that your mother's driving is not unfair to others and do nothing, perhaps she will cause an accident resulting in injury or death to someone; but it will be an accident, not your fault. If you think her driving is unfair to others and restrict it or take her car away, and her mental health deteriorates, that too will not be your fault.

Finally, do what you can to sustain your mother's faith and strengthen her hope. How well elderly people accept their inevitable limitations and losses as they decline partly depends on what, if anything, continues to give their lives meaning. While suffering never is pleasant, Christians waiting in joyful hope for heaven can patiently endure far more than people who lack lively hope or, even worse, foresee nothing but continuing and increasing decline.

43: Is it wrong to wish for death?

I do volunteer work with some of the elderly Catholic residents at a nursing home. Few if any of them ever will leave. I got involved when I started serving as a eucharistic minister for the home two years ago, and discovered that some of the people to whom I bring Communion have other visitors only rarely if ever. I visit these people regularly, bring them little gifts, try to make friends with them, pray with them and encourage them to pray more, and, in general, try to brighten their lives. Some other volunteers have been working with the home's administrators to provide more opportunities for worthwhile activities for long-term patients who are not terminally ill. I have encouraged the people I visit to participate in the new activities, and some are doing that and spending less time watching television.

Still, many of these elderly friends are bored and have little to look forward to in this life. Most are not dying or even sick with anything in particular. But they are debilitated, burdened with various handicaps and health problems, and more or less depressed. Some regularly speak of death and clearly look forward to it. Some who are devout pray to die soon.

I know wishing for something can be a sin of thought. Wishing to commit adultery is adultery in the heart, and wishing an enemy would get killed certainly seems to be a serious sin of hatred. Is it also wrong for these elderly friends of mine to wish for death? I am not asking whether they are sinning, for I realize only God knows that, but whether what they are doing is wrong in itself. If it is, what should I do?

---

139. Persson, ibid., 91, makes the point that "alternatives to driving are essential" and says the challenge is "to take over the driving function without taking over other functions."

Another point. Federal law requires the nursing home to give residents information about their rights to refuse treatment and to give advance directives excluding life-sustaining treatment in case they become terminally ill. Most have signed the directives. One of my friends told me signing makes sense because "we are just waiting here to die and don't want to be kept alive longer than necessary." Not knowing what to say, I changed the subject. What should I have said?

Analysis:

There are two related but distinct moral questions here. The first is whether wishing for death is the matter of a sin. The answer depends on whether the wish for death involves an unreasonable act of the will. The act of the will involved in a wish for death is reasonable if death is only accepted as a side effect or understood as a necessary condition in a choice or readiness to choose to act for an intelligible good. The act of the will involved in a wish for death can be unreasonable in either of two ways: if it is a conditional intention to kill oneself or if it endorses an unreasonable emotional desire to die. Thus, an adequate response to the question must clarify those two wrongful will acts. The second question presented here is how one ought to deal with persons whose state of mind seems to involve one of those wrongful will acts. The answer is that one should try to help them stop willing wrongly, if indeed they are, and encourage them to wish rightly for death.

The reply could be along the following lines:

I assume that, in saying your elderly friends are "more or less depressed," you do not mean all of them are suffering from some degree of psychological illness. However, I suggest that you familiarize yourself, if you have not already done so, with the signs of depression, so that you will be able to encourage any needing treatment to get it. On this matter, of course, you should look for guidance to those responsible for the health care of the home's residents. But it also would be helpful to call their attention to anyone whose apparent depression they seem to have overlooked.[140]

Many elderly people in nursing homes are victims of grave injustices. Some have been entirely or largely abandoned by their children and/or others who should be taking care of them or, at least, taking a greater interest in them, and such elderly people often are aware of the injustice and sometimes embittered by it. But many others are not even conscious that they are victims: they suffer not only from the attitudes and practices of a society that measures personal worth by economic productivity and consumption, vigor, attractiveness, and status, but from a self-appraisal, based on those false standards, that makes them feel

---

140. Primary care physicians often fail to diagnose depression; see Leon Eisenberg, "Treating Depression and Anxiety in Primary Care: Closing the Gap between Knowledge and Practice," *New England Journal of Medicine,* 326 (1992): 1080–84. A helpful booklet on depression: Depression Guideline Panel, *Depression in Primary Care: Detection, Diagnosis, and Treatment,* Quick Reference Guide for Clinicians, no. 5, AHCPR pub. no. 93–0552 (Rockville, Md.: U.S. Department of Health and Human Services, Public Health Service, Agency for Health Care Policy and Research; Apr. 1993). Practitioners should first use volumes one and two of *Depression in Primary Care: Clinical Practice Guideline,* publications 93–0550 and 93–0551.

useless, worthless, undeserving of care, and even guilty for continuing to live and burden others. In most cases, you probably can do little or nothing to overcome these injustices. But by gently asking appropriate questions and being a sympathetic listener, you can help your elderly friends articulate their experiences of injustice, acknowledge their feelings about them, accept those feelings as appropriate, gain self-esteem, and forgive those who have wronged them.

You are doing a good thing in visiting these elderly people, making friends with them, praying with them and encouraging them to pray, trying to cheer them up, and encouraging them to spend less time on television and more on worthwhile activities. The questions you raise about their attitudes concerning death are not incidental to your relationship with them. Indeed, these questions ought to be central to your effort to understand and help them. Since nothing is more important than that they go to heaven, you can do nothing better for them than help them live well and prepare properly for death—for example, by receiving the sacraments, learning to join their suffering to Jesus' passion, and making peace with enemies. Still, do not focus exclusively on the prospect of their death, constantly initiate discussion of it, or stop doing any of the good things you have been doing. But do keep in view the all-important benefit to your elderly friends of being prepared to die in God's love, do nothing incompatible with their sharing in this benefit, and try to do everything else you do for them in a way conducive to this benefit.

I entirely agree with you that wishes have moral significance. You also are right in distinguishing between asking whether someone wishing for something is sinning, which only God knows, and whether the wishing is wrong in itself. Of course, deliberately to wish wrongly is to commit a sin, and anyone guilty of an unrepented sin is responsible for bad wishes arising from that sin, even if the wishes themselves are not deliberate. But most people, even those who are virtuous, very likely wish for many things that they should not, without ever choosing to do so. A wish simply comes to mind and is entertained, without the person ever asking: Is it wrong for me to wish this?

Nevertheless, your question remains important. Wishing wrongly, like any other kind of objectively bad act, is harmful at least to the one wishing, and is morally perilous even when not sinful, since bad wishes may eventually tempt one to make choices known to be wrong. Therefore, it is preferable that people reflect on the moral quality of their wishing and choose to set aside wishes that cannot be rightly entertained.

Since human life is a person's concrete reality, it always retains its intrinsic goodness; since death is the privation of life, it is always bad. Therefore, in any straightforward choice between life and death, one always ought to choose life and may never choose to do anything precisely to bring about death (see *LCL,* 460–67).

Still, someone willing and acting for various goods that truly fulfill human beings may foresee that his or her own death will be an inevitable side effect or a necessary condition, or both, of attaining them, and so may and even should be willing to die, without ever intending death as an end, choosing it as a means, or doing anything to bring it about. When this willingness to die is allied with positive feelings toward some foreseen effect of death, such a person can be said to wish to die. Thus, St. Maximilian Kolbe can be said to have wished to die inasmuch as he chose to take a condemned man's place; many martyrs wish to die inasmuch as they prefer death to infidelity and welcome it as an opportunity to bear witness to their faith; and every good Christian wishes to die inasmuch as he or she hopes for heaven, since only by dying is one born again to eternal life.

On this basis, many devout people, having prepared well for death, long for it and earnestly beg God to take them to himself. Thus, St. Paul says: "To me, living is Christ and dying is gain" (Phil 1.21), and: "We would rather be away from the body and at home with the Lord" (2 Cor 5.8). Yet Paul plainly judges death, as not itself something good, but only a necessary condition for the fulfillment of Christian hope: "I want to know Christ and the power of his resurrection and the sharing of his sufferings by becoming like him in his death, *if somehow I may attain the resurrection from the dead*" (Phil 3.10–11, emphasis added), and: "While we are still in this tent, we groan under our burden, because we wish not to be unclothed [deprived of our bodies by death] but to be further clothed, so that what is mortal may be swallowed up by life" (2 Cor 5.4).

Moreover, inasmuch as death itself, as the privation of the great good of life, is a real evil, the process of dying that ends in death also is evil, and one can rightly wish it not to be prolonged. Similarly, faced with death, one can rightly wish that the stressful period of anticipating it be short. Thus Jesus, anticipating his passion and death, said: "I have a baptism with which to be baptized, and what stress I am under until it is completed!" (Lk 12.50). Still, Jesus by no means regarded the suffering and death he foresaw as good; he only accepted them and endured the cross "for the sake of the joy that was set before him" (Heb 12.2).

Plainly, both Paul and Jesus wished principally for life. Yet as part of their wish for life they wished for death: the gateway to resurrection and the life of the world to come. In the same way, every faithful Christian, hoping for heaven, rightly wishes for death.

But it also is possible to wish wrongly for death. One can do wrong in conditionally accepting death by taking unreasonable risks and engaging in self-destructive behavior, thinking that death, if it results, will be welcome. One can conditionally choose to kill oneself or can refuse care not only foreseeing death but intending to bring it about.

Moreover, one can wrongly wish for death by accepting and endorsing an unreasonable emotional desire to die. Life always includes various sorts of suffering: physical pain, boredom, frustration, fruitless anger, grief over losses, and so on. Most people during most of their lives feel that various satisfactions and enjoyments more or less outweigh sufferings or at least balance them, so that life seems "worth living." However, for some people at each stage of life and for many elderly people, satisfactions are few and sufferings many, so that life as a whole may seem empty and meaningless. At this point, death begins to seem attractive as a way to escape suffering, and this apparent attractiveness generates an emotional desire for death. This psychology is understandable, but such a desire is unreasonable insofar as it is based on false judgments: that life no longer is worth living, that pain and suffering are evils to be escaped at all costs, or that death itself can be good.[141] Therefore, nobody should willingly entertain that desire and in that way wish for death. Moreover, if one does, one approves the unreasonable motive and, having approved it, is likely to be tempted to follow it out in action, that is, by choosing to do or omit doing something in order to die, or, at least, conditionally choosing to end one's life. In either case, one commits suicide in one's heart, and in both cases one may actually carry out the choice and kill oneself.

Someone might argue that one can rightly regard death as good and wish for it as a way of escaping suffering by pointing out that saintly Christians who wish for death as the gateway to eternal life look forward to freedom from pain and suffering as one of heaven's blessings. Certainly, when devout people anticipate death they often speak about being freed of suffering, and, in general, Christians are aware that death will in fact put an end to earthly suffering, regard that as an advantage, and hope for it. This is very different, however, from thinking of death as a *way* of escaping suffering—as a possible means that could be rightly regarded as good. Saintly Christians realize that death always is bad: "God did not make death, and he does not delight in the death of the living. For he created all things so that they might exist" (Wis 1.13–14). Unlike the ungodly, devout Christians, though rightly wishing for death, do not consider it "a friend" (Wis 1.16), but "the last enemy to be destroyed" (1 Cor 15.26).

The preceding explanation makes clear the possible ambiguity in a wish for death. When rooted in hope for heaven and accompanied by docility to God's providential plan, the wish is good and in no way at odds with reverence for life and determination to preserve it and make the most of it. But when rooted in sadness and/or anger about the poor quality of daily experience and accompanied by a will unsubmissive to God's plan, the wish for death is bad and is the seed of the contralife will that uses death as a means to escape suffering. Doing that is suicide, which, freely chosen despite awareness of its gravity and unrepented, leads to hell. In your relationships with the elderly, therefore, encourage and support their uprightly wishing for death but avoid in any way fostering or condoning their wrongly wishing for it.

Someone might object that the alternatives just mentioned are not exhaustive, since a person's wish for death, though rooted in negative feelings toward the poor quality of his or her daily experience, can be accompanied by docility to God's law forbidding suicide. But such a wish is confused: objectively bad inasmuch as not rooted in hope for heaven, but subjectively blameless inasmuch as limited by an upright will to avoid sin. With such a confused wish, a person will be vulnerable to the temptation to choose suicide, perhaps persuading himself or herself that God will understand. The suicidal choice sometimes will take the form of an unreasonable decision to refuse treatment, rationalized by excluding death-dealing behavior: "Though I never would do anything to kill myself, that treatment would only prevent nature from taking her course."

---

141. On the falsity of these judgments, see John Paul II, *Evangelium vitae,* 34–39, *AAS* 87 (1995) 438–44, *OR,* 5 Apr. 1995, vii–viii. On the relationship of pain and suffering to what is truly evil, see *CMP,* 119–20; *LCL,* 31–32, including n. 54.

The appropriate response to your elderly friends' expressions of a wish for death will vary in particular situations, depending on precisely what someone says, his or her beliefs and problems, and how you think you can help. Your friend's explanation of signing advance directives excluding life-sustaining treatment—"We are just waiting here to die and don't want to be kept alive longer than necessary"—perhaps expresses a feeling of uselessness. *Just waiting* suggests that nothing of value remains to be done. That certainly is a mistake. Those capable of doing so should exercise their creative gifts, help care for themselves and one another, and so on. No matter how severely handicapped and debilitated, anyone able to communicate with others can share in intrinsically valuable communion with them, and even when the ability to communicate is lost, a person may be able to pray and offer up his or her suffering. However, *just waiting* also might express not only negative feelings but a wrongful wish for death and even an immoral choice to forgo treatment as a means of hastening death. In the latter case, your friend has chosen suicide—though probably without sufficient reflection, and so probably without the guilt of mortal sin.

Confronted with ambiguity of this sort, your first responsibility as a friend is to be a good and sympathetic listener, to show interest proportionate to the great importance of what has been said, and then very gently to draw out the thinking and feelings behind the remark. If these turn out to be morally acceptable, try to reinforce and perfect them. But if they point to a morally unacceptable conditional intention or unreasonable emotional motive, kindly admonish the apparent sinner, leading him or her to see the wrongness of that wishing, to repent it, and to replace it with hope for heaven and a commitment to make the most of his or her remaining life.

Your goal in every case should be to get your friends eventually to say sincerely: "We remain here in order to finish the work God has given us; we are living out the life of good deeds he prepared for us in advance; still, since we hope to go to heaven, we would welcome death." Given that outlook and attitude, an elderly person often may forgo medical treatment because of its costliness or other serious disadvantages, not arrogantly choosing to escape suffering by suicide but humbly willing to complete suffering by accepting its consummation in death: "Master, now you are dismissing your servant in peace, according to your word" (Lk 2.29). To help your friends come to this way of thinking, your message should contain the following ideas.

God is a loving Father who always knows what is best for us. We would not remain alive if there were no good reason for us to be here. Up to now and at this moment, God wants us to continue to live for some purpose. We must try to see what that purpose is and do our best to cooperate in realizing it. Perhaps a spouse or someone else still needs us, and we may not abandon that person. But even if not, as long as we are able to control our thoughts, one thing we can do is pray for ourselves and others, and offer our difficult lives as a sacrifice in union with Jesus' suffering. God may be calling us to save someone's soul in that way. There may be other ways in which we can help others less blessed than we are, and God also may be calling us to those forms of service. In any case, God is calling each of us to continue living a good Christian life, and in doing so to become the saints he wants us to be, not only by growing in faith and love, but by becoming exactly the way we are to be forever in heaven—unique saints who persevered through the precise set of difficulties each of us faces and who, by God's grace, won the victory. Thus, we should look at ebbing life with the eye of hope: "So we do not lose heart. Even though our outer nature is wasting away, our inner nature is being renewed day by day. For this slight momentary affliction is preparing us for an eternal weight of glory beyond all measure" (2 Cor 4.16–17).

At the same time, we rightly long to enjoy that glory. Having prepared ourselves to die in God's friendship, we look forward to death with hope of heaven. But heaven is God's to give, not ours to take, and we must not despise this present life or let ourselves become impatient, much less even think of doing or omitting anything in order to hasten death. Rather, as in other things, so also in this, we must submit entirely to God: "We do not live to ourselves, and we do not die to ourselves. If we live, we live to the Lord, and if we die, we die to the Lord; so then, whether we live or whether we die, we are the Lord's" (Rom 14.7–8). With this attitude, we rightly pray for death, not at a time of our choosing, but in God's good time.

These Christian ideas contrast sharply with the secularist views spread by proponents of assisted suicide and euthanasia. When they talk about "quality of life," they mean, not a person's holiness and readiness to do God's will, but only the proportion between his or her enjoyable experiences and sufferings. Insofar as suffering becomes unavoidable and cannot be eased, they consider it as meaningless, useless, degrading. And so they advocate "death with dignity," by which they mean ending life when and as one chooses so as to avoid physical pain, debility, bowel and bladder incontinence, and so on[142]—harms that, despite their repulsiveness and unfittingness for persons, cannot detract from anyone's essential human dignity.

Such secularist views are widespread, and both the staff and the residents of the nursing home undoubtedly are being influenced by them. You must counter them, especially by reminding your friends of the dignity with which Jesus suffered and died, of the salvific meaning of his doing so, and of the Easter glory to which his obedience brought him. Made in God's image and likeness, and called to share in Jesus' glory, we too enjoy a dignity that cannot be taken from us—though we can violate it by sin, not least the terrible sin of deliberately ending human life, whether another's or our own (see *CCC*, 2268, 2276–83). And we too, invited by Jesus to take up our cross and follow him, can accept unavoidable suffering as part of our noble vocation, share by that acceptance in the salvific meaning of Jesus' suffering, and hope confidently to share in his glory.[143]

---

142. For a concise and sound treatment of how to deal with such problems, see Cicely Saunders and Mary Baines, *Living with Dying: The Management of Terminal Disease,* 2nd ed. (Oxford: Oxford University Press, 1989).

143. See John Paul II, *Salvifici doloris (On the Christian Meaning of Human Suffering),* 19–27, *AAS* 76 (1984) 225–42, *OR,* 20 Feb. 1984, 4–7. With regard to advanced directives, see *LCL,* 528–30, and q. 44, below.

44: What must an elderly person do to stay
alive and healthy?

I am a widow, seventy-one-years old; my husband died of Parkinson's disease two years ago at seventy-four. I have adjusted fairly well, and keep busy working around the house, visiting with family and friends, and helping out at our parish. My income is adequate, and I have no real worries about future needs. Still, life no longer means as much to me as it did when my husband was alive. I think more about heaven than I used to, and it seems more real as I look forward to it. This hope has made me less anxious about most other things.

I had a major operation five years ago and another about a year ago. They were successful, but the tests beforehand and the aftermath were extremely difficult both times, and taking care of myself as I recuperated last year was very hard. During the past few years I also have been bothered with three smaller health problems for which there is no treatment, as I learned in each case after unpleasant and complicated tests. The operations and the tests cost a great deal. Though most of the expense was covered by Medicare or my supplemental insurance, those big bills bother me, because other people eventually have to bear the cost. That, along with everything else, has set me thinking.

It occurs to me that perhaps I may—and maybe even should—do without most health care from now on, and let nature take its course. My grandparents and other elderly people did that when I was young, though of course they had little choice. I would continue taking medicine I know I need, getting flu shots, and doing other simple things, but I would do without more difficult and costly things. Would there be anything wrong with that? If it would be all right, where should I draw the line?

Of course, if it would be all right and I do cut back, there might come a time when I no longer can make these decisions for myself. Then I would want done only what it would be wrong not to go along with. I have looked at different forms of a living will (sometimes called an "advance directive"), but did not feel sure about them, and so have not signed any. I wonder if one or another of them would suit my purpose.

I have talked with several friends about my idea. They don't like it and don't want it to get around. If some senior citizens voluntarily start doing without most examinations and operations, they say, the government is likely to decide that all elderly people can do without them, and then Medicare will stop covering such things. One of my friends pointed out that some writers already are claiming that the elderly are getting more than their fair share of health care, and arguing for a cutoff after a certain age.

I also have a question about eating. About ten years ago, both my husband and I had high cholesterol. Rather than take medicine, we began to walk more and changed to a strict, low-fat diet. I never have been overweight and am not about to make a pig of myself now. But the diet limits what I can offer guests and eat when I visit others, and often is inconvenient in other ways, such as requiring more frequent shopping. I would like to forget it and take a more relaxed approach. I might not live as long, but do I have to be so careful?

Analysis:

This inquiry includes three distinct questions. The basic question bears upon the extent and limits of an elderly person's obligation to employ various means of health care. In principle, the answer is the same for the elderly as for everyone else. One may not omit health care with the intention of ending one's life, and one should try to survive and function long enough to fulfill one's other responsibilities. But within these limits, one should consider the benefits and burdens of available means of health care and conscientiously judge whether to accept what is available. A subordinate problem is whether the questioner could ensure, by some sort of living will, that her policy of limiting health care would be followed if she became incompetent. The answer is no. Since judgment is needed to compare the benefits and burdens of means under consideration, only a suitable proxy is likely to be able to safeguard her interests. The third question concerns the obligation to diet. For younger people, other responsibilities generally require limiting health risks; but for people without other responsibilities, temperance calls only for reasonable moderation in eating. So, the relaxation of diet proposed by this elderly questioner also could be morally acceptable.

The reply could be along the following lines:

Your reference to your grandparents and others of their generation points to one factor contributing to the problem that concerns you. Health care technology has developed with increasing rapidity during the twentieth century; many new operations, tests, and so on are available today; hospitals and diagnostic centers are filled with more sophisticated equipment; and highly trained specialists deliver far more of the care. Economic obstacles to using this vast technology have been dealt with by private insurance and government programs that have relieved many individuals and families of much of the cost.[144]

Partly for this reason, partly because many physicians make decisions on narrowly technical grounds, partly due to their defensiveness about malpractice lawsuits, and partly due to their fundamentally sound commitment to promote their patients' health and preserve their lives, practitioners often recommend or even insist on trying every means of health care that offers any prospective benefit, with little or no regard to its cost or its burdensomeness to the patient. Docilely accepting their physicians' unilateral judgments, many patients, probably most, gladly abdicate their own primary responsibility to care for themselves. Even many people who want to make their own health care decisions have been intimidated by professionals' expertise and the wizardry of their techniques. Moreover, the increasingly high valuation placed in affluent societies upon survival, healthful functioning, and freedom from pain has tended to detach these goods from other elements of human well-being and even to absolutize them, so that more people now than in the past are likely to make health care decisions without reference to their impact on the rest of the patient's life and on the legitimate interests of others. Much more can be done today to keep elderly persons alive, and

144. See William L. Kissick, *Medicine's Dilemmas: Infinite Needs versus Finite Resources* (New Haven, Conn.: Yale University Press, 1994), 1–10, 23–32.

both physicians and patients also are more likely to suppose that whatever can be done must be done.

By contrast, you have been thinking about how health care fits into your life as a whole. Moreover, while people all too often ignore the fact that doing everything possible can become unfair to others, you rightly recognize that care paid for by government programs and private insurance ultimately imposes costs on other people and these costs should be taken into account. Thus, you perceive a moral issue: How far should you go in trying to stay alive and healthy?

Besides the limit fairness sets to seeking care, every decision about health care should meet two other definite requirements. First, since suicide is always wrong, one may never choose to do or omit anything so as to bring about one's death—for instance, to relieve others of burdens or to forestall further suffering. Second, one should try to be healthy enough and survive long enough to fulfill all one's other duties. The first norm can be violated by those who choose to limit treatment for the sake of "death with dignity," for they can be seeking death as a way to avoid so-called indignity, and choosing to refuse treatment as a means of bringing about death. Nothing you say suggests you are thinking of suicide. The second norm can be violated by people who still have pressing responsibilities to fulfill—family, work, something else—or who need time to prepare for death and put their affairs in order. It seems that you no longer have exigent responsibilities to others, and I assume you are prepared spiritually and in other ways for death, and will take care to remain so.

People lacking hope are likely either to cling to life too greedily or else to regard death unreasonably as an escape to which they are entitled when they no longer find life worth living. But no matter how old and debilitated one is, life is God's gift, which always remains a blessing. And, though death always is an evil that may never be sought, Christians not only should resign themselves to it but spiritually prepare for it and anticipate it with joy, insofar as it is the ultimate opportunity to share in Jesus' sacrifice and the only gateway to heaven (see q. 43, above). Therefore, your more detached attitude toward this present life and more intense hope for heaven seem to me entirely sound.

Within the definite limits already explained, you and other elderly people should judge what health care to accept in the same way younger people should, namely, in terms of prospective benefits and burdens (see *LCL,* 524–32). The prospective benefits of any available means of health care are its likely contributions to promoting or protecting intelligible goods; its prospective burdens are its likely adverse effects in terms of intelligible goods. Each time you have a decision to make, you must exclude unreasonable motives (such as fear recognized as excessive and the sadness of depression), consider and compare the reasons for and against accepting treatment in terms of its prospective benefits and burdens, and judge which set of reasons makes a better case.

While nobody can make that judgment for you, I can indicate the limits and what to take into account.

Since life and health are good in themselves, not merely as conditions for pursuing other goods, prolonging life and maintaining or restoring healthful functioning always are benefits. In several ways, however, aging tends to reduce the cogency of reasons for accepting many sorts of health care. The older one gets, the less time one has left, no matter what steps one takes to extend life, and the fewer possibilities of healthful functioning remain. Thus, the prospects for developing one's gifts and using them to serve others gradually lessen. Moreover, generally even the most successful operations and best remedies only slow one's decline rather than reverse it; health care more and more staves off death rather than restores functioning. Then too, though anyone who can think and make choices always can do things of great human value, such as pray, the possibilities of attaining many goods inevitably decrease with aging, so that life and health have less instrumental value. Thus, though you have adjusted fairly well, your widowhood makes a significant difference. Marital responsibilities no longer require you to take care of your health and preserve your life; you now have more freedom to accept death because your husband no longer needs your companionship and help, and you spend your time in activities that are not exigent responsibilities—working about the house, visiting with family and friends, and helping out at your parish. Besides, since your life is less rich and your life expectancy is growing ever shorter, the benefits of lifesaving procedures are fewer for you than when you were younger and had more to look forward to in this world.

Health care also always involves burdens, several of which you mention. Many means involve risks of death or disability, suppress or interfere with normal functioning for some time, and/or are painful. Many also have bad side effects for other goods by preventing one from moving about freely, isolating one from family and friends, and/or interfering with one's inner life. As one ages, burdens usually grow more serious as the ability to deal with them decreases due to diminishing personal powers and decreasing help from loved ones, who also decline and die. And all health care imposes economic costs, for the most part, usually, on other people. Even if accepting these costs is fair, Christians often may and sometimes should forgo health care to which they are entitled so that the resources will be available for others in need.

In view of the many ways aging tends to decrease the prospective benefits and increase the prospective burdens of many means of health care, it seems to me that people like you, whose other, stringent responsibilities no longer require efforts to stay alive and healthy, might well judge that a difficult and costly major operation or examination is not appropriate for them. So, you might well conclude that it is appropriate to forgo some currently available, technological means of health care. If you do, there will be nothing wrong in doing without them. However, no clear line can be drawn, since no general policy could take into account the impact on you of the shifting combinations of more and less foreseeable burdens and benefits of diverse means that might be used to diagnose or treat more and less serious health problems. Therefore, a fresh judgment will be needed each time you must make a choice.

Obviously, to judge properly, you must have relevant information. To gather facts, you must continue to have regular checkups and at least obtain an initial assessment of any new symptoms. Moreover, since many conditions that are easily treated if caught in time become far more serious if neglected, it would be a great mistake to neglect or put off seeing your primary care physician. However, when that physician proposes that you see a specialist, undergo a further test or examination, or go into a hospital, you can ask about the pros and cons, and then decide whether to accept the proposal. Similarly, you can insist on explanations so that you can judge for yourself whether to take the advice of specialists to submit to difficult tests and examinations, undergo surgery, or be hospitalized. Even if you become gravely ill and some professional care is indispensable, you can consider alternatives to hospitalization, such as nursing care in your own residence or terminal care in a hospice.

Someone might object that what I have said would allow you to decide to forgo examinations such as sigmoidoscopies and mammograms, which are ordinary means of detecting early cancer, and simple, lifesaving major surgery such as a hysterectomy to deal with uterine cancer. Three things can be said in reply.

First, at present you very likely would decide that all or some of the procedures mentioned as examples are appropriate, and you probably will refuse them only if changing circumstances lead you to consider their prospective benefits less and their prospective burdens greater than at present. Who would argue that a permanently bedridden, ninety-year-old woman has a moral obligation to continue undergoing regular sigmoidoscopies and mammograms, or to submit to a hysterectomy and other aggressive treatment of incipient cervical cancer? Between that woman's condition and yours at present, however, lie a continuum of conditions each differing only infinitesimally from the next. Somewhere a line must be drawn, and I simply have said that only you can rightly draw it for yourself.

Second, if you thought you could spend your retirement more peacefully and comfortably on a remote tropical isle that happens to lack modern health care services, I doubt that anyone would consider your choice to move there morally wrong. But if you could rightly forgo such services in avoiding the distractions of life in an affluent society, why should it be wrong to forgo them to avoid the various burdens they entail?

Third, to say such examinations and surgery are "ordinary" means is ambiguous. If that signifies *common* in affluent societies, I concede, but no ethical conclusion follows. If it means *always morally obligatory,* I deny, and the objection simply begs the question at issue.

How should you answer your friends' objections? If they still have exigent family or other responsibilities—for example, toward grandchildren who are not being brought up well, toward friends who need spiritual help—make it clear that they still have a reason to take care of themselves that you no longer share. Make it clear, as well, that you still consider your life a precious gift of God and have no intention of killing yourself by neglect, but only of forgoing health care you judge excessively burdensome for you.

The public authorities could not soundly use the explanation I have given as an argument for denying difficult and expensive tests and surgery to elderly people. Elderly people do receive a larger than average share of health care, but that does not show that any elderly person is receiving more than his or her fair share, since fairness depends on factors such as need and potential benefit. Using age as a criterion for denying or rationing health care would be unjust, since age does not of itself specify anyone's responsibility to tend to health problems or affect the burdens and benefits of the various means available.[145] Indeed, as has been explained, no general criteria can adequately guide reasonable health care decisions. Thus, if self-denial by some were used as an excuse for official denial to all, government would preempt individuals' responsibility to judge what is suitable for themselves. Furthermore, insofar as mercy toward others is part of one's motive for forgoing health care to which one is entitled, to limit everyone similarly would unjustly impose what should be an act of free self-giving.

In the absence of a sound argument for using age as a criterion for rationing health care, doing so would be manifestly discriminatory. Recognizing themselves as victims of discrimination, the elderly would pose a formidable threat to any officeholder or candidate tempted to treat them unfairly. Thus, your friends' worries almost certainly are excessive.[146] At the same time, if elderly people are just and merciful in using available resources, younger people are less likely to resent the cost of sustaining them and more likely to respect their rights.

The factors requiring judgment about what health care to accept and making it impossible to draw a clear line also make it impossible to draw up a satisfactory living will (advance directive) limiting what will be done for you and to you if you become incapable of making decisions for yourself. Any such directive will be so vague in some respects as to leave the judgment to care givers, and so specific in other respects as to allow many things a reasonable person might well refuse while perhaps excluding some things such a person would accept in certain circumstances. Moreover, a living will is likely to be interpreted too broadly by some health care providers, especially as euthanasia becomes more common, and to be ignored by others, who will provide unwanted care unless a court orders them to desist.

There is an alternative to signing a living will, namely, designating someone you trust to make health care judgments and choices on your behalf when you no longer can do so, and then discussing your views about the burdens and benefits of various sorts of means with the person you designate, so that he or she will gain

145. This proposition is entirely consistent with what I have said above about the significance of aging. People age at different rates, so that some eighty-year-old persons can get greater real benefit from various health care measures than most people who are only sixty. So, making seventy the cut off for any particular form of health care would be unreasonable. Thus, I disagree with Daniel Callahan, *Setting Limits: Medical Goals in an Aging Society* (New York: Simon and Schuster, 1988), 115–58, who argues that age can be a valid principle for cutting off governmental support for various forms of health care. However, if fairly applied, a criterion based on life expectancy could be reasonable—e.g., that for those whose life expectancy is less than six months, public programs will pay only for palliative care. But such a criterion would apply to everyone regardless of age.

146. This statement probably is not true for people in some countries other than the United States. In some affluent nations, age already is being used as a basis for discrimination with respect to health care, employment, and other matters. Under such conditions, elderly individuals renouncing health care that they could rightly seek or accept should do what they can to prevent their action from indirectly contributing to injustice against other elderly people.

insight into your thinking and desires (see *LCL,* 528–29). You would do well to consider this approach.

As for your low-fat diet, you no longer have the reason to follow it that you had while your husband was alive. When taking meals with others, you plainly have a good reason to set it aside and accept somewhat greater health risks from higher cholesterol. Temperance in eating requires only reasonable moderation, not the healthiest possible diet, and you intend not to eat so much as to become overweight. Therefore, it seems to me that you need not be as careful as you have been. At the same time, you might regard the reasonable restraint still necessary as a sort of fast in preparation for the heavenly wedding banquet!

Finally, though you can rightly limit your efforts to sustain your life, never regard the time that remains to you as useless. Even if your capacities gradually fail, you will be able to do much good for yourself and others—for example, by praying for the living and the dead, and offering your sufferings for the needs of the Church and the world.

Among those you pray for, please include me and my work. I pray that your hope will be fulfilled and you will rejoin your husband in heaven.

45: Will one spouse's rejection of euthanasia for the other violate the Golden Rule?

You may be surprised to receive this letter from the Netherlands. A law student—a real Catholic—who met you last year is helping me write it. He will send it from his computer, and I hope you will be able to answer quickly.

My husband, Pieter, is sixty-three. Five months ago he had a stroke. At first it did not seem so bad, and we hoped he would even be able to walk. But three weeks later it happened again, and the damage was more severe. Pieter probably will never be able to walk and can use only his left hand. Still, after six more weeks I was able to bring him home.

With a nurse who comes for the day, I can care for Pieter. Though he cannot speak well, he has some words. We understand each other, and he prays with me. But taking care of him is not easy. He knows it, and during the first month or so at home he was very sad. He was sorry to be such a burden to me and wished he had died in the hospital.

For more than a month now Pieter has had a cough. Dr. Klaussen has come every week, but the cough is not getting better. He says it is not yet pneumonia but probably will come to that. Yesterday the doctor asked me to step outside, and he talked about euthanasia. He told me one need no longer have any qualms about it, that it is perfectly legal. He wants to do it, and seems to want my consent. He said "it is the right time for us to help Pieter be released from his useless body."

That upset me. This morning I went to talk about it with the pastoral worker who brings Communion. I thought she was a real Catholic, because she does everything just as it is in the book, and earlier she encouraged Pieter when he was sad.

I told the pastoral worker I do not think it would be right for me to agree with the doctor to kill Pieter. She said Dr. Klaussen is a good physician, and I should go along with what he thinks best. I questioned that, and she pointed out that we Catholics believe "life is changed, not ended" at death, and that St. Paul says "we would rather be away from the body and at home with the Lord" (2 Cor 5.8). She also asked me: "Would you want to be in your husband's condition?" I said no. But if I make Pieter go on as he is, she said, I will be making him be as I do not want to be myself, and that would be against the Lord's word, "Do to others . . .." I wondered if we should ask Pieter what he wants. She said no; that would upset him uselessly and put too much of a burden on him.

I am not sure what to say to Dr. Klaussen next week when he comes. I still do not want to have him kill Pieter. But neither do I want to go against the Lord's word.

Analysis:

This question concerns the proper application of the Golden Rule. Since it is a moral principle for evaluating one's actions affecting others, not for evaluating their situations or conditions, the relevant issue is whether the questioner would want euthanasia. That killing would be wrong, however, and she should not want it for herself. Even if she did, the Golden Rule would not justify killing her husband—which she rightly does not want done. The response should include a refutation of the pastoral worker's unsound arguments. The doctor may be a technically good physician, but his training and expertise lend no authority to his judgments about killing, since killing not only is wrong in itself but outside medical competence. The legalization of euthanasia does not affect its intrinsic immorality. Asking a person whether he or she wanted euthanasia would be scandalous in the strict sense.

The reply could be along the following lines:

The Lord's word mentioned by the pastoral worker, which often is called *the Golden Rule,* is: "Do to others as you would have them do to you" (Mt 7.12, Lk 6.31). This principle concerns what one does and what one would have others do, not people's situations or conditions and whether one would want to be in them. So, the pastoral worker's question, "Would you want to be in your husband's condition," was misleading. Nobody wants to be severely handicapped, but that does not imply everyone should help do away with those who are.[147]

The pastoral worker's question would not have been misleading had she straightforwardly asked: "If you were in your husband's condition, would you want to be killed?" Not thinking that right, you would have said no. Then it would have been clear that you will not violate the Golden Rule by rejecting Dr. Klaussen's

---

147. For an argument against legalizing euthanasia, see Germain Grisez and Joseph M. Boyle, Jr., *Life and Death with Liberty and Justice: A Contribution to the Euthanasia Debate* (Notre Dame, Ind.: University of Notre Dame Press, 1979), 86–250. Also see The New York State Task Force on Life and the Law, *When Death Is Sought: Assisted Suicide and Euthanasia in the Medical Context* (New York, N.Y.: May 1994); this body made a careful study and, despite the great diversity of its members, reached a unanimous and cogently argued conclusion against legalization. Michael Burleigh, *Death and Deliverance: 'Euthanasia' in Germany, c. 1900–1945* (Cambridge, England: Cambridge University Press, 1994), provides an unbiased history of euthanasia in Germany under the Nazi regime; despite the unique features of that history, Burleigh's account helps clarify various aspects of the mentality and arguments of those who now favor euthanasia.

proposal to kill Pieter. Thus, the pastoral worker's argument that you should consent was fallacious. She assumed that euthanasia is morally acceptable, which was the precise point at issue.

Even if you agreed that you would want to be killed if you were handicapped as Pieter is, you would not be bound by the Lord's word to consent to euthanasia for him. The Golden Rule assumes that those to whom it is addressed act rightly toward themselves, so that they would not have anyone do anything to them against any of the Lord's words. But choosing to kill an innocent person or consenting to another's proposal to do so, even as a means of ending the person's suffering, is against God's commandment, "You shall not kill," which Jesus reaffirmed and the Church has held and taught constantly and most firmly.[148] Nobody violates the Golden Rule by refusing to consent to euthanasia, and, indeed, anyone who consents to it violates the Golden Rule.

The pastoral worker's argument also was fallacious in supposing that, if you do not consent to euthanasia, you will "make Pieter go on as he is." That implies you would be at fault for not ending his suffering. But that would be true only if your refusal of consent were a wrongful omission—that is, if you had an obligation to consent to euthanasia to end Pieter's suffering and failed to fulfill it. Thus, once again, the pastoral worker's argument assumed what it was meant to prove.

Moreover, though killing your husband would end the suffering he experiences due to the damage from the strokes, Dr. Klaussen erred in saying euthanasia would "help Pieter be released from his useless body." That supposes a person is some sort of spiritual being who only has and uses his or her body, so that death can be liberation, a good and great benefit to the person. But the human person is a bodily being, for whom death cannot be a benefit.[149] As St. Paul teaches, death will remain a great evil until the end of time: "The last enemy to be destroyed is death" (1 Cor 15.26).

Of course, we also believe that the soul, the spiritual part of the person, survives death. But the separated soul is not the whole person, as St. Thomas says in explaining the need for bodily resurrection: "Now, since the soul is part of the human body, it is not the entire human being, and my soul is not I. So, even if the soul reached salvation in another life, neither I nor any human being would thereby do so."[150] Though ending Pieter's life would end his suffering and his soul would survive, only God's gift of resurrection life will release Pieter himself not only from all suffering but from the far greater evil of death.

---

148. Ex 20.13, Dt 5.17, Mt 19.18, Mk 10.19, Lk 18.20; cf. *CCC,* 2268, 2276–83; John Paul II, *Veritatis splendor,* 6, 13, 15, 17, 52, *AAS* 85 (1993) 1138, 1143, 1145, 1147, 1175–76, *OR,* 6 Oct. 1993, ii, iii, viii; *Evangelium vitae,* 64–67, *AAS* 87 (1995) 474–80, *OR,* 5 Apr. 1995, xii–xiii. Also see, *LCL,* 459–88; Luke Gormally, ed., *Euthanasia, Clinical Practice and the Law* (London: The Linacre Centre, 1994), 37–58, 118–33.

149. See *CCC,* 362–65; John Finnis, Joseph M. Boyle, Jr., and Germain Grisez, *Nuclear Deterrence, Morality and Realism* (Oxford: Oxford University Press, 1987), 304–9; Patrick Lee, "Human Beings Are Animals," in *Natural Law and Moral Inquiry: Ethics, Metaphysics, and Politics in the Thought of Germain Grisez,* ed. Robert P. George, forthcoming.

150. St. Thomas, *Super primam epistolam ad Corinthios lectura,* commenting on 1 Cor 15.19; see *LCL,* 464–67.

The phrase "life is changed, not ended" expresses a truth of Christian faith, but it does not support the view that the person is a spiritual being who is liberated by death. Rather, it expresses Christian hope in bodily resurrection, which overcomes the evil of death by restoring the bodily person to a better, an immortal life:

> In him, who rose from the dead, our hope of resurrection dawned.
> The sadness of death gives way to the bright promise of immortality.
> Lord, for your faithful people life is changed, not ended.
> When the body of our earthly dwelling lies in death
> we gain an everlasting dwelling place in heaven.[151]

Likewise, St. Paul's Christian preference for being away from the body and at home with the Lord does not imply that the human person is a spirit who is liberated by death. A few verses before the one cited by the pastoral worker, Paul clearly expresses the Christian hope, which is not to be free from a body, but to be more perfectly embodied:

> For we know that if the earthly tent we live in is destroyed, we have a building from God, a house not made with hands, eternal in the heavens. For in this tent we groan, longing to be clothed with our heavenly dwelling—if indeed, when we have taken it off we will not be found naked. For while we are still in this tent, we groan under our burden, because we wish not to be unclothed but to be further clothed, so that what is mortal may be swallowed up by life. (2 Cor 5.1–4)

And, immediately after saying "we would rather be away from the body and at home with the Lord" (2 Cor 5.8), Paul makes it clear that this preference must be subordinated to God's will: "So whether we are at home or away, we make it our aim to please him. For all of us must appear before the judgment seat of Christ, so that each may receive recompense for what has been done in the body, whether good or evil" (2 Cor 5.9–10; cf. Rom 14.7–8). Therefore, Paul's Christian preference for being away from the body and at home with the Lord should not be taken to mean a person is liberated by death nor used to argue for euthanasia.

Dr. Klaussen may be a capable physician. But perhaps, thinking euthanasia will solve the problem, he is failing to treat Pieter's cough as vigorously as he might. Even if he is not falling short in that respect, physicians' judgments are authoritative only on matters within their competence, which is to sustain life and promote health. Killing obviously does neither. So, even if euthanasia were morally permissible, a decision about it would be beyond Dr. Klaussen's competence. Moreover, his technical capabilities as a physician do not lend authority to his moral judgments. The legalization of euthanasia, to which he appeals, in no way eliminates or lessens its intrinsic immorality.[152] Therefore, the pastoral worker also is mistaken in supposing you "should go along with what he thinks best."

---

151. *The Roman Missal: The Sacramentary,* Preface of Christian Death I.

152. Strictly speaking, euthanasia has not been legalized in the Netherlands. However, court decisions and governmental actions have generated a state of affairs in which physicians are not punished for killing patients even without their consent. Drawing on a Dutch governmental report (the Remmelink Report) of 1991, Richard Fenigsen, "Euthanasia in the Netherlands," in *Encyclopedia of U.S. Biomedical Policy,* ed. Robert H. Blank and Janna C. Merrick (Westport, Conn.: Greenwood Press, 1996), 72–76, states that in 1990 the rule that active euthanasia can only be carried out at the request of the patient was followed in 5,859 cases and disregarded in 5,941 cases;

Now that he wishes to kill Pieter, Dr. Klaussen is a threat to his life, and no longer a good physician for him. A good physician cooperates with patients in protecting and promoting life and health, and always limits what he or she does by each patient's judgment as to what is acceptable. By contrast, Dr. Klaussen is prepared to kill your husband without his consent. If possible, then, keep the doctor from getting near him again, just as you would keep any other would-be killer away. Besides, if Dr. Klaussen is not providing the care Pieter needs, it would be appropriate to replace him with someone who would vigorously treat the cough and possible pneumonia. So, if you can, and even at the cost of considerable inconvenience and expense, you ought to replace this dangerous person with a competent physician who absolutely excludes euthanasia.

But perhaps you have no alternative to accepting Dr. Klaussen's medical service. In that case, make it very clear to him that you reject his offer of euthanasia as a proposal to kill your husband and try to elicit his promise not to carry it out. But do not rely on that promise. Someone willing to kill is likely to be willing to lie. Closely watch anything he does and check out anything he prescribes as carefully as you can.

Ironically, the pastoral worker was right about one thing: You should not ask your husband what he wants with regard to euthanasia. Severely handicapped and suffering, he might well consider euthanasia and be tempted to request it, so that asking him what he wants would be scandalous in the strict sense—it would gravely risk leading him into temptation and sin (see *LCL,* 232–39). Moreover, raising the question would suggest you are willing to have him killed, and he might interpret that as an indication that you no longer are unconditionally committed to him as a faithful wife should be, but have come to regard him as a problem to be solved, a burden to be got rid of.

Still, if you cannot replace Dr. Klaussen, it might be appropriate—only you can judge—to warn Pieter that the doctor proposed euthanasia, tell him you absolutely rejected that proposal and will never consent to it, and urge him to tell the doctor something like: I want God, not you, to decide when it is time for me to die; please do not take it upon yourself to murder me.

You also probably should seek better pastoral care for Pieter. Since the pastoral worker supports killing him, she may urge him to consider and request euthanasia. Even if she does not, her acceptance of euthanasia is likely to prevent her from

---

when patients' lives were terminated without their request, consultations with other doctors were omitted in 52% of the cases and except in one case doctors did not state the truth in the death certificate. John Keown, "Further Reflections on Euthanasia in The Netherlands in the Light of The Remmelink Report and The Van Der Maas Survey," in Gormally, ed., op. cit., 219–40, analyzes the same document in greater detail, but comes (236) to essentially the same conclusion: "Doctors have killed with impunity. And on a scale previously only guessed at: the Survey discloses that it was the primary purpose of doctors to shorten the lives of over 10,000 patients in 1990, the majority without the patient's explicit request." Herbert Hendin, *Seduced by Death: Doctors, Patients, and the Dutch Cure* (New York: W. W. Norton, 1997), 21–134, provides evidence, including detailed reports of interviews with leading Dutch advocates and practictioners of euthanasia, supporting Fenigsen's and Keown's analyses and revealing the disingenuousness of attempts to explain away the facts.

providing him with the spiritual support he needs to persevere in faith and hope despite his hardships. But if you cannot arrange for a more faithful person to replace her, do not leave Pieter alone with her unless he requests it.

Finally, I would like to make a suggestion that goes beyond your question. You say taking care of Pieter is not easy, and probably it will become harder as time goes by. You also say he was sorry to be a burden to you and wished he had died in the hospital. Even if that feeling and wish have subsided, they are likely to return. But you and Pieter can still communicate with each other and pray together. I suggest that, in your prayers, you meditate on the fact that our Lord Jesus suffered for us.

This *for us* is mysterious and rich in meaning, but at least partly it means this: Jesus accepted suffering and death because only in them could he love us as fully as a man can love his brothers and sisters, only by them could he draw us most strongly to himself, and only through them could he reach the glory of his resurrection and bring us, if we but follow him, to share in that glory. The situation in which you and Pieter find yourselves inevitably seems a burden to be resented, and by no means a blessing to be welcomed. But perhaps you already realize that, in allowing both of you to suffer, God is calling you to love each other more perfectly and become more intimate with his Son. Try to accept your hard situation, and encourage Pieter to accept it, as an opportunity to bear witness to your faith and hope, to grow in love and holiness, and to merit for yourselves unending life together in heaven. With that acceptance, the miserable burden, no longer only yours but also Jesus', will, as he promised, become light for you, strengthened by the power that raised him to heavenly glory.

46: Should a wife consent to removing her husband's respirator "to get it over with"?

My husband, Roger, is seventy-one. He smoked heavily for many years and retired from his job as a lithographer nine years ago because of health problems. Six years ago he had surgery to improve circulation in his legs, finally quit smoking, and was better for a while. But in the past year or two he has had more and more problems. Hating hospitals as he did, Roger put off dealing with his problems as long as he could. In the end, the doctors said he needed a multiple bypass and an operation on his right carotid artery. Two weeks ago today, the surgeon worked on Roger about six hours. Something went wrong, and he has been in intensive care since then. He breathes with a respirator, is fed through a tube to his stomach, and receives all sorts of medications intravenously.

The doctor had warned us that, even if Roger's surgery went well, his recovery would be difficult, because he has so many health problems. But whatever went wrong during the surgery damaged his brain. He is not what they call "brain dead," but they say he has not come to. Still, when I talk to him and stroke his forehead, I sense that he responds. A tear comes to his eye and his face softens, as if he were about to smile.

On the fifth day they did an encephalogram. It was "very abnormal." The next day, which was our golden wedding anniversary, a brain scan was done, and the doctors talked with me. The neurologist told me the scan showed many damaged spots on both sides of Roger's brain and in different parts of it, and said he would never regain consciousness. When I said he responds to me, the surgeon said I am imagining it. He argued that if Roger were conscious, he would show signs of needing the sedation that had to be withdrawn on the third day (to exclude it as a possible cause of his not waking up). The neurologist and the surgeon also agreed that, even if Roger regained consciousness, he never would enjoy any "real quality of life." The intensive care doctor took the same view and urged that the respirator be removed "to get it over with."

I could not accept that, and the children also were very upset. Our eldest son is involved in a prolife organization whose chairman, Dr. Levi, is a believing Jew who happens to be a neurologist. We got him to come down to the hospital to look at the report on the scan and examine Roger. Dr. Levi also thinks Roger is unconscious, probably never will wake up, and almost certainly will die within a few weeks no matter what is done for him. He told me it does not seem possible that Roger responds as I think he does, but, with a person in his condition, nobody can say for certain. And, though Dr. Levi spoke very gently, he said that, if Roger did wake up, he would be demented, blind, have little or no ability to use language, be unable to recognize things, and be completely or almost completely paralyzed. I asked what to do about the respirator. Dr. Levi said Roger might be able to do without it if he were weaned from it gradually. But he did not want to tell me what to do, since I am not a Jew. So, I talked with the Catholic chaplain at the hospital, who suggested I talk with you.

I hope you can help me make the right decision. The intensive care doctors have said over and over that Roger could survive for a long time, but will die of something sooner or later, and in his condition, it might as well be sooner. Yet I still cannot bring myself to agree. At the same time, though Roger never told anyone what he would want in this sort of situation, I am sure he would not want to go on with intensive care without hope of recovering. The intensive care unit seems to me more intensive than caring; I sometimes imagine it is a horrible laboratory where mad scientists are experimenting on people. Going on also will be difficult for me. Even though Medicare will cover most of the cost, the bills will add up. Then too, I have to be driven to the hospital, which is in the city, forty miles away, because I have never got used to driving in heavy traffic.

Perhaps you should know that Roger is not a Catholic. He was raised as a Baptist and always has been a good man and a serious Christian. But because he smoked and drank, his church refused to baptize him, and, except for special occasions such as weddings and funerals, he never would go into a church again. Still, he supported me in raising our children as Catholics, and I must confess that since the last of our children left home ten years ago, he has been more faithful to religion than I have. He has continued spending every Sunday morning reading the Bible and praying, while I have been going to Mass only occasionally.

Analysis:

The question is what sort of care is morally required and appropriate for this patient. The questioner rightly rejects the homicidal proposal to remove the respirator so as "to get it over with." Though intensive care benefits the patient insofar as it helps him survive, it also imposes significant burdens. To remove the respirator in order to avoid such burdens would not be homicidal. However, withdrawing the respirator suddenly would be morally questionable, since that would deprive the patient of all care and risk leading others in similar cases to engage in homicide. A morally acceptable alternative would be to remove the patient from intensive care and attempt to wean him from the respirator. The questioner should be encouraged to have her husband baptized as soon as possible and to repent her neglect of her faith.

The reply could be along the following lines:

Despite the great difficulty of your painful situation, you have put the question very clearly. I can respond briefly and directly. First, I agree with you that the respirator should not be removed unless Roger is weaned from it gradually. Second, you should consider removing him from intensive care. Third, if Roger is removed from intensive care, other care appropriate to his present condition should be continued. I shall explain each of these three points.

The physician who urged that Roger's respirator be removed "to get it over with" apparently thinks its rapid removal would bring about death and that would be a good thing—not, of course, in itself but as a means of resolving the present situation. Believing Roger never will enjoy "real quality of life," he and the other physicians think his life should be ended. Removing the respirator would do that as surely and promptly as anything else, and undoubtedly it would be more psychologically acceptable to the physicians than, say, giving Roger a deadly drug. Moreover, if you agreed, they could remove the respirator without risking professional and/or legal sanctions. Still, it seems clear that the proposal to remove Roger's respirator was homicidal. Since consenting would have been consenting to murder, you rightly rejected it.

By contrast with the physicians' thinking, yours is sound and reasonable. Desiring that Roger live, and expecting that removing the respirator would lead promptly to his death, you cannot bring yourself to agree. Yet you believe Roger "would not want to go on with intensive care without hope of recovering," and you are quite reasonably concerned about its mounting costs and other burdens on you and others.[153]

I believe someone thinking about a similar case *could* decide to remove the respirator without judging that the patient's quality of life warranted ending it and adopting the proposal to do so. The choice could be simply to end all care of the

---

153. The questioner's statement, "The intensive care unit seems to me more intensive than caring; I sometimes imagine it is a horrible laboratory where mad scientists are experimenting on people," forcefully expresses repugnance to inappropriate, ongoing intensive care. However, it obviously is not an accurate general description of intensive care units and the professionals who staff them. Their skilled and dedicated work generally provides great benefits for suitable patients.

patient so as to avoid the burdens of continuing it. In that choice, the patient's foreseen death would not be intended, but only accepted as a side effect. Even if not homicidal, however, a choice to end all care for anyone is morally questionable for at least two reasons.

First, ending all care would be appropriate only if nothing that could be done for the person would promise any benefit worth the trouble of pursuing it. But even when a patient is in Roger's condition, various measures far short of the intensive care he is receiving can offer significant benefits. One of these is sustaining the patient's life briefly in a more humane environment, until death results less abruptly from underlying pathological conditions. Then too, care can manifest respect and love for the patient as a person, and so provide the benefits inherent in a good interpersonal relationship, both to the one cared for and to everyone who respect-fully and lovingly wants the care to be provided or helps provide it.[154]

Second, even if the intention in ending all care is not homicidal, that step brings about death so surely and abruptly that people generally will find it difficult, even impossible, to distinguish it from homicide. Failing to make a clear distinction, some will go on to approve and even carry out homicidal choices, while only psychological inhibitions will keep some others from doing so. In my judgment, then, a choice to end all care is warranted only if it is morally obligatory—for example, if a shortage of respirators meant continuing care for a patient with very poor prospects would unfairly deprive another patient with far better prospects of care he or she needed to survive and recover.

Dr. Levi plainly doubts that Roger responds to your voice and presence as you think he does, yet he grants—and I agree with him—that nobody can know for certain. In deciding what to do, therefore, take into account your belief that Roger is somewhat aware. If he is, keeping up a losing fight to sustain his life may be imposing an awful burden on him. Put yourself in his place and, bearing in mind his dislike of hospitals, ask whether he would wish to go on with that fight. If not, loving him as you do, you will want a different approach.

Without ending all care for Roger, you could direct that he be moved out of the intensive care unit. Intensive care ordinarily is supplied temporarily to sustain only the lives of people who have some reasonable prospect of recovering sufficiently to go on without it. It is extremely expensive and, even if Medicare covers most of the cost, it burdens taxpayers, and the copayment on the physicians' fees burdens you. Moreover, intensive care facilities are more or less limited and should be available to those likely to benefit more from them. And, as you point out, unless there is some significant likelihood of eventual recovery, this form of care is repugnant both to those who undergo it and to their loved ones. So, intensive care certainly is not morally required for patients unlikely to recover. Therefore, you can rightly have Roger removed from intensive care, and so end the constant monitoring and multiple medications being administered intravenously. In doing that, you need not at once have the respirator removed. But if you have not done

---

154. See Germain Grisez, "Should Nutrition and Hydration Be Provided to Permanently Unconscious and Other Mentally Disabled Persons?" *Linacre Quarterly,* 57:2 (May 1990): 30–43.

so already, you could direct that no emergency measures—resuscitation, emergency surgery, and so on—be taken to sustain his life.

You also can rightly direct that he be weaned from the respirator, so that the machine will not be an obstacle to you and your family and friends being with him as he dies. At the same time, you can direct the attending physicians to leave the stomach tube in place to supply water, nutrition, and any medications he regularly takes by mouth that still would help sustain him. And, given your belief that he is not completely unconscious, it would be reasonable to ask that medication be administered regularly to mitigate his possible suffering, while taking care to avoid suppressing respiration.

In giving these instructions, your intention should be to continue appropriate care until Roger dies from the illness that has caused both him and you so much trouble and suffering, while giving up the clearly hopeless battle indefinitely to sustain his life.

That is not surrendering unconditionally to sickness and death. We look for the resurrection of the dead and the life of the world to come. The care Roger needs most is not for his bodily life but for his soul. Without delay and before removing him from intensive care, tell the hospital chaplain that, though Roger had wanted to be baptized and regularly prayed and read the Bible, he never was baptized. Even if he never chose to become a Catholic, he plainly is a man of faith who desired baptism and showed that he was committed to living a Christian life (see *CIC*, c. 865, §2). If you cannot reach the chaplain or he hesitates to baptize Roger, you can and should do it yourself.

Having seen to Roger's baptism, you will be able to hope that he will soon be in heaven. Wanting, as you surely will, to look forward to joining him there, you should examine yourself and identify the ways you have not been faithful in fulfilling your religious duties, repent and confess those shortcomings as well as any other serious sins, and recommit yourself to a devout Catholic life. I hope and pray that you and Roger will gain by these spiritual means what medical technology cannot give: restored, rich, carefree, and unending life together.

47: May a husband consent to stopping feeding his permanently unconscious wife?

Just over a year ago, my wife, Martha, was operated on for a brain tumor. I rejoiced when the doctor said it was not malignant. But ten days later, due to complications from the first operation, she had to undergo brain surgery again. Something went badly wrong, and she has not regained consciousness, though she did recover, in the sense that in a few weeks her condition stabilized and I was able to have her moved from the hospital to a nursing home. She breathes on her own, is fed through a tube leading directly into her stomach, and goes through a sleeping-waking cycle.

At first I thought Martha sometimes knew when the children and I were there and sometimes smiled when we talked with her. But the doctors, nurses, and chaplain all believed she never was really responsive, and after a few weeks I realized that they were right. The neurologists recently told me they are convinced Martha is in what they call a "persistent vegetative state," from which patients do not recover. Now I no longer expect Martha ever to wake up.

I have come to accept this as God's will. Many people in our parish have been praying for her recovery at particular times each week, so all this time someone has been praying for her from early morning until late at night. But I am not expecting a miracle and feel God has been answering the prayers by strengthening me and blessing the children. We have five, ranging now from eighteen down to six. Despite everything, they are all doing well, caring for one another and even for me, and various relatives, friends, neighbors, and fellow parishioners have given us generous help when we needed it.

They take good care of Martha at the nursing home, keeping her clean, regularly turning her from side to side, monitoring her temperature and so on, treating any sign of infection, and dealing with other health problems just as they do with patients who are alert and responsive. The problem is the cost—more than a hundred dollars a day. The insurance ran out early on. Hoping to get some help with this expense, I had a law firm that specializes in medical malpractice cases look into Martha's operations. The lawyers and their doctor got her records and examined them (for which they did not charge me), but found no grounds for a case against the doctors or the hospital. Since the insurance ran out, I have used more than thirty-five thousand dollars of our savings. If that goes on, the savings will be exhausted within another year, and Medicaid will begin paying most of the bill. But then there will be nothing left for the children's education or for retirement or anything else.

I love my wife, have always been faithful to her, and always will be. The children love their mother and miss her. We certainly do not want her to die. But I do wonder whether there is some way out. A few years ago, she signed a sort of living will, saying that in case of terminal illness she did not wish to be kept alive by means other than those morally required. Does that document give me the right to decide, either now or at some point in the future, that the care she is getting should be stopped? If I do have that right, our family doctor suggested I could end the care most easily by having the feeding tube removed. I know this sounds drastic, but since I now believe Martha never will regain consciousness, it seems to me that she no longer has a life worth living.

Analysis:

The question is what sort of care is morally required and appropriate for this patient. Since removing the feeding tube would save the cost of skilled nursing care as a whole only by bringing about the woman's death, the choice to remove the tube would be homicidal. Since she did not renounce her right to the care appropriate in her present condition, withholding all care would signify lack of love for her and lack of respect for her dignity. Still, the benefits of continuing care in the nursing home are limited and the financial burden is great. So, the questioner is not obliged to continue caring for his wife in that way. The morally acceptable alternative would be to take her elsewhere and care for her within the limits of the human and financial resources that can be reasonably allocated for this purpose.

The reply could be along the following lines:

While I can only dimly imagine your suffering during the past year, I sympathize with you and desire to help you. Nevertheless, I must begin by saying your last remark is mistaken.

Of course, as matters stand, your wife's life has little or no emotional appeal, since your feelings of repugnance toward her present condition quite naturally engulf your feelings about her very survival, taking away your joy in it and negating your desire for it. Moreover, the expression "persistent vegetative state," used to describe her condition, falsely suggests that, since her life no longer serves as the basis for feelings and thoughts and actions, it is now no better than the life of a vegetable.

No human life is a merely instrumental good, however, for a human life is the concrete reality of a living human body, and a person's living body *is* the bodily person (see qq. 43 and 45, above). To deny this is to accept some sort of dualistic theory of human persons—that is, a theory that they actually are bodiless beings who only have, inhabit, and use bodies (see q. 45, above). Therefore, the prospect of sustaining and prolonging any person's life always is a reason for taking measures to do so.[155] It is not always a decisive reason, however, because life is only one among many goods that together comprise a human being's fulfillment, and people's duty to preserve their own and others' lives is limited by the needs of other people and the claims of other goods. In sum, since your wife remains a living person, her life retains its inherent goodness and is a reason, though not necessarily a decisive one, to continue caring for her.

You implicitly acknowledge the goodness of her life in saying you do not want her to die. Though she no longer can actively live her life, she does still have a life worthwhile in itself. Moreover, she has your love and faithfulness, the children's love, the committed care of her nurses, and the good will of others, such as those who pray for her. Some fully conscious people have a good deal less of true human value.

You ask about stopping the care your wife is now receiving and how that might be done, and say your family doctor has suggested removing the tube through which she is fed and given water.[156] I do not know whether the administrators of the

155. In a critique of a preliminary version of this question, Kevin D. O'Rourke, O.P., "Withdrawal of Life Support: Mistaken Assumptions," *Health Progress,* 77:6 (Nov.–Dec. 1996): 61, begs the question by assuming that life is only instrumentally good, denies that prolonging the life of a permanently unconscious person benefits the person, and holds that the "abstract concept of 'intrinsic goodness'" is irrelevant to moral decision making.

156. Council on Ethical and Judicial Affairs, American Medical Association, *Code of Medical Ethics: Current Opinions with Annotations,* 1996–97 ed. (Chicago: American Medical Association, 1996), 2.20, lists (p. 39–40) artificial nutrition and hydration as included in life-sustaining medical treatment and asserts (p. 41): "Even if the patient is not terminally ill or permanently unconscious, it is not unethical to discontinue all means of life-sustaining medical treatment in accordance with a proper substituted judgment or

nursing home would accept such a directive from you. Be that as it may, it seems to me that, morally speaking, you have no right to direct that the tube be removed.

I say this because I think that in giving such a directive you would be reluctantly choosing—though without fully realizing it—to kill your wife. I believe you when you say you and your children do not want your wife to die, and your purpose in giving the directive would be, not to end her life, but to save the cost of caring for her, so that the money saved would be available for other responsibilities. What you cannot afford, however, are not the tube feedings, in themselves not very expensive, but her care in the nursing home as a whole. Removing the feeding tube will solve that problem only by bringing about your wife's death. So, it seems to me, the directive to remove the tube would be a reluctant choice to end her life as a means of ending her costly care, and that choice would be homicidal. If that is correct, though you may end your wife's costly care, you must do so in a different way.

The document your wife signed is not helpful, since it provides directions only about what to do when she is terminally ill. One cannot reasonably call someone "terminally ill" unless he or she either is plainly dying, so that death in a very short time can be predicted with certainty, or is suffering from some disease or injury that predictably will be the cause of death.[157] Neither of those conditions is verified in your wife's case. Rather than being terminally ill, she is very severely handicapped. Her handicap is similar to, though more extreme than, that of a severely retarded person who will never be able to make a choice or even control his or her stream of consciousness.[158] Besides being irrelevant, the document your wife signed is unhelpful in saying that only morally required means shall be used in sustaining life. After all, your question precisely is: What is morally required?

Unfortunately, the Church's explicit teaching provides no clear answer to it. The bishops of the United States have taught: "There should be a presumption in favor of providing nutrition and hydration to all patients, including patients who require medically assisted nutrition and hydration, as long as this is of sufficient benefit to outweigh the burdens involved to the patient."[159] As has been explained, the care

---

best interests analysis." But this opinion is inadequate insofar as it fails to consider the intention with which life-sustaining treatment is discontinued.

157. O'Rourke, op. cit., 60, rejects this definition of *terminally ill* and proposes instead: "A more nuanced concept maintains that a terminal illness is one from which death will result if medical means to prevent or delay death are not used." But this "nuanced concept" plainly is much too broad, since many people who would die without medical intervention recover, and many people who suffer from chronic diseases would die without medical interventions that keep them alive and functioning, though with impairment, for many years.

158. See Stephen L. Mikochik, "When Life Becomes Optional: A Comment on Kevin O'Rourke's Approach to Forgoing Life Support," *Issues in Law and Medicine,* 10 (1994): 343–51; also see Kenneth R. Mitchell and Terence J. Lovat, "Permanently Unconscious Patients and the Ethical Controversies Surrounding Artificial Nutrition and Hydration: Getting the Facts Straight," *Linacre Quarterly,* 60:1 (Feb. 1993): 75–90.

159. National Conference of Catholic Bishops, *Ethical and Religious Directives for Catholic Health Care Services* (Washington, D.C.: United States Catholic Conference, 1995), directive 58; cf. U.S. Bishops' Pro–Life Committee, "Nutrition and Hydration: Moral and Pastoral Reflections," *Origins* 21:44 (9 Apr. 1992): 705–12.

your wife is receiving does benefit her by sustaining her life and in other ways, and it hardly can be thought to burden her. So, you should presume that the feeding tube should not be removed from your wife. But that presumption does not settle the matter, for burdens to others of continuing to provide such care might be so great that it could be rightly ended. For example, in a disaster situation where continuing to provide nutrition and hydration for someone in your wife's condition would prevent helping a person with a good prospect of recovering, a choice to help the latter person surely would not be wrong. Therefore, a line must be drawn, and the question is how and where to draw it.

To clarify what you should do, I shall first explain both the ground and the limits of the obligation to provide life-sustaining care to people who need it.[160]

Since being alive is a condition for participating in other human goods, people ordinarily have strong reasons to do what they can to sustain life. Still, the use of any life-sustaining means imposes some burdens, at least its costs in time and energy, and the resources used to sustain one person's life usually also could be used to sustain another's and perhaps for various other good purposes. Thus, there are limits to the means one need use, or even can rightly use, to sustain any person's life.

When someone is in your wife's condition, most reasons for doing what can be done to sustain his or her life—rather than using the resources for other good purposes—have dropped away, since remaining alive no longer enables the person to share in those goods that involve or presuppose normal consciousness. Since life is inherently good, there still is a reason to sustain it and to care for the gravely debilitated person in every appropriate way; but this reason cannot be considered decisive in determining moral responsibility. Otherwise everyone always would be obligated to use every available means to sustain any person's life. But sound principles of morality do not entail such an exceptionless obligation, in practice nobody acts on it, and the Church implies that it does not exist by teaching that some means can be considered extraordinary and nonobligatory.[161] Therefore, when resources that could be used to sustain someone's life are needed to meet some other serious responsibility, one may use them for that other purpose, provided there is not some reason in addition to human life's inherent goodness for using them to sustain life.

---

160. I previously have treated this question to some extent (*LCL,* 284–86 and 530–32), and shall not repeat that discussion here.

161. Congregation for the Doctrine of the Faith, *Declaration on Euthanasia, AAS* 72 (1980) 549–50, Flannery, 2:514–16, restates previous theological and magisterial teaching that some means of life-sustaining treatment are ordinary and morally required while others can be extraordinary and nonobligatory; this document adds a terminological clarification, according to which *ordinary* and *extraordinary* may be replaced with *proportionate* and *disproportionate,* and immediately explains that the distinction between the two is to be made by comparing burdens and benefits: "In any case, it will be possible to make a correct judgment as to the means by studying the type of treatment to be used, its degree of complexity or risk, its cost and the possibilities of using it, and comparing these elements with the result that can be expected, taking into account the state of the sick person and his or her physical and moral resources" (*AAS* 550, Flannery, 515).

Applying this position to your problem, I think you need not use all your remaining savings and a large part of your future income to continue paying for the care your wife has been receiving, but may use these resources for the other good purposes you mention: your children's education and your retirement savings. If the neurologists are right, your wife never will regain consciousness, and ending skilled nursing will not deprive her of anything that presupposes awareness, though, of course, it probably will shorten her life.[162]

Still, you should do what you reasonably can to care for your wife. Care for anyone in need ordinarily maintains and manifests solidarity with that person: respect and love for him or her as a person. By the same token, failing to do what one can for those in need constitutes and manifests alienation from them: lack of respect and love for them as persons. As Christians, we are called to that love, and failing the least of Jesus' brothers and sisters is failing him (see Mt 25.41–46, 1 Jn 3.17). Hence, life-sustaining care for people in your wife's condition and for others who are very severely handicapped ordinarily does have a human and Christian significance in addition to the one it would derive precisely from the inherent goodness of their lives. This additional significance is not symbolic, in the sense of being a mere gesture effecting no real benefit, but profoundly real, just as is the significance of your faithfulness to your wife, which continues to benefit not only you but her inasmuch as the two of you remain, until death, one flesh.

However, while neither spouse may rightly forgo the other's fidelity, a person sometimes can uprightly choose not to receive care. Lacking an obligation to seek or accept care but having a right to it, one might choose to forgo it, not as a suicidal act but as an act of merciful self-denial—to allow the money and effort that would be devoted to one's care to be used instead for others' benefit. But nobody else, not even a spouse, can perform a merciful act of self-denial on someone's behalf. Still, when someone does uprightly choose to forgo care, those who abstain from providing it, far from being alienated, maintain solidarity and manifest respect and love for him or her as a person.[163]

On this basis, I have maintained that a person who foresees the possibility of becoming unconscious, with no reasonable hope of recovering consciousness (the condition the neurologists believe your wife now is in) could rightly direct that, if he or she ever were in that condition, *no* care be given, in order to save others the costs and other burdens of giving it (see *LCL,* 530–31).

162. The unconsciousness of persons said to be in a "persistent vegetative state" is in principle not demonstrable, and some call it into question; see, e.g., Chris Borthwick, "The Proof of the Vegetable: A Commentary on Medical Futility," *Journal of Medical Ethics,* 21 (1995): 205–8. The diagnosis of vegetative state also may be mistaken; Keith Andrews et al., "Misdiagnosis of the Vegetative State: Retrospective Study in a Rehabilitation Unit," *British Medical Journal,* 313 (6 July 1996): 13–16, report that of forty patients referred to a rehabilitation unit as being in vegetative state between 1992 and 1995, seventeen (43%) were considered as having been misdiagnosed, and seven of these had been presumed vegetative for more than one year, including three for over four years.

163. O'Rourke, op. cit., 61, misrepresents me as holding that the moral right to make health care decisions on behalf of an incapacitated person depends on civil law; he simply ignores the moral significance of a person's expressing (or not expressing) a merciful choice to forgo care to which he or she is entitled.

Had your wife taken that position, I think you could rightly direct the nursing home to abide by it and to do *nothing* more for her. In doing so you would not be choosing to end her life, though stopping the tube feeding along with all other care certainly would soon result in her death. However, she did not sign a directive concerning the present situation, but one concerning what to do if she were terminally ill, which does not show what she would want in the situation you face. And, as I have explained, it seems to me that, if you were to direct the removal of your wife's feeding tube, you would choose, reluctantly but homicidally, to end her life.[164]

In sum, in my judgment: (1) you may not direct that your wife's feeding tube be removed, (2) you need not continue to provide for her care in the nursing home, and (3) you should not simply stop all care. What, then, are you to do? Do the best you can. Care for your wife as well as you reasonably can while keeping the costs within your means. To cut costs, you will have to take her out of the nursing home. Perhaps you should bring her home, though you should look into alternatives and may be able to make some other suitable arrangement.

Supposing you bring her home, how can you care for her and what should you do for her? Having neither the nursing home's facilities nor the professional skills of its staff, you cannot continue to meet the standards of the care she has been receiving. However, you and your children should do what you can, consistent with other responsibilities, to care for your wife and their mother. Let your relatives, friends, neighbors, and fellow parishioners know what you are doing; some probably will offer to help, and you should accept such offers while trying not to divert people from their other responsibilities. If physicians, nurses, or other health care personnel volunteer their help and advice, accept it.

You should establish a budget so that your total expenditures in caring for your wife will be consistent with meeting other family members' needs. If problems arise with the tube feeding or she seems ill—for example, if she becomes feverish—obtain professional help and medications insofar as the budget permits, while making use of any available insurance coverage. Keep her warm in winter and as clean as you can. Provide restraints so that she does not fall out of bed, turn her from side to side regularly if you can, and so on. Ideally, you should arrange to

---

164. For a further explanation of the position that nutrition and hydration generally should be provided for permanently unconscious people who did not make it clear that, if ever in that condition, they wished to forgo all care, see Germain Grisez, "Should Nutrition and Hydration Be Provided to Permanently Comatose and Other Mentally Disabled Persons?" *Linacre Quarterly,* 57:2 (May 1990): 30–43. In this article I criticize an argument offered by Kevin D. O'Rourke, O.P., for the view that nutrition and hydration may be withdrawn from all permanently comatose people. O'Rourke, op. cit., and also "Prolonging Life: A Traditional Interpretation," *Linacre Quarterly,* 58:2 (May 1991): 12–26, has reaffirmed his view but not responded to my criticisms. For another articulation of the two opposed views, see the debate, "Hydration and Nutrition: Medical, Legal, and Ethical Obligations," in Donald G. McCarthy, ed., *Scarce Medical Resources and Justice,* Proceedings of the Bishops' Workshop, Feb. 9–13, 1987 (Braintree, Mass.: The Pope John Center, 1987), which includes Mark Siegler, "I) A Physician's Perspective" (133–41); Dennis J. Horan, "II) Legal Reflections on the Role of Church Teaching" (141–58); Benedict M. Ashley, O.P., "III) Ethical Obligations" (159–65); and discussion involving the three presenters in response to bishops' questions (179–94).

have someone with her at all times—with the help of relatives, friends, neighbors, and fellow parishioners—but if that is impossible, you need not exceed the budget in order to hire someone, and may leave her alone when necessary.

In short, you should make a genuine effort to care for your wife, just as good Christian families always did for their helpless and debilitated members. But also go on with your lives, not slighting other responsibilities, and limit expenditures for your wife's care to a reasonable level. With such care, your wife's condition will not be as good as it would have been had she remained in the nursing home, and she probably will die sooner than if she had stayed there. However, you will no more have killed her, and will have loved her no less, than if you had continued to pay for her care in the nursing home at the cost of the children's education and saving for your own retirement.

Caring for your wife at home certainly will be physically and emotionally burdensome for you and your children. I expect it will be especially painful to experience the consequences for your wife of the comparatively inadequate care you will be able to provide for her. It would be much easier to solve the problem quickly and neatly by taking your family doctor's advice and having the feeding tube removed. However, by accepting suffering, you will avoid choosing to kill your wife. And bearing that suffering, along with all the other burdens of caring for her at home, will be a work of faithful love. By that work of love you will bear powerful witness to truths often questioned and denied today: that people in your wife's condition enjoy no less dignity than anyone else, that human bodily life is always good, and that we ought to care for our loved ones rather than kill them even when they no longer can consciously live their lives and may even seem not to have a life worth living.

As for the children, while there are reasonable limits to the help that should be asked of them, children should do what they can to care for their parents when help is needed. Yours may well find fulfilling their responsibilities toward their mother a hardship, but it will be only fair that they accept rather heavy burdens, since part of the money saved by bringing her home will be used for their education. Moreover, helping care for their mother will be morally beneficial to them. They will be the first to benefit by the witness you and they together will bear to their mother's equal human dignity, the preciousness of her life, and the appropriateness of continuing to love and care for her to the end. If you tried to spare your children this cross, you would not really be considerate of them. Rather, you would deprive them of the last lesson God wished their mother to teach them, a lesson that will remain with them their whole lives, guiding them to follow Jesus and so rejoin her in heaven.

48: May a woman agree to inducing delivery of her nonviable defective baby?

We married last year and were very happy when I became pregnant. Now I am nearly five months along. Two weeks ago, my obstetrician did an examination, including various tests, and yesterday he had us come in about the results. He said our baby, a girl, is seriously defective, and even if I went to term she would not survive long, probably only a few hours and certainly not more than a few days. I have diabetes, and, though the pregnancy has not been going too badly, the doctor had planned from the beginning to deliver the baby about a month early. But since she will not live long anyway, he wanted to induce labor at once. He explained that he thinks it best, when the mother is diabetic, "to terminate the pregnancy as soon as it becomes clear that the baby has nothing to lose."

We were surprised, since we picked this obstetrician partly because he was recommended by prolife friends. He left us alone for a while, and we talked it over. When he returned, we told him we would not have an abortion even to save my life, both because we believe abortion is wrong and because we want our baby to be born alive. We want to have her baptized and give her all the love and care we can, no matter how short her life is. The doctor said he never does abortions, but in cases like mine he does not regard inducing labor early as abortion. He also said the baby almost certainly would be born alive, so that she could be baptized, though she might live only a few minutes. And he told us that it would risk my life to go on with the pregnancy and he would not be responsible for what might happen if I do not follow his advice. We told him we needed more time to think it over.

We talked with our parish priest about it, and he referred us to a Sister Luke, who has studied health care ethics and works in the chaplain's office at the local Catholic hospital. After listening to our story, she told us to follow the obstetrician's advice and get the pregnancy over with. That is the right thing to do, she explained, because there is "a proportionate reason." If we were sure her advice is sound, we would follow it. However, we are not sure, because my husband read that the Pope condemned something called "proportionalism" in his encyclical, *Veritatis splendor.* We want advice about what to do, and we want to make sure we do not get mixed up in something the Pope condemned.

Analysis:

The question is whether it would be morally acceptable to induce labor at once in this case. Even if a baby never will be viable, it is abortion to induce labor in order to end his or her life, and it is unjust to do anything without a grave reason that will result in shortening an unborn baby's life. So, if the pregnancy can be continued until near term without grave risk to the questioner, she should not consent to the induction of early labor. If early delivery were necessary to save the mother's life, her consenting in order to save her own life would not involve the intention to kill the baby or shorten her life. Saving the mother's life could be called a "proportionate reason" for accepting the baby's somewhat accelerated death. This use of the expression *proportionate reason* differs from that of the proportionalists whose opinion John Paul II condemned in *Veritatis splendor.*

The reply could be along the following lines:

Your letter is deeply moving. So often you speak of *we!* It is a sign of the love with which you, less than a year married, joyfully welcomed the prospect of your first child and now, with grief but evident faith, face the prospect of losing her so soon. Telling the doctor you would not have an abortion even to save your life also showed courageous and praiseworthy readiness to accept martyrdom. Moreover, you show your Catholic sense of values: you picked an obstetrician recommended by prolife friends; you want your baby to be born alive and baptized; you sought advice from your parish priest and Sister Luke to whom he referred you; and you question the soundness of the advice, which you otherwise would follow, because you fear it might be inconsistent with papal teaching.

There seems to be an increasing tendency for obstetricians to recommend the abortion of babies found to be seriously defective. As you have discovered, even some physicians who usually reject abortion consider it morally acceptable to induce early labor as soon as it becomes clear that the baby probably will not live long even if the pregnancy goes to term.[165] Often they give the excuse that the "baby has nothing to lose." That, of course, is false. The baby loses his or her life, and life, even of a very severely handicapped or dying person, remains good and is sacred. Moreover, in most such cases, labor is induced to achieve some purpose precisely by ending the baby's life—for example, the pregnancy is terminated to spare parents psychological stress. With such an intention, inducing labor early simply is a method of abortion.[166]

165. National Conference of Catholic Bishops, *Ethical and Religious Directives for Catholic Health Care Services* (Washington, D.C.: United States Catholic Conference, 1995), directive 45: "Abortion (that is, the directly intended termination of pregnancy before viability or the directly intended destruction of a viable fetus) is never permitted. Every procedure whose sole immediate effect is the termination of pregnancy before viability is an abortion . . .."

166. Jean deBlois, C.S.J., Patrick Norris, O.P., and Kevin O'Rourke, O.P, *A Primer for Health Care Ethics: Essays for a Pluralistic Society* (Washington, D.C.: Georgetown University Press, 1994), 235–38, note that pregnancy with an anencephalic fetus can put the mother at a somewhat increased risk and that the emotional trauma to the couple of a diagnosis of anencephaly can be considerable, assert (236) that the "condition uniformly is fatal, death usually occurring hours after birth from cardiorespiratory arrest," claim (237) that "viability has no meaning as a moral marker in such cases" and that once the defect occurs integrated development is impossible due to absence of the cerebral cortex, and conclude (237): "On the basis of the above analysis it seems that once the diagnosis of anencephaly has been made the pregnancy may be terminated at any time." This position is rejected—I believe rightly—by the Committee on Doctrine, National Conference of Catholic Bishops, "Moral Principles Concerning Infants with Anencephaly," *Origins*, 26:17 (10 Oct. 1996): 276: "Hence, it is clear that before 'viability' it is never permitted to terminate the gestation of an anencephalic child as the *means* of avoiding psychological or physical risks to the mother. Nor is such termination permitted after 'viability' if early delivery endangers the child's life due to complications of prematurity." Peter J. McCullagh, *Brain Dead, Brain Absent, Brain Donors: Human Subjects or Human Objects?* (New York: John Wiley and Sons, 1993), 105–42, and a child neurologist, D. Alan Shewmon, "Anencephaly: Selected Medical Aspects," *Hastings Center Report*, 18:5 (Oct.–Nov. 1988): 11–15, make it clear that the diagnosis of anencephaly sometimes is mistaken and the extent of the affliction varies; if anencephalic babies are born alive, many live more than a day and a few a month or more; some such infants behave in many ways like normal babies and may be conscious; and the cause of death varies. For infants afflicted with anencephaly who could not possibly survive long after birth, viability is irrelevant as a moral marker, but that irrelevance does not entail that aborting those infants is permissible, since the relevance of viability as a marker is that, what would have been abortion before viability may be a permissible early induction of labor after it. The fact that anencephalic infants develop a more or less perfect body (apart from their brain defect) shows that the cerebral cortex is not

Your physician has a more serious reason. Your diabetes could make continuing the pregnancy seriously harmful to you. Your question, therefore, really amounts to asking whether inducing labor now so as to forestall that harm must be regarded as abortion and excluded.

In my judgment, the answer partly depends on whether going on with the pregnancy would be risking your life. Without adequate knowledge of the facts and lacking medical expertise, I cannot say how much basis there is for your obstetrician's concern. However, it is possible that what he told you is unduly pessimistic, and he may also be taking too dim a view of your baby's prospects. Therefore, the first thing I think you should do is obtain a second medical opinion. That is your right, and in no way calls into question the competence of the physician you have been seeing. Though he told you he would not be responsible for what might happen if you do not follow his advice—which seems to me to have put you under undue pressure—he should and probably will cooperate with you in obtaining a second opinion by sending your clinical records and test results to the physician you choose to review the situation. That should be an obstetrician who practices in full accord with Catholic teaching. To identify such a person, you might try calling the offices of the obstetricians on the staff of the Catholic hospital and asking: "Does the doctor prescribe contraceptives?" If the answer is yes, ask if he or she knows any obstetrician who refuses to do so. If this approach does not succeed, tell your parish priest about the difficulty and ask him to help you—and, if necessary, to get an appropriate diocesan office to help you—find the right doctor. Do not hesitate to press your parish priest and diocesan officials on this matter; you are prepared to lay down your life, if necessary, in order to do what is right, and you have a special claim to their help. Having identified a suitable obstetrician, tell him or her you need a second opinion, and explain the situation. After obtaining and studying your medical records and the test results, this physician probably will examine you and perhaps order additional tests. Then he or she will give you a fresh, independent evaluation and explain your options.

I hope the second opinion will be that any problems likely to develop probably can be dealt with easily or even forestalled, without significant risk of serious and lasting harm to you. If so, your problem will be solved. Perhaps, however, there will be a serious problem, impossible to forestall and difficult to deal with, that will impose some risk of harm on you. Even so, the second obstetrician may be able to suggest a plan of care and treatment that, without gravely risking your life, will delay inducing labor until the pregnancy reaches the stage at which inducing labor for a good reason is regarded as acceptable by all Catholic moralists. In that case, accept the plan and carefully cooperate in carrying it out, even if it is unlikely to result in your baby being born alive.

Someone might disagree and argue that the point at which a baby normally is viable is irrelevant in your case, because your daughter is so seriously defective

---

essential for integrated development. I conclude that choosing to terminate pregnancy when anencephaly is diagnosed is homicidal if the intended end is to reduce parental emotional trauma and is unfairly discriminatory against the baby if the intended end is to avoid the slightly increased risk of a properly managed pregnancy and natural birth.

that even if you go to term she will die shortly after she is born. Assuming the accuracy of what your obstetrician has told you about your daughter's prospects, her life after birth will be extremely brief. However, her life remains good and she probably can live within your womb until the end of the normal period of pregnancy. Therefore, inducing labor early would deprive her of what little life she is likely to enjoy, and your responsibility is to bear and nurture her, if possible, until she is ready to be born.

I think it quite unlikely that both obstetricians will agree that you and your baby both probably will die unless labor is induced early. But suppose that is their judgment? Even in that case, unless the danger of death is imminent, you should not agree to proceed at once, but should delay, hoping and praying for a good outcome. In that way, you will prolong your baby's life and keep open the possibility that, despite the dire predictions, things will work out so that no life-or-death choice becomes necessary. But if the time does come when you must choose between risking your life, which also would cause your baby's death, and inducing labor early, then, I think, you should choose the latter. That choice plainly will not be to end or shorten the baby's life, for, though she probably will die sooner outside your womb than within it, your reason for inducing early labor will be to prevent your own death and, if possible, to provide your baby with the benefits of living briefly outside your womb, namely, baptism and a brief period of loving care. Thus, you will not be choosing to shorten your baby's life, but only accepting that as an unwanted side effect. That will be fair to her, not only because your life also will be preserved but because she, too, will benefit.

Because this motive for accepting the shortening of your baby's life would be fair to her, one can call it "a proportionate reason." Perhaps that is what Sister Luke meant—though, it seems to me, her advice was defective insofar as she neglected to suggest that you obtain a second opinion and put off a life-or-death choice. A proportionate reason in this sense, however, differs from what is called "a proportionate reason" by the proportionalists whose theory John Paul II condemned in his encyclical, *Veritatis splendor.* Since you are anxious to avoid confusing the two, I shall try to explain the distinction.

The Pope's main purpose was to reaffirm *"the universality and immutability of the moral commandments,* particularly those which prohibit always and without exception *intrinsically evil acts."*[167] The relevant commandment, of course, is "You shall not kill," which always and without exception prohibits killing by private individuals—capital punishment and killing in just wars are a separate problem (see *LCL,* 469–81, 890–94, 897–911). The prohibited, intrinsically evil act of killing, however, is to be understood, not merely as an outward performance resulting in someone's death, but as a freely chosen kind of behavior characterized by its *"'object' rationally chosen by the deliberate will"* or, in other words, by "the proximate end of a deliberate decision which determines the act of willing on the part of the acting person."[168] Now, if, in the life-and-death crisis described above,

167. John Paul II, *Veritatis splendor,* 115, *AAS* 85 (1993) 1223, *OR,* 6 Oct. 1993, xviii.
168. Ibid., 78, *AAS* 1196, *OR,* xii.

you agree to induce labor early, you will not be rationally choosing by deliberate will to kill your baby or shorten her life; your act of willing will not be a deliberate decision that she die sooner rather than later. That harm, as already explained, will only be accepted as a side effect of what you will be choosing: preventing your own death and bringing about her birth so that she will live, though briefly, outside your womb.

The proportionalists whose theory the Pope condemned also might recommend accepting your obstetrician's advice, though probably without delay and certainly on a different basis. Instead of focusing on the object of the act and asking, for example, whether the shortening of life is only accepted as a side effect or is the proximate end of one's choice, proportionalism "by weighing the various values and goods being sought, focuses rather on the proportion acknowledged between the good and bad effects of that choice, with a view to the 'greater good' or 'lesser evil' actually possible in a particular situation."[169] Thus, proportionalists deny that there are intrinsically evil acts; they say, for example, that, while it is generally wrong to kill, exceptions can be justified when killing is the "lesser evil."[170] Proportionalists, however, "are not faithful to the Church's teaching, when they believe they can justify, as morally good, deliberate choices of kinds of behavior contrary to the commandments of the divine and natural law."[171] Moreover, they do not use a moral standard, such as fairness, to compare goods and bads; rather, they think benefits and harms, considered as premoral, can be compared directly. That suggestion, however, is absurd, for, as the Pope points out, "everyone recognizes the difficulty, or rather the impossibility, of evaluating all the good and evil consequences and effects—defined as pre-moral—of one's own acts: an exhaustive rational calculation is not possible."[172]

In sum, if Sister Luke meant by *proportionate reason* what proportionalists mean by it, she thinks you would be justified, not only in accepting the shortening of your baby's life in inducing labor at once, but even in choosing to kill her, on the theory that her death would be a lesser evil than the harm your obstetrician predicts you will suffer if your pregnancy proceeds. Since goods and bads cannot be rationally commensurated in that way, however, *lesser evil* here can have no definite meaning. It expresses only a subjective opinion based on feelings. On this basis, a proportionalist may regard an abortion as justified whenever the baby is expected not to live long after birth.

Your minds may be boggled by the preceding explanation of the difference between the proportionalism the Pope condemns and the legitimate use of *proportionate reason.* If so, do not worry about the details, for I am sure you will grasp the fact that the two are different. Looking at the matter in your clear-eyed way, you were prepared to stake your life on one of the truths proportionalists deny—that abortion is always wrong—but perhaps would have followed Sister Luke's advice had your husband not read about the Pope's condemnation of proportionalism.

169. Ibid., 75, *AAS* 1193, *OR,* xi.
170. See ibid.
171. Ibid., 76, *AAS* 1194, *OR,* xii.
172. Ibid., 77, *AAS* 1195, *OR,* xii.

Without articulating the point, you saw correctly that, though choosing to kill a baby always would be a terrible wrong, accepting the baby's death as a side effect could be right. Still, I hope and pray the crisis will not confront you, so that there will be no need to consent to inducing labor until your pregnancy is near term.

49: Must life support, once begun, be continued?

My husband, Steve, has Lou Gehrig's disease, which causes its victims gradually to lose the use of all their muscles and inevitably leads to increasing paralysis and death. At present he is confined to a wheel chair but still has some use of his hands. Eventually the breathing muscles will deteriorate to the point where he will die from lack of oxygen unless put on a ventilator. We are looking ahead to that situation and considering what to do when it comes. In particular, we wonder whether it would be wrong for Steve to go on the ventilator for a while, with a view to discontinuing it at some later time.

We have come to terms with the disease and are facing the future calmly. We have time, at least several weeks and perhaps a few months, to make this decision. The community in which we live has been very supportive, and, for the most part, Steve has been at home, where I have been able to care for him with some help. Both of us want to continue in this way to the end, partly because we want to go through this together and partly because we want to keep the costs down to limit the impact on Steve's associates—a rather small group with whom we have our health coverage.

While caring for Steve at home will not rule out his going on a ventilator, it will, of course, make things harder for both of us and the hardship will increase as his condition deteriorates. We expect that the time will come when the ventilator will seem not so much a helpful appliance as an annoying contraption. As his condition deteriorates, however, we will be able to communicate less and less, so I may have to decide alone when to discontinue the ventilator—if it is to be discontinued. The decision will be hard, because at that stage of the disease discontinuing the ventilator will result in death in minutes, whereas continuing it could delay death for many more days or weeks.

So, as I said, we are wondering whether it would be wrong for Steve to go on the ventilator and stay on it as long as it seems to us worthwhile, then discontinue it and allow him to die.

There is one other thing. Some of our friends have been praying for a miracle. So far, Steve and I have not been doing that. From the beginning, we have prayed only that God's will be done, and that Steve and I and our children will meet again in heaven. Do you think it would be better to ask also for a miracle? Or should we leave that up to God, as we have been doing? Should the possibility of a miracle come into our thinking about Steve's going on the ventilator and, possibly, discontinuing it?

Analysis:

Two questions are asked: whether it is morally acceptable to go on a ventilator for a time with a view to eventually discontinuing it, and whether to pray for a miracle. Before deciding whether to use any specific means of prolonging life, three prior moral requirements must be satisfied. (1) One may have a moral obligation to use a means necessary for prolonging life so as to fulfill some important responsibility. (2) If using some means to stay alive is unfair to others, one should not use them. (3) One may never choose to do or omit anything in order to bring about death. If these three requirements are satisfied, the questioner and her husband should consider the reasons, grounded in likely benefits and burdens, for and against going on the respirator, and judge which set of reasons makes a stronger case. As burdens and benefits shift, they should reconsider the question. If and when they judge it appropriate to discontinue the ventilator, they may rightly do so despite foreseeing that death will result in minutes. Whether to pray for a miracle is a question for their discernment, and the possibility of a miracle need not be taken into account in their decisions about the ventilator.

The reply could be along the following lines:

You and Steve show your faith and hope by your conscientiousness and calmness in accepting suffering. Do not miss any of the religious value of this cross. Since God has permitted it and you cannot avoid it, it is a part of your vocation—a part which, like any other, you should obediently accept and commit yourself to fulfilling, as, indeed, you apparently have done. Commitment to such an element of one's vocation means seeking ways to make the most of it and faithfully carrying out its responsibilities to the end. Besides dealing rightly with the problems immediately presented by the disease and its care, these responsibilities include using the opportunities for witness—giving others an example of faith and humility—and offering your suffering in prayer for others' benefit.

Like any other new element of a Christian vocation, this sort of calling must be considered together with all the other elements of your vocation and integrated with them. Therefore, one criterion for your decision about the ventilator, as for other life-and-death decisions, is whether any unfulfilled responsibility—for example, some duty pertaining to work or family, or the need to prepare for death—requires that Steve try to stay alive, so that using the means necessary to do so would be obligatory. Presumably, though, at this point he has met all his responsibilities and would gladly accept and stay on the ventilator if that were necessary to remain alive so as to meet any others.

Responsibilities to other people include not only affirmative ones but also negative ones. In the present case, perhaps a time will come when some form of care will impose excessive burdens on others. For example, perhaps you will be unable to deal with some crisis at home and the mounting costs of hospitalization will begin to impinge unfairly on the other members of the group with which Steve is insured. If that happened, it would be necessary for him to leave the hospital in order to avoid injustice, even if that would lead quickly to death. This is not putting a dollar value on a person's life; but even when life is at stake, there are limits to the burdens that can be imposed fairly on others. I am confident that in this respect, too, neither of you would be reluctant to forgo what you should.

Turning now to your specific question, I think the key to answering it correctly lies in focusing on the intention behind refusing or limiting some form of care. Someone who initially accepted a ventilator might decide to have it removed precisely in order to bring about speedy death. That would be wrong, since it would be a decision to commit suicide. Notice, though, that someone also might choose not to go on the ventilator in the first place (or might refuse some other life-sustaining means) for the same unacceptable reason. While neither you nor Steve is likely to embrace a suicidal option, both of you should clearly understand what that option is; you also should be aware that, when suffering mounts, the temptation might arise to end it by seeking death, and that temptation must be resisted firmly.

Nevertheless, while foreseeing death either eventually or almost immediately, someone might refuse to go on a ventilator or choose to discontinue it (or any other life-sustaining means), not in order to bring about death, but for some other reason—for example, to limit the cost of ongoing care or to avoid some other bad aspect or effect of accepting or continuing with it. In that case, refusing or discontinuing a ventilator would not be a choice to commit suicide.[173]

Before I go further, let me summarize what I have said thus far. There are three definite limits: (1) one should try to keep oneself alive long enough to fulfill all one's duties; (2) one may not do something to stay alive when doing it is unfair to another or others; and (3) one may not choose to do or omit anything in order to bring about death, even as a means of avoiding further suffering. Your question therefore can be restated: How do Steve and you judge within those three definite limits whether he should go on the ventilator, and if he does go on it, whether at some time to discontinue it?

Begin by examining your feelings. Naturally, you always will feel some fear of death and reluctance to forgo anything that might prolong life; but at some point such feelings no longer will be reasonable, and will have to be set aside. Other feelings imperfectly integrated with your better selves also must be recognized. Having done that, consider the reasons for and against. The reasons for going on the ventilator are the prospective benefits of doing so. If Steve does not go on the ventilator, I assume his breathing will become more and more of a struggle until he finally suffocates. The ventilator will forestall that, and his dying will be easier if he remains on it at least until his condition deteriorates to the point that he could not breath at all without it. Then too, initially, at least, it not only will sustain his life but enable him to continue doing various worthwhile things, such as maintaining family ties by communicating with you and the children, and engaging in religious acts such as praying and offering his suffering. The example he will give to others also may be an important benefit of his staying alive. Even initially, however, going on the ventilator will impose certain burdens. It will cost something; it will make his life more of a struggle; and it will require you, as care giver, to work harder. As long as he is on it, regular lung pumping will be required, and

---

173. Choosing to do or omit something to bring about death so as to end burdensome life is euthanasia, which always is wrong; choosing to forgo some sorts of treatment because they have become too burdensome is not euthanasia and sometimes is justified; see *LCL,* 469–88, and qq. 45 and 47, above.

the family always will be anxious that the machine might break down or the power go out. These burdens also must be considered. They provide serious reasons to forgo the ventilator.

Having considered the reasons for and against, how do you decide? There is no norm to tell you what to do. Both using and forgoing the ventilator could be appropriate. Consider the reasons for both possibilities, that is, both the benefits and the burdens of using the ventilator. Then, since the two sets of reasons are disparate and not commensurable with each other, you will have to judge which set of reasons constitutes the stronger case.

I expect that initially you will judge it appropriate for Steve to go on the ventilator. As you point out, however, if he does, the benefits will decrease as the disease progresses and the burdens will increase: he will be able to do less and less, while the costs will mount and you will tire. Therefore, you should regularly reconsider the benefits and burdens. Considering everything, you always will have some reason (at least that his life remains good and his death will be bad) to continue the ventilator and some reason (at least that continuing it costs money and requires effort) to discontinue it. You will have to judge at each stage whether to continue.

While that decision cannot be made in advance, you and Steve would do well to discuss now how much importance to give to certain stages of his decline whose significance he may be unable to discuss with you once they have occurred. If he thinks it probably will be better to forgo the ventilator and accept death at some such stage of decreasing benefits, in order to end the mounting expense and other burdens of his care on you and others, you are likely to find your judgment when the time comes more confident and less painful to act upon.

If the law where you live allows people to appoint someone to make health care decisions when they cannot do so for themselves, Steve would be wise to take advantage of that law and appoint you (see *LCL,* 528–30). Having legal authority over his health care, you will be far less likely to encounter resistance to your decision by anyone, such as hospital administrators if Steve happens to be in the hospital when you decide the time has come to discontinue the ventilator.

Some Catholic ethicists who adhere to the Church's teachings would say that you should use the ventilator as long as it is an *ordinary* means of preserving Steve's life, but may discontinue it when it becomes an *extraordinary* means. In practice, however, one cannot distinguish an ordinary means from an extraordinary one except by reflection along the lines sketched above. As has been explained, that reflection, while presupposing several norms, finally requires a judgment whether to use means for the sake of their benefits or to forgo them so as to avoid their burdens. Thus, the preceding reply did not speak of ordinary and extraordinary means, since speaking of them would not have been helpful.[174]

---

174. Congregation for the Doctrine of the Faith, *Declaration on Euthanasia, AAS* 72 (1980) 549–50, Flannery, 2, 514–16, restates previous theological and magisterial teaching that some means of life-sustaining treatment are ordinary and morally required while others can be extraordinary and nonobligatory; this document adds a terminological clarification, according to which *ordinary* and *extraordinary* may be replaced with *proportionate* and *disproportionate*.

As for praying for a miracle, that is a matter for your discernment. You should pray over the question, arouse the feelings associated with your faith and other commitments pertaining to personal vocation, and use those feelings to discern which possibility and set of reasons is more harmonious with your Christian selves (see *LCL,* 291–93). But perhaps the following thoughts will be helpful.

Surely, praying as you have been is good. Jesus taught us to pray that God's will be done, told us to seek heaven first of all, and promised that God would provide everything else we need. But praying for a miracle also would be good. Jesus said that we should be childlike, and, as you very well know, children ask for exactly what they want. Besides the benefits for Steve, you, and your children, a miraculous cure would manifest God's goodness and power, arouse faith in some people and strengthen it in many others, and perhaps be a confirmation of the holiness of a person through whose intercession you sought the miracle. Praying through an intercessor would not be necessary, of course, but it would be good, as Catholic tradition makes clear. As an intercessor, you might choose someone whom the Church has declared venerable or blessed, or, perhaps, someone deceased whose holiness you know about at firsthand, such as a devout and faithful grandparent or parent.

Of course, anyone who prays for a miracle must be ready to accept God's will. Though Jesus told us to ask for whatever we need and promised we would receive what we ask for, he plainly did not mean that we always would receive what we want in the form we think best. And even if God responds to your prayers with a miracle, that cure will only delay Steve's death. Eventually all of us will die, and the prayer for life of those who persevere in grace will be fulfilled, not by a temporary extension of life in this world, but by unending life in heaven.

The possibility of a miracle should not influence your decisions about using a ventilator. If you pray for a miracle, be confident that God will do what is best, whichever conscientious decision you make. As I have explained, your decision should be made on the basis of the reasons available to you. Whether you pray for a miracle or not, be confident that Steve, even if he die, will live. And hope confidently, too, that you and your children will meet him again in heaven.

50: May a person with kidney failure accept a transplant?

I am thirty-five, married, with four children, aged twelve, nine, seven, and three. I have a serious kidney disease, and, after suffering from chronic renal inadequacy for many years, I am now experiencing end-stage renal failure. I depend on hemodialysis, which has considerably improved my health, and I can expect to remain about the same.

I am able to function reasonably well on dialysis, which I manage at home, connecting myself to the machine three times a week for four hours each time. The treatment is not painful once I have cannulated a large vein in my arm with the two needles that allow the blood to flow through the machine and back. The major problem is the time commitment, not only for me but for my wife, who must assist during the treatment. The setting up of the machine, the time spent connected to it, and cleaning up afterwards involves both of us for about eighteen hours every week, during which I can do little work and she cannot leave the house. In addition, the machine sometimes requires repair, which delays things until a technician comes; this uncertainty also limits employment possibilities.

Given these drawbacks, my physician is urging me to accept a kidney transplant. I would, except that I am worried about whether it is the right thing to do. If I receive a kidney, it must come from either a supposed cadaver or a live donor willing to sacrifice a kidney for my sake. There are serious reasons for reservations about both of these possibilities.

I never have been entirely convinced by the idea that people really are dead when they suffer so-called brain death—that is, the complete and irreversible cessation of all brain function. Moreover, I know how to use a medical library and have looked into the ways doctors go about determining that people are "brain dead." As a result of this research, I now have serious questions about both the adequacy of the criteria used in determining "brain death" and how carefully they are applied in practice. My conclusion is that even if "brain death" really is death, many people may actually be killed by the removal of their organs. So, I am not willing to accept a kidney that may well have been taken from someone falsely pronounced dead.

Several of my brothers and sisters have offered to give me one of their kidneys. In particular, one of my brothers took the initiative in getting tissue typed, and we match well. He regularly restates his offer and tells me to let him know whenever I decide to accept it. I know most theologians think such donations can be morally good and the Church has not said they are wrong. But there are risks, both of trouble connected with the operation itself and of future difficulty, in case at some point the donor suffers impaired kidney functioning. I appreciate my brother's offer, but since he has a family, I am not sure I ought to accept it.

In itself, the disease I have is no blessing, yet in some ways it has been good for me, not least by making me acutely aware of the fragility of life. While many people today seem to have forgotten about heaven and hell, I never forget. I am more concerned to do the right thing than to stay alive or have an easier time of it, and shall be grateful for straightforward advice.

Analysis:

The question is whether to accept a transplant, and a sound reply can only articulate considerations that the questioner should take into account. His unwillingness to accept a kidney that may well have been taken from someone falsely pronounced dead seems reasonable. In my judgment, however, he probably could uprightly accept a kidney from his brother. If a living person who is well informed offers with full freedom to donate a kidney, the offer may be accepted, assuming the potential donor is morally free to make it. The questioner's brother is morally free to donate a kidney, provided his wife wholeheartedly supports his doing so and appropriate medical examination reveals no special risk. If these conditions are met, the donating brother and his wife would benefit morally by doing that work of mercy, and that benefit provides some reason to accept their offer.

The reply could be along the following lines:

I wish everyone who proposed difficult moral questions shared your clearheadedness and eagerness to get at the truth. May the Lord help you persevere in your sound attitude.

You do not say whether you have talked this problem over with your wife. If not, it seems to me you should. Even your children, especially the eldest, deserve to have their thoughts and feelings considered, since you have taken responsibility for them, and your well-being is vital to theirs. Therefore, I hope you will share my reply with your wife and, insofar as feasible, with your children.

Given that you function reasonably well on dialysis and given your grounds for hesitation about accepting a kidney transplant, I do not think you have any obligation to accept it—certainly not at the present time, perhaps not ever.

Unlike you, I have regarded the concept of brain death—meaning the irreversible cessation of *all* brain functions—as acceptable in principle.[175] Still, some reasonable objections to it have been advanced.[176] Moreover, though one cannot know for certain how often the criteria for determining death on this basis are either inadequate or misapplied, it is clear that some, and perhaps even most, determinations of brain death would not meet adequate criteria properly applied.[177] That being so, your unwillingness to accept a kidney that may have been taken from someone falsely pronounced dead seems to me reasonable.[178]

You might consider publicizing your position on this matter and your reasons for it, not only by communicating personally with relatives, friends, and acquaintances but also in other feasible ways. That would bear witness to the sanctity of human life and provide an example for people tempted to violate it. Moreover, you could call many people's attention to the arguability of the concept of brain death, the inadequacy of some methods of trying to determine it, and possible abuses in applying the methods that have been adopted. That in turn might lead to wider discussion of these problems, clarification of what is going on, and needed corrections. Of course, such publicity could make severe demands on you and your

175. On the concept of brain death, see Germain Grisez and Joseph M. Boyle, Jr., *Life and Death with Liberty and Justice: A Contribution to the Euthanasia Debate* (Notre Dame, Ind.: University of Notre Dame Press, 1979), 59–78; Working Group of the Pontifical Academy of Sciences, *The Determination of Brain Death and Its Relationship to Human Death* (10–14 Dec. 1989), ed. R. J. White, H. Angstwurm, and I. Carrasco de Paula (Vatican City: Pontifical Academy of Sciences, 1992), 81–82.

176. See Paul A. Byrne et al., "Brain Death: The Patient, the Physician, and Society," *Gonzaga Law Review,* 18:3 (1982–83): 429–516; Josef Seifert, "Is 'Brain Death' Actually Death? A Critique of Redefining Man's Death in Terms of 'Brain Death'," in Working Group of the Pontifical Academy of Sciences, op. cit., 95–143; D. Alan Shewmon, "Recovery from 'Brain Death': A Neurologist's *Apologia,*" *Linacre Quarterly,* 64:1 (Feb. 1997): 30-96.

177. On the application of inadequate criteria, see Peter J. McCullagh, *Brain Dead, Brain Absent, Brain Donors: Human Subjects or Human Objects?* (New York: John Wiley and Sons, 1993), 7–103, 225–47.

178. In stating this conclusion and assuming it to be decisive for the questioner, I do not mean to settle the issue of whether other patients could rightly accept the transplant of an organ that might have been taken from someone wrongly pronounced dead. In view of present (Jan. 1997) uncertainties about relevant facts, I believe that upright people can reach and act on different reasonable judgments on this matter.

loved ones, and information about questionable practices might distress people who have received organs taken from donors perhaps not yet dead as well as such donors' families and friends. So, you might conclude that most of the possible ways of making your stand known would not promise sufficient benefits to warrant accepting the foreseeable burdens.

As for transplantation from a live donor, no potential kidney recipient should assume that every relative's or friend's offer to donate can be taken seriously. Even if all conditions are ideal, the donor's self-sacrifice goes beyond duty and is called for only as an act of generous love, that is, as a work of mercy. Family members and friends may feel constrained to offer a kidney or may even be manipulated into doing so; such offers also sometimes are made impulsively, without due delibera-tion about risks and burdens.[179] But so great a work of mercy ought to flow from sufficient reflection and full freedom of choice. Before accepting any offer, the potential recipient should make certain it has been made after careful deliberation and with full freedom. This condition is not met until the potential donor has been informed of the burdens and risks involved in the operation.[180]

Still, since your brother has regularly repeated his offer, I think it likely that you could rightly accept a transplant from him.[181] I say "I think it likely" because at least two conditions must be fulfilled. First, in view of the responsibilities your brother assumed in marrying and having children, it surely would be wrong for him to proceed with the donation if his wife were opposed or even ambivalent. But since he has made and regularly repeated his offer, I assume he has his wife's whole-hearted approval and support. Second, your brother almost certainly would not be accepted as a donor by the physicians concerned and certainly should not proceed without a thorough physical examination, including a careful medical history, ruling out possible reasons for thinking his giving you a kidney would involve a risk other than the risks always accepted by healthy kidney donors.

Assuming these conditions are met, I think your reasons for hesitating to accept your brother's offer are sound, but not so morally compelling that accepting would be wrong. There is a certain risk for your brother, and he and his wife should place a very high priority on their responsibility to work together in raising their children. Still, the risk to your brother and his family probably would not be great, while the benefit to you and your family probably would be great.

179. Helpful works on diverse aspects of donation by a living person: Renée C. Fox and Judith P. Swazey, *Spare Parts: Organ Replacement in American Society* (New York: Oxford University Press, 1992), 31–48; Marc D. Smith et al., "Living–Related Kidney Donors: A Multicenter Study of Donor Education, Socioeconomic Adjustment, and Rehabilitation," *Ameri-can Journal of Kidney Diseases,* 8:4 (1986): 223–33.

180. Once donors have recovered from the operation, their risk in living with only one kidney does not appear to be great; see Barry M. Brenner, ed., *The Kidney,* 5th ed., vol. 2 (Philadelphia: W. B. Saunders, 1996), 2036, and the studies cited.

181. On the moral acceptability of such transplants, see National Conference of Catholic Bishops, *Ethical and Religious Directives for Catholic Health Care Services* (Washington, D.C.: United States Catholic Conference, 1995), directives 29 (with n. 16) and 30; *LCL,* 544, including n. 147; Donald G. McCarthy and Edward J. Bayer, eds., *Handbook on Critical Life Issues,* rev. ed. (Braintree, Mass.: Pope John Center, 1988), 122–34; William E. May, "The Ethics of Organ Transplants," *Ethics and Medics,* 21:7 (July 1996): 1–2.

Moreover, if the conditions have been met, an additional consideration in favor of accepting your brother's offer can come into play, namely, that he and his wife also stand to benefit. Since they love you, the improvement in your functioning would be a benefit for them. Besides, assuming their full and free agreement to donating the kidney, they already have become better as individuals and as a couple by making so generous an offer. In transforming their benevolence into beneficence—their good will into a good deed—they would make an additional sacrifice and deepen their love for you and for each other. Indeed, the potential moral benefits to them, perhaps even more than the health benefit to you, provide you with good reason to accept their offer with grateful love.

51: Should a woman try to bear her dead sister's frozen embryo?

You do not know me, but a friend of mine told me you are working on unusual moral questions, and I hope you can answer mine.

My eldest sister, Susan, fell away from the Church when she went to business school at Harvard. She pursued her career for ten years, had several affairs and abortions, then quit work and married two years ago at thirty-five. She wanted a baby, thinking it would cement her marriage. But there was a complicated fertility problem, and they decided to try in vitro fertilization (IVF) using donor semen. Several of Sue's eggs were fertilized successfully, but the first attempt to make her pregnant failed. One 'spare' embryo had been frozen, but before a second attempt was made, Sue's husband left her for his secretary. Feeling she had nothing to live for, she killed herself six weeks ago.

She left behind a long, bitter note with messages for her husband, Mom, Dad, and various other people, including me. She recalled that, when I was thirteen, I tried to talk her out of having an abortion by arguing that every new individual is a tiny baby from the very beginning. She wrote: "Annie, if you still believe that, you can keep my appointment next month with the IVF clinic, and try to be a mother to my 'tiny baby,' who is currently residing in the deep freeze!"

Sue was being sarcastic, of course, and at first the message struck me as just another bad line in her whole miserable act. But a couple of weeks ago I recalled what she said and began thinking about doing it. After praying over it for a few days and talking it over with Mom, I felt at peace with the idea. I looked into it, and now know I can try to save this baby. It will not be as simple as just keeping Sue's appointment, but the IVF clinic is asking for only three things: a release from her husband, payment in advance, and a waiver of liability from me. Sue's husband is willing to sign the release, and Dad is willing to put up the money. The clinic wants me to waive liability because, if in doubt, they ordinarily take no chances and discard the embryo. When they explained that, I told them I am not interested in having a perfect baby but in trying to save *this* one and so would want them to go through with the transfer even if they have doubts about the embryo's condition and prospects of developing normally. They then said the consent form would have to spell out my instructions and waive liability, and I have no problem with that.

Still, I am not sure whether to go ahead. If nothing is done, the embryo will be at the disposal of the IVF clinic. They refuse to say what they will do with "it," but I am afraid they will either discard the embryo or turn him or her over to someone to experiment on. A priest I talked with told me the Church has ruled out IVF and surrogate motherhood, and he thinks that decision might apply to me, though he did not want to say for sure. Also, if I became pregnant, I would give the baby up for adoption. I am twenty-two and healthy but am not married. I would like to marry and have children eventually, but I'm not ready for that yet, and don't want to be a single mother.

What do you think? Should I do it or not?

Analysis:

This question requires the derivation of a new specific moral norm. The teaching of the Church excludes IVF and surrogate motherhood, but the proposal being considered by the questioner is different: to try to save the embryo's life by receiving this tiny individual in her womb and nurturing him or her until birth. The end of saving the baby is good, and the chosen means of transferring him or her from freezer to womb is not at odds with human life, the transmission of life, or the good of marriage. So, in itself, this action would be morally acceptable. Though it would involve cooperation with the IVF clinic and might be used by other women to rationalize immoral actions, these circumstances need not make it wrong.

The reply could be along the following lines:

Since legislators can choose whether to make a rule of law and, within limits, what rule of law to make, the legality of doing various sorts of things often depends on legislators' choices. But whether doing something is morally good or evil does not depend on anyone's choice. Rather, it depends on the act's relationships to fundamental human goods and to loving God and neighbor (see *CMP,* 184–89 and 603–6). Therefore, on moral questions the Church does not attempt to legislate; rather, in the light of God's word, she teaches what she believes to be the truth about what is really good for human beings, who are fallen but redeemed and called to heavenly glory. Thus, it is misleading to say the Church has *ruled out* IVF and surrogate motherhood. To be precise, one should say the Church has examined these sorts of action and *found them to be gravely wrong* (see *CCC,* 2376–77; *LCL,* 684).

Your argument against abortion was sound. The frozen embryo truly is a tiny baby. Even though this baby should not have been brought into being as he or she was, now that this new person exists, he or she—like a baby conceived as a result of fornication, adultery, rape, or incest—has the same immeasurable worth and deserves the same respect and loving care as every other human being. The loving care of bearing this baby in your womb is what you propose to try to give. Still, reflecting on the Church's teaching, you rightly wish to make sure that what you propose to do is not somehow morally wrong.

IVF always is wrong, because it brings a new human individual into being, and deals with him or her, as a product of technology rather than as a person enjoying the same essential dignity as his or her human originators. If the product fills the order, the baby may be accepted and loved as a person; but the individual also may be found defective and be scrapped, or eventually be discarded as surplus. In any case, he or she is not procreated as a fruit of love, given by God in answer to an act of marital love cooperating humbly with his own love.[182] Done with donor semen, IVF is wrong for additional reasons. It violates the exclusivity of the marital communion and deprives the child of the normal human relationship to his or her parents.[183]

The surrogate mother is impregnated either by transferring to her an embryo resulting from IVF or by fertilizing her own ovum with semen from a man who is not her husband, and she bears the child as part of an arrangement with someone to whom the baby will be surrendered shortly after birth. This procedure is wrong not only because both IVF and artificial insemination are wrong but also because it violates the good of marriage and uses both the surrogate mother and the baby as mere means to providing a child for the person or couple who want one.[184]

Obviously, though, what you propose to do would not involve artificial insemination. And though the embryo came to be by IVF, your sister, her husband, and the people at the IVF clinic did what they did some time ago, and what you are considering doing cannot in any way contribute to their past acts carrying out IVF. Moreover, you are proposing to bear the child not on anyone else's behalf but simply to save his or her life. So—supposing your project succeeds—even if you think it best to give the baby up for adoption, you would not be acting as a surrogate mother.[185] Rather, you would be acting in much the same way as a mother who volunteers to nurse at her own breast a foundling conceived out of wedlock, abandoned by his or her natural mother, and awaiting adoption by a suitable couple. Like that mother's nursing, the nurture you hope to give will in no way involve you in the wrongs previously done to the baby and will be offered to him or her for his or her own sake, not done as a service to anyone else. Therefore, you certainly can try to save the baby without acting contrary to what the Church has taught regarding IVF and surrogate motherhood.[186]

Moreover, in my judgment, you could do it without acting contrary to any other moral norm. Plainly, your end would be good: to try to save the baby's life. So, your project cannot be intrinsically wrong unless the necessary means is immoral. The chosen means would be to have the embryo moved from the freezer into your womb and to nurture him or her there, as any upright pregnant woman nurtures her

182. See Congregation for the Doctrine of the Faith, *Donum vitae,* II, B, 5; *AAS* 80 (1988) 92–94, *OR,* 16 Mar. 1987, 5–6; also see *LCL,* 267–68; q. 52, below.

183. Ibid., II, A, 2; *AAS* 88–89, *OR,* 4–5.

184. Ibid., II, A, 3; *AAS* 89, *OR,* 5.

185. The preceding facts are essential presuppositions of the subsequent conclusion that the questioner may, and perhaps even should, try to bear her sister's baby. Therefore, my answer should not be taken to mean that the end of making babies available to adoptive parents could justify doing anything to promote IVF.

186. William B. Smith, "Response," *Homiletic and Pastoral Review,* 96:11–12 (Aug.–Sept. 1996): 16–17, insists that a woman who bears someone else's frozen embryo would be a surrogate mother. He ignores the fact that bearing *on another's behalf* is part of the very definition of surrogacy.

child.[187] Nurturing the baby in your womb surely will not be wrong; if someone transferred an embryo to your womb without your consent, abortion would be wrong, and it would be your duty to nurture the baby, just as it is the duty of a woman who has been raped and finds herself pregnant. Thus, if anything makes your project intrinsically wrong, it must be having the embryo moved from the freezer into your womb. But that is not at odds with any basic human good. It protects life rather than violates it; since the new person already exists, it does not violate the transmission of life; and it has nothing to do with the good of marriage, because it is not a sexual act, and the relationship between you and the baby is neither marital nor a perverse alternative to the marital relationship.

To be sure, embryo transfer usually is an integral part of the project of obtaining a baby by means of IVF, and that project as a whole is immoral. But in your case, the transfer of the embryo would be part of an entirely different project: rescuing this person in distress.[188] Though superficially similar to acts violating various goods involved in marriage and procreation, what you propose to do is not the same as any of them. In choosing to receive the embryo into your womb, you would be committing yourself to only one thing: trying to save his or her life.

Someone might grant that what you propose to do would not involve IVF or surrogate motherhood and would not be wrong in virtue of either the end of saving the baby's life or the means of having him or her transferred from the freezer into your womb, yet argue that your project would be wrong for another reason: You would be cooperating with the IVF clinic's operators, who regard babies as a product, and setting an example that will be followed by single women and couples in the market for that product.[189] In reality, however, the IVF clinic's operators

187. Geoffrey Surtees, "Adoption of a Frozen Embryo," *Homiletic and Pastoral Review,* 96:11–12 (Aug.–Sept. 1996): 11–13, thinks only a woman prepared to adopt the child should have an embryo moved to her womb, and says the object of the act is adoption. However, even if a couple wishing to adopt a frozen, embryonic child were in question, their necessary means would be to have the embryo transferred from the freezer to the wife's womb, and their plan to adopt, pertaining to that act's end, would lie outside its precise object.

188. William B. Smith, "Rescue the Frozen?" *Homiletic and Pastoral Review,* 96:1 (Oct. 1995): 72 and 74, takes a contrary position, but for the most part, it seems to me, builds his case on confusing the wrongs others have done with the precise act of the rescuer. Smith, however, does quote and argue from one seemingly relevant sentence of Congregation for the Doctrine of the Faith, *Donum vitae,* I, 5; *AAS* 80 (1988) 84, *OR,* 16 Mar. 1987, 4: "In consequence of the fact that they have been produced *in vitro,* those embryos which are not transferred into the body of the mother and are called 'spare' are exposed to an absurd fate, with no possibility of their being offered safe means of survival which can be licitly pursued." Smith goes on: "No safe means that *can be licitly pursued!* Perhaps, the CDF did not intend to address this precise case, but I read here a first principled insight indicating that this volunteer 'rescue' is *not* a licit option." But the sentence Smith relies upon ends a section concerned with using embryos produced in vitro for research, and is immediately preceded by a condemnation of deliberately exposing such embryos to death. In my judgment, therefore, the sentence Smith quotes should not be understood as referring to the action of a rescuer who has in no way participated in the wrongs that have brought the embryonic persons to be and left them to their absurd fate, but to the options available to those wrongly involved in IVF. For a fuller argument against Smith's use of this passage, see Surtees, op. cit., 8–9.

189. Maurizio P. Faggioni, O.F.M., "The Question of Frozen Embryos," *OR,* 21 Aug. 1966, 5, seems to concede that the prenatal adoption of a frozen embryo would be permissible in

would be cooperating with you in dealing with the embryo as a baby rather than as a product, and nothing you did would contribute to any of their other, wrongful acts. And while people who wanted a baby not for his or her sake but to satisfy their own desires might use your example to rationalize their very different project, you could rightly accept that bad effect of your very different choice, insofar as you could not prevent it; and you could try to forestall it by your witness to the truth about the relevant goods.

The positive value of that witness and the danger that your action would be misunderstood would be cogent reasons for explaining carefully whenever possible what you were doing and why. If you proceed, therefore, you should do your best to make three things clear: (1) you are convinced that both IVF and surrogate motherhood are wrong in themselves and unjust to the babies involved; (2) you are certain that all human embryos, including those produced by IVF, are tiny persons and that, like every person, they should be loved for their own sakes, not regarded as products or mere means to other people's ends; and (3) you believe it right to try to save the life of your sister's baby, and that is all you are interested in.

Against what you propose, it also has been argued that only a couple who can and will adopt and raise the baby can appropriately have an embryo transferred to the wife's womb. The argument is that a single woman who plans to rescue and give the child up for adoption would treat him or her as "an object or item to be transferred about as a mere temporary possession," and that the child needs and deserves "a family which vows to meet the obligations, responsibilities, and duties any family must live up to."[190] This argument is not sound. No more than a loving wet nurse or foster parents of an infant awaiting adoption do you propose to treat the baby as an object, item, or temporary possession.

Still, perhaps you know or can find a faithful Catholic married couple who would make good parents for this baby and would be prepared not only to try to save this child but to receive him or her into the wife's womb and at once commit themselves to fulfilling all parental responsibilities. Generous as it would be for such a couple to adopt the baby after he or she was born, it would be more appropriate for them to assume parental responsibilities now if they can. That would constitute a more integrated parental principle. Therefore, if Sue's husband and the IVF clinic will cooperate and a suitable couple wish to try to save the baby, you should not, in my judgment, carry out your plan.

Your way of putting your question, "Should I do it or not?" suggests a further question, though one you probably did not have in mind: Supposing nobody better qualified attempts to bear your sister's baby, would you have some obligation to do so?

Very often, not only those whose job it is to rescue others (fire fighters, life guards, and so on) but someone who puts another into a dangerous situation can

---

itself, but raises "serious questions" about circumstantial factors that might morally exclude such adoption as a general "solution, suggested as an *extrema ratio* to save embryos abandoned to certain death."

190. Surtees, op. cit., 13; but cf. 16, n. 23, where he concedes that being rescued and given up for adoption is better for the baby than being left in the freezer.

have a strict obligation to attempt a rescue. But you are not responsible for the coming to be of your sister's embryo or for his or her present perilous situation. You are more like a passerby who, noticing a child drowning or trapped in a burning house, considers attempting a rescue. Therefore, you have no such strict obligation to undertake this service.

Still, since at times everyone needs and wants a passerby's help, the Golden Rule can require one to be a Good Samaritan. And since we Christians believe that we have been saved by Jesus, who freely accepted death for our sakes, we must extend like mercy to others. So, if the passerby could attempt the rescue without unreasonable cost, difficulty, or risk, he or she might have an obligation to try to help; if he or she is a Christian, that obligation could require significant self-sacrifice. At the same time, grave risks to the potential rescuer, small prospects of success, or responsibilities to others might well provide cogent moral reasons why the passerby need not, or even should not, try to help. Only he or she could consider the pros and cons, and conscientiously judge whether either option was obligatory.

Obviously, carrying a baby and giving birth always involve significant burdens and risks, and the chance of saving an embryonic individual produced in a laboratory is poor. So, you have good reasons not to make the attempt. Still, if the burdens and risks to you are set aside, those reasons are hardly conclusive. Therefore, it seems to me that, unless someone else attempts to bear your sister's embryo or some unmentioned responsibility precludes your doing so, you might well have an obligation of Christian mercy to try to bear him or her.

Finally, if you undertake this responsibility, be on guard against a possible temptation to harbor resentment toward your sister. While rightly deploring some of the things she did, you should forgive her for the pain she has caused. Pray that God also will forgive her; he alone knows how responsible she was for her life and death. Having forgiven your sister and prayed for her, you will be able to try to save her tiny baby as a pure act of love for him or her, an act you could also offer as a sacrifice for your sister.

52: May an infertile married couple try tubal ovum transfer with sperm?

We have been married five years and have no children. The first two or three years, we were not concerned, but then we began seeking medical help. Wishing to follow the Church's teaching, we have gone only to Catholic doctors. Our family doctor thought that NFP might solve our problem, and she taught us how to use it. After we had tried that unsuccessfully, the gynecologist my wife used to see thought in vitro fertilization might work for us, but we found out that the Church says it is wrong, and neither of us liked the idea very much anyway.

Now we have another doctor who has told us about something called "TOTS" (tubal ovum transfer with sperm), which is different from in vitro fertilization.[191]

191. The procedure described sometimes is called GIFT, but some people use *GIFT* to refer to a slightly different procedure; see Nicholas Tonti-Filippini, "'Donum Vitae' and Gamete

Working through a very small opening in the wife's abdomen, the doctor removes an ovum from the surface of her ovary. The couple have intercourse using a special kind of condom with a small hole in its tip; part of the semen is caught and part of it leaks into the vagina. (We did this once before to provide a semen sample for testing and were assured by a very solid priest that it is morally all right.) The doctor prepares the ovum and the semen, then puts them both into a thin tube with an air bubble between to keep them apart until they are injected into the wife's fallopian tube, where, if all goes well, conception occurs just as it normally does.

We are not very enthusiastic about this either, but, unlike in vitro fertilization, it does not involve making several babies and then, perhaps, discarding or freezing some of them. The doctor tells us the Church has never said tubal ovum transfer is wrong and some theologians who support the Church's teaching on contraception think there is no moral problem with it. What do you think?

Analysis:

This question calls for the derivation of a moral norm regarding TOTS. Since the ovum and semen used in TOTS do not pertain to any act of marital intercourse, this procedure, when successful, produces a baby by technology rather than contributes to a marital act's fruitfulness. Whenever babies are produced by technology, they are intended by those who want them as means to parental fulfillment. Using technical means to assist the marital act's natural fruitfulness is morally acceptable, but doing so to satisfy desire for a prospective child as a means to parental fulfillment vitiates any use of technical means.

The reply could be along the following lines:

You not only manifest your faith by your commitment to follow the Church's teaching but conscientiousness by your readiness to question the moral acceptability of a procedure whose morality has not been addressed by Church teaching.[192] Though you are not very enthusiastic about either IVF or TOTS, it is clear that no one has explained to you why IVF is wrong and how TOTS compares to it. Yet understanding these matters is essential to answering your question. Therefore, I will try to explain them and will begin by discussing the desire for children.

It is natural for people who marry to hope for children. The good of marriage is centered in one-flesh communion, whose natural basis is the exercise and fulfillment of the reproductive function (see *LCL,* 555–74). Hence, having a baby does fulfill the couple precisely as a married couple. Human instincts and feelings naturally and strongly favor this fulfillment, especially in the case of women, whose erotic inclination tends toward not only engaging in intercourse but nurturing a

---

Intra–Fallopian Tube Transfer," *Linacre Quarterly,* 57:2 (May 1990): 68–89, not only for terminological clarifications but for a moral analysis of the procedure.

192. For discussion, see Donald G. McCarthy, "TOTS Is for Kids," *Ethics and Medics,* 13:12 (Dec. 1988): 1–2; Donald T. DeMarco, "Catholic Moral Teaching and TOT/GIFT," in *Reproductive Technologies, Marriage and the Church,* ed. Donald G. McCarthy (Braintree, Mass.: The Pope John Center, 1988), 122–39; Donald G. McCarthy, "Response," in the same book, 140–45; John M. Haas, "Gift? No!" *Ethics and Medics,* 18:9 (Sept. 1993): 1–3; Donald G. McCarthy, "Gift? Yes!" in the same issue, 3–4.

baby in the womb and at the breast. These emotions coalesce with the marital commitment, the husband's and wife's mutual willing of the good of marriage for themselves and each other. So, a married couple naturally and reasonably want children and hope for them as part of their own fulfillment precisely as a married couple.

There is no entitlement to children, however. Sometimes couples who find themselves infertile feel not merely disappointed and unfulfilled but actually cheated, as if they had a right to beget and bear offspring. Couples able to marry, have children, and bring them up no doubt have a right to do so in the sense that other people and communities, such as political society, should respect and support marriage and family life, not suppress or interfere with them. But fertility is a gift of God, who owes nothing to anyone. Since no one has a duty to provide married couples with children, they can have no right to have them.

Moreover, married couples' natural desire for children can be partially fulfilled in other ways (see *CCC*, 1654, 2379). Adopting children and raising them exercise many of the couple's specific capacities and fulfill them in many respects: the moral unity resulting from their mutual consent to marriage, their capacity to nurture and care for new human beings, and their cooperation with God in raising children for him. In other words, marriage as the fount of life is partially fulfilled by raising adopted children. But in one respect it is not fulfilled: No adopted child is precisely part of the fulfillment of marriage as a one-flesh unity, and the feeling motivating toward this fulfillment remains unsatisfied. Then, too, adoption may not be an option for some people. It may be impeded by the lack of a baby to adopt or other factors, or a couple may rightly judge that their negative feelings toward adopting would make it too risky for a prospective adopted child, and so rule it out. Still, every married couple can exercise their capacity for parenting by helping other parents in some way or by doing other things analogous to parenting, such as helping to care for retarded, handicapped, or elderly people who cannot care for themselves or need help in doing so.

Of course, some sterile couples will remain deeply dissatisfied. In general, however, there are many prospective goods for which we can act; and usually, having encountered a serious obstacle to accomplishing anything, we give up after a certain point—unless there is a strict obligation to press on—and start using our available resources of time, energy, and money in the pursuit of some other purpose with better prospects of success. Consequently, while it is understandable and right that couples with fertility problems make some effort to overcome them with medical help, it is hard to see any good reason for going to the great lengths that some do. In some cases it appears that the emotion involved is so strong that a couple become fixated on the goal of having a baby from their own flesh.

That fixation is morally questionable. The emotional focus is on having the prospective baby as a concrete state of affairs—a goal, a desired object. Volitionally, a baby may be sought to satisfy this intense emotional desire and to fulfill the married couple precisely insofar as that fulfillment is their own good. If so, the baby is not willed for his or her own sake, but as an instrumental good. This motivation is different from the normal case of a couple uprightly choosing to marry and have a family. They too, of course, can experience a strong desire to have a baby. But for such a couple, having and raising children are included in the benefits of marital fulfillment, and they hope for this whole, complex good of marriage as an end. Thus, the couple need not and usually do not seek a prospective child precisely as a goal instrumental to an ulterior benefit for themselves.

Your motivation in seeking to have a baby seems sound. Your dislike of IVF and TOTS may arise from a suspicion that both are used wrongly to satisfy a morally questionable desire for a baby. If so, I believe the suspicion is correct and points to the answer to your question: No couple entirely clearheaded about these methods could choose either with upright intentions. With both techniques, the baby is produced by technology to satisfy the couple's desire, and his or her coming to be cannot fulfill their one-flesh unity since it is not the fruit of a marital act. That is obvious in IVF, where the ova are taken from the wife's body, the semen obtained (even if from the husband) by masturbation, and the two combined in the laboratory. It is less obvious, but still the case, with TOTS.[193]

Since with TOTS the ovum is taken from the wife's body prior to intercourse, that act of intercourse could not fertilize it, and since the semen used to fertilize the ovum is the portion of the ejaculate that is intentionally gathered by the sheath, it could not pertain to marital intercourse, as did the ejaculate which, leaking into the vagina through the hole in the sheath, constituted their act as intercourse. The latter point can be further explained. If there were no hole in the sheath, no semen would reach the vagina, and so the act, not making the couple one flesh, would not be intercourse. The semen that is intentionally prevented from reaching the vagina obviously does not pertain to intercourse but is incidental to it.

Thus, a child's coming to be by means of TOTS cannot fulfill the couple's one-flesh unity, for that child is in biological continuity with his or her parents, not insofar as they are one flesh, but only insofar as they are two distinct sources of the elements used by the technician. Not being the fulfillment of the couple as a one-flesh unity, the baby's coming to be cannot be willed by them as an aspect of their willing of that benefit, and so (assuming they clearly understand what they are doing) they cannot hope for the baby as a gift in hoping for fulfillment of their one-flesh unity. Rather, when a couple choose to use technology to produce a wanted baby, they seek his or her coming to be, not as part of their fulfillment as parents, but as a goal subordinated and merely instrumental to that fulfillment.

Someone might object that the couple, though acting to satisfy their desire to have a baby of their own, can hope for the child, not as instrumental to their own fulfillment, but as a great good, entirely separate and distinct from any fulfillment

---

193. Though I think my position on TOTS is not only true but implied by what the Church already teaches about IVF, Catholics who think the matter through, conclude that TOTS is morally acceptable, and act on that judgment do not thereby violate anything the Church expressly teaches (as of Jan. 1997). In my judgment, the procedure usually called *GIFT,* if distinct from TOTS, is morally objectionable for the same reasons as TOTS and perhaps for other reasons too; see Benedict M. Ashley, O.P., and Kevin D. O'Rourke, O.P., *Healthcare Ethics: A Theological Analysis,* 3rd ed. (St. Louis: Catholic Health Association of the United States, 1989), 284–86. IVF, of course, also is gravely immoral inasmuch as "spare" embryos are discarded, frozen, or used for experimentation.

of themselves. But that is impossible. One always realizes oneself by acting, and so never acts without self-fulfillment in view. Therefore, one can love the good of another person only insofar as that good is not entirely separate and distinct from one's own fulfillment but is joined with it in a common good. If the baby's good were entirely separate and distinct, however, the couple and the child would have no good in common, and so the couple would have no reason to act for the child as an end in himself or herself.

The opponent might object: The adopted child can no more fulfill the couple's one-flesh unity than the child conceived through TOTS; therefore, if the argument were sound, it would exclude not only TOTS but adoption. But adoptive parents can act with a common good in view: community with the already-existing child who needs parents. In seeking to produce a child by technical means, however, people cannot be acting for the sake of community with that child, since there is, as yet, no one with whom to initiate community. Hence, in seeking to produce a child, a couple must be acting for their own fulfillment as parents, and since the child to be produced is, as such, extrinsic to that, it is inevitable that he or she initially be sought as an instrumental good, not loved for his or her own sake.

Technical means sometimes are used, not to produce a baby, but to assist the marital act by removing obstacles to its fruitfulness, just as technique is used to assist other bodily functions when abnormal conditions interfere with them. In assessing the morality of technical assistance to the marital act, one must consider both the intrinsic character of what is done and the motives for doing it.

Assisting the marital act is not wrong in itself, so long as the couple engage in a genuine marital act that remains the real cause of the child's conception. Instead of the actual procedure used in TOTS, suppose that after the couple engaged in a normal act of intercourse, the semen were taken from the vagina and/or the ovum from the ovary, and one or both elements, perhaps after treatment of some pathological condition or conditions, were moved to the fallopian tube where they could meet. Provided the intention motivating such procedures were precisely to assist the marital act, these steps would do that. Somewhat similar technical maneuvers, however, could violate rather than assist the marital act, if they were intended, for example, merely as a scientific experiment or as a way to delay conception by freezing the elements so that the couple might choose to have a child later.

Such complex procedures may or may not be possible. If they become available, couples still should examine their motives. Those who are not trying to produce a baby by technical means but are only using technique to assist marital intercourse, and even those who are engaging only in unassisted intercourse, may nevertheless be acting with the unsound motivation, inherent in IVF and TOTS, of wanting a child for their self-fulfillment. In times past, parents who did not love children for themselves sometimes wanted them merely as heirs to carry on the family line or as hands to work the land. Today, economic considerations are more likely to motivate contraception and abortion, but perhaps more people than in former times have other motives, such as the prospect of emotional gratification, for wanting a child without loving him or her as a distinct, unique person. All married couples who desire a child should examine their motives and criticize them, to ensure that they are not interested in the baby as one among the many things they consider necessary or helpful for their self-fulfillment. They should hope for a baby as a gift who, while making their love fruitful, will be loved for his or her own sake. Having intercourse with that hope in mind is not using the marital act as a means of producing a child.

53: May a woman whose uterus is badly damaged have a hysterectomy?

I have been pregnant seven times, have had four miscarriages, and have three children, all delivered by caesarean section. Now I am pregnant again. I am being cared for by Dr. Brown, the same obstetrician who cared for me last time, when the pregnancy went to term and we had our first son. Like all the earlier pregnancies, this one has been difficult, but now there are only six weeks to go.

Yesterday Dr. Brown, who is a devout Catholic and prolife, told my husband and me that he thinks my tubes should be tied when he delivers the baby. He knows that we have followed the Church's teaching and used natural family planning (NFP), and that I quit my previous doctor when he insisted I be sterilized or find another doctor. But Dr. Brown says he thinks tying my tubes would not go against the Church's teaching.

He explained it to us this way. My uterus, he said, is in such bad shape that another pregnancy might well end in disaster, and so removing it would be in order. But to remove it, he would have to tie and cut my tubes. Once that was done, however, pregnancy would be impossible, and so actually removing the uterus would be unnecessary. Dr. Brown says even theologians who accept the Church's teaching against sterilization have said that tying the tubes in such a case is something different, called "uterine isolation."

My husband and I have talked this over and are not sure it makes sense. Something else also has occurred to me. If it would be morally acceptable to remove my uterus, I think I might prefer that anyway. I plan to take estrogen after menopause, and I understand it is simpler for a woman whose uterus has been removed. Also, my eldest sister and two other relatives on my mother's side of the family have died of cancer of the uterus and, while there is no sign that I have cancer, I would just as soon not run the risk. Therefore, I think I'd rather have my uterus removed, if Dr. Brown agrees.

What do you think about both things. Do you consider "uterine isolation" different from sterilization? If so, would it be morally acceptable for me to go all the way and have my uterus removed rather than just having my tubes tied?

Analysis:

This question calls for the application of moral norms and a judgment regarding the acceptability of a hysterectomy. Recently, the Church has taught that so-called uterine isolation is direct sterilization. But since the questioner's purposes are entirely distinct from preventing conception, she could choose to have a hysterectomy while only accepting sterility as a side effect. The health benefits she hopes to gain ordinarily would not warrant accepting sterility and the burdens of having a hysterectomy. But she could rightly accept sterility inasmuch as she has a good and perhaps obligatory reason no longer to exercise her capacity to procreate. The prospective benefits of the hysterectomy will not be offset by such surgery's usual burdens, most of which will be entailed by the caesarean section.

The reply could be along the following lines:

As Dr. Brown told you, some faithful theologians have said that so-called uterine isolation differs from other sterilization and is morally acceptable.[194] However, the Congregation for the Doctrine of the Faith has issued a document, approved and ordered published by John Paul II, in which both this procedure and hysterectomy in the same circumstances are judged to be direct sterilization.[195]

The Church's teaching on this matter is easily explained. The damaged condition of your uterus does not in itself medically indicate that it needs to be removed. If it did, Dr. Brown would be saying you need the hysterectomy rather than proposing uterine isolation. Tying your tubes will forestall a possible disaster, not by improving the condition of your uterus, but only by preventing conception. Therefore, in uterine isolation, the chosen means of forestalling disaster is preventing conception, and the choice to prevent conception by tying the tubes is contraceptive sterilization.

Nevertheless, in my judgment you could choose to have your uterus removed without choosing to prevent pregnancy and without violating any moral norm. Your concerns—to simplify estrogen replacement therapy and to eliminate the risk of uterine cancer—are in themselves grounded in the intelligible good of health. For most women, of course, it would be unreasonable to have major surgery for those purposes alone. In your situation, however, satisfying these concerns by choosing hysterectomy could be reasonable, because the operation would involve few additional burdens. You would already be undergoing the major surgery required for a caesarean delivery, and the loss of your capacity to procreate would be insignificant inasmuch as you have a good, and perhaps even obligatory, reason no longer to exercise that capacity. So, I think you may tell Dr. Brown that, provided he sees no medical indication against a hysterectomy, you wish him to do it in order to eliminate the risk of uterine cancer and facilitate estrogen replacement therapy after menopause.

I must point out, though, that if the advice I have offered you is regarded legalistically, it is likely to be abused by others. Your question makes it clear that you and your husband have followed the Church's teaching and withstood your previous physician's insistence that you be sterilized. Plainly, in raising the possi-

194. See Thomas J. O'Donnell, S.J., *Medicine and Christian Morality,* 2nd ed. rev. (New York: Alba House, 1991), 138–44; but see the same author's "'Uterine Isolation' Unacceptable in Catholic Teaching," *Linacre Quarterly,* 61:3 (Aug. 1994): 58–61, in which he retracts that opinion in view of the judgment of the magisterium on the matter.

195. See Congregation for the Doctrine of the Faith, "Responses to questions proposed concerning 'uterine isolation' and related matters" (31 July 1993), *AAS* 86 (1994) 820–21, *OR,* 3 Aug. 1994, 2.

bility of hysterectomy, you really are motivated by the concerns you state, which provide reasons for choosing a hysterectomy, and these concerns are entirely separate and distinct from preventing conception. Indeed, if you already were past menopause and undergoing abdominal surgery for some other reason, those same concerns could motivate you to have a hysterectomy. Others, however, desiring a hysterectomy for the purpose of sterilization, might insincerely use such considerations as an excuse, rationalizing their choice rather than justifying it. So, I do not say any woman whose uterus is so seriously damaged that another pregnancy might end in disaster and who is about to undergo a caesarean section may rightly use such considerations as a ground for having a hysterectomy. Rather, I am saying only that you—or a woman in your situation and with your ends in view—may choose a hysterectomy unless her physician judges that there are medical indications against it.

Finally, if the hysterectomy is performed, you and your husband probably will be glad you no longer need practice NFP. Someone might say such gladness either is wrong in itself or a sign that the hysterectomy was contraceptive. Neither will be true. With your purposes, the hysterectomy will not be contraceptive, though sterility will result as a side effect. And it will no more be wrong for you to rejoice over the advantageous aspects of that sterility than it is wrong for couples to rejoice over the advantageous aspects of the normal sterility during each cycle and after menopause.

54: May a tubal ligation be done on a woman who is severely retarded?

I serve as a volunteer with an organization that works with pregnant women and encourages them to choose a morally acceptable alternative to abortion. A few weeks ago a prolife nurse, whom I'll call Ann, came to us bringing a beautiful twenty-four-year-old woman, whom I'll call Jane. Due to her mother's alcoholism, Jane is severely retarded; mentally she could be a preadolescent child. Otherwise she is healthy, psychologically normal, even tempered, and affectionate. She is not institutionalized but lives in a shelter operated by the city for people who need help caring for themselves.

Jane was pregnant for the fourth time. Her previous pregnancies had been terminated by abortions, and her social worker was arranging another abortion after Jane missed her period and tested positive on a pregnancy test. Ann and I did our best to get Jane to understand her situation, and she then wanted to have the baby. I managed to prevent the scheduled abortion and took Jane to my own obstetrician, but about two weeks later she miscarried.

That was ten days ago, and since then Ann and I have been thinking about Jane's future. She almost certainly will get pregnant repeatedly, and her social worker almost certainly will arrange repeated abortions, at least some of them probably beyond our ability to prevent. We feel sure that when Jane has sexual intercourse, her grasp on what she is doing is insufficient for her to refuse it, so that she is not committing a sin of adultery or fornication. Rather, she is being played with by men who are retarded or taken advantage of by men who should know better. In other words, although a friendly, nonthreatening man need not use force to get Jane to have intercourse with him, she is being raped, morally speaking, since she really cannot consent—using *consent* in the relevant sense.

A chaplain at the Catholic hospital where Ann works told her that, while a woman who has been raped may not have an abortion, not only she but a woman who anticipates being raped may try to prevent conception. But if contraception depended on Jane, it would not work, while the IUD or anovulants not only might have bad side effects for her but sometimes are abortifacient. Since her retardation is a permanent condition, contraception, if it is permissible, would better be permanent. Therefore, Ann and I are wondering whether it would be all right to suggest that Jane's social worker arrange a tubal ligation for her.

Analysis:

This question concerns the application of the norm that excludes direct sterilization. If doing a tubal ligation on a severely retarded woman were intended to prevent conception, not insofar as it is the beginning of a new person, but insofar as it is the fullness of wrongful sexual union, that act, in my judgment, would not be an instance of the sterilization which the Church condemns. Moreover, if the act were not wrong on other grounds, its suppression of the woman's reproductive function could be a morally acceptable side effect rather than intentional mutilation. Nevertheless, doing a tubal ligation on a woman who is retarded would be wrong if those responsible for her care neglect any of their duties with regard to her sexual activity. Moreover, if they allow sexual activity and seek only to prevent conception, a tubal ligation would be an instance of sterilization, and therefore both contralife and an intentional mutilation. The tubal ligation also would be wrong if it is possible that the woman eventually will become capable of marital consent, or if there is some medical or psychological factor indicating it will not be in her best interests.

The reply could be along the following lines:

Even when every reasonable measure is taken to protect women who are retarded from being sexually abused, intercourse may occur and, if it does, occasionally pregnancy will result. But even if a woman is retarded to such an extent that she cannot consent to intercourse, her pregnancy and giving birth are not in themselves bad, and the child to whom she gives birth is a human person, with the same immeasurable dignity we all enjoy. Sometimes such children's mothers could help care for them; sometimes the children would have to be raised entirely by others. Both solutions can be good, and one of them always ought to be preferred to abortion.

You did well to prevent the abortion of Jane's baby. Killing unborn babies never is justified, even when pregnancy results from rape. The rapist gravely wrongs his victim, but the baby is entirely innocent and has the right to live and to be loved and cared for. Killing this innocent person only adds wrong to wrong. Moreover, even for victims of rape and incest who are capable of choosing to have an abortion, undergoing it is both physically and psychologically traumatic.[196] In Jane's case, aborting her three previous babies was, in my judgment, at least as great an injury and injustice to her as the sexual abuse from which their conceptions resulted.

You ask whether a tubal ligation may be arranged for Jane, to prevent probable future rapes from culminating in the conception of children who may well be aborted. Since you leave unclear how severe Jane's retardation is, and leave unstated various other circumstances that might dictate a negative answer, I shall not say yes or no. Instead, I shall articulate the considerations I think relevant and the moral norms I think should be followed, and leave it to you to apply the norms to Jane's case after ascertaining and considering the relevant facts.

First, nobody should take it for granted that persons who are retarded cannot appreciate the value of sexual purity, control themselves, and resist lustful advances. Like most young children of average intelligence, most people who are retarded have such capacities and can realize them, provided they receive suitable instruction and encouragement. Those in a position to provide the necessary help should do so.

Second, adults who cannot protect themselves from various sorts of mistreatment, including sexual abuse, should live in a sheltered community, with sufficient care and supervision to forestall most abuse, whether by persons within the community or by outsiders. Even apart from ulterior bad consequences, the sexual abuse of a person who is retarded, like similar abuse of a child, is a grave evil, and its victims also are likely to suffer greatly. While persons who are retarded should enjoy the freedom required to participate in authentic human goods according to their capacities, it is gravely wrong for those responsible for them to neglect to protect them from sexual activities with one another and from being abused by other people who know the wrongness of doing so.

Third, they do grave wrong who, regarding the abuse itself as no great evil and allowing it, seek only to prevent consequences they consider undesirable for themselves or society. If such wrongdoers try to prevent women who are retarded from becoming pregnant by giving them the pill or having their tubes tied, they plainly intend their actions to impede new life and so, in my judgment, they engage in the acts of contraception and sterilization that the Church condemns.

Fourth, a man who engages with sufficient reflection and consent in nonmarital sexual intercourse with a woman incapable of giving or withholding her consent commits the mortal sin of rape (even if he need use no force because his victim offers no resistance or even welcomes his advances). Those who commit such a sin of rape generally also commit a crime. The resources of the law should be used as fully in pursuing and punishing these criminals as in pursuing and punishing those who commit similar crimes against people of greater mental ability and higher

196. For some psychological evidence that abortion is not beneficial to victims of rape and incest: Sandra Kathleen Mahkorn, "Pregnancy and Sexual Assault," and George E. Maloof, "The Consequences of Incest: Giving and Taking Life," in *The Psychological Aspects of Abortion,* ed. David Mall and Walter F. Watts (Washington, D.C.: University Publications of America, 1979), 53–110. For some personal accounts by victims of rape or incest who underwent abortion: David C. Reardon, *Aborted Women: Silent No More* (Chicago: Loyola University Press, 1987), 206–18.

social status. Equally important, those who may be tempted to commit such crimes—including all who regularly come into contact with retarded persons—should be warned that they will be prosecuted if they do.

Fifth, papal teaching has neither affirmed nor denied that trying to prevent conception that might result from rape violates the moral norm excluding contraception as intrinsically evil. However, the U.S. bishops have recently taught—and I agree—that trying to prevent conception that might result from rape is consistent with the Church's teaching.[197] In explaining this position, I presuppose that sexual intercourse should realize and perfect marital communion, which unites spouses so intimately that they truly are one flesh. On this view, conception resulting from marital intercourse is not only the beginning of a new person but the ultimate fulfillment of the spouses' communion. So, chosen by the married, contraception is both contralife and a mutilation of intercourse that prevents it from actualizing marital communion (see *LCL*, 506–19 and 634–39). Chosen to forestall a conception resulting from rape, however, preventing conception is a specifically different kind of moral act. Mutilation of marital intercourse is not in question, and preventing conception need not be contralife, because conception resulting from rape has a special significance. It consummates the wrongfully imposed intimate union (which, of course, is one reason why some people, ignoring the child's distinct being and inherent dignity, mistakenly think abortion uniquely justifiable in cases of rape). Accordingly, I have proposed an explanation of the moral significance of preventing conception due to rape:

> Rape is the imposition of intimate, bodily union upon someone without her or his consent, and anyone who is raped rightly resists so far as possible. Moreover, the victim (or potential victim) is right to resist not only insofar as he or she is subjected to unjust force, but insofar as that force imposes the special wrong of uniquely intimate bodily contact. It can scarcely be doubted that someone who cannot prevent the initiation of this intimacy is morally justified in resisting its continuation; for example, a woman who awakes and finds herself being penetrated by a rapist need not permit her attacker to ejaculate in her vagina if she can make him withdraw. On the same basis, if they cannot prevent the wrongful intimacy itself, women who are victims (or potential victims) of rape and those trying to help them are morally justified in trying to prevent conception insofar as it is the fullness of sexual union.
>
> The measures taken in this case are a defense of the woman's ovum (insofar as it is a part of her person) against the rapist's sperms (insofar as they are parts of his person). By contrast, if the intimate, bodily union of intercourse is not imposed on the woman but sought or willingly permitted, neither she nor anyone who permits the union can intend at the same time that it not occur. Hence, rape

---

197. National Conference of Catholic Bishops, *Ethical and Religious Directives for Catholic Health Care Services* (Washington, D.C.: United States Catholic Conference, 1995), directive 36, provides: "A female who has been raped should be able to defend herself against a potential conception from the sexual assault. If, after appropriate testing, there is no evidence that conception has occurred already, she may be treated with medications that would prevent ovulation, sperm capacitation, or fertilization. It is not permissible, however, to initiate or to recommend treatments that have as their purpose or direct effect the removal, destruction, or interference with the implantation of a fertilized ovum."

apart, contraceptive measures are chosen to prevent conception not insofar as it is the ultimate completion of intimate bodily union but insofar as it is the beginning of a new and unwanted person. (*LCL*, 512)[198]

Sixth, since a person's bodily integrity, which is damaged by mutilation, is an aspect of the basic good of life, it always is wrong to choose precisely to mutilate a person, that is, to remove some bodily part or suppress some bodily function. So, sterilization is wrong as a method of contraception, not only as other forms of contraception are, but also as mutilating (see *LCL*, 544–45).[199] But it can be right to choose to do something of itself good which at the same time mutilates—for example, to remove a cancerous limb or organ, or even to suppress a function healthy in itself that is gravely harming the body as a whole (see *LCL*, 542–43). In my judgment, if an attempt to prevent conception that might result from rape were justified, choosing as a means to tie the tubes of a woman who will never be able to consent to intercourse would be choosing, not precisely to mutilate her, but to protect her against the fullness of sexual intimacy—to stop a rapist's sperm from reaching her ovum and penetrating it.

Seventh, many persons are capable of marital consent despite being somewhat retarded. They have the same right to marry as anyone else, although they may need special help to find a suitable spouse and to carry on their marriage and family life. To sterilize such a person would be a grave injustice toward him or her.

In sum, it seems to me that, if those responsible for the care of a woman so retarded she cannot consent to sexual intercourse have done and continue to do all they should to protect her from abuse, and if it nevertheless remains likely that she will become pregnant again, they could choose to have her tubes tied so as to prevent conception, not insofar as it is the coming to be of a new person, but insofar as it is the fullness of sexual union. In my judgment, that would not be the sterilization the Church condemns and its choice would not *necessarily* be morally wrong. Even so, tying the woman's tubes would be morally wrong if she might eventually be capable of marital consent or if there were some medical or psychological factor indicating that the operation was not in her interests.[200]

---

198. With regard to attempts to prevent conception after a rape has occurred, see q. 64, below.

199. Pius XII, *Vegliare con sollecitudine* (Allocution to the Italian Union of Midwives), *AAS* 43 (1951) 843–44, *Catholic Mind*, 50 (Jan. 1952): 55, precisely defines the sterilization that always is immoral: "Direct sterilization, that which aims at making procreation impossible as both means and end, is a grave violation of the moral law, and therefore illicit."

200. A routine practice of sterilizing women who are retarded is a grave injustice in itself and an even greater injustice toward those capable of marital consent and intentionally deprived of motherhood in a fruitful marriage. I suspect that the conditions I have stated in this proposed reply are seldom met, and that most sterilizations of women who are retarded facilitate neglect and are meant to prevent conception precisely as the beginning of new life. Catholic institutions responsible for the retarded should not, in my judgment, have a woman sterilized; rather, they should provide care and supervision adequate to forestall almost all sexual abuse. Moreover, individuals acting in the name of Catholic entities should not, in my judgment, authorize or consent to sterilization. Such cooperation inevitably would be perceived by many people as approval of sterilization as a method of birth control, and that perception would cloud the Church's witness to the relevant moral truth and give scandal by contributing to the rationalization of sterilization.

55: Should a hospital agree to a hysterectomy on a mentally handicapped girl?

I am the chaplain at a Catholic hospital and serve on its ethics committee. At our next meeting, we will be dealing with an unusual case.

The patient, a girl of fourteen, has been shown through chromosome studies to be afflicted with a rare genetic disease. Though mentally deficient and incapable of speech, she has some mental capacity, has been able to communicate to some extent with her parents, is receiving special education, and has learned some sign language.

This patient, whose reproductive system is normal, began menstruating a year ago June. Her periods are normal and have become very regular. From the onset, it was clear that the young woman is very uncomfortable with menstruation, and, as time went by, she became increasingly upset and irritable during her periods. She expresses her anger by sign language and body language, sometimes kicking her parents and teachers. Often she must be taken home from school because of her behavior and discomfort. Her psychological reaction does not seem to result from premenstrual syndrome, but from cramps and, perhaps, local discomfort, since keeping her clean and dry while she is menstruating is difficult.

Our staff psychiatrists referred the case to a psychologist who has worked successfully with people who are severely mentally handicapped. He saw the young woman frequently, but gave up after two months, saying he did not think he could communicate with her sufficiently to be of any help. Now her parents have asked a gynecologist on the hospital's staff to do a hysterectomy to eliminate her menstruation and the problems it leads to. He persuaded the parents to accept a delay and gave the patient an injection of a drug he hopes will suppress menstruation for a few months. In his opinion, if that treatment is effective, it probably can be continued indefinitely without serious side effects.

But, talking with me, the parents said they regard medical suppression of their daughter's periods as a stopgap rather than a long-term solution. I suspected they might have mixed motives in seeking the hysterectomy, and pointed out that the young woman eventually might manifest enough maturity to marry and then would have the right to do so, despite what I understand to be a fifty percent chance that any offspring would inherit her affliction. The parents said they think it very unlikely that she ever will be able to marry. My impression is that they love her very much, are trying to do what they believe is best for her, and really do wish to end the distress and trouble her periods are causing her and them, rather than to eliminate the possibility that she will get pregnant.

I make every effort to advise other members of the committee in accord with the Church's teaching. In this case, however, it seems to me that nothing in that teaching indicates what the hospital should do. What advice do you think I should give?

+ + +

Analysis:

The question is whether doing a hysterectomy is morally acceptable in this case. If the intention to prevent pregnancy is excluded, the Church's teaching does not answer the question. The judgment whether to use this means of eliminating the troublesome menstrual periods must be made by considering the reasons, grounded in prospective benefits and burdens, for and against doing the hysterectomy. In my opinion, the operation is not warranted at present. If developments strengthen the case for doing it, an effort should be made to determine whether the woman will eventually be capable of marital consent. If she will be, consideration must be given to whether it would be fair to deprive her of fertility.

The reply could be along the following lines:

I think you should test your impression that the parents are not trying to prevent pregnancy by gently but straightforwardly asking them, if you have not already, whether they are seeking the hysterectomy, at least in part, because they fear that their daughter eventually might either become pregnant due to rape or marry and transmit her affliction to a child. Intending the hysterectomy to prevent pregnancy within marriage, even if that were only one motive among several, would turn the act into contraceptive sterilization, which is always wrong. Intending it to eliminate the risk of pregnancy resulting from rape might not be contraceptive sterilization, but even so might be morally questionable (see q. 54, above). In any case, do your best to make sure the parents do not proceed with unexamined mixed motives, for if they were to act in bad faith they would incur guilt for a serious sin they might persist in rationalizing and never repent.

If their request for a hysterectomy is not motivated by a concern to prevent pregnancy, I agree with you that nothing in the Church's teaching indicates what should be done in this case. It seems to me the gynecologist on the hospital's staff acted rightly in persuading the parents to delay and giving the young woman a drug he hopes will suppress menstruation temporarily. If this treatment succeeds initially and can be continued for a time without undue side effects, the young woman might mature sufficiently and/or become receptive to psychological counseling, so that menstruation will not be a serious problem. Or other ways of treating her problem might become available. Thus, the alternatives are not necessarily limited to lifelong medical suppression of her periods by means of the drug or an immediate hysterectomy. Moreover, the costs and risks of a hysterectomy argue strongly against using this permanent and radical treatment to deal with a problem that might be transient, and for which a stopgap might be adequate. Therefore, I would tell the parents that it is unreasonable, and therefore morally unjustifiable, to do the hysterectomy if the problem can be dealt with medically.

They may well find it hard to accept this advice. Try to help them do so, but proceed carefully. While they, like any parents, would fail gravely to meet their responsibilities if they did not love their daughter and try to do what is best for her, their care for her is commendable because it is so demanding on them. You and I cannot imagine their grief upon learning of their daughter's affliction, their years of struggle and frustration with her many unusual problems, and all the other sufferings she has brought them. Carrying so heavy a cross, they naturally experience each new problem as a great burden, so that anything that seems to offer a permanent solution to a problem has strong emotional appeal. Bear all this in mind and try to awaken their hope, so that they will realize as clearly as possible that this life as a whole is temporary, stopgaps often are appropriate, and heaven alone holds the lasting solution to their problems.

But what if the drug fails to suppress menstruation as the gynecologist hopes, or it has unexpected and unacceptable side effects, or eventual attempts to allow normal menstruation indicate that this patient is likely to have problems with her periods until menopause? Then, it seems to me, a careful study should be made to determine whether she ever will be capable of marital consent. If it is virtually certain she will not, if the intention to sterilize her is excluded, and if the costs and risks of a hysterectomy, including the possible psychological effects of the operation on her, seem warranted, I think the choice to perform a hysterectomy would be reasonable and appropriate.[201] If, however, there is some possibility that the young woman will become psychologically and morally mature enough to marry, that possibility must be taken into account. It must not be ruled out of consideration by assuming that mentally handicapped people cannot be good spouses and parents, though special support generally is needed. Moreover, as I said at the outset, a hysterectomy may not be chosen to prevent pregnancy within marriage, even if that were only one intention among others, because that would be sterilization. But even if the intention to sterilize is entirely excluded, it might be unfair to this woman to do the hysterectomy; for, if she eventually becomes capable of marriage, she will have the same right as anyone else to marry, and the hysterectomy would deprive her marriage of its appropriate fulfillment in children.

In judging whether doing the hysterectomy to eliminate her periods would be fair to her, I believe that, besides the degree of probability that she eventually will be able to marry, all the burdens and benefits to everyone concerned of both alternatives (that is, doing the hysterectomy and refraining from doing it in order to preserve her reproductive capacity) should be taken into account: the factors that weigh against continuing with medical suppression of her periods, the expected hardships for her and others due to her regular menstruation until menopause, the fulfillment children would bring to the marriage, the burdens parenthood would impose on the couple and on others, and so on. Having considered all the relevant factors, those making the judgment must imagine that the young woman eventually will marry, put themselves in her place, and ask whether they would understand what had been done, consider it reasonable, and accept it without resentment.[202]

201. Renée Mirkes, O.S.F., "Sex and Trisomy 21—Part One," *Ethics and Medics,* 15:5 (May 1990): 2–3, discusses a similar case and also thinks that the hysterectomy could be morally acceptable.

202. This case illustrates a subtle point. It might seem that the preceding analysis falls into proportionalism insofar as it allows the burdens as well as the benefits of prospective parenthood to be taken into account in deciding whether to do something that, in fact, will eliminate a person's reproductive capacity. However, provided the hysterectomy were not

56: May an HIV-positive student keep her infection secret?

I am a woman, twenty-one, beginning vacation after my third year of college. I have tested and retested positive for HIV. The fact that I'm perfectly healthy right now and the hope that better treatments will be found are some consolation. I've told my parents, and it already has been decided that I shall return to school in the fall. That leads to my question: May I keep my condition secret from the college's administrators and my fellow students?

If I say nothing, I will live in a dormitory suite with three other women, all close friends, sharing a bath and kitchenette. Also, I will be playing basketball, since I have a full basketball scholarship. The doctors tell me that if I am careful, the living arrangement will involve virtually no risk for the others, but continuing to play will involve minimal risk, though a real one, since players occasionally do bleed and get blood on one another. If I tell the school, I'm not sure what they'll do, but my guess is they will ask me to live in a one-person unit and not play basketball, while continuing my scholarship and keeping my condition confidential. If I don't tell the school but tell all the other students with whom I'll be in close contact, I don't know how they'll react, but probably someone will talk and soon everybody on campus will know.

I want to do the right thing. But many people react irrationally to anyone known to be HIV positive, and it's not easy to see what is right.

Analysis:

The moral issue the questioner raises is: How much risk to others can she fairly accept so as to keep her secret and continue her usual, legitimate activities? The answer should be sought by considering all the relevant facts and applying the Golden Rule. Also, mercy calls a Christian to put others' interests first unless some moral obligation forbids doing so. If the HIV infection resulted from drug abuse or illicit sexual activity, the questioner should repent and amend her life, if she has not already done so. If others were involved in such activity, she also should warn them and urge them to repent and to seek appropriate assistance.

The reply could be along the following lines:

While I shall do my best to answer your question, you surely will need far more moral guidance and spiritual help than I can give you. So, unless you already have a suitable person to talk with, I urge you to try to find someone who is faithful to the Church's teaching and a good listener—probably a priest—to provide that guidance and help.

You do not say what caused you to become HIV positive. Perhaps there was no wrongdoing on your part. But if there was, you should consider sacrificing your privacy and publicly bearing witness to relevant moral truths. Mistakenly imagining themselves to be invulnerable, many young people recklessly engage in

---

intended to prevent pregnancy, it would not be wrong in itself, and all the prospective burdens and benefits of parenthood would be considered solely as side effects, rightly taken into account in judging whether the act need be excluded as unfair or may be chosen for its genuine benefits to her and as fair to all concerned.

behavior that is both sinful and risky. Unless consideration for your family and friends requires you not to make your experience public, you might do great good by sharing it.

Then too, people in certain situations might have a right that the law would recognize to be told you have tested positive for HIV. I do not know whether that is so, but I suggest you look into the possibility. If the law very probably would recognize such a right, you should presume that you are morally obliged to respect it.

Perhaps neither of the preceding considerations provides a compelling reason for you to forgo secrecy about your condition—at least, not vis-à-vis the college administration and your fellow students. In that case, your question stands as you present it, and I respond as follows.

In principle, your problem is no different from that of many other people who cannot fulfill their responsibilities by engaging in activities good in themselves without accepting some risk of serious harm to others. The problem arises for anyone afflicted with a communicable or hereditary disease. In every such case, the moral question is whether it is fair to carry on one's usual, legitimate activities or whether one is required to modify them so as not to expose others. That can be decided only by applying the Golden Rule.

In doing so, one must take into account the interests of everyone concerned and all the ways their various goods are at stake. Then one must try to put oneself in others' places. When not prevented by some moral responsibility, a Christian also should be merciful, which means putting others before oneself.

Playing well in any sport is worthwhile in itself and so is personally fulfilling. Since you have a scholarship for basketball, you obviously play it well. So, to give up playing the game would be a sacrifice, even if it would not result in the loss of the scholarship. You say the doctors have told you that the risk for others involved in your continuing to play will be minimal but real. Its extent depends on many factors: how much hard contact is likely to occur in the games you would play, whether you play a position in which you are more or less likely to be involved in such contact, whether wounded players who might exchange blood are promptly taken out of the game and kept out, and so on. You must honestly consider all such factors and judge what is fair. No one else can do that for you.

It does seem to me, however, that, unless the risk of infecting others is almost nil or your responsibility to continue playing involves more than your personal commitment to the sport, you should stop playing basketball. On the assumption that, if you tell your college's administrators, you will be asked not to play but will not lose your scholarship, continuing to play is not required by any duty to either the school or others, such as your parents, who presumably would have to pay your tuition if you lost your scholarship. I doubt that the risk is almost nil; the doctors acknowledged some risk and probably did not exaggerate it. Granted, some people react irrationally to those known to be HIV positive. But can you honestly say it would be unreasonable for other basketball players to prefer to avoid the risk your playing would impose on them? Furthermore, like all of us, you desire others' compassion. Does not mercy, then, require you to give others' welfare the benefit of any residual doubt, rather than exercise your own questionable right to continue to play?

Someone might suggest that you could go on playing, provided you told your teammates and the members of opposing teams about your condition. I do not think that would solve the problem. Plainly, if you shared the information with that many people, it would become common knowledge. Moreover, school administrators or league officials might intervene and stop you from playing. And even if you were able to continue, telling other players about your condition probably would mean that some would refuse to accept the risk of playing the game with you, while, for those who did play, it would reduce but not eliminate the risk to them. Then too, if your opponents knew you are HIV positive, they almost certainly would try to avoid contact with you, and that would give you an unfair advantage over them.

With respect to your living arrangements, you say the doctors tell you that, if you are careful, you will impose virtually no risk on your three friends by living with them in a dormitory suite, with a shared bath and kitchenette.[203] If you do share in that way, it seems to me you should confide in your three friends about having tested HIV positive. Even if the risk of living with you is virtually nil, it hardly would be friendly to deny them the opportunity to decide for themselves whether they wish to take the risk. Then too, if they know, by taking precautions they can almost eliminate any residual risk to themselves—for instance, by being careful never to use anything that might have your blood on it, such as your toothbrush, nail clippers, or razor. Moreover, friendship calls for sharing one's concerns, not hiding them. If you do not take your friends into your confidence, you not only will deprive yourself of their support but will deprive them of the opportunity to grow by being loyal to you in this difficult situation.

Therefore, though I do not wish to substitute my attempt to apply the Golden Rule for your own conscientious and merciful application of it, it seems to me you should share your secret both with your three friends and the college administration. If you reach the same conclusion, I suggest you first have confidential talks with your three friends, and try to secure their agreement to carry out your plan to live together. All may agree, and almost certainly at least one will. You then can approach an appropriate school official and, before divulging your secret, request that the conversation be kept in the strictest confidence. Having received that assurance and explained that you have tested HIV positive, you should share the advice your doctors gave you as well as your friends' response to you. On that basis, you can try to work out an agreement to give up playing basketball, continue to receive your scholarship, and live with all or at least one of your friends.

Of course, if you accept this suggestion, carrying it out will involve some risk. One or more of your friends might violate your confidence and spread word about your condition. Also, contrary to your expectation, the college might not only ask

---

203. A summary of information about the epidemiology of HIV: John G. Bartlett and Ann K. Finkbeiner, *The Guide to Living with HIV Infection,* developed at the Johns Hopkins AIDS clinic, 3rd ed. (Baltimore: Johns Hopkins University Press, 1996), 28–40; this volume summarizes a great deal of information that would be helpful to a person infected with HIV, but offers morally unsound recommendations on matters such as contraception and abortion.

you to stop playing basketball but take away your athletic scholarship. But do not overestimate the significance of these risks. That others know you are infected need not prevent you from living a good life in the time remaining to you, and, even if the college takes away your scholarship, both compassion for you and public relations considerations are likely to motivate it to find another way to help you complete your education. So, you can hope for the best in accepting the unavoidable risks in doing the right thing—which you commendably want to do.

If your infection with HIV resulted from drug abuse or nonmarital sexual intercourse, I hope you have repented that misbehavior as well as any other grave sins of which you were guilty and have firmly committed yourself to amending your life. Nothing is more important than that you live blamelessly before the Lord from now on so that you will die in his love. Moreover, if the infection resulted from wrongful activity with others whom you can identify, you ought to tell them you have tested positive, and urge them to repent, amend their lives, and obtain appropriate medical, psychological, and spiritual help. Finally, no matter how you became infected, you owe it to others to do what you reasonably can to minimize the risk of infecting them, especially to avoid all wrongdoing that might transmit the infection.

57: May a woman have a face-lift to gain a more youthful appearance?

I am a woman in my fifties. A little over a year ago, a checkup showed that my cholesterol had risen dramatically, and, since I no longer am ovulating, my doctor recommended I go on estrogen therapy. After looking into it, however, I decided not to, and instead took up a regular exercise program. My husband and I also changed our diet by drastically reducing saturated fats, so that now we are virtually vegetarians. As a result, my cholesterol has come down, and both of us have lost a lot of weight.

My husband feels and looks better than he has in years, and I feel five years younger. But, unlike him, I look ten years older, especially in the face. Careful makeup helps, but it cannot hide the pouches and wrinkles, and I am thinking of having a face-lift. A friend of mine had one a few months ago and looks years younger. She was very pleased with the surgeon who did it and with the hospital, where it was done on an outpatient basis. She needed only two or three weeks to recover, though she does have a couple of permanently numb spots where nerves were cut.

My husband, agreeable and supportive as always, says he will be happy with whatever I decide. He also told me he will love me just as much without as with a new face, since I still seem beautiful to him. Though I don't still seem beautiful to me, I know he meant it; he does not waste words and always means what he says. Then too, while I have a job outside our home, my appearance has no effect on my work. In short, I cannot say I *need* the face-lift. The total cost would be around ten thousand dollars, and my health insurance would not cover any of it. Still, I would like to look younger, and wonder whether that is a good enough reason to go ahead.

Analysis:

The questioner asks whether she may spend ten thousand dollars for a face-lift. If necessary to fulfill one's responsibilities, one could have a moral obligation to have such surgery. The questioner, however, is considering a face-lift simply to conceal the evidences of aging. Prizing youthful appearance for itself reflects conventional secularist values rather than sound human and Christian ones; it also manifests the wish to relate to others on the basis of a deceptive appearance. Rather than using ten thousand dollars for a face-lift, the questioner has an obligation, which in my judgment is grave, to use the money to meet genuine needs—if not her and her dependents' needs, then those of others.

The reply could be along the following lines:

While it is not quite true that beauty is in the eye of the beholder, perceptible beauty is relative to the perceptual capacities of those who perceive it. In some respects, these capacities are determined by nature, and to that extent people tend to agree in their judgments about beauty. For example, since bright, clear colors and regular, balanced shapes provide a good visual stimulus and are easily taken in, they are agreeable to anyone with normal visual perception, and so are regarded as beautiful by just about everyone. In other respects, however, perceptual capacities are determined by experience, which varies and whose shaping is influenced by emotions, and to that extent people disagree about what is beautiful. For example, those who lack experience of people belonging to other races or are prejudiced against them often find members of other races ugly, since they look so different from the way people "should" look. At the same time, individuals always look like themselves, and so they seem to appear just as they should to those who know them well, love them, and perceive them as the unique persons they are rather than as more or less good instances of some type. Since your husband perceives you in this way, you still seem beautiful to him.

Cosmetic measures, such as beauty treatments and makeup, serve at least four diverse purposes.

First, every culture develops certain conventions of personal appearance, some applying generally and others only to people in certain roles or on certain special occasions. These conventions usually involve wearing certain sorts of clothing and/or jewelry, and often involve cosmetic measures by either men or women, or both. Second, cosmetic measures can be used to enhance already satisfactory appearance in accord with either an individual's personal taste or commonly accepted esthetic standards, or both. Styling the hair and using cosmetics to highlight attractive facial features are examples. Since I do not think either of these purposes is among your motives for considering a face-lift, I shall not discuss them further.

Third, both makeup and cosmetic surgery can be used to correct or conceal abnormalities or blemishes. Since these can be repugnant to others, correcting or concealing them can facilitate interpersonal relations. It also can reduce feelings of embarrassment and increase self-confidence, thus improving a person's ability to function well. Cosmetic measures appropriate for such purposes are justified in themselves, though their use should be limited by other responsibilities. While cosmetic surgery often is used for this purpose, you do not say your appearance is abnormal for your age, and so I set this purpose aside.

That leaves only the fourth purpose: to conceal the evidences of the normal aging process, which are felt to be undesirable for two reasons. First, since aging causes deterioration and ends in death, its signs are repugnant; thus, appearing to be elderly is undesirable to both men and women, and people who appear to be older than sixty or sixty-five tend to be seen as diverging from the person-in-the-prime-of-life type. Second, since a woman's capacity and opportunity to mate is greatest shortly after she sexually matures, evolution has made the nubile young woman erotically appealing to men, with the result that many men see every woman who might be considered a possible sexual partner in terms of the nubile-young-woman type. By these ideals, beauty fades with age, and even middle-aged women who no longer appear youthful are more or less ugly.[204]

Thus, face-lifts often are used to conceal the evidences of aging and restore a youthful appearance, and this seems to be your motive. You say that, after losing weight, you "look ten years older" and your friend, after a face-lift, "looks years younger." Perceiving yourself as neither in the prime of life nor a nubile young woman, you no longer seem beautiful to yourself, and "would like to look younger." For several reasons, I do not think you should act on this motive.

In the first place, we Christians should both hope for everlasting life and habitually regard others and ourselves as complete, unique persons rather than mere instances of types such as *healthy adult* and *sexually attractive female (male)*. Our sense of self-worth should be based on those things in us that we know God values highly. The reasons that cause many people to feel that signs of aging are unattractive should not affect our self-esteem as Christians. Still, they do affect it because our perceptual standards are skewed by our corrupt culture—with its prejudice against the aged and obsession with sex—and our virtues of hope and modesty are imperfect. On this score, I suggest that, instead of getting a face-lift, you should resist the biases of our culture, bear in mind the gifts that accompany growing old, and try to see and value yourself as your husband does—as the unique person you are—rather than as an aging woman (see Prv 31.25–30). After all, you have no need to attract a mate or impress people with youthful vitality.

In the second place, people who get face-lifts, wishing to seem younger than they are, generally prefer that others not know about the operation. If others know, they do not regard the more youthful appearance as natural but are likely to see the renovated face as a mask, perhaps faintly ludicrous, perhaps pitiful. Concealment is necessary, both for effective deception and to forestall seeming vain. In this matter as in others, however, honesty is the best policy. Avoiding all deception and vanity, and allowing others to know one's true self enables one to live with them in more authentic communion.

---

204. Linda A. Jackson, *Physical Appearance and Gender: Sociobiological and Sociocultural Perspectives* (Albany, N.Y.: State University of New York Press, 1992), 65–67, supports this point and summarizes research showing that middle-aged men are considered more attractive than younger ones while middle-aged women are considered less attractive than younger ones.

The questionable purpose aside, getting a face-lift probably also would be more or less ineffective and perhaps even self-defeating for you. Facial pouches and wrinkles are not the only signs of aging; in their absence, other telltale signs sometimes become even more noticeable, and the discrepancy between a youthful face and other aspects of one's behavior and appearance can seem ugly. The apparent effectiveness of cosmetic surgery for entertainers and certain other public figures is somewhat misleading; makeup applied by experts and careful photography complement the surgeon's work and conceal any telltale signs and other incongruities. Moreover, a person's skin continues to age, so that after a few years the face no longer seems so youthful. And, like any surgery, a face-lift involves risks; you might suffer more serious consequences than your friend's couple of numb spots.

Does it follow that you also should avoid using makeup, as you have been, to mitigate the appearance of aging? No. Though makeup sometimes is a sign of vanity, its judicious use serves legitimate purposes other than trying to hide the signs of aging. You lost a good deal of weight suddenly, and your present appearance also is not normal for you. But this "abnormality" will be corrected naturally as time passes, for you and the people who know you will become accustomed to the new you. Meanwhile, inasmuch as you are justifiably using makeup for other reasons, you may use it insofar as you can to subtly mitigate your suddenly changed appearance.

Someone might say that, if you may rightly hide some abnormal signs of aging with makeup, you may regard all such signs as abnormal, so that you would be justified in getting a face-lift to correct or conceal them to the fullest possible extent.[205] That argument would be unsound, however, since not all signs of aging are abnormal. Moreover, your stated purpose in considering a face-lift was to gain a more youthful appearance. So, you should resist any tempting suggestion to let considerations about correcting or concealing abnormalities play a role in your deliberations. Bringing in such fresh considerations at this point would be mere rationalization.

Suppose you were widowed or changing jobs, and thought a more youthful appearance would help you remarry suitably or find a satisfactory job. Would getting a face-lift then be justifiable? Perhaps. Since a face-lift for the sake of appearing more youthful is not intrinsically evil, it can reasonably be chosen as a means to an ulterior good end. Still, even with such an end, one is surrendering to cultural pressures and reinforcing the biases that underlie them in trying to appear more youthful than one is. Therefore, it seems to me, only those whose personal vocation requires it are justified in having a face-lift to gain a more youthful appearance. In other words, getting a face-lift never is morally optional; either it is appropriate to fulfill one's responsibilities or it is morally excluded.

Finally, one factor makes your obligation not to get a face-lift be, in my judgment, a grave matter: the ten thousand dollars it would cost. Perhaps this money

---

205. This line of argument is a common rationalization of cosmetic surgeons and their patients; see Diana Dull and Candace West, "Accounting for Cosmetic Surgery: The Accomplishment of Gender," *Social Problems*, 38 (1991): 54–70.

should be used to meet some of your own or your dependents' current or predictable needs. If so, you should not use it for a face-lift, which you really do not need. If not, though, you should use this money to meet others' needs (see *LCL,* 780–82, 789–92, 800–806, 811–14). For instance, you might donate it to an organization that would use it to fund plastic surgery for some poor child born with serious facial deformities. Jesus teaches that, on the day of judgment, he will say to those who failed to meet others' needs: "'Truly I tell you, just as you did not do it to one of the least of these, you did not do it to me.' And these will go away into eternal punishment" (Mt 25.45–46). Instead of investing in a face-lift for yourself, invest in the kingdom of heaven, where alone we can hope to remain forever youthful.

58: May physicians, to protect themselves, order unnecessary examinations?

I practice family medicine in a small midwestern city—one large enough, however, to have good health care facilities. There is a small but well-managed hospital and an independent diagnostic center with well-trained technicians, a good lab, and up-to-date equipment, including equipment for CAT scans and MRIs. The diagnostic center is owned and operated by a consortium of local physicians, not including me—this arrangement already existed when I established my practice here three years ago.

Patients frequently come in with problems requiring sophisticated diagnosis, and I regularly use the diagnostic center. Usually this involves no problem, but sometimes I feel pressured to order X rays, CAT scans, and especially MRIs whose justification for diagnostic purposes is marginal at best. For example, recently I had a patient who was experiencing intermittent hearing loss and had a history and set of symptoms that virtually ruled out the possibility of an auditory nerve tumor. Still, there was a very small chance that examination at the diagnostic center would discover such a tumor. I could have ordered a CAT scan, costing about three hundred dollars, but if there actually were a tumor—which I estimate might be the case once in twenty thousand times or fewer—a CAT scan offers only about a sixty-five percent probability of detecting it, while an MRI, costing fifteen hundred dollars, increases that probability to about ninety-five percent. Although I felt even the CAT scan would be diagnostic overkill, I reluctantly ordered the MRI.

I did that because the alternative was to render myself vulnerable to a malpractice lawsuit. Patients today expect doctors to use every state-of-the-art method of diagnosis and treatment, and whenever a physician's effort fails to produce the results a patient hopes for—a complete and quick cure with no trouble or hardship—he or she is likely to begin talking to a malpractice lawyer. Confronted with this situation, nearly every physician and hospital administrator orders more tests, keeps more records, and takes various other precautions. Now, malpractice is defined by falling short of the common standard of practice adhered to by competent physicians engaged in similar practice in the same geographical area. Since other physicians in this city order more tests than I otherwise would, I have been forced to follow suit. The situation is made worse here by the understandable tendency of the physicians in the consortium that owns and operates the diagnostic center to make use of its facilities. I am not saying they order examinations and tests *solely* to make more money, but, in my judgment, they do order them in many cases where they would not if they did not have a stake in the diagnostic center. Consequently, their pattern of ordering examinations has ratcheted up the standard, and I have no choice but to conform.

I would be even more concerned except that virtually all the charges are paid on behalf of patients by either private insurance, Medicare, or Medicaid. Then too, sophisticated exams and tests sometimes do turn up significant and totally unexpected information. For example, the MRI that I ordered provides a complete brain scan, which is studied carefully by the radiologist who interprets it before he or she reads the referring physician's order indicating precisely what is to be checked out. With that method, the exam could result in early diagnosis of some serious pathology and thereby save a patient's life.

All the same, it seems unreasonable that anxiety about malpractice suits should drive medical practice to the extent it does.

Analysis:

This question is about the moral acceptability of reluctantly conforming to a false standard of good practice. That most charges are paid on behalf of patients does not justify conforming to the false standard. Nor is conformity justified by occasional, unexpected, diagnostic benefits. Physicians should defend themselves against malpractice litigation by reducing patients' unrealistic expectations, teaching them to understand the physician's role in helping patients care for themselves, and leaving many decisions to them, including those about matters where the fear of malpractice has contributed to a false standard of good practice.

The reply could be along the following lines:

Your explanation of the constantly rising standard of so-called good practice in your area indicates that an important factor is self-referral by the physicians involved in the consortium. Assuming you are correct in saying that they order examinations and tests "in many cases where they would not if they did not have a stake in the diagnostic center," their behavior is seriously flawed due to their conflict of interest. The patient cannot be justly billed for an examination or treatment that would not be ordered except for the physician's financial self-interest. When the principal benefit of ordering such examinations or treatments is to the physician rather than the patient, the physician profits by fraud—morally, at least, if not legally. Moreover, any unnecessary examination or treatment is itself burdensome to the patient who undergoes it, and so is an abuse of the patient and a grave betrayal of the trust that ought to be the basis of the physician-patient relationship. Then too, this basic evil of self-interested self-referral by certain physicians leads to many further evils, including the distortion of standards of good practice that has attracted your attention and concern.

The physicians involved might argue that setting up and managing the diagnostic center was justified by the lack of such facilities in your city and was reasonable for them, since their investment offered hope of a fair return from an enterprise they were especially well qualified to organize and conduct. I grant that, if there were no other way to obtain needed facilities, they had good reason to finance them and set them up. However, retaining an interest was bound to be an occasion of sin, constantly skewing judgments that ought to be made disinterestedly for patients' well-being. So, financial arrangements should have been made in such a way as to ensure that the use of the diagnostic facility made by physicians in the consortium would not affect the return on their investment.[206] If they wanted an investment opportunity, they could have chosen a different sort of vehicle or even invested in a similar facility in another town, where they would have had no conflict of interest.

The medical profession should act to prevent not only such conflicts of interest but their bad effects, especially exploitation of patients.[207] You share this responsibility. You should talk with your colleagues who belong to the consortium and urge them to end their conflict of interest. Whether or not that effort succeeds, you also should bring this problem, which is recurrent, to the attention of your medical society and urge steps to deal with it. Perhaps, too, you should discuss the matter with members of your state's legislature and encourage them to consider appropriate regulatory legislation.

Even if the abuse of self-referral were eliminated, however, the problem caused by a false standard of good practice arising from anxieties about malpractice suits would remain. When you say, referring to that false standard, "I have no choice but to conform," I must disagree. To explain the alternative, I shall begin by criticizing the two considerations you mention as lessening your concern about the problem.

Excusing diagnostic overkill on the grounds that private insurance and government programs pay the bills is mere rationalization. Insurance companies do not create money from nothing; they receive it from policy holders and pay it out—after taking a substantial percentage for overhead and, usually, for profit. The more they pay out, the more they are going to charge their policy holders. As for government programs, they are funded by taxpayers. Thus, everyone pays the bill for diagnostic overkill. It also is one of the factors that make adequate health care prohibitively expensive for many people who are not covered by insurance or a government program. Moreover, in most cases patients themselves directly pay some portion of the charge, often an amount large enough to constitute grave matter. Thus, the ordering of each unnecessary examination is likely to be a grave injustice to the patient concerned, and a policy of ordering such examinations also is unjust to payers of private insurance premiums and to the public at large.

206. That could have been accomplished in various ways, which I shall not describe here. Council on Ethical and Judicial Affairs, American Medical Association, *Code of Medical Ethics: Current Opinions with Annotations,* 1996–97 ed. (Chicago: American Medical Association, 1996), 8.032 (pp. 108–9), holds that, *in general,* physicians should not refer patients to a facility in which they have an investment interest, at which they do not provide care and treatment, and which is outside their offices; yet allows physicians to invest in a genuinely needed facility to which they will refer, provided there is no satisfactory alternative and various safeguards are met.

207. See Jean M. Mitchell, "Physician Joint Ventures and Self-Referral: An Empirical Perspective," in Roy G. Spece, Jr., et al., *Conflicts of Interest in Clinical Practice and Research* (New York: Oxford University Press, 1996), 300–317.

In considering the other excuse, I take it for granted that there often are legitimate differences among reasonable professional opinions about the medical indications for using various tests. However, the argument that a sophisticated examination such as an MRI brain scan occasionally leads to early diagnosis of some unsuspected serious pathology is not an adequate excuse for ordering it when, admittedly, no medically relevant indication really calls for it. The test then is being used as if it were so easy and cheap that it could be an appropriate part of a routine checkup. No doubt, the threat of malpractice suits puts conscientious and competent physicians under unjust pressure. But most patients are in no way responsible for that injustice, and it is not fair for physicians to shift the burdens it imposes on them to their patients.[208] Therefore, when you reluctantly ordered the MRI, motivated by a concern about your vulnerability to a malpractice suit, the test's occasional unexpected benefits did not compensate your patient for the cost and inconvenience.

But how can you deal with patients' unreasonable expectations and their tendency to sue for damages when physicians fail to satisfy them?

First, you must teach them to expect no more of you than you can give. That requires a systematic effort to reduce their exaggerated idea of your ability to a realistic level and lower their expectations that technology can work miracles. When unsure about your diagnosis or plan of treatment, make it clear to the patient that you are unsure. When your prudent judgment is that the best available treatment will have only poor results, warn the patient. The primary responsibility for your patients' survival and health is theirs, and they must understand that you can do no more than help them in limited, often ineffective ways. Teaching patients this also will motivate them to take better care of themselves and cooperate more fully with diet, regimen, and medical treatment you propose. Having entered into this type of physician-patient relationship, they are more likely to hold themselves responsible than to blame you for an unsatisfactory outcome.

Second, in properly carrying on this type of relationship, you will explain to patients, at a level they can understand, their health problems and possible ways of dealing with them. When there are medically acceptable and practically feasible alternative ways of dealing with problems, you will explain their pros and cons, and encourage patients to judge what is appropriate for them, considering their concrete circumstances and personal responsibilities.[209] When not all competent

---

208. Malpractice in health care occurs far more often than most people realize, and only a small proportion of physicians and others guilty of it are ever held accountable for the injuries and deaths they cause. Though some awards for damages no doubt are excessive, others are inadequate. Though malpractice insurers vigorously defend many cases, they make large profits. See Harvey F. Wachman with Steven Alschuler, *Lethal Medicine: The Epidemic of Medical Malpractice in America* (New York: Henry Holt, 1993); Paul C. Weiler et al., *Measure of Malpractice: Litigation and Patient Compensation* (Cambridge, Mass.: Harvard University Press, 1993).

209. Eric J. Cassell, *The Nature of Suffering and the Goals of Medicine* (New York: Oxford University Press, 1991), points out that many physicians focus almost exclusively on disease processes and fail to take into account the patient's wider perspective. Though not everything Cassell says is consonant with Catholic teaching, his reflections contain many sound insights that Catholic physicians should take into account.

and conscientious physicians would regard a test or examination as essential for a patient, you will describe it sufficiently so that he or she can evaluate its potential usefulness and burdens, and decide whether to accept it. Moreover, you often will remind patients of their right to seek a second opinion and will encourage doing so whenever you think it in the patient's interest.

Where fear of malpractice is a factor, you will say so frankly: "Many physicians would order this test (examination), but in this case, I think, they would do that mainly for fear of being sued in the unlikely event that its result would have been important for proper treatment. Personally, I do not think it worthwhile, but the choice, as usual, is yours." If a patient accepts your advice, you need only make and keep a record of your reasoning, and, if you think it necessary, ask the patient to sign a release indicating the purpose of the possible test or examination, and stating that it was offered and declined. When patients insist on questionable tests, the responsibility for the waste will be theirs.

The medical profession also has a responsibility, which you share, to work to rectify abuses motivated by anxiety about malpractice. Within the profession, excesses can be discussed and appropriate limits set and agreed upon, so that evidence of a reasonable standard of good practice will be available. Where excesses occur due to patient irresponsibility, insurers and other payers, including the government, should be told about problems so that they can take action. The professional also can promote appropriate legislation to regulate malpractice lawsuits, not merely to limit the size of awards (sometimes probably too low rather than too high), but to ensure that damages awarded are reasonably proportioned to the harm done and, perhaps even more important, to help the courts identify authentic standards of good practice.

At this point, some physicians are likely to object that following such advice would completely transform their professional work. They would spend a large part of their time telling people about their options and persuading them to consent to tests, examinations, and treatment that the standard of good practice requires and any competent physician would prescribe without hesitation. They also would use much more time than now dealing with colleagues and public officials. They simply would not have time to care for all their patients, with the bad results that some might not be so well cared for and the physicians' income would shrink significantly.

Part of my response to such objections is that the demands my advice imposes on physicians must not be pushed to absurd extremes. The time spent with a patient on a particular matter need not be great if its potential impact on his or her life is slight. Then too, taking into account—as they may and should do—various patients' differing abilities to understand the advantages and disadvantages of alternatives, physicians need not burden patients with information they simply cannot use in judging what is more appropriate for themselves. Again, a physician need not waste time explaining differences that are highly technical and affect only the probability of a favorable clinical outcome, rather than other aspects of a patient's life. Moreover, if an authentic standard of good practice really requires that a physician prescribe something, no technically acceptable alternative will be available, and reasonable patients generally will accept their physician's authority once the situation is explained.

Even so, I grant that following my advice would largely transform some physicians' professional work. (I trust and hope that in most respects the transformation would bring them into line with what you already are doing.) They would use their professional authority in a Christian way, serving patients by focusing on their best interests rather than serving the physicians' self-protection and convenience. These physicians would cooperate with their patients, on the basis of mutual understanding and shared purposes, not work on them as veterinarians work on animals.[210] They would spend more of their time being *doctors* (Latin: teachers) of medicine and health, and somewhat less being technicians. In short, they would be better physicians, practicing medicine as it should be practiced and providing patients with all the benefits to which they are entitled and which competent and conscientious physicians can help them obtain. They also would be doing their part to fulfill their responsibilities both as members of the medical profession, which should regulate itself and deal with its own problems, and as citizens who have the professional knowledge and skills to help legislators fulfill their responsibilities bearing on people's health and the health care professions.

All this would require some reallocation of many physicians' time, and no doubt they could not see as many patients. But the demands patients would make on their time should not be overestimated, since once the physician-patient relationship was reformed, long conversations would be necessary only occasionally, and patients, taking more responsibility for themselves and perhaps being in better health, would need to see physicians less often. Some of their present patients probably would prefer to find other doctors who would not care for them so well, but those who remained their patients would receive far better care–the sort of medical service every patient always deserves but quite a few never get. Though longer sessions with patients would warrant a higher fee per visit, physicians' income probably would shrink somewhat, but that would be a small price to pay for being good people as well as good doctors.

Of course, you are not held to do the impossible. But do not define what is possible by assuming that what would be very hard is impossible or that commonly accepted standards of practice need not change. Unfortunately, commonly accepted standards can be structures of sin, embodying the prevailing level of selfishness among members of a profession. It is the business of Christian moral reflection and conscience to bring such sin to light, so that we can stop being conformed to the world and instead be transformed by the renewing of our minds (see Rom 12.2). Naturally, to such light, darkness sometimes seems preferable. Transformation means giving up an existing, familiar self in exchange for a new self, known and

---

210. Sheila Cassidy, *Sharing the Darkness: The Spirituality of Caring* (Maryknoll, N.Y: Orbis Books, 1991), 18, remarks with respect to the physician-patient relationship: "We have to learn to be whole-person doctors because our patients are whole persons. It takes so much more time and energy. It is destroying our protective hierarchies, our sense of omnipotence. Our corridors of power have been invaded and we are having to learn humility!"

loved by God, but as yet unknown and so unappealing to ourselves: "If any want to become my followers, let them deny themselves and take up their cross and follow me" (Mk 8.34; cf. Mt 10.38, Lk 14.27).

59: Must a physician tell patients the whole truth about their bad prospects?

As an oncologist, a physician who specializes in treating people suffering from cancer, I do not believe in telling patients how bleak their prospects really are. I agree that it is wrong to lie to people, even "for their own good," but I also think it is wrong to be brutally frank. For example, when a worried patient asks, "What are my prospects?" I never lay out the statistical probabilities: "In your type of case and at this stage of the disease's progression, about fifty percent die within one year and nearly all within three." Instead I say something like: "Well, all of us will die sooner or later, but you still have some good time left, and if you cooperate fully with my treatment plan, we'll stretch that out as much as possible." Even in cases where treatment is quite successful, we know that very often a recurrence is probable. If patients don't ask, I say nothing, though, of course, I schedule regular checkups. If they ask, I tell them: "There is no guarantee that anybody will stay healthy, but in cases like yours, patients sometimes live to a ripe old age with no more signs of cancer. And, with regular checkups, we'll catch any problems before they develop very far."

Some of my colleagues think my approach is dishonestly evasive and "paternalistic." The trouble with telling the whole truth, however, is that it distresses all patients and their families, kills the incurable patient's hope, and causes the successfully treated patient years of unnecessary anxiety—and there is evidence that anxiety worsens a cancer patient's prognosis. As for so-called paternalism, I am not ashamed to take a fatherly attitude toward patients, whose illness often is too much for them. Even with my approach, moreover, conversations about patients' prospects often are very time consuming and unpleasant, and, frankly, I have no desire to make my life more difficult.

So, my question is: Where should we draw the line?

Analysis:

This question concerns the duty of candor. Competent patients have the right to be in charge of their own health care, so as to integrate it with other legitimate concerns, which are comparatively more important as life wanes. Physicians should provide patients with the information they need to come to terms with reality and make important decisions. Therefore, communicating adequately with patients is an essential professional responsibility. In evading incurable patients' questions about their prospects, the questioner wrongly precludes their choice about whether to accept treatment and prevents them from considering other things they perhaps should do. In reassuring successfully treated patients about the possibility of a recurrence, the questioner lies to them and deprives them of information they need.

The reply could be along the following lines:

I shall refer, as you do, to your partner in communication as the *patient,* but this use of the word must be clarified. Even if they are elderly or severely debilitated, competent adults are primarily responsible not only for their health care but for the whole of their lives, and physicians ordinarily should communicate directly with them. Sometimes, however, the person being treated is a minor or an adult unable to make decisions on his or her own behalf, and the physician must talk with one or both parents, a guardian, or some other person having the authority to make decisions for the individual. Very often, too, competent adults, especially but not only the elderly and severely debilitated, wish to discuss such important matters with someone else present—a spouse, one or more other family members, a friend, or some other trusted person. When the involvement of such persons is desired or freely accepted by the patient, the physician should welcome and even encourage it. However, as long as the patient is competent, a physician should not substitute communication with anyone else for talking with the patient, since the patient is entitled to direct communication with his or her physician and indirect communication makes misunderstandings and errors more likely. Moreover, patients should not evade their responsibility to make their own decisions; family members should not usurp the patient's role in this matter; and a physician should not be a party to any such evasion or usurpation.

A physician always should bear in mind what a reasonable patient inquiring about his or her prospects really needs, namely, the information essential to come to terms with reality, to plan, and to make important decisions. Distressing details about a disease's later stages that would not at present contribute to a patient's practical reflection can be covered in very general terms or even omitted entirely, unless the patient asks specifically about them. Still, I agree with your colleagues who consider your approach evasive and paternalistic. While you rightly exclude lying to people, even "for their own good," you are not supplying them with important information they need—information you have and should communicate—and you probably often seriously mislead them about their condition and prospects.

Of course, you should try to choose the best time and circumstances for talking with patients about their prospects. Avoid hurried conversations, situations where outsiders will overhear, or talking with patients when they are partially sedated or exhausted by prolonged or stressful examinations.

Then too, before saying anything, remind yourself of the limits of your knowledge and the virtual impossibility of foreseeing the course of any individual's disease and suffering in precise detail and with absolute certainty. By humbly communicating to your patients a realistic awareness of your uncertainty about their prospects, you not only will avoid misleading them but will soften the harshness of bad news, whereas announcing it with dogmatic assurance is bound to cause greater distress.

You should clearly inform patients who have only a short time to live about their poor prospects, even if they do not ask, since they need that information to prepare in various ways for death—for example, by hoping more eagerly for heaven, receiving the sacraments, learning to join their suffering to Jesus' passion, making peace with enemies, offering advice to loved ones, bidding them goodbye, paying debts, making a will, or planning a modest funeral. Deliberately withholding such needed information without some compelling reason is a very grave wrong—and I doubt that many physicians will encounter such a compelling reason even once in the whole of their professional practice.

When patients ask about their chances, an honest answer must include a statement of statistical probabilities. But because the mathematical neatness of a statistical statement is likely to convey specious clarity and precision, you should warn them that, since each case is unique, they should not draw overly firm conclusions from the statistics.

A patient asking about his or her prospects is cheated when you say: "Well, all of us will die sooner or later, but you still have some good time left, and if you cooperate fully with my treatment plan, we'll stretch that out as much as possible." Though this signals that the patient probably will die of cancer, it prevents a patient who will die soon from realizing the urgency of settling his or her affairs and preparing for death, and tends to preempt the choice he or she has the right to make about whether to accept and cooperate with your treatment plan. Plainly, whatever its benefits, cooperating with it also will involve considerable expense and other burdens, so that an incurable patient might prefer, not unreasonably, to forgo aggressive treatment and accept only palliative care, staying out of the hospital and meeting death, though somewhat sooner, in a residential hospice or at home amidst family and friends.

I also think you are being unfair to successfully treated patients who might suffer a recurrence in not telling them about that possibility when they do not ask and responding evasively when they do. You say, "We'll catch any problems before they develop very far" but even with regular checkups, you will be unable to catch some problems before it is too late. Thus, while I trust you are sincere in saying you believe it wrong to lie to people, it seems to me that in this case you cross the line between withholding information and making statements you know to be false.

Besides, having been kept in ignorance by you, such patients are impeded in whatever planning and decision making they might wish to undertake. Furthermore, some of your patients undoubtedly move away or for other reasons do not return to you for scheduled checkups. Lacking a clear understanding of why these are important, some probably neglect them entirely or delay them too long, paying a high price for freedom from the anxiety you mean to spare them.

No doubt, when patients and their families are candidly informed of bad prospects, they sometimes do experience distress that evasions could have averted. I agree that such distress cannot be brushed aside as insignificant. However, patients and their families also sometimes are distressed by continuing vagueness and uncertainty, and are relieved when given clear and definite information, even about a fatal condition. Moreover, patients who find it hard to cope with their feelings, especially those who become depressed, can and should be offered suitable treatment and, if necessary, referred to a psychiatrist for appropriate help.[211]

Telling incurable patients the truth can involve a risk of killing their hope, and of course that is undesirable; but its undesirability does not warrant sustaining false hopes. Incurable patients need to be assured that you care about them, that you will do your best to ease their pain and alleviate other symptoms, and that you will never abandon them but will help and care for them to the end. Even more important, people whose prospects are very bad from the point of view of your technical capacities can have good prospects in other respects. You should encourage and help all patients to make the most of the time that remains to them, and remind Catholics and others who believe in an afterlife that their prospects for happiness are not limited to this life, and that they can hope for life beyond death.

Communicating honestly with patients about their prospects does take valuable time, and such conversations can be as difficult for physicians as for patients. But communicating with patients, not least about their prospects, is just as much part of sound medical practice as careful examination and skillful treatment. To omit appropriate communication is to withhold part of the service for which the physician is being paid, and that is a form of theft. You have a strict duty to invest the time and accept the stress of communicating to patients the truth to which they have a right.

The underlying point is that you, as a physician, are not in charge of your patients' lives and their health. True, you are an authority, in the sense of having extensive education and experience, and it would be foolish and self-defeating for any patient to ignore your observations and advice. But patients also are in authority in their relationship with you, in the sense that they employ you and, within the bounds of morality, have every right to choose among the options your professional skills can offer them. Always, too, and not least when afflicted with a fatal illness, patients have important concerns other than life and health—their relationships with God and with other people, family and work responsibilities, and so on. They, not you, can and must decide how to integrate these other concerns, which you do not share with them, with their concern about survival and health, which you do share.

Someone might object that when patients' lives are at stake, their other concerns pale in significance, so that physicians who meet all the standards of good medical practice can make any appropriate decision about treatment, without burdening patients with information they hardly will be able to absorb, understand, and use. In fact, however, reasonable people whose lives are waning realize that death is inevitable and resign themselves to it, with the result that the importance of some other concerns becomes comparatively greater, not less. As good servants, physicians and other health care providers should support and cooperate with such reasonable resignation rather than unilaterally make decisions about treatment. While physicians certainly should meet the standards of good medical practice,

---

211. See The New York State Task Force on Life and the Law, *When Death Is Sought: Assisted Suicide and Euthanasia in the Medical Context* (New York, N.Y.: May 1994), 13–16, 175–77, 197–208.

doing so includes giving patients the information about their prospects which they need if they are to judge for themselves the value of further treatment.

In sum. Should you tell patients the whole truth? No, insofar as you simply do not know the whole truth, and again no, insofar as some of the horrible truth you know will not be of any possible use to a patient. But while you need not and should not be brutally frank, you must not be evasive. Taking a fatherly attitude is entirely appropriate, provided you help patients come to terms with reality and respect their right to live their own lives, as would a good father of an adult son or daughter. Your role is to serve your patients' true interest in caring for their health and dealing with the problems disease confronts them with, and fulfilling that role can require you not to spare their feelings. You must respect their dignity as free and responsible persons, entitled to the information they need both to choose how far they wish to go in accepting your professional help and to shape their own lives in other respects.[212] In a word, do not reduce any person who uses your professional services to the status of a mere patient, but bear in mind that all your patients are also, and primarily, agents, bearing primary responsibility for their own health care and also for other matters, some of which, such as saving their souls, are more important than life itself.[213]

60: May a physician prescribe a placebo for an anxious patient?

I specialize in internal medicine and serve as primary care physician for most of my patients. Since I really do believe in informed consent, in general I make a genuine effort to tell my patients about their condition and prospects, explain their options, and encourage them to make decisions about their care. However, I confess that sometimes in unusual cases I compromise my general principle. This seems justifiable, but I am open to being shown otherwise.

Here is an example. An elderly woman recently moved here to live with her daughter and son-in-law, who have been my patients for years. She was running low on several prescription drugs and wanted me to write prescriptions for refills. I prescribed only enough to last her six weeks and persuaded her to come in for a thorough general physical. At my request, she had her records sent me by her previous physicians—a general practitioner and three specialists. I also had her bring in all the drugs she has been using, prescription and over-the-counter.

212. On this view, though patient autonomy is only instrumentally good, it serves the intrinsic goods of authentic cooperation between physician and patient, and the upright patient's sound choices regarding other aspects of his or her life; for elaboration of a similar view, see Edmund D. Pellegrino and David C. Thomasma, *The Virtues in Medical Practice* (New York: Oxford University Press, 1993), 95–97, 122–24, 129–33, and 193–94.

213. Naoko T. Miyaji, "The Power of Compassion: Truth-Telling among American Doctors in the Care of Dying Patients," *Social Science and Medicine,* 36 (1993): 249–64, reports research showing that the questioner is typical; many American physicians tell patients the diagnosis and propose treatment without telling them about their prognosis unless they ask questions. Sheila Cassidy, *Sharing the Darkness: The Spirituality of Caring* (Maryknoll, N.Y: Orbis Books, 1991), 30–32, points out that British patients often are not told the truth about their prospects and illustrates by a telling example the injury caused by lying and evasion.

Reviewing this patient's history and the results of the physical, I concluded that she definitely would be better off with an alternative to one prescription drug she has been taking, with a reduced dosage of another, and entirely without two others; and that she probably would be better off without most of the other things she has been using.

When I talked the matter over with her, she was open to my recommendations to reduce the dosage of one of her medications and to replace another with a different drug. However, she was reluctant entirely to give up anything she has been taking, although I explained the reasons, and her daughter joined me in promising we would keep an eye out for any problems. Finally, she consented, but two days later her son-in-law called and said his mother-in-law had become so anxious she could hardly sleep or eat. Since the anxiety could not have resulted directly from any of the changes in medication, I decided it was merely psychological and prescribed a placebo, instructing him to tell his mother-in-law that I was giving her this prescription as a "replacement" for the discontinued drugs.

That was a month ago. Last week I saw this patient again. She says she has been feeling better than she had in years, and her daughter says she has become far more alert and outgoing. Their impressions were confirmed by my examination and the results of tests, which came back today.

Do you agree that it was appropriate to make this exception to the norm requiring informed consent?

Analysis:

This question involves two distinct moral issues: about deception and about informed consent. One can prescribe placebos without lying. The questioner, however, intended to lead the patient to believe the placebo replaced other medications in the precise sense in which it did not. Like any lie, this one was unjustifiable. Granting for the sake of a more complete reply that the questioner did not lie, one can consider the justifiability of making an exception to the norm requiring informed consent. That norm is not absolute; in some cases, proceeding without a patient's informed consent might be justified.

The reply could be along the following lines:

Before addressing your specific question, I wish to make two preliminary, general points.

One concerns our relationships with elderly persons. They generally are less able physically than they once were, and often are more distracted, confused, and anxious than younger people. As a result, others, including their own children and physicians, are tempted to treat them as if they were hardly more able than small children to make decisions about important matters. This temptation should be resisted lest elderly people be treated unjustly, and their personal dignity thereby violated, on the basis of disabilities that, though significant, are compatible with continuing competence to shape their own lives. Of course, many elderly people do gradually become less competent, and as this occurs they may be competent with respect to some matters but not others, as is the case with children. Still, with respect to any particular matter, every elderly person should be presumed competent unless and until the contrary becomes obvious to those helping care for him or her.

Your question also points up the widespread failure to coordinate the treatment of patients and the tendency to overmedicate many of them, not least the elderly. Your review of a new patient's medications is wisely calculated to deal with this shortcoming. But the problem you encountered with this patient makes it clear that her previous physicians fell short quite seriously in the matter.

Your explicit question about informed consent is distinct from a closely related issue regarding deception, which I shall consider first. In prescribing the placebo, did you tell the women's son-in-law to lie to her?

One can use a placebo without lying. Consider situations in which people care for themselves and their children. When experiencing minor health problems, such as colds, many sophisticated people resort to traditional home remedies, saying something like: "Plain tap water undoubtedly would be just as good for me, but my mother always gave us hot tea when we caught a cold, and it does make me feel better." The tea is consciously used as a placebo, and yet it works. Again, many parents care for a small child's minor scrape or bruise by kissing it "to make it better," and some administer a pink soothing syrup made of sugar water and red food coloring as a remedy for minor complaints. The kiss or the spoonful of syrup does make the child feel better. Because they manifest love and offer reassurance, such placebos work; and provided parents make no other, false claim ("This syrup will kill the nasty bug that is making your nose run"), no deception need be involved. Similarly, when patients ask for futile and possibly harmful medication— say, powerful antibiotics for a common cold—a physician, while refusing, can offer a placebo: "I cannot prescribe that, because it would not help, and unnecessarily using it has long-term disadvantages; but, if you insist, I can give you something I am sure won't do any harm that you can take while the ailment runs its course." The physician leaves the placebo's mode of action unstated, and the patient may be deceived by drawing an unwarranted conclusion. But the physician says nothing false; the patient need not be deceived; and, even for the sophisticated patient who realizes that the remedy may be a placebo, it can have its psychologically beneficial effect, just as the hot tea and soothing syrup do.[214]

You might say you proceeded in exactly the same way in communicating to your elderly patient that the placebo was a "replacement" for all the discontinued drugs. The placebo did psychologically replace them, and you could argue that you asserted nothing more. That argument, however, seems to me unsound. While in other contexts *replacement* might ambiguously signify either a placebo or an effective medication, and while the placebo might work even if the patient were not deceived, your elderly patient had become anxious precisely because she was giving up what seemed to her effective medications. In this context, you must have realized that you could not alleviate her anxiety unless she accepted the placebo,

214. See Mary Crenshaw Rawlinson, "Truth-Telling and Paternalism in the Clinic: Philosophical Reflections on the Use of Placebos in Medical Practice," in *Placebo: Theory, Research, and Mechanisms,* ed. Leonard White et al. (New York: Guilford Press, 1985), 410–11, and studies cited. In Rawlinson's article as a whole (403–418), however, she attempts to justify deception.

just as she previously accepted the substitute you recommended for one of her drugs, as an effective drug replacing those you considered unnecessary.

If this analysis is correct, you deceived your elderly patient into continuing to get along without the discontinued drugs by telling her son-in-law to lie to her. That was unjustifiable despite the fact that the placebo worked, since lying is wrong and telling others to lie is doubly wrong. Someone might argue that, even if you lied, the lie was justified inasmuch as it benefited the patient and was necessary. But good ends never justify bad means, and lying always is wrong (see *LCL,* 405–12). Moreover, the lie was not "necessary" since there was an alternative. You could have dealt straightforwardly with the patient's anxiety, perhaps by offering her a mild tranquilizer for a few days but if necessary by referring her to a specialist for counseling to help her overcome her unreasonable emotional dependency on the drugs she had been taking. That would have enhanced her self-control and so made her more able to make necessary decisions and live her own life.

Still, you might say your elderly patient was seeking only reassurance rather than effective medication, consider my analysis unsound, and deny that what you said was a lie. Though not conceding that, I turn to your original question: Was using a placebo to quiet your elderly patient's anxiety a justifiable exception to your general policy of obtaining patients' informed consent?

Someone might argue that you made no exception because the patient did in fact consent to taking the placebo you prescribed, and her consent was sufficiently informed. When did she consent? Proponents of this view could answer that she consented implicitly by seeking your services as her physician, agreeing, albeit reluctantly, to follow your advice with regard to her medications, and accepting the placebo as a "replacement" for the discontinued drugs. Her consent was informed, the argument would go, not by any one thing you told her, but by your entire effort to communicate with her so that she could willingly cooperate in carrying out your decisions about changes in her medications. Since the placebo was not an effective medication with potentially serious side effects, it might be argued that the consent you received was sufficiently, even if not fully, informed.

In my judgment, however, that argument is not sound. A placebo has no potentially serious side effects, of course, but the patient's need to take side effects into consideration is only one reason for the requirement of informed consent. While your patient no doubt gave informed consent to changing her medications, she took the placebo under the illusion it was an effective drug. So, even if what you said, to make her think that, was not a lie, her consent to taking the placebo was not informed. While she willingly cooperated in carrying out your decisions, she did not, with regard to the placebo, make her own decision or understand yours. To that extent, you did make an exception to your general policy, and the question remains as to that exception's justifiability.

One argument that the exception could not be justified is based on the concept of patient autonomy, namely, the view that, provided a patient is competent, his or her decisions by themselves determine what health care providers may do to and for him or her. In making the exception, the argument would go, you tried to determine what was good for the patient, despite her contrary view of the matter.

Against this argument, one way of trying to justify the exception would be to say that, while this patient is competent in general, her competence did not extend to deciding how to deal with her anxiety. The treatment of choice, the placebo, could relieve her anxiety only by providing the illusion that the discontinued medications were being replaced by another effective drug. So, someone might conclude, your elderly patient was not competent to decide about the placebo, and you rightly decided on her behalf, just as you rightly decide on behalf of unconscious accident victims to take the steps appropriate to save their lives.

This attempted justification, however, is unsound. True, people competent in general can lack competence about alternatives that transcend their comprehension and ability to evaluate. Competence, however, is an individual's moral capacity to shape his or her own life, and this capacity is not limited by the fact that, when one cannot allay inappropriate feelings by knowingly using a placebo, only deception by another will make it effective.

In sum, your elderly patient was competent and you did make an exception to your general policy on informed consent. However, assuming you did not lie to or wrongly deceive her—which I do not concede—giving her the placebo without her informed consent might be justified on the grounds that it benefited her and was not unfair to her. That line of argument is possible, it seems to me, because—in reply to the question with which you began—the informed consent requirement is not a moral absolute, but only a general duty open to exceptions. Its ethical basis is not that patient autonomy, understood as a patient's capacity to determine what is good for himself or herself, is an overriding value; in fact, autonomy, so understood, is an instance of the error of subjectivism.[215] In truth, the duty to obtain the informed consent of competent patients is grounded in the facts that only they can mediate among their own interests, integrate medical treatment with other aspects of their lives, limit it in accord with their other responsibilities, and effectively carry out their own part in it. Whenever proceeding without informed consent may adversely affect these purposes, making an exception is likely to be unfair, and so unjustifiable. But making an exception is fair if that surely will not adversely affect these purposes or otherwise harm the patient and if it seems likely to benefit him or her in some way.

Still, this incident must not establish a pattern in which this elderly patient's own decisions will be replaced by your judgments made in cooperation with her daughter and son-in-law. For that reason it seems to me that you should frankly tell her you gave her a placebo, and promise you will never prescribe one for her again. In this way, she will learn from the experience and be better able in the future to shape her own care and deal with any anxieties related to it.

+   +   +

---

215. Edmund D. Pellegrino and David C. Thomasma, *The Christian Virtues in Medical Practice* (Washington, D.C.: Georgetown University Press, 1996), 117–25, provide a fuller criticism of the exaggerated notion of patient autonomy.

61: May a physician treat a wife's syphilis without her informed consent?

Some years ago, in the days before AIDS, I was the only physician serving a remote, island community. The nearest hospital with surgeons and other specialists was in a city on the mainland, a half day's trip from my clinic. Having been trained for family practice, I took care of everything I could. People always were reluctant to go to the mainland for care, and I sent them off only if they needed surgery or better facilities were essential for adequate diagnosis and treatment. While serving that community, I once had a case that seemed to me to involve a real conflict of duties, and I would like to know what you think of the way I handled it.

Since the islanders were culturally conservative and quite religious, I had been there more than three years before encountering a case of venereal disease. Then one of my patients, a married man, turned up with syphilis. The couple were middle-aged, and the man was quiet, hardworking, and generally a decent person. He did not know what he had, and, when the test results came back and I told him, he was reluctant to discuss how he could have become infected. Wanting to find out whether there were likely to be other cases on the island, I pressed him, and he finally told me. Four months before, while in the city for a few days on business, he had stayed with a wealthy friend, an old college roommate who had been recently divorced. Late one night while the men were drinking, two attractive young women arrived. Since the friend had arranged the party without asking him, my patient was caught off guard and, he shamefacedly admitted, he spent the rest of the night with one of the women.

I started the patient on the usual course of treatment with penicillin, explained the importance of carrying it through fully, and made a follow-up appointment. One problem remained—he probably had infected his wife. He was terrified that she would find out and seemed sincerely repentant. He swore he had not been unfaithful before or since, and never would be again. I believed he meant it. Fortunately, the wife was due to come in soon for her annual checkup. When I examined her, I found the typical chancre of first stage syphilis. Like her husband, she had no difficulty taking penicillin, so I also started her on the usual course of treatment.

I told her only that she had an infection that would have become very serious without treatment, but we had caught it in good time. As with her husband, I emphasized the importance of carrying the treatment through fully, and made a follow-up appointment.

While my explanation was true, it hardly provided the information I usually would have thought it necessary to give a patient. However, the woman asked no questions, and I expected that, if I told her the whole truth, she would draw the obvious conclusion that her husband had been unfaithful, and he would feel I had betrayed his confidence. Moreover, she was a fastidious woman and devoted wife, and I felt sure she would be devastated if she learned of her husband's infidelity.

Analysis:

This question concerns conflicting duties: to preserve the secret confided by the unfaithful husband and to inform the wife about the infection as a basis for obtaining her consent to treatment. Neither duty is absolute. Consideration of the two duties' grounds and their relevance in the situation suggests that the questioner's solution probably was morally acceptable. However, the questioner should, but may not, have taken special care to forestall possible bad consequences of not fully informing the wife.

The reply could be along the following lines:

Someone might argue that telling the wife she had been infected with syphilis would not, strictly speaking, have betrayed the husband's confidence, but would only have provided her with information regarding herself to which she was entitled—information only incidentally enabling her to infer her husband's infidelity. However, while she was entitled to information about her condition, that right was no greater than your duty to inform her; and normally you would be breaking confidentiality in exposing a patient's secret by giving a third party information from which it is likely to be inferred. The argument would err by focusing on one relevant duty and ignoring the other; and it seems to me you are right to think you had conflicting duties.

Still, neither duty is absolute, as consideration of their grounds makes clear.

Normally, you should keep patients' confidences. Besides the basic obligation everyone has to protect others' privacy by keeping their secrets, you have a special and much stronger professional responsibility. If patients had to worry about confidentiality, their communication with physicians would be greatly impeded, and effective cooperation requires free communication (see q. 70, below).

Normally, too, you should inform competent patients rather fully of your diagnosis and proposed treatment. They bear primary responsibility for their own health care, while your role as a physician is only to assist them. Patients usually need to be informed in order to make decisions both about their health care and other aspects of their lives—for example, whether to consult another professional, whether to accept the treatment you propose despite its impact on their lives as a whole, how meticulously to follow your directions, and whether to regard possible side effects or recurrent symptoms as indications that they must see you again. Failing to provide patients with adequate information generally is likely both to impede their efforts to deal with their health problems and to infringe upon their authority over their own lives, whose other dimensions they must integrate with their health, the proper object of your concern, and their interest in caring for it.

Though lying to conceal adultery would be wrong, married people who have been unfaithful without raising their spouses' suspicions are not obliged to confess the infidelity to them.[216] Moreover, the man's reluctant admission to you is exactly

---

216. This has been the common view of Catholic moral theologians. In general, one has no moral obligation to communicate secrets, and should not communicate them when that is unlikely to benefit anyone. Though one spouse's adultery gravely injures the other even if the latter does

the kind of thing patients are least likely to communicate unless they trust their physician. Thus it is the sort of secret in regard to which the duty of confidentiality is most relevant and most stringent. Then too, though you may have been wrong in assuming the wife would be devastated if she learned of her husband's unfaithfulness, there undoubtedly was a significant risk of serious consequences for their marriage. So, it seems to me, you had good reasons to try to maintain confidentiality. Still, the course you adopted involved the risk that the wife would ask questions. Had she done so, you could not have lied, since lying is always wrong (see *LCL*, 405–12).

As it turned out, you were able both to keep the man's secret and to provide appropriate care for your other patient, his wife. Even if you had told her more about her infection, she would have had no reason to see another physician or any realistic alternative to the standard treatment you offered, which, moreover, is not risky or otherwise difficult. So, it was not as important as usual to provide her with information about her condition. Therefore, the solution you adopted, in my judgment, probably was morally acceptable.

I say *probably*, because a patient treated for syphilis ordinarily should be warned to watch for symptoms that the infection has not been completely eliminated, and you also should have made the usual subsequent tests. I suppose that, in instructing the husband, you told him also to watch his wife for problems, and perhaps you remained on the island long enough to be sure the couple were entirely free of the disease. If not, contact the man and urge him to arrange tests for both himself and his wife. If he has died and she is still living, take whatever steps are necessary to ensure that she has received or receives adequate treatment, even if that requires informing her now of the nature of the infection.

62: How freely should physicians prescribe psychoactive drugs?

We are three specialists in internal medicine, practicing as a group. Many of our patients are covered by a managed choice insurance plan; for them, we provide primary care. Working together, we can see patients when they need us at any hour on any day, and we frequently see one another's patients. On the whole, the arrangement works well. However, in one area we find ourselves frequently and seriously disagreeing. Our conflict concerns different philosophies on prescribing pain killers and drugs such as tranquilizers, stimulants, and antidepressants.[217]

We all agree that our primary responsibility is to diagnose and treat the causes of physical dysfunctions. But one of us, jokingly dubbed "Dr. Feelgood," considers it equally important to see to it that patients experience no pain and suffer no distress that can be counteracted by means of medication. Another of our group, dubbed "Dr. Letemsuffer," argues that the merely subjective experiences of patients are not

---

not learn of it, the guilty person's obligation to repent and make up for the injury can be fulfilled without confessing to his or her innocent and unsuspecting spouse.

217. *Psychoactive drugs* refers to all these, and, in general, to anything introduced into the body for the purpose of affecting the nervous system and how one feels.

our concern except insofar as they are symptoms of underlying conditions we can do something about. I, the writer, am the middle-of-the-roader, but on a common sense basis rather than any general principle.

If our disagreement were over some issue within the purview of scientific medicine, we could study the question and work things out. In this case, though, we have found no way of doing that, and so are beginning to think the problem is more one of philosophy. How can we resolve our differences? Are there some principles to help us do that?

Analysis:

This question calls for the derivation of moral norms for prescribing psychoactive drugs. The two extreme approaches are unsound. Emotional disorders call for health care, and severe pain should be treated; but trying to eliminate light or moderate pain and normal psychological distress interferes with healthful functioning and encourages drug abuse. Managing physical pain must be distinguished from treating emotional problems. Physicians should know current techniques of pain management, and should prescribe analgesics carefully but sufficiently to meet patients' needs. Patients unreasonably demanding psychoactive drugs or experiencing severe and/or continuous psychological problems should be referred to an appropriate specialist, whose plan of treatment the questioner's group should follow.

The reply could be along the following lines:

Your responsibility as physicians is to help your patients not only to sustain their lives but to maintain healthful functioning. The relevant functioning is not only physical but psychic, insofar as psychic functioning pertains to the nature of the human person as a sentient organism. While your area of concern as physicians excludes the mind's functioning as logical, the will's as moral, and the person's as skillful, it surely includes the functioning of the psyche as an inseparable dimension of the human body (see *LCL,* 519–21). People are not vegetables; sensory cognition—not least the awareness of pain—and emotional reactions are among a human person's natural functions, and disorders in them call for health care no less than do diseases of the circulatory or digestive systems.

On this basis, Dr. Letemsuffer seems to be taking too narrow a view of your responsibility. He surely is right to insist that patients' experiences be viewed as important symptoms, so that underlying dysfunctional conditions will be discovered and effectively treated. Many physicians who are more psychologically oriented seriously fail in this regard, tending too quickly to prescribe pain killers, tranquilizers, and so forth when patients really need treatment for their blood pressure, digestion, renal functioning, and so on. Still, pain and suffering must not be dismissed as merely "subjective" experiences. In many cases, they not only are signs of underlying dysfunction but are themselves an important, and even the primary, part of the dysfunction calling for your help. For instance, severe pain is an integral part of migraine headache, and emotional distress is the primary part of the psychological shock of an unexpected disaster, such as the sudden loss of a loved one.

At the same time, Dr. Feelgood's approach errs in regarding light or moderate pain and normal psychological distress as if they were pathologies, whereas in reality they usually are integral parts of healthful functioning. Light and moderate pain ordinarily are helpful signals of the need to limit and regulate behavior that otherwise would damage the organism or interfere with its functioning, while normal emotional distress is an effective motive for appropriately dealing with and adjusting to reality—both the physical and social environments, and ultimate evils such as death and sin. Feelgood's efforts to ensure that patients experience no pain and suffer no distress do not help patients function well but instead interfere with healthful functioning. Moreover, though patients no doubt often request, and probably usually are grateful for, prescriptions given in accord with his philosophy, it seems certain that his approach sometimes initiates and often supports irresponsible uses of psychoactive substances to promote desired experiences as ends in themselves. Making experiences a goal in this way, without regard to their significance for psychosomatic functioning, interferes with appropriate functioning and evades reality. Consequently, Feelgood's approach not only is medically faulty, insofar as it interferes with rather than supports health, but is a morally indefensible abuse of his power to prescribe, insofar as he encourages patients' irresponsible use of psychoactive substances (see *LCL,* 534–40).

In contrast with your colleagues, your middle-of-the-road approach seems to me nearer the truth. Perhaps I can help you articulate what you have accepted as a matter of common sense. In trying to do this, I think it will be helpful to distinguish between managing physical pain—that is, the sensation of pain in its many diverse degrees and modalities—and dealing with emotional distress: anxiety, depression, and so on.

Pain management is a specialized medical field, and I cannot pretend to tell you how to do it; still, I can say a few things.[218]

First, many physicians apparently have not been trained adequately in pain management. If that is the case with all or some of you, additional study is in order. Current approaches to pain management include various new techniques, such as biofeedback and meditation, though analgesics (that is, pain relieving drugs) continue to play an important role in most cases.

Second, while some physicians, like Feelgood, inappropriately prescribe analgesics, especially narcotics, studies indicate that many physicians, like Letemsuffer, tend to underprescribe analgesics, even to patients experiencing intense pain. Some physicians simply are unsympathetic to their patients' suffering; they violate

218. A two-volume work for health care professionals: John J. Bonica, ed., *The Management of Pain,* 2nd ed. (Philadelphia: Lea and Febiger, 1990). On the possibilities of satisfactory pain (and psychological stress) management and the multiple reasons for inadequacies in such management, see Kathleen M. Foley, "The Relationship of Pain and Symptom Management to Patient Requests for Physician-Assisted Suicide," *Journal of Pain and Symptom Management,* 6 (July 1991): 289–97; The New York State Task Force on Life and the Law, *When Death Is Sought: Assisted Suicide and Euthanasia in the Medical Context* (New York, N.Y.: May 1994), 43–47, 158–75; A. Jacox et al., *Management of Cancer Pain: Clinical Practice Guideline No. 9,* AHCPR Publication No. 94–0592 (Rockville, Md.: Agency for Health Care Policy and Research, U.S. Department of Health and Human Services, Public Health Service; 1994), 7–21.

the Golden Rule, allowing patients to undergo pain they would not accept for themselves or their loved ones. This is because they fail to regard their patients as persons with whose efforts to care for themselves the physician should cooperate, and instead regard them as organic systems to be tended and repaired. Other physicians either do not realize or actually forget that individuals' pain tolerance greatly differs, and wrongly assume that everyone can easily bear what they themselves can. Still others seem overly nervous about possible addiction. They fail to see that appropriate therapeutic uses of analgesics do not involve the motivation of seeking desired experiences for their own sake, which belongs to the psychological component of addiction. Perhaps they also are ignorant of the fact that a merely physical addiction is rather easily treated, and so should not be considered a disaster to be avoided at all costs. Consequently, while the risk of addiction should not be ignored when prescribing analgesics, and while narcotics, especially, should be prescribed with care, the risk usually is reasonably accepted when relieving severe pain will contribute to a patient's functioning.[219]

Third, patients often are seriously harmed by physicians' failure to prescribe needed analgesics. Even Letemsuffer should acknowledge and act on the evidence that pain, especially when severe and prolonged, interferes with organic functioning and impedes healing. But such pain also calls for relief insofar as it interferes with psychological and behavioral functioning—for example, by increasing irritability or depression, and impeding concentration and mobility.

Fourth, contrary to Feelgood's one-sided view, sound pain management does not always mean trying to eliminate or minimize pain. Sometimes effective pain relief would render a patient languid or unconscious, and he or she should tolerate as much pain as necessary so as to be conscious and alert in order to fulfill some responsibility. Again, since pain's function is to signal physical threats and regulate behavior to forestall damage, suppressing it—for example, so that an injured athlete can compete—can impede healing or lead to more serious injury.

Beyond these general reflections, I suggest that you and your colleagues work together to sort out the kinds of cases in which you disagree about pain management, if necessary seek the advice of specialists in that field about how to deal with each type of case, and try to work out a common policy.

But how can you deal with what for you probably is the more difficult challenge: treating your patients' emotional distress? While this problem seems formidable, once the mistaken elements of the approaches of Feelgood and Letemsuffer are excluded, the right approach will be obvious and rather simple.

Patients sometimes will show signs of psychological addiction to psychoactive substances, including alcohol, or will experience severe or ongoing distress, suggesting an underlying psychological illness. In such cases, you should not delay in referring the patient to an appropriate specialist. Once that physician has diagnosed the problem and worked out an appropriate treatment plan, your role will be to cooperate in carrying it out. Collaborating in accord with another

---

219. Some physicians deny adequate pain relief to terminally ill patients, fearing that it would shorten their lives; regarding this, see *LCL,* 530.

specialist's more expert judgments, the members of your group should experience no conflicts among themselves.

In other cases, patients' psychological distress is episodic and arises from understandable causes. Unusual traumatic situations—the death of a loved one, a major operation, or a serious business crisis—can cause severe psychological distress for which short-term use of a psychoactive drug may be appropriate. More common, but still episodic, occurrences also may call for occasional use of such drugs—for example, to promote sleep when traveling. When neither of these two grounds exists for prescribing a psychoactive drug, yet a patient nevertheless persists in demanding it, he or she should be refused the prescription and referred for evaluation to a mental health specialist.

If your group follows the policy outlined, occasions of conflict among you will be virtually eliminated. At the same time, the three of you will be guiding your patients in the reasonable use of analgesics and other psychoactive prescription drugs and discouraging their abuse.

63: Under what conditions may surgeons attempt to separate Siamese twins?

As a resident in pediatric surgery, I am fascinated by the problem of separating Siamese twins. Eventually, I may have the opportunity to participate in such operations. There seems to be no moral problem in the less challenging cases. The connection between the babies is limited, separating them promises similar benefits to both, the likelihood of success is high, and the risks are minimal. But in many of the more interesting cases, there are moral problems.

Take, for example, the case of Amy and Angela Lakeberg, who were born 29 June 1993 at Loyola University Medical Center in Chicago. Joined at the chest, the babies shared a single liver and an abnormal, six-chambered heart. Because of the way they were joined, they could not breath normally and were soon put on a ventilator. Had they remained together and been given optimum care—an option apparently not thought worth considering by the Loyola ethics consultation committee—it seems they would have had to remain on the respirator and died before long of congestive heart failure. The babies were transferred to Philadelphia Children's Hospital for surgery to separate them. Though Angela was expected to survive the operation, her prospects were poor. It was doubted that she would ever be able to do without the ventilator and thought likely that she would die without ever leaving the hospital. Amy, the weaker twin, was to die in the operation, since it would deprive her entirely of the shared heart and liver. The surgery was carried out 20 August 1993. After that, Angela's mother visited her only three times and held her only once; the baby never left the hospital or breathed without the ventilator, and she died 9 June 1994 of pneumonia and cardiorespiratory failure.[220]

220. The history of the case is drawn from David C. Thomasma et al., "The Ethics of Caring for Conjoined Twins: The Lakeberg Twins," *Hastings Center Report,* 26:4 (July–Aug. 1996): 4–12. This article is not well written, and I cannot recommend the ethical analysis attempted in it.

Many other problematic cases differ in various ways from that of the Lakeberg babies. I would be interested in knowing what you think about that case, but my question is more general: How can surgeons identify cases in which they may try to separate Siamese twins?

Analysis:

This question calls for specific norms by which to judge the moral acceptability of surgery to separate conjoined twins. At least three norms apply. First, an attempt to separate conjoined twins is unreasonable unless it is fair to everyone concerned. Second, the attempt is unjust to the babies if the prospective benefits to them are not sufficient to ground the argument for proceeding. Third, an attempt to separate conjoined twins that holds out different prospects for the two babies is unfair to the one whose prospects are poorer unless the detriment to that baby is slight and the benefit to his or her twin considerable. Applied to the case of the Lakeberg twins, each of these three norms would, in my judgment, have been sufficient to exclude the attempt to separate them.

The reply could be along the following lines:

In general, whether it is reasonable to undertake and/or continue a health care measure depends on a consideration of its prospective burdens and benefits. Individuals able to make decisions for themselves rightly refuse health care when they consider the prospective benefits to themselves inadequate to offset the expected burdens to themselves and others; and they unfairly choose measures whose prospective burdens on others they would not judge to be offset by their prospective benefits to themselves if it were a question of burdens on themselves and benefits to strangers. For the sake of prospective benefits to others, individuals may choose out of merciful love of neighbor to undergo experimental measures upon themselves that they could rightly reject as too burdensome. However, nobody may rightly choose experimental measures for a noncompetent person unless the prospective benefits to that very person seem adequate to offset the burdens, including the risks, to him or her.

The preceding general norms can be specified to guide decisions about surgery to separate conjoined twins. First, a surgeon cannot reasonably undertake such an operation unless the prospective benefits to the babies and others are sufficient to offset the burdens to everyone concerned. Second, a surgeon cannot justly try to separate conjoined twins unless the prospective benefits to the babies themselves are sufficient to offset the burdens imposed on them.

Since the prospective benefits and burdens of surgery to separate conjoined twins (like any other sort of health care) are diverse in kind and subject to no common measure, one cannot rationally commensurate them. Norms that seem to require doing that actually call for something else, namely, conscientious judgment, which presupposes excluding unreasonable motives and appraises the cases that can be made for each option.

The application of the two norms stated above in decisions about surgery to separate conjoined twins, therefore, requires that two things be clarified: the unreasonable motives likely to be operative and the intelligible goods, to which one can be rightly committed, involved in the peculiar benefit to the twins of their being separated rather than remaining conjoined.

Saying you are "fascinated by the problem of separating Siamese twins" and characterizing difficult cases as "challenging" and "interesting" point to one possible unreasonable motive that must be excluded. Since surgery requires special gifts and great skill, surgeons, like many other skilled people, take special interest in projects allowing them to innovate, perform outstandingly, improve their professional status, and/or increase their future income. Unlike people who work on subhuman materials, however, surgeons work on human persons and should put their skill entirely at their patients' service. So, though surgeons are likely to be tempted to treat challenging cases as other creative people treat challenging projects involving subhuman material, the professional commitment to serve patients and patients' personal dignity both require that surgeons' interest in professional accomplishment be excluded as an unreasonable motive when considering whether to undertake an operation.

Another motive possibly operative is the prospect of developing surgical technique by experimentation so as to improve the prospects for other pairs of conjoined twins. Insofar as it bears on a genuine benefit, this motive could legitimately be taken into account as offsetting burdens to others (for example, costs to the public), but it cannot legitimately affect the estimation of burdens and benefits to the children themselves, which the second norm stated above requires. Being incapable of self-sacrifice, no pair of conjoined babies may be treated as an opportunity to experiment for others' eventual benefit.

Surgery to separate conjoined twins sometimes offers a prospect of prolonged survival or improved functioning for both of them or at least one. It also usually enables the two persons to live independently of each other, a genuine benefit inasmuch as remaining conjoined is likely to impede (if not prevent) their efforts to pursue and enjoy various authentic goods, including the intimate communion of marriage and other friendships—not least, that with each other based upon their relationship as brothers or sisters. But the benefit of separation should not be absolutized. Like other serious handicaps, remaining a conjoined twin does not detract from an individual's personal dignity and need not prevent him or her from living a good and holy life.

With the preceding clarifications in mind, the two norms stated above can be applied to the case of the Lakeberg twins. The burdens of the surgery included the immediate death of the weaker twin, the risk of shortening the life of the stronger twin, suffering for the children and their family, and the use of considerable resources at great expense. The prospective benefits were a slight possibility of significantly prolonging the life of the stronger twin and, perhaps, experience that might be helpful for dealing with similar future cases. The value of the experience was limited, however, for there are very few similar cases in which even the most successful technique could ever be applied.[221] Thus, the prospective benefits to everyone concerned were not, in my judgment, sufficient to offset the whole set of

221. Ibid., 5.

burdens, as the first norm requires. I suspect that the decision to proceed partly hinged on a mistaken absolutizing or, at least, overestimation of the benefit of separation and/or an inappropriate interest of the surgeons in this challenging case. Even if the decision did not violate the first norm, however, I think it clearly violated the second, which excludes consideration of prospective benefits except to the babies themselves. There was no prospect of benefit to the weaker baby and very little prospect of benefit to the stronger. The weaker was certain to lose her life at once, the stronger certain to suffer greatly and unlikely to ever enjoy health or leave the hospital.

Besides the general norms for decisions regarding health care, norms of fairness govern actions affecting two persons. In general, apart from cases in which one person has some special duty to sacrifice himself or herself for another's benefit, it often is unfair to subordinate one person's interests to those of another—that is, to seek benefits for one at the cost of detriments to the other. How is the judgment of fairness to be made? As usual, by applying the Golden Rule. If one were in the place of one of the persons but did not know which, would one think it plainly reasonable to seek the benefit regardless of whose place one turned out to be in? One very likely would say no unless the prospective benefit to one individual is substantial and the detriment to the other negligible.

So, in a case of conjoined twins, where neither baby can have any duty to the other or be capable of self-sacrifice, a third norm for any attempt to separate them is: If the surgery will not be beneficial to both, it will be unfair to the baby whose prospects are poorer unless the detriment to that baby is slight and the benefit to his or her twin considerable. Therefore, in my judgment, if one baby certainly or probably will not survive the surgery, the attempt will be unfair to that one unless two conditions are met: (1) without the surgery, the abnormality of the babies' shared organ(s) is likely to result soon in the death of both, and (2) with the surgery, the prospective survivor's prospects are greatly improved. Since the second condition apparently was not met in the Lakeberg case, I believe that this norm, too, was violated.

Some who commented on the attempt to separate the Lakeberg twins held that it was intrinsically wrong.[222] One argument for this view was that, since cutting the shared heart away from the weaker twin deprived her of her blood supply and immediately killed her, killing her was a means to provide an adequate heart for her sister. So, the argument concluded, the attempt to separate these twins involved the intrinsically wrong act of directly killing an innocent person.

I hold that directly killing an innocent human being is always wrong, provided *direct* killing is understood as killing intended as an end or chosen as a means to some other end (see *LCL,* 475–79). I also grant that the attempt to separate the Lakeberg twins involved the physically immediate causing of the weaker twin's death, so that the surgeon directly killed her in the sense that the surgery of itself

---

222. See, e.g., Albert S. Moraczewski, O.P., "What Nature Has Misjoined Together," *Ethics and Medics,* 18:11 (Nov. 1993): 1–2, who asserts (2) what I deny: "In effect, the heart is taken from one individual and given to another," and proceeds by (what I will argue is an unsound) analogy with taking a vital organ from one nonconjoined twin and giving it to another.

straightaway brought about her death. However, there is no reason to think the surgeon intended the weaker twin's death as an end and there was no need to choose her death as a means. The shared heart and liver were not exclusively the organs of either twin; the chosen means to fashion an adequate heart for the stronger was to cut away the shared heart from the weaker and the chosen means to provide a liver from the stronger was to cut it away from the weaker. That, of course, resulted in her death, but her death was an effect of chosen means that in no way contributed to the end sought.[223] Therefore, in my judgment, the operation was not intrinsically wrong as it would have been had it involved a choice to kill the weaker twin. Nevertheless, as explained above, the surgery did involve the wrongful killing of the weaker twin inasmuch as the surgeon should not have accepted her death, there being little chance the operation would significantly benefit her sister.

To challenge my view that the operation to separate the Lakeberg twins did not involve the intrinsically wrong choice to kill the weaker, someone might propose the following argument. Suppose identical twins who were not conjoined were born afflicted with similar heart defects, so that neither was likely to survive without heart surgery, and suppose the surgeon removed the weaker twin's heart and used it to fashion a more adequate heart for the stronger. Since the weaker baby's death, though an effect of removing his or her heart, would in no way contribute to the end sought, even this operation would not involve the intentional killing of an innocent human being. Yet, the argument would proceed, removing the weaker baby's heart surely would be intrinsically wrong; if not, there would be nothing wrong in transplanting vital organs from dying persons without waiting for them to die. So, the argument would conclude, the attempt to separate the Lakeberg twins did involve a choice to kill the weaker.

I concede that on my analysis removing the weaker twin's heart and transplanting vital organs from dying persons would not necessarily involve intentional *killing*. But I maintain that such operations would be intrinsically wrong, since they would involve an intentional violation of functional bodily integrity. The surgery would involve two distinct procedures: (1) to take from certain persons organs needed for some function, and (2) to give those organs and their functioning to others. The first procedure would be chosen as a means, and the choice would include depriving persons of a function. By contrast, separating the Lakeberg twins involved only a single procedure: cutting away the stronger twin, together with the heart and liver both babies had shared, from her weaker sister. So, it seems to me, the operation did not involve intending the violation of the weaker twin's bodily

223. See *LCL*, 470–74. William B. Smith, "A Single Heart?" *Homiletic and Pastoral Review*, 94:6 (Mar. 1994), 68, says: "That death is perhaps not directly intended as an 'end,' but it is surely foreseen and intended as a 'means,' as a necessary and causative condition of the hoped-for outcome here." However, had a suitable heart and liver been available and been transplanted to the weaker twin, she might have survived; if so, that would have had no effect whatsoever on the hoped-for outcome for the stronger twin. Therefore, though no such transplant was attempted, the death of the weaker twin was not a necessary and causative condition of the operation's success.

integrity, but only accepting her being deprived of her share in organs that had been parts of both her sister and herself.[224]

In sum, the attempt to separate the Lakeberg twins involved, in my judgment, neither intentional killing of the weaker baby nor intentional violation of her bodily integrity, and was not intrinsically wrong. However, the operation failed to satisfy three other relevant norms, largely because there was little prospect of benefit even to the stronger baby. Therefore, I think similar surgery could be morally acceptable in a case in which, without it, both children probably would soon die, while with it one of them probably would survive indefinitely.

64: May a physician working in an emergency unit embrace "emergency ethics"?

More than nine times out of ten, my work as a physician in a hospital emergency room differs little from that of a general practitioner and presents no special moral problems. But sometimes, making the best of desperate situations, emergency physicians must do things that would be malpractice if done by another doctor. Similarly, it seems to me, in this practice it sometimes is right to do things that would be immoral in other situations. Here are three kinds of cases that illustrate this point. In regard to each, I would like to know whether you agree with me.

(1) Tests we routinely make often show that the driver of a vehicle involved in a traffic accident is intoxicated in the legal sense. Unless compelled by law to reveal this information, physicians are directed by professional ethics to treat it as confidential, just as they would if a patient asked for help in dealing with his or her alcohol problem. But the information is vital to public prosecutors, who should hold drunken drivers responsible for the carnage they cause, and to innocent victims and/or their families, who are entitled to compensation. When people involved in traffic accidents are legally intoxicated, I regularly give the information to the police and others involved in the accident, or their families, so that they can take whatever action they consider appropriate.

(2) Some emergency room fatalities resulting from accidents, heart attacks, and so forth are conscious when brought in. Usually, until these people lose consciousness, they suffer a good deal before we can do much about it. Their families and friends must be given the devastating news. A loved one, who was (or seemed) fine such a short time before, is dead and gone forever. They ask: "Did he (she) suffer?" The simple answer always would be yes, and the completely honest answer often would be to describe excruciating pain, groans, pleas for relief, and so forth. But that never would do any good and would only

---

224. Moraczewski, op. cit., 1, says: "But in that very same procedure, the other twin is deprived of her rightful share of the single heart"; Smith, op. cit., 68, says: "But, this causal act does deprive the other twin of her rightful share of the single heart, and the same act does cause her death." But precisely the point at issue is whether the weaker twin had a rightful share of a single heart inadequate to sustain both persons and whether causing her death was intended or only accepted as a side effect.

add to their grief. I reply: "Not really. He (She) died quickly despite everything we tried to do, and so hardly was aware of what was happening."

(3) During the emergency room evaluation, most women who are victims of rape voice concern about possible conception. Many express a determination to abort should they become pregnant. Quite a few have no gynecologist of their own, and most will not see another physician about the rape after they leave the emergency room. After twenty-four hours, the morning-after pill is less effective or ineffective, so it must be given at once if it is going to be given. Unless the woman plainly is pregnant, I routinely do a pregnancy test; if the result is positive, the conception cannot have resulted from the rape, since there would not have been time for the embryo to implant, and so I do not dispense any medication. However, if the result is negative, the standard treatment is to offer two tablets of Ovral at once and two more twelve hours later. The effect depends on the timing of the woman's menstrual cycle. If she is preovulatory, the drug prevents conception; if postovulatory, pregnancy is impossible, and the drug has no effect; if ovulatory, conception is possible, and, assuming it has occurred, the drug is abortifacient, but in such a way that neither the victim nor anyone else ever knows. I present these facts in an objective way, and dispense the pill to the woman if she wants it. My reasoning is that most often no harm is done, and that when, occasionally, the medication has an abortifacient effect, that is not as bad as it would be if the woman, finding herself pregnant a couple of months later, followed through then on her determination to have the baby aborted.

Analysis:

The question is whether the relevant norms admit of exception. (1) Maintaining confidentiality facilitates trusting communication by patients with their physicians, but exceptions may be made for sufficient reasons. (2) Lying is always wrong, and the questioner plainly lies to families and friends who ask about the suffering of deceased loved ones. (3) Conditionally intending to abort human individuals, even at the earliest stage of their development, involves the intention to kill innocent persons, which no good end can justify.

The reply could be along the following lines:

While most moral norms, like most rules of good medical practice, admit of exception in unusual situations, some are exceptionless. Any violation of such a norm violates some good intrinsic to the human person, and so the conditions of your practice do not justify making exceptions. The requirement of confidentiality does admit of exception in some cases, but the norms excluding lying and intentional killing do not.

(1) Your professional responsibility as a physician mainly concerns safeguarding human life and promoting health. Only for this reason do patients provide information they would prefer to keep secret or allow you to gather it by examinations and tests. To do your work, you need this information about patients, and communication by patients themselves and/or others almost always is necessary or helpful to obtain it. The practice of confidentiality by health care professionals facilitates that communication, which very often would be inhibited if people

feared that what they tell physicians and other health care providers would be divulged and result in embarrassment or injury to them. Making unnecessary exceptions will tend to arouse people's anxiety. Moreover, when opportunity offers, you should speak with drunken drivers before they are discharged from the hospital and urge them to obtain any help they need to forestall driving while intoxicated again; but they will be less likely to take such advice if they think you may have voluntarily acted against their interests. Therefore, you ought to maintain confidentiality unless there is a very strong reason for making an exception.

I do not see how the need of public prosecutors for information regarding the condition of drivers involved in traffic accidents can justify any exception. Since this need is neither unusual nor unpredictable, lawmakers perhaps have established—and, if not, should establish—appropriate procedures to meet it. If you think appropriate procedures have not been established, you should act as a citizen to deal with the problem. I suggest you begin by discussing it with a public prosecutor, who probably will be able to clarify what needs doing and how you can help. If appropriate procedures already exist, you, of course, should know and follow them. These might well include requiring physicians to report evidence of alcohol or drugs in the blood of certain persons involved in accidents. Reporting such findings only because and insofar as required by law, you would not make any unnecessary exception to confidentiality; indeed, such reporting, as you say, is permitted by the existing norm of professional ethics.[225] Moreover, this legally mandated exception to confidentiality is unlikely to arouse people's anxiety about confiding in their physicians, because the professional relationship of physicians who staff emergency rooms with drunken drivers is itself unusual. These patients do not choose an emergency room physician as their caregiver and deliberately confide in him or her, but are brought to the emergency room and found to be intoxicated in the course of a routine test.

As to providing information useful to accident victims and their families in obtaining fair settlements, that also should be regulated by law, and you should look into that matter. However, existing legal regulations may not be adequate to satisfy private citizens' just needs for such information. So, occasionally you may have reason to believe that persons who were seriously injured or killed were innocent victims, and that they or their families may not take appropriate steps to obtain compensation due them unless you tell them that available information might support a legal case. If so, you should put yourself in the place of each of the parties involved and apply the Golden Rule. If you judge that fairness to victims or their families requires an exception to confidentiality, you may make it—but only insofar as necessary for the good purpose to be served. For example, you should not divulge precise clinical data but only tell those concerned that you think the other party perhaps should not have been driving and that the hospital's records will contain evidence that might be helpful in a lawsuit.

225. Council on Ethical and Judicial Affairs, American Medical Association, *Code of Medical Ethics: Current Opinions with Annotations,* 1996–97 ed. (Chicago: American Medical Association, 1996), 5.05 (p. 77): "The physician should not reveal confidential communications or information without the express consent of the patient, unless required to do so by law."

(2) It plainly is a lie to tell people a loved one who suffered greatly did not really suffer. Likewise, saying someone died quickly and was hardly aware of what was happening is truthful only if it accurately describes what occurred, which certainly is not so in the circumstances you describe. Lying always is wrong (see *LCL*, 405–12), and lying by physicians undermines trust in the profession. Moreover, lying meant to spare people's feelings condescendingly assumes that they are too immature to face the truth, and it often injures them, either by concealing truth that would benefit them, or by undermining their confidence in related, truthful statements, or in both ways. If an accident victim's loved ones even suspect you have lied to them about one thing, they are likely to wonder whether you are not concealing something else. Such suspicions might well intensify their grief.

When you are asked whether a loved one suffered, you can give an entirely truthful answer without including all the unpleasant, heart-rending details. Provided one tells no lies and withholds no truths to which others are entitled, one is candid, that is, completely honest. The candid person can leave unmentioned facts that are likely only to hurt others, because nobody is entitled to such information. Even if a question as stated calls for a yes or no answer, one always can reply with a truthful but indirect statement, supplying less information—and so less likely to hurt—than a straightforward yes or no.

In considering how to respond to bereaved relatives' and friends' queries about the suffering of their loved ones, focus on the underlying concerns behind such questions and take into account the possibility that evils other than suffering usually motivate survivors' grief. To most people, avoidable suffering probably is more abhorrent than suffering that is inevitable, and the fact that a loved one is dead and gone forever is, as you suggest, more significant than that he or she briefly suffered. So, an honest response pointing out that suffering was unavoidable and making the evil of death seem less by focusing on its side effect of ending suffering is likely to be consoling: "Given what happened, some suffering was inevitable, but we did what we could to help, and his/her suffering is over now."

Sometimes dying persons, despite their suffering, display courageous self-control and/or express love for those near and dear. In such cases, try to console survivors by telling them how the dying person acted and what he or she said. In doing that you may be able to evade the question about suffering and leave it unanswered. Such information will not be entirely beside the point either, since it will assure survivors that their loved one, even in suffering, acted in a significant way they are likely to find consoling. Similarly, in some cases, the facts of a case will allow you to ignore questions about suffering and tell survivors: "He (she) had time to make his/her peace with God."

If survivors press their questions about suffering, in some cases you may be able to lessen their anguish without dishonesty by taking advantage of our ignorance about the conscious experience of people under extraordinary stress. As you doubtless know, survivors of serious injuries whose outward behavior seemed to manifest severe suffering sometimes say later that, though conscious, they experienced little or no pain for many minutes or even hours. In appropriate cases, you might say: "We will never know. He (She) was conscious but in shock, and so perhaps felt very little."

(3) From conception, a new human individual's life is sacred (see *LCL*, 460–67, 489–97). Even if one cannot demonstrate theoretically beyond all question that such a tiny human being is a person, all those who are recognized as persons have nothing else in common beyond being living, human individuals, and there is no evidence or cogent reason for denying the incipient human individual's personhood. So, deliberately killing such an individual involves intending to kill an innocent person (see *LCL*, 497–98). Such intentional killing, therefore, is a great evil, and no good end ever justifies it.[226]

You say you objectively explain how Ovral works to women who have been raped, and then dispense the drug to those who want it.[227]

A physician intending to avoid legal liability rather than intending to encourage acceptance and use of the drug might deal with such patients just as you do. In doing so, such a physician would not need to intend that the woman take Ovral and that it be effective. Even so, explaining the situation and offering Ovral as you do would lead many women to take the tablets with a twofold conditional intention: to prevent conception, if that is possible, and, if it is not, to abort any embryo that may have been conceived, or may be conceived, as a result of the rape. Moreover, regularly supplying the tablets to women who want them sooner or later will result in the destruction of some incipient persons who otherwise would survive. Therefore, though such a physician could act without an intention to kill, he or she would lead patients to act at least with a conditional intention to kill, and also sooner or later would cause the death of some incipient persons. In leading patients to act with a conditional intent to kill, such a physician would be giving grave scandal. And, inasmuch as such a physician, to avoid legal liability, accepted the death of some incipient persons, he or she would be doing a grave injustice.

Your moral situation is worse. You plainly intend that victims of rape who fear pregnancy take the Ovral tablets for both their contraceptive and abortifacient effects. Therefore, you conditionally intend abortion and, by proceeding as you do, you encourage women who have been raped also to intend it conditionally.[228] The condition, moreover, does not limit willingness to abort; morally, your intentions and those of the women who, sharing them, ask you for the drug are no different from those of women who regularly use some method of contraception while planning to abort the unexpected pregnancy if the contraceptive method fails. The only difference is that, in prescribing and taking Ovral, the intentions to contracept and, if need be, to abort are carried out by one and the same outward performance.

The moral evil in such a conditional intention of abortion is always present, even if the condition for actually bringing about an abortion never happens to be fulfilled.

226. See John Paul II, *Evangelium vitae,* 58–63, *AAS* 87 (1995) 466–74, *OR,* 5 Apr. 1995, xi–xii; *LCL,* 498–504; *CMP,* 141–71.

227. For a medical evaluation of the use of Ovral, see Eugene F. Diamond, "Rape Protocol," *Linacre Quarterly,* 60:3 (Aug. 1993): 8–19.

228. On conditional intentions, see John Finnis, "On Conditional Intentions and Preparatory Intentions," in *Moral Truth and Moral Tradition: Essays in Honour of Peter Geach and Elizabeth Anscombe,* ed. Luke Gormally (Portland, Oreg.: Four Courts Press, 1994), 165–70.

In no way is that intention's moral evil mitigated by the fact that you and the women do not know whether the Ovral had any effect at all and whether it was abortifacient. Furthermore, though the physical and psychological trauma of other methods of abortion might be greater, the moral evil of intending abortion in using Ovral is the same in kind as that of intending abortion in a later choice to use some other method. Indeed, in one respect, an induced abortion of which a woman remains unaware is a greater evil. Her ignorance is likely to facilitate self-deception, preventing salutary guilt feelings that could lead to repentance.

Therefore, you ought to change your present practice in this matter, and at once stop instructing rape victims as you do and dispensing Ovral in the way you do. If you can determine, by the history you take together with appropriate examinations and tests, that a woman is preovulatory, you can rightly offer a drug appropriate to inhibit ovulation, sperm capacitation, or fertilization and in the circumstances unlikely to act as an abortifacient.[229] Your intention in offering the drug should be only to prevent conception, and to prevent it not as the beginning of a new life, but as the completion of the rape. Inhibiting ovulation, sperm capacitation, or fertilization in a woman who has been raped is morally similar to pushing the rapist away so that he ejaculates outside her vagina rather than within it.[230]

But what if you have no way of determining that the victim of rape is preovulatory or, even worse, find evidence that she is ovulatory? Then it is worth bearing in mind that very few women become pregnant as a result of rape. I suggest that you acquaint yourself with relevant studies and reassure anxious women by providing this factual information.[231] If some women nevertheless ask for medication effective as an abortifacient, you should try to persuade them to forgo it; if a woman insists, you should refuse to provide it.

229. Eugene F. Diamond, "Ovral in Rape Protocols," *Ethics and Medics,* 21:10 (Oct. 1996): 2, says that determining the stage of the cycle "will require objective laboratory evidence such as the *Ovutest* to detect the LH surge, urine pregnanediol, and serum progesterone levels."

230. National Conference of Catholic Bishops, *Ethical and Religious Directives for Catholic Health Care Services* (Washington, D.C.: United States Catholic Conference, 1995), directive 36, provides: "A female who has been raped should be able to defend herself against a potential conception from the sexual assault. If, after appropriate testing, there is no evidence that conception has occurred already, she may be treated with medications that would prevent ovulation, sperm capacitation, or fertilization. It is not permissible, however, to initiate or to recommend treatments that have as their purpose or direct effect the removal, destruction, or interference with the implantation of a fertilized ovum." If the attempt to prevent conception carried with it some slight risk of abortion, that could rightly be accepted as a side effect: see Joint Committee on Bioethical Issues of the Bishops' Conferences of England, Wales, Scotland and Ireland, "Use of the 'Morning-After Pill' in Cases of Rape," *Origins,* 15 (13 Mar. 1986): 633, 635–38; "A Reply: Use of the Morning-After Pill in Cases of Rape," *Origins,* 16 (11 Sept. 1986): 237–38; *LCL,* 512, note 103.

231. Many recent articles assert that five or more percent of women who have been raped thereby become pregnant; see, e.g., Mary P. Koss, "Rape: Scope, Impact, Interventions, and Public Policy Responses," *American Psychologist,* 48 (1993): 1065: "Pregnancy results from rape in approximately 5% of the cases"; L. L. Heise, "Gender-Based Violence and Women's Reproductive Health," *International Journal of Gynecology and Obstetrics,* 46 (1994): 223: "In the United States, the chances of becoming pregnant from a rape are estimated at 5%." But a study (by a physician associated with Planned Parenthood) showed that the chance of pregnancy from *any* single unprotected intercourse is two to four percent; see Christopher Tietze, "Probability of

In some jurisdictions, that refusal might make you vulnerable to a lawsuit. I suggest you discuss that possibility with a lawyer who is faithful to the Church's teaching and competent in such matters, and try to find a morally sound way of forestalling unacceptable legal consequences. Someone at the hospital may urge you to tell rape victims to whom other physicians would give Ovral that pregnancy is a possibility, and refer them to another physician who will explain their options and provide Ovral to those who choose it. Acting in this way would make you a reluctant accomplice in the intentional destruction of incipient persons, for you still would be leading rape victims to take Ovral (see q. 66, below). Moreover, even if you could be involved in that way without intending the use of the drug, you hardly would find similar involvement by someone else in killing you or someone you loved to be acceptable, and so it would be unjust. Therefore, if you cannot avoid excessive legal liability without such involvement, in my judgment you must stop practicing emergency medicine.

If that sacrifice is necessary, however, you should work to obtain legislation to protect you and other conscientious physicians from coercion to prescribe abortifacients. In this effort, you might seek the help of prolife organizations, which very likely will be glad to cooperate with you.

65: How should a physician advise possible carriers of genetic diseases?

I am a physician just beginning my practice as a specialist in obstetrics and gynecology. I will take a very extensive medical history from every woman who comes to me, including questions about grandparents, parents, siblings, any children she already has, and other close relatives. While not routinely obtaining a similar history from every patient's husband, I will do that when there are infertility problems or other reasons for the man to see me professionally. These histories sometimes will indicate or lead me to suspect that any child the couple might have is more or less likely to be afflicted with some severe genetic disease.

Some physicians avoid dealing with the problem by routinely referring patients for genetic counseling. I plan not to do that, mainly because I am concerned about some of the advice patients would get from anyone to whom I could refer them. But I do have a reliable counselor whom I can consult. So, I plan to consult often and refer rarely.

Many physicians who approve of sterilization and abortion tell anyone who might be a carrier of a genetic disease to be tested. If the chances of handing it on are great, they recommend sterilization; and they have every fetus checked for defective genes and advise abortion when they think it warranted. However, I plan

---

Pregnancy Resulting from a Single Unprotected Coitus," *Fertility and Sterility,* 11 (1960): 485–88; other studies have shown that the chance of pregnancy from rape is considerably less: see Eugene F. Diamond, "Rape Protocol," 11–12. Pregnancy is less likely to result from rape than from a single act of consensual intercourse without contraception partly because sexual dysfunction is more common among rapists than among men engaging in consensual intercourse and partly because the rape victim's fertility is reduced by her lack of sexual arousal and emotional reaction to the violence.

to practice in accord with the Church's teachings on sterilization and abortion—and contraception too. I intend to tell everyone who comes to me where I stand, though I will explain my position, not in religious terms, but as part of a philosophy of medical practice that I believe to be both valid and appealing to many people, whether or not they have faith. This philosophy stresses preventative medicine, exercise, diet, and so on rather than merely diagnosing ailments and prescribing drugs. It also prefers cooperation with nature to the aggressive use of technique. Thus, it excludes abortion and sterilization as violent and manipulative, and favors natural family planning (NFP).[232]

Within this framework, what should I do when I know or suspect that a couple may pass on some severe genetic disease? Urge them to be tested, and, if the outlook is bad, try to dissuade them from having children? Should I offer tests during pregnancy to determine whether a baby will be seriously defective?

Analysis:

This question calls for the derivation of specific moral norms. The basic question is whether patients themselves should choose tests if they have reason to suspect they might transmit a severe genetic disease. If such people are considering marriage, or are already married and considering having a baby, they generally should choose tests, so as to obtain information bearing on their decision. Tests during pregnancy should never be chosen with a view to possible abortion. Tests with a view to the child's well-being might be obligatory. Tests to end the parents' anxiety are acceptable if they do not involve significant risk to the child, are accurate, and are not too expensive. In the preceding matters, physicians' responsibilities correspond to those of patients, but some cases present additional problems. If a woman or couple concerned about a genetic problem are determined to have an abortion and the physician's effort to dissuade them fails, he or she should recommend tests that might save the child's life by excluding the feared condition. If a woman or couple are determined to get tests with a view to having or considering an abortion, and efforts to dissuade them from getting such tests fail, the physician should adopt the course of action, consistent with other moral obligations, that he or she judges offers the best chance of saving the child.

The reply could be along the following lines:

Since competent adults bear the primary responsibility for their own health and functioning, including their reproductivity, your role as a physician is to serve those who come to you by helping them fulfill their responsibility. So, a good professional relationship with your patients will involve cooperation based on shared understandings and common purposes. Therefore, the primary question is, not what you should do about these matters, but what your patients should do.[233]

---

232. For a fuller, technical account of how practice might be conducted along these lines, see Thomas W. Hilgers, *The Medical Applications of Natural Family Planning: A Contemporary Approach to Women's Health Care* (Omaha, Nebr.: Pope Paul VI Institute Press, 1991).

233. This response should be read in conjunction with that to q. 66, below. Jeffrey Blustein and Alan R. Fleischman, "The Pro-Life Maternal-Fetal Medicine Physician: A Problem of Integrity," *Hastings Center Report*, 25:1 (Jan.–Feb. 1995): 22–26, articulate the issues and discuss

But though you should cooperate with your patients, you will be fully responsible for all of your own actions. Since you plan to practice in accord with relevant Church teachings, as a faithful Catholic should, you rightly mean to explain your commitment to all potential patients—an instance of the openness essential for a good physician-patient relationship. That openness also is necessary to forestall misunderstandings on the part of patients who might otherwise expect you to conform to the standards of physicians who consider contraception, sterilization, and abortion to be part of good reproductive health care. Unfortunately, as you doubtless are aware, the courts might use those false standards to define your legal duties and liabilities as a physician. So, since you will not be conforming to those standards, I suggest you obtain competent legal advice to protect yourself.

You may be able to minimize your vulnerability arising from your nonconformity by not only telling those who come to you where you stand but having them read, and perhaps even sign, a carefully drafted summary of your position on matters where your standards of good practice will diverge from those the courts would be likely to use. Without anticipating the legal advice you will receive, I think such a summary probably should include a clear statement that, as a matter of principle, you will not prescribe contraceptives, do sterilizations, or perform abortions; you will give no medical advice regarding these matters and no information about their availability; and in respect to these matters you will not refer patients to others from whom they might obtain any service, advice, or information that, as a matter of principle, you will not provide personally.

I now turn to the questions you raised, which must be considered within the kind of cooperative relationship I have described. So, I will look first at the patient's responsibilities.

Should couples with reason to suspect they might transmit some severe genetic disease to offspring undergo a test? If they are considering marriage or are already married, I think they should, assuming the test is not dangerous, too expensive, or otherwise seriously burdensome. For a couple not yet married, a test's results would either remove a reason for concern or establish a reason, not conclusive but worthy of serious consideration, for abstaining from marriage or choosing to marry someone else. For a couple already married, negative results again would remove a reason for concern—a possibly serious deterrent from having a family—while results indicating a significant likelihood that a child would suffer from a serious disease would contribute to responsible deliberation concerning whether to engage in marital intercourse that might result in conception.

In general, married couples should be conscientious in deciding whether to have a child or another child. They should begin with a presumption in favor of doing so, because "the true practice of conjugal love and the whole meaning of the family life which results from it have this aim: that the couple be ready with stout hearts

---

options for the prolife physician. But not being prolife, their preferred solution (25) is for the prolife physician not to think that "his strong anti-abortion convictions must *trump* the values and responsibilities that attach to his role as maternal-fetal physician" (italics theirs). Thus, they assume that being prolife is extrinsic to the physician's role, whose values and responsibilities are to be defined as including the acceptance of abortion.

to cooperate with the love of the creator and savior, who through them will enlarge and enrich his own family day by day" (GS 50). The object of the deliberation should be to discover God's will, and that certainly will not be that they impose unfairly on others, fail to fulfill already-existing responsibilities, or assume new responsibilities they cannot reasonably expect to fulfill. Therefore, they should take into account the many factors that might be relevant: their physical, psychological, economic, and social conditions; the good of their present and future children; the needs of their extended families, of society as a whole, and of the Church.[234]

In times past, some faithful Catholics thought (and a few still think) that a couple can be sure of acting in accord with God's will by engaging in marital intercourse whenever they wish and trusting in providence. Certainly married couples should trust in providence; but God has given the Christian couple reason enlightened by faith and the power to act in accord with it (see q. 31, above). Neglecting these gifts is not pious submission to providence, even though many people misled by bad pastoral advice no doubt sincerely thought it was.[235]

Suppose a married couple undergo genetic testing and the results reveal a significant probability—say, one chance in four—that a child would suffer from a serious genetic disease. Should they abstain from intercourse that might be fertile? In many and perhaps in most cases, yes, for either running the risk would be unfair to others or having a child afflicted with the disease would entail responsibilities the couple either could not fulfill or would be seriously tempted to omit fulfilling. In some cases, however, the answer is no. Foreseeing no morally cogent reason to avoid having an afflicted child, they may courageously agree to accept the risk, at the same time firmly committing themselves to carry out this element of their vocation should it be part of God's plan for them.

Many people will disagree with this position, thinking that deliberately taking a high risk of having a child afflicted with some terrible disease is plainly an injustice to the child. However, deliberately taking such a risk must not be confused with causing a similar injury to an already-existing person. The child who comes

---

234. See *LCL,* 681–84, and the documents of the magisterium cited there. Paul VI, *Humanae vitae,* 10, *AAS* 60 (1968) 487, *PE,* 277:10, teaches: "With regard to physical, economic, psychological and social conditions, responsible parenthood is exercised by those who prudently and generously decide to have more children, and by those who, for serious reasons and with due respect for moral precepts, decide not to have additional children for either a certain or an indefinite period of time."

235. Paul J. McDonald, "Accept the Children God Sends," letter to the editor, *Homiletic and Pastoral Review,* 96:3 (Dec. 1995), 6, denies that couples ought to judge conscientiously whether and when to have a baby or another baby, and misinterprets me as holding that "it is a sin not to practice NFP!" In criticizing my treatment of this matter (see *LCL,* 681–90), McDonald ignores not only most of what I say but the documents of the magisterium I cite, which support my view. To these may be added a recent, balanced statement: John Paul II, "Sunday Angelus Meditation" (17 July 1994), 2, *OR,* 20 July 1994, 1: "Truly, in begetting life the spouses fulfill one of the highest dimensions of their calling: they are *God's co-workers.* Precisely for this reason they must have an extremely responsible attitude. In deciding whether or not to have a child, they must not be motivated by selfishness or carelessness, but a prudent, conscious generosity that weighs the possibilities and circumstances, and especially gives priority to the welfare of the unborn child. Therefore, when there is a reason not to procreate, this choice is permissible and may even be necessary."

to be with an affliction would otherwise not have come to be at all. For a person, however, having come to be means living forever, with an opportunity for happiness that no affliction, however severe, can impede, lessen, or bring to an end. Thus, the child himself or herself remains a great good, and no one can rationally judge that any amount of foreseeable suffering—for the child and others involved—outweighs that good (see q. 33, above).

Again, some people will argue that taking the risk always will be unfair to those who will be burdened with the costs of special care, not least health care, not only for the child but for his or her descendants. But that is far from clear unless taking the risk is wrong on other grounds. Since much health care would be unneeded if people behaved temperately and chastely, imposing a burden by doing something otherwise morally good hardly seems unfair. Moreover, the possible benefits of the child's life for other people should not be ignored, and the burdens should not be projected overconfidently. Those burdens might be eliminated or reduced significantly by advances in treating the disease and/or the defect that causes it, and the child will not have any descendants without future choices that should not be anticipated. And other arguments based on fairness—for example, to children the couple already have—can be answered similarly. Though duties to others no doubt often will preclude taking a high risk of having a child afflicted with a serious disease, such a child is not only burden but gift, and sometimes, all things considered, the burden is fairly accepted for the sake of the gift.

So, one cannot rule out the possibility that a couple could rightly decide that they need not abstain from possibly fertile intercourse, despite the probability that a child will be afflicted with a severe disease, genetic or other. Moreover, in the case of genetic diseases, a couple accept only more or less risk; avoiding parenthood on this basis means also forgoing children who would themselves be healthy, though perhaps carriers of the genetic defect.

What about genetic tests during pregnancy?[236] Three factors must be considered: the intended purpose of such a test, its accuracy, and burdens such as risk to the child and cost. It is always wrong for the parents to seek a test with a view to aborting or even considering aborting a child found to be afflicted with a disease. On the other hand, if done with a view to treating the child or mother, or making necessary preparations to care for the child, a test, especially if very accurate, would be justified if the prospective benefit to the child warranted any risks to him or her. Trying simply to end the parents' suspense—so that they will be freed of unnecessary anxiety if the test is negative and able to adjust to their child's condition if it is positive would not justify a test involving significant risk to the child. But if a

---

236. See *CCC*, 2274; John Paul II, *Evangelium vitae*, 63, *AAS* 87 (1995) 473, *OR*, 5 Apr. 1995, xii; National Conference of Catholic Bishops, *Ethical and Religious Directives for Catholic Health Care Services* (Washington, D.C.: United States Catholic Conference, 1995), directive 50. On this question in general, see Benedict M. Ashley, O.P., and Kevin D. O'Rourke, O.P., *Healthcare Ethics: A Theological Analysis,* 3rd ed. (St. Louis: Catholic Health Association of the United States, 1989), 320–27; Agneta Sutton, *Prenatal Diagnosis: Confronting the Ethical Issues* (London: Linacre Centre, 1990).

test were accurate and with very little risk to the child, easing parental suspense might well justify the cost. Testing merely to satisfy parental curiosity is unreasonable inasmuch as it wastes health care resources, and is unjust if all or part of the cost is covered by insurance or a public program and so passed on to others.[237]

If the preceding analysis correctly articulates a couple's responsibilities, what are yours as a physician?

In general, having entered into a professional relationship with your patients, you must make your expertise available to them and you owe them candor. Therefore, if you learn something and the patient or couple could use the information for any legitimate purpose, you may not withhold it but must communicate it. At the same time, however, you should not try to replace with your advice a patient's or couple's own conscientious reflection about options that might be morally acceptable for them. You cannot know anyone else's vocation and situation as a whole, and so you cannot judge and discern for others. Attempting to do so is likely to result in shaping others' lives by your reasonable priorities for your own or even by your biases. Very often, patients or couples, confronting difficult questions, will want such inappropriate direction. Be careful not to give it, and bear in mind that your facial expression and tone of voice in talking about possibilities can convey as much as saying, "In your place, I would do such-and-such"—which often would suffice to settle an issue. If pressed for your opinion on such issues that lie beyond your professional competence, explain frankly: I cannot say what I would do if I were in your place, because my life and situation are so different from yours that I really cannot put myself in your place.

What about cases in which you have provided information and a couple must make a decision but disagree with each other? If both positions could be morally acceptable for the couple, the decision remains their responsibility and beyond your competence to make. So, you should not take sides. However, insofar as the couple's disagreement affects your ability to cooperate with them, you ought to try to help them resolve it by acting as a nondirective mediator, helping them become conscious of and share their feelings, articulate their thoughts, and listen to each other.

What about your responsibilities in particular?

Having reasons to suspect unmarried individuals or couples may carry a severe genetic disease, you should inform them about the possible problem and offer any tests they could rightly choose. But, having explained the reasons for such tests and any adverse factors, leave the decision to them. If they decide to have tests, you should not only inform them of the results, but, if they are positive, fully explain their implications and make a serious effort to ensure that this important explanation is well understood and accepted. Whether such people should marry is not a matter within your competence as a physician, and so you should not presume to offer professional advice for or against.

---

237. Though generally unrelated to genetic problems, costly examinations and tests to determine an expected baby's sex seldom provide any real benefit and so generally are unreasonable and unjust.

You should proceed similarly in dealing with married couples, except that the practical implications of a positive test result obviously will be different. Except in cases in which pregnancy and childbirth are themselves strongly contraindicated by health considerations, physicians as such never should advise people whether to have children, because the chief goods at stake in that decision are the child and the couple's potential fulfillment in parenthood, and these goods transcend the proper end of medical practice. However, you should help couples to foresee accurately the various burdens and hardships the disease would impose on the child, themselves, and others. More important, however, is to help couples who think they ought to avoid pregnancy learn how most effectively to practice NFP, as should be done by those who judge that they have a grave obligation, for genetic reasons or others, to avoid having a child.[238]

As for tests during pregnancy, always bear in mind that the unborn child is also your patient and you are responsible for his or her life and health. This responsibility might call for steps by you that otherwise would be at odds with the requirements of a sound physician-patient relationship with the child's mother. Three broad kinds of cases must be distinguished.

In some cases, the woman or the couple raise no question about abortion. When you have reason to suspect that the child may inherit a genetic defect or disease, there is a prospect of benefiting either the child or the parent(s) or both, and there is no prospect of harm or significant risk to either, you should offer tests, making clear the limits of their accuracy and any adverse factors. But you should not go further and recommend testing unless the results are needed for some morally acceptable medical decision.

In certain other cases, fearing that the expected child will suffer from some genetic disease, a woman or couple will have decided on abortion before discussing the matter with you and will not ask about testing. If in these circumstances other efforts at persuading her or them to reconsider fail, I believe you should recommend testing that might rule out the feared condition and save the child's life. In such a case, the woman's or couple's choice of testing would be with a view to possibly accepting the child, and so would not be wrong in itself, even though the test's results, if unfavorable, would tend to confirm their previous wrongful decision to abort the child. Of course, if the test result was unfavorable, you would try to get the couple to change their minds and accept the child. If that effort failed, you would, in my judgment, be obliged to recall the basis on which you had accepted the woman as a patient, point out that you had excluded having anything to do with abortion, and terminate your professional relationship. Doing that would be your last service to the unborn child, while not doing it would be a serious failure to bear witness to the truth.

Finally, in still other cases, a couple will be interested in testing with a view to having or considering having an abortion if the test discloses a defect. In such cases,

238. The most effective practice of NFP reduces the probability of having an unexpected baby to not more than one percent per year. See Thomas W. McGovern, "More about Effectiveness," in John F. Kippley and Sheila K. Kippley, *The Art of Natural Family Planning,* 4th ed. (Cincinnati, Ohio: Couple to Couple League, 1996), 139–52.

too, you will try to persuade the couple to accept the baby regardless of any defect or disease that might afflict him or her, and, unless test results will be needed for some morally acceptable medical decision, you will try to persuade the couple to forgo them. What if they insist on getting tests? Their insistence would violate the relationship they had formed with you. Still, as the unborn child's physician, you should adopt the course of action, consistent with your other moral obligations, that you think would offer the best chance of saving the child.

I can think of two such possible courses of action, though there may be others. If you think your best chance of saving the child is to tell the parents that you cannot continue serving as the woman's physician unless the couple change their minds, you must make that threat. Then, if the threat proves ineffective, you will have to carry it out—to bluff would be to lie, and lying is always wrong. If you think your best chance of saving the child is to agree to obtain the tests the couple insist on, you must agree to get them. The chosen means—the testing—will not be intrinsically evil, and your intended end can be to prevent the couple from receiving unfavorable test results from someone who would advise, facilitate, or do an abortion; and instead to present the results yourself and, if they are unfavorable, to take advantage of that final opportunity to try to save the child. If that effort failed, you would, in my judgment, be obliged to proceed as in other cases in which a couple are determined to obtain an abortion.

In every case, you should pray for your patients, not least for unborn children. And you should hope that God's mercy will bring into the light and save those you tried but failed to dissuade from killing and preserve from being killed.

66: May a physician refer patients who desire morally excluded services?

I am a Catholic obstetrician-gynecologist, committed to carrying on my practice in strict accord with the Church's teachings. Over the years, that has resulted in an increasingly wide gap between what I am prepared to do and what many other competent physicians regard as good medical practice.

When a woman straightforwardly asks for contraception, sterilization, or abortion, I can refuse to accept her as a patient or tell her I no longer wish to care for her. I have done that many times. Sometimes, however, circumstances make things more difficult. Instead of a straightforward request, I am confronted with a situation in which offering and recommending contraception, sterilization, or abortion would be considered appropriate by most fellow specialists practicing in this region. In not proceeding as colleagues would in such cases, I could be regarded as falling short of the standard of good practice, and that makes me vulnerable to being sued for malpractice. For example, serious health conditions sometimes indicate that a woman should avoid pregnancy, while past experience makes it clear she and her husband will not effectively use NFP. Most of my fellow specialists would recommend tubal ligation if the problem is permanent and contraception by anovulants—unless something precludes prescribing them—if it is temporary. Again, many colleagues routinely check every pregnancy for congenital defects and, finding any, more or less strongly suggest abortion, depending on the defect's seriousness.

One such problem is dealt with explicitly by the AMA *Code of Medical Ethics*. In a section on genetic counseling that allows for physicians whose consciences and moral values lead them to limit or avoid "genetic services," the Council on Ethical and Judicial Affairs adds: "However, the physician who is so disposed is nevertheless obligated to alert prospective parents when a potential genetic problem does exist, so that the patient may decide whether to seek further genetic counseling from another qualified specialist."[239]

Can I fulfill that "obligation" and those like it in other sorts of cases, such as those I have mentioned, without violating the Church's teachings? It seems to me hypocritical to say to a patient: "In a case like this, most of my colleagues would recommend abortion. But I think abortion is wrong, even in a case like yours, so I am not recommending it. At the same time, I don't want you to go to the neighborhood abortion clinic. Therefore, if you want an abortion, I suggest that you see Dr. . . .." But, then, what should I say instead?

Analysis:

This question calls for the derivation of a specific moral norm. Physicians usually formally cooperate with the services for which they refer. So, cooperating materially with morally unacceptable services by referring patients to physicians who will provide them would undercut the questioner's witness and good example, and might cause scandal. If a pregnant patient wants a morally unacceptable option, the questioner should try to save the child. If that effort is rejected or if a nonpregnant patient wants a morally unacceptable option, the questioner should decline to serve any longer as that patient's physician and should warn her against any foreseeable, dangerous action or omission. If necessary to forestall professional sanctions or civil liability, the questioner may inform the patient about an available referral service.

The reply could be along the following lines:

Whether or not it is hypocritical to give the advice as you formulate it, I think your instincts are entirely correct in rejecting that formulation. If you provide a referral to a particular physician, your advice will be unhelpful, and seem to the patient dishonest, unless that physician will provide the service you regard as morally excluded. But if your advice directs the patient to someone who you expect will provide the morally excluded service, giving the referral will strongly suggest that your own stand is weak and superficial. Since physicians making referrals ordinarily intend that the patient receive the service for which he or she is referred, a patient so referred and others hearing about it would reasonably think: "This physician does not wish to dirty his/her own hands with things like abortion but

---

239. Council on Ethical and Judicial Affairs, American Medical Association, *Code of Medical Ethics: Current Opinions with Annotations,* 1996–97 ed. (Chicago: American Medical Association, 1996), 2.12 (p. 22).

does not mind having others do them." In other words, your witness and good example would be undercut and a bad example given in their place.

As to the opinion of the AMA's Council on Ethical and Judicial Affairs regarding genetic services, I see no special problem. Your principles are entirely compatible with offering appropriate genetic services.[240] To do so, however, and also to deal appropriately with analogous problems, I believe you must take care in establishing your relationship with each new patient to tell her at the outset what your principles are and that you intend to practice exclusively in accord with them. Patients unwilling to accept your services on this basis will go elsewhere. But when your services are accepted on this basis, it establishes the common understanding and sharing of purposes essential for the true cooperation that should characterize every authentic physician-patient relationship.[241]

Even within this framework, though, cases will arise in which most other competent specialists in your field would recommend contraception, sterilization, or abortion. What should you do?

In many cases, patients themselves will think of those options, or other people will call them to their attention. It is appropriate for you to face them frankly and make the case against them. Say: "Here is the problem. Physicians who see nothing wrong with contraception (sterilization, abortion) very likely would recommend that way of solving the problem. But, as you know, I consider contraception (sterilization, abortion) wrong and reject it. Instead I recommend such and such, for such and such reasons." Having established a clear framework for your relationship with your patients and now recommending an approach within that framework, you may reasonably expect that your advice will be accepted.

If not? Then you should remind the patient of the basis on which your relationship was established, and try to persuade her to continue on the same basis. If that fails and the woman is pregnant, the baby also is your patient, and you should do what you can, consistent with other moral obligations, to try to save him or her (see q. 65, above). But if that effort also is futile or the woman is not pregnant, gently inform her that you no longer will serve as her physician. In saying that, you perhaps will foresee the danger that the patient will fail to obtain necessary care or will act inappropriately and dangerously. You may advise the patient not to neglect her problem and/or warn her against some inappropriate action, for example: "You must not let this go, so you should see someone else as soon as possible" or "Don't march off to the neighborhood abortion clinic, for they will simply do an abortion, while ignoring other aspects of your problem."

If nothing more is necessary to save you from serious professional or civil liability, I see no reason why you should offer any further advice. But let us suppose

240. Of course, when genetic tests indicate problems, those who consider sterilization and abortion morally acceptable may think it appropriate to recommend them—see, e.g., Richard West, "Ethical Aspects of Genetic Disease and Genetic Counseling," *Journal of Medical Ethics,* 14 (1988): 194–97. But a faithful Catholic will never consider those options appropriate; see q. 65, above; John M. Haas, "Human Genetics," *Ethics and Medics,* 21:2 (Feb. 1996): 1–3.

241. Legal counsel may advise a physician to present patients with a written statement of his or her principles, and perhaps also to obtain each patient's written consent to be cared for in accord with them (see q. 65, above).

that stopping at this point would open you to disciplinary action or a malpractice suit. Given such pressure, I think you may go one step further. Without recommending any particular physician, you could tell the patient about available medical referral services, for example: "Since you no longer will be seeing me, no doubt you will wish to find another physician. If you do not know whom to see, you can call such and such a referral service for suggestions."

This formula, unlike the one you articulated and we both rejected, does not suggest that you approve of what is morally excluded and desire only to avoid doing it yourself. So, this advice will not undercut your witness or give bad example, especially if you point out that you are giving it only because of professional and/or legal pressures. Moreover, telling patients about a referral service does not greatly increase the likelihood that they will act on their plan to do what they should not. Then too, in some cases the physician to whom they are referred may at least offer for consideration a morally acceptable approach and perhaps even recommend it. Finally, referring in this indirect way is unlikely to weaken your own commitment and lead you to intend anything you should not. Hence, it seems to me morally acceptable to tell such a patient about available medical referral services when that is necessary to avoid serious problems.

67: May a physician prescribe contraceptives?

I am a Catholic physician working under contract for a health maintenance organization (HMO) and providing primary care to some patients enrolled in it. Some are Catholic; many are not.

In principle, primary care includes family planning. But I am not expected to fit diaphragms, do sterilizations, or perform abortions; women who want those services can and do go directly to a gynecologist. I offer natural family planning (NFP) to all my patients who need help with birth regulation, and some accept it. But many do not, and they often ask me to prescribe birth control pills. Up to now, I have done so only infrequently and quite reluctantly for non-Catholic patients. Should I be refusing all contraceptive aid except NFP, regardless of the patient's personal convictions? Does it make a difference if the patient is a Catholic who does not accept the Church's teaching?

I have gotten different answers from the several priests with whom I have discussed this matter. All said that opinions among theologians vary, and one told me some bishops do not think contraception is wrong. But I realize that theologians and even bishops who disagree with the pope cannot change the Church's teaching. I would like to forget about the problem, but it continues to worry me.

I have another question, less urgent but related. The pill has certain therapeutic benefits distinct from its contraceptive effect, and these sometimes make it appropriate to prescribe it. As you probably are aware, its primary action is to suppress ovulation, but there is a significant chance of breakthrough ovulation, so that the pill achieves its high rate of effectiveness by acting as an abortifacient perhaps one time in fifty (or more often, depending on which version of the pill is used). Should this secondary action of the pill be taken into account in prescribing it for noncontraceptive purposes?

Finally, in some cases it is hard to decide whether using the pill would be contraceptive. For example, one patient, over forty, has had seven deliveries, five by caesarean section. According to the gynecologist who saw her, this patient's uterus is not fit for another pregnancy. He said if he were in private practice, he would do a hysterectomy; but the HMO's policy is to minimize surgery, and so he prescribed the pill. Now, in a case like this, where the pill is used as the alternative to hysterectomy, it seems to be therapeutic. But is it also contraceptive?

Analysis:

The questioner asks three distinct questions, which can be dealt with in reverse order. The third concerns the application of the norm excluding contraception. Though pregnancy avoidance is therapeutic for the patient, the hysterectomy's purpose would be to sterilize her; so, using the pill as an alternative to hysterectomy is contraceptive. The second concerns the acceptability of side effects. When the pill is used for genuinely therapeutic purposes, the risk that it will act as an abortifacient is an unintended side effect, which perhaps can be rightly accepted, but only if that will be fair to any embryonic individual whose life may be lost. The first concerns formal and material cooperation. Respect for others' consciences never calls on one to set aside one's responsibility for one's own actions. Prescribing the pill as a contraceptive generally is formal cooperation in contraception. In my judgment, even when it is only material and is reluctant, it is wrong.

The reply could be along the following lines:

While I do not doubt your account of what priests told you about varying opinions of theologians and even dissent by some bishops, this conflict and confusion in no way undercut the truth of the Church's constant and most firm teaching. It remains precisely what it always has been: Contracepting is always gravely evil (see *LCL,* 506–19, 634–36). Catholics who, like you, wish to be faithful to their commitment to live in the light of the moral truth taught by the Church should follow without compromise that teaching excluding contraception.

Laws, such as the former requirement that Catholics abstain from meat on Friday, do not apply to everyone, but only to people subject to the authority that enacted them. Hence, in dealing with people, one must take into account whether a law applies to them or not. For example, in years gone by it would have been wrong to encourage a Catholic to eat meat on Friday, but one might rightly have encouraged some non-Catholics to do so. By contrast, negative, exceptionless moral norms, such as the norm excluding contraception, identify actions at odds with every person's human fulfillment, and so apply to everyone, though some people, being ignorant of them, violate them guiltlessly. Thus, the Church's teaching that contraception is wrong is not a law, binding Catholics only. It is a moral norm, true for all people, though not everyone recognizes its truth.

Respect for others' consciences can require that one neither prevent them from doing what they believe they should nor urge them to do what they believe they should not, and generally requires that one not coerce them into doing what they believe wrong (see DH 2). But respect for others' consciences never calls on one to set aside one's responsibility for one's own actions. So, in every case you are responsible for your own actions, and you may never do anything you believe wrong. Therefore, in judging what you yourself may and may not do—with respect to contraception and every other moral question—it makes no difference whether your patient is a Catholic whose conscience is formed by the Church's teaching or someone, Catholic or not, who thinks an action Catholic teaching rejects as immoral would be permissible or even obligatory for himself or herself, or for you.

Someone might object that the preceding paragraph is at odds with the patient's right to choose among ways of handling medical problems.[242] But while physicians always should respect patients' freedom to choose among possibilities that are both morally acceptable and technically feasible, neither a physician nor a patient who differ in their sincere moral judgments may act contrary to conscience, and neither should expect the other to do so. Refusal to cooperate with patients' use of contraceptives, therefore, is entirely consistent with a general policy of informing patients about morally acceptable and technically feasible options and respecting their preferences.

Now I shall deal with your three questions, but in reverse order.

Your final question, about prescribing the pill to a woman whose uterus has been severely damaged, actually involves no special problem. In this case, the hysterectomy's immediate purpose would be to sterilize the woman. One can easily see the point by asking oneself: If the patient were no longer fertile or were not sexually active—for example, if she were now past menopause or a chaste widow—would the gynecologist have considered a hysterectomy or prescribed the pill? Obviously not. So, while an important medical indication makes it reasonable for this woman to avoid any future pregnancy, the intention of the gynecologist in prescribing the pill plainly was to prevent future conception. And even though avoiding pregnancy would serve a therapeutic purpose in this case, using contraception as a means to prevent pregnancy cannot be justified by that good end or any other.

Your second question, about prescribing one of the pills for therapeutic benefits independent of its contraceptive effect, poses a real and special problem that confronts many physicians. If the patient is known to be sterile or does not engage in sexual intercourse, prescribing one of these drugs involves no moral questions other than those raised in prescribing any other medication. But if the patient does engage in sexual intercourse and is reasonably presumed to be fertile, the possibility of unfairness to embryonic individuals who might be killed must be taken into account.

The possible bad side effects that argue against prescribing many drugs in various other cases almost always are far less significant than risk to a third party's life. So, if a presumably fertile patient engages in intercourse, the reasons for therapeutic use of one of the pills must be serious indeed to warrant it. When the condition being treated is relatively minor or you could use adequate alternative therapy with less serious side effects, prescribing the pill plainly would unfairly risk abortion. In less clear cases, the Golden Rule must be applied carefully, taking

242. See qq. 44, 58, 59, 60, 65, above; q. 72, below.

fully into account the personhood of the embryonic human individual even at the very earliest stage of his or her life. On this basis, a risk of the abortifacient side effect would be justified if, for example, the therapy would forestall an even greater risk to the mother's life.

But what about cases falling between these extremes? One rule of thumb might be this: Do not prescribe one of the pills for its therapeutic benefits when you are confident that not prescribing it would not be considered malpractice by omission. Most of your professional colleagues whose judgments constitute the standard of good practice clearly do not share your concern about possible abortifacient effects of prescribing the pill. So, if not prescribing it meets even their standard of practice, it surely should meet yours.

However, their standard plainly is not a sufficient criterion of fairness toward the embryonic persons whose lives are at risk. In cases of persistent and serious pathology, if surgery would be considered an acceptable option by your specialist colleagues, you might recommend that approach.[243] Again, you sometimes might be able to prescribe a type of medication that would minimize the potential abortifacient side effect; that very small risk could then be fairly accepted for the sake of significant and highly probable benefits to the woman's health. Or, if you can estimate the probable time of breakthrough ovulation, you could minimize the risk of abortion with patients who practice NFP by instructing them to abstain during the relevant stretch.

What about a case in which the HMO's policies and an uncooperative patient leave you with no workable alternative to prescribing the pill as therapy, and with a risk of abortion that you judge, prescinding from consequences to yourself, to be unfair and, therefore, unacceptable? In such a case, you may take into account the likely consequences to yourself—say, of giving up your contract with the HMO or accepting a risk of being sued for malpractice—and reconsider the fairness of accepting the possibly abortifacient side effect. But this will not, by itself, solve the problem. As with other difficult fairness questions, you must consider all the facts from the point of view of every person involved—including, of course, the embryonic individual whose life may be at risk—apply the Golden Rule, and judge as honestly as you can what you may and should do.

As to the first of your three questions: Physicians prescribing the pill for contraception ordinarily thereby advise and direct patients to use it. When they write the prescription, "Take one pill each day . . .," they normally intend that it be followed. They therefore share, and sometimes even induce, the patient's choice to contracept. Regardless of patients' beliefs or opinions, conscientious or not, that is wrong, because a physician is responsible, not only for the patient's action, but for his or her own. Intending the contraceptive to be used, the physician who realizes that contraception is wrong yet prescribes it not only has the contralife will characteristic of contraception but unjustifiably accepts the abortifacient risk of using any of the contraceptive pills.

243. See Thomas W. Hilgers, *The Medical Applications of Natural Family Planning: A Contemporary Approach to Women's Health Care* (Omaha, Nebr.: Pope Paul VI Institute Press, 1991), for indications of legitimate ways to deal with some common problems.

You say you prescribe the pill only reluctantly and when asked to do so by a patient. Further, perhaps you urge the patient to reconsider, explain the pill's bad side effects, including the risk of abortion, point out the advantages of NFP, conduct a careful examination to try to find some medical contraindication ruling out the pill, and so on; and only if the patient persists in her request after all this do you at last give in and write the prescription. Can someone who cooperates only with such reluctance be said in any real sense to *intend* the contraceptive use of the pill? Yes, just as a victim of blackmail who reluctantly commits treason really does intend to help the enemy. Moreover, in writing the prescription and instructing the patient, even a physician proceeding in that manner ordinarily hopes the patient will use the pill effectively, not encounter side effects that will interfere with doing so, not make mistakes and experience an accidental pregnancy (which might end in abortion), and so on. Such hopes are indications of the contraceptive intention involved in even reluctantly prescribing the pill.

Are there any situations in which a physician could avoid intending the pill's use as a contraceptive while prescribing it for someone who meant to use it in that way? The answer depends on what is meant by *prescribe*. Suppose someone who wanted to use the pill as a contraceptive put a gun to a physician's head and said, "Write a prescription for the pill or I'll kill you." Under such a threat, the physician, without intending the contraceptive use, could write the prescription; his or her intention would be to avoid being killed, and the use of the pill and its contraceptive and potentially abortifacient effects could be accepted as a side effect. Moreover, it seems to me that in this case the physician could plausibly and honestly apply the Golden Rule and say: "It is fair enough for me to write this prescription." Then too, writing it would not be likely to lead the physician to share the contraceptive intention or to tempt others to contracept. In other words, the physician not only could write the prescription without intending the drug's use but writing it could be justifiable. Yet even in this case a physician not impeded by other responsibilities from laying down his or her life might rightly consider himself or herself called to bear witness to the moral truth about contraception by refusing to write the prescription.

Coercion by less serious threats—for example, the threat of the loss of one's job with an HMO or one's share in a group practice—also could bring it about that writing a prescription for a patient who demanded the pill would not involve intending that the drug be used. The patient, having already determined to use the pill as a contraceptive, would regard the prescription she sought, not as a directive, but only as a legally required means of obtaining the pill from a pharmacy. In such a case, the physician, anticipating that the patient would have no trouble obtaining the necessary prescription from some other physician and intending to avoid threatened harms, could write the prescription, regarding it solely as a certificate that no recognized medical indication precluded the patient's use of the pill. Under these conditions, the physician's reluctant cooperation would not involve a contralife will.

But can such cooperation be morally acceptable? I think not. In the first place, writing such prescriptions, however reluctantly, is almost certain to be understood by patients and others as approval of the pill's use. That perception of approval—especially approval by a physician who, like you, usually tries to follow the Church's teaching—will reinforce the self-deception and rationalization involved in the dissenting opinions you described. By contrast, taking a clear stand and refusing to have anything to do with the pill's contraceptive use offers a necessary witness and example for patients and other physicians. Second, in the ongoing physician-patient relationship, a physician's prescribing the pill, together with his or her concern for the patient's well-being, is all too likely to lead to intending the drug's effective use. Third, using the pill involves risking the lives of embryonic persons, a risk that becomes a certainty when the pill is used not briefly by a single patient but for long stretches by many. So, unless all the patients would obtain the prescription elsewhere if not from you, prescribing the pill is virtually certain to result in the death of some embryonic persons who otherwise would survive. That side effect, in my judgment, cannot be fairly accepted merely to avoid economic hardship, even of a severe sort. Fourth, and finally, if in the absence of extreme pressure you prescribe drugs without intending their effective use, you cease being a responsible professional and become a mere functionary who makes a living by giving people what they want.

In sum, you should not prescribe the pill as a contraceptive to any of your patients. Insofar as you have been doing that, you should stop at once, and not just try to work out some way of stopping or wait until your contract with the HMO expires, so that you can decide whether to renew it. If the contract does not clearly require you to prescribe contraceptives, you should resist any pressure either to do so or to give up your position. Giving in to such pressure would set a bad example and weaken the position of others who follow the Church's teaching with upright consciences. If, however, your contract does clearly require you to prescribe contraceptives, that provision does not morally bind you, since nobody has an obligation to keep a promise to do something wrong. Perhaps you will be able to negotiate a contract amendment that will exempt you from prescribing the pill. Still, very likely you will not be able to continue working for the HMO while avoiding doing what you have contracted to do, and so will have to terminate your relationship with it. In that case, unless you have some compelling reason for going quietly, you should object strenuously to the unjust coercion, in the hope that objecting will serve as witness to the truth of the Church's teaching, a good example to other physicians and patients, and a contribution to the struggle to protect all health care professionals against coercion to participate in contralife activities, beginning with contraception but extending to abortion and euthanasia.

You do not explain why you raise these questions only now, when you already are working under contract with an HMO. Perhaps until recently you were misled about the Church's teaching concerning contraception or failed to take it seriously, and only now are coming to see and accept its implications for your practice. But if no such development has occurred, you should have considered what the work would involve before contracting to do it. I realize that this advice is of no help to you with your present problems. But you should examine your conscience about what you have done and failed to do until now and, if necessary, make a good confession.

Finally, if doing what you must reduces your income or results in legal problems, regard those unfortunate consequences as a small price to pay for the everlasting life promised Christians who are faithful until death. In rectifying your practice you are joining the small but splendid band of Catholic physicians who courageously and consistently have said no to contraception, sterilization, and abortion. Their witness is especially valuable because it is being given despite theological dissent and clerical confusion. And it is a witness to the truth about not only the good of human life and the sins against it but the heavenly kingdom. People without hope do not willingly accept so much loss and suffering.

68: May a physician remain in a group that provides morally excluded services?

I am a physician in family practice with a small health maintenance group. It includes three primary care physicians (one an internist), a pediatrician, an obstetrician-gynecologist, a general surgeon, and a psychiatrist. All of us are at least nominal Catholics. We use a community hospital (not Catholic) and refer when necessary to specialists in a nearby larger city, where there also is a well-equipped hospital. But we can take care of most of our patients' needs, and in most respects the arrangement has worked well.

When we set up the group some years ago, we agreed to adhere to the U.S. Bishops' *Ethical and Religious Directives* and to tell patients who asked about contraception, sterilization, or abortion: "We do not offer that sort of thing." In his previous practice, the obstetrician-gynecologist, Dr. Xander, had refused on medical grounds to prescribe oral contraceptives or IUDs. But he insisted upon—and all of us recognized—the need to help our patients with birth regulation. Since the others were not interested, the pediatrician, Dr. White, and I accepted responsibility for teaching natural family planning (NFP).

Soon, though, White and I realized that Xander was fitting diaphragms and recommending nonprescription contraceptives to many women. When confronted, he admitted "cheating a little on our agreement." But he defended what he was doing as "the least of three evils" for couples who will not practice NFP consistently. If he did not help them limit their families satisfactorily, he argued, many would leave our group and go elsewhere for oral contraception, sterilization, and abortion. Since the group needed an obstetrician-gynecologist and it would have been very difficult to replace Xander, the others did not wish to press the issue, and White and I reluctantly let it drop.

Recently, however, Xander began prescribing oral contraceptives. White and I again confronted him, and he said that, on his reading of the more recent literature, the low-dosage oral contraceptives are medically acceptable. Xander also argued that the group must offer "more satisfactory family planning services" to retain an adequate clientele. White and I objected that all oral contraceptives, and especially the low-dosage ones, sometimes act as abortifacients, but the others sided with

Xander and agreed that he not only could prescribe them but do sterilizations and, when he thinks it appropriate, refer patients for abortion to a physician outside the group. They also decided, despite our protests, that from now on no one in the group would say we do not offer that sort of thing; instead, everyone would direct patients "needing" contraception, sterilization, or abortion to Xander. Even White reluctantly agreed to go along. I said I would think about it, and they let it go at that until next month.

I either must go along or leave the group. That would be difficult for me personally, since all of the patients belong to the group as a whole, and I would not be able to take any of them with me. I would have to uproot my wife and children, and begin practice all over again somewhere else. Up to now, I have been trying to work out a modus vivendi. I continue to advocate NFP and, believing that nobody *needs* contraception, sterilization, or abortion, never bring them up. No patient has brought up abortion with me; not only do most of our patients know where I stand, but those who are pregnant, or think they might be, can go directly to Xander and normally do. A few have asked about contraception, and I say: "I don't want to have anything to do with that sort of thing, but you can see Dr. Xander about it."

I think this approach will satisfy the others, but my conscience is bothering me. Also, I really am worried about whether I could say the same thing if someone does bring up sterilization or abortion.

Analysis:

This question concerns material cooperation in wrongdoing. The obstetrician-gynecologist is, or will be, doing sterilizations and formally cooperating in contraception and abortion. Though the questioner's cooperation need not be formal, the usual norms regarding material cooperation must be applied. Doing so indicates that, even if the cooperation remains as limited as the questioner now proposes, it will be morally unacceptable. He should investigate alternatives to the two he mentions. If he can find no workable and acceptable alternative, in my judgment he must leave.

The reply could be along the following lines:

In prescribing oral contraceptives, which he regards as an appropriate method of birth regulation, Dr. Xander certainly intends that they be used effectively, and he perhaps also intends, but certainly at least wrongly accepts, their sometimes-abortifacient mode of action. Xander is or will be doing sterilizations. And, in referring patients for abortion, which he regards as an element of adequate family planning services, he will intend to make that option available.

In directing patients who ask about contraception, sterilization, and abortion to Dr. Xander, you will be cooperating with him in these matters. Of course, your involvement could remain limited. Holding that these contralife procedures are not appropriate methods of family planning and that nobody needs them, you do not bring them up. Thus far, you have told only those patients who ask about contraception that you do not want to have anything to do with that sort of thing but that they can see Xander about it, and you are considering saying the same thing to those who bring up sterilization or abortion. In saying this, you need not intend that patients see Xander, much less that he or they do anything immoral. Your intention can be, and undoubtedly is and would be, simply to make true statements required of you as a condition for remaining in the group. So, in responding to patients' inquiries, your cooperation with Xander's wrongdoing need not involve willing anything he or the patient wrongly wills. Still, even such cooperation is morally unacceptable if it is likely to lead one to cooperate more fully, if it gives scandal or impedes bearing witness as one should, or if it is unfair to anyone.

You might suppose that you may refer patients to Xander, much as a physician who is not in a group but under other pressures may refer patients—at least by suggesting a referral service—to someone who will accommodate them (see q. 66, above). But your situation is different. Since you and the other physicians are a group, your professional work and theirs ordinarily is wholehearted cooperation for common purposes, which include your patients' well-being and community among yourselves both in your professional activities and in sharing their benefits, not least their financial proceeds. This close association is understood by everyone concerned, and the patients you refer to Xander also will remain yours. When you refer someone to him, you know what he will do, and the patient knows that you know. This state of affairs will profoundly affect the significance of your involvement.

At times you certainly will be tempted to intend the same thing Xander wrongly intends. Caring for the same patients, you cannot help joining him in the intention that they survive and enjoy good health. Knowing that wrong things are being done, you will try to forestall some of their injurious effects. If Xander prescribes a contraceptive, you will be concerned that the patient take it correctly and deal appropriately with side effects; if he is planning to do a sterilization, you will be concerned that the couple understand what sterilization is and that the patient not be coerced; and if Xander refers someone for an abortion, you will be concerned that it not be late in pregnancy, when it would be more dangerous to the mother. Caring for your patients even as they engage in contralife acts, you surely will sometimes be tempted to join them in intending the bad means of attaining their ulterior good ends.

Even if you can avoid intending bad means, your involvement in Xander's wrongdoing, which inevitably will be extensive, is likely to lead at least some of your patients who otherwise would resist temptation to give in to it. Since you have adhered to Catholic teaching up to now, for you to go along with the group's change of policy will strongly suggest that contraception, sterilization, and abortion are not so wrong after all, and this suggestion will encourage people to rationalize choosing what they previously regarded as wrong. At the same time, you will be inhibited from bearing credible witness to the truth—that is, saying clearly what you believe about these contralife actions and acting in unambiguous harmony with what you say.

The point is especially clear and serious with respect to abortion. Someone is certain to bring it up sooner or later. If you say, "I don't want to have anything to do with that sort of thing but you can see Dr. Xander about it," you will give the impression that you regard abortion, not as wrong in itself, but only as repugnant to you. Yet all of the patients served by the group and, indeed, the wider community need to be reminded constantly that human life is sacred and abortion is its wanton destruction. And even though others continue doing that, the fact that you no longer do will undermine their witness.

Moreover, even your limited involvement in abortion will raise a very serious question of fairness to the unborn child. If you were in his or her place, would you not wish a prolife physician your mother consulted to do everything possible to dissuade her from killing you? Nor is involvement in prescribing oral contraceptives free of the issue of fairness. As you and White argued, they sometimes work as abortifacients. Moreover, they do not always work, and then a child comes to be as unwanted and is in danger of being either aborted or resented and, perhaps, abused (see *LCL*, 514–16).

Consequently, it seems clear to me that you may not comply with the decision of the others even within the limits you have set. But it is not clear to me that your only alternative is simply to leave and begin a new practice elsewhere. While you might be forced to do that, it should be a last resort. You owe it to your patients, including those not yet born, to help them preserve their lives and promote their health. Before leaving, you should communicate with your partners, one by one, in an effort to persuade at least some of them, and especially Dr. White, to insist on keeping to the terms of the original contract. If you win back at least three of your partners, that majority can save and restore the group's original purpose of providing good care in accord with sound morality. Your patients, who came to the group on that basis, deserve nothing less.

Even if you do not persuade enough—or any—of your partners, in my judgment you should not go quietly, but should consult a competent lawyer, unless you already have done so, about possible legal steps. Perhaps the agreement you made in setting up the group—to practice in accord with the Church's teaching—remains legally binding on the others, so that they cannot amend it without your consent. In that case, you can insist that they abide by it. Perhaps the status of the agreement is not so clear, but their position could not be easily defended. In that case, perhaps you can refuse to leave, refuse to cooperate with the new policy, and even openly oppose it. The resulting conflict will be painful for all concerned and may lead the others to offer you some sort of fair settlement. Even if the conflict drags on for a long time, your refusal to refer patients to Xander for immoral procedures and your open opposition would change the significance of your involvement, so that, if you were careful, you could avoid doing anything morally unacceptable.

But perhaps the legal situation is clear, so that you plainly must either cooperate, at least at the level you propose, or leave. In that case, I believe you must leave. Losing your share in this practice certainly will be a great sacrifice. However, you should compare it with the greater sacrifices, including life itself, that many other Christians gladly have made in order to keep the faith.[244] You still will have your training and experience in a very remunerative profession. Even if you establish a new practice in some community too poor and/or small to have a physician up to

---

244. See John Paul II, *Veritatis splendor,* 90–94, *AAS* 85 (1993) 1205–8, *OR,* 6 Oct. 1993, xiv; *LCL,* 112.

now, you probably will be able to live as well as your neighbors, and Christians dedicated to service should be willing to share, insofar as necessary, the lot of those they serve. Moreover, in due time, you will be compensated very well for your deprivation: "Blessed are those who are persecuted for righteousness' sake, for theirs is the kingdom of heaven" (Mt 5.10).

69: May a physician help unmarried couples achieve pregnancy?

I am one of the few women in obstetrics and gynecology, a specialty ironically dominated by men, and I have a moral question to which I have not been able to find an answer. It is about cases in which a woman not really married but involved in an ongoing relationship asks for help to achieve a pregnancy desired by both her and her partner.

A great many couples today are not really married. Besides those simply living together, many of whom may eventually marry, there are Catholic couples who are only civilly married and, no doubt, many couples, whether non-Catholic or Catholic, who are divorced and remarried invalidly. Of course, I often have no way of knowing whether a patient is really married, and then I assume she is. But I know that certain of my sexually active patients are not. I am sure it is right not only to provide them with the gynecological care that even single women need but to see them through their pregnancies and deliveries, since they and their babies need care, regardless of their marital status. I also try, in a motherly way, to encourage unmarried women involved in ongoing relationships to end them or straighten them out, though I must be careful in bringing up the issue, since some patients are edgy and likely to feel that it is none of my business. I suppose that is true, strictly speaking, but in a few cases my meddling has encouraged a well-matched couple to marry, or a woman to end a bad relationship.

Even with non-Catholic couples, I never prescribe contraceptives. I point out the unsatisfactory aspects of oral contraceptives, including their bad side effects and possible abortifacient mode of action, and offer natural family planning (NFP). Taught properly, it is highly effective and is acceptable to a surprising percentage of couples (though some no doubt cheat by using nonprescription contraceptives during their fertile periods). However, teaching NFP to unmarried couples has bothered me a bit, since it facilitates their continuing illicit relations.

In dealing with infertility, I offer only diagnostic procedures and remedies that are in accord with the Church's teaching.[245] The diagnosis and treatment of the underlying causes of sterility seldom are simple. Occasionally, however, infertility is a symptom of pathology that would require treatment in any case. If such pathology is ruled out, the problem may be that a couple's timing or other factors

---

245. For a summary of some morally acceptable steps, see Thomas W. Hilgers, *The Medical Applications of Natural Family Planning: A Contemporary Approach to Women's Health Care* (Omaha, Nebr.: Pope Paul VI Institute Press, 1991), 123–49; John F. Kippley and Sheila K. Kippley, *The Art of Natural Family Planning,* 4th ed. (Cincinnati, Ohio: Couple to Couple League, 1996), 297–99 and 305–15.

are unfavorable for conception, so that use of NFP and other simple adjustments can solve the problem. In trying to help couples have the babies they want, therefore, I almost always discuss their sexual activity with them, teach them fertility awareness, and instruct them when to engage in intercourse. Doing this for unmarried couples bothers me more than teaching them NFP as birth regulation, since in this case I am both telling an unmarried couple when to have intercourse instead of when to abstain from it and helping them bring into the world a baby who probably will be deprived of the stable parental cooperation children deserve.

If I did not help couples who are not married reach their goals of avoiding or achieving pregnancy, someone else would, and in the process very likely would offer and use morally unacceptable techniques. Still, I know that a good end does not justify doing anything wrong in itself, and so I am concerned that I may be going too far, especially in helping unmarried couples achieve pregnancy.

Analysis:

Several distinct moral questions are presented here. First, is teaching an unmarried couple how to practice NFP formal or wrongful material cooperation with their illicit sexual activity? Second, is helping an unmarried couple achieve pregnancy formal or wrongful material cooperation with their illicit sexual activity and/or their wrongful intention to have a child? In both cases, I think, the cooperation need not be formal and is unlikely to be so for this physician. But is the material cooperation justifiable? In the first case, it seems to me the material cooperation generally would be justified. Helping unmarried couples achieve pregnancy is more questionable, but I think even such material cooperation can be justified in some cases.

The reply could be along the following lines:

When an unmarried patient is involved in an ongoing sexual relationship and the couple wish to avoid pregnancy, you can teach them NFP without doing anything wrong in itself. You need not intend their illicit intercourse as an end or choose it as a means, but can merely accept it as a given. Teaching NFP to help the couple avoid pregnancy is an objectively good end inasmuch as, not being married, they should not have children. Your means also is good: teaching fertility awareness, including various methods of identifying fertile and infertile times. In most cases, your help probably does not in fact facilitate the couple's illicit sexual relations. Even if you did not help them, couples involved in ongoing relationships very likely would continue their sexual activity, either irresponsibly risking pregnancy or using contraception to prevent it. However, if your help occasionally does have this result, you surely do not intend or choose it, but only accept it as a side effect.

Of course, though not wrong in itself, such involvement in others' objectively wrongful behavior can be and often is wrong. Sometimes it is the occasion of oneself willing the wrong; sometimes it is unfair to those injured by the wrongful behavior; sometimes it leads others into sin or impairs witness to moral truth. However, teaching NFP to unmarried couples is hardly likely to lead you to will their illicit relations, that is, to intend them as an end or choose them as a means. Your involvement is neither unfair to the couple, who voluntarily injure themselves and each other by their wrongdoing, nor to any child they might have, since by teaching them NFP you reduce the likelihood of a child's coming to be outside marriage. Finally, in most cases your involvement will not encourage the couple to sin and, indeed, will give you an opportunity to encourage them to repent—an opportunity of which you take advantage by your "meddling." Moreover, in teaching NFP, you can propose sound attitudes both toward sexual intimacy itself and toward possible offspring, and thus help an unmarried couple gain insight into the inappropriateness of their intimate relationship and the wrongness of accepting any risk of procreating an unwanted baby. Moreover, even couples in illicit relationships who begin to practice NFP must exercise certain good habits, and doing so may lead to their ending the relationship or transforming it into a chaste friendship or marriage.

Still, in certain circumstances, teaching a couple NFP might encourage them to continue their illicit behavior and impair your witness to the truth about it. That could be so, for instance, if the couple's or woman's relationship with you were not merely that of patient with physician but that of a friend or relative whose illicit behavior you had a special responsibility to discourage. If you then judged that your involvement would be taken as approval, you probably would be obliged to make your disapproval clear by refusing all cooperation.

Though helping unmarried couples achieve pregnancy is more questionable than helping them avoid it, I do not think your effort to help an unmarried couple overcome infertility requires you to intend either their illicit sexual activity or the morally unacceptable aspects of their effort to procreate. The sexual activity of such a couple is habitual behavior in which they presumably will persist no matter what you do. So, though you teach fertility awareness and instruct them when to engage in intercourse, you intend only that they choose this time rather than that for intercourse; you take for granted, rather than choose or intend, their acts of intercourse themselves. As for the morally unacceptable aspects of their efforts to procreate, you need not will them. Nothing you do is specified by their being unmarried; indeed, your intention and choices can be precisely the same as when you help a couple whom you assume to be married while being ignorant of their true marital status.

The preceding point will be clarified by considering a possible objection. In helping an unmarried couple achieve pregnancy, you intend to satisfy their desire, and they desire not merely healthful functioning but its fruit, namely, a baby who will fulfill their sexual union. Now, the couple cannot rightly will that fulfillment, because their sexual intimacy, not being marital, is bad. So, the objection will conclude, in helping an unmarried couple achieve pregnancy, you intend part of what makes their act bad, and so share in their wrong willing. It is true that, in helping the couple overcome infertility, you do share their intention insofar as both they and you intend that a child be conceived. Note, though, that the child's conception fulfills an unmarried couple's sexual union in two ways: first, insofar as it is the natural consequence of healthy reproductive functioning; second, insofar as it is the desired culmination of an interpersonal relationship constituted by objectively bad human acts. As a physician dealing with the couple's infertility, you necessarily intend the first, which is an intelligible good, but need not intend —indeed, need not even be aware of—the second, which is morally defective. Thus, in helping an unmarried couple overcome infertility, you need not will the morally unacceptable aspects of their effort.

Still, you could intend what the patient wrongly intends—for example, if you helped an unmarried woman achieve pregnancy so that her restless partner would continue their relationship. In view of your conscientious attitude, however, I assume you would refuse to cooperate in a case you knew to be of that sort.

Is your assistance to unmarried couples in achieving pregnancy unfair to the children who come to be? It might seem so, since an unmarried couple do an injustice to a child by procreating him or her out of wedlock. Your actions, however, do not cause or contribute to the consequence that the parent's defective relationship has for the child (being born out of wedlock) but only to the consequence that their healthy reproductive functioning has for him or her (coming to be). Since it is good to be, the child's coming to be, considered in itself, is good, not bad. Thus, unless your assistance is detrimental to the child in some other way, what you do benefits, not injures, him or her, and so is not unfair.

Will your assistance encourage unmarried couples to persist in their wrongful activity or impair your witness to relevant moral truths? Here, it seems to me, distinctions must be made regarding what you do, characteristics of the couple's relationship, and their attitude toward the child who might be conceived.

Insofar as you try to discover and treat pathological causes of infertility whether or not the couple wish to have a baby, what you do pertains directly to your professional duty. You could not continue to serve patients while omitting care like this, and providing such care is not likely to lead those you treat or others into sin. At the same time, retaining such patients allows you to try to influence them for the good. So, it seems to me, such assistance is morally acceptable.

If a couple do not consider themselves married and are not regarded by others as a married couple, doing anything precisely to help them overcome infertility is likely to encourage them to persist in their relationship and wrongful sexual activities, and will tend to undermine the credibility of your witness to relevant moral truths. In such cases, it seems to me, your assistance to them would not be justifiable.

However, when a nonmarital relationship is regarded by the couple themselves and most other people as marital, you probably will not know—though you might suspect—that they are not married. But even if you are certain they are not, your further professional help in overcoming infertility is unlikely to have the bad effects that preclude helping other unmarried couples.

Still, such a couple or even a couple who are truly married might manifest an immoral attitude toward the child who might be conceived—for instance, by planning to have pregnancy tests and abort any fetus deemed unsatisfactory, wanting a baby to cement a troubled relationship, or desiring an otherwise unwanted baby solely to satisfy others' expectations. In such cases and others in which desire for a child is patently immoral, helping the couple achieve pregnancy would, I believe, be unjustifiable, for it might well encourage them and others to sin or persist in sin, and certainly would impede your witness to the child's inherent dignity.

70: Must a company physician maintain the confidentiality of employee-patients?

I am a salaried employee of a small corporation, working at its headquarters. My services as primary care physician are available to the company's employees and their families without charge. The company also provides a health and hospital insurance plan to complement my service.

While I refer patients to specialists when necessary, I need not refer as often as many doctors do, because, after good medical training, I practiced for ten years as the sole physician in a poor southern county. Also, having had extensive training in psychiatry, though unable to complete my residency, I can deal with many of my patients' psychological problems.

My situation raises two special questions about confidentiality. First, the company wants to require all its employees who are my patients to sign a general release, allowing the personnel department access to information bearing on job performance and sick leave. Should I cooperate? The question is especially troubling because few employees feel it practical to go elsewhere—and pay—for primary medical care. Second, management thinks I should be prepared to make an exception to confidentiality, even beyond any release, when the company's well-being is at stake, much as physicians generally are prepared to do when it is a question of the common good of society as such. Should I accept this view?

Analysis:

This question concerns the application of the norm requiring that secrets be kept. In general, adequate communication by patients to physicians demands trust that confidentiality will be maintained. But since patients may reveal their secrets, physicians should release confidential information at their request. Since the proposal of the questioner's employer would tend to undermine patient trust that secrets will be kept, the questioner should resist its implementation. But if it is implemented, the questioner must either resign in protest or respect the access employees authorize. Apart from releasing information with a patient's authorization and making exceptions in accord with the norms of official medical ethics, the questioner almost always should maintain confidentiality. Still, in my judgment, fairness to the company's interests might in rare cases require the questioner to make an exception.

The reply could be along the following lines:

The AMA's basic norm on confidentiality is: "The information disclosed to a physician during the course of the relationship between physician and patient is confidential to the greatest possible degree. . . . The physician should not reveal confidential communications or information without the express consent of the patient, unless required to do so by law." Still, the norm allows for "certain exceptions, which are ethically and legally justified because of overriding social considerations."[246] Two classes of exceptions are mentioned explicitly: the legally required reporting of communicable diseases and of gunshot and knife wounds, and the divulging of information necessary to protect the intended victim of a patient's credible threat to do serious bodily harm.

The reasons for confidentiality also are clearly stated: "The patient should feel free to make a full disclosure of information to the physician in order that the physician may most effectively provide needed services. The patient should be able to make this disclosure with the knowledge that the physician will respect the confidential nature of the communication."[247]

Another provision deals specifically with the problem of confidentiality as it affects physicians in industry. If a physician's service is limited to doing preemployment physical examinations or examinations to determine whether an employee who has been sick or injured is able to return to work, a physician-patient relationship does not exist, and the physician may provide the employer with relevant information. However: "A physician-patient relationship does exist when a physician renders treatment to an employee, even though the physician is paid by the employer." Thus, except as required by workers' compensation laws, the physician may not "discuss the employee's health condition with the employer without the employee's consent or, in the event of the employee's incapacity, the family's consent."[248]

These provisions seem reasonable. Though the norm admits of some exceptions, others' secrets generally ought to be kept (see *LCL,* 415–18), and the fact that an effective physician-patient relationship depends on the patient's trust that the physician will keep secrets provides an additional, specific reason why physicians should keep them. Moreover, confidentiality is especially necessary for patients inasmuch as health problems and suffering tend to increase people's vulnerability and tendency to reveal secrets, including some the physician need not hear. Still, some important social interests embodied in laws and the interests of potential victims justify certain limits even to professional confidentiality. Also, since anyone may divulge his or her own secrets, physicians do not violate the trust placed in them when they act upon a patient's authorization to supply information to others. Finally, even if an employer offers employees medical services without charge by directly paying a physician to supply them, this arrangement does not change the grounds for a physician's duty of confidentiality or alter its reasonable limits.

Given this framework, how should you respond to the company's proposals with respect to medical information about your patients, who are among its employees and their families? The two proposals must be considered separately.

The first is "to require all its employees who are [your] patients to sign a general release, allowing the personnel department access to information bearing on job

246. Council on Ethical and Judicial Affairs, American Medical Association, *Code of Medical Ethics: Current Opinions with Annotations,* 1996–97 ed. (Chicago: American Medical Association, 1996), 5.05 (p. 77).

247. Ibid.

248. Ibid., 5.09 (p. 93).

performance and sick leave." Should you cooperate? The question is not clear, because your cooperation might be at either of two stages: (1) in drafting the release form, encouraging your patients to sign it, and helping to develop a system by which the personnel department will access employee medical records; (2) in supplying management with information from the medical records of an employee who has signed a release in accord with that employee's authorization.

It seems to me you should not cooperate with management at the first stage. A general release giving the employer access to employee medical records will damage the good purpose of confidentiality, namely, patients' readiness to confide in you as their physician, and that effect will be the more deleterious insofar as your services include the delicate matter of your patients' psychological problems. Moreover, management's plan to require current employees—as distinct from new ones at the time of their employment—either to sign the general release or seek primary medical care elsewhere at their own expense would unfairly penalize those who do not surrender the confidentiality to which they are entitled.

Rather than cooperate in implementing this injustice, you should work against it. Tell management that compromising confidentiality will hamper your service to all of your patients and that its proposal is unfair. If your advice is not accepted, oppose the plan even at some risk to yourself. Encourage other employees to seek legal advice about thwarting it and, even if that is not feasible, to agree only to the release of specific information, which you would then provide on the same basis as do other physicians, not employed by the company, who care for employees under the complementary insurance plan.

If management persists and succeeds in putting the plan into effect despite opposition from you and others, consider resigning in protest. That would be warranted by the company's manifest violation of the physician-patient relationship, contrary not only to its employees' rights but to the autonomy due you as a professional committed to serving your patients. Your resignation might compel management to reconsider. However, that course of action may be excluded by your need for your position and/or loyalty to your patients. If so, at the second stage, you will be obliged to provide access to information about patients who have authorized it. In doing that, you will be cooperating with the company's wrongdoing. But you will be cooperating with the company only indirectly by cooperating with patients, whose directives you must honor. Moreover, by making clear to everyone concerned your reasons for cooperating, you can greatly mitigate the bad effects of doing so.

Your second question is whether you should make an exception to confidentiality, even beyond any release, when the company's well-being is at stake, much as physicians generally are prepared to do in view of overriding social considerations. Again, the question is not clear. It perhaps means: Should you provide management with information as required by workers' compensation or other laws, or warn the public authorities and management if an employee credibly threatens to do serious violence to a co-worker? Then the answer is yes, but, as has been explained, medical ethics already provides for such exceptions. But more likely the question means: Should you agree to make exceptions to confidentiality and reveal employees' secrets to management whenever you think that will help safeguard important company interests? To this, the general answer is no, since such a policy, like a general release, will violate your patients' rights and militate against the good purpose of confidentiality.

Nevertheless, it seems to me that you (and any other physician) could be compelled at times to choose between breaching confidentiality and permitting a patient to inflict harm on others as grave as, or even graver than, serious bodily harm to individuals, and that in such a case fairness can demand an exception to confidentiality (see *CCC*, 2491). Some harms to a business would very gravely harm persons, including some or all of the owners, managers, employees, customers, suppliers, and the dependents of any of these. So, I think, you might rightly make an exception to confidentiality to prevent an employee from wrongly causing some harm to the company that would be likely to gravely harm persons. For example, if the treasurer's wife, seeking a prescription for a tranquilizer, revealed that her husband was doing something that would bankrupt the company—for example, embezzling and gambling away millions of dollars of its funds—you might have an adequate reason to breach confidentiality. Even so, you first should try to persuade the patient to deal appropriately with the problem, so that you will have no need to reveal confidential information. Moreover, I do not think such an exception should be made without solid grounds for thinking that great harm probably will thereby be averted.

71: May a pathologist examine tissue from immoral procedures?

I am a pathologist practicing as a member of a private group of pathologists in a community hospital. Several moral questions connected with my work concern me.

Medically, we distinguish between spontaneous abortions (miscarriages) and induced abortions (terminating pregnancy on purpose). Induced abortion is the destruction of an unborn human being, and I see no reason to consider it any less wrong than killing anyone else. Of course, as a pathologist, I am not asked to perform abortions, since I do not perform any operations at all. However, is it improper to examine the tissue, which includes the remains of the fetus, from an induced abortion? I think it is wrong, because the main purpose of the examination is to verify the abortion's success, that is, make sure the entire fetus and all the accessory tissues have been removed. But what if my partners felt they could examine the tissue? Would I be obliged to quit the group or would it be enough if I avoided doing those examinations and left them to my partners?

Other questions concerning proximity to abortion: Is it permissible to provide other lab work—such as blood and urine testing—for clinics that do nothing but abortions? I think it is not. But is it also improper to provide these services for gynecologists who do some abortions while also providing various sorts of appropriate health care to women—caring for pregnant women and delivering babies, doing regular checkups, and so forth?

Following the teaching of the Church, I consider sterilizations—tubal ligations on women and vasectomies on men—morally wrong. As with abortions, I'm not asked to do them. However, on a daily basis I do verify the ligations by tissue studies. Is this cooperating too closely in sterilizations?

I discussed the abortion and sterilization questions with the hospital chaplain. Having conferred with some other priests and theologians, he said they felt I was not morally obliged to avoid doing this lab work. I assume they have their reasons, but in good conscience I still do not want to examine tissue from abortions. Also, I do not want to provide any other laboratory services to abortion clinics.

At this time, most of our work comes from the hospital, and, so far as I know, no induced abortions are done in it. Fortunately, my present partners respect my position on abortion, and have agreed not to solicit any outside work related to induced abortions. But there is a possibility that the rules at the hospital are going to change. Suppose that happens and the tissue from abortions is sent to us. Would I be required to quit the staff? Or could I leave it to my partners to examine the abortion tissue?

With regard to sterilizations, I've been following the chaplain's advice. The procedures are so ubiquitous that it would be next to impossible to practice pathology and avoid them. I realize that this fact by itself does not make doing the examinations right, but I think I'm not in morally questionable territory, since sterilization does not involve killing someone as abortion does.

Analysis:

The questions presented here concern cooperation with wrongdoing. The questioner cooperates only materially and is not likely to be tempted to cooperate formally. Still, judged by the usual criteria, the material cooperation with sterilization is morally questionable; since the tissue study can lead to a second attempt, doing it impedes witness. Still, I think the questioner may tolerate his or her partners doing that work, and, if the alternative is giving up his or her profession, may even continue to do it personally. As for the partners' examining tissue from abortions, even tolerating that would be morally questionable. If employment were available in a situation free of abortions, the questioner would, in my judgment, be obliged to accept it.

The reply could be along the following lines:

Your questions manifest conscientiousness in doing your professional work. Like you, and in accord with the constant and most firm teaching of the Catholic Church, I believe that both induced abortion and sterilization are always wrong. So, in replying to your questions, I shall presuppose the truth of the moral norms absolutely excluding operations of both kinds. Examining the questions you raise from various points of view, I shall apply several distinct ethical criteria. Just as you might identify pathology in a sample of tissue by only one of several studies you make, so my analysis will show that in one respect, though not in others, the lab work you describe is morally unsound.

Your proper role as a pathologist is to examine tissues in order to answer specific factual questions about them, and then to report your findings accurately to those who sent the tissues to you. Plainly, the actions you must do to fulfill that role are not in themselves wrong, are conducive to knowledge of the truth, and ordinarily serve health as well. However, while your work ordinarily contributes to other physicians' efforts to save lives and promote health, examining tissues from abortions and sterilizations contributes to other physicians' killing babies and destroying people's reproductive capacity. Thus, your questions require examination of your intentions and of various side effects. I shall consider both and, as will become clear, find some difficulties with the latter.

Though pathologists do not arrange operations or direct those who perform them, some pathologists perhaps desire that induced abortions and sterilizations be done so that they will derive income from work consequent upon these procedures. Plainly, you do not share that wrongful desire. Moreover, you do not do tissue studies to verify the success of induced abortions, although you do perform such studies to verify sterilizations. But even a pathologist doing studies in both kinds of cases need not intend the operations themselves, for, after others have undertaken them, someone might seek to verify their success with upright intentions of two sorts. First, as you of course know, an abortion in which parts of the fetus or accessory tissues are left behind can be life threatening to the woman, and so the pathology studies needed to verify the completeness of abortions can be chosen to preserve women's lives. Second, carrying on the practice of pathology to make a living and serve patients in other sorts of cases might require that a practitioner verify the success of various procedures that should not have been done. (Apparently, your reasons for verifying sterilizations are of this second sort.) Of course, if your tissue study does not verify the success of a sterilization, your report is likely to lead to a second attempt. However, while foreseeing that result, you need not intend it. Consequently, it seems to me that the hospital chaplain's advice—you need not avoid doing this lab work—is sound in the respect that such work need not involve a wrong intention.

Not personally doing anything inherently wrong and not sharing the objectively wrongful intentions of those who choose to do induced abortions and sterilizations, you contribute at most only incidentally to what they are doing. Your main questions thus reduce to the moral acceptability of the side effects of what you are doing (verifying sterilizations) or might do in the future (continue to participate in a group practice whose other members examine tissue from induced abortions).

Your involvement would be an occasion of sin for you if it were likely to tempt you to share the wrongful intentions of those doing induced abortions and sterilizations. That seems unlikely, and so this possible side effect can be set aside. Your involvement would constitute scandal—that is, it would wrongly risk leading others into sin—if it were likely to lead others to choose to perform or undergo induced abortions or sterilizations, or to cooperate wrongly in them. That also seems unlikely, not only because your work as a pathologist begins only after these operations are undertaken but also because it is carried on behind the scenes, hardly noticed by anyone except other professionals, who very likely already have taken their own stands on these matters.

Though the preceding tests have revealed no moral pathology, the examination is not yet complete.

You say it would be "virtually impossible" to practice pathology and avoid verifying sterilizations. But since doing so leads to a second attempt when the first is unsuccessful, it does contribute to bringing about the procedure's illegitimate goal. Moreover, insofar as possible, everyone should bear witness to moral truth in word and deed. Even incidental involvement in what you believe wrong impedes your witness before your partners and other professionals. Therefore, it seems to me you should try to desist from this work. However, tolerating your partners' doing it would distance you from it and so, I think, would be compatible with your own witness against sterilization. But if your partners will not cooperate in freeing you from verifying sterilizations, I do not think you must give up your profession so as to avoid doing so.

The requirement of witness to moral truth about induced abortion also argues against even remote, incidental involvement in it. Also, and perhaps even more cogently, against such involvement is its contribution, however minimal and indirect, to the killing of unborn children. One must apply the Golden Rule and ask: If one's own life or that of someone near and dear were at stake, would one regard a similar degree of involvement by others as excusable, or would one want them to refuse to be involved? On this basis, it seems to me, you are rightly unwilling to examine tissue from abortions or to do other laboratory services for abortion clinics. If the hospital's rules change and your partners decide to examine tissue from abortions, tolerating their doing such work would be harder to justify than tolerating their verifying sterilizations. If you could find employment in a situation that excluded examining tissue from abortions, it seems to me you would be obliged to take it, in order to bear witness to the truth about the sanctity of human life.

As for doing lab work, such as blood and urine testing, for gynecologists who do some abortions but also provide various sorts of appropriate health care for women involving the very same kinds of tests, the incidental involvement in abortion seems to me so slight and remote that you need not be morally concerned about it.

72: May a hospital give blood transfusions despite patients' conscientious refusal?

I am the administrator of a teaching hospital at a major university. We have a problem with the management of Jehovah's Witnesses as patients. Sometimes these people refuse on religious grounds to consent to blood transfusions, even transfusions that would use their own blood and even those that seem necessary to save their lives. Some staff physicians do not accept these patients, others do. That in itself is no problem for us, but a problem does arise because almost all of our anesthesiologists are unwilling to agree to withhold blood.

A current case was referred to our hospital ethics committee, and they have sent me their recommendation, which I am free to follow or not. The case presentation states the facts as follows. A twenty-three-year-old mother of two wants to deliver her third child at our hospital. Though a caesarean section might be necessary, she is not willing to consent to a blood transfusion, and her obstetrician has agreed to proceed on that basis. He hopes for a vaginal delivery; but if the caesarean becomes necessary, withholding blood would not imperil the baby, and he feels the woman is entitled to run the risk to herself. When he contacted our anesthesiology department to arrange for caudal anesthesia, however, he learned that few obstetrical anesthesiologists are willing to care for the woman on her terms, so that there might not be an anesthesiologist available when needed. Some who refuse explain that withholding an intervention so simple as a blood transfusion would violate their standard of practice and/or that they could not in good conscience agree to stand by while such a patient died, especially when she would leave children motherless.

In discussing the case, members of the ethics committee agreed that people unwilling to accept care in accord with our staff's conscientious convictions should be asked to go elsewhere. But that will not solve the problem, because we must deal with emergency cases, where neither we nor the patients have a choice about their being here. For such cases, it would be best to have available an anesthesiologist willing to care for these patients on their terms. However, guaranteeing that would require having such a person not only always on duty but always standing by, and that is not feasible. Inevitably, then, we sometimes will have such patients when there is no anesthesiologist available to care for them on their terms. Then, the committee majority argued, whoever does care for them cannot be expected to compromise his or her principles, since a physician's conscience deserves no less respect than a patient's. The hospital's lawyer supported this view, pointing out that almost all lawsuits against hospitals and physicians brought by Jehovah's Witnesses given blood against their will either have been decided for the defendant or settled by a rather small payment to the patient.

The ethics committee concluded: "When all efforts to find care commensurate with the patient's wishes have failed, there is no choice but to proceed according to the values of the physicians delivering the care."

If I endorse that conclusion, we would state our policy very clearly and warn those who might be affected to go elsewhere if they can. Still, I am not comfortable with this approach, because of the problem with emergency patients. We would be making it hospital policy to impose blood transfusions on some of them not only without their consent but despite their express refusal. But what alternative have I, other than trying to coerce members of our staff to act against their consciences?

Analysis:

This question concerns norms for the cooperation of health care providers with patients. Since the relationship between a patient and any care provider should be a free cooperation, neither party should be expected to act against his or her conscience. But, with certain exceptions, care providers may not act on patients without their informed, actual or reasonably presumed consent, and so a care provider can be required to refrain from doing something otherwise required by professional ethics and/or personal moral standards. In emergencies, an anesthesiologist should do all that can be done consistently with both his or her own standards and the patient's consent.

The reply could be along the following lines:

In responding, I shall assume that, as in your example, no one else's life will be at risk; if it were, that would be a different problem.[249] I also shall assume that, while Jehovah's Witnesses are mistaken in thinking that God forbids blood transfusions, their belief is sincere and important to them. Given these assumptions, I do not agree with the ethics committee's recommendation.

It seems to me the committee's discussion is flawed in two ways: by presupposing a false view of the relationship between patients and care providers (I use *care providers* here to refer not only to physicians but to hospital administrators and other health care personnel), and by ignoring a vital distinction between acting and refraining. The relationship between patients and care providers should be a free cooperation. Since the consciences of both physicians and patients deserve the same respect, neither party to this cooperative relationship should be expected to act against his or her conscience. Still, the patient's unwillingness to proceed can require that a care provider refrain from acting as his or her conscience otherwise would require. I therefore disagree with the statement in the ethics committee's conclusion: "When all efforts to find care commensurate with the patient's wishes have failed, there is no choice but to proceed according to the values of the physicians delivering the care." My analysis of the problem is as follows.

On the one hand, patients are not merely cases on which expert care providers exercise their technical skills in accord with their own professional and moral standards. Competent adults are acting persons responsible for their own life and health, and care providers are potential assistants, to be engaged and cooperated with by mutual consent. Except in certain special cases provided for by law (for example, immunizations to prevent epidemics), no sort of health care ever should be imposed upon competent adults without their actual or reasonably presumed consent. That consent should not be a blank check, licensing care providers to do whatever they consider appropriate, but should be informed and specific, so that the patient can limit the cooperation in accord with morally acceptable interests other than that in health and survival—not least, the interest in obeying what is sincerely believed to be God's will. Therefore, it seems to me, imposing care on a competent adult against his or her will is doing violence to that person. It follows that anyone who gives a blood transfusion to a Jehovah's Witness against the patient's will commits an offense against her or him, and that you, as hospital administrator, should do your best to prevent such an offense. Warning potential patients who do not want blood transfusions to go elsewhere if they can will not

---

249. The problem regarding children already born, as it confronts a state legislator, is dealt with in q. 197, below. I do not deal with the problem regarding unborn children, which should be handled in the same way as if they were already born. Of course, those who assume that abortion is acceptable will regard it as a quite different, and difficult, problem; see Ruth Macklin, "The Inner Workings of an Ethics Committee: Latest Battle Over Jehovah's Witnesses," *Hastings Center Report,* 18 (Feb.–Mar. 1988): 15–20.

adequately safeguard patients' rights, since, as you say, some people will have no choice about being in your hospital.

On the other hand, care providers are bound not only by the standards of good practice and professional ethics but by their personal moral convictions. In carrying out their professional responsibilities, they never should be required to do anything they believe wrong. Moreover, except when their action is limited by others' rights, they should not be required to provide professional services under conditions that would prevent them from doing what they consider required by professional standards.

In emergency situations, those available should do what they can ("can" being limited by their conscientious convictions as well as by other limits on their capacity to act) to meet urgent needs, even if they are prevented by a patient's refusal from doing some things they otherwise would consider obligatory. In dealing with Jehovah's Witnesses, everything except giving blood can be carried out in full accord with the anesthesiologist's professional standards. So, if nobody else is available to provide essential service, an on-duty anesthesiologist who considers it wrong to allow a Jehovah's Witness to die for want of a blood transfusion should do all these other things for the patient while refraining from doing that to which the patient refuses consent. However, when someone willing to cooperate with a Jehovah's Witness becomes available or the emergency ends, any institution or individual providing service on an emergency basis should be free to avoid further involvement—for example, by discharging the patient from the hospital or withdrawing from the case.

Someone might object that, in caring for any patient, an anesthesiologist would commit a sin of omission by not giving a transfusion he or she judged should be given. But nobody commits a sin of omission except by failing to do something he or she both can and ought to do. To give the transfusion despite the patient's refusal would not be to cooperate with a competent adult but would be to violate that adult's rights by unilaterally acting on him or her. So, the anesthesiologist, lacking the patient's authorization to give the transfusion, cannot rightly do so. Consequently, his or her refraining is not a sin of omission.

Nevertheless, if a court were to order blood transfusions for a patient despite his or her refusal, an anesthesiologist who judged the transfusions appropriate could rightly provide them. In such cases, the blood transfusion presumably is lifesaving and the court presumably acts for some public interest—for example, in forestalling the need to care for orphans. Even if the hospital and/or the anesthesiologist sought the court order, in carrying it out the anesthesiologist would act as an obedient citizen rather than as a physician cooperating with and serving a patient.[250]

250. However, if a court were to order someone to do an abortion or other act against life or health, that person would be obliged to refuse: "We must obey God rather than any human authority" (Acts 5.29). Many health care providers who do not share the belief of Jehovah's Witnesses that it is wrong to accept blood transfusions have no problem of conscience in cooperating with these patients within the limits they set. Such people should make known their readiness to care for Jehovah's Witnesses.

73: May a hospital serve a patient who refuses food in order to die?

I am chief administrator of a Catholic hospital. We have a patient, Miss Thornton, aged forty-three, whose condition currently is deteriorating. Thornton has refused to give her consent to medically indicated treatment and has said she no longer wants to go on living. For the past two days, she has been refusing to eat. However, she wants not only the nursing care that would be appropriate in any case, but certain other things required by her peculiar project, in particular, medication to alleviate her hunger pangs. A patient always is free to refuse medical treatment, and we cannot impose anything on Thornton against her will without incurring legal liability. But caring for her within the limits she has set seems to me to be helping her commit suicide.

Our hospital ethicist points out, however, that people foolishly, and sometimes irresponsibly, refuse treatment for other reasons. For example, a man under forty with a large family was admitted a few months ago. Tests showed he needed heart surgery, but he had the notion he would get well without it and was afraid of it because his father had died some years ago while undergoing similar surgery. Neither reassurances about progress since then nor pastoral counseling could alleviate his anxiety, and warnings about the risk he was running failed to move him. His wife pleaded with him, but still he would not consent to the surgery. We considered the possibility that his anxiety manifested psychopathology, but concluded that he was competent and that we had to accept his refusal of treatment. Still, we did everything we could to save him until he died, and nobody thought we should have done otherwise in that case. Therefore, our ethicist argues, while doing what we can for Thornton, we may observe the limits she sets on her treatment even though we think her refusal of treatment is wrong.

I am not sure what to make of that argument. But if it is unsound and I am right in feeling we should not go along with Thornton, I still am not sure what we should do. Of course, our options may be limited by legal considerations, and I shall consult our lawyers. But my question is: What should we do if we can?

Analysis:

This question concerns material cooperation. Assuming the patient is refusing treatment and food in order to end her life, the questioner is correct in thinking the hospital would be cooperating with suicide if it continues to care for her as she wishes. While the cooperation would not be formal, material cooperation probably would be wrong in this case. In the case of the man cited by the hospital ethicist, the hospital in no way cooperated in doing anything morally unacceptable in itself; rather, it formally cooperated with the patient in attempting to survive despite his unreasonable, but not suicidal, refusal of surgery.

The reply could be along the following lines:

Whenever a patient expresses a seemingly suicidal intention or, with any motive, refuses treatment or food that physicians or hospital staff consider appropriate, they should make a suitable effort to communicate with the patient and generally also with available family members or others close to the patient. The main purposes should be to correct any factual mistakes or misunderstandings, attend to any unmet needs for pain relief or any other sort of support, discover the patient's real intentions, and persuade him or her to rectify them if necessary. Of course, the possibility that the patient is depressed or otherwise mentally ill also must be considered and ruled out. You seem to have fulfilled these responsibilities in the case of the man whose excessive fear led him to refuse indicated heart surgery. You may also have done so in the case of Miss Thornton, but that is not clear.

Perhaps her statement that she does not want to go on living really manifests feelings of depression or some nonsuicidal, though ill-expressed and perhaps mistaken, volition. If so, you should deal with her much as you did with the man who refused heart surgery. If you are convinced that Thornton really has chosen to commit suicide, arrange for her to be counseled and urged to change her mind.

Treatment that health care providers consider medically indicated sometimes promises such small benefits and/or entails such great burdens to the patient that he or she can rightly refuse it. Dying persons sometimes lose their appetites and reasonably refuse to eat. So, even if Thornton really is intent on suicide and should be exhorted to repent of that wrongful intent, she also should be supported in any morally acceptable alternative, including choosing on legitimate grounds to refuse anything she can rightly refuse.

If you have met your responsibility to communicate with Thornton and are convinced that she remains intent upon killing herself, you are right that caring for her as she wishes would constitute cooperating with her wrongdoing. Some ethicists faithful to the Church's teaching probably would assert that giving her medication that would alleviate hunger pangs, or providing her with other care not required if she were not killing herself, necessarily would involve intending to bring about her death. But that is not so. Of course, some hospitals and their personnel might provide such care precisely to help patients intent on suicide attain their end—for example, offering medication to relieve hunger pangs so that a patient starving himself or herself to death would not give in to the urge to eat. That would be sharing her will to end her life, which would be morally wrong in itself, though it might be subjectively blameless for some or all of those involved due to their lack of sufficient reflection. However, I assume your hospital and its personnel would give Thornton the care she desires, including medication that would ease her hunger pangs, for other, legitimate reasons—to make her comfortable, dispose her to accept counseling that might lead her to change her mind, avoid legal problems. Even though Thornton needs some elements of that care only because she is refusing food and appropriate treatment, acting on any of those reasons would be morally permissible in itself. In providing the care she desires, therefore, your hospital and its personnel, though facilitating her suicide, would intend only to mitigate some of the bad side effects of her method of killing herself.

Still, doing anything that facilitates a gravely evil act often is morally unacceptable. Sometimes that is so because it occasions wholehearted cooperation in the sin; but you hardly are likely to be tempted to intend anything, whether as an end or as a means, that would contribute to Thornton's death, and you could explain to hospital personnel the legitimate reasons for giving her the care she desires while warning them against being moved by sympathy to do anything precisely to help her bring about her death. Sometimes doing what facilitates an evil act is morally excluded inasmuch as it is unfair to third parties; but Thornton's death may not injure anyone else, and even if her suicide does wrong others, your reluctant and limited contribution to what she is doing may not be unfair to them. Sometimes, though, such involvement in an evil act is morally unacceptable for yet another reason. It impedes one's witness to the moral truth about the wrongdoing and may even encourage other people to embrace that sort of wrong. Those bad consequences are likely to follow if you voluntarily continue to serve Thornton as she starves herself to death. Therefore, in my judgment, you must resist doing so.

This point can be clarified by comparing this case with that of the man who refused indicated heart surgery. He plainly did not intend to kill himself but unrealistically expected to get well. You intended to help him try to survive without thereby facilitating any wrongdoing, since, even though his refusing surgery was unreasonable, it was not suicidal; he intended only to avoid surgery he mistakenly regarded as too risky. But I am assuming that Thornton does intend to kill herself. Thus, continuing to serve the man in no way impeded clear witness to the sanctity of life and the wrongness of suicide, whereas continuing to serve Thornton, by helping her mitigate the bad side effects of her chosen method of killing herself, might well suggest that life of poor quality is valueless and suicide can be appropriate in such a case. Moreover, your effort to save the man's life despite his refusal of surgery surely did not encourage anyone else to refuse appropriate surgery. But mitigating Thornton's hunger pangs and other unpleasant side effects would enhance the appeal of her suicidal project to people tempted to end their lives and might well encourage them to follow her bad example. If, however, you strongly resist involving the hospital in her suicide and explain your stand in terms of the hospital's commitment to the intrinsic goodness of every person's life, regardless of his or her condition, you will bear clear witness and do what you can to deter others from committing suicide.

What, then, should you do? Begin by asking Thornton to leave the hospital. If she does not wish to leave, explain to her that the hospital's purpose is to promote health and protect life, that she was admitted for services in accord with that purpose, and that her refusal to cooperate in receiving those services has eliminated her reason for being in the hospital and her right to stay. Now she is imposing on hospitality, and impeding the hospital from carrying on its proper work to benefit people who need and want what it offers. Point out, too, that her wish that the hospital help her kill herself is unfair. The hospital and its patients cooperate voluntarily. Just as the hospital cannot justly compel patients to accept services they consider inappropriate, so patients cannot justly expect the hospital to provide services it considers inappropriate.

If Thornton refuses to leave, warn her that the hospital will do everything it can to disassociate itself from her project. Of course, you must consult your lawyers about what you can do. But I suggest that, in consulting them, you investigate not only the hospital's possible legal vulnerability but also the possibility of obtaining a court order requiring Thornton either to accept food and the treatment she needs or to leave the hospital.

Even if the court is unlikely to issue such an order, seeking it would afford an opportunity to publicize the hospital's commitment to human life and witness to the wrongness of suicide. Similarly, if a court order compels the hospital to provide Thornton with palliative care, you certainly should publicize the fact that this involvement is not voluntary, thereby making the public aware that the hospital is acting under protest due to legal duress. That will mitigate damage to the credibility of the hospital's commitment and witness.

74: May physicians and dentists try to maximize income?

I am finishing the first year of medical school, and my studies are going well. My dad is a physician, and I plan to follow in his footsteps, because medicine is a good profession, offering the satisfaction of helping people, the freedom to work as one's own boss, and adequate income.

My brother, who is finishing his training in orthodontics, brought home a booklet put out by one of the companies that makes dental equipment. The booklet tells people planning to set up their practice in dentistry or one of its specialties how to maximize their income, within parameters set by their other desires regarding the kind of place they want to live. It breaks the whole country down by states and counties, and provides statistics that make it possible to pick out places where dentists and dental specialists are most likely to be able to develop a sizable practice with comparatively high fees. My brother, who is thinking about where to practice, spent a lot of time during the holidays picking out twenty-five counties that promise high income and evaluating them by some of the criteria used in a recent study identifying the fifty U.S. cities offering the best living conditions.

Since I hope to marry and, like my dad, become the father of a large family, I expect to need a good income. Still, it seemed to me that my brother's approach involved the wrong priorities. We always enjoy a good argument, so I challenged him, taking the position that a better approach—which is much simpler and the one I actually will follow—would be to think first in terms of raising a family. Begin with the study identifying the fifty cities that are good places to live, then use the booklet's statistics to rank them by their promise of a large practice with high fees, so as to take into account, but only secondarily, each city's potential for maximizing income.

Starting from what our mother often points out, that as Christians our first concern should be to try to see what is morally right, we agreed that in a question of this sort, where neither alternative violates any of the Commandments, the morally right approach is the one involving the right priorities. Then we argued about whether his approach or mine does that. Needless to say, neither of us convinced the other. Since you are looking for difficult moral questions, I am sending you this one: Should physicians and dentists put maximizing income ahead of practicing where conditions are good for raising a family, as my brother thinks, or the other way around, as I think?

Analysis:

This question calls for clarification of health care service as a possible element of the questioner's personal vocation, and an explanation of how other possible elements of his vocation—in particular, marriage and family life—can be integrated with a genuinely Christian commitment to professional service. The questioner should make his vocational commitments and use them as the standard for determining how much income to seek and how to use it. He should use available information to see where needs are great and the likelihood that others will meet them is small. Money is only an instrumental good, which always should be subordinated to the basic human goods that fulfill persons: life and health, marriage and family, and so on. So, he should not try to maximize income, but should seek only as much as necessary to fulfill his vocational commitments.

The reply could be along the following lines:

It is commendable that you wish to follow your mother's advice by trying first to find out what is morally right. Moreover, you have the better of it in your argument with your brother. Money never should be the first consideration for Christians, as it so often is for us as well as for our nonbelieving neighbors. Money and the things it can buy are, after all, only means, while raising a family is something good in itself; and, certainly, basic human goods deserve priority over instrumental ones. Your parents obviously have tried to bring you up as Christians, and their effort has borne some fruit in you. It sounds, though, as if your brother may not have taken in Jesus' warning about how hard it is for the wealthy to enter the kingdom of heaven (see Mt 19.24, Lk 18.24–25).

While you have a more authentic sense of values, however, I am afraid you still tend to think too much about your self-interest in relation to those values. Is it significant that, in saying why the medical profession is good, you speak of the satisfaction of helping people rather than the benefit to them? Then too, while a man called to be a husband and father certainly ought to consider the likely impact that decisions regarding his profession will have on the good of family life, it is wrong for anyone to regard his or her work as a mere means of making a living, so that others' needs for the work's products or services are inadequately considered or even overlooked entirely. Finally, and most importantly, nothing in your question indicates that you have ever seriously asked yourself what God is calling you to do, what his plan for your life is, and how you should follow Jesus, who came not to be served but to serve.[251]

To hear what God is calling you to do, you must consider, on the one hand, what your gifts are (and also your limitations), and, on the other hand, what needs people have that you could help meet by putting your gifts to work. Comparing the two, and taking into account the likelihood or unlikelihood that others will help people meet their needs if you do not, you will discern rather easily, I believe, the part God is offering you in carrying out his plan for the preparation in this world of material for his heavenly kingdom (see GS 38–39).

---

251. Personal vocation has been treated in general and more fully in *LCL*, 113–29.

Since you are doing well in the first year of medical school, your vocation probably does include caring for people and helping them fulfill their responsibility to sustain life and promote and protect health in themselves, their children, and others. When the medical profession is considered in this way, the booklet's statistics about various localities will be a helpful index to where you should establish your practice. You should use the statistics, though, not as your brother did or as you proposed to do, but to see where potential for income is poor, for in many such places needs for service will be great and the likelihood that others will come to meet them will be low.

Of course, in deciding where to set up a practice, you also must take into account the requirements of other elements of your vocation. Your hope to marry and raise a large family suggests these might be part of it. At least, however, you should consider the possibility that your gifts for medicine and people's needs for your service are so great that God is calling you to forgo marrying or to delay having your own family so that you can offer greater and more selfless service to other families. Having considered the question as you should, though, you still may be confident that marrying and raising many children belong to your calling. If so, be sure to consider them in that way, not merely as contributions to your self-satisfaction. Doing that, you will be careful about whom you marry and will have a sound principle for decisions about regulating births.

A most important part of discerning God's will for your life will be seeing how central elements of your vocation—especially profession, on the one hand, and, on the other, marriage and fatherhood—are to be integrated harmoniously, each complementing the other. Of course, there are other elements: religious responsibilities, civic duties, friendships, recreation, and so on; indeed, personal vocation includes every sphere of activity and even conditions beyond one's control. So, you must discover every part of the life of good deeds God has prepared for you and then weave all of those elements together into a seamless whole.

Having begun to understand your life in this way, and not before, you will begin to be able to judge what financial and other resources you need to fulfill your vocational responsibilities. Only then will you be in a position to consider how to obtain those resources. Of course, if marriage and family life are part of your vocation, you will need to live where conditions are suitable for raising your children. But a suitable place need not be among the "fifty cities that are good places to live."

Unless you find that you are called to practice medicine in some very poor locality, you probably will be able to earn the money you need in return for your services.[252] Indeed, your problem may well be how best to limit your income to

252. Joel H. Goldberg, "Doctors Struggle to Keep Their Earnings Up," *Medical Economics,* 72:17 (11 Sept. 1995): 184–86, 189–92, 201–2, reports the results of a survey of the 1994 net, pretax earnings of U.S. physicians in office-based private practice. The median for all was $148,890; for general practitioners (the field with lowest earnings), $100,240. In a later article further analyzing the same survey results—"Why Some Doctors Make a Lot, and Some Make Little," *Medical Economics,* 73:6 (25 Mar. 1996): 142–44, 149, 153–54, 157—Goldberg explains the differences in income; some low earners, who are more likely to be female or over sixty-five, work fewer hours; some low earners take capitation; and so on.

that justly due you. Since there is no real market in medical services, competition usually does not serve as an effective brake on fees. Those who supply medical care greatly influence people's judgments whether they need it, and when patients think they need care, they have little choice but to get it if they can. Moreover, the supply of care often is quite limited, and the conditions under which it is provided make it virtually impossible for people to shop for good values for price. Then too, patients generally cannot obtain the information they would need to evaluate available providers, and once a provider has been chosen, changing is often difficult. Under these conditions, physicians in the United States, and perhaps in other affluent nations, have been very well compensated. In defense of their fees, physicians often point to their costly education, additional years of training at low pay, high overhead, large insurance premiums, long hours, and so on. Even taking all those factors into account, however, most physicians' net income appears more than adequate. How, then, are you to tell how much to ask for your services?

The answer will depend upon who is paying and from what resources the payment is to be made. Where government programs and/or insurance provide a certain amount, I doubt that you will have any reasonable basis for charging any but wealthy patients more than the required copayments. At the same time, I think you can justly accept what such payers provide; if the payment is excessive, the structure determining it is not of your making and is so complex and shot through with injustices that you cannot reasonably be expected to rectify it case by case. However, when you serve the uninsured working poor who must personally pay your fee or go without care, you should charge only what they can pay without giving up other necessities—an adequate diet, decent shelter, and the other things you regard as essential for yourself and your family. Of course, if some of your patients are wealthy people who are ready, willing, and able to pay what generally are regarded as reasonable and customary fees, you may charge accordingly and use that income to meet your responsibilities.

You perhaps have the gifts and will find opportunities to work toward reforming the medical profession so as to subordinate it, as it should be subordinated, to people's needs and accommodate it justly to their means. Therefore, consider the possibility of working in professional associations and/or trying to influence legislation as ways of bringing about needed reforms.

What should you do if, proceeding as I have outlined, you find the income from your practice either exceeding or falling short of your own true needs? If the former, you may simply assign the excess to meeting the responsibility to help others in need. If the latter, you should seek other sources of funding, such as governmental subsidies or foundation grants. Finding no such sources, you should share the poverty of those you serve insofar as you can do so in good conscience—considering, for example, family responsibilities—and then, if necessary, shape your professional practice to serve a sufficient proportion of more prosperous people so that you will earn the income you need.

I realize my reply offers far more advice than you asked for. Still, I hope you will take what I have written to heart and, having done so, share it with your brother and your fellow medical students. I also hope it will help him and at least some of them to think more uprightly about their profession. Yet I fear you might say: "If I undertake to follow your advice, I might as well become a monk and take a vow of poverty!"

Not so. Jesus' teaching about relationships with others is: "You shall love your neighbor as yourself" (Mt 22.39) and "Love one another as I have loved you" (Jn 15.12)—that is, with an other-serving, self-sacrificing love. Applied to matters of income and wealth, this teaching makes radical demands on Christians, especially the affluent (see *LCL,* 780–82, 789–92, 800–806, 811–14). Following so-called common sense, of course, most of us, including many who have taken a vow of poverty, do not take those demands seriously. But even though Jesus' reply to the rich young man was not in keeping with his listeners' common sense, it was part of the saving good news he preached. That young man went away sad, but he would have been more sensible and also happier had he followed Jesus' advice, which all Christians, not only an elite, are called to follow.[253] Considered as a whole, that advice is nothing less than a prescription for a good and holy life, in which alone one also finds true self-fulfillment. Just as Jesus endured the cross not only for our salvation but for the joy that was set before him (see Heb 12.2), so we, if faithful to his gifts, will deserve and receive a payment that will never lose its value: "Come, you that are blessed by my Father, inherit the kingdom prepared for you from the foundation of the world" (Mt 25.34).

75: May a physician waive coinsurance payments required by insurers?

My wife and I practice family medicine in a small midwestern city. Many of our patients have health coverage (usually under contracts between their employers and the insurance companies) requiring them to pay a portion (generally twenty percent) of most fees and other charges as coinsurance. Because these coinsurance payments are meant to discourage excessive use of health care services, the insurance companies do not want providers to waive them. This system probably works fine with people who are better off, but the payments oftentimes are very difficult for poorer families. When we know a family would have trouble paying the coinsurance, we do not bill it, partly to lighten the financial burden but more importantly to make it easier for those people to get care when they should—before small problems become serious and when proper care requires a follow-up visit or ongoing treatment.

Almost all the insurance plans now set our charges for us, saying exactly how much they will allow for office visits, procedures, and so forth. When we waive a coinsurance payment, we do not receive more than we otherwise would. We have only been forgoing some income to which we are entitled, and have not been cheating the insurance companies.

Now some insurers are writing into their contracts with providers or including on their claim forms language ruling out the waiving of coinsurance payments. If

---

253. See John Paul II, *Veritatis splendor,* 16–24, *AAS* 85 (1993) 1146–53, *OR,* 6 Oct. 1993, iii–iv.

we sign such contracts or forms, I suppose we will be agreeing to conform to the companies' rules or stating that we have done so in the particular case. Yet we do not wish to begin requiring coinsurance payments from families that cannot afford them, and it seems to us the insurers are being unreasonable. May we sign the contracts and forms but continue waiving the payments?

Analysis:

This question concerns the application of the norm excluding lying. It is unjust for insurers to insist that coinsurance payments be collected even from poorer families. But the norm forbidding lying excludes agreeing without reservation not to waive coinsurance payments while intending to do so, and also excludes stating that the rules were followed when they were not. Though there may be no workable resolution of the conflict between the insurers' rules and the physicians' policy, alternatives can be suggested for further investigation. It also should be pointed out that the policy of forgoing coinsurance payments by poorer families could occasion abuses by the physicians and/or their patients.

The reply could be along the following lines:

As you may know, an influential code of professional ethics deals with the problem you raise, without providing a solution. On the one hand, it favors the policy you have been following: "When a copayment is a barrier to needed care because of financial hardship, physicians should forgive or waive the copayment." On the other hand, it warns you not only to avoid fraud but to conform to agreements with insurers: "Routine forgiveness or waiver of copayments may constitute fraud under state and federal law. Physicians should ensure that their policies on copayments are consistent with applicable law and with the requirements of their agreements with insurers."[254] Thus, your question truly is difficult, and cannot be answered without additional ethical reflection.

Applied to affluent families, the requirement of coinsurance payments probably does not impede the appropriate use of health care resources and may be a reasonable deterrent to frivolous and wasteful use. But, as you suggest, for many less well-to-do families, requiring coinsurance payments probably does deter appropriate use of these resources. This likely adverse impact makes it gravely inequitable for insurers to insist that these payments never be waived. Moreover, unless health care providers are themselves needy, it is appropriate that they reduce charges to patients who cannot afford them, since that enables such patients to seek and obtain needed services. Therefore, the insurers' efforts to compel you to collect coinsurance payments from your poorer patients unjustly impede you from fulfilling your professional responsibility to serve the poor, insofar as you can, without placing heavy financial burdens on them.

Nevertheless, lying is always wrong. Presented with a contract including the unjust requirement not to waive coinsurance payments, you may not agree without

254. Council on Ethical and Judicial Affairs, American Medical Association, *Code of Medical Ethics: Current Opinions with Annotations,* 1996–97 ed. (Chicago: American Medical Association, 1996), 6.12 (p. 100).

reservation while planning to continue waiving the payments. That would be making a promise you did not intend to keep, saying "I will do X" while thinking "I will not do X"—a lie. Likewise, you may not subscribe to a claim form including the statement that you have followed the insurance company's rule requiring a coinsurance payment when you have not done so, since that would be lying. Moreover, violating the terms of a contract with an insurance company or lying in making insurance claims might render you vulnerable to a lawsuit.

I am not sure there is any workable solution to the problem. However, there are several possible approaches you might investigate and consider trying.

First, since your policy of waiving coinsurance payments by poorer families is reasonable while it is unjust for insurers to require that you never waive them, you might communicate straightforwardly with the insurers and try to convince them to allow providers to waive all or at least part of the payments for poorer patients. That would have the advantage of admonishing the insurers about the wrong they are doing to many people besides you and your patients; also, in taking this approach you might seek the cooperation of other health care providers, advocacy groups, and so on. Moreover, this straightforward approach undoubtedly would clarify some possible abuses, and, if it succeeded, the outcome probably would include provisions to limit abuses.

You also might invoke public authority. Since the insurers' unjust requirement no doubt affects all health care providers and insured persons throughout your state, you might seek action by some state regulatory body or by the legislature to protect the right of providers to waive coinsurance payments by patients otherwise likely to be impeded from seeking and obtaining needed services. If successful, this not only would solve the problem for everyone but, like the first approach, would include the opportunity to clarify and limit possible abuses.

If neither of these approaches is feasible and successful, the language in the contracts and on the claim forms may leave room for you honestly to subscribe to them while in practice circumventing the insurers' intent. One tactic would be to bill poorer families for the portion of the insurers' approved charges designated as coinsurance while at the same time assuring them that you will not press them to pay these bills. Then, in due course, you would write off those that remain unpaid as bad debts. Another tactic would be to establish a special charitable fund, perhaps administered by a church near your office, from which poorer families could obtain the money for their copayments. You could contribute to the fund, and disbursements from it could be made by a check payable to both the patient and you. To investigate such possibilities, you undoubtedly will need legal and tax advice.

Again, in signing contracts forbidding you to waive coinsurance payments, you might send along a covering letter saying you mean to adhere carefully to the rules insofar as that is consistent with meeting your obligations to your patients. Similarly, when signing claim forms, you could strike out the statement that you are not waiving the coinsurance payment, without making the strike out any more noticeable than necessary to make it unambiguous. In expressing your reservation in these ways you would avoid lying, yet the reservation might be overlooked by insurers. The difficulty, of course, is that this approach is hardly likely to succeed in every instance.

If you find a way to continue forgoing coinsurance payments, you should take care to resist the abuses that could occasion. In general, insurance companies have a good reason for requiring coinsurance payments. Families for whom you waive the payments might be tempted to waste health care resources, including your time, and thereby impose unfair burdens on those who, sooner or later, will have to pay higher insurance premiums. You must keep track of your patients' use of your services and correct any who begin to be wasteful.

Finally, as you point out, your present practice of waiving coinsurance payments by needy families means you lose some income. This could lead you to be tempted to compensate by doing additional procedures which, though not medically point-less, go beyond what you would consider appropriate for the same patients if they could afford the coinsurance. You also might be tempted to recoup the income by increasing your fees to other families, when no schedule of payments applies. That could be wrong, since it might arbitrarily impose burdens on people hardly more able to bear them than the families whose poverty comes to your attention. Doing such an injustice would be practicing false mercy.

But you seem well aware of the demands of mercy. You have been sacrificing income to serve your patients well. You have not been trying to enlarge your practice, but serving patients as you do may well have that effect, and so be to your own advantage. Even if it reduces your income, however, you can hope to profit in the long run: "Make purses for yourselves that do not wear out, an unfailing treasure in heaven, where no thief comes near and no moth destroys. For where your treasure is, there your heart will be also" (Lk 12.33–34; cf. Mt 6.19–21).

76: May a dentist do costly work before
patients' insurance ends?

My professional work as a dentist sometimes raises an ethical problem con-cerning the treatment of patients whose insurance is about to end, usually because their employers are eliminating dental care from their benefits, but sometimes because the patient is opting out. In deciding on a course of treatment, can I take the insurance situation into account? Or is that dishonest, even when all the information required by the insurance company is fully and accurately stated? Here are two examples.

A female patient in her fifties had multiple amalgam fillings in several molars. None required immediate replacement, though crowning all those teeth would be desirable, and might eventually be necessary. Her insurance coverage included the full cost of amalgam fillings and fifty percent of the cost of crowns. Since it was ending, I pointed out to her that doing the crowns now would be comparatively economical and would forestall problems for many years to come. I would have given the same advice if she had been wealthy and asked for the best possible treatment. However, she was of moderate means. If she had either been without insurance or were going to continue to be insured, I would not have urged her to go ahead at once. But, since her insurance was ending, I told her what I thought was in her best interests, all things considered.

The other case concerns a very prosperous businessman in his late thirties. I had restored two adjacent teeth in January, and when he returned in July he reported being bothered by a good deal of sensitivity to heat and cold in both. Examination did not reveal an abscess. Ordinarily my policy in such cases is conservative: Wait and see whether the sensitivity clears up or an abscess develops. I began to tell him what symptoms to watch for, but he explained that he was opting out of dental coverage as of the end of August, and asked me about the chances of an abscess developing and what would have to be done if it did. I told him that in roughly half the cases like his, an abscess will develop requiring root canal therapy and further restoration in at least one tooth. I went on to explain why I take a conservative approach. He had nothing to lose in waiting to see if an abscess develops, but unnecessary root canal therapy might be unsuccessful, and then one or both teeth would have to be extracted, which would be a great loss. He asked whether doing the root canals was likely to have a bad outcome in his case, and I had to admit it was not. Given this information, he said he liked the odds and insisted that I do root canal therapy on both teeth at once. Against my better judgment, I did. Fortunately, the outcome seems to be good.

Analysis:

This question calls for the derivation of specific norms. Provided all the information required by the insurer is truthfully supplied, it is not inherently wrong when making decisions about treatment to take into account that a patient's insurance coverage will begin or end. Even when patients desire it, however, dentists, like other health care professionals, should never do anything they judge to be unreasonable, and it is unjust to accept an insurance payment for work one considered it unreasonable to do.

The reply could be along the following lines:

Adults bear the primary responsibility for their own health care, including dental care. The role of the dentist, like other health care professionals, is to help people fulfill their responsibility to care for themselves. In view of their other legitimate interests and limited resources, people often set reasonable limits on how far they will go in pursuing or promoting their health. You must abide by the limits a patient sets insofar as you believe them reasonable, either because you can see that they are or because the patient is trustworthy. In practicing your profession, however, you should fulfill a commitment to promote dental health by using sound technical means, and so should never do anything you believe inappropriate or technically bad, even if an unreasonable patient desires it.

In setting premiums and administering policies, insurance companies no doubt take into account that people whose dental coverage will soon end and their dentists sometimes make decisions about treatment influenced by that prospect. Hence, when all the information required by the insurance company is fully and accurately stated, I see nothing inherently wrong in taking the insurance situation into account. That can be wrong, however, if it leads to a decision that, all things considered, is unreasonable. Moreover, when a decision is unreasonable, accepting the insurance payment is unfair, for, while paying unreasonable claims is a cost of doing business that insurance companies pass on to those who pay the premiums, the latter bear a burden unreasonably imposed by those who receive payment on unreasonable claims, and thus suffer an injustice similar to having to help bear the cost of fraudulent claims.

Regarding the first case you describe—crowning molars restored with multiple amalgam fillings that did not require immediate replacement—you suggest as a standard what you would have advised the woman had she been wealthy and wanted the best possible treatment. That might not be an appropriate standard, however, since wealthy people sometimes desire more health care than is reasonable.

Your usual policy, which seems to me sounder, apparently is to provide every patient with good treatment within the limits he or she reasonably sets. On this basis, given the discrepancy between the insurance's full coverage for amalgam fillings and its fifty percent coverage for crowns, you would not recommend crowns if this patient's coverage were continuing, since that treatment is not urgent, but instead would assume it reasonable that the patient make do with the existing fillings. With her insurance coverage ending, however, it might well be reasonable for her to invest now in the crowns instead of waiting until they become necessary. So, it seems to me your advice to her was sound from both the technical and the moral points of view.

In the second case—root canal therapy on two sensitive teeth of a very prosperous young man who was ending his dental insurance—your usual policy would have been to avoid treatment that might be unnecessary and could even be seriously harmful. Making an exception in this case meant taking a very significant risk of doing unnecessary root canal therapy on at least one tooth and, supposing it unnecessary, a small chance of the patient's losing one or both teeth when otherwise he would not have lost them. In this case you should have followed your better judgment rather than the patient's wishes, and, in my opinion, complying was doubly wrong.

First, in the perspective of the good to which you are committed—namely, the patient's dental health—the young man's decision to proceed with possibly unnecessary root canal therapy, accepting a small chance of a bad outcome, was unreasonable. Of course, he had a reason. He was opting out of his insurance yet wanted it to pay for the work instead of risking having to pay for it himself. But I think that, being very prosperous, he should have avoided the possibly unnecessary root canal therapy and the risk of losing the teeth. You apparently agree, since you say you proceeded against your better judgment.

Second, carrying out the decision to do the root canal therapy at once did not reduce its cost, but simply shifted it from the young man to the group of people and/or employers whose premiums make it profitable—or, at least, possible—for the insurance company to provide dental coverage despite such cost shifting. Since the purpose of insurance is to spread risks individuals cannot reasonably accept among a large group, policy holders should not seek insurance payments to avoid taking risks they ought to accept. Thus, the young man's cost shifting was unfair, and the injustice was the greater inasmuch as he was very prosperous. Since the payment you received belongs by right to those who paid the premiums, you have money you should not have and ought to make restitution. Must you reimburse the insurance company for the full amount you received? Perhaps, but not necessarily. The young man also should make restitution, though he probably will not. In any case, you must do what is fair, considering all things as they now are (see *LCL,* 444–58).

Someone might object that, since the sensitivity in the two teeth was caused by necessary work that had been covered by the insurance, it was only fair that root canal therapy to eliminate that sensitivity be carried out before the insurance terminated. That argument would be sound if it had been reasonable for the young man to insist on having the root canal therapy at once. However, as has been argued, the reasonable option would have been to wait and see whether the therapy proved necessary.

Nevertheless, in some clinically similar cases, doing root canal therapy could be reasonable and accepting the insurance payment fair. First, suppose a patient without insurance had a similar problem, was about to spend a year in a foreign country where dental care is very poor, and wanted you to do the therapy so that the work would not be botched. Clearly, that request would be reasonable, and you would rightly make an exception to your usual, conservative policy. Next, suppose a situation similar to the first, except that the patient's dental insurance would terminate when he or she went abroad. The request would be no less reasonable, the exception no less justified, and the insurance payment fairly accepted. Finally, then, suppose a patient with the same dental problem who was going to lose his or her insurance coverage due to unemployment or inability to pay the premiums. If he or she had little prospect of obtaining root canal therapy when it might be needed, the request that you do it at once also would be reasonable, and so you could accept the insurance payment without unfairness to those whose premiums would cover the cost.

Even in this last case, though, you would provide better health care for your impoverished patient by adhering to your usual policy, promising to do the root canal therapy if it became necessary, and deferring payment until the patient could afford to pay. Assuming the risk—perhaps virtual certainty—of never being paid would be the merciful thing to do. If you could afford it without slighting some other obligation, that might well be your duty as a Christian, since mercy is the justice of the kingdom.

77: Should a nurse stay on in a hospital to oppose injustices against patients?

When I finished nursing training last year, I came to work here in this public hospital. Many of our patients are poor, uneducated people, cared for almost entirely by residents and interns, though nominally assigned staff physicians. The way they are treated is appalling in many respects, but what bothers me most is that consent is nothing but a formality. They routinely sign forms at admission, so we have consent to anything and everything that might be done to them while here. The doctors, with few exceptions, hardly talk to patients except for diagnostic purposes, brush their questions aside, and put them through examinations, treatments, and even major surgery without explaining what is going on or giving either them or their families any real chance to refuse. I try to answer their questions when I can, and in a few cases have gone so far as to suggest to a patient that he or she need not go along with what a doctor was planning. For doing this, I have been scolded repeatedly for wasting time, and doctors several times have told me to mind my own business. Yesterday the head nurse called me in and reprimanded me. I pointed out that many other nurses share my dissatisfactions and constantly gripe about how the doctors deal with patients and ignore their rights. She admitted that not everything is done here "in the ideal way," but excused the doctors because they are tired and overworked, and said informed consent is meaningless for most of the patients we deal with.

I do not know what I should do, but I do know I cannot just stay here, do as I am told, and go along with the way things are done. I could quit and go to work elsewhere, and that is what I am inclined to do. I am the kind of person who likes to get along with everyone, and I always was an obedient daughter and a "good girl" in school. Still, when I put myself in the place of my patients, I feel as though I should do something about this situation. But the thought of fighting for better treatment for my patients really frightens me. Besides, I do not know what I could do that would make any real difference.

Analysis:

Though patients are being dealt with unjustly in the hospital where the questioner works, she can do her own work without wronging her patients, and so need not quit and go elsewhere. At the same time, though she could remain and work to mitigate the evil, she apparently has no strict duty to do that. Therefore, the question calls for discernment between two morally acceptable options—staying and quitting. Since the questioner seems well aware of factors pointing to a decision to quit, her discernment can be assisted by calling attention to factors pointing to a decision to stay and sketching out steps she might begin to take to try to obtain justice for her patients.

The reply could be along the following lines:

Obviously, patients' limited ability to understand options and their limited freedom due to psychological factors can make them more or less incapable of consenting to various forms of care and treatment. However, failing to obtain truly informed and specific consent, insofar as patients are capable of it, gravely violates their fundamental human and legal rights: both their right to decide what potentially burdensome things will be done to them and their right to shape their health care so that it will be harmonious with other aspects of their lives. Moreover, patients whose informed consent is not obtained are ill served, for they are not helped to understand their problems and assume responsibility for them as they must if they are to care for themselves, with their families' or others' help, after being discharged from the hospital. It is gravely dishonest to reduce obtaining patients' consent to a mere formality, since the purpose of getting their signature is to provide evidence, if it becomes needed, that genuine consent was given. Finally, using the patients' poverty and lack of education to rationalize this abuse manifests willingness to discriminate against them in a way that gravely violates their essential human dignity. Therefore, it is a great evil to make these patients' consent a mere formality.

Even so, you need not personally share in the guilt for the mistreatment of your patients, provided you do all you can under the circumstances to care for them properly and refuse to lie or do anything else wrong in itself. But while you should not feel obliged to quit, nothing in your letter indicates that you have any obligation to remain, and so you could in good conscience go to work elsewhere. Your personality and limited professional experience might make it pointless for you to try to do more about the situation than you already have; perhaps you would do well to accept your inability to remedy these evils, at least here and now, and move on. But perhaps you are being called to rise above yourself and do more to serve your patients. Consequently, your question can be answered only by discernment.

You are understandably anxious and hesitant, but those feelings may not reflect the requirements of the real situation and your better self. You prefer to be docile, but you are spirited enough to feel you should do something. Remember that even Jesus was anxious in the Garden of Gethsemane, and try to put your anxiety aside as you seek to discover God's will in the matter.

In discerning, gather the facts about your options, and consider them calmly and carefully. Consider all your gifts and limitations, the possibilities of serving in a different situation and perhaps developing your ability to deal with problems similar to those that have aroused your concern, the possibility that you will be able to do something toward meeting your present patients' needs, and the likelihood that someone else will do what you will not if you go elsewhere. Then, praying for the light to discover God's plan for you and calmly reflecting, compare your feelings about your employment options with the feelings integrated with your Christian faith and professional commitment, and choose the option—staying or moving on—that seems preferable.

To help with your discernment, you would do well to seek the advice of an older colleague of good character and long experience—someone you trust and admire, perhaps a former teacher or someone you served under during your training. Such a mentor could not only provide information you lack but help you put your present experience and dissatisfactions in perspective. Should you decide to remain in your present job, such a person also would be a great help in planning how to carry on the struggle.

While not presuming to discern for you, I note that you seem to be focusing on reasons to leave, and I urge you also to consider everything pointing to a decision to stay. On the one hand, reform in the hospital is badly needed, and your account offers no ground for optimism that others will strive to meet that need. On the other hand, you have certain gifts necessary to work to rectify the abuse. You have clear insight into the injustice and hate it, while others resignedly tolerate or even endorse and defend it. You do not think of yourself as aggressive, but your persistent efforts to vindicate patients' rights manifest courage, and this character trait will grow as you exercise it. Since how patients are treated is your business and answering their legitimate questions is an appropriate use of your time, the scoldings and reprimand you have received plainly were unfair, and their very unfairness would count in your favor if the conflict generated by your behavior became public. Finally, since you have other appealing employment opportunities, you can risk your job without fearing that losing it will prevent you from meeting your responsibilities to care for yourself and your dependents, if any.

How might you proceed if you do opt to stay and struggle for better treatment for your patients? You say you do not know what you could do that would make any real difference, and if you take too broad and long a view, you are indeed likely to find the prospect daunting. I suggest that, at least at the outset, you focus instead on simple things you can do at once, and start doing them day by day.

Begin by thinking about your relationships with your fellow workers and determining your stance toward them.

Some have opposed your efforts to serve patients as they should be served. Their attitudes and actions plainly are wrongful, but only God knows how great the physicians' and head nurse's responsibility is. It probably is true that the physicians are tired and overworked. Residents and interns in many hospitals work absurdly long hours, and staff physicians often are responsible for more patients than they can serve adequately. In many cases, nurses should explain treatment options to patients and answer their questions, but the head nurse's reprimand perhaps is a sign that staffing is inadequate to carry out properly both this duty and others she regards as more essential. Very likely, your hospital's budget restrictions and screening procedures effectively ration health care for poor and uneducated people, so that they cannot obtain the minimum level of service to which they are entitled in strict justice. That structural injustice almost compels personnel working within the system to compromise professional standards and violate patients' rights. The only adequate remedy for the bad practices you describe, therefore, would involve not merely changes in individual physicians' and nurses' attitudes and behavior but a more adequate budget and better administration as well.

Therefore, you should regard these fellow workers neither with hatred and anger nor with fear and submissiveness. Deal with them as you do with patients who present problems. Be unfailingly polite and friendly; focus on the business at hand and the purposes you wish to achieve; ignore anything unpleasant they say or do unless it will have practical consequences; and find appropriate ways to deal with anything significant they say and do. For example, if you think the head nurse's reprimand was mere talk, you need not make an issue of it; but if you think it was a threat to discharge you if you do not stop doing what you believe your professional responsibility toward your patients requires, perhaps you should write the hospital administrator a letter (with a copy to the head nurse) laying out the problem and asking for guidance.

You indicate that a few exceptional doctors deal with patients more appropriately than the rest, and that many other nurses share your dissatisfactions. Regard all these people as potential allies. Discuss your concerns with them, ask them to share their views with you, and listen carefully to what they have to say; after all, you have been at the hospital only a year or so, and probably have much to learn. As you get to know them and their reasonable dissatisfactions with the situation, do not let your conversations become bogged down in sterile griping. Instead, ask what they think might be done to improve matters. If some seem able to speak out against abuses, urge them to do so, since even a small chorus of criticism is much harder to disregard or silence than an isolated voice. If someone seems more suited than you to exercise leadership, urge that person to take on that role and promise to help him or her enlist others.

Probably many of your fellow workers who conform to the common pattern are not antagonistic toward you and others who deviate from it. Gently sound out these people about their attitudes. In some cases you will find that they share your views and deplore the injustice toward patients, but have resigned themselves to it, hopelessly feeling that nothing can be done to improve matters. Try to arouse their dormant professional idealism and encourage them, if not to act and speak out, at least to support you and others who do. If they respond at all, show your appreciation. The moral support of this seemingly inert mass of people is likely to be critical if your work for reform eventually provokes serious retaliation from the hospital administration.

Support also might be available from other quarters. Some members of the governing board might be sympathetic and willing at least to investigate the situation. If you belong to a nurses' union, the union might help you defend the profession's standards and safeguard your position. If the hospital has a quality-control committee or an ethics committee, providing it with factual information about especially egregious cases could provoke action that would lead to more general reforms. Perhaps the staff and its auxiliaries include social workers, psychological counselors, patient advocates, chaplains, or others concerned with patients as persons and with their families. They are likely to include some natural allies who could bring pressure to bear on the administration and/or the clinical staff.

You also might try to form an interreligious prayer group with the faithful Catholics and other devout Christians among your fellow workers. With such a group, you could begin to try to develop a dialogue about conditions in the hospital, focusing first on the facts, then reflecting on them in the light of faith and the norm of love of neighbor, and prayerfully considering even the smallest concrete steps that might be taken to improve matters.

Moreover, it is likely that nearly everyone working in the hospital shares a common interest in obtaining more funding. Whenever you have the chance, you could make an effort to further this cause—serve on committees, testify at hearings, write letters to the editor, and so on. In this way, your fellow workers would come to think of you as someone dedicated to the common interest rather than as a mere troublemaker.

Under suitable conditions—and perhaps as a last resort—you might even look outside the hospital for help. If there are any large benefactors, you might arouse their interest in the matters that concern you. Careful documentation of abuses could lead some relevant official body to investigate the hospital's policies and practices. The editor of the local newspaper might be willing to speak with you confidentially; if so, you could provide him or her with factual information that could lead to a journalistic exposé. You might be able to enlist a public interest group or leader of a minority to assume an advocacy role for your patients. Perhaps a public official or one of the politicians who deals with the hospital's budget would be sympathetic to your concerns.

If you stay at the hospital and struggle to improve conditions, you surely will suffer. To endure that suffering without resentment toward those responsible, you will have to draw close to Jesus and learn from him how to love and forgive them. Strengthened by prayer and the Eucharist, you will be able to bear your cross. Choose a suitable saint, someone like Peter Claver, as the patron of your struggle; learn about your patron, become his or her friend, ask for this friend's intercession, and confidently expect the heavenly help you will need.

Above all, be firm in hope. Measure your success, not against the ideal the hospital should meet, but against the worse treatment this or that particular patient would endure if you were not carrying on your struggle. Each time you confer some small benefit on one patient or prevent some small harm to another you will achieve something of great worth. Every one of your poor and uneducated patients has been called to be a member of Jesus' body, and you do for Jesus what you do for each of them (see Mt 25.40).

78: Must a nurse report a patient's plan to commit suicide?

I quit nursing when we began having our children, but now the youngest is six, and my husband is good with them. I have gone back to nursing part time, working in a home for the aged overnight Friday-Saturday and again Saturday-Sunday. Since many residents need no care at night, my duties are light. When otherwise free, I make a habit of staying with one or another of those who cannot sleep, listening a lot and talking a bit.

Many of these people are extremely lonely, especially at night, and having someone to talk with means a great deal to them. They trust me and tell me all sorts of things, even their deepest secrets. Naturally, many talk about death, and I try to encourage them to take the right attitude. One gratifying thing about my job is that I have been able to encourage several people to get straightened around spiritually. Fortunately, the priest who cares for this home is capable and devout, and when someone is ready to see him, he is always available, friendly, and patient.

The day before yesterday—Thursday afternoon—a chronically depressed resident committed suicide, and when I came in last evening everyone was discussing it. Around three this morning, I was talking with a patient, whom I'll call Alan, who has no surviving family and never has visitors. He is a fallen-away Catholic; I've talked with him several times before, and thought we were making progress. He is undergoing treatment that will be completed in two weeks, and after that will be evaluated for major surgery. He confided that if the surgeon decides to operate, he will kill himself. Naturally, I told him that was not a good idea and he need not be so afraid of the operation.

When Alan entered the home, they changed his medications, and he still has some of the old pills. He showed them to me, and I believe they will kill him if he takes them all at once. As he talked, it also became clear that he has thought the matter through. He does not seem depressed, and his records do not mention any history of suicidal tendencies or any other psychological problem. Ordinarily, I make a note on anything special that comes up and in the morning call it to the attention of Dr. Young, the residents' primary care physician, when she comes in. My first thought was to do that. But, having confided in me as a friend, Alan expects me not to betray his confidence, and I think he will be very hurt and angry if I do. So, I talked with the priest about Alan without mentioning his name or that he will be evaluated for surgery.

Father was not sure what I should do and suggested I call you. He agrees it would be unfortunate for me to antagonize Alan but also thinks his telling me about his plan was an urgent "cry for help." May I keep the secret and continue talking with Alan in the hope that he will give up his plan and agree to see the priest? Or must I report what he told me? If so, I could call Dr. Young now or wait until I see her tomorrow morning.

Analysis:

This question calls for judgment to resolve a conflict of responsibilities. Preventing suicide is part of the questioner's professional responsibility as his nurse, but she also has a serious reason to keep the patient's secret. She should talk with him tonight, explain that he can refuse the surgery whose prospect he finds repugnant, promise to do what she can to ensure that he receives adequate pain relief, and try to persuade him to give up both his plan to kill himself and his cache of pills. If necessary, the questioner should try to confiscate the pills. If she fails to persuade the patient to give them up, her duty as his nurse and the poor prospects of helping him spiritually argue for reporting what has happened. But if the patient is persuaded and gives the nurse the pills, she should, in my judgment, keep his secret both for the sake of her personal relationship with him and the benefits she hopes to achieve by maintaining it.

The reply could be along the following lines:

I agree with the priest that Alan was crying for help when he told you of his conditional intention to commit suicide. He would not have confided in you had he not hoped to benefit in some way by doing so. However, he may have been seeking various kinds of help: action to prevent his suicide, moral support to carry out his plan, companionship to mitigate his loneliness in facing death, or something else. No matter what Alan wanted, however, it is most important that his intention to kill himself change. If unchanged, that intention not only is likely to be carried out sooner or later, but it endangers his soul. Therefore, no matter what else you do, pray for Alan and ask the priest to join in that prayer.

Using your spare time while on duty to visit and talk with lonely patients is the sort of service our Lord commends: "I was sick and you took care of me" (Mt 25.36). By helping patients spiritually prepare for death, you carry on your professional work as a genuine apostolate, caring for each person as a whole, not only for a malfunctioning organism. Your care for patients as persons makes you value your personal relationship with them, and that concern underlies your question. You risk forfeiting Alan's trust and losing his friendship if you violate his confidences, and unless you maintain your friendly relationship with him, you will be unable to help him spiritually. So, while your duty of confidentiality toward patients who share their secrets with you is not exceptionless, you have a special reason to keep Alan's secret.

At the same time, his seriousness about committing suicide is shown by the fact that he is not merely talking about it but has a definite plan and the means to carry it out. While saving Alan's soul is far more important than keeping him alive, preventing his suicide not only must be assumed to be necessary to save his soul but is important in itself and falls directly within the sphere of your professional responsibility. Therefore, I think most physicians and nurses would say reporting what Alan told you is your duty not only to him but to the other members of the team responsible for his care and to the nursing home itself.

Still, since you did not report it this morning and will be seeing Dr. Young tomorrow morning, it seems to me you may wait at least until then rather than call her at once. Meanwhile, you can talk with Alan tonight. In doing so, I think you should discuss the possible surgery that concerns him and try to persuade him to put aside his plan of committing suicide and give you his cache of pills. Pray for guidance and gather your thoughts for this important conversation. I shall sketch out the points I think you should cover, but you must decide what to say and how best to say it as the conversation unfolds.

Perhaps you have too easily accepted the surgeon's outlook and assumed that, when surgery seems indicated, it must be done, whether the patient wants it or not. But since Alan is living in a home for the aged, I assume he need not try to stay alive in order to fulfill obligations toward dependents or others; since he will have to be evaluated for surgery, I assume its appropriateness will not be immediately obvious; and since he finds the prospect of the surgery very repugnant, I assume it would be quite burdensome for him, not to mention the costs that someone—if only the taxpayers—will have to bear. I strongly suspect, therefore, that he has no moral obligation to accept the surgery, and could rightly refuse it and insist on receiving only palliative care.

If so, and assuming you would refuse the surgery if you were in his place, I think that is the first thing you should tell him. But if you judge that he ought to accept the surgery, I think you should tell him that and explain why—it offers very significant benefits, and the burdens for him will be comparatively insignificant. If he responds by restating his plan to kill himself, I think you may then tell him that he has the legal right to refuse the surgery and cannot be compelled to undergo it. Also, undoubtedly at least part, and perhaps most, of Alan's motivation to kill himself rather than undergo surgery is fear of pain and suffering. Therefore, in discussing the options with him, assure him you will do everything you can to make sure he receives adequate pain medication and other care necessary to make him comfortable.

Perhaps the alternative of refusing the surgery, or your reassurances, will be sufficient to get Alan to set aside his plan to commit suicide. But he also needs to recognize that suicide is wrong, and that he must surrender the pills he is planning to use. So, whether or not he says he will reject the surgery, I think you should explain why you believe suicide would be wrong and try to get him to give you the pills.

How should you make the case against suicide? Certainly, you should point out to Alan that his life still has value, that he still can do worthwhile things, and that his death would be a loss to you. But more important, I think, is to tell him you believe in heaven and hell, hope he will go to heaven, and fear what might become of him if he kills himself.

Having made the case against suicide as best you can, explain to Alan that, as an employee of the home and only one member of the team that cares for him, you are not free to deal with him as you might deal with an elderly family member you were caring for in your own home. Then tell him that, though he told you about his plan in confidence, you cannot in good conscience let him keep the means for carrying it out. If you did nothing and he killed himself, you would have failed him as his nurse, and would consider yourself at fault for not having prevented his suicide.

On that basis, ask him as your friend to set aside his plan and give you the pills. What if he will not? In telling him that you cannot in good conscience allow him to keep the means of killing himself, you must be truthful; thus, having made that subtle threat, you must carry it out. So, if Alan will not surrender the pills and you can confiscate them without doing him violence, you should take them, while telling him you hate to do it but believe you must. For the same reason, if Alan has hidden the pills or resists your attempt to take them, you definitely ought to report what has happened to Dr. Young as soon as she comes in.

Suppose you get the pills. Should you report what has happened or keep Alan's secret, at least for a while?

There is a case for reporting. Even if Alan gives you his pills, he might find some other way to attempt suicide. If he tries to kill himself and you have not reported what has already happened, your omission might come to light, particularly if he survived the attempt. In that case, as you may realize, you might be vulnerable to accusations of professional misconduct and civil or even criminal negligence. Because nurses' rights and duties regarding patients' confidential communications are ethically and legally unclear, the outcome of any action against you would be unpredictable.

Moreover, members of the team caring for residents in the home doubtless usually share with one another confidential information bearing on patient's problems. So, though you would be expected not to divulge patients' confidences to other patients or outsiders, you would be expected to report anything about a patient that might call for attention by others responsible for his or her care. Apart from those who support assisted suicide and euthanasia, most health care professionals would consider anyone's plan to commit suicide a probable symptom of problems calling for investigation and treatment. You say that Alan does not seem depressed and that his records do not mention any history of suicidal tendencies or other psychological problems. But your past experience and familiarity with Alan's personality and moods may not suffice for reasonable assurance.[255] Despite appearances, he may need psychological counseling and/or medication—matters you are not competent to evaluate.

If Alan refuses to give you the pills and you must confiscate them, that will suggest he probably will go on considering suicide and perhaps eventually attempt it. Moreover, his refusal to hand over the pills would indicate that he probably has not been receptive to your efforts to help him spiritually, so that your confiscating the pills almost certainly will antagonize him. Thus, any prospects your effort may have had will be greatly dimmed. Taking into account your own vulnerability and your professional duty, then, if you must confiscate Alan's pills, I think you definitely should fully inform Dr. Young tomorrow morning about what Alan told you and the steps you will have taken.

The considerations already articulated, especially with regard to your professional responsibility, may seem to show that your duty to inform Dr. Young will be no different even if Alan voluntarily surrenders the pills. However, you also have a more-than-professional, personal relationship with him, and it is not obvious that you should regard your professional role as the sole determinant of your responsibility toward him. If he responds to your persuasion by giving up the pills, the prospects for him and your relationship with him will be far better than if you must take them from him. Telling the doctor what has happened will violate Alan's confidences and forfeit his trust, and so will impede your effort to encourage him to receive the sacraments. Moreover, it hardly would be right to restrain him indefinitely so as to prevent him from committing suicide. So, if his plan to do so was deliberate rather than a product of psychological factors beyond his control, the problem really is to get him to repent and face the future with hope, and you and/or the priest probably are more likely than any health care professional to succeed in helping with that.

Two things favor giving the priest Alan's name and asking him to deal with the problem: he may be more able than you to persuade Alan to give up thoughts of suicide, and, if his attempt goes well, it might lead Alan to receive the sacraments. But Alan, being alienated ("fallen-away") from the Church, probably is not yet ready to listen to a priest, and if the priest's contact with him goes badly, you, having violated his confidences and betrayed his trust, may be unable to encourage him to prepare his soul for death. Moreover, the priest may well be less able than you to work with him, for even if he has more experience and skill than you in dealing with people in need of spiritual help, he lacks your established, friendly relationship with Alan. So, I am inclined to think you should not give him Alan's name at this time.

---

255. Many people who are suicidal suffer from some psychological condition, often treatable depression; see The New York State Task Force on Life and the Law, *When Death Is Sought: Assisted Suicide and Euthanasia in the Medical Context* (New York, N.Y.: May 1994), 13–16, 175–77, 197–208.

Therefore, though I realize that some reasonable people will disagree, it seems to me that, if you succeed in persuading Alan voluntarily to surrender the pills, you probably should not report at once what has happened. Instead, I think you should keep his secret and continue talking with him, hoping and praying that he will reaffirm his faith and die with the dignity of a child of God.

79: Must a nurse give up her hospital job to avoid assisting at abortions?

I have been employed for seven years as a nurse at a small community hospital, which is the only hospital in this county. Not many abortions are performed here, but two doctors do them occasionally. Shortly after I came here, I was scheduled to assist in one—that is, to prepare the patient, assist in surgery, and provide aftercare—and I refused. The hospital administrator was not happy about that, but he gave in to the extent of agreeing not to schedule abortions in the afternoons and evenings, when I normally work. Still, three times in the seven years, I had to fill in for another nurse on a morning when an abortion happened to be scheduled. Each time I assisted under protest.

Though all but one of the other nurses here have been and are prolife, nobody but me has resisted. One of them told me assisting in abortions was classified as licit material cooperation in an ethics course at her Catholic nursing school, but the same professor approved of sterilization. The one who favors abortion says I lack sisterly feelings and would think differently if I had ever been pregnant. I do sympathize with women who have problems, but I cannot help feeling for the baby too and think abortion is always wrong. Being involved in any abortion bothers my conscience, and I really want to avoid it completely.

Now the hospital administrator has told me abortions no longer will be scheduled to "accommodate" me. I will be replaced unless I assist when I am on duty. I talked with a lawyer active in our state right-to-life organization. He looked into the problem and told me no statute protects nurses in this hospital who refuse to assist in abortions. I could ignore the administrator and sue the hospital if the administrator dismisses me, but I probably would not win.

Apart from this one problem, I enjoy my work and get along fine with almost everyone, even the difficult patients. Must I give up my hospital job?

If I quit or am let go, I will not be able to move where I could get another hospital job, since I live with my elderly mother, and she could not bear leaving the home she has lived in for sixty years. But the public high school here needs a nurse for its dispensary, and the job does not involve giving out contraceptives or anything else that would be a problem. The principal would like me to start immediately, but has given me until next week to decide. The hours would not be so good, since on school days, which are about half the days of the year, I would have to work during the hours my mother needs me most. Changing jobs also would mean benefits a lot less adequate and a reduction of about forty percent in annual take-home pay. But I could make up some of that during the summer, and we could get by, since my mother still has enough income to pay her share of the bills.

Analysis:

This question concerns cooperation in wrongdoing. The questioner says being involved in abortion "bothers my conscience." If that means she chose to assist at abortions despite judging it morally wrong, she should repent having done so, and may not again assist at an abortion unless further reflection leads her to judge it morally permissible. Though recent Church teaching might be taken to mean that a nurse may not assist at abortions, I do not think that teaching should be interpreted as forbidding it if the usual requirements for morally acceptable cooperation are met. Under certain conditions, a nurse's involvement could be formal cooperation, but this nurse may be able to avoid it. If formal cooperation is excluded, however, the usual norms regarding material cooperation must be applied. The steps the questioner would need to take to avoid scandal and bear witness to the truth about abortion might well lead to her dismissal unless the other prolife nurses cooperate with her. Unless they do, therefore, it seems to me she should accept the available alternative employment.

The reply could be along the following lines:

You are right in holding that abortion itself is always gravely wrong.[256] In saying that being involved in it "bothers" your conscience, perhaps you mean only that assisting at abortions has given you guilt feelings, even though you thought it morally permissible to do it under the circumstances. In that case, your involvement was not sinful. But perhaps you mean you thought it morally wrong to assist at the three abortions, but did it anyway. In that case, your involvement was sinful, and you should repent it. Even if what one does is not objectively wrong, one always sins in choosing to do what one believes morally wrong.

Of course, if you need to repent, you must have a firm purpose of amendment. Does that mean committing yourself never again to assist at an abortion, regardless of the consequences? Not necessarily. You must commit yourself never again to act contrary to your conscience, regardless of consequences. But, as I shall explain, it could be morally permissible for you to assist at abortions, and, if you already believe it is or become convinced of that, choosing to assist would not be sinful. If it still made you feel guilty, that feeling would not be appropriate, though feelings of regret and sadness would be. Any false guilt feelings would then have to be dealt with in the same way as feelings of anxiety when there really is nothing to be afraid of.

Someone might argue that recent Church teaching provides a clear answer to your question. John Paul II, listing those who share responsibility for abortion, says: "Doctors *and nurses* are also responsible, when they place at the service of death skills which were acquired for promoting life" (italics added).[257] And

256. See John Paul II, *Evangelium vitae,* 58–63; *AAS* 87 (1995) 466–74, *OR,* 5 Apr. 1995, xi–xii; *LCL,* 488–505.

257. Op. cit., 59, *AAS* 468, *OR,* xi.

speaking of the responsibilities of health care personnel, including nurses, he says: "Absolute respect for every innocent human life also requires the *exercise of conscientious objection* in relation to procured abortion and euthanasia."[258] Moreover, having pointed out that one may not conform to laws allowing abortion, the Pontifical Council for the Pastoral Assistance of Health Care Workers says: "As a result, doctors and nurses are obliged to be *conscientious objectors.* The great, fundamental value of life makes this obligation a grave moral duty for medical personnel who are encouraged by the law to carry out abortions or to cooperate proximately in direct abortion."[259]

Plainly, these statements absolutely exclude doing abortions and wrongly cooperating in them. They also call for the exercise of conscientious objection, which, however, can take different forms. When called on to do anything intrinsically immoral, one must refuse no matter what the consequences. When called on to assist in an abortion, nurses and other health care workers should bear witness to the truth about abortion by objecting and taking advantage of laws and regulations that protect them against sanctions for refusing to be involved. However, I do not think these statements directly address your question. You have conscientiously objected, and relevant laws and regulations apparently give you no protection. Some faithful Catholic moralists—ones who did not dissent from any teaching of the Church—held that in such a case a nurse's assisting in abortion could be morally acceptable material cooperation.[260] It seems to me that if recent teachings were meant to exclude that opinion, they would have done so more clearly. Therefore, it is reasonable to suppose that your question remains to be answered.

Ordinarily, when nurses assist in any procedure they intend it to be carried out successfully. Your involvement in abortion would be absolutely wrong if you chose to assist with that end in view. That would be so if, in doing at least something that you did, you intended to help bring the abortion about. It also would be so if you had some discretion about your contribution to the procedure and had to make one or more choices in view of the goal of getting the abortion done. For example, suppose a physician decided to do an abortion by inducing labor before the fetus was viable, and you were directed to administer medication to induce labor, beginning with a certain dosage and increasing it gradually until it had the desired effect; or suppose you were assisting at a surgical abortion and were required to use your judgment in selecting implements or regulating a machine in order to help bring about the abortion. You could not carry out such directives without intending to effect the abortion, which nothing could ever justify.

Clearly, however, you do not want any abortion to be done. And when you are assigned to assist at an abortion, perhaps you have no choice about what you are to do. That is so if your involvement consists either in following routines (for example, in preparing the patient) or in obeying particular orders (hand me

---

258. Ibid., 89, *AAS* 502, *OR*, xvi.

259. Pontifical Council for Pastoral Assistance to Health Care Workers, *Charter for Health Care Workers* (Boston: Pauline Books and Media, 1994), 143 (p. 123).

260. See, e.g., Gerald Kelly, S.J., *Medico-Moral Problems* (St. Louis: The Catholic Hospital Association, 1958), 332–35.

such-and-such an instrument, adjust the light)—in either case, behavior you could perform without making any choice regarding abortion. If so, you could do all the things you do without knowing an abortion was taking place, except, perhaps, for the fact that the word *abortion* may be used in naming a routine (for example, in preparing the patient or setting up the operating room), no element of which, considered in itself, need be directed by you toward bringing about the abortion. Under these conditions, even if the abortion could not be done without your doing your duties as a nurse, in performing them you need only accept, and in no way intend, the bad use of your services, which will remain good in themselves.

Yet even such limited involvement in abortion often is wrong. That is so when it is likely to lead one into a wrong intention or choice, when it is likely to scandalize others, when it is unfair to the baby who will be killed, or when it impairs the witness one should give to the truth about abortion.

A person's limited involvement in abortion would be likely to lead to intending the abortion if she or he regarded abortion as somehow desirable (for example, supported so-called reproductive freedom or made a living by working at an abortion clinic) or if the limited involvement were likely in some circumstances to compel the person either to intend abortion or to choose an extremely repugnant alternative (for example, if a gynecologist could not continue after beginning an abortion, a resident involved by assisting at it would be compelled to choose either to finish destroying the baby or to refuse and accept the consequences). Plainly, your involvement in abortion is not likely to lead you in either of these ways to intending it.

A nurse's involvement might scandalize others—that is, lead them to commit the sin of abortion—if it seemed to manifest approval of abortion. That would be so if the nurse's involvement included behavior that contributed with physical directness to bringing about the abortion, for instance, if he or she switched on the suction machine or administered the abortion pill. However, what nurses do in preparing abortion patients, assisting in surgery, and providing aftercare need not manifest approval. Moreover, women who seek abortion, physicians who do it, and others involved who intend it generally have made their choices before nurses start to carry out their duties.

Still, a real and important possibility of scandal remains in the case of women who are ambivalent about getting an abortion. Such patients may not be easy to recognize; and the behavior of nurses who carry out their routine duties just as if they were participating in health care rather than homicide could provide them with reassurance that there is nothing exceptionable about abortion. Nurses who, like you, reluctantly assist at an abortion could forestall scandal in such cases only by clearly stating their position to each patient and anyone else involved who seems to assume or desire their approval, encouragement, and/or psychological support. But that might well be judged to violate patient care standards and lead to your dismissal.

Applying the Golden Rule makes it clear that a nurse's involvement would be unfair to the baby being killed if the nurse's refusal to be involved would not merely briefly delay the abortion but prevent it and save the baby's life. That probably does not apply in your case. Assisting at abortions also is unfair, in my judgment, for those who offer no resistance. But unlike the other prolife nurses, who have no problem being involved in abortion, you have resisted. Assisting also is unfair for nurses who could avoid it without making a significant sacrifice. On the one hand, if you lose your job for refusing to assist, some important benefits will be lost. You will no longer engage in hospital nursing, for which you seem to have a special gift, and, though you have been pressed to participate in abortion on three occasions in seven years, almost all your work in the hospital serves genuine human goods in an important way. You will have to give up a substantial part not only of your income but of your capacity to meet your mother's needs. On the other hand, you do have the offer of a job that would be adequate, and working in the school's dispensary might afford you many opportunities to be a good influence on young people.

Finally, a nurse's involvement impairs the witness he or she should give to the truth about abortion if it prevents communicating that truth credibly. You could take advantage of your reluctance to assist at abortions to give credible witness.

To begin with, you might try to help the other prolife nurses see that assisting at abortions should be a problem for them and that they should join in your protest. If they do not, I doubt you will be able to bear witness to the truth about abortion without giving up your job at the hospital. If they do, however, you could work out a common policy about what to say to a woman as one of you prepares her for an abortion or provides aftercare. Beforehand, certainly, no encouragement should be given to proceed. It would be appropriate to talk with the patient to make sure she understands what abortion is and knows about its many possible bad effects on her. If a woman expresses any hesitations, she should be assured that she can change her mind and will be supported. Moreover, it might become clear in some cases that the woman is less than wholehearted, is ignorant of what abortion does, or has not thought about alternatives, so that appropriate information and support can be offered. Afterwards, no assurance should be given that everything bad about the abortion is past; and, if a woman expresses any remorse, she should be encouraged to repent and assured that divine forgiveness is available. A nurse who has listened sympathetically to the motives and regrets of a woman who has rid herself of her baby often will have an opportunity to suggest tactfully that she seek the spiritual healing she needs.

You also could write a letter to the hospital administrator, with copies to the physicians who perform abortions, stating that from now on you will assist when assigned, but under protest and only because of the administrator's ultimatum; and that you regard the ultimatum as unjust inasmuch as it requires you to assist in killing babies—not only a great injustice to them but a betrayal of the commitment of every health care professional. The hospital administrator probably will not dare to take action against you for writing that letter. The injustice of retaliating against a frank statement of your position would be manifest even to many people who would not see the injustice of compelling you to assist at abortions. If you think being discharged from your present job would prejudice future employment, however, you might judge the risk of protesting excessive, even if in itself not great.

In sum, your involvement when assigned to assist in abortion might not require you to intend the abortion or choose to do anything wrong in itself. But the steps that would be necessary to prevent scandal and bear witness to the truth about abortion might well lead to your dismissal, especially if the other prolife nurses do not join in your protest. Moreover, you can obtain other adequate employment, and so, unless you do everything you can to prevent scandal and bear witness, assisting in abortions might well be unfair to the babies who will be killed.

Only you can say whether you can entirely avoid sinful intentions and choices, take the steps necessary to both prevent scandal and bear witness to the truth, and assist in killing unborn babies without violating the Golden Rule. However, if you seriously try to meet all those requirements, I think you very likely will be dismissed unless the other prolife nurses join you in resisting abortion and dealing with women obtaining abortions along the lines I have sketched out. Therefore, unless you reasonably hope to obtain their cooperation, I believe you should accept the job as a school nurse.

The law should include provisions to protect everyone, including nurses and other health care workers, from being pressured into assisting in abortion and other procedures they consider morally wrong—sterilization, assisted suicide, artificial insemination, the taking of organs for transplantation from people who are still alive, and so forth. Ideally, these provisions should not require that the moral judgment be based on religious faith, but simply that it be a serious judgment based on deeply held convictions. They should protect not only against criminal and civil liability, but also against loss of any public benefit, or of one's job or professional status, or of any opportunity for education or employment or professional advancement. In view of the advice you received from the prolife lawyer you consulted, I assume there are no such provisions in your state's law, and that the relevant federal statute does not apply to your hospital.[261] You should enlist others' help and do all you reasonably can to get your state legislature and, if possible, the U.S. Congress to act on the matter. Your own experience will be a valuable source for your testimony. Even if you fail, you will call many people's attention to the injustice both of abortion and of pressuring people to be involved in it. That will encourage resistance and probably save at least some babies' lives.

80: Should nurses inform the bishop of a hospital's wrongly made decision?

I am head nurse in a Catholic hospital's pediatric unit. A recent case is still troubling both me and other nurses involved, including my superior, the chief of the hospital's nursing service. We wonder whether we should have gone to the

---

261. While the lawyer's advice may be sound in this particular case, in many places nurses enjoy a right to refuse to participate in abortion, either under a state law or under a federal statute that protects all health care personnel whose employers receive moneys under certain federal programs: 42 U.S.C. 300 A–7. Therefore, any nurse pressed to participate in abortion should ascertain whether such a legal right exists where she or he works and, if it does, should take appropriate steps to exercise it.

bishop about it. It is too late now for that baby, but we probably will have similar cases in the future.

When baby Agnes was born, it was obvious that she had serious congenital defects. Still, everyone went all out for her until the diagnosis was confirmed—a genetic disorder, one far more severe than Down's syndrome, and usually fatal within a year. When the diagnosis was confirmed, Agnes was on a respirator. When the pediatrician told her father about the diagnosis, he at once demanded that the respirator be removed. The hospital administrator called a staff meeting for the next morning to decide how to proceed. In preparing, I talked with my superior and every nurse in my unit, and all of us felt we should continue to care for Agnes, who was not dying, even though she had many problems and a poor prognosis.

At the meeting, the pediatrician produced a statement signed by both parents directing that the respirator be removed. He also said the patient's respiratory deficiency was so severe that she would not long survive removal of the respirator; still, he favored removing it, because he felt the baby had no prospect of meaningful life. A staff psychiatrist, who had interviewed the parents, said the father rejected the child as abnormal, and the mother, while showing some ambivalence, agreed that the respirator should be removed. He judged that the family would experience severe stress if the baby eventually were brought home, so that it would be best if death came about quickly by removing the respirator. At the same time, he made it clear that, for the mother's sake, everyone who talked with the parents should stress that the baby's underlying problems were the cause of her death.

The administrator had consulted the hospital's lawyers, who advised complying with the parents' desires. They said no legal liability would be incurred by doing so, while continuing care against their wishes might lead to trouble unless the hospital obtained a court order. The hospital administrator and the pediatrician shared concerns about the likelihood that prolonged care for the baby would involve substantial costs that probably would never be recovered, since the family is not wealthy and has limited insurance coverage. I, of course, stated my own view and reported that my superior and all the nurses in the unit agreed with me. The administrator said he understood how I and the other nurses felt, and the psychiatrist commented that we naturally had motherly feelings toward the baby. But the administrator and the pediatrician agreed with each other that, all things considered, the practical course was to remove the respirator.

At the end of the meeting, the pediatrician went directly to the nursery and removed it. Then he went out for coffee, Agnes stopped breathing, and he returned and pronounced her dead.

My superior and I were not only sad but angry. We began wondering what we could have done. We do not think it would have done any good to go to the public authorities, since a nearby university hospital has been very open about selecting defective newborns for nontreatment, and the authorities have done nothing about it. But the bishop has shown an interest in the hospital and insisted that no sterilizations be done here. That makes us think we could have appealed to him.

Analysis:

This question concerns the duty to report wrongdoing within an organization to a competent authority. The decision to remove Agnes's respirator was based on unsound reasoning. Still, though Agnes was denied procedural justice, removing the respirator may not have been wrong. The judgment should have been made by considering both the benefits and the burdens to her and to others of carrying out alternative plans of care. The administrator's unfair handling of the case shows that he is either ignorant of relevant Catholic teaching or uncommitted to following it. Without waiting for another case to arise, the questioner and her superior should call this case to the bishop's attention and ask him to take appropriate preventative measures.

The reply could be along the following lines:

In my judgment, the basis on which Agnes's respirator was removed was morally unacceptable. The decision was carried out so quickly, however, that you probably did not have enough time to reach the bishop and get him to intervene. In any case, you did your best at the time and should not blame yourself for not doing more.

Even if there were no reason to expect another similar case in the future, what happened in this case calls for guidance by the bishop, since it not only manifests a few persons' ethical insensitivity and confusion but surely has weakened some others' moral stance. But no doubt you are right that there will be more such cases, and if the hospital administrator proceeds in the same way, similarly questionable decisions are likely to be made and quickly executed. Moreover, you and others who opposed what was done may not have an opportunity to take action in the next case. So, I do not think you and your superior should wait until another case arises before appealing to the bishop. Instead, I suggest you report to him precisely what happened so that he can take appropriate preventative measures. The following reflections may help you clarify your thoughts as you prepare to communicate with him. Or, if you wish, you may pass them on to him to help him in evaluating the situation.

The decision to remove Agnes's respirator must be criticized apart from considering what should have been done. For, though it might have been right to remove the respirator on other grounds, in this instance the decision was vitiated by the reasoning on which it was based. First I shall criticize that reasoning, then discuss how the case should have been handled.

The pediatrician quickly decided that his patient did not deserve prolonged care. His reason for wishing to remove the respirator may well have been homicidal. His argument—Agnes "had no prospect of meaningful life"—presupposes that human life itself is not a fundamental good of the person but only a necessary condition for some other human good or goods. That presupposition is false, since a human person is an organism whose life, being his or her concrete reality, is intrinsically good.[262] Moreover, since one cannot judge to be meaningless the lives of people afflicted with handicaps, such as severe genetic disorders, without applying a

---

262. See John Paul II, *Evangelium vitae,* 34, 68; *AAS* 87 (1995) 438–40 and 480, *OR,* 5 Apr. 1995, vii and xiii; *LCL,* 460–67; see qq. 43 and 45, above.

nonrational standard of adequate quality of life, the pediatrician's argument depended on a nonrational standard; and so it involved unjust discrimination against this severely handicapped baby. The pediatrician's main concern seems to have been to obtain the mother's authorization and the hospital's agreement to do as he wished. Perhaps he communicated his discriminatory attitude to Agnes's father or at least confirmed the father's inclination to evade paternal responsibility. The father "rejected the child as abnormal," according to the psychiatrist's report, as if only normal babies were entitled to acceptance and care by their parents.

The psychiatrist altogether ignored Agnes's personal good and rights, and his argument turned solely on the psychological stress he thought her parents would suffer if she were brought home. That argument assumed not only that the psychological stress would be a very serious evil but that it could not be borne or appropriately dealt with except by ensuring that Agnes would never be taken home. To that end, the psychiatrist judged "that it would be best if death came about quickly by removing the respirator." That reasoning was homicidal, for according to it the respirator was to be removed in order to bring about the child's death, which, in turn, was to be a means of forestalling the parental distress of having the child at home. The psychiatrist apparently was more or less conscious that removing the respirator would be, morally speaking, the chosen method of murdering Agnes, for he urged everyone to cooperate in distracting her mother from that fact by stressing Agnes's underlying problems as the physiological cause of her death. Moreover, the psychiatrist apparently was very considerate of the father's rejection of Agnes but paid little heed to the mother's ambivalence, perhaps assuming that any sensitivity on the mother's part deserved no respect. Then too, rather than acknowledge that the nurses' "motherly feelings" might be a sound response to Agnes's human dignity and right to care, the psychiatrist referred to them only in making a sophistic excuse for brushing aside the nurses' reasons to continue caring for Agnes.

Though the hospital administrator's primary concern should be the well-being of patients and his primary duty is to hold physicians and others to technically and morally sound standards of practice, he apparently was mainly interested in limiting costs and supporting the pediatrician's decision. Accepted at face value, the parents' signed statement directing that the respirator be removed and the advice of the hospital's lawyers that a court order would be needed to continue treatment indicated a possible limit on the hospital's capacity to care for Agnes. But that possible limit should not have entered into the hospital administrator's deliberation until he first decided on morally acceptable grounds whether to try to keep Agnes on the respirator. If he had concluded that this small and severely handicapped patient could not rightly be deprived of the respirator, at least at that time, he should have sought the necessary court order.

The unanimous judgment of the nurses in your unit that you should do no less than you had been doing in caring for Agnes was sound insofar as it rejected homicidal intentions and unjust discrimination against her. The confirmation of the diagnosis of a severe genetic disorder did not of itself warrant any reduction in care. Still, Agnes's poor prognosis could not be ignored in judging what sort of care to give her.

In sum, Agnes at least was denied the procedural justice—fair consideration of her case—to which every person is entitled. The grounds for the pediatrician's and hospital administrator's decision to remove the respirator were unsound. Nevertheless, the fact that Agnes was not dying did not of itself require that she be kept on it. So, the question remains: Should Agnes have been kept on the respirator? Or could she rightly have been deprived of it, even though her death was foreseen?

Your account does not include sufficient information to answer that question. The Church's teaching indicates what would have been the only morally acceptable way to answer it: to judge what would have been fair both to Agnes and to others by considering the benefits and burdens to her and others that probably would have been involved in carrying out alternative plans of care.[263]

Keeping Agnes on the respirator and using other technical means to deal with her problems would have kept her alive, and sustaining her life would have been a benefit to her, one that deserved consideration despite her handicap and poor prognosis. Caring for Agnes also would have provided some personal and professional fulfillment to you and the other nurses who wished to do so.

The means used to preserve Agnes's life, however, might well have been burdensome to her. And the provision of an adequate level of care also would have imposed considerable burdens on others, including the costs discussed by Agnes's pediatrician and the hospital administrator. Yet they apparently were concerned about the costs only because they did not expect them to be covered by insurance and so feared the bills would never be paid. From a less selfish viewpoint, the costs of care ought to be considered even if they will be covered by private insurance or a public program, for even then some people must bear the costs, and their capacity to bear them not only is absolutely limited by their resources but morally limited by other responsibilities.

Considering the case this way, I think more information about Agnes's prognosis was needed to decide how aggressively to care for her. On the one hand, the psychiatrist's concern about the stress the family would experience if the child eventually were brought home might suggest that there was some prospect of her condition stabilizing so that she could leave the hospital. In that case, the costs of her care might not have been so great as to impose unfair burdens on others, and, with the care parents typically can provide, she could have enjoyed an abbreviated life as an infant member of a family, if not with her parents, then perhaps in a foster home. On the other hand, Agnes's poor prognosis perhaps indicates that she never could have lived without the respirator and other, increasingly complex life support measures, so that the costs of her care would have imposed far greater burdens, while she would have remained in the hospital and experienced only a patient's

---

263. Congregation for the Doctrine of the Faith, *Declaration on Euthanasia, AAS* 72 (1980) 550, Flannery, 2:515: "It will be possible to make a correct judgment as to the means by studying the type of treatment to be used, its degree of complexity or risk, its cost and the possibilities of using it, and comparing these elements with the result that can be expected, taking into account the state of the sick person and his or her physical and moral resources."

life. The limited burdens and considerable benefits of the former prospect might well have warranted keeping Agnes on the respirator, while the far greater burdens and more limited benefits of the latter might well have justified removing it. But even if, as is likely, the actual prognosis was more complex and less clear than either of the alternatives I have sketched out, a sound consideration of the prospective burdens and benefits for Agnes and others would have been necessary to apply the Golden Rule and reach a just decision, whether to keep her on the respirator or to remove it.

The hospital administrator's unfair handling of this case shows that he either is ignorant of relevant Catholic teaching or uncommitted to following it. The way this decision was made is unlikely to be an isolated instance of ethical malpractice; similar bad decisions probably are being made throughout the hospital. Therefore, you should report to the bishop not only on this case but on anything else you have observed at odds with the hospital's claim to be Catholic, and urge him to provide sound instruction and guidance not only to the administrator but to the hospital's lawyers and other personnel, especially those who participate in life-and-death decisions.

If the administrator is responsive, he should be ready to make whatever changes are necessary—including changes in procedures and in the hospital's staff, legal counsel, and employees—to maintain its Catholic character. If he proves unresponsive, the bishop might be able to get the hospital's board or sponsoring religious congregation to replace him with someone who understands relevant Catholic moral teaching and is committed to putting it into practice, so that the hospital will be able to offer its services as an authentic Catholic health care apostolate.

If the administrator is unresponsive and it is impossible to get him replaced, the hospital should not be permitted to betray its mission of health care as an apostolate, defraud potential donors, and mislead its personnel and the public by misrepresenting itself as Catholic when it no longer is. As John Paul II teaches with respect to Catholic institutions, including those concerned with health care: "Bishops are never relieved of their own personal obligations. It falls to them, in communion with the Holy See, both to grant the title 'Catholic' to Church-related . . . health-care facilities and counselling services, and, in cases of a serious failure to live up to that title, to take it away."[264]

81: May a computer programmer help produce deceptive statistical reports?

As a computer programmer employed by a hospital with a very large organ transplant program, I have the task of computing the life-table statistics on our transplant patients. The surgeons who do these operations are very competitive, and are as anxious as athletes to have good numbers, because good numbers mean professional prestige and money. Moreover, the success of the transplant program is judged not only by the United Network for Organ Sharing—the agency that

---

264. John Paul II, *Veritatis splendor,* 116, *AAS* 85 (1993) 1224, *OR,* 6 Oct. 1993, xviii.

matches available organs with patients waiting for them—but by the health insurance companies, which direct patients into one program or another.

Wanting to be conscientious about my work, I studied the relevant federal guidelines on statistical reporting. On a number of key points the methods of reporting the surgeons have been using do not conform. There are many ways to "sandpaper" statistics, and while the surgeons are not exactly lying, they are hardly being candid. As a result, the statistical reports I generate are deceptive—they make the hospital's program look more successful than it is.

At a meeting yesterday afternoon with the surgeons and the hospital administrator, I brought this matter up. Everybody admitted that the methods used diverge from the guidelines and result in deceptive reports, but they were unanimously against changing. The surgeons' response, basically, was: It is our business to provide the data and yours to compile the reports; don't worry about the guidelines and mind your own business. The hospital administrator argued that competing programs at other hospitals also diverge from the guidelines. I do not have any firsthand knowledge about that, but have no trouble believing it, since there must be similar motivations and opportunities to deceive everywhere.

May I do as I have been told and go on compiling these deceptive reports? If I refuse, I am sure to be fired, probably for insubordination, and given a negative recommendation. Even so, there is a lot of demand for programmers, and my previous record is good enough that I could expect rather quickly to get another job without these problems, though probably with fewer benefits than I have now. Also, the hospital administrator will have no trouble finding a programmer to do things his way, since most programmers have no qualms about using whatever data are given them, just as most secretaries do not hesitate to type up whatever the boss dictates.

Analysis:

This question concerns cooperation in deception. The administrator's argument that reporting by other programs also diverges from the guidelines at best claims that diverging from the universal practice in reporting would make the hospital's transplant program appear comparatively less effective than it really is. But even so, life-table statistics on transplants as a whole would seriously mislead potential recipients, referring physicians, and others unaware of the practice. If the questioner must intend to bring about the deception or certify that the methodology conforms to the guidelines, he or she formally cooperates in the wrong and must refuse to continue doing so. Otherwise, the cooperation is only material and under certain conditions would be morally acceptable. However, since the questioner expects to get another adequate job very easily, he or she almost certainly ought not to continue following orders and, in my judgment, should try to bring an end to the deception.

The reply could be along the following lines:

In answering your question, I first shall explain why programmers sometimes should have qualms about using the data supplied them. Then I shall clarify the reality and gravity of the surgeons' deception, discuss your involvement, and suggest what you should or might do.

At the Last Supper, Jesus said to his apostles: "You are my friends if you do what I command you. I do not call you servants any longer, because the servant does not know what the master is doing; but I have called you friends, because I have made known to you everything that I have heard from my Father" (Jn 15.14–15). While Jesus' work and his apostles' cooperation in it were unique in their character and importance, the relationship Jesus established with his apostles provides a model for the relationships between superiors and subordinate workers in any situation. When workers and superiors are "friends," their community can realize human and Christian values that would be impeded or entirely blocked by a master-servant relationship.

The computer programmer and secretary who know what their "master" is about can look toward the ulterior end of their work. Provided the enterprise is morally sound, they can intend the benefits not only of their personal contribution but of the enterprise as a whole for the people it serves. Understanding and intending these benefits, workers who are their superiors' "friends" need not follow orders blindly but are able to adjust their work when necessary so that it effectively serves its real purpose. The work then has more meaning for those who do it, and gives them greater personal fulfillment and psychological satisfaction. Most important, however, is that such workers, their superiors, and the people the enterprise serves can form a true community pursuing a common good and willing one another's benefits through sharing in it.

Friendship, of course, depends on mutual good will; workers cannot unilaterally establish it. In conscientiously studying the federal guidelines for statistical reporting, you looked beyond the technical goal of programming to the real benefits to which it should contribute; you were not thinking as a mere servant. From what you say, it seems that, when the surgeons told you to mind your own business and forget about the guidelines, they were telling you to be a mere servant. Christians, however, finding themselves involved in injustices to others, should resist and try to overcome them, not simply resign themselves to them. You rightly have qualms, since your work should serve the survival and health of transplant patients.

The hospital administrator's argument that reporting by competing programs at other hospitals also diverges from the guidelines can be interpreted in two ways.

He might be granting that the life-table statistics on the hospital's transplant program really are deceptive but assuming a patently false premise—for example, "A common practice cannot be wrong" or "Competitors need be fair only to one another." Such an attempt at justification obviously fails.

However, he might be making a more interesting claim: that the common practice in reporting, not that specified in the guidelines, must be followed in order to provide an accurate statement of the comparative success of the hospital's program; otherwise, it would be measured by higher standards than those used to measure other hospitals' programs. The result very likely would be that both the United Network for Organ Sharing and the insurance companies that direct patients into programs—not to mention potential financial supporters—would at times mistakenly prefer other hospitals' programs. If this is the administrator's argument, it attempts to show that the life-table statistics accurately assert the success of the hospital's transplant program relative to competing programs.

However, the argument depends on the premise that reporting by all the other competing programs diverges from the guidelines to the same extent this hospital's does. It is hard to imagine how the administrator could know that, though he may well have anecdotal evidence about similar deception by some other places. More important, even if the argument is sound, it fails to justify a practice that makes all transplant programs seem more successful than they really are. For choices are made, not only among transplant programs, but between seeking a transplant and not seeking it. Potential patients and the physicians who refer people to transplant programs compare the burdens and benefits of such treatment with those of alternatives, including palliative care until the death that even the most successful transplant can only postpone. Consequently, overly optimistic statistical reports seriously mislead at least some people who are considering transplants and their referring physicians, as well as the programs' supporters. This deception is gravely evil. It defrauds at least a few patients of the alternatives they would have preferred had they and their physicians been accurately informed, and imposes the very substantial costs of transplants that otherwise would not be chosen on those who ultimately pay them, namely, others paying insurance premiums and/or the taxpayers.

How are you involved in this gravely evil deception? If you had to adjust your procedure in order to make the hospital's program seem more successful than it is, you would have to intend the deception. Likewise, if you asserted that the guidelines were followed in gathering the material for the statistical reports you generate, as an auditor certifies that appropriate accounting procedures have been followed in auditing a financial statement, you would make a false assertion. In either case, while not sharing all of the surgeons' and/or hospital administrator's purposes, you would share their immediate purpose of deceiving, and so participate fully, even if reluctantly, in the deception. If so, you would be obliged to refuse to do your job, regardless of the consequences.

However, your statement of the problem suggests that, even knowing what you do, you need not share the purpose of deceiving. You do your work, I take it, just as you would if the surgeons were entirely candid. I assume you are not expected to certify the accuracy of your reports. On these assumptions, it seems to me that, while your work helps bring about the deception, you do not intend it or choose to do anything so as to bring it about, and you might rightly do as you have been told and continue compiling the deceptive reports. That surely would be so, I believe, only if three conditions were met: (1) you needed your job to fulfill your responsibility to support yourself and your dependents; (2) your refusal would result in your being fired; and (3) the deception with all its bad effects on patients most likely would continue even if you gave up the job.

You say, though, that you expect to get another job quickly, even if you are discharged for insubordination and given a negative recommendation. This prospect certainly requires you to consider alternatives to doing as you have been told. Indeed, I believe that you almost certainly should adopt an alternative. I shall sketch out some, though you very likely will think of variations.

First, you might simply resign and take another job where you could use your talents to provide people with real benefits and there would be a better prospect of being your superiors' friend rather than their servant. This would minimize your personal sacrifice, since it would be unlikely to provoke your present employer and would free you from trying to end the deception.

However, if you think there is even a remote chance of persuading the hospital administrator and/or the surgeons to change their minds, I think you should take that chance out of concern for their souls and fairness toward those the deception harms. In that case, a second alternative seems the least you should do: Tell the hospital administrator you have decided not to continue compiling deceptive reports, explain your reasons, and ask him to cooperate with you in ending the deception. The focus of your argument should be on the deception's unfairness to patients and those who pay for transplants, the real harms they suffer, and the betrayal of professional responsibility by both him and the surgeons in preferring their own interests to the interests of those they promised to serve in undertaking their professional roles. In making it clear to the administrator that his attempted justification fails, you need not question his claim that competing hospitals do the same. Rather, you can challenge him to use the information he has to work for broad reform by demanding that his counterparts in other hospitals cooperate in ending the deceptive practice. You might communicate with the administrator along these lines without resigning. But if you judge that such an appeal almost certainly would result in your dismissal, you might consider it preferable to resign, using the occasion to bear witness to the truth about the deception and exhort those responsible to reform.

If the deception is not ended, you probably should bring it to the attention of outsiders. Doing that probably should be your last resort, unless it appears that first speaking directly with those responsible would hurt its chances of succeeding or involve serious risks to you. Various outsiders could be approached. You might urge the relevant federal authorities to investigate the practice of deceptive reporting and take steps to correct it, ask federal and state prosecutors to explore the possibility that those responsible for the deception are violating criminal laws, inform at least the major insurance companies concerned and the United Network for Organ Sharing, and/or inform relevant consumer groups or the public media.

While pursuing such alternatives no doubt would be burdensome to you, you would be carrying out your responsibility as a Christian to bear witness to the truth and share in Jesus' struggle against the Father of Lies. If your efforts succeeded, those wronged by the deception would be benefited. Even if they failed, your love for those neighbors would not be pointless, since it would contribute to your own sanctification and prepare material for the kingdom (see GS 38–39).

+ + +

82: May medical trainees participate in immoral procedures?

I am a medical student in my third year. Soon I will be interning and then doing a residency, probably in family practice. I accept the Church's teaching on contraception and abortion, and expect to encounter pressures as I finish my training to participate in immoral procedures. I have read that formal cooperation always is wrong and material cooperation sometimes is permissible, but do not understand how to draw the line. Perhaps you could show how to do that in three situations described to me by doctors who experienced crises of conscience at one or another stage of their training.

As a student during the 1960s in a Catholic medical school, one physician was expected, during a two-week obstetrics rotation at a public hospital, to do a postpartum physical exam to make sure there was no medical reason why the women—mostly teenage blacks—should not be given a birth control method, usually the pill or an IUD. A black resident from another university then selected the method and supplied it, although she regarded the program as an attack on women and on her race. When the resident said this, the student decided to refuse to do the exam; the physician in charge of the program asked if he meant to report the matter to the authorities at his Catholic medical school. He said no, and the physician in charge did not insist he do the exam. Now, years later, he wonders whether he did the right thing. In promising under pressure not to report the matter, he tolerated the program. Was that justified by his fear of failing that segment of his training if he pressed his position that contraception is wrong, especially when it is virtually forced on women?

A second physician, interning in a non-Catholic hospital, was expected to scrub up and assist at various operations, including abortions and surgical sterilizations by hysterectomy, which were done on various pretexts. Because he was not specializing, his actual involvement was limited; he never was asked to wield the instruments that actually destroy a baby or remove a woman's uterus. Afraid of being dismissed from the internship, he did what he was told to do. Had he been dismissed, he might never have completed his training and gone into practice, since he already had been dismissed from a previous internship for criticizing what he believed to be unjustified obstetrical aggressiveness—inducing labor as soon as a woman was a few days beyond her "due date," using heavy sedation during labor followed by a forceps delivery, and a very high percentage of caesarean sections. He wonders now if he should have refused to scrub up and assist, even at the sacrifice of his medical career.

A third physician was dismissed from her nearly completed residency in psychiatry for opposing the chief of service and a nurse over aborting a retarded woman. The patient, twenty-four years old with the intelligence of an average child of ten, eighteen weeks into her fifth pregnancy with three previous abortions, was brought to the psychiatric emergency service where the resident was on duty. The patient wanted the baby, especially since she had been forced to give up her two-year-old son about ten months before, and had been grieving his loss until she again became pregnant. She was sent to psychiatric services to be tranquilized and persuaded to accept an abortion. The nurse said this was how the chief of service would want the case handled and prepared the tranquilizer. But the resident thought that the tranquilizer might cause fetal damage and that the chief's policy wrongly anticipated such patients' decisions. She also judged that an abortion might endanger the woman's life by disposing her to commit suicide. The resident therefore refused to administer the tranquilizer; instead, she calmed the pregnant woman by talking with her and then encouraged her not to change her mind. Next day, the chief of service confronted the resident; she refused to back down, insisting that abortion not only is wrong but would be dangerous for this particular patient; and she was dismissed. This physician now is in general practice, and she still thinks she did the right thing. I wonder: Could she have taken another way out?

Analysis:

This question concerns cooperation in the immoral procedures. In the first case, the medical student probably should have reported the contraception program to the authorities at his Catholic medical school. However, had he been compelled to choose between failing that segment of his training or doing the examination, the latter would have been material cooperation with the contraceptive program; judged by the usual criteria, that material cooperation could have been justified. In the second case, the resident's involvement in abortions and sterilizations by hysterectomy was, in my judgment, morally unacceptable material cooperation, and he ought to have sacrificed his career, if necessary, to avoid it. In the third case, the resident's compliance with the wishes of the chief of service would have been formal cooperation in abortion. Still, she could have remained silent about the intrinsic evil of abortion and taken her stand on the risk that the mentally handicapped patient would commit suicide and on her right to bear her baby.

The reply could be along the following lines:

You are wise to consider in advance moral problems likely to arise as you complete your medical training. All too often, people fail to think ahead, with the bad result that they confront grave moral challenges with no prior preparation and little time to reflect. Then they are likely either to give in where they should not or to take stands where they need not, and also are likely in later years to feel guilty or have doubts about what they did and did not do.[265]

I turn first to the case of the medical student who promised under pressure not to report a virtually compulsory contraceptive program, conducted in a public hospital, to the authorities at his Catholic medical school. It seems to me he should not have made the promise and had no obligation to keep it. His fear of failing that segment of his program probably was excessive, since he was entitled to his own medical school's protection against retaliation. The authorities there were responsible for arranging the rotation to this public hospital,

265. Anyone confronted with pressure to participate in immoral procedures should obtain advice from a competent, prolife lawyer. In many hospitals receiving money under federal programs, physicians, including interns and residents, who refuse to be involved in sterilization and abortion are protected by federal law (see 42 U.S.C. 300 A–7.); state law also may offer protection.

and they should have been told what their students were being asked to do there. While it very likely would not have blocked the program if the student had reported what was going on, his doing so might have led to the termination of the Catholic medical school's involvement.

What should the student have done if compelled to choose between doing such an examination and failing that segment of his training? Considered in itself, doing the examination was not wrong, for it involved nothing more than observing and truthfully reporting. In context, the examination cleared the way for the main business of the program: imposing contraception on women, mostly teenage blacks. Thus, what the student was called on to do was an instance of material cooperation in wrongdoing. The material cooperator does not share, even reluctantly, the wrongful will of those who do the wrong to which his or her action contributes. Rather, he or she only accepts the contribution that his or her action, good in itself, makes to another's wrongdoing. Material cooperation is sometimes morally excluded but sometimes acceptable. In this case, it seems to me, it would have been morally acceptable for the student to do the examination, especially since he then would have had the opportunity and duty to look carefully for medical contraindications and to protect women from being given contraceptives likely to harm them. At the same time, his refusal to do the examination was a courageous act of witness to his belief that contraception is gravely wrong and a serious injustice when virtually forced on women.

What about the resident who carried out her assigned role though regarding the program as an attack on women and on her race? Someone fulfilling her role could hardly avoid instructing patients how to use the chosen method of contraception and encouraging them to use it effectively. Though the resident may have lacked sufficient reflection about the immorality of contraception, in choosing to do her assigned part in the program, she shared its contralife intention. So, her cooperation was formal. Moreover, for someone who considered the program an attack on women and her race, cooperating with it meant reluctantly participating in those injustices—a serious moral compromise.

Your second case is that of an intern in a non-Catholic hospital who was expected to scrub up and assist in abortions and surgical sterilizations by hysterectomy. Had he refused, he might never have completed his training and gone into practice, since he had been dismissed from a previous internship. My first comment is that this doctor's earlier criticism of what he considered unjustified obstetrical aggressiveness, while perhaps medically sound, probably was not morally required. His primary responsibility was to complete his studies, and it seldom is reasonable to expect that a single student's criticism will bring about reforms in an established program. Therefore, I think he should have kept quiet rather than risked provoking those in charge.

Assisting at abortions and hysterectomies (where the latter are not medically necessary but are done as a method of sterilization) is far more questionable, morally speaking, than is doing a postpartum physical examination in the context of a contraception program. Abortion is a very grave injustice to the unborn individual who is killed, and hysterectomy as a method of sterilization is both wrong in itself and more mutilating than necessary for the purpose. Moreover, even though assisting in such operations did not require that the intern wield the instruments used to destroy the baby or remove the uterus, his involvement was closer and his contribution more direct than that of the intern doing the postpartum exam in the contraception program.

That closer involvement and more direct contribution were morally significant in several ways. First, while the student doing the examination was unlikely to be called on to go further, the intern in some circumstances, such as an emergency, might well have been expected to take a more direct part in the surgery; and then he would have been strongly tempted to participate so closely that he could not have avoided intending its success, and so formally cooperating in the killing or mutilation. Again, the intern's behavior was more likely than the medical student's to be taken by others as a model, and so lead them into sinful participation in abortion and sterilization. Then too, the intern's involvement was more at odds than the student's with clear and credible witness to relevant moral truths. Finally, since anyone totally innocent and defenseless facing death would want most others who recognize the injustice to refuse to participate closely, the intern's involvement in the abortions almost certainly was unfair. Therefore, even if the intern's assisting was not formal but only material cooperation (as I think it probably was), I do not think it was morally justifiable.

The main lesson for you in this case is to do what you can to plan and arrange your further training so as to avoid being pressured to assist in morally unacceptable operations. Even if refusing to participate so closely in such operations would mean risking your medical career, I believe that would be the right thing to do. If you do refuse and are threatened with unjust consequences, I advise you to put up as strong a fight as possible, not only for yourself but in the hope that your effort will help limit the serious injustice that those in charge of training programs do in forcing trainees to choose between their careers and their consciences. Also, if worse comes to worst and you must sacrifice your career, I think you should use every available means to publicize your decision, so that it will serve as a good example for others.

Your third case is that of a physician dismissed from her nearly completed residency in psychiatry for refusing to administer a tranquilizer and persuade a retarded woman to accept an abortion. The resident could not have given in to this pressure without intending, however reluctantly, that the patient agree to the abortion; thus, she would have formally cooperated in trying to bring about the abortion, and so she had no morally acceptable option but to refuse.

While her refusal was morally necessary and notably courageous, I wonder whether she fully followed through by fighting the dismissal and publicizing her decision and its consequences. If not, I think she should have, unless she had compelling reasons not to. By being dismissed, she was freed to bear strong witness, just as St. Thomas More was by being unjustly convicted. Since Christian life should be apostolic, a person who does so good a deed should make its light shine, both to enlighten others and to encourage them to resist evil.

It also seems to me that the chief of service's policy of using a tranquilizer to get patients to undergo abortion is medically indefensible and constitutes a very grave wrong to patients, which would call for professional disciplinary action and warrant a lawsuit on behalf of a victim. In the particular case, the danger that abortion might lead the patient to commit suicide provided an additional argument against following that policy. Without conceding the acceptability of abortion, the resident could have focused on those points and made them the central issue, while keeping to herself her conviction that abortion as such is evil. Perhaps in this way she could have avoided the dismissal without giving in to the pressure to act against her conscience. Doing that would not have involved any moral compromise and would have enabled her to continue to fulfill what she had accepted as her vocation. Consequently, though it would not have borne witness to the evil of abortion, it would not have violated the duty to bear witness.

The moral to be drawn from this case: Living among wolves, those undergoing professional training must "be wise as serpents and innocent as doves" (Mt 10.16). A Christian should invoke commonly accepted standards when they are compatible with moral truth and helpful in safeguarding his or her vocation, but when necessary should absolutely refuse to conform to those standards.

83: May pharmacists dispense pills to be used for ending human lives?

I am a pharmacist working in a large chain drugstore. Part of my job is to keep an eye out for circumstances in which there might be some reason for not filling a prescription, but otherwise I am expected to dispense whatever is prescribed. That includes birth control pills, although I reject contraception. Knowing that the pills have an abortifacient dimension, I have not liked doing this. But theologians usually faithful to the Church's teaching have said it is acceptable material cooperation, and so I have done it. It would be virtually impossible to work as a pharmacist otherwise unless one owned the store. Today very few pharmacists can do that, and most, like me, are simply employees.

Still, I am worried about future developments. I feel sure that eventually abortion pills will be available by prescription, and probably suicide pills as well. In most ways, this does not seem to me to differ much from dispensing contraceptive pills, but my gut feeling is that it is much worse, and I cannot see myself doing it. What should I do if my fears are realized?

One other thing worries me. I know that prescriptions for birth control pills sometimes are being written with instructions regarding dosage and timing that make it clear they are being prescribed as morning-after pills. Physicians around here do not seem to be doing this, and up to now I have not been asked to fill such a prescription. But I expect I will be sooner or later. What should I do when that happens?

Analysis:

This question concerns problems of cooperation with wrongdoing, which must be treated by applying the usual criteria. Dispensing contraceptives is at odds with a pharmacist's professional commitment rightly understood. In my judgment, a pharmacist who owns his or her own pharmacy engages in morally unacceptable cooperation in stocking and selling contraceptives or any other merchandise customers could want only for some objectively immoral use. However, when pharmacists who do not own their own business dispense drugs, even those that sometimes are abortifacient, for use as contraceptives, they can be engaging in morally acceptable material cooperation. The wrong of using abortion and suicide pills would be greater and more obvious than the wrong of using contraceptive drugs. Though pharmacists' cooperation in the killing could remain strictly material, it would, in my judgment, be morally unacceptable even for employee-pharmacists. The very grave injustice of abortion grounds an especially cogent case against dispensing abortion pills. Dispensing contraceptive drugs for use as morning-after pills would involve material cooperation in their use with the twofold intention of preventing conception and preventing implantation—and so with a conditional intent to kill. This cooperation, in my judgment, would be morally similar to that involved in dispensing a drug specifically designed for killing. Rather than dispense either sort of drug, pharmacists should, I believe, give up their profession if necessary.

The reply could be along the following lines:

Serving alongside physicians, nurses, dentists, and so on, members of your profession make an important contribution to meeting people's health care needs. That is why you rightly "keep an eye out for circumstances in which there might be some reason for not filling a prescription." As your profession's official ethics code makes clear, you have not undertaken merely to be a salesperson who dispenses drugs, while taking care to avoid mistakes, in order to make an honest living. You also have undertaken to help those you serve "achieve optimum benefit from their medications, to be committed to their welfare, and to maintain their trust."[266] Therefore, you should watch out for inappropriate or incompatible prescriptions and normally should do what you can to educate people who come to you, so that they will use prescribed drugs as directed and be alert for dangerous side effects. When possible, you also should offer prudent advice concerning nonprescription medications, discourage people from overmedicating with them, and try to offset excessive and misleading advertising claims.

Since at least some pills usually prescribed for contraception also can be used both in ways that certainly are morally acceptable and as morning-after pills, I shall first deal with cases in which you know the drug is being prescribed for use as a contraceptive, though it also sometimes acts as an abortifacient. Then I shall treat your question about dispensing drugs specifically designed for abortion and suicide when they are plainly prescribed for those purposes. Finally, I shall treat your question about dispensing contraceptive drugs for use as morning-after pills.

In dispensing contraceptive pills and encouraging women to use them effectively, your colleagues who see nothing wrong with contraception doubtless think they are acting in accord with pharmacists' professional commitment to the welfare

---

266. American Pharmaceutical Association, *Code of Ethics for Pharmacists* (27 Oct. 1994), I.

of those they serve. However, like the use of abortion pills and suicide pills, the use of contraceptives is contrary to the good of human life. Of course, contraceptives sometimes are used to prevent pregnancies that should be avoided, and those who suppose that a good end can be a proportionate reason for choosing to prevent life judge that in such cases encouraging women to use contraceptives effectively really does promote their welfare. However, such judgments about welfare overlook the implications for human welfare adequately understood, which includes moral goodness, of choosing—and approving or sharing in others' choices—to prevent human life or, more generally, to destroy, damage, or impede any good intrinsic to human persons. There can be no proportionate reason for making such a choice (see *CMP*, 141–71). And using contraceptives never effectively promotes anyone's true welfare. So, providing contraceptives of any kind is not in accord, but rather at odds, with your professional commitment rightly understood. That is especially clear when you dispense contraceptive drugs that, though primarily meant to prevent conception, sometimes work as abortifacients. You are right to dislike doing this, for it not only reduces you to the role of a salesperson who dispenses drugs, but makes you reluctantly play a part in ending some incipient human lives.

What about the advice some theologians have given you—dispensing birth control pills is acceptable material cooperation for a pharmacist? I think a distinction should be made between pharmacists who own their own businesses and those who do not.

In my judgment, if you owned your own pharmacy, it would be wrong for you to dispense contraceptives or sell any other merchandise (such as pornographic magazines and books) that customers could want only for some objectively immoral use. Intending customers' use of such products would be willing their wrongful acts, and the owner of a business usually promotes sales and always intends the use of whatever is promoted. Still, in filling prescriptions for contraceptives, a pharmacy owner might be able to avoid sharing the will that they be used, since he or she does not lead the purchaser to take the drug; that decision already has been made by the patient and the prescribing physician. But even if pharmacy owners who sell products they know will be put to a morally unacceptable use can avoid intending their use, they still should forgo such sales. Even their material cooperation is unjustifiable, not least because it inevitably tempts them to cooperate formally by promoting the use of such profitable products. Moreover, in dispensing birth control pills, as has been explained, the pharmacist acts at odds with his or her professional commitment and becomes a mere salesperson who dispenses drugs. Pharmacists who own their own pharmacies are less likely than those who are "simply employees" to be considered mere salespersons. So, their action in dispensing birth control pills is certain to undercut their witness to the truth that one should not use these drugs, and also is likely to cause scandal by contributing to users' rationalizations.

In some places even pharmacists who do not own the business but are employees, as you are, can practice their profession without dispensing contraceptive drugs; either the employer has a policy of not stocking contraceptives or respects the consciences of employees who object to filling prescriptions for contraceptive drugs. In such a situation, a pharmacist should bear witness by refusing to dispense contraceptives. However, where there is no such opportunity, I think it possible that in dispensing contraceptives employee-pharmacists can avoid morally unacceptable cooperation.

Because employee-pharmacists normally have no responsibility for advertising and other forms of promotion, they avoid intending the use of the drugs they dispense more easily than owners do. Moreover, the material cooperation of employee-pharmacists who reluctantly dispense contraceptive drugs probably can be morally acceptable. If they clearly recognize the evil of using the drugs and wish to avoid wrongly cooperating, they are not likely to be tempted to cooperate formally. The risk of scandal also can be minimal, because the woman whose prescription is filled has already decided to use the pill and filling the prescription is hardly likely to lead anyone else to decide to use it. Then too, filling prescriptions for contraceptive pills is consistent with plausibly bearing witness to the evil of contraception, since people do not suppose that employee-pharmacists personally recommend or approve the use of everything they dispense. And refusing to dispense contraceptive pills so as to bear witness against their abortifacient dimension is hardly likely to be effective. Since the pills generally are not being used with the intention of causing abortion, their occasional, invisible abortifacient effect would not trouble most people, even if it were fully explained to them. Finally, the pill's abortifacient dimension does not render the employee-pharmacist's material cooperation with its use unfair to the unborn. Since most pharmacists dispense the pill and hardly anyone who uses it is likely to be concerned about its abortifacient dimension, refusing to dispense it is not likely to save lives.

In dispensing contraceptive pills, however, if you have reason to think pointing out the possibly abortifacient mode of action of a prescribed contraceptive might deter a particular purchaser from using it, you should point out and explain the language in the package insert indicating that possibility. Moreover, you must never fulfill the pharmacist's usual responsibility of encouraging effective use of the drug. In this case, you cannot have such a responsibility, for you could not encourage effective use of contraceptive pills without intending that they be used effectively, and that intent, being contraceptive, would be evil. But you should keep an eye out, as usual, for contraindications the prescribing physician may have overlooked, and alert purchasers to side effects that may require the physician's attention. When you can do so without risking your job, you also should throw away or put out of sight displays and other materials advertising contraceptives and promoting their use.

Someone might suggest that, rather than filling the prescription for a drug you know is being prescribed for contraception, you should contact the prescribing physician, just as you would about any other prescription of a drug likely to harm the user and perhaps even kill her unborn child. Unless you thought the physician had made a mistake, however, contacting him or her would be pointless, since the moral question that concerns us does not trouble the prescribing physician.

I believe you are right in thinking that dispensing abortion or suicide pills would be similar in important respects to dispensing contraceptive drugs. Your cooperation would differ in similar ways from the cooperation of the physician prescribing the drugs, and, as an employee-pharmacist, you could easily avoid formal cooperation. Moreover, I believe that your material cooperation would be no more likely to tempt you to cooperate formally. But I also think your gut feeling is right—dispensing abortion or suicide pills would be worse than dispensing contraceptives.

Though the wrong involved in contraceptives' use (the evil of contraception and the risk of an abortifacient effect) is grave, it is less obvious and less certain than the wrong involved in using abortion or suicide pills (the evil of intending to kill and the virtual certainty that the drug will be effective). While the limited material cooperation of the employee-pharmacist in the former evil can be morally acceptable, that is hardly the case with similar material cooperation in the latter, more obvious and more certain evil. Dispensing drugs specifically designed to kill would be plainly contrary to a pharmacist's proper role and professional commitment. Therefore, dispensing abortion and suicide pills would more likely convey the pharmacist's approval and undercut his or her prolife witness.

Moreover, even if most pharmacists will dispense pills specifically designed to kill, with the result that people who want them will be able to get them elsewhere, refusing to fill prescriptions for these drugs would bear significant witness to the truth about them. Their sole intended effect will be to kill, and clearheaded users will have that intention. Pointing out the evil of using them, and if necessary sacrificing one's livelihood to do so, will call those planning to use them to repent and those tempted, to resist. At least with respect to abortion pills, bearing witness in this way will be, in my judgment, a strict obligation for pharmacists. Putting oneself in the place of innocent and defenseless unborn persons, one can hardly deny the duty to do what one can to save at least a few of their lives. And putting oneself in the place of potential suicides, who might die in mortal sin, one can hardly doubt that Christian mercy calls for considerable sacrifice to save at least some of their souls.

When drugs usually used for contraception are prescribed for genuinely thera-peutic purposes, your moral responsibility is determined by the drug's use rather than by its pharmacological characteristics. Similarly, when you are asked to dispense drugs usually used for contraception prescribed as morning-after pills, your moral responsibility will be determined by the precise intention with which they are prescribed and used. But while the phrase, *morning-after pills,* indicates that the drug is to be used after intercourse, it does not specify whether the intention is to prevent pregnancy by preventing conception (as contraceptive pills generally do) or by preventing either conception or the implanting of the early embryo in the uterus, as the case may be. Even if some slight chance that the drug might prevent implantation is accepted by the prescribing physician and/or user, pills to be taken after intercourse with the reasonable expectation and intention of preventing conception would not, in my judgment, pose for you a problem different from that posed by the common use of the contraceptive pill.[267] However, the medical literature and discussion in the mass media may make it clear that physicians who prescribe morning-after pills and women who use them typically mean to do whatever is necessary to prevent pregnancy, and so act with a twofold intention: to prevent conception when that is possible and, if it is too late, to prevent the implantation of the early embryo.[268] That, I take it, is the situation you anticipate and ask about toward the end of your question. In that situation, you will have to assume that any prescription presented to you for a morning-after pill will pose the problem of helping implement an abortifacient intention.

No factual evidence or philosophical argument provides reasonable grounds for denying that the new human individuals who sometimes will be intentionally killed by morning-after pills are tiny persons. The Church clearly and most firmly teaches that such an individual must be regarded as a new human being, whose "rights as a person must be recognized, among which in the first place is the inviolable right of every innocent human being to life."[269] So, when contraceptive pills are used as morning-after pills, one of their intended effects is to kill an individual who must be regarded as a person, and those who prescribe and use them with the twofold intention explained above intend what should be considered homicide. Therefore, if you dispense morning-after pills, you will knowingly help people commit intentional homicide.

What, then, should you do if you are asked to dispense them? You should, in my judgment, draw the line at this and refuse. Though those acting with the conditional abortifacient intention will be unaware of the instances in which the condition is fulfilled, their wills will be morally similar to those of people who prescribe and use drugs specifically designed to kill. Thus, there is the same possibility and need for witness to the truth about the morning-after pill as about drugs specifically designed to kill, and the duty to try to save lives also is similar.

Someone might object that, even if dispensing morning-after pills is similar in the way explained to dispensing pills specifically designed for abortion, filling a prescription for morning-after pills could be morally acceptable material cooperation. The argument would be that the woman taking the pill seldom will be pregnant, never will know that she is, and very often either will not understand that taking the pill will prevent the implantation of a new individual or will not agree that the new individual is a person. But these subjective factors in no way affect the fact that whenever the morning-after pill prevents implantation a tiny person dies. Moreover, the very factors that might prevent or lessen guilt for the killing also facilitate rationalization and self-deception, which can impede repentance for doing something confusedly recognized as gravely wrong. Thus, witness to the truth about morning-after pills is no less morally required—and perhaps even more

---

267. A reasonable expectation and intention of preventing conception would presuppose evidence that the woman was not already pregnant and was in the preovulatory stage of her cycle; see q. 64, above.

268. See, e.g., Leon Jaroff, "Rx: 'Morning After' Pills," *Time*, 148:4 (15 July 1996): 59.

269. John Paul II, *Evangelium vitae*, 60, *AAS* 87 (1995) 469, *OR*, 5 Apr. 1995, xii; cf. *LCL*, 495–98.

so—than is witness to the truth about drugs specifically designed to kill. Therefore, the differences between the two do not imply that the material cooperation with killing involved in dispensing morning-after pills can be morally acceptable.

You may be able to avoid dispensing pills specifically designed to kill and morning-after pills by finding employment in a pharmacy whose owner either will not stock them or will respect a conscientious objection to dispensing them. If not, you must, in my judgment, refuse to dispense them, explain why, and, if necessary, give up your profession.

Since that plainly would be a great sacrifice, you should try to organize other pharmacists to work together—and in cooperation with other health care professionals—to obtain provisions in relevant laws, governmental regulations, and codes of professional ethics to exempt individuals who regard intentional killing as wrong from cooperating in this growing evil.[270] I do not believe that this effort's objective should be the kind of conscience clause that would wrongly suggest that some special moral or religious ground is needed to justify refusing to participate in killing the innocent. Rather, the objective should be language guaranteeing the full freedom of anyone and everyone to choose not to participate in any way in such killing (see q. 79, above). Morally speaking, that freedom requires no justification, and those who rightly desire to exercise it should resist demands to offer any.

Considering the great need for such protections, you and other health care professionals have a serious and urgent responsibility to work for them. Do not delay in getting to work. I hope your effort will be successful.

84: May one certify that one has counseled a woman seeking an abortion?

In some places where abortion has been legalized, the laws require women seeking abortions to accept counseling about the availability of alternatives. This requirement should ensure that women will receive at least some information that might lead them to change their minds. The results of counseling are mixed; most women do not change their minds, but some do.

They are more likely to do so if counseled by people who consider abortion morally unacceptable. This suggests that prolife people should serve as preabortion counselors whenever they can. The qualifications required vary from place to place, but in many places prolife physicians, nurses, social workers, and/or others can become counselors.

But there is a problem. Since the law requires counseling as a condition for obtaining a legal abortion, a woman who decides to go through with the abortion despite the counseling must be able to show she has been counseled. Jurisdictions requiring counseling therefore require counselors to give each woman they counsel a legally prescribed form certifying that the requirement has been

---

270. On the right to opt out, see *Evangelium vitae*, 74, *AAS* 487–88, *OR,* xiv.

met. The woman gives this certificate to the abortionist, for whom it serves, in effect, as a legal license to do the abortion.

Some Catholics have asked whether they may serve as counselors and provide the certificate, and I am not sure whether doing so would be morally unacceptable cooperation with abortion. I am asking various moral theologians for an opinion, and would be glad to have yours.

One point must be clarified to obviate a possible misunderstanding. In some jurisdictions whose laws permit abortions only on certain "justifying" indications, an abortion can be done lawfully only if a social worker, psychiatrist, physician, or individual of another officially designated type certifies that at least one specified indication obtains. The certification at issue in the present question differs. The counselor certifies only that the woman has been counseled about the availability of alternatives to abortion.

Analysis:

This question concerns cooperation in abortion. Some hold that counselors who provide the legally required certificate formally cooperate in the abortion. They argue that in providing the certificate counselors intend to do what the law authorizing abortion requires, and so share that law's intention to facilitate abortion. This argument is not sound. Though counselors do intend to fulfill the law's requirements regarding counseling when they provide the certificate, and though having the certificate is a legally required condition for obtaining a lawful abortion, counselors need not intend abortion in providing the certificate. For the committed prolife counselor, counseling is a means of changing women's minds about getting an abortion; promising women the counseling will be certified is a means to motivate them to accept it; and providing the certificate when counseling fails to dissuade is keeping the promise. By providing the certificate, therefore, the counselor cooperates in the abortion only materially, and this material cooperation can be justified.

The reply could be along the following lines:

Some moral analysts (moral theologians or ethicists), whose position on this matter I do not accept, hold that counseling women about abortion in this context and providing them with certificates that they have been counseled constitute formal cooperation—which never can be morally acceptable—in the gravely evil act of abortion. They acknowledge that prolife people undertake such counseling for the sake of the good end of trying to dissuade women from going through with their plan, and also that counselors often can provide women not only with information about alternatives but with at least some reasons to choose them. Yet they argue that, in agreeing to provide certificates to women who are not dissuaded, counselors share the intention of facilitating abortion. Therefore, they conclude, in agreeing to provide the certificate, counselors choose a bad means to their good end.

In trying to show that preabortion counselors share the intention of facilitating abortion, such moral analysts point out that most, if not all, women who want abortions submit to counseling only in order to obtain the certificate, which they regard as nothing but a means of obtaining an abortion. Also, these analysts point out, though those wishing to be appointed or recognized as qualified counselors hope to prevent abortions, they choose as their means the role of preabortion counselor as defined by the relevant laws. The purpose of those laws is clear, they argue: They were enacted to replace laws forbidding abortion so that at least some women who want abortions could obtain them legally. So, they reason, in agreeing to provide certificates to women who are not dissuaded, counselors commit themselves to meeting a requirement for a lawful abortion, precisely as that requirement is specified by the laws legalizing and regulating it, and thus share the intention of facilitating abortion, which was the reason for enacting those laws. Therefore, these analysts conclude, in undertaking to certify that the counseling requirement has been met—a necessary condition for obtaining an abortion legally—even prolife counselors intend to facilitate abortion, and thus formally cooperate in it.

It seems to me that this analysis includes four sound points. First, if committing oneself to providing the certificate needed to get a lawful abortion is formal cooperation in abortion, making that commitment cannot be justified even by the laudable purpose of dissuading women from abortion. A good end cannot justify a means immoral in itself. Second, the wish of prolife counselors that no law would permit abortion and no woman they counsel would go through with her plan need not preclude their sharing the intention of facilitating abortion; for an agent's intention in choosing to do something is specified, not by what is wished for, but by precisely what is chosen, that is, the object of the act proposed through practical reasoning.[271] Third, the woman intent on abortion generally submits to counseling solely to obtain the certificate, which for her and the abortionist is no more than a necessary condition for lawful abortion. Fourth, prolife people who undertake to do the counseling required by law in order to dissuade women from getting abortions do choose as their means to fulfill the role of preabortion counselor as defined by relevant laws, and that role does include providing the certificate those laws prescribe as a necessary condition for obtaining a lawful abortion.

Nevertheless, I think the analysis confuses the obvious intention of women bent on an abortion and provisions in laws facilitating it with those laws' other provisions regarding counseling and its certification. The latter provisions do not thereby facilitate abortion, although the laws' more central provisions do just that. The counseling requirement limits the number of abortions by giving every woman seeking an abortion an alternative—that is, some information and motivation to change her mind. The legislation (or, in some cases, later administrative policy) required certificates because few if any women seeking an abortion would accept the counseling unless forced to prove they had done so by producing a certificate. Thus, while the woman intent on an abortion and the abortionist regard the certificate merely as a necessary means for getting an abortion and doing it lawfully, prolife counselors can agree to give the certificate solely because that

271. See John Paul II, *Veritatis splendor,* 78, *AAS* 85 (1993) 1196, *OR,* 6 Oct. 1993, xii; cf, appendix 1, below.

is a necessary means to obtaining the opportunity to counsel women and getting them to accept counseling which, in turn, is a means of preventing abortions—despite the laws' other provisions facilitating them.

The point can be clarified in two ways.

The first is by comparing the situation in countries requiring counseling and its certification with the situation in the United States, where the Supreme Court legalized abortion by judicial fiat, and proponents of women's so-called right to choose abortion have strongly opposed much milder restrictions than the one under discussion here. If a state legislature passed a law requiring every woman seeking an abortion to accept counseling, the law would be pointless if it allowed women to obtain a lawful abortion without being counseled, and so it also would have to require certification of counseling by the counselors. While this whole law, including its certification requirement, would be condemned vehemently by proponents of the "right" to abortion, they would be mollified if some court struck down the certification requirement but left the rest of the law standing as a dead letter.

The point can be clarified in a second way by comparing the requirement of counseling and its certification with the requirement in some jurisdictions that there be certification of some supposedly justifying indication for abortion. Laws specifying indications and requiring their certification do thereby facilitate abortion. Replacing laws entirely forbidding abortion, those authorizing it in some cases required certification of indications to identify those cases while also continuing to prohibit it in others. Determining whether an indication exists does nothing to lead a woman who wants an abortion to change her mind, and the deliberation that ends in giving or refusing the certificate simply applies the law authorizing abortions to a particular case. Not only abortionists and women seeking abortions but the people doing such certifications must regard certifying an indication as licensing an abortion.

Someone might object that in some places both counseling and indications requirements are in force, and the same individuals certify both simultaneously. But the fact that in some jurisdictions the two things are combined in a single process does not eliminate their significant distinction in those jurisdictions where counseling focuses exclusively on alternatives to abortion.

Having distinguished between, on the one hand, what the laws are meant to bring about in requiring the certification of counseling and, on the other hand, their provisions legalizing abortion and the intention of women who accept counseling solely to obtain a certificate, it is easy to see the sharp difference between the woman's and the counselor's intentions, provided one bears in mind what the certificate is. It is not a statement that an abortion is indicated or justified, but only a statement, in prescribed form, that the required counseling has been done. True, a woman bent on abortion submits to counseling in order to obtain the certificate as a means to getting an abortion; but that intention need not enter into the counselor's practical reasoning. For the counselor, counseling is a means of informing women, changing some of their minds, and so saving some babies; undertaking to certify counseling and promising women that it will be certified are means to obtain the opportunity of counseling and to motivate women to accept counseling; and providing a certificate when counseling fails to dissuade a woman from having an abortion is fulfilling the undertaking and keeping the promise.

Providing a woman with a certificate does enable her to get an abortion, but only because the counselor's effort at dissuading her has failed. The counselor in no way intends to facilitate abortion, but only materially cooperates with women who have not been dissuaded. Sometimes material cooperation is not morally acceptable, but in the present case it seems to me it can be justified. Though someone who thinks that abortion is sometimes morally acceptable is likely to slip into formal cooperation with at least some of the women seeking an abortion, that temptation hardly will arise with counselors who are convinced that abortion is always gravely wrong. For such counselors, who are firmly committed to saving babies' lives, the point of the material cooperation is to make it possible to bear witness to the mother in the hope that she will change her mind. Moreover, giving the certificate will not motivate any woman to have an abortion, and carrying out the counseling precisely in order to save unborn babies whose lives are at risk is fair to them. Indeed, considering that some of those lives will be saved if committed prolife counselors do the counseling and putting oneself in the babies' place, one can see that the Golden Rule calls for an effort to dissuade women from abortion.

It might be objected that, since the obligation to keep promises is not absolute, the Golden Rule also demands that the counselor break the promise and not provide the certificate, so as to save babies' lives. That objection fails for two reasons. First, while breaking promises sometimes can be justified, lying never can be, and making a promise one intends to break is a lie. Counselors must mean to keep their promise when they make it—that is, people who undertake to give preabortion counseling must intend to provide the expected certificate if their counseling fails. Second, regularly breaking the promise would result in the counselor's dismissal, and doing so in a particular case generally would not stop a woman bent on abortion. Still, if a counselor, having sincerely promised to provide the certificate, were to discover in some case that breaking the promise very likely would save the baby's life, then, in my judgment, he or she should break it.

Again, someone might object: Suppose a law both forbade suicide unless those wishing to commit it accepted counseling and also required that counselors who failed to dissuade someone from suicide end the session by dispensing a cyanide capsule for use as the sole lawful means of committing suicide. Would it be morally acceptable for a prolife person to seek the role of presuicide counselor as defined by that law?

My answer is no. But not because providing cyanide capsules at the end of such prolife, presuicide counseling would necessarily be formal cooperation in suicide. The prolife counselor would give the capsule in order to keep his or her promise—a promise made in order to get suicidal people into counseling. So, the cooperation still would be only material. Even so, giving the cyanide capsule would be morally unacceptable material cooperation in suicide, chiefly because it always would be scandalous. People—primarily but not only those counseled—would think the legislators who set up this system and the counselors who participated in it regarded suicide as morally acceptable for those who undertook it deliberately rather than rashly or as a result of some treatable psychological condition. That interpretation, while not strictly necessary, would be plausible, because the requirement of counseling could be enforced adequately by requiring a certificate. So, the requirement that counselors dispense cyanide capsules, which are in themselves deadly, would suggest that the counseling had a different purpose: not to deter suicide as such, but only to forestall rash acts of suicide.

By contrast, certification that preabortion counseling has taken place is a necessary condition for any effective counseling requirement, since without certification the counseling would become optional and the counseling requirement would pose no obstacle to obtaining an abortion. Therefore, giving a woman a certificate of preabortion counseling is not scandalous, since people realize why the law provides for it and know that prolife counselors who do it consider abortion morally unacceptable and are trying to dissuade every woman from it, no matter how deliberately a woman is acting.

85: May a researcher use tissue from deliberately aborted fetuses?

I am a medical scientist teaching and doing research in the graduate school of a major non-Catholic university. I have been invited to participate in a research project which, if successful, could lead to significant advances in our knowledge of the causes of certain prenatal, developmental abnormalities, and, eventually, our ability to prevent and/or treat them. Studying the draft of a proposal for the project, I see only one problem. The tissue required as material will have to be fresh (not preserved or frozen). Obtaining fresh tissue from spontaneously aborted fetuses will not be feasible, as I have concluded reluctantly after looking into that possibility. The university hospital's department of obstetrics and gynecology will supply the tissue, and it will come from deliberately aborted fetuses.

I believe abortion is wrong and have worked actively in our state's citizens-for-life organization and often spoken out here at the university. But I would like to participate in this research project. Nobody in the obstetrics and gynecology department will be involved in it, and no abortions will be done that would not have been done anyway. All the tissue used would otherwise be disposed of along with other hospital waste. If I refuse the invitation, it will go to a colleague, and the project probably will proceed. In that case, however, the chances of success will be somewhat less, since I am better qualified by previous research experience—which, of course, is why I am being invited first to participate and would like to participate.

Also, if I refuse the invitation and my colleague accepts, as I am quite sure he will, I expect that he will seek my advice regularly on an informal basis. If I am not going to give it, I think I should tell him that before he commits himself. I would appreciate having your opinion on this problem too.

Analysis:

This questioner's problem about involvement in induced abortion is similar to a problem about cooperation. Even if participants in the project can entirely avoid cooperating in the abortions from which the tissue will come, they necessarily will be associated with those abortions. This complicity will be wrong for several reasons, and agreeing now to give the colleague advice would be wrong for similar reasons. Still, if the questioner expressly refuses to participate in the project as a matter of principle and it nevertheless goes forward, he or she may, in my judgment, consider giving the colleague some advice. But doing that could be justified only if the questioner observed certain limits so that complicity with abortion would be avoided.

The reply could be along the following lines:

Many people involved in abortion deny that unborn babies are persons. But since you believe that abortion is wrong, I assume you hold that the new human individual is—or, at least, should be presumed to be—a person from fertilization (see *LCL,* 488–98). Holding that, you should be disposed to see the force of arguments against accepting the invitation to participate in this otherwise appealing research project.

Even if no member of the department of obstetrics and gynecology will be involved in the project, you or others participating in it necessarily will become involved in that department insofar as it is doing the abortions. For surely you will not receive the tissue in the precise condition it would be in when dumped into the incinerator. Rather, at a minimum, you will have to arrange that it be kept apart, handled with special care, and delivered to you in timely fashion. Very likely, further arrangements will be needed affecting the methods and timing of abortions. So, researchers, perhaps including you, will have to become involved in the activities of those doing abortions insofar as those activities will serve your research project. Such involvement, I believe, would constitute the "complicity in deliberate abortion" condemned by the Church's teaching.[272] This complicity in deliberate abortion would be morally wrong for at least four reasons.

In the first place, it could lead you to share the evil will of abortionists. For instance, intending to carry the project to successful completion—something impossible unless abortions are done regularly in timely fashion—you might at some point ask that an abortion be scheduled as soon as possible and thus intend that it be done, not merely accept it as given that abortions are done more or less regularly.

Second, even if you avoided sharing abortionists' evil will, your complicity would be scandalous in the strict sense. By enabling abortionists to feel that they are contributing to science, it would provide them with an excuse of a kind especially important in a university hospital where there might otherwise be some

---

272. I think the phrase *complicity in abortion (cum abortu volontario societatem)* refers to all morally unacceptable involvement with abortion, whether that be cooperation, strictly speaking, or not; see Congregation for the Doctrine of the Faith, *Donum vitae,* I, 4, *AAS* 80 (1988) 83, *OR,* 16 Mar. 1987, 3; cf. Joseph Boyle, "Moral Outrage and Medical Benefits," *Ethics and Medics,* 16:4 (Apr. 1991): 3–4.

repugnance to doing many abortions. The research project also probably would be used to reassure women seeking abortion that terminating their pregnancies is not so bad, inasmuch as it would benefit other babies.

Third, this complicity in abortion would make it seem that those participating in the research were not opposed to abortion. In the case of someone like you, who has publicly opposed abortion and joined in efforts against it, your involvement would suggest that your opposition was not deep and sincere but merely superficial. Participation in the research project would thus undercut your prolife witness.

Fourth, from the point of view of the aborted unborn individuals, your involvement also would be unfair. If you were about to be killed unjustly, you surely would regard the plan to make use of your remains as a seal of doom, forestalling possible reconsideration and more energetic opposition by those interested in your welfare. So, you would want everyone to make it clear that he or she would reject any benefit from anyone's killing you. You would be especially upset if even those who had recognized and decried the injustice being done to you betrayed you by their complicity with those perpetrating it, as if little were at stake. Then too, the use of human remains ordinarily requires consent, either in advance by the individual or after death by next of kin acting on behalf of the deceased. Aborted babies obviously cannot have consented, and their mothers, by choosing abortion, forfeit the authority to act in their interests.

Therefore, you should reject this invitation. But your second question remains: If your colleague agrees to participate, as you expect, should you advise him?

I think it would be wrong for you to tell your colleague you will help and advise him. Doing that would have many of the negative features of participating yourself, not least that of making the project's funding and execution more likely. By contrast, telling your colleague you will give him no advice would both reduce the likelihood that the project will go forward and maximize the clarity of your witness. Moreover, since researchers tend to follow up on successful projects, giving no advice, by reducing the likelihood that this project will succeed, might reduce the incentive for other projects using tissue from aborted fetuses.

However, refusing entirely to give advice also might have a significant disadvantage. If the project goes forward despite your refusal to participate, it might be better for it to be more rather than less fruitful, and, if you do not give any advice, it probably will be less fruitful. Therefore, it seems to me, you could stop short of telling your colleague you will give him no advice, and simply say your refusal to participate in the project is a matter of principle—being convinced that abortion is wrong, you want no part in it. By saying that, you would do nothing to encourage the project.

Nevertheless, if and when it is actually under way, you could consider three things: (1) the likelihood that giving advice would indirectly encourage other researchers to use tissue from deliberately aborted fetuses, (2) the extent to which your colleague becomes involved in the abortions, and (3) the likelihood that the project really will benefit other babies. If you judged acceptable the risk that giving advice would indirectly encourage others to use tissue from aborted babies, found your colleague's complicity in abortion to be minimal, and believed the likely

benefits of advising him would be substantial, you might, without directly participating in the project, provide advice that would contribute to its benefits.

In doing so, however, you would, in my judgment, have to observe at least three
limiting conditions. First, you could not become physically involved in any way
with the fetal tissue; or, to put the point affirmatively and perhaps overly simply,
you could advise only in your office, not in the laboratory. Second, you could give
advice only on questions that would be the same if the tissue had been obtained
from spontaneously aborted babies. You could not, for example, help your colleague resolve problems arising from the scheduling of abortions. Third, you could
not allow your name to be listed as an adviser to the project or accept any stipend,
but would have to keep your contribution entirely informal.

With these limits, advising your colleague would have few if any of the bad
features of directly participating in the project. You would avoid sharing in your
colleague's complicity in abortion, and your name would not be identified with the
project. From the point of view of fairness, even the victims of abortion would have
to admit that your advice to your colleague was not so much injurious to them as
it was beneficial to other babies, whom you hoped to help protect from developmental anomalies.

86: May a person work for an organization that funds research using fetal tissue?

For many years I have been working as an administrative assistant for the local
chapter of a national organization whose purpose is to educate the public about a
certain disease, help those afflicted with it, and support research directed toward
improved treatment and some way of preventing or curing the disease. Much of
my work consists in answering the telephone, and very often this involves talking
with people whose family members are seriously ill, trying to console them, and
referring them to support groups and individuals who can help them. To improve
my work, I took a college evening course in counseling at my own expense, and I
also have read several books and articles on the disease as well as all the educational
materials the organization provides.

Within the last year, the national organization started funding research involving
the use of human fetal tissue obtained from induced abortions. I am firmly
convinced we should not be funding this research, because using the tissue is wrong
and because funding such research is likely to cost the organization the support of
prolife donors. I have made my views known to my superiors here and to the
national president. It did no good, except that my immediate superior told me that,
if anyone asked me about this matter, I could frankly say I disapprove of what is
being done, and refer any further questions to him.

Should I quit? That would mean giving up my work on the telephone, which
I personally find very rewarding and believe does a lot of good. But part of my
work (ten to fifteen percent of my time) does help the national organization's
fund raising—for example, mailing acknowledgments of donations we receive
locally, sending information to people who contact us about donating, and so on.

Most of the funds raised are used for good purposes, but the funding for fetal research will be about two percent of next year's budget. Also, by referring people who ask questions to my superior, I am helping him handle the problem this funding is causing.

Analysis:

This question concerns material cooperation in raising funds, part of which support research that is involved with abortion. By funding research that uses tissue obtained in abortions, the organization becomes involved in the abortions. Applying the usual criteria, this complicity is wrong, and people should not donate to the organization without some special reason. The questioner, however, mainly engages in morally good work that not only serves others but is self-fulfilling; she or he cooperates only materially in the organization's fund raising. Applying the usual criteria, I believe this material cooperation probably is morally acceptable. Still, perhaps the questioner should quit and attempt to get the organization to end its support for the morally objectionable research.

The reply could be along the following lines:

In trying to improve your work by taking a course in counseling at your own expense and studying several books on the disease with which your organization is concerned, you manifested your dedication to serving both people afflicted with the disease and their families. While this dedication is morally required of people doing work like yours, not everyone in such a position is conscientious enough to attend to the requirement and make the necessary commitment. Too many, not caring enough for those who need help, are content to do only what they must to earn their pay.

In funding research using fetal tissue, your organization intends the research and becomes associated with abortion (see q. 85, above). Since the good of health is part of the good of life itself, in supporting such research the organization undercuts its witness to its own laudable, general purpose. Moreover, deriving from abortion what most people are likely to suppose is an important benefit, the organization's research funding makes killing the unborn less repugnant, which, in turn, encourages people to have abortions. Therefore, I believe you are right about the organization's responsibility. It should not be funding research that involves it in induced abortion. From this it follows that potential donors with no compelling reason to donate to the organization should not do so, but should instead support other worthy organizations whose activities include none that are morally tainted.

If you were engaged directly in the fund raising—for example, by personally urging people to donate—you would share fully in the organization's objectively wrong effort to encourage potential donors to do what they should not. In that case, I would say you should stop doing that work and, if necessary, quit your job. However, your involvement in the fund raising apparently consists merely in fulfilling a secretary's normal responsibilities: mailing acknowledgments, sending out requested information, and referring people to a superior when they ask questions about the organization's research funding. It thus appears that you need only assist indirectly in the organization's fund raising, which itself is involved only indirectly in abortions. Being further removed from the evil of abortion than the organization itself and having been authorized to inform callers of your position, you can continue to bear plausible personal witness to the truth about abortion, and you do almost nothing toward making it respectable. Moreover, you probably can keep your job without unfairness to babies who might be aborted, because you have good reasons for keeping it, while quitting probably would not save even one baby's life. Consequently, it seems to me you need not quit your job and probably should keep it.

Suppose, however, you thought you could get the organization to end its wrongful research funding by resigning and campaigning publicly against this part of its program. Then, you might have a duty to take that course, not only for the sake of victims of abortion, but for the sake of the organization. Motivating it to end its wrongdoing would be an act of loyalty, promoting its true good: fidelity to its own purpose and retaining the support of its prolife donors. Even so, of course, you might have a duty to keep your job—for example, if you thought it unlikely that you would find another adequate to meet your genuine needs and/or thought it unlikely that the organization could replace you with someone who would give as much help as you do to people in serious need of it. Again, you might have other responsibilities incompatible with campaigning against the organization's funding of the objectionable research, so that quitting would be pointless.

In sum, while I can imagine conditions under which you should quit, I do not think what you have told me about your work and its circumstances points to an obligation to do so. Indeed, I am inclined to think you should not, but rather should continue giving dedicated service to people who need your help.

If you were not doing good work or the organization did not value your work, I doubt that your immediate superior would have told you that you may tell anyone who asks about the organization's funding of the objectionable research that you do not approve of it. So, it seems likely that your position is secure enough for you to continue to urge your local superiors and the national president to reconsider the decision to fund research using tissue from induced abortions. You might, for example, draw up a petition and get as many of your fellow employees as possible to sign it. Still, you may have compelling reasons for not engaging in such activities. Consequently, just as I cannot answer your original question with a simple yes or no, so I cannot say you ought to do more than you have already done to try to get the organization to reconsider.

If you do decide to give up your job, look for another where you can use your gifts, especially your preparation and experience in counseling, in meeting people's serious need. Indeed, the likelihood of finding such a position should be a consideration in your deliberation about whether to quit your present job.

+ + +

87: How far may Catholic hospitals cooperate with providers of immoral services?

As you may know, the religious institute of women to which I belong always has been committed to health care. We regard it as an apostolate that continues in our day an essential part of Jesus' own ministry during his earthly life. At present, our various provinces operate hospitals in many communities and several states.

In times past, we carried on our work autonomously, ignoring most other health care providers while allowing some non-Catholics to work in our hospitals under conditions we set. Today, however, mutually agreeable cooperative relationships with those who do not share our faith and ethical views are becoming increasingly vital. There are four reasons: the increasing complexity of health care, which requires many forms of cooperation to meet the needs of the people we serve; the need to eliminate duplication in order to limit escalating costs; the demands of payers (the government and insurance companies) that we meet their conditions with respect to benefits and adapt to their arrangements for financing them; and the resistance of non-Catholics (and also of Catholics who do not agree with some of the Church's teachings) to the U.S. bishops' *Ethical and Religious Directives.* Given the trends of the time, our hospitals either will participate in various sorts of cooperative relationships or will become increasingly marginalized and ultimately financially nonviable.

Recognizing this dilemma, our superiors have established an interprovincial committee, of which I am a member, to develop guidelines for various types of cooperative arrangements. While difficult to sort out and classify, these appear to fall into four broad groups, though with some overlap: (1) simple contractual arrangements with other hospitals, diagnostic facilities, individual physicians, and so forth; (2) integrated delivery networks, that is, broad affiliations with other institutions and providers to deliver the complete spectrum of health care in a particular locality; (3) cosponsored health maintenance organizations or similar deliverers of health care to certain groups of insured people; and (4) arrangements assuming responsibility for a purchased portion of the practices of a group of physicians and/or other providers who, at the same time, will remain free to offer the same or other clientele services in which we feel we cannot participate.

The recently revised *Ethical and Religious Directives* and the committee's initial discussions seem to indicate that, where the ethical aspects are concerned, two matters will be central.

First, while our commitment to the health care apostolate requires that we do whatever is necessary under rapidly changing conditions to continue delivering quality services, we must find ways to maintain our institutions' Catholic identity even as we surrender some of our traditional autonomy and legal control.

Second, though we will not sponsor any forbidden procedures (such as sterilizations and abortions) in our own hospitals, we necessarily will cooperate with those who perform them; therefore, we must clarify the ways in which formal cooperation might arise in the delivery of services under various arrangements, and try to limit our hospitals' involvement to material cooperation.

Though I know you probably will not be able to say much on the basis of such a general description of the problems we face, I will be grateful for any suggestions you can offer regarding their ethical aspects.

Analysis:

The questioner seeks fuller answers to two closely related questions touched on briefly in the 1994 revision of the *Ethical and Religious Directives*. The first question concerns the Catholic identity of Catholic hospitals, and calls for a clarification of the concept of the health care apostolate and the likely impact on it of entering into and carrying on the sorts of arrangements described. The second question concerns formal and material cooperation. An adequate response must explain two things. (1) Formal cooperation can occur not only in carrying on a cooperative arrangement but also, and even especially, in setting it up. (2) Material cooperation also can be wrong, and a Catholic hospital's material cooperation with the provision of morally unacceptable services is likely to be wrong. Catholic hospitals that avoid all wrongful cooperation and maintain their identity may not be economically viable. Therefore, Catholics committed to health care as an apostolate may have to look for other, better ways of carrying it on.[273]

The reply could be along the following lines:

As you say, I cannot provide specific moral advice in response to a general question. However, I will sketch out some considerations that I think the administrators of your hospitals should keep in mind as they deliberate about entering into any cooperative arrangement with other providers.

First, because Catholic identity is maintained by living up to the moral requirements of faith and is obscured, and ultimately abandoned, by living as nonbelievers do, the questions about Catholic identity and the moral limits of cooperation are not separable. Clarifying the concept of the apostolate of health care and its roots in Jesus' ministry will help answer both questions.

Since death is humankind's last enemy (see 1 Cor 15.26) and is part of the punishment for sin (see DS 1511/788), Jesus' redemptive mission was to overcome not only sin but death by making available resurrection and everlasting life. As health perfects life, disease detracts from it and ends in death. Thus, Jesus raised the dead and cured people of diseases. Yet, though these miracles no doubt were motivated partly by compassion for the suffering individuals he helped, Jesus' principal intention in healing people was to provide signs and foretastes of the coming of God's kingdom. Had he been committed to providing health care, having the power to cure everyone and raise all the dead, he would have done so. This consideration makes it clear that simply delivering quality health care services, as even some nonbelievers do, does not carry on an essential part of Jesus' ministry.

In commending the health care service of consecrated persons, John Paul II clarifies what is required if such work is to be a genuine apostolate:

---

273. Appendix 2 is especially relevant to this question; its last two sections comment on the appendix on formal and material cooperation in the 1994 revision of the *ERDs* and the moral significance of various sorts of pressure—"duress" in a wide sense.

The church looks with admiration and gratitude upon the many consecrated persons who, by caring for the sick and the suffering, contribute in a significant way to her mission. They carry on the ministry of mercy of Christ, who "went about doing good and healing all [who were oppressed by the devil]" (Acts 10.38). In the footsteps of the Divine Samaritan, physician of souls and bodies, and following the example of their respective founders and foundresses, those consecrated persons committed to this ministry by the charism of their Institute should persevere in their witness of love towards the sick, devoting themselves to them with profound understanding and compassion. They should give a special place in their ministry to the poorest and most abandoned of the sick, such as the elderly, and those who are handicapped, marginalized, or terminally ill, and to the victims of drug abuse and the new contagious diseases. Consecrated persons should encourage the sick themselves to offer their sufferings in Communion with Christ, crucified and glorified for the salvation of all. Indeed they should strengthen in the sick the awareness of being able to *carry out a pastoral ministry of their own* through the specific charism of the Cross, by means of their prayer and their testimony in word and deed.

Moreover, the Church reminds consecrated men and women that a part of their mission is *to evangelize the health-care centers* in which they work, striving to spread the light of Gospel values to the way of living, suffering and dying of the people of our day. They should endeavor to make the practice of medicine more human, and increase their knowledge of bioethics at the service of the Gospel of life. Above all therefore they should foster respect for the person and for human life from conception to its natural end, in full conformity with the moral teaching of the Church. For this purpose, they should set up centers of formation and cooperate closely with those ecclesial bodies entrusted with the pastoral ministry of health care.[274]

Thus, to be an apostolate that carries on Jesus' ministry of mercy, Catholic hospitals must not only deliver quality health care but provide service to "the poorest and most abandoned of the sick," give religious instruction and encouragement along with health care, explicitly evangelize, strive to humanize medical practice, fully conform to the Church's moral teaching, and supply sound formation in that teaching. Of course, even isolated individuals' work in the field of health care can qualify as a lay apostolate, in the same way as other morally acceptable occupations Christians might undertake, if carried out in a way that struggles against the evils that afflict such work and restores it in the light of the gospel, manifests Christian mercy, and bears clear witness to faith (see AA 5–7; *LCL,* 102–13). However, Catholic hospitals will have lost their identity unless they meet all the conditions for carrying on Jesus' mission of mercy.[275]

274. John Paul II, *Vita consecrata,* 83 (notes omitted), *AAS* 88 (1996) 460–61, *OR,* 3 Apr. 1996, xvi.

275. Richard McCormick, S.J., "The Catholic Hospital Today: Mission Impossible?" *Origins,* 24 (1995): 648–53, proposes several characteristics of the context in which health care is now being delivered as grounds for suggesting (though he does not firmly assert) that "the heart of the Catholic health care culture is gone. The mission has become impossible" (649). An illustration of the tension between mission and financial viability for one (unnamed) Catholic hospital: Marie Wolff, "'No Margin, No Mission': Challenge to Institutional Ethics," *Business and Professional Ethics Journal,* 12:2 (Summer 1993): 39–50.

The challenge they face must not be underestimated. A hospital is not simply a formal, institutional structure; it is a community whose corporate identity and character depend on the people who make it up. Thus, a Catholic hospital's special apostolate requires that the critical mass of participants be not only practicing Catholics but people whose professional work is permeated by faith and Christian mercy. However, most religious institutes operating hospitals have experienced a decline in new members, and now can staff only a few positions in their hospitals while filling a few others with Catholics who have the necessary characteristics. Hence, even if Catholic hospitals could retain the autonomy they formerly enjoyed, their ability to carry on their special apostolate, and so their very Catholic identity, would be in question.

Second, those entering into cooperative arrangements should not take too narrow a view of the actual and potential problem areas. These are by no means limited to sterilization and abortion. Prescribing contraceptives and helping people use them normally involve formal cooperation with contraception, and even material cooperation, especially with forms of contraception whose mode of action sometimes is abortifacient, can be gravely wrong. Genetic counseling to assist deliberation about contraception, sterilization, and abortion normally involves formal cooperation in those immoral activities. The treatment of sterility often involves formal cooperation in masturbation. In vitro fertilization is morally unacceptable in itself, and procedures such as TOT and GIFT are morally question-able.[276] While treatment often can be rightly limited or withdrawn, either can be a method of suicide or homicide, and both are likely to be abused by coming attempts to ration care on the basis of so-called quality of life, with the result that the elderly, the severely retarded, and others will be unjustly discriminated against and many of them will be victims of homicide by nontreatment and neglect. Active euthanasia also is likely to be legalized, at first by permitting assisted suicide, but eventually by authorizing euthanasia for many people, including some incapable of consent, whose lives others do not consider worth living.

Third, you realize you must "try to limit" your hospitals' involvement in "forbidden procedures" to material cooperation, and say: "We will not sponsor any forbidden procedures (such as sterilizations and abortions) in our own hospitals." You rightly note the importance of clarifying "the ways in which formal coopera-tion might arise in the delivery of services under various arrangements." But you also say that "our commitment to the health care apostolate requires that we do whatever is necessary under rapidly changing conditions to continue delivering quality services." This way of putting the matter suggests that you consider continuing to operate your hospitals as the essential objective and consider avoid-ing wrongdoing as an incidental, though important, concern. Firmly committed to continuing to deliver quality services, you will try to avoid formal cooperation in sterilization and abortion.[277] However, doing God's will and entirely avoiding

276. In my judgment, they are morally similar to the "simple case" of in vitro fertilization; see q. 52, above.

277. Patricia A. Cahill, "Response to 'The Principles of Cooperation and Their Application to the Present State of Health Care Evolution,'" in *The Splendor of Truth and Health Care,*

wrongdoing are at the heart of anything that can be called an apostolate. Do not regard actions such as sterilization and abortion merely as forbidden procedures and do not think of wrongful cooperation with them merely as rule breaking, to be avoided if possible. Recognize such acts as grave injuries to persons or their very destruction, and thus contrary to Christian love and entirely incompatible with your apostolate.

Someone might argue that you can easily avoid formal cooperation if you reluctantly work with non-Catholic providers only insofar as you must in order to continue operating your hospitals. Acting under duress, it might be argued, your participation in necessary cooperative arrangements will not be formal cooperation; it will be like the submission of a woman threatened with death by a would-be rapist: in order to save her life, the woman obeys his orders to undress and assume a certain position. Plainly such a woman chooses only to do things morally acceptable in themselves for the good end of saving her life, and she neither intends sexual intercourse with the rapist as an end nor chooses it as a means. So, the argument could conclude, your hospitals need neither intend nor choose any forbidden procedure. They need only choose to take the morally acceptable steps they must take to survive.

True, duress can lead one to choose to carry out another's orders by doing things that, though not wrong in themselves, ordinarily would be chosen only if one wished to cooperate in a wrongful common action. But duress also can lead one to choose reluctantly to adopt an immoral way of life and cooperate in common actions. The desperate woman who reluctantly chooses to become a prostitute as a way of earning her living formally cooperates in immoral acts, though with considerably mitigated guilt. Unlike the rape victim, who chooses to submit passively to violence, and like the desperate woman who chooses prostitution, your hospitals, though under duress, may well come to cooperate formally in the immoral activities of other parties to the complex arrangements into which the hospitals are constrained to enter.

Since sponsoring acts of mutilation and killing in your own hospitals plainly would be formal cooperation with those evils, you rightly reject doing so. But even without sponsoring immoral procedures carried out in a hospital, those responsible

---

Proceedings of the Fourteenth Workshop for Bishops, ed. Russell E. Smith (Braintree, Mass: The Pope John Center, 1995), 238–42, makes the point (239): "The majority of joint ventures, networks, mergers and affiliations which have occurred and which are on the drawing board are, from my observation, driven from a business or economic perspective. The leaders responsible for consummating these arrangements understand the business world well. They also understand and support fully the fact that no proscribed services may be offered by their own Catholic institution. However, when the transaction under consideration is between the Catholic provider and a non-Catholic provider and its consummation promises improved fiscal well-being for the Catholic partner, attention sometimes shifts from strict adherence to the *Ethical and Religious Directives* to a tone of compromise which recognizes the ethical perspective of the non-Catholic provider and softens the principle to achieve the desired outcome. These are not people who intend to do wrong but they are people who have not necessarily had the theological and philosophical preparation to address appropriately the material cooperation questions before them. They hear the term 'material cooperation' but do not understand its philosophical underpinnings and rationale and thus, in my opinion, are ill equipped to apply the principle to the matter at hand."

for the hospital can formally cooperate with such procedures. Indeed, if a hospital is involved in a cooperative arrangement with providers who do immoral procedures, its administrators can formally cooperate in those procedures even if they are done elsewhere and without using any of their hospital's facilities.

Unlike people who manage a hotel, the administrators of a hospital ordinarily do sponsor the things done in it. Since a hospital exists to provide health care services, administrators ordinarily intend each and every procedure carried out using its facilities. Of course, if a hospital's administrators were blamelessly unaware of wrong things done in it, they would not cooperate with them, and they might avoid formally cooperating even with certain wrongful activities done in the hospital they knew about but neither initiated nor facilitated. However, administrators hardly can avoid cooperating formally with procedures such as sterilization and abortion done using their hospital's facilities. They must ensure that patients, having been adequately informed, genuinely consent, and must see to it that the procedures are carried out correctly. Therefore, when such a procedure is done in a hospital, even if its administrators not only avoid sponsoring it but are very displeased about its being done, they are likely to cooperate formally in it.

Formal cooperation also can occur without a hospital's facilities being used when the hospital is involved in a cooperative arrangement with providers of sterilization, abortion, and other evils. Suppose that the arrangement to provide the complete spectrum of health care in a locality or all services for participants in a health maintenance organization includes some immoral activity of at least one of the other providers involved in this joint enterprise. In that case, all who share responsibility for managing the enterprise will formally cooperate in that activity insofar as they must ensure that patients give informed consent and that those directly involved meet professional standards. Therefore, if your hospitals enter an arrangement with providers of any evil, they either must avoid all responsibility for managing the joint enterprise or entirely exclude from it the evils other parties provide.

Moreover, your hospitals will be involved not just in delivering services after an arrangement has been made but in making the arrangement.[278] Moral norms can be violated at this stage.

Suppose, for instance, a governmental agency, insurer, or non-Catholic health care provider sought to create an entity to provide the full range of services that at least some of the prospective clientele and parties to the cooperative arrangement think pertain to health care. Suppose a Catholic hospital was a potential party to the prospective arrangement. The negotiators might agree that nothing contrary to the *Ethical and Religious Directives* would be done in the Catholic hospital or sponsored by it; they might even arrange that providers working in the Catholic hospital would never be called on to refer for excluded services or follow up on them. To ensure that the Catholic hospital would be able to avoid such unacceptable cooperation, they also would agree that one of the other parties to the arrangement

---

278. William B. Smith, "Cooperation in Health Care," *Homiletic and Pastoral Review,* 96:9 (July 1996): 70–72, agrees in questioning the possibility of avoiding formal cooperation with other parties' wrongdoing when setting up the joint arrangement.

would provide the excluded services for clients who wanted them. This arrangement seemingly would neatly divide responsibility, isolating the Catholic hospital from immoral activities.

In making the arrangement, however, the Catholic negotiators, intending to avoid providing the immoral services in their hospital, would have intended that another party supply them. So, making the arrangement would be formal cooperation in the other party's supplying them. Moreover, when those authorized to act on behalf of the Catholic hospital signed the contract, the hospital would be agreeing to all its provisions and intending its doing so to motivate the other parties to agree to the contract and do as they agreed. So, since one of the other contracting parties would have undertaken to provide immoral services, the hospital would be formally cooperating in that undertaking and its execution as long as the contract remained in force.

Someone might object that nothing the Catholic hospital did would bring about anything immoral. The governmental agency, insurer, or non-Catholic health care provider initiating negotiations might well have decided beforehand that certain services, such as sterilization, would be provided, "either because the market 'necessitates' this or because the government will mandate a basic benefits package which will require provision of all services." And, indeed, the immoral services would be provided even if the Catholic hospital did not participate—the arrangement "designed this way will neither increase nor decrease the number of prohibited procedures." Moreover, the objection will continue: "The 'moral object' of the Catholic provider is the provision of health care as a Gospel mission." So: "The moral object of creating [the entity] is precisely *not* to provide prohibited procedures." Therefore, the objection will conclude: "Since our intention is *not* to provide services we deem immoral, cooperation seems to be *material.*"[279]

The problem with this argument is that it treats the Catholic hospital's intended end—providing health care as an apostolate without being involved in immoral procedures—as the moral object of its choice to participate in the arrangement. But the object of that choice precisely is to make an arrangement for "provision of all services," and in choosing to make this arrangement, each contracting party intends the others to make and carry out the undertakings required of them by the arrangement. Therefore, to achieve its good end the Catholic hospital chooses a bad means: to have the immoral procedures provided by another party to the arrangement. Even if no more immoral procedures are done than would have been done in the absence of the arrangement, the Catholic hospital will have intended to arrange that the immoral procedures be done as a necessary means to "the provision of health care as a Gospel mission."

But, it might be argued, this formal cooperation could be avoided. Your hospitals could refuse to agree to anything more than this: "We are only going to do together what all partners agree is appropriate and anything deemed

279. The quotations in the argument are from Russell E. Smith, "The Principles of Cooperation and Their Application to the Present State of Health Care Evolution," in *The Splendor of Truth and Health Care,* 228–29.

inappropriate must be the private project of that proponent."[280] Thus, the contract would omit all reference to immoral activities except to make it clear that the Catholic provider would not provide them and that the cooperative arrangement in no way concerned them. The Catholic negotiators could require that the contract not specify that any party to it would provide any immoral service. They could even require that the contract's effectiveness not be contingent on any agreement between the other parties for the provision of any immoral service.

One can imagine making agreements with provisions of that sort, and such agreements could be made and carried out without formally cooperating in another party's immoral procedures. But an agreement with such provisions hardly would satisfy those who "mandate a basic benefits package which will require provision of all services." To satisfy them, negotiators might work out an arrangement to provide all services but agree to formalize it in two or more legal documents so that the Catholic party would not be required to sign any contract that made reference to immoral procedures except in specifying that the Catholic party would not provide them. However, if the set of documents gave effect to the whole arrangement, the choices of all parties in signing any of them would depend on one another's undertakings in the same way as they would if a single contract straight-forwardly implemented the agreement to provide all services, and the Catholic hospital would formally cooperate in providing all of them.

In sum, entirely avoiding formal cooperation in immoral practices will be difficult indeed. It can arise in ways that are not obvious and it seems unavoidable in any arrangement that would satisfy a mandate to provide all services. Though I have pointed out some of the problems, there might well be others.

Fourth, avoiding formal cooperation in wrongdoing is not enough. Even if it can be avoided, your hospitals will materially cooperate with all the services by other providers in any way facilitated by a cooperative arrangement. Such material cooperation can be morally unacceptable for several reasons. It can occasion a sin of formal cooperation; it can be scandalous; materially cooperating with wrongdoing can impair the capacity to give credible witness against it; and it can be unfair to those injured by the wrongdoing.

In providing health care, one who materially cooperates in wrongdoing often will be tempted to cooperate formally for three closely related reasons. Health care providers ordinarily share the intentions of those they serve; particular services ordinarily must be integrated into a comprehensive pattern of care; and the problem with morally excluded services very often is that a bad means is chosen to attain an appropriate end. For example, if a woman's or family's physical and/or psycho-logical health calls for birth regulation and the woman refuses morally acceptable means, any health care provider sharing responsibility for her care will be tempted not only to refer her to someone who will prescribe other means but to try to ensure that she uses her chosen means regularly and effectively. Even if a Catholic

280. Russell E. Smith, "Ethical Quandary: Forming Hospital Partnerships," *Linacre Quarterly,* 63:2 (May 1996): 90.

hospital's policy excludes such formal cooperation, members of its staff and some other personnel—some and perhaps many of whom do not accept the truth the Church teaches on such matters—almost certainly will be drawn into it.

If a Catholic hospital is to carry on its work as an apostolate, its board members and administrators should deal with formal cooperation in various evils by its personnel. If those responsible instead studiously avoid noticing such formal cooperation or decide to tolerate it, they at least materially cooperate in it in a way that hardly can be justified. As a community committed to an apostolate, the hospital will have betrayed itself even if its board members and administrators manage to stop just short of letting its own complicity in evil become formal cooperation.

Material cooperation with wrongdoing can be scandalous in the strict sense: It can lead people to sin by encouraging them in rationalization and self-deception (which do not free them of guilt) regarding the wrongdoing. The scandal would not be prevented by a Catholic institution's prohibition of morally unacceptable procedures within the domain remaining to it, even if that policy is well publicized. For to most non-Catholics and many Catholics the material cooperation would seem to imply that those procedures are not wrong in themselves but merely forbidden to Catholics, as eating meat on Friday used to be. Moreover, other things being equal, a Catholic institution's material cooperation is much more likely to be scandalous than an individual Catholic's. The institution's acts are presumed to be fully deliberate and free, not the product of ignorance or weakness, as an individual's might be. And since the institution claims to be distinguished from others by being Catholic, whatever it does is taken by many non-Catholics and even unsophisticated Catholics to be the Church's own act.

In various ways, a Catholic institution's significant, obvious, voluntary cooperation in wrongdoing inevitably will impair and probably even negate its capacity to provide credible witness. For example, commingled with the service of secularized providers, its activities will become less identifiable and less distinctively Catholic. Again, the closer association with health care providers whose practice violates moral norms taught by the Church often will make it harder for a Catholic institution's administrators and staff to speak out for the truth of those norms and work against their violation. Its partnership in an integrated delivery network or cosponsorship of an HMO providing sterilization, abortion, or euthanasia will strongly suggest that the Catholic Church does not really and firmly reject these evils but only maintains an insincere official opposition. For those engaged in health care as an apostolate to impair their witness in these and other ways would be utterly self-defeating, since, to repeat, the essence of apostolate is not only to promote a human good such as health but to practice Christian love and bear witness to the gospel's truth, including love for the tiniest and the most debilitated of Jesus' sisters and brothers, and the moral truths regarding how they are to be dealt with.

The material cooperation itself, together with the scandal and impairment of witness, will have consequences. Some individuals will die or suffer lesser injuries that might have been prevented if those who profess the sacredness of life and the dignity of persons consistently avoided complicity in wrongful behavior. Accepting these bad consequences is likely to be unfair unless the victims themselves freely consent to what they suffer. Like individuals, institutions should be prepared to make great sacrifices rather than allow anything they do to bring about the death of—or grave injury to—an innocent person.

Someone might argue that many health care providers who do not accept Catholic moral teaching are convinced that what they are doing is right, and if those with whom a Catholic hospital cooperates act out of sincere consciences, their good faith calls for respect that can justify otherwise excluded material cooperation. But Catholic hospital administrators are responsible for their own acts. The apparent sincerity of conscience of others—their actual consciences are unavailable to us—does call for respect and sometimes justifies toleration of objective wrongdoing. But their apparent good faith may even increase the temptation to cooperate formally with them by making such cooperation seem less repugnant. And if some who appear to be acting in good faith actually are rationalizing and deceiving themselves, cooperating with them can give very serious scandal by making it more difficult for them to acknowledge the truth and repent. Similarly, cooperating with others presumed to be in good faith makes it not easier but in some ways more difficult to bear clear witness to the truth about what they are doing. And even real good faith cannot reduce the unfairness to third parties involved in helping bring about effects injurious or destructive to them.

In view of these considerations, it seems to me that limited material cooperation with non-Catholic providers is least likely to be morally excluded from the first and fourth of the types of cooperative arrangements you mention: specific forms of cooperation with other providers, and purchasing and administering the morally acceptable services of other providers. As for the second and third types of cooperative arrangements, even if a Catholic hospital can participate in an integrated delivery network or cooperatively operated health maintenance organization with others who provide immoral procedures while avoiding formal cooperation in them, I doubt that it can justifiably engage in the material cooperation that any such arrangement would require of it. Moreover, operating within the cooperative arrangement, the Catholic hospital's distinctive characteristics and practices would be likely to be marginalized or even completely suppressed, so that even if it maintained its juridical ties with the Church, it will no longer carry on Jesus' ministry of mercy and will have lost its Catholic identity.

Fifth, the preceding considerations make it clear that you cannot assume that you always will be able to enter into the arrangements necessary to keep a hospital financially viable while entirely avoiding wrongful cooperation. Therefore, you ought to be prepared to give up at least some—and eventually, perhaps, all—of your hospitals. In bearing witness, individual Christians are expected to sacrifice even life itself when that is necessary. Should not your institute be ready to bear witness by giving up its hospitals and finding other ways of carrying on its apostolate under today's changing conditions?

Many dedicated and generous women and men put their money and effort into building the system of Catholic hospitals founded and operated by your institute and others. Health care fully integrated with Catholic faith, moral teaching, and pastoral care would otherwise have been unavailable; some cities and towns would have lacked hospitals; and many poor people would have been deprived of hospital care. Without Catholic teaching hospitals, Catholics would not have had the opportunity to be trained as physicians and nurses in full harmony with their faith and in a way that helped many of them carry on their professional work as a true apostolate.

Since Catholic hospital administrators today are, as it were, trustees for those who built the system, your superiors rightly wish to adapt to the changed situation and carry on the apostolate, if possible. But they would betray their trust in saving their hospitals by changing them in ways their founders and their supporters would not approve. Institutions like hospitals are only means for carrying out a health care apostolate. Like other means, their usefulness is limited. Remaining attached to them as their usefulness diminishes will entail infidelity to the good they formerly served.

Many of the benefits that flowed in the past from operating Catholic hospitals will no longer be realized if they are merged into the secularized health care system, and some of those benefits could be realized even without Catholic hospitals. To provide health care fully integrated with Catholic faith, moral teaching, and pastoral care surely is a noble ideal. But how likely is it to be realized by a Catholic hospital whose services are merged into an integrated delivery network or HMO cosponsored by secularized providers? Do Catholic hospitals really do better than secular providers by people with financial problems, and, if so, can this difference be maintained within a cooperative arrangement? Catholic teaching hospitals offer a valuable opportunity for Catholics to be trained in full accord with their faith only if their programs are consistently Catholic, and if nurses and doctors completing those programs will be able to practice without moral compromise in the fields for which they trained. But where such principled practice remains possible, the technical training for it is likely to be available outside Catholic teaching hospitals, and individuals can acquire their indispensable moral and spiritual formation by private study and from faithful Catholic mentors whose concerns extend to health care.

Finally, just as individuals maintain their Christian identity by constantly seeking, accepting, and faithfully fulfilling their personal vocations, so groups of Christians who make up associations maintain their identity as Christian communities only by fidelity to their proper missions. Fidelity precludes questioning basic commitments, such as the vows by which you and other members of your institute have consecrated your lives. But it also calls for periodic reconsideration of all projects undertaken to implement those basic commitments. Like discernment pertaining to vocation, this reconsideration should seek to match gifts and resources with the opportunities to serve others by meeting their genuine needs, not only for temporal goods but for spiritual ones. In carrying on such reconsideration, members of your institute might ask: What health care needs are now unmet and likely to remain unmet by others? And what gifts equip us for meeting some of those needs?

Today, I believe, clearheaded and courageous reflection may well point toward refusing to accept a subordinate role for your hospitals in a secularized health care system and instead adopting more suitable means of serving people most in need and least served by the secularized system. Candidates for your service include the terminally ill who need appropriate care to die with true dignity rather than by the indignity of suicide or homicide,[281] handicapped individuals whose quality of life falls below some arbitrarily set limit, unborn babies whose abortions the system would provide and whose mothers need help to choose an alternative, couples who need instruction in natural family planning, the working poor who lack health insurance, people too disorganized to make use of the health care system, the mentally ill who have been "freed" from institutions to wander in the streets, and other victims of selfishness and ideological fashions. By serving these "poorest and most abandoned" and joining explicit catechesis and evangelization to that service, your institute could in truth continue to carry on Jesus' ministry of mercy.

88: Should a head nurse cooperate with her hospital's United Way campaign?

I am a laywoman and the head nurse in a large Catholic hospital. The administrator, Sister Jane, and I disagree about participation in the local United Way campaign.[282] In the past, no organization providing abortion services was included; this year, Planned Parenthood, which operates abortion clinics here, is listed. That might not seem a problem, since donors can designate the organizations they want to receive their contributions. But that is unlikely to make any real difference, because designation has an effect only if the total designated for an organization is greater than the amount it would receive as its budgeted share of the total amount donated in the campaign[283]—which seldom happens in this city, because most people do not designate. Consequently, our local right-to-life organization is urging people who oppose abortion to refuse to contribute to United Way unless and until it takes Planned Parenthood off the list, and instead to contribute directly to organizations of their choice. Personally, that is what I am going to do.

The hospital gets some money from United Way, though, and Sister Jane insists that we must urge everyone on the payroll to contribute enough to reach the target set for us by the United Way guidelines. Otherwise, she argues, the hospital will seem deficient in community spirit, with potentially disastrous consequences. Though the hospital has won a broad base of support by serving the

---

281. Sheila Cassidy, *Sharing the Darkness: The Spirituality of Caring* (Maryknoll, N.Y: Orbis Books, 1991), shows both how providing hospice care can be a true apostolate and how great the need is for such care; as the culture of death intensifies, the need and apostolic potential of such work will increase. For a fuller understanding of hospices and how they differ from hospitals, see Sandol Stoddard, *The Hospice Movement: A Better Way of Caring for the Dying,* rev. ed. (New York: Vintage Books, 1992).

282. A United Way campaign is a method of fund raising for many charitable and welfare organizations in a particular city or metropolitan region. By participating in a common effort, the organizations reduce the costs of fund raising. The rules for dividing the funds raised differ somewhat in various places.

283. The possibilities and effects of designation by donors to United Way campaigns have varied at different times and in different places; see Eleanor L. Brilliant, *The United Way: Dilemmas of Organized Charity* (New York: Columbia University Press, 1990), 103–9.

whole community (most of our patients are not Catholics), she is afraid that being perceived as sectarian will cost us some support, so that we may not be able to balance our budget. Although I told her I am not going to contribute to United Way, she is pressing me to cooperate with the campaign. I feel that would be hypocritical and told her so. She cannot compel me to cooperate but is quite angry with me. Do you think I should cooperate? If not, can you give me any arguments that might change Sister Jane's mind?

Analysis:

This question concerns material cooperation in abortion. Though participating in a United Way campaign that helps fund abortion providers need not be formal cooperation in abortion, even as material cooperation it would be morally unacceptable, in my judgment, in the absence of compelling reasons. Sister Jane argues that there are compelling reasons for the hospital to cooperate. But the questioner sees no compelling reasons to cooperate personally, and so rightly refuses. Sister Jane might argue that the questioner's conscience is in error, and that the hospital's common good provides her and other loyal employees with a compelling reason to cooperate. However, contributing to civic causes pertains to people's responsibility as citizens rather than as employees, and the common good of the civic community is not served by participating in a United Way campaign that funds abortion providers.

The reply could be along the following lines:

Even though it is likely that a portion of every contribution to the United Way campaign you describe funds abortions through funding Planned Parenthood, organizations such as your hospital could cooperate with the campaign without intending that abortions be done; so, too, could individuals such as you. The sole intention could be to serve good purposes, including assisting worthy recipients, while only accepting as an unwanted side effect the use of part of each contribution for killing unborn babies. Participation on that basis would not be wrong in itself. Yet, in the absence of compelling reasons, it seems to me such participation would be unjustifiable.

In the first place, it is easily avoidable. Nobody wishing to contribute to worthy organizations needs to channel contributions through United Way. Then too, even if contributing to the United Way campaign probably will provide little funding for abortions, doing so tends to undercut the clear witness that should be given to the truth about abortion. By suggesting it is not as horrible as it is, contributing could lead some women to have abortions who otherwise would not do so. Moreover, in the absence of compelling reasons, donating money that facilitates abortions is fair neither to the babies who will be killed nor to people whose genuine needs would be served by channeling one's donations more appropriately.

Considering your question in this perspective, I think reformulating it as two questions will clarify your disagreement with Sister Jane. Are there compelling reasons for the hospital to cooperate with the United Way campaign? Are there compelling reasons for you and other employees to contribute? She argues that there are compelling reasons for the hospital to cooperate—not doing so will weaken the community support it needs. You personally see no compelling reason to contribute, however, and so you rightly refuse. Assuming other employees also lack compelling reasons, you cannot consistently urge them to contribute. That would not be hypocrisy—a pretense of virtue by someone lacking it—but a more serious sin, since advising others to do what you consider wrong would be scandal, that is, leading them into sin.

If you explain your position in these terms to Sister Jane, she may see that your refusal to cooperate with her in administering the United Way campaign is principled and may stop pressing you to act against your conscience. But she may argue that your conscience is erroneous. Thus far, her argument to you has been that the hospital's common good depends on broad-based public support, to retain which employees must contribute enough to meet the hospital's United Way quota. To complete this argument, she could supply some missing premises: You and other employees should be loyal, and loyal employees should protect and promote the hospital's good. Therefore, she might conclude, you and other employees have a compelling reason to contribute.

The first point to make in reply is that, while loyal employees certainly should act for the sake of the hospital's good insofar as they are members of this health care community, they also have other roles and responsibilities. Voluntarily contributing within their means to worthy causes in the local civic community pertains to their role as citizens, not to their role as participants in the hospital's health care community. So, in pressing you to cooperate with her in carrying on the United Way campaign in the hospital, Sister Jane is abusing her authority. Moreover, in deciding whether to contribute despite the campaign's funding of Planned Parenthood's baby-killing activities, you and other hospital employees, like all citizens, should consider, not the hospital's common good, but the common good of the civic community. That good is corrupted rather than served when the community actively assists abortion. Therefore, neither hospital employees nor other citizens should contribute to a United Way campaign that helps fund abortions.

Furthermore, you and other hospital employees can question whether reaching the hospital's quota in order to maintain broad-based community support actually will serve the hospital's true common good. If the community really needs it, the hospital probably will be given the means to continue providing service, even if its current Catholic sponsors and administrators lose public support and have to turn it over to the city or some other sponsoring body. It is likely that some employees—and perhaps many—have no commitment to health care as a Catholic apostolate; for them, a change in the hospital's sponsorship and administration might seem no harm or even a benefit. Other employees, no doubt, do have such a commitment; but, understanding the hospital's good in terms of apostolate, they can reasonably deny that its cooperation in this campaign really will serve its good. How can a Catholic hospital cooperate even remotely in killing babies without betraying itself so utterly that it would do far better to bear witness faithfully by ceasing to exist? Martyrdom can be required of any individual Christian. Why not also of Christian institutions?

Nevertheless, while martyrdom should be accepted joyfully when it is inevitable, it may be avoided provided there is an acceptable way of doing that. Perhaps then there is a way for the hospital to retain both its integrity and the broad-based support it needs. In concert with the hospital's board of directors, for instance, Sister Jane could state publicly that the hospital cannot cooperate in this year's United Way campaign because its funding of Planned Parenthood's baby killing is not only wicked but wholly repugnant to the hospital's purpose. At the same time, having prepared a plan with the hospital's employees and perhaps with other employers in the community, she could announce that the hospital will encourage and facilitate contributions by its employees to a separate fund, to be distributed to acceptable United Way beneficiaries. In this way, the hospital would bear witness to the truth about abortion while manifesting appropriate community spirit.

Sister Jane might argue that this alternative would not retain the support the hospital needs. But if that is so, the hospital must have already deeply compromised its Catholic character: not by serving non-Catholics, since extending its apostolate to everyone, especially the poor, is its very reason for being; but by soft-pedaling its Catholic character to get money from sources that do not respect its religious commitment. Thus it has become the agent of contributors who wish it to provide services, not as a Catholic health care apostolate, but on some other, incompatible basis. If that is not the case, members of the community who have supported the hospital will continue to do so, for they will not expect its administration and those of its employees who are committed to a Catholic health care apostolate to violate their consciences in fulfilling civic responsibilities, and will be satisfied with the plan for a separate fund.

If Sister Jane accepts the proposal I have sketched out, the hospital (and any other employers that collaborate in setting up a separate fund) will conform to the advice of your local right-to-life group that everyone refuse to contribute to United Way and instead contribute directly to organizations of their choice. Unfortunately, that advice and the publicity likely to result from acting on it may have the bad effect of increasing Planned Parenthood's funding from the United Way campaign. For proponents of "abortion rights" can be expected to respond by urging people to designate Planned Parenthood to receive all or a large part of their contributions, and the total designated for it may well exceed its share of the total amount raised by United Way. But this prospect is not a sound argument for cooperating with the United Way campaign, because the argument against is not based on the desirability of depriving Planned Parenthood of funds but on the undesirability of helping to provide those funds. Killing is profitable in money, but bearing witness to the truth about killing and defending life as best one can are profitable in everlasting wealth (see Mt 16.26, Mk 8.36, Lk 9.25).

+ + +

89: May NFP programs inform clients of alternatives so as to obtain funding?

I am head of an international organization that promotes and supports the teaching of natural family planning (NFP)—that is, birth regulation by means of periodic abstinence from intercourse and the breast feeding of infants. We cooperate with programs for teaching NFP in many third-world nations. Virtually all are directed by people who believe contraceptive birth control and sterilization are immoral, and some are under the direct auspices of the Catholic Church.

The United States Agency for International Development (AID) financially assists a wide variety of birth control programs in third-world nations. However, no funding is granted to any program whose directors do not agree to provide clients with "information about access to a broad range of family planning methods and services." In this context, "family planning methods and services" does not include abortion. In practice, the requirement means that all clients of an NFP program would have to be given a leaflet listing all nearby providers of contraception and sterilization.

Funding is hard to come by. Can directors of programs seeking funding from AID agree to and fulfill this condition without violating their own conscientious convictions that exclude contraception and sterilization?

Analysis:

This question concerns cooperation in sterilization and contraception. In agreeing to provide information about immoral alternatives and providing it, directors of NFP programs and those who work in them need not intend that the information be used, much less that any client choose contraception or sterilization. So, the cooperation involved is not formal, and the usual criteria for evaluating material cooperation are to be applied. If the program is not an activity of the Church herself or any of her agencies, it is morally acceptable, in my judgment, to provide the information. But Church agencies should not, in my judgment, provide information about the availability of immoral methods of birth regulation, because that would compromise the Church's primary mission—bearing witness to God's truth—and might well give scandal.

The reply could be along the following lines:

Applicants for funding who reluctantly agree to provide clients with "information about access to a broad range of family planning methods and services" need only intend to fulfill the agreement insofar as necessary to obtain the funding: to give each client a leaflet listing nearby providers of contraception and sterilization. For applicants to achieve their end it is not necessary that anyone use that information. So, they need not intend to do anything to encourage anyone to contact providers, much less try to get anyone to practice contraception or be sterilized. Thus, the directors of NFP programs who apply for AID funding, intending to persuade everyone to use NFP rather than any immoral method, could meet the requirement to obtain AID funding without intending the use of immoral methods of birth regulation. In what follows, then, I assume that cooperation involving a wrongful intention is not in question.

Because doing anything that might contribute to abortion is likely to be unfair to the person who is unjustly killed, such an action is much more likely to be wrong than doing something that might contribute to contraception or sterilization. It also is crucial that, in the context you describe, abortion is not among the things referred to by "family planning methods and services." Still, IUDs and the various forms of anovulant drugs sometimes act as abortifacients in preventing births, and this fact must be taken into account.

Administrators and workers in NFP programs who provide clients with information about where to obtain contraceptives or be sterilized do call attention to the immoral alternatives. Even if it is unlikely that clients will use the information, the choice to provide it necessarily includes accepting as a side effect the risk of its being used. Thus, providing the information could contribute to the wrongdoing of those offering the immoral methods.

Still, I think meeting this requirement for funding can be justified for public or private programs that are activities neither of the Church herself nor of any of her official agencies. Several considerations support this judgment.

Providing the information is not likely to tempt administrators and workers in NFP programs to share in the immorality of contraception and sterilization by promoting the immoral alternatives. Moreover, the workers are likely to do their best to prevent scandal, that is, leading people into sin. I assume that in distributing the leaflet they will try to forestall misunderstanding by pointing out that it is required by law to obtain funding, will carefully avoid explaining the leaflet in ways likely to encourage its use, and also will take the occasion to instruct clients about the many disadvantages of contraception and sterilization in comparison with NFP.

But can they fairly accept the risk that some clients will use the list of nearby providers to obtain contraceptives that sometimes act as abortifacients, use them, and thus bring about the death of incipient persons? In my judgment, that risk is acceptable. Very often, people seeking help from those providing NFP already have excluded immoral methods. If not, however, the help with NFP that they receive is likely to enlighten and motivate them to commit themselves firmly to family planning consistent with all the relevant goods and moral norms, and to reject the immoral methods that they otherwise might have come to accept. Moreover, even if those directing and working in NFP programs did not provide information about where to obtain immoral methods of birth regulation, people prepared to adopt such methods probably usually would gain access to them. Finally, obtaining AID funding has two sorts of good effects. First, those sponsoring NFP programs are providing an important service to their clients, and the sponsors need funding to carry on their work. Second, if they do not obtain funding from AID, the money, having already been assigned to promote birth regulation, is likely to be used to promote immoral methods.

Someone might object that in the circumstances described administrators and workers in NFP programs are cooperating with the morally excluded services, much as physicians do who refer patients to other physicians to obtain such services (see q. 66, above). The two kinds of cases are similar in some ways, but they also differ in several morally significant respects. First, when physicians refer patients for morally unacceptable services, the physicians no longer can try to persuade the patients to choose a morally acceptable way of dealing with their problems. By contrast, when administrators and workers in NFP programs give a client information about the availability of morally unacceptable services, they obtain an opportunity to try to persuade the client to use NFP. Second, physicians who refer patients for morally unacceptable services do more than provide information; they recommend someone else who will provide a specific service a patient wants and they do not wish to provide themselves. By contrast, administrators and workers in NFP programs do not recommend anyone else to meet the client's need for help in regulating births, but offer to meet that need themselves. Third, because physicians normally intend that the patient obtain the service for which they give a referral, a physician's referral for a morally excluded service is likely to be understood as approval and support for the patient's obtaining it. By contrast, for administrators and workers in NFP programs to provide the required information is an action of a distinct kind, and under the circumstances it will not connote approval and support for using the immoral alternatives.

What about cases in which NFP programs are conducted by a Church agency? May it provide information about access to immoral methods of birth regulation, or may bishops authorize Church agencies to do so? In my judgment, no.

The Church's primary responsibility is to bear witness to God's truth and make the sacraments available. Her mission does include action for social justice and work to promote other human goods, but this responsibility is secondary. If a Church agency were to provide information about where to obtain contraceptives and sterilization, that would tend to obscure and render ambiguous the Church's teaching on birth regulation. In some situations, the agency's providing such information could lead someone into sin and be scandalous in the strict sense. But scandal apart, in my judgment a Church agency should never compromise the Church's primary responsibility, even if it seems necessary to do so in fulfilling her secondary responsibility.

If in certain regions, therefore, Church agencies are providing information about access to immoral methods of birth regulation in order to obtain AID funding for NFP programs, I think one of two things should be done so that the Church will no longer be involved. Either an entity with no institutional or juridical ties to the Church should be established to conduct those programs, or no information should be given regarding immoral methods of birth regulation and the necessary funding should be sought elsewhere.

+ + +

90: What should a patient do about a physician who made a serious mistake?

Two months ago, an examination by a specialist showed that my bones are getting less dense. Her report recommended several things, including another test that involved collecting my urine for twenty-four hours. Having seen my general practitioner, Dr. Robert Burns, I went ahead with that, and, when the results were in, he asked me and my husband to come in and go over them. Dr. Burns told us the urine-sample test showed abnormally high levels of calcium and certain proteins, and said this meant that, despite my apparent good health, I was in the early stages of multiple myeloma, a type of blood cancer that affects the bones. He told us my long-term outlook was not good. Though chemotherapy would keep me going for a while after the disease took hold, treatment probably would not keep it at bay for more than a couple of years. Then it would be out of control; my bones would break up, and I would probably die in a year or two.

He arranged an examination, called a bone scan, for me at the hospital in a nearby city, and I had it the following week. They injected something in a blood vein, and a couple of hours later X–rayed my whole body. Another week, then another visit to Dr. Burns. He said the bone scan had not been any help, and I would have to see a cancer specialist. He set up the appointment for two weeks later.

We were really upset by then, and did not want to wait the two weeks to find out more about what we were up against. My husband has a cousin in California who recently finished medical school and is interning at a university hospital. We got in touch with him, and he told me to fax him the report on the urine-sample test. Dr. Burns did not want to let us have the report, but my husband insisted, and we had it faxed. That evening the cousin called from the office of a medical school professor, who, he told me, is a leading cancer specialist.

The professor was very kind. She told me at once that nothing in the report gave any reason to think I had multiple myeloma or any other sort of cancer. She explained that the report said the sample had no monoclonal proteins, which rules out multiple myeloma rather than points to it. She asked whether I had been put on any new medication or given any treatment, and I said no, but told her about the inconclusive bone scan. She said Dr. Burns should not have sent me for it, even if he'd had some real reason to think I had multiple myeloma. She asked questions about the urine-sample test, and it turned out that the directions Dr. Burns had given me were not clear, and I had mistakenly included urine from two mornings. The professor said that mistake probably partly accounted for the higher-than-normal levels of calcium and proteins. She asked whether I'd ever had any kidney problems, and I said no. She said the lab that did the urine test had included in its report a reference to a medical journal article about diagnosing certain kidney problems, and the article discussed elevated calcium and protein levels as a possible symptom. If I did have a kidney problem, she said, it might not be serious, but I should get it checked out. She told me to cancel the appointment with the cancer specialist and get a new doctor. I told her I have a good gynecologist, whose office is in the city, and the professor said I should ask the gynecologist to recommend someone trained in internal medicine. The professor even gave me her name and phone number, and told me to call her back if I had any more questions. And though she talked to me for over half an hour, she never sent us a bill.

I followed her advice and saw my new doctor two weeks later, the same day I would have been seeing the cancer specialist. When I told my new doctor that Dr. Burns thought I had multiple myeloma, he looked at the report of the urine-sample test and said the same thing the professor had. He had me redo that test, drew blood for some other tests, and gave me the most thorough physical I've ever had. A week ago we saw him to get the results, and he reported that I have no kidney problem and everything else is fine. He started me on a new medication to help the bone density problem, which apparently is common in women my age.

I had been going to Dr. Burns since he came here after finishing his training seven years ago. He is a fellow parishioner. I felt I should tell him why I quit so suddenly. I thought he would be glad to know everything turned out all right. But I also thought I should let him know he'd made a mistake. Of course, no great damage was done, though we had a bad couple of weeks and I got the useless bone scan. But he needs to be more careful.

I called him and told him I don't have multiple myeloma after all. Since he did not seem to believe me, I started telling him about talking with the professor in California. He got angry at that, made a derogatory remark about women doctors and medical school professors, and said nobody could make a sound diagnosis over the telephone without examining me and having my complete record. I told him my new doctor, who is a man, agreed that the urine-sample test did not indicate cancer, but only a possible kidney problem, and as it turned out not even that, since I had not done the test right because the directions had not been clear. He replied that he did not want to hear such criticism and did not need to talk to me, since I am no longer his patient. Then he said emphatically: "But you had better see a cancer specialist," and hung up.

My husband and I were very surprised and began wondering what to do. My husband thinks that since doctors are terribly afraid of being sued, perhaps we ought to see a lawyer and sue him: "That would wake him up, and maybe we'd get something for the two weeks he put us through." I am not eager to sue Dr. Burns, and, thinking it over, am not sure it would be right. Being sued might just make him angry and more set in his ways. Then too, personally, I do not want to be involved in a lawsuit, and that may be influencing me too much. I am thinking of just sending Dr. Burns a letter that would not even mention suing him, but would simply describe how we felt when we thought I had multiple myeloma and ask him to put himself in the place of his patients, and think about his work and his attitude. My husband does not think that would have much effect. He says—and I see his point—that Dr. Burns probably will throw the letter in the waste basket without even reading it, or else will skim it, feel glad at not being threatened, and ignore the rest.

Meanwhile, I decided to call the professor in California to tell her how well everything worked out. She was pleased to hear my good news. When I told her about Dr. Burns's reaction, including his derogatory remark about women doctors and medical school professors, she said he is arrogant and is going to kill a lot of people if he doesn't change. I told her about the disagreement between my husband and me, and she said she would send us a memorandum we could use, whatever we decided to do. The memorandum, which came today, makes clear exactly what happened. The professor reports the intern's first conversation with her, their discussion of the urine-test report, and her first conversation with me, which she seems to have taken down almost word for word.

But I still do not know what I should do.

Analysis:

This question concerns the duty to admonish. The physician may or may not be guilty of serious sin, but objectively he not only fell short in carrying out his professional responsibilities but manifested serious character flaws. Because the well-being of his other patients is at stake and the questioner apparently is free to make the effort, she has a serious obligation, which she recognizes, to try to induce the physician to examine his conscience, repent, change his attitude, and carry on his practice more carefully. However, neither suing him nor merely writing to him along the lines the questioner outlines is likely to help him. Society provides channels, such as medical review boards, through which action could be taken; but it is questionable whether such action would help. So, before using such a channel, the questioner should make another attempt at private communication. The physician might be induced to cooperate in such communication with some suitable third party, or an intermediary might induce him to take seriously a letter from the questioner. If such efforts fail, the questioner should consider using the socially provided channel to file a complaint.

The reply could be along the following lines:

Plainly, Dr. Burns's performance and, even more, his attitude and reaction to you were seriously defective. It was imprudent and uncaring to communicate so awful a diagnosis to you and your husband without making certain it was correct; he should have either verified it first or referred you at once to the cancer specialist to check out a "possible problem," without specifying what he suspected. Moreover, his closed-minded and defensive reaction to your telephone call manifests serious character flaws: overvaluation of professional status, overconfidence about competence, inadequate commitment to serving patients, and neglect of self-criticism and self-correction. Such defects endanger patients and are bad for this physician.

Professionals, public officials, and others whose poor performance can greatly endanger other people's vital interests or the common good sometimes fall so far short of fulfilling their responsibilities that, if a choice must be made, those concerned should concentrate, not on helping them, but on helping their victims. In such cases, all morally acceptable means should be used to limit the injuries reasonably anticipated from their continuing defective performances, even if that probably will have the bad side effect of making them less likely to repent and reform. In my judgment, you should ask yourself whether your concern should be focused more on Dr. Burns's present and future patients than on him.

Since you do not say whether he has made devastating mistakes in other cases, I assume you know of none. The public health department or medical society in your state probably has some sort of process by which instances of alleged professional misconduct and questionable performance, including those patients complain of, are studied by a body that can initiate disciplinary action against a physician, and perhaps even withdraw his or her license to practice. You could inquire of that disciplinary body whether any complaints are pending or any disciplinary action ever has been taken against Dr. Burns. You also could inquire discreetly around town to find out if others have had bad experiences with him. Avoid leading questions, and ask neutrally: "You have been going to Dr. Burns, haven't you? Are you happy with him and his work?" "Didn't Dr. Burns take care of your [deceased loved one] during his/her last illness? Would you recommend him for a similar case?" If what you find out indicates that Dr. Burns probably should not be allowed to continue practicing as he has been, I think you should gather up the evidence pointing to this conclusion and make it available to the disciplinary body. Moreover, if you do that, then, with legal advice about your responsibilities and the risks involved, you also should consider taking legal action (probably, as I shall explain, in small claims court), and informing the local media as well as any of his patients whom you know personally. Of course, in initiating any or all of these possible courses of action, you should be prepared to carry the process through to its conclusion.

However, if you do not conclude such drastic action would be warranted, your present plan seems to me right: to do what you can to encourage Dr. Burns to examine himself and his work, identify what needs correcting, and commit himself to making the changes needed to be better both as a person and as a physician. Your awareness of your responsibility in this matter is commendable; all too many people in such situations think only of getting what they can for themselves rather than helping the erring person and safeguarding others.

Since you have a clear idea of what you should do and are trying to determine how to do it, you will have no difficulty grasping the chief norm that should guide your planning: Proceed in ways most likely to be beneficial to Dr. Burns (see *LCL,* 231). Flowing from this norm is another: Follow the sequence of steps the gospel recommends (see Mt 18.15–17). Begin by talking personally and privately with the one who seems at fault, involve another or a few others only if necessary, involve the wider community only as a last resort. You acted in accord with these norms in calling Dr. Burns to tell him he had made a mistake and should be more careful, and you still are thinking in accord with them in looking for a way to communicate that message more effectively.

Writing a letter may be the best you can do. But I agree with your husband that, given the doctor's attitude, a letter probably would not be effective. Face-to-face communication, under conditions that would motivate him to pay attention to your concerns about his patients' good and his own, seems more likely to work. In trying to bring about such conditions, do your best not to threaten and embarrass him more than necessary. Otherwise he is likely to become more defensive, and obdurately resist self-examination and repentance.

In view of that danger, suing him would be a mistake. As you say, it probably would make him angry and more set in his ways. Besides, almost certainly he has insurance against malpractice suits, and the insurance almost certainly requires him to report even the first threat of a lawsuit to the insurance carrier, refuse to communicate directly with anyone who seems likely to sue, and refer any such person's attempt at communication to the insurer. A lawsuit probably would make the needed communication impossible.

As you remark, too, no great damage was done, though you suffered two weeks of unnecessary distress and underwent a useless X–ray examination. To some extent, serious damage was avoided because of the nature of Dr. Burns's mistakes—making an erroneous diagnosis and ordering an inappropriate test. Mistakes like that cause distress and a great deal of waste, but by themselves they seldom kill or seriously injure patients. Consequently, even though he was insensitive and careless, what he did may not have been malpractice as the law understands it. Even if it was, punitive damages probably would not be awarded and compensatory damages would be minimal due to the small amount of actual harm. Probably, then, the only practical legal recourse in this case would be to file in small claims court. Unless you judge that you should use all morally acceptable means to prevent Dr. Burns from carrying on his practice as he has, however, even that might very well impede your purpose rather than serve it.

How could you bring about an effective private admonition—a personal communication that would motivate Dr. Burns to consider your concern for him and his patients and respond as he should? It is questionable whether you can accomplish this by yourself. Having already lost his temper with you and refused to converse, he probably would be no more willing to do so now than to pay attention to a letter from you. However, you may be able to enlist another person to admonish him—someone who can do so effectively.

Consider talking the matter over confidentially with your pastor if you have not already. Since Dr. Burns is a parishioner, the pastor may know a good deal about him. Do not ask him about that, though; instead, tell him, as accurately as you can, what happened and express your concerns for Dr. Burns and his patients. If the pastor shows serious interest in the problem—he should, but may not—you might ask him to try to talk with Dr. Burns, and, if the pastor is willing, you could share with him the memorandum from the California physician. Another possible intermediary would be a professional colleague of Dr. Burns, a nearby physician in a somewhat similar practice. In broaching the matter to such a physician, you could share the California physician's memorandum and seek advice about the appropriateness of filing a complaint with the local disciplinary body. If the physician urges you not to do that, you might then ask him or her to communicate your concerns privately and informally to Dr. Burns. And, of course, you may know of some other possible intermediary, such as a good mutual friend.[284]

---

284. In some jurisdictions, a governmental agency provides a mediation service, designed to forestall litigation and to settle conflicts for which legal action is not feasible or seems inappropriate; where such a service exists, it might be useful in a case of this kind.

The way you presented the matter to me also would be adequate, I think, for anyone you might approach as a possible intermediary. If you enlist someone to attempt the task, offer to write a letter to Dr. Burns, which the intermediary at least might use as a resource and might decide to deliver.

Perhaps using an intermediary will not seem feasible, or you will not find one. If so, writing Dr. Burns a letter probably is your best option, even though it offers slim hope of achieving your good purpose. In the letter you might mention that you are not planning legal action and, trying not to give offense, explain your reasons. After describing what happened as you experienced it, you might frame your admonition quite simply, appealing to Dr. Burns as a fellow parishioner to put himself in his patients' place and do as Jesus commanded: "Do unto others as you would have them do unto you."

Whether you communicate your concerns to Dr. Burns through an intermediary or, if that is not feasible, by sending a letter, I think you will have fulfilled your responsibility to admonish. If he receives the admonition and takes it to heart as he should, he ought to offer you an apology.

And if you hear nothing? If your inquiry found no evidence of other instances in which he was seriously at fault, let the matter rest, pray for him, and hope for the best. But if you learn of other instances in which people have had serious problems with him, but lack sufficient evidence to convince you he should not be practicing, consider filing a complaint with the appropriate disciplinary body.

If you do that, of course, Dr. Burns is likely to become angry, but he also may be more careful in the future. On the same basis, it seems to me that, if you file a complaint against him, you also might take action against him in small claims court.

91: May one get health care one would forgo if one had to pay its full cost?

Looking back over my medical records from last year, I noticed that most of the smaller charges were for seeing my regular doctor, prescriptions, and other things I would have wanted and paid for myself if I had no insurance. But I would never have had done several expensive things without insurance to cover at least eighty percent of the cost. I had no trouble getting these things done even though my insurance is under a managed care arrangement, so that I receive full coverage only if my regular doctor gives me a referral to some physician or facility listed as a participating provider.

Here are two examples. My prostate is gradually growing larger, as virtually every man's does, and last year I began to notice symptoms. They were not very serious, and I imagine most men would have ignored them. But since I had met my deductible, additional care was not going to cost me much. I saw my regular doctor and got a referral to a urologist, who sent me for tests, then saw me again to go over the results. I had reasons for doing this: to talk with a specialist whose answers to my questions would be more dependable, to make absolutely sure the condition was not more serious than I thought, and to establish a basis for comparison in a future diagnosis when surgery might be in question. To me, it was worth the seventy dollars I ended up paying but not worth the three-hundred-plus dollars the insurance paid. Again, one Thursday night I slipped off a curb and twisted my ankle; Friday morning it was swollen and painful. Usually I would have put an ice pack on it, taken some pain killers, and waited until Monday to see whether it would quiet down. But I was planning to go away that weekend, and did not want to take the trip only to find myself in an out-of-town emergency room—which my insurance probably would not have covered, since it has very strict rules about using emergency rooms. I checked in with my doctor, who sent me for X rays, then on to a specialist, who told me to put an ice pack on the ankle and take some pain killers, supplied a lace-up brace, and said to stay off my feet as much as possible during my weekend excursion. All this cost me only around forty dollars, but the insurance paid over two hundred.

My parents, who have retired and are covered by Medicare and a medigap policy, also obtain a great deal of care they would never get—though they have a good income from their pensions and social security—if they had to pay all the bills themselves. For instance, for several months last winter my mother had a cough. It didn't actually bother her much, and she would have put up with it, but my dad felt that would be foolish, since most of the cost would be covered, and, as he said: "We have nothing more important to do than look after our health and plenty of time to do that." Having gone to the doctor, my mother was referred to several specialists, who sent her for X rays, an MRI, and a bronchoscopy, and did various other tests, including a long series for allergies and a psychological evaluation. They never did figure out what was causing the cough, and it finally got better.

I am of two minds about this sort of thing. I do not see how I or my parents did anything wrong. We followed the rules and got what our health coverage entitles us to. But I do not like the ever growing insurance premiums and budget deficits that result from other people with coverage doing the same, and I wish they took less advantage of coverage than my parents and I do. It seems we are being unfair at least to those who do take less advantage. But how can we be unfair if we are not doing anything wrong?

Analysis:

This question concerns the application of the Golden Rule. Taking advantage of health insurance coverage is wrong and unfair if in seeking care one is motivated by mere feelings rather than reasons; it also can be unfair if one deliberately exaggerates symptoms or is not wholly candid in providing information that might limit care. In the instances described, however, there seem to have been reasons for seeking care. If so, and if those seeking the care were not only truthful but appropriately candid, they did not act unfairly. The appearance of unfairness results from a defect in the social structure of the health care system, which lacks suitable controls to shape cooperation toward the common good.

The reply could be along the following lines:

Many people do unfairly abuse the health care coverage provided by private insurance or public programs.

Sometimes a mere emotion, rather than a reason, moves people to obtain covered services. They may disguise this by rationalization—usually referring to the basic good of health—but their real motive for seeing a doctor, seeking referral to a specialist, or wanting various examinations and tests is not rational. They are not hypochondriacs—people who suffer from neurotic anxieties—but they are excessively afraid of death and anxious about their health, so that they see the doctor about every small symptom. Some people with chronic, untreatable conditions regularly use professional services as a placebo or with unreasonable hope of obtaining relief. Again, some people feel they must make use of coverage lest they not get what they regard as their share of health care service, and so they keep an eye peeled for problems they would otherwise ignore: "I will see the doctor about this knee ache; after all, I hardly ever have a chance to use my high-priced health insurance."

Sometimes, too, not only people with merely emotional motives but some who have a reason for seeking health care deliberately exaggerate their symptoms in order to obtain service, or more or speedier service. People do this for diverse reasons. Some people, lacking confidence in their primary care physician, almost always wish to be referred to a specialist and/or have the reassurance of additional tests. Some, thinking the newer always is better, are dissatisfied unless the most up-to-date equipment is used to diagnose and treat their problems. Some, abusing prescription drugs for their psychological effects, seek unneeded medication. And, of course, some people feign illness to obtain a medical excuse for absence from work or school, or failure to fulfill some other duty. Whatever the motives, such deliberate exaggerations are lies and, as such, always are wrong.

Patients should develop a cooperative relationship with physicians who can be trusted to serve their true interests. They should be not just truthful but entirely candid—for example, by providing information about their past medical history or a symptom's development that might lead the physician to delay expensive examinations or decide against a referral to a specialist. Unfortunately, managed care insurance plans and other health care systems in which primary care physicians act as gatekeepers for access to specialists and hospital services create a conflict of interests for those physicians. They must try to serve both the patients' interest in obtaining appropriate services and the interest of the organizations paying for services in limiting costs.[285] Patients dealing with such physicians can rightly keep information to themselves if they fear providing it might give the physicians an excuse for denying them access to services they think they need.

Your stated reasons for obtaining a referral to a urologist and the tests for which he sent you may well have been your actual motive. (I put it that way because people whose motives are mere feelings sometimes rationalize them in similar terms.) Only you can identify your own motives, and I shall assume they were sound. The persistence of your mother's cough certainly gave her a reason to see her primary care physician, though the reasonableness of your father's view of the matter is

---

285. See Marc A. Rodwin, "Physicians' Conflicts of Interest in HMOs and Hospitals," in *Conflicts of Interest in Clinical Practice and Research,* ed. Roy G. Spece, Jr., et al. (New York: Oxford University Press, 1996), 197–227.

questionable. Perhaps you or your mother exaggerated symptoms or were not appropriately candid. But assuming you and she did nothing wrong in these respects, both of you obtained service to which your health coverage entitles you, and both acted fairly. In obtaining care for your twisted ankle, you were partly motivated by a rational concern to decide about your weekend plans and partly by a rational interest in avoiding the uncovered cost of emergency room treatment. As often happens, in this instance a rule meant to limit unnecessary use of a costly facility was self-defeating for the insurer. But, again, assuming you were not only truthful but appropriately candid, you acted fairly.

What about your other concern—the ever rising insurance premiums and budget deficits resulting partly from the heavy use of health coverage? The answer is twofold. First, many people do abuse their coverage, as already explained, and it is entirely fair for anyone who does not, to wish the abusers would desist. Second, here as in many other matters, tension between the common good and individuals' rational self-interest generates a paradox. Everyone can reasonably wish that everyone would make more conservative use of covered health care services, even while no one has a good reason to do so.

Before the introduction of health insurance and public health care programs, most people purchased health care, as they do food and other necessities, with their own funds. People who lacked funds and urgently needed care often obtained it free from providers, including hospitals sponsored by churches, and sometimes care for the poor and indigents was paid for by local charitable and relief agencies, which were close to their clients. Nonrational use of health care was rare, and people who paid for their own care, as well as providers or agencies supplying care to those who could not pay, set limits even to the rational use of available services. Generally with the counsel of the physician involved, they considered the relationship between benefits and costs, and made hard choices between the benefits to be expected and other needs. But health insurance and public programs not only removed the financial incentive to use health care services rationally, and to limit even that use, but lowered the threshold at which taking advantage of health care resources is rational, eliminated the main disincentive to rational use, enabled providers to increase their charges, and ensured that they usually would be paid in full.[286] No longer was there the same convergence between the proper interests of health care consumers and providers, on the one hand, and, on the other, their common interest in preventing waste and limiting costs.

An imaginary case analogous to the present problem will help clarify it. Imagine a tropical isle whose native population regards its grove of palm trees, like the plentiful fish in the sea, as a common resource freely available to all. The palms provide all the coconuts anyone wants, and a mature tree occasionally is cut and used as material for a new fishing boat. Building boats is hard work, however, so that families delay until their old boat no longer can be repaired and absolutely has to be replaced; as a result, the palm grove is not endangered by the occasional cutting. But suppose some ingenious fellow invents a new technique for building

286. See George J. Annas et al., *American Health Law* (Boston: Little, Brown, 1990), 121–26.

boats much more easily. Fascinated by the new technique, some families build extra boats they seldom use; their tree cutting is wasteful and unfair. Most build only boats they will use regularly, but they now build a new one as soon as their present boat becomes less serviceable and begins needing repairs; and although their tree cutting is neither wasteful nor unfair, the average family now builds a new fishing boat twice as often as previously. Three times as many mature palm trees are cut, the supply of coconuts is no longer adequate, and thoughtful people begin to worry about the grove. Every family wishes boats were built less often, as in the old days, but no one family's decision to delay building will save the palm grove.

Such a problem can be solved only by the cooperation of everyone involved, and authority is necessary to organize and direct cooperation. *Authority* need not mean a single decision maker or bureau, but it does mean some way of guiding decisions in accord with the common good. The islanders need a way of guiding decisions that not only will prevent waste but limit even rational boat building, so that there will continue to be enough palm trees to meet everyone's needs.

Similarly, people in affluent societies who use health care services paid for by insurance and public programs have a problem requiring cooperation and the authority necessary to organize and direct it. Everyone involved would benefit if the nonrational use of health care services were eliminated, and most would benefit from the savings realized if even their rational use were somewhat limited. But as long as services are not effectively restricted, individuals with reasons for using them will take advantage of their availability. They cannot be faulted for doing so, since no individual's restraint would serve the common good by reducing the costs of insurance and public programs.

Moreover, unlike the need for food, which is finite, the need for means of preventing, curing, and struggling with disease and accidental damage to the human organism is as limitless as human ability to invent such means. From that point of view, there is no way of setting a term to the expansion of health care resources. In reality, though, health care technology and services cannot go on expanding indefinitely; otherwise, there soon will be no resources to meet other needs. Consequently, health care services somehow must be limited and rationed.

Health plans requiring coinsurance payments and the payment of a deductible before coverage begins attempt to preserve or restore something of the discipline that existed before the development of health insurance and public programs.[287] As your examples make clear, the attempted discipline is inadequate. Many insurance companies, health maintenance organizations, and some public programs have tried to solve the problem, as your managed care plan has, by using primary care physicians as gatekeepers who limit access to specialists, hospitalization, and so on. As has been explained, however, that generates a conflict of interest, and

---

287. If a person or family with health insurance receives a service the insurance covers but is required to pay part of the bill, that payment is a coinsurance payment. If the insured person or family must pay the entire bill for covered services until a certain level of total payments has been made in a given period—e.g., $500.00 in the current year—that total payment is the deductible. This method of limiting the use of health care is common in the U.S. Nations with a more socialized system of health care try to achieve the goal in other ways—e.g., by making patients wait, setting budgets for providers, and limiting the availability of expensive services.

sometimes the conflict is aggravated by financially rewarding those gatekeepers who limit services more drastically while penalizing those who limit them less. Usually, too, the gatekeepers must obtain approval from another, more remote authority for at least some of their decisions. Thus, the system generates a costly bureaucracy and gives considerable power to people whose only role is limiting care and whose knowledge of patients and their needs is at second hand. Even so, to the extent gatekeepers and managers conscientiously try not to deny essential services, many people, like you and your mother, will receive a great deal of health care whose utility is marginal in view of its great cost and rather small benefits.

What should we do about this problem? First, not unfairly use the health care coverage that insurance and public programs provide. Second, resist all so-called reforms that continue or increase the use of primary care physicians as gatekeepers, since that cannot solve the problem and may even aggravate it. Third, not oppose the rationing of health care services, which is inevitable, but oppose unfair methods of rationing—for example, denying care to the working poor who lack insurance, as the U.S. system effectively does, or on the basis of age, as the British system does with respect to certain procedures. Fourth, take advantage of opportunities to clarify the problem for others. Fifth, encourage and support systemic changes that you think would contribute to the common good.[288]

92: Should a veterinarian provide futile treatment demanded by pet owners?

I am bothered by a problem that comes up regularly in my practice as a veterinarian. A pet, usually a cat or dog, becomes seriously ill or is badly injured, and the owner brings it to me for treatment. If I think there is any chance of success, I offer a treatment plan and estimate its cost, then let the owner decide. When I am certain that medical treatment and/or surgery would be futile, I say so and suggest putting the animal out of its misery. This is where the problem arises. Many owners are so attached to their pets that they cannot bear losing them; quite a few simply refuse to listen to reason and demand that everything possible be done, including complex and difficult surgery. Some people also think that, since they own their pets, they have the right to have done to them whatever they want, and that, as long as they are willing to pay, I should carry out their wishes despite my misgivings.

Nothing in the law or my code of professional ethics forbids giving treatment I know to be futile. From a purely business point of view, it would be to my advantage in such cases simply to warn the owner of the virtually certain outcome, make sure of payment, and go ahead. Many of my colleagues do that. However, it goes against the grain, not only because futile treatment is wasteful, but because the animal is my patient and has the right to be treated properly. My duty is to provide that patient with good care, including putting it out of its misery when appropriate. But if I refuse to do what owners want, they are likely to find someone else who will, while I lose customers and income.

---

288. Having tried to clarify the ethical elements of this problem, I deliberately abstain from discussing various proposals for trying to mitigate or solve it.

Analysis:

This question calls for the derivation of a specific moral norm. Though animals, not being persons, have no rights, they ought to be treated with respect. A veterinarian should provide animals with the medical treatment and surgery reasonably desired by their owners, but should not cooperate with an owner's unreasonable demands. To provide futile treatment is wrong not only because it is wasteful but because it is cruel to the animal. Therefore, the questioner ought to try to dissuade owners who want futile treatment for their pets and should decline to carry out such requests even at the sacrifice of some income and future business. However, the duty to decline is not a moral absolute.

The reply could be along the following lines:

You say "the animal is my patient and has the right to be treated properly." You are right to take a serious view of your profession, but that way of describing your relationship to the animals you treat is not, strictly speaking, correct, for it implies that pets are like children and your veterinary practice little different from a pediatrician's. Animals, however, not being persons, have no rights, and their lives lack the dignity of human life. That is precisely why it can be appropriate deliberately to kill them, not only to put them out of their misery but to serve any significant human interest.[289]

Nevertheless, animals do have their own special value. Like everything else God created, they are good in themselves; like beautiful features of the natural landscape and flowers, they arouse our wonder and lead us to admire, praise, and thank their creator (see Ps 148). Reverence toward God requires us to respect their value. Just as it would be wrong wantonly to pollute a stream or crush a wild flower, so it is wrong wantonly to injure any animal (see *CCC,* 2415–16). Indeed, since animals are creatures of a higher metaphysical order than streams and flowers, the wrong is greater, other things being equal.[290]

Moreover, since we human beings, though rational, also are sentient creatures, we have natural sympathy toward animals, as is especially obvious in small children's feeling for any baby animal that seems to be separated from its parent, sick, injured, hungry, or thirsty. By the same token, people who treat animals cruelly display a flaw of personality that also will vitiate their relationships with other people. The natural sympathy toward animals underlies the close emotional bonds people develop with their pets. This sympathy is good in itself, and an individual's or family's affection for a pet also can be good, provided it is well integrated with

289. See Gn 9.1–3; *CCC,* 2417; *LCL,* 782–88. The reply to this question is relevant to current ethical concerns within the veterinary profession in the United States and, perhaps, elsewhere; see Jerrold Tannenbaum, "Veterinary Medical Ethics: A Focus of Conflicting Interests," *Journal of Social Issues,* 49:1 (1993): 143–56.

290. The fact that animals, like all God's creatures, are good in themselves does not mean that their being and welfare are basic human goods, that is, reasons per se for human action. The moral goodness or sinfulness of human acts bearing on subhuman goods is determined by relevant human goods: religion (failure to respect the goodness of subhuman creatures is irreverent toward God) and fairness toward others (spoiling and wasting subhuman creatures almost always is likely to deprive others unreasonably of potential benefits).

practical reason so that it never interferes with fulfilling responsibilities toward God and human persons, including oneself.

Your work as a veterinarian primarily is to provide appropriate medical treatment and surgery for animals. What is appropriate, however, depends not only on an animal's condition but on its owner's reasonable choice, and owners rightly exercise far greater discretion in dealing with pets than parents in dealing with children. For example, owners who prefer that their pets not reproduce rightly have them sterilized, and unwanted animals, including even healthy newborns, can rightly be killed painlessly. Still, pet owners sometimes are unreasonable, and then you should not cooperate with them. Therefore, veterinarians must try to establish good relationships with the owners of the pets they treat and try to encourage the owners and their families to form sound attitudes and make reasonable decisions. In fulfilling this element of your professional responsibility, you will help many of the people you deal with, especially children, develop the relevant facet of good character.

The preceding explanation makes clear how mistaken people are in thinking owners have the right to have done to their pets whatever they wish. Like owners of any other property, pet owners are entitled only to the reasonable enjoyment and use of their animals. And like other professionals, veterinarians must shape their work by relevant moral norms, not do whatever people are prepared to pay for.

Having sketched out the necessary presuppositions, I now turn to your question. May you comply with owners' unreasonable demands to do everything possible, often including complex and difficult surgery, to sustain a pet's life? You say that "goes against the grain"—which I take to mean disturbs your conscience—and offer two reasons.

First, you mention waste, presumably of people's money and your work, and perhaps also of facilities and materials that could be put to other uses. In my judgment, this consideration is valid and in many cases will be sufficient in itself to make it gravely wrong to provide futile treatment to animals. In passing, however, it is worth noting that some animals would never have come to be or would long since have passed away were they not kept as pets by people with no good reason for having them, and the goods and services used for such animals are wasted. So, even some of your work that really benefits a particular animal is wasted.[291]

The second reason you mention is the point I began with. You regard the animal as a patient with a right to be treated properly. As I have explained, I consider that reason, understood strictly, to be unsound. However, it seems to me to point to a valid and profound moral consideration, which can be articulated more accurately by focusing on the owner's unreasonable attachment to the pet. In one way, that attachment is excessive affection, which makes it difficult to part with the pet even though that would be reasonable. In another way, paradoxically, it is lack of respect for the animal, which ought to be put out of its misery, but is made to suffer

---

291. *CCC,* 2418: "It is contrary to human dignity to cause animals to suffer or die needlessly. It is likewise unworthy to spend money on them that should as a priority go to the relief of human misery."

pointlessly in order to satisfy the owner's feelings. In this way, the owner's unreasonable attachment results in cruelty to the animal.[292]

If you give in to the demand for futile treatment, you assist in disrespectfully using the animal to satisfy the owner's unreasonable feelings. That morally injures the owner, something not only wrong in itself but inconsistent with your professional responsibility to teach and encourage people to adopt sound attitudes toward animals. Your obligation is especially strong when children are involved, since wrongly using animals to satisfy affectionate feelings is likely to misshape a child's attitudes toward his or her friends and partners in human relationships, not least eventual intimate ones.

Consequently, when owners insist on treatment you judge futile, you should not acquiesce. Often, vividly describing the suffering the treatment is likely to impose on the pet should suffice to dissuade the owner, but I assume you already make as much use of that tactic as you can. When it fails, I think you should decline to carry out the request for unreasonable treatment, and not only pass by that opportunity for income but risk losing some future business.

Nevertheless, since animals have no rights and you need not intend their owners' unreasonableness, your obligation to withhold futile treatment is not a moral absolute, such that you would have to do without necessities or give up your profession if that were the only way to avoid providing such treatment. I gather from your letter, though, that only a portion of your potential income is at stake. Moreover, you may stand to lose less than you suppose. With sensible pet owners, refusing to provide futile care will gain you a reputation for competence and trustworthiness that probably will help you build a good clientele. But even if a principled approach involves some financial sacrifice, you will retain your professional integrity, help people you serve develop a facet of good character through upright attitudes toward animals, and exercise reverence toward God, the creator of animals and the Lord who made humankind responsible for them.

93: May islanders using primitive methods slaughter whales for food?

We live on an island in Oceania. Each year since colonial times when whales come near, people here have herded some of them into our small harbor and slaughtered them. These whales are not leviathans, but one of the smaller species. Still, using only simple tools, we cannot do the work gently and efficiently. The slaughter is messy and rather wasteful.

---

292. James Serpell, *In the Company of Animals: A Study of Human-Animal Relationships* (New York: Basil Blackwell, 1986), 19–116, describes a variety of bad and good relationships between people and their pets; among them, he notes (28) the type of relationship exemplified here: Some people "are prepared to make costly, humiliating or even heroic sacrifices on their behalf, they dress them up and indulge them sometimes to the point of cruelty, and they may be crippled with remorse when they die."

Nobody here ever had any moral qualms about the annual whale kill. The meat always has been an important part of our diet. Nobody would starve without it, but people here are not wealthy, and we would miss it.

Lately, however, outsiders have objected to our whale kill, using several arguments. First, they say it is cruel to slaughter any animal by cutting it apart alive, as we do the whales. Second, they point out that we keep much less of each animal than professional whalers do, and accuse us of outrageous waste. Third, they claim that, with human populations increasing, the unnecessary killing of these animals soon will endanger the species, if it has not already done so, and so is unfair to future generations.

What do you think of these arguments?

Analysis:

This question concerns the application both of the norm forbidding cruelty to animals and of the Golden Rule. The annual whale kill is not cruel and wasteful if the islanders cannot reasonably obtain the tools required to carry it out more gently and efficiently. The whale kill is unfair if islanders, to obtain its benefits, definitely would not accept for themselves the sorts of harm it does to outsiders; it is unfair to future generations if it is likely to contribute to extinguishing the species. If the annual whale kill is not unfair to anyone and it is not feasible for the islanders to obtain better tools, they may continue conducting it as they have.

The reply could be along the following lines:

You say nothing about the lawfulness of the annual whale kill. If applicable laws prohibit it, they should be presumed just, and, not needing the whale meat for an adequate diet, you islanders almost certainly should obey them. But in the remainder of this reply, I shall assume that those participating in the whale kill do nothing against the law.

You say outsiders accuse you of great waste because you keep less of each whale than the professionals do. Perhaps you could quite easily take and use more of the animal, even with the tools you have, to meet others' needs, if not your own. If you could, you of course should, but I shall assume in what follows that you are doing the best you can with the tools you have.

Some people today would condemn you on the ground that everyone should practice vegetarianism. However, Christians always have held that animals may be used for food, provided the meat contributes to a healthful and temperate diet.[293] Of course, in the Old Testament, certain kinds of animals were considered unclean, but the New Testament makes it clear that there is nothing inherently wrong in eating any kind of meat (see Acts 10.10–16, 11.2–10, 15.6–20).

Since the whale kill provides a legitimate and important part of your diet, it serves the fundamental human good of health. Moreover, if you were a group of native people, your critics probably would regard what you do as a tribal tradition, and many would defend or, at least, tolerate it. But a double standard should not be

---

293. Despite some contemporary opinion to the contrary, the Catholic Church approves using animals for food, clothing, and medical or scientific research (see *CCC,* 2417).

applied, and, as a communal activity carried on for many years, the annual whale kill is part of your culture, comparable to certain practices of native peoples. Like those folkways, it contributes not only to your standard of living but to the good of social solidarity among those who participate and benefit.

Since those who treat animals cruelly act both against natural sympathy without a good reason to do so—which injures their own character—and irreverently toward God, nobody should treat animals cruelly (see *CCC*, 2416; *LCL*, 785–86; q. 92, above). Cruelty, however, is not simply inflicting pain; one surely may, for example, inflict pain on animals, as on fellow humans, for their own good and also in legitimate self-defense. Taking pleasure in an animal's suffering or negligently accepting it in doing something that is morally wrong on other grounds is cruel, since neither serves any human good. For instance, bearbaiting, which makes sport of an animal's misery, is cruel; so is accepting the suffering of pets which are kept without good reason and neglected. Moreover, even in doing something in itself good, accepting an animal's suffering that could be avoided or prevented without undue difficulty is cruel.

You say those conducting the kill cut the whales apart alive—and, it seems, without first stunning them to prevent their suffering. This is cruel if the animals first could be killed or stunned without sacrificing any significant human interest. You also say the slaughter is rather wasteful. Certainly, wasting any material good not only is irreverent toward God but likely to be disadvantageous to those involved or others, and the whale kill is wasteful if carrying it out more efficiently is required by reasonable self-concern or the Golden Rule. Thus, one question raised by your long-standing practice is whether it would be possible and not too difficult to obtain more adequate tools, so that the kill could be done more gently and efficiently.

But how far must you go in trying to obtain better tools? Suppose you were faced with the choice between entirely forgoing the practice and making it more efficient by getting better tools and sharing the expense—a long-term investment that would benefit islanders immediately and for many years to come. If, facing those alternatives, you would choose to obtain better tools, it would be wasteful, it seems to me, to continue the annual whale kill as it has been conducted in the past. Suppose that, without significantly compromising any legitimate interest of the community's members, you could get the tools needed to kill or stun the animals before cutting them apart. In that case, it would be cruel not to do so. I believe, therefore, that you should look into obtaining more adequate tools. In doing so, you might ask critics of the annual whale kill for constructive advice and, perhaps, financial aid.

The third argument proposed by the outsiders raises a further question: Would you be justified in slaughtering these whales for food even if you did it more gently and efficiently? The answer depends in part on information you have not supplied. The mere fact that human populations are increasing does not imply that you are acting unfairly, and the prospect that this species may be endangered at some future time does not exclude using the whales now, as people use other renewable natural resources. However, the annual whale kill is unfair if islanders, to obtain its benefits, definitely would not accept for themselves the sorts of harm it does to outsiders—for example, if it deprives some people of the food they need to survive or deprives professional whalers of their livelihood. Moreover, if this species of whale becomes actually endangered, and if you could help save the species for the enjoyment and use of future generations by forgoing this food, continuing the slaughter, in my judgment, would be unfair to the people whom you would deprive of these creatures in the future.

Suppose the annual whale kill is neither unfair to anyone now living nor an actual threat to the species, yet there is no feasible way to obtain better tools, or tools can be obtained only to make the slaughter either gentler or more efficient but not both. May you continue conducting it, at least partly, as in the past? Yes. The slaughter inflicts pain on the animals, but that is cruel only if the pain can be avoided without significantly compromising legitimate human interests. And while the slaughter is inefficient, insofar as a large part of each animal goes unused, inefficiency is waste strictly so-called only if reasonable self-concern or fairness requires that one do what is necessary to be more efficient.

What if you must choose between making the slaughter gentler or more efficient? In that case, the animals' suffering could be mitigated only by compromising some of the slaughter's benefits to the community, which, as explained, justify accepting that suffering. So, if you must make that choice, you should, in my judgment, make the slaughter more efficient.

94: May a retiree accept a job to get extra money for optional expenditures?

I have no immediate family. My husband was killed in an accident a few months after our wedding, and I never remarried. My parents, brothers, and a sister also have died. Four years ago I retired from my lifelong work as a public high school teacher. Though not covered by social security, I do receive a teacher's pension from the state. It is not indexed, but so far it has been enough to cover all the necessities—rent, utilities, food, clothing, transportation, health care, insurance, incidentals—with a fair amount left over to donate to the Church and various charities.

I enjoy a variety of free or inexpensive activities, such as visiting with friends, and using public libraries and museums. I also do volunteer work here and there, and write letters to editors, government officials, managers of businesses, and so on, calling their attention to situations I consider unjust or otherwise wrong. Still, having done some traveling and photography before I retired, I'd very much like to do more of those things now. For financing, I could go to work part time, editing and desktop publishing an in-house newsletter for a nearby hospital. I sometimes have helped the hospital administrator's secretary with the work on a volunteer basis, but it has been taking too much of her time, and now they are offering to pay me to do the whole job. I would enjoy the work, and the income would not affect my pension.

However, having thought long and hard about Jesus' teaching on our duties toward people in need—"When I was hungry" and so forth—I wonder whether I may take this job and use the extra money as I would like. I would no longer have the time and energy to do volunteer work, which is one way I can help people less fortunate than I am. And I would be filling a job that could be done during school hours by some working mother who needs income for family necessities. Finally, I would be using this extra income for luxuries, while many people in the world are starving. All these things lead me to ask whether I may take this job. Of course, if I do, I could give part of the extra income to the poor and use only part of it for travel and photography. In that case, what would the right division be?

I also have U.S. government savings bonds, now worth about one hundred thousand dollars, that I bought over the years. I could cash some of them, both to finance travel and photography and to help the poor. However, I have been keeping the bonds in case inflation reduces the buying power of my pension so much that it no longer will cover all the necessities, and I am reluctant to give up this safety net. Am I being miserly?

Analysis:

This questioner's problem is partly one of justice in the use of resources and partly one of vocation: to discover the way God wishes her to use her gifts in serving others and fulfilling herself. She might be able to combine activities in such a way as to satisfy all her concerns and objectives. Not all recreation is a luxury; travel and photography can serve genuine human goods. In judging how much one may spend on recreational activities, one must consider others' needs as well as one's own, and apply the Golden Rule.

The reply could be along the following lines:

People all too often regard retirement as an endless vacation that frees them of any further responsibility to serve others. Accepting this view, many retirees take it for granted that they have the right to work for extra income to spend on recreation or any other extras they choose. You do well to continue listening for God's call during your retirement years, as every Christian should, so that you can continue finding and following your vocation as it unfolds. Moreover, the concerns you express manifest a spirit of loving service and a Christian attitude toward money. You also are following the norms for discovering moral truth by treating your options as a matter for moral inquiry, though none of the options is in itself morally evil.

I do not think you are miserly in keeping your savings. Like other financially independent members of society, you have the duty to try to provide for your own continuing needs, and it would be wrong to take a great risk, without any morally compelling reason, of shifting that burden to others. Most advisers on retirement planning recommend taking inflation into account, and, living as you do on a fixed pension, you do need a hedge against future inflation. In my judgment, moreover, your savings are not excessive for that purpose. However, if you have not already done so, I suggest you consider bequeathing anything that might remain of your savings when you die to a worthy cause. Assuming you have no obligation to provide for anyone else, such a bequest, it seems to me, would fully meet your responsibility to put your savings to good use.

Part of your concern about accepting the offer of part-time work for the hospital is that it might deprive a mother of needed work. That concern is laudable, but your not taking the job would not ensure that such a person would get it. Perhaps it would go to someone similar to you, who planned to use the income less responsibly. Your concern about forgoing the volunteer work that you have been doing is more substantial, since working for the hospital will require much of your time and energy, and will displace volunteer work.

Perhaps you could meet both concerns effectively as follows. You would do the editing and desktop publishing of the hospital's newsletter by yourself until you fully mastered the work. Then, without additional cost to the hospital, you would search for and select a suitable person, such as a mother who needed the income but could work only during school hours, and teach her to do the work. When she proved herself capable and was doing a significant part of the work, you would let her take over the job, but continue advising and assisting her until she mastered it. The cooperation involved in helping someone in this way might well also initiate a good friendship.

So, rather than contributing part of the income from your work, you would be giving up the job itself. Having thus achieved your purpose of making the job available for someone who needed it and having contributed some volunteer work to that cause, you could use the extra money you had earned for travel and photography. Of course, if the project succeeded, you could look for other, somewhat similar, part-time jobs and do the same thing repeatedly.[294]

There remains your concern about spending money on luxuries while people are starving. It seems to me that this concern results, in part, from a mistaken assumption that all recreational activity is a luxury. Actually, while people often indulge themselves in luxurious recreation, everyone needs some recreation, and activities that really serve that purpose also serve other interests, such as gaining knowledge, having experiences valuable for their own sake, and exercising various skills. You might even be able to put your travel and photography to work in serving the poor. For example, you might visit places in this country and abroad where you could gain firsthand experience of human misery, capture its images on film, and thus gather material to enclose in your letters or illustrate talks and/or articles intended to raise others' social consciousness. Dollars spent traveling in less prosperous places also constitute earnings for the local economy and so, in a small way, help to alleviate poverty, especially if one patronizes locally owned and operated businesses.

To judge whether a recreational activity is justified, considering that many people in the world are starving, you must reflect on two things: how it would benefit you and others—that is, enable you and them to participate in the various basic human goods, which really fulfill persons—and how forgoing it would enable you to mitigate the evils from which other people are suffering and, at the same time, fulfill yourself by serving others. Then, considering your lifestyle as a whole,

---

294. This suggestion might not apply in countries other than the U.S.; in most parts of the world, even skilled and able elderly persons cannot easily find jobs. In such a case, the questioner and the person she trained might share the job on an ongoing basis.

rather than one or another activity in isolation, you must apply the Golden Rule (see *LCL,* 282–86). When you have done this, I believe you will be able to judge in good conscience that you may spend at least some of the extra money you earn for some reasonably priced travel and photography—forms of recreation that can embody genuine human goods and that, as I have suggested, you also might use as means of working for social justice.[295]

95: Must charitable giving involve an immediate personal relationship?

My husband and I never give to street beggars or people who come to us asking for a handout, and, except for a few cases involving relatives and friends, we have not responded to individuals' pleas for financial help.

We have various reasons for this policy. We recognize that people struggling with problems they have brought on themselves deserve help, but we often suspect that a handout would simply support deliberate idleness or perpetuate habitual misbehavior, such as compulsive gambling or the abuse of alcohol or drugs. Even when the money would be put to better uses, those seeking help may be lying about their situation and needs, so that helping them would encourage them and others to continue defrauding people. In this country, people with serious, legitimate needs usually can get help from a public agency. No one can investigate every request and identify the few cases in which his or her money would meet a real and urgent need that otherwise will go unmet. Moreover, since donations to individuals are not tax deductible, one can help more needy people by giving exclusively to qualified charitable organizations.

That is what we have been doing. Since the last of our children got out of high school, I have been selling real estate. I do well at it, and my husband's income as a certified public accountant also has grown over the years. As our income grew and our expenses shrank, we substantially increased our donations to the parish and diocesan collections, especially those to help the poor. Then, thinking that many people in poorer countries are far more in need of the things money can buy than almost anyone in this country, we looked for other channels, and started donating to organizations that help people abroad: Catholic Relief Services, Catholic Near East Welfare Association, Mother Teresa's Missionaries of Charity, and Aid to the Church in Need.

---

295. The ideas underlying the preceding suggestions for solving this problem can be applied to many other cases. When confronting options none of which is in itself morally evil, one should reflect in the perspective of vocation, and the question is how best to use one's gifts and resources. The particular goals that arouse one's desire often are too limited and exclude richer possibilities. Yet many people focus on a few definite goals that they happen to have in mind and regard everything else as mere means to obtaining them. Instead, one should focus on possible benefits to people—others and oneself—and try to discover goals that will bring about those benefits as fully and richly as possible. In the face of what appear to be alternatives for serving various goods and persons, a bit of ingenuity often enables one to find some way of combining activities into an integrated whole, so that everyone concerned and all the relevant goods can be served simultaneously.

This year we will donate a little over thirty percent of our income before taxes and other deductions. I am not saying this to boast; we live quite comfortably and probably should be giving more. My point is that our practice of not responding to personal requests for money has been based on the reasons stated, not on unwillingness to give.

Last month we went on a retreat that focused on the corporal works of mercy. The conferences were based on St. Luke's Gospel and the writings of some of the Church Fathers. One central idea, which we agreed with, was that the Christian way of dealing with wealth and poverty is neither Marxist revolution nor the welfare state, but voluntary cooperation between materially needy people and those with excess wealth. The point was stressed that political approaches at best redistribute wealth in a depersonalized way, while the Christian approach transforms people and their relationships, making strangers into neighbors. It is important that the needs of the poor be met from the resources of the wealthy, the retreat master explained, but it is far more important that the poor person and the wealthy person be Christ to each other and respond to Christ in each other.

What he said next seemed to be aimed directly at us. Even Church-affiliated organizations that collect and distribute money, he said, turn charity into an impersonal financial transaction. He contrasted their methods with scriptural teaching about almsgiving in which the immediate personal relationship is uppermost. Is not the sacrifice God prefers "to share your bread with the hungry, and bring the homeless poor into your house; when you see the naked, to cover them, and not to hide yourself from your own kin?" (Is 58.7). Refusing a face-to-face request, he said, hurtfully rejects the person making it: "Do not grieve the hungry, or anger one in need. Do not add to the troubles of the desperate, or delay giving to the needy. Do not reject a suppliant in distress, or turn your face away from the poor" (Sir 4.2–4). The retreat master also argued that it is better to be cheated occasionally, or even often, than to risk refusing someone in need: "Many refuse to lend, not because of meanness, but from fear of being defrauded needlessly. Nevertheless, be patient with someone in humble circumstances, and do not keep him waiting for your alms. Help the poor for the commandment's sake, and in their need do not send them away empty-handed" (Sir 29.7–9). Then too, he quoted from several Church Fathers who excoriate those who refuse to help the needy person who encounters them along the road or comes to their door.

Have we been doing the right thing in rejecting personal requests and channeling our donations through organizations?

Analysis:

This question concerns a proposed norm requiring—or, at least, favoring—charitable giving that involves an immediate personal relationship. The Church's practice and teaching, beginning with St. Paul, do not support the view that it is wrong to channel donations through organizations while rejecting most personal requests. The apparent support that view has in the tradition can be accounted for. Thus, the questioners' reasons for channeling donations through organizations are acceptable, and they need not change their policy. Still, when directly responding to personal requests contributes to an immediate personal relationship, it can yield benefits unavailable or less available from giving alms to distant recipients through charitable organizations.

The reply could be along the following lines:

Few people donate as large a percentage of their income as you to charity, but probably many who are similarly sincere, though perhaps not so generous, have wondered about the question you pose. So, though people who are merely looking for an excuse to refuse personal requests do not deserve encouragement, I am happy to explore this matter.

As Jesus warns, almsgiving can be perverted by bad motives so that it is not really an act of charity (see Mt 6.1–4). Sometimes people less interested in helping others than in obtaining tax deductions assume that all the poor they meet are undeserving; on that basis, they prefer impersonal almsgiving. Occasionally, a crying need demands an immediate response (see Lk 10.29–37; Jas 2.15–16), and certain types of needy people, such as pregnant women who might be pressed to have abortions, should not be abandoned to public agencies.

But organizations that collect and distribute money to needy people do not ipso facto turn charity into an impersonal financial transaction. Organized relief has a long Christian history. Disciples in Antioch—the first people to be called "Christians"—organized a collection for the relief of believers living in Judea, and St. Paul and St. Barnabas delivered the proceeds (see Acts 11.25–30). Later, Paul organized much more extensive collections of alms from Gentile converts for delivery to Jerusalem (see Acts 24.17, Rom 15.25–28, Gal 2.10, 1 Cor 16.1–3).

In appealing to the people of Corinth for contributions, Paul makes it abundantly clear that helping distant recipients through an organized effort can be a genuinely religious and charitable act (see 2 Cor 8.1–9.15).[296] He characterizes as a divine grace the Macedonians' contribution to this organized effort (see 2 Cor 8.1; cf. 9.15), and says he administers the grace of this project for the Lord's glory (see 2 Cor 8.19). Contributing "not only supplies the needs of the saints but also overflows with many thanksgivings to God" (2 Cor 9.12). Paul also says the collection is a "ministry to the saints" (2 Cor 8.4, 9.1) in which the donors themselves benefit (see 2 Cor 8.4–5). Contributing is an act of Christian *koinonia* (participation or fellowship) (see Rom 15.26–27; 2 Cor 8.4, 9.13). The collection will test and prove the Corinthians' love, and Paul makes clear the sort of love he has in mind by referring to the supreme act of charity: Jesus' self-sacrifice for us (see 2 Cor 8.8–9, 24).

The Church has continued what St. Paul began.[297] In an encyclical calling on his brother bishops to solicit their people's prayers and alms for the Irish people, who were afflicted with famine and disease, Pius IX asserts that he is following the example of many predecessors; he also regards as relevant, and quotes, the praise

---

296. On this passage, see Victor Paul Furnish, *II Corinthians: Translated with Introduction, Notes, and Commentary,* The Anchor Bible, 32A (Garden City, N.Y.: Doubleday, 1984), 398–453.

297. Regarding this history, see M. Scaduto, "Charity, Works of," *New Catholic Encyclopedia,* 3:480–97.

of several Church Fathers for almsgiving.[298] This sort of organized charitable giving to distant recipients is regularly carried on in the Catholic Church today by various means: the Peter's Pence collection, earmarked for charitable distribution by the Holy See, and many organizations, including those you mention, operating either directly under ecclesiastical authority or with papal and/or episcopal approval and encouragement.

Much of the Church's modern social teaching bears on the activities of governments, businesses, and other organizations. When it deals directly with the activities of individuals and families, it encourages charitable help for people in need, and certainly does not exclude those who personally seek one's help. But I have not found any Church teaching to support the view that charitable giving must involve an immediate personal relationship. Treating the place of almsgiving in a Christian democratic society, Leo XIII looks back to postapostolic times, when "those who embraced Christianity originated that wonderful variety of institutions for alleviating the miseries by which mankind is afflicted," defends against socialist criticism the practice of almsgiving to alleviate immediate need, and commends as an appropriate work of charity the "establishment of permanent institutions" to help the poor.[299]

Therefore, though the retreat master is right in saying that meeting people's needs for material goods is less important than that the parties be Christ to each other and respond to Christ in each other, he is mistaken in claiming that this requires an immediate personal relationship. What it requires is that alms be given to meet genuine needs and that both the giving and the receiving be acts of charity. For an organization to collect and distribute alms need not impede charity, and can in fact facilitate it, as St. Paul's teaching makes clear.

The retreat master's argument that refusing a face-to-face request hurtfully rejects the person also is unsound. Refusing a request, whether made face-to-face or not, rejects the one who made it only if the refusal violates love for that person—either because the request should have received a favorable response, or because the refusal is motivated by hatred, or because the manner of refusing is discourteous. However, one can decline a face-to-face request for help without violating love, and then the person is not rejected. Indeed, in refusing face-to-face requests, one sometimes can affirm those making them—for example, by directing them to some agency that can evaluate their needs and provide appropriate help.

The retreat master also seems to have misunderstood one of the Scripture passages you quote, namely: "Many refuse to lend, not because of meanness, but from fear of being defrauded needlessly. Nevertheless, be patient with someone in humble circumstances, and do not keep him waiting for your alms. Help the poor for the commandment's sake, and in their need do not send them away empty-handed" (Sir 29.7–9). This passage's first verse is not about almsgiving but lending, and it acknowledges the reasonableness of concern about possible fraud. The latter

---

298. See Pius IX, *Praedecessores nostros, Acta Pii IX,* I, 1:32–37, *PE* 41.
299. See Leo XIII, *Graves de communi re, ASS* 33 (1900–1901) 391–93, *PE* 154.15–17.

two verses, which are about almsgiving, assume that the need to be met is evident, so that concern about fraud is irrelevant.[300]

This passage and the two others you quote from the Bible do focus on direct help to someone who is present, and no doubt many passages from the Church Fathers and other reliable Christian writers have the same focus. However, such passages say nothing about almsgiving through an organization, perhaps because there were few such organizations in those days. Since they do not compare the two kinds of cases, they should not be taken to mean that almsgiving without an immediate personal relationship is defective.

Of course, various factors can give someone who personally asks for help a special claim on one's charity. Most obvious is the special claim of family, friends, and others to whom one should be grateful for past benefits. One of the Scripture passages you quote mentions "kin," and, other things being equal, one should prefer relatives to others when giving alms (see *LCL*, 309–10). Similarly, any other bond of community provides some reason for people to help one another, and that reason will be decisive when other things are equal. But other things are almost never equal. As you point out, most people in poorer countries are far needier with respect to material goods than nearly anyone in our country; and people here prepared to donate money hardly ever are directly asked for help by anyone with a need as great and urgent as that of many people who might be helped through organizations.

Moreover, in times past, factors now seldom present often made it more reasonable to respond to personal requests. Many people knew very little about the needs of anyone outside their locality; the modern media of communication have changed that. Many needy people had no recourse except to private charity; public relief and welfare programs have changed that. Most people with surplus resources regularly encountered people in evident, urgent, and desperate need; economic and social developments in affluent countries have changed that. And when most people lived in rural areas and small towns, those personally asked for help usually were acquainted with those seeking it and either knew or could verify their need; urbanization, mobility, and the complexity of the modern economy have changed that.

Then too, there could be morally bad reasons for limiting giving to persons with whom one has an immediate personal relationship. For instance, the motive might be a selfish desire for condescending emotional gratification or relief from the embarrassment and annoyance of saying no. Then too, when the needs of people far away are much greater than those close at hand, responding to the latter rather than the former can be a grave violation of one's strict duty to make right use of one's resources. The relative anonymity of those who receive alms from an organization also can help maintain their self-respect.

In sum, one certainly can give with genuine charity to people with whom one does not have any immediate personal relationship, and people living in affluent nations today often can reasonably judge that the greater need of poor people abroad

---

300. See Alexander A. DiLella, O.F.M., *The Wisdom of Ben Sira: Introduction and Commentary,* The Anchor Bible, 39 (New York: Doubleday, 1987), 370–71.

prevails over any special claim others might have on their charity. Your reasons for not responding to personal requests for help are grounded in contemporary conditions, which differ from the conditions in times past reflected in many Christian statements that focused on direct help to someone present. Under current conditions, your policy is reasonable. So, in my judgment, you have not been doing something wrong.

Still, by directly responding to personal requests, one can achieve benefits that you and those you help through organizations entirely or largely miss out on. When a transaction establishes or enhances a worthwhile personal relationship, that bond's specific qualities have their own, irreducible value. The direct communication facilitates the parties' cooperation, so that the intended help can be more appropriate and effective, and therefore more satisfactory to both. The giver's emotional involvement is likely to motivate greater generosity, not only in the quantity of goods bestowed but in their variety. The recipient is more likely to make good use of what is given and to respond with appropriate gratitude. Insofar as the relationship involves a greater exchange of spiritual goods, the giver of alms profits more and the recipient is ennobled by contributing more. Thus, the parties' emotional bonds can stimulate and encourage their mutual good will, and so dispose them to more perfect charity.

Therefore, I suggest that you and your husband consider looking for, and even inviting, some deserving personal requests for help. In your work and other activities, and in conversations with relatives, friends, and neighbors, be alert for evident or verifiable cases of need that your help can meet and that are likely to go unmet otherwise. You could obtain the tax deduction on your help by channeling it through an appropriate qualified entity, which in some cases might be your parish or diocese. Or you might tell your pastor that you will welcome requests to help people who otherwise might do grave wrongs—for example, women who might get abortions—and donate to the parish to meet at least some such needs. Again, you might both donate to a local relief agency and participate as volunteers in its work, so that you would come to know those helped by your money.[301]

An alternative would be to continue directing virtually all your donations to needy people abroad, but to give through only one organization for some ongoing program in a particular place. You could then learn about that program and involve yourselves in it, beyond donating money. Eventually, you might visit the place where the program operates and develop a personal relationship with those who manage it and some of those it serves.

Provided you pursued only the genuine benefits of immediate personal relationship and avoided condescension, either of these approaches could offer most of the

---

301. John Paul II, *Salvifici doloris*, 29, *AAS* 76 (1984) 246, *OR*, 20 Feb. 1984, 8, teaches: "The eloquence of the parable of the Good Samaritan, and of the whole Gospel, is especially this: every individual must feel as if *called personally* to bear witness to love in suffering. The institutions are very important and indispensable; nevertheless, no institution can by itself replace the human heart, human compassion, human love or human initiative, when it is a question of dealing with the sufferings of another." However, though everyone should personally help others who are suffering and doing so sometimes requires almsgiving, this obligation very often is best fulfilled by personal services rather than by giving money.

advantages, while avoiding most of the disadvantages, of the approach you have been using and the alternative advocated by the retreat master. However, even if you continue, and appropriately increase, your donations without in any way modifying your present policy, you can be doing genuine acts of charity. The essence of such acts is doing what is necessary to meet others' real needs by carrying out a good intention and choice, which themselves are gifts flowing from the love of God. The immediate personal relationship that seemed not to exist in this life will perhaps be revealed later. For, as Jesus suggests, those who do good to others benefit him without realizing it: "Lord, when was it that we saw you hungry and gave you food, or thirsty and gave you something to drink?" (Mt 25.37). Through the Lord we can hope to enjoy intimacy with those we love now at a distance and help through organizations.

96: Should a man donate to the very poor rather than to a college?

This has been an extraordinary year. In January, my wife began having problems that turned out to be symptoms of brain cancer. She died in August, leaving me to raise our six children, the eldest fifteen and the baby just over a year old. I have been making a decent living selling insurance, but the cost of hiring good help seemed to dictate a drastic cut in our standard of living. Suddenly, though, I am a wealthy man, winner of the ten-million-dollar jackpot in the October state lottery. They will pay me a half million every year for twenty years. When I learned I had won, I took a week off and went on a retreat to think about what to do. By the end of the retreat I had reached some decisions. Among them is that I will give fifty percent of each annual payment to charity. I think it only right to share this windfall with others, and, anyway, the tax collectors otherwise would take about half of it.

My first thought was to help the poorest of the poor. Most poor people in this country receive some sort of assistance, and donations to individuals and foreign charities are not tax-exempt, so I began looking into agencies based in the U.S. that help the very poor in other countries. So far, Catholic Relief Services (CRS) looks like the best channel for my purpose. It appears from an initial discussion that by working through them I could save many children from death and hopelessness by providing some extremely poor families with basic necessities and helping their children get a start in life. I would not have to pledge to continue donating to CRS year after year, but could review the matter each year and find an alternative if I had doubts about how they were using my donations.

But there is a complication. I graduated from a nearby Catholic college, to which I also plan to send my children. When the president asked to talk with me about the school's plans for development, I agreed to see him, and he visited me a few days ago. I told him what I am thinking of doing, and he acknowledged that it would be good, but he urged me instead to help build the school's new auditorium. Today he brought me architect's drawings, a description of the project, and a formal request for the donation, together with documents ready for me to review and, he hopes, sign. Some funds already have been raised for the project. If I make an irrevocable commitment to donate the quarter-million dollars annually for twenty years, the college could get advantageous financing and start construction in a few months.

The school does need the new auditorium. The gymnasium makes a poor auditorium; and many guest lectures and some other events have been in the chapel, but the new chaplain says it should not be used for anything but liturgy, devotions, and sacred music. An auditorium with proper lighting and backstage facilities also would make it possible for the college to expand its performing arts programs and related extracurricular activities. There is no similar facility in the area, so the auditorium could be rented out often enough to cover its operating costs and maintenance.

Having kept in touch with the college over the years, I know that, while far from perfect, it has stayed more Catholic than most. This president has made a number of changes for the better. For instance, he replaced the dean of students and tightened the rules for dormitory life. He also got the bishop to appoint the new chaplain, a middle-aged priest who is orthodox but personable, extremely hardworking, and very good with young people. The president even has managed to get rid of several nontenured faculty members, including two in theology who openly dissented from the Church's moral teaching and whose replacements openly support it.

The idea of giving the money for the auditorium appeals to me. If I commit to it, the project can be completed within three years, by the time my eldest child begins her first year at the college, and the building would be dedicated as a memorial to my wife. I also would be given a seat on the college's board of directors. Still, I am not sure what to do. An auditorium, no matter how needed it may be, will not save anyone's life, and it seems I would be paying for an auditorium at the cost of human lives. Jesus told us to feed the hungry, clothe the naked, and shelter the homeless, not provide facilities for colleges whose students are not and never have been hungry, naked, or homeless.

You will appreciate that I've never confronted anything like this before. What do you think I should do?

Analysis:

This question calls for the derivation and application of a norm regarding the use of surplus resources to meet others' needs. Anyone with such resources should select a beneficiary who cannot meet a genuine need without help and whose need will not be met excessively with the help to be given. The possibility that hoped-for benefits will not be realized also should be considered. In light of these considerations, the questioner might conclude that he ought to try to help the very poor rather than the college. If not, his concern that the subsistence needs of the very poor may demand preference over others' need for education is not decisive. Therefore, if he judges after due inquiry and reflection that giving to Catholic Relief Services and to the college would both be good, he must discover which God is calling him to do by discerning which is more appropriate for him—though it might be even more appropriate that he develop an option for simultaneously helping both the college and the very poor.

The reply could be along the following lines:

Despite your conscientious effort—unusual, but entirely appropriate—to discover your responsibility for using the lottery prize, someone might argue that, lacking true charity, you are ungenerous and selfish in being concerned about the tax implications of the possible donations and about your personal connections with the college. In fact, however, the former concern shows that you really care about the well-being of those in need, to whom you would have less to give if you paid more taxes than you must. Only if one believed the government likely to make better use of one's surplus money than those to whom one might give it would it be reasonable to ignore possible tax breaks, and in that case one should donate all one's surplus wealth to the government. As for your concern about your involvement with the college, far from evidencing selfishness, it is entirely compatible with genuine charity toward those to whom you are closely bound. To disregard such special ties, especially those with your family, would be incompatible with charity (see *LCL,* 309–10).

While your problem is unique, anyone with surplus resources that should be used to meet others' needs faces a similar problem. Resources are limited, and apparent unmet needs are virtually endless. To identify suitable beneficiaries, several questions must be answered.

Is an apparent need genuine? People do not have genuine needs for everything they want or think they need. Genuine needs are marked out by the basic human goods, which are intelligible reasons for action, considered as the object of a will toward integral human fulfillment (see *LCL,* 801). So, *genuine needs* refers not only to the basic necessities but to the less obvious yet real needs for religious, moral, and cultural goods. What *genuine* excludes are mere objects of emotional desire and anything that would be obtained, used, or enjoyed sinfully. On this basis, one should not meet needs artificially created by advertising or a revolutionary's need for weapons to be employed in terroristic attacks on innocent persons.

Could the need be met adequately by the effort and parsimony of the individual or group who will be benefited? One should help those who cannot sufficiently help themselves, not those whose need results from ongoing unwillingness to do what they can and should be doing. On this basis, St. Paul points out: "Anyone unwilling to work should not eat" (2 Thes 3.10).

Will the help one might give meet the need adequately and moderately, or more than adequately and, perhaps, extravagantly or luxuriously? Adequacy and moderation are specified by the precise need to be met. Concerns about comfort and convenience can lead to excess, and the influence of mixed, nonrational motives often results in extravagance and luxury. For instance, one should not supply a few hungry people with choice and expensive food rather than many with a palatable diet or provide one institution with sumptuous facilities rather than several with serviceable ones.

Plainly, the needs of the very poor that you could try to meet by donating to Catholic Relief Services are genuine; even with your help, those needs would be met only moderately. The needs of the college's students and others for education also are genuine. The auditorium's intended uses presumably would help meet those needs, though some incidental uses of the building probably would be bad ones. Presumably, too, the students and their parents, who would be the main beneficiaries of your donations, cannot afford the whole cost of the students' education. Your judgment is that the auditorium really is needed, and presumably it would be serviceable, not sumptuous.

Of course, on further inquiry and reflection, you might come to think that most of the genuine needs to be served by the auditorium probably could be met, though less conveniently and pleasantly, with existing facilities or improvements to them funded by a tuition increase. By contrast, the needs to be met by Catholic Relief Services might come to seem more exigent and the potential beneficiaries more clearly deserving of your help. Moreover, committing yourself irrevocably to giving the college money annually for twenty years would involve considerable risk. The present president may not remain in office; laws affecting religiously oriented colleges may change; and for these or other reasons the school might deteriorate in respect to its Catholic commitment or otherwise, perhaps so drastically that you would rather not support it or send your children to it. Considering all these things, you might conclude that, with people dying of hunger and malnutrition, building the auditorium either would be an indulgent extravagance or would offer insufficiently certain benefits or both. If that is your conclusion, it would be unreasonable to accept the president's proposal in place of your tentative plan to help the very poor.

But perhaps, having carefully considered all the relevant facts, you will conclude that both sets of needs are genuine, each project would attempt to meet needs moderately, both potential sets of beneficiaries are deserving, and the risk involved in donating to the college is acceptable. In what follows I shall respond on the assumption that you will reach that conclusion. Also, I shall take it for granted that fairness and Christian mercy require using surplus resources to meet others' genuine needs (see *LCL,* 780–82, 789–92, 800–806, 811–14).

But does any reason require you to prefer trying to meet the needs of the poorest of the poor? It might be argued that subsistence needs should take priority over others, such as the needs for education and wholesome entertainment, and you therefore should prefer to donate to Catholic Relief Services. Indeed, you articulate that argument in tentatively judging that you would be financing the auditorium's benefits at the cost of human lives, and you theologically support that tentative conclusion by invoking Jesus' teaching.

Subsistence needs sometimes do deserve priority, because remaining alive is a necessary condition for participating in many other human goods. Thus, an individual has a strong reason to try first to meet his or her own subsistence needs, and a family or other tight-knit community whose members are united in solidarity by biological ties or other close bonds, has an analogous reason for preferring to meet its members' subsistence needs. For example, suppose a family expects to meet many religious, moral, and cultural needs of all its members, provided all survive, but a famine threatens the very survival of some. In such a case, everyone in the family should put aside other concerns for a time and devote the family's resources to ensuring the survival of all.

Sometimes, however, subsistence needs do not deserve priority. For example, meeting in moderate ways the religious, moral, and cultural needs of one's own children takes priority over feeding someone else's, even if the latter are starving; parents are not free to be merciful at their children's expense. Moreover, Jesus defended the action of a woman who anointed him against criticism that the costly ointment should have been sold to help the poor (see Mk 14.3–9), and Christians surely may support missionary activity rather than feed the starving. In all such cases, the fundamental reason why other needs may be preferred is that meeting diverse genuine needs contributes in incommensurable ways to the well-being and fulfillment of persons, so that the choice to meet any genuine need is the willing of at least some person's good—which is an act of love—and the meeting of any one sort of genuine need is not in and of itself better and more loving than the meeting of another.

Moreover, even if the money you could donate to Catholic Relief Services would save the lives of people who otherwise would die, you will not finance the auditorium's benefits at the cost of those lives by giving the money to the college instead. You neither will have willed those people to die—for example, by choosing to kill them as a means to some other end—nor judged their lives of less worth than the benefits of the auditorium. You only will have reluctantly accepted their deaths as a side effect of promoting the other good. And, provided you can choose that other good fairly, you need not be unreasonable in choosing it—not as better, but simply as the irreplaceable good it is. (This is on the assumption—I repeat—that you have concluded after careful consideration that both sets of needs are genuine, that each of the projects would attempt to meet one of them moderately, that both potential sets of beneficiaries are deserving, and that the risk involved in donating to the college is not too great.)

True, Jesus taught about meeting the subsistence needs of the poor, not about providing facilities for colleges. But colleges as we know them did not exist in New Testament times. The opportunities for advanced education, which were quite limited, generally were available only to the wealthy. The charitable works Jesus mentions are clear-cut examples relevant in every culture and historical epoch. But tradition has not regarded Jesus' list as exhaustive or exclusive of other possibilities, so that, besides meeting the bodily needs of the poor, Christians have been exhorted to perform so-called spiritual works of mercy, including instructing the ignorant (see *CCC*, 2447).

Still, the Golden Rule requires that, other things being equal, one use surplus resources in ways that more clearly and certainly will meet genuine needs of deserving people in a moderate way. In my judgment, then, one reasonably donates money, other things being equal, to a trustworthy agency to feed the starving rather than to a college to add to its facilities.

Other things are not equal, however, in the alternatives you are considering. You already have some special ties with the college; you are an alumnus and hope to use it for educating your children; the building would be a memorial to your wife; and your appointment to the board, in response to your donation, would enable you to participate in directing the college toward its good purpose. Though these considerations could appeal to mere sentiment or even to vanity, they also refer to intelligible goods, and your clearheaded reflection and evident desire to make the right choice indicate that you regard these goods as reasons for accepting the president's proposal.

Therefore, on the assumptions explained previously, you could rightly choose to donate the money for the new auditorium, just as you certainly also could rightly carry out your tentative plan to donate it to Catholic Relief Services. If both options would be morally good choices for you, however, nobody can say you should choose this one or that. To learn God's will, you must consider both options prayerfully and discern which is appropriate for you (see *LCL,* 291–93).

But I suggest you also consider some additional options. For example, you might divide your donation, evenly or unevenly, between Catholic Relief Services and the college. That might not make it possible for the college to start building the auditorium at once, but it would help with the project or otherwise provide students with significant benefits.

Again, you might consider giving the whole donation to the college, not for an auditorium, but for one or more programs that also would help the poor: a new program of studies to prepare generous and dedicated young people to carry out some kind of service to the poor, or a fund to help some very needy, academically promising young people attend the college. You probably could help the college in ways like these while making it more likely that your donations would bring about genuine benefits for deserving individuals in a moderate way. Indeed, you probably could become acquainted with those whose studies your donations subsidized, and you might be able to give them your personal, fatherly guidance and encouragement. Such an option also might have the advantage of not involving any irrevocable commitment to continue your donations, regardless of changes in the college. And your contribution could still serve as a memorial to your wife, and perhaps would still bring you a seat on the board, which I trust you would use, not for mere self-aggrandizement, but to promote the college's continuing improvement.

97: What costs and risks may a man impose in launching an apostolic business venture?

I believe this country needs a large, efficient distributor of Catholic literature and audiovisual materials—books, pamphlets, tapes, movies, film strips, CD ROM disks, and so forth. The service I have in mind would handle only doctrinally sound materials, but it would try to handle everything sound and of decent quality available in English or Spanish—though I realize that is not literally possible. All materials would be listed and described in a widely distributed catalogue, also supplied on computer disk and available on-line. Orders would be accepted both by mail and through a 24-hour toll-free number. An important goal would be to ship orders within one day with very few exceptions, though meeting that goal would require a large stock. Ideally, substantial discounts would be offered, and packing and shipping charges would be limited to a small, fixed fee for each order.

The point would be to support study, evangelization, and catechesis faithful to the Church's teachings by making sound and good quality materials widely and easily available. Such materials might then compete more effectively with the unfaithful, unsound, and poor quality materials that now have a distinct advantage in channels of distribution as well as in favorable publicity in the secular media—and even in many so-called Catholic media.

For thirty years, I have managed my own small mail-order company, specializing in items businesses sometimes need but cannot get from most stores handling business supplies. Meanwhile, I have kept up with what is going on in the Church and been active in a lay organization that supports faithful catechesis. I now am sixty-two and I could retire. But the prospect of retiring lost its appeal when my wife died several years ago. Since we had no children, though we hoped for them, and I have no other family responsibilities, I am quite free. By liquidating all my assets—the business, our home, my retirement plan, investments—I could realize about two million dollars after taxes. I could then set up a nonprofit corporation and capitalize it by irrevocably transferring my assets to it.

I could rent suitable warehouse and office space, and equip the office with the facilities minimally required for me to live there. I also could cut my expenses by doing without a car and dropping all my insurance. Initially, I could live on my social security income, while taking advantage of food stamps and other programs for the poor. Working constantly, I would be able to keep the payroll to a minimum.

Especially at the beginning, extensive advertising and direct mail promotion would be necessary. That would be a substantial investment, and I cannot predict the response. Beyond that, to carry the project through the critical period—from start-up to the point where it became self-sustaining—I would need substantial donations and/or some loans, with the first payment deferred at least two years. While I already have a few promises of help, I would have to count on additional backers coming forward as the project became known. In merely human terms, then, the likelihood that this venture would succeed is not great. But many saints have taken risks in starting or expanding their apostolic projects, and it seems to me I should be able to undertake this project even though doing something like this as an ordinary business venture would be foolhardy.

If the project succeeds, I will take a modest salary so that I will be able to do without help from public programs for the poor. Of course, if the project fails, I will be left with nothing. I am ready to accept that risk; I expect I would find a way to support myself for some years, and then, if need be, I could make do on social security, food stamps, and so on. However, failure also would affect others adversely. Backers would lose the money they donated or loaned; employees would be out of work; suppliers who extended credit would go unpaid; and my personal needs would be met from the public purse, a cost that might be substantial if, for example, I live out my life in a nursing home with Medicaid paying the bill. Also, to maximize the chances of success, I would have to keep the operation going as long as possible, even if the chances of bankruptcy became great.

Provided I do not lie to anyone, may I accept these risks of adverse consequences to others in undertaking an apostolate I am convinced is needed and would benefit many people?

Analysis:

This question primarily concerns the moral permissibility of accepting risks of harm to others as a side effect of undertaking an apostolic project. With respect to private individuals and groups, the question can be answered by applying the Golden Rule; with respect to the public at large, it requires consideration of the project's bearing on the nation's common good. The questioner not only must refrain from lying but must at all stages take care to obtain the fully informed consent of potential supporters, employees, and suppliers and to comply with laws that justly apply. A secondary, implicit question concerns the role supernatural hope legitimately plays in judging acceptable risks when undertaking an apostolic project. Answering this implied question requires clarifying the proper object of hope—the heavenly kingdom—which does not ensure the earthly success of any apostolic project.

The reply could be along the following lines:

Noting that many saints have taken great risks in undertaking apostolates, you suggest that the apostolic character of your plan provides a ground for hope absent in an ordinary business venture. Of course, many good apostolic projects fail, and many wicked business ventures succeed. Yet if you undertake this project, I think you do have a ground for special hope, namely, your readiness to put everything you have into it. Surely, your evangelical generosity will be met by corresponding divine generosity. Still, supernatural hope bears primarily and directly, not on desired results in this world, but on the kingdom (see *LCL,* 85–86; q. 6, above). You can be confident of finding the good fruit of your effort in heaven (see GS 38–39), but that hope is relevant to judging the morality of accepting the risks involved only insofar as they are risks to yourself or others who share your reasons for being ready to accept them. Some saints who took great risks in launching apostolic projects may have violated this norm; if so, that was wrong, though presumably sinless due to lack of sufficient reflection.

Everyone has a duty to provide for his or her own genuine needs, and no one may set aside this responsibility in making any commitment, however good. Still, in committing oneself to any element of one's vocation, one must forgo some goods in which one has shared or might share, and risk suffering some evils one could otherwise avoid. Even in committing oneself to an apostolic project such as you have in mind, one still should provide with minimal adequacy for oneself, and that seems to be your plan. Having done that, one can rightly give up comfort and risk security, even health and life, if the prospective benefits make great sacrifice reasonable. Though you judge that your proposed venture is not likely to succeed, its prospective benefits would be very great. Therefore, in my judgment, you may proceed despite the risk of losing everything and the other costs to yourself. Foolish by worldly standards, such a commitment can be an appropriate response to Jesus' call to set aside everything else to join him in service to the kingdom (see Lk 12.32–34, 18.18–30).

Not lying is an important and necessary, but not sufficient, condition for establishing just relationships with others. In seeking people's cooperation in any apostolic work, one also must avoid misleading them, so that their consent to cooperate will be adequately informed. Indeed, not only honesty but candor is necessary whenever one foresees that failing to provide information or answer questions straightforwardly is likely to generate unrealistic expectations. In seeking backing for your project, hiring and dealing with employees, and doing business with suppliers, your enthusiasm for and commitment to the undertaking could lead you to ignore or brush aside various obstacles, exaggerate the prospects for success, and make implicit promises—for example, of ongoing employment or of payment of bills—without there being reasonable grounds for confidence that the promises can be kept. Before considering the acceptability of risking adverse consequences to others, you first must firmly commit yourself to be honest and candid with them. Likewise, you should consider the legitimacy of imposing burdens and risks on the public only after first meeting the more basic and obvious responsibility to inform yourself about relevant laws and committing yourself to abide by those that justly apply.

The chances of your imposing unfair risks on other individuals and organizations will be greatly reduced if they give adequately informed consent to their cooperation with you, not only initially but at every subsequent stage. For instance, no matter how great the prospect of bankruptcy, you are unlikely to impose unfair risks on suppliers if you are always entirely candid with them about your operation's condition and prospects. To determine whether you may accept any remaining risks of adverse consequences to them and others, you need only apply the Golden Rule. But putting yourself in others' places should not extend to their moral defects, so that, for example, you ought not to consider it fair to accept credit from a supplier or a loan from a supporter who should not be advancing the credit or should be keeping the money to meet some other obligation. Also, when applying the Golden Rule, you should leave behind your enthusiasm for the project and your commitment to it, and consider the acceptability of risks to others in the light of their own true interests and responsibilities.

Since laws normally are designed to safeguard the common good, conforming to all justly applicable laws will greatly reduce the chances of wronging the public at large by voluntarily impoverishing yourself, taking advantage of programs for the poor, and obliging the taxpayers to meet the cost, perhaps substantial, of supporting you.

Someone might argue that to impoverish yourself voluntarily would be an unjust imposition on society. However, impoverishing oneself need not be unjust in itself, and it seems to me you would be justified in doing so. To determine whether you are morally free to accept the social costs and risks you can lawfully accept, you need only consider how what you are doing is related to the nation's common good. That means comparing your project's potential risks and costs with its potential benefits for the nation. Though a political society's constitution perhaps rightly forbids the state to promote religious truth, patriotic citizens ought to use nonpolitical means to promote it, for their nation's sake among other reasons (see *LCL*, 840–42). As you say, "this country needs a large, efficient distributor of Catholic literature and audiovisual materials." Your service, if successful, will help the country learn about Catholic truth and resist socially corrosive secularism. Its potential benefits for the nation, therefore, argue for the acceptability of its social costs and risks. Therefore, provided you abide by the law, I think you may take for granted that the social costs and risks involved in carrying out your plan are morally acceptable.

Someone might reject the preceding argument's claim that your project will benefit the nation's common good, and argue that taking advantage of programs to aid the poor will be unfair to fellow citizens who do not share your faith. I do not concede the soundness of that argument. But even granting its premise, an argument can be made that impoverishing yourself will not be unfair to fellow citizens. The public programs of which you plan to take advantage indiscriminately benefit all who meet their requirements. That includes many people who have contributed little or nothing to society and some whose need is a product of their own irresponsibility, perhaps even their criminal activities. I assume that you, by contrast, have been a law-abiding citizen, have paid your taxes, and have contributed in other ways to the common good.

Besides the responsibilities on which your question focuses, you have another important one that you may have overlooked: to investigate and take into account how your undertaking might affect others' apostolates. Since every authentic apostolate is a way of cooperating in the Church's single mission, sound dedication to any apostolate presupposes ecclesial spirit: the determination to harmonize one's effort with others' somewhat similar projects and avoid working at cross-purposes.

For this reason, it seems to me, before proceeding with your plan you should seek episcopal review of it. I do not mean that you must obtain formal episcopal approval, but that you should ask for episcopal criticisms and suggestions, with a view to harmonizing your apostolic effort with theirs and other related operations. Since your undertaking will have a nationwide impact, communication at least with all the ordinaries—if not also with the auxiliaries and retired bishops—would be appropriate. Many probably will not reply, but some will, and you will gain useful insights. Moreover, your demonstration of ecclesial spirit, the potential value of your apostolic undertaking, and your own dedication to it are likely to gain some episcopal approval and support.

A final suggestion, though you may well have thought of it already. Before proceeding, seek comments on your plan from publishers who will be among your suppliers and from others already engaged in somewhat similar apostolates. For example, the Daughters of St. Paul operate a chain of bookstores that sell both their own and others' publications faithful to the Church's teachings. You should forestall damaging competition with their apostolate, and perhaps should try to work out some form of collaboration. Again, this preliminary consultation is likely to prevent various problems from arising, lay a foundation for cooperation, and enable you to improve your plan and perhaps significantly increase its chances of succeeding.

98: What percentage of donations may fund raisers spend on overhead?

I am the president of a Church-affiliated, nonprofit organization whose sole function is to raise and distribute funds for missionary activity. Raising money costs money for staff, offices, advertising, and so forth. Most contributors to nonprofit organizations probably do not realize that these overhead costs often take a large part of what they contribute. Before I became president, our board of directors had considered this problem and decided that eighty cents of every dollar we raise must actually go to the missions and not more than twenty percent may be used for overhead. I am wondering whether I should urge the board to increase the percentage I may use for overhead, and, if so, by how much.

The case for making the increase is quite simple and straightforward. Last year we raised nearly ten million dollars, and our total overhead was just over $1,800,000—which was a little under 19%. Advertising accounted for more than half the overhead, just under one million. An advertising agency we use has worked up a convincing study showing that, if we double our advertising budget, we can expect to raise two to four million more. That would give us about one to three million more to distribute, since distributing the money costs virtually nothing and other elements of our overhead would hardly increase at all. At worst, our total overhead would be 25% of twelve million raised and at best under 21.5% of fourteen million raised.

The same sort of argument can of course be made for increasing the advertising budget even more, to the point at which any further increase would no longer bring in contributions adequate to cover it. That strategy, adopted by some fund raisers, often results in overhead of fifty percent, seventy-five percent, or even more. Personally, I feel adopting that strategy would not be keeping faith with our contributors, but I do not feel the same way about the proposal to double our advertising budget. But if we do that, where do we draw the line?

In considering my question, you may find it helpful to know that at present we are not required to tell contributors about overhead costs and never do so unless asked. When asked, we send a brochure that includes a detailed statement for the previous year and an easy-to-understand explanation justifying our overhead. The explanation points out that, while all our advertising is meant to raise money, it does incidentally educate people about the missions and their needs, including their need for vocations and prayers. Thus, our advertising has some nonmonetary benefits, sometimes even when it brings in no contribution.

On this basis, we could adopt a device used by many fund-raising organizations. Instead of saying that more than eighty cents of every dollar received goes to the missions and less than twenty cents for overhead, we could introduce "educational programs" (the advertising budget) as a third category. Then we could say that more than so much of every dollar is either distributed to the missions or used for educational programs, while the remainder, ascribed to overhead, would be a much smaller percentage than now, and would shrink proportionately as our advertising budget increased.

Of course, we could make this change whether or not we raise the present limit. I would therefore appreciate it if you would consider as a distinct question: May we adopt the device of attributing our advertising costs to "educational programs" so as to reduce the proportion of contributions apparently going for overhead?

Analysis:

The first question—What percentage of the money donated may be used for overhead?—admits of no precise answer, and reasonable judgments must take into account diverse circumstances. Fund raisers defraud donors if overhead takes a significantly larger portion of donations than thoughtful donors would expect. Fund raisers also must be fair to other fund raisers and their causes. The present policy of the questioner's organization limiting overhead to twenty percent does not clearly violate these norms. However, in my judgment, raising that limit would be questionable. Investigation could determine recent donors' expectations regarding overhead. If those expectations are to be exceeded, all appeals for donations at least should state clearly that a substantial portion of donations is used for fund-raising costs and that a detailed statement is available on request. The second question—May this organization's advertising costs be attributed to "educational programs"?—can be answered definitely: no. Because all of the organization's advertising is directed primarily to fund raising, attributing advertising costs to educational programs would be deceptive.

The reply could be along the following lines:

I do not think there is any precise answer to the question: What percentage of donated money may be used for overhead? But one can articulate some relevant norms indicating the outer limits of moral acceptability. For organizations making a first effort at fund raising, those whose purpose is to raise funds adequate to meet some well-defined need or set of needs, those with unpopular causes, or those with substantial management expenses other than fund-raising costs, the norms would be somewhat different from those for organizations which, like yours, are well-established, are seeking funds to meet open-ended needs, have a cause acceptable to many members of an easily identified community, and have few other management expenses. So, while some of the following norms are true for every fund-raising organization, not all are.

First, fund raisers must be dedicated, not merely self-serving. Claiming to serve the good cause for which they seek funds, they must intend to serve it, not simply to make a living for themselves. Of course, they may take fair recompense for their service, but the good cause, not self-interest, must remain the end shaping their decisions about fund-raising strategies and how much to spend on overhead.

Second, in seeking donations, a fund raiser implicitly assures potential donors that their money will be used for the purposes described. Everyone who thinks about it knows there will be some overhead, so fund raisers need not make a point of that unless it exceeds what potential donors would expect. Unless told otherwise, people asked to donate for a particular purpose surely expect that most of what they might give would be used for that purpose. So, a fund-raising strategy resulting in undisclosed overhead of fifty percent or more plainly would be fraudulent. That would not be so if the high overhead were fully disclosed to all potential donors, but then of course the campaign would not be likely to succeed.

Third, in many situations, a strategy resulting in overhead even less than fifty percent would be fraudulent, since expectations are based on people's past experience. For instance, many Catholics' expectations regarding fund raising are shaped by their experience with parish and diocesan collections, such as Catholic charities, where the overhead is very low. Of course, anyone who thinks about the matter should realize that the overhead for virtually any other sort of fund raising inevitably will be greater. Still, when the costs of fund raising for Catholic causes are significantly greater than most thoughtful Catholics would expect, fund raisers defraud people unless all appeals for donations include a fair warning about overhead costs.

Fourth, fund raisers must be not only honest with potential donors but fair to other fund raisers and their causes. Some strategies might encourage people to give more overall, but others are more likely to lead them to redirect part or all of what they donate. In the latter case, even if relatively high undisclosed overhead is not fraudulent, it can be unfair to competing fund raisers and causes. Most bishops and pastors of parishes, for instance, probably would regard any Catholic organization spending a quarter of what it raises for overhead as unfair competition, unless the organization encouraged people to regard what they give it as a complement to, rather than as a substitute for, their contributions to diocesan and parish collections.

Applying these norms to the current policy of your organization, I think it clearly meets the requirements of the first two. Whether it meets the requirement of the third is not so clear, yet I do not think it clearly violates that norm, and your practice of responding fully and honestly to inquiries about overhead costs is reassuring. Without analyzing the literature you now send out, I cannot guess whether your present strategy meets the requirement of the fourth norm. But since your purpose is to raise and distribute funds for missionary activity, you can easily avoid unfair competition with parish and diocesan collections by focusing your appeals on the responsibility of all Catholics to contribute not only to their own parish and diocese but to the Church's worldwide apostolate—especially to spreading and supporting the faith where the Church is not yet well enough established to sustain herself.

What about the proposal to double your advertising budget, so as to increase the amount you will raise and distribute to the missions, while also increasing your overhead, perhaps to nearly twenty-five percent? Assuming all or much of the increase in donations would result from acquiring new donors, the additional advertising cost might well be fruitful in future years.[302] Still, I suspect that increasing your overhead would put it beyond donors' reasonable expectations. To

302. James M. Greenfield, *Fund-Raising: Evaluating and Managing the Fund Development Process* (New York: John Wiley and Sons, 1991), 45–47, offers as reasonable guidelines for fund-raising cost-effectiveness $1.00 to $1.25 per dollar raised for direct mail acquisition and $.20 per dollar raised for direct mail renewal.

find out whether it would, you could have an independent organization poll a representative sample of your recent donors. Those polled would be asked to guess the costs of fund raising by various causes on a list including the missions among others. I think the inquiry will show that increasing the advertising budget, and perhaps even maintaining it at the present level, will violate the third norm unless you begin to inform all current and potential donors about overhead costs, at least by clearly stating that a significant part of every donation goes for overhead and offering to send your detailed statement and explanation to anyone who wants it.

What about calling advertising expenditures "education?" Unless the primary purpose of the advertising really is to educate, introducing so-called educational programs as a third category would be fraudulent. All sound advertising to raise money for good causes does teach people about responsibilities pertaining to justice and mercy. But this teaching is strictly subordinate to fund raising. Some organizations, of course, not only raise money for a certain purpose (for example, research to cure or treat some disease) but carry on distinct programs intended to educate both donors and the general public (for example, how to watch for signs of the disease); their budgets rightly include educational programs as a category separate from overhead. Since the purpose of a program determines what it is, an honest description of any particular expenditure requires that it be charged to one or another category according to the main intention in making it. Expenses intended for both purposes should be divided appropriately between the two categories. Since the content of any advertisement or literature an organization distributes reveals the intention behind the material, one might seek advice from a panel of impartial people in deciding how to allocate the costs of such materials between overhead and educational programs.

If it is literally true, however, that your organization's "sole function," as you put it, "is to raise and distribute funds for missionary activity," then all your advertising is intended to raise money, and it would be dishonest to attribute any part of its cost to educational programs. Yet the educational benefits from your advertising, even when it elicits no contribution, do help justify its costs, and so you rightly point out those benefits in explaining your statement of income, expenses, and funds distributed to the missions.

99: What moral norms should one follow in tipping?

While we have always had a decent income, we have lived conservatively, avoiding credit, paying off our mortgage and improving our house rather than moving up to a bigger and fancier one, saving for the children's education, and so on. We seldom ate in restaurants, and when we traveled we either camped out or stayed at one of the less expensive motels. Now our last child is finishing college, and our economies over the years are paying off. We have no debts and, with both of us working, our income is more than twice our expenses. Last autumn we decided to loosen up and live a little before we get too old to enjoy it. We have been eating out and staying at better places. Just after Christmas we took an eight-day Caribbean cruise, and we are planning our first overseas trip, a three-week vacation in Europe this summer.

With this change in our lifestyle, we are fairly often in situations where tipping is expected. Since the vacations we are taking are expensive, we do not want to tip more than necessary, and we wonder what our obligations are. Books on etiquette and some travel books deal with tipping, but they only say what is expected. We want to know what is morally required.

For instance, a tip presumably is for good service, so not giving a tip is legitimate when service is poor. But how poor must it be? Again, especially in hotels, attendants sometimes insist on doing things, such as handling luggage, that we would just as soon do ourselves. Is it necessary to tip for such unwanted service? Then too, on the cruise they gave us a list of "recommended gratuities" adding up to a lot of money. There also is a problem with tipping in restaurants. Assuming the usual fifteen-percent tip, waitresses and waiters in inexpensive places get three dollars on a twenty-dollar check while in fancier places, for providing essentially the same service, they expect fifteen dollars on a hundred-dollar check, which seems excessive.

Another problem concerns tipping in other countries. Presumably Jesus' "Do unto others" applies to tipping as it does to any other question about how to treat people. But in many situations, its implications are far from clear. The European travel books we have been looking at indicate that the customary tips are not the same there as here. In their place, we would want to be tipped as Americans usually are, and, applying "Do unto others," it seems to follow that we should tip in Europe as we would here.

Last but not least, some people argue that the whole system of tipping should be done away with, and we are inclined to agree with them. But if that would be right, perpetuating the bad system seems wrong to us. In that case, wouldn't it be right never to tip at all? This idea, though, is so attractive that there probably is something wrong with it!

Analysis:

This question calls for both the derivation of specific norms regarding tipping and an explanation of how to apply the Golden Rule. A tip can be either compensation required in justice, a gratuity, or both. The practice of tipping often is an occasion of sin for both parties; also it often leads to objective injustice because many patrons or customers cannot know whether and how much they ought to tip. So, in my judgment, tipping should be done away with. But until it is, one ought to provide just tips for services rendered. In applying the Golden Rule to determine whether and how much to tip, one should take local practice into account. Unusually good service calls for a supplement, especially if the person being tipped is not so well off as oneself. Unwanted services can be refused, and then, if provided, not compensated unless mercy requires it. If someone providing service seriously fails to do his or her duty, compensation is not due in justice, but Christian mercy may call for giving both the tip and an admonition. The issue of the right use of wealth is not raised by the questioner, but ought to be addressed; otherwise the casuistry of tipping is likely to be applied in a legalistic way.

The reply could be along the following lines:

What is tipping?[303] It is a way of paying people for particular performances of certain sorts of services, generally ones supplied in earlier times by a proprietor's slaves or servants rather than by professionals or other independent contractors. The payment provided by a tip involves one or both of two elements: compensation justly due for a service rendered by someone who otherwise will not receive adequate compensation, and a bonus or gratuitous amount given for one or more reasons—for example, as a reward for especially pleasing service, as alms given poorly paid workers by comparatively prosperous recipients of service, as a way of sharing the joy of a celebration with those providing services, and as a way of marking the superiority in socioeconomic status of those served to those who serve. Peculiar to tipping is that even the element that is due in strict justice cannot be legally exacted, so that its payment depends on the honesty of the service's recipient.

This definition makes it clear that the practice of tipping can raise two moral issues: about fairness in compensation for services rendered and about rightness of intention in giving a bonus in excess of fair compensation. I shall not consider the latter issue, however, since your question focuses exclusively on the former.

When patrons or customers know precisely what is expected—especially when they frequent an establishment regularly and receive service from the same people, so that the parties become well acquainted—tipping may result in fair compensation. When it works well, the practice has certain moral advantages over a system that specifies required service charges. People who tip appropriately must exercise more consideration for others and good will toward them than those who merely pay fixed charges, while people of good will who provide services compensated by tips also have greater opportunities to develop various virtues, such as meekness and patience, than those whose compensation is fixed. When both parties act uprightly, their interpersonal relationship, even if ephemeral, has the human depth of friendly cooperation. Moreover, the practice facilitates adjustments in compensation both by way of a supplement given for any good reason and by way of a downward adjustment in costs for people of severely limited means.

Still, I am inclined to agree with those who maintain that tipping should be done away with. The fundamental flaw is that it often requires people to decide how much to pay for services, without the information needed to make that judgment. Thus, the system can lead to objective injustice even when those concerned are subjectively upright. It also can be an occasion of sin for both parties. Those who serve are sometimes motivated to act unauthentically and react resentfully, while those served sometimes exploit the situation for their own psychological gratification. Moreover, the latter sometimes evade paying what they owe, while those providing service sometimes practice deception to elicit a gratuity. Then too, people

303. The conceptual answer given here can be supplemented by empirical data; see Michael Lynn et al., "Consumer Tipping: A Cross-Country Study," *Journal of Consumer Research,* 20 (1993): 478–88; Mary B. Harris, "Waiters, Customers, and Service: Some Tips about Tipping," *Journal of Applied Social Psychology,* 25 (1995): 725–44, which includes references to many previous studies.

who get tips sometimes cheat one another and/or cheat on their taxes. Further, the practice sometimes overlaps with bribery and extortion. Tips are given in exchange for unfair advantage over other customers in obtaining service or goods, or are demanded for the delivery of something already due in justice. Consequently, it seems to me that everyone should urge the proprietors of enterprises whose employees still depend on tips for just compensation to do away with the practice. This they could do either by specifying a service charge in their bill or including the cost of service in their basic prices, and informing patrons that their employees are paid adequate wages and tipping is not expected.

But as long as the practice of tipping persists, both parties can do their parts virtuously, and anyone receiving a service of a sort for which a tip might be expected has a moral obligation to judge whether and how much to tip. Even if someone considers tipping an unjust social structure, he or she is bound to do justice within that unjust structure rather than deprive workers who depend on tips of just compensation. To withhold a tip that is strictly due is a form of theft. And even where tipping has been eliminated as a method of providing just compensation, gratuitous supplementary compensation can be appropriate, just as it may be when receiving especially good service from someone plying a trade whose basic compensation normally is not paid by tipping.

Since practices regarding tipping are subject to change and also differ greatly in various places—especially in different countries—I shall not attempt to say whether tips for various services are strictly due and how much they ought to be. Helpful information of that sort can be found in recently published travel guides and works on etiquette, or you can consult travel agents or friends more experienced than you in the matter. The suggestions of proprietors, such as the management of the ship on which you cruised, are less trustworthy and may well be on the high side. Here I shall offer only a few points of clarification.

In putting oneself in another's position when applying the Golden Rule, one should take along one's capacity to make sound moral judgments—all the truth one knows, one's moral responsibilities, one's ability to reason, and one's normal feelings with regard to the matters at issue—but leave behind all other attributes and aspects of one's situation. What an American would want to be tipped is not the standard to use in other countries. Rather, take into account the customs of the place. For example, in restaurants and sometimes in other establishments in some countries, a charge for service on the bill often constitutes all or most of the payment due those who provide it, and the customary tip is small change if that. Even in America, though waiters and others who provide services receive little or no compensation except tips in some establishments, in others, anyone providing a service receives at least a living wage even before counting tips. Again, in some places the person who receives a tip can keep it; in others, it is collected by the proprietor or shared with other workers.

Applying the Golden Rule, one will find, I think, that unusually good service calls for a supplement, particularly when the basic tip otherwise would be small and the person providing the service is not so well off as oneself. But whether or not one happens to be feeling cheerful and expansive should not affect how much one tips.

It is common practice in some situations to provide customers with services they would rather not have, just so that they will tip. Usually this can be avoided by patronizing more or less modest establishments or by firmly declining such services before they are performed. If employees of a modest establishment insist on providing a service anyway, no tip is strictly due, since one owes nothing for services one has refused, just as one owes nothing for unordered products sent by organizations hoping for a donation. Still, if the person providing the service seems needy, mercy can call for at least the customary tip.

As for the difference between tips at the customary rate in more and less expensive restaurants, the usual tip may well be inadequate to provide just compensation for waitresses and waiters in inexpensive restaurants. Though many people do such work on a part-time basis for supplemental income, if you regularly eat at certain inexpensive establishments, you might discuss the matter frankly with the manager and/or those providing service, try to find out how large a tip would be needed to provide your fair share of a full-time worker's living wage, and tip at least at that level. At the same time, the larger tip on the larger bill in a more expensive restaurant may not result in excessive compensation. The amount of employee time devoted to each patron usually is greater, and many expensive establishments divide tips among all who contribute to the service. One also expects better service in such establishments, and those skilled and dedicated enough to provide it merit somewhat greater compensation. Then too, many people working in expensive restaurants make a career of it, and so deserve appropriate compensation, including adequate income for retirement. Of course, by choosing moderately priced restaurants, one avoids having to give large tips.

In general, one cannot expect flawless service, and so the quality of service must be judged by how those providing it handle any problems that arise. Insofar as a tip is just compensation for a service, even poor service must be paid for with a tip proportionate to the service received. One also should distinguish between defects that are the fault of the person providing the service and those that are others' fault, and not penalize one person for others' failings. For example, if a restaurant serves poor food, one should refuse it or request an adjustment in the check rather than withhold the waiter's tip, unless he or she shared responsibility by recommending a dish while certainly knowing it to be defective or spoiled. When service of any sort is abnormally delayed, one should ask for an explanation, accept reasonable excuses, and complain to superiors when a satisfactory explanation is not forthcoming, rather than arbitrarily withhold a tip that may be due in justice.

Occasionally, someone providing service for which a tip usually is expected misbehaves significantly or plainly is responsible for grossly inadequate service. For example, two waiters chat while food ready to be served grows cold; an inquisitive taxi driver asks prying, personal questions and vulgarly insults a passenger who politely declines to answer. In such cases, it seems to me, one can justly withhold the tip, but, if possible, should politely and clearly explain why. It is often more appropriate in such cases, however, to exercise Christian mercy by trying to overcome the evil and improve the human relationship—while giving the customary tip, gently point out the fault in service and exhort the individual to avoid it, for his or her own sake and for the sake of other patrons.

Having responded as well as I can to your specific question about tipping, I shall also sketch out the broader perspective in which Christians should think about such matters. Repeating constant and very firm Catholic teaching, Vatican II articulates the principle:

> God has destined the earth and all it contains for the use of all human individuals and peoples, in such a way that, under the direction of justice accompanied by charity, created goods ought to flow abundantly to everyone on a fair basis [note omitted]. One must always bear this universal destination of goods in mind, no matter what forms property may take, as it is adapted, in accordance with diverse and changeable circumstances, to the legitimate institutions of peoples. (GS 69)[304]

Overlooking or ignoring this broader perspective could lead to a legalistic use of ethical norms, so that, while you would be neither parsimonious nor profligate in tipping, you might be at once miserly and self-indulgently wasteful in much more important decisions about your wealth.

Your past economies were wise. Frugality has been an appropriate part of your Christian style of life. It helped you to fulfill the responsibilities pertaining to your vocation, not least providing for your children's education. Our sole standard in using material resources as well as time and energy should be our calling from God; and now that your children are grown up, you should be trying to find new opportunities to serve people's needs and other new dimensions of your vocation.

Travel for pleasure and other recreation certainly can play a subordinate part in a Christian couple's life. Now it might well be justified that you "loosen up and live a little." But you must be vigilant to resist the temptations regarding property and money to which many more or less affluent, middle-aged and elderly people succumb: I mean hoarding wealth in the futile pursuit of absolute security and wasting money in the unreasonable pursuit of emotional gratification. Bearing in mind the universal destination of goods, think about others' needs, and the possibility that some of your wealth ought to be used to meet them (see *LCL,* 780–82, 789–92, 800–806, 811–14).

Therefore, without presuming to criticize your Caribbean cruise, I suggest you examine your conscience about it. Consider the dire needs of those poorest of the poor that you could have met by donating what you spent on that cruise to a suitable charity. Then ask yourself whether you had good reasons to choose the cruise, or whether it was merely self-indulgence. If the latter, you failed to do justice to the poor and should now consider conscientiously what to do by way of restitution (see *LCL,* 444–58). Even if you had good reasons for choosing the cruise, could you have forgone it without slighting any of your responsibilities, and used the money

---

304. Justo L. González, *Faith and Wealth: A History of Early Christian Ideas on the Origin, Significance, and Use of Money* (San Francisco: Harper and Row, 1990), describes the socioeconomic background against which this Christian teaching was articulated, shows its sources in the New Testament, and illustrates its development by the Fathers of the Church.

in works of mercy? If so, you fell short of the self-sacrifice for which Christian love of neighbor calls.

In the future, too, such questions will be relevant whenever you are making similar plans and choices. In answering them, bear in mind another question: "How does God's love abide in anyone who has the world's goods and sees a brother or sister in need and yet refuses help?" (1 Jn 3.17).

100: Should a pharmaceutical firm develop a drug as a philanthropic act?

I am an outside member of the board of a midsized pharmaceutical company. The employees receive excellent pay and benefits; their team spirit is high; personnel turnover is very low. The business has been consistently profitable, and annual profits have exceeded twenty-five percent of book value since three drugs the company developed for veterinary medicine became big winners. Indeed, even without the drugs marketed for veterinary medicine, the balance sheet would have been in the black every year.

One of the veterinary drugs cures a disease in cattle caused by a parasite. This disease is so debilitating that animals afflicted with it used to be destroyed. Now, an initial course of heavy medication eliminates the parasite; the animal recovers completely; and a low, maintenance dose administered for the rest of its life protects it against any further invasion.

In some very poor tropical countries, but nowhere else, a similar parasite afflicts humans with equally devastating effects. The researchers who developed the veterinary drug worked up a proposal to modify and test it for human use. If people in affluent countries were afflicted with this disease, it would be good business to go ahead. In this case, though, the people who need the drug will not be able to pay for it. Management studied the probable costs of development, manufacturing, and distribution. Sources of funding were investigated—our own government, various international agencies, several foundations, and so forth—with negative results. The conclusion was that this project inevitably would lose money, reducing after-tax profit by around ten percent for two to three years. The board unanimously decided not to proceed.

Two further developments have reopened the question. First, some members of the research team and certain other employees offered to donate overtime work to the project, which would significantly reduce development costs. Second, when they learned of the employees' offer, the company's public relations consultants worked up an attractive proposal to use the project in advertising to improve the company's image and win good will from an influential segment of the public, including opinion leaders in the media and government.

Management's analysis of the question makes several points clear. (1) The project is feasible and almost certain to result in a drug that will cure hundreds of thousands of people. (2) Accepting the employees' offer would be in line with the company's highly successful employee-relations policy, but not accepting it probably would not cause any lasting harm. (3) The project's usefulness for public relations, while not precisely calculable, would be significant; the favorable publicity would strengthen the company's position in any future situation where public opinion was a factor. (4) Nevertheless, even considering long-term benefits to the company, the project cannot be justified on an economic basis alone.

If we approve going forward with this project, then, we are committing the company to a substantial act of philanthropy. Since the corporation is publicly held, this work of mercy will reduce the return of stockholders who, presumably, invested to make money, not do works of mercy. Still, I am personally inclined to vote in favor, for I think a business should be more than a money-making engine. It must make a profit, of course, but I believe any business, and above all a pharmaceutical firm, should serve human needs and contribute as a good member to the larger community, and this project undeniably would fulfill these wider responsibilities.

Analysis:

This question calls for the derivation of a specific moral norm regarding the philanthropic activity of profit-making businesses. The common end of every voluntary association is determined by its participants' mutual understanding and consent. A profit-making business is a voluntary association of the persons who cooperate in the specific activities for which it was organized, in order to achieve various economic benefits. The common good of participants in a business is the principle grounding and limiting the authority of those entrusted with the decision making that shapes their cooperation. So, like the people who exercise authority in any other voluntary association, the directors and managers of a business should not elect to use its resources for purposes that, however good in themselves, do not contribute to its common good. Therefore, though the proposed project, considered in itself, would be good, the directors should not vote to proceed with it as a philanthropic act. However, they and others should try to carry out the project by the voluntary cooperation of participants in the business and other parties able and willing to contribute.

The reply could be along the following lines:

To see how a director should vote on this issue, one first must consider the principle underlying all the responsibilities of members of a profit-making corporation's board of directors. It is neither maximum profit for shareholders nor the interests of everyone who affects and is affected by the business's actions—the various individuals and groups collectively called "stakeholders" by some theorists.[305] Rather, it is the common good of the business as a community of persons freely cooperating in the specific activities for which it was organized.

Though many people think a profit-making enterprise's sole end is profit, which its directors and managers should use every lawful means to maximize, I agree with

---

305. R. Edward Freeman, *Strategic Management: A Stakeholder Approach* (Boston: Pitman, 1984), 46: "A stakeholder in an organization is (by definition) any group or individual who can affect or is affected by the achievement of the organization's objectives." Since Freeman focuses more on effective management strategies than on ethics (see Part II of his book, 83–192), he does not attempt to distinguish among directors' and managers' moral responsibilities to various kinds of stakeholders.

you that "a business should be more than a money-making engine." While a profit-making corporation considered as a legal entity primarily represents and limits shareholders' interests and involvement in the enterprise, the shareholders themselves—and, therefore, the directors and managers—have moral responsibilities to others. They should not regard other peoples' activities essential for the business's success as mere means for making profits.

Investment deserves a fair return, but work has priority over capital (see *LCL*, 763). Money is not a basic human good but only a means; it does not fulfill persons, but only enables them to do things—which fulfill or, perhaps, injure themselves and/or others. By contrast, work is both a basic human good, inasmuch as it realizes certain basic potentialities of workers, and is the principal efficient cause of valuable results. Moreover, insofar as more or less regular suppliers of materials and services, and purchasers of the business's products or services contribute to the business's success by their morally upright activities, they too should be considered participants in the enterprise. Their cooperation should not be regarded as a mere means to protecting and rewarding the shareholders' investment.

But even though maximum profit for shareholders is too narrow a goal to serve as a morally acceptable principle for directors' decisions, maximizing the interests of as many stakeholders as possible is too wide.[306]

Of course, the directors and managers of a profit-making business are bound by not only the legal requirements but the moral norms binding all groups and individuals. They may not intend as either an end or a means that the business's activities injure anyone or any community; they may not unfairly accept side effects harmful to anyone; they must see to it that the business fairly plays its part in wider communities to which it belongs—for example, by avoiding unfair competition and obeying just laws. So, the directors and managers do have some moral responsibilities toward every individual and group affected by the business's activities. Moreover, directors and managers can be morally required to act for outsiders' interests insofar as that is conducive to the business's own survival and flourishing. Thus, the public relations value of the project would justify part of its cost.[307]

306. Freemen, op. cit., 249, does not assert, but calls for research into, the proposition that managers are fiduciaries to all stakeholders rather than to the stockholders or owners alone—"a concept of management whereby the manager *must* act in the interests of the stakeholders of the organization." Thomas Donaldson and Lee E. Preston, "The Stakeholder Theory of the Corporation: Concepts, Evidence, and Implications," *Academy of Management Review,* 20 (1995): 65–91 (including an extensive bibliography), advocate the stakeholder approach, reject (85–87) some ways of identifying legitimate stakeholders as too loose, but provide no criterion and fail to distinguish between the rights of participants in the business and the claims of nonparticipants to fair treatment.

307. Much corporate giving, even the sort called "charitable investing," is motivated (and justified) by the interests of businesses themselves; see John W. Dienhart and Saundra I. Foderick, "Ethical and Conceptual Issues in Charitable Investments, Cause Related Marketing, and Advertising," *Business and Professional Ethics Journal,* 7:3–4 (Fall-Winter 1988): 47–59; Kenneth A. Bertsch, *Corporate Philanthropy* (Washington, D.C.: Investor Responsibility Research Center, 1982), 20–27.

Still, in making decisions, directors and managers of a business may not use as a principle the best interests of all those who will be (or could be) affected by what the business does. It is easy to see why.

Everyone has a set of moral responsibilities, usually including duties to care properly for himself or herself, to care for dependents, help friends, do some sort of work, pay taxes, and so on. This set of responsibilities limits each person's freedom to do things good in themselves, including things that otherwise would be obligatory and greatly beneficial to others. So, good people never form or enter into any voluntary association without assuring themselves that its activities involving them and affecting their interests will be consonant with their already-existing responsibilities. Taking advantage of this necessary social practice, even people who are not so good, being jealous of their own interests, demand assurances that any voluntary association in which they participate will limit its activities to pursuing its specific, agreed upon purpose or purposes. Consequently, each voluntary association is organized for a limited and definite common good, and the authority of those who make its decisions is limited to using its resources and shaping its cooperation toward that good.

Sometimes a voluntary association's common good and the limits it imposes are explicitly formulated in a written constitution, legally binding contracts, or some other way. Whether or not such a formulation exists, an association's authority is morally limited by participants' mutual understanding and agreement, and while these often are unclear and disputable, they sometimes are clear beyond reasonable doubt and often more restrictive than any explicit formulation indicates. For example, a neighborhood garden club may have no written constitution or a constitution that does not limit the purposes for which its funds can be spent or that can be amended by two-thirds of the members present at any meeting. Still, if two-thirds of its members happen to be Catholics, they act unfairly in deciding, without other members' unanimous agreement, to use the surplus in the club treasury to buy a new set of hymnals for their parish church.

Like any other voluntary association, a profit-making business is organized for a limited specific good. Because it is an association for ongoing cooperation by which money, work, services, and products are contributed by and distributed among various groups of participants, its common good is effective economic cooperation and fairness to all participants. Some businesses, however, are organized wholly or partly to benefit individuals or groups who do not contribute to the economic cooperation, or to benefit some contributors more generously than their contributions warrant. Unless all participants at least implicitly agree to such a gratuitous arrangement, fairness requires distributing all benefits to participants in such a way that what they get is proportionate to what they contribute. Generally speaking, of course, participants in most businesses do not agree to a gratuitous arrangement. Their duties may rule that out, or they may prefer other means of benefiting others gratuitously, or they may be selfish.

Your question implies that the pharmaceutical company on whose board you serve is organized without any gratuitous arrangement for providing benefits to anyone who does not contribute. If that is so, the preceding explanation makes it clear that the principle that should shape directors' and managers' decisions is the common good of all who actively participate in the business by cooperating in its proper activities. There are five such groups: investors who provide the needed capital, managers whose activity directs and coordinates the other parties' activities, nonmanagement employees who create and distribute the company's products, more or less regular suppliers of materials and services, and more or less regular purchasers of the business's products. The members of all five groups should benefit insofar as the enterprise is successful and its common good is realized: investors by receiving a reasonable rate of return; managers, besides sharing in the benefits accruing to other employees, by enjoying self-fulfillment in their role of service and receiving the respect and gratitude of those they serve; employees by doing fulfilling work under decent conditions and receiving fair wages and benefits in return for what they do; suppliers by receiving fair prices, with some assurance of a market for their goods and services; and wholesale purchasers and ultimate buyers by receiving good products at fair prices, with some assurance of a dependable source of supply.

You ask whether to support a project to supply a drug that will cure a devastating disease in hundreds of thousands of very poor people, even though this project is likely to lose money, reducing profit over two or three years. My answer is no. The reduction in profit either will be unfair to investors or not. If it is, that unfairness excludes this use of the company's resources. If not, then the return investors otherwise would receive must be excessive; and in that case, other participants in the business are getting less benefit than they should for their contributions or paying more than they should for the company's products, and that unfairness should be corrected.

Assume the reduction in profits would be unfair to at least some investors—for example, recent ones, who purchased their shares at or near current market value, which has taken the company's anticipated profits into account. Some of them surely are not well-to-do individuals; they may be retired people living off the modest income from their investments or nonprofit organizations that depend on investments for essential income. If you and the other directors reduce their investment income by doing the proposed philanthropic work, you will not be doing a work of mercy—since mercy is not done at others' expense—but robbing one group of needy people and organizations to benefit some even needier people.

But assume, instead, that the reduction in profits and dividends would not be unfair to investors, and that suppliers, managers, other employees, and wholesale buyers already are being fairly treated. In that case, the ultimate buyers of the company's products are being charged higher prices than necessary, and those excessive prices would fund this project. But the group paying the excessive prices includes not only wealthy people but poor people and businesses hard pressed by the cost of health insurance. Such buyers plainly have no obligation to fund this project for the benefit of other poor people.

Someone might argue that the company's products cannot be overpriced, because people freely choose to pay the prices charged for them. Like other elements of health care, however, prescription drugs normally are a necessity, often a very urgent one, and purchasers seldom have much choice about whether to buy a particular drug. People's willingness to pay whatever they can afford for pharmaceuticals is no indication of fair pricing, especially in the case of drugs still under patent. Moreover, there almost certainly are at least a few people who now forgo buying the company's products but would enjoy their benefits if the prices were slightly lower.

Again, someone will object that the preceding argument assumes an unrealistic precision about what is fair, given the complexity of the transactions among participants in the business and the unpredictability of the economic factors affecting it. In reality, the objection will continue, it is impossible precisely to calculate or foresee what would constitute a fair share of contributions and benefits for the various participants, so that without being unfair to anyone, the business as a whole could absorb the cost of the philanthropic project, just as it must absorb the cost of various contingencies—new governmental regulations or taxes, the unfavorable outcome of a lawsuit, an unexpected problem with a drug requiring its withdrawal from the market, and so forth. Recalling that the philanthropic project almost certainly would bear fruit in a drug that would benefit hundreds of thousands of people, the objection will conclude that the directors should approve it and allow the business to absorb its cost.

It is true that what is fair to various participants in the business cannot be precisely calculated and various contingencies cannot be forestalled. But those responsible for the business need not and ought not make decisions they know are at odds with its common good. If the directors of a profit-making business use its resources for a philanthropic project not fully justified by anticipated economic benefits to the business, they exceed their authority and misappropriate the resources entrusted to them, just as the employees in charge of warehousing and shipping the company's products would if they made an unauthorized gift of drugs to a clinic in a poor country.

Finally, someone might argue that this firm ought to develop and distribute this drug because otherwise hundreds of thousands of people almost certainly will continue to suffer the devastating effects of the disease. Even if one has charge of a unique capacity to meet a vital need, however, one may not use the capacity to meet the need if that would violate some prior responsibility. Parents of modest means, for example, may not donate part of the money they could use to meet any genuine need of their own children to famine relief that would save the lives of other children.

But even though the firm as such should not undertake this philanthropic project, it seems to me that the directors and managers should try to bring about this work of mercy. Although earlier efforts failed to turn up outside funding, the employees' offer to donate overtime work that would significantly reduce development costs might well evoke support previously denied the project. So, in my judgment, you and the other directors should try again to obtain some sort of foundation grant or public subsidy. In doing so, you can explain why the company may not proceed by itself but is prepared to make a significant contribution to the project. Whether or not that effort succeeds, the employees' offer also points to an interesting possibility. You and the other directors might offer voluntary donations of your own money, and invite the rest of the employees and other groups—the investors, suppliers, wholesale buyers, and retail customers—to help with voluntary contributions of work, supplies, or money. If the project gets favorable publicity, the public at large also might be invited to support it. If this strategy succeeds well enough that either the project's cost probably will be fully covered or, at least, its impact on profit will be offset by its probable public relations value, you can support it without unfairness to anyone and should do so for the sake of those who will benefit.

101: Should an exasperated manager quit or stay to shield his subordinates?

My whole career has been in the marketing division of a major business machines manufacturer. For the past five years I have been in charge of the government and education sales section. During my tenure, our section has increased its market share and profitability, while the other sections have declined. My people, especially my branch office managers, deserve the credit. Our section's employee turnover has been less than half that of the rest of the division, and this has made for solid customer relations. The section already had good team spirit when I took it over; I built on that by getting to know our people and taking a personal interest in each of them, so that all of them know we will do everything we can for them, and they, in turn, have given their best.

Earlier this year the vice-president for marketing resigned to become chief executive officer of our second largest competitor. I hoped to succeed him. Instead, the job went to Ms. Constance Crane, who had done well as head of the advertising section. Before her promotion was announced, the president took me to lunch and explained the situation. Since virtually all our top people are white men, the company can no longer resist pressures to promote or bring in some women and blacks. Still, the positions in question are too important to fill with unqualified people, and qualified women and blacks are few, and the demand for them is great. When this vice-presidency opened up, he decided it had to go to Crane. I agreed that she is qualified, but pointed out that my record not only is longer and richer in relevant experience but at least as good as hers in other respects. He frankly admitted that I "definitely would have been better qualified in other respects," but said being a woman or a black has become an important qualification. He asked me to help Crane succeed for the good of the company. My bonus arrangement was sweetened, and I accepted the situation.

The day before yesterday, the president and Ms. Crane informed me that the board has decided on a restructuring. The plan is to merge the three sales sections and eliminate their separate heads, so that the managers of the consolidated branch offices will report directly to Crane. They are asking me to oversee the restructuring, then to take over as sales manager of what will be our largest branch office in Washington, D.C.

The news was not particularly good, but it was not really bad for me personally. The job in Washington would be neither a promotion nor a demotion. Relocating also would have both pluses and minuses for me and my family. Still, I am considering quitting. When I did not get the vice-presidency, I put out a few feelers, and I have an offer from a manufacturer of major appliances to manage its marketing division. This also would be a lateral move, since they would match the package I now have. But there would be some possibility of eventual promotion.

Two other things also incline me to take the offer and resign. First, while I understand the reason for the restructuring—operating economies that will improve the company's profitability in the short run—I think it will harm profitability in the long run by losing the advantages in customer service for which the separate sections were created. Eventually that will hurt my own income. Second, the decision to restructure was made without ever consulting me. Coming on top of the decision to give Ms. Crane the vice-presidency, it makes me wonder about the company's future as well as my own.

One thing inclines me to stay. The restructuring not only is going to break up my winning team but will mean trouble for many of my best people. Their pain is likely to be a lot worse if Ms. Crane oversees the restructuring than if I stay on to do it.

Analysis:

Since both of the questioner's options—staying and changing jobs—are morally acceptable, the problem requires discernment. Emotional motives should be examined and discounted insofar as they are not integrated with the intelligible goods at stake. Because the options pertain to the questioner's vocation, he should focus on the opportunities each offers to use his gifts in service. His relationship with his people is good in itself, and he should consider the effect his quitting would have on them, and on the company's customers as well. If he decides to change jobs, he should take care when explaining his decision to avoid leading any of his people to make decisions against their own best interests.

The reply could be along the following lines:

When you put this problem to me, looking for help in sorting things out, you did not present it as a moral question. Many people would say it is not. And it is true that neither quitting nor staying would be morally wrong, and I will not try to tell you which to do. As I told you, however, my field is Christian ethics, and I take a broad view of what that includes, namely, thinking reasonably in the light of faith about any choice a Christian makes. So, as I promised, I mulled over the alternatives you face, and here are my reflections.

Since you are being asked to manage a restructuring of the whole marketing division that will greatly affect people under you and your own work, you surely should have been consulted before the decision was made. Perhaps you should make your case against the restructuring to the president and urge him to ask the board to reconsider. Still, you seem to think the decision is final, and I shall suppose it is.

Plainly, your prospects are not what they were only a short time ago. With your hope for a promotion frustrated, you no longer are looking forward to developing your talents in a more challenging position. What you have experienced understandably has diminished your enthusiasm for your work, and you can hardly foresee whether you will regain it. Moreover, you regard your treatment as a symptom of a serious defect in higher management, which, in turn, grounds your pessimistic view of the company's prospects and, unless you resign, yours too.

But are you allowing your feelings to affect your judgment more than they should? Naturally, you were saddened by the treatment you received and angry at those responsible. You did not mention those feelings, but you would be extraordinarily meek if you did not have them. That you put out feelers when passed over for the vice-presidency suggests that disappointment motivated your initial thoughts of quitting. But your understandable feelings about that are only an emotional motive, not a reason, for quitting. Sort out your motives, and acknowledge your feelings, but discount any feelings that are not harmonious with the intelligible goods at stake.

In every aspect of life, Christians should try to discover God's plan and will, and respond to his call (see *LCL,* 113–29). One's talents and resources are God's gifts, to be used in serving others, and thereby to fulfill oneself. So, in making career choices, Christians in business and the professions should not focus on their individual economic advantage or their status among peers, but on how best to use their gifts in service. Of course, one must earn enough to provide for one's needs and those of one's dependents, but that requirement apparently will be met no matter which alternative you choose.

Focusing on individual economic advantage and status encourages mobility, since people generally cannot take full advantage of opportunities for career advancement without repeatedly severing relationships and establishing new ones. The underlying individualistic focus and the prospect that business and professional relationships may not last long lead to considering them as mere means rather than as special forms of community, in some ways like friendships, valuable in themselves. By contrast, while a focus on serving others in response to God's call does not rule out career changes, it does encourage one to regard relationships as valuable in themselves and so gives rise to commitments and bonds of loyalty that make for stability.

Therefore, in reflecting on your options, your main concern ought to be to discover what God is calling you to do. You will find the answer by considering others' needs, on the one hand, and your capacities and gifts, on the other. You should regard the possibilities before you as different opportunities for service.

The warm way you speak about those you call "my people" suggests that your relationship with them is more than merely functional. You got to know and took a personal interest in each of them. That was not merely a management tactic using a clever technique of psychological manipulation; you were leading them in a genuinely cooperative effort to achieve common purposes, not least providing good service for the company's customers. Prizing the community you have built up with your people, you are disposed to be loyal to them and inclined to stay through the restructuring in order to minimize its bad effects on them. In line with this reason for staying, you also should consider the impact your leaving would have on them even after the restructuring.

Closely allied to this consideration is another you did not mention: the impact your quitting would have on the company's customers, both during the transition and afterwards. You explain that the restructuring itself will sacrifice important advantages for customer service. Would your quitting at this time aggravate the situation? If so, having built up solid relations with the customers your division served, you may fall short of your commitment to them if you quit.

In my judgment, a society more just than ours would require all employers to afford equal opportunities to candidates for jobs and promotions regardless of such factors as sex and race, and would not exert pressure on any employer to discriminate against white males. However, given the pressures your employer is under, the company's interests may well have required giving Ms. Crane the vice-presidency you otherwise would have deserved. If so, though you are a victim of unjust discrimination, neither the company nor Ms. Crane is guilty (see q. 110, below). Patience in suffering injustice is an important Christian virtue (see *CMP*, 637–39), and it becomes a strict obligation when the alternative is seriously injuring people who are innocent by failing to fulfill some responsibility to them.

In sum, though the reasons you offer in favor of quitting are weighty, they do not seem to me to constitute a compelling case for quitting now. The prospect that the company will not do well in the future and that its decline will adversely affect your income does not seem to require you to leave at once, since even if you are right, its short run profitability, as you also point out, will be improved by the restructuring. If you owned stock in the company, would you sell it now? If not, it hardly seems you need quit now. You do have the offer of another job, but you do not seem to find it highly attractive. Of course, if taking that offer were the only way to meet your need for a secure income—for example, if you anticipated being discharged when you complete your work on the restructuring—you would have a cogent reason to resign now.

If you stay long enough at least to oversee the restructuring, you will be able to reassess the situation at the appropriate time. By then, your prospects with the company may seem brighter, perhaps even with regard to the possibility of promotion—after all, one or more of your superiors could decide to leave or be discharged, and everybody is mortal. But even if it then seems best to quit, you will be able to make a concerted effort to find a position where you could put your gifts to better use. Considering what to do in that light, however, the company's prospects might seem better, and you may decide to stay on indefinitely.

Still, your reflection and discernment might well lead you to judge that you should quit now or plan to leave as soon as the restructuring is completed. If so, you no doubt will share with your people something of your view of the restructuring and the company's prospects, and perhaps will tell them about your own plans. Overstating the case for a pessimistic view might encourage many who trust your judgment to move out. But that might not be in their own best interests and could seriously affect service to customers and so damage the company as a whole.

So, even if you decide to quit, you should bear in mind in talking with your people the differences between yourself and them, and the element of uncertainty in your view of the company's prospects, and should avoid signaling that the time has come for everyone to abandon ship. Nevertheless, loyalty requires that you not only avoid deceiving them about the restructuring and your own plans but candidly answer their questions about their prospects.

102: May an entrepreneur locate a factory in a third-world country?

The good news is that I have a product that looks like a winner. It is a line of construction sets designed for children in different age groups and made of very tough plastic. I had ten thousand sets manufactured and test marketed them in one city; they sold extremely well. Of course, I incurred a substantial loss on the test, but it was expected. It is not the bad news. That, instead, is that there is no way to make the product profitable unless it is manufactured outside the United States.

Costs here for both physical plant and labor are high. By locating in an economically less developed nation—I shall call the country, not yet selected, *Elden*—I can acquire suitable factory space and hire workers far more cheaply. The savings will be partly offset by the costs of setting up there, sending key personnel, training workers, freight, export-import taxes, and so on. But the manufacturing-cost differential will still be great, largely because wages in Elden are comparatively low and business is far less burdened with governmental regulations, such as costly U.S. requirements regarding environmental impact and workers' health and safety. Moreover, in Elden people can be hired strictly on the basis of suitability for the job and retained strictly on the basis of productivity; a business need not comply with U.S. civil rights and labor laws, and the possibility of unionization is not a constant threat.

Critics no doubt will say locating in Elden for the sake of such advantages is unjust both to the people there and to fellow Americans. But I see no other way to set up this business.

Analysis:

The moral issues raised by this question concern the justice to fellow Americans and to Eldenians of manufacturing the product in Elden. Provided the questioner complies with all relevant U.S. laws, locating the factory in Elden is unlikely to be unfair to fellow Americans. However, the questioner's statement of the economic advantage of locating in Elden suggests that doing so will involve injustices against that nation and the factory's employees. The questioner must not only meet the just requirements of Elden's laws but fairly treat everyone employed there and in all other respects act fully in accord with the Golden Rule.

The reply could be along the following lines:

You assert without qualification "that there is no way to make the product profitable unless it is manufactured outside the United States." Are you absolutely sure? There are places in the U.S. where many people are unemployed, few workers are unionized, inexpensive factory space is available, state and/or local governments offer subsidies and/or tax breaks to attract businesses, and state and local regulations are not very burdensome. Since your test marketing went well, I am not convinced you could not manufacture the product, entirely or at least partly, in the U.S. with reasonable hope of making some profit. So, I reformulate the question: If at least part of the manufacturing could be done profitably in the U.S., could you be justified in doing all of it in Elden in order to reduce the venture's risk and make it more profitable? I shall reply by considering, first, the question of justice to fellow Americans and, then, the question of justice toward Eldenians. (Still, if there really is no way to make the product profitable without manufacturing it outside the U.S., my reply would be the same.)

Assuming you comply with all relevant U.S. laws, I do not think locating the factory in Elden is likely to be unjust to fellow Americans. Your operation and the marketing of the product in the U.S. will employ some Americans and generate some tax revenues. American retailers will make a profit on the product, and, if you price it fairly, you will pass on some of the benefits to American consumers. Besides, import taxes and part of the cost of freight will contribute to the U.S. economy, and your key personnel who spend time in Elden may benefit from the experience. Furthermore, while Americans are rightly concerned about their own national economy, they and other comparatively affluent people have responsibilities toward poorer nations, whose citizens also are neighbors in the worldwide human community. Provided you do no injustice to Eldenians, those who work for you will benefit from training and jobs, and that will contribute to fulfilling Americans' responsibility toward less developed nations. At the same time, even the poorest, unemployed U.S. workers you might employ in this country probably suffer less deprivation than the unemployed people you would employ in Elden. So, locating your factory there need not be unfair to fellow Americans.

Whether you can avoid treating Eldenians unfairly seems more questionable. You say the economic advantage will result largely from the fact that "wages in Elden are comparatively low and business is far less burdened with governmental regulations." That statement is alarming, because a situation like that is an opportunity for injustice—for example, grossly exploiting nonunionized workers. Ask yourself whether it is morally acceptable to take advantage of Elden's comparatively low wages and lack of regulations. In considering this question, bear in mind that many of the relevant American regulations were designed to protect the environment and workers' health and safety, prevent unjust discrimination and unfair labor practices, and safeguard workers' rights to organize and bargain collectively.

Still, if you pay just wages and provide good working conditions and reasonable benefits, it could be morally acceptable to take advantage, within certain limits, of Elden's freedom from regulations.

To begin with, though most regulations in force in the U.S. were meant for good purposes, what they actually require can be unfair, especially insofar as all their requirements, which are not always fully harmonious, must be met simultaneously. Like most laws, these probably were not perfect even at the outset, and their original value may have been lessened by changed economic and social conditions, perhaps calling for their amendment or even, in some cases, their repeal. Moreover, like all laws, these regulations were designed for typical cases. So, sometimes—namely, when their requirements are not just—it would be morally acceptable even for businesses in the U.S. to do what the regulations forbid, except for the moral duty in most cases to conform even to unjust requirements of law. Now, if such regulations do not exist in Elden and justice does not require them there, plainly there is nothing wrong in taking advantage of the situation.

Besides, some regulations that are reasonable in the U.S., a relatively prosperous nation with its own problems and its unique set of capacities and opportunities for economic and social development, would not be reasonable in Elden. For example, if the cost of living is far less in Elden than in the U.S., an entirely adequate family wage there might be less than the U.S. minimum wage. Then too, due to social and cultural differences, different injustices afflict different nations. Elden may not need laws like those in the U.S. forbidding unjust discrimination and dealing with unfair labor practices, and businesses operating in Elden, without acting unjustly, avoid some of the burdens of complying with relevant U.S. laws. Furthermore, it would be morally acceptable for a business there to do things U.S. regulations justly forbid, insofar as in Elden those actions are just. For example, it can be just in the U.S. to require using resources that otherwise would go for luxuries to protect the environment and to minimize risks to workers' health and safety, but in Elden it would be unjust to require that resources necessary for people's survival be used for anything less urgent.

Nevertheless, there are limits. Even though not constrained by law, a business operating in Elden should avoid policies and actions that unfairly damage the environment or risk workers' health and safety, involve unjust discrimination, lead to unfair working conditions, prevent workers from exercising their right to organize, or are unfair to anyone or any group in any other way. To judge what is unfair, it is not enough to look to prevailing practices or to learn by experience what the Eldenian government will tolerate or its people will accept without argument or complaint. Rather, as always in applying the Golden Rule, you must consider all the relevant facts of the situation, including facts which most Eldenians ignore or care little or nothing about, and imagine yourself or your loved ones in the places of each of those affected by any choice you consider making. For example, bring to bear all available information about sociocultural anthropology, ecology, and the causes of disease in considering impacts on Eldenian society, the environment, and workers' health; then imagine your grandchildren as part of the country's future generations and yourself or your spouse as a worker in the factory.

Suppose you conclude that you would be justified in setting up production in any of several less affluent nations. In that case, your choice should not be guided solely by considerations of self-interest. Rather, you ought to take into account the legitimate interests of everyone else involved. For example, other things being equal, a nation with a greater need for jobs and tax revenue would benefit more by having your factory located there.

Suppose, on the other hand, that, having conscientiously considered what justice toward Eldenians will require, you conclude that the prospect of profitability would not be improved by locating your factory there—in other words, to make manufacturing your product in Elden worthwhile, it would be necessary to exploit the nation in general and/or your workers in particular. Must you then give up your project, which in other respects would do much good? If you cannot carry it on anywhere without injustice, yes, you must give it up. All the requirements of justice are gathered up in love of neighbor (see Rom 13.8–10), and "those who do not love a brother or sister whom they have seen, cannot love God whom they have not seen" (1 Jn 4.20). Those who do not love God will of course suffer eternal loss, compared with which no earthly profit matters.

103: What should a factory owner have done about downstream environmental harm?

I own a factory that employs about a hundred people and is located on the bank of a small river just north of a state line. The river flows south, across the line and through a state recreation area. For many years the neighboring state has stocked the river with fish, and there are several motels and other facilities along the highway south of the recreation area.

My factory always has drawn water from the river and then returned it, no worse for our using it. About three years ago, however, it became clear that, to remain competitive with factories in other parts of the country, we would have to change our process and make far more use of the river water. The new process does not pollute the river; in fact, nothing whatsoever is added to the water when we return it. But we do take out virtually all the oxygen, and the river only gradually regains sufficient oxygen to support fish. It still can be stocked in the southern portion of the recreation area, but most of the popular fishing spots were in the north, near us. Thus, the change in our process has had a deleterious impact on the recreation area and the businesses that serve it.

Before changing the process, we made certain that doing so would not violate federal, state, or local laws or regulations, not least those regarding environmental impact. We knew the changes would have some adverse effect on our neighbors' businesses, but we did not realize how much.

Despite what I did foresee about the impact, I had to go ahead; the alternative was closing the factory. Not only would I have lost my investment but our employees would have been put out of work. The factory is not just the largest local employer but the only one on our side of the state line that brings money into the area rather than taking it out, and closing down would have undermined other businesses serving our employees. For selfish reasons and also out of responsibility to my employees and others who would have suffered if the factory closed, I had no choice but to change the process.

Like most people around here, I've enjoyed using the neighboring recreation area and I'm acquainted with many of the business people who have been adversely affected by what I've done. Needless to say, their attitude toward me is decidedly cool, and in some cases hostile. Fortunately, since our businesses are so different and we operate in different states, we are not members of the same associations and do not have to do business with one another.

Nevertheless, when a motel owner I know down there asked me, "How would you like it if you were in my place?" I had to admit I would not like it at all. I sympathize with her and others who have been hurt. But, knowing she is a fair-minded woman, I asked her, "What would you have done if you had been in my place?" Though she said I at least should have talked my plans over with them before going ahead, she candidly but reluctantly admitted that she would have changed the process to save the business. It seems as though we both have the Golden Rule against us!

I also have been criticized by some environmentalists. They admit that I did not violate any law or regulation regarding environmental impact, but they claim I took advantage of a gap in the law to do something plainly wrong by adopting a process that interferes with nature by removing oxygen naturally present in the river.

I do not think what I have done is wrong, but I wonder whether I have overlooked something. If you think so, what must I do?

Analysis:

This question raises two distinct issues of fairness, one regarding the procedure followed in making the change, the other regarding accepting its adverse impact on neighbors. The motel owner's admission that she also would have changed the process suggests that doing so and accepting the adverse impact was not in itself unfair. However, the questioner should have enlisted the cooperation of those affected in looking for a mutually acceptable way to deal with the problem, and acting unilaterally was unfair to them. That unfairness should be rectified through an effort to work with those who have been adversely affected to find some way of mitigating the harm. The environmentalists' argument is unsound insofar as it assumes that interfering with nature is wrong in itself.

The reply could be along the following lines:

In changing your process, you foresaw but did not intend some adverse impact on your neighbors' businesses. The first question is whether you acted fairly in accepting that side effect. In describing the problem, you indicate how much was at stake from your point of view: your investment, the jobs of your hundred employees, and the survival of some other businesses that serve them. But you do not say how much was at stake for those adversely affected. Perhaps you should have foreseen that their loss would be far greater than the goods you hoped to preserve; but even if you could not have foreseen how much they would lose, perhaps you now realize that your change's negative impact on them greatly exceeds its benefits to you and others. If so, you should put yourself in the place of those adversely affected, acknowledge any unfairness to them, and consider how to make amends. However, since the fair-minded motel owner admitted that in your place she would have done what you did, I shall assume that what is at stake on both sides is at least roughly comparable or even greater on your side. On that assumption, you are not necessarily acting unfairly in accepting your operation's adverse impact, and in this respect the motel owner had the Golden Rule against her.

Nevertheless, while you may have been compelled to change your process, it is possible that you had, or could have found, some alternative that did not have such an adverse impact on your neighbors. Having foreseen harm, though not its magnitude, you should have regarded the problem as one in which they shared. Thus, the motel owner was right in saying you should have talked your plans over with her and others who would be adversely affected before going ahead. While you and they do not belong to the same associations, you could and should have arranged a meeting with them, explained the problem, and sought their help in searching for a mutually satisfactory solution. Moreover, you should have done that when you first realized you needed to make more extensive use of the river water, and your obligation to do it became graver when you saw that the harm to your neighbors would be greater than you had expected. Insofar as you fell short in this matter, you had the Golden Rule against you.

Therefore, while I think both the motel owner and you have the Golden Rule against you, the paradox is dissolved by distinguishing between what you did in changing your process and what you failed to do in acting unilaterally rather than cooperatively.

Having failed to organize a timely cooperative effort to deal with the problem, you now should acknowledge that omission to those adversely affected and do what you can to rectify it. Perhaps, even now, you and they might still work together to find some way of mitigating the adverse impact. In this effort, both sides could seek help from their respective state and local governments. Preliminary studies and preparation of petitions to governmental bodies will be needed. Keeping in mind that you are comparatively prosperous while your neighbors have suffered serious losses as a result of what you have done, you should bear the cost of this effort, at least initially. Fairness might also require you to provide some additional assistance to your neighbors. Even if your cooperative effort does not lead to a solution and any additional assistance you can give them does little to mitigate the damage they have suffered, your conscientious attempt to rectify your omission probably will soften their attitude toward you and improve your relationship with them—benefits of great value in human and Christian terms.

As for the environmentalists' argument, I do not think you should be moved by it. Moral issues about environmental impact are reducible to questions about reverence toward God, the author of nature, and fairness toward fellow human beings (see *CCC,* 2415; *LCL,* 771–82). The subhuman world, which was created for human persons, is not sacred in itself; there is nothing inherently wrong in interfering with it. Human beings rightly use natural things, and fulfill both themselves and those things in using them. Still, every such use somehow "interferes" with nature. The neighboring state interferes with nature in stocking the river with fish, and the fishermen interfere again when they catch them. Moreover, since human beings are part of the natural world and deliberately altering other parts of it is natural to them, the impact of human activities on nature is no more unnatural than is the impact of other natural phenomena: animals' eating and moving about, volcanoes' eruptions, tropical storms, and so forth.

Very often, of course, the interests of people who are only remotely affected, including future generations, are slighted or overlooked entirely. But the problem you present seems not to involve any question of irreverence or any effects on people other than those previously considered.

104: May businesses try to drive competitors out of business?

"Love your enemies" may be a law of Christian morality, but it is not easy to see how it applies to the owner of a business dealing with unprincipled competitors.

Having completed my education with an M.B.A., I recently inherited my father's Chevrolet-Geo dealership in my home town. Toward the end, Dad let the business deteriorate, tolerating laziness by the two salesmen and poor work by the foreman and three mechanics in the shop. I replaced three of these people, got the others to shape up, and am gradually rebuilding the business by working hard to make sales and working personally as foreman of the shop, which now provides good and honest service at fair prices.

My most important competitors, located in a somewhat larger town nearby, are less than honest. They operate a franchise of a well-known national tire chain. They sell and install good tires, and they get other business by offering a deal on wheel balance and alignment that allows customers to have the job redone without an additional charge every five thousand miles as long as they own the car. But when customers return for that service, the manager talks them into unnecessary work— replacing perfectly good struts, relining brakes that are only half worn, and so on—by falsely claiming safety requires it.

I talked with the county prosecutor about the problem and worked out a plan with him to build a case against these competitors. A friend of mine who is a Ford dealer in town and I will check our records to identify our regular service customers who have not had wheel balancing or alignment done in two years and will discreetly ask some of them whether they have bought the deal at the dishonest service department. We will offer those who have a free safety inspection, to be made just before next taking his or her car for wheel alignment and balancing. If work of the kind involved is needed, we will do it at the competitors' prices. If no work seems necessary, we will ask the customer to let the dishonest service department do whatever the manager there claims is necessary for safety; then, having kept careful records, we will help the customer file a complaint with the prosecutor.

To encourage cooperation by the customers we select, we plan to promise to check out any unneeded work done at the dishonest shop, rebate the full cost of the work, and redo it without charge if it was not done properly, and to provide the free wheel balancing and alignment the customer had been getting at the dishonest service department. We are not doing all this simply as a public service. We hope to put an end to competition by the dishonest shop by driving it out of business, and we plan to do all we can to dramatize the case. I expect to turn to the prosecutor and to friends in the local media for help on that.

I realize my approach to the problem is hardly loving, but what else am I to do? After all, business is business.

Analysis:

This question calls for the derivation of a moral norm. One may never choose to destroy an instance of a basic human good, and a business is an instance of the basic good of community. So, one may not try to drive competitors out of business. Therefore, the questioner's proposal is morally unacceptable. However, the questioner and his or her friend have a morally acceptable alternative: to work with the prosecutor to achieve the good end of proving the competitors' fraud and putting a stop to it. In doing this, they may seek the ulterior end of benefit to their own businesses, and they can rightly accept as side effects both the failure of their competitors' business and its bad consequences for innocent third parties.

The reply could be along the following lines:

Insofar as a business is a specific kind of human association, it is not just an instrument for attaining other goods, but itself instantiates the basic human good of community. So, to try precisely to drive someone out of business is to choose to destroy an instance of a basic human good. Such a choice always is wrong, and no ulterior end, however good, can justify it (see *CMP*, 141–71, 215–22).

Of course, something called "a business" may be nothing more than a group of individuals, such as a band of thieves, sharing no common commitment to any basic human good, not even the commitment to treat one another fairly. They may arrange to coordinate their behavior so that it better serves their various goals, but their interrelationships do not constitute a community. Choosing to drive such a group out of business would not be contrary to a human good and might well be justifiable.

Then too, someone who is not choosing precisely to destroy an enterprise as a human community might be said to be trying to drive it out of business. The prosecutor you have talked with might intend solely to stop fraud, yet could say he is trying to put the franchise out of business, assuming that it would no longer be viable if all its fraudulent practices were ended, and accepting its failure as a side effect of stopping the fraud. However, you and your friend, the Ford dealer, apparently are motivated by resentment and also want to drive the franchise out of business as a means to eliminating its competition.

Acting vindictively always is wrong. Nor may one ever seek others' injury as a means to an ulterior end. You also should foresee that if you succeed in driving your competitors out of business, their suppliers, employees, and customers are likely to suffer losses: the suppliers may lose business, the employees might not easily find other jobs, and most customers probably will lose the service still due them under their contracts for wheel alignment and balancing. Since you and your friend will be at fault, you cannot rightly accept any of this harm to third parties, and so will be guilty of the injustice of bringing about all of it.

You might argue that the dishonest shop's employees, being involved in its wrongdoing, deserve to lose their jobs, while its customers' loss of the service due them will be compensated by their no longer being defrauded. But are you sure every one of the employees shares moral responsibility for the shop's fraud? Even if you are, you cannot be sure every one of the customers who stand to lose out on the service due them would have been vulnerable to the fraud.

You and your friend have a morally acceptable alternative, however, which you should choose.

Considered in itself, your plan to obtain evidence of the franchise shop's fraud and provide the evidence to the public prosecutor is morally acceptable. However, your purposes should be to help the law do justice and to compel your competitors to do business honestly. If you and your friend act for these legitimate purposes, you probably will behave somewhat differently. For example, you might tell the owners of the franchise shop that you know about its wrongdoing and try to encourage them to repent and make fair restitution to those they have defrauded, making it clear you will not let the matter rest unless the fraudulent practices are eliminated completely and permanently. Then, if you must go through with the plan you describe, you will not try to injure your competitors by getting the prosecutor and your media friends to dramatize the case.

If the dishonest shop ends its wrongdoing, makes restitution, and survives, you and your friend presumably will benefit by not having to contend with the advantage your competitors enjoyed as a result of dishonest practices, and you may rightly seek that benefit as the ulterior end of your public service. Perhaps your competitors will not survive exposure, but if your purposes are limited to bringing them to justice and compelling them to do business honestly, you can rightly accept that outcome and its harmful effects on third parties as a consequence of doing something good.

105: Must a man make up for various losses resulting from his bankruptcy?

I had an auto body shop in a suburban area, but lost my lease and had to move to a small city almost twenty-five miles away. I did everything I could to succeed at the new location, but the shop didn't draw enough work, and the business, which was incorporated, went bankrupt after struggling a year.

I was behind in paying my employees. All of them knew how badly we were doing, but they kept working because they had no good job opportunities elsewhere and, like me, were trying to make a go of the business. Four of them were members of my wife's family or mine, and I paid them off out of my own pocket. But I had a mechanic and a painter who were not related to us, and I did not pay them off. They learned that they had been treated differently and complained that I cheated them.

The court settled everything. Some pieces of equipment I was making payments on were returned to the company I had bought it from. When I closed down, no cash was left. The payments from insurance companies that came in after the shop closed went for legal expenses and taxes.

That was not quite two years ago now. I quickly got a job managing a body shop at a large dealership. My two best mechanics and I had paid off our home mortgages, and six months ago we remortgaged our houses, quit the dealership, and opened our own shop, which is already beginning to turn a good profit.

During the bankruptcy, I did not want to commit perjury, so in talking with my lawyer and in court I told the truth and answered questions honestly. Still, my conscience is bothering me. The other day one of our suppliers called because he had not received our check, though it was mailed on time. He reminded me that two years ago I was telling him (as, of course, I was telling everybody) that "the check is in the mail." I began thinking about those days and recalled that, when we closed, some customers who had problems with work we had done were never taken care of. One lady even threatened to sue me, though nothing ever came of it. She had skidded on ice and rammed a utility pole, but was saved by the airbag. Though she never knew it, her car would have been totaled, but for the sake of getting the job I kept the estimate down and did the work.[308] I knew there might be problems. If the shop had stayed in business, I would have taken care of everything and tried to collect something more from her insurance company for the extra work. When we closed down, she had to get the additional work done elsewhere, which cost her nearly a thousand dollars, and her insurance refused to pay any of it. Besides that situation, I am wondering whether I ought to pay off my two former employees.

What must I do to straighten all this out? If I have to make good on everything, I cannot do it all at once. What should I do first?

Analysis:

This question calls for clarification of the factors that could call for restitution and application of the Golden Rule to each case that requires restitution. Probably the questioner defrauded some of his creditors; he must reimburse them for what they lost through his fraud, with interest at a reasonable rate. Similarly, he owes restitution to the woman he wronged by deliberately giving a low estimate. A fair settlement can be determined only by considering all the facts of the case and applying the Golden Rule. He also owes restitution to other customers who suffered losses due to imperfect work if he accepted their jobs unfairly in view of looming bankruptcy. Perhaps he cheated the two employees he never paid off, perhaps not. If the family members were paid what was due them as employees, other employees were due the same. But if what he paid the family members was a gift not owed them as employees, he did not cheat the other two. The questioner can determine the proper order for making restitution only by applying the Golden Rule to the whole set of cases in which he owes it.

---

308. *Totaled* means that the insurance company would have exercised its contractual right to declare the car a complete loss, pay the insured its estimated market value immediately preceding the accident, and, in exchange for that payment, receive the wreck and the right to the proceeds from its salvage. Thus, had the questioner given an honest estimate for repairing the car of, say, $10,000, and the estimated value before the accident been $9,500, the insurance company would have paid the woman $9,500 and taken the wreck. To get the work, the questioner kept the estimate for repair down to, say, $9,300. Presumably, all necessary work was completed as well as possible. But, as is common with such extensive jobs, additional work was found to be needed afterwards.

The reply could be along the following lines:

I assume not only that you were entirely honest in carrying out the bankruptcy proceeding but that the failure of the business was not your fault. If so, the bankruptcy itself was blameless, and you need only compensate someone who suffered a loss as a result if you either wronged that party in some specific way or had a special relationship that makes absorbing some or all of that loss appropriate for you.[309]

Not only owners but employees, customers, and suppliers are true participants in a business. All should cooperate for their common good, and cooperation presupposes candid communication. If all parties communicate candidly and cooperate fairly, none owes the others restitution should their common enterprise fail. However, if owners and/or managers regard some of the other parties as outsiders and omit candid communication, injustices calling for restitution are likely. Then too, in a common enterprise characterized by genuine cooperation, fairness and mercy can require that more affluent participants accept greater burdens, including a larger share of losses if things go badly.

Obtaining anything on credit involves a promise to pay, and that promise is untruthful unless the person making it expects to be able to pay. You say that when the business was failing, you were telling creditors, such as the supplier who pricked your conscience, that payment was imminent when, in fact, it was not. That was a lie, and I assume it was a means to obtain continuing credit. If so, or even if you simply continued buying things on credit when you no longer expected to be able to pay, you wrongfully caused creditors to suffer losses they otherwise would have avoided.

Suppliers and others who extended credit to your business undoubtedly knew in general that they might suffer losses from bad debts, and most such creditors probably do not make a practice of cutting off credit at the first sign of a debtor's difficulty. So, at least some of your creditors' losses probably resulted from their forbearance rather than your fraud. You owe no compensation for such losses. However, the mere fact that businesses extending credit foresee and allow for bad debts, and sometimes even deliberately accept significant risks of loss, in no way reduces your responsibility for any loss a creditor suffered due to your dishonesty. Moreover, dishonesty that results in creditors' losses entails the moral duty of restitution even if it would not constitute fraud in a legal sense.

Losses due to a debtor's dishonesty are no different from losses resulting from other sorts of fraud. They call for restitution (see *LCL*, 444–58). You should examine the facts about your transactions with each creditor who lost money when you went bankrupt, judge conscientiously whether and how much of the loss resulted from your dishonesty, and commit yourself to repaying that amount, with

---

309. Some might challenge the justice of laws permitting businesses to limit liability by incorporating and allowing both businesses and individuals to escape indebtedness by bankruptcy. These deeper issues, not treated in this question, must be acknowledged. But I shall assume that the structural injustices involved in these laws, if any, cannot reasonably be taken into account by the questioner in determining his obligations to make restitution.

interest at a reasonable rate—for example, the rate creditors would have had to pay on money they owed their creditors during the same period.

Similarly, if your wrongdoing caused a loss to any customer after the shop closed, you personally ought to compensate that customer, with interest at a reasonable rate. In the case of the woman who threatened to sue, you clearly sinned at least by deliberately underestimating the damage, since that underestimate was a lie to her and her insurance company. Perhaps you also had in mind eventually getting more from the insurance company than it really owed. Then too, it appears that you deliberately imposed on the customer the risk, which she otherwise would have avoided, of the loss she eventually suffered. You owe her restitution.

But how much did she lose? You cannot assume it was no more than the nearly one thousand dollars she paid for additional repairs; much less can you assume it was simply the difference between what the insurance company paid out and what it would have paid had your estimate been honest. An honest estimate would have permitted (and even compelled) the woman to part with the car in exchange for the insurance payment, and she would not have had her subsequent problems with that car. It seems to me you should investigate—perhaps simply by asking the woman, perhaps in some less direct way—what she suffered by continuing to own that car. If all went well after she paid for the additional repairs, I think you could fairly take, as a basis for determining your debt to her, what she paid for those repairs plus a fair allowance for her time and inconvenience. But if she experienced additional harms and losses, I think the fair basis for your restitution will be greater. To establish the amount, consider everything and apply the Golden Rule. Provided the woman is still alive and is fair-minded, that probably can best be done by dealing directly with her. You could begin by telling her your conscience has been bothering you, and you wish to make up to her the losses you caused. If she cooperates, you can discuss her problems with the car and arrive at a settlement you both consider fair.

What about other customers who suffered losses due to imperfect work that had to be completed and/or corrected by others? Plainly, if you knowingly cut corners, you should compensate them for their additional cost to have it finished. But what about cases where you did your best? No doubt, every auto body shop sometimes does work that happens to be defective in some way and calls for correction without additional charge. If some customers' losses resulted from such defects, you are not responsible for their extra costs unless you accepted those jobs even though you foresaw, or reasonably should have foreseen, that your business was at such risk of failing that, in the customer's place, you would have taken the work elsewhere had you known how things stood.

Employees who lacked options but deliberately remained with the failing business freely chose to risk the loss of pay they eventually suffered. But perhaps the two employees you did not pay off were right in claiming you cheated them. You say you "paid off" out of your own pocket the employees who were members of your wife's family or yours. Why did you do that?

Perhaps you had been cheating all your employees, but made restitution only to family members. Owner-managers of failing businesses sometimes continue to draw all or most of their own salaries while cutting employees' wages or delaying paying them. That is unfair. Insofar as owner-managers draw salaries, they are employees no different from others, and should share the sacrifices other employees make by reducing their own salaries at least proportionately and delaying payments to themselves at least as long. If you treated yourself better than your employees, you certainly owed them restitution based on what they would have received had you treated them as you did yourself. And if you made such restitution to some, you should have made it to all.

Again, perhaps you paid off those you did because you realized you had a moral obligation, though not a legally enforceable duty, to do so. Incorporation limited your legal liability, so that you did not have to draw upon your personal wealth and possessions to pay your debts when the business went bankrupt. But you may have recognized that the personal loyalty of your employees, who cooperated in a valiant though unsuccessful effort to save the business, demanded that you compensate them out of some of your wealth, which probably came from profits they had helped you make during the years when the business was doing well. If your motivation was of that sort, then, again, all your employees deserved the same consideration, and you ought now to make restitution to the two you cheated.

However, perhaps you "paid off" family members because, despite the personal setback when the business failed, you remained better off than they, and this was a way of sharing your remaining wealth with people close to you who were experiencing hard times. Perhaps you would have given them similar help even if you all had been working together in someone else's shop. Or, perhaps, the payment was really a gift meant to keep peace in the family. If motivated by any of those considerations, the payment was not really delayed wages, and the two employees who did not get it were not cheated, though you could and should have forestalled their resentment by making clear the nature of the payment.

In paying whatever compensation you owe, draw only on your personal funds, and do not charge off any of the cost to your new company. It is a separate and distinct entity, and your new partners are in no way responsible for your prior obligations. Moreover, it would be tax fraud to treat your restitution as an expense of your new business.

Assuming you cannot at once make all the restitution you should, in what order should you pay? There is no simple answer. Consider everything, put yourself in the place of each of the other parties involved, and apply the Golden Rule. Among the things to consider is whether the basis of your obligation is the same or different in each case. It seems to me that, other things being equal, those deliberately defrauded should be paid before any who were not. If any of the parties needs what you owe more urgently than others, that too is an important consideration. Other things being equal, you can take into account your personal interests and the interests of your new business. For example, if you owe something to the supplier who pricked your conscience, your new business perhaps will benefit by settling quite soon with him.

In dealing with each party, do your best not only to determine what you owe and arrange to pay it, but to restore or heal the good relationship destroyed or wounded by your wrongdoing. All or most of those parties knew they were wronged, probably were justifiably angry at you, and perhaps hate you. You need not explain to them the precise nature of the wrongs they suffered, but you should admit frankly that you wronged them, express sincere sorrow, and humbly beg forgiveness. That, along with treating them fairly, is likely to bring about reconciliation.

Someone might object that in trying to make matters right with people you defrauded you will remind them of what they suffered and admit responsibility, which might well lead at least some of them to sue you personally. But I doubt that risk is great. None of the people you wronged sought legal redress, and your offer of compensation hardly will be provocative. Whatever risk exists can be minimized by carefully avoiding explaining precisely how you wronged each party, and focusing on your desire to put your conscience at rest and remove their ground for dissatisfaction with you. Some risk will remain, of course, but fulfilling the obligation to make peace with those one has wronged always involves some risk. One simply must accept that irreducible risk as part of the price of having wronged others.

The preceding explanations constitute a guide for clarifying your guilty conscience. As with any more routine examination of conscience, begin by praying for the Holy Spirit's light and strength, and proceed to sincere contrition and a firm purpose of amendment. Since you almost certainly committed sins at least grave in themselves, even if not fully deliberate, you have a good reason to confess them along with any other grave sins you may have committed since your last good confession (see *LCL,* 202–16). In this way, you will enjoy the help both of your confessor and of the sacrament's grace.

Profit by this experience and prepare to resist future temptations to cheat in your business. Unfairness generates grave obligations of restitution that do not fade with passing years. Indeed, because fairness demands paying interest for the period others were deprived of what was due to them, the amount to be paid back grows steadily as the years pass.

106: What know-how may people use in serving their employers' competitors?

I am president of my own management consulting firm, which specializes in helping small businesses obtain technical information and engineering assistance. More and more of our clients are new companies set up in third-world countries to supply products to those countries' domestic markets at lower prices than comparable imports. In most cases, we obtain needed information from sources accessible to everyone—libraries, data bases, governmental agencies, and academic experts—and we deal with engineering problems by identifying firms or self-employed engineers with whom our clients can contract for needed help. Generally, the only troubling ethical problem has involved an occasional conflict of interest on our part, and we now avoid that by adhering to a strict rule never to accept clients who are or are likely to be in competition with one another.

Sometimes, though, the best source of information and help for a client is a competitor's past or present employee. Such people are useful precisely because of what they have learned on the job. We do recognize some definite limits on how far we can go in using such sources. Bribing or deceiving a competitor's employees to obtain its secrets and other methods of industrial espionage plainly are wrong. But after excluding such methods and the use of information and techniques that clearly are proprietary, we still regularly find ourselves in situations where it is hard to identify the ethical limits.

I suspect most people who confront this problem draw the line at what they think would be likely to provoke a lawsuit they cannot afford to lose. But that standard seems too loose in many cases and too tight in some. It is too loose when the source is a former employee of a company that probably either will not sue or will be unable to prove its proprietary information and techniques have been stolen. It is too tight when the source is a present employee of a company that jealously guards its rights with frequent lawsuits and claims they extend to absolutely everything its employees learn from the day they are hired. Just as employees have the right to quit their jobs and use their experience in new ones, so they surely have the right to use it in outside consulting, provided that does not interfere with what they are being paid to do during their working hours.

I would appreciate any help you can give me in drawing an ethical line between the legitimate and illegitimate uses of the experience of past or present employees of our clients' competitors. Probably there is no simple rule for the many diverse cases, but perhaps you can suggest guidelines.

Analysis:

This question calls for the derivation of moral norms. Unless obligated by a valid and applicable contract not to do so, people who developed their talents while working for one company are free to use them in serving another. They also may continue to use commonly available information and techniques familiar to people in their field. But a company's present employees should be loyal, and so generally should not help its competitors even in ways that would be permissible if they were former employees. With some exceptions, then, the questioner should not serve a client by drawing on its competitors' current employees. The moral acceptability of using the expertise that sources have gained in their employment, whether past or present, depends on two things: whether they make available information and techniques that are the property of the previous employer, and, if they do, whether the previous employer can fairly forbid that use or require compensation for it. So, sound norms presuppose clarification both of the conditions that constitute ownership of information and techniques, and the limits owners can fairly set to others' use of this peculiar sort of property.

The reply could be along the following lines:

No company owns everything its employees learn while working for it. To a great extent, their employment experience develops their personal abilities to gather information, organize material, plan tasks, solve problems, and so on. Such personal development would be the employer's property only if the employees themselves could be property—that is, if they truly were slaves. Of course, the institution of slavery can exist as an unjust social structure, but, morally speaking, persons cannot be owned. Moreover, by their on-the-job experience, employees become aware of much commonly available information and learn commonly used techniques, and these acquisitions plainly do not belong to the employer. Thus, I agree with you in rejecting the view that an employer's rights extend to everything employees learn from the day they are hired. Anyone who legitimately terminates his or her employment or is discharged from it may in general use acquired expertise in work performed for a new employer, even if the two employers are competitors.

By contrast, a company's current employees generally should be committed to promoting and safeguarding its legitimate interests. Helping a competitor by supplying service not otherwise readily available to it generally would violate that commitment and constitute grave disloyalty. Many employers try to forestall this by requiring employees to promise to avoid such behavior or by threatening to dismiss anyone found guilty of it. But even without any explicit contractual requirement or other enforcement measure, employees ordinarily assume an obligation of loyalty to their employer simply by accepting employment.

Someone might point out that lawyers and accountants may provide professional services for competing firms, provided the specific matters they handle generate no conflict of interest. So—it might be argued by analogy—current employees may do work for a company's competitors on the same basis as former employees, provided all specific duties pertaining to both jobs are fulfilled. But lawyers and accountants are engaged to supply services that they and others in their professions openly offer to all clients on the same basis; thus, their duty of loyalty to a client, though no less serious, is different from that of a company's employees. Since employees are one of the groups that constitute a business—by cooperating with investors, managers, customers, and suppliers—the company's common good calls for a commitment and loyal service. That commitment bars employees from significantly serving competitors by providing any technical information and engineering assistance not otherwise readily available.

Of course, in exceptional circumstances a current employee can rightly help a company's competitor, even when a contractual obligation forbids it. A company's employee sometimes can serve its competitor without disloyalty if the employer-employee relationship is seriously unjust and the employee is the victim of exploitation, though even in such a case helping a competitor could be unfair to fellow employees and/or some other participants in the business. Again, at times an employer might not be injured and might even be benefited by an employee's helping a competitor; then the employer's permission should be obtained unless it can be confidently presumed. The overriding claims of the common good of the wider society also could lead patriotic people to help their employer's competitors in order to meet an urgent need—of the society as a whole or of some fellow citizens—for a good or service.

In sum, with some exceptions, a company's present employees should not significantly help a competitor by supplying a service not otherwise readily available to it. Now, it would be wrong for you to intend that anyone you use to serve your clients do what he or she should not do. Therefore, you generally should not use current employees of your clients' competitors. You may not make exceptions unless confident that special circumstances allow an individual to serve his or her employer's competitor without being disloyal. Moreover, even when a company's current employees are rightly serving a competitor, they have the same obligations toward the company as former employees have. Your question focuses mainly on those obligations, which I shall now consider.

To begin with, like current employees, former employees may be barred by contract, at least for a certain stretch of time, from communicating specific information to anyone outside the company or from working for a competitor. Of course, such contractual constraints are not absolute. Sometimes they are unreasonable, and courts might find them to be invalid. In other cases, though reasonable in general, they admit exceptions as other promises do (see *LCL*, 412–14). Still, you should not intend that anyone you enlist to serve a client violate any contract with a former or present employer unless you are convinced that the contract is invalid or that its relevant provision is inapplicable in a particular case so that an exception to it will be morally justified.

In making such judgments, two possible sources of confusion must be kept in mind. First, if a company's former employees have not been justly compensated for their contributions to the enterprise's discoveries and innovations, or have some other just claim against their former employer, they deserve appropriate compensation. But even though they might be eager to obtain it by serving the former employer's competitor, that might well be unjust. You should not use such persons to serve your clients unless convinced they can rightly do so. Second, a company's former employees sometimes help its competitor duplicate some discovery or technical innovation without explicitly communicating it—for example, by pointing out which commonly available information and generally used techniques are relevant to the discovery or innovation and which are not. But such indirect communication is wrong if intended to evade their responsibility to refrain from communication.

The problem about proprietary information and techniques can be more clearly defined by referring to two other things. On the one hand, as I noted at the beginning, a previous employer has no right to the development of employees' talents resulting from their work or to the commonly available information and widely used techniques they appropriated while employees. On the other hand, industrial espionage often is used to obtain a company's secrets—for example, plans to raise or lower prices, increase or reduce production, file or settle a lawsuit. Such information is not so much a company's property as part of its inner self, much as individuals' private thoughts and intentions pertain to their persons rather than belong to them as property does. Since you provide clients with technical information and engineering assistance, your question about ethical limits does not concern company secrets. Putting aside as irrelevant these two things, then, shall focus on information and techniques that could reasonably be regarded as a previous employer's property. The problem is how to draw lines when such property rights are not clear.

Basic human goods and other factors antecedent to law provide a foundation for property rights and responsibilities, but they must be specified by authoritative social judgments and choices (see *LCL,* 795–99). To identify something as the property of a particular individual or organization, relevant legal provisions must be taken into account. Such legal provisions, therefore, are among the criteria for identifying information and techniques as a company's property. The relevant provisions are found not only in statutes but in case law—in the decisions that might serve as precedents in a lawsuit alleging a violation of property rights. So, in judging whether the information and techniques a person has acquired while working for a particular company are its property, one must consider whether it would have a sound legal basis for asserting a proprietary interest in that information and those techniques.

As you say, it would be wrong to draw the line only at what you think would be likely to provoke a lawsuit you could not risk losing, since circumstances irrelevant to the merits of a claim of ownership often make its enforcement at law impractical or even impossible. But if existing law probably would not support a company's claim that certain information and techniques were its property, it would be reasonable to assume that they were not. On the other hand, if existing law probably would support the claim, it almost certainly should be considered valid.

Someone might object that the existing, relevant law might be unjust. It should be presumed just, however, unless the contrary can be shown. And showing that involves special difficulties. This sort of property and the conflicts that arise regarding it are remote from people's everyday experience, and only statutes and the adjudication of conflicting claims will have specified the conditions under which information and techniques can and do belong to people's former employers.

What about cases in which neither existing law nor relevant contracts and patents make it clear whether certain information and/or techniques belong to a former employer? In general, when an enterprise leads to fresh discoveries or the creative development of technology, these fruits belong to the people whose efforts brought them about, unless they did what they did as justly compensated employment, in which case the fruits belong to the enterprise's owners. But if commonly available information and techniques are used to obtain some new result, the result's newness does not justify the assertion of an exclusive claim to that information and those techniques. Moreover, if a company's employees make discoveries or creatively develop techniques partly in fulfilling their duty as employees and partly as a result of their own uncompensated or inadequately compensated efforts, those fruits of the enterprise belong partly to the owners and partly to the employees.

Even when information and techniques clearly belong to a company, it might not be justified in trying to keep such property to itself. In general, owning property does not entail an unlimited right to forbid its use or be compensated for it (see *LCL,* 800–806, 811–14). Owners of technical discoveries and technological advances have some right to their use, but they also have a responsibility fairly to administer the use to meet genuine human needs. This could morally oblige company to share its proprietary information and processes with others, perhaps even with competitors, with or perhaps without compensation. Suppose, for example, a company developed a way of generating electrical power more cheaply and with less adverse environmental impact than any current method; suppose also that it could exploit the new technology to meet the needs of only a small part of the world's people. It ought to share its advance with others able to use it to meet everyone's needs; and although the company may be entitled to compensation, the amount must be limited to what is fair and should not exclude the very poor from enjoying the new technology's benefits.

To some extent, no doubt, these considerations about ownership responsibilities and the limits they impose upon a company's rights in respect to its technical discoveries and technological advances are taken into account by the same body of law that helps define and identify such property. But existing U.S. law may not allow adequately for international socioeconomic structures and relevant differences between third-world and domestic companies. So, at least in certain cases, you might be justified in recruiting a competitor's former employee to help a third-world client though not a domestic client.[310] Only after taking all the circumstances into account, however, could you judge a client entitled to uncompensated use of its competitor's proprietary information and processes. Of course, in making such a judgment, you must not let your own interest in serving your client lead you to rationalize conduct that would amount to stealing proprietary information and techniques.

107: May a company's president discharge a colleague to obtain his stock?

Until three years ago, I worked for a large consulting firm that had fallen on hard times. Four co-workers and I became convinced that its days were numbered. We also were dissatisfied with its practices, which had become increasingly questionable from an ethical point of view. (As it happened, the firm survived and rebounded, but that is another story.) I took the initiative in finding venture capitalists and forming a new company. My four co-workers joined me, and we have been providing consulting service, specializing in marketing problems.

Initially, my colleagues and I each invested fifty thousand dollars, and five venture capitalists each invested three hundred and fifty thousand dollars, for a total of two million. We incorporated and divided the stock. Each of the venture capitalists received eleven percent; as president, I received fifteen percent, and each of my colleagues received seven-and-one-half percent. The ten of us constituted the board of directors, with me as chairman. My four colleagues and I each drew a salary of ten thousand per month. Our employment contracts provide that,

---

310. Paul Steidlmeier, "The Moral Legitimacy of Intellectual Property Claims: American Business and Developing Country Perspectives," *Journal of Business Ethics,* 12 (1993): 157–64, describes the conflict between a view that tends to absolutize owners' claims to intellectual property and a view that limits those claims—as Catholic social teaching does—by other peoples' rights to livelihood and development. But he neither criticizes the former view nor notices that ownership claims which are just in the U.S. might be unjust in a third-world country.

if any of us withdraws or is terminated, the firm has the right to buy back his stock at current market value.

Since it would have been unethical to try to take our former employer's clients with us, we made no attempt to do that and got off to a slow start. However, a few old clients sought us out, and we slowly have picked up new ones. At the same time, our overhead is substantial, since we have ten employees—junior associates and staff—and our office is in downtown Chicago. Also, cash flow is difficult, since we often must pay suppliers for work done on a project three months or so before receiving the client's payment. Consequently, we have yet to show a profit, and my colleagues and I sometimes have had to treat part of the salary due us as a loan to the firm.

Early in the second year, I found that one of my colleagues was defrauding the firm by receiving part of a client's payments on the side. He admitted it, agreed to forgo what we otherwise would have owed him in back salary and severance pay, and left quietly. At that point, his stock had no market value, and so we got it back for nothing. However, one of our venture capitalists loaned us two hundred thousand dollars at no interest in exchange for that stock, thus providing desperately needed cash. Six months later, another colleague accepted a major corporation's vice-presidency for marketing, and he also surrendered his stock, which we used to obtain a similar loan, netting around one hundred thousand dollars after settling his severance.

I am now considering discharging another member of the original group, Brian. During the first year, his contribution was substantial; in fact, we would not have survived without him. Since then, however, he has not produced enough to cover his salary. All the other directors and a senior member of the staff have talked the matter over with me informally and favor letting him go, both to reduce the payroll and to obtain his stock, which, as in the other cases, would be exchanged for a loan sufficient to settle his severance and provide needed cash.

Three things argue against discharging Brian. First, he was with me from the beginning, has done nothing wrong, and has done his best. Second, he needs the job, probably will not easily get another, and so will not go willingly. Third, to some extent his poor performance has been due to circumstances beyond his control: family problems, including his wife's ill health, and his lengthy commute, which he would have reduced by relocating if the business had been more successful.

This is the most difficult dilemma of my life. I feel I have to discharge Brian for the good of the business. But he has been a good friend, and if our positions were reversed, I would consider him disloyal, especially insofar as the discharge was meant to obtain my stock. My wife, who knows Brian's wife well, thinks discharging him would be outrageous.

Analysis:

This question concerns a conflict of responsibilities. The questioner must distinguish between his responsibilities as company president and as the colleague's friend, and fulfill both sets of responsibilities. Even the business relationship calls for loyalty. If the business were flourishing, it would be wrong to discharge the colleague without first trying to help him deal with his problems. But if the common good of the business requires that he be discharged, the questioner, as president, should discharge him, at the same time making a reasonable effort to help him during transition and, as friend, offering appropriate assistance.

The reply could be along the following lines:

The last paragraph of your letter, in which you speak of the tension between your roles as the company's president and as Brian's friend, points to your need to distinguish carefully between your responsibilities in each role.

As the company's president, you are responsible for its common good: the efficient cooperation of all concerned—suppliers, employees, clients, investors, your associates, and yourself—and a fair distribution among them of the burdens involved in that cooperation and the benefits accruing from it. In fulfilling that role, you should exclude from consideration your personal friendship with Brian, which existed before you formed the company and which, no doubt, you have carried on by communications and activities that contributed nothing to the business. You also should exclude your wife's strong views. To compromise or even slightly risk the common good of the business by giving Brian special consideration on these bases would be an injustice to all the other participants.

Still, as Brian's friend, you owe him the same sorts of advice, encouragement, and help you owe other, similar friends. Yet whatever you owe him as your friend must be supplied from your personal resources, not those of the business. Consequently, after judging what the common good of the business requires you to do about Brian, you will also have to decide how much of your own time and money you should devote to his needs.

First among the things you owe him as a friend is a clear statement of your conscientious distinction between your two relationships with him, together with an earnest request that he, too, keep this distinction in mind. Then your friendship may be preserved even if your business relationship must be changed or ended.

While you must not make the business decision on the basis of personal friendship, you must not exclude considerations of loyalty proper to the business relationship itself. Setting the friendship aside, I think you have indicated some legitimate business considerations that argue against discharging Brian. He stands to lose both his job and his investment of time and money as one of the original associates in the business; his contribution at the beginning was substantial and vital, and even now the good will he enjoys with some clients may make his contribution greater than it appears. Family problems and a lengthy commute partly account for deficiencies in his recent performance, so that you have reason to expect his performance to improve if he can relocate and/or his wife's health improves. If the business were flourishing, considerations like these, quite apart from friendship, would oblige you to keep Brian on, at least another year or so, while making a reasonable effort to help him deal with his problems. Therefore, though you must identify your motivations as his friend and set them aside, your loyalty to him as a business associate surely precludes discharging him at this time unless the common good of the business requires it.

Does it? You say: "I feel I have to discharge Brian for the good of the business." But if the very survival of the business immediately required that he be discharged, I imagine the venture capitalists, who hold the controlling interest in the business and have much to lose, would insist that you act at once. Thus far, however, the other directors have done no more than tell you informally that they favor letting him go. Therefore, before discharging him, you ought to look for possible alternatives and consider each carefully. In doing this, you almost certainly should tell him frankly what is on your mind and ask him to contribute to your deliberation by both making the best possible case against discharging him and trying to find a mutually acceptable alternative.

Perhaps Brian could be retained at a salary reduced in proportion to his current contribution. Could the business afford that? Could he make do? Could you, Brian, and your other colleague each give up some of your stock, perhaps in different proportions, to obtain the cash the business needs? Could Brian increase his contribution by assuming enough of the duties of the least able of the junior associates to allow you to lay off that person?

If no such solution can be found and you become convinced that the good of the business requires discharging Brian, fairness to him may well demand that the business do more than just pay his back salary and severance pay. In view of his contribution to the business and his loyal service, the company very likely owes him help in finding another job and perhaps should provide other forms of assistance during the transition, such as office space and secretarial services, continued health coverage, and so on.

If you do discharge Brian, your friendship with him will require that you personally help him in any way you reasonably can. If he needs help with the work of packing up and moving, you might offer to pitch in. If your personal wealth and financial situation permit, you might offer some money as a gift or, perhaps, a larger amount as a loan.

Though you say the stock you wish to get back from him has no current market value, it plainly is not entirely worthless. The venture capitalist is willing to risk another large, interest-free loan to the company in order to get it. Moreover, though the stock originally owned by you and your four colleagues was contractually linked to your and their employment status, it represented a substantial financial contribution to setting up the company. I suppose the associate who was defrauding the firm was willing to give up all his claims on it in order to settle its claim against him, and the colleague who resigned to take another job fully understood his options and was under no constraints in agreeing to the settlement he received. But since you say Brian will not go willingly, it is clear that, if you discharge him, he will have no choice but to accept the terms of his separation. Therefore, it seems to me, his stock morally may not be taken back unless the company makes some sort of commitment to compensate him for it. It could take different forms—for example, a guarantee of a certain amount of money if the company ever becomes profitable or a promise of some portion of future profits, if any, for a certain number of years.

Unfortunately, even if you treat Brian fairly as company president and are kind and generous as his friend, he may well be angry and bitter toward you, and respond by saying and doing inappropriate things. Be prepared to suffer that meekly, to continue to treat him gently, to forgive him any hurt he does you, and to fulfill all of the company's and your personal responsibilities toward him, not least to pray for him and his wife. Then, even if your long-standing relationship is destroyed, you may hope to find it again, one day, in heaven, not only restored but perfected, so that it will be fit to continue forever.

108: What should an executive do about superiors' misuse of corporate resources?

While still in high school, I began working part time as an office boy at one of the regional offices of a large, nationwide, nonprofit organization. Upon graduation, I became a full-time employee, and worked my way up to regional manager while studying in the evenings for a B.A. and then an M.B.A. I believe wholeheartedly in the organization's purpose, and working for it has been gratifying. Moreover, I always have been treated very well.

In January, after six good years as a regional manager, I was transferred to the national headquarters and promoted to administrator for the eight regional offices. Since regional managers have a certain degree of autonomy, that does not quite make me the regional offices' general manager, but I now am the organization's top executive after the president and three vice-presidents. All of them have been supportive, and I have had no problem settling into my new job.

However, I have encountered an unexpected ethical issue. I knew the organization took a lavish approach when people from here visit the regional offices or regional managers come here for semiannual meetings. Believing less extravagant arrangements would be more appropriate for a nonprofit organization, I hoped to get everyone involved to agree to cut back. But after taking over here, I discovered that I had seen only the tip of the iceberg. There are many other instances of extravagance in doing essentially legitimate things, and the officers, whose salaries are quite adequate, enjoy remarkably generous fringe benefits, authorized by the board. But there also is something far more troubling. All the officers are diverting resources from the organization for their personal benefit.

I don't just suspect this. I know it is going on. The president has talked to me quite freely about some of these matters, and I cannot help overhearing other things. Having become good friends with the accountant, I asked him about the situation, and he confessed to knowing about it for over three years and becoming increasingly anxious about it. During that time, the abuses have grown steadily and currently include the following. The president and his wife regularly take vacations and entertain relatives and personal friends at the organization's expense. All the officers frequently charge to their budgets items of office furniture, equipment, and supplies sent as gifts to relatives and personal friends, or taken home permanently for family use. One of the president's secretaries spends most of her time working on his and his wife's family histories and other nonbusiness affairs, including activities involving the officers' children and help with their school and college assignments. Three other people on the payroll seldom come to the office; they almost always are at one of the officers' homes doing maintenance, yard work, housekeeping, and so forth. Over the past twelve months, these and other, smaller abuses have cost the organization more than two hundred thousand dollars. The figure for this calendar year will be significantly higher, because the officers (except one vice-president) are going to take their wives on a European vacation in October. As cover, they are arranging some brief meetings with leaders of counterpart organizations in each of the six capital cities they will visit. These meetings will serve no real purpose, and the junket will cost over a hundred thousand dollars.

Though I am now responsible for the extravagant arrangements for meetings with the regional offices, my office has not been involved in any of the clear-cut abuses and will have nothing to do with the European vacation. I also declined when the president invited me and my wife to go along on that trip, saying I felt I should stay here to back up the vice-president who will remain on duty. And, though my predecessor personally participated in some abuses, I have not taken advantage of any opportunity to do so. But what the officers are doing is troubling, and I have been wondering what if anything to do about it.

I often deal directly with the president. I could talk privately with him about my concerns, to which he seems oblivious. But I very much doubt that I could get him to do anything. He obviously is accustomed to these perks and is hardly likely to welcome the idea of giving them up. Moreover, even though he is the prime culprit, he is not in the least embarrassed about what he and the others are doing. If I put the matter to him gently, I am sure he would brush it aside and send me off with a friendly pat on the shoulder. Only a sharp confrontation would get him to take my concerns seriously. But anybody who gets into a sharp confrontation with him is likely to lose both the argument and his or her job. Even though he has treated me as a protégé since we met seven years ago, it could happen to me.

I feel torn by my feelings toward the president. I am saddened by his venality and afraid of what he might do to me, but I still like him and am enormously indebted to him. I would not want to betray his trust. But if I confronted him and he reacted as I expect, I could threaten to tell the state's attorney everything I know unless the abuses are stopped.

My personal feelings aside, there are good reasons for not making that threat. If it worked, my relationship with the president and the other three officers would be so strained that continuing to work with them, if possible at all, would be difficult and unpleasant. And if the threat didn't work, I would have only two alternatives: not carry it out or carry it out. Not carrying out the threat would leave things here just as they are—except that I would, at best, have strained relationships and probably even no job—while carrying out the threat almost certainly would lead to a criminal investigation and prosecution. That would not only ruin the lives of all four officers but greatly disrupt my own life and, most important, produce devastating publicity for the organization. Eighty percent of its income comes in small donations from middle-class people, who are likely to react by finding other beneficiaries for their philanthropy.

I do not know what to do, and am beginning to think maybe I should just get on with my job and ignore the abuses.

Analysis:

This question calls for clarification of a duty pertaining to the questioner's role in the organization. The abuses constitute a grave breach of trust by the organization's officers. They should be stopped. The questioner is well informed about the problem and has the highest managerial position in the organization after the officers, all of whom share guilt. Therefore, it is the questioner's duty to stop the abuses. If the questioner judges that he need not at once tell relevant public officials about the abuses, he probably should bring the matter to the attention of the organization's board, which can deal with it decisively. If the board is reluctant to act, he should be prepared to communicate with other parties interested in the organization and, if necessary, with public officials.

The reply could be along the following lines:

Apparently, God is calling you to imitate Jesus, who was sent into our corrupt situation to redeem us. Since even he shrank from suffering and death, your thought that you might ignore the abuses and simply get on with your job is understandable. Still, I think you should regard it as a temptation to which you must not give in. Probably several, perhaps most, of your colleagues experienced a similar temptation and gave in. If you did, you would miss a unique opportunity to try to save the organization you work for and, almost inevitably, would be drawn into the corruption that imperils it.[311]

Morally, at least, the abuses not only constitute a regular practice of theft, very similar to embezzlement, but are a very serious betrayal of the organization. It has a purpose—its common good—for which different groups of people should cooperate in diverse ways: those people the organization is meant to serve, by gratefully accepting and making good use of benefits; suitable potential donors, by generously supplying necessary means; and employees, by efficiently using donated means to deliver benefits. Corresponding to each group's contribution to the common good is its own legitimate interest in the organization. Those it serves enjoy the benefits they receive; donors make good use of some of their wealth and receive an appropriate recompense (honor, gratitude, growth in virtue, and/or merit with God); employees do worthwhile and fulfilling work for which they receive appropriate compensation.

Any corporation should have policies and procedures to protect its common good and forestall problems of the sort that concern you. Your organization has a special need for such safeguards. Abuses of its resources betray donors and cheat those they meant to help. But apparently the needed policies and procedures are lacking. At the appropriate time, you ought to do what you can to remedy this defect.

311. Though the officers' misbehavior differs from that of William Aramony as president of United Way of America, his subordinates' motives for not taking action were like those that incline the questioner to get on with his job and ignore the abuses; see John S. Glaser, *The United Way Scandal: An Insider's Account of What Went Wrong and Why* (New York: John Wiley and Sons, 1994), 98–121.

By diverting resources for their personal benefit, the officers act contrary to their fiduciary responsibility to use donated means efficiently in order to provide benefits. Thus, they violate the organization's good and directly deprive other participants of part of their legitimate interest. Some potential beneficiaries either are not served or benefit less than they otherwise would; donors' intentions are partially frustrated; and the good efforts of other employees become somewhat less fruitful. Moreover, as you point out, publicity might greatly injure the organization, and the prospect of such publicity is hardly negligible, since the abuses are ongoing, increasing, carried on openly, and known to various employees. So, besides the direct harm they are doing, the officers are taking a grave and unjustifiable risk of additional injury to the organization and all who have a stake in it. Their abuses should be stopped.

Of the considerations you mention in favor of tolerating the abuses, only one is grounded in the organization's good: the prospect of harmful publicity. In my judgment, it should not prevail in your thinking. The abuses already violate the organization's good and injure those involved. Action adequate to stop them might be possible without publicity. And even if they cannot be stopped without publicity that harms the organization, the damage is likely to be less if the abuses are brought to light sooner rather than later and not allowed to continue and increase. Moreover, if you can end the abuses without deliberately publicizing them, the likelihood of harmful publicity over the long term may well be significantly lessened.

You also mention your personal feelings for the president and the prospect of losing your job, straining your working relationships with the president and other officers, and suffering great disruption of your life. But both true self-interest and duty argue against simply getting on with your job while tolerating the abuses.

If you fail to act now, you probably will be pressed eventually to facilitate and conceal the officers' wrongdoing, even if you refuse personally to take part in it. Then too, your long-range career prospects may be far better if you take prompt and vigorous action to stop the abuses. If you do nothing and they eventually are brought to light by someone else, you might lose your job; if you take action and the present officers are discharged, you might be promoted or, at least, retained by new officers, with whom you might develop a good working relationship.

Your personal relationship with the president and your duty to be loyal to him do not require tolerating his wrongdoing. As long as he continues peacefully to enjoy its fruits, he is hardly likely to repent and very likely to become increasingly obdurate. Your ties with him demand that you seek his true welfare by putting a stop to his abuses and encouraging him in genuine repentance.

Furthermore, in accepting your present position, you assumed a responsibility for the organization as a whole. That responsibility should prevail over self-interest and your personal relationship with the president. When the officers cannot or will not do something essential for the organization's good, their responsibility devolves on you as the next ranking executive. Since all of them are involved in the abuses, they cannot be expected to put a stop to them. And while in other matters lack of information or power might keep you from acting, you make it clear that you are well informed about this matter and can act in various ways. So, putting a stop to the abuses falls within your sphere of responsibility.

Given that responsibility, failing to take action would be, morally speaking, a grave omission, and you might also incur legal liability, criminal and/or civil, for the abuses. With a view to taking action, you obviously must be ready to make your case and to protect yourself against possible false accusations. For these reasons, you probably should get a lawyer's advice, which may lead you to conclude that you ought to communicate at once with a suitable public official. But, if it does not, the following thoughts might be helpful.

Since your friend, the accountant, has known about the abuses for over three years, he almost certainly has failed to fulfill his legal responsibilities—for instance, his duty to present accurate information to the auditors. He probably should consult his own lawyer. But since he shared information about the situation with you and both of you are anxious about it, you might be able to work together to rectify it. If feasible and successful, such cooperation would be mutually advantageous. The accountant could extricate himself without paying too high a price, and you could avoid the onus of acting alone.

Whether or not you get the accountant's cooperation, you must proceed without delay. If you judge that you need not communicate at once with a public official, you must try to terminate and rectify the abuses by taking action within the organization. I see two ways of doing this. You have a strict moral duty, in my judgment, to attempt at least the first. Yet I do not consider it entirely adequate, and I also suspect that your legal duty will require the second—though, of course, that also is a matter on which you will need legal advice.

You could forcefully communicate to the president, and perhaps to the other officers, your deep concern as a loyal colleague and good friend. To avoid sharply confronting the president, you could prepare a careful memorandum for him and perhaps some or all of the other officers, pointing out that confidentiality often is breached and many people know about various things that have gone on in the past and about the planned vacation. You need not judge and condemn; you could simply sketch out how these things would be perceived by the media, by people who support the organization, and by various governmental officials. You could call attention to the great risk the officers are taking, both to themselves and to the organization, and add that you also are anxious about possible bad consequences for other employees, including yourself. Without including any explicit threat, such a careful, written statement would focus attention on the issue. If addressed to at least two of the officers, it certainly would lead them to discuss the problem. Undoubtedly, they would be anxious about what you might do, but for that very reason might hesitate to dismiss you. And once the officers focused their attention on the risk they are taking, they might well put a stop to the abuses.

In my judgment, though, that would not be sufficient to rectify the situation and vindicate the organization's interests. The officers and your predecessor owe the organization full restitution, with interest, for the resources they have wrongly diverted, and they are not likely to be willing to repay all they should. They probably also would wish to treat any repayments as tax-exempt donations, but that would be tax fraud, to which the organization should not be a party. Moreover, because these abuses constitute a grave breach of trust, indicating that the officers are not fit to continue in their positions, they should be replaced, something that cannot be done without action by the organization's board.

Therefore, it seems to me you should not take the first approach, but should address your memorandum to the board. It should be carefully drafted, so that you could swear to the truth of everything it says. It should list only clear abuses, not extravagances in carrying on the organization's legitimate business. It should be as specific as possible, including dates and the names not only of those profiting from the abuses and involved in them but of everyone who could give testimony about them. Briefly sketch the probable disastrous consequences for the organization if the abuses continue and become public knowledge, and point out the board's legal responsibility to take decisive action, including replacing the officers and requiring full restitution. When you send the memorandum to the board, whether or not all the officers are on it, you probably ought to hand them copies and do your best to express your personal concern for their true well-being and encourage them to fulfill their responsibilities voluntarily by resigning and making restitution.

What if they refuse and the board is reluctant to act? The regional managers, with whom you deal regularly, plainly have a significant share in responsibility for the organization. Presumably they would be interested in the problem and inclined to trust you. Even if they are not members of the board, they might well be able to influence it. Somewhat similarly, some large contributors are likely to be both concerned and influential with board members. Moreover, both the regional managers and large contributors would have motives similar to yours for avoiding or minimizing bad publicity. Therefore, you might seek their support, if necessary, to motivate the board.

If such private efforts do not succeed, I think you should communicate with an appropriate public official, despite the publicity that would result. Of course, you should also try to mitigate the bad effects of the publicity, and should enlist the cooperation of others to do that.

109: May attractive people be preferred for certain jobs?

For some years, I have been involved in managing a large, successful, consistently top-rated restaurant. Our patrons can afford the best in food, wines, ambience, and service, and they expect nothing less. We seldom if ever disappoint them and charge accordingly. Now I have acquired the controlling interest and, while inclined to keep most things just as they are, I am considering certain changes. One concerns hiring standards. Many other businesses have similar problems, so your discussion of my question would be of wider interest than it might seem. The problem is where to draw the line between unfair and justifiable discrimination when setting the qualifications for waiters and waitresses.

Until now, nobody has been hired for these positions who has not matched a very tight image: white, male, above average in height, below average in weight, clean-cut, handsome, pleasant but dignified, articulate and well-spoken, imperturbable—and, of course, accurate, energetic, and dexterous. Since nobody hired has lacked extensive experience and good references, our waiters range in age from forty to sixty-five. Despite these hiring standards, we have not had any trouble keeping the place fully staffed with excellent waiters—the restaurant always draws high praise for service—partly because working conditions and benefits are much better here than in most restaurants, and partly because our waiters earn top dollar and enjoy an excellent esprit de corps that makes their work rather easy and pleasant.

Nevertheless, past policy on hiring plainly must change. Even if I wanted to continue hiring none but white males, such discrimination is illegal, and it is only due to happenstance that we have not already been compelled to hire women, blacks, orientals, and hispanics; besides, I consider discrimination on the basis of race, sex, and ethnic background grossly unjust, so that I have opposed it right along and would end it even if there were no outside pressure.

At the same time, several of the existing standards seem to me necessary for the good of the business and entirely justifiable as qualifications for the job. People who are not accurate, energetic, dexterous, and able to communicate clearly and easily should not be serving in any restaurant. In a restaurant of quality and style, I think it also is entirely reasonable to hire as waiters and waitresses only people with the right kind of personality. They must be pleasant but not overly friendly, with the attitude of a capable and self-respecting employee toward his or her employer; and they must not show the slightest impatience or irritation, no matter what a patron says or does.

What I am asking, then, is whether I am justified in continuing past standards in respect to other elements of the image—elements that could be summed up as *immediate attractiveness*. Here, too, it seems obvious that there is nothing wrong in employing only people who keep themselves neat, clean, and well groomed. And, I hasten to say, I do not mean sex appeal; all our waiters and waitresses will be clothed conservatively and modestly. But some people are handsome, beautiful, or, at least, nice looking, while others are less attractive: too fat, too short, with irregular features, bad skin, visible scars or birthmarks, poor teeth, and so on. Some people have pleasant voices, while others speak with a lisp, stutter, or rasp—unpleasant features they can do nothing about.

I have no doubt our customers would rather be served by attractive people, and it is likely that business will suffer if we do not maintain this standard. Because our payroll and expenses are high, our margin is not great. A fifteen percent decline in receipts would render the business unprofitable. Nevertheless, unattractive individuals also need jobs, and people in general probably should be more accepting of them. In short, is discrimination on the basis of attractiveness justified or not?

Analysis:

This question concerns the application of the Golden Rule. It would be unfair to favor applicants on the basis of attractiveness unless it is relevant to the job's requirements. Whether it is fair to count among job requirements a potential employee's effect on others' feelings and reactions is the question. It does not seem unreasonable that the questioner's patrons expect an esthetically pleasing ambience and the assurance of wholesome offerings, and attractive waiters and waitresses are better able to satisfy these expectations. So, it seems fair to take into account at least some elements of immediate personal attractiveness in hiring for this job. However, our culture's standard for personal attractiveness seems in part unreasonable; moreover, patrons are likely to be satisfied with waiters and waitresses who are not attractive provided they are not more or less repellent. Therefore, the questioner should not exclude applicants who are neither attractive nor repellent, but may exclude applicants patrons would find repellent.

The reply could be along the following lines:

Someone might claim that employing otherwise well-qualified but unattractive people as waiters and waitresses would not adversely affect your profit. Possibly you should reconsider your contrary view, but since I know almost nothing about the restaurant business, I must take your word for the factual presuppositions of the problem you present. Accepting those presuppositions, I find your question interesting and well formulated. You insist on several qualifications that surely are reasonable for anyone to be a waiter or waitress, and exclude discrimination on the grounds of sex, race, and ethnicity. In this way, you clarify your question: Is it just to discriminate among applicants for this position on the basis of their immediate attractiveness?

Someone might argue that discrimination as such is unjust, and hold that every individual, sharing equally in human dignity, should be offered the same opportunity you now are going to make available to women, blacks, and members of various ethnic groups. But such an argument would be unsound. Employers reasonably discriminate by criteria relevant to applicants' capacity to fulfill job requirements. Sex, race, and ethnicity are objectionable bases for discrimination in hiring people to serve in a restaurant such as yours[312] because these characteristics either are irrelevant to an individual's capacity to do the job or are relevant only in virtue of erroneous beliefs and unreasonable attitudes—on the part of managers, other employees, or patrons—which ought to change and cannot be taken fairly into account.

However, it seems reasonable to include as qualifications for serving in your restaurant certain other traits that, though they will not directly affect an employee's performance, will affect patrons' feelings.[313] For instance, among the qualifications you include are several personality traits that seem to be reasonable requirements. With regard to potential employees' immediate personal attractiveness, many other businesses, as you say, have problems similar to yours, since certain employees' immediate personal attractiveness often greatly affects the first impres-

312. I say "restaurant such as yours" to leave open the possibility that special characteristics of a restaurant or its clientele might provide rational ground for at least some discrimination that otherwise would be unjust.

313. Whether it is morally acceptable for those evaluating job applicants' qualifications to take into account others' reactions to attributes of individuals doing the job is a question of fairness. It must be answered in each sort of case by considering all the facts and applying the Golden Rule; there seems to be no plausible, simple, general norm to guide this judgment; see Alan Wertheimer, "Jobs, Qualifications, and Preferences," *Ethics,* 94 (Oct. 1983): 99–112.

sion a business makes and, thereby, its effectiveness in marketing its products and/or services. That undoubtedly is why businesses hire attractive people to serve as receptionists, product demonstrators, and so on. When hiring for such positions, it seems to me, businesses fairly take immediate personal attractiveness into account. So, it seems legitimate to ask about the relevance that various elements of attractiveness have to the reasonable requirements of the job of waiters and waitresses in your restaurant.

Arguably, certain attributes, such as height and weight, which you regard as elements of attractiveness, can function like race and sex as grounds for unjust discrimination.[314] I shall not take a position on the issue of the relevance of these and other elements of attractiveness for waiters and waitresses, but suggest that, in developing the new policy, you consider the elements one by one. I take it for granted you also will take into account any pertinent legislation or court decisions.

In reflecting on your question, two considerations must be set aside. The first is that, at least to some extent, attractiveness is in the eye of the beholder, and so is likely to be socially or culturally relative. While that may be so, you and most of your customers probably have similar tastes in this matter, so you can discriminate well enough among job applicants to exclude those who would be unattractive to your customers. The second is that the attractiveness or unattractiveness of job applicants no doubt often influences hiring decisions, even when it has little or no relevance to a business's success; that influence is as rationally indefensible as it is widespread. But your question concerns intentionally using immediate attractiveness to patrons as a criterion for hiring those who will wait on them, and, what is more, you do offer a reason for doing so, namely, the likelihood that business will suffer otherwise.

In some respects, the impression receptionists and product demonstrators make in a very brief encounter can be even more vital to other businesses than the impression made by waiters and waitresses on restaurant patrons. Still, because many people have an emotional, visceral reaction of distaste toward unattractive individuals, the issue no doubt is in some ways more pressing for you, as manager of a restaurant, than for many other businesses that take immediate attractiveness into account. Patrons of expensive restaurants expect an esthetically pleasing ambience, and the appearance of any employee they encounter is important to their satisfaction. Moreover, while people with certain unattractive features—for example, some skin conditions—may be hale and hearty, they are likely to appear unhealthy, and that is likely to make customers uneasy about the wholesomeness of the restaurant's offerings. Though these attitudes of your patrons are not based on reflective judgments, it is not clear to me that they are unreasonable, as racial prejudice, for instance, plainly is.

As I explained above, it would be unfair to take applicants' immediate personal attractiveness into account if it were simply irrelevant to their job. But the preceding

---

314. See Stephen M. Crow and Dinah Payne, "Affirmative Action for a Face Only a Mother Could Love?" *Journal of Business Ethics,* 11 (1992): 869–75; however, these authors fail to consider an argument like that proposed here defending the moral acceptability of preference on the basis of attractiveness.

considerations suggest that, though unattractive individuals might be as able as attractive ones to provide service in other respects, they are not so able to satisfy certain expectations—which, though not based on reasons, are not entirely unreasonable—of patrons of expensive restaurants. Therefore, you will not be unfair, in my judgment, if you maintain some standard regarding the immediate impression made by applicants for the job of waiter or waitress.

However, especially in respect to women, our culture's standards of personal attractiveness, it seems obvious to me, are confused with erotic appeal and irrational bias toward youth. Moreover, a mature person of pleasing personality who at first seems neither attractive nor repellent but who provides polished service through the course of a meal will by its end make a good impression on patrons, lend a distinctively personal note to their experience as a whole, and perhaps even enhance the esthetic impact of the restaurant's decor, food, and so on—as a small irregularity enhances the beauty of someone whose features are otherwise perfect. Thus, I doubt that the good of the business requires choosing only those who are definitely attractive, while excluding not only the unattractive but those who, because they are no longer youthful or for other reasons, make no definite impression either way, and I therefore think it would be unfair to do so. It seems to me you may rightly exclude only those applicants whose unattractiveness is so marked that a significant number of your patrons would be likely to find them more or less repellent.

You rightly note that unattractive people also need jobs and people in general should be more accepting of them. Therefore, do not allow an applicant's unattractiveness to prejudice other hiring decisions, when that quality will have little or no relevance to the success of your business. Indeed, it seems to me, employers who intentionally take immediate attractiveness into account in filling positions for which this quality contributes to the success of their business may, and perhaps should, compensate when filling other positions, including those that pay well, by preferring less attractive applicants, other things being equal. In this way, both the need to present an attractive face to the public and the need of unattractive people for work can be met, to the benefit of both groups and the detriment of neither.

Having responded to your specific question, I propose a more fundamental one on which I think you should reflect.

In a world where many people are starving or otherwise in dire need, a relatively small number of affluent people use a large part of the world's goods. When measured by their own genuine human needs, furthermore, much of that use is self-destructive or, at least, wasteful; while much of the rest, though not wasteful, is crassly self-indulgent and unjust—or, at least, incompatible with Christian mercy—in view of others' unmet needs (see *LCL,* 780–82, 789–92, 800–806, 811–14). Therefore, much consumption by the affluent is gravely sinful.

You describe your restaurant as an expensive one patronized by the affluent, who, very likely, spend a good deal there on luxurious foods and fine wines. In operating your business, you must promote and thereby intend that sort of consumption. Can you honestly judge that all of it, or at least enough of it to make your business profitable, is morally justifiable? If not, you intend what is unjustifiable, and you need to repent and change the character of your business so that it will provide a truly needed, and so legitimate, service.

110: Should a manager voluntarily adopt an affirmative action plan?

I am general manager of a company providing parts and service for a wide variety of small appliances. Founded just after World War II, the business flourished and expanded, so that now we operate in three locations and have nearly one hundred employees. Members of the founding family own all the stock, but it has been more than ten years since any of the owners took an active interest in the business. I was the first executive hired by the family, initially on a part-time basis to take care of legal and financial matters. As the founders retired and their children and grandchildren continued to receive a satisfactory rate of return while pursuing other interests, the family entrusted more and more responsibility to me. For all practical purposes, I now am solely responsible for making policy decisions.

Employee relations have been good, and our employees are not unionized. All of them receive a generous benefits package. Our key employees, the service technicians, receive a percentage of the labor charges on the work they do; during the thirty-day-guarantee period, they are required to make good any defects in their work without additional compensation. Other employees are paid at going rates, but our benefits package gives us a competitive edge in getting and holding good people.

In the early days, the family hired relatives and friends, and practiced a great deal of favoritism among employees. As my role increased, I put in place a simple and straightforward employment policy: Do what the law requires in offering equal employment opportunities and nondiscriminatory treatment of employees, but hire strictly on the basis of an individual's qualifications, and advance employees strictly on the basis of performance. The unintended result is that more than two-thirds of our employees, including all but two of our service technicians, are white males.

Now we are under some pressure to hire more women, blacks, and members of other minorities. Some of the pressure comes from advocacy groups, some from certain of our institutional customers (whose business is vital to us), some from the threat of bad publicity, and some from vulnerability to lawsuits. I am considering a range of options. One is to seek for any job that opens up a woman, a black, or a member of another minority better qualified than any white male applicant, and perhaps even offer a premium if necessary. Another is to give preference to women and minorities when applicants' qualifications are roughly equal. A third is to put a virtual freeze on hiring white males, making exceptions only when no other minimally-qualified applicant can be found.

I also need to rethink our policy on advancing employees. Changing it would be a more delicate matter than changing hiring policy, because most employees will resent it if someone whose job performance is inferior moves ahead of them.

In deciding what to do I have to consider the law and each option's probable consequences for long-term profitability. But I also know there has been a good deal of debate about the ethical aspects of so-called affirmative action, and I want to adopt a policy that will be compatible with the requirements of Catholic teaching.

Analysis:

This question concerns the duty of a business to help overcome injustice in the wider society. The principles for answering this question are the business's legal obligations and its own common good: efficient cooperation and fairness to all participants. The business should fulfill its legal obligations and remedy any injustices of which it has been guilty, but should not voluntarily attempt to remedy others' injustices. Moreover, programs of affirmative action that systematically prefer others to white males are neither just nor an effective remedy for past and ongoing injustices against women and members of minority groups. Therefore, the questioner should not adopt a voluntary affirmative action program. However, even if the pressures the questioner describes are unreasonable, he or she should hire more women, blacks, and members of other minorities insofar as the good of the business itself requires doing so.

The reply could be along the following lines:

Catholic teaching does not offer any decisive answer to your question, but I shall sketch out a view I believe consonant with it.

The common good of the business is the basis of your managerial authority— that is, of your right and duty to make decisions, including those shaping company policy on hiring and promotions. The business is a cooperation among the owners, customers, employees, suppliers, and, of course, you as manager. The common good of this ongoing cooperation is its efficiency together with justice in all participants' interrelationships, including their fair sharing in the burdens and benefits accruing from their cooperation.

Like any other member of civil society, the business should obey just laws and conform even to unjust ones when that is required by the common good either of society at large or of the business itself (see *LCL,* 874–83). Moreover, the business must rectify any injustice it has done. Insofar as it is a cooperation limited by its specific, agreed upon purpose, however, its common good forbids you, as manager, to undertake voluntarily to remedy past or ongoing injustices for which it is not itself responsible (see q. 100, above).

Someone will object that this position belittles the vast injustices to which women, blacks, and others have been and, in some cases, still are being subjected, and shows little compassion. That is not so. The enslavement of blacks, the spoliation of native peoples, and the murder of many members of both groups were terrible crimes, and probably most descendants of the victims still suffer from the consequences of past, and perhaps also ongoing, injustices. Many members of other minorities—for example, orientals—and many women also have been victims of social and economic injustices. Victims of injustices deserve vindication, and all injustices should be rectified insofar as possible. But your company's responsibility for doing that is limited to the injustices of which it has been guilty, except insofar as presumably just laws might require it to help fulfill the duty of society as a whole to rectify other injustices.

Moreover, programs of affirmative action that systematically prefer others to white males in hiring and promoting are neither a just nor even an effective means for political society to use in trying to rectify injustices.[315] In the first place, they give preference to entire groups, though some members of those groups are not at an equal—or, indeed, even any—disadvantage due to past or ongoing injustices, and it is irrational to try to remedy an injustice by giving preference to individuals who are not among its actual victims. Second, such affirmative action imposes very light burdens, or none at all, on wealthy people who probably have profited most from past injustices while imposing very heavy burdens on white males who are in direct competition with preferred individuals for jobs and advancement. Yet some of these men and their families are themselves gravely disadvantaged, and not all bear significant responsibility for past injustices or have benefited significantly from them. Third, such affirmative action does nothing to rectify, and may even aggravate, socioeconomic injustices suffered by people discriminated against on grounds that have not received political and social recognition—for example, those who hold unpopular religious beliefs or have unattractive physical traits. Fourth, insofar as affirmative action imposes the burden of rectifying socioeconomic injustices on businesses, a disproportionate share of that burden must be borne by their neediest customers, least well-paid employees, hardest-pressed suppliers, and least prosperous investors.

Christian morality is not individualistic; it recognizes the value of people's different gifts and potentialities for cooperation, and insists on the inherent value of community (see *CCC*, 1936–37; *LCL*, 353–56, 359–60). Excluding consequentialism, it condemns treating any person as a mere means to the advantage of others (see *CCC*, 1929; *LCL*, 380–88). By these Christian standards, the efforts of secularists to rectify social injustices generally fall short in at least three ways. They often tend toward egalitarianism and fail to take adequate account of people's diverse gifts and potentialities. They frequently overlook the value inherent in community itself and so enlarge the role of political society to the detriment of smaller communities, including businesses and families. And, presupposing some sort of consequentialism, they assume that the good end of rectifying past injustices justifies any politically feasible means that seems likely to be effective.

In my judgment, then, you should not embrace a voluntary affirmative action program, but should ask yourself two questions. Has the business, by its past policies of hiring and promotion, been responsible for any injustice you now can

315. Some of the following arguments are supported and/or developed—though together with other arguments not entirely sound—in recent works: Terry Eastland, *Ending Affirmative Action: The Case for Colorblind Justice* (New York: Basic Books, 1996); Clint Bolick, *The Affirmative Action Fraud: Can We Restore the American Civil Rights Vision?* (Washington, D.C.: Cato Institute, 1996); Bob Zelnick, *Backfire: A Reporter's Look at Affirmative Action* (Washington, D.C.: Regnery, 1996). The benefits of affirmative action to those preferred also is questionable; see, for example, Shelby Steele, *The Content of Our Character: A New Vision of Race in America* (New York: St. Martin's Press, 1990), 111–25.

and should rectify? Is there any reason why you should change your present hiring and promotion policies more drastically than law requires so as to increase the proportion of women, blacks, and members of other minorities among your employees as a whole and also among those in better-paying positions?

You say that in the early days the family hired relatives and friends. Was that original hiring policy unjust? Perhaps, but I doubt it. In founding the enterprise, the family was creating new jobs, and these were made available to individuals to whom the family recognized duties of kinship and friendship. Those existing communities had their human value and offered a natural basis for developing an economic cooperation with good prospects of the camaraderie and mutual loyalty conducive to its success. The family's members and most of those they employed probably belonged to the same religious and ethnic groups, whose parents may have been discriminated against—for example, Catholics frequently have been excluded from employment or denied equal opportunities for certain sorts of jobs.[316]

You also say that in the early days the family practiced a great deal of favoritism among employees. Favoritism is an injustice common in family businesses, where ties of kinship and friendship are allowed to distort the relationships proper to the enterprise. But that injustice did not affect hiring. It involved only such matters as wages and promotion, and probably it has been overcome by your long-standing policy of promoting strictly on the basis of job performance. Moreover, as the result of your nondiscriminatory hiring policy makes clear, the family's favoritism, even at its worst, mainly worked to the disadvantage of some white males in comparison with others, rather than to the disadvantage of women, blacks, or members of other minorities in comparison with white males.

The hiring policy you put in place was to comply with relevant, presumably just laws in offering equal employment opportunities, and within that framework to hire strictly on the basis of an individual's qualifications to do the job. Many employers, of course, purported to operate on such a policy, while in reality systematically discriminating against certain groups, such as blacks. But provided you not only stated but really adhered to that policy, I see no injustice in what you did (see *CCC*, 2433).

Hiring individuals on the basis of their qualifications undoubtedly furthered not only the common good of the business, for which you as manager are responsible, but the good of those hired. Less-qualified individuals whom you did not hire may well have suffered no disadvantage thereby. Perhaps they found other, more suitable employment; people generally find work for which they are well qualified more fulfilling and rewarding. However, even less-qualified individuals who would have been better off had you hired them did not suffer any injustice by your preferring better-qualified individuals; some preference was inevitable and yours was reasonable.

---

316. See Andrew M. Greeley, *An Ugly Little Secret: Anti-Catholicism in North America* (Kansas City, Mo.: Sheed, Andrews and McMeel, 1977), and the works he cites in chap. 2, n. 2 (117–18).

Someone is likely to object that the injustice of your past hiring policy is manifest from its result—more than two-thirds of your employees, including all but two of your service technicians, are white males. That argument is unsound. Undoubtedly, both historical and contemporary injustices are at least partly responsible for the difference between blacks and whites as groups in their qualification for various desirable jobs. But the business you manage neither caused those injustices nor benefited from them, and so you would have acted wrongly if you had voluntarily assumed the burden of remedying them at the expense of the business's owners, customers, suppliers, and other employees. Somewhat similarly, both historical and contemporary social and cultural differences between female and male roles account at least partly for the difference between women and men as groups in their interest in and qualification for various jobs. However, not only is the business you manage not responsible for those differences in roles, but in many respects they result, not from any injustice, but from the natural and humanly good complementarity of men and women in marriage and family life—a complementarity that should be respected and safeguarded for the good of individuals themselves, their families, and society as a whole (see *LCL,* 387–88, 626–33).

Should you now change your existing hiring policy in ways not mandated by law in order to increase the proportion of women and minorities among your employees as a whole and among those in better-paying positions? Very likely you should, but not with the intention of rectifying injustices committed by others. Rather, the pressures you describe—from advocacy groups, institutional customers, bad publicity, and harassing lawsuits—are part of the socioeconomic environment affecting the capacity of every business to operate efficiently and perhaps to survive. Even if those pressures are unjust, you may not ignore them, but, while avoiding doing anything wrong in itself, must take them into account for the good of the business.

Plainly, in filling every job, you should try to attract and identify well-qualified applicants whose hiring would mitigate the pressures. It would be wrong in any case not to hire such an applicant when he or she is better qualified than any white male applicant. If you do not already advertise the basis on which service technicians are compensated, perhaps doing so would attract well-qualified applicants other than white males for those key positions. Often, of course, applicants' qualifications are not entirely comparable. One is better qualified in some respects, another in others, and a choice must be made. In such cases, too, it will be reasonable for you to prefer those whose hiring will help solve your problem. Similarly, when a woman, a black, or a member of some other preferred minority is both available for advancement and more deserving, you will have no reason to promote anyone else; and when the claims of different employees for advancement are not comparable, you should take into account the business's need to respond to pressures.

What if the preceding measures do not suffice? While you might reimburse moving expenses or the like to enable and encourage appropriate, qualified applicants to come to work for you, I do not think you should pay other employees more than white males for doing the same work. Violating the principle of equal pay for equal work would provoke justified resentment on the part of white males; and paying a premium to attract more than your share of well-qualified women and members of minority groups would pass on the difficulty you face to other employers. Similarly, promoting less-qualified employees would be unfair to those whose superior performance merits advancement, and probably also would be unfair to other groups involved in the business, not least your customers.

Therefore, insofar as the good of the business requires you to employ more members of the preferred groups, it seems to me you should hire such people, though less qualified than white male applicants, as trainees at somewhat reduced pay, then provide special training and supervision so that they will do their jobs satisfactorily and, if all goes well, eventually realize their full potential for the work.

Doing this, of course, you also should avoid dishonesty and unfairness. For example, misleading white males into applying for jobs for which they certainly will not be hired would be both dishonest and unfair; if you expect to hire few white males, your ads should make it clear that others will be strongly preferred. Misrepresenting your hiring policy to your present employees or to customers would be dishonest; you may not pretend to employ only the best-qualified people available if you no longer can do so. Resenting the less-qualified people you reluctantly hire and treating them unkindly would be unfair to them. Hiring less-qualified people but failing to train and supervise them so that they perform adequately would be unfair both to them and to others involved in the business, especially your customers, who would be inconvenienced and deprived of the quality of service they expect.

111: May a major stockholder dump his holdings in a troubled firm?

I have a problem of conscience with which I would like help, but I am not free to divulge the facts of the situation, and I have constructed a fictional case instead. If it is the sort of moral question you are interested in treating, feel free to publish it, provided you keep its source confidential.

G–G, Inc., a manufacturer of small appliances, was formerly a partnership of two men, Goetz and Graham, but went public about ten years ago. The former partners still control the business, each owning twenty-six percent of the stock and holding seats on the board. The firm, which has conducted its morally sound business in a morally upright fashion, did well until two years ago. Then a downturn in business began. That happened just as its largest plant was severely damaged by flooding that closed it down and required costly repairs, not covered by insurance. Since then, the company's quarterly accounts have been deep in the red, its credit has been restricted, and it is failing to maintain adequate cash flow. Goetz and Graham are talking with the company's lawyers about going into bankruptcy, in hopes of reorganizing the business and restoring profitability.

The chances of succeeding and saving the business are perhaps fifty-fifty. Up to now, however, the company's stock has not declined as drastically as one might expect, and the quarterly report to be issued next week will be less bleak than the previous eight. But new problems are emerging, and the next report is sure to be the worst thus far. Graham is considering his options. He can sit tight through the bankruptcy, as he is sure Goetz will, and hope the reorganization succeeds. Or he can tell his broker to sell his stock piecemeal but as soon as possible after next week's quarterly report appears. If Graham sits tight, his chances are one in two of preserving and enhancing his investment, and the same that he will lose everything. If he sells, he can be sure of salvaging a large part of his investment. Thinking a bird in hand is worth two in the bush, he calls his broker.

He does this fully expecting that the investment community will take it as a sign the business is doomed, and that will drive down the price of its stock, ruin its credit, force it at once into bankruptcy, and greatly reduce chances of a successful reorganization. But, he reasons, I have the right to sell my stock any day I choose.

Is Graham being fair to Goetz and the other stockholders?

Analysis:

This question calls for the application of the norm regarding promise keeping and judgment in accord with the Golden Rule. Graham plainly is not being fair to Goetz and the other shareholders. First, Graham is betraying Goetz's trust. Second, as a director of the business, Graham shares fiduciary responsibility for it; preferring his personal interests to its common good is a grave betrayal of trust. Third, taking advantage of inside information unavailable to those who rely entirely on the company's quarterly reports, Graham is unfair to those who purchase his stock. Fourth, even if he neither shared fiduciary responsibilities nor took advantage of inside information, he would have a moral duty to other participants in the company to protect its common good at some risk to his own interests, and his motive for selling appears to disregard that duty.

The reply could be along the following lines:

The answer clearly is no. Graham is sure Goetz will sit tight through the bankruptcy, doing his best to save the business. Instead of dumping his holdings, he should cooperate in Goetz's effort. As former partners and now colleagues in the business, the two have undertaken and built up a relationship of trust that Graham's betrayal will destroy.

Moreover, along with Goetz, Graham is in control of the company and has a fiduciary responsibility for it. As the captain of a sinking ship should be the last to save himself, so a person who controls a business may not prefer his or her personal interests to its common good; and in his role as a director, Graham is responsible for that common good, which includes the just interests of all shareholders, employees, and other participants who will be adversely affected if the company does not survive and flourish. Let Graham put himself in the position of any of these people, especially the shareholders who purchased stock since the company went public, and he will easily see what he is doing as they will: a betrayal of trust. In saying, "I have the right to sell my stock any day I choose," he ignores his fiduciary responsibility and focuses exclusively on his self-interest. The argument is fallacious, a mere rationalization.

Even if Graham did not share in the control of the business and in fiduciary responsibility for it, his sale of his stock would remain unjust. If, before calling his broker, he let it be known publicly that he was about to sell all his stock and explained why, it either would not sell or would sell for very little. But he makes no such announcement and acts instead on his inside information about the company's condition and prospects, and about his intention to sell all his stock. Lacking access to this information, those who buy the stock, especially in the early stages of the sale, act on a false assumption they could do nothing to correct. Graham makes his profit by taking advantage of them; and morally speaking, at least, for him to sell in this way is fraud. He may have the right to sell his stock any day he chooses, but he does not have the moral right to sell it on the basis of inside information. (I believe doing so also would violate the law, but I leave that to legal counsel.)

Furthermore, even if Graham were neither managing the company nor acting on inside information, it would remain morally questionable and, I believe, probably unjust for him to sell the stock. Owning something does not carry with it a moral right to do with it whatever one wishes. Rather, ownership entails moral responsibility to care for property, administer its good use, and avoid wasting it, so that it will help meet not only the needs of the owner and his or her dependents but others' needs as well (see *LCL,* 800–806, 811–14). Accordingly, even if Graham had no established association with Goetz, no share in control of the business, and no inside information, he would not be justified in acting solely out of a desire to salvage as much of his investment as he can. He also would be obliged to take into account the interests of other shareholders (who hold seventy-four percent of the stock), the company's employees (probably not so well off as he is), and so on. All these interests considered, it seems clear to me that he is prepared to accept such great harm to others only because selling his stock suits his self-interest, which he considers overriding only because it is his.

Graham might object: If I urgently needed money, I would be justified in selling some stock, even if I foresaw it would hurt the business and others with interests in it; so, what I am doing now can be justified, provided I put the investment I salvage to good use. However, Graham's sale of his stock does not seem to meet the conditions specified by this objection. And even if the conditions were met, the argument shows no more than that Graham may not be violating his general responsibility as an investor in the business. Still, it remains the case that he is betraying Goetz, violating his fiduciary responsibility, and taking unfair advantage of inside information.

112: May one invest in morally tainted businesses?

May one invest in businesses that supply various good products or services but also supply some things one considers seriously immoral to use? The answer seems clear: Don't do it. But when investing in a mutual fund holding stock in scores of companies, what responsibility does an individual investor have to try to track down all the products or services of all those companies? With multinational companies, take-overs, mergers, and so on, it is very hard to determine who makes what. Foreign firms are particularly hard to get information on. Would it be morally wrong to invest without even considering whether bad products or services are involved?

Again, if one learns that one or two companies among the many represented in a mutual fund provide bad products or services, does that mean that investing in that fund is wrong?

What about holding stock in a company that sponsors immoral television shows or funds organizations that promote unjust public policies? Occasionally I have written to companies to protest such activities, but we still hold their stock.

A few years ago, when banks were paying better interest on certificates of deposit, people like us were not in the stock market, and such questions wouldn't have occurred to us. But as I'm near retirement, my wife and I are trying to plan for the future, when we will need an adequate income. At the same time, we would rather starve than sell our souls.

Analysis:

This question concerns cooperation in the wrongdoing of businesses in which one invests. People who invest directly in the stock of a particular business normally intend that it do all they are aware of its doing to make its profit, and so normally cooperate formally in any of its profit-making wrongdoing that they are aware of. People who invest in a mutual equity fund holding many different stocks can intend to profit from the presumably morally clean businesses and only accept the tainted profits that accrue. Applying the criteria for evaluating material cooperation, I judge that the questioner may invest in mutual equity funds provided (1) he judges he has no morally preferable way adequately to meet reasonably anticipated needs, (2) he makes a reasonable effort to investigate various funds and excludes any whose policies tend to select companies that profit by wrongdoing, (3) he resists the temptation to cooperate formally in wrongdoing he knows about and profits from, and (4) he does what he can to persuade management to right wrongs that come to his attention. Holding stock in companies whose wrongful activities do not contribute significantly to its profits is morally questionable but not clearly wrong.

The reply could be along the following lines:

Before thinking about the morality of particular investments, one should consider several prior questions.

First, is it appropriate to invest this money? I do not mean to ask whether you should spend the money on your own and your dependents' present needs—I assume these are being met adequately—but whether you should use it to help others. Even understanding the question in this way, though, some people with management expertise and a great deal of money might well reply: Yes, I should invest the money, for in that way I hope to provide greater benefits for the poor in the long run, and meanwhile to provide jobs for people who need them, a good product or service for people who can use it, and so on. But assuming you are not in that position, the question for you becomes more specific: Should I invest this money so as to provide for my future needs and those of my dependents or should I donate it to help other people who are in need?

Even most Christians share the individualistic notion that, having earned money or come by it in some other legitimate way, people may keep it for themselves or do with it as they please. The authentically Christian and more reasonable view is that possessing wealth entails the responsibility to see that it is used fairly to meet human needs, and that others' urgent present needs often should take priority over investment of any sort (see *LCL*, 780–82, 789–92, 800–806, 811–14). To judge whether investing is justifiable, one must apply the Golden Rule, not only imagining one's own position if one's available money is not invested but putting oneself in the place of those whose needs will go unmet if the money is invested, and asking: If I were in such need, would I find acceptable such investment by people with prospective needs no more certainly foreseen and no greater than mine?

If one's conscientious conclusion is that one should invest, one next should ask what kind or kinds of investment will adequately meet the future needs that justify investing. People very often fail to do this, instead taking for granted the desirability of obtaining a high rate of return. However, the higher an investment's rate of return, the higher the risk it generally involves, and accepting unnecessary risk is wrong insofar as it is incompatible with fulfilling the responsibility that justifies investing. So, high rates of return should not be sought for their own sake; need, not greed, should dictate investment decisions. By this standard, investment in the stock market, whether directly or by way of mutual funds, might not be appropriate for someone nearing retirement, especially if the investment is to provide income for the near future. Other investment vehicles should be considered and perhaps should be preferred to investment in mutual equity funds.

Moreover, it would be preferable to invest in ways very likely to promote genuine human goods, even at the sacrifice of part of the profit otherwise available. Therefore, if you have not already done so, I think you should seek investment advice from several honest persons with expertise in various types of investment, and should consider investment opportunities that would not only avoid involvement in evil but positively benefit others. While such opportunities can be found in the public securities markets, they also exist elsewhere—for example, in privately held enterprises and real estate.

Then too, in thinking about possible moral problems involved in investing in a business, one should consider not only the moral quality of its product or service, its advertising, its impact on the natural and social environments, and other things about it affecting people outside the business but also the moral quality of the business as a community organized by relationships among owners, employees, suppliers, customers or clients, and managers (who, of course, also are owners and/or employees).[317]

---

317. John Paul II, *Centesimus annus*, 35, *AAS* 83 (1991) 837, *OR*, 6 May 1991, 11, teaches that while a business must make a profit, doing so is not sufficient: "In fact, the purpose of a business firm is not simply to make a profit, but is to be found in its very existence as a *community of persons* who in various ways are endeavoring to satisfy their basic needs, and who form a particular group at the service of the whole of society."

Any business that primarily serves the interests its owners and high-level managers have in profit and high compensation—while treating others involved in the business no better than is required by laws, contracts, and market forces—is likely to do immoralities at least as grave, though seldom as obvious, as those of companies that supply products or services with no morally acceptable use. For example, a company distributes wholesome foods, advertises unobjectionably, and so on, but exploits its agricultural workers with low pay, no benefits, and wretched working conditions. Or a large retailer, morally clean in most respects, encourages suppliers to develop specialized capacities they cannot otherwise profitably use and then takes advantage of their dependence to minimize the prices it pays for what they produce. Or an insurance company, morally above reproach in most respects, deliberately trains its sales agents to deceive potential buyers about their need for insurance and cost-effective ways of meeting that need with a view to maximizing profit for the company and commissions to agents.

In searching for appropriate investments, you may find help in various publications that evaluate the ethical aspects of various businesses. Some investment advisers also present themselves as specialists in applying ethical criteria among others in recommending investments. In either case, of course, you will be able to trust advice only if you are reasonably confident that the moral criteria employed are themselves sound.

Having considered preliminary matters, I turn now to your explicit question about investing in the stock of various companies by purchasing shares in mutual equity funds.

In investing directly in the stock of a particular business, one buys a share in it; in investing in a mutual fund holding stocks in many businesses, one does not buy a share in any of those businesses.[318] Of course, even if one invests directly, a very small share in a business gives one no real power to shape its policies and actions. Still, there is an important ethical difference between the two cases. One normally has no reason to invest directly in a particular company's stock unless one expects and intends one's money to be used to make a profit, and one normally cannot intend that without intending that the company do all that one is aware of its doing to make its profit: treat people in certain ways, encourage potential customers to choose its products or services, and so on. Thus, those who directly invest in a company normally intend it to do efficiently all they are aware of its doing to make its profits. If some of the company's profit-enhancing policies and actions are immoral, the investor normally intends the immorality and so shares moral responsibility for it.

By contrast, just as one can buy certificates of deposit from banks that lend money to all sorts of people and businesses, some of which use the borrowed funds immorally, so one can invest in a mutual equity fund in order to profit from the presumably morally clean operations of diverse businesses represented in the fund, and not intend to gain, but only accept, the tainted profits accruing from businesses that provide bad goods and services. Still, though without sharing others' bad

---

318. Investing in the stock of conglomerates or holding companies often is very similar to investing in mutual funds.

intentions, by reluctantly becoming involved in certain questionable businesses, you would contribute to others' wrongdoing. Of course, accepting the bad consequences of investing in that way also can be wrong—for example, if it is unfair to someone, or gives bad example, or is likely to be an occasion of sin for oneself, or impedes one's witness to relevant moral truths. But sometimes doing something that contributes to others' wrongdoing is justified, inasmuch as it is necessary to fulfill various responsibilities and its bad effects are slight.

Taking into account the preceding points and the ways in which it could be wrong for you to invest in mutual equity funds, I think it probably would not be wrong, provided certain conditions are met.

First, you may invest in this way only if: (a) you conscientiously judge that you have a need that justifies investing in some way, (b) you have made a reasonable effort to investigate various ways of meeting that need, and (c) you have concluded either that this is the only form of investment adequate to meet the need or that investing in any adequate alternative is at least as problematic as investing in certain mutual funds.

Second, as you suggest, it probably is not feasible for you to try to find out about all the products, policies, and activities of all the businesses represented in the various mutual funds among which you might choose; and even if it were feasible, the information would not solve your problem, since most funds' holdings frequently change. However, you should use any information you have or can easily obtain to steer clear of mutual funds whose holdings seem especially heavy in seriously tainted industries or firms. Therefore, you may invest in a particular mutual fund or funds only if: (a) you have made a reasonable effort to investigate various mutual funds, and (b) you have excluded from consideration any whose policies seem especially likely to lead to the selection of the stocks of businesses that profit from wrongdoing. Certain mutual funds call themselves "socially responsible" and the like, suggesting that their managers use moral criteria in selecting stocks, but the criteria often are secularist rather than Christian. Do not trust such labels unless your study of the criteria, as stated in the fund's prospectus, makes it clear these correspond to sound morality, including the Church's social teaching.

Third, insofar as the profitability of one or more businesses held by a mutual fund in which you have invested depends on something immoral, you may be tempted not only reluctantly to accept that immorality but to take into account the profit from it in making investment decisions or, at least, to wish that those businesses continue making money as they do. Be on guard against those temptations and take care to resist them.

Fourth, if you learn of blatant wrongdoing by companies whose stock is held by a mutual fund in which you have invested, inform the managers of the fund that you object to investments in companies that do such things and do what you reasonably can (such as writing letters of protest) to persuade the offending company's management to right the wrong.

You also ask about holding stock in companies that sponsor immoral television shows or promote unjust public policies. If a company's profits depend on such activities, direct investors in its stock generally intend them. But if one reasonably judges that such activities and/or a company's bad products and services are unnecessary for a company's profitability and will contribute little to expected income, direct investment need not be wrong, and one could have a good reason to buy the stock despite the company's wrongdoing. For example, some individuals and groups have invested in such companies' stock in order to gain standing to criticize their activities and work for reform.

Finally, besides investing money to provide for your material needs, in planning for retirement you should consider carefully how you will use your remaining years and other resources. No doubt, you can rightly spend somewhat more time on rest and recreation. But many retired people waste a lot of time on passive entertainment, especially watching junk television. Avoid doing that. Ask yourself instead: How can I use my gifts to serve others? What is God's will for me now? For in his will you will find your peace, not only in what remains to you of this life but in the endless life to come.

113: Is it morally wrong to increase efficiency
at the cost of jobs?

I work in a field called "engineering economy" that studies mutually exclusive alternatives for achieving a result, such as providing a service. The measures are in terms of dollars; the tools are a careful analysis of costs and benefits, and evaluation by an economic model showing cash flow over time.

The analysis frequently concerns mechanizing a labor-intensive process. Usually, the benefits result from reducing the number of employees needed to produce goods or provide a service. The payback period, in which all the costs will be recovered by the reduction in payroll, generally is only a few years, and the cost after that may be cut by half or more. Jobs eliminated in this way often are low-paying positions—telephone operators, data entry clerks, cashiers.

Mechanization has been a very important factor in the economic development of every prosperous nation. Can you imagine having all our telephone calls handled manually? But in certain segments of our own economy and in the less affluent parts of the world, job creation or retention might be more important than economic efficiency. Considering the value of the work to the workers and their need for income, it seems to me there must be some point at which replacing workers with machines becomes immoral. How do I recognize that point if I reach it in my work? When, if ever, must I give up my job?

Analysis:

The questioner's work is good in itself; harm to displaced workers is a foreseen but unintended side effect. So, this question calls for judgment with regard to accepting the bad side effect and for norms of justice and mercy to shape that judgment and the questioner's action based on it. Though those norms are the same in both affluent and poor nations, their concrete demands depend on all the relevant facts, and so differ in different situations. Employers who use new technology to increase efficiency have a limited duty to give displaced workers other jobs, retrain them, or help them obtain other employment; displaced workers also often deserve public assistance. The questioner need not give up his or her line of work, but should take appropriate action to encourage employers and governments to fulfill their responsibilities toward displaced workers. In a particular case, nevertheless, fairness or mercy toward workers threatened with egregious injustice could require that the questioner quit a job in protest.

The reply could be along the following lines:

You are right to be concerned. Management decisions adversely affecting many employees all too often are made solely with a view to maximizing profits. But work is a good that fulfills persons while capital and profit on investment are only instrumentally good (see *LCL,* 756, 763). So, the effects of your work in engineering economy upon displaced workers surely deserve consideration.

Before addressing your question, I shall deal briefly with two related matters.

First, some enterprises are radically flawed. They provide an immoral product or service, such as pornography or abortion, or else their essential policies are gravely unjust—for example, by deliberately violating just and applicable laws, exploiting workers, defrauding customers or suppliers, or unreasonably damaging the environment. I assume you are alert to such moral flaws and would refuse to serve any enterprise in which you found them present, unless doing so helped reverse the unjust policy.

Second, trying to provide a product or service "more efficiently" sometimes really means compromising its quality. That compromise is likely to be unfair to consumers, particularly if most of the savings are taken as profit rather than passed on. However, since you say nothing about this matter, I assume in what follows that your work does not reduce quality.

Turning to your question, I think you do have some responsibility for the adverse effects of what you do on workers. But I think your responsibility is more complex than merely identifying a point at which your work would be immoral and quitting your job if you reach that point.

Obtaining desired, morally acceptable results with less work certainly eliminates drudgery and frees people for leisure and/or other, more productive work. Moreover, the new process always opens up some new jobs requiring greater skill and offering more rewards, financial and other. Plainly, then, there is nothing inherently wrong either in constantly trying to provide a useful, morally acceptable product or service more efficiently, or in what you do, namely, finding more efficient means to desired, morally acceptable results.[319] Any harm to workers who are displaced is a side effect, which you need not intend. Indeed, though the managers who employ you plainly do intend to cut their payrolls, they are hardly

---

319. Technological advances in many ways benefit workers, though some workers lose ground in some respects; see Scott Ralls, *Integrating Technology with Workers in the New American Workplace* (Washington, D.C.: U.S. Department of Labor, Office of the American Workplace, 1994).

likely to intend that displaced workers remain unemployed. Thus, the moral question concerns accepting unemployment as a side effect.

Displaced workers do not always suffer unemployment or other harm; they may even be benefited by finding other, better ways to use their abilities. But in many cases, workers do suffer unemployment and consequent harm, and the question is whether those who determine policy can fairly accept this side effect and you can fairly participate in bringing it about.

People who are unemployed due to mechanization or other causes sometimes are more or less responsible for the hardship they and their families experience. That is so if they imprudently failed to save or even went needlessly into debt, improvidently counting on greater employment security than they could reasonably expect. Occasionally, too, workers make unreasonable demands that provoke management into finding technological ways of displacing them. People also have a lifelong obligation to educate themselves so that their talents will provide good service to others. Unemployed people who cannot do available work because they have neglected to develop their capacities share responsibility for their situation. But granting all that, even many people who have done their best to husband their resources and develop themselves are badly injured when technological advances eliminate their jobs.

Whether or not the workers who are about to suffer such injury were treated fairly in the past, the relevant question is: How will they be treated when an innovation leads to their displacement? An employer has some responsibility to reassign or retrain them, or to try to help them find other jobs. But this responsibility is limited, because the company also has responsibilities to its other employees, customers, suppliers, and investors, and can fairly care for displaced workers only insofar as that is compatible with a reasonable allocation of resources for employee benefits.[320] Moreover, when displaced workers need more help than businesses and private agencies can provide, public authorities have considerable responsibility in this matter.

At the same time, it seems to me, you have some responsibility to urge higher management and/or public officials to mitigate the hardships of displaced workers and to give them suggestions for doing that. Of course, many other people besides you share that responsibility, and your duty, especially with regard to the company or companies for which you do your work, may be limited by reasonable concern not to risk your livelihood unduly, especially if you are responsible for supporting a family and/or other dependents. Still, you do have a special set of gifts and opportunities, which very likely make it possible for you to bring to others' attention and clarify any injustice being done to displaced workers, propose ways of overcoming it, and perhaps even organize pressure of one sort or another to bring about appropriate action by those capable of it.

---

320. However, by promoting continual learning by employees, businesses often can adapt to changing market forces and new technologies, and thus avoid displacing workers without incurring unreasonable costs; see David Stern, "Institutions and Incentives for Developing Work-Related Knowledge and Skill," in *Technology and the Future of Work,* ed. Paul S. Adler (New York: Oxford University Press, 1992), 168–80.

Suppose, though, you do what you can, but management and public authorities do not meet their responsibilities. Must you give up your line of work? No, since that will do nothing to mitigate the injustice to those who suffer it, and continuing to do your work presumably will bring about real economic benefits for your employers' or clients' customers, suppliers, owners, and many of their employees. Moreover, you very likely have adequate reasons, such as your own need for a job, to do your work and accept the bad side effects on displaced workers of others' failure to treat them justly. Still, you could have an obligation to terminate your relationship with a particular employer or client who planned to treat displaced employees with egregious injustice, and, being in a position to quit in protest without neglecting your other responsibilities, you judged that quitting might prevent or significantly mitigate the injustice.

The better your work, the more in demand your services will be; and the more in demand your services, the more likely people you work for are to listen patiently to your concerns about fairness to displaced workers. Strive therefore for eminence in your field, not for the sake of mere prestige or financial rewards, but for greater power to promote justice.

The norms of fairness and mercy I have outlined are applicable equally in affluent nations and less wealthy parts of the world. Where wages are lower, however, savings from mechanizing labor-intensive processes will be relatively less, and the hardships imposed on displaced workers very likely will be greater. Under such conditions, both employers and governments probably should be more cautious about pressing for or permitting changes to increase efficiency, and more energetic in striving to soften their harmful effects on displaced workers. If these responsibilities go unmet, the suffering of poorer and more vulnerable displaced workers probably will require you to do and risk more to help the victims of injustice.

For you to raise this question manifests your concern for those adversely affected by your work. It takes courage to think about anything that might require one to limit opportunities for practicing one's profession or even to give up one's career. Those who habitually act with such compassion and courage can hope one day to be welcomed by our Lord into his heavenly kingdom (see Mt 25.34).

114: May a manager use lie detector tests to deal with employee fraud?

I own and manage a company whose main offices are outside the United States and whose representatives, working out of various cities, are on the road most of the time. In recent years, despite getting an outside accounting firm's advice and tightening up my whole operation as much as possible, the company has experienced increasing losses due to employee dishonesty. At a meeting last week with my counterparts from several other companies, I learned that my problem is far from unique. Apparently, employee dishonesty has become a major cost of doing business and a leading cause of rapidly increasing prices.

Virtually all of my counterparts agree that something must be done. The only apparently cost-effective tactic anyone proposed, however, is the use of polygraph testing (so-called lie detector tests). I find the idea repugnant and I know that my employees, most of whom are honest, will find it equally so. In the first place, polygraphs do not detect lies, but only indicate signs of stress that, at best, provide ground for suspicion that a person is lying. More important, in my view, resorting to polygraph testing would be an act of desperation, admitting defeat in my effort to build my business on mutual respect, team spirit, and honest dealing. But there seems to be no alternative. The business has been losing money and will fail in the next year or two unless I can regain profitability, and a half-dozen incidents within the past eighteen months have made it clear to me that abuses by employees constitute a major component of my financial problem.

If I institute polygraph tests, testing cannot be voluntary, for otherwise it would be ineffective. My employees will have to be given the choice between submitting to regular tests and resigning. Presented with that option myself, I would feel that my integrity was being questioned, my privacy invaded, and my will coerced. But what alternative is there if the business is not to go down the drain, leaving not only me but my honest employees high and dry?

Analysis:

This question calls for the derivation of norms regarding polygraph testing. Any legal restrictions on it should be presumed just and almost certainly should be obeyed. The employer-employee relationship should be real community, based on mutual understanding and commitments faithfully fulfilled in genuine cooperation. Difficulties troubling the relationship should be dealt with by dialogue, mutual correction, self-improvement, and reconciliation. Polygraph testing is hardly likely to build up community and may further impair it. So, before resorting to such testing, the questioner should make a serious attempt to enlist employee cooperation in solving the problem. Moreover, if polygraph testing is to be used, the employees' cooperation should be sought in working out a plan to minimize its detrimental effects on genuine community, and that plan should exclude treating the results of such testing as evidence of guilt.

The reply could be along the following lines:

In the United States, the law severely restricts the use of polygraph testing in dealing with problems like yours.[321] I assume you have looked into relevant law where you operate and found it to be permissive or less restrictive. If not, find out what the law requires before proceeding; you should presume its requirements just and, almost certainly, should comply with them.

I agree that instituting polygraph testing is repugnant and would be an act of desperation in the face of the breakdown of the good interpersonal relationships

---

321. On the political and legislative history of the U.S. Employee Privacy Protection Act 1988) see Priscilla M. Regan, *Legislating Privacy: Technology, Social Values, and Public Policy* (Chapel Hill, N.C.: University of North Carolina Press, 1995), 144–67; the law prohibits most private employers from using polygraph testing except in specific investigations of loss or injury to the business (n. 99, 288–89).

you had hoped to build and enjoy with your employees. Real community requires cooperation, involving faithful fulfillment of commitments, and based on mutual understanding and shared purposes. Failures and conflicts are inevitable, of course, but partners in authentic community handle these by dialogue, mutual correction, self-improvement, and reconciliation. Using a technical device such as the polygraph to enforce honesty is a miserable way of salvaging a remnant of community—the outward behavior that should be involved in true cooperation. It makes no direct contribution to healing and building up community and, indeed, may even further damage it.

While profitability is indispensable for your business, genuine community also is necessary and, humanly speaking, far more valuable; it requires the mutual respect, team spirit, and honest dealing on which you have sought to build your business. Without these, your relationships with your employees and their relationships with one another will be no more than crass pursuit of self-interest and mutual exploitation, and such bad relationships are likely to lead to the failure of any business. Therefore, for the sake of a real, long-term solution to your problem as well as for the intrinsic human value of genuine community, make every effort to proceed in a way that builds up community or, at least, avoids further damaging it.

I suggest that, before instituting polygraph tests, you give community another chance. Communicate with your employees and enlist their cooperation in solving the problem so that you can avoid resorting to that repugnant technique. If feasible, the best way would be by calling them together for face-to-face discussion, since that would make for more effective communication, not only between you and them but among themselves.

You might begin by pointing out the company's financial peril and explaining the role of employee dishonesty in it. Make it clear that the company cannot survive and everyone will be out of work unless the abuse is corrected, so that all understand that those behaving irresponsibly are injuring each and every honest participant in the business. Next, tell them you have considered initiating polygraph examinations, and how repugnant you find the prospect and why. Propose, as far better, an approach that will rely upon, build up, and restore genuine community.

You should explain that each member of the company must do his or her part for such an approach to work. Those who have behaved wrongly must stop and, insofar as they can, repay what they have taken or otherwise make up for the damage they have done. If you have set a bad example by using the company's resources for personal amenities, you should acknowledge the error of your ways and provide the model for amendment. Even those who have not contributed in any serious way to creating the problem must help solve it. They must resist temptations to join in the wrongdoing; if they know someone who has succumbed, they must demand that he or she reform and make restitution. They also must keep an eye out for misbehavior, move at once to correct it, and report to higher management anyone who persists despite their efforts. Make it clear that anyone whose future misbehavior is established will be dealt with severely, and that where the amount involved exceeds a certain specified sum, this will include both dismissal and, whenever possible, criminal prosecution and a legally enforced demand for full restitution.

In concluding, ask your employees to discuss what you have said among themselves and tell you what they think, and especially to give you any constructive ideas they might have for dealing with the problem. Finally, listen to their reactions and suggestions, think them over carefully, and act as quickly and openly as possible on any that seem likely to help.

Why do I suggest specifying a sum that will trigger dismissal and legal proceedings? Not because minor theft is morally acceptable; it is not. Rather because most employees at least occasionally cheat their employers in some small, tolerable ways, so that not all misbehavior can or should be treated as equally significant. Those guilty of gross misconduct do not recognize this distinction and regularly rationalize what they do by saying: "Everyone does it." The embezzler of a million dollars, for example, points a finger at a secretary who used the office postage meter to mail an urgent personal letter. You need to draw a clear line to mark the boundary of your readiness to tolerate minor misbehavior.

If this approach does not sufficiently reduce the problem, I believe you nevertheless can maintain the communitarian spirit behind it even if you decide you must institute polygraph examinations. In taking that step, you could communicate again with your employees, preferably by calling them together, explain your decision and your reasons, and invite their cooperation in working out a procedure that will minimize detrimental effects on your relationship with them.

Of course, you must be prepared to offer a tentative plan. I think it should be along the following lines. First, everyone, including you, should be expected to take the same examination on a regular basis, so that being tested will not call anyone's integrity into question. Second, only questions about outward behavior that harms the company's profitability should be asked, so that everyone's privacy will be respected and there will be no prying into anyone's thoughts, feelings, and intimate affairs. Third, no questions will be asked about petty amounts, so that nobody will be expected to be perfect, and attention will be focused exclusively on gross and deliberate misconduct damaging to the company and unfair to everyone involved in it. Fourth, signs of lying detected by a polygraph test will not be used as a ground for dismissal or otherwise treated as evidence of guilt, but will serve only as grounds for suspicion warranting investigation and close oversight. No action will be taken against any employee except on the basis of hard evidence. Fifth, tests should be administered by a well-trained and experienced examiner.[322]

Stating and adhering to a set of conditions along these lines will minimize the negative impact of polygraph tests on genuine community. That, along with inviting everyone's cooperation, will make it possible for you to proceed with this technical device, if it proves unavoidable, without being unfair to anyone. In this way, you can hope to overcome the problem, restore profitability, and at least preserve what remains of the genuine community you and your honest employees desire.

322. This condition is necessary for polygraph validity and reliability; see Stan Abrams, *The Complete Polygraph Handbook* (Lexington, Mass.: Lexington Books, 1989), 179–201.

115: What measures may a business take to deal with employee fraud?

My family owns a retail business. At a single location, we operate a combined hardware and building supply store, lumber yard, and garden center—each of these units the largest of its kind in the city. Though we now have over a hundred employees, management-employee relations still are very relaxed and informal. Dad always has encouraged those working on the floor and around the lots to follow his own example: be familiar with all the merchandise and help customers find everything they need for even a large and complex project. Our sales people move about freely, and only those with special skills in filling certain sorts of orders are tied to particular departments.

A few months ago we began to experience an unusual and significant shrinkage of our inventory in several departments. After our accountants studied the problem and we ruled out other explanations, we were forced to conclude that either outsiders in collusion with some of our employees or some employees acting alone are systematically stealing from us. Our first move was to talk about the problem with a dozen of our oldest and most trustworthy people. None could help, and though we asked them to keep their eyes open, they have not come up with anything. After two months, with the problem continuing and even growing worse, we reluctantly talked with the police. They told us they would need evidence pointing to one or more definite individuals before taking action. We then hired a private detective agency. It sent in a number of plainclothes operatives posing as customers, some just browsing and others making purchases, with instructions to watch out for anything amiss. A month has passed, and this approach also has been fruitless.

Yesterday, Dad and I reviewed the situation with the head of the detective agency. He suggested several other steps: have some of his agents offer cash to people working on the dock to see if any of them will load goods without a ticket; advertise three upcoming openings as usual, but "hire" his agents, so that they can gain the confidence of "fellow" employees; put video cameras in strategic places; install numerous hidden microphones, not only where business is transacted but in the employees' snack bar and locker rooms, and at the outside locations where the smokers take their breaks; have some of our suppliers package a sensor strip with certain small and relatively costly items that have been especially hard hit, so that the removal of those items from the premises can be detected.

Dad said he felt sick at the thought of doing such things, but we could not let matters slide. He told the head of the agency and me to work things out. Some of the suggestions seem shady to me, and none of them is appealing. I am wondering about their ethical acceptability.

Analysis:

This question calls for the application of relevant moral norms. Packaging sensor strips with valuable items would be morally acceptable. Provided privacy is respected, installing video cameras (without microphones) also seems acceptable.

Offering cash to employees to see if they will cooperate in theft intentionally tempts them to sin, which is gravely immoral. Hiring detectives to pose as employees is unfair to real applicants and will involve readiness to lie. Installing hidden microphones to eavesdrop on unsuspecting employees is unjust, and eavesdropping on unsuspecting customers invades their privacy. Perhaps more helpful than any of these techniques would be revisions in personnel management, supervision, and incentives that would strengthen cooperative relationships and foster employee responsibility.

The reply could be along the following lines:

Packaging sensor strips with valuable items vulnerable to theft seems to me an excellent proposal. I assume it would help detect theft by customers as well as employees. No ethical consideration I can think of argues against this technique, which neither tempts anyone to steal, nor puts innocent people under suspicion, nor invades anyone's privacy. It seems to me you should adopt this idea. Such electronic measures can be used without warning to try to catch thieves or with warning to deter thefts. But since your employees will soon learn that electronic measures are being taken, it seems best to me that you give them—and perhaps your customers as well—fair warning regarding what is being done. Still, a case can be made for giving no warning. The sensor strips might expose an unsuspecting culprit, so that he or she could be brought to justice. In any case, it may be necessary to limit the routes by which employees may exit the premises, but that should not bother or upset anyone provided the limits apply to everyone without exception.

Installing video cameras (without microphones) in strategic places, provided these do not include restrooms or other areas where people's privacy would be invaded, does not seem to me morally objectionable in itself, although it might interfere with easy communication and good interpersonal relationships, since awareness of being observed makes many people self-conscious and anxious even about innocent behavior. However, this measure might help deter systematic theft if the cameras provided virtually constant surveillance of critical areas. Moreover, if that surveillance served other legitimate purposes, such as detecting accidents and fires, these benefits could be explained to employees, and the system might be better accepted by them.

Some of the other suggested steps are inherently and gravely immoral. They should not be adopted under any circumstances. Among these is offering cash to people working on the dock to see if any of them will load goods without a ticket. This technique of entrapping possible wrongdoers would tempt people to sin, which is scandal in the strict sense—an extremely serious offense against justice and love of neighbor (see *LCL,* 236). Using this technique might even corrupt previously innocent people. The head of the detective agency might argue that law enforcement authorities often use such methods, and their success often is applauded. True, and they also are guilty of scandal if they tempt suspects to commit crimes.[323]

---

323. Superficially similar methods of gathering evidence against persons known to be habitual criminals—for example, purchasing illegal drugs from those known to be offering them for sale—do not involve tempting anyone to do wrong and can be employed uprightly.

Another excluded technique is hiring detectives to pose as employees, gain other employees' confidence, and spy on them. "Hiring" the detectives would be unfair to real applicants, who, having been deceived about the availability of work, would waste time and effort in applying. Moreover, the project probably would not succeed unless the detectives maintained the deception by lying to other employees—if asked, for example, where they worked before and why they changed jobs. So, the detectives would have to be prepared to lie if necessary. Then too, if the use of these spies became known to honest employees, many would be offended, and their resentment surely would injure your relationship with them.

Installing hidden microphones in locker rooms, snack bars, and smoking areas to eavesdrop on unsuspecting employees would be unjust. Installing them in places to which customers have access would invade their privacy, since even when they are in a public place, people, noticing no one about to overhear, sometimes communicate confidences, and the hidden microphones would pick up such conversations.

Having plainclothes operatives act as customers, as you already have done, is a common practice in retailing, and need not be unjust in itself. People walk about stores for many reasons, often with no intention of purchasing anything. The detectives need tell no lies; they have legitimate business in the store, and their presence can discourage theft even if no one is deceived. However, this technique seems not to have helped.

Perhaps more helpful than any of the detective agency's suggested techniques or others like them would be revising your way of dealing with employees and managing their work. On this, you probably would do well to consult someone with appropriate expertise. However, I shall offer a few thoughts to illustrate what I have in mind.[324]

Many newer employees probably regard your oldest and most trustworthy employees as part of management, and it is not surprising that they could not help solve the problem. Neither should they be considered entirely above suspicion—one or more might be involved in the thefts—nor should all the other employees be regarded as potential suspects. Most surely are innocent, and some might help solve your problem. Therefore, I suggest that your father and/or you call all the employees together, fully and accurately describe the relevant facts, explain their impact on the business and the employees' own interests, and enlist their cooperation. Ask for suggestions. Explain why all employees have a duty to report any wrongdoing they observe, and why they should not childishly regard that as tattling: Everyone involved in the business will be injured if the thefts continue; criminals do not deserve support; people who keep secrets about ongoing criminal activities share responsibility for the crimes.

While it would be a mistake to supervise employees so closely that they cannot use their own judgment in helping customers, your practice of encouraging most

---

324. Screening job applicants with integrity-honesty tests would not help solve the immediate problem, but would be legitimate and perhaps helpful in the long run; see H. John Bernardin and Donna K. Cooke, "Validity of an Honesty Test in Predicting Theft among Convenience Store Employees," *Academy of Management Journal,* 36 (1993): 1097–1108.

to move about freely may have prevented you from developing the structures required for effective cooperation among a group as large as a hundred. If each employee belonged to a particular department, he or she would more likely take responsibility for it. Probably your "very relaxed and informal" management-employee relations deprive some, and perhaps many, employees of the conditions they need to work responsibly. Forgetting people's weakness and asking too much of them puts them in an occasion of sin, which is unfair to them. You probably should more clearly define each employee's sphere of responsibility, limit the mobility of most, and minimize their opportunities not only to steal but to behave irresponsibly in other ways, such as handling merchandise carelessly, wasting supplies, and so on.

In earlier times, when employees were fewer, emotional ties with them probably were closer and more familial. Since the business has grown, however, most employees apparently are not in the same category as your dozen "oldest and most trustworthy people." The other employees' feelings toward you and your father no doubt correspond to your feelings toward them. You need to find new and better ways to develop sound cooperative relationships and genuine community with all your employees. For example, you might consider introducing a profit-sharing plan, offering bonuses for employees in departments that achieve or maintain a level of profitability impossible if thefts continue, and giving employees a role in deliberation before making important decisions affecting the business.

116: Is it fair to fire a sexually harassed woman for vengeful industrial sabotage?

I recently was hired as Director of Human Resources at a large assembly plant, and I find myself facing a problem unlike any I had to deal with in my former job. The plant has had an extraordinary number of returns under warranty of a particular item. Engineering found the same defect in nearly every case. The defect, which causes the unit to overheat under certain conditions, results from a mistake on the assembly line that can be made easily but is impossible for inspection to detect. Everyone who works on that line is taught to be careful to avoid this mistake.

We identified one line worker, Denise, as responsible. Until this misbehavior, she had been an excellent employee since she was hired last year. I called her in, told her we knew she had been making this mistake regularly, and asked her if she could explain why. She broke down and admitted she was doing it on purpose, not realizing we could identify her. She said the line foreman was sexually harassing her, and she was making the mistake to get him in trouble, hoping he would be fired.

At first, I doubted her story. That foreman, though new here, worked for the company at another plant for twelve years and had a clean record. But I talked at once with each of the other women working on the line with Denise, and all of them told me the same thing. While the foreman had never bothered them, on many occasions they had seen him putting his hands into Denise's smock and had seen her pushing him away. Several times she had shouted at him and spat in his face.

Once she managed to give him a knee in the groin, but within a few days he was bothering her again.

I called him in and handed him signed statements of every woman working on his line. His excuse was his wife had separated from him; Denise at first was "friendly"; he became crazy about her and could not keep his hands off her; he felt sure she would "come around." I fired him, pointing out that his behavior violated company policy, which forbids a foreman to touch a worker unless necessary in doing the job. (That rule was made years ago, and was meant to prohibit foremen from physically disciplining workers; to the best of my knowledge, it never has been applied to sexual harassment, but surely is broad enough to cover it.)

I have talked again with Denise and asked her why she did not complain to the shift supervisor or come to Human Resources with her problem—which is what all workers are told to do whenever they feel a foreman is mistreating them in any way. She could not explain, except to say she hated the foreman and wanted to get him fired. When I pointed out that what she had done had already inconvenienced and irritated hundreds of our customers and cost the company tens of thousands of dollars, she said she had not thought about that and was sorry.

There was a time when I would have fired Denise as quickly as I fired the foreman and also would have reported what she had done to the police. Being more aware of the seriousness of sexual harassment, though, I have decided, with the approval of the company's president, not to treat this as a crime. I wonder whether it even would be fair to fire Denise or whether we should give her a second chance.

Analysis:

This question calls for the derivation and application of norms for the questioner's treatment of employees who misbehave. Though provoked by a grave wrong, Denise's behavior was not justified. She acted from hatred, without regard to the interests of her employer and the company's customers. However, the company probably shares some responsibility for what happened, and there are strong reasons for retaining Denise and trying to help her become a better person and a better worker. On the same basis, the foreman, too, should perhaps be offered a second chance and similar help. In general, insofar as employees' moral character affects the company's common good, the questioner, in managing personnel, should undertake the responsibilities of a moral teacher and guide.

The reply could be along the following lines:

You certainly have reasons to fire Denise. Apparently, her intention was not merely to put an end to the foreman's harassment. She could have tried to do that by using the means of redress the company provides and instructs employees to use. Rather, moved by anger and hatred, she deliberately sabotaged her work to get the foreman fired—not for his wrongdoing that deserved punishment but for something that was not his fault—while entirely ignoring her responsibilities to the company and its customers, whose right to good products does not depend on employees' working conditions of which they know nothing. To excuse her misbehavior because the foreman's wrongdoing provoked it would be unreasonable; to give her another chance merely because she is a woman would be to discriminate unjustly in her favor.

Still, there is a strong case against firing Denise. To her, the foreman represented the company that had placed him over her, and she may well have doubted that her grievance would be sympathetically received and fairly handled. Management's policies and past behavior plainly did not lead the other women to urge her to complain and/or to complain on her behalf. Despite the ongoing harassment and her vigorous response, the shift supervisor was oblivious to the foreman's misbehavior or tolerated it; in either case, he hardly seems to have been exercising appropriate oversight. These considerations strongly suggest that until now the company has failed to develop policies and procedures appropriate to discourage sexual harassment and detect it when it occurs. So, the company itself probably shares responsibility for what provoked Denise. Moreover, prior to the harassment, she had been an excellent employee, and the motive for her wrongdoing is now removed. Therefore, it seems you should not fire her and should proceed more vigorously to forestall and deal with harassment.[325]

I also think you should do more for Denise than merely give her a second chance. For the company's sake and hers, counsel her so that she understands very clearly not only that what she did was gravely wrong and why, but also why anger and hatred can never justify trying to hurt someone (see *CMP*, 215–16). Confront her with some actual cases of the trouble and inconvenience she caused customers, and try to get her to put herself in their place. To get her to grasp the seriousness of what she did, you might point out that, had the company reported it to the police, she might well be in prison. In short, do your best to encourage her to repent her wrongdoing and firmly commit herself never to repeat it.

Unless you judge that the company's responsibility for the situation or something else rules out requiring Denise to make restitution, you should seek it. For example, you might, if possible, ask her to forgo a portion of each pay, but allow her to earn that portion by working overtime so as not to impose too great a burden on her. Perhaps the overtime work could take the form of helping you teach other employees about sexual harassment and how to deal with it. Moreover, you not only should work with Denise and other employees to develop better policies and procedures regarding sexual harassment but should make it clear to all employees that while in the workplace they must resist temptations to act on their sexual impulses and try to avoid provoking others' lust (see q. 165, below).

Perhaps, too, you should offer the foreman a second chance—assuming a job is available that will not bring him into contact with Denise but will be appropriate for him in other respects. He had a good record for twelve years. Since he did not harass the other women on the line, his mistreatment of Denise probably was occasioned by something special about her or about their relationship. Separation from his wife by no means justified his romantic interest in Denise, much less his lustful behavior, but his marital troubles do help explain the infatuation that

---

325. A helpful summary of relevant law with practical guidance for dealing with the problem: William Petrocelli and Barbara Kate Repa, *Sexual Harassment on the Job,* 2nd ed. (Berkeley, Calif.: Nolo Press, 1995).

occasioned his wrongdoing. Moreover, unless he has obtained a comparable or better job elsewhere, his firing probably has severely harmed not only him but his wife and children, if any. Finally, if he can be rehabilitated, that might well be in the company's own best interests.

Therefore, you might contact the foreman and offer to reconsider his dismissal. If he wishes to be rehired, begin by explaining to him very clearly why what he did was gravely wrong. Point out to him that he seems to share a widespread view of erotic desire as a primal urge that cannot be denied, and explain that, though many in our society—for example, proponents of so-called safe sex—take this view for granted, it is false. People who really cannot control themselves need to be locked away for the protection of others, but normal adults can choose to restrain themselves. His marital difficulties call for continence, not adulterous behavior. Confront him, too, with actual cases of the unforeseen harm that resulted from provoking Denise's retaliation. Again, you should try to elicit sincere repentance and encourage a firm commitment to behave properly in the future.

If the foreman seems repentant and determined to reform, you could rehire him on a probationary basis. If you do, require him to make appropriate restitution both to Denise and to the company for the losses it incurred due to his wrongdoing. His superiors should be told to keep an eye on him, and he should be told they will. Point out to him that his behavior toward Denise violated the law, and warn him that you not only will report any repetition to the police but will encourage the victim to cooperate with the public prosecutor.

In sum, I advise you to assume, as it were, a pastoral role toward both these people, and to act as their moral teacher and guide. Some will object that this would be presumptuous paternalism on your part. However, to do good work and cooperate well with others, employees must think prudently about what they do in the workplace. Therefore, personnel management—an expression preferable to *human resources,* which suggests that employees are nothing more than assets to be used—rightly includes relevant moral formation, while respecting employees' privacy in regard to aspects of their lives and character not manifested in the workplace. Dealing with employees fairly, you can strive to overcome the evils inevitable in their working relationships and so build up a more genuine community with and among them. I believe that approach will not only be good business but an appropriate way of fulfilling your responsibility as a lay apostle to penetrate and transform the workplace with the light of the gospel and the healing touch of Jesus (see AA 5–8).

117: Should a woman who tried to use sex as a bribe be denied a promotion?

I have over eleven hundred people in my data processing department. Except for Sundays and a few major holidays, we operate twenty-four hours a day. On the night shift, we have nearly three hundred people. The night supervisor will be retiring in about two months, and I will promote one of his three assistants. All of them have been with us five to ten years, and, on paper, all are qualified. Each, of course, has his or her own pluses and minuses, so that, as usual, it does not make sense to say either that they are equally well qualified or that one is absolutely better qualified than the others. It comes down to a judgment call.

Last week our night supervisor was taking a week of the vacation he has coming before he retires. Because this position is so important to our operation, I filled in for him, so as to observe firsthand how the assistants perform, interact with one another, and deal with problems. While I was at it, I also had each of the three in my office for a leisurely, open-ended interview, during which I asked what problems they saw in the night operation as it has been managed up to now, and what they thought could be done to improve it.

All three assistants are white; two are men, the other a woman. My inclination was to promote the woman, since more than three-fourths of the night crew are women. I interviewed the two men first and was better impressed by one of them; he also seemed to me slightly more effective on the floor. Finally, I interviewed the woman, and for nearly an hour it went well. She is not as technically proficient as either of the men, but she seems good at handling the women who work under her, and the interview showed that she has some promising ideas for solving a couple of problems in the night operation. She also was straightforward in underlining her own strengths and saying she is eager for this promotion, and I respected her frankness.

My inclination to promote her had virtually become a decision by the time I stood up to end the interview and show her out. Then, she asked if she might bring up "something personal." I agreed, and she said that, since both of us have been "celibates" for the past year—around the time my wife died of cancer, this woman was separated from her husband and now has her divorce—she wondered whether I might be ready for some "companionship." Taken by surprise and wishing to be gentle, I answered honestly that, while I found her appealing and have begun dating, I have been limiting it to widows around my own age. As a Catholic, I explained, I do not believe in remarriage after divorce. She smiled, took my hand in both of hers, pressed up against me, and said that she was not proposing marriage, "only a relationship, since we will be working more closely together when I become night supervisor." Pretending not to understand, I replied that I had not yet decided whom to promote and quickly showed her out.

Her behavior was so repugnant to me that now I am inclined to promote the better of the two men instead of her. But since she would have got the job if she had not tried to bribe me by using sex, I wonder whether it is fair to make this business decision on the basis of my personal values. Then too, policy requires explaining the decision in a report to the Director of Human Resources. Referring to that incident could invite trouble.

Analysis:

This question calls for the derivation of a norm. The questioner's narrative makes it clear that the woman offered sexual favors as a bribe. Generally, a person who offers a bribe of any sort to obtain a promotion manifests several character flaws that probably will impede his or her proper and effective exercise of a managerial position's responsibilities. So, taking the attempted bribe into account in deciding whether to promote the woman would not be making the decision on the basis of "personal values" but using a relevant criterion. If the character flaws exist, the current night supervisor would have observed other behavior manifesting them, and so should be able to verify them. Therefore, unless the questioner has reason to distrust the night supervisor, he should ask him about all three candidates' character, and take his testimony into account in making the decision.

The reply could be along the following lines:

The timing and specific details of the woman's words and behavior, assuming you have reported them accurately, leave no room for reasonable doubt that she was offering sexual favors and offering them as a bribe so that you would promote her rather than one of her competitors. Someone might say that, in pretending not to understand, you acted deceptively. Under the circumstances, though, your reaction may well have been a mere expression of shock or embarrassment. Even if intentional, the pretense was ambiguous, and you undoubtedly expected it would serve its purpose even if the woman, not being deceived, correctly understood it as an unqualified rejection of her offer. I see no dishonesty in that pretense.

Your account gives no indication of impropriety on your part that might have evoked the woman's attempt. Still, she may have suspected you had something in mind other than business in inviting her to your office for a leisurely interview, which took place at night when, presumably, your secretary was not on duty and no one else was likely to interrupt. My first suggestion is that you reflect on your past treatment of female employees in general and this woman in particular to see whether you provided any reasonable ground for her to think you would be susceptible to sexual bribery.[326] And examine yourself as carefully as you can to see whether something you imprudently said or did before or during the interview triggered her behavior. If you were at fault, repent and amend your life.

Assuming nothing for which you were responsible occasioned this woman's behavior, her attempt at bribery was a serious affront to you. But more is at stake than your personal values and honor. Unusual circumstances—desperate need for the means of survival or well-grounded fear for the safety of a loved one—might tempt even a woman of good character to try to bribe someone with sex. Under the circumstances you describe, however, this subordinate's offer probably manifested the same character defects that one of the men would have manifested had he offered you, say, five thousand dollars.

Under ordinary circumstances, a person who offers any sort of bribe to obtain a promotion shows several things about himself or herself. First, the behavior evidences lack of solidarity with others and a disposition to treat them as mere means instead of cooperating with them as persons who are respected co-workers. Second, it shows lack of integrity, the readiness to violate relevant norms and use

---

326. Andrea P. Baridon and David R. Eyler, *Working Together: The New Rules and Realities for Managing Men and Women at Work* (New York: McGraw–Hill, 1994), 125–69, propose for men and women who share a workplace a contemporary business etiquette that could serve as a checklist for the questioner.

bad means. Third, its self-centeredness shows lack of a spirit of fairness toward competitors and lack of commitment to the organization's common good. Fourth, it indicates lack of appropriate self-confidence and self-respect—personality defects likely to occasion mistreatment of others. A person with such defects of character and personality is ill equipped to supervise the work of nearly three hundred people, which should involve gaining their respect and good will, encouraging their cooperation, and fairly resolving their disagreements and problems. Furthermore, giving a promotion to someone who offered a bribe to obtain it would tend to confirm and reinforce the flaws revealed by the act, with the likely bad result that the person would make a practice of abusing his or her power, thereby injuring both subordinates and the organization as a whole.

If this woman's character is defective in these ways, that surely will have manifested itself in the years she has worked under the present night supervisor. Unless you have a good reason for distrusting him, I suggest you question him closely, if you have not already, about his three subordinates' character, without first telling him about the incident. Probably he will provide various examples confirming the character traits manifested by the incident.

If so, you should consider these defects relevant to the question of whether the woman is qualified for the position, and they would show that she is not as well qualified for it as you had thought. On that basis, rather than on the basis of your "personal values," it would be clear, I think, that you should promote the better-qualified man rather than her.

If the night supervisor's experience with the woman does not confirm the implications of your experience with her or if for other reasons you decide to promote her, it still would be prudent to forestall any misunderstanding or misrepresentation by mentioning the incident in your report to the Director of Human Resources and explaining why you have decided on the promotion anyway. Then talk frankly with her, explaining how you perceived what she did and warning her to avoid similar behavior in the future. Explain what such behavior usually implies about the character of someone who engages in it, and how unsuitable such traits are in anyone in a supervisory position. Finally, make it clear you hope her performance will show that promoting her was not a mistake.

And if you decide not to promote this woman? I suggest you call her in and—in your secretary's earshot—confront her about the incident. Tell her frankly that it raised questions about her character, which suggested that she was not qualified for the position. Very likely she will offer some excuse or propose a less damning interpretation of what she did. Without conceding its plausibility, you can tell her that further inquiry prompted by the incident turned up other examples of inappropriate behavior. In discussing them with her, your intention should be to encourage her to reflect on the mistaken beliefs and bad attitudes they reveal, see the point in changing, and do so, at least insofar as her character flaws affect her performance at work and her relationships with others in the department.

Then in your report to the Director of Human Resources, include a summary of what you learned about the woman's character from the night supervisor, use her attempt at sexual bribery as an example, summarize your conversation with her about the matter, and indicate that, except for her serious character flaws, you would have considered her well qualified and promoted her. Presented in this way, your report not only might forestall questions about your decision but provide a basis for defending yourself, if necessary, against her possible claim that you initiated the personal conversation, made improper demands, and denied her the promotion when she rebuffed you.

118: May a manager discharge a good employee at another's unreasonable demand?

I am the vice-president for finance and personnel of a privately owned company that makes precision parts for other manufacturers. Due to an expansion five years ago, the company is heavily in debt at rather high interest rates. Orders have not increased rapidly enough for us to use our enlarged capacity efficiently. By cutting costs in every possible way, we have managed to avoid bankruptcy, but just barely. We are walking a fiscal tightrope; any misstep is likely to put us in serious trouble.

Our employees are not unionized. We have forestalled that by paying them well and treating them right. Recently, however, I have been under a lot of pressure to cut labor costs and have done so, sometimes in ways I do not like. Still, I have tried to be fair in spreading the pain. For instance, I have insisted that the company's officers give up salary and benefits proportionate to the cuts imposed on other employees. But now I face a serious dilemma.

Yesterday, the first day after the holiday weekend, one of our key workers, Ray, came to my office demanding that we fire a fellow worker, Joe. Both have worked here more than twenty years but they have never gotten along. Last Friday after work they got into a quarrel outside a bar. Ray told me Joe assaulted him and he no longer is willing to run the risk of working in the same place with "such a maniac." My initial reaction to Ray's demand was that, since the fight happened somewhere else, it is no concern of ours, and since I have no complaints about Joe's job performance, I have no reason to discharge him. I also called in Joe to hear his side. He said Ray started the fight, and three other trustworthy employees who were there supported his story. I then told Ray I was not going to discharge Joe. He replied with an ultimatum: Either fire Joe by Friday or that will be his own last day here.

I am quite sure Ray is not making an idle threat. He has had recent offers of other jobs that we considered it worthwhile to match. Still, I do not believe management ever should give in to any employee's arbitrary demand. Also, while Joe is a less skilled worker, he does everything we ask of him, and losing his job here will be hard on him. He has a family to support and will not easily find a job with comparable pay and benefits. If we were not in such perilous shape financially, I would be happy to tell Ray goodbye. However, he would be very hard to replace, while Joe could be replaced easily and, in fact, would have been laid off by now except that he is a good employee with more seniority than those we have laid off. Moreover, while we were finding Ray's replacement and breaking him in, we would have to pay overtime to other workers in that section, and the new man inevitably would make a certain number of costly mistakes before mastering the job.

I really am perplexed. Our lawyer foresees no problem if we discharge Joe, but that seems to me obviously unjust. At the same time, considering the serious consequences for the company, taking the risk of losing Ray seems obviously irresponsible. What to do?

Analysis:

This question calls for the application of norms regarding lying and promise keeping, and judgment in accord with the Golden Rule. Even if it becomes clear that the well-being of the company as a whole requires that Joe be dismissed, the questioner must not falsely suggest that he has given cause to be discharged or tell any other lie to placate Ray. Moreover, inasmuch as Joe has been an entirely satisfactory employee for many years, the company has at least implicitly promised him job security. Therefore, if he is dismissed, he has a moral right to a fair severance settlement even if he has no legally enforceable right to ongoing employment. What fairness requires must be determined by considering all the relevant facts and applying the Golden Rule.

The reply could be along the following lines:

Before making a decision, you ought to consider not only the problem of fairness to Joe but all the prospective disadvantages of giving in to Ray's arbitrary demand. Although he is a twenty-year employee, he plainly cares nothing about the company's good and is trying to exploit its need for his services to extort compliance with his unjust demand. If you give in, you can expect more demands from him. And since he has no loyalty and his threat to leave is credible, do not count on him to stay even if you meet all his demands. So, even if you dismiss Joe, you must prepare to replace Ray. Moreover, giving in to him will more or less undo your effort to build good employee relations by treating employees right. It will provide a bad example for other disloyal employees and will weaken loyal employees' confidence in you and the company, perhaps even alienating many of them.

These considerations suggest that you should not give in to Ray's demand. If you nevertheless judge that you cannot now take the risk of letting him go, you should seek an alternative resolution. One possibility would be to offer him a substantial raise to stay. This would have the advantage of not only motivating him to withdraw his demand for Joe's dismissal but countering other motives he might have for leaving. You also might be able to change Joe's work assignment so that the two men will have little or no contact with each other. At the same time, you could begin to get ready to replace Ray as soon as possible.

If neither this proposal nor any other you can think of provides a workable solution, one thing you certainly may not do is fire Joe—that is, not only dismiss him but allege that he deserved it. Your statement of the facts makes it clear that he has done nothing to give cause for dismissing him; therefore, to say or imply that he has, would be to calumniate him, a very grave wrong. Moreover, this wrong probably would make the company legally vulnerable.[327] Of course, you need not tell Ray you are not going to fire Joe, and probably he is not interested in the terms under which Joe leaves so long as he does leave. But if this should become an issue, you may not lie about Joe regardless of the consequences—even, for example, if the company's president ordered you to lie and your own job was at stake.

Can you fairly terminate Joe's employment in some other way? There would be nothing wrong with offering him an incentive adequate to motivate him to leave voluntarily. But what if you cannot do that? Even if he has no legally enforceable right to his job, his long and faithful service with the company has built up a valuable human relationship and created reasonable expectations on his part that the company will continue to employ him if it can. In view of that bond and those expectations, terminating his employment would be breaking an implicit promise to him. Yet, like the obligation of keeping explicit promises, the duty to keep such an implicit one is not absolute but limited by various conditions, which surely include the need to discharge the employee for the well-being of the company as a whole—the same condition that justifies laying off good and loyal workers. Thus, it seems to me you may terminate Joe's employment, provided you do that without either lying about him or failing to give him a fair severance settlement. In saying this, I am not telling you to discharge Joe; I am only saying that, if you conclude that the company's common good requires that he be discharged, you must proceed honestly and must be fair to him.

It would not be fair simply to discharge Joe, since the obligation of the company's implicit promise to him must be considered in the context of his long and satisfactory service. When promises are unfairly broken, the communion established between the parties by their mutual promises and built up by their faithful cooperation is damaged or destroyed. So, to discharge Joe fairly, you must keep faith with him. In effect, try to see to it that he goes away only sad, rather than justifiably mad, by doing what fairness requires, all things considered, to mitigate the harm he will suffer.

Certainly you not only should give Joe as full and favorable a recommendation as you honestly can, but should make an effort to help him find employment elsewhere—for example, by contacting your counterparts in other companies who might have a job for him. Beyond this, you must consider all the relevant facts, including the following: what he has contributed to the company by long and loyal service; what that contribution has cost him not only in hard work but, perhaps, in other ways, such as forgone opportunities to work elsewhere; what harm, not only monetary but psychological, he and his family will suffer by his being discharged; and what the company's present and possible future capability is to mitigate that harm. Then you must apply the Golden Rule by asking yourself what you would regard as a reasonable severance settlement if you were in Joe's place. Not knowing the outcome of that reflection, I cannot say precisely what you should do. But I can offer a few suggestions.

---

327. At least in some places, even dismissing Joe under the circumstances described would make the company legally vulnerable; but the questioner already received legal advice on that issue, and I presume it was sound.

One important harm resulting from Joe's discharge will be the psychological impact on him and his family. It may be greater if they do not know that he is faultless, that you are acting under constraint, and that you wish to make up to them fairly for discharging him. So, I suggest you meet with Joe and his wife, fully and honestly explain the situation, and invite them to help you work out a plan as satisfactory as possible to them. If you can, for example, you might offer a severance bonus, the temporary continuation at company expense of important benefits such as health insurance, and/or reimbursement of expenses related to job hunting and moving, if that turns out to be necessary. You also might promise Joe that, if and when conditions permit, you will reinstate him in his job with full seniority and other benefits.[328]

119: Should a supervisor make a labor-saving suggestion to management?

I am supervisor of the packing and shipping department of a manufacturing company. I used to be a foreman with a much larger company. From the time I began this job, the operation here seemed to me comparatively inefficient. But the problems are different from where I worked before, and I did not know how the setup could be improved. Early on, I talked with the plant superintendent about it. He in effect told me to mind my own business and stick with established procedures. I've made only a few changes, mostly to cut down the risk of accidents and injuries to my crew. These changes have improved efficiency very little if at all.

While on vacation recently, I was talking shop with my wife's cousin who manages the maintenance department at a similar plant operated by one of our competitors. He took me there and showed me around, and I had a good look at their packing and shipping department. Their setup really is ingenious, and now I see how we could make ours a lot more efficient. What's more, I believe we could do it in the space we have and without getting any costly new equipment. The changes' only significant costs would be for moving things around and training the crew in some new procedures.

Still, I am wondering whether I should go back to the plant superintendent about this or, perhaps, to higher management. There are pros and cons.

I feel sure suggesting improvements that could be carried out so easily would not hurt my future with this company. However, the changes would keep my crew working more steadily, and practically eliminate their overtime. Not being union-ized, they will not be able to do much about that, but they will not appreciate it. That will make supervising them harder and less pleasant. Which means that if I

---

328. The answer to this question points to a more general norm that should be followed in many similar cases. While promise breaking may be justified, one nevertheless always must keep faith with those to whom the promise was made—that is, do whatever one reasonably can to maintain the bonds of community that are strained by justifiable breaking of promises. Thus, while a business's common good can require its managers to break various promises—to investors, suppliers, customers, or employees—they should do what they reasonably can to compensate those adversely affected. That is not generosity but a requirement of fairness.

push for the changes and get them adopted, I probably stand to gain something for myself, but not much.

There also are two sides to this thing from a broader point of view. I hate to go on wasting the crew's time and energy doing the job the hard way when it could be done so much better. But my people are used to the take-home pay they have been getting, and it is going to be hard on them if they are cut back.

Analysis:

This question concerns a duty pertaining to the supervisor's role. The answer flows from the fact that cutting waste and increasing efficiency pertain to the common good of the business considered as a community, of which both workers and managers are members. The questioner has a duty to suggest the changes to make the common enterprise more efficient, and the workers should accept them. Because of the workers' interest in the matter, the questioner, in my judgment, should seek to enlist their cooperation in proposing the changes. But whether he gains it or not, he ought to propose the changes to higher management, and in doing so should point out that the workers deserve a fair share in the savings that will result.

The reply could be along the following lines:

Companies often have policies that provide some guidance for dealing with questions like yours. My first suggestion is that you find out whether such guidelines and/or provisions exist where you work. If they do, presume them just and conform to them unless the presumption favoring them is overcome by convincing reasons. In the remainder of my response, however, I shall assume that such guidelines and provisions are lacking; if any exist, my suggestions will need to be modified appropriately.

Cutting waste and increasing efficiency lower costs and improve productivity. These benefits enable management simultaneously to increase profits, reduce prices, and retain or increase market share. Efficient workers also make it possible for their employers to maintain or even improve their pay; inefficient workers are likely sooner or later to be displaced by machines or by competing companies' less costly workers. Moreover, other things being equal, more efficient work is better and more fulfilling to workers. Cutting waste and increasing efficiency, therefore, are important elements of the common good of any enterprise. Since that common good is the ground for the authority of the enterprise's managers, it is an essential and important responsibility of managers to reduce waste and promote efficiency. Consequently, you are right to be concerned about the inefficiency of the packing and shipping department, and as its supervisor you have a duty to suggest the change you describe. But since that duty might be subject to exception if fulfilling it would involve serious risk to yourself and/or harm to others, your question remains to be considered.

Making changes so that members of your crew work more steadily will not, considered in itself, injure them, assuming you allow them adequate breaks for rest. Provided they are properly trained in the new procedures, the only direct harm likely to result from your labor-saving suggestions is elimination of their overtime.[329] Even that, however, will not in itself harm them; not having to spend so many hours at their workplace, they will be able to spend more time with their families and will be free to do other things. The real problem is the loss of the extra pay. Though the workers are not entitled to work overtime, they naturally are interested in maintaining their present level of income, and it hardly would be fair to ignore that interest. Therefore, in making your suggestions for improvements, do what you can to maintain a good relationship with the workers and to safeguard their interest in maintaining their present income. The question is: How?

Though you will have to decide, taking into account your knowledge of your crew and your relationship with them, my suggestion is that you try from the outset to collaborate with them in dealing with the matter. You might begin by calling them together, explaining how you think the setup can be improved, saying you plan to suggest these improvements to higher management, and pointing out the advantages of doing better work with less wasted effort. At the same time, make it clear that the improvements would mean less overtime work, and you are concerned about how that will affect them. Encourage the workers to express their views, and invite their suggestions on how to approach higher management. As discussion develops, commend comments and suggestions that, going beyond narrow self-interest, express readiness to work together to make changes that will benefit everyone concerned.

If this initial discussion goes reasonably well, ask the workers to join with you in proposing the improvements to management. Develop a proposal that assures them a reasonable share in the prospective benefits of their increased productivity. If feasible, propose reducing the crew's size by attrition or transferring some workers to other departments, so that those who remain still will have opportunities for overtime work during busy periods.

And if the initial discussion does not go well? Since the plant superintendent rebuffed your previous effort to discuss the problem, higher management presumably does not see it as significant. There being no apparent urgency for you to proceed, it seems to me you can delay for a time, work quietly to win over the more reasonable members of the crew, and so try to develop consensus. If it becomes clear that the effort will not succeed, however, I think you should suggest the improvements by yourself.

With or without the workers' cooperation, you should be careful about how you approach your superiors. In explaining how the company would benefit from the changes you propose, point out that sharing the savings with the workers will be both fair to them and in the company's long-term interest. Indeed, you might begin by saying something along these lines: "Some members of my crew and I think we can accomplish the same work we do now with less overtime or even none. If we are right, will you be fair-minded enough to share with the workers the savings that will be realized by their increased productivity?"

---

329. If the workers were likely to suffer greater loss—for example, termination of employ-ment—the remainder of the response would be different. For consideration of such a problem, though from a different viewpoint, see q. 113, above.

Even if you proceed without the workers' cooperation, your efforts to work with them and safeguard their interests are likely to limit their resentment and help you retain their good will. But the company may adopt your suggestions without fairly sharing the savings. If so, assuming you do not need additional compensation to support your family or fulfill other pressing responsibilities, you should, as a matter of Christian mercy, ask management to distribute the increase in pay it would give you among the members of your crew. In doing that, you will not only mitigate their suffering due to the unfairness but bear witness to it before management and provide the workers with evidence of your good will, thereby probably lessening their resentment. Of course, whether or not the company agrees to your proposal, some workers are likely to react in ways that will make it more difficult for you to supervise them. Be ready to accept that difficulty as part of the price you must pay for doing your duty.

I assume the plant superintendent is your immediate superior and would be involved in making and implementing a decision to change the setup in your department. If so, it seems to me you should not exclude him from any approach you make to management, though perhaps you should offer your suggestion simultaneously to him and to one or more other superiors. In your earlier discussion with him, you had no alternative to your department's present setup to propose; now that you do, he is likely to be more receptive.

Finally, the efficient setup at the shop operated by your employer's competitor might be its property. That would be so if it could be patented or if its development involved significant expenditures and/or work. In that case, adopting it without its owner's permission and/or appropriate compensation would be a form of theft. Therefore, do not suggest that this setup be adopted at your plant without making the source of your ideas clear and calling attention to the competitor's possible legal and/or moral rights to be compensated.

120: Should a union member who considers a strike unjust be a scab?

I am a unionized factory worker. There is going to be a strike, and I am trying to decide whether to take part or break ranks and accept an offer to continue working—be what we call a "scab."

Negotiations went on for two months, until management claimed they had gone as far as they could and presented a final offer many of us wanted to accept. But when we met to vote, the president argued that the company could give us a lot more, and a motion to accept the offer was defeated. The old contract still had three weeks to go. We could have gone back to the table. But the negotiating team said that would be useless, and the majority voted to strike when the old contract runs out unless by then management agrees to everything in our last offer. Nobody expects that, and everybody thinks the strike will be a long one.

Maybe the company could give us everything we are demanding, but our president admitted its offer was better than most of the agreements made at other companies. Besides, this strike is going to be hard on some of us. Some people will be able to manage with their strike pay and what they can make at temporary jobs. The younger people without families don't have the bills to pay, and many older ones have wives or husbands who work elsewhere. But husbands and wives who both work here and those of us who have big house payments and wives who stay home and take care of the kids will not be able to make ends meet. We can't afford a strike.

If we do go out, everybody in the union will be assigned times for strike duty. People who don't show up won't get any strike pay. But the strike duty will involve carrying signs or passing out leaflets claiming that the company refused to bargain in good faith, the strike was unavoidable, and so forth. Since I see things differently, I really don't want to be involved in that.

Something else also is bothering me. Yesterday morning the stewards passed the word that starting Monday we are going to soften up management by working to rule for the two weeks until we go out. That officially means doing everything exactly according to the book, but it really means a slowdown. Without doing anything a foreman can show is a violation, the workers take turns delaying things so the line has to be stopped every few minutes. Tools disappear; somebody puts a part in the wrong way; a compressor begins leaking oil, and nobody notices until it shuts down. One day, everybody qualified for certain essential jobs calls in sick; another day, there are long lines at the infirmary to get specks removed from eyes, little cuts cleaned and bandaged, "bruised" toes X–rayed, and so forth. Many people actually enjoy playing these games and make life miserable for anyone who doesn't. But I don't want to get involved in this sort of thing when I am not enthusiastic about going on strike anyway.

The managers are planning to keep the plant in limited operation for one eleven-hour shift, as they've done before, using nonunion employees with experience on the line. But this time they also are trying something new. They called in a group of us at the end of the shift this afternoon and offered to make us foremen from now until the strike ends. Temporary promotions to nonunion jobs often are necessary to fill in for someone who is on vacation or off work for some other reason, and union rules provide that membership terminates with a temporary promotion and automatically resumes (without affecting seniority) when the promotion ends. This offer means that I and the others would help the regular foremen deal with the slowdown and, of course, work as scabs during the strike.

I don't know whether to accept. If I do, most of my fellow union members, many of them relatives or lifelong friends, will think I'm a Judas and treat me accordingly. I live in this town, and people who are my neighbors might never forgive me. But for the reasons I've explained, I don't want to go along with the slowdown and the strike. Besides, there is a big difference between strike pay and what I would make working eleven hours a day as a foreman, and my wife and I really could use that money.

Analysis:

This question involves two distinct issues. (1) Would it be right to break ranks with fellow union members and accept the opportunity to work during the strike?

(2) Would it be morally acceptable to participate actively, in the ways described, in the slowdown and strike? The answer to (1) depends in part on whether the strike will be just. Unless the questioner judges that the strike probably will be unjust, he almost certainly should not accept the opportunity to work during it. But even if he reaches that judgment, he perhaps should refuse to work. If he judges that the strike probably will be just, the answer to (2) depends on the moral character of the specific acts of participation in the slowdown and strike. But if he judges that the strike may be or certainly will be unjust, the character of those acts as material cooperation in a possibly or certainly unjust common action also must be taken into account.

The reply could be along the following lines:

Sometimes neither side in a dispute is in the right, and one may not cooperate fully with either. And even if one side is acting rightly, one's other responsibilities can limit or even rule out involvement on that side. So, do not take it for granted, as you seem to, that you may either take part in the strike or accept the offer to continue working, for involvement on either side would raise moral questions that must be considered separately. I shall first discuss whether you should accept the offer to work during the strike, then whether and to what extent you may participate actively in the slowdown and the strike.

Like members of other communities, members of a union ought to cooperate for their common good and not act contrary to it. A strike can be just and necessary for the union's common good. Of course, unless convinced after careful reflection that a strike would be just, union members should not vote for it. But if a union, by due process, justly decides to strike, all members ordinarily should obey that decision, not act contrary to it by accepting the employer's offer to work during the strike. While it often is hard to tell whether a decision to strike is just (see *CCC,* 2435; *LCL,* 770–71), union members, including those who opposed the decision, should begin by presuming that they owe it obedience, and should set aside that presumption only if they reach a well-considered judgment that striking probably is unjust—that is, more likely unjust than just.

Can that condition be met in this case? Perhaps. You foresee a lengthy strike, imposing severe hardship on you and some of your fellow workers and quite possibly doing severe injury to various other participants in the company—owners, suppliers, customers, and so on. These adverse effects could make striking unjust, as other factors, such as unlikelihood of success, also might. Moreover, among the reasons you offer for opposing the strike is that the union's president admitted that the company's offer "was better than most of the agreements made at other companies." That may mean you think the offer was fair, and those who voted against accepting it acted unreasonably, motivated by greed aroused by the president's argument "that the company could give us a lot more." If so, you should consider whether you have such clear and convincing evidence that, had it been available to you at the time, you could not have voted in good conscience to go on strike. Almost certainly, you should not accept the offer to work during the strike unless conscientious reflection leads you to believe it was wrong to vote as the majority did (even though some people did so guiltlessly due to an honest mistake).

Why do I say "almost certainly," leaving open the possibility that you might rightly accept the offer to work even if you conclude that it was not wrong to vote as the majority did? Because other responsibilities could require you to continue working—for example, if your family otherwise would be compelled to suffer hardships that fair-minded fellow union members, putting themselves in your place, would regard as intolerable (see *LCL,* 760–61). In that case, acting contrary to the common good of your fellow union members would not be disloyal, and your relatives and friends, if fair-minded, would not hold it against you. You do indicate other responsibilities—"this strike is going to be hard on some of us," who "will not be able to make ends meet." But apparently this does not mean that those responsibilities are so exigent that you ought to work. Rather, you seem only to be saying they were reasonable grounds for voting to accept the proposed contract. If that is all they were, the responsibilities in question hardly can justify working during the strike unless you believe it was wrong to vote as the majority did. Moreover, you should not suppose the majority ought to have taken the hardship that the strike would involve for some as a decisive reason to forgo it, for any community's common good often requires that some members accept considerable burdens.

Even if you judge that the strike probably will be unjust, so that it was wrong for the majority to vote as it did, you should consider your other responsibilities. Even if the union will be striking unjustifiably, nothing you say suggests it has been consistently unjust. Perhaps it has been a good association that continues to deserve its members' support. If so, your duty as a member might forbid working for the company as a scab, since that would injure the union and reduce or destroy your capacity to participate in it and influence its future decisions and actions for the better.

Similarly, quite apart from your being a fellow union member, your relatives and friends involved in this conflict deserve your loyalty as a relative or friend. You realize that they will deeply resent it if you work as a scab and are considering the price you will pay. But have you considered that the relationships of family and friendship you share with them are great goods for both them and you, that you ought to protect these goods, and that failing to do so without a serious reason would be wrong? This obligation might well rule out your accepting the injury to these relationships that you anticipate will result from doing what you foresee will be considered a profound betrayal.

Again, you must conscientiously consider the relevant facts and, of course, make your own judgment. If the majority of the union's members are habitually greedy and the union regularly abuses its power by enforcing their unreasonable demands, perhaps it does not deserve your support; if your relatives and friends care little for you and only want to exploit your relationships with them so that you will cooperate in their injustice, you may have an obligation to resist them. Then, provided you are not aware of anything else that makes it wrong to accept the company's offer, your responsibility to support your family by honest work could require you to be a scab. I say "could require," since even on those assumptions, you might have another acceptable possibility, such as reducing your standard of living, and perhaps even a preferable one, such as working elsewhere.

If you do not accept the offer to work during the strike, may you participate actively in the slowdown and the strike itself? If so, in what ways?

Whether or not they judge their union's action to be just, union members should never do anything wrong in itself, even if it seems a necessary or highly effective means of compelling an employer to settle a dispute. In my judgment, this general norm morally excludes participating in the tactics of the slowdown you describe. To begin with, it would be virtually impossible to conduct the slowdown without lying (calling in sick when not sick, seeking first aid for feigned problems), and lying is always wrong. Inducing real minor illnesses or injuries is intentionally damaging health or bodily integrity, which also always is wrong, even if the damage intended is very slight. Deliberately misplacing tools or mistreating equipment violates the company's property rights. Even more important, though *working to rule* might refer to actions that could be morally acceptable, the acts implementing the slowdown you describe will carry out the intention to work inefficiently and wastefully. That intention is bad, not only because carrying it out deprives the company of the production to which it is contractually entitled and for which it must pay, but because it is contrary to the good of work itself (see *LCL,* 759). Work is one of the basic human goods (see *LCL,* 756–57), and acts whose very object is to violate it are always wrong—though not necessarily always gravely so.

Some actions wrong in themselves also might be demanded of union members as part of their strike "duty"—for example, intentionally injuring strikebreakers or lying to law enforcement officials. But nonviolent picketing and carrying signs or distributing literature expressing the union's view are methods of enlisting support morally acceptable in themselves. However, if you are told to carry a sign or hand out a leaflet with a message you regard as false, you could not obey without lying, since those addressed would reasonably assume that you were not only delivering the union's message but personally asserting it.

Even if picketing union members personally convey no message they believe false, any who regard a strike as unjust help bring about what they think bad, namely, the perpetration of the injustice. Such cooperation in bringing about an injustice often is wrong, because it can lead one to intend the injustice, lead others into sin, impair one's witness to relevant moral truth, or be unfair to those who suffer the injustice. If you judge the strike to be unjust, the participation involved in picketing, even without conveying false information, would seriously impair your witness to the truth about it. It also would contribute to the damage that the injustice would do to the company and could encourage others to will it. In my judgment, such participation would therefore be wrong.

If you conscientiously refuse both to participate in the slowdown and to perform assigned strike duty, and also conscientiously reject the company's offer to work during the strike, your fellow union members should not allow you and your family to suffer the consequences of losing strike pay. I suggest you explain your stand to your relatives and friends, ask them for the support your loyalty to them deserves, and try to get them to join with you in demanding from the union's wider membership and leadership either strike pay or equivalent compensation, perhaps for helping with union business unrelated to the strike. Your solidarity with fellow union members, proved by your refusal to break ranks with them even though you conscientiously object to the course they have chosen, surely would call for that corresponding solidarity with you.

If it is not forthcoming and your family responsibilities do not demand that you work as a scab, you ought to accept the hard consequences not only for yourself but for your family. In doing so, keep in mind our Lord's promise: "Blessed are those who are persecuted for righteousness' sake, for theirs is the kingdom of heaven" (Mt 5.10). Having put the kingdom first, trust his assurance about the Father's providential care with regard to the necessities of life: "Do not worry about your life, what you will eat or what you will drink, or about your body, what you will wear. . . . Your heavenly Father knows that you need all these things. But strive first for the kingdom of God and his righteousness, and all these things will be given you as well" (Mt 6.25, 32–33).

121: May a union leader bargain for what he or she considers unreasonable?

There are many fiercely competing independent companies in the industry I work in. Each employs between three and five hundred skilled workers who have organized their own union, and all these autonomous unions act independently, imitating management. There is a clear need for some cooperation. But, though I am union president at one of the larger companies, I have not been able to get the other unions to work with us.

This competitive situation underlies the problem I now face. In two months our contract will run out, and next week we start negotiations on a new one. If we simply renewed the present contract, pay and benefits would remain above average for the industry. But since the other companies and unions either already have completed their negotiations or have contracts that do not run out this year, management here is vulnerable. If we go out on strike, the competition will grab the company's share of the market, and business may never recover. Knowing this, many of our people have become convinced that now is the time to demand a raise that would give us by far the highest pay in the industry, as well as changes in benefits to make our package as good as any.

I and my colleagues in the union's leadership thought that such demands would be unreasonable. The company already has serious financial problems. If it gave in to the demands, it probably would be driven into bankruptcy before the new contract runs out. But when we tried to explain the situation to the membership at a general meeting, we immediately ran into heavy opposition, led by the man I replaced as president. Among other things, he seriously accused us of selling out to management, and, even though I got a vote of confidence in the current leadership, some people half believed the charge. As a result, I could not persuade enough of the rank and file that it would be foolish to demand too much, and the majority not only approved the demands but voted to go out on strike unless every one of them is met.

I then tried to win over some key people whose support I had expected but didn't get. Only a few have changed their minds. Those who haven't are mainly younger men who could relocate and think they can get jobs somewhere if the strike is prolonged or the company goes under. They may be right, but most of the people supporting me have more seniority and other ties here, and will face serious problems.

With negotiations about to begin, I do not know what to do. If I do not get management to give in to the unreasonable demands, I will call another meeting and try to get the membership to consider a compromise. But the opposition probably will prevail, and I am still convinced a strike will seriously damage the company and perhaps even destroy it. If I do get management to give in, the result will be even more certainly disastrous for the company. In either case, many of the rank and file are liable to lose more than they stand to gain—although too few of them see that. As the union's leader, too, I'm expected to try to convince management our demands are reasonable—it would be in the company's best interests to give in—but I cannot honestly make that argument. I've thought of resigning, but I'm sure the leader of the opposition would be elected to replace me. He will take a hard line with management right from the start: "Either agree to every one of our demands or we strike." He will refuse even to consider a compromise and will call the people out on strike without giving them a chance to reconsider. Those who have supported me are entitled to that chance, and it would not be right to break faith with them.

It looks as if whatever I do will be wrong. Am I missing a way out?

Analysis:

The questioner is perplexed—both available options seem morally unacceptable (see *LCL,* 290–91). The perplexity's main cause lies in the fact that at least one presupposed moral norm admitting of exception is mistakenly being regarded as absolute. While the union's president is obliged to represent its membership in the negotiation, the questioner has not defined what that duty entails and must clarify it. If it can be fulfilled without asserting anything false or trying to obtain an unjust contract, the questioner may present the union's demands. But if the questioner's understanding of his or her duties as president precludes carrying them out in good conscience, he or she should resign and will not break faith with supporters by doing so.

The reply could be along the following lines:

Moral norms guide us in carrying out God's wise and loving plan for our lives, and God never asks the impossible (see DS 1536/804). So, it cannot be true that whatever one does will be wrong. A morally acceptable option always is available. While none of your options is appealing, at least one surely is morally acceptable. Though the information you have provided is insufficient to judge what you should do, I hope the following considerations will clarify matters so you can reach a sound judgment by your own conscientious reflection.

You say you are supposed to try to convince management that the union's demands are reasonable—that it would be in the company's best interests to give in—but you cannot honestly argue for that. I take that to mean that ordinarily, at least, your duty in dealing with management is to put aside your personal views about what the union's position should be and try to achieve the members' objectives. However, the strictness of that duty depends on the terms of the commitment you made to the union's members in accepting the office of president.

What exactly are the terms? The union's written constitution and bylaws no doubt provide some indications, but previous presidents have interpreted them by their habitual practice. Insofar as the members have known how your predecessors carried out their duties, and have found it satisfactory, that clarifies and supplements the written formulation of duties. Perhaps you also made some further written or oral pledge that helped get you elected. You must consider all these things and then ask yourself whether, given the peculiarities of the situation, you can fulfill all your duties as president without lying or trying to bring about what you regard as unjust. If so, continue in office; if not, resign.

Given that your judgment and the majority's vote are in conflict, how could you fulfill your duty to represent the union's membership in the negotiation without asserting anything false or intending to obtain an unjust contract? I am not really sure, but I can sketch out some suggestions that might be helpful.

Even if you shared the majority's position, you might well begin the negotiation with a simple recital of the relevant facts. The union's membership has voted to make this set of demands and to strike if management does not meet them; since other companies will not be negotiating simultaneously, the company is vulnerable to a strike; and you believe the majority of your members will vote to carry out that threat rather than accept any counteroffer. Even though you regard the majority's view as mistaken, you still can make that argument, and I doubt that as president you are obliged to give any other. An attempt to show the reasonableness of the demands—which surely would not convince management—could hardly represent the majority's position more effectively. And honesty does not require that you state your personal judgment, only that you not lie about it.

What if management challenges the reasonableness of the demands? You might respond, truthfully, that arguing about that is hardly likely to be fruitful, and management must face and deal with reality (as, indeed, it must)—the union's members want what they want and are determined to get it. Probably management will respond by reciting the company's financial problems and pointing out that meeting the union's demands would bankrupt it. You might truthfully report that the membership had been told all that before voting. You also might consider it compatible with your duty as president to ask management to document its claims as fully and clearly as possible, and promise to share that evidence with the members. Again, you might suggest to management that they make their case directly to the membership or, perhaps, propose some other cooperative way of getting the members to understand the company's problems.

What if management presses you to express your personal judgment: "Do you really believe it would be in the workers' own best interests for us to meet these demands?" It may be clear that management knows your judgment is in conflict with the majority's position; if so, lying would undermine your credibility and effectiveness, and you will have to judge whether it would be better to admit the conflict or evade the question. You probably could do the latter in one of two ways—point out that your personal views are irrelevant inasmuch as your role in the negotiation is to represent the union's members or simply repeat that the workers have made up their minds and are hardly likely to be impressed by anyone else's views about what is in their best interests.

With this approach, you might present the union's position very much as the former president would do if conducting the negotiation, though both his manner of acting and his intention would be entirely different from yours. He surely would be belligerent; his hard line would challenge management. You could be pleasant and calm; your dispassionate recital of relevant facts would invite a counterproposal that might win the majority's acceptance. So, your precise intention could be to elicit such an offer. Your understanding of your duties might not prevent you, at some point, from suggesting terms the company could grant and the workers might accept—for example, substituting for the pay raise a profit-sharing arrangement offering workers the prospect of even greater compensation over the term of the contract without immediately placing an excessive financial burden on the company. But even if you do not think you may make such a suggestion, you might be able to cooperate with management in shaping any proposal it offers to increase its chances of being accepted.

Proceeding in this manner might lead management to agree to the union's demands or in some other way concede more than it should. Still, you need not intend to elicit such an offer, and, if it were made, you could oppose its acceptance even as you conducted the meeting at which you presented it and the majority accepted it. You may succeed in eliciting an offer that is both compatible with the company's survival and appealing, even in unexpected ways, to many of your members. If so, you can advocate accepting it, not least by pointing out how much many workers will lose if they go on strike, and perhaps you will succeed in averting the disaster you foresee.

On the other hand, your understanding of your duties might prevent you from undertaking the negotiation along the lines I have sketched or, at some point, from continuing as president. If so, you ought to resign. Since one never can have an obligation to sin, no commitment to anyone can require continuing in an office one believes one can no longer uprightly fulfill. In resigning, you would be choosing to avoid both violating your commitment as president to represent the union's members and violating your conscience in fulfilling the office's duties. You would not intend, but only accept as an unwanted but inevitable side effect, the bad consequences you foresee for both the company and the workers as a whole. Since you will have done all you ought to do on behalf of those who supported you, you will not be breaking faith with them. If they ought to have a chance to reconsider the decision to strike before they act on it, the person who replaces you, not you, will wrongly deny them that chance.

Finally, if you preside over a meeting at which the majority reaffirms the decision to strike, it seems to me you would be obliged to resign unless you become convinced the strike is just, for I do not see how a union's president can preside over a strike without intending it to be carried on. If you resign then or earlier, you and other members of the union who regard the strike as unjust ought not to cooperate in it in any way that would involve intending either the strike itself or its success.

Indeed, in that event, you should consider the possibility that you ought to part company with the majority and offer to lead the minority in an effort to break the strike so as to save the company and the jobs of those who are less mobile. Union members owe one another solidarity not in the greedy pursuit of unjust objectives but in the reasonable pursuit of legitimate interests. By disclosing that you are considering leading an effort to break the strike, you might move enough of those in the majority to change sides so that the decision to strike could be reversed. Of course, you may well have other responsibilities that would exclude such a course. If not, however, both the union's common good, which includes the authentic interests of all the participants in the company, and your loyalty to those who have supported you might require you to put your unique talents to work by assuming the odious role of leading strikebreakers.

122: Should a pilot resign to avoid involvement in the airline's immoralities?

The air transport business used to be cleaner than most, and the airline I work for as a pilot used to be among the best. Deregulation changed all that. Unrestricted competition resulted in a rising tide of red ink, and that led management to cut corners and use all sorts of questionable tactics to reduce costs and increase the load factor.

Six months ago, our maintenance department was nailed for several violations. Naturally, management said we were not guilty, promised to prevent any future violations, and paid the fine. But I hear on the grape vine that maintenance is still cheating, and, assuming that is true, it is frightening. Also, twice in the last six weeks flights were delayed, one time more than three hours, while we waited for freight to arrive and be loaded. But I was ordered to tell passengers there was a problem that prevented closing the cargo door.

Marketing also has changed. We advertise reduced fares, but often their availability is so limited that the advertising is a classic case of bait-and-switch. And to fill as many seats as possible at the highest possible prices, clerks are now trained to answer callers' questions in ways that come very close to lying.

Recently, each seat in the first and business class sections of the planes I fly has been fitted with an individual video monitor. Passengers have a choice of movies, including X–rated ones. At the same time, by manipulating flight-crew schedules, the company is staffing those sections with female flight attendants with the least seniority, so that they are generally more vulnerable to exploitation besides being younger. The uniform these young women used to wear has been replaced with a sexier one, and they have been motivated—by a so-called reward-for-excellence program under which passengers rate flight attendants—to put up with what would be regarded as sexual harassment in most other jobs. If the trend keeps up, the captain of an airliner soon will be the proprietor of a whore house.

I find the whole business so disgusting I have been thinking of quitting. Lacking an acceptable employment option, most pilots would find that virtually unthinkable. However, I have only a few years until retirement and do have an employment alternative that would be adequate, though the work would be harder and the income less.

Analysis:

This question calls for clarification of the duties of a pilot as captain of an airliner and application of the norm excluding lying. A captain should serve passengers and fellow crew members by working to overcome conditions that threaten their safety or well-being while on the aircraft. So, before quitting, the questioner at least should make a serious effort to deal with the abuses touching closely on a captain's responsibilities, especially the rumored cheating on maintenance. Since it is a lie to tell passengers that a deliberate delay is caused by difficulty in closing the cargo door, the questioner should refuse to give that deceptive explanation. The questioner is not closely involved in any of the company's other immoralities and bears little or no responsibility with regard to them.

The reply could be along the following lines:

In likening your position prospectively to that of proprietor of a house of prostitution, you exaggerate the depths to which management is likely to sink. You also exaggerate your personal involvement in the company's use of pornography and exploitation of the female flight attendants to promote sales of the more costly seats. That marketing tactic, of course, is gravely evil, but you need neither intend it—as you plainly do not—nor contribute to it. By contrast, the proprietor of a house of prostitution necessarily intends all the sinful behavior from which he or she profits.

Moreover, except for delaying departures to load freight, you are not closely involved in perpetrating management's other wrongdoing and are not likely to be tempted to become more involved in it. Your continuing to work for the company is not likely to encourage anyone else to participate in its wrongdoing, and your quitting would be unlikely to inhibit it. Consequently, while your understandable disgust is a sign of your Christian conscience's opposition to immorality, your moral feelings do not indicate that you have an obligation to quit.

Quite the contrary. In undertaking to be an airline pilot, you should have committed yourself to use your gifts to serve your passengers and fellow crew members. I assume you did. The people you pledged to serve are now being badly treated by management. Since you have the prospect of other acceptable employment, you are in a strong position to seek appropriate ways of overcoming the evils you describe. So, it would be wrong for you to quit, in my judgment, at least until you have made a serious effort to stop the abuses that touch closely on a captain's responsibilities. Reform always is possible, and as a Christian you should resist moral corruption, not surrender to it even by fleeing, unless duty requires that you flee. By resisting the abuses, you will not only fulfill your job's responsibilities but exercise a valuable form of Christian apostolate. In that way, your fond recollections of past times in the face of increasing corruption will not be pointless, as nostalgia usually is.

Of the various evils you describe, one directly and very significantly concerns your duty as captain: the rumored ongoing cheating on maintenance. Lives are at stake, and, as captain, you are responsible for the safety of your passengers, crew, and yourself. You should refuse to take off if there is any unreasonable risk in doing so. Existing maintenance requirements should be presumed reasonable, and cheating on them should be presumed to entail unreasonable risk. Therefore, you and other captains should insist that the requirements be met in every instance. If you judge the rumors of ongoing cheating credible, and it seems you do, you have so strict a moral obligation to take action that even prospective unemployment would not justify tolerating the cheating—but I note that you have an acceptable employment alternative, if it comes to that.

To ensure your plane's airworthiness before a flight, you should check out possible faults in maintenance or have someone else do so, if that is possible. If not, refuse to fly until adequately reassured that maintenance is being carried out as it should be. If you judge that this is what you must do, do everything you can to ensure that your fellow captains do the same, so that the airline's operations will be halted. I assume you can act through your pilots' association. If necessary, however, you should use other available channels: government agencies, the company's insurers, the public media, and so on.

When a flight is delayed to accommodate freight, telling passengers there is a problem in closing the cargo door will not mollify them unless that ambiguous statement deceives them into supposing it refers to a mechanical problem. That statement by you therefore is a lie, and the lie will be grave matter if it imposes seriously unfair burdens on passengers—for instance, by preventing them from taking timely steps to deal with problems resulting from their delayed arrival, or seeking alternative transportation, or even canceling their trips, if that is what they would prefer to do. In the future, you must refuse to make that or any other deceptive excuse for delays. I suggest you warn management that you will no longer lie to passengers, but will explain delays either truthfully or not at all.

The flight attendants are being sexually exploited. Management is rewarding them for arousing passengers' lust and cooperating in their own degradation. In this respect, your analogy with a house of prostitution is sound, though the managers responsible, not you, are its proprietors. Talk with the flight attendants, appeal to their self-respect, and urge them to refuse to cooperate in this indecency. You no doubt know older flight attendants whom you might encourage to oppose management in this matter; quite possibly they could work through their own union, even enlist feminist organizations and propagandists in the struggle. You also should be alert for any incident involving a passenger's misbehavior with a flight attendant that might be criminal, annoying to other passengers, or disruptive of the crew's work. If such an incident occurs, make as large an issue of it as you can, and try to use it to arouse the concern of government agencies and others. If you hear any passengers criticize the sexual exploitation of the flight attendants, you might encourage them to complain to management.

Not knowing the technical aspects of the system for providing pornographic movies, I cannot say much about how you might work against that evil. If there were some feasible way to sabotage the objectionable recordings and you had no reason to refrain, that would not be wrong; it would free passengers from an occasion of grave sin, and the airline can have no moral right to such material. However, I suppose such a direct approach might provoke disciplinary action and, perhaps, criminal penalties. But perhaps you could organize a protest against this pornography in the workplace by crew members who share your moral judgment.

More remote from your sphere of responsibility are the abuses you describe in advertising and sales. Of course, there are similar abuses in the marketing methods of competing airlines and many other businesses, but that by no means lessens their gravity. The public at large has an interest in correcting deceptive advertising and dishonest communication by sales agents. Anonymously providing information about these abuses to journalists, consumer groups, and so on might help remedy this evil.

Besides the preceding reasons for fulfilling your various responsibilities, an additional, general duty provides a cogent reason for doing so in an exemplary way. You are a senior member of your profession, and others look to you as a role model. By bearing clear and unflinching witness to the moral truth about your professional responsibilities, you will help all your colleagues, especially those just beginning service, to shape their own work as they should.

The state of affairs you describe also needs to be considered from a broader perspective. As you say, a rising tide of red ink motivates management to use immoral methods of cutting costs and increasing sales. But air transport is an important industry, whose service is essential to many people and useful to most others. Surely, the problems management faces could and should be dealt with in other, morally legitimate ways. Perhaps you could make some contribution to identifying what should be done, work with others, through professional associations or otherwise, in making constructive suggestions to management, or become active in politics so as to promote appropriate governmental action.

Even if you do not quit your job or lose it, you will retire in a few years. In either case, you might be able to continue to work against immoralities like those you describe and in support of the cleaner business you remember. Among other possibilities, you might consider writing and publishing your memoirs, to make known your reflections on management practices that surely will do the industry as a whole no good in the long run.

+   +   +

123: May a mechanic continue working for a business that cheats people?

After taking a course in auto mechanics, I got a job in a shop specializing in exhaust systems, brakes, shock absorbers, and so forth. As far as I can tell, we install good parts, do jobs right, and charge fair prices. But the service manager regularly talks customers into having unnecessary work done "for safety's sake." So, I often find myself replacing brake cylinders, struts, and other parts that are perfectly okay. Fortunately, since I never talk with the customers, I do not have to argue with them or lie to them. Still, I don't like replacing parts that are perfectly okay.

But when I tried to talk with the service manager about what he does, he smiled and said: "Son, it's my job to deal with customers and your job to do the work on the service order, not argue with me about it." He made it clear that's how it is if I want to keep my job.

I do need the job. Will it be wrong for me to keep it?

Analysis:

This question concerns cooperation in fraud. Assuming the service manager is defrauding customers, the questioner need not be formally cooperating. Still, his material cooperation is morally questionable. He is likely eventually to be tempted to cooperate formally, and if his need for the job is not great, his cooperation may be unfair to defrauded customers, especially the neediest. He must judge whether he needs the job badly enough to justify keeping it and continuing to cooperate materially in the fraud. If he judges that he may not, simply quitting would end the occasion of sin for him but would not help those being defrauded. To do that, he should make a serious effort to stop the fraud.

The reply could be along the following lines:

The service manager presumably has much more experience than you do. Is it possible that you are mistaken and are misjudging him? If it is, do nothing until you are certain of the fraud you allege. But if you are sure of it, I offer the following advice.

Assuming the service manager is defrauding customers, you are closely involved in grave injustices. Still, you need not share the service manager's sinful will. You are only trying to make a living, and what you do to earn your pay is exactly the same as when customers themselves, being overcautious, categorically tell the service manager they want certain work done "whether or not you think it could be put off," and it turns out to be equally unnecessary. In carrying out the customer's order in such a case, the shop does him or her no injustice. And in both cases, your intentions can be the same: to do the work well, not only to earn your pay but for the customers' benefit, since, assuming unnecessary work is going to be done, properly installing the parts does benefit customers, while not doing so could lead to serious accidents or other harm.

Still, you at least are contributing to the success of the service manager's wrongdoing. I say "at least," because you also may be tempted to intend part of what he wrongly intends. For example, on occasion you probably will be called on to talk with customers—for example, if the service manager steps out briefly and a suspicious customer questions you—and then you will have to choose between sharing in the deception and risking your job by being honest. In that case, you are likely to be tempted to take part in the wrongdoing itself by choosing to maintain the deception.

Moreover, you must ask yourself whether your involvement in the fraud is fair to the customers. Putting yourself in the place of the neediest of those being defrauded, consider what you would want a conscientious person in your place to do. You say you need the job. If someone else's need for his or her job were a matter of life and death, or even a matter of staying out of jail or something of comparable importance, out of sympathy you would no doubt regard his or her similar involvement in an injustice to you as acceptable. But if your need for your job is not urgent, would you not want a person in your place to do what he or she could to save you from being defrauded?

What should you do if you judge that you must not go on contributing to the fraud and accepting the bad consequences of doing so? If your sole responsibility were to avoid the occasion of sinning, you could simply give up your job. But you would be replaced, and the fraudulent operation would continue. So, quitting would not by itself save anyone from being defrauded. Therefore, if you conclude that you must not continue as you have been, in my judgment you need not at once quit. Instead, you should accept the risk of losing the job while making a serious attempt to put an end to the service manager's wrongdoing.

Only you, knowing the facts of the situation and your own strengths and limitations, can decide what action to take. But several possibilities deserve consideration. First, you might talk over the problem with the shop's owner or another superior of the service manager, if any. But perhaps you have no opportunity to speak with a superior, or it appears that any accessible superior also is involved in the fraud. If this approach seems unpromising or does not resolve the problem, you could communicate confidentially with some agency or person who could prove the shop's fraudulent practice and put a stop to it—for example, with the police or other, appropriate public authority. If that does not lead to action that stops the fraud and you still have the job, you could take a crusading approach—for example, carefully select several cases in which the work you do is extensive and the parts removed plainly do not need replacement, save the parts and tag them with the vehicle's license number, and deliver this evidence, along with an explanation of its significance, to a consumer advocacy group or the local newspaper.

124: Must clerical employees give up jobs that involve cheating people?

An old friend and I work for two different mortgage loan companies. A few day. ago, she told me her conscience has been bothering her about her work, and we started comparing notes.

When these companies make a conditional commitment for a loan, they guarantee the interest rate for as long as two months. When rates go up during that time the companies make little or no profit on loans they must make at the locked-in, lower rate. For that reason, when a rate increase is announced, the companies want to delay as many closings as they can until the deadline for the guarantee has passed.

My friend's company is straightforward about delaying closings. One way is to demand a reappraisal—several grounds are mentioned in the fine print of the loan commitment. Another way is to remove from the file and shred one of the harder-to-get required verifications—for instance, one explaining why previous employment ended or showing that a third party's error affected the applicant's credit rating. When the file is checked just before the time set for the closing, it is "found" to be incomplete, and the borrower is asked to supply the missing item. The delay usually means a rescheduled closing at the higher rate.

Every borrower also is assigned to someone in the office and told to contact him or her about any questions. When the company wishes to delay loans, the contact person never is available, questions aren't answered, and the borrowers often make mistakes that delay things. Those who call repeatedly or ask to speak with a supervisor get excuses and are told their contact person will call back in a day or so. The contact person waits two days, then takes steps *not* to reach the borrower— for example, calling his or her home during working hours and leaving a message.

Subtler methods are used where I work. We are not told to remove anything from a file or deceive people. But when an increase is announced, we are required to double check all pending files to make sure each borrower has done everything perfectly. Even the smallest question must be resolved before the loan is made. If there is any gap in the information or a missing verification, or if names and dates do not match up perfectly, we notify the borrower by mail rather than telephone, as we normally would. Preparing the letter usually takes one working day, but when we are busy it can take longer, and then the letter is in the mail a day or two and sometimes more. The letter explains what the problem is and tells the borrower what to do. But it does not mention that failure to act promptly could delay closing beyond the deadline for the locked-in rate. A surprising percentage of people who get such letters ignore them entirely or delay too long in answering, and some get the problem only partly cleared up, requiring another letter and more delay.

My friend and I both deal with borrowers. She finds it very hard being a contact person. People often get angry and act as if the delays were her fault. She cannot explain what is going on and must tell fibs to cover up. Since they don't have the same system where I work, I don't find talking with borrowers particularly unpleasant. But we both feel sorry for people who get loans at a higher rate than they had locked in. Over the mortgage's term, the difference usually adds up to thousands of dollars of additional interest. Still, we need our jobs, though she needs hers more than I need mine. (I used to be the girl Friday for a real estate broker who has several offices in the area, and he has offered me a job as office manager across town at slightly better pay than I now get. But the work would be harder and the commute longer.)

Can we continue doing as we are told so that we can keep our jobs? Or should I change jobs and must my friend start looking for something else?

Analysis:

This question concerns cooperation in fraud. Plainly, the company at which the friend works is gravely violating its promises and defrauding borrowers. Her work involves wrongs—of lying and destroying items in applicant's files—that surely constitute grave matter. She should repent those acts at once, amend her life, and somehow fairly contribute to the restitution due those she has helped defraud. The company at which the questioner works uses procedures each of which could be chosen as means to a legitimate end. But since they are chosen precisely as ways of delaying closings, this company's intent also is to defraud borrowers, but the questioner probably need not cooperate formally. Still, even material cooperation can be wrong, and the questioner almost certainly should change jobs.

The reply could be along the following lines:

A conditional commitment to make a mortgage loan at a guaranteed rate is, morally speaking, a promise. In exchange, applicants pay an application fee; relying on the promise, they seldom seek funding elsewhere. Nevertheless, under certain conditions, anticipated by neither party, a mortgage company might break its promise without injustice—for example, if there were an economic crisis and interest rates suddenly doubled, so that fulfilling loan commitments would be ruinous. When rates increase within normal expectations, however, intentionally delaying closings to avoid making loans at the guaranteed rate deprives borrowers of precisely what they bargained for.[330] Therefore, in trying to delay closings, both companies intend to defraud borrowers, and, morally speaking, when they succeed they steal the extra interest from borrowers.

Apparently wishing to avoid legal liability for its fraudulent practices, your employer limits its delaying tactics to procedures each of which might be used without wrongful intent. Carefully scrutinizing applications and insisting on every detail might be a way of screening out weak or fraudulent applications. It might be cheaper or more effective, though usually slower, to send borrowers letters about problems than to make telephone calls. But any such purposes would be just as relevant when rates are holding steady as when they are rising. So, using these procedures only in the latter circumstance manifests fraudulent intent. Supposing the extra interest imposed on borrowers to be the same, the injustice of the theft is no less than if your employer used the grosser delaying tactics of your friend's company.

Your employer's delaying tactics are such that you can do as you are told without personally doing anything inherently wrong. Though your work contributes to the company's fraud, you need not share its bad intention—to delay closings and defraud borrowers—but can intend simply to earn your pay by applying rules, detecting problems, drafting letters, and so forth.

Even such involvement in another's wrongdoing can be immoral, however, because it can lead to sharing bad intentions, lead others into sin, impair one's

---

330. And what they will pay for—the points and rate specified in the loan commitment include a hedge adequate to cover the risk of an increase in the interest rate; see Stephen R. Rigsbee et al., "Pricing for Profits," *Mortgage Banking,* 52:5 (Feb. 1992): 65–71.

witness to relevant moral truth, and/or be unfair to those injured by the wrongdoing to which it contributes. Your superiors do not direct you and others to remove anything from a file or lie to people, but they make their purpose clear. An employee who wanted to please them might well be tempted, not simply to follow instructions, but to find new ways of delaying closings, thus sharing management's wrongful intention and its guilt for the injustice being done to borrowers. Moreover, even if you do not give in to that temptation, you hardly can openly criticize what management is doing and warn your fellow employees against sharing management's wrongful intention. Your apparently complacent participation might lead those who regard you as a good person to rationalize wholehearted cooperation. And put yourself in the place of borrowers. Wouldn't you think someone in your position—aware of the injustice and able to change jobs rather easily—should make some effort to stop the fraud?

Your friend's moral situation is even worse. She intentionally wrongs borrowers in lying to them and destroying items in their files. Someone might argue that she need not intend to delay closings, but could be doing as she is told just to keep her job, so that her lying and destruction of documents might be only light matter. But I doubt that she can do her job without intending, at least in some cases, to delay the closing. And even if she could, an injustice is not light matter unless a reasonable person suffering it would regard it as negligible (see *LCL,* 319–20). Hardly any defrauded borrower would consider the injury done him or her by your friend's wrongful acts negligible, since they substantially contribute to her employer's fraud.

Besides, even if she could follow orders without precisely intending to defraud borrowers, she could not justify accepting any of the bad effects of her acts which, being morally wrong, cannot themselves be justified. These bad effects include not only the injustice to the borrowers but likely bad consequences of the kinds, already described, resulting from your contribution to your employer's subtler methods. Indeed, some of those consequences are even more likely to follow from your friend's participation in her employer's wrongdoing. She is more likely than you to begin sharing her employer's intention to delay closings, if she has not already. And her involvement is more likely than yours to encourage others, not least her superiors, to rationalize their wrongdoing. Then too—though she might need a lawyer's advice on this point—her own acts perhaps violate laws or governmental regulations. If so, disobeying those laws or regulations almost certainly is grave matter.

I think these considerations make it clear that both of you ought to change jobs. In any case, your friend must never again cooperate in her employer's fraud by doing anything that can be done only with wrongful intent. If either of you think talking with your employer about the fraudulent practices might lead the company either to assign you to other, morally acceptable work or to reform its practices, you should consider that approach. But I assume both of you either will not find it feasible or will not succeed in getting your employers to do either thing.

Perhaps interest rates have not risen recently, so that neither you nor your friend is currently involved in fraudulent practices. In that case, you have some time to look for other jobs. But if your friend currently is involved, prospective hardships, no matter how great, cannot justify continuing the wrongdoing even for one day—even for a minute. I trust she will understand and accept her responsibility to desist at once, since she manifested her concern to avoid sin by telling you her conscience has been bothering her.

Even if your employer is currently engaged in its fraudulent practices, your moral situation is not as bad as your friend's. You may have done nothing wrong or, if you have, you might be able to repent without at once changing jobs. But unless you consider it worthwhile to talk with your employer, I see no reason to delay in accepting the other job available to you, even though it is less desirable in some respects.

Besides changing jobs, you and your friend should try to rectify the injustices in which you have participated. Her obligation is more definite and greater than yours. Having personally wronged borrowers, she ought to contribute to the restitution to which they are entitled—probably by helping them obtain it, but perhaps by paying her fair share of it. Moreover, her employer's fraud, being easier to prove, is more likely to be redressed by legal processes. Both of you may need legal advice. But three possible approaches, not necessarily mutually exclusive, seem worth considering. First, you might—and your friend, given her duty to make restitution, probably should—communicate directly with borrowers who have been recent victims of the fraud, and offer to testify in court if called upon to do so. Second, both of you could present your information about the fraudulent practices to the state's attorney and/or some other public official, if there is one, responsible for regulating the mortgage loan business. Third, you could make the information available to local news media, and perhaps even let them identify you. The latter course would include public repentance of your involvement. It would be quite painful, but it might bring the fraud to an end and lead to rectification of past wrongs. And it would bear credible witness to the relevant moral truth.

125: May a woman take a job handling complaints evasively?

After three years as a secretary in the main office of this city's largest retailer of home furnishings, I have been offered a position handling customer complaints and adjustments at one of the company's stores. I would like to take the job, because it would be nearer to where I live and my take-home pay would be about thirty percent higher.

The company's procedure for handling complaints has four stages, but my job would include only the first two. At first, the customer gets a very cordial hearing, but at the same time every effort is made to put him or her off. In most cases, the customer is advised to study any instructions that came with the item and/or told that the apparent defect or malfunction very likely is normal (which, I have been assured, is statistically correct). If it seems serious, the advice is to seek an adjustment directly from the manufacturer under the warranty. Customers who persist are asked to come in with their paperwork and fill out a form so that "we can look into the problem." But the form is simply filed away, and no action is taken unless the customer presses the complaint. About half do not.

At the second stage, customers who actually press complaints are asked what would satisfy them, then offered a minimal adjustment. The amount never exceeds the company's profit. There is no attempt to judge the merits of a complaint unless that offer is refused and the customer shows real determination—for example, by threatening legal action. That leads to the third stage, where my superior from the main office would step in, examine the complaint and the facts, and try to satisfy the customer with no more than he or she would be likely to win in court. If that fails, the fourth and final stage is to ask the company's legal counsel for advice on minimizing total anticipated costs, including legal fees.

The rationale for all this is that it is economically necessary to be somewhat evasive in handling complaints. They told me that many complaints are either caused by the customer's failure to read and follow directions, or are unreasonable or fraudulent. It is the manufacturer's responsibility, not ours, to resolve any major problems resulting from defects in materials and workmanship, they said. They also assured me that customers whose complaints have substance are likely to press them. Since not only satisfying every demand for an adjustment but even examining every complaint's merits would be too expensive, the first two stages try either to get the customer to drop the matter or, if necessary, resolve it at minimal cost. That would be my job. I have been assured that this procedure has kept litigation to a minimum and resulted in very few interventions on customers' behalf by the state's Consumer Affairs Division. Management thinks this indicates the policy is reasonably fair.

Do you think the procedure is sufficiently fair? Even if it is not fair, could I take the job anyway?

Analysis:

This question calls for application of the norm excluding lying and judgment in accord with the Golden Rule. Though businesses must find efficient ways of dealing with ill-grounded complaints, they must not lie and must be fair to customers with legitimate complaints. The company's procedure for handling complaints is deceptive and unfair to customers with legitimate complaints. Management's argument in defense of the morally flawed procedure is an instance of consequentialism used to rationalize injustice and lying. The job could not be done without deceiving customers and intending to induce some of them to accept unjust settlements, and it often would be an occasion of the sin of lying. So, the questioner may not accept it.

The reply could be along the following lines:

No doubt, many complaints are due to customers' failure to read and follow directions, their unreasonable expectations, or their dishonesty. In establishing policies for handling complaints, the managers of any business therefore must find ways to limit the cost of dealing with those that are ill-grounded in order to safeguard the interests of other participants in the business—other customers, owners, employees, and so on. Still, a morally acceptable method for handling complaints must exclude lying and extend fair treatment to customers, including the less determined ones, with legitimate complaints.

The managers of a business should regard their relationship with customers as cooperative. Authentic cooperation involves mutual understanding, which depends on communication, and that, in turn, requires mutual trust and candor. So, a procedure for handling customers' complaints should involve honest communication, and its stages should facilitate effective cooperation.[331] The description of a procedure meeting these standards could be made available to anyone who needs to file a complaint. But some elements of your employer's approach purposely exclude cooperation with customers in resolving complaints, and the process works only because customers do not realize they are being manipulated.

For upright people, fair is fair. That management regards its policy's success in forestalling legal problems as evidence that it is reasonably fair is a clear sign that the managers regard fairness toward customers, not as a moral requirement, but merely as part of the problem to be dealt with. Holding that view of fairness, management argues that, since its method of handling complaints has sufficed for its own interests, it is reasonably fair. While you would not be asking for moral advice if you were not a conscientious person, management's view seems to have influenced even your thinking, since you ask whether the procedure for handling complaints is sufficiently fair.

Still, I think the real question behind your inquiry is: Does the company's way of handling complaints measure up to moral standards, including the Golden Rule? The answer is no. Anyone can see why by imagining himself or herself in the place of an unassertive, trusting, and uninformed customer with a well-grounded, urgent, and serious complaint.

First, the procedure is deceptive. Saying that an apparent defect or malfunction "very likely" is normal would be truthful if the facts about the particular case warranted it. But when the only basis for making the statement is statistical, it is intended to convey what may well be false. Again, when customers who persist are told to come in and fill out a form so their problem can be looked into, they are led to believe that step will initiate cooperation in resolving the problem; yet the form is filed away and nothing is done unless the customer presses the complaint.

Second, the procedure discriminates among customers, favoring those who are knowledgeable, articulate, and aggressive. Customers must persist and press their complaints to obtain any sort of settlement. The initial settlement offer, not being based on the complaint's merits, inevitably will fall short of fairness in some cases, but only customers who threaten legal action or otherwise show real determination obtain a review.

Third, the procedure plainly is not meant to give customers their due, but to minimize the cost of placating them sufficiently to forestall trouble. Consideration of the merits of complaints is delayed to cut costs; only customers who pose a threat to the company's self-interest are likely to receive satisfaction; complaints, regardless of their merits, are met with resistance; and the prospect of losing a lawsuit, in

---

331. Such a procedure also is necessary to retain or regain customers with complaints; see Rodney L. Cron, *Assuring Customer Satisfaction: A Guide for Business and Industry* (New York: Van Nostrand Reinhold, 1974), especially the treatment of the sources and solutions to customer problems (90–108).

which an injustice could be proved, is the standard used in resolving even the most persistent customers' undeniably legitimate complaints.

The defense of this policy offered by management exemplifies the use of consequentialism to rationalize injustice and lying. The assumption is that treating customers fairly would not be cost effective (it would be "too expensive"), and so profitability, presumed to be a good end, is taken to justify the bad means of manipulating customers. The procedure for handling complaints meets the company's requirements because the deception involved often succeeds and, if it does not, customers whose dissatisfaction would be likely to damage the business usually are satisfied. While the complaints of some customers manifest their own carelessness, unreasonableness, and/or dishonesty, those problems, which have led management to adopt this procedure, obviously cannot justify following it in dealing with reasonable, honest, and careful customers with well-grounded complaints.

May you accept the job despite the system's unfairness? No. You could not succeed without intending to lead customers, by means of the deceptive procedure, to accept settlements that in some cases certainly would be less than fair. Moreover, in some of those cases the matter will be grave. Then too, in carrying out your role, you often would be tempted to lie, since some people would ask you to explain why their complaints were not being dealt with more straightforwardly, and a truthful answer would undermine the procedure.

If your present secretarial work does not require you to participate in the company's wrongdoing, you need not resign. Still, you should consider whether your other responsibilities would permit you to risk your job or give it up. If so, you should perhaps explain to your superiors why you are not accepting the promotion and urge them to adopt a fair procedure for handling complaints in place of the present one. If that seems pointless or has no effect, consider trying to stop the injustice—for example, by reporting what is going on to appropriate public officials, calling it to the attention of consumer groups, or urging the public media to investigate. Indeed, even if you dare not risk your job, you might communicate anonymously or confidentially with the state's Consumer Affairs Division or some other agency that could put a stop to the wrongdoing.

126: May a desk clerk implement a hotel's devious pricing strategy?

I work weekends at the front desk of a large hotel in a major city. This is a second job, but I really need it, because my wife had to quit work to stay home and take care of our baby. However, I have some qualms of conscience about the way this hotel and many others use discounts to boost occupancy rates.

Every unit that goes unoccupied for a night represents an irrecoverable loss of income to a hotel. Low occupancy also cuts profits, or even results in losses, on food and beverage services, and reduces other revenue. In the short run, renting rooms or suites at anything over the cost of making them up and handling the accounts produces more—sometimes much more—income than not renting at all.

Still, no hotel wants to appear entirely flexible about rates, or else everyone would demand a very low rate whenever space is plentiful.

A unit's full listed price is called the "rack rate." Most people realize it is subject to various discounts. But few realize that many hotels, including this one, will extend discounts beyond their stated conditions if necessary to improve occupancy. For example, when we have plenty of units available, you need not be employed by any government to get the "government employees' rate." There also is a rock-bottom rate, at this hotel called "the Manager's Award rate."

Even when we do not expect to fill up—and we seldom fill up on weekends—many people have advance reservations at an agreed price, and they usually pose no problem. But if people looking for a bargain call us directly to register for the same night or come to the desk without a guaranteed reservation, we try to register them at the highest rate we can. People vary a lot in aggressiveness and sophistication about bargaining. Ordinarily, no matter how many open units we have, we first offer the rack rate. Many accept it, or just ask for discounts always given to people who qualify and ask for them—for example, the ten percent discount for AAA and AARP members. Others insist on a better rate or say they will try elsewhere if we do not give them a more attractive deal. So, as necessary, we offer to register them at a deeper discount or on a half-price plan, even if they do not meet the conditions. Occasionally, people ignore the rack rate, or don't even ask about it, and simply tell us what accommodations they want and how much they are prepared to pay, and we offer a rate somewhat above their proposal, generally for a better unit. The policy is not to give the Manager's Award rate to most people. But when space is plentiful, we offer it as a last resort to register people whose patronage we particularly want: those who are obviously well off or whose previous record with us suggests they will run up a sizable bill.

We have been trained never to lie about rates. Saying "I can give you (or: We have available) such and such a unit at so many dollars per night" neither invites bargaining nor rules it out. But the results often seem unfair. During one half-hour stretch last Saturday afternoon I put an elderly couple without a reservation in a standard double at $161.10 (the rack rate of $179 less ten percent seniors' discount), checked a couple with two children into a similar room they had reserved two weeks in advance and prepaid at a weekend rate of $109, and was bargained down to a half-price deal, $99.50 for a deluxe room, by someone calling on the direct line from the airport. Then I gave the Manager's Award rate of $79 for a suite ($499 rack rate) to a man who turned down other offers; he was well dressed and wearing an expensive watch, and the doorman told me on the intercom that a woman in a mink jacket was waiting outside in their new Mercedes convertible.

This sort of thing never used to trouble my conscience, though I sometimes have been tempted to let people know they could get a better rate. But recently I went on a retreat. The theme was love of neighbor, and it occurred to me that treating people so differently, based on how aggressive and sophisticated they happen to be, does not seem in line with loving them as I love myself. The retreat included some group discussion, and I brought up the problem. A businessman making the retreat with me argued that hotels are not taking advantage of people who do not get the better deals but are being taken advantage of by those who do, just as creditors strapped for cash are taken advantage of by debtors who know of the problem and demand deep discounts for paying what they owe. I am not sure what to think about that, but I still feel uneasy.

Analysis:

This question concerns cooperation in deception. Hotels that propose negotiable rates as if they were fixed are unfair to people insofar as that marketing strategy is deceptive. Given that the questioner does not lie to people who ask him about the hotel's rates, however, what he does in implementing the hotel's marketing strategy is to be evaluated by the usual norms for cooperation. It does not seem to be formal cooperation, and as material cooperation it might be morally acceptable. In general, he should do his job as he has agreed, but when he judges it fair to all concerned he should give people who fail to bargain the discounts they could get by bargaining. Love of neighbor perhaps also should impel him to do something to overcome or mitigate the unjust structure in which he is involved.

The reply could be along the following lines:

The view that people who bargain aggressively take advantage of the hotel implies that they get unfairly low rates. That would be so if an insolvent hotel's vulnerability were exploited by hard bargainers to rent space for less than the hotel could obtain if its cash flow were adequate. In that case, the businessman's analogy would be sound. However, it does not hold true for the situation you describe, which depends on the economic condition of the commodity rather than the need of a party to the transaction. Even the most profitable business is vulnerable to bargaining if supplies of its products or services obviously exceed demands, and this vulnerability is accentuated whenever the service or product will quickly lose its value if not sold. For example, merchants selling highly perishable foods in great oversupply must either reduce prices for quick sale, donate the merchandise, or let it spoil. The vulnerability of hotels during periods of light occupancy is similar. Of course, like other profitable businesses confronting a similar problem, most hotels can charge enough when the good they market is scarce to make up for their discounts when it is in oversupply.

The hotel need not be taking advantage of people merely by offering similar accommodations at diverse prices, even though some pay considerably more than others.[332] The differences can be justified insofar as they are necessary to make a reasonable profit under various conditions affecting the volume and predictability of sales and payments. Marketing hotel units is similar in this respect to marketing airline seats. The difference is that your hotel, like many others, regularly undercuts its own published rates in the ways you explain, whereas the airlines, though they sometimes engage in other ethically questionable marketing practices, for the most part adhere to their published fares. To obtain a certain airfare, one almost always must meet and accept the stated conditions, and ad hoc bargaining is generally excluded; but when space is plentiful, rates for many hotel units, though proposed

---

332. On why justice does not require the same prices for everyone, see q. 146, below.

to the public as if they were fixed prices, are only a point of departure for bargaining by well-informed people prepared to bargain.[333] This marketing strategy, in my judgment, is unfair to people unaware that the seemingly fixed prices actually are negotiable.

Someone might argue that this strategy, used by many hotels, differs little from that used by other businesses whose list prices, though open to bargaining, are stated without any indication that other offers will be considered. But even though many businesses do not call attention to the fact that they are prepared to bargain, some do nothing to deceive anyone about that possibility, so that it is generally understood. By contrast, the marketing strategy you describe (which some businesses other than hotels also employ), by offering various discounted rates subject to specific conditions, intentionally suggests that lower rates are unavailable unless the stated conditions are met. Therefore, this strategy is deceptive, and, as you say, unsophisticated people are likely to be deceived.

Like any other business, a hotel should regard its patrons as associates cooperating in a common economic enterprise. Cooperation presupposes candid communication, and a hotel using a deceptive marketing strategy should replace it with a forthright one. Its goal should be to maximize occupancy in order to increase not only income but service to the public, by minimizing the waste that occurs when usable space goes unused.[334]

Of course, as an employee without managerial authority, you cannot make the ethically required change in the hotel's policy. Meanwhile, you need this weekend job. May you keep it and continue implementing the hotel's morally flawed policy?

You would have to give up the job if you were required to lie, but you say you are trained not to do that. You answer honestly if someone asks for the lowest available rate for a certain type of accommodation. Besides not lying, however, you must not share management's intention to deceive. You carry out the hotel's marketing strategy by proposing rates in the same way whether or not bargains are available, and by bargaining only when asked to do so. However, you need not choose to do anything to deceive potential guests or keep them unaware that they could bargain. Rather, you accept their deception as an existing condition, within which you work. Therefore, though your work implements the company's deceptive strategy, you need not intend the deception.

Such involvement in others' wrongdoing also can be wrong, of course, because it can lead one to intend the wrong, lead others into sin, impair one's witness to relevant moral truth, or be unfair to those injured by the wrong. Given your conscientious concern, however, I do not think your involvement is likely to develop into sharing your employer's bad intention. Because the wrong involved in the deception is embedded in the hotel's policy, what you do in implementing it

333. For an explanation of the marketing strategy, see C. DeWitt Coffman, *Marketing for a Full House: A Complete Guide to Profitable Hotel/Motel Operational Planning,* ed. Helen J. Recknagel (Ithaca, N.Y.: Cornell University School of Hotel Administration, 1972), 149–62.

334. Comparing the workability and profitability of possible forthright alternatives, including those currently employed by some hotels and/or other businesses, pertains to management technique rather than ethics.

is not likely to lead others into sin or impair your witness. And because you need your job and giving it up would not affect the hotel's unfairness, your involvement in its wrongdoing does not seem unfair to the victims.

You speak of being tempted to let people know they could get a better rate. Realizing now that the hotel's marketing strategy is unjust, that temptation is likely to grow stronger. In general, do not give in to it. If you regularly give people lower rates, management surely will begin asking questions. Lying would be wrong, and admitting that you regularly violate the rules is likely to cause you to lose the job, which you need to support your wife and baby. Moreover, having undertaken to follow the rules, regularly violating them would be a breach of faith with your employer, not justified by the fact that the rules implement an unjust strategy. Inasmuch as what you do is justifiable, having promised to do it, you should keep your promise. Still, a promise may be broken if doing so is fair to all concerned, and occasionally it will be clear that potential patrons need a rate lower than the rate they would be willing to accept, that your employer would wrong those particular people by exacting the higher rate, and that you can help them obtain what they deserve without unduly risking your job. Only in such cases should you give the lower rate.

More generally, you probably should try to do something about the deceptive marketing strategy itself. As with other injustices, if you can rather easily take some action likely to overcome or significantly mitigate it, you should do so out of love of neighbor. For example, if your employer welcomes employee suggestions, you might consider saying that a more candid marketing strategy might serve and satisfy larger numbers of people, thereby winning their continuing patronage and increasing the hotel's regular clientele. Again, when enough people learn about the deceptive marketing strategy, it no longer will be effective, and you might help hasten that day by looking for ways of publicizing it. You can judge whether you ought to take any such action by considering its probable burdens for you and benefits to the public, and applying the Golden Rule.

127: May employees allow an employer's defects or wrongdoing to hurt others?

I am a bookkeeper in a real estate office where the broker has had a problem with alcohol that has been getting worse during the five years I've worked for him. Young men and women planning to start their careers here invest time, energy, and money in getting their real estate licenses, only to discover that they did not make the wisest choice. What should I do when someone asks about coming to work in our office? Am I obligated to tell the truth and say "If I were you I'd run for my life"? Is it my obligation to protect my employer's business or is it my responsibility to try to warn these young agents? My head tells me to go with my employer, my heart with the young agents.

I have a friend with a similar problem. She is office manager for an electrical contractor struggling to stay in business, who makes low bids on jobs he cannot do properly for his price, then cheats to make a profit. That sometimes means bribing an inspector to approve work that violates the code. The cheating on larger jobs can run into thousands of dollars. My friend manages to avoid lying to people by listening to their complaints, noting them, and referring them to her employer. But she wonders whether she should say something to customers who are being cheated that would help them get what they paid for without having to pay more than they originally agreed.

These problems are not easy for us. I am a widow and my friend is single. We must support ourselves, and so we do not feel we can simply quit and start looking for better jobs. Anyway, we might face very similar problems with other employers.

Analysis:

This question calls for application of the norms regarding admonishing apparent sinners and lying; with respect to the friend, there also is a question about cooperating in fraud. Though the broker may be failing to fulfill some of his responsibilities, the questioner is not cooperating in his wrongdoing. The electrical contractor is defrauding customers, and the questioner's friend is cooperating at least materially. Both employees should admonish their employers. If the questioner's employer is alcoholic, she probably should make additional efforts to motivate him to acknowledge and deal with his problem. Meanwhile, if potential employees ask questions, she may not lie, but she need not advise anyone against accepting employment. Applying the criteria for evaluating material cooperation, the questioner's friend may not continue cooperating with her employer's fraud.

The reply could be along the following lines:

While your problem and your friend's are similar in some respects, they also differ in ways that are, morally speaking, crucial. Your employer's alcohol problem may prevent him from fulfilling some of his responsibilities to young agents and other people, and that may more or less seriously inconvenience or harm those concerned. But he is not committing fraud as your friend's employer is, assuming you describe the situation accurately. Moreover, while as bookkeeper you need not be directly involved in the relationship between your employer and the young agents and others, your friend, as office manager, becomes directly involved in the relationship between her employer and his defrauded customers when she handles their complaints.

Still, you and your friend have one common responsibility: to admonish these apparent sinners (see *LCL*, 227–32). You should talk with your employers about the problems you perceive. For both seem to be sinning in different ways, with consequent harm to others, themselves, and their businesses. The broker's alcohol abuse not only hurts the young agents and perhaps others with whom he does business but is self-destructive, while the contractor's cheating injures customers, risks criminal prosecution, undermines his self-respect as a skilled project manager, and will destroy his reputation, without which his business can hardly do well in the long run. Each of you therefore should talk matters over with your employer at a time when he is likely to be receptive and the conversation will not be overheard or interrupted. The advice should be to face up to the misbehavior and rectify it—which, in your friend's case, would require ending the fraud and making restitution to all those who have been cheated. Both of you should avoid being or sounding self-righteous, reproachful, or threatening; your tone should be concerned, realistic about the problem, and constructive, pointing hopefully toward the prospective benefits of following your advice—benefits for your employers, their businesses, and the people they deal with.

What if you admonish, or already have admonished, your employer about his alcohol abuse without effect? You say he has "a problem with alcohol," but that can describe a broad spectrum of behavior. Since you still are and, apparently, expect to be employed in this broker's office, his problem plainly is not so incapacitating that he no longer functions at all. Have you perhaps misjudged the seriousness of his problem so that you now are exaggerating it? If that is a possibility, you should learn more about alcoholism. If it is already clear to you, or becomes clear from further investigation, that your employer really is an alcoholic who needs help, it may be that you should confidentially communicate that conclusion, along with your concrete reasons for it, to his family and/or others closer to him than you are. Then they, or they and you acting in concert, might effectively confront him about his problem and motivate him to get the help he needs.

Whatever the broker's drinking problem may be—genuine alcoholism or something else—you have some responsibility as an associate to try to help him and as an employee to protect the business. You will be acting on those responsibilities by doing what you can and should do to help him acknowledge and deal appropriately with the problem.

Meanwhile, when someone asks about coming to work there, you certainly should not lie to them, for example, by saying: "There is no reason to be concerned," when you believe there is. It is not clear, however, that you would be telling the truth if you said, "If I were you I'd run for my life," since you have not done that yourself. Like you, at least some of the young agents might have adequate reasons to accept work with this broker, even if they foresaw problems, since they may have no better opportunity, at least until they get some experience. Therefore, respond to their worries honestly, but with the reserve of a loyal employee, saying something like: "It's not my place to advise you about coming to work here; you need to evaluate the significance of whatever has aroused your concern and make your own decision." That would reveal little, but it would be genuinely helpful, since it would implicitly acknowledge that there are grounds for reservations about coming to work in this office, while suggesting that these need not necessarily be considered conclusive.

Morally speaking, your friend's situation is far more perilous than yours. She is closely involved in her employer's fraud and may be tempted to further it. If she chooses not to do something she should do to expose it, she incurs some moral responsibility for it; if she chooses to do anything to prevent its detection while nothing is being done to end it, she intends that it succeed and shares in her employer's bad will. Even if she does nothing to further the fraud, not doing what she can to put an end to it is, in my judgment, unfair to the victims. When inspectors must be bribed to pass defective electrical work, not only property but people are endangered. Then too, the fraudulent practices almost certainly violate the law, and she might even be charged as an accomplice. And while it is true that she is likely to encounter some moral problems no matter where she works, it is not true that every business involves its office manager in fraudulent practices. Therefore, if your friend fails to persuade her employer to stop defrauding customers and to begin making restitution to everyone he has cheated, she should promptly discuss his activities with the police and/or other relevant authorities—such as a licensing body or consumer affairs department—in hopes of putting a stop to his fraud, and, whether that effort succeeds or not, should get a job elsewhere. That might have bad consequences for her, but the alternative—complicity in serious injustice—is likely to have worse consequences: "Do you not know that wrongdoers will not inherit the kingdom of God?" (1 Cor 6.9).

128: Must an engineer warn the government about a life-threatening safety problem?

I help design airplanes. My company is the design subcontractor for an airframe manufacturer now about to start building and delivering a new, wide-bodied plane we have been helping develop for six years. Despite the fact that the plane is about to be certified by the Federal Aviation Administration (FAA), I am convinced it has a design defect that, if not corrected, probably will result sooner or later in serious accidents.

I made my concerns known to my superiors from the earliest stages, and our company's management met our obligations as a subcontractor by urging the manufacturer to correct the problem. We were rebuffed, but my analysis was verified by an accident that happened while a prototype was being tested on the ground. That led to some modifications, but I consider them worse than inadequate; in some ways they actually increase the risk.

When the certification process was about to begin, I once more summarized the problem for my immediate superior; he agreed with my analysis, and again made the case to our top management. They again urged the airframe manufacturer to correct the defect, and again were rebuffed. Our people are not happy with the situation, but feel there is nothing more they can do, since our contract makes it clear that the manufacturer bears sole responsibility for ultimate design decisions, and forbids our company to communicate directly with the government authorities.

I hoped the FAA would refuse certification, but now it is clear that the manufacturer has sold them on the plane's safety and they are going to certify. I fear that will mean the death of some people, perhaps hundreds. Within my company, there is nothing more I can do; my only course would be to violate company policy by going directly to the FAA. If I do, I might as well also contact the communications media. I think there would be some—but not much—chance the FAA will delay certification until adequate modifications have been made.

Must I personally take responsibility for trying to stop certification by giving my analysis of the design defect to the FAA? I probably would lose my job. Openings in my field are few, and an individual known to have unilaterally violated a company's policies is hardly likely to get one. I am forty-five, and my four children are lined up to go to college.

I have no desire to be a hero and will make this sacrifice only if convinced I must. My wife says not to do it. But I hate the prospect of hearing on the news: "An airliner has crashed with the loss of everyone aboard, three hundred and . . .."

Analysis:

The moral issue for this questioner is one of fairness. He should consider not only the diverse goods at stake but the likelihood that lives will be saved or lost, on the one hand, and that his family will be harmed or protected, on the other, assuming he proceeds on each of the available options. He should then judge between (or among) the options by applying the Golden Rule, and act according to that judgment. If he judges that fairness requires him to try to prevent certification, it will not be supererogatory self-sacrifice but his duty to do that; if, judging that he should protect his family's interests, he refrains from acting and the defect results in a disaster, he will not be responsible for the lost lives.

The reply could be along the following lines:

You do well to ask this question, and it really is difficult.[335] Since far more people sometimes fly on airplanes than ever support their families by work like yours, most people probably would tell you that you plainly must make the sacrifice. At the same time, people in positions like yours all too often take it for granted that moral responsibilities in connection with their work end when they have carried out the duties in their job description. While love of neighbor does not demand that you forget your responsibilities toward your family, it plainly calls for the broader view of work related responsibilities that you are taking.

Perhaps your employer should have violated the terms of its contract with the airframe manufacturer and delivered your case against certification to the FAA. But even if the company failed to do its duty, it does not follow that you have a duty to try to save the lives at risk. If your employer is neglecting its duty, not only are its responsibility and yours separate and distinct but what you did should have been sufficient to prevent its negligence. And though your employer perhaps could have stopped the certification, your chances of stopping it are poorer.

Generally, a company's employees should obey its policies and cooperate in fulfilling its contracts with other firms. Provided the policies and contracts are in themselves just, only serious reasons can override an employee's responsibilities and justify him or her in taking independent action. Loyal employees bear their responsibilities in mind and do not lightly set them aside. As you point out, your superiors, having decided to do nothing more about the problem, are

335. The question as stated is fictional but drawn (with simplifications of the technical and other complexities) from a real case; see Paul Eddy, Elaine Potter, and Bruce Page, *Destination Disaster: From the Tri-Motor to the DC–10: The Risk of Flying* (New York: Quadrangle, 1976), esp. 122–251. For a fuller and worthwhile discussion of the general problem the question presents, with sound criticism of alternative responses, see Mike W. Martin, "Whistleblowing: Professionalism, Personal Life, and Shared Responsibility for Safety in Engineering," *Business and Professional Ethics Journal,* 11:2 (Summer 1992): 21–40.

likely to regard further action by you as disloyal, and so would the managers of other companies in your field.

However, loyalty is not merely steadfastness but a virtue, and as such it never requires anything at odds with other moral responsibilities. If there truly is a significant probability that your going directly to the FAA would save many peoples' lives, it seems to me you would not be disloyal in violating company policy and the terms of its contract with the airframe manufacturer. But, besides the issue of loyalty, your question raises an issue of fairness between your family and the people who might die in a disaster. To judge what you should do, you must consider two things distinctly and very carefully: the likelihood that your intervention would save lives and the likelihood that it would seriously harm your family. Then you must apply the Golden Rule.

First, just how likely is it that your going directly to the FAA would save lives? Presumably the officials who are about to certify the plane have considered the problem with some care, and people who have made up their minds about such matters generally are not easily dissuaded from acting on their conclusions. I think you should ask yourself whether you may be mistaken about one or more of three things: the seriousness of the safety problem, the probability that it will cause the loss of lives if the plane is certified, and the likelihood that your intervention at this stage will keep the plane from being certified until the problem is corrected.

Second, just how likely is it that your going directly to the FAA will lead to great harm to your family? The chances of losing your job and being unable to get another in your field may be great if you act openly and do not warn your superiors. But if the government authorities are receptive to what you tell them, they may do what they can to protect you, and the managers of your company, if they truly are unhappy with the situation, might be prepared to tolerate your doing what you believe you must. These considerations suggest that you might communicate confidentially with the government authorities; or you might take into your confidence the highest manager in your company you have confidence in and can speak with, and warn him or her that you believe you must try to block certification. Also, even if you do lose your present job, you might be more successful than you expect in finding other suitable employment.

Having determined (as well as you can) how likely independent action by you is to save lives and how likely it is to result in great harm to your family, you must apply the Golden Rule. Of course, if you think of more than one way to try to prevent certification and the two (or more) differ in potential effectiveness and/or riskiness, you should consider each separately.

Perhaps, with respect to some possible way of acting, you will judge that someone like you in an analogous situation would be obliged to accept the risk of similar harm to his or her own family in order to save the lives of many strangers including your loved ones. Then it will be your duty to act either in that way or some other more likely to be effective; and doing so will not be optional heroism beyond the call of duty. In such a case you should act, entrusting your family to God's providence.

But perhaps you will judge, with respect to every way of acting you can think of, that another person in a similar situation would be obliged to put his or her family's interests first, even though taking action might prevent the death of many people, including your loved ones. Then you should refrain from acting and entrust those whose lives will be at risk to God's providence. If a disaster does occur, do not consider it your fault but rather the fault of others whose responsibility for the airplane's safety is more immediate and greater than yours—the managers of the airframe manufacturing company seeking certification, the government officials granting it, and even the management of your company.

129: May an employee obediently carry on a pointless and wasteful dispute?

I work for a large contractor. Most of our contracts are with the federal government. The projects we participate in always involve other primary contractors—neither of us is the other's subcontractor. Coordination problems often come up, and my job is to deal with them. I am the first woman this company has hired for this job, and I am determined to succeed.

Generally, all the primary contractors are paid on a cost-plus basis, which results in a great deal of waste.[336] That bothers me, and I feel somewhat guilty whenever I am directly involved.

Here is a current example. We and another contractor have been arguing about whether we owe them one-half of an outside consultant's fee. Our superintendent at a job site agreed to their getting the consultant's opinion on a problem affecting both of us, but nothing was said about the fee, and they simply assumed we would reimburse them for half. The amount at issue is $987.50, and the time spent investigating what happened and carrying on the dispute already has cost each side more than that. Either of us could charge off the disputed amount along with all the other reimbursable costs. But because the government is paying for carrying on the dispute, neither cares to give in. I will meet next Monday with my counterpart to deal with a number of issues. The $987.50 item is on the agenda, and, once more, the accounting department has instructed me not to concede it. But if we did, we would make our usual profit on the item, and it would cost us nothing but the profit we are making on the cost of carrying on the dispute and wasting the taxpayers' money. So, plainly, we ought to concede the item.

But what am I to do? If I concede it despite instructions, the head of accounting will be irritated. Nothing will come of it this time. I have been doing a good job resolving many real problems, and the company is cautious about disciplining female employees. But every meeting's agenda includes one or two items that ought to be conceded, and if I regularly violate instructions, eventually I will be fired. If I am, that will have no effect on the waste. It obviously is a pervasive part of doing business when payment is on a cost-plus basis, and my replacement almost certainly would accept the waste without a qualm.

336. *Cost-plus basis:* a method of determining the amount contractors will be paid for goods and/or services; the contractor is reimbursed its costs plus a specified rate of profit.

Analysis:

This question concerns cooperation in waste. If carrying out the managers' unreasonable instructions requires intrinsically evil actions, the questioner must not carry them out and, if necessary, must give up her job. If the managers continue to give irrational instructions and the questioner can carry them out without doing anything intrinsically evil, in my opinion she can rightly accept the waste as a side effect, though the managers wrongly accept it. She materially cooperates in actions that are objectively wrong, but this cooperation seems justified.

The reply could be along the following lines:

You do not say whether you can carry out the instructions without doing anything wrong in itself, such as lying. If you cannot, you must not do as instructed, regardless of the consequences, even if they include giving up your job. What follows presupposes that you need not do anything wrong in itself, and your only concern is the irrationality of some of your instructions.

Like any waste, the waste that concerns you is morally evil for several reasons. Anything wasted should have been put to other, better use. The costs are unfairly imposed on some person or group, and some person or group is deprived of the benefits of a right use of what is wasted. Moreover, and most important, since all the means we sometimes waste are provided by God for good uses, wasting them always is irreverent toward God.

Wastefully carrying on pointless disputes of the sort you describe is so obviously irrational that I wonder whether the people directing your work have reasons they do not share with you for pressing the issues. If you have not tried to communicate with the managers about their seemingly irrational instructions, you should. Without challenging their authority or contesting their instructions about particular matters, you could tell them you assume they have reasons you have not understood for pressing issues when doing so seems wasteful, and point out that you could do a better job for them if you better understood their intentions. You also might tell them you have been troubled by having to dispute items whose payment by the company would be reimbursed by the government and would earn the usual profit.

Since you have done a good job resolving many problems, the managers probably will not react negatively. Instead, they may either explain the reasons for your instructions or stop having you carry on pointless disputes. But you may already have approached the managers and either not received an explanation or had it verified that, sometimes, at least, the instructions really are irrational but will not be changed. Must you give up your job? I do not think so.

Acting as your company's advocate, you need only intend to make the strongest honest case possible for its position and to try to resolve the problems to its advantage. If pressing certain issues is wasteful, you need not intend the waste, since it is a side effect of what you do. Those who give you unreasonable instructions do wrong, at least objectively, in accepting that side effect. But you have a good reason to accept it—you must do as you are told to keep your job and contribute to the good that comes from resolving real problems.

Of course, insofar as you carry out the unreasonable instructions, your work contributes to the managers' objectively wrongful action, and such involvement in others' wrongdoing can be wrong. It can lead one to share the wrongdoers' bad intentions, lead others into sin, be unfair to those injured by the wrong, and/or impair one's witness to relevant moral truth. But you are hardly likely to share the managers' unreasonable intentions, and playing your role in the wasteful system—a well-established, sinful social structure—is not likely to lead others to sin. Since the common good suffers from the waste, it is unfair to the taxpayers; but since you do other needed work and giving up your job would not reduce the waste, you do not contribute to that unfairness. Then too, continuing in your job and excelling in it will permit you to bear witness as credibly as possible within the company to the truth that is being ignored—that waste should be eliminated—while quitting would hardly affect the existing corporate culture.

At the same time, your firsthand experience of the waste, your insight into its unfairness to taxpayers, and your articulateness put you in a good position to bring this matter to public attention, and public awareness of the evil might generate demands for corrective measures. As a citizen, you ought to promote the common good. Try, then, to find effective ways of publicizing the waste and calling for its elimination. Of course, this responsibility should be carried out in harmony with your other responsibilities, so that among possible courses of action you must conscientiously judge which is or are appropriate for you to pursue.

130: Must an employee abide by an agreement limiting postemployment activities?

I am employed by a family business—not my own family, I hasten to add. We act as intermediaries between European and Japanese suppliers and U.S. buyers, mainly smaller manufacturers and wholesale distributors, but also some large, independent retailers. I am vice-president in charge of the section handling home furnishings, decorating accessories, and fabrics. We do not buy and sell goods, but serve as agent; negotiate contracts, make shipping and delivery arrangements, and so on. Usually we are paid by the vendor, who includes our commission in the selling price; occasionally we serve as a buyer's agent, and are paid for our time and expenses.

I went to work here right after graduating from college seventeen years ago. After eight years' experience, I got my present position when the son who was being groomed for it broke with the family and went to work elsewhere. Now two of my staff and I are thinking about leaving and starting our own import brokerage, specializing in the sorts of goods our section handles. If we do, I expect that about a dozen other employees—most of the people in our section—will want to join us.

There are several reasons for leaving. Younger members of the family are coming into the business, and, while I am not worried about being let go, I have no prospect of advancement. Then too, when I became a vice-president, I asked the owners to base my pay on my section's profitability. But they said no, and my pay has gone up less than half as fast as the section's profit, much of which is due to business I personally brought in. Though I will earn over two hundred thousand dollars this year, the company gives few benefits and is strict with my expenses. Last year they did away with company cars, and I had to buy one for myself, since my wife and children need the family car. Meanwhile, family members draw high pay, write off exorbitant expenses, and take out all the profit rather than reinvesting to expand the business. Moreover, the owners always have been autocratic, and in recent years they have frequently overruled my business decisions.

The only problem with starting our own brokerage is a "Trade Secrets Agreement." One Monday morning, about five years after I came to work here, the owners presented every employee with a document by that name, and told us that, if we did not sign by Wednesday, we would be given thirty days notice. Things were going well at the time, and I signed without much concern. Since then, all new employees have been required to sign the same document as a condition of employment. It includes this statement: "During my employment and for two years after its termination, I will not call on, solicit or take away, or attempt to call on, solicit or take away any of the clients of [the firm] with whom I become acquainted or of whom I learn during my employment, either on my own behalf or on behalf of any other person, firm or corporation." The word *clients* is defined to include all parties to any transaction in which the brokerage has served or is serving as broker or agent.

Adhered to strictly, this agreement would keep me from doing business for two years with any of the suppliers and buyers who know and respect me. However, I have been told by a lawyer that though the agreement is legally valid, the family probably would not win a lawsuit to enforce it. Still, I want to do the right thing. Must I abide by the agreement?

Analysis:

This question concerns the moral obligation to keep a contractual promise. Various conditions can make breaking a promise morally acceptable, but none of those conditions seems to be fulfilled in this case. If there are grounds for thinking that keeping the promise would be unfairly burdensome, the questioner in evaluating them should exclude inappropriate feelings. The moral obligation to abide by a contractual agreement does not depend on its enforceability at law. However, precisely what was promised does depend on the meaning of the agreement's wording, and a reasonable interpretation of that wording, which probably can be found in relevant case law, will clarify the obligation the questioner undertook in signing the agreement. He also should consider alternatives to either continuing in his present job or violating the agreement.

The reply could be along the following lines:

In signing the Trade Secrets Agreement, you made a promise to your employer in contractual form. Your main question is: Would it be morally wrong to break it? Fairness generally requires keeping promises, not least those in contractual form, but various things can justify or require breaking even such a promise (see *LCL,* 412–14). In your case, however, only two of them seem to me relevant—that the promise might have been made under duress and that keeping it might be unfairly burdensome, due to a great change in the conditions you reasonably anticipated when you made it.

Were you coerced into making the promise? Your employer did present you with a choice between signing and giving up your job. But, in my judgment, that did not constitute coercion. Very often, a contracting party's alternative to making an agreement is repugnant, but that constitutes coercion only if the other party takes unfair advantage of the lack of a better alternative, and apparently your employers were not doing that. The commitment you were asked to make merely specified your general responsibilities to be a loyal employee and refrain from using your position to enrich yourself at your employer's expense beyond your agreed compensation for your work. Moreover, you were not disinclined to sign; as you say, things were going well and you signed without much concern. Then too, you had two days to consider the matter, and had you chosen to give up your job, you would have had a month to look for another.

Are conditions now so different from those you reasonably anticipated back then that keeping the agreement would impose an unfair burden on you? Nothing you say indicates that. There has been a change, but it is in your relationship with the owners and your job satisfaction, not in other conditions that make keeping your promise more onerous.

You might argue that the owners have been treating you unfairly, that their unfairness requires you to give up your job, that your responsibilities require you to earn an amount available only if you start your own brokerage, that you cannot successfully do that if you abide by the agreement, and that you could not reasonably have anticipated this situation. That argument would be sound if its premises were true, but I very much doubt that the facts support them all. Perhaps the owners are greedy and disagreeable, but have they been treating you unfairly? If so, why have you not sought other employment during the twelve years since you signed the agreement? Any unfairness you are suffering may be tolerable—with an income over two hundred thousand dollars a year, you should be able to tolerate a good deal. But even if the situation becomes intolerable, you might be able to earn adequate income without starting your own brokerage, or else by doing so without breaking your promise. Moreover, and most important, it seems to me that, in signing the agreement, you almost certainly should have anticipated precisely the sort of situation you now confront.

Of course, there may be facts besides those you have mentioned that incline you to think changed conditions have made it unfairly burdensome to abide by your agreement. If so, you must apply the Golden Rule and conscientiously judge whether you, as owner of a similar business, would consider your employees dispensed from keeping a similar promise in a similar situation. In making that judgment, take care to exclude feelings that might bias it: resentment toward your employers, envy of their wealth, the sheer desire to increase your income (see *CCC,* 2535–40; *LCL,* 781–82).

The lawyer's opinion, that the owners probably would not win a lawsuit to enforce the agreement, calls for two comments. First, even if the contract is not legally enforceable, you may have a moral duty to abide by it, since moral responsibilities pertaining to legal duties often extend beyond what could be legally enforced. Second, even successfully defending yourself against a legal action could cost so much time, energy, and money that your attempt to start your own brokerage would be hampered, perhaps fatally, with great damage to you and your associates.

However, good legal advice probably would help in a different way to clarify your moral responsibility. In signing the document, you promised no less, but also no more, than the words on the page signify. That language or language quite similar to it probably has been used in similar agreements that have been adjudicated. Since the document plainly was meant to create a legal obligation, you can reasonably take the law's interpretation of the language as its real meaning. Thus, careful research in the relevant case law probably would determine precisely what you promised, and so indicate what you might do without breaking your promise.

That would be helpful. It would clarify the precise moral obligation you assumed in signing the agreement. It might reveal that you are mistaken in supposing the agreement bars you from doing business with the buyers and suppliers who know and respect you. For example, perhaps the agreement does not prevent you from sending a simple notice announcing your new brokerage and describing its services to many potential suppliers and buyers, including your present employer's clients. The agreement also might allow you to maintain contacts and cultivate relationships with clients during the two-year period, so that when it was up you could immediately start doing business with them. Even if the agreement precludes such things, perhaps it would not bar you from doing business with clients who spontaneously approached you after learning from some third party, not your agent, that you had gone into business for yourself.

If starting your own brokerage while abiding by your contractual agreement seems hopeless, consider alternatives. You could try again to negotiate more satisfactory terms of employment with the family, or look for a more suitable position with some other employer for whom you could use your talents and experience without violating the agreement. You might be able to start an independent import brokerage specializing in products your present employer does not handle, and serving other suppliers and buyers.

Negotiating before a conflict occurs almost always is more consonant with love of neighbor than taking action likely to generate a conflict that will antagonize and burden both parties. So, if you decide to try to start your own brokerage, you probably should try first to obtain the family's consent. For a share in your future profits or some other price, they might allow you and your associates to separate your division from their company. The prospects of that probably will be helped if well-researched legal advice makes it clear that the agreement you signed would be difficult to enforce, though it would be wrong to use that difficulty to obtain a new agreement that a fair-minded partner in the negotiation would not otherwise make with you.

Finally, God plainly has given you a great deal of talent, and you should be doing your best to use it well, not only to provide for your family but to serve others. If you do start your own brokerage, do not make maximizing profit the supreme end of the enterprise. Conduct your business as a form of lay apostolate, seek above all to bear witness to your Christian faith and hope, and put love into action (see AA 7–8, 16–17). Certainly you must seek a fair return for your work and on your investment, but you also should strive for efficient cooperation among all those involved in the business—employees, clients, and so on—and a fair share of benefits for each. Moreover, if you are the sole owner and chief manager, go beyond the requirements of justice to the extent that your responsibilities to others permit, and exercise Christian mercy. For example, you might offer your services to suppliers in third-world nations, even if their business would be less profitable than the business of first-world suppliers you are accustomed to dealing with.

131: May a man use an executive-training program to prepare for another job?

I am completing my Master of Business Administration degree and am engaged to a wonderful woman. She is the only surviving child in her family, because her three brothers and a sister were killed two years ago when a small plane, piloted by the eldest brother, crashed. Her father owns and manages a fairly large business, and he already has told me he hopes I will come to work for him and eventually take over as chief executive officer. But first, he thinks, I should work elsewhere for a few years to get experience.

There are various possibilities. The most appealing would be a stint with a major corporation in its executive-training program. I probably could make more money elsewhere while still gaining useful experience, but I doubt that anything else would provide such a solid background. My professors assure me that with my record and their recommendations, I am almost certain to get more than one attractive offer from corporations with good training programs.

Many executive trainees switch jobs when they have a few years experience, just as their training begins to pay off for the employer, and I am sure I would do enough useful work to earn my pay. Still, training programs and the opportunities to which they lead obviously are not meant to give people experience so that they can take over their in-laws' businesses, and I plainly would not do enough work to compensate my employer for the cost of training me. I have some qualms of conscience about going this route, but would like to do it. Frankly, I hope you will tell me there is no moral problem!

Analysis:

This question calls for application of norms excluding lying and deception, and judgment by the Golden Rule. The questioner's expectation that he will go to work for his prospective father-in-law does not of itself morally exclude as unfair applying to corporations with good training programs. However, in the application process, the questioner not only must not lie but should communicate candidly to any company that makes it clear it wants to know about his plans. Moreover, he should not apply for any job that probably will generate serious conflicts of interest and duty for him if and when he resigns to work for his father-in-law. Therefore, the questioner should consider the other, less appealing possibilities he refers to but does not describe.

The reply could be along the following lines:

I do not think it necessarily would be unfair for you to apply for a place in an executive-training program while planning eventually to go to work for your prospective father-in-law.

Like many young people, you seem confident that you can look into the future and plan your life, much as you might plan some fairly simple project, such as a vacation. In reality, our lives are subject to many contingencies, and God alone is in a position to plan them for us. By constantly trying to discover God's plan, we can learn enough to take the next step in following it. We must do this constantly, year by year and even day by day (see *LCL,* 113–29). It is a mistake to imagine one can know with certainty what the future holds.

Perhaps God not only is calling you and your fiancée to marry and form a family of your own but will call you and her father to form a business relationship in which you can put your talents to good use serving all those in any way involved in the business. If both things really are elements of your vocation, your working elsewhere for a time would contribute to your subsequent career only as a way of obtaining training and gaining experience. At present, however, you need a job and your prospective father-in-law is not offering you one. You must look elsewhere, taking into account that the future may not work out as you expect.

I do not suggest that there is anything wrong with your hopes to marry your fiancée, gain business experience, go to work for her father, and eventually take over the management of his business. After your marriage, though, you and/or your father-in-law may have second thoughts. Your better-informed assessment of the prospective benefits and burdens of working for him, based on how your relation-ship with him develops and affects your marriage, might lead you to judge that it would be better for your marriage if he and you avoided a business relationship, given that tensions in such a relationship could be stressful to your wife and any serious difficulty would be heartrending for her. At the same time, your father-in-law's better-informed assessment of your talents, based on longer acquaintance and your development as you gain experience, might persuade him that the business and you both would be better off if you continued to work elsewhere.

These contingencies would be in play even if your fiancée had been an only child, but as matters stand I believe there is an additional reason for uncertainty. Her parents suffered a terrible loss. The death of even one child brings on a special grief, hard for anyone who has not experienced it to understand, comparable to suffering the loss of part of oneself. Far more painful to your fiancée's parents, I am sure, was the loss at once of four children, including all their sons, whom they had raised and cherished for many years. Even without that grief, they no doubt would hope that their daughter's marrying you would mean their gaining a son; but considering the grief they have experienced, it is virtually inevitable that some of their hopes for their lost sons are being transferred to you, so that your future father-in-law is likely to expect far more of you than he otherwise would. You may not be able to satisfy his expectations or perhaps even willing to try.

Not only that possibility but others should be taken into account. The marriage you now plan might never take place; your father-in-law's business might fail; your work with the company that first employs you might be so satisfying that you decide to remain with it rather than going to work for your father-in-law. I repeat: I do not wish to discourage you about your prospects. My point simply is that you are more confident that you foresee the future than you have any reason to be. In this respect, your enthusiasm and optimism, which lead you to suppose you can make calculations about the future, are generating a false moral problem for you, much as many people offer specious solutions for real moral problems on the mistaken assumption that they can calculate future benefits and harms. Set aside that mistaken assumption, and you will partly overcome what looks to you like the inevitable unfairness of going to work for a corporation with a good executive-training program, for you will no longer say: "I plainly would not do enough work to compensate my employer for the cost of training me."

Perhaps the rest of the basis for your supposing that you will inevitably act unfairly can be removed by considering the limited nature of the implicit commitments expected of people who enter such training programs. There is great mobility in contemporary business; a morally questionable individualism is pervasive, and stability in relationships is not expected. All this surely is taken into account by corporations running executive-training programs. They gamble on holding good people whom they train. If they ask for no explicit commitment that trainees will stay for a certain length of time, that no doubt is because doing so would only exclude some of the most desirable candidates: those both creative and candid enough not to feign a commitment they do not seriously undertake. Then too, corporations wish to avoid committing themselves to retaining trainees who turn out less satisfactorily. And if this is why no commitment is sought, then surely the same assumption will rule out the existence of some sort of implicit commitment making it unfair for you to seek a place in an executive-training program.

But even if you need not be unfair, still you are likely to encounter moral problems in applying for a place in an executive-training program while planning to work for your prospective father-in-law. You say: "There are various possibilities," but you describe only one. Whatever the other possibilities are, I suggest you examine them very carefully and perhaps choose one that would serve your purpose about as well, without morally problematic features. Moreover, if you do apply for a place in an executive-training program, take care to anticipate and forestall the moral problems.

In the first place, in applying for positions and being interviewed, you are likely to be asked about your career goals, your expectations of the corporation's training program, and so on. Your answers must be strictly truthful. You may not deceive a potential employer about your plans. If anyone asks you for an explicit commitment to remain for a certain period provided the results of the training program are mutually satisfactory, do not make that commitment unless you believe you can keep it and really intend to do so. Moreover, you not only must refrain from lying about your plans. You also must speak candidly and describe your prospects, including their contingency, as accurately as you can whenever the interviewer's questions or other elements of a selection process make it clear that this information is wanted. In entering into a relationship that calls for mutual commitment and ongoing cooperation, not only lying but evasiveness would be gravely unjust both to the employer who might thereby be misled into hiring you and to a competitor who might miss out on a position you would win by dishonesty.

In the second place, you should take into account and, probably, discuss with your prospective father-in-law your duties to the corporation where you might obtain your training and experience. Since you already foresee the likelihood of resigning after only a few years, you ought to take into account the harm that might do to all the participants in the company that will train you, and plan ahead to limit it. Moreover, you may not appropriate that company's secrets and proper expertise; you must not abuse the opportunity it gives you by betraying its legitimate interests. Therefore, shaping your plans in view of the probable demands your prospective father-in-law's business will make on you, you should not apply for any job you foresee is likely to generate serious conflicts of interest and duty for you.

132: May an employee keep expense money saved by economizing?

I work for a company in a city near Chicago, and like many of my fellow employees, I often am sent to Chicago to work there for the day. We always get overtime on these assignments, and the company gives us seventy dollars in cash, as an "advance against expenses," to cover transportation and lunch. When I started on the job a few months ago, the supervisor said unused expense money "is supposed to be returned," and I have been giving him back whatever I did not use—usually only about five or ten dollars but sometimes more. Other employees tell me they never return anything.

Now my wife is pregnant with our first baby. Soon she will have to quit working. When the baby comes, our health insurance will leave us with a bill of over eight hundred dollars, and we have almost no savings. My wife thinks I am being too scrupulous about the expense money. She summed it up like this: "The company ought to pay you more than they do, and we need the unused expense money more than they do." Would it be all right to keep it? If so, I could cut back on expenses by taking along something to snack on instead of buying lunch, and be at least twenty dollars to the good every day I spend in Chicago.

Analysis:

This question calls for application of norms regarding lying, theft, the use of resources provided by an employer, and payment of income taxes. Keeping unused expense money perhaps requires lying, and lying is always wrong. If no lying is required, the company's real policy, which perhaps differs from its stated policy, should be ascertained. If the real policy is that unused expense money is to be returned, it almost certainly should be. Occasionally, an unjustly treated employee or a needy one could be justified in keeping it, but the temptation to rationalize theft should be clarified and excluded. Money for expenses also should be used for that purpose insofar as that is likely to contribute to the quantity or quality of an employee's work. If any unused expense money is retained, this income probably is subject to taxation.

The reply could be along the following lines:

Many employees whose consciences have been dulled by practices of petty fraud that employers cannot easily prevent would never even think about the question you raise. You have retained your moral sensitivity despite your need for money. Still, the outlook of all too many employees is detectable in the fact that you only thought of economizing on your expenses when it occurred to you to keep some of the money. Even if employees cannot rightly keep expense money for themselves, they ought to economize when they reasonably can for the common good of the business, all of whose participants should work together to achieve its purposes efficiently and fairly share the burdens and benefits of doing so.

Many employers provide a fixed sum for meals and/or lodging with the understanding that the employee is responsible for excess expenditures but may retain anything saved by economizing. If your employer provided a certain part of the expense money on that basis to be used for lunch, your proposal to economize by carrying food to snack on would be morally acceptable provided the diet was adequate, so that your work did not suffer. Apparently, though, your employer has not done that, for otherwise company policy would be clear.

Perhaps it would be impossible to keep any unused expense money without lying—for instance, if the company requires you to account for the use of money not returned or to assert in a general statement that such money was used for the designated expenses. Perhaps the company intends to allow a certain amount toward lunch, regardless of its actual cost, but requires an account or statement regarding the remainder. In any case, since lying is always wrong, you certainly may not keep any unused expense money unless you can do so without lying. Therefore, in what follows I shall assume that lying is excluded.

Supposing, then, that you can keep all or some unused money without lying, the lack of any requirement to say what was done with it strongly suggests that management does not seriously expect any money to be returned. Yet even if management does not expect that, it still may be the real policy that it should be, while the supervisor tolerates violations to avoid various consequences of enforcing it, such as unpleasant confrontations and employee unrest. In that case, you receive the money in trust to pay expenses, and you almost certainly ought to return what you do not use. Moreover, even if the policy is not being enforced, adhering to it might well be in your own long-term interest since, other things being equal, a trustworthy employee is more likely than those who cheat their employer to be retained and promoted.

Still, the supervisor's statement that unused money "is supposed to be returned" may have expressed a policy no longer in force—one replaced in practice by a tacit understanding that employees can keep unused expense money. If such a policy change really has occurred, you may be able to find that out by discussing the history of the policy and its application with your supervisor. If you asked him directly, "What is the company's current, real policy on returning unused expense money?" he probably would simply repeat that it is supposed to be returned, and your question might even provoke a tightening of existing practice. But if you take a less direct approach, such as casually mentioning that practices at this company in regard to expense money seem quite different from elsewhere, the conversation might be more illuminating. Talking further with other employees also might help.

If you become morally certain that the policy really has changed, you can rightly take advantage of the company's real present policy. But if the actual policy differs from a tolerated practice, some or all of the employees taking advantage of the latter may falsely signify that they are adhering to the former, yet think they are not being dishonest because the supervisor knows what they are doing and cannot be deceived about it. Still, if deceptive conduct or false statements are necessary, they are dishonest, for even if the supervisor knows they are deceptive or false and not intended to deceive him or her, they are untruthful and are meant to deceive whoever must be deceived for the whole arrangement to work—for example, higher management, auditors, and/or tax collectors.

Also, expense money should be used for the specified purpose insofar as that is likely to contribute to the quantity or quality of an employee's work. For instance, even if an employer permits employees to keep unused expense money, it would be wrong for an employee to waste time on the job by taking a bus instead of a taxi in order to save money and increase the amount he or she retains. On the same basis, even if no other consideration precludes your keeping all or some of the unused expense money, you should not cut back on expenses by not buying lunch if that would detract from your work, for example, by reducing your energy or alertness.

Occasionally employees have no feasible way of collecting what their employer certainly owes them except by taking it, and occasionally employees cannot meet some urgent need except by taking what belongs to an employer who can well afford its loss. In such cases, the taking can be just (see *LCL,* 825). But employees who have an opportunity to steal—for example, by cheating on expenses—often turn these justifications into rationalizations by extending them to situations in which their strict conditions are not met. Consider conscientiously whether either of those justifications is operative in your situation. If not, do not let them, or vague thoughts akin to them, confuse your thinking.

Finally, any expense money you keep will be income to you, and it probably will be taxable. If you judge that you may keep any, you should pay whatever taxes may be due on it.

+ + +

133: May a man claim the hours his wife spends helping with his work?

I work for a book publisher, doing the final editing of manuscripts and preparing them for publication. When work is heavy, I am expected to put in a great deal of overtime, and, with my employer's approval, I always have brought overtime work home. A few years ago, the whole operation was computerized, and my job was expanded to include typesetting the books I edit. Since a desktop publishing program is used for typesetting, that work is done on a personal computer, and a laser printer is adequate to generate the preliminary proofs. My employer supplied me with equipment to use at home that duplicates the setup at the office.

My wife was the secretary of the English department where I did my graduate work. We married when I completed my degree, and she stopped working outside the home just before our first baby was born. Being very skillful with a computer, she helped me master the typesetting program when I first brought that work home. Then she took over doing enough of the typesetting during the day so that I no longer have to spend any of my time at home on it. The result, gratifying to both of us, is that we can spend our time at home together in activities with the children and things like housework, shopping, and cooking.

My wife does the typesetting better and faster than I can. I have been reporting her actual hours, but only them, as "overtime at home." My employer has been pleased enough with my work as a whole that both last year and this year I have received the largest raises of anyone in the department. My conscience bothers me slightly about reporting my wife's work as mine, but if I told my employer what I have been doing, he probably would feel obliged by law to list my wife as a separate employee. I do not wish to invite trouble by telling him and seeking his approval.

Analysis:

This question calls for application of norms regarding lying, fraud, tax evasion, unfair competition, economic exploitation of a spouse, and restitution for injustices. Granting the assumptions of modern individualism, the questioner lies to his employer in reporting as his the hours his wife works, defrauds both his employer and the government, competes unfairly with fellow employees, and deprives his wife of recognition for her work. But on communitarian assumptions, family members—especially spouses—personally do whatever productive work they accomplish with one another's help. On this communitarian position, the questioner is not lying to his employer nor cheating him or the government. His competition with fellow workers is fair, and he does not wrongly deprive his wife of due recognition. If the questioner is convinced that this communitarian view is true, he may act on it. If not, he might seek his employer's approval for the arrangement. If approval is refused, he should desist and make appropriate restitution to him. Whether or not the employer approves, the questioner may owe restitution to one or more of the other parties.

The reply could be along the following lines:

I am sure many conscientious people would say very confidently that what you have been doing is gravely wrong. They would maintain that you have been lying by reporting as "overtime at home" many hours that you did not really work; deceiving your employer by having your wife do work you are paid to do; cheating your employer by collecting payment at your overtime rate for work done by your wife on a part-time basis; perhaps cheating the government out of the difference between the payroll taxes withheld from your wages and those that would be withheld if your wages and your wife's were separated as they should be; competing unfairly with fellow employees who to your employer seem comparatively less capable, thus causing them to miss out on the merit raises you receive in virtue of your wife's excellent work; and depriving your wife of the recognition she deserves. On this analysis, you must not only immediately stop what you have been doing but make appropriate restitution to all the parties you have been injuring.

That analysis no doubt is sound if one grants the individualistic assumptions underlying most modern social and economic theories and much modern practice. However, those assumptions are questionable, especially in their application to work done within a household by family members. In carrying out all their tasks, family members who love one another as they should naturally pitch in to help one another whenever help is needed and they can give it, and they do not keep track of their individual contributions to doing various jobs. While each one has primary responsibility for certain work, that responsibility is discharged adequately whether he or she completes everything with assistance or without it. With persons living, not individualistically, but in genuine communion, the two or more distinct individuals become *we,* so that there are no sharp boundaries between "my work" and "your work." This is true especially of the husband and wife, who in marrying become, as it were, one new person: mutual help is part of the good of marriage (see *LCL,* 555–71). Consequently, there is a true sense in which family members in general, and spouses especially, do personally not only the productive work they individually accomplish but also whatever they do with one another's help.

Consider a family that makes its living operating a convenience store. Dad is mainly responsible for the business, mother is mainly the homemaker and nurse for the little children, and the older children are mainly engaged in their schoolwork. Still, dad helps mother around the house and helps the children with their studies; mother does the paper work for the store, takes orders over the telephone, and even clerks when dad must be away; and the children also help out, not only by taking care of themselves when mother is busy with the store, but by delivering orders, stocking the shelves, and so on. Nobody keeps track of how many hours each family member spends doing this or that; nobody is overburdened or mistreated. In filing tax returns, mother reports the profit from the store as dad's income and calculates self-employment taxes on that basis. No doubt, that violates the letter of the law, according to which she and each child working in the store should be treated as employees, with respect to whom dad would have to meet all laws and regulations regarding not only taxes but equal employment opportunity, minimum wage, child labor, and so on.

Now, like other laws, those this family technically violates should be presumed just and, with few exceptions, obeyed. Still, laws must be interpreted and applied reasonably. Assuming all the profit from the business is reported, would it be reasonable for the authorities to insist the father treat his wife and children as employees or to charge this family with tax fraud? I do not think so. Indeed, it seems to me that not condoning such a deviation from the letter of the law would unjustly impose upon a healthily functioning family an individualistic structure damaging to the family's excellent communion. Of course, you are not operating a family business, and so your situation differs in various ways from that in the example. The point is, though, that within the family the individualism considered normal in modern economic and social relationships plainly is unhealthy, and the authorities, rather than spreading that disease, should condone the activities of families resistant to it.

Are you lying to, deceiving, and cheating your employer? On communitarian assumptions, you are doing the productive work you accomplish at home with your wife's help. You accurately report the hours worked at home, and those hours are over and above the time you put in at the office. So, it seems to me, you are not lying to or deceiving your employer. Moreover, since your wife does the work better and faster than you can, your employer, rather than being cheated, is doing well from this mutually beneficial arrangement.

If you are not cheating your employer, neither are you cheating the government out of taxes, even on the assumption that they would be higher if you and your wife were listed on your employer's payroll as two separate employees and compensated individually. As with the father of the family with the convenience store, you reasonably report the income resulting from all the common productive work within your household.

But what about the advantage this arrangement gives you over your fellow workers? It is real, but I do not think it is in any way unfair. Getting work done is not like competing in a sport or game in which individuals are matched against individuals. Even in the workplace structured by individualism, people help one another to some extent, and often the most productive are those who know how to get others' cooperation and support. Nobody thinks a successful executive with productive assistants and excellent secretaries deserves less compensation and status than less successful competitors who do more of the work themselves. The advantage over fellow workers that you enjoy by having your wife's help seems to me no less fair. You contribute more than they to the common good of the business, and how you accomplish this within your family circle is no concern of theirs.

What about depriving your wife of recognition for her excellent work? Certainly, she deserves recognition for it, and you should give it to her in abundance. But if you do and she is satisfied with your affection and gratitude and the children's, I see nothing wrong in her voluntarily forgoing others' recognition.

While I am persuaded by the preceding considerations, other reasonable people might disagree, and you should not act on my view unless really convinced of its truth. If you are not, what I have said thus far will not provide the help you need in forming your conscience. In that case, how might you proceed?

You could tell your employer about your wife's computer skills and the help she gave you in learning the desktop publishing program, and ask whether there would be any objection to her doing the desktop publishing tasks you take home. If your employer objects, you will have to desist and make appropriate restitution to him. Moreover, if you believe that you have wronged your fellow employees, cheated the government, and deprived your wife of due recognition, you also will owe restitution to them. If your employer agrees, however, you can reasonably assume that what you have been doing has been fair to him and go on doing it without making restitution to him. Nevertheless, you will have to judge conscientiously whether the arrangement has been and will be fair to your fellow employees, the government, and your wife. Unless you are convinced it is, you must at once begin to treat all parties as they deserve and you also will owe appropriate restitution to the party or parties you judge you have treated unfairly.

I admire your wife and you for your way of life. Though very skillful with a computer, she quit working outside your home just before your first baby was born. She pitches in to help you with the typesetting so that you need not spend time on it at home. In this way, you enjoy the gratifying experience of spending your time at home together in activities with the children, housework, shopping, cooking, and so on. How blessed it is when a couple live together in such communion! Hope and pray the Holy Spirit will continue to enrich and strengthen your love, so that you will rejoice in it until death parts you and then, when resurrection rejoins you, forever and ever.

134: May salespeople push products on which extra commission is paid?

I am one of the salespeople in a large, privately owned furniture store. We work on commission, usually five percent of the pretax total of every sale we make; we also receive a guaranteed, semimonthly, minimum salary. It would be too little to live on, but it provides a basis for vacation pay and sick leave as well as a floor when business is slow. As in many other businesses where salespeople work on commission, management sometimes offers us extra commission, most often another five percent but sometimes more or less. Extra commission sometimes is on accessories, such as lamps, sold with a suite of furniture. I have no problem with that. But very often it is on certain lines or particular items, and not on alternatives that would bring only the basic commission. Manufacturers or distributors often arrange for this by giving retailers a discount, part of which is passed on in this way to the salespeople. Sometimes the store itself offers extra commission to promote more profitable merchandise or reduce excess inventory.

To obtain extra commissions, some of the other salespeople push products by lying—for example, saying the line or item is made better than others we sell, when it really is no better and perhaps even not as good. I will not do that. But even without lying, you can push a line or product—for example, by drawing a customer's attention to it at the right moment, calling former customers who might be interested in it, and so on.

Short of lying, just how far may a salesperson go in pushing a line or item in order to obtain extra commission?

Analysis:

This question calls for the derivation of norms for the work of salespersons. Merchants and customers should genuinely cooperate in mutually beneficial transactions fair to both parties. Since a salesperson acts as both the merchant's agent and the buyer's assistant, he or she should try to establish the necessary conditions for that cooperation. So, salespeople should be not only truthful but candid. They should entirely avoid deception and supply the information potential customers require if they are to choose, from what the merchant can supply, those items that will best meet their needs. But since a salesperson remains the merchant's agent, he or she generally need not tell potential customers they could do better by buying from a different merchant. In pushing items, salespersons also must avoid unfairness.

The reply could be along the following lines:

Modern institutions often were shaped by a false philosophy of the human person, according to which individuality is natural and fundamental while community is artificial and secondary. This false philosophy also exaggerated the average person's ability to identify and rationally pursue his or her self-interest. Moreover, many of those involved in organizing modern and contemporary markets for goods and services have been powerful people bent on increasing their status and wealth. Therefore, in some respects these markets embody unrealistic and unjust social structures. Among these is the assumption expressed by the slogan "caveat emptor" ("let the buyer beware") as it usually is understood: that a merchant has no duty to ensure the fairness of the sales contract to which he or she is a party but is obliged only to carry out its terms.

Contrary to this assumption, merchants and their customers should engage in genuine cooperation rather than in one-sided or even mutual exploitation. Cooperation occurs only when parties whose actions are interrelated share a common understanding of what they are doing and freely choose to act for the sake of a common good. The common good of a merchant and a customer is a relationship including transactions that are not only beneficial to both parties but mutually fair, that is, in accord with the Golden Rule.

A salesperson acts not only as the merchant's agent but as the customer's assistant, as is suggested by the question often used in greeting potential customers: "May I help you?" Serving in this twofold capacity, the salesperson bears a special responsibility for bringing about a truly cooperative transaction. Therefore, the salesperson should strive to establish the necessary conditions for cooperation. He or she does this by communicating honestly and sufficiently to bring about a common understanding of what is involved in the transaction, helping potential customers learn about and choose what will benefit them, and completing a transaction only if he or she believes it to be fair to both parties. These responsibilities are especially exigent when a salesperson deals with a child or an unusually defenseless adult.

Plainly, lying by salespeople is excluded not only as wrong in itself but as a betrayal of their proper role. Lying turns selling into manipulation by preventing mutual understanding and facilitating unfairness toward the customer. By refusing to be dishonest as some of your co-workers are, you maintain your integrity not only as a person but as a salesperson. Still, your question rightly suggests that in pushing one line or item rather than another for the sake of extra commission, salespeople not only must avoid lying but should observe other limits implicit in the responsibilities proper to their role. It seems to me these other limits are threefold.

First, some forms of deliberate deception, as distinct from lying, may be practiced in certain kinds of situations, such as games and warfare (see *LCL,* 409). In the present context, however, deliberate deception is as manipulative and unfair as outright lying, and so should be altogether excluded.

Second, in helping customers understand what will benefit them and encouraging them to choose only that, salespeople should try to ascertain each potential customer's needs, then give all relevant information about merchandise their employer can provide to meet those needs. Therefore, in pushing one thing, a salesperson may not withhold information that might lead a potential customer to judge an alternative line or item preferable. In particular, if a salesperson believes a certain line or item is a better value and/or will meet a need better than any alternative, he or she should say so and give the reasons, even if that encourages the customer to choose something on which no extra commission is available.

Suppose a competitor offers better value or can provide merchandise that would better meet a potential customer's need. Must a salesperson who knows that say so? In general, no. The salesperson remains the merchant's agent, and fairness does not require, nor does the public expect, that a business's agents impartially serve its competitors. Still, fairness can require a salesperson to turn away potential customers whose needs he or she cannot satisfactorily meet; and the poor deserve special consideration in judging what will be satisfactory.

Third, a salesperson should apply the Golden Rule to any tactic that might be used in pushing something, by asking whether it would seem objectionable for others to use a similar tactic on himself, herself, or a loved one; he or she should do nothing that fails this test. In pushing anything, therefore, a salesperson should not encourage potential customers to act contrary to their own best interests—for example, by burdening themselves with excessive debt.

These limits are not necessarily violated by the two tactics you mention: drawing a customer's attention at the right psychological moment to something on which extra commission is available and notifying former customers who might be interested in it. However, I do not think even these tactics will be morally acceptable in every instance. Nor do I believe it possible to specify any other tactic that cannot be abused.

Someone might object that the norms proposed here are too idealistic, failing to take realistic account of a salesperson's need to make a living and of most potential customers' own moral defects. Three things can be said about that.

First, in this matter, as in others, the norms of Christian morality do seem very strict by conventional standards. But conventional standards, being an aspect of the fallen human condition, are distorted by avarice and are inadequate for people enlightened by Jesus' gospel and raised up by his grace. Aware that humankind is called to be God's family, Christian salespeople, following the law of love, should treat each potential customer as a brother or sister in Christ.

Second, many potential customers have their own moral defects, including some detrimental to merchants and salespeople. For example, some waste a salesperson's time with no intention of doing business; some take delivery on merchandise, use it to meet a temporary need, then return it; some fail to pay what they owe. However, such injustices toward merchants and salespeople are not likely to be provoked or worsened by salespeople's fidelity to their role. Indeed, a salesperson who does his or her best to establish and maintain a genuinely cooperative relationship with potential customers provides good example and motivation for them to respond in kind.

Third, competent and hardworking salespeople generally can earn a living without making moral compromises, since potential customers who are well-treated are likely to respond with trust and gratitude, become regular customers, and recommend such salespersons to others.

135: Is it fair to price substantially similar products very differently?

I am a middle manager in the marketing division of a major supplier of home products and toiletries. The company has been consistently profitable, and usually has done better than its major competitors.

Among other things, I participate in setting the wholesale prices for our products. Costs seldom bear much relationship to prices in this business. For example, we manufacture a liquid detergent that does a good job dissolving grease without being hard on people's skin. It can be used for many purposes—bathing the baby, shampooing hair, hand washing dishes. We market it for those purposes and several others, and there is absolutely no difference among the apparently diverse products except colors, perfumes, and, of course, packaging. The different colors and perfumes do not significantly differ in cost, but different packages do, especially since we do not package the different items in the same range of sizes, and packaging five gallons of detergent for institutional use in hand-washing dispensers is a lot more efficient than packaging eight ounces for bathing the baby. That difference, however, only accounts for a small part of the difference in wholesale prices. For example, using for comparison the wholesale price of this product as a hand dish-washing detergent and assuming other factors affecting price remain the same, its wholesale price as a shampoo for women is 114 percent more, as a shampoo for men 157 percent more, and as a baby bath 343 percent more.

Not only that, in packaging this detergent and other products as house brands for large retail chains, we price them at forty to sixty percent less than when we package and distribute them as our own brands. (My wife buys it in the largest size of a house brand packaged for hand washing dishes, and we and our children use it for everything.)

There is nothing illegal about this pricing. Effective marketing of a product requires promoting its use for various specific purposes, and features that make it suitable for those different purposes must be advertised. Once the product is differentiated, prices are largely determined by consumers' perceptions of value and different levels of competition in the marketplace. Thus, the shampoo for men has less competition than that for women. And when we began selling the detergent for bathing babies, market tests at several price levels showed it sold better if priced above rather than below competing brands, and nearly as well (and far more profitably) if priced above than if priced about the same.[337]

Our advertising includes no false statements. Our products are as good as any on the market. Similar pricing practices prevail throughout the industry. Still, if I were not in the business and found out how we price products, I am sure I would feel cheated. At the same time, it would be futile for me to criticize our pricing strategy without having a viable alternative to propose.

Analysis:

This inquiry includes two questions: about the fairness of the employer's marketing strategy and about the acceptability of the questioner's participation in it. Businesses should cooperate with their customers, and cooperation presupposes candid communication. The questioner's employer is not communicating candidly; it withholds information its customers could use and deliberately gives an illusory value to is products. Therefore, its marketing strategy is unjust. The questioner's own application of the Golden Rule identifies this injustice, and he formally cooperates in it by intending the success of the market strategy. The amount unfairly taken by this strategy is cumulatively substantial, and so the injustice is grave. Therefore, unless his employer is willing to change, the questioner must give up his present job. He also owes appropriate restitution, which he can make by giving alms for the spiritual benefit of customers and by doing what he can to expose and overcome the injustice.

The reply could be along the following lines:

The moral issue you raise usually is not recognized and acknowledged. As you say, differences in the costs of packaging do justify some differences in price among essentially similar products. Your advertising and rebate costs in marketing your own brands perhaps warrant charging more for them than for the same products packaged as house brands. Moreover, marketing various products with different profit margins and marketing the same products with changing prices under

---

337. The explanation for this paradoxical situation is that most people fear using inferior products for their babies. So, if most baby bath products sell for, say, two dollars, and a new product priced about the same is purchased by ten people, pricing it at one dollar may reduce sales to five, while pricing it at three dollars may reduce sales only to eight. If the cost of supply is fifty cents per package, pricing at one dollar yields a profit of $2.50, pricing at the competitors' price yields a profit of $15.00, and pricing at three dollars a profit of $20.00. (This example deliberately simplifies by omitting many costs that affect retail prices.)

different conditions, as permitted and required by competition in the marketplace, may be necessary to maintain a reasonable level of profit on the whole, and is not unfair in itself (see q. 146, below). At the retail level, handling and transaction costs also help account for price differences.

Still, even taking various justifications for price differentials into account, when the price of a small package seems disproportionately high by comparison with a larger size of the very same product, one suspects sellers are taking advantage of customers who need only a small amount or are too poor to shop economically. Moreover, advertising, often using lust, acquisitiveness, and status seeking as motives, can establish brand differentiation, especially for luxury products, so that one brand may be sold at a far higher price than others from which it has no discernible difference at all. Your question, therefore, points to only some of the closely related features of ethically questionable marketing strategies.[338]

A business should organize economic cooperation among several groups. One of these is its customers. But cooperation presupposes candid communication and a mutual commitment to further one another's true interests by working together for a common good. By this standard, your company's marketing strategy is unethical. It would be in the true interests of many people to know that they could use a large-sized container of your detergent to meet a variety of needs, but you do not provide this helpful information.

Of course, pricing strategies such as yours are not entirely secret. People can learn about them by studying the publications of consumer organizations, books that criticize advertising, and so on. Such well-informed people can experiment with available products, identify those that meet their needs more efficiently, and make better-informed buying decisions according to their own interests. Someone therefore might argue that consumers are deceived due to their own negligence, and you have no obligation to give them more information. But the entire culture of consumerism, to which contemporary marketing techniques have greatly contributed, has weakened many people's critical capacity and motivation in making judgments and decisions about spending their money, so that any relevant negligence of theirs is less their fault than the fault of companies like yours. Moreover, people differ greatly in ability. Those who are better educated, with time to read and study, can and should become prudent consumers, seldom needing to depend on advertising when comparing the value of products. But many people lack either the ability, the time, or both to develop such skill. Your marketing strategy, directed toward the public at large, takes unfair advantage of them.

It also relies on giving an illusory value to its products. Unless informed otherwise, people suppose they get what they pay for. They think, for example, that the detergent marketed for bathing babies is a formula especially suited to the purpose, whose costly ingredients justify its high price. Thus, even if your advertising includes no false statements, it is deceptive. It leads the public to think the differences among essentially similar products are more significant than they are.

338. For a detailed description of methods of pricing to maximize profits, see Thomas T. Nagle and Reed K. Holden, *The Strategy and Tactics of Pricing: A Guide to Profitable Decision Making,* 2nd ed. (Englewood Cliffs, N.J.: Prentice Hall, 1995).

Is there a viable alternative? The alternative is to stop misleading the public, provide potential customers with the information they need to make decisions in their own true interests, and market products in ways calculated to meet the needs of prudent customers. You might, for example, make the basic detergent available without added color or scent, frankly advertise that it is substantially the same product you have been marketing for a variety of uses, and assure customers that for all those uses the basic detergent will be just as safe and effective as its colored and scented versions. The detergent could be packaged as simply as possible in various sizes, including small, easy-to-use, refillable containers and large containers with reusable spouts or taps designed for convenience in refilling the small ones. The product could be promoted for its environmental and health advantages: no dyes and perfumes that waste resources and trigger allergies in some people; less packaging which saves scarce resources and reduces trash disposal; and reduced environmental impact in manufacturing the product and packaging it.

I expect your superiors and colleagues will say that even if the detergent were marketed in this way, many people still would prefer the familiar and higher priced products. Probably so, but being candid with the public, the company could justly make meeting the ongoing demand for those products part of its alternative strategy. Thus understood, is the alternative viable? If it were viable from the point of view of the industry's policy makers, presumably the practice you describe would not prevail. Yet being more candid with consumers than any of your competitors might well gain new credibility and good will for your company, and increase your market share sufficiently to make the new strategy viable.

If your employer is unwilling to change, what is your moral responsibility? You yourself have applied the Golden Rule: If you were not in the business and you found out how your products are priced, you are sure you would feel cheated. In my judgment, that feeling is reasonable, and the marketing strategy of which the pricing policy is an integral part is unfair to customers. In implementing this unfair strategy, you collaborate with others in your firm to make it succeed. Since you would not be doing your job satisfactorily if the strategy failed, in helping implement it you cannot avoid intending that customers be deceived and cheated. Though the amount unjustly taken by each retail sale is small, those of you who collaborate in implementing the strategy also make every effort to retain buyers' loyalty to your brands, and so intend that the company profit not simply on each sale individually but on the whole set of sales to each and every customer over time. The amount involved in the injustice is cumulatively substantial, and the matter therefore is grave; if you continue doing your job as you have in the past while acknowledging the injustice, you will be committing a grave sin. Consequently, if you accept this conclusion, you must at once either transfer to a job that does not require you to intend that customers be deceived and cheated, or resign from the company.

Moreover, if you now acknowledge that you have been helping to perpetrate a serious injustice, you should not only end your complicity in it but make restitution to its victims. Plainly you cannot do that by repaying your fair share of what the many buyers of your company's products have paid in excess of what would have been fair prices. However, within limits set by your other responsibilities, you could give alms for the spiritual benefit of customers. You also could help them, at least by confidentially supplying information about the industry's practices to consumer groups and/or anonymously writing and publishing a detailed exposé of the practices that, as you say, prevail throughout the industry. If you must resign, you might try developing a career as a consumer advocate and industry critic, working for laws that would regulate marketing so that advertising would have to provide the information potential consumers need to make intelligent choices among competing products (see q. 149, below).

In thinking through your question and responding, I have been aware of the severe hardship you and your family are likely to experience if you accept the conclusion and act on it. The industry's marketing strategy has been shaped over many years by the practices of people less morally sensitive than you—people more interested in maximizing profits than in cooperating with customers. You have been working within an unjust social structure that no doubt seemed to you something given and permanent. Though your moral sensitivity led you to question what you have been doing, you probably never expected the preceding reply. While in many cases people working within such a structure need not intend any injustice and can avoid personal guilt, your role, unfortunately, has required you to intend that customers be deceived and cheated. To free yourself from continuing slavery to the corrupt world, you must deny yourself radically. To gather the courage to take up your cross, remember that "we will reap at harvesttime, if we do not give up" (Gal 6.9).

136: Should a business pay a higher price out of loyalty to a good supplier?

One of our new products required an electronic subassembly that we could not engineer and produce in house. I identified possible suppliers, gave them our specifications, and ordered, not from the one that bid lowest, but from the one that seemed most likely to meet our requirements fully and deliver on time. That supplier gave us excellent service, including extra help with integrating the subassembly into our product design.

The product sold well, and we are now getting ready for a second and much larger production run. The pressure is on to minimize costs. There are two ways to go on that subassembly. One would be to reorder from our original supplier; the other, to order from a supplier with no engineering department and lower overhead. My department head decided to ask the original supplier and several of its low-overhead competitors for bids, which are now in. The lowest acceptable bid is just under three percent lower than the original supplier's.

Changing suppliers would involve no legal problem, since the design of the subassembly is legally ours. I am confident the low-bidding supplier will satisfactorily duplicate the subassembly and deliver on schedule, so that getting the better price need not sacrifice quality or risk production delays. But the saving works out to less than one-tenth of one percent of the wholesale price of this product, and our projected profit margin on it is over six percent.

Under these conditions, I wonder how fair it is to switch after having used our original supplier's service. My department head and I disagree. He sees no problem, pointing out that if suppliers wanted to, they could either recover the full costs of their engineering service on the initial order or patent and license their designs. Furthermore, he says similar things are done all the time. People go to a store that stocks cameras or computers to check out the goods, then buy from a mail-order house; they go to a large dealership to look at new cars and get a price, then order from a small dealer willing to meet the price; they shop retailers that provide good displays and buying advice, identify the wholesaler of the product they want, and purchase directly.

Analysis:

This question concerns the duty of loyalty and calls for application of the Golden Rule. Suppliers should be considered cooperators in a business, especially if they provide special service. Fairness requires loyalty toward cooperators, and, though the demands of loyalty are limited, in this case changing suppliers seems unfair. Moreover, the industry's common good requires suppliers that offer full service, and participants in the industry should do their share in serving its common good; so, the questioner's company has some responsibility to support its full-service supplier. The argument by analogy proposed by the questioner's department head is not sound.

The reply could be along the following lines:

I think you are right in being concerned about the fairness of switching suppliers. I lean toward your side in your disagreement with your department head.

In the first place, any business should count its suppliers among the cooperators in the enterprise, along with investors, employees, and customers. Even purchasing a standard component, and selecting a supplier strictly on the basis of price and guaranteed delivery, involves some cooperation with the supplier and establishes a relationship, albeit minimal. Purchasing a custom designed component from a supplier whose special skills and commitment are important to ensure good quality involves more cooperation and establishes a more significant relationship.

The supplier to whom you gave your initial order for the subassembly cooperated with you by providing excellent service, including extra help in integrating the subassembly into your product design. No doubt, that contributed to the product's success. Moreover, you surely realized that the supplier was motivated by a hope for additional orders if the product succeeded, and you profited by taking advantage of that hope. Trusting you to respond in kind to its good will, the supplier did not patent the subassembly. So, while buying from another supplier would not violate the law or any written agreement, it would violate the relationship you established by accepting the supplier's cooperation, and that relationship is intrinsically valuable. Then too, while switching to another supplier would realize small short-run savings, maintaining your relationship with the original supplier may be good business in the long run, since that supplier probably will continue to try hard to fulfill its commitments and meet your needs when extra effort is required. Therefore, I think you should be loyal to your original supplier.

The demands of such loyalty, of course, are limited, as are the demands of loyalty toward good employees, who sometimes must be laid off when business is poor. In both cases, you cannot ignore the legitimate interests of investors, customers, and other participants in the business. It might well be fair to change suppliers if necessary to maintain the product's profitability or if the price differential were not so small. What you have told me, however, seems to indicate that properly applying the Golden Rule will make clear the unfairness of changing suppliers.

Someone might object that the supposed value of a company's relationship with its suppliers is intangible, and should not be allowed to influence purchasing decisions, which ought to be based solely on calculable factors such as price. Otherwise, the objector might argue, personal feelings of friendship inevitably will influence purchasing decisions, resulting in increased costs, so that either the product's price will have to be raised or owners will be deprived of part of the profit to which they are entitled or both. The answer is that, while personal relationships should not be allowed to influence purchasing decisions contrary to the company's true interests, good business relationships with suppliers, as with employees and customers, pertain to the company's good. Moreover, while owners are entitled to a fair profit, they are not deprived of it when profit is reduced by treating suppliers, employees, and customers fairly.

Another consideration also argues against changing suppliers in this case. The alternative supplier, whose overhead is lower, is, as it were, taking advantage of the lack of structures to protect the common good in your industry. If no supplier could have provided the full service you needed, you could not have launched your product, and the same is true of others trying to launch new products. So, as a community of businesses, your industry needs suppliers providing full service. Since the cost of sustaining them must be met and should be met fairly, you have some responsibility to sustain your full-service supplier. Besides, failing to meet such responsibilities is likely to harm the entire industry in the long run.

Your department head might object that other companies are not doing their share to sustain full-service suppliers. But the unfairness of others does not cancel out one's duties as a participant in an industry, unless it so undermines the conditions essential for the industry's well-being that fulfilling one's responsibilities becomes pointless.

The argument by analogy proposed by your department head is unsound, since there are ethically significant differences between his examples and switching suppliers. The most obvious is that the shoppers in his examples need not have established a relationship by previous transactions with the merchants whose services they use. Another important difference is that shoppers generally do not establish a relationship with vendors similar to yours with your initial supplier.

In a market economy, vendors expect potential buyers to shop around. Many businesses, therefore, offer free information about the availability and prices of their goods and services, display goods, and welcome anyone who wishes to inspect them. Retailers, of course, intend only to help potential customers, but they foresee and accept that others will take advantage of their promotional services. Moreover, even though they intend to buy elsewhere, shoppers examining items displayed by a full-service store or large dealership offer the retailer an opportunity to persuade them to change their purchasing strategy or, at least, to remember helpful salespeople, recommend the store or dealership to other potential customers, or buy from it another time. In some cases, too, distributors and retailers help one another in promoting a certain brand of product, so that all retailers of the product benefit by providing good sales service to the public. Therefore, using services offered to shoppers hardly is unfair unless it imposes significant burdens—for example, by asking for a "sample" of something one has no interest in buying, carelessly damaging displays and demonstrator products, or wasting the time of the sales staff and impeding sales to others, which, in many cases, is unfair both to the salesperson and other shoppers.

Someone might say your department head's view differs from the one articulated here not in morality but only in effectiveness—the department head's view is simply shortsighted, while maintaining relationships with good suppliers is good business that will pay off in the long term. Indeed, it may pay off, but there is no guarantee it will, and the only compelling grounds for rejecting the department head's view concern fairness, not profits. That consideration of fairness, however, may not seem to be a matter of morality, since it does not turn on any hard-edged norm of the sort that excludes stealing and promise breaking. Still, between individuals, less hard-edged duties, such as gratitude for gifts and loyalty to friends, certainly also are moral responsibilities. These have their analogues in relationships even among nations, and certainly also in those between businesses and their suppliers.

137: May customers take advantage of generous guarantees?

Some businesses advertise that they guarantee their customers' satisfaction and offer a full refund to anyone not completely satisfied with their goods or services. I see nothing wrong in watching for such guarantees, interpreting them strictly, and taking advantage of them. My wife thinks that is dishonest.

Last year a local supermarket chain advertised specials on their house brand of turkeys. The guarantee was that any family that had one of their turkeys for Christmas and did not consider it as good as any turkey they ever had, could return the leftovers the next day and get a full refund. For several years we have been getting our turkeys from a farmer; they are premium birds and cost a bit more, but undoubtedly are the best turkey we or any of our guests have ever eaten. The store's offer was too good to resist, though, so I bought a twenty-five-pound turkey there. We had it for Christmas dinner and had sandwiches off it for lunch the next day. Everyone agreed it was very good, but not quite as good as the turkey we usually have. That evening I took the remains back to the store with the cash register receipt and got the full refund. My wife thought this was definitely going too far.

Here's another example. One of the motel chains advertises a free night's lodging if a guest is not completely satisfied. We stayed last summer at one of their motels, and the air conditioner quit in the middle of the night. We opened the windows and, fortunately, were reasonably comfortable. In the morning, though, the noise from the parking lot was loud and clear through the open windows, which prevented us from sleeping late, as we had planned. I would have complained to any place about the air conditioner, so I had no qualms invoking the guarantee. My wife agreed that a complaint was in order but argued that people generally would not expect free lodging for something the management probably could not help.

As long as a person tells the truth, it seems to me there is nothing wrong in holding a business to the letter of its guarantee. My wife's view is that customers should ask for a full refund or waiver of charges only if they are so dissatisfied they would feel entitled to some adjustment even if a business did not advertise a guarantee. What do you think?

Analysis:

This question calls for application of norms excluding lying and fraud, and for judgment by the Golden Rule. In taking advantage of guarantees, one must not lie and may ask only for what the guarantee promised. If these conditions were met, the questioner did nothing dishonest in the cases described. Still, it probably would be a sign of avarice for someone who lives comfortably to buy something while expecting to take advantage of a money-back guarantee. By contrast, I see no reason to think taking advantage of the motel chain's guarantee was morally questionable. Still, differences between the parties' economic status could require a Christian to forgo his or her rights.

The reply could be along the following lines:

Your position about taking advantage of guarantees includes a limiting clause: "as long as a person tells the truth." One might be tempted to violate that condition—for example, by saying this turkey is not as good as any we ever had when, in fact, one cannot recall ever having a better one. Lying to take advantage of a guarantee plainly would be fraud, and both the lie and the fraud would be grave matter if the amount were significant. So, in responding to your question, I shall presuppose that no false statements are made in taking advantage of guarantees.

Similarly, you say you interpret guarantees "strictly." It is essential to be consistent in doing so, since consistently strict interpretation will exclude potential abuses. For example, some mail-order companies guarantee complete satisfaction and promise to refund, no questions asked, the full price of returned merchandise even after it has been in service. One might be tempted to buy camping equipment, use it for a time with complete satisfaction, and then return it. Even though the no-questions-asked policy would let one do that without lying, it almost always would constitute theft. The guarantee is that unsatisfactory merchandise may be returned, and so one dishonestly takes what the guarantee did not promise by invoking it without a reason for dissatisfaction. In what follows, I also shall assume that all the terms of guarantees are interpreted strictly.

Given these assumptions, I think your wife is mistaken in regarding what you did in the cases you describe as dishonest.

Even so, she could claim that in the first case, even if not dishonest, you treated the store unfairly in taking advantage of its guarantee. You were virtually certain the store's turkey would not measure up to the premium birds you have been getting. So, she might argue, you did not give the store the fair chance you want others involved in transactions to give you.

That argument, however, is unsound. True, you want others involved in transactions to give you a better chance of benefiting from the exchange than you gave the store, but you are not operating a business and do not enjoy the benefits businesses gain by making generous guarantees. Businesses do that only because it is in their own interest. Many people are motivated to try the guaranteed merchandise or service, and some will adopt it as their preference. The promotion is cost effective because not many people demand that the guarantee be fulfilled, for, even if the product is not as good as promised, returning the unused portion requires not only some thought, time, and effort but unembarrassed assertiveness. Thus, a business that makes a generous guarantee freely undertakes to accept the cost of satisfying those who honestly require its fulfillment. Those who freely undertake something are not treated unfairly when they are held to do as they agreed. Therefore, provided the merchandise really is not as promised, there is nothing unfair in demanding that the guarantee be fulfilled.

Your wife might argue that, even if you would have been justified in returning the turkey after Christmas dinner, you went too far by doing so only after having lunched off it the next day. That argument, however, also would be unsound. Having the turkey for another meal did not violate the terms of the guarantee, and returning more of it than you did would not have benefited anyone. Since the store could not resell the leftover portion, and its managers and employees hardly would use it, it simply would have gone to waste.

But even granting all that, it probably would be a sign of avarice for someone who lives comfortably to buy a turkey, as you did, while expecting to take advantage of the store's guarantee. Unless you must struggle to make ends meet, your wife may be reasonably concerned about your character, and you should ask yourself whether your attitude toward money is as upright and merciful as it should be. In particular, are you attentive to the rights of the poor who need your help (see *LCL,* 780–82, 789–92, 800–806, 811–14)? Are you as ready to do your duty toward them as you are to exact your rights under generous guarantees? If you are not as careful in fulfilling your responsibility to the poor as you are in exacting your rights under generous guarantees, your attitude toward money is at least somewhat avaricious.

Even if taking advantage of the guarantee did not cheat the merchant, supposing you acted out of avarice what you did was incompatible with your responsibility as a participant in the business—along with its owners, employees, and so on—to cooperate for its common good. The more involved in the business you were, the more serious this wrong would be. Thus, avariciously taking advantage of the generous guarantee of a business that regularly gave you excellent service at reasonable prices could be grave matter.

By contrast, a family fallen on hard times might find camping equipment purchased in better days unsatisfactory only because they can no longer afford to use it. Even so, the family would not, in my judgment, do an injustice by taking advantage of a prosperous mail-order company's no-questions-asked guarantee and returning the equipment for credit toward desperately needed winter coats for the children (see *CCC*, 2408). But would it be honest to obtain a refund under such a guarantee for goods satisfactory in themselves and unsatisfactory only in the sense that the family could no longer afford to use them? I think so. Companies offer such a guarantee to motivate potential customers to buy despite all sorts of reasons for hesitating. Among those reasons are not only doubts about goods' intrinsic qualities but doubts about their utility to purchasers, all things considered. The family's inability to use the goods due to its changed economic circumstances certainly does affect utility, and therefore satisfaction, in this sense.

In the second case, it seems to me, there is no plausible reason to think asking the motel to forgo payment for the night's lodging was morally wrong. Your wife may well have been mistaken in assuming the motel's management could not have prevented the problem with the air conditioning. If properly maintained, regularly checked, and replaced before it entirely wears out, good equipment very seldom breaks down without warning. If an establishment saves money by replacing equipment at long intervals or limiting preventative maintenance and inspections, fairness requires that it share its savings with patrons inconvenienced by breakdowns. Moreover, whether the establishment was at fault or not, its failure to provide the air conditioning and restful quiet it promised was a breach of contract, so that, even in the absence of any special guarantee, you would have been entitled to a substantial reduction in the price. Given your right to that, you plainly had the right to invoke the chain's guarantee of full satisfaction to avoid paying for the night's lodging. No doubt your wife was correct in saying many people would not have done that. But that fact merely shows that many people overlook their own rights or prefer not to vindicate them.

As with other matters of justice involving property and money, however, differences in the parties' economic status sometimes require Christians to forgo their rights. Thus, if a struggling merchant is pressed by cutthroat competition to offer a generous guarantee, financially secure people would be merciless in taking full advantage of it.

138: May one ever violate the terms of a computer software license?

Many computer software programs come with a license to which the purchaser agrees by opening the software package. These licenses generally exclude installing and/or using the program on two or more computers at the same time. However, copying the software and even the instruction books that come with it is easy, and it is hard to enforce these licensing agreements. So, they are very often ignored.

I think most people who use software programs recognize limits to violating the agreements. They would not buy a program, make extra copies, and sell them; nor would they knowingly purchase a program from someone who sold it in violation of the provisions of the license. They would not consider it right for a business or other organization with many employees working at many computers to buy only one or a few copies of a program, and make unlicensed use of it. But I wonder about certain more limited violations.

First, consider a large family with two or more computers. When one family member purchases a software program, it may be installed on both or all the computers in the house, so that all family members use it on occasion. But some—the smaller children, for instance—get very little use from it, and the whole family's combined use does not amount to that of many individuals who perfectly abide by the licensing agreement. For a family of moderate means, furthermore, the realistic alternative would not be buying two or more copies of the same program, but limiting their convenient use of it, by putting it on only one computer, simply in order to abide by the letter of the licensing agreement.

To be sure, the family does violate the letter of the license. But software makers must realize that many people do this sort of thing, yet they never try to enforce their licenses' terms in such cases. Doesn't it seem reasonable and fair enough for a family to buy only one copy of a program and then use it without worrying about the letter of the agreement?

Second, consider a volunteer who edits newsletters for a parent organization, a women's prolife counseling center, and a parish religious education program, and who also prepares the bulletin and liturgy booklets for her parish. She is not paid for any of this; indeed, the volunteer work costs her money for computer supplies and babysitting. Intending to help her, a fellow parishioner who has upgraded his desktop publishing program gives her the old version—both the program disks and the manuals—which he otherwise would simply discard. The program helps her improve her work and speed it up considerably, and is entirely adequate to her needs.

She does not think using the program is theft. The software maker is losing nothing, and if she were to buy a program now, she says, it would be a different, cheaper one, not the one she is using, which would cost over five hundred dollars. However, she wonders how she would like it if she were in the software maker's position, and that makes her uneasy. A friend who is a spiritual confidante tells her: "Regard the program as a gift, and the problem, if any, not as yours but as the giver's." Her confessor says: "Software makers get rich enough from their sales to users who can charge off purchases as an expense. It's only fair that the industry and such users subsidize people who donate their services for worthy causes, which are always short of money."

Analysis:

This question calls for application of the norm excluding theft. Copying, using, or transferring commercially marketed software in violation of the license's terms generally should be considered theft. Titles to property are not absolute, however, and a poor person or group who can verify that certain conditions are fulfilled is morally justified in violating the terms of a computer software license so as to meet a need that cannot otherwise be met. Again, a person or group that has been treated unjustly by a software publisher and can verify that certain conditions are fulfilled is morally justified in taking fair compensation by a proportionate violation of license terms. Moreover, in some cases the copyright holder's permission to violate the express terms of the license can be reasonably presumed. Though it is plausible that a software publisher would take a tolerant view of some license violations by families, the questioner argues unsoundly from the absence of attempts by software publishers to enforce their rights against such violations. Again, though the use of an earlier version of a program might not violate the terms of the software license, the arguments offered to justify accepting the gift are unsound.

The reply could be along the following lines:

For a long time, copyright laws have provided authors and/or publishers of books, sheet music, records, films, and so on with protection of their interest in receiving a fair return for their work and other investment that make such items available to those who can benefit from their use. At least in their general lines, copyright laws surely are reasonable, and fair-minded people recognize that they should be respected. Software programs also are protected by copyright laws, but many people who would never copy a book owned by a friend regularly acquire software programs in that way.

This question concerns only commercial software, which is most of the software sold by software publishers, computer stores, and other vendors. However, it will be helpful to understand three other types: public domain software, freeware, and shareware.

The creators of public domain software deliberately give up their copyright and make their product freely available by clearly marking it as such; everyone may copy and use both the software itself and any documentation accompanying it. The creators of freeware retain their copyright but use it to forbid others to profit from their work. Thus, freeware may be copied for one's own use and also given, but not sold, to others. The creators of shareware offer it for everyone's free trial, distributing it either personally or through intermediaries who specialize in doing that. However, the intention is to establish a cooperative relationship with those who find a program useful, so that, in exchange for a registration fee, users receive benefits such as bound manuals, updates, technical support, and the opportunity to try additional programs. Someone who makes continuing use of a shareware program without paying the registration fee violates the copyright. While that right seldom is legally enforced in the case of shareware, those abusing it take unfair advantage of the creator's reasonable offer to cooperate with users.

Companies that market commercial software programs hold the rights to them, having either developed these products or purchased the rights to them. In marketing a program, such companies do not actually offer the software and its accompanying documentation for sale; rather they offer for sale only the use of copies within specified contractual limits, stated in a license. The license packaged with the software usually permits the purchaser to load it on only one computer, and to make only one copy as a backup. (Sometimes a license specifies that the software may be loaded on two computers, provided they never are used simultaneously. Many vendors also offer special licenses to those who wish to use the same software on many machines; it is necessary to contact each vendor directly for information about the availability and terms of such licenses.)

The typical license packaged with a program states that original purchasers may transfer the software and license to someone else only if they give the software up entirely, retaining no copy of it whatsoever. Partly to prevent unauthorized copying, the licensee also is forbidden, without the copyright owner's consent, temporarily to transfer licensed software by renting, leasing, or lending it to another party.

In the U.S., unauthorized copying of commercially marketed software is a federal crime if done "willfully and for purposes of commercial advantage or private financial gain."[339] However, even if the copies are not sold but are given away or retained for the copier's own use, unauthorized copying, though not a crime, infringes the right of the copyright holder, who can seek redress by suing.

What about the morality of this copyright infringement? Except when a property owner's consent can be reasonably presumed, using his or her property in any way that goes beyond his or her expressed, limited permission is using it contrary to his or her will; and using anything contrary to its owner's will is the same kind of act, morally speaking, as taking something from an owner contrary to his or her will. Provided the owner's will in the matter is reasonable—which is to be presumed unless the contrary is established—the using is unfair and constitutes theft. Thus, copying, using, or transferring commercially marketed software in violation of the terms of the license generally should be considered theft. Moreover, such theft generally is a grave matter, because people do not consider most comparable infringements insignificant (see *LCL*, 319–20).

Many people who would not violate an author's or publisher's copyright by copying a book or a musical composition seem to see nothing wrong in making or accepting and using unauthorized copies of computer software. There are at least three reasons for this difference in perception.

First, software licensing is comparatively new, and software makers do not adequately publicize the limits they set on the use of their products; for instance, these generally go unmentioned in advertising and other promotional materials. In the case of other products, documents drafted by lawyers and packaged with them or included in purchase agreements usually limit buyers' rights to remedies if the product proves unsatisfactory but do not limit their rights to do with it whatever they wish. So, most people never read fine print unless they encounter some problem. Since a software license is virtually unique in limiting buyers' rights to use the product, many people ignore the license terms and assume that, having bought the package, they are free to do with it as they see fit. It is worth noting that such people lack sufficient reflection, and so their moral guilt for not respecting software license terms is mitigated or even nonexistent.

Second, having bought a software package, many people feel that the restrictions specified in the license are nothing but an attempt by the software company to maximize its profits by arbitrarily limiting their use of it. In one sense, of course,

---

339. 17 U.S.C. §506(a), possible penalties in 18 U.S.C. §2319(b). The gain need not be realized, but violations of copyright without commercial advantage or financial gain in view are not crimes. Still, copyright holders can sue and may be awarded substantial punitive damages.

the restrictions are arbitrary—those setting them do so freely, and could (and, indeed, generally do) offer to sell different and broader rights. This arbitrariness, however, is no different from that of the owner of a furnished dwelling who rents it out for specified periods, stipulating in the contract when tenants are to take possession and vacate it, restrictions on the use of appliances and furnishings, and so forth. In both cases, owners have the right to decide how far they wish to go in offering the use of what is theirs in exchange for payment; anyone who thinks the required payment excessive need not accept the offer, but those who, having accepted it, go beyond the stipulated limits take more than they bargained for and purchased.

Third, computer software seems excessively expensive to many people. Perhaps that is because copying a software program, unlike copying a book, costs very little in relation to the price of the original, and the copy—again unlike many book copies—often is almost as useful as the original. But this difference does not show that computer software is unfairly overpriced. The price mainly covers, not the cost of manufacturing the software package, but the outlay for purchasing or developing and testing the product; losses on other, unsuccessful projects; marketing expenses, including advertising, packaging, and shipping; the cost of technical support and customer service; and other business expenses, including legal fees, insurance, taxes, and interest on borrowed funds.

Moreover, two considerations suggest that, with some exceptions, computer software is not overpriced. First, people want software programs precisely because they are powerful tools that save them valuable time and enable them to get results otherwise beyond their reach. The cost of a program seldom is great in proportion to the benefits. Second, the market for the most part is free and competitive, so that alternatives to many successful products quickly appear, and prices usually are held down and often reduced. Competition also has led to rapid improvement in most sorts of software, to the benefit of users; copyright infringement, however, impedes innovation by lessening profitability and thus reducing competition.

Defending limited violations like those in question here, people sometimes argue along the following lines. Software makers surely realize that the licenses' terms will be widely violated, and undoubtedly they set their prices high enough to compensate for that. Therefore, they cannot reasonably expect customers to abide strictly by the licenses' terms, for those who did would not only put themselves at a comparative disadvantage but forgo benefits for which they already have paid. However, even when victims of theft can pass on the cost of their loss—as most merchants pass on the cost of shoplifting—the theft remains unjust. If software makers do not bear the cost of license violations, each and every one of their customers does. Violators therefore impose extra costs on software users who either have no occasion or opportunity to cheat, or are conscientious enough not to do so; violators are unfair to such other users, just as shoplifters are to other customers. Then too, since a person normally makes a contract in buying and opening the software package, people who violate the license's terms usually break a promise; and even though the duty to keep promises is not absolute, breaking them merely to avoid the disadvantage of keeping them is dishonest and unfair.

Still, titles to property are not absolute. As Vatican II teaches: "God has destined the earth and all it contains for the use of all human individuals and peoples, in such a way that, under the direction of justice accompanied by charity, created goods ought to flow abundantly to everyone on a fair basis" (GS 69). This divine plan for material goods is basic, and private property is just only insofar as it implements God's intention that everyone's genuine needs be met equitably. Therefore, it sometimes is morally justified to take what belongs to others, even if that is plainly against their will and forbidden by law, because the owners' will to retain what they have is unreasonable, and taking it in violation of the law is both fair and compatible with one's other moral responsibilities (see *LCL*, 824–25, 878–82). On this basis, in certain circumstances some people may, without moral fault, ignore the copyright of a licenser of computer software, just as, in similar circumstances, some people may ignore others' legally recognized claims to other possessions.

Circumstances of the relevant sort exist in a society whose property system carefully protects the rights of the powerful and wealthy while providing inadequately for the basic needs of the powerless who are poor, with the bad result that the wealthy live luxuriously while the poor, even with parsimony and hard work, cannot meet all their basic needs. Then the poor can be morally justified in violating the law and using or taking what legally belongs to the wealthy, not just to survive, but to meet any genuine need that cannot otherwise be met. Thus, a poor person, family, or other group needing a software program marketed by a prosperous company could be morally justified in obtaining and using an unauthorized copy. Insofar as this justification can exist, the promise given in opening a software package is not to keep the license's terms as offered by the copyright holder but as amended so as to be fair to the poor. But one should first be sure the conditions that would justify proceeding in this way really do exist.

As in other highly competitive businesses, many companies that market commercial software are not prosperous; some are struggling to establish themselves and some, though long established, are losing money or making little profit. For even poor persons to violate the copyrights of such companies plainly is unfair to all who have a stake in them: employees, customers, suppliers, and owners.

Again, those who can meet their needs by working hard and economizing are not poor, and associations and nonprofit organizations whose resources and capacity to raise money are adequate to meet other expenses do not suddenly become poor when they need computer software. Most people who think nothing of using an unauthorized copy of a software program would never take a program from a store without paying for it. There is a difference, of course—not in the justifiability of the taking, however, but only in the likelihood of getting caught. Upright people do not allow themselves to be affected by that difference and respect others' property rights even when violations would go unnoticed.

Very often, too, poor people can obtain public domain software, freeware, or inexpensive shareware adequate to meet their needs. Families with multiple computers often can meet their needs in this way, especially because children's needs usually are limited. Moreover, rather than making several copies of an expensive program, a family often can make do with one copy used in conjunction with an inexpensive or free program. It generally takes only a few minutes to import, check, reformat, and print out in a powerful word-processing program a file a child has spent many hours creating in a simple and cheap program, which might not itself be adequate to generate a satisfactory hard copy.

Circumstances that justify violating the conditions specified in a license for a software program also can exist when the copyright holder has done an injustice to the licensee, and the unauthorized copying and use of the program is appropriate as restitution or compensation (this is an instance of what classical moralists called "occult compensation"). Some companies that market software plainly do treat their customers unfairly: by misleading advertising, failing to deliver products when promised after taking orders and payment, failing to provide promised help, refusing to admit defects in programs that seriously limit their claimed usefulness, making grossly excessive profits from indispensable software on which a company has a virtual monopoly, and so forth. Copyright violation may be the only way that users who suffer such injustices have of obtaining compensation for the harm they have suffered. When this justification exists, it also justifies breaking the promise made in opening the software package. Once again, one must know the justification's conditions are fulfilled in order to judge that it exists.

One may not take something to compensate for an injustice unless certain its possessor really has done an injustice. Software users all too often judge a program defective when the problem arises from their own failure to study the manual and learn how to use the program, and some real problems are due to hardware rather than software. Moreover, one generally should not take something to compensate for an injustice without first calling the injustice to the attention of those responsible and seeking voluntary restitution, since by doing that one calls on them to do better and, if they respond suitably, strengthens genuine community with them. Finally, it is stealing to take more than is fair to compensate for an injustice—for example, making for a friend an unauthorized copy of an expensive program on the mere excuse that some rather insignificant feature of it does not work as advertised.

Someone might argue that software users are entitled to violate the terms of licenses in ways exemplified in the question, since virtually all software companies treat potential customers unfairly. The argument would be that, since vendors sell only a restricted license, they should make that policy clear in their advertising. Potential buyers are unfairly treated by advertising that stresses the advantages of products while saying nothing about the severe restrictions in licensing agreements. So, the argument would conclude, while buyers should not grossly violate licensing agreements, they need not abide by their letter.

My answer is that buyers of software who understand the licensing system are not unfairly treated by advertising that makes no mention of the restrictions. Less sophisticated buyers, who learn of the restrictions only after purchasing a software package, have been treated unfairly, even if they have the option of returning the package for full credit, since it is burdensome to buy, prepare to use, and then return a package. In my judgment, such less sophisticated buyers can justifiably violate in minor ways the first licensing agreement they encounter, and nobody who has innocently violated a software license owes restitution for doing so. But experienced software purchasers should not rationalize ongoing violations on this basis.

Besides justifiable exceptions of the preceding two kinds, sometimes the copyright holder's permission to make an exception to a license's provisions can reasonably be presumed. For example, if a user who is enthusiastic about a program temporarily installs it on friends' computers to demonstrate that it would be worth buying and removes it completely at the end of each demonstration session, he or she reasonably presumes the software maker's permission. Similarly, it seems to me, when the computer on which a program is permanently installed is temporarily not in use—for example, when it is out of order—permission may be presumed to install the program temporarily on another computer, making it available solely for the licensee's use. Again, if a licensee's printer is out of order, it seems to me that permission may be presumed to install the program temporarily on another computer so as to print out a file.

One might argue that, even where a license expressly limits installation to one machine, individuals who buy the package for their personal use may presume permission to install it on two or more computers that they alone use—for example, a desktop used at home and a laptop used on the road. One could comply with the letter of the license, the argument goes, by regularly removing the program from each computer and installing it on the other; but that would waste time and benefit nobody. I think this argument is plausible.

Similarly, in regard to the first example proposed in the question, one might argue that a family of modest means with several children and two computers reasonably presumes permission to install on both a program that a family member purchases if the only alternative is, not to purchase another copy of the program, but to limit its use to meeting the more urgent need when two or more family members want to use it at the same time. I am not certain that this argument is sound, but it is plausible that any reasonable software publisher would take a tolerant view of such a violation. And what a reasonable publisher would tolerate is the appropriate moral—and legal—standard to follow.[340] However, I think it is unsound to argue, as in the question, that families may presume permission to install programs on two or more computers merely because software makers never try to enforce their licenses' terms against families who do this. Trying to enforce the terms in such cases usually would be impractical, because evidence would be virtually impossible to obtain and legal action usually would be costly in comparison with the damages that might be won. Yet those who make no effort to enforce rights whose enforcement is impractical need not concede them, and seldom do. For example, people who make unsecured loans to friends and relatives in amounts ranging up to several hundred dollars seldom try to compel repayment, yet they often consider themselves gravely cheated if not repaid as they were promised. So,

---

340. Most instances in which the copyright holder's permission is justly presumed are instances of what is, legally speaking, "fair use"; see L. Ray Patterson and Stanley W. Lindberg, *The Nature of Copyright: A Law of Users' Rights* (Athens, Ga.: University of Georgia Press, 1991), 218–22.

that software makers do not enforce their rights against minor violations is not a sign their permission can be presumed.

What about the other question, concerning the volunteer who uses a desktop publishing program given her by someone who had purchased an updated version? The wording of licenses varies with respect to earlier versions that have been replaced with upgrades. Many exclude the transfer of earlier versions of the program; some say earlier versions may be transferred to specified sorts of recipients; still others say nothing explicit on the matter. In the last case, if the update package includes a license bearing a number different from the original, one may give the earlier version to someone else, provided one does not violate the license's terms in making the gift; but if the update package is made available under the original license, one almost certainly violates its terms by giving the earlier package to someone else while using the later version oneself. Therefore, more information would be needed to know whether the license's terms excluded the gift. If they did, the volunteer's use of the program is theft, unless one of the conditions justifying an exception to an owner's property rights is present or the copyright holder's permission can be presumed reasonably.

In any case, the three considerations offered to justify the volunteer's use of the software are fallacious.

First, it is not sound to argue that copyright infringement is not theft because the owner does not lose anything. Ordinarily, owners of copyrights lose something every time their rights are infringed: the income they would receive if others respected their rights in regard to each copy. Even if the practical alternative to copyright infringement is not using copyrighted material (and perhaps using something else instead), the unauthorized copy still is used without compensating its actual owner.

Second, generally, one may accept a gift one is offered without questioning the giver's ownership. However, if there is some reason to suspect that accepting a proffered gift will be cooperating in theft, one should not accept it without putting the doubt to rest, since one cannot receive as a gift something that, belonging to another, is not the offerer's to give. Considering how often the limits specified in computer software licenses are violated, anyone offered a copy of a commercially marketed program—even an earlier version of one that has been upgraded—does have reason for suspecting it cannot be rightly given, and should not accept it without making sure that doing so is compatible with the license.

Third, the generalization, "Software makers get rich enough from their sales to users who can charge off purchases as an expense," is not sound. Unless one knows a particular copyright holder is prospering, one unfairly risks taking from another who can ill afford the loss. Moreover, many people who cannot obtain reimbursement for the cost of a program are fully able to pay for it and should do so.

Finally, Christians using computer software should not overlook their first and overarching responsibility toward others: to love them, even if they are enemies, as Jesus has loved all fallen humankind. When dealing with a corporation, one easily forgets that the transaction will affect the individual persons who are involved in the business. Those persons include not only the business's owners—

among whom may be nonprofit corporations and people living meagerly on their investment income—but its suppliers, employees, other customers, and so on. Each of these anonymous persons is called to share in the same heavenly family life for which a Christian hopes, and so should be regarded as a brother or sister. Therefore, just as with all other requirements of justice, one's moral responsibilities with respect to the rights of software vendors not only are a product of reasonable rules but an implication of Christian love.

139: May one retain certain payments from insurance companies?

My daughter has been taking acrobatics at a private school that specializes in that sort of thing. One class was on the front handspring, which she had never done before. When she tried to do it, she landed wrong and broke her left leg. The doctors' and hospital's bills were covered by our family health insurance, except for the policy's deductible and coinsurance. Last week, when my daughter returned to class, the manager of the school spontaneously said he thought the accident had resulted from negligence by the instructor, and he asked me to submit all the bills and a statement of other costs, including my daughter's lost pay from her part-time job. I did, and the school's liability insurance company has offered to reimburse us for everything, provided we agree to forgo any further claim. May I accept that offer and keep both the partial payment of the bills from our own insurance and the full reimbursement from theirs?

Another case. Five years ago my husband had to stop suddenly at a pedestrian crossing and was hit in the rear by a truck. His injuries put him in the hospital for a week. Afterwards, he still had to go for therapy for his neck. The trucking company's insurer offered to cover everything, plus twenty thousand dollars, if my husband agreed to forgo any further claim, and he did. Within another month the therapy was completed; he felt fine and has had no problems since. Obviously, they paid him the twenty thousand thinking he might have further problems. Since he didn't, he wonders whether he ought to refund some or all of it.

Analysis:

This question calls for application of the norms regarding lying and candor. To make a just claim on insurance, one must truthfully supply all required information. Assuming this couple did that, they may try to negotiate a larger settlement than has been offered by the school's liability insurance carrier and keep the settlement paid by the trucking company's insurer. In the first case, the settlement should be, and in the second it was, not only for the damage clearly done to the injured parties but for the residual risk of later ill effects. If medical expenses for the daughter's injury were paid by the health insurance on the basis of a statement by the questioner that turns out to have been false, she should correct the mistake. If not, she should find out whether the family's health insurance excludes payments for injuries covered by other insurance; if it seems to exclude them, she should inform her health insurance carrier of the settlement by the school's insurer as soon as it is paid.

The reply could be along the following lines:

In asking these questions, you and your husband manifest sensitive and sound consciences. Moral questions about insurance claims are hardly likely to arise unless a significant amount is at stake. Hence, questions in this field regularly concern grave matter. Nevertheless, some people who are honest in dealings with individuals and most organizations have no qualms about defrauding an insurance company, reasoning that it is wealthy and will suffer little harm. Like other business expenses, however, the costs of fraudulent claims are distributed by insurance companies among policyholders, so that cheating on a claim eventually burdens other people.[341]

The first requirement in making an insurance claim is to be completely honest. It is dishonest not only to lie but to withhold relevant information requested on a claim form or by a claims adjuster—for example, to omit some fact that might disqualify the claim. If one has been honest, however, one almost always may accept any payments or settlements offered, since insurers take great care in interpreting their own policies, evaluating any claims arising under them, and protecting their own interests. In responding to the questions raised by the two cases you describe, I shall assume you were completely honest.

The settlement offered by the school's liability insurance company in the first case is not merely to pay the medical and hospital costs already reimbursed by your health insurance. Rather, the insurer is using those bills and other costs, including your daughter's lost income, as a basis for settling a potential claim based on negligence. That claim might eventually be for a far greater amount, if your daughter later has serious problems that could be traced back to the injury. If you accept the payment offered, you will be forgoing the right to additional payment in such an eventuality. For that reason, I believe you would be justified in trying to negotiate a larger payment. You certainly will not do the company an injustice in accepting the settlement.

At the same time, your health insurance perhaps also covers the medical and hospital bills for your daughter's broken leg. If so, you need not refund the payment made by that insurance company. I say "perhaps also covers," because many health insurance contracts exclude coverage for injuries due to accidents when the costs are otherwise covered, as they may be in this case. If your health insurance policy includes that provision, you probably stated in making your claim that the injury was not otherwise covered. Though such a statement would have been truthful at the time you made it, you now know it may have been mistaken, and, if you made it, you may have a duty to correct it.

But what if you made no such statement? If you tell your health insurer about the settlement offer, they might ask you to refund their payment even if you are

---

341. Michael Clarke, "The Control of Insurance Fraud: A Comparative View," *British Journal of Criminology,* 30 (1990): 1–7, describes the rationalization of insurance fraud and explains why insurers may prefer to pass on the cost of fraud rather than to resist it vigorously.

entitled to keep the money. Still, you should at least try to examine the policy to find out whether it requires repayment. If your health insurance is provided by your employer, perhaps you do not have a copy of the policy itself. In that case, unless the policy is available to an employee who asks to see it, the insurer has chosen in its own interests to limit the information available to you, so I think you may decide what to do on the basis of your study of whatever materials the insurer and your employer do provide.

In the second case, again assuming your husband was completely honest, he did nothing wrong in accepting the settlement offered by the trucking company's insurer. The insurer thereby forestalled the risk of having to pay out far more if your husband's injuries led to ongoing, serious medical problems, while he accepted the corresponding risk of receiving far too little. Provided such a settlement is made freely by two parties competent to judge their own interests, there is no reason to doubt its fairness. In this case, the insurance company's agent almost certainly was better able than your husband to estimate appropriate compensation for the risk he assumed. So if your husband took the first offer instead of bargaining for the maximum the company was prepared to pay for a settlement, he probably settled too easily and got less than he should have. Moreover, even after five years, he still lives with the risk he accepted, since he cannot be certain he will never have any problems resulting from that injury.

140: May a farmer continue planting tobacco?

I make a living and support my family by growing tobacco, but I know regular use is deadly. I quit years ago. Since then, I have discouraged my family and friends from starting and have urged the smokers among them to quit.

I sell my crop to a major tobacco company; most of it goes into cigarettes, some into other products. The company advertises in a way plainly meant not only to win smokers from other brands but to get young people to take up smoking. I could not do that in good conscience.

Nevertheless, I've continued planting tobacco up to now. If I could make an adequate income from a different crop or could sell the farm and support my wife and children in some other way, I would. But I've explored the possibilities, and none of them is promising.

I have reasons for thinking it is not wrong to continue planting tobacco. First, I cannot stop the company from advertising as it does, and so I am not responsible for that. Second, people have been warned about the risks of using tobacco, and nobody has to do it. Third, if I quit planting tobacco, I honestly do not believe it would save even one life. Fourth, some people do use tobacco only occasionally, and there is no evidence they are taking any significant risk; so, it's not as though there were no possible legitimate use for what I produce. Finally, the government has not done what it should: put an end to tobacco advertising, do everything possible to discourage young people from starting to smoke, and tax cigarettes more heavily.

A neighbor who retired two years ago says all my reasons are just rationalizations. He is sorry he did not quit growing tobacco years ago. That worries me, since, though he is not a Catholic, he is probably the most decent and Christian man I know.

Analysis:

This question concerns cooperation in gravely self-injurious behavior. The regular and typical use of tobacco is morally wrong, and, because deadly, always grave matter in my judgment. The first three reasons the questioner gives for judging it not wrong to continue planting tobacco do show that doing so is not unfair to tobacco users. But even if some people use tobacco legitimately, the questioner cooperates with typical users. If he carefully avoids in any way contributing to the promotion of regular and typical use, he does not cooperate formally. Because his material cooperation impedes his witness against typical tobacco use, he should try again to find an alternative way of making a minimally adequate living. But if he cannot, he may, in my judgment, continue planting tobacco.

The reply could be along the following lines:

I doubt that your reflections are mere rationalizations. Your moral earnestness in questioning what you have been doing strongly suggests that up to now you have not chosen to act against your conscience in growing and selling your crop. Like growers back through the generations, you have worked hard and made an honest living. Unaware of tobacco's deadliness, they were innocent of wrongdoing; you have become aware of the consequences of using tobacco and are asking questions because your conscience is sound.[342]

If using tobacco ever was rational, surely today there are stronger reasons for not using it: the danger of addiction, the risk of very bad effects on health, the financial cost, and the impact on others—both those who imitate the bad example and those who are harmed by others' tobacco use or simply find it objectionable.[343] Therefore, in my judgment, using tobacco not only is foolish but morally wrong. How wrong? As you say, regular and typical use of tobacco is deadly. For that reason alone, I believe, such use, as against occasional light use, always is grave matter.[344] Moreover, the gravity of typical tobacco use often is aggravated by other factors, such as bad example to young people.

The first three reasons you propose for judging it not wrong for you to continue planting and selling tobacco bear on whether doing that is unfair to tobacco users. You plainly are not responsible for the despicable advertising of the tobacco company to which you sell your crop, and nothing you can do would stop it. While you do grow and sell tobacco knowing that people will misuse it, they have been

342. The tobacco companies, rather than the growers, reap most of the profits and are morally responsible for intending cigarette smoking; see Richard Kluger, *Ashes to Ashes: America's Hundred-Year Cigarette War, the Public Health, and the Unabashed Triumph of Philip Morris* (New York: Alfred A. Knopf, 1996).

343. See *Smoking Tobacco and Health: A Factbook*, DHHS Publication No. (CDC) 87–8397, rev. ed. (Washington, D.C.: U.S. Department of Health and Human Services, Public Health Service, Center for Disease Control, 1989); Richard Peto et al., *Mortality from Smoking in Developed Countries 1950–2000: Indirect Estimates from National Vital Statistics* (New York: Oxford University Press, 1994).

344. See *LCL*, 537–38, including n. 136.

warned, as you point out, and will get it from others if not from you. Everything considered, I agree that you are not being unfair to users—that is, you are not violating the Golden Rule—by continuing to plant and sell tobacco.

The requirement of fairness, however, is not the only form moral responsibility takes; you also should think about the bad consequences of continuing to grow and market tobacco, not least for typical tobacco users. You could respond with your fourth point: There might be a legitimate use of tobacco, that is, light and occasional use, which has not been shown to be harmful. For the sake of argument, I grant the factual claim that there are people whose use of tobacco is harmless. But such light users certainly are few, and you cannot cause your crop to be used only by them. Therefore, in growing and marketing tobacco, you almost always cooperate with the seriously self-destructive, and so objectively gravely wrong, behavior of typical smokers.

What is your moral responsibility with respect to this cooperation? It is grave if you intend the wrongful behavior. That would be so if you did anything in order to maintain the market for your product—for example, if you supported legislation that would protect tobacco companies against lawsuits or worked against measures, such as increased cigarette taxes, that would discourage smoking. But if, while avoiding such activities, you merely accept as a given the typical use of tobacco that creates a profitable market for it and strictly limit your involvement in the industry to growing and selling your crop, you need not intend the wrongful use people make of the tobacco you market.

But even if you do not intend tobacco users' self-destructive behavior, are you justified in contributing to it? The other considerations I have mentioned do not, in my judgment, preclude your continuing to plant tobacco. However, effective witness against its use is needed, and your witness, which could save some people's lives, would be especially credible. You do well to discourage your family and friends from starting smoking tobacco and to urge the smokers among them to quit. But you should not limit your concern to those near and dear; you should extend the same witness to other people insofar as you can. People who do not know you well are hardly likely to believe that you really think using tobacco is wrong as long as you continue making your living from it. You would convey the message more effectively if you stopped planting and explained your reasons for doing so. In my judgment, therefore, you should explore more carefully other ways of making a living, and should be prepared to accept a lower standard of living and take significant risks to extricate yourself from the tobacco industry so that you will be able to work more effectively against its typical use.

Nevertheless, provided you carefully avoid doing anything that would involve intending the typical use of tobacco, I do not think you and other tobacco farmers are obliged to quit if you really have no other way of earning enough to meet the genuine needs of yourselves and your families.

Someone might argue that alcohol abuse does even more harm than tobacco use, so that, if the preceding analysis is correct, any conscientious person who now encourages the use of alcoholic beverages also must stop doing that. The argument, however, is fallacious because the analogy is not sound. Alcoholic beverages can be and often are used rightly; their abuse, though widespread, is incidental, so that people who promote alcohol use need not intend its abuse. Of course, some do intend it, and they should repent. Perhaps some could not profit without promoting alcohol abuse and so cannot help intending it. They ought to give up their profitable involvement with alcohol. People who need not and do not intend the abuse of alcohol, however, may continue to promote and profit from its use, provided they do what they reasonably can to prevent and discourage abuse.

141: May a company pay a bribe to obtain a third-world government contract?

I am a project manager for an Australian construction company. Last month I was sent to the capital city of a Latin American nation to bid on a major governmental project. If we get the contract, we will build six buildings during the next three years.

Bidding here is open; it amounts to an auction. According to law, nevertheless, the ministry responsible for the project may choose among the three low bidders. Our bid of just under four hundred million dollars is the lowest and objectively, I am convinced, the best. We have the experience, financing, and human resources to do the work well and on schedule, and we can offer the best price because we happen to be completing a similar project in a nearby country and will avoid certain costs that our competitors would incur.

This morning a go-between told me that, despite its merits, our bid will have no chance of being chosen unless I agree to employ a "consultant"—the husband of the niece of the minister who will make the decision. His "fee" would be one-half of one percent of all payments we receive under the contract, and his sole role would be "to assist in processing legally required paper work with the ministry." One might view the arrangement as a sort of unofficial tax on doing business with this government, but, as far as I am concerned, it is nothing but a bribe, and our company has a strict rule against paying bribes.

If I refuse, we seem certain to lose this contract, which we need to utilize our present employees and other assets during the next four years. If I accept, I will be breaking the law here and violating company policy. However, I have left room in the bid for unexpected expenses at this level, so there still would be enough profit to make getting the job well worth our while. Should I refuse to pay the bribe or agree to it?

Analysis:

This question concerns cooperation in wrongdoing; it also calls for derivation of norms for the questioner's action as the company's agent. If the questioner judges it more likely that the project itself will not serve the nation's common good than that it will, the company's contracting to carry it out would be formal cooperation in wrongdoing, and he or she should refuse to pay the bribe. If the questioner judges that the project more likely will serve the nation's common good than not, then he or she should neither disobey company policy by agreeing to pay the bribe without authorization nor refer the issue to his or her superiors before judging whether paying it would be morally acceptable. Paying the bribe would be wrong if it requires actions evil in themselves, such as lying, and probably would be wrong if it violates Australian law. Even if not morally excluded on any of the preceding grounds, paying the bribe might be wrong insofar as it would be material cooperation with the corrupt practices of the local leaders—practices contrary to the nation's common good and unjust to its people. If the questioner concludes that paying the bribe would be wrong, he or she should not refer the issue to higher management but should simply refuse, thus avoiding tempting superiors to sin and forestalling the possibility of being ordered to act contrary to conscience. If the questioner concludes that paying the bribe would be morally acceptable, he or she should refer the problem to higher management.

The reply could be along the following lines:

In considering whether to pay the bribe, you need to look at the relationship between the nation's common good and the project.[345] Will the project serve the nation's common good? Or will it serve only the corrupt leadership and the people they represent? If you judge it more likely that the project will not serve the nation's common good than that it will, making the contract to carry it out, even if bribery were not an issue, would be wrong. For if the project will not serve the common good, the corrupt leaders' decision to carry it out will be a choice to defraud the nation's people of the resources that will be misused for the project. In contracting with the corrupt leaders, your company not only will undertake to carry out their project but will intend their wrongful contractual commitment as the necessary means for getting the work and profiting from it. But to intend another's gravely wrongful choice is gravely wrong. Therefore, if you judge that the project will not serve the nation's common good, you should deliberately lose the contract by refusing to pay the bribe. But assuming you judge that the project more probably will serve the nation's common good than not, I offer the following considerations about the possible moral acceptability of paying the bribe.

One who offers a bribe to someone who neither asked for it nor is known to expect it plainly intends to motivate the person to prefer self-interest to the duties pertaining to his or her proper role. That intention constitutes a sin of scandal unless it would be immoral for that individual to fulfill his or her duties—for example, the duty of a Mafia gunman to kill people. But your question concerns a bribe solicited by another. Paying such a bribe is not always wrong, since the one who pays it neither leads the other person into sin nor does the injustice, but rather is its victim.[346]

---

345. In discussions of foreign corrupt practices, the common good of the foreign nation and the interests of its people are usually ignored; see, e.g., Bill Shaw, "Foreign Corrupt Practices Act A Legal and Moral Analysis," *Journal of Business Ethics,* 7 (1988): 789–95.

346. The U.S. has antibribery legislation—principally the Foreign Corrupt Practices Act of 1977—that would prohibit an American company from paying the solicited bribe. Though doubtless sometimes violated, the law has significantly reduced the volume of business by U.S. companies in nations where bribery is prevalent; see James R. Hines, Jr., *Forbidden Payment*

I do not think you should immediately take at face value the message delivered by the person you call a go-between. First, make inquiries to verify that winning the contract really is contingent on paying the bribe. Two possible ways of doing this occur to me, and there may be others. Considering the amount of money at stake, you might try a direct approach—seek a private appointment with the responsible minister and, if you get it, tell him about the message you received and see how he reacts. Or you might consult people who lately have done business with the same ministry: more experienced local agents of international businesses that are not competing for the contract.

Assuming your inquiries indicate that the message is reliable, you actually have at least three options, not two. Acting on the authority you have been given, you could agree to pay the bribe, or you could refuse to pay it, or you could refer the matter to higher management in your company for their decision.

It seems to me that the first option is morally excluded. As an agent of your company, you should do your work within the framework of its policy unless you have a compelling reason to do otherwise. While the company's interests appear to be gravely at stake in this situation, so that an exception to its official policy (assuming the action involved would be otherwise morally acceptable) might be warranted, I see no reason why you need to make this exception, and in principle it would be more appropriate that those responsible for the company as a whole make it. Moreover, if you unilaterally agree to pay the bribe, you perhaps will have to report those payments to your superiors as consultant's fees, and that reporting would be misleading and untruthful because intended to deceive higher management about payments that violate company policy.

That seems to point to the third option: to refer the matter to higher management. In that case, you may be ordered to pay the bribe. That will be no problem if you can obey in good conscience. But if not, you will have both occasioned your superiors' doing what you judge wrong and put yourself in an occasion of sin, since you will have to choose between refusing to carry out their decision and violating your conscience. Now, therefore, before communicating with higher management, you should consider and judge whether the company may pay the bribe or should abide by its existing policy and refuse. If you conclude that the company should stand by its policy, exercise your authority in accord with that policy and refuse to pay the bribe. If you conclude that paying the bribe would be morally acceptable, refer the matter to higher management.

To bribe someone to do something wrong always is wrong. If an honest minister would not award the contract to your company, it would be wrong to obtain it by bribery. However, you say your bid ought to be accepted. If so, you would be bribing a corrupt official to do what he ought to do anyway. Still, paying the bribe might be wrong for other reasons. First, it might be impossible without violating Australian laws your company should obey, either because they are just and

---

Foreign Bribery and American Business after 1977, NBER Working Paper 5266 (Cambridge, Mass.: National Bureau of Economic Research, 1995). A thorough treatment of the problem as it was just before the enactment of the 1977 law: Neil H. Jacoby et al., *Bribery and Extortion in World Business: A Study of Corporate Political Payments Abroad* (New York: Macmillan, 1977).

applicable laws or because they call for your company's compliance despite being unjust and/or inapplicable (see *LCL,* 874–83). Second, paying the bribe might involve doing something always wrong, such as lying. Third, even if governmental corruption is widespread there, it might be unjustifiable for your company to violate local laws.

Assuming the first two are not problems, why might violating local laws be unjustifiable? It should be presumed that these laws protect the society's common good. The corrupt officials' demand on your company might seem to be only a sort of unofficial tax, another cost of doing business. But the corrupt practices of these officials impose the burden of ongoing bad government on their own citizens. Those who cannot afford to pay bribes are deprived of their rights. Officials should carry out their duties as a service to the common good; in taking bribes, they are motivated by self-interest hardly likely to coincide with the common good. Real competition for the government's business is undermined, and officials defraud their nation of far more than the amount of the bribes they receive. By paying the bribe, your company would sustain and contribute to that unjust structure.

Could that cooperation be justified? Perhaps. You say the company needs this contract to utilize employees and other assets during the next four years. Presumably, employees otherwise will lose their jobs, investors will be deprived of profit on their investment, and so on. Furthermore, perhaps giving the bribe will make it possible for the project to go forward on terms that will minimize its cost to the country's people and be unlikely to worsen or prolong the government's corruption, while refusing to give it is likely to increase the project's cost and unlikely to improve the corrupt system, hasten its end, or mitigate the lot of citizens. If so, cooperation within the unjust structure would be morally acceptable.

If, having judged that paying the bribe would be morally acceptable, you refer the problem to higher management and they order you to pay it, you of course should try to negotiate more favorable terms, as you do with other suppliers of goods and services. Proceed carefully, too, and gather evidence of the government's corruption. In this way, you will be prepared to resist additional extortionate demands, and perhaps will be in a position at the end of the project to expose the government's corruption, thereby making some small contribution to ending it.

142: How far may a taxi driver go in cooperating with patrons' immoralities?

Six months ago I lost the only job I ever had—doing precision grinding in a shop that made machine tools. The company folded, and no other outfit had an opening. We had savings, and I bought into a contract deal with Suburban Taxi and invested in a cab. They provide the license and dispatching service for a monthly fee plus one dollar per dispatch. Everything else I take in over expenses is mine, and I can work whatever hours I want. The first two months I did not make as much as I had been getting in unemployment compensation, and I thought I had made a disastrous mistake. Driving seven days a week and averaging ten hours a day, I also miss the time my wife and I used to have together on weekends. But now I am catching on to the business. I think I can make a go of it and might even be able to make a fairly decent living.

In this business, I meet all kinds of people and see the seamier side of life, and a few things are bothering my conscience.

Sometimes people want to use the cab as a place to do something immoral. They give me a destination or just tell me to drive around a quiet neighborhood, and along the way I realize they are taking drugs or having sex. They may ask me to take them to a quiet place and park for a while, so that they can do what they want. Youngsters especially ask for that, and, having kids of my own, I hate to do it.

Sometimes a man wants me to cruise around until he spots someone to try to pick up or buy drugs from. One guy even wanted me to help him find someone to mug and offered to share the take. (I refused and told him to get out!)

A lot of my best business comes from several large hotels where conventions are held and people stay when they are in town on business. The best deal is a run into downtown. From there I always can go to the airport and get a fare back to my suburban base. And, even with the wait in line at the airport, the round trip really pays. In the evening, a fare often wants to head downtown for sex or drugs. Of course, if they give me any definite destination in the county, the law requires me to take them to it. I could lose my license if I refused, so I don't have much choice. But sometimes they tell me what they are after and want me to take them where they are likely to find it, or even to suggest a place, such as a "good" strip club.

I am learning fast. Some drivers get something for delivering business to the strip clubs, massage parlors, drug dealers, and so forth. I am not about to make any deals like that. But to support my family I do need all the income I can get. To tell the truth, I want to go just as far as I can. But I am afraid I have been going too far, and that is why my conscience is bothering me.

Analysis:

This question concerns cooperation in wrongdoing and the responsibilities to admonish, bear witness, and report crimes. The questioner has refused to cooperate formally in wrongdoing, and his problems mainly concern material cooperation. He may comply with the law and take passengers to definite destinations, even if they tell him that they plan to do something immoral there. But under suitable conditions he should admonish and try to divert passengers who reveal immoral intentions. Providing information about how to carry out an immoral intention might remain material cooperation; but, applying the usual criteria, such cooperation, in my judgment, almost always would be morally unacceptable. The same must be said of cruising about or finding a suitable place to park so that passengers can engage in specified immoral activities. Civic responsibility, limited by reasonable self-concern, requires reporting crimes and trying to prevent them. The questioner also should admonish minors who behave immorally in his cab, especially if they are sure to realize that he is aware of what they are doing.

The reply could be along the following lines:

Usually, when people ask how far they can go without sinning, I respond by criticizing their legalism and urging them to commit themselves to more generous service and the pursuit of holiness. But you have good reason for wanting to know precisely where your moral obligations lie—you must support your family and already are working hard to fulfill that responsibility. Under the circumstances, the fact that your conscience is bothering you is a sign of appropriate moral sensitivity. So: Precisely how far may a taxi driver go in these matters?

To a great extent, your problem is one of cooperation. Cooperation in wrongdoing that involves sharing the wrongdoer's bad will is always wrong. Any taxi driver who makes a deal, such as you rightly reject, with a purveyor of vice—for example, a strip club operator or drug dealer—to deliver prospective patrons must intend that they and the proprietors of the establishments do business. By intending that, a driver endorses the evil intentions of both parties to those transactions and thus wrongly cooperates with them. Similarly, you could not have helped the mugger find a victim in exchange for a share in the take without also sharing the mugger's bad intention. That would have been not only immoral cooperation but a criminal act of your own, and so you rightly refused.

It seems to me you should report to the public authorities the information that commissions are being paid to taxi drivers for delivering business to certain unlawful enterprises. While your report may well be ignored, it might help the authorities deal with those unlawful activities or encourage them to undertake such an effort. Reporting the intending mugger to the police probably would have been pointless. But in refusing his proposal, you also should have explained why you would not do such a thing and urged him to repent. That admonition might have been fruitless too, but very likely you had nothing to lose by it, and, reinforced with a prayer, it might have borne fruit.

The law requiring you to take passengers to any destination they specify within the county presumably is just, and only serious reasons would justify refusing to comply. In abiding by it and so taking passengers wherever they wish to go, you need only share their intention to reach their destination. If a passenger tells you he or she wishes to reach a certain destination in order to commit some sin there, you need not intend the sinning as an end and you can choose to transport the passenger as a means to earning the fare, while only accepting the fact that it facilitates the sin. People who do not state their plans perhaps intend nothing wrong in going to a destination, no matter what it is. For example, a woman going to an abortion clinic could be planning to intercept and dissuade people from having abortions there.

Still, even in taking people to definite destinations in compliance with the law, you may be tempted to approve of their immoral desires. Needing all the income you can get, when business is slow you might wish that a group of people attending a convention would decide to go to town for sinful purposes. Deliberately entertaining that wish would involve willing their immorality. You must guard your thoughts so as to avoid sinful wishes—which also would be profitless, since your wishing does not affect others' choices.

Moreover, even when people ask to be taken to a definite destination, if you have good reason to think their plans are immoral, and especially if they tell you of their immoral plans, you should try to divert them or urge them to change their minds. For instance, if someone wishes to be taken "for a night on the town" to a district where immoral entertainment and prostitutes are available, you might point out that the neighborhood is crime ridden and the prostitutes may well be diseased, and suggest other, morally acceptable entertainment as a better alternative.

In making such efforts, of course, you may not tell lies, and your duty to admonish passengers is not absolute. You need say nothing unless you think speaking up might be effective, and you can proceed in ways unlikely to deprive you of needed income. For example, rather than admonishing a passenger before you arrive at a destination and receive the fare and a tip, you might carry cards with brief, carefully prepared exhortations suitable for various situations, and give them to passengers after settling with them. For instance, for women going to an abortion clinic:

Is abortion a necessary evil?
It *is* bad. An abortion wipes out a tiny baby.
But it is *never* necessary.
Birthright helps a woman make a better choice!
Call: [telephone number].

If someone who wants to do something immoral does not tell you to go to a definite destination but asks you to select or suggest a place, he or she is seeking your help, not only as a taxi driver, but also as a possible source of information about opportunities to fulfill illicit desires. Though you could supply such information without intending the wrongdoing, the cooperation almost always would be wrong due to its bad consequences. You might be tempted to encourage the person to go where you suggest, and you hardly would be in a position to bear witness or try to deter him or her. Therefore, it seems to me, in such cases you almost always should refuse to cooperate, ask passengers to state a definite destination, and, if necessary, take them back to where you picked them up. Of course, if someone forced you to provide information about where to satisfy illicit desires—for example, by threatening you with a gun—you could do so not only without intending that they satisfy them but without wrongly accepting bad consequences. But it seems to me you may not provide such information under ordinary conditions, even if you cannot otherwise make adequate income as a taxi driver.

My judgment is the same with respect to requests to cruise about or identify a suitable place to park for specified immoral purposes. However, if someone wishes to cruise in a particular neighborhood without specifying any immoral purpose, you may comply and need not ask about his or her intentions. I suggest you have in mind various places unsuitable for sexual activity and/or drug abuse but suitable for a quiet conversation or a pleasant stroll. Then, if someone tells you to go to a quiet place and park without specifying an immoral purpose, you can drive to or suggest one of those places.

Your problem is more complex when someone simply directs you to a particular quiet place and asks you to park, or without asking permission takes advantage of your cab's comparative privacy to engage in morally illicit behavior. Generally, I believe, you should respect passengers' privacy and ignore what they do and say to one another in your cab. But if you notice people engaging in what you believe to be criminal activity in your cab, you have a civic responsibility, limited by reasonable concern about your own safety, to try to prevent the crime. If you think reporting the incident to the public authorities might help, you ought to do that.

Moreover, if you notice minors engaging in seriously immoral behavior, such as sex play, in your cab, tell them you have children of your own and admonish them. If they do not desist, do what you can, consistent with your legal responsibilities, to cut short their ride. This obligation will be the greater if the misbehaving young people are sure to realize that you are aware of what they are doing, for then your toleration will seem to condone their wrongdoing. Even in the case of adults, if silence would seem to condone the wrongdoing, it would be appropriate for you to express disapproval.

The moral problems might tempt you to stop trying to make a living by driving a cab. This service, however, usually meets a real and legitimate public need. I doubt that observing moral limits will prevent you from doing well in the business, particularly if you keep your cab clean and comfortable, and provide dependable and courteous service to regular customers.

Carried out in a Christian way, taxi driving offers many opportunities for witness and spiritual growth. Many drivers display personal items; you might get an icon or crucifix whose artistic quality would appeal even to nonbelievers and mount it on your dashboard where passengers will see it. When people ask questions or talk about it, or otherwise provide suitable opportunities, you can tell them about your faith. During your long hours of work and many periods of waiting for a fare, you have a good deal of time to use as you see fit. I am sure you will use some of it in thinking about family problems and making plans. I suggest some be used for spiritual reading and regular prayer, not least for your passengers: that at the end of their lives all will safely reach the right destination.

143: May a club owner book acts with morally questionable elements?

I have been married thirty-five years and am the father of eight, two of whom still depend on me for support. I support my family by owning and managing a combination cafe and nightclub. We put on music and comedy acts, both local and nationally touring ones. During the last several years, I have grown increasingly worried about the content of some of this programming.

Occasionally we have a program suitable for families, but for the club to make money, most programs have to be aimed at adults. Nationally touring shows are booked through promoters, whose better offers often involve a package of two or more acts. I usually know pretty much what an act will be like, but sometimes I am surprised.

It is easy to exclude certain types of acts—for example, heavy metal, satanic "music." Even if a promoter is pushing this sort of thing, I turn it down: "It brings in a rowdy crowd, with a real risk of damage to my place." My concern is with programming that is harder to censor: immodest attire by performers, lyrics or skit that ridicule sound values, irreverence toward God and things religious, acts meant to appeal to gays and lesbians, witchcraft (it came as a surprise from a booked singer), approval and encouragement of hedonism, and so forth.

Besides providing a living for us, the business has another good aspect. Often after a show is over, and occasionally at other times, I get a chance to talk seriously with performers and others involved in the business. Many times, I can explain my faith and defend it. Not always, but often, people have shown more respect, at least while here, and a few performers have told me they see the point and will permanently eliminate objectionable elements from their acts.

If I program only acts I am certain are morally sound, I will soon be out of business. Those I deal with regard me as selective, and others in the business see me as setting the tone of the club, which they consider quite restrained. I do want to maintain a decent tone in my place, but freedom of speech and rejection of censorship put limits on what I can do.

What is my responsibility? If I sold the club, someone interested only in making money might book programming that would do even more harm to audiences. Would I be responsible for that, so that I may not sell? If I simply closed the club, it would be a great financial loss, since we not only make our living from it but have most of our money tied up in it and our home. Should I keep on walking this tightrope, trying to keep the club more or less decent, even while the acts available become more questionable year by year?

Analysis:

This question mainly concerns scandal, which the questioner must avoid. While he may intentionally book acts objectionable on various grounds, he should not intentionally program anything that appeals to patrons by involving objective immorality, supplying material for their sins, or confirming them in a sinful way of life. This responsibility requires a reasonable effort before booking any act to ascertain that it will be morally acceptable. If an act includes unexpected objectionable content, even though other responsibilities may justify the questioner's tolerating what it would have been wrong for him to program intentionally, he should not tolerate a performance likely to lead some patrons into grave sin and/or undercut his Christian witness. If he examines his conscience and judges he has been transgressing the moral limits, he should stop doing so at once and reform the business so that it is operating morally. Then, but only then, may he sell it.

The reply could be along the following lines:

In general, you obviously take a sound attitude toward your business. You do not regard it simply as a way of making a living, but as an opportunity to bear witness to your faith, and you are concerned, as you should be, about the moral effect on patrons of the entertainment you offer. Since leading others into a grave sin, even a sin to which they are predisposed, is a grave sin of scandal, you have good reason for that concern.

You perhaps should extend it a bit further, beyond not doing your customers moral injury to benefiting them as much as possible. To do this, you must consider how good entertainment should fit into their lives. It should help them to relax, to celebrate, to communicate with one another, and so strengthen them and their relationships, and should send them back to their other responsibilities—at work, home, school, and so on—more ready to fulfill them.

In considering the morally questionable characteristics of entertainment available for booking, first make a distinction between (1) what is tasteless, vulgar, or religiously insensitive, and (2) what appeals to some members of the audience precisely by involving objective immorality (such as blasphemy or witchcraft) or by supplying material for sin (such as pornography) or by confirming them in a sinful way of life (such as entertainment meant to appeal to homosexually active persons by implicitly or explicitly approving their behavior). In trying to book programs that will be profitable, you may if necessary include some involving only the first. But the second you may not intentionally program, since in doing that you would intentionally lead your customers into sin by seeking their approval and enjoyment of the material, which either would be gravely sinful in itself or a near occasion of grave sin.

What does *may not intentionally program* mean? I do not think it means you must be certain every act you book is of good moral value. It means that when you know an act bases its appeal on something unacceptable, you may not book it. It also means you must try to find out whether an unfamiliar act will be unacceptable, and, if that seems likely, not book it.

Until you have made a contract, I see no reason why you should consider yourself constrained by concerns about freedom of speech and censorship. As the owner of the place, you have every right, not only morally but legally, to decide what you will and will not book; you are responsible for the tone of your place and have the right to be selective. Moreover, I am confident that a competent lawyer could draw up language for the contracts you make when booking acts requiring performers to observe your standards and to exclude specific sorts of behavior you consider morally unacceptable.

Even if you take due precautions and book only what you believe will be morally acceptable, a performer may confront you with content you could not have booked in good conscience. In that case, you could tolerate the performance and accept its morally bad effect on patrons without intending that evil. The prospect of serious financial and/or other injury to you and your family might justify such toleration within limits. But your tolerance must end if it seems to you likely some of your patrons will suffer grave moral injury and/or your Christian witness will be undercut. For example, you would be obliged to cancel an act if it unexpectedly included straightforward pornography.

Obviously, you are devoted to your faith and are conscientious. If not, you would never have sent me this question. Moreover, I take seriously your point that besides providing income for your family, you value your business as a channel for bearing witness to your faith. Still, you have been increasingly uneasy about the entertainment you have been providing, and you must now try to make a sound judgment of conscience. Bring to bear every bit of faith and devotion you have, remembering Jesus' warning: What does it profit if one gains the whole world but loses one's very soul (see Mt 16.26, Mk 8.36, Lk 9.25)? Plainly, if the whole world is not worth the price paid for sinning, your business is not worth it, though it has been of great significance to you and your family.

What must you do if, after thinking over what you have been doing, you find you certainly or probably have been transgressing the moral limits? Stop transgressing them at once. May you sell the club? If you wish to sell it because you judge it to be immoral, the answer depends on precisely what you would be selling.

It would be right for you to sell the morally indifferent or good elements of the business: not only the building and fixtures but the patronage of people who are satisfied with morally acceptable entertainment. But it would be wrong for you to sell contracts to provide morally questionable entertainment during the coming months and/or the patronage of people accustomed to such entertainment. Since such "assets" owe their "value" to the moral evil they involve, they should not be sold, just as sinful sexual acts should not be bought and sold. So, if you cannot sell only the business's moral elements, you may not sell it.

But you could try to reform your place to bring it within moral limits. This need not mean offering only bland, so-called family entertainment, as that is understood today. Surely there can be morally acceptable and even constructive entertainment suited and pleasing to a variety of adults with differing tastes and levels of sophistication. You might try to appeal to a new audience, such as senior citizens, whose tastes are more easily satisfied with morally acceptable material. If there is no nearby theater for live performances, you might obtain the patronage of audiences by allowing amateur companies to perform in your club. You also might experiment with the forms of entertainment that made an old-fashioned pub attractive.

If you use your imagination and try to make your place appealing in new ways to fresh customers, that might lead to greater success than you anticipate. However, if your best efforts fail and the place is no longer profitable, you could then put it on the market and, as is usual in selling anything, ask no questions about potential buyers' plans for it. You would be proceeding like the repentant owners of a house of prostitution who turn it into a rooming house but find it no longer profitable; they may sell it without asking potential buyers what they plan to do with it.

144: Must sellers and buyers reveal relevant information?

As a real estate broker, I often encounter moral problems that center on whether one party can legitimately take advantage of information unavailable to the other. Lying plainly is wrong, and concealing facts that affect the value of the property to be sold seems tantamount to lying. But what about a case where one party has information the other lacks? Here, it seems to me, finer lines are needed. Consider three examples.

Betty, who is single, is promoted and receives a substantial raise. She decides to offer to buy the house she has been renting from Ben, who has been working abroad for several years. Since he left the country, the opening of a technology park that brought many new jobs to the area has caused properties in the neighborhood to appreciate by about twenty percent, though real estate prices in the United States as a whole have been stagnant. Betty sends Ben a contract offering $134,950—

about $10,000 dollars more than the house was worth when he left the country. Expecting he will check out current prices and make a counteroffer somewhat above $150,000, she hopes they will agree on a price between the two figures. But Ben simply signs the contract Betty sent, and so accepts substantially less than he could have got for the house.

The second case. Cecilia has been operating a very successful independent pizza shop in a rather remote, but growing, suburb of a large city; her profit on the investment and compensation for her time have increased every year. Still, because she is in her mid-sixties and has adequate savings, she has been toying with the idea of selling the business. The local newspaper reports the sale of a nearby piece of property to the Clemens Corporation, which Cecilia happens to know is a large franchiser for a major pizza chain. The competition is likely to result in at least a temporary drop in sales and may make her business unprofitable. Cecilia investigates and learns that construction will begin in six months. She decides the time has come to sell.

In advertising the business and talking with prospective buyers, Cecilia discloses all information relevant to her own operation, neither exaggerating nor concealing anything. She shows how well the business has grown and how profitable it now is, but she also makes it clear that many of her regular customers are friends and neighbors, who enjoy the highly personalized service she has provided by varying ingredients and recipes to satisfy each family's preferences. She answers every question asked of her with complete and accurate information. But nobody asks about possible future competition, and she says nothing about what she has learned.

The third case. The county's zoning commission has been divided three to two against rezoning a parcel of agricultural land for multifamily dwellings. The parcel is about one-half mile beyond local water and sewer lines; if it is rezoned, service will be extended. The commissioners who up to now have opposed rezoning decide the time has come. Their decision is entirely honest. They have no personal interest, but more housing is needed, and the would-be developer is making a proposal that seems fair to the community. The rezoning will be unexpected, since the three commissioners have just met informally and arrived at their decision, which they will announce in two weeks, when the commission next meets. However, talking with elderly neighbors thinking of selling their house and moving into a rather unsatisfactory apartment, one of the three, Donald, tells them new apartments will be available within a year on the parcel whose rezoning is imminent.

The neighbors mention this conversation to their nephew, Ed, who owns a home on the road along which the local sewer and water lines will be extended. Naturally, he considers the impact of the extension. Up to now, the scattered homes on that stretch of road have had wells and septic systems, and have required one-acre lots; now owners will be able to tie in to sewer and water lines, and can subdivide their lots. While each owner will have to pay assessments for the new service, Ed calculates that by subdividing he will make a great deal of money.

A neighboring couple have just listed their home for sale. Ed is about to tell them what he knows, so that they can hold off until the rezoning goes through, but he decides instead to explain the situation to his wife's sister and her husband, who have been looking for a house to buy, so that they can contract at once to purchase the property, contingent on obtaining the necessary financing, with a view to profiting from the property's expected increase in value.

Are Betty, Cecilia, and/or Ed violating any moral standard by not revealing information relevant to the transaction in which they are interested?

Analysis:

This question calls for application of the norm requiring candor and clarification of the proper application of the Golden Rule. Market prices, though generally perceived to be fair, often are unfair, especially to the poor. A price negotiated by bargaining in the absence of a market or an optimum market may be fair even though it differs from the price in a market that is not available or in a hypothetical, better market. Lying is common in negotiating and is always wrong. Withholding relevant information sometimes is justified, but also can be wrong. A prior relationship may ground a duty of candor; the end for which the information is withheld may be bad; or the transaction may be unfair. Mercy also may be required of Christians. Since love of neighbor requires taking differences among persons into account, and not treating everyone alike, one cannot soundly apply the Golden Rule without considering everything one knows about a possible action's impact on everyone concerned.

The reply could be along the following lines:

If buyers and sellers are said to be *better off* when they think their wants are more adequately satisfied, a buyer and a seller both hope to be better off by means of the transaction than they otherwise would be. Differences in skill in bargaining, eagerness to deal, and the ability to appraise the qualities of items to be sold and bought can enable one of the parties to get more than the other out of the transaction. But when a market exists—that is, when many potential buyers and sellers of similar items can make and compare tentative offers before dealing—the difference between the advantages gained by the parties to each transaction tends to decrease. Generally, buyers and sellers who consider the mutual advantages gained from a transaction to be roughly equal regard it as fair, and they would be willing to trade places if their current wants were those of the other party to the transaction. Therefore, a market tends to result in transactions perceived as fair.

But market prices in many cases are not just. Major participants in a market sometimes manipulate prices; holders of copyrights and patents sometimes exact excessive prices; both producers who exploit workers and importers who exploit poor communities unfairly drive down prices; and some people's self-indulgent and/or wasteful consumption of items whose supply is inelastic unjustly raises their prices. Though the parties to particular transactions often can be fair to each other even in a market shaped by injustices, those who wrongly contribute to those injustices cannot fairly obtain any advantage resulting from them. Thus, when they do take advantage, the market prices at which they sell are unjustly high and those at which they buy are unjustly low.

The behavior of wealthy people generally affects a market more than that of poor people. The wealthy not only have and exercise more economic power but sell and consume more than the poor do. So, the wealthy are generally responsible for market injustice and the poor are generally its victims. Then too, since being cheated out of a given amount of money injures a poor person more than a wealthy one, injustices shaping a market result in more harm, and so do greater injustice, to the poor than to the wealthy.

Sometimes no market for an item exists or is available to a buyer or seller. Items to be sold and bought may be unique, or no one may be competing to engage in a transaction with a potential seller, buyer, or both. Available markets also may more or less lack features required for an optimum market. Various potential sellers may offer items that, though more or less similar, also differ significantly; communication about available alternatives to a potential transaction may be impeded; the participants in the market may not be numerous and diverse enough to exclude the effect on market prices of characteristics that would make no difference in a large market with participants more nearly representative of everyone who might be interested in buying or selling similar items.

When a market is unavailable or the available market is lacking in some respect, bargaining to negotiate a price is common and sometimes necessary. People sometimes suppose that a price reached by negotiation is unfair if it differs from either the actual price of a similar item in some unavailable market or the price they suppose would be reached in a market free from limitations such as those mentioned in the preceding paragraph. Such suppositions are not likely to be sound. As has been explained, in a market free of such limitations, prices may be unfair, especially to the poor. Then too, getting access to a market that is unavailable or improving an existing market can require time, effort, risks, and costs whose avoidance sometimes fairly compensates those who negotiate less advantageous prices. Moreover, the features required for an optimum market that can be more or less lacking may offset one another, so that improving a market in one respect might lead to or increase unfairness rather than reduce or eliminate it.

In bargaining, people often lie to or deliberately deceive the other party about the availability or unavailability of alternative transactions or about features of the item to be conveyed. Since lying and deliberate deception are wrong in themselves, they may not be used even to limit the other party's injustice. But since withholding relevant information is not wrong in itself, one is justified in doing so provided (1) one has no duty arising from one's role in some existing relationship to convey the information, (2) one withholds it for a morally acceptable end, and (3) one reasonably judges that the transaction will be fair. Justifiably withholding information should not be regarded as an omission, since *omission* implies a duty to communicate. Of course, Christians should practice mercy; when they can fulfill their other responsibilities while conceding their rights they should concede them if doing so seems likely to overcome or mitigate some evil.

Consequently, no simple answer can be given to your question. By not revealing information relevant to the transaction in which they are interested, Betty, Cecilia, and Ed may or may not be violating a moral standard and, if not, may or may not be acting with appropriate mercy. However, by applying the preceding explanation in discussing your three examples, I shall try to show how reasonable judgments can be reached in such cases.

If any of the three had the relevant information in virtue of holding a position of trust—as, for instance, Donald, the zoning commissioner, does—she or he might have a duty not to use it for personal or family advantage. (Note that Donald should not have divulged his and his colleagues' change of mind to anyone before it was announced officially.) But none of them has such a responsibility not to use the information she or he has.

Ben should have known Betty's initial offer was likely to be low. Perhaps he was aware that he might get less than the property's market value by accepting it, but preferred to save the trouble and expense of engaging an agent to obtain an appraisal and negotiate a fair price. So, it hardly seems that Betty took unfair advantage of his ignorance.

But suppose he was a soldier assigned to overseas duty, she was comparatively well off, the two had known each other since childhood, and they had agreed to handle their tenant-landlord relationship directly to save Ben the cost of an agent. He has regularly taken her word for the costs of maintenance and repairs deducted from the rent. Within the context of such a relationship, based on Ben's trust, Betty, in my judgment, would violate the Golden Rule by acting as she did, even though her action did not violate their agreement, inasmuch as purchasing the property did not pertain to Betty's role as a tenant.

In many situations similar to Cecilia's, sellers who disclose information that would discourage buyers still can obtain a good price by assuming or limiting the buyer's risk—for example, a seller might provide some sort of warranty or insurance policy to cover the risk. Cecilia could do that, but I do not think she must. If potential buyers of Cecilia's pizza business can afford investment risk and are as shrewd as people making such an investment typically are, she does not seem to violate the Golden Rule by remaining silent about the prospective competition.

For one thing, such buyers would realize that in a growing suburb a business like this probably will have competition before long. A prudent potential buyer would check recent real estate transactions and ask the major chains whether a franchise is available for that town, and so probably would learn what Cecilia already knows, since the information is publicly available.

In the second place, the effect of competition on Cecilia's business is not entirely predictable. The new competitor might not so much cut into her market as generate more business with its somewhat different product; its advertising also might stimulate more hunger for pizza and boost sales volume for both shops. Besides, as Cecilia warns potential buyers, her business has been built on personalized service; if a buyer fully heeds that warning, he or she may be able to compete very effectively with a franchise offering only standard service. And even if Cecilia's successor in the business suffers a short-term decline in business that makes the shop unprofitable for a time, the business might well regain profitability before too long as the suburb continues to grow.

Someone might object that Cecilia's silence will be to her advantage only if it causes a potential purchaser to misjudge the true value of the business, which would be determined by the bids of fully informed parties. That, however, assumes an optimum market in which real values are established by many free and fully informed parties' offers to buy and sell, but the real market never is optimum. In this context, the original question can be restated: Does the Golden Rule require Cecilia to supply the information she has to improve the market? In my judgment, it does not, since she cannot reasonably expect others to be entirely rational and/or to cooperate in creating an optimum market. Some potential buyers might over-estimate the significance of the coming competition, and others might see possibilities Cecilia has overlooked for making the business more profitable or have some other information she lacks indicating that it is potentially more valuable than she realizes.

Nevertheless, she should be alert to the special circumstances of some potential buyers making it unfair for her to sell her business to them without either helping them succeed or telling them about the prospective competition. Suppose the first acceptable offer comes from a rather unsophisticated young couple who have worked very hard—they met when both took second jobs, working evenings and weekends at a pizza parlor in a nearby town. Having saved only enough for a down payment, they plan to mortgage the business so as to buy it, and could easily lose everything if profits fall significantly even for a year or two. Considering Cecilia's comparative affluence, she hardly can judge that she will meet the standard set by the Golden Rule in selling to them, taking the proceeds, and leaving them to discover their problem and struggle to keep the business going.

What if such a sale were not unfair? Assuming Cecilia is a faithful Christian, mercy and the opportunity to bear witness to her hope for more than worldly goods should lead her to prefer to her own interests the well-being of any potential buyer who would be likely to be hurt, for she apparently is reasonably secure and free of responsibilities to others.

Someone might point out that she will be unable to investigate the financial condition and business experience of everyone who expresses an interest in buying her business, and argue that she should therefore ignore differences among potential buyers, and simply ask a "fair" price. To set a fair price, though, Cecilia must put herself in the place of potential buyers, and so must make some assumptions about their capacity to operate the business successfully. Knowing nothing about their differences, she would be compelled to base her assumptions entirely on generalities. True, her information about the differences among poten-tial buyers will be limited; but in dealing with them, she may well learn a good deal about them. If she learns anything that will greatly reduce the value of the business to some potential buyer, to ignore that would be to refuse to put herself in the other's place, and so would be unfair.

If one assumes Ed's neighbors and his in-laws are about equally able to meet their respective responsibilities, he does seem to violate the Golden Rule by sharing the information he happens to have with his in-laws rather than passing it on to his neighbors. Though he does not have that information about a prospective increase in the property's value by virtue of holding a position of trust and did no wrong in acquiring it, and though he and his in-laws can use it without lying or deceiving anyone, the information is not publicly available, and Donald should not have divulged it. If neither Ed nor his neighbors knew about the impending rezoning, it may be that no one would purchase the neighbors' property before its increase in value became known. When Ed learns that he will enjoy a windfall by subdividing his own property, his first impulse is to help his neighbors share in the windfall. Family partiality, however, apparently motivates Ed to tell his in-laws so that they can purchase the property before the neighbors find out what is happening.

Nevertheless, in this case, too, I believe factors significantly differentiating the situations of the neighbors and the in-laws could make a difference so that Ed's action would be fair. Suppose, for example, that the in-laws have several children, including one who is severely handicapped and requires a great deal of care and special education; suppose, too, that this family lives very modestly and needs a house like the neighbors' place but can afford only something less adequate; and suppose Ed's wife helps her sister when possible and could do that more effectively and more often if the family moved into the neighbors' place. And suppose the neighboring couple, by contrast, are childless by choice, are moving to a larger and fancier house in the country, regularly entertain lavishly and take expensive vacations, drive a Porsche and a Mercedes, and both have highly paid jobs that make their lifestyle possible but by no means require it. In this case, Ed may have put himself in his neighbors' and in-laws' places, set aside his neighbors' materialistic values, and judged that the neighbors should be willing to settle for the price they were expecting and allow the windfall to go to meet Ed's in-laws' genuine needs. If that was the basis on which Ed decided to give his in-laws the information rather than reveal it to the neighbors, it seems to me his second thought is motivated, not by partiality, but by reasonable considerations, which make it clear to him that his neighborly impulse need not settle the question.

Someone might argue that, since Donald should not have divulged his decision before announcing it officially, nobody learning of the imminent rezoning can use the information without being unfair to people not aware of it. But that hardly seems true. If Ed told his neighbors, would they be unfair to potential buyers in taking their property off the market until the rezoning is announced and then repricing it in accord with its increased value? I do not think so.

Again, someone might object that Ed cannot compare his neighbors' situation with that of his in-laws without judging and condemning the neighbors—something Christians are forbidden to do. It might also be argued that the neighbors could have good reasons for living as they do and financial obligations of which Ed knows nothing. The answer to the first point is that the prohibition of judging others must be correctly understood: "God alone is the judge and searcher of hearts; for that reason he forbids us to make judgments about the *internal guilt* of anyone" (GS 28; emphasis added). Ed need not judge his neighbors' internal guilt to conclude that they have chosen to avoid parental responsibilities, are very prosperous, and live luxuriously, while his in-laws are devoted parents hard pressed to meet their children's needs. The answer to the second point is that, while Ed's information about his neighbors' financial situation may be imperfect, it can be adequate for reasonable judgment, and while the neighbors may not be blameworthy for living as they do, their lifestyle is objectively self-indulgent and unjustifiable.

Someone might object to all three answers: Betty need not tell Ben the value of his property even if she is better off and their relationship has been based on trust; Cecilia need not tell the unsophisticated young couple more than she ought to tell everyone; and Ed should act the same even if his neighbor's and in-law's financial situations are very different. The argument: Sound morality, being a matter of objective truth, is not relative to diverse situations; so, all buyers and sellers ought to be treated alike. This is true up to a point: Sound morality is a matter of objective truth, and some moral norms—for example, never intentionally kill the innocent—must be followed regardless of any situational differences. But love of neighbor requires that one take into account differences among relationships and persons, not treat everyone exactly alike. One always ought to love every neighbor, but fairness and mercy to various persons requires paying attention to differences and treating each person appropriately. For example, professionals rightly bill people well able to pay them at their regular rates, but reduce these rates for the poor and provide service without charge to the indigent. Similarly, if buyers and sellers are aware of and can take into account relevant differences among those with whom they deal, they generally may and sometimes ought to do so.

A final objection: Christian love of neighbor requires the same treatment by Cecilia toward all potential buyers and by Ed toward his neighbors and his in-laws. The argument: Christians should love all those called to the kingdom—and that includes everyone, even the worst sinners—as brothers and sisters, and no decent person would treat his or her own brother or sister less well than someone else. This, again, is true up to a point: Love efficaciously wills goods to those loved, and Christian love wills that everyone enjoy all the blessings of heaven. Still, a Christian need not—and must not—efficaciously will that anyone and everyone enjoy any particular good he or she owes others. Thus, a Christian husband does not owe every woman the affection and care he owes his wife. And Christians do not owe everyone the consideration the more vulnerable deserve, or owe others the help they should give to extended family members.

145: Must one tell potential buyers that a car's engine needs to be replaced?

My car is a little over four years old and has sixty thousand miles on it. It never has been in an accident, and I have taken good care of it. So, in many ways it is in excellent shape. But despite regular oil changes and no abuse, when it was in for regular maintenance the mechanic—whom I've known for years and am sure I can trust—discovered that the engine is going bad and will need to be replaced. I had hoped to get a few more years out of the car. But now I've decided to get rid of it and buy a new one.

I could trade it in on the new car. If I do, I do not think I have to tell the dealership the engine is going bad until the sale is completed. Then I would warn them about the problem so that they could replace the engine before reselling the car. But in the past I always have been able to find buyers for my old cars who would pay more than the dealer would give me. I would like to do that with this car, and if I do, I know I must give honest answers to any questions people ask. But if they don't ask, must I tell them about the engine? If I don't, most people will not notice anything wrong, because the symptoms are not yet obvious.

Analysis:

This question calls for application of norms requiring truthfulness and candor; it also requires judgment by the Golden Rule. If the questioner directly sells the car, he or she probably may not sell it for more than its market value, and should carefully estimate how much that is. In making a sale, lying always is excluded, fairness always is required, and neighborliness should not be neglected. The questioner's responsibilities will depend partly on local practices regarding such transactions and partly on his or her own financial condition and that of potential buyers. Christian mercy may require the questioner, especially if he or she is prosperous, to be more candid than most upright people would be and to sell the car for less than its estimated value.

The reply could be along the following lines:

There is a possibility you do not mention: to sell the car on an auction lot where buyers and sellers meet, if at all, only after vehicles are sold. I suppose customs and expectations differ at various auto auctions, but at least some, conducted with the understanding that sellers give no assurances, are frequented by sophisticated buyers, who examine beforehand the vehicles in which they are interested. I see no moral problem in offering a car such as yours for sale on an auction lot like that.

I also agree with you that, if you trade your car in, you need not tell the dealer about its engine until the transaction is completed. Considering why that is so will throw some light on the conditions under which it might be fair for you to sell the car directly to a private buyer.

To begin with, it is not likely that you could take advantage of the automobile dealer even if you wished to. Dealers generally are knowledgeable about the market value of cars, and before making an offer they can obtain the expert advice of their own mechanics in assessing the condition of a car offered as a trade-in. Then too, paying wholesale prices for parts and labor, the dealer could replace the engine at minimal cost and market your car, otherwise in excellent shape, at a premium price. Moreover, since the dealer's offer for any trade-in leaves a margin for occasional errors of judgment, any offer you accept will be low enough to help ensure that the dealer's losses on some transactions, including that one, will be offset by its profits on others. Considering all these things, I agree with you that, if you traded in your old car, the dealer could not reasonably expect you to volunteer what you know about its engine. Provided you told no lies and did nothing to conceal the engine problem, trading in the car would not be unfair to the dealer.

By contrast, if you sell it directly, you probably will be passing your problem on to someone no better able to deal with it than you are. The buyer might well be unable to assess the car's value accurately; in replacing the engine, he or she probably would pay retail prices for parts and labor; and someone who suffered a loss by buying your car could not write it off as an expected expense. Therefore, it generally would be unfair for you to sell your old car directly for more than its market value (see *LCL*, 832–33). To see the point, you need only apply the Golden Rule by putting yourself in a buyer's place.

But how do you estimate the market value? Begin by determining as well as you can the current price in private sales of typical, similarly equipped vehicles of that make, model, and year. Subtract from that the probable cost of replacing the engine, including a reasonable allowance for temporary loss of service. Finally, adjust that price upward, taking into account the car's excellent general condition and the fact that the new engine will run longer than a typical engine in a car like yours would. These calculations should result in a reasonable estimate, from which other reasonable estimates would differ within a rather narrow range.

How should you go about making the sale? This question calls for more than one answer, depending both on local practices regarding such transactions and on your own financial condition.

Suppose people selling and buying used cars where you live generally bargain aggressively: sellers ask more than they think their cars are worth, claim they have received other offers, exaggerate their cars' good qualities, evade disclosure of defects (and perhaps even lie about these matters); buyers offer less than they think a car is worth, claim better deals are available, and affect disdain for the car. Suppose, too, that you are not well off and need to get all that you fairly can for your car. If this is your situation, you may proceed as people usually do except in three respects. First, you may not lie—though initially asking more than you think your car is worth and speaking of it with the usual puffery will not be lying.[347] Second, you may not in the end accept more for the car than you judge fair—though you might rightly judge it fair to accept more than your estimate of the car's market value from someone clearly more prosperous than you are. Third, you may not unfairly sell the car to certain persons even for what you estimated to be its market value—for example, to an unsophisticated person who could not afford to replace the engine and would be likely to suffer grave harm if he or she bought your car, even at a price reflecting its true value.

If practices where you live are as I have described but you are well off, so that you can risk getting somewhat less for your car than it is worth, you should proceed differently. The usual practices are a social structure distorted by sin. They occasion sins in violation of the three respects, just mentioned, in which an upright person should depart from them. They impede neighborliness and generally result in transactions in which true cooperation is absent or minimal. All too often, such practices also lead to serious injustices against the vulnerable. You should exercise Christian mercy by opposing these evils. You might do that in various ways. One

---

347. *Puffery* refers to exaggerated commendation of someone or something for promotional purposes. Using it is not lying in a situation where such exaggerations are common enough that one can reasonably expect the hearer not to misunderstand them as factual claims that would be false. But like other exaggeration, puffery is lying in a situation where it expresses false claims, which are likely to deceive hearers.

way would be to offer your car for sale at what you estimate to be its market value, fully explain how you reached that price to anyone interested in buying, refuse to bargain significantly and explain why, take the risk that some potential buyers will be put off and go away, and accept less than your estimated value from—or even offer a discount to—someone who genuinely needs the car but cannot afford it at that price.

To the extent that local practices are less distorted by sin, such a way of acting on the part of prosperous sellers would be less a matter of mercy and more a requirement of fairness and neighborliness. But if you are not well off and need to get all you fairly can for your car, you need not take the risk of putting off potential buyers by disclosing the engine's condition. Moreover, you could rightly ask initially slightly more for the car than its estimated value and accept that full price from a prosperous buyer, though not from others. Still, you must not lie to anyone, and puffery would be lying. Then too, if a potential buyer's comments and questions make it clear that he or she wants or needs the information you do not initially volunteer, you should be straightforward, not evasive. Moreover, if you suspect that someone about to buy the car for what you estimate to be its market value would experience serious hardship in replacing the engine, you should frankly explain the problem in order to avoid taking unfair advantage of him or her.

146: May someone who buys used goods take advantage of sellers' ignorance?

Recently I was able to take over the jewelry shop where I have worked part time for the last eight years. A small but significant part of the business is buying used items. Sometimes the sellers are heirs who do not care to keep inherited items or divorced women who want to get rid of jewelry their ex-husbands gave them. But often they are people who simply need money and would probably pawn the items if there were a pawn shop nearby.

People generally don't know the value of what they want to sell. Those who know the purchase price of a piece of jewelry usually have a grossly exaggerated idea of its value, while those who don't, often are willing to accept a minimal offer. The former owner took advantage of such opportunities, and so do I. But I am not always entirely at ease about it.

I don't lie. If someone asks: "How much is this item worth?" I do not answer directly, but explain that many factors affect the value of jewelry, and ask whether the person is offering to sell the item. When someone wants an appraisal—for instance, to determine how much insurance coverage to buy—I help them without charge if I can; it builds good will for the business. But if someone wants to sell something, my usual practice is to begin by offering about half of what I think I can get for it. When I make the offer—"I can give you so many dollars for this item"—I also frankly say it might bring more elsewhere, especially if the owner can sell it directly to someone who wants it. Most people accept my offer or make an acceptable counteroffer; I never pay more than I am certain I can get. The result almost always is profitable, sometimes very much so.

For instance, recently a young man brought in a large gold medal he had just inherited from his mother; it was a foreign military decoration handed down in her family. I weighed it, estimated I could get about six hundred dollars for the gold, and offered him three hundred. He resisted, we bargained, and I bought it for five hundred. I suspected the medallion might be valuable, and it turned out to be a collectors' item. I got six thousand dollars from its sale by a New York auction house, and am well satisfied with the deal.

Still, as I said, I sometimes have qualms, particularly when dealing with people who simply need money. A while back, a middle-aged couple in financial straits brought in the wife's diamond engagement ring. Unlike most people, they realized that used jewelry is worth only a fraction of its purchase price. I estimated that the stones would bring me at least nine hundred dollars and the gold about one hundred, and offered five hundred. The husband asked whether they would get as much from a pawn shop in the city. If I had thought so, I would have encouraged them to go there. But I was quite sure they would not. The wife hesitated, obviously hating to part with her ring. Imagining how my own wife would feel, I told them my price would hold for ten days if they wished to try elsewhere or think about it. But they accepted my offer, and the ring brought just under twelve hundred dollars.

Analysis:

Given the questioner's exclusion of lying, this ethical question has three parts: whether the practice described is deceptive, otherwise fair, and merciful. It does not seem deceptive, since the nature of the situation and the warnings the questioner gives should be sufficient to alert most people that bargaining is appropriate and they might obtain a better price elsewhere. In other respects, the fairness of the practice depends on whether it fulfills or violates a previously established relationship with the seller. By this criterion, the practice does seem acceptable in dealing with sellers with whom the shopkeeper has not done other business, but not in dealing with trusting customers whose expectations have been shaped by transactions of other sorts. Finally, if he can afford to be merciful, people plainly in need should be treated more generously.

The reply could be along the following lines:

In dealing with your customers, you manifest virtues not always shown by people engaged in similar activities. You not only avoid lying but provide at least some information to help customers look after their legitimate interests. You also were decent in offering the married couple time to seek a better price for the ring. And the sensitivity of conscience that leads you to raise these questions is commendable.

Problems like yours arise in many other businesses. Dealers buy used books, antiques, art objects, and so forth; different sellers vary greatly in sophistication and determination to find the best market for their goods; values are seldom easy to determine, and prices are set by bargaining. Many dealers follow essentially the policy you do, and I do not think what they do is generally regarded as unethical, provided they tell no lies.

But dealers sometimes deceive people even without lying—for example, by proceeding in ways that deliberately forestall bargaining by falsely suggesting an item's value is more definite and certain than it is. Still, your practice as you describe it does not seem deceptive. Explaining that many factors affect an item's value and clarifying the nature of the potential transaction should warn people that your initial offer is for bargaining purposes. By doing nothing to persuade people that their items certainly are not worth more than your offer, you avoid deceiving them, even when you benefit from their ignorance, as you did in purchasing the gold medallion. And saying an item might bring a better price elsewhere should alert them that they might be wise to investigate further.

Someone might argue that it is unfair of you to begin bargaining by offering only about half what you think an item is worth. In the absence of deception, however, making an initial low offer is not unfair in a bargaining situation. Any business that buys used items must limit how much it pays for them so that the expected sale price will yield a reasonable profit after covering all the costs of doing business: interest on investment, overhead, insurance, taxes, and so on.[348] I assume you also occasionally make a costly mistake, and run some risk, impossible to eliminate, of being defrauded by someone disposing of a stolen item.

Again, someone looking at the matter only from the perspective of isolated transactions might argue that to retain a greater-than-average—and especially a greater-than-expected—profit from any transaction necessarily is unfair. But individual transactions are possible only if a business survives, and it can do that only if it makes a reasonable profit over time. Transactions that yield little or no profit or even result in a loss must be offset by others yielding a greater-than-average profit. And transactions that result in unexpected profits are offset by others that result in unexpected losses.

It might seem that taking advantage of ignorance, as you did in purchasing the medallion, is unfair even if not deceptive. Of course, it is unfair to take advantage of people so immature or mentally handicapped that they are incompetent to do business. Moreover, people who previously have had you do repair work and/or purchased items from you may have established a relationship with you based on trust that you will use your expertise to their advantage, charging for your merchandise and services only enough to make a fair profit on each transaction. Since such customers naturally expect you to act consistently within your established relationship with them, you abuse trust, in my judgment, if you make significantly more than your usual margin of profit on items of extraordinary value that you purchase from them. Thus, if the young man who sold you the medallion previously had done business with the shop and on that basis expected to be treated differently than he was, you should have handled the transaction differently, and now should share the proceeds with him on the basis of the profit margin in previous dealings with him.

In future cases of this sort, you could serve your customers fairly by proposing to act as their agent in disposing of items of uncertain value, setting a reasonable

---

348. On the just limits to profit, see *LCL,* 832.

commission, and fully sharing with them the benefits of your expertise and their trust. That also might well help build good will for your business and so be to your own advantage in the long run.

However, competent people who have not previously done business with you and sell you items without first investigating their value have no basis for expecting you to act differently than people usually do in bargaining situations, and so they freely choose to risk getting significantly less than they might. Since they could obtain a professional appraisal of any item they wish to sell and look into other markets for it, they are responsible for their own ignorance. Therefore, taking advantage of it need not be unfair.

This can be confirmed by considering somewhat similar transactions in which knowledgeable collectors buy items from businesses or other sellers unaware of their true value. Suppose the man who sold you the medallion had instead hired an auctioneer to sell it and other items he inherited. If a collector aware of the medallion's value successfully bid five hundred dollars for it, no reasonable person would regard that as unfair to the seller. Again, few people would condemn a collector of rare books who finds one worth a thousand dollars in a used book store and buys it from the prosperous shopkeeper who, failing to recognize its value, has priced it at only ten.

Financially distressed people are due special consideration. It is unjust to take advantage of such a person's need by driving a harder bargain than with someone less pressed for cash. Moreover, if your other responsibilities permit, you should be merciful to those in special need. For example, even if the couple who sold you the wife's engagement ring had not previously done business with you, you might have promised them that, if the ring brought more than the estimate on which you based your five-hundred-dollar offer, you would send them an additional payment. And, having received nearly two hundred dollars more than the minimum you expected, you should consider giving them this extra profit or, if you cannot afford that, at least sharing part of it with them.

147: Should landlords concern themselves with tenants' lifestyles?

Adjacent to our home, my wife and I have three rental homes that we rent out seven months each year, during the summer and winter tourist seasons, and we also operate an eighteen-space mobile-home park. We find renters easily; everything is always full. We conform to federal, state, and local laws excluding many types of discrimination and try to be fair when selecting renters. Within these limits, we ask prospective tenants various questions and try to select applicants we think will not cause problems for us or our other tenants.

Sometimes, after a single person has rented and moved in, we find out he or she is living with an unmarried partner, either of the opposite sex or the same sex. The laws virtually rule out getting rid of such people. Still, we don't like to rent to them, since we would like to keep a wholesome, family-type community.

How accepting can we be of such couples without compromising our own moral standards? Morally, should we be concerned with a tenant's private lifestyle? Or should we simply try to ignore what people do privately?

Personally, I feel that as landlords we do not have the right to inquire into tenants' private lives. Many nonmarried couples seem to see nothing wrong in their arrangements. Then, too, Scripture says, "Do not judge." Sometimes young people seek our advice, since we are an older couple, whom many of them treat like grandparents. But I don't like to offer advice unasked.

Analysis:

This question calls for derivation of norms for landlords. The objective of maintaining a wholesome, family-type community is legitimate. To achieve it, the landlords may take various reasonable measures, within the limits of the law, in accepting tenants and renting to them. Once tenants are accepted, the landlords should assume they are behaving in an upright way unless evidence to the contrary comes to their attention. If tenants misbehave in a way that probably violates the law and it seems appropriate to call the police, the landlords should do so. If tenants' lawful behavior annoys others or is indecent, the landlords should require them, within the limits of the law, to behave better or leave. If tenants' sole indiscretion is in speaking openly about their immoral relationships, the landlords should give them sound moral advice.

The reply could be along the following lines:

A landlord cannot prevent tenants from committing various sorts of sins in the space they occupy, and, in general, need not try. Of course, it plainly is wrong for a landlord intentionally to facilitate immorality in order to profit from it, as some motel owners do—for example, by renting rooms to prostitutes at special, hourly rates. But there is no question of that in your case. You like to keep a wholesome, family-type community. Within the limits of the law, you apparently try, as you should, to do everything possible to achieve that goal. Since you have no problem keeping everything full, you certainly should not compromise that policy to maximize profits, and, if you can afford it, you might even sacrifice some profit to further the policy—for example, by minimizing rent increases to desirable tenants, not least to large or less affluent families, in order to encourage them to stay with you or come back.

Someone might object that charging desirable tenants less than others would be unfair to the latter. However, if your regular charges are fair, you will do no injustice in sacrificing some of your profit to promote tenancy by people you prefer, assuming your preference has a morally acceptable basis, as seems the case.

I assume that in renting your units the laws you mention prevent you from discriminating on racial and ethnic grounds, which certainly would be unjust. If the laws permit you to favor senior citizens and families with children, however, you might find it helpful for your purposes to restrict occupancy to families with at least one member over a certain age or under a certain age—for example, over sixty or under sixteen—and I see no reason why such discrimination need be unjust.

You are likely to be better able to maintain a wholesome community if you fully inform prospective tenants of your standards of behavior and as a condition of renting to them obtain their commitment to observe those standards. It also may be helpful, if the law allows it, to require prospective tenants to list the names and ages of each person who will reside in the unit, and to prohibit unregistered overnight guests.

Once renters have been accepted, I do not think landlords, managers of hotels, and so forth have an obligation—or even a right—to ask who is going to bed with whom after the doors are closed and the shades drawn. You should assume that people are behaving in an upright way, as some surely are, unless you have evidence to the contrary. Tenants who are behaving improperly should not commit additional sins of immodesty and disrespect for others' moral sensibilities. Unless they commit such additional sins, there is no evidence of impropriety and, therefore, no problem for you. But what if tenants do not behave discreetly?

In some cases, their behavior may violate the law; know what to watch for and call the police when appropriate, just as you would if you had reason to believe a tenant was committing robberies or other crimes. In other cases, behavior is not unlawful but annoys others and/or damages your property. Then you, as landlord, have a right and duty, within the law, to require such tenants to behave better or leave. Even when the law severely limits your options, you can and should ask undesirable tenants to leave or discourage them from returning.

In still other cases, the only indiscretion of tenants is to speak openly about their immoral relationships. If they speak thus to you, it is not invading their privacy to offer moral counsel. Indeed, doing that is a Christian duty that used to be called "fraternal correction," but is better called "admonishing apparent sinners" (see *LCL,* 227–32). By fulfilling this duty, one can help others avoid hell. Nor should anyone be deterred from admonishing wrongdoers by Jesus' warning not to judge, since it concerns others' internal guilt rather than the objective immorality of their actions (see GS 28; *S.t.,* 2–2, q. 60, a. 2, ad 1).

A couple who flaunt their immoral relationship sometimes consciously or, perhaps, unconsciously desire others' acceptance and approval, either to lessen their own sense of shame and guilt, or to overcome social hindrances to their behavior, or both. Admonishing them makes it clear that you will not give the acceptance and approval they seek.

Any admonition, however, must be delivered gently and in a constructive spirit; self-righteousness and castigation should be avoided. For the two purposes of admonishing others are to help them understand moral truth, so that in its light they can see how its violation injures themselves and others, and to encourage them to live according to moral truth, so that they will fulfill themselves in genuine communion with others. Thus, it also follows that your responsibility to admonish tenants who seem to be sinning comes to an end as soon as it is clear that doing so is fruitless or even counterproductive—for example, by provoking greater or more blatant wrongdoing.

Finally, people living in immoral relationships generally have deeper moral and spiritual problems. Do what you can to help with these by praying for your tenants, giving them good example, being receptive to their confidences, offering friendly advice, and bearing witness to your faith whenever you can.

148: May one use unordered merchandise and reuse uncanceled postage stamps?

My questions are not the most earthshaking, but they do concern me, and they are easily stated.

Groups often mail me items such as cards or address labels, sometimes with a request for a donation and sometimes to solicit an order. I used to return such items, but now I use them without donating or ordering. Do you see anything wrong with that?

Also, when the post office misses a letter or parcel so that the stamps are not just lightly canceled but completely uncanceled, many people (I confess I am one) steam or float off the uncanceled stamps, let them dry, and reuse them. Is there anything wrong with this? If the post office did not cancel stamps but simply forbade their reuse, I would think it wrong. But I know of no postal regulation saying people cannot reuse uncanceled stamps and, since it is their job to cancel stamps, it seems only fair to use those they miss.

Sometimes, too, such stamps could be sold to a collector or a business that handles stamps for collectors. I know they usually pay more for uncanceled stamps than for canceled ones. Would there be anything wrong in doing that?

Analysis:

This question calls for application of the Golden Rule and several norms. If unordered merchandise is delivered by mistake, one should apply the Golden Rule and do what is fair. If such merchandise is intentionally delivered, it may be treated as if it were a gift or free sample. Still, some moral norm can forbid its use, and mercy can require one to request a worthy organization to remove one's name from its mailing list. One may sell uncanceled stamps to a collector or stamp dealer. Where the law forbids reusing them for postage, that law should be presumed just, and no justifiable exception to the duty to obey it is likely. A similar question can be asked with regard to using or seeking a refund for an uncanceled or uncollected ticket. In general, doing so is a theft of service. As in other cases of taking what belongs to others, however, certain exceptions can be justified.

The reply could be along the following lines:

If you receive unordered merchandise, ask yourself whether the sender intended that you get it. If the delivery to you was not intended but was a mistake, apply the Golden Rule. Usually, that will lead you to return the goods, send them on to the intended recipient, or at least notify one of the two parties, sender or intended recipient, to claim them. However, it is not wrong to keep or throw away something of such little value that performing that service for the sender or recipient costs more in time and trouble than the item is worth.

If the sender did intend that you receive the unordered merchandise, the purpose was to gain your attention and, perhaps, make you feel that you should respond.

Confronted with psychological manipulation, you should resist. Still, you may judge a cause worthy and send a donation or consider the merchandise desirable and order it. If not, you have no moral obligation whatsoever to return what you did not order and may throw it away or use it in any appropriate way. So, items like cards and address labels, sent with a request for a donation or an order, may be treated as you would treat a gift, and generally may be used even if you do not respond.

That is not always so, however. Certain cards, for instance, say you have enrolled those to whom you send them in an association whose members will share in the benefit of Masses offered for their intentions; the accompanying material makes it clear that enrollment requires a donation. You may not give the card to someone without sending the donation, since otherwise you would be making a false statement—that is, lying—to the person. Still, even in such a case, there would be nothing wrong in using the remainder of the card and the envelope if you removed the statement that could not be made truthfully.

However, when one decides not to respond favorably to repeated solicitations, Christian mercy may require that one ask the organization to remove one's name from its mailing list. In many cases, of course, lists are sold or shared, and trying to have one's name removed would be futile. But if one has contributed previously to an apparently worthy organization or somehow been associated with it, a note stating one's decision not, or no longer, to respond favorably can be helpful.

As for stamps, the last part of your question can be answered easily. There is nothing wrong in selling such stamps to a stamp company or a collector. Of course, such buyers will not pay face value for currently available stamps; and they consider stamps without the original glue to be used, and so worth little if any more than similar specimens that have been lightly canceled.

At least in the United States, the law addresses the first part of your question about stamps—it is a federal crime to reuse a stamp, whether canceled or not.[349]

From a moral point of view, your question can be extended to other similar cases. For example, when a ticket purchased for transportation or admission is not collected or punched and remains valid, may one use it again or request the refund for an unused ticket? This extension makes your question more interesting, since significant amounts of money often are at stake in such cases.

The basic answer emerges clearly when one considers that in buying and using a stamp or a ticket one is paying a price for a service. Assuming the price is fair, even if the stamp or ticket is not canceled or collected, the price nevertheless was owed. In reusing the stamp or ticket, however, one avoids paying for the second instance of the service and so deprives the provider of what one owes for it. That plainly is unjust: a theft of service. Therefore, the basic answer is that one should not reuse such items or seek refunds as if they were unused. One's duty in this matter, being an aspect of one's duty to pay a fair price for services rendered, in no way is affected by the failure of the post office to cancel stamps or of organizations selling tickets to collect or cancel them.

349. U.S.C., title 18, §1720.

As is generally the case with matters of justice concerning property and money, however, there are some exceptions (see *LCL,* 824–25).

First, if one has suffered an injustice for which no legal remedy is available, one sometimes is justified in taking fair compensation. Although that may be excluded by various foreseeable bad consequences, such as scandal, injury to community, or risk to oneself, reusing an uncanceled or uncollected ticket is unlikely to have such consequences. Organizations selling tickets for transportation or admission sometimes treat people unjustly in ways that call for compensation at least equivalent to the value of a ticket, and then, if no legal remedy is reasonably available, reuse of the ticket can be justified.

Second, provided the poor have done everything they should to earn their living and avoided unnecessary spending, and provided they avoid wrongly violating just laws and doing anything wrong in itself (such as telling lies), they may take from the prosperous what they require not only to satisfy urgent needs but to satisfy any genuine need that otherwise will go unmet (see *LCL,* 825). Thus, except in cases in which the provider of the service also is poor—for example, an airline in bankruptcy—the poor could be justified in reusing uncanceled or uncollected tickets.

Can exceptions to the norm forbidding the reuse of uncanceled postage stamps be justified? Leaving aside the fact that the work involved in reusing stamps might be a waste of time, the answer would be yes, in my judgment, if there were no law forbidding it. As noted above, however, there is such a law in the United States (and, I suppose, in other countries). That law should be presumed just, and just laws ought to be obeyed unless an exception is either required for the common good itself or justified because obeying the law would prevent fulfilling some other duty weighty enough to take precedence over abiding by the law (see *LCL.* 878–79). I cannot imagine a situation in which the common good would require reusing an uncanceled postage stamp, and usually there is so little to be saved by doing so that it is very unlikely that even an extremely poor person would have any duty he or she could fulfill only by violating this law. So, even though one might imagine some situation in which a person could justifiably violate the law and reuse an uncanceled postage stamp, it seems to me that the norm against doing so will admit of almost no exceptions.

149: To what extent may advertisers appeal to subconscious motives?

I am vice-president for marketing of one of the largest and oldest manufacturers of windows in the United States. Our products are available nationwide and are used chiefly in residential construction and remodeling. Cheaper windows are available, but ours are well designed, made of good materials, carefully crafted and inspected, and marketed solely through honest and well-managed distributors. In short, we have emphasized quality, and, as a result, our name is respected by architects, builders, renovators, and the public.

Our advertising strategy has not changed in nearly half a century. Central to it is a brochure that includes photographs of some fine uses of our products, but mainly consists of factual information about their quality features, different styles, available options, sizes, and so on. We mail this brochure to anyone who asks for it, with a covering letter and information about dealers in their area. To attract attention and stimulate requests for the brochure, we have advertised in journals and magazines directed toward both professionals and consumers interested in residential construction and renovation. We also have taken space at builders' conventions and at home shows open to the public. Our displays, as well as our journal and magazine ads, have been similar to our brochure, simply presenting our products attractively and providing factual information, though, of course, less of that than the brochure.

Recently, we decided to increase our advertising budget substantially and begin using television in an effort to increase our market share. Our advertising agency account executive just retired and his successor, a bright young woman, Ms. Grey, urged us to take an entirely new tack. Underlying her proposal is a general theory based on psychological research. In the past, she points out, our ads assumed that rational considerations motivate people to buy our products. While such considerations are significant in buyers' choices about features, type, and size, she argues, their preferring one brand to another is due almost entirely to emotional factors, and our television ads should focus on selling our brand.

Consequently, Grey proposes that our new ads and brochure use certain images that research proves attract attention, put our product in settings whose architecture and furniture manifest affluence and high fashion, feature paid endorsements by celebrities, emphasize sunlight (which, of course, comes through any opening in a wall as well as through our windows), and so forth. While the brochure still would contain plenty of factual information, the emphasis in our advertising as a whole no longer would be on showing that our products are of high quality but on appeals to subconscious motives—"pushing the right buttons," as Grey puts it.

Personally, while wanting to increase our advertising budget, I had reservations about the rest of her proposal. Our past strategy has served us well, and I am anxious to avoid doing anything that would damage the company's reputation. Therefore, I proposed an alternative to the management committee: reduce prices by cutting costs without compromising quality, and make "The same familiar quality at a new low price" the theme of our TV advertising. But the management committee decided not to invest in the new equipment needed to cut costs. I then argued that we increase our advertising without using television or departing from our traditional approach, but the decision was made to adopt the new strategy. Still, I retain ultimate authority to decide what will and will not go into the ads and the new brochure.

It seems to me that "pushing the right buttons" sometimes is nothing but a way of manipulating people, and I am anxious to avoid mistreating our potential customers. How can I draw reasonable lines to limit our use of the methods of persuasion Grey advocates, so as to keep this new approach from going overboard?

Analysis:

This question calls for the derivation of norms for advertisers. Advertising intended to arouse emotions is morally acceptable only if it is meant to contribute to a morally good response to the persuasion. This norm is violated in various ways: the motivated action itself is wrong for all or some; the motivating imagery is deceptive; intense emotion is meant to displace or interfere with rational reflection and choice; or the emotional motive is irrelevant. Advertising has two distinct though closely related motivational goals: to attract attention and to motivate a specific decision. In pursuing either, advertising can motivate wrongly. In advertising windows that will be used in ordinary settings, using architecture and furniture that manifest affluence and high fashion is generally intended to arouse emotions allied with false values. Since all testimonials should reflect the real choice of a competent judge, it is wrong to purchase a testimonial from a celebrity who has not used the product.

The reply could be along the following lines:

You are right to want to avoid harming your company's good name. Its reputation, earned by competence and honesty, is of great value in attracting new customers and retaining the business of old ones. Managers intent solely on short-term profits all too often ignore this value. But even if short-term profits increase, they are likely to harm their companies' long-run profitability.

Even apart from how it affects subconscious motives, advertising can go wrong by deceiving the public, encouraging self-indulgence and waste, and representing immoral attitudes and behavior as acceptable, clever, or funny. At the same time, persuasion playing on subconscious motives is not necessarily wrong. In presenting your products attractively, the brochure you have been using already strives to give a good impression. And a good impression, rather than being the conclusion of an argument, is a subconsciously motivated response to perceived features of objects or persons. Indeed, persuasive arguments usually include and are accompanied by various elements aimed at eliciting an emotional response: certain tones of voice or graphic styles, a presentation organized to maximize its psychological impact, figures of speech, appealing examples, and so on.

Still, playing wrongly on subconscious motives almost always is an important element of morally questionable advertising. Morally good persuasion arouses emotions that could lead to or be part of an intelligent and morally good response to the persuasion. Advertising playing on subconscious motives is morally unacceptable if the emotional response it arouses would not be part of a morally well-integrated evaluation of what is being promoted or of a reasonable response to the advertiser's message. Thus, morally acceptable advertising arouses emotions that lead people to consider using a product or service that might help them fulfill some of the responsibilities of their vocation, while morally unacceptable advertising arouses emotions that do not serve that purpose but are more or less directly at odds with it.

Sometimes the product or service cannot be rightly used by anyone—for example, pornography or the service of a prostitute—and any attempt to arouse emotions to purchase it is wrong. Sometimes the service or product could be rightly used by some people but not others—for example, various medical treatments and drugs, including tranquilizers and analgesics—and an attempt to arouse emotions in those who should not use it is wrong. Sometimes the play on subconscious motives uses images that deceive, without asserting anything false. For example, deceptive packaging can generate the false impression that a brand offers better value for price than it really does; trick photography can create an illusion that a product has more desirable attributes than it has; clever imagery can suggest misleadingly that using a product will meet subconscious desires and interests. Sometimes persuasion aims at arousing emotions so as to lead to action without adequate reflection, and thus attempts to forestall the contrary choice that some people should make. For example, easy credit and various sorts of insurance often are promoted by arousing desire and fear while the information required to make a prudent decision is omitted or carefully concealed. Sometimes the emotions aroused are simply irrelevant to the product or service being promoted. Erotic desire is used to draw favorable attention to all sorts of things, and doing so is wrong not only because deliberately attempting to arouse that desire is wrong except within marital intimacy but because it has nothing to do with reasonable consideration of most products or services, preference for them, or use of them.[350]

In applying the norm just explained in order to avoid wrongly using nonrational means of persuasion, one should distinguish between two motivational goals of any advertisement or, more generally, of any instance of persuasive communication. The first is to attract the attention of the intended audience, encourage receptivity, and effectively communicate (get the message across). The second is to induce a specific interest and decision—for example, an interest in a particular brand and the decision to buy a product of that brand rather than a competitor's. While some features of a communication can serve both goals simultaneously, something might be justified as serving one goal that would be unjustifiable if meant to serve the other. For example, certain photographs that might legitimately be included in a brochure describing a medical textbook in order to show the quality of its graphics might be abused in a medical journal advertisement as an attention-getting device. Conversely, using carefully selected colors or graphics in an ad is reasonable insofar as it helps get the message across, but unjustifiable if it in any way wrongly motivates interest and decision. This can happen when a product is deceptively packaged to resemble a different brand, when colors and graphics are chosen as part of motivation inconsistent with reason (for instance, when novelty in advertising a new line of products is used to suggest that they are desirable for their novelty), and so on.

The preceding analysis can be applied to Grey's proposals that you mention. Unless an image shown by research to attract attention arouses emotions inappro-

---

350. Various sorts of abuses of advertising are described by William Meyers, *The Image Makers: Power and Persuasion on Madison Avenue* (New York: Times Books, 1984); many instances of unethical emotional motivation in advertising are discussed with considerable psychological insight by Carol Moog, *"Are They Selling Her Lips?": Advertising and Identity* (New York: William Morrow, 1990).

priately, it can be used to help get your message across. Emphasizing sunlight also seems legitimate. While any opening in a wall admits light as well as your windows do, it goes without saying that a good window admits light without the disadvantages of other kinds of opening. Of course, deception must be avoided. For example, it would be wrong to suggest that your windows admit more light than others comparable to them and wrong for a photographer to use artificial light to give the impression that windows will do more than they can to brighten a room.

What about presenting your products in settings far richer than those in which they ordinarily will be used? That might be done, as will be explained below, to provide one premise of a rational argument to prefer your brand. But what if it is done independently of any rational argument? Wealth, social status, and stylishness are not fundamental human goods, and people who regard them as if they were have false values. Feelings allied with those false values simply cannot be integrated with a reasonable response to your products. So, it would be an abuse to appeal to those feelings by using architecture and furniture that manifest affluence and high fashion in order to interest people in your products. Contrast this abuse with showing tasteful furnishings in modest rooms featuring your products—for example, a family dining room with the table laid to celebrate a holiday, birthday, or some other special occasion—the scene bathed in sunlight coming through several of your windows. The feelings evoked by such a presentation can be integrated with a reasonable plan and choice to use your products in building or remodeling a home.

Someone might argue that people expect ads to show products like yours, not as they will appear in an average-priced home's typical room, furnished and decorated for a few thousand dollars, but as they would look in a stunning room of a luxurious house, with furniture and decoration costing far more. People like to see products in attractive settings, the argument will continue, yet know very well that the setting is just part of the ad. Nobody thinks buying a few good windows will turn an average house into an opulent mansion. So, the argument will conclude, there is nothing wrong with using the setting proposed.

People do expect to see advertised products in luxurious settings because ads often use such settings; but the precise question is whether their use is morally acceptable. If an affluent and stylish setting does not motivate people, using it is pointless; if it does motivate them, its specific features must arouse their feelings. True, using such a setting need not make an ad deceptive. But can the feelings its features arouse be allied with a reasonable choice to use the product in the typical room of an average home? Do not such feelings belong to someone always restless for more and better material things, whose choices of products feed that insatiable desire?

What about paid endorsements by celebrities? Employing as a spokesperson someone well known to an audience can help get a message across, and an individual with a familiar persona can project the "personality" of the advertiser. However, the use of celebrities and their testimonials not only sometimes appeals to false values, such as wealth and status, but often is deceptive—for example, because the advertiser knows that the celebrity does not believe his or her testimonial to the product. Advertising should project what the company truly is and aspires to be, not merely whatever seems likely to appeal to some segment of the market. Moreover, any testimonial should be truthful.

Considered together, the two norms rule out purchasing the endorsement of a celebrity who has not used a product. However, you could conduct a market survey among celebrities to identify some who have recently installed your products or purchased properties that have them. Since the windows are good, your survey is likely to find some well-known people who are delighted with them. You could solicit honest testimonials from among them. Nor do I see any reason why it would be wrong to pay celebrities a reasonable fee for any time and effort involved as well as for allowing use of their names, photographs, and so on.

If you find some celebrity who chose your windows when building or remodeling a magnificent mansion, your advertising could legitimately show them in that setting and draw the true conclusion that their fine qualities motivated even a person of such means to prefer them to other available windows. Of course, such an ad also would motivate viewers subconsciously, by evoking favorable feelings related to wealth, social status, and stylishness. This psychological effect, however, need not vitiate showing the windows in that setting. In making a sound argument for preferring your windows, you can legitimately accept its effect of causing those feelings, which you could not rightly intend to arouse.

150: What advertising aimed at children should an organization oppose?

We are an organization that seeks to defend the integrity of the family and its values against the incursions of the economic system and the media, which so dominate contemporary culture. A committee studying the negative effects of advertising on the parent-child relationship has concluded that we ought to oppose most persuasive advertising targeted at children with the intention of influencing parents' buying decisions. However, the committee has not been able to articulate a principle for distinguishing morally objectionable instances of such persuasion from acceptable ones.

Plainly, deceptive advertising aimed at children—for example, telling them that eating a certain cereal will make them star athletes—is objectionable since it uses lying to mislead them into pressuring their parents to make buying decisions rather than providing rational grounds for those decisions. At the same time, advertising that tries to persuade children to influence their parents to do what they should, for a reason at least including some benefit to the children themselves, seems morally unobjectionable. Thus, there does not appear to be a problem with an advertisement by a public health authority urging children to tell their parents to stop smoking in the home: "Your smoking harms us kids." But many ads fall between these two extremes. They neither are deceptive nor are they supportive of commonly recognized values; they are simply intended to increase the sales of various products by getting children to influence their parents' choices.

Are all such ads morally objectionable or are some acceptable, and why?

Analysis:

This question calls for the derivation of norms for advertising directed to children who cannot make their own decisions. Such advertising is not intended to provide information, but only to persuade. Persuasion directed toward either adults or children can be morally flawed in several different ways. If not flawed in any of those ways, advertising meant to persuade children to motivate their parents to act in the children's true interests is morally acceptable. But advertising otherwise acceptable is morally objectionable if meant to motivate parents to prefer a product that either offers children no real benefit or a benefit no greater than an available alternative. Its specific moral defect is that it violates the parent-child relationship by using children, not in their own interests, but in the interests of third parties to bring about parental action that is motivated emotionally rather than rationally.

The reply could be along the following lines:

Advertising aimed at adults and others mature enough to make their own decisions and act on them has two distinct and even separable purposes: to provide information—for example, about the availability and price of a product or service—and to persuade. Advertisers who merely provide information assume that those addressed already have relevant interests and are prepared to act on them; advertisers engaging in persuasion try to arouse interests and influence behavior. By contrast, advertising directed toward children too young to make their own decisions never simply provides information, even when it appears to do only that, since advertisers take for granted that the children are not in a position to use information. Rather, such advertising attempts to motivate children to motivate their parents.

Some people argue that every effort to persuade children of anything is wrong, since they cannot recognize persuasive discourse for what it is, criticize it, and resist the persuasion. They think any advertising addressed to children necessarily is a sheer imposition on the child's plastic personality and so is inherently manipulative.[351] But parents and others caring for children often try to persuade them, and such efforts surely are not wrong when undertaken for the child's true benefit. The idea that such persuasion imposes on children is confused. It recognizes their lack of adult capacities but demands that they be treated as if they were adults. What actually is required is that persuasion directed toward children seek their true benefit rather than use them as means to others' ends. On this basis, I think you are right in seeing nothing wrong in ads aimed at children that are morally acceptable in other respects and are meant to motivate children to influence their parents to do something parents should do, at least partly for the children's benefit.

351. Assuming something like this argument, Dale Kunkel and Donald Roberts, "Young Minds and Marketplace Values: Issues in Children's Television Advertising," *Journal of Social Issues,* 47 (1991): 57–72, summarize research on young children's responses to television advertising, which shows that they do not understand its persuasive intent and are very susceptible to its commercial message; Kunkel and Roberts deplore the failure of the research to shape policy regulating such advertising. My criticism of the argument suggests that research should be directed to the negative effect of such advertising on the parent-child relationship.

You certainly are right in observing that many ads aimed at children, like many aimed at adults, are morally unacceptable because they are deceptive. Often, too, they are bad because they are meant to motivate children to motivate their parents to do what the parents should not do—for example, serve them cereals less likely to contribute to a balanced diet and more conducive to developing bad dietary habits than alternatives that are equally or even more economical. Moreover, without being deceptive or seeking to motivate wrongful behavior, advertising aimed at children as at others can be, and often is, wrong inasmuch as it seeks to arouse emotions that are simply irrelevant.

Many people would argue that, if advertising directed toward children is not wrong in one of the ways referred to in the preceding paragraph, it is morally acceptable. However, I believe you are right to focus attention on the parent-child relationship. It obviously is strained whenever parents must resist a child's advertising induced pressure to do what they should not do. But even if not wrong in this way, ads aimed at children often deliberately violate the parent-child relationship and are wrong precisely for that reason.

These are the specific sort of ads your committee should concentrate on: those aimed at children and intended to get them to motivate their parents' buying decisions so that they will choose one product or service rather than another from among a number that either offer no real benefit to the children or else do not differ significantly in the benefit offered. Such ads violate the parent-child relationship.[352]

Their sole beneficiary is the advertiser, who increases profits by increasing sales and, in a competitive situation, market share. The parents do not benefit; indeed, they are motivated to make a choice, not on rational grounds, but by the pressure the advertiser's persuasion applies to them through their children. Nor do the children benefit, since, even if the products or services advertised do benefit them, the persuasion's specific purpose is not that benefit but the choice of the advertiser's product or service rather than an alternative. For example, ads for cereal perhaps encourage children to get their parents to serve breakfast, which is good for children; but the advertiser's specific aim is to cause parents to choose this brand rather than that, and advertised differences, if not actually detrimental, make no significant difference to children's well-being.

Since the sole beneficiary of this sort of advertising is the advertiser, neither the child nor the parent is treated as a person; both are used as instruments. The child's motivational capacity is actuated as a mere means to motivating the parent, while the parent, as has been explained, is induced through the use of the child to make a choice without rational grounds. This use of the child—to emotionally motivate his or her parents' preference—intentionally damages the parent-child relationship. Instead of helping and encouraging the parent to benefit the child, the advertiser uses the child to motivate the parent to act in the advertiser's interest. In effect, the advertiser works to invert the appropriate relationship between

---

352. Studies suggest that many parents experience and resent this violation: see Brian M. Young, *Television Advertising and Children* (Oxford: Oxford University Press, 1990), 140–47. Young's book as a whole provides factual background for the ethical question dealt with here.

parent and child, so that parents, rather than guiding their children will follow their children's nonrational preference.

A cereal manufacturer advertising in this way might argue that the advertising really is intended to benefit children and not merely use them. It includes persuasion that children eat cereal for breakfast, while, the argument might claim, studies show that many children either have no breakfast at all or eat something less nutritious than cereal. But even if the persuasion does benefit children in this way, its specific point is to bring about, not that benefit, but the choice of one cereal rather than another for the particular advertiser's benefit. Otherwise, the advertiser would limit the content to persuading the child to eat a good breakfast, including not only cereal but other appropriate nutrients, and there would be no need to mention any particular brand of cereal.

If cereal manufacturers really had children's interests at heart, and respected the sanctity of the parent-child relationship, they would set up a trade association that would advertise to children with precisely that objective, and would direct advertising for their particular brands exclusively to parents. Assuming that parents need to be encouraged to feed breakfast to their children and that cereal ought to be part of it, the advertising directed to children would be morally acceptable. It would do nothing more than to move them to move their parents to fulfill their duty to provide their children with a proper diet. At the same time, the cereal manufacturers could rightly seek as their ulterior end that, by persuading children to eat nutritious breakfasts, the advertising would expand the market for cereal, and that ulterior end could justify them as managers of their businesses in doing a public service.

151: May a public affairs firm serve a government that mistreats its citizens?

Located in Washington, D.C., our firm helps clients deal with the U.S. government and the public. We provide information, facilitate contacts, lobby, arrange mail handling, manage advertising campaigns, organize press conferences, and so forth. Among our clients are American and foreign businesses, nonprofit organizations, various associations, and governments. Our governmental accounts—two foreign governments, three U.S. cities, and one state—have been among the most lucrative. Recently another foreign government's representative, whom I'll call Mr. Que, approached us to look into our services. Not only human rights organizations but U.S. officials consider this government one of the world's worst in the treatment of its own people. My four partners and I have no doubt it condones and even foments gross and widespread violations of fundamental human rights.

Que talked freely about his government's problems with the U.S. government and the American public. His government's "public persona," Que said, is bad, and this has adversely affected tourism, outside investment, trade, and so forth. Some public officials and the more "enlightened" members of his country's upper class (including, of course, Que himself), deplore the policies and practices Americans find so repugnant and wish to change them. But even he and his like-minded compatriots regard the typical American reaction as excessive and think it largely due to lack of sympathy for a nation so different in culture and traditions.

Drawing on past experience, my colleagues and I offered many examples of services we could supply, but we proposed no definite plan. At the end of the session, Que asked us to draw up a comprehensive plan and agreed to pay us at our usual rate for doing so, with the understanding that the payment would be credited against future services if his government accepted our plan and engaged us. We agreed, and Que at once gave us a substantial deposit.

Two of my partners feel we cannot afford to pass up this account and strongly favor developing a comprehensive plan to improve the government's "public persona"—that is, its image. One of them, while not proposing that we violate our policy not to lie on behalf of clients, argues that this government is being tried and condemned in the court of public opinion, and is entitled to our services, much as common criminals are entitled to the services of a lawyer to make the best possible case for them. Another partner thinks our involvement with this government is a mistake that will hurt us in the long run; he urges that we renege on our agreement and return the deposit. Between the two extremes, another partner and I think that, while some caution is necessary in our own interests, we should prepare and undertake to implement a limited plan—limited in that it would entirely pass over the government's abhorrent practices and bad image, and focus instead on the nation's underlying good features, with a view to helping it in specific areas like tourism and foreign economic relationships.

What do you think of these three options?

Analysis:

This question concerns cooperation in governmental abuses. The questioner's firm may not seek to improve Mr. Que's government's image; that would betray the firm's professional responsibility and involve grave dishonesty. If the firm provides even limited service, it will materially cooperate with the government's abuses; this material cooperation might be morally excluded, especially inasmuch as it could well be unfair to that nation's citizens. But if limited service is not morally excluded, it could have several good effects. The firm might realize many of the benefits of providing limited service to the government without actually doing so by offering to serve one or more privately owned businesses or nongovernmental organizations in Que's country.

The reply could be along the following lines:

I believe most decent people in your profession try to forestall moral problems by working exclusively for organizations or individuals whose purposes and programs they judge morally acceptable. Having taken this precaution, however, they tend to regard themselves primarily as advocates for those they represent. When the employer or client makes a decision, the public relations adviser usually does not question its morality. Like an attorney who considers that even the guilty deserve an effective defense, the adviser reasons: "The ethics of my profession both permits and requires me to make the best possible case for my employer or clients even if I privately think what they are doing is wrong. It is not my job to second guess or criticize their policies and decisions, but to sell them to the media and the public." Of course, any decent public relations person will draw the line at some point (only the morally corrupt will stop at nothing), and most try to avoid gross dishonesty, not just because it is morally repugnant but (a perhaps more compelling consideration for them) because it is more likely to hurt than help an employer's or client's long-term interests as well as their own. Still, serving clients' interests within some moral limits seems to most people in your profession to exhaust their professional responsibilities.[353]

This understanding of your profession apparently is shared by your partner who argues that Mr. Que's government is entitled to your services, much as any criminal is entitled to the services of a lawyer. I believe that view is profoundly mistaken, and your partner's talk of Que's government being "tried and convicted in the court of public opinion" is a misleading metaphor. There is an essential disanalogy between the defense attorney and the public relations person. A criminal's lawyer plays only one part in an adversarial system, while others play other parts. The prosecutor makes the best possible case against the defendant, the judge referees so that other participants proceed according to the rules, and so on. This structured system as a whole is meant to result in a judgment on the merits, based on sound interpretation of relevant law and on the truth about what was done and other relevant matters. Moreover, if defense attorneys properly play their part in the system, they are subject to various constraints that do not affect public relations advisers.

If defense attorneys were their clients' advisers in communicating with others, they could not proceed as they do within the adversarial system of criminal law without being grossly immoral. Since the public relations adviser does not work in an adversarial system, an exclusive focus on the employer's or client's interests is certain to lead to the abuse of techniques of communication to manipulate the thinking and behavior of those addressed. Communication, however, ought not simply to aim at motivating others so that their opinions and behavior will facilitate or, at least, not impede the communicator's purposes. It should instead be directed toward common understanding with those addressed as a basis for mutually advantageous cooperation in authentic community. Consequently, public relations people should commit themselves to serving not only their employers or clients but those they address, helping each side understand and respect the views and legitimate interests of the other. For this reason, public relations advisers should not serve employers and clients except insofar as the latter are prepared to be partners in genuine communication.[354]

353. Thomas H. Bivins, "Public Relations, Professionalism, and the Public Interest," *Journal of Business Ethics,* 12 (1993): 117–26, points out the inadequacy of the ethical standards of many who practice public relations. He holds that professional responsibility requires them to promote public debate of issues, but does not consider whether it requires them to facilitate cooperation based on genuine communication.

354. A significant contribution to the ethics of public relations thus conceived: Lee W. Baker, *The Credibility Factor: Putting Ethics to Work in Public Relations* (Homewood, Ill.: Business One Irwin, 1993). Baker stresses the value of credibility and shows that candor is needed to gain and retain it; he provides many examples of self-defeating manipulativeness.

Your colleague who proposed the analogy I have been criticizing might respond: "Working to bring about authentic communication would make sense in an ideal world. But the situation we work in, though not as structured as the legal system, is every bit as adversarial. The human rights organizations have indicted Que's government; certain media representatives have played the role of prosecutor; and U.S. government officials are sitting in judgment. Que's government is confronted by the real world, and we should serve as its advocate." My answer: Perhaps the sole intention of the groups and individuals that criticized Que's government has been to communicate the truth about its wrongdoing in order to stop or impede it. If so, though in a sense they have become adversaries of Que's government, the legal analogy plainly remains unsound. Perhaps, though, those groups and individuals at least to some extent have assumed an inappropriate adversarial role. If so, they have wronged both Que's government and the public. However, that wrong would not justify responding in kind, if for no other reason, then because that, too, would wrong the public.

Your account makes it clear that Que wants you to help improve the bad image his country has acquired due to its government's unjust policies and activities. But since you and your partners agree that his government not only tolerates but foments grave violations of fundamental human rights, you could not do what he asks without striving to mislead the American public about what is going on in the country. That would be not only gravely dishonest but an utter betrayal of your professional responsibility. Consequently, you are right to exclude the option supported by two of your partners, including the one who argues that Que's government is entitled to your services in defending it before American public opinion. You may not develop a comprehensive plan to improve that government's image, no matter what consequences refusing might have for your firm.

By contrast, several ethical considerations support the position of your partner who thinks your involvement with Que's government is a mistake and urges returning his deposit. A case also can be made for the option you favor: offering Que a limited plan. I do not find the information you supply sufficient to exclude either possibility, so I shall sketch out the cases for both. Taking into account everything you know and reflecting conscientiously, you may find the argument against your view convincing. If not and you judge both possibilities morally acceptable, you will have to discern between them (and perhaps others), and choose the option more consonant with the unique qualities of your firm considered as a whole.

Against serving Que's government is that any work you would do for it would contribute to its ongoing grave injustices. This involvement might well be very important, since it would reduce the pressure on the regime to behave less badly and help it remain in power, perhaps offsetting the force of world opinion that otherwise might be decisive. Moreover, merely to accept this government as a client would not only prevent you from bearing witness on behalf of its victims but would contribute to the semblance of respectability it desires—a semblance of respectability that might well lead other Americans to engage in more questionable or even plainly immoral cooperation with Que's government. Perhaps even more important, since the account will be lucrative, you will be tempted to share, albeit reluctantly, at least some of the client's wicked intentions—if not its intention to violate fundamental human rights, at least its intention to avoid paying the price that deserves. Finally, the preceding considerations all point to a final one. Serving this government might well be unfair to its victims. Could you have accepted Nazi Germany as a client in 1938 without being unfair to the people the Nazis were abusing and killing? If not, is Que's government significantly less evil, or do other relevant factors distinguish the two cases?

You proposed the option of serving Que's government within limits. In doing that, you could intend, not to support its wrongdoing, but to promote the nation's common good. For no matter how bad the government is, the nation it badly rules has legitimate interests that need good service, which you might provide by dealing with the government in power. The limits should exclude not only dealing with the government's bad image and abhorrent practices but promoting anything that directly contributes to its injustices—for example, trade in weapons of guerrilla warfare or implements of torture, foreign investment in enterprises that use slave labor, or tours to visit government approved houses of prostitution.

If your firm observes those limits and recommends nothing but strictly truthful communication, the possibilities of scandal and temptations to become more deeply involved in the wrongdoing would be minimized. And, of course, if your firm does not serve this government, another public relations firm probably will, and very likely without observing the morally necessary limits. Moreover, your help in promoting foreign investment, trade, and tourism could have some good effects. First, expansion in these areas would benefit many citizens of Que's country, including, surely, some who are victims rather than perpetrators of the government's injustices. Second, while your own business would be the first to profit, it would not be the only one. The activities of American citizens that your work would encourage presumably would be in their own interests and so, probably, beneficial to them and to others in the U.S. Third, increasing economic relationships with the U.S. might press Que's government toward reforms that would further the nation's common good by at least mitigating some of the government's injustices. Fourth, in serving the government, you might be able to persuade its leaders that human rights violations are bad from a public relations standpoint and, therefore, not in their own interests. You might even persuade the client to institute real reforms that you could legitimately publicize. While reform motivated solely by self-interest does not make wicked people just, it does reduce the number of victims.

If you judge that you probably should avoid further involvement with Que's government, your firm should give him no plan at all and should promptly return his deposit. I would not call doing that "reneging on the agreement." *Reneging* connotes unfairness, and there is nothing unfair in breaking a promise one judges cannot be fulfilled without wrongdoing. Indeed, even if the only reason for withdrawing and returning the deposit were your partner's pragmatic concern that involvement with Que's government will hurt your business in the long run, I do not think it would be unfair to break this promise, provided you do so promptly.

If your firm undertakes to serve Que's government on a limited basis, keep in view the potential good and bad effects of your service, and try to promote the former and minimize the latter insofar as you can.

Finally, perhaps your firm can realize many of the good aspects of providing limited service to Que's government without actually involving itself with that bad regime. How? By refusing to serve Que's government but at the same time offering to serve in suitably limited ways one or more privately owned businesses and/or other independent organizations in his country. Might Que even be willing to help you negotiate a contract with a consortium of such clients having legitimate interests in promoting investment, trade, and tourism by Americans? If you choose this option and succeed in carrying it out, you will be able to avoid dealing with his bad government while promoting his nation's common good.

152: May a spokesman defend something he considers wrong?

I am director of communications for a nationwide, nonprofit membership organization. Since I unqualifiedly share its good purposes, and since its leaders believe in honest communication, I seldom encounter moral problems in my work. But recently a controversy has arisen among members of the organization, and the leaders probably will resolve it in a way I consider both wrong in itself and unfair to a substantial portion of the membership. While I could resign over the issue and my wife is inclined to think I should, I cannot see how a public protest by me would have any good effect. Therefore, I would rather continue to serve this organization, provided I can do that without moral compromise. But I am not sure that I can.

The source of the problem is that certain members, including well-known public figures, have taken positions and supported movements that, judged by the organization's own standards, are morally unacceptable. Considering their statements and actions inconsistent with continuing membership, other members have sought their expulsion. The leaders, who could expel those under criticism, agree that they are in the wrong. In confidential discussions, I have argued that their expulsion is morally required, despite the price the organization would pay, both by reducing its membership and in terms of public opinion, which generally would side with those expelled. But the leaders not only are reluctant to pay that price but also are coming to think—sincerely, I believe—that they do not have the right to judge the erring members' wrongdoing incompatible with membership. I consider that view mistaken, but it is plausible, since the same problem exists throughout the wider community in which the organization is based, and the leaders of that wider community, while aware of this widespread misbehavior, have done virtually nothing about it.

If the leaders decide as I expect, it will be my job to communicate their decision as favorably as possible, both to our members and to the press. In what ways may I defend the leaders' decision, assuming they sincerely consider it right while I consider it wrong? In particular, without lying, how can I help them communicate their sincerely held views that I consider mistaken?

Analysis:

This question calls for application of the norms regarding truthfulness and for judgment on cooperation in an action the questioner judges to be objectively wrong. Formal cooperation with the leaders' objectively wrong actions must be avoided, but at least some material cooperation will be permissible. The intended end of that material cooperation can be understanding and *acceptance*—as distinct from *approval*—of the decision by members who will disagree with it, since that end is not bad in itself and can serve the organization's true good. In at least certain sorts of situations, the questioner, without personally asserting anything he believes false, not only can help the leaders articulate their views but act as the organization's spokesperson in presenting its position.

The reply could be along the following lines:

Your question would be easy to answer if your organization's leaders were insincere, for then honest communication would not serve their purpose and your duty would be clear: to refuse to share in their wrongdoing and, if necessary, resign. But the leaders apparently are doing their best to make a morally correct decision, and you have good reasons—your commitment to serve this organization whose good purposes you share—for wishing to carry on with your work insofar as your conscience permits. So, while legalistic minimalism always is to be avoided, you rightly wish to find a way through this moral thicket, and I shall identify some distinctions that may be helpful.

Granting, as you do, the plausibility of your superiors' view, you first should reconsider the matter at issue. Plainly, it is not simple and straightforward, and the organization's leaders, not you, have the authority to make the decision. Is it possible that their judgment is correct and yours mistaken?

If the leaders make the expected decision and you remain convinced it is wrong, you could ask to be excused on this one occasion from fulfilling your usual responsibilities. No doubt the organization could find someone to replace you temporarily if you were taken ill. If the leaders value your services and are themselves as conscientious as your narrative suggests, they might agree that your absence would be no less appropriate in this situation and let you take a vacation or, at least, a leave of absence without pay while someone else handles this matter.

What if your request to be excused is rejected, or you think it better to handle the problem yourself? Then you must judge to what extent and in what ways you may deal with the public relations problems resulting from what you believe to be an objective violation of the organization's common good and an injustice to members who sought the expulsion of those publicly doing wrong.

To make this judgment, bear in mind that when what one does contributes to others' objectively wrong action, one must entirely avoid sharing their wrongful intention. Thus, in helping the leaders deal with the public relations problems resulting from their decision, you may share their intentions only insofar as you believe these to be objectively right. And some of the leaders' intentions may be objectively right, since the wrong will be in their decision itself, which will be prior to and distinct from any public relations effort regarding it. Therefore, the first question you must try to answer is: In what respects will the measures the leaders wish taken to support their decision be truly morally acceptable? In trying to answer this question, we must bear in mind that the leaders' sincerity, though decisive for their responsibility in the matter, does not settle your responsibility.

The answer will depend on the shape the public relations effort takes, and you must do your best to shape it. From your statement of the facts, it seems that the public at large is likely to approve of the decision, but some members of your organization are likely to resist it. I shall assume it will be better for the organization as a whole if the decision, having been made, is generally accepted—that is, if members who disagree remain loyal members and do nothing to oppose the decision inconsistent with the organization's constitution and procedures. On that assumption, the members' understanding and *acceptance* of the leaders' decision, as distinct from their *approval,* will be objectively good, and you may intend their acceptance as the purpose of your public relations effort. Consequently, you must try to persuade the leadership to let you make the case, not that their decision is objectively correct, but that they have done their best and even those who consider the decision mistaken should recognize that the organization's good now requires closing ranks. This approach not only will allow you to function as spokesperson without violating your conscience but will mitigate the antagonism of members who share your disappointment with the decision.

Even if the leadership agrees to shape the public relations effort in this way, however, they are likely to wish to communicate their own sincere view to at least some members and some segments of the wider public, and to work for approval, not merely acceptance, of their decision. If so, you will be enlisted to help communicate what you consider false and achieve what you consider wrong. The relevant questions will be: (1) Can you help communicate positions you consider false without personally asserting them? (2) What can you do without sharing the leaders' objectively wrong intention? (3) Will some other grounds morally exclude doing what you can? I shall begin by considering together the first and second questions.

Doubtless part of your work will be preparing materials, such as a press release and a letter from the leaders to the members, and part will be communicating directly with the press and members, either in conferences, or by individual conversations or letters, or both. These various activities may present somewhat differing problems.

In preparing materials to be issued in the leaders' name or in the name of the organization as such, you may state the decision, explain it, and point to the leaders' grounds for it. Though those grounds will include the leaders' reasons for approving the decision, you need not intend to induce members to approve it. Rather your intention can be to help the leaders communicate their own view, so that members will accept the decision not merely as a fait accompli but as the leaders' sincere, even if mistaken, attempt to do the right thing. Moreover, if you draft a letter to be signed by one of your superiors, you can without lying include in it statements you believe false but the sender believes true. For you do not assert any of the statements in the letter, but only formulate them as a proposed expression of what your superior wishes to communicate.

Probably your role as spokesperson also will require you to defend the decision in other ways, involving direct communication on your part. Your own objective, of course, must remain limited to the legitimate one of gaining understanding and acceptance for the leaders' decision rather than approval of it, and you may not seek approval for the decision as a way of gaining acceptance for it. Within this framework, will you be limited to saying only what you believe true? Obviously, without lying you can write and speak in the third person, presenting the matter as a whole from the leaders' point of view, while also asserting without qualification propositions you personally consider true. But can you go beyond this? Provided it is clear to those addressed that you are communicating as spokesperson, I think you can, at least when addressing an indeterminate group—for example, by issuing a press release, sending a newsletter you write to the membership at large, or speaking before a press conference or a general membership meeting. In these circumstances, those addressed do not—or, at least, cannot reasonably—expect to be getting your personal views but those of the organization, since you are speaking not for yourself but for it. Therefore, it seems to me, you may speak in the first person, using not *I* but *we,* without thereby referring to yourself, and so without personally asserting elements of the organization's view that you consider mistaken.

Could you take the same approach in replying over your own signature to individuals' letters or in conversing with individuals or small groups especially interested in the problem and decision? In some instances, especially in correspondence, you might be able to make it clear that you are expressing the organization's position without personally asserting it. But in others, I think, such situations will prove more problematic. The closer relationship existing between the parties to such communications makes it less likely they will distinguish between what you personally think and what you assert in your role as spokesperson. If you try to maintain the distinction, that is likely to indicate that your personal view differs from the official position, and that may provoke questions about your view. These, of course, you could decline to answer, but that would tend to lessen your effectiveness as spokesperson on the matter. Therefore, I think you should try to avoid answering letters over your own signature and engaging in conversations with individuals and small groups. Considering the decision's obvious importance to the organization and your difference with the leaders, they may be willing to do these things themselves—of course, with your help in drafting letters and so on.

With respect to the third question—whether what you can do without sharing the leaders' objectively wrong intentions might be morally excluded on other grounds—it seems likely to me that this probably will not be the case. In the first place, as has been explained, you can intend an acceptable end and avoid sharing the leaders' objectively wrong intention. The leaders no doubt will go beyond the goal of the public relations effort and seek approval for their decision. But given your clearheadedness and commitment, you are not likely to be tempted by your involvement to choose to do anything you judge wrong. In the second place, the risk of scandal is lessened by the facts that the decision will already have been made and that the wider community's leadership already has taken a similar stance in respect to the problem. In the third place, if you are right in thinking that your resignation and public protest would have no good effect, your work on this matter will not affect your capacity to bear witness to the truth about it, since one cannot both serve as an organization's spokesperson and openly oppose its leadership. Finally, your cooperation with the leaders very likely will not be unfair to anyone. If you did not carry out the public relations effort, the leadership surely would find someone to replace you, and that person would be less likely to shape it toward only the limited goal of gaining acceptance for the decision.

You might wonder: "What if the situation were different in only one respect —I doubted the soundness of the leaders' decision rather than considered it mistaken? Might I then promote not only its acceptance but approval?" No. Unless you judge the leaders' decision more probably morally sound than not, you must proceed on the assumption that it may well be unsound and so entitled to no more than acceptance.

153: May an adviser adjust advice on one matter to gain a hearing on another?

I am a public health physician with specialized training in obstetrics and gynecology, but have never practiced in that field. However, the bishop has asked me for confidential advice on a complex and difficult problem involving the department of obstetrics and gynecology at a local Catholic hospital. He described the problem to me and asked me to think it over and help him decide what he ought to do. When I am ready to advise him on the matter, he said, he would like me to come to his home for dinner and an open-ended session. I readily agreed to do what I can to help with the problem, though I really am much more concerned that he take seriously my advice about a different matter, namely, health considerations, including sex education, in our Catholic schools. (I have been working on this for some time with the diocesan superintendent of schools, who is preparing a plan he will deliver to the bishop next month.)

Up to now I haven't met the bishop, but I am told that, though devout and hardworking, he is thin-skinned and disposed to ignore bad news. What I shall have to tell him will not be good news, and it will point to some serious mistakes he already has made in handling the problem. If I speak clearly and straightforwardly, I expect he will not be so receptive to my advice regarding the schools. But unless I am blunt, I am afraid he will miss the point.

I never have advised a bishop before and know you have. How would you handle this?

Analysis:

The question concerns the responsibilities of a person who has agreed to provide advice. The relevant general norm is: One should fulfill a commitment unless one has a reason adequate to break it without being unfair. This norm must be specified by pointing out that lack of candor would be deceptive and also can be specified by explicating what is involved in advising well. The physician should not let his concern that his advice on a different matter be accepted affect either the substance of the advice to be given on this occasion or the case for following it. Suggestions also can be offered for dealing with the bishop's possible unreceptiveness to sound advice.

The reply could be along the following lines:

In agreeing to give the bishop advice, you committed yourself to making a reasonable effort to be what he needs, namely, a good adviser. If you had a good reason not to carry out your undertaking—for example, the conflicting claims of other, more pressing responsibilities—you might fairly break your commitment and provide no advice at all. If you do give advice, however, you must fulfill your commitment by trying to be a good adviser. Otherwise, you would deceive the bishop. He would suppose that you were doing your best to advise him well, while you really would be shaping your advice on this matter so as to dispose him to be receptive to your advice on the other, in which you happen to be more interested.

Good advisers try to help those they advise judge truly and act rightly. They do their best to communicate effectively, in order to make their advice less likely to be misunderstood and more likely to be taken into account. Your responsibility is graver than in most cases of giving advice. The matter itself probably is important; the bishop is exercising his office in the Church; and you, as a member of the Church with expertise he lacks, have a special duty to help him fulfill his responsibility (see LG 37; *CIC,* c. 212, §3).

Advising is not merely providing information but helping someone arrive at practical truth by sound practical reasoning. Moreover, in advising the bishop, the reasoning to be assisted is not merely technical reflection about how to achieve a particular goal but moral reflection about how to fulfill his responsibilities. So, in thinking out your advice for the bishop, keep in mind his responsibilities, capacities, and limitations, and try to contribute to the reflection you believe he must carry through if he is to see what he really ought to do. Possible alternatives also must be considered and the reasons against them stated within the framework of what is morally possible for him and required of him. Be ready to listen to the bishop until you thoroughly understand his problem and his possibilities for dealing with it, and only then venture to offer advice.

Prepare well. Pray that the Holy Spirit enlighten and strengthen you and the bishop—you to develop and give good advice and the bishop to receive and make use of it. If necessary, you should refresh your knowledge about any nonmedical aspects of the matter. You might be tempted not to do the necessary work, since you are not enthusiastic about advising on this problem and, perhaps, do not expect to be paid. Having agreed to advise, however, you should take the task as seriously as its inherent significance requires. In agreeing to think over the problem the bishop outlined, you implicitly promised to refresh your knowledge on the subject and do any research you judge warranted. Since you cannot expect him to be familiar with technical terminology and scientific presuppositions you usually take for granted, be ready to supply necessary background information and explain matters in ordinary language. Perhaps you should prepare a brief written and/or graphic presentation of essential points, if you think that would help him understand them. In sum, you should prepare as seriously as you would if you were preparing to make a professional presentation to an important audience; you should not do less for the bishop than you would for the chief public official under whom you work.

In planning what advice to give and preparing the case for following it, set aside your concern about the bishop's future openness to the advice you expect to give him on the other matter, and focus on advising well on this occasion. To alter in any way the substance of your advice on this occasion in view of your greater interest in the other matter would be to deceive the bishop and betray the confidence he is placing in you. You could only think such trimming reasonable insofar as it seemed conducive to a better outcome on the whole and in the long run. But you cannot know that—you cannot even know how interested the bishop is in your advice on each of the two matters—and so you are in no position to foresee and commensurate the goods likely to result from either setting aside your concern about the other matter or letting it affect your advice on this one. That being so, trimming now would be altogether unreasonable.

Still, without doing that, try insofar as possible to avoid offense. You may do this partly in view of your interest in his being receptive to your advice on the other matter. But you should do it, in any case, in order to increase the chances of having your present advice understood and taken into account. Talk about the problem as an objective state of affairs and avoid emphasizing his personal involvement. When you must mention his mistakes, you can avoid underlining the point that they are his if you use the passive voice or speak impersonally about "things done inappropriately," "a policy that had best be discontinued," and so on. If mentioning his responsibility for a mistake cannot be avoided, make it clear that you take it for granted he did his best and any missteps were understandable.

You also might try to prevent your advice here and now from dimming prospects for your advice on the other matter by speaking frankly to the bishop during dinner. Assure him that you realize the problem he has asked you about is only one of many complex and difficult matters he must deal with. Tell him of your deep concern regarding health considerations in the Catholic schools, your temptation to soften your advice on the present problem in view of that concern, and your decision not to do that. Then, express the hope that your present effort will not prevent him from taking full account of your work on the other matter. That straightforward approach might dispose him to understand and sympathize with your concern.

In talking with the bishop and trying to understand his view of the problem, your perspective inevitably will change somewhat in the course of the conversation. Be ready to revise and correct what you have said previously as your grasp of the problem improves. Toward the end of the session, if possible, reorganize and restate your advice from your final perspective. I also suggest that you prepare a careful memorandum as soon as possible afterwards and send it to him, so that he will have your best thinking in written form to reflect upon and share with other advisers.

The diocesan superintendent of schools, a good pastor, or some other mature and well-balanced diocesan priest will have had experience in dealing with the bishop, and should be able to give you helpful information about him. I suggest that, in preparing for your session with him, you ask one or more such priests the question you have asked me, though without mentioning, even in general terms, the subject on which the bishop is seeking your advice.

154: May a librarian select morally objectionable and propagandistic books?

Three weeks ago I started my new job as the acquisitions and cataloging librarian for this small city's public library. Cataloging presents no moral problem, and I am experienced in doing it. But as acquisitions librarian, I shall decide which new books to order—except those for the reference section and the young people's room, whose librarians do their own ordering. Here I have a moral problem.

Surveying the present collection, I have found a great deal of soft pornography and a preponderance of nonfiction favoring secularist views. There are serious gaps in the collection of classical works of fiction and drama. Nonfiction sympathetic to traditional religious views is quite sparse. I want to make changes for the better.

Formally, my authority is only limited by the library board, the head librarian, and the annual budget.

The library board, appointed by the mayor with the approval of the city council, has ultimate authority over our entire operation. But I understand that, rather than involving themselves in the librarians' professional work, board members have confined themselves to naming the head librarian, reading the staff's annual report and discussing it with them, making decisions about physical plant and employees' wages and benefits, and recommending a budget to the mayor and council. I shall have to write up an account of how I am handling acquisitions for the annual report to the board. However, I do not expect binding directives from the board but informal suggestions at most.

If she wished, the head librarian could tell me to order particular items or she could review my decisions and veto them. But she has explained that, in her judgment, professionals should be as self-directing as possible. She manages the other librarians' work by providing only general direction, encouraging everyone to share ideas, mediating such conflicts as arise, and "retaining on staff only people who work well together."

Portions of the acquisitions budget are designated for the reference section and young people's room, and for replacing missing, mutilated, and worn-out volumes. But currently that leaves enough for me to add about twenty-five hundred new books a year to our collection—a good number for the community we serve. Consequently, though the other librarians sometimes will suggest books and I will get many requests from patrons, I actually will have considerable freedom in choosing almost fifty new books a week.

Most librarians in my place would order just about every book on the best-seller lists, but I am reluctant to do that, because many of these books are morally objectionable. Much of the fiction published today, even by the most reputable houses, is soft pornography; most new novels and collections of short stories include passages of needlessly graphic sex and/or violence. I object to such material as sexually arousing or morbidly exciting, and degrading to people, usually to women. Also, a significant segment of the nonfiction, even that published by university presses, is propaganda—for abortion, euthanasia, alternative lifestyles, and other causes—posing as journalism or scholarship.

Nevertheless, it already is clear that most of the books requested by patrons and suggested by other librarians will be best sellers or works opposed to traditional positions on controversial issues. It is not feasible for me regularly to ignore these requests and suggestions. For one thing, it would not seem fair to many patrons, since citizens pay for the library with their taxes and expect it to have many of the books they want. Also, if too many patrons and my colleagues become dissatisfied and begin complaining, I am sure the head librarian eventually will let me go. Personally, I could accept that, for even though I took this job partly because I like the city and thought the work would be a new challenge, I am sure I could find another cataloging job somewhere. However, I also wanted the chance to select better books than many of the ones I was cataloging where I used to work—a concern that probably would not be shared by anyone who replaced me here.

I have two questions. First, what moral limits must one observe in selecting books for a public library? Second, are there any other considerations I ought to take into account? Don't hesitate to offer suggestions about how to do my job, since the troubling part of it is entirely new to me. But bear in mind that other librarians will do all the ordering for the reference section and young people's room. The reference section here includes the newspapers and adult magazines, and the young people's room includes all materials for boys and girls under fifteen. I shall not be ordering any periodicals, but shall be ordering books for adolescents roughly fifteen and older as well as for adults.

Analysis:

This question calls for the derivation of norms for the questioner's selection of books. A public library should serve a certain element of the common good: the availability to all members of the community of many books they can use in pursuing or promoting various authentic goods for themselves and others. This principle implies a negative norm regarding acquisitions: No book should be selected unless it is likely to serve a legitimate purpose for an adequate number of community members. Probably this norm seldom excludes acquisition of a best seller. However, several affirmative norms can be articulated: Choose fiction of good literary quality; seek to balance holdings not only on particular controversial issues but on fundamental philosophical and religious questions; take into account the vulnerability of adolescents and young adults in selecting books of special interest to them; and try to serve the needs of many less sophisticated members of the community.

The reply could be along the following lines:

Insofar as acquisitions librarians are public servants, the principle for their work is a certain aspect of the common good of the communities they serve, namely, the availability to everyone of many books useful for wholesome recreation and entertainment, authentic esthetic experience, and gaining knowledge and the ability to use it. It would be wrong for someone responsible for acquisitions to select a book he or she thought would fail to give one or more of those benefits to an adequate number of potential patrons.

This norm plainly excludes both pornographic material, which harms everyone and benefits no one, and anything so incompetently researched and/or badly written that nobody would profit by reading it. But it also excludes books useful to too few people. Other things being equal, an acquisitions librarian using public funds clearly ought to prefer a book that would benefit many patrons to one that would benefit few, even in the long run. So, as a necessary condition for ordering any book, he or she should anticipate that a certain number of people will be interested in it—how many will depend on the library's budget, its patrons' interests, and the number and variety of good books available. Librarians can be tempted to select books useful to very few or even none of the library's patrons, not only to serve their own interests and those of their friends and loved ones, or the unusual interests of particular patrons, but simply so that the library will have books considered of unusual merit—in other words, to engage in the hobby of book collecting at public expense, while depriving patrons of a portion of the service to which they are entitled.

Will the norm ever absolutely exclude selecting a best seller? Perhaps, but I expect that very seldom will be the case. It is hard to think of a best-selling book so bad it cannot be of legitimate interest to some people, who might at least criticize it as an example of cultural depravity, bad argument, or the like.

I agree that many best-selling works of fiction are morally objectionable inasmuch as they include needlessly graphic sex and violence. But best sellers usually are written well enough to offer something more than titillation, and mature persons who have developed the virtue of modesty, by quickly skimming the objectionable passages, can read them without sinning.

I also agree that a significant segment of nonfiction is propaganda. But, again, most nonfiction best sellers can be read with profit by some people. Anyone seriously interested in a controversial topic needs to examine the opposing views and the arguments for them, including the alleged facts on which those arguments depend. In this way, thoughtful people can exercise critical judgment, develop a well-grounded position, become able to explain and defend it, and respond effectively to other, unsound or less sound views. Indeed, people who do not examine and understand the propaganda for erroneous positions are likely to be seduced into absorbing false claims and unsound arguments from mass public opinion, where they float about disconnected from their sources and not easily identifiable.

Among newly published works of fiction, you obviously should select books of solid literary quality, even if they also have some morally objectionable passages. If you order one copy of many best-selling novels, the library will not be ignoring popular demand, while patrons already keen to read them will keep these single copies in constant use for a long time, so that they will be unavailable to more casual readers, including most adolescents and young adults. Moreover, older fiction, much of it rich both in literary and moral qualities, sometimes is available in inexpensive editions. You can acquire, and make available as new, some books of this sort that are both readable and missing from the library's collection. They probably will not be so heavily used in the short run as the current best sellers, but they may get more use in the long run.

Someone might object that such a policy would not serve the public adequately. Ordering only a single copy of a best-selling book hardly responds to popular demand; many patrons must wait a long time for the book and so are deprived of it precisely when they want it. But though the policy is not fully responsive to popular demand, it can serve the public's needs. Very popular books generally are inexpensive or soon become available in cheap editions, so that most people who want them can acquire them. The library more appropriately serves the public by providing works of lasting interest, which may never become available in cheap editions but in the long run will be useful to a large number of people.

In selecting nonfiction on controversial issues, reject shallow treatments and prefer those that are more solidly researched and well argued. Since there generally is a great deal of duplication and overlap in this sort of literature, it should suffice to acquire a few comprehensive works each year representing each position on a particular topic; when a controversy continues, prefer works that move the debate forward in some significant way. Though books opposing traditional views generally are more effectively promoted and widely publicized, you are in a position to provide balance by identifying and acquiring books that best represent and support the tradition, many of which, again, will not be current publications. In choosing books on controversial topics, take into account how you will catalogue them, so that balance will be achieved insofar as possible not only on the whole but in the diverse classifications into which works on various aspects of a controversy will fall. In this way, readers looking for a book on one side of a certain aspect of a controversy—say, on the medical or legal or philosophical aspect of abortion—often will encounter on the same shelf a work on the other side.

With nonfiction, as with fiction, look for gaps in the library's collection that can be filled with sound and readable older works available in inexpensive editions or through used book dealers. Since secularist prejudices often shape public libraries' holdings, you are likely to find little good material representing traditional views, not only on particular controversial issues but on the broader questions of perennial interest. Besides theological and philosophical books accessible to nonprofessionals, sound works in history and biography are especially important in making the theistic tradition available for serious consideration as an alternative to contemporary, antireligious thought. In looking for such materials, be scrupulously fair in acquiring sound and readable books by non-Catholic authors as well as Catholics. For this purpose, you might ask local non-Catholic religious leaders for advice.

Your patrons of high school and college age are especially vulnerable to morally objectionable passages in fiction and to propaganda in nonfiction. Be very careful in choosing among books likely to appeal especially to them. Most books you decide not to acquire despite popular demand for them should be ones that are either morally objectionable or propagandistic, and that have special appeal to youthful readers. You also should familiarize yourself with what young people are encountering in their studies, so that you can build on whatever wholesome interests they may be developing and provide balance where possible to the secularistic indoctrination they may be receiving.

Many people in the community who seldom read a book will appreciate your work and support you if they know you are trying to supply the books they want—about auto repair, growing roses, travel, health problems, cooking, taxes, refinishing furniture, caring for babies, and so on. Instead of talking only with the comparatively small group of rather sophisticated people who request particular books or otherwise bring themselves to your attention, strive to communicate with a broader spectrum of library patrons and even with those who have seldom or never taken advantage of this community resource. Encourage members of this wider public to request the books they want, and keep a record of every such request you satisfy. Expanding the library's usefulness in this way not only will be fairer to the public it serves but will strengthen your position against those who might object to other aspects of your acquisitions policy.

As each new book is received, you might post a brief, annotated notice about it on a "New Books" bulletin board near the circulation desk or main entrance. Similarly, you might be able to provide a local newspaper and/or broadcasting station with a weekly "New Books" column and/or program. Through the same media, you could invite advice and suggestions, not just about particular books to acquire but about areas of interest people think have been neglected. You might even be able to arrange a more or less formal community survey to learn about needs the library could serve better.

In writing your part of the annual report to the library board, you no doubt will wish to forestall problems by explaining what you are trying to accomplish. Without lying, put your explanation in terms likely to be acceptable. For example, make the point that you are trying to ensure that the library's holdings will meet the needs of a broader spectrum of community members and more fairly represent diverse points of view on controversial issues. Say that, while selecting fewer works of current fiction, you are ordering many highly readable older works, and trying to ensure that all books selected are of good literary quality. Have in mind examples of your selections that illustrate each point you make or respond to each criticism you anticipate. Though you may not have space enough to include the examples in your report, you will be able to use them in conversations with fellow librarians and other interested parties.

+ + +

155: Must a student do his best in every subject?

My sister, Anne, and I talked about some of the moral questions that came up in the course she took with you last year. Now I have a question you might be interested in, and Anne has helped me write it up for you.

I am beginning high school at St. Benet's Prep. My dad is an engineer, and I want to be one too. Dad thinks I can do it, and that I should try to get into one of the top engineering schools. For me to do that, my grades and aptitude test scores will have to be very good, but my math and science grades and math aptitude score will have to be almost perfect. They grade hard at St. Benet's, and hardly anybody gets an *A* in every subject. Math and science are easy for me, but I'm afraid that if I go all out on other subjects, my record might not be good enough for the top engineering schools. I have been planning to do my best in math and science, and to work for a *B* or a *B*+ in everything else.

At freshman orientation this morning the headmaster talked about studying. His main point was that we should do our best in every subject. He said one of the biggest mistakes students make is not doing their best in subjects they find difficult or think unimportant. He told us that if we did that we would be cheating our parents by wasting part of the tuition they pay and cheating ourselves by wasting part of the chance St. Benet's offers to build a solid foundation for our future lives. He said the young man who wastes any part of that chance is like a carpenter building a vacation home for himself in a dry climate, who does less than his best putting in the drainage around the footings. Because the job involves masonry, it is difficult for the carpenter; and because the site is so dry, the drainage does not seem very important. But just because the carpenter finds masonry difficult, the headmaster said, he should try twice as hard to do his best with the drainage, remembering that a house without adequate drainage eventually will be undermined by the heavy rains that fall occasionally even in the desert.

All that makes sense. Even if I will not need other subjects as much as math and science, my whole record must be very good, and I will not get the grades I need in some other subjects unless I work even harder on them than on math and science. But will I be cheating my parents and myself if I do not go all out on those other subjects?

Analysis:

This question calls for help in making a sound judgment about allocating effort to different subjects. Because students' duties flow primarily from the good they can hope to realize by developing their gifts, the questioner can be helped by clarifying that good. At least three points should be made. First, as students embark on any phase of their education, the good to be realized by developing their gifts remains obscure. The earlier the phase, the greater the obscurity. Second, that good includes benefits, to the students themselves and others, not only of their future professional work but of carrying out other elements of their vocation. Third, no matter what else students are called to, they are called to be students, and should not ignore or undervalue the immediate benefits to be anticipated in doing good work as students. Taking these clarifications into account, the questioner should judge whether his responsibility to prepare for a career as an engineer warrants his planned allocation of effort.

The reply could be along the following lines:

Accepting the requirement that students do their best in every subject as sound, you are wondering whether you would violate it by settling for grades of *B* or *B+* in subjects other than mathematics and science. Of course, many students simply tend to neglect subjects they enjoy less. But you make it clear that you are conscientious and have no intention of neglecting the other subjects, though you find them more difficult and/or consider them less important. So, you present a real moral question well worth trying to answer.

"Do your best in every subject" might be taken to mean: In every subject do all you might if you had no other responsibility to fulfill. But that would be absurd, so it cannot be what the headmaster meant. He plainly thinks hard work on every subject is necessary for your education as a whole, and you are not questioning that. So, I take for granted that you are prepared to do what you can in each subject without slighting your other responsibilities.

Of course, you have many responsibilities that do not pertain to your life as a student: those bearing on religion, civic life, family, and friendships; those regarding your own health and well-being; and still others, such as occasionally helping a stranger in need. I shall take it for granted that you will fulfill those responsibilities—which include appropriate rest and recreation—and know how to balance them with the responsibilities pertaining to your life as a student. Therefore, your question can be restated: If you do not go all out on subjects other than mathematics and science, will you violate your responsibility to strive to master every subject? To help you answer this question, I shall try to clarify the latter responsibility.

I shall not argue, however, either that you should seek similar grades in every subject or that you may settle for grades of *B* and *B+* in subjects other than mathematics and science. At best, grades only signify teachers' judgments about students' achievement in comparison with one another, and discussing grades will not explain why you should try to achieve anything. You do owe it to your parents and teachers to make good use of the opportunity they are giving you, but only because it is an opportunity for something inherently worthwhile: the good you can realize by developing your talents. Having received your talents from God so as to realize that good, you owe it to him to develop them (see Mt 25.14–30). Therefore, you will better understand your responsibility as a student by reflecting on the fruit to be anticipated from your education. I propose three points for your reflection.

First, at present you are not in a position to appreciate or even foresee many, perhaps most, of the benefits that will accrue from your education for yourself and others. You almost certainly have talents of which you are not yet aware, and you surely have many of which you are only imperfectly aware. You have some idea how you might exercise some talents of which you are more or less conscious, but that possibility will become clearer as your education proceeds, and new opportunities probably will emerge or at least will come to your attention.

Second, no matter what you do, your desire to become an engineer could be frustrated, and proficiency in mathematics and science may turn out not to be as important for you as you now suppose. If you do become an engineer, doing the work well will involve using talents, such as the ability to communicate, developed mainly by studying other subjects. Moreover, not all the benefits to be anticipated from your education will be realized in and through your work. God has blessed you with faith, citizenship, and membership in your family; perhaps he will call you to be a husband and a father. He certainly wants you to be an active Catholic, citizen, and family member; and if you marry and have children, he will want you to lead your own family. You should develop your talents to carry out all these roles, and subjects other than mathematics and science will be important for that purpose.

Third, some of the good fruit of education becomes available and can be enjoyed at once. You should not study now only for the sake of what that will enable you to do later but also for the benefits, for yourself and others, of being a good student. Knowledge of God's creation and appreciation of the good and beautiful things human beings have made are valuable in themselves, and your preparatory school years can greatly enrich you in that knowledge and appreciation. Moreover, a good student's work, like all work, is good in itself (see *LCL,* 754–58); the self-discipline and exercise of other virtues involved are good in themselves; the fellowship and cooperation with teachers and other students are good in themselves. Accepting the work as your present vocation, doing it as a witness to your faith, offering it in the Eucharist with Jesus' sacrifice, and so making it available as material for the kingdom (see GS 38–39)—all these are good in themselves.

These three reflections make it clear that you should expect extremely rich and varied fruit from your education. You are not yet in a position to appreciate or even clearly foresee much of it. As you go on with your education, the benefits received and to be anticipated will gradually become clearer but always will remain somewhat obscure. Indeed, only toward the end of a good life, if even then, can one know, by looking back, what one received and achieved, and appreciate the value of one's education. Of course, despite the obscurity, eventually you will have to make commitments and concentrate your studies more and more narrowly. You will be in a much better position to do this, however, as you learn more about your gifts and the opportunities for using them by further developing and exper- imenting with them.

These reflections do not conclusively show that not going all out on subjects other than mathematics and science would violate the norm that students should do their best in every subject (assuming a reasonable understanding of the norm— one that takes their other responsibilities into account). Only you can judge when the time is right to begin focusing your efforts to prepare for the specific kind of work you will do. In making that judgment, however, consider the whole range of benefits at stake and keep in mind the inevitable and irrevocable sacrifice of other benefits that any decision to prepare for a specific kind of work entails.

In making such judgments and others regarding their education, many students begin by considering what they want in life. Then they try to calculate which available option is likely to yield more of what they want. Faithful Christians seeking first the kingdom, begin by considering what God wants; they try to discern what he is calling them to, not only for their own fulfillment but as service to others (see *LCL,* 113–29). Therefore, in deciding whether it is time to begin focusing your efforts, gather all the relevant information, talk the problem over with those who can help you think it through, rouse your faith, ask for the light of the Holy Spirit, consider everything prayerfully, make your judgment, and concentrate your effort or not, as seems right. That will be doing your best in every subject.

156: May a student cheat when a teacher plainly expects it?

I am fifteen and just beginning my last year of middle school. My problem is about cheating. We are divided into different groups for our math course. Math isn't my best subject, so I am in the bottom group. The teacher probably knows a lot of math, but he does not explain things so that we can understand them. One of the girls has an older brother who is really good at math. He does her homework for her, and all the other kids copy it. I don't want to cheat, so I haven't done that, but even though I have been spending a lot of time on homework, I'm afraid I'm not doing too well.

The first test will be in two weeks. When this teacher gives a test, he gets it started, then leaves the room and doesn't come back until near the end of the period. Also, he uses a lot of the same problems he has used before, and the answers are passed down every year. When the teacher leaves, the kids check out the problems, line up the answers to the old ones, and work on the new ones together. They get some wrong, of course, but everybody does pretty well.

The teacher must know what is going on. If I don't go along with it, I probably will fail and have to take the course over in summer school. I won't learn any more there, but I will pass. In summer school everybody passes that comes to class regularly. Maybe I should go along with the rest of the class. But I don't like doing that, because I never cheated before.

Analysis:

This question calls for application of norms regarding cheating, scandal, and the work of students. Cheating, properly so-called, is a form of fraud, and so is always wrong. But if the facts of this case have been stated accurately, the teacher plainly intends and invites his students to behave as they do, so that they are not really being dishonest, though he is. For two reasons, however, the questioner should not conform to the pattern set by other students. First, that is likely to lead to real cheating in other cases. Second, even if teachers behave irresponsibly, students ought to develop their talents, and so should try to obtain the best education they can. Therefore, rather than conforming to the usual practice of students in this bad situation, the questioner should do what is possible to master the material and change the situation for the better.

The reply could be along the following lines:

Cheating by a student in doing his or her assignments and taking tests is wrong for four reasons. It is dishonest; it is unfair to others, especially to honest students whose work seems poorer by comparison; the bad example encourages others to cheat, not only in school but in other situations; moreover, it is a self-defeating way of evading the responsibility to learn what one needs to know and develop one's abilities.[355]

Students often exaggerate how badly teachers are behaving and how wide-spread cheating is among their fellow students. If I thought you were exaggerating, I would simply tell you: Study hard and don't cheat. However, if your account is entirely true, as I trust it is, you are right in saying this math teacher must know what is going on. In fact, he plainly expects students to deal with homework and tests in the ways you describe. That being so, the students are not deceiving him in presenting others' work as if it were their own, and so are not, strictly speaking, cheating. It is the teacher, who is only pretending to do his job, who is cheating. Moreover, you would not be unfair to your fellow students if you acted as they do.

Still, there are two reasons why you should not go along with the rest of the class in this matter.

First, even though it would not really be cheating, many of your fellow students no doubt think they are cheating. Thinking that, they mistakenly suppose cheating properly so-called is justified in this case. But if it were, it might be justifiable in other cases, and the temptation to cheat would be stronger. So, if you were to go along with the rest of the class, you would be reinforcing the temptation to cheat and contributing to real cheating by less clearheaded and conscientious students. By refusing to conform, you will bear witness to the truth that cheating is always wrong and avoid giving bad example to those all-too-ready to cheat (see *LCL,* 233).

Second, even if going along with the rest of the class would enable you to pass the course without going to summer school, you would not learn the mathematics the course is supposed to help you learn. That lack might very well handicap you in the future. In general, learning is good for you and important, because without knowledge and skills you will be unable to use the gifts God has given you, and will fall short of what he is calling you to be. As a result, you will do less interesting and rewarding work than if you were better educated, and you will be less able to contribute to others' well-being and to fulfill your responsibilities to people who will depend on you. In the present instance, moreover, learning the material of the course is especially important because you already are weak in mathematics.

I realize that failing the course is not an appealing alternative, especially because you do not expect to learn more by retaking it in summer school. You might be able to pass the course without entirely going along with the other students. Perhaps your family or some more able fellow student could help you master the material rather than simply complete the assignments. Then too, preparing for the exam by working over tests given previously and allowed by

---

355. Fred Schab, "Schooling without Learning: Thirty Years of Cheating in High School," *Adolescence,* 26 (1991): 839–47, reports the results of a survey of high school students regarding cheating, first taken in 1969 and repeated in 1979 and 1989. Cheating on tests and homework increased, and dishonesty was increasingly viewed as necessary. Cheating was especially common in mathematics and science courses, and motivated mainly by fear of failure.

teachers to circulate would not be cheating, and you could participate in that but avoid cooperating with what goes on during the exam itself. You also might be able to learn more in summer school than you think. I assume you would have a different teacher and time to concentrate on the one course.

Still, I think there is something more you ought to do. This teacher, who is only pretending to do his job, needs to change his ways, not only for your sake and the sake of the other students, but even for his own sake. Do what you can to bring about that change. That probably will not be easy for you, but it will be truly good for everyone concerned, including you.

Where to begin? I suggest you tell the teacher you are concerned about your progress in the course and ask him for special help. If he responds well to that request, you could tell him about other students' cheating, without naming names, and ask him to do what he can to prevent it, so that the work of students who are unwilling to cheat will not seem poor by comparison.

Frankly, though, I do not expect that this teacher will respond well. If he does not, or you decide not to talk with him, tell your parents at once exactly what has been going on and what you tried to do about it. You might show them your letter to me and my reply. You also should try to help some of your fellow students understand that they are being cheated. If they see that, you may be able to get them to talk about it with their parents. Then, all of you can ask your parents to talk over the problem with one another. I suggest that they, in turn, talk with the teacher and the person responsible for evaluating his work (probably the school's principal). In these conversations, the parents should make it clear that they want more effective teaching and properly conducted examinations, which are as necessary to evaluate the teacher's work as his students' progress. If their initial efforts do not lead to the needed reforms, the parents should not hesitate to go to the appropriate school authorities.

What if your parents are unwilling to talk with the teacher and those over him? In that case, I think you should tell someone at the school—perhaps a counselor or a good teacher—about the situation and your efforts to deal with it, and ask that person for help. If possible, get at least one, and preferably two or three, of your fellow students to join you in this appeal.

If you do not succeed in bringing about the needed changes, you still should do everything you can to learn what ought to be learned in the course. Learning is good, and you must pursue it as best you can. Teachers can and should help you, but if they do not, you still should do your best to learn. Again, you should ask your parents for help. If they cannot help you themselves, perhaps they will be able to find someone to help you understand the material well enough for you to do the work.

I know that what I am telling you may seem very hard. But you are no longer a little child, and I believe you can do what you should.

+ + +

157: May students use former students' notes and say in tests what they believe false?

Having begun graduate work in religious studies at a Catholic university, I have a couple of moral problems.

One of my courses is an excellent seminar on the Church's social teaching. Every week we read one of the main magisterial documents, and each student writes a short paper answering one of a set of assigned questions on the reading. During the session, each of us summarizes his or her paper and everyone discusses it; then the professor calls attention to important points we have overlooked and sketches out more adequate answers to the whole set of questions.

The problem is that this seminar is offered annually, and the assigned questions do not vary greatly from year to year. Several students who did well in previous years made their notes available. The professor probably knows about it, and he did not tell us not to use them. Up to now, I haven't, feeling that would be cheating. But students who use the notes in preparing their papers seem more knowledgeable, and I am naturally concerned how their competition will affect my grade. May I use the notes?

Another course is a survey of contemporary Catholic theology. The professor is a good lecturer, but she maintains that there are many inconsistencies in the Church's teachings. She supports dissenting views, ridicules theologians who are not in the "mainstream," and claims that "development of dogma" is a dishonest way of camouflaging the abandonment of outdated dogmas. Class discussion is minimal. The grade will be based on a final exam and a term paper summarizing some aspect of the thought of a contemporary theologian of one's choice and evaluating criticisms of that aspect of the theologian's work.

Older students tell me anybody whose final or term paper reveals any disagreement with this professor's views will get a C (for practical purposes a failing grade). I never have written anything in a test or term paper that I did not believe to be true. But since I deeply disagree with this professor on many things, I do not see how I can satisfy her without lying and virtually denying my faith.

Both questions are troubling me, but especially the second one.

Analysis:

This question calls for application of norms regarding the work of students, cheating, lying, and bearing witness. If using previous students' notes has not been forbidden, students who use them do not cheat. However, a sound commitment to the goods served by study requires that students use any such aid as a supplementary means of learning rather than as a substitute for doing the assigned work as well as possible. Unless students writing examinations are asked to assert their personal beliefs, they tell no lies in answering questions in ways they consider likely to meet examiners' standards. Similarly, a term paper or dissertation almost always can be written in a way that will manifest the writer's competence while concealing his or her beliefs. However, if a professor directly challenges a student's convictions, the student should bear courageous witness.

The reply could be along the following lines:

First, let me offer you some general advice to help you deal with these and other problems you will encounter as you carry on your graduate work. Since religious studies should not be separated from a devout life, you should pray and receive the sacraments regularly, and you would do well to try to find a faithful and wise priest to be your spiritual director and confessor. In your personal life and relationships, maintain your moral standards and avoid self-indulgence. Be friendly with all your fellow students, but cultivate close friendships among those who are faithful. A friend who is faithful and has succeeded in the program for a year or more will be your best source of advice. One of the older students who has warned you of possible trouble might turn out to be a good mentor. But be careful, since some students exaggerate problems to rationalize their own deficiencies, and most professors, I believe, grade by standards that are independent of whether students agree with them.

Sometimes the practice of using previous students' notes is entirely open and even encouraged, and occasionally a professor's syllabus or a graduate program's specific norms clarify students' responsibilities in this matter. So, if there is no relevant norm and the professor has said nothing about it, students reasonably assume that what is not forbidden in this regard is permitted. Therefore, provided you have not overlooked a prohibition, using the notes, as others do, would not be cheating.

Of course, as with other sources, so with other students' notes, one should not adopt passages from them without acknowledging the source. However, that requirement will not impede appropriate use of the notes, which should serve only as an additional aid for your study, not as a substitute for it.

Concern about grades is reasonable, since they do have important practical consequences. Still, unless good grades indicate solid accomplishment, they are nothing but deceptive signs, and, creating expectations that those who receive them are unable to fulfill, they are likely to be self-defeating. In doing your graduate work, your primary concern should not be grades but increasing your knowledge and developing your abilities. Regard each course as an opportunity to learn more—to become more able to find truth and communicate it effectively. Bearing in mind that students never get more out of a course than they put into it, do not try to minimize your work but to make it as fruitful as possible.

Consequently, I suggest you do the assigned reading and write a draft of your weekly paper as carefully as you can before looking at previous students' notes. Then use the notes for limited purposes: to find points in the reading that you have overlooked, to check your interpretation of obscure passages, and to identify any mistakes you may have made. Even in doing these things, use the notes only to raise questions; rely on the document itself and your own reflection on it to provide the answers. Finally, revise your paper in the light of what you have learned by using the notes.

Having done this, you not only will appear more knowledgeable, but really will have learned more than you otherwise would. You will provide the professor with evidence of your real progress and not evade the work he has assigned. Then too, if asked whether you had used previous students' notes, you could answer honestly—as you would be obliged to do—without discrediting yourself, for you could explain your reasonable way of using them.

Examinations are an academic exercise meant to determine the extent to which students have achieved the goals, set by professors, of courses or other elements of a program. In this context, unless the contrary is clearly indicated, questions should not be understood as asking students to manifest their beliefs. Rather, the questions call for specific performances to show that a student is familiar with a certain body of supposed facts, opinions, arguments, analyses, and so on; and that he or she can articulate this material and intellectually deal with it in certain approved ways. An academically experienced person reading or hearing examinations does not assume those being examined assert the statements they make. Every response is understood as if in quotation marks, introduced by: *Here is some evidence of what I can do with this question.* Therefore, provided questions do not plainly call for a statement of personal opinion and those taking examinations avoid expressions that indicate personal adherence to any proposition they do not believe true, they tell no lies by giving answers they think will be acceptable, even if some or all of the statements in the answers are contrary to what they believe true.

In examinations, potential problems often can be forestalled by employing certain formulations that enable one to articulate views to which the teacher is committed without sharing that commitment. For example, "The accepted view among many theologians is that . . ."; "It often is argued that . . ."; and "So-and-so [the teacher's favorite theologian] explains the matter in this way." Such expressions indicate that one is not asserting positions one considers false but do not manifest disagreement with them.

Term papers sometimes are assigned as exercises very similar to examinations; a precise topic is designated, and specific instructions make it clear that students are not expected to develop and express original views. Even though the assignment you describe leaves some scope for personal initiative, you should be able to do the assignment to the professor's satisfaction without misrepresenting your real beliefs. You can show your competence while concealing the convictions likely to provoke biased grading by choosing a suitable theologian and treating his or her work honestly but within strict limits.

For example, you might choose a leading American moral theologian who accepts proportionalism and dissents from the exceptionlessness of certain norms taught by the Church. If you take care to understand fully that person's version of proportionalism, and to present it accurately and dispassionately, you will seem sympathetic to the view. In the literature, you will find many criticisms of proportionalism, some flawed in ways pointed out either by some of the more careful critics of the view or by proportionalists themselves. In your paper, you can deal exclusively with such flawed criticisms, and point out their fallacies—of course, taking care to give due credit for ideas you adopt from other authors.

By doing a paper along these lines, you will learn part of what you need to know about an important topic and adequately show your scholarly ability and objectivity. You also will satisfy your professor's requirement without saying anything you think false, while, by leaving unsaid much that you think, you will avoid provoking a biased evaluation.

In general, in writing term papers and dissertations, capable students usually can satisfy a professor with whom they profoundly disagree by explicitly labeling as *presuppositions* the set of propositions that the professor insists upon and they consider false. For example, a student can take up a view acceptable to his or her professor, explain its bases without criticizing them, and state that the propositions comprising this view will be used as "working hypotheses." Having clearly stated this limiting condition, the student can employ that group of propositions as if they were true, without asserting them and so without dishonesty. Of course, this strategy should not be used if the finished work will be published without revision or is likely to become available in some other way to readers it might seriously injure—for example, by leading them into error on some matter of faith or morals.

Following these suggestions may seem cowardly. But the primary responsibility of students is to develop their abilities and complete the program they have undertaken, not to carry on probably fruitless controversies with their professors. Following one's apprenticeship as a scholar, one will have plenty of time for controversy. Meanwhile, a student will have many opportunities to articulate and defend his or her convictions in discussions with other students, who often will be more receptive than professors to unfamiliar and even unwelcome truths.

Because a professor dogmatically committed to an ideology usually wishes to seem fair and open-minded, he or she is unlikely directly to challenge students' faith or other convictions. So, I doubt that your professor will question you straightforwardly about your faith or otherwise press you to deny it. If that should happen, however, you would be obliged to bear witness to what you believe.

In that event, it would be wrong to try to soften the truth by asserting it as if it were a mere personal opinion. Tactically, moreover, it might be more effective both to define and to depersonalize the issue, insofar as possible, by referring to the relevant Church teaching and affirming your belief in its truth. For example, if your professor pressed you to agree with her views about development of dogma, you might say: "I believe what Vatican I teaches on that matter in chapter four of *Dei Filius* and what Vatican II teaches on it in chapter two of *Dei Verbum.*" You also could promise to consider her views carefully, something you must do both to learn how to expose the errors they contain and to disengage any truth that may be in them.

Professors who grade ideologically, not on the basis of students' knowledge and performance, but on the basis of their sharing the professors' opinions, do a grave injustice. As in other cases of injustice, those who suffer or observe this injustice should try to resist and rectify it. Familiarize yourself with any appeals process available to students, and consider using it. Being affirmative, however, the obligation to resist and try to rectify injustices is not absolute (see *CMP,* 256–59). Sometimes even great personal sacrifice is likely to produce little benefit, and an individual rightly suffers in silence or tolerates the injustice done to others. That is particularly so when ideologues have gained so much power over a field of study that they are able to maintain social structures that systematically, though subtly, discriminate against those who do not share their so-called mainstream consensus.

In sum, you and other faithful students should try to follow Jesus' advice: "Be wise as serpents and innocent as doves" (Mt 10.16). Still, even that might not enable you to survive in the program. So, be prepared to give up what you hoped to attain by undertaking it. If that sacrifice becomes necessary, make it without regret. You may be able to continue graduate studies elsewhere. If not, you can be sure your vocation does not require an advanced degree.

158: How can Catholics in a secularized school avoid being of their world?

We are twins, a sister and brother, and are writing this letter not just for ourselves, but for six friends of ours, too. We all went through St. Philomena's together, and all of us are now in the first year at the local public high school. It has its good points, but it also has a lot of problems, and I want to tell you about the problems.

They don't try to teach the kids *why* they should not do bad things, like use drugs, but they try really hard to catch and punish anybody who breaks the rules. They take it for granted that all the kids are "sexually active" and seem to have no problem with that. They give out condoms to anybody who asks for them. There is a lot of violence, and they don't do much to protect smaller kids from the bigger ones. A lot of kids are afraid all the time. But a friend of ours who had seen two older girls beat up another first year girl brought along a hunting knife to defend herself just in case, and they expelled her. She never used it on anybody or even took it out of her book bag, and they only found it because they were searching for drugs, which she's not into. But they said carrying a concealed weapon is against the law and there is a rule, which they had never said anything about, that a student caught breaking that law has to be expelled.

Even so, we can handle all those things pretty well. Mostly, it's just a matter of behaving ourselves, not being in the wrong place at the wrong time, and sticking together. It is harder to deal with what the teachers are trying to get us to believe. You get a poor grade from some teachers if you say something in class that lets them know you don't go along with them. Some of the teachers are really anti-Christian. They made fun of some Protestant kids who were eating lunch and reading the Bible together, and they keep going after the Catholic Church—about the Inquisition, priests who misbehave, and the Church's teaching on sex, among other things. Those teachers are in favor of abortion. Our English teacher talks about having three of them herself, like she deserved a medal or something.

The school organizes all sorts of activities, and the counselors put a lot of pressure on everybody to get involved. Most kids get into the activities, so that you are practically an outsider if you don't. But if you do, the school becomes your whole life. We are not sure whether to get involved.

Another thing is that, in the academic courses, they want everybody to be a high achiever who will make a lot of money and get ahead of others. They never talk about what a person shouldn't do to get ahead, as if nothing mattered but success. We don't think that can be right.

Our six friends and the two of us have talked with our parents about these things. They listened but didn't seem to know what to do. We all go to the religion class our parish provides for students going to public high school, and the priest takes our class once each month. We brought this up with him. He listened too, but in the end just said we have to be "in the world but not of it," and need to figure out for ourselves how to do that. We sure could use some help!

Analysis:

This question calls for the application of several norms, especially those regarding cultivating and protecting faith, bearing witness, practicing ecumenism, and seeking and accepting one's personal vocation. Living in the secularist world of their public school, these young people must reject unbelief, keep and grow in their faith, and bear witness to it when appropriate. They should work together and cooperate with their believing classmates when possible. They should continue to talk with their parents and try to get them to collaborate with other parents in dealing with specific problems at the school. They may have good reason for participating in some activities organized by the school, but also should organize activities of their own and spend some time in solitude. While rightly questioning the false ideal of high achievement proposed to them, they should work hard to develop their God-given talents and prepare themselves for service to others and authentic self-fulfillment in good work.

The reply could be along the following lines:

By saying you must be in the world but not of it, the priest meant you must live your faith by doing what it calls for in your situation. That truly is very difficult. Since there is no formula for it, he was right to say you must figure it out for yourselves. You already have made a great deal of progress. You see clearly what you are up against, you are judging what you see by the light of faith, and you are asking what to do about it. I wish all young people in your place were doing as well. Without the right questions, you would never find sound answers, and very likely you would begin to believe what your teachers want you to believe.

Do not suppose that all the bad things you face are problems you should be able to solve. Perhaps you have heard the so-called serenity prayer: "God, grant me the serenity to accept the things I cannot change, the courage to change the things I can, and the wisdom to know the difference." That prayer seems to assume one always ought to change what can be changed, whereas doing that sometimes destroys or damages good things or makes bad things even worse. But you do need, and should pray for, something like the attitude expressed by the serenity prayer: patience to put up with some bad things, courage to resist and oppose others, and wisdom to tell which to put up with and which to resist and oppose.

To a great extent, what you are encountering is the "world" that Jesus talks about in St. John's Gospel: people living in the fallen human condition who reject faith and live as though God did not exist. Today this way of thinking and living takes the form of secularism. It has become dominant in our society: in government, in business, in the mass media, and, not least, in education. Secularists claim to value pluralism and promote liberty, but they really value only secularist alternatives to the traditional Judeo-Christian world view and they are interested in promoting liberty for ways of living shaped by some secularist alternative to that traditional world view. Despite constitutional guarantees of religious freedom, many laws and public policies in so-called liberal democratic countries today favor secularism.

In the United States and some other nations, many public school systems have become increasingly secularistic and systematically propagate that world view. Of course, in some public schools the majority of administrators and teachers are believing Jews or Christians. Even in schools where secularism dominates, some administrators and teachers may not be secularists, but some who are not, go with the trend out of weakness and/or because they have uncritically accepted slogans about pluralistic democracy, separation of church and state, and so on.[356] Thus, in many public schools, some or all of the teachers, as you have discovered, imagine that education must reshape the minds and hearts of believing young people to fit into the secularist mould.

Jesus predicted that the nonbelieving world would hate those faithful to him: "If you belonged to the world, the world would love you as its own. Because you do not belong to the world, but I have chosen you out of the world—therefore the world hates you" (Jn 15.19). Still, Jesus explains that he wants his followers to live in the world. Just as the Father sent him into the world, so he sends his followers (see Jn 17.18). Carrying on Jesus' mission, his followers are not alone. When they ask the Father in Jesus' name for anything they need, the Father will give them what they ask (see Jn 16.23–24), and Jesus himself asks the Father to protect them (see Jn 17.15). Moreover, Jesus assures his followers that, in enduring the world's hatred and standing against it, they are not fighting a losing battle: "In the world you face persecution. But take courage; I have conquered the world!" (Jn 16.33).

---

356. For evidence and arguments showing that to a very considerable extent public school textbooks and curricula are not religiously neutral but shaped by secularist assumptions, see Warren A. Nord, *Religion and American Education: Rethinking a National Dilemma* (Chapel Hill, N.C.: University of North Carolina Press, 1995), 138–91; Charles L. Glenn, "Religion, Textbooks, and the Common School," *Public Interest,* 88 (Summer 1987): 28–47. John Stuart Mill, one of the most important nineteenth century secularist thinkers, strongly insisted on pluralism and public neutrality on the differences among religious and secular world views. He held that political society should require all parents to educate their children, and should pay part or even all the cost of educating the poor. But he argued—*On Liberty,* V, in *Essential Works of John Stuart Mill,* ed. Max Lerner (New York: Bantam, 1961), 351–52—that the state should not provide education: "That the whole or any large part of the education of the people should be in State hands, I go as far as any one in deprecating. All that has been said of the importance of individuality of character, and diversity in opinions and modes of conduct, involves, as of the same unspeakable importance, diversity of education. A general State education is a mere contrivance for moulding people to be exactly like one another: and as the mould in which it casts them is that which pleases the predominant power in the government, whether this be a monarch, a priesthood, an aristocracy, or the majority of the existing generation, in proportion as it is efficient and successful, it establishes a despotism over the mind, leading by natural tendency to one over the body." Today, many public school systems are doing precisely what Mill said such a system would do. But since secularists are in control, they no longer object.

Christians undergoing persecution must be clearheaded. Nonbelieving authorities, even wicked ones, must be respected and, in general, obeyed: "For the Lord's sake accept the authority of every human institution, whether of the emperor as supreme, or of governors, as sent by him to punish those who do wrong and to praise those who do right. For it is God's will that by doing right you should silence the ignorance of the foolish" (1 Pt 2.13–15). But if the person in authority abuses it and demands that something wrong be done, the Christian must refuse: "We must obey God rather than any human authority" (Acts 5.29). Respect and obey your nonbelieving teachers, but always ask yourself whether what they are telling you to do is wrong. If you believe it is, do not do as they tell you in that particular matter.

Sometimes, you should plan and work together to challenge your teachers' views—for example, on abortion. From a local prolife organization you might obtain pictures of unborn babies (not ones that obviously have been aborted) at twelve to sixteen weeks of development, show these to other students, and tell them it is as bad to allow these people to be killed, just because they are very small, as it was to allow Africans to be captured and enslaved, just because they happened to be black. You even can and should challenge your teachers openly. They can suppress and retaliate against one or two students, but they cannot deal so easily with a group of ten or twelve who share a common view and speak up in support of one another.

Still, in general, you need not challenge your teachers and risk getting a poor grade by letting them know you do not agree with what they want you to believe. Of course, you must never deny your faith or lie. Moreover, Jesus has sent you into the world—into this school—to carry on his mission. He told people the truth about God and themselves, poked holes in their attempts to evade it, and showed he meant what he said by the way he acted. You and your friends can and must do that too, especially when you are with other students. Try to help them get at the truth by telling them what you believe and showing you mean it by the way you act. This will make some of them begin to think, and the seed you plant may bear fruit—if not now, later, perhaps even many years later.

When teachers say something (or have you read or watch something) that seems at odds with faith or against the Church, discuss the problem with your friends after class and tell others what you think. Most high school students will be receptive to fellow students' disagreement with a teacher, and so many will listen to what you have to say. If you are not sure what to think, talk about the problem with your parents and, if necessary, with your religion teacher or the priest, then discuss it with your friends. If the religion teacher and priest are not helpful or do not seem able to clear up problems, try to find another priest or other well-informed Catholic adult who can help.

Unfortunately, not all intelligent and well-educated Catholics are entirely faithful to the Church's teaching, and you need help from someone entirely faithful. You can find out whether a priest or other possible source of help is faithful by posing some of the questions raised by what your teachers are saying about sexual activity. *Is it ever okay to have intercourse before marriage?* The answer should be no, without hesitation. *How far may I go on a date?* The answer to this should make it clear that it is wrong to do anything in order sexually to excite oneself or the other party. A helpful person may mention some specific things to avoid: uncovering or touching parts of the body that usually remain covered even in a swimming pool, hugging and kissing repeatedly or at length, spending time alone together where nobody else is likely to interrupt, and so on. *Why is it wrong to go farther?* A good answer is likely to be complicated, but it should include the point that to go farther is to prepare for or lead up to intercourse, and so is appropriate only for a married couple. If a priest or other intelligent and well-educated Catholic gives sound answers to such questions, his or her further explanations are likely to be reliable.[357]

It would be good for you and your Catholic friends regularly to pray together for the Holy Spirit's help in dealing with your common problems. When the eight of you pray together, Jesus will be among you, and with him as the ninth, you can be sure your prayers will be heard. It also would be good, with the help of a faithful priest or other adult Catholic, to try to do more than can be done in the religion class to improve your knowledge of the faith and the history of the Church, and to learn how to defend both against misunderstandings and unfair criticisms. One way to do this is by reading together and discussing good books.[358]

Don't limit yourselves to Catholic friends though. Be as friendly as you can with all your classmates. Try especially to get to know the Protestants whose Bible reading provoked ridicule, and talk with them about problems that come up in class. You will find that in many cases all of you will agree, and you will be able to work together in sharing your Christian view with other students.

Though your parents have not been too helpful up to now, tell them when there is a specific problem they might be able to help with and ask for their help. For instance, the violence you describe should get parents' attention. Police, school officials, and teachers never can prevent all forms of physical mistreatment of some students by others, but students should not have to worry constantly about their safety, and those in charge should be able to prevent persistent bullying and almost all violence likely to result in serious injury. All of you should talk about this problem with your parents, and ask them to get together and go to the principal. Since not only Christians are threatened, talk it over not only with your Catholic and Protestant friends, but with other students anxious about their safety. If some parents already have discussed the situation with the principal and it has not improved, as many parents as possible should contact the school authorities and local public officials (the mayor and city council or the people with similar responsibilities where you live), and demand appropriate action.

Inept as they may be, the school's efforts to catch and punish students who break rules no doubt are meant to deal with some of the other problems that concern you.

---

357. A book on sex and marriage that might be helpful to these young people: Mary Beth Bonacci, *Real Love* (San Francisco: Ignatius Press, 1996).

358. E.g., three books by Edward J. Hayes, Paul J. Hayes, and James J. Drummey: *Catholicism and Reason: The Creed and Apologetics; Catholicism and Life: Commandments and Sacraments;* and *Catholicism and Society: Marriage, Family, and Social Issues* (Norwood, Mass. C. R. Publications, 1996–97). Both the books and Leader's/Catechist's manuals for them may be ordered from the publisher: 345 Prospect Street; Norwood, MA 02062.

You are right that it is more important for a school to teach all its students why it is wrong to do bad things than to catch and punish a few who break rules. But secularists find it hard to explain such matters, since they do not agree on any solid grounds for the set of rules by which a society tries to control behavior. So, the school is handicapped when it comes to explaining why anything is wrong.

Your friend should not have been carrying a hunting knife. If she had tried to use it, she might have killed or seriously injured someone, or the weapon might have been used on her. Still, unless there is more to the story than you have told, her bad judgment hardly warranted expulsion. In trying to get action against violence at the school, parents might consider making an issue of this case. They could argue that it was not fair to impose such a drastic penalty for violating a rule not previously made known and that the girl would never have provided so unwisely for her self-defense if those in charge had been fulfilling their responsibility to prevent violence and maintain peace in the school. Such arguments, in my judgment, would impress many secularists, and also might appeal to the local newspaper or other media. Unfavorable publicity might motivate public officials to take more vigorous action to deal with the violence.

The school's multiplicity of organized activities and the pressure to participate in them are part of its project of moulding young people. The activities very likely are set up so that virtually everyone can seem to excel in something. If the organizers give plenty of rewards for this sort of success, participation easily becomes the norm, and most students are virtually compelled to take part. The organizers probably are aided and abetted by parents who prefer that their children not come home after school and/or who look for psychological gratification in their children's successes.

In my judgment, you and your friends will do well to limit your involvement in activities organized by the school. In the first place, not all your time should be spent in activities. You should save some time to spend by yourselves—reading, praying, thinking things through, planning for the future. In the second place, you often will get more out of an activity if you organize it. In doing that, you can build up closer friendship among participants and develop more of your gifts, not least those involved in organizing and managing something yourselves. Of course, you will need a place to gather and other facilities; perhaps the priest will make parish facilities available.

Still, if one or another activity organized by the school offers an opportunity to do something worthwhile, do not rule out participating. When you do participate, try to excel, not for personal glory but in order to strengthen your position for bearing witness to your faith. A star athlete, for example, is likely to influence many other students and unlikely to be suppressed by school authorities.

Also, joining with Protestant and believing non-Christian classmates in some activities, such as hobbies and sports organized independently of the school, probably would be mutually beneficial. But even though you should be friendly with your Protestant classmates and should work together with them whenever possible, you and other Catholics probably should not participate in any study, prayer, or social group connected with a Protestant church. Protestants and believing non-Christians have much in common with us—especially by contrast with secularists—but important differences remain, and you need to mature in your Catholic faith, prayer, and sacramental life, and develop Catholic boy-girl friendships, which later might lead to good marriages for some of you.

You are quite right to reject the goal of becoming a high achiever, when that is taken to mean making a great deal of money and doing anything and everything to get ahead. Money is necessary but not good in itself. It is not something to take as one's goal in life. Likewise, getting ahead of others is not important in itself, and nobody should use questionable means of doing it, nor even aim at it except in competitive sports and games—and even then, athletes and players should focus more on performing well than on defeating their opponents.

But you should take your studies very seriously and do your best in them, though for a different reason—to develop the talents God has given you, so that you can serve others and fulfill yourself: "For we are what [God] has made us, created in Christ Jesus for good works, which God prepared beforehand to be our way of life" (Eph 2.10; cf. *LCL,* 113–29). In living such a good life, working well with others almost certainly will be very important, and you should aim at that. It also is worthwhile in itself. People who work together in doing what God asks of them can look forward to the highest possible achievement: reaching heaven and sharing in the joy of the wedding feast that will never end (see Rv 19.6–9).

159: How should a professor of comparative religion bear witness to his faith?

My Ph.D. was in modern languages, but I have been in the foreign service, and only began teaching a year ago when I retired. I now teach a course in comparative religions—a subject in which I always have been interested—in the religious studies department of a community college. The course is an elective, and many of the students it attracts are less interested in the subject matter than in thinking through their own religious problems. I have good rapport with them—they've benignly nicknamed me "Granddad"—and spend considerable time after class and in the office talking with groups or individuals about their personal religious concerns. Since these discussions may make a great difference in their lives, I consider them important and am anxious to do the right thing. But I am not always clear about what that is, since the problems posed by dealing with the students are different from those I was accustomed to handling in my previous career.

Some of my students, for instance, are Jews or Muslims from nonobservant families. They are interested in Judaism or Islam as a cultural tradition but antagonistic toward the beliefs and practices of conservative and orthodox Jews or Muslims. I have tended to try to arouse their religious interest in their own tradition and in some cases that has led to their making contact with a rabbi or imam and becoming more or less observant. This seems a realistic approach, since I doubt that I could lead these students into the Catholic faith, and I question whether attempting it would be in keeping with my responsibilities as a teacher.

Students brought up as evangelical Protestants present a somewhat different problem. They are struggling to work out their own position regarding the faith in which they have been raised. Their problem is complicated by the real defects in this form of Christianity, but many of their difficulties arise from the conflict between our secularized culture and the requirements of Christian faith as such. Trying to help them sort things out, I often find myself explaining to them what they should believe and do to be faithful Protestants, even when that is inconsistent with what I as a Catholic think.

You taught philosophy for some years to students from a variety of backgrounds, and you may have encountered and thought through problems similar to those that concern me. In any case, I'll be teaching this course every semester, and I would appreciate any thoughts you might have to clarify these matters.

Analysis:

This question calls for the derivation of norms for the questioner's work of teaching this course. The purpose of the course should include both students' appropriation of the truth about the subject matter and their use of that truth for personal development. So, the same norms should be observed in all intellectual exchange with them. Though the questioner should bear clear witness to his faith in legitimate ways, he should not try to evangelize his students. In class, he should present accurate information about the various religions as sympathetically as possible; he should not hide his own faith, but should deal with Catholicism only in due course. Outside class, he should not try to guide students toward specific religious convictions but should help them deal with the obstacles they immediately confront in pursuing religious truth.

The reply could be along the following lines:

In undertaking the responsibility of teaching the course in comparative religions, you enter into cooperation with those who take it. This cooperation must be shaped by the purpose you and the students share and by a mutual understanding about how to pursue it. The shared purpose is knowledge of truth, specified by the course's subject matter: comparative religions. *Knowledge of truth,* however, does not refer only to the sort of thing on which students can be tested at the end of the semester —what you call "the subject matter." It refers as well to something far more important but inaccessible to any test: their appropriation of what they learn and their use of it for their own authentic development, part of which is what you call "thinking through their own religious problems." Therefore, my first suggestion is that you think of this second aspect of knowing the truth about comparative religions as an integral part of the purpose of the course, rather than something incidental. Looking at the matter this way should help you with the problems you raise by bringing all of your intellectual exchange with your students under a single set of norms governing your responsibilities, so that different norms will not come into play when you discuss their personal religious concerns with them.

As a teacher, you are not an apologist or minister of the gospel; students do not come to your class to be evangelized or catechized, and it would be wrong for you to attempt these things. Moreover, while you should be friendly with all of your students and some of them will become your friends, as a teacher you are not their friend. Students do not come to you to be asked the personal questions and given the unsolicited advice friends freely and rightly ask and give, and it would be wrong for you to try to direct your students' spiritual lives or urge them to become Catholics. You should, of course, bear witness to your Catholic faith, but as a teacher you will do that by fulfilling, not only faithfully but generously, all the responsibilities you have undertaken toward your students, never in the slightest way misusing your power as a teacher, and then, when occasion offers, explaining in terms of your faith why you act as you do.

Your first lecture setting up the course at the beginning of the semester is extremely important. Prepare it with care, making sure you not only say what needs to be said but say it with the greatest possible precision and clarity. I suggest you cover at least the following four points.

First, the purpose of the course is to study various religions, so as to understand their similarities and differences, partly to grasp the elements of truth and value characteristic of each, and partly to contribute to a better understanding and appreciation of religion as such. Since this is a college course, it also aims to help students as they study its particular subject matter to improve their intellectual abilities—reading comprehension, clear thought and sound reasoning, skillful oral and written expression.

Second, the study of comparative religions is interesting to you and probably to most of the students because it can help an individual think through the religious questions that personally concern him or her. When such questions touch on matters of interest to most students, they can be discussed in class. But inasmuch as each student's personal religious quest is unique, not much class time can be devoted to questions of great concern only to particular students. And inasmuch as students have the right to maintain their privacy about their intimate spiritual life, no student will need to discuss such matters to fulfill any requirement of the course. Nevertheless, you consider it part of your responsibility as a teacher to discuss such questions with students who wish to do so, and you will be available for that purpose after class and in the office. Your intent in such discussions will be to help students clarify their own questions, not tell them about questions that concern you, and then to help them find accurate information and think soundly about their questions, not tell them what you have come to believe through trying to answer your own questions.

Third, many people today say one religion is as good as another, or any person's religion is fine as long as he or she finds it satisfying. Such views are forms of religious relativism or subjectivism, and some people embrace them partly because they suppose that the only alternative is unthinking commitment to one's own religion and intolerance toward every other. But relativism and subjectivism are mistaken. Different religions take incompatible positions on many important issues, and incompatible positions cannot both (or all) be true, although it may be that both are false yet embody important elements of truth. Insofar as a religion takes false positions on important issues, it is not good for its adherents, since i fails to put them in touch with reality and does not help them respond to reality appropriately. For example, the different views held by different religions about what happens to people after they die cannot all be right, and only those who believe what is true about the matter will be in a position to shape their lives realistically.

Furthermore, if relativism and subjectivism were right, those who hold these positions would nevertheless have to assent to their falsity. For though some religions are more or less syncretistic, and so seemingly compatible with relativism and subjectivism, others firmly reject such views—and the relativist or subjectivist cannot consistently claim that only syncretistic religions are acceptable. Therefore, in religious matters, no less, say, than in matters dealing with the natural world, relativism and subjectivism are to be rejected.

Nor are unthinking commitments and intolerance the only alternative. Just as in dealing with the world of nature, so in dealing with the spiritual world, one can and should try to discover the truth—find out how things really are—and, when one thinks one has found it, accept it and live in accord with it. Of course, one does not discover all religious truth at once any more than one immediately uncovers all truth about the world in exploring nature, and one sometimes makes mistakes that must be corrected by further inquiry. So, there is no room for intolerance, but there is a need for people with different religious beliefs to try to help one another find the truth.

Fourth, you are a Roman Catholic, not in virtue of an unthinking commitment, but because your own effort to find and accept religious truth has led you to conclude that one ought to be a Catholic. As you said before, you recognize elements of truth and value in other religions, but you believe Catholicism entirely avoids mistakes on important issues while no other religion does. Believing as you do, you naturally also believe that if all other people had the means and the will to carry their own religious quest through to the end, they would eventually become Catholics. However, students need not be afraid that you will try to force or trick them into agreeing with your Catholic beliefs. Convinced that truth is at stake, you also are convinced that force and trickery are counterproductive, and only an individual's serious effort to pursue the quest for himself or herself can be fruitful. Thus, you meant what you said earlier: You will do your best to deal with the subject matter accurately and fairly, and will be available to students who want your help in thinking out the religious questions that actually concern them.

In line with this opening lecture, in setting up the course, you might give students an option of doing a modest research paper, to be graded by the usual standards, or maintaining a journal during the semester, to be graded solely on the quality of the thought and writing, where they would record their reflections on the significance to them of the material they studied class by class.

Make every effort in the course to present the subject matter accurately. Do not hesitate to present as sympathetically as possible everything true and good in each religion. Whenever possible, in describing and explaining the various religions, use materials that are approved by or would be acceptable to their adherents. It probably would be wise to use as a text a book by a non-Catholic that you judge sound in scholarship and fair-minded—qualities you will discern, at least partly, by the way it deals with Catholicism. When students ask what you personally think, do not be evasive, but answer briefly and refer to the segment of the course in which Catholicism will be treated. Your main effort should focus on helping them sort out information, grasp facts, clarify their ideas, reason soundly, recognize and deal with inconsistencies, and so on.

Talking with students outside class about religious questions that personally concern them, you should try to help them deal with the obstacles they immediately confront so that they can take the next step on the way to religious truth. Very often, this will mean helping students of a certain religious background to perfect their understanding of it and take it more seriously. If you think a nonobservant Jew or Muslim would be helped to find sound answers to questions he or she has by attending a rabbi's or imam's instruction sessions, suggest that he or she do so. But your intention should not be that the student become an observant Jew or Muslim, but rather that he or she make progress in the quest for the truth.

Bear in mind at all times that you do not have the power to bring any of your students to the Catholic faith. Only God's grace and an individual's own free choices can accomplish that. If you were a priest, you would do your part by preaching the gospel. As a teacher, you do your part by teaching your course and helping your students overcome some obstacles to finding the truth. And, of course, you bear witness to your faith by the way you fulfill your responsibilities and conduct yourself around the college, and you pray for your students and colleagues.

If you proceed with the restraint I have suggested, I do not believe you will be compromising your Catholic faith in any way or falling short in professing it. Indeed, by demonstrating that professional competence and evenhandedness in dealing with students are entirely compatible with firm and unembarrassed Catholic faith, you will bear powerful witness to it, refuting without ever mentioning the widespread suspicion—and occasional calumny—that only nonbelievers can be genuine scholars and fair-minded teachers. Nevertheless, the recommended approach could involve a risk of scandal, by giving the false impression that, after all, what is characteristic of Catholicism is not very important, and religious indifferentism is somehow acceptable. To offset that risk, profess your faith very openly, making it clear to everyone at the college that you believe everything the Catholic Church believes and teaches, not least those teachings some Catholics have denied or questioned in recent years. Practice your faith publicly when there is a suitable opportunity—for instance, by declining meat on Fridays (a form of penance still recommended though no longer obligatory) and having in your office a religious statue or picture chosen to foster and manifest your own devotion but with esthetic quality that will make it appealing to reasonable nonbelievers.

Finally, sometimes a current or former student will say or do something that makes it clear he or she wishes to relate to you in a legitimate way transcending the student-professor relationship. Some will seek your friendship, and a few probably will want you to help them receive or grow in the gift of Catholic faith. If you judge it appropriate to respond, make sure both the student and you are entirely clear about what the two of you are undertaking, so that there will be no misunderstanding. Even then, you must take care not to compromise the student-professor relationship if it still exists. But you will no longer be inhibited by it, and will be free to proceed according to the norms proper to the newly developing relationship. In many cases, that will mean introducing your student or former student to one or more other Catholics, who will carry on the good work you have begun.

160: Must teachers try to tell their students the whole truth?

I teach a Sunday school class for teenagers at our parish and also teach history in a public high school five days a week. Due to different sorts of constraints, I have encountered problems in both situations about answering students' questions. Of course, I try to tell them the truth. But even though I would like to tell them the whole truth, I must often settle for a good deal less, then wonder whether I've done the right thing.

Recently, for example, my Sunday school class asked about euthanasia. I gave a fairly detailed presentation of the Church's teaching. Then, toward the end of the class, somebody asked about the Church's position on abortion when the life of the mother is at risk. I was about to respond by explaining the principle of double effect, but the kids' eyes already were glazed from trying to understand what I had said about euthanasia. Their attention span was used up, and I knew I would lose them completely if I tried to explain double effect. I said the Church in general does not oppose abortion if the mother's life is genuinely in danger and there is no other way to save it.

I am often in this situation when teaching. I want to give a detailed and thorough answer, but the class dynamic or the students' capacity restricts me. I hate giving an answer I know is simplistic or too broad, but sometimes it seems one must choose between keeping students' attention while giving a flawed answer and giving a thorough answer but not reaching them at all.

Teaching history in a public school, I face additional constraints. Students naturally are curious about what teachers personally believe and about their motivations. Moreover, some of my students are very bright, and their probing questions often press beyond the carefully drawn, antiseptically neutral boundaries of the textbooks, and bring to light the ultimate religious and philosophical issues at the heart of so many historical developments. Naturally, I would like to tell them the whole truth as I see it, but I am sure I could never get away with that.

Most of the teachers at my school are either liberal Protestants or complete nonbelievers. Their outlook corresponds pretty well to the world views prevailing among parents in this wealthy suburban district. From what students tell me and from what these teachers themselves say, it is clear that they don't hesitate to tell students what they believe, advocate their own values (often amounting to what I regard as vices of self-indulgence, status seeking, greed, and so forth), and belittle traditional religious faith and its values. But if I—or any traditional Catholic, evangelical Protestant, conservative Jew, or devout Muslim—were to express and promote his or her beliefs and values just as freely, I am sure some parents, other teachers, and the administration would condemn it as religious proselytizing, a violation of the separation of church and state, and so forth.

But even if I could get away it, I wonder whether it would be right. My history students do not come to me to be catechized, as my Sunday school students do. The public school is supposed to be religiously neutral, and in undertaking to teach there, it seems I have implicitly agreed to accept some constraints.

How far may I go in expressing my beliefs and promoting my values in the classroom, and just where should I draw the line?

Analysis:

This question calls for the derivation of norms for the questioner's teaching activities. When children ask teachers questions they cannot adequately answer under the circumstances, they must take care to avoid saying not only what is false but what would be likely to mislead, that is, generate an erroneous opinion. Public school teachers should answer questions about their personal beliefs and state briefly their reasons for holding them. However, the questioner should behave better than colleagues in several ways: refrain from evangelizing students, present others' beliefs accurately and fairly, respect students' rights, and help students develop their intellectual capacities so that they can fulfill their own responsibility to pursue the truth about ultimate questions.

The reply could be along the following lines:

Your first question is one all teachers, including parents, constantly confront. Students, especially curious children, ask many questions that one cannot answer by presenting all the information one has and giving the fullest explanation available. There is a limit, set by the capacity of the questioner, circumstances such as lack of time, or both.

In such cases, try not to mislead the questioner or other members of the class. One misleads not only by saying something one considers false but by saying something one foresees is likely to lead students to accept an unsound argument or an erroneous position. Teachers, who know a great deal more than their students, seldom can tell them the whole truth. But one always can try to communicate as much as possible without misleading. Simplified and broad answers are sometimes necessary, but they can be labeled clearly as such, so that they will not be likely to mislead.

I realize you did not mean to mislead your Sunday school students, but I am afraid you did just that in saying "the Church in general does not oppose abortion if the mother's life is genuinely in danger and there is no other way to save it." That formulation is bound to be understood as meaning that the choice to destroy an unborn child is morally acceptable if it is made for the good end of saving the mother's life—a position incompatible with the Church's clear teaching that no choice to destroy an unborn child ever can be justified, regardless of the good end sought.[359]

Asked by eighth graders about the Church's position on abortion when the mother's life is at risk, I would have answered along the following lines:

---

359. See John Paul II, *Evangelium vitae*, 58–63, *AAS* 87 (1995) 466–74, *OR*, 5 Apr. 1995, xi–xii; *LCL*, 488–505.

Since time is running out, I cannot answer your question as fully as I would like, but I will say this. The Church holds that nobody may ever kill an unborn baby for any reason whatsoever. So, the Church teaches that everything possible should be done to save both the mother and the child, and that killing either of them on purpose always is wrong. Sometimes, of course, it is impossible to save both, and, in trying to do the best they can, doctors do something with a chance of saving one that also leads to the death of the other. That is not killing on purpose, and, even if it leads to the baby's death, the Church's teaching against abortion does not apply to it.

While such an answer does not fully explain what the Church teaches and avoids technical language about double effect, it calls attention to its own incompleteness and, so far as it goes, is not misleading. Often, in giving such an answer, it also is appropriate to offer to explain the matter more thoroughly to interested students after class, to recommend a good reading on the topic, or to promise a fuller answer in a later class. (In that case, of course, you must make good on the promise!)

I also think teachers sometimes do well to respond to questions with abbreviated, technical answers they do not expect most students to understand. Of course, one must be careful to avoid insulting and frustrating them. But such an answer, presented with respect and as a challenge, can arouse students' curiosity and stimulate at least some to learn far more than they otherwise would.

The other problem, about the constraints under which you operate as a history teacher in a public high school, seems to me more difficult.

When the subject matter leads students to ask probing questions, teachers should be free not only to express their beliefs and acknowledge their values but explain them, and in this way, at least, promote them. In doing this, teachers committed to some form of traditional religious faith should not compromise it by suggesting that other beliefs are equally valid for those who hold them or that all beliefs are a mere matter of personal opinion or feelings; those are expressions of relativism and subjectivism incompatible with every form of monotheistic, religious faith. Moreover, when students assert or take for granted some form of relativism or subjectivism, teachers with faith should not let their views go unchallenged. Rather, it is a teacher's duty to point out that, though many questions have no single right answer, still, of any two conflicting positions at least one surely is false, and its falsity must be discovered and established so as to work toward truth (see q. 159, above).

Still, as you seem to realize, you should not take the propagandizing of your liberal Protestant and nonbelieving colleagues as a model. The professional role you have accepted as a public school teacher does limit how you can express your personal beliefs and profess your Catholic faith. This limitation applies not only to teachers, but to many other professionals, such as lawyers and judges, physicians and nurses, and so on. In many instances, a devout and thoughtful Catholic can bear witness to his or her faith only by relating to others in a virtuous way and fulfilling professional responsibilities that leave no room for any explicit statement of faith.

Even if you were teaching in a Catholic school, your professional role as a history teacher would set certain limits. You would owe it to your students to inform them about various historical accounts and interpretations, and the evidence and arguments that support them. While you would say what you think true and why, you could not forbid your students to express other views. In no case would it be right to penalize a student, by a grade or otherwise, for disagreeing with you or rejecting Catholic teaching. Your primary responsibility would be to help students acquire the commonly accepted information and major views on important disputed issues, and assist them in developing their intellectual capacities so that they could assimilate and organize the material, think clearly and critically, and resist fallacies. Even when students held beliefs you regarded as false, you would have to help them articulate their beliefs, consistently draw out their implications, and explain them as well as possible.

Teaching in a public school where traditional religious faith and values are the exception rather than the rule, you are of course under additional constraints—for example, from the set syllabus and assigned textbooks. For several years I taught philosophy in a public university in Canada and experienced somewhat similar constraints. I found that organizing a legitimate course plan and sticking to it won the confidence of students and colleagues who did not share my faith. Acknowledging elements of truth in views with which one disagrees and frankly admitting difficulties in one's own views also help to allay suspicions of bias. When questions not strictly relevant (including those regarding my own beliefs and thinking) came up in class, I regularly pointed out their irrelevance and answered very briefly, adding an invitation to anyone interested to discuss the matter after class. This strategy often led to lively discussions outside class; I do not think any student open to the witness I had to offer was deprived of it.

However, in describing the freedom with which your fellow teachers express their liberal Protestant or secular humanist beliefs and values, you point to a fundamental fallacy underlying the public school system in the United States, namely, the myth of neutrality. Thus, I think you are mistaken in saying that the textbooks you use remain within "antiseptically neutral" boundaries.[360] In fact, there is no way to be neutral between a world view that regards human (and, perhaps, also subhuman animal) feelings and interests as ultimate principles of all truth and value, and one that regards God's wisdom and love as ultimate. All schools and school systems implicitly favor some sort of religious faith or some alternative world view by their methods of discipline, ways of motivating students, selection of textbooks, choices of subjects to be included in (and excluded from) their curricula, and so on. But disingenuously ignoring reality, majorities of the U.S. Supreme Court have decided repeatedly since 1945 against traditional theism and in favor of secularism.[361]

---

360. For evidence and arguments showing that to a considerable extent public school textbooks and curricula are not religiously neutral but are shaped by secularist assumptions, see Warren A. Nord, *Religion and American Education: Rethinking a National Dilemma* (Chapel Hill, N.C.: University of North Carolina Press, 1995), 138–91.

361. See Germain Grisez and Joseph M. Boyle, Jr., *Life and Death with Liberty and Justice: A Contribution to the Euthanasia Debate* (Notre Dame, Ind.: University of Notre Dame Press, 1979), 313–31.

In sum, you work within a radically unjust social structure that you are powerless to change. You cannot expect to do everything you want to do for your students or everything you would be obliged to do if you had the freedom you ought to enjoy. Do not blame yourself. Do the best you can under the circumstances, pray for your students, and hope to be satisfied along with others who hunger and thirst for justice from a tribunal superior to any this world calls "Supreme."

161: How candid should one be in writing letters of recommendation?

Three years ago, I finished my Ph.D. and began teaching both undergraduates and graduate students. Quite often a graduating student or a former student asks for a letter of recommendation, expecting that I will support his or her application for a job or for admission to a more advanced educational program. Sometimes it is easy, even pleasant; to comply, since the student is so gifted and accomplished that it would be hard to exaggerate his or her good qualities and attainments. Occasionally, too, a student is so poor that I simply refuse to write the letter. Of course, the student is likely to be irritated, but I explain, as gently as possible, that anything I could write with a good conscience probably would do him or her more harm than good.

Most cases fall in between. They try my conscience. I avoid outright lying, of course, though sometimes I am sorely tempted, especially when recommendation forms include questions suggesting that a criterion I consider inappropriate is being used to sort out applicants. But many people write recommendation letters filled with extravagant and unqualified praise, and language in this context has become debased, so that it is hard to know what constitutes lying. If I am too cautious, I might well spoil a good student's chances by offering an entirely honest, accurate, and balanced evaluation pointing out weaknesses as well as strengths. It seems unjust for a good student to lose out because others writing on behalf of competing applicants are willing to be dishonest.

I am sure you have faced the same dilemma over the years. How do you think it should be dealt with?

Analysis:

This question calls for the derivation of norms for writing letters of recommendation. These are needed because in writing such letters professors have conflicting interests and responsibilities. The general norms of truthfulness and fairness are relevant, but they must be specified appropriately. To do this, the purposes of letters of recommendation and the relationships among the parties involved should be clarified. Someone asked to write a recommendation and unable to write favorably sometimes should write unfavorably. Even debased language retains some meaning and can be used to make truthful statements, but it often occasions further abuse, and those committed to speaking truthfully must resist the temptation. To ensure insofar as possible that honesty does not impose unfair hardships on those recommended, one must communicate as effectively as one can whatever favors a candidate.

The reply could be along the following lines:

As a basis for answering your question, one must consider the complex relationships among the various parties in the situation.

Professors and those to whom they write letters of recommendation are colleagues or collaborators in an established educational-economic system for whose good functioning they share responsibility. This good functioning, in which many people have important and legitimate interests, requires that opportunities for education and jobs be matched with applicants' qualifications. So, in writing a letter of recommendation, a professor should try to help not only that particular applicant but those seeking the best-qualified applicant.

Educational institutions and professors also often benefit, even tangibly, by their students' advancement to the jobs or further educational opportunities they desire. Programs that succeed in placing their graduates usually flourish, and flourishing programs usually provide more advantageous conditions of employment for administrators and faculty. Also, success in placing graduates tends to increase the influence and prestige of the institution and the professor. But there also are important intangible benefits; professors often take a personal interest in their students and sometimes develop a quasi-parental affection for them, so that their advancement gratifies the professors much as it does parents. With these and perhaps other motives, educational institutions and professors often make implicit, and sometimes explicit, promises to place their students well.

In these circumstances, professors who undertake to write letters of recommendation have a serious conflict of interests. As members of the wider system, they should provide all relevant information, favorable and unfavorable, to help decision makers identify the best qualified applicants; as members of a particular academic community with a commitment to place its students, they should help the students obtain what they are applying for—a responsibility reinforced by self-interest. This conflict of interests explains your dilemma and the debasement of language you mention.

A partial solution is to be completely honest with students. That requires not offering specious guarantees of placement or making insincere promises of support. But it requires more. A professor must be careful not to lead students to think he or she will help them obtain a job or other placement except by communicating truthfully about their qualifications.

Lowering students' unreasonable expectations in this way would help, but it would not entirely solve the problem. A more adequate solution would be for employers and advanced educational programs to stop requiring applicants to obtain letters of recommendation from professors. Those who wished to support applicants still might do so, but it would be clear that their recommendations were promotional material extraneous to the completed application. The change would be no great loss, in my judgment, since these letters generally provide little useful information, and a great deal of time certainly would be saved by those who currently write them and read them.[362]

The conflict of interests I have mentioned should be obvious to everyone concerned. As matters now stand, those who require that students applying for jobs and admission to advanced educational programs supply letters of recommendation from professors cannot reasonably expect to get entirely disinterested and objective appraisals. But because the students, those to whom they apply, and competing applicants all stand to gain or lose a great deal, a professor writing a recommendation letter assumes a grave obligation to be just. The obligation can be specified by at least six norms, which those who require letters of recommendation and those asking to be recommended should be able to expect professors to follow.

First, professors should not support an individual's application if they believe he or she probably will not succeed in the job or educational program. The individual will be better off in the long run doing something for which he or she is better fitted, and good will toward him or her should be enough to rule out giving a favorable recommendation. Reinforcing that motive is fairness toward more able competitors, who will be gravely wronged if the opportunity goes to someone not only less able but perhaps even incapable of taking advantage of it.

Second, though professors cannot help caring more for some students than others, they should not take their feelings toward a student into account in judging how strongly to recommend him or her. Doing that is as truly unfair as making affection the basis for grading students or giving them opportunities. Professors who are fair to all their students will at least be consistent in their recommendations, so that those who read them regularly will learn how to interpret them.

Third, sometimes a professor should write an unfavorable letter. Occasionally a poor student insists that a professor write a letter, and honesty requires that it be unfavorable. Such a letter need not point out the applicant's poor qualities, but can make its point simply by stating facts while omitting customary expressions of praise or limiting them to the candidate's few—and probably less relevant—good qualities. On rare occasions, a professor has negative information that will enable those considering the application to avoid very serious burdens. He or she then should apply the Golden Rule: If I were receiving the application, would I expect fair warning? And if I were a fair-minded student, would I acknowledge that sending the unfavorable letter was justified? If the answer is yes, the professor should communicate the information by writing the letter, unless there is another adequate and more appropriate way to communicate it.

Fourth, since lying always is wrong, it must be excluded absolutely. But one must bear in mind how what one says will be understood by those one addresses. It is not lying to use language that in other contexts would express a false proposition while reasonably expecting it to be understood by those addressed as

---

362. Carter Zeleznik et al., "Levels of Recommendation for Students and Academic Performance in Medical School," *Psychological Reports,* 52 (1983): 851–58, report the result of a small study showing that the level of recommendation did not help predict performance in medical school. A much larger and broader study of this sort might help clarify the matter and end or greatly limit the practice of requiring letters of recommendation.

expressing a true proposition. Thus, even debased language can be used to make both truthful and deceptive statements. Making truthful statements requires distinguishing between two kinds of expressions. Some—for example, "upper ten percent" and "my best ever"—have definite meanings, and one cannot reasonably expect them to be understood otherwise. Even though letters of recommendation may often abuse them, one should only use them if they correspond to the facts. Other expressions—"excellent," "outstanding," "one of our better students"—are vague; their abuse has given them special meanings in letters of recommendation. Still, readers can reasonably be expected to understand them at least to mean *above average*. A writer who says, "John Smith is excellent, outstanding, one of our better students," lies if Smith is only marginal but could be telling the truth if he is at least above average.

It is understandable that someone confronted with a question suggesting that an inappropriate criterion is being used to sort out applicants should be tempted to lie. But a questioner's possible or even certain unfairness does not justify lying. One may either ignore questions that seem unfair or, if it seems appropriate, explicitly refuse to answer and explain why. In any case, the applicant's attention should be called to such signs of unfairness on the part of the organization, since they may point to more trouble further down the line.

Fifth, since few who write letters of recommendation are candid, a professor's candor can seriously harm applicants he or she recommends. Rather than revealing all relevant information, one is justified in passing over things likely to put an applicant at a disadvantage. Therefore, since people reading recommendations generally are on the lookout for anything unfavorable, but few writers say anything of the sort, one should avoid suggesting anything unfavorable to the applicant unless fairness (as explained in the third norm, above) or truthfulness requires it.

Sixth, in the absence of a contrary agreement, rule, or customary practice, a professor generally should supply students with copies of letters written for them. If a letter is entirely favorable, the applicant can make the most of it; if not, he or she will have a chance to try to offset it. This norm is not exceptionless; applicants are not entitled to all the protections enjoyed by defendants in criminal trials, and occasionally it is fair to communicate unfavorable evidence confidentially—for example, to prevent retaliation. In such a case, of course, the professor must take special care to be clear and accurate, and not to assert anything unqualifiedly unless absolutely certain of it.

In my experience, certain techniques also help lighten the burden of writing recommendations conforming to the preceding norms.

A professor writing a favorable recommendation must gather all information that will be helpful to the applicant and communicate it as effectively as possible. For types of recommendations that recur regularly, one can make comprehensive check lists of relevant information. Those about whom letters are to be written can be required to supply the information, though it should be verified, if necessary, before the letter is written.

In making an evaluation, one can identify and focus on something both good and unusual about an applicant—for example, his or her effective handling of some handicap or obstacle. Without exaggerating, this calls favorable attention to the applicant. Besides evaluating an applicant's personality, character, and attainments, one can provide helpful descriptive information: facts indicating his or her suitability for the opportunity. Favorable letters are likely to be more effective if they avoid obvious efforts at persuasion. Mentioning some irrelevant imperfection and/or admitting one's personal friendliness toward an applicant can engender confidence in the recommendation.

Honest professors using such techniques greatly mitigate the damage their honesty otherwise might do to applicants they support. Eventually, those who are consistently conscientious probably will be recognized as trustworthy by regular readers of their letters, so that their recommendations will be far more influential than most others. But it should not be supposed that, pragmatically speaking, in the fallen human condition honesty always is the best policy. Sometimes, it will result in better-qualified applicants losing out to those whose dishonest supporters were believed. There may be no remedy in this world for such injustices, but in due course the Lord will rectify them, along with all others.

162: May scholars republish the same material?

Certain practices of some academics engaged in research and publication seem to me worth discussing.

Some publish the same article twice under different titles, often at more or less the same time, simply to lengthen their list of publications. This seems intentionally deceptive, both with regard to those who will use publications lists in professional evaluations and in regard to journals that ask for assurance that a manuscript has not been published and is not under consideration for publication elsewhere. Then again, some academics, especially in the social sciences, talk about "idioplagiarism" (that is, self-plagiarism), which means publishing the same research data in two or more places—for example, the results of a sociological survey or psychological study might be used in several articles. A rank-and-tenure committee sometimes detects this and reacts negatively.

A related practice is using one's own previously published material in a new work. Sometimes, one has written something well enough that there is little point in rephrasing it. Should one seek permission of the copyright holder? What about reusing in an article the same passages from other scholars' writings that one previously used in a book?

Another problem that often comes up involves making copies of copyrighted books and articles. People say: "I wouldn't have bought the book anyway, so I photocopied it"; "The book is out of print, so I photocopied it." In this case, do law and Christian morality coincide?

Analysis:

This question calls for the derivation of norms regarding scholarly publication and for application of norms regarding theft to use of material under copyright. Duplicate publishing of the various sorts described is not wrong in itself. Often it serves good purposes and is morally acceptable or even obligatory. But it also often is vitiated by bad intentions and/or injustices. Merely emotional motives sometimes lead to publication that serves no intelligible good. Duplicate publishing sometimes involves deception, unfair competition with colleagues, a waste of publishing capacity, and/or cheating buyers of journals and books. Copyright law is complex; scholars should know it insofar as it is relevant to their work and should presume it just. Still, like other just laws, under certain conditions copyright law can be violated without moral wrong.

The reply could be along the following lines:

In dealing with this question, I shall take for granted that the common norms for scholarly writing and publication are known and followed. One must clearly identify whatever one draws from others' work and give them due credit for it; one must adhere to accepted practices in many fields that forbid simultaneously submitting the same manuscript to two or more potential publishers without telling them; when one submits to an editor a work substantially the same as something one published previously, one must make its status clear; a reprinting or revision of a previous publication, whether under the same title or a different one, should be identified as such in any list of publications likely to be used for professional evaluation; except when the principle of fair use allows copyrighted material to be used without permission, one must obtain permission to use it.

Similar moral issues are raised by all the various sorts of duplicate publishing you mention in your question: publishing the same article in various places, republishing in a new form material one previously published, publishing the same research data in different places, and using the same quotations or citations in various publications.

Until modern times, not only duplicate publishing but what we would regard as plagiarism were quite common and seldom or never questioned. To some extent, I think, that was because people regarded truth and literary expressions of it as goods to be shared freely rather than as property. But to some extent it was because authors and copiers of works in former times seldom needed to recover costs and obtain fair compensation as modern writers and publishers generally do. Hence, today there often are good reasons for constraints on duplicate publishing.

Still, looking into the publications of most leading twentieth century scholars, one finds a great deal of duplicate publishing; while this does not demonstrate that the practices you mention are morally acceptable—perhaps corruption is pervasive in the scholarly community!—it does require that anyone who claims they are always wrong should show why. Considering the matter, I see no reason why any of the things you mention would be wrong in itself; none of them need violate truth, justice, or any other good. Thus, the moral issues seem to concern injustices and bad intentions.

One can imagine all sorts of possible bad intentions. For example, a greedy person might publish many books solely to make money; a status seeker might publish solely to make a name; someone might get psychological satisfaction out of having publications appear, and so publish solely for the enjoyable feeling. Such intentions could motivate, and so morally vitiate, any act of publishing, and they and other nonrational motives can lead to publishing that serves no intelligible good. Thus, they very likely account for some duplicate publishing. But that does not have to be so in any particular case, so duplicate publishing is not always wrong on this score.

It likewise is easy to imagine a variety of injustices. If duplicate publishing is a device to build up one's list of publications in order to gain academic advancement, it will not work except by deliberate deception in grave matter. It very likely also will be unfair to competitors, who will appear less productive by comparison. Moreover, unless there is some good reason for it, by filling up available space in journals and other media, duplicate publishing unfairly impedes others who have good reasons for wishing to use that space. Again, it can cheat people who buy books and subscribe to journals by delivering the same old thing when the circumstances of a publication and/or the methods of promoting it promise something new. Then too, if editors are not given fair warning that a proffered work will be a republication, they may be deceived, and the publisher may suffer a financial loss and/or injury to its reputation.

Nevertheless, the legitimate point of publishing is to communicate something one thinks worth communicating to a particular audience, in order to bring about some genuine benefit, usually including a benefit to those who will receive the communication; and duplicate publishing often serves that legitimate point. For example, the same article published in different places can reach (perhaps with very little overlap) and benefit two different audiences. Scholars often test their work by publishing it first in journals read mainly by fellow scholars, then revise it in view of criticism and republish it for a wider audience in books or other media. Again, republishing the same material in a new form not only can make it more widely available but put it into a new context, so that the message is developed, refined, corrected. As for research data, the same material can be used over and over to make different points as well as in presentations at diverse levels of sophistication suited to different audiences. And when one has a good reason to publish something and quotations or citations that have been used before will be helpful to its audience, using them again surely is appropriate; indeed, I do not understand why anyone would think it problematic.

In short, I think there can be good reasons for various sorts of duplicate publishing, and then, absent any bad intention or injustice, I do not see why it would be wrong. Indeed, I think it often is obligatory in order to fulfill one's responsibilities as a scholar and teacher.

Copyright law is complex, and this is not the place to summarize it.[363] Every academic has an obligation to try to understand it insofar as it applies to his or her teaching and research (see q. 138, above). I cannot think of any use of material permitted by copyright law that would itself be unjust, although, of course, there are many ways of treating other scholars unfairly without violating any copyright. In general, there is a presumption in favor of obeying laws, and so in general

---

363. Helpful summaries of the law: Ellen M. Kozak, *Every Writer's Guide to Copyright and Publishing Law,* 2nd ed. (New York: Henry Holt, 1996); Stephen Fishman, *The Copyright Handbook: How to Protect and Use Written Works,* 3rd ed. (Berkeley, Calif.: Nolo Press, 1996).

copyright law should be obeyed. That one would not buy a particular book does not excuse making an unauthorized copy: doing so makes unauthorized, uncompensated use of another's property.

In some cases, however, there can be a moral justification for making use of materials without the copyright holder's permission. For example, I think that copying for personal use out-of-print materials, including whole books needed for one's work, can sometimes meet the test of the Golden Rule and other relevant moral norms, as well as the legal principle of fair use.[364] Also, even if making a copy is not permitted by the principle of fair use, it sometimes really is reasonable to presume permission, and then one can proceed without actually obtaining it. For example, if the textbook a professor adopts for a course fails to arrive on time, he or she might reasonably supply students with copies of a section to get the class under way, provided they will be required to purchase books when they arrive. Finally, the poor who need some copyrighted work but cannot obtain it without violating the copyright can be justified in doing so.

163: How should a Catholic college tighten its rules of student conduct?

I am a professor at a nominally Catholic college and have just been named one of the two faculty members on the student affairs committee. This coming year we are going to do a complete revision of the student handbook, which contains all the college's disciplinary policies and rules of student conduct. We also will consider other relevant college policies and arrangements, and modify them as necessary to make the rules more realistic and effective. While we will be considering everything, for the initial stage of our work, we have divided ourselves into two subcommittees. The other group will be considering violence against persons, theft, property destruction, drug abuse, and academic offenses, such as cheating on tests and plagiarism. My group will deal with the more contentious matters, especially alcohol abuse and sexual activity.

Years ago, neither was a problem. Students were not permitted to have or use alcohol on campus. It was a women's school, and no men were allowed to visit the dormitory floors of the residence halls. Sisters on the faculty lived among the students in the residence halls. Things changed during the 1960s. The legal age for drinking in this state was reduced to eighteen, and alcohol was permitted on campus; at first there were narrow limits, but these were quickly eliminated either officially or at least in practice. The school went coed and grew larger, and the resident portion of the student body increased to around seventy-five percent. Women and men were housed in the same buildings, though on different floors or in different wings; and visitation was permitted from ten in the morning until midnight (or, on weekends, two in the morning). The number of nuns declined drastically as some quit religious life and others died or were given other assign-

---

364. For an explanation of this important limit on copyright, see L. Ray Patterson and Stanley W. Lindberg, *The Nature of Copyright: A Law of Users' Rights* (Athens, Ga.: University of Georgia Press, 1991), 190–218.

ments. Those who remained stopped living in the residence halls, and the only authority figures regularly present there were resident assistants, that is, students chosen from among the more responsible seniors to do what they could to keep order and deal with problems.

The school continued to grow in the 1970s. Some old residence halls were remodeled for other uses, and new housing was built to accommodate most seniors and juniors. Unlike traditional dorms, the new buildings were designed as an apartment complex. Each unit has two double rooms, a bath, a fully equipped kitchenette, and a living-dining area. Dozens of students often crowd into these apartments for parties, which on weekends typically feature kegs of beer and go on until morning. Around 1985, the drinking age in this state was moved back up to twenty-one, but that has not made much difference; older students turn their apartments into pubs for the younger ones. Most students party, and about half of those partying intentionally get drunk at least one night a week. In the apartments, twenty-four-hour visitation is permitted. Men and women are officially assigned to different units, but the students rearrange themselves so that roughly a third of the units soon are occupied by two mixed couples per apartment. Resident assistants are mainly concerned with limiting property damage and calling campus security to deal with emergencies. When students are in residence, administrators and faculty members stay away from the apartment buildings, and the security people go in only when called, see and do as little as possible, and get out quickly.

Most faculty members and administrators seem to have no moral problem with drunkenness or fornication as such; a few, myself included, definitely do. But the majority of the faculty and many of our more able and committed students do object to the quality of campus life to the extent that, as matters stand, only the most self-disciplined and committed students are getting an education, and even they learn less than they otherwise would because of distractions resulting from sexual misbehavior and alcohol abuse—the constant noise and the emotional turmoil of their fellow students. Some administrators, including our newly installed president, see the problem as a serious obstacle to raising the academic quality of the college. The president also is very concerned about the costly consequences of alcohol abuse: sexual assaults and other crimes of violence, theft and vandalism, and the need to spend so much on student health care, safety and security, and liability insurance. Therefore, it is likely that we will be able do something toward tightening up student discipline, not only on paper but in reality.

Even so, most students, many faculty members, the administrators directly concerned with student activities, and, ironically, the people involved in the college chaplaincy will oppose any tightening up. They will base their case on respect for the students' right as adults to make their own choices, the limits of the college's authority to make rules and its power to enforce them, and the pointlessness of trying to foster good character by strict rules governing outward behavior: "Even in the old days, many students kept a hidden bottle, and boys and girls who were so inclined always found some place to sleep together; so, the old system fostered hypocrisy rather than virtue."

I trust you will be on my side. What tightening up do you think I should argue for, and what arguments would you offer for those changes?

Analysis:

This question calls for a clarification of the principle for just rules and policies of student conduct in a Catholic college. The college's common good rather than students' personal welfare should be the principle of its rules and policies. The elements of the common good are cooperation in cultivating and sharing intellectual virtues and knowledge of truth, including faith and faith's truth; justice and charity among all members of the college community; and the religious significance of their common enterprise. Grounding the rules on the college's common good will enable the committee to answer objections based on students' rights and the limits of the college's authority. The college's rules need not violate students' rights; since the rules are included in a contract students freely accept, obeying them is a responsibility of membership in the college. Though covert violation of the rules by some students and merely outward conformity by some others will limit the rules' benefits, good rules will promote the college's common good and support students' sound commitments.

The reply could be along the following lines:

In making and revising rules to regulate student behavior, bear in mind that for the most part good rules produce benefits independently of their enforcement. They are effective by bearing witness to the goods to which they direct action, teaching members of the community how to act, and providing an objective, interpersonal structure that validates and reinforces the commitments of individuals to the common good and to the means necessary to it. Rules need to be enforced only when the reasonable effort they embody to shape cooperation fails, and enforcement seems likely to redress and limit the harm done to the community by an individual's or group's misbehavior.

Hence, it is very important that the college's rules be reasonable, that they be clearly explained, and that as many students as possible understand and accept the explanation. Moreover, though students should not share in the power of determining rules, their suggestions and comments on proposed changes should be invited and carefully considered. In this way, many reasonable refinements will be made and ambiguities eliminated.

Many schools no longer seek to educate students who wish to be educated, but instead merely try to supply clients—tax payers or paying customers, as the case may be—with whatever training and information they want, so that they can pursue whatever arbitrary goals they choose. Faculty members cease to be professionals and are reduced to giving students what they want, rather like some physicians who, no longer committed to their patients' health, use medical technique and drugs to help people do whatever they wish with their bodies and psyches.

But a college should try to educate its students, and any real effort to educate—that is, to help develop various human potentialities—presupposes some definite conception of what fulfills those potentialities. A Catholic college appropriately draws its conception of human fulfillment from natural law illuminated by Catholic faith and defines its principal purpose, which is its common good, in terms of human fulfillment thus conceived.

The central elements of the common good of a Catholic academic community are three: first, effective cooperation among faculty and students in cultivating and sharing intellectual virtues and knowledge of truth, including the virtue of Catholic faith and faith's truth; second, justice and charity among all involved; third, the religious significance of the common enterprise considered as cooperation in a particular part of God's creative, redemptive, and sanctifying work. The fundamental principle of the college's authority to regulate student behavior is its common good. Therefore, the college can rightly regulate students' use of alcohol and their interpersonal sexual behavior insofar as these impede effective cooperation in teaching and learning, in living as a just and loving community, and in realizing various aspects of the common religious value, such as the Christian witness that the college's common life should provide to members and outsiders.

The law setting twenty-one as the drinking age should be presumed just, and college policy should conform to it. Habitual drunkenness, as you and others have observed, impedes education, not only by its direct effects on mental functioning but also, and perhaps more importantly, by substituting escapism and self-indulgence for the self-discipline required for intellectual development. When older students give or sell alcoholic beverages to younger ones, all involved violate the law, and their cooperation in wrongdoing violates mutual charity. As you note, alcohol abuse also is costly for the college in several ways, and it is unjust to impose these costs on the college community.[365] Plainly, too, if alcohol abuse is an integral feature of the culture of a Catholic college campus, the community will not be markedly better—and may be markedly worse—in this respect than the surrounding secular society. To that extent, it will be incapable of bearing witness.

Intimate sexual relationships distract unmarried young people from their studies and displace other activities that would contribute to their development. Fornicators not only wrong their own bodies but injure each other; their sin violates charity, and so is incompatible with any form of Christian community (see 1 Cor 6.13–20; *LCL,* 648–68). Like alcohol abuse, sexual self-indulgence is at odds with the self-discipline essential for moral maturity and with a Christian culture capable of giving witness.

In my judgment, student living accommodations must be designed to promote such an environment if a college is to regulate student behavior as reasonably and effectively as possible. Imagine a college where each student has his or her private room, with just enough space to store personal belongings, sleep, study, and engage in other individual activities. Abundant common areas would be provided, indoors and out, for the use of groups of various sizes, ranging from couples to the entire student body. These common areas would be arranged and divided so that each group could carry on its own activities, neither disturbing others nor being disturbed

---

365. For the facts about the extent and bad effects of alcohol abuse on U.S. campuses, see Commission on Substance Abuse at Colleges and Universities, *Rethinking Rites of Passage: Substance Abuse on America's Campuses* (New York: Center on Addiction and Substance Abuse at Columbia University, 1994), 12–26.

or overheard. However, in indoor common spaces, glass dividing walls and windows would keep all couples' and groups' activities open to the view of others. With such accommodations, the imaginary college's rules bearing on student alcohol use, sexual activity, and noise could be simple, along the following lines.

> Students under the legal age for drinking may not possess or use alcohol on the campus. Nobody on campus may supply underage students with alcohol, and doing so will be considered a very serious infraction. Outside their rooms, students of drinking age may consume alcohol on campus only if it is supplied by a college facility or, on an approved occasion, by the college's food and beverage service. (The only facilities regularly serving alcohol are arranged for eating and/or conversation, without any amplified sound; weeks during which an approved occasion occurs are the exception rather than the rule.)
>
> Students may not publicly do anything inconsistent with Christian modesty in sexual matters. Students may not have guests in their private rooms.

This rule would impede not only illicit sexual activity but a great deal of time-wasting talk and socializing; it would promote study and prayer by protecting students from constant interruptions. It also would prevent residents from making unfair use of one another's space—a common abuse facilitated by peer pressure against claiming one's right to privacy.

> Students may not intentionally cause any sound in their private rooms annoying to others. Amplified sound may never be audible outside a student's room. Within common areas, the level of sounds, other than those specifically authorized by the college administration, may never be so high as to be perceptible in any chapel, library, classroom, study hall, office, or private room on the campus.
>
> The common areas are supervised by mature adults who are authorized to exercise the college's disciplinary authority. Campus security officers regularly patrol residence halls and common areas, both for everyone's safety and to discourage and deal with violations of rules.

Obviously, though unfortunately, the living accommodations on your campus are such that your rules of student behavior cannot be so simple and strict. In particular, the apartment complex you describe seems to have been very poorly designed for housing students on a Catholic college campus. Almost certainly, too, the college lacks adequate common areas. You must therefore propose rules adapted to the conditions on your campus.

Men and women should be housed in separate buildings or in parts of buildings remodeled to preclude inside access to one another. Visiting hours should be limited, say, from nine in the morning until nine in the evening. Students should be required to reside in their assigned units. The number of visitors to a residence unit should be limited, so that it never exceeds, say, twice the number of residents present. Moreover, the consent of all residents present in a unit should be required for any guest; each student sharing a room or apartment should have a strict and strongly enforced right to require at any time that any or all visitors leave the unit at once. For the sake of worthwhile gatherings, classrooms and public areas should be made available to groups of students who wish to study together or engage in extracurricular activities.

Severe restrictions on alcohol use and noise remain possible. You should argue for them. It is especially important to forbid selling or giving alcohol to underage students, and firmly to punish infractions. Amplified sound in residence units, whether conventional dormitory rooms or apartments, must be limited. As some localities' ordinances have done, the college's rules should set maximum levels of noise permitted at various times.

Having answered your direct question about the tightening up I would argue for and the arguments I would propose, I turn to the counterarguments, several of which you have sketched out. You must be prepared to answer them.

The first will be that the old idea that a college stands in loco parentis is out of date and the students, as adults, have the right to make their own choices, provided, of course, they do not seriously injure one another or damage college property.

Begin by dismissing as a red herring talk of the college standing in loco parentis. That phrase referred to deputed parental authority, which boarding schools and colleges exercised over young people for their personal welfare—in matters of morality such as censoring reading materials, in matters of health and hygiene such as requiring adequate rest and a balanced diet, in matters of safety such as ruling dangerous parts of town off limits, and so forth. On that basis, students might have been penalized precisely for having liquor on campus or getting drunk, even if they were of age to drink; for fornicating, even if they did it off campus; for possessing a recording with obscene lyrics, even if nobody heard them play it; and so on.

Unfortunately, since the demise of their responsibility in loco parentis, "most colleges and universities have failed to devise a comprehensive and consistent model that both defines their relationship with the students and poses clear guidelines for student and campus policy."[366] The policy proposed above is intended to supply the needed model; according to it, the college would regulate students' behavior precisely insofar as necessary to promote the campus sociocultural environment required by the college's common good. Students would be assisted and encouraged to foster certain aspects of their personal good. But the college's rules would require them to do so only insofar as some aspects of their personal good also pertain to the common good.

Go on to grant that students have the right to make their own choices, but argue that this right is limited by morality and the common good. Nobody has a moral right to get drunk, fornicate, or immerse himself or herself and others in mind-numbing and spiritually debilitating noise. True, it is not for the college to enforce the whole of morality, but when immoral behavior also impedes its common good, rules against that behavior do not infringe students' rights but protect them. Moreover, students contract freely with the college, and it includes its rules of behavior in the contract. When students accept the contract and become members of the college, they should keep their contractual promises, which now are responsibilities of membership.

The second counterargument will be that both the college's authority to make rules and its power to enforce them are limited.

366. Ibid., 32.

Grant that the college's authority is limited, but argue that the proposed tightening up in no way exceeds that limit, since the college's common good rationally requires it. Strict rules cannot be enforced perfectly, but committed administrators can enforce them earnestly by providing enough suitable persons to exercise the college's disciplinary authority, and by regularly imposing the stated penalties on those proved guilty of infractions.

Some faculty members no doubt will say that the objectives of the proposed tightening up are unrealistic. Campus life nowhere is what it once was, and students in Catholic schools no longer differ significantly from their counterparts in secular schools. So, they will conclude, the college must accept the way things are. If that argument were sound, the college might as well close down or, at least, honestly admit that it no longer is Catholic. But you can point to a few Catholic colleges with strict rules that are doing well. In the name of realism, administrators also may object that the college cannot afford to try to tighten up, since many students would rebel and withdraw. But even though some current students will withdraw if the college adopts and widely advertises strict but reasonable rules, they will be replaced by others better prepared to cooperate in the appropriate work of a Catholic college, and the institution's academic quality will make a quantum leap in a short time.[367]

The third counterargument will be that strict rules governing outward behavior are pointless, since they do not foster good character but, instead, tend to foster hypocrisy.

Begin by noting that this argument is beside the point. Tightening up the rules of student behavior is intended, not to foster the good character of individual students, but to contribute to the college's common good. You also can point out that it need not be hypocritical for people outwardly to conform to social norms they have not appropriated. People are hypocrites, strictly speaking, only if they pretend that their good behavior manifests good character they lack.

Having said that, you should go on to answer the argument directly. Every social effort to regulate behavior does risk some hypocrisy as an unwanted side effect. The question is whether this bad side effect ought to be accepted. You must argue that it is not too great an evil to accept. Subject anecdotal evidence and casual appeals to history—how things were in Catholic colleges in the old days—to critical examination. And point out, too, that nobody is proposing a return to the old days. Still, the former, stricter rules not only maintained various conditions conducive to a college's common good but removed many unnecessary occasions of serious sin and other foolishness. They were a real help to many young people who were not bad willed but weak. Now, by contrast, the college both defeats its own purpose and actively scandalizes its students. Indeed, many schools today

---

367. Henry Wechsler et al., "The Adverse Impact of Heavy Episodic Drinkers on Other College Students," *Journal of Studies on Alcohol,* 56 (1995): 628–34, report the results of a survey of 17,592 students at 140 American colleges showing that many students who do not drink heavily suffer seriously due to others' heavy drinking, especially on campuses where it is prevalent. Advertising the results of such studies along with a college's strict rules would encourage applications by individuals who plan not to drink heavily.

officially engage in serious hypocrisy, pretending to be Catholic while allowing themselves to become, or even deliberately making themselves, less and less distinguishable from otherwise similar secular institutions.

The college chaplaincy's preaching, catechesis, and counseling should promote right attitudes and action with respect to the goods that sound discipline will try to safeguard and, in its own way, promote. If those involved in the chaplaincy will oppose any tightening up, I suggest you urge their replacement as quickly as possible. Very likely they teach dissenting theological opinions on moral questions and apply them in their pastoral practice, thus contributing greatly to the college's scandalizing of its students. Even if this happens not to be true, people who see no need to curb the works of the flesh in order to facilitate the works of the spirit do not belong in a Catholic college chaplaincy.

Another challenge you are likely to encounter is that basing rules of student behavior on the common good of the college as Catholic is unfair to non-Catholic students and at odds with the church-state separation that must be respected insofar as the institution depends on public assistance (at least in guaranteeing student loans if not in other ways). Your first point should be that, while the proposed rules will be conducive to the common good of the college as Catholic, their content also pertains to the natural law, and so neither is unfair to any student nor involves anything specifically Catholic. Moreover, even if non-Catholic students were held to something specifically Catholic, they would suffer no injustice, provided the school makes its commitment and policies clear to applicants, who then can freely choose whether to enter its community and conform to its rules. As for church-state separation, not even the U.S. Supreme Court's school aid decisions impede tightening up the rules along the lines I have sketched.[368]

Some probably will protest that, if stricter rules are adopted and enforced, the college will become a monastery, with the students deprived of a normal social life and isolated in lonely silence. Certainly the change would help create an atmosphere conducive to study—an atmosphere the students will need if the faculty make higher academic demands and enforce them. But the students would not be deprived of wholesome social life or isolated in silence. The rules would allow for decent social events of many kinds, and the college should sponsor or encourage all sorts of morally acceptable activities. There should be a great variety and adequate quantity of games and sports equipment, and many sorts of associations should be encouraged based on common interests in academic matters, hobbies, and so on. Moreover, studying together, in and outside classrooms, should provide the foundation for any college community, and fitting liturgy should be the nucleus of a Catholic college's common life. Thus, the students should have rich opportunities to enjoy appropriate camaraderie and participate in a genuine community.

Undoubtedly, you will encounter a great deal of opposition in trying to promote a cultural environment more appropriate in a Catholic college. I hope you will neither compromise too quickly nor become discouraged. Even if you make little

---

368. See Kenneth D. Whitehead, *Catholic Colleges and Federal Funding* (San Francisco: Ignatius Press, 1988).

visible headway and your college remains a stumbling block to most of its students, your effort itself will bear witness to the kingdom and provide material for it, as does every good work of those who obey the Lord (see GS 38–39). Carry on the struggle not only with the hope of improving your college but also, and even more, with the hope of contributing to a better, a heavenly college, and enjoying tenure in it.

164: Should a college dismiss a misbehaving professor?

I am academic dean of a Catholic college facing a difficult personnel matter. Professor Russell, as I shall call him, ought to be fired, and I wish to do just that. While the college president seems to understand my point of view, he feels we must give Russell a substantial settlement to get him to go quietly.

Russell was hired not long after both the president and I came here, thirteen years ago. He was then a priest and well-regarded mainstream theologian, and we brought him in to head our religious studies program. Hired as an associate professor, he came on a three-year contract with the agreement that, if all went well, he would make full professor and receive tenure. All did go well until midway in his fourth year. Then it came out that he and the wife of the bright, young chairman of our chemistry department had been having a discreet affair almost from the day Russell stepped on the campus.

At the time the affair surfaced, we looked hard at the possibility of getting rid of Russell. Some of our faculty and staff were outraged, as were the majority of the board, the alumni who made their feelings known, and some important donors. But we reluctantly came to the conclusion that we could not fire him. Our policy, with which the president and I had concurred, was that strictly academic standards should be used in all matters concerning faculty status. Meetings with representatives of the American Association of University Professors (AAUP) and the faculty association's lawyer made it clear that Russell's personal life could not be used as a ground for action against him. Our own lawyer told us that if we fired him and he sued, he almost certainly would win and we might well be ordered to pay his legal bills. So, the chemistry chairman's wife got a divorce, Russell quit the priesthood, the two civilly married, and the couple became part of our happy college community.

Starting shortly thereafter and increasing little by little, we experienced other reasons for dissatisfaction with Russell.

His formerly excellent rate of publication slowed. Now it is barely a trickle, though he keeps it looking stronger than it really is by various dodges: listing himself as author of a book he merely edited, listing a book as published that nobody ever has seen and that has never appeared in *Books in Print,* listing as publications with no credit to anyone else an important series of articles of which he was only one of several coauthors, and so forth.

While that was going on, Russell also gradually became less visible on the campus: unavailable for meetings, seldom in his office even during posted office hours, frequently absent from class (though he sometimes had someone stand in for him to screen a film or conduct an informal discussion among the students on a topic of their choice). He sometimes failed to provide syllabi of his courses, which I request from all faculty members. Students also increasingly complained that he did not adhere to the syllabi he gave them, made no comments on their written assignments and papers, and behaved erratically, often spending an entire class period venting his feelings about problems in the Church completely irrelevant to the subject matter of the course and sometimes becoming abusive to students who dared to disagree.

Recently, we discovered the explanation for Russell's increasingly unsatisfactory performance. Just after he quit the priesthood, he founded a rehabilitation center for ex-priests and religious. Gradually he developed it into a multimillion dollar psychological counseling business. Though the center is about seventy miles from here, he manages that business on a day-to-day basis. We have hard evidence about this operation, supplied by some of its dissatisfied clients. Moreover, we now have discovered that, adding malfeasance to his gross neglect of duty, Russell once made an arrangement with a secretary in the psychology department, now no longer with us, to refer to his center applicants for a somewhat similar program that our psychologists were trying to set up.

This time, both the law and recognized criteria for academic behavior are on our side. Neither Russell's contractual rights nor the AAUP's standards can be used to defend his pursuit of his business interests in direct conflict with his responsibilities to the college. In view of the facts, I am convinced we should fire him. We should not pay him and we should tell him to stay off the campus or be treated as a trespasser. I hold that this is a matter of principle, since he has been defrauding the college and our students for ten years, and should not be given a dime for getting out.

The president says he understands my point of view and sympathizes, and I believe he does. Moreover, our lawyers have advised that if it comes to a court battle, we have an excellent chance of winning in the end, even though the fight could be hard and messy.

However, Russell has made it clear that, if we fire him as I propose, he will sue, and, through the faculty association's lawyer, he has telegraphed his strategy. He will use the media against us, claiming we are waging a vendetta against him because he left the priesthood and married. Despite everything, many of the faculty support him, as faculty always do, partly because they think, "There but for the grace of God go I."

The president wants to avoid messy litigation and bad publicity. He is concerned primarily because the college is having mild, but worrisome, problems recruiting students, and we are in the midst of an important fund-raising campaign.

Russell has told us that, if we pay him the equivalent of four years' salary and benefits in a lump sum at the end of this academic year, he will go quietly. The president has concluded that, all things considered, we should do that. I feel we should not let him get away with what he has done. Reflecting on this as a moral question, do you agree that we must fire Russell? If so, how would you articulate the argument?

Analysis:

This question primarily calls for judgment regarding accepting bad side effects; it also requires application of norms regarding fair procedure and restitution. In my judgment, a college ought to dismiss any professor who behaves as badly as this one has. He has no right to the money he is demanding, and giving it to him would waste funds that should be put to other uses. Even more important, giving in would encourage other faculty members to behave similarly and would set a bad precedent, which would lower the standard of faculty behavior. Still, the college should offer Russell some sort of fair hearing and take care in dismissing him to meet its own institutional standards. Whether the college dismisses him or not, it has been negligent with respect to the students he defrauded and owes them restitution.

The reply could be along the following lines:

In my judgment, you and the president made a major mistake when you concurred in the policy that all matters regarding faculty should be decided by "strictly academic standards." What that really means is the systematic but arbitrary exclusion of other considerations equally vital for an authentically Catholic faculty: whether someone rejects what the Catholic Church proposes as revealed truth, or systematically and publicly follows a lifestyle at odds with Catholic moral teaching, or carries out all of his or her academic responsibilities just as if he or she were a nonbeliever rather than a Catholic. With these considerations excluded, you are bound to have a faculty no different from any secular college. But no college is more Catholic than its faculty. So, you have collaborated in secularizing what once was a Catholic institution, even if you have managed to keep up some appearance of Catholicism for the benefit of those parents, alumni, and donors who care.

I am not saying that academic standards are less essential than Catholicism in matters bearing on faculty status. No Catholic college will be good unless it has an academically well-qualified faculty. But standards of Catholicism are equally essential. No college can be a good Catholic college unless the preponderant part of its faculty is well-formed in Catholic faith and devout in practicing it. Had you insisted on this necessary condition for a Catholic college, you would have included in your contracts with Russell and every other faculty member provisions permitting the dismissal of anyone who publicly violated the college's Catholic character. Acting on those provisions, you would have got rid of Russell years ago. Lacking them, you could neither dismiss him nor, I suppose, do anything about many other less egregious cases.

But you still have your problem, and it requires a sound solution, just as it would if the question came from the academic dean of any other secular college. Though the president's view of the issue plainly is based on practical considerations that cannot be ignored, I believe yours is substantially correct. As you requested, I shall concentrate on articulating the argument for your view, only incidentally responding to the president's concerns, which I assume you will deal with more adequately.

Your argument seems to me sound so far as it goes. Russell's actions and negligence, as you describe them, clearly have defrauded the college and its students, and he has no reason for a lawsuit except its nuisance value. In other words, he has no right to the money he is demanding, and the college has no reason to give it except getting him to go away quietly without causing the harm he unjustly threatens. Sometimes it is reasonable to forestall an unjust lawsuit in order to avoid the costs and other bad consequences of litigation, but Russell's threat seems to me morally indistinguishable from extortion, to which it would be wrong for the college to surrender. Meeting Russell's unjust demand not only would waste college funds that should be used to bring about other benefits to which various people are entitled, but also would encourage other faculty members to engage in similar tactics.

Another consideration offers an additional reason for resisting his demand. Since the college has a policy of adhering strictly to academic standards in dealing with matters affecting faculty status, the president at least should do that in this case. Russell's behavior has fallen below the very lowest tolerable level. If the college tolerates it, you will further lower a standard, prevailing in virtually all universities and colleges, that already accommodates a certain number of tenured people who somewhere along the way have stopped working hard and developing their talents. Think what it will be like if the college in the future is dragged down by as many Russells, brazenly acting on their conflicting interests and defrauding the college and its students, as it now is by lazy people. The college would be doing itself a tremendous, long-term injury in accepting such a development. Then too, the college would be likely to fare less well in litigation involving Russell's imitators, other things being equal, if it gives in to him, than it will fare if it resists and finds itself involved in litigation against him. What your college does in this matter also could set a new low standard for more or less similar cases in many other colleges. Therefore, you owe it to them as well as to your own college's future members not to do that.

So, I would urge the president to dismiss Russell. However, the college must first offer him a fair hearing. It must at least meet your own institution's standards in dealing with employees generally; it need not necessarily meet the standards of the AAUP, unless the college has committed itself to doing that even in a case like this. When the hearing reaches its predictable outcome, dismiss Russell, and let him sue. Be prepared to file a countersuit for breach of contract to recover the portion of his salary he has not earned during the past ten years. He owes the college that money in strict justice as restitution, and the college has a good case, inasmuch as his performance fell below what hitherto was the lowest tolerated level, set by lazy professors. You might also try to recover the income Russell's counseling program diverted from the college, damages for the injury he has done the college's reputation, and punitive damages both to make clear the outrageous injustice Russell has done and to deter others from following his bad example.

If the president properly lays out the case to members of the board and potential donors, they may well be glad to see him acting decisively and getting rid of someone who is not carrying his weight. Many people who might donate to the college are convinced that academic institutions suffer very heavily from dead weight. They are right. Making it clear to faculty members just how far Russell has fallen below the level of the worst of them, and how gross his wrongdoing has been, will help them realize that they are not threatened. Moreover, as academic dean, you can tell them that very straightforwardly.

Those concerned about the Catholic character of the college very likely have reason to despair of it. I am not advising you or the president to deceive them. Yet even they will feel better if you get rid of Russell, and their support will help the college weather the storm.

Finally, though the evidence you present about Russell's misbehavior constitutes a strong case against him, it also points to serious negligence by the college toward its students. Much of Russell's decade-long failure to fulfill his obligations toward his students has been known to you and/or other administrators, but little has been done to rectify the situation and vindicate students' rights. Therefore, no matter what the college does about Russell, it owes fair restitution to the defrauded students. The amount owed and the manner of paying can be determined only by considering all the relevant facts, putting yourself in the place of Russell's students, and applying the Golden Rule.

165: How should a Catholic college deal with employees' sexual misbehavior?

I am president of a midsized Catholic college. Besides various undergraduate programs, we have a few programs leading to masters' degrees. Our student handbook includes policies regarding students' sexual behavior among themselves. Nobody is calling them into question at present, but last year we had two unrelated cases of inappropriate sexual behavior involving other members of the college community.

One involved a young man who teaches psychology and has been voted an outstanding professor by his undergraduate students at the end of each of the seven semesters he has taught here. A female graduate student to whom he gave a *C* in a required course in the M.S. in Social Services program accused him of downgrading her because she refused to have sexual intercourse with him. He admitted that they had been dating and that she had broken off the relationship, but claimed he had never tried, or even wanted, to have intercourse with her. The faculty affairs committee conducted a hearing, found nothing to support the accuser's claim, observed that the school's existing policies were not violated even if the professor did seek intercourse with the student, and recommended unanimously that the case be dismissed. I approved the recommendation, and most faculty members and students were satisfied. However, the case was widely publicized, and an intense debate took place, both on campus and in the local media, about the propriety of such a relationship between a professor and a student. Concerned about the publicity, the board discussed the matter and asked me to develop a policy on sexual intimacies involving students with other members of the college community—not only faculty members but other employees.

The other case involved a male food service supervisor. One of his female staff accused him of repeatedly squeezing her breasts. He denied the accusation, claiming the woman was angry because he had reprimanded her for violating sanitary food-handling procedures. We asked an attractive young woman, whom we had just hired as assistant director of campus security, to work temporarily in food service; in a few days the supervisor began squeezing her breasts, and we fired him. The story spread around the campus, and WAMD (Women against Male Domination, pronounced "whammed"), a campus feminist society, began campaigning for an explicit policy on sexual harassment. Their key demands were that every complaint be heard by a panel of two women elected by female members of the college community and one man elected by the males, that when it is her-word-against-his the panel should presume the woman is telling the truth, and that any employee found guilty by the panel should be terminated at once.

I set up an ad hoc committee of five to study both matters and suggest a comprehensive policy on inappropriate sexual behavior by administrators, faculty, and staff. The committee represented not only the different segments of the college community but different points of view. I directed it to examine both sexual harassment and employees' sexual behavior with consenting parties, whether other employees or students. The committee worked hard throughout the year, gathering information about relevant policies on other campuses, holding extensive hearings, and thoroughly debating the problems and possible solutions. Now they have delivered the results: a brief common report reviewing the committee's activity and summarizing the issues that emerged, and five lengthy individual reports offering somewhat overlapping but largely inconsistent policy proposals.

One committee member argues that intimate relationships involving a superior and subordinate employee, or an employee and a student, should be excluded absolutely, because subordinates and students are likely to be exploited. Another would exclude all intimate relationships involving an employee on the ground that Christians not married to each other should not be involved in any intimate relationship. Another committee member holds that there should be no rules against intimate relationships between or among consenting adults, since people should be free to do as they please, and the college has no business enforcing traditional moral norms; cases of exploitation are an entirely different matter and should be dealt with as harassment. A fourth member wishes to draw lines depending on how far mutually agreeable activities go, so that dating would be permitted, sexual behavior that does not involve any exposure of genitals would be tolerated in some cases but not in others, and other behavior would be excluded. The fifth wishes to draw lines on a different basis. All sorts of intimacies between consenting parties would be acceptable unless they were currently related as female subordinate and male superior or female student and male professor.

The committee is similarly divided over what constitutes sexual harassment and how to deal with it. One member holds that the college should consider only legally wrongful behavior to be harassment; he proposes that we help anyone who complains of harassment to file a complaint with the police and/or a lawsuit, and discharge anyone found guilty or ordered by a court to pay damages. Another holds that sexual harassment cannot be defined in general terms and argues that the college community as a whole should act as a legislative body, one vote for each person, to enact a code of interpersonal behavior prohibiting specified performances and setting punishments for individuals found guilty of violations; he also proposes that a college court be established to hear and decide cases, and that it follow procedures and use standards of evidence similar to those of state criminal courts. Still another committee member argues that any verbal or physical conduct of a sexual nature is harassment if it (1) relates to some action affecting the other party's status, advancement, or evaluation; (2) interferes with the other party's work or educational performance; or (3) tends to create an intimidating or offensive living, working, or learning environment. While proposing that complaints of harassment be dealt with initially by the informal procedures we have followed in the past, this member also recommends that a harassment board be established to conduct formal hearings on complaints not settled to the satisfaction of the complainants. The procedure in such hearings would be similar to that of a civil lawsuit, with the decision based on the preponderance of the evidence; penalties would range from a formal reprimand to dismissal. Finally, two committee members subscribe to the WAMD demands about how to deal with harassment, and hold that it occurs whenever a man's behavior either would be considered offensive by the average woman or is considered offensive by a particular woman and repeated after she has told the man not to do it again.

I have asked our lawyers to review the committee's report and advise me what the college must do to comply with all relevant laws in these matters and minimize our liability. I am asking you and two other Christian ethicists what we must do to comply with the Church's teaching and fulfill our moral responsibilities to all members of the college community.

Analysis:

This question calls for clarification of the principles from which sound rules can be derived. The principle of all college policies should be the common good of the community as a Catholic college. The college should not attempt to enforce traditional Christian moral norms considered insofar as they guide individuals to their proper good. But its policies certainly should exclude all sexual behavior that is both likely to impede cooperation for its common good or otherwise injure it. Injustice associated with a violation should be considered an aggravating circumstance. To be fair, the college's policies should exclude inappropriate sexual behavior not only of heterosexual males but of heterosexual women and homosexuals as well. Behavior of specifically excluded types should be subject to sanction even if it occurs only once and nobody involved objects. Not all violations of the norms will be equally grave, and only very serious or repeated violations warrant dismissal. A formal procedure is needed for receiving, investigating, and adjudicating instances of alleged misbehavior.

The reply could be along the following lines:

Since a community's leaders should shape its members' cooperation toward their common good, that good is the principle of the norms a leader should articulate and enforce. So, try to articulate norms and policies regarding employees' sexual behavior in view of the college's common good. Since not even virtuous sexual behavior pertains to academic life, the college's norms and policies will limit sexual behavior rather than positively direct it, and the college should prohibit any sexual behavior by employees that would unreasonably impede their cooperation for the common good or otherwise injure it.

The central components of a Catholic college's common good are three: (1) effective cooperation among faculty and students in cultivating and sharing knowledge of truth and intellectual virtues, (2) justice and charity among all members of the community, and (3) the religious value of the common enterprise considered as cooperation in a particular part of God's creative, redemptive, and sanctifying work. That religious value primarily is realized in the cooperation of members of the college community in its specifically academic life, insofar as that cooperation is shaped by the Gospel's truth and bears consistent witness to it.[369]

It appears from the views of some committee members that they have not accepted the college's common good as the principle for making policy. Given this principle, however, the college indeed can rightly limit individuals' freedom to do as they please, can describe in general terms what behavior is excluded, and can articulate objective norms, rather than using the subjective standard of offensiveness, whether to the average woman or to a particular woman.

Since civil law, especially in a secularized society, is not grounded on the components of the college's common good, it can tolerate some behavior college policy should exclude. Moreover, while the college's procedures for applying and enforcing its policy should be fair, that does not require all elements of legal due process. Some in fact would be so costly and time consuming that trying to implement them would be self-defeating, and so detrimental to the common good of the college.

For various reasons, not all members of a college community are equally able to shape the common effort toward the common good. Moreover, different sorts of members are involved in the community on different bases, and some have far greater stakes in it than others. Therefore, though the college's governance can include democratic elements, on the whole it cannot be democratic, as most participants in the community usually acknowledge. Still, as in other matters, so in this case norms of sexual behavior articulated and enforced by the administration are likely to be effective only if most of the community's reasonable and committed members see their appropriateness and put them into practice.

The problem of sexual harassment now exists in Catholic colleges largely as a consequence of the so-called sexual revolution—that is, the widespread rejection, especially since the early 1960s, of traditional Judeo-Christian norms of sexual conduct. Perceptions of sexual misbehavior also have changed, in some ways for the better due to greater sensitivity to injustice, but in other ways for the worse due to dulled sensitivity to the goods of chaste friendship and marriage. Today, people who see nothing to object to in interpersonal behavior that is objectively wrong, inasmuch as it is unchaste or immodest, frequently initiate such behavior and/or are receptive to it. The behavior, then, often is mutually agreeable, and it has become more or less common, even in a community such as a Catholic college.

369. See AA 5–8; John Paul II, *Ex corde ecclesiae,* I, 13–14, 21, 27, 33, 48–49, *AAS* 82 (1990) 483–84, 1488, 1490–91, 1494, 1500–1501, *OR,* 1 Oct. 1990, 4–6.

Still, everyone agrees on the need for regulation when the behavior either abuses power or is not mutually agreeable, and so sexual exploitation by people in positions of authority and the repetition of unchaste or immodest behavior by one party despite another's objection have become essential criteria for defining offenses. Instead of censuring unchaste and immodest behavior as such, people now adopt the language of governmental guidelines and talk about "an intimidating and hostile environment" or "an offensive learning, working, or living environment."[370] The fact is, though, that even truly consensual and mutually agreeable unchaste and immodest behavior is morally unacceptable in itself, and for someone to persist in such behavior despite another's objection to it is only an aggravation of its inherent wrongness.

To deal with sexual harassment, therefore, a Catholic college must begin by teaching the truth about the requirements of charity and justice in all interpersonal relationships, not least intimate ones, as well as the norms of chastity and modesty. Moreover, the college's facilities and activities should be arranged to foster a wholesome atmosphere conducive to a Christian style of life, and the college should support its members who wish to avoid temptation and live good and holy lives (see q. 163, above).

However, not all violations of the norms of Christian morality bearing on sexual activity affect the college's common good. Not only employees' sins of thought and secret unchaste solitary acts are outside the college's jurisdiction, but also some sexual wrongdoing that becomes known and involves couples. For example, it should not concern the college if a food service supervisor openly lives in a lawful nonmarital relationship with the manager of the campus bookstore, provided they behave modestly around the college and their relationship does not adversely affect either their job performance or their working relationships with each other and co-workers. Again, an administrator's or faculty member's isolated sexual sin with someone outside the college community is unlikely to have any serious impact on the college unless the act also violates the law. However, college policy plainly should exclude all violations of the norms of Christian sexual morality at odds with the college's common good. College policy even may exclude sexual activity morally acceptable in itself if it is likely to interfere with attainment of the college's common good.

The contracts the college makes with its employees, including administrators and faculty members, should and perhaps do allow it to impose appropriate sanctions for proven violations of its policies, including the prospective policy regarding sexual activity. If existing contracts do not include the necessary provisions, legal problems might limit the sanctions the college can impose. But I shall assume that the college can enforce the policies required for its common good, even by dismissing administrators and tenured faculty members.

---

370. This understanding of sexual harassment informs even the more moderate and competent treatments of it in the academic context; see, e.g., Bernice R. Sandler and Robert J. Shoop, eds. *Sexual Harassment on Campus: A Guide for Administrators, Faculty, and Students* (Boston: Allyn and Bacon, 1997); still, this work includes much relevant information and practical suggestions worth thoughtful consideration by Catholic college administrators.

In formulating the college's policies and norms, various classes of activities should be distinguished, though the same behavior may fall into two or more of these.

One major kind is immodest behavior that detracts from the college's cultural environment. Modesty disposes one to forestall, avoid, and escape occasions of sexual sins for oneself and not to generate them for others (see *CCC,* 2521–24). Behavior that intentionally or, if not intentionally, foreseeably and unjustifiably tends to arouse others' lustful thoughts and desires is immodest. Such behavior, especially if flagrant, is contrary to any community's common good, since it violates justice and charity by tempting people to commit grave sins. In a college, even subtly immodest behavior in public also seriously detracts from the cultural environment by distracting attention from intellectual pursuits and recollection. In a Catholic college, it also impedes the effectiveness of the community's witness to Christian values. So, the college should promote modesty and prohibit all its members from doing things likely to lead others into sin—for example, by dressing, speaking, or behaving in sexually provocative ways; or by displaying indecent images, distributing pornographic literature, or playing indecent recordings so loudly that others have to hear them.

A second major kind of activity that must be dealt with comprises certain unchaste forms of behavior to which participants consent. Of course, if it is carried on secretly and never becomes known to the college community, the behavior never becomes an issue. Also, as suggested above, not all habitual sexual immorality of employees adversely affects the college's common good. But those who directly cooperate in providing the college's educational service—members of the faculty and administration—should contribute to its witness to Christian values, especially by being models for students. Where such employees are concerned, the college should never tolerate grave and habitual sexual immorality, including living in a nonmarital sexual relationship, whether with another member of the college community or someone outside it.

An important subclass of this second kind of activity comprises unchaste activities by two or more consenting members of the college community that are likely to adversely affect their or others' cooperation for the college's common good. For example, even an isolated instance of unchaste sexual activity involving employees related as superior and subordinate is likely to distort their working relationship and, if it becomes known, to generate tensions with other employees, who will suspect favoritism. Similarly, and more seriously, even isolated instances of unchaste sexual activity by faculty members or administrators with students lead the latter into sin instead of encouraging them to grow in virtue. They also provide bad example for other students, damage the college's witness to Christian values, and adversely affect its cultural environment by creating expectations, or fears, of more such romantic relationships. Such expectations in turn generate ambiguities in academic relationships and inhibit appropriate camaraderie among faculty and students in their academic pursuits. Not just intercourse but any behavior intended to bring about or maintain sexual arousal or cause sexual satisfaction should be excluded.

For the same reason, a student's actual academic relationship with a faculty member—for example, as a current member of his or her class—should not be considered a necessary condition for an offense, but should be an aggravating circumstance. Another common, and very important, aggravating circumstance is injustice associated with the unchaste behavior—for example, the demand for sexual favors to obtain a deserved promotion or grade, or the offer of an undeserved promotion or grade in exchange for sexual favors, or the offer of sexual favors as a bribe. Even if mutually agreeable to those involved, such transactions are unjust. Things that should not be exchanged are exchanged, subordinates and students are exploited or exposed to exploitation, and an irrelevant criterion is used for evaluations that will reflect unfairly on other employees or students.

A third major kind of behavior that must be dealt with comprises unchaste or immodest activities injurious and objectionable to one or more of the persons involved. Sexual assault, ranging from an immodest touch to rape, is an important subclass (see *LCL,* 545–49); and, though they are often less serious, unchaste proposals and any sort of immodesty that is an unwanted occasion of sin for others involve violations of justice and charity analogous to those in sexual assault. When both parties are members of the college community, such wrongs also injure its common good by impeding cooperation. But even if the victim is not a member of the college community, such wrongful behavior involving administrators and faculty members—and even other employees or students, if the behavior is unlawful—will injure the college's common good by damaging its reputation and witness to Christian values. Since such behavior is at odds with the common good of the college in every instance, it should be excluded in all cases, not subjected to sanction only if someone persists after having been informed that it is objectionable. The persistence that constitutes harassment should be considered an aggravating circumstance, not a necessary condition for the offense.

A fourth major kind of behavior can be called "sexual" only by analogy. It comprises activities neither unchaste nor immodest but unjust and offensive inasmuch as they violate the equal respect owed to persons of both sexes: jokes ridiculing persons of either sex on the basis of sex-related characteristics, insults referring to sex-specific organs or bodily features, derogatory generalizations about women or men. Also included in this kind of behavior are activities that violate the equal respect due homosexual persons despite the unchaste activities in which they perhaps engage. Behavior of this kind should not be treated as sexual harassment but should be reprimanded and, if necessary, punished as other instances of disrespect are.

A fifth major kind of behavior comprises activities morally acceptable in themselves, but detrimental to the college's common good. These can be subdivided into activities mutually agreeable to the parties involved and those objectionable to one or more of the persons affected.

Chaste expressions of erotic affection between engaged couples are an example of activities both morally acceptable in themselves and mutually agreeable. Carried on in public, nevertheless, such activities in some situations are detrimental to the college's common good by being distractions from the work at hand. Carried on by a member of the administration or faculty with a student, they also would create at least the appearance of impropriety. So, the college can rightly require discretion on the part of those who engage in these legitimate activities. Such romantic activities must be distinguished from appropriate signs and tokens of friendship among members of the college community, including those between administrators or faculty members and students of both sexes. These must not be discouraged, for they not only are legitimate in themselves but pertain to relationships generally harmonious with the college's common good and often conducive to it.

Various sorts of activities morally acceptable in themselves but objectionable to one or more persons affected also can be detrimental to the college's common good. Suppose two college employees, Dan and Sharon, are free to initiate a romantic relationship. Dan persistently seeks to become better acquainted despite Sharon's repeated refusals, and she objects to this persistence, though it involves nothing unchaste, immodest, or insulting. As a matter of courtesy Dan should desist, while persisting is likely to interfere with the working relationship between the two employees. So, the college can rightly require Dan to desist. In such cases, an individual's persistence in the annoying behavior constitutes harassment, and that is the defining feature of his or her offense.

In formulating and promulgating norms forbidding inappropriate sexual behavior, the college should specify the possible sanctions. These should vary, since not all violations will be equally detrimental to the common good. Not only do different sorts of wrongful behavior vary in their inherent gravity, but circumstances can greatly affect their seriousness. For example, sexual intercourse by a professor with a student who consents is not inherently as grave an offense as a professor's raping a student; however, if a professor accepted a student's invitation to have intercourse in return for a better grade, the mutually agreeable intercourse might be considered so injurious to the college's good as to be punishable by the same penalty, namely, the professor's dismissal. For most offenses, other circumstances also should be taken into account: whether the wrongful activity involved (even incipient) marital infidelity or sacrilege, whether it was an isolated instance of misbehavior or part of a pattern, whether the offender's guilt was mitigated by subjective factors limiting his or her responsibility, whether the victim in some way shared responsibility for the wrongdoing, and so on. For example, though one person's immodesty by no means justifies another's sexual assault or invitation to engage in unchaste activity, a victim's immodesty, though it should not lead to condoning an offense, should count as a mitigating factor in evaluating it. Similarly, an insult blurted out in anger should be considered a very minor offense by comparison with a calculated injustice, such as an actual or proposed transaction involving the exchange of sexual favors and an undeserved grade or promotion.

Since every member of the college community shares responsibility for its common good, the policies should exclude inappropriate sexual behavior not only by heterosexual males but by heterosexual women and homosexuals. For the same reason, when the norms exclude activities by consenting participants, any member of the college community involved in such an activity should be recognized as an offender, even though the differing guilt of particular participants also should be taken into account. For example, if a professor and a student exchange a high grade for sexual favors, both violate the college's common good and deserve punishment, even though the professor deserves to be punished more severely. Of course, since members of the faculty and administration have a far greater stake in the college than students and staff, dismissal, the most severe sanction available to the college, is likely to be a far greater penalty for a professor or administrator than for a student or staff employee.

In designing the procedures for dealing with offenses, you should of course obtain legal advice. I offer the following ideas only with the thought that they may be helpful.

It seems to me that informal procedures can be used to deal with some violations, especially many less serious ones, without sacrificing the college's interest or violating individuals' rights. But to safeguard the common good and individuals' rights, a formal procedure for receiving, investigating, and adjudicating alleged violations will be needed, especially in cases that could lead to severe sanctions or might render the college liable for damages or subject to penalties if not handled properly. The formal process need not embody all features of public criminal process, but it should be fair to the accused.

A fair process should include features providing reasonable assurance that it will result in judgments based on the truth (see q. 167, below). That precludes finding anyone guilty unless his or her guilt is established beyond reasonable doubt. WAMD's demand that a woman be presumed to be telling the truth whenever her assertion contradicts a man's is unacceptable because the presumption would unfairly prejudice judgment. WAMD's demands regarding the composition of the panel to hear complaints and its members' election are unacceptable since they would discriminate unfairly against men as such.

166: How should a Catholic college set employees' wages and benefits?

Right after graduating from this Catholic college nearly twenty years ago, I went to work for admissions doing recruiting. After a few years I became secretary to the vice-president for finance and administration and worked for him until last year. Then I was promoted to my present job: administrative assistant to the academic vice-president—which makes me a member of the administration, though just barely. This year I have been appointed to the wages and benefits committee. Within the limits set by the overall budget, it has the job of recommending to the president changes in the pay and fringe benefits of everyone from the president himself down to the students we employ part time. On the committee, which is chaired by my former boss, are three members of the administration (including him and me), three faculty members, and three people from the "staff"—that is, all the other people who work in the offices, maintenance, food service, housekeeping, security, and so forth.

We have been in a budget crunch for the past several years and still are. The college has done everything possible to meet enrollment targets, but registration have fallen short, and tuition and other charges cannot be raised without worsening the situation. As usual, too, the cost of health insurance is going up—this year so much that, if the college picked up the total increase, that alone would take the whole three percent available for increases in pay and benefits. In the past three years, the college has taken on about one-third of the increased cost of health insurance, given all full-time employees a total increase of four-and-one-half percent, and, of course, increased the pay of individuals who were promoted. Part-time employees, mostly our own students or high school students, are paid the minimum wage and receive no benefits.

The budget crunch has been hardest on staff members. Some of the best people have left. Many staff vacancies have not been filled, so the people who remain have had to work harder to get their jobs done. Wherever possible, part timers have been used to fill in, to avoid paying overtime to staff members. Formerly generous holidays and vacation time have been cut back, and even their modest Christmas bonus has been eliminated. With the small percentage increases in wages, the lowest-paid staff members, including most of the people in housekeeping and food service, actually are taking home less today than they were three years ago, due to the increase in FICA tax, their pension contribution, and, especially, the deduction for health insurance.

No segment of our staff is unionized, and it would be exaggerating to say the staff people are demanding a better deal. They are unhappy, however, and a couple of the more articulate ones are arguing that the staff as a whole is not being treated fairly. One of them spoke up at a community forum the president held in September, pointing out that a Catholic college should follow the Church's teaching on a family wage, and that the lowest-paid staff have been falling behind for several years, while top administrators and faculty, who already were making enough to live on and whose children also can enroll in the college without paying tuition, have received raises of thousands of dollars. (I happen to know this is true. Over the past five years, the president's salary has gone up by a sum greater than the wages of one of our lowest-paid, full-time employees.) While recognizing the college's financial difficulties, this articulate staff member argued that, as long as the budget crunch continues, the limited funds available for increases in pay and benefits should be divided equally among full-time employees rather than distributed unequally in proportion to present wages, which range from as little as twelve thousand dollars per year to over two hundred thousand.

The vice-president for finance and administration acknowledged the problems of the lowest-paid employees and said he would like them at least to stay even. But he maintained that financial realities limit what the college can do. It would be easy enough to distribute available funds equally—for instance, by applying the whole amount available for increases this year to the increased cost of health insurance, so that no one's deductions and paycheck would change. But doing that repeatedly, he argued, would soon cause essential employees to resign. Already some of the electricians, carpenters, and other better-paid staff have quit, and others soon will unless the college offers wages and benefits competitive with other employers in the vicinity. The same is true of faculty and administrators. The most capable people are very mobile, and are unlikely to stay here long if their compensation does not keep pace with that of colleagues in other colleges and universities.

Seeing the point of both arguments, I have what seems to me a very difficult problem: What position should I take when these issues come up in the committee? I suspect I was appointed because my old boss assumed I would be a safe vote yet credible with staff people, having gotten to know most of them over the years and being on friendly terms with them. But my sympathies are with them, and I am personally inclined to come down on their side. If I have a clear position and can make a good case for it, I am sure all three staff members on the committee will support it, so that, if I can win over one of the three faculty members, we would have a majority. While the president need not follow the committee's recommendation, he always has done so in the past, and I think he would this year too. Of course, if I do this, I probably will not be on the committee next year!

Analysis:

This question calls for application of the norm regarding just wages, judgment according to the Golden Rule, and the derivation of norms for the questioner's work on the committee. The committee's primary objective should be to determine what the college community owes its members in justice. If committee members acknowledge that even a single person without dependents cannot live decently on wages of twelve thousand dollars per year, they should determine how much the college owes its lowest paid full-time employees, and recommend that the available funds be used to satisfy that debt. If any funds remain, applying the Golden Rule probably will indicate that they should be used to maintain take-home pay for those employees less able to bear the increased deduction for health insurance. If the available funds are insufficient to fulfill the college's strict obligations toward its employees, the questioner should urge the committee to recommend that the budget be revised and the necessary funds be raised. The questioner should recommend that a more representative body be established to consider both the long-term problem of just pay and benefits, and the question of how to make appropriate restitution for underpayment to current and past employees.

The reply could be along the following lines:

Members of a community asked for advice on important matters or given an opportunity to influence policy all too often think only about the interests of their own segment of the community, take their responsibilities lightly, or mute their contribution so as to maintain their position of influence. Your attitude is commendable insofar as you are concerned about the staff people falling behind, are conscientious about the committee's work, and are not anxious about whether you will be on it again next year.

The principle of authority in the college is its common good. That should be the basis for all policies and decisions, including those regarding employees' pay and benefits. As with any community, just relationships among all who share in the college's life and work are essential to its common good. In a Catholic college, moreover, as in every Catholic community, justice should be transformed by charity so as to become mercy—the justice of the kingdom (see *LCL*, 360–71). The college's financial problems are important but subordinate; they concern necessary means, not ends. Urge the committee first to consider what the community owes all its members, and only then how to solve its financial problems so that it can fulfill its obligations to its employees.

While the Church teaches that all workers should receive a family wage, that teaching does not mean every employer must pay each adult, full-time employee enough to support a family. Families' needs can be met in part by tax breaks and public assistance programs.[371] However, the absolutely minimum just wage for a full-time worker surely must provide at least sufficient benefits and take-home pay to meet all of an individual's genuine needs, that is, everything required to live a morally good life: food, housing, utilities, health care, clothing, transportation, retirement savings, and at least a minimal level of participation in religious activities, civic life, interpersonal relationships with relatives and friends, personal cultural development, and recreation (see GS 67; *LCL,* 801).

You say the lowest-paid, full-time college employees receive twelve thousand dollars per year in salary, plus benefits, including part of the cost of their health insurance, and opportunities for overtime have been eliminated by filling in with part-time workers. Though that no doubt meets the college's legal obligations, you should ask the members of the committee to put themselves in the place of those making twelve thousand dollars a year and ask whether that level of pay would seem to them adequate as a living wage. I doubt that they will be able honestly to say yes. If not, the first priority should be to determine the minimum that must be paid each full-time employee to bring his or her compensation for next year to the amount surely required by justice.

If any funds remain, I suggest you next ask the committee to put themselves in the place of other low-paid, full-time employees, and consider whether a reduction in take-home pay would be acceptable. I doubt that any will be able honestly to say yes. If not, the next priority should be to determine how to allocate the remaining funds so as to maintain this year's level of take-home pay for employees who cannot easily bear the increased deduction for health insurance, or, at least, to minimize for them the reduction in take-home pay that the budget inevitably will impose on some.

What if there is not enough money in the budget to cover the pay increases due the lowest-paid employees? Urge the committee to recommend that all available funds be used for this purpose and that the budget be revised to provide at least enough additional funds to achieve it. If the necessary funds cannot be raised in

---

371. John D. Callahan, *The Catholic Attitude toward a Familial Minimum Wage* (Washington, D.C.: The Catholic University of America, 1936), argued that all adult, male, full-time workers deserve a wage adequate to support a family. However, though employers ought to make a substantial contribution to the support of male, full-time workers' families, the Church's teaching does not clearly specify the employers' obligation beyond that of paying at least a living wage to each individual employed full time (see *LCL,* 765–67). Moreover, social and economic changes since the 1930s have complicated the matter; see Bryce Christensen et al., *The Family Wage: Work, Gender, and Children in the Modern Economy* (Rockford, Ill.: The Rockford Institute, 1988). Though these matters deserve fuller treatment, I set them aside here, and insist only on the demand of strict justice that every worker be paid at least an individual's living wage.

some other way, you might suggest a special fund-raising effort. If the college's need for funds to do justice to its lowest-paid, full-time employees is explained clearly to all its better-paid employees, alumni, students, students' parents, and friends, the necessary funds probably can be raised.

What if your efforts fail and there is little or no improvement in the way staff employees are compensated? Your account suggests that the employment market is least favorable to them, so that they lack the leverage to obtain more favorable consideration. Perhaps you should suggest to some of your friends among the staff employees that they examine the possibility of organizing a union. They certainly have both a legal and a moral right to do that. Still, taking such an initiative might not be worthwhile, for it would involve risks, the most serious being that one or more ineffective or corrupt unions would organize the employees, with little or no benefit to staff members and, perhaps, much injury to the college as a whole.

I also think you should urge your committee or some more appropriate body to recommend that a special committee be established to study the long-term problem of pay and benefits for all employees. It should be charged with developing proposals to assure wage scales that are both just to all employees and sufficient to retain desirable employees for whose services other potential employers are likely to compete. Its charge also should include studying the college's obligation to make restitution for past injustice in underpaying employees and proposing a plan for fulfilling that obligation.[372]

If your college is like most with which I am acquainted, one reason why it is difficult to do justice to all members of the community is that the administration tries to manage the community's finances unilaterally instead of organizing cooperation to deliberate about common problems and find mutually acceptable solutions. Staff members, especially, are not treated as community members but servants. Therefore, I also would propose that the special committee be elected by all segments of the college community so as to be truly representative, and that its charge be presented to it as a common concern of all—a problem to be dealt with by everyone's sharing in sincere dialogue.

Generous cooperation by all members of the community will be necessary to solve the problem. If the better-paid employees—administrators and senior faculty—agree to a fairer distribution of the college's payroll and settle for somewhat less pay than they might receive elsewhere, they will put into practice the justice to which most well-educated Christians pay at least verbal respect. Administrators could cut their own expenses and work harder, so that they will be able to reduce the size and cost of the administration by attrition. Faculty members, likewise, could eliminate nonessential expenditures and accept a somewhat heavier teaching load. In their quarters and around the campus, students could be neater, more careful, and more considerate, thereby lessening the work load of

---

372. Since the obligation to make restitution is only to do now what is fair, all things considered (see *LCL*, 452–57), the college's capacity to rectify past injustice, both with respect to present and past employees, limits its duty to do so. Also, restitution, at least in some cases, would not need to be by cash payments but could take the form of credits toward tuition.

staff people and allowing reduction by attrition to continue without overburdening those who remain.

167: Should law violations on a college campus be reported to the police?

I just became the top administrator for student affairs at a small Catholic university (until recently we called ourselves "college"). While I will not single-handedly make policy on student affairs, I will have a large role in the process. My problem concerns student misconduct that violates not only our institutional norms but, in a more or less serious way, public laws: rape, sexual and other assault, arson, theft, intentional property destruction, drug offenses, and so on.[373]

My main question is whether it should be our general policy to report incidents of such misconduct to the police. But I do not think this question can be answered without simultaneously answering a number of related questions. Should we encourage students to report such incidents to the police, and, if so, before or after reporting them to us? Should we have a uniform policy on this matter for all members of the college community—not only students, but faculty, administrators, maintenance people, office staff, and so forth? When there is only some reason to think someone has violated the law, should we proceed in the same way as when it is fairly certain or even obvious that an offense has occurred? Should we differentiate sharply between various kinds of offenses, say, by having different policies for offenses against persons and against property and so-called victimless crimes, such as drug offenses?

Closely related to these questions are certain others. Often, misconduct that violates the law also violates institutional norms, and then both the law and our own disciplinary process can come into play. In many respects, our disciplinary process does not meet the requirements of due process in criminal proceedings, and, for this and other reasons, we sometimes find students guilty of infractions and impose penalties in situations where the public authorities would—or actually do—decline to prosecute, or would deal with a serious offense by treating it as a misdemeanor, or would fail to obtain an indictment.

Our past policy has not been clear, and our practice has not been consistent. There has been considerable reluctance to call the police. Students have not been told not to report violations of the law to public authorities, but they have not been encouraged to do so; indeed, my predecessor frowned on anyone's "going public" and wanted virtually all problems to be "kept within the college community." It would have been considered disloyal to go to the public authorities before ap-proaching the college administration about virtually any misconduct short of a serious crime against a person, still in the process of being committed.

---

373. This question concerns an institution located in the United States. Some universities in other countries enjoy certain immunities from the public criminal justice system and exercise, within limits, police and judicial power on their own campuses. In the case of such an institution, some of the response to this question would be irrelevant or would apply differently.

As a result of all this, violations of the law were not reported to the public authorities unless it was virtually certain a violation had occurred; the nature of the offense made little or no difference.

There has been no policy for dealing with misconduct by members of the college community other than students. It seems to have been assumed that members of the administration and faculty never violate the law, and other employees have been treated very much as they would be by the management of any business.

Finally, some of my fellow administrators and many students think our own disciplinary process should have all the features of criminal due process. They consider it unfair for the institution to impose penalties on students for misconduct that was reported to the police yet was not punished by the law even though it could have been. Personally, I am inclined to take the contrary view.

Analysis:

The questioner raises a set of complicated, specific questions to which there probably is no single set of right answers. But the issues can be clarified and the limits of morally acceptable positions indicated. Private groups and their members are not exempt from public law, and citizens ought to report crimes. But this duty admits exceptions, so that the authorities in private groups often rightly rely on internal disciplinary processes to deal with wrongful behavior. In general, college and university administrators should deal with unlawful behavior on campus much as management does in a factory or place of business. This does not require reporting all crimes, but does require always reporting known or probable crimes of certain types, which ought to be specified. Students should not be encouraged to report all incidents to police, but they should not be inhibited from communicating with public authorities. Internal disciplinary processes must be fair but need not have all the safeguards of due process in criminal law. Everyone on campus should be treated alike when it comes to reporting unlawful behavior, but internal disciplinary processes must take into account the differing rights of different groups within the community.

The reply could be along the following lines:

Your questions are very specific. You say nothing about your university's wider policies and practices regarding student conduct on campus. I hope they are subordinated to an effort to build an authentic Christian community. If students and other members of the university community considered themselves "dead to sin but alive to God in Christ Jesus" (Rom 6.11), you would not have a problem about which on-campus crimes to report to the police. Moreover, any Christian community's sound moral instruction and pastoral care of its members should help them form and reform themselves so that the remedies of its internal discipline and public criminal process will not often be required.

Reporting violations of the law to police obviously has a different significance where the laws and legal procedures are regarded as just than where these are considered unjust. In responding to your question, therefore, I shall assume that the laws whose violation is in question are those of a generally just polity—for example, one of the liberal democracies—not those of a thoroughly oppressive regime, such as Hitler's Germany.

The set of questions you propose really is complicated, since it involves complex relationships among individuals, a voluntary association to which they belong, that community's authorities, the wider society, and the public authorities. The common goods of both the university community and the wider society must be respected and served; and the goods of justice and fellowship are at stake in diverse ways. Probably there is no single set of right answers. but, plainly, there are some wrong ones. I shall try here to clarify the issues and mark out some boundaries. Within those boundaries, colleges and universities (from now on, for brevity's sake, "colleges") reasonably differ in their policies and procedures.

Some might argue that mercy should characterize a Catholic college's handling of its members' criminal misbehavior, so that most offenses will be treated leniently, offenders who seem contrite almost always will be given another chance, and sympathy for the individual often will prevail over the requirements of rules and laws. It is true that Christian mercy rightly understood—love overcoming evil—should motivate and shape what the college does in this as in other matters. But authentic mercy never sets aside the requirements of the common good or the rights of victims and potential victims (see q. 18, above). Therefore, a Catholic college's policies and procedures for dealing with criminal misbehavior should not be permissive, indulgent, or arbitrary. Only by being a model of justice will they be truly merciful.

Moreover, members of a Catholic community charged with protecting rights and the common good should not be deterred from seeking justice by the fear of being, or seeming to be, judgmental (see *LCL,* 312–13). Though God "forbids us to make judgments about the internal guilt of anyone" (GS 28), he gives some the authority to articulate and enforce just standards of outward behavior (see Rom 13.1–5). If those entrusted with that authority fail to exercise it, they themselves share responsibility not only for the wrongdoing invited by their negligence but for its many foreseeable bad consequences in this world and the next.

College administrators should of course obtain legal advice in developing policies and designing procedures. They also should involve both local public authorities and all segments of the college community as fully as possible, and should do their best to reconcile opposing views, so that the results will be supported by a very broad and firm consensus. Only with such a foundation is a policy or procedure likely to enjoy the general respect it will need if it is to be conducive to the common good.

All private groups—families, churches, business organizations, and so on— have their own internal discipline, including a set of more or less clearly articulated norms and processes for enforcing them. While directed toward the private group's limited common good, this discipline is analogous to the criminal law of political society and to some extent overlaps with it. For, although the common good of political society and that of a private group, being distinct, set many different requirements for their members' behavior, any group whatsoever must insist on certain requirements if it is to be a decent human community.

No private group within a political society is an enclave exempt from public laws and legal processes. The jurisdiction of public authorities extends to crimes committed in the privacy of one's home, in a house of worship, in a factory or place of business, on a college campus, and so on. In general, citizens should cooperate with the criminal justice system. An important element of this responsibility is the moral duty—which sometimes also is a legal duty—to report not only known criminal activities but even probable ones.

This duty, however, is not absolute. It is limited by certain exceptions, two categories of which are relevant to your questions. First, often because of a policy based on practical considerations, though rarely because of the letter of the law, prosecutors and police allow a crime's victim to decide in certain types of cases whether the violator will be prosecuted, that is, they let the victim decide whether to "press charges." In types of cases where that is known to be the public prosecutor's practice, a victim persuaded that prosecution will not be in the true interests of those concerned need not inform public authorities of the crime, and others aware of the crime also have no responsibility to report it. Second, even conscientious people who are aware of many sorts of illegal activities by members of their own families and by various associates often put off informing the public authorities while admonishing the criminal to repent, make amends, and abide by the law in the future. Such a delay in reporting seldom is treated as a violation of legal duty.

In view of these exceptions to the duty to report criminal activities, those exercising authority in any private group use their own internal disciplinary process to deal with much—and perhaps even most—of the unlawful behavior among their members. In practice, the public authorities are called upon only when that is necessary to provide protection against outsiders, to reinforce the limited power of the group's internal discipline, and to deal with crimes so serious that not to report them might itself be regarded as a crime or an injustice to members of the larger community.

In colleges, the general tendency to deal privately with unlawful behavior was reinforced in times past by the assumptions that students are minors, not fully responsible for their own behavior, and that a college's administrators exercise guardianship over its students on their parents' behalf. College discipline extended to many aspects of students' lives, being directed not only to the common good of the academic community but to each student's personal welfare. Since the 1960s, however, people of college age have come to be classed as adults, with the result that much of the traditional discipline has vanished from college campuses. This development can be considered reasonable only if it is carried through consistently, so that students who enjoy all the rights and privileges of adults are not extended the indulgence and special protections appropriate only for children (see q. 163, above). Consequently, there no longer is a special reason for a college to shelter students who commit crimes from the workings of the criminal justice system. In general, college administrators should deal with unlawful behavior on campus much as management does in a factory or place of business. Such a general policy, of course, in no way negates a college's responsibility, flowing from its specific common good, to discipline its students and other members in ways very different from those appropriate in a factory or office.

On this basis, should a college's general policy be to report all unlawful behavior to the public authorities? I doubt it, for if that were the policy, it probably would be appropriate to make exceptions to it more often than to adhere to it. Many violations will be of a sort that public authorities do not prosecute unless the victim presses charges, and the victim, whether a member of the college community or the community itself often will prefer not to do so. In still other cases, where public authorities tolerate having members of groups remain silent about other members' unlawful behavior while trying to bring about their reform, a college's authorities often will prefer this approach, especially when, as often happens, the circumstances seem to mitigate a student's responsibility for an infraction. In other cases, however, either the common good of political society or of the college itself, or fairness to individuals who have been or might be gravely harmed by unlawful behavior, or the criminal's own true self-interest will require that he or she be subjected to the sanctions of criminal law. Then it will be unjustifiable to make any exception to the duty to report unlawful activity. Moreover, if the college chooses not to use its own disciplinary process to deal with unlawful behavior or that process proves ineffective, indefinite delay in reporting criminal activity is unjustifiable. For example, if colleges tolerate continuing violent and destructive behavior by students, they fail to fulfill their responsibilities not only to their own common good and that of the larger society but their duty to protect and correct their members.

In view of the complexity of the matter, it probably should be the college's policy always to report to the public authorities only certain specified types of unlawful behavior, and to make sure everyone on campus knows and understands this policy; at the same time, the college must keep open the option of reporting other instances of unlawful behavior when its internal discipline proves inadequate to cope with them or a reasonable effort to induce a wrongdoer to reform is fruitless. Where a policy of this sort is in place, I think it will be appropriate to report to the public authorities every instance in which there is a good reason to believe unlawful behavior of any of the specified types has occurred, and not just cases in which this is obvious or virtually certain. For deciding whether someone probably has committed a crime should be left to the public authorities, who are assigned that responsibility by law.

In specifying the types of unlawful behavior that will be reported, I do not think it would be helpful to use broad categories, such as crimes against persons, crimes against property, and so-called victimless crimes. Crimes against persons include both assault with a deadly weapon and simple assault or battery; surely the former always should be reported, while probably the latter usually should not be, since that would mean calling the police every time a student is slightly injured in a fight with another student. Again, vandalism, a crime against property, varies in seriousness according to the extent of the damage; probably a line should be drawn, so that serious instances (for example, slashing tires) always will be reported but not every minor incident (for example, smashing a light bulb in a dormitory hall).

Similarly, it is one thing for a student to use an illegal drug, another for someone on campus to stock and distribute illegal drugs.

Besides, in specifying some types of unlawful behavior that always will be reported, a sound policy will take into account the importance of mutual respect between students, faculty, administrators, and other college employees. A fist fight involving two students is one thing; similar behavior involving a student and some other member of the college community is quite another. In a Catholic institution, moreover, the policy on reporting offenses should take into account the religious significance of criminal behavior that aggravates its gravity by the standards of the college community even if not by those of the wider society. For example, vandalism that involves sacrilege—such as the desecration of the chapel or a crucifix in a classroom—regardless of the monetary value of the damage could rightly be listed as a crime not only to be dealt with severely by the college's disciplinary process but always to be reported to the public authorities.

Should students be encouraged to report incidents to police? Considering how private groups usually operate, I do not think you should encourage them to report every law violation, but only instances of the kinds specified by the established policy. However, they should be told that their status as students in no way limits their right to invoke the police power of the state and they always should feel free to report anything they believe to be unlawful behavior, whether it occurs on or off campus. Certainly, the college's fear of bad publicity should not lead to discouraging students from reporting law violations, and nobody should be made to feel disloyal to the college community for calling the police about an incident on campus.

Obviously, a college's internal disciplinary process will be morally acceptable only if it involves a serious effort to be fair to everyone concerned and a reasonable likelihood of arriving at judgments based on the truth. These conditions require at least that those alleging violations be heard respectfully and treated as gently as possible; that the accused be presumed innocent, notified of the charges and possible penalties, given reasonable time to prepare to respond, given access to evidence and/or testimony supporting the charge, and permitted to present evidence and/or testimony tending to rebut the accusation or mitigate the offense; that no case be heard by a party to it; that the person presiding over the process seek to ensure its fairness; that a single accuser's unsupported testimony be presumed insufficient to find an accused guilty; that those adjudicating a case reach their decision solely on the basis of relevant evidence, testimony, and arguments; that the accused be informed of the decision reached and the reasons for it; that the proceedings be conducted in private and remain confidential so as to minimize burdens and injury to victims and other innocent parties; and that a record (though not necessarily a recording or transcript) of the process be made for use by the college president or other person empowered to consider an appeal, the public authorities, and others with a right to the information.

Nevertheless, I think you are right in rejecting the view that your disciplinary process should have all the features of due process in criminal law. It must be sufficiently workable, economical, and efficient to serve the common good of the college community, and it could not do this if it were as cumbersome as criminal due process—for example, with respect to the right to counsel and the admissibility of confessions and evidence. A less elaborate process can be fair, especially since the ultimate sanction—a student's expulsion or an employee's dismissal—is not so severe as the ultimate sanctions of criminal law. So, when unlawful behavior of the more serious kinds regularly reported to the public authorities also violates the college's standards, I see no injustice if the perpetrator is found guilty and punished by the college's disciplinary process even while escaping the sanctions of criminal law. At the same time, in dealing with serious crimes, the inevitable limits of the disciplinary system—not least, its sanctions—point to the inappropriateness of trying to use it in place of criminal law and its processes.

Finally, it seems to me that all members of the college community—students, faculty, administrators, and other employees—should be treated alike in the matter of reporting unlawful behavior to the public authorities. Moreover, the college should not apply its own discipline against criminal misbehavior by some members (for example, students or employees) while tolerating the same kinds of misbehavior by others (for example, faculty or administrators). Still, members of each group have different roles and responsibilities within the institution, so that its common good calls for somewhat diverse internal disciplinary processes and rules for each group. Trying to apply the same internal disciplinary process and rules to everyone also would conflict with procedures generally accepted in the academic world for dealing with the misbehavior of faculty members and, perhaps, with rules governing the treatment of unionized employees.

168: May a whole group be held liable for the wrongdoing of some?

As dean of students, I have a question to which I have never found a satisfactory solution: When some members of a group of students, a few or many as the case may be, are not behaving properly, is it fair to punish everyone or, at least, make the entire group suffer the consequences? Most students, naturally, say it is unfair. But there are various kinds of cases in which faculty members or administrators argue that it is fair.

Last year, for instance, the librarian, who has the power to impose fines of up to fifty dollars for any abuse of library privileges, fined every graduate student twenty-five dollars. Previously only staff and faculty had access to the room where recent issues of periodicals are stored until bound, but last year all graduate students were given keys. Despite being warned not to leave the door unlocked, some apparently were careless, and during the fall semester undergraduates often were found in the room. Nothing was missing and no damage was done, but the librarian was determined to keep the undergraduates out. At the beginning of the spring semester he fined all the graduate students and warned them he would do the same thing every semester unless the door was kept locked. It worked, but the graduate students complained bitterly to me.

Another example occurred a few years ago when my predecessor punished the whole senior class by canceling their baccalaureate dinner dance. That was a drastic move, and I do not think I would have done it; the members of that class have consistently given less than any other to annual alumni fund raising. Still, I understand his motivation. That class always had been unruly, and the administration had been forced to take unusual measures to try to keep some semblance of order at its events. Despite all precautions, the class's last scheduled affair before the dinner dance, an April Fools masked ball, ended in disaster when some of the fools got into a fight, campus security was called, and a melee ensued in which the guards were beaten up and one of them was seriously injured. There also was more than twenty thousand dollars worth of damage to the gym.

Still another example is the way our basketball coach trains his players to avoid fouls. All the players detest calisthenics. The coach does not schedule them at the beginning of practice sessions, as most coaches do, but instead has the squad playing basketball right from the start. Whenever a player makes a mistake that would draw a foul in a game, though, the coach makes everyone stop and do ten push-ups or sit-ups or some other exercise. Then all the players get after the offender. At first some players complain bitterly that the coach is being unfair, but his approach seems to work, and complaints die down when the team begins winning games.

Then there are things that are not exactly punishment, but involve more or less the same problem. For example, many professors would like to limit examinations to the final and avoid quizzes. But they give reading assignments students must do to prepare for class. Finding that some students come to class unprepared, they reluctantly begin quizzing the class on the readings. Many of our better students resent this, feeling that they are being treated like school children merely because other students are too lazy or disorganized to do the reading assignments regularly.

Last but not least is the perennial problem about billing students for damage in the residence halls. Of course, there is no problem when those responsible come forward or are identified. But very often it is impossible to identify the guilty party. Undoubtedly, students often know who the culprits are, but they are reluctant to tell on one another. We therefore put it in the housing contract that the cost of repairing damage inside a unit will be divided among all those sharing it, the cost of damage on a corridor will be divided among those living there, and the cost of damage in any other area will be divided among everyone in the building. Many students regard this as unfair, especially when charged for damage that may well have been done by a student living elsewhere or even by a visitor from off campus. Still, someone must pay. Students often argue we should charge it off to general operating expenses. But then every student would pay an equal share, and that hardly seems fair, since different groups of students tend to concentrate in certain places, and there are consistent differences in the levels of damage in the various dorms.

Though there is nothing in the rules about damage to the gym, my predecessor charged the whole senior class for the cost of repairing the damage resulting from the April Fools affair mentioned above. Many students were especially bitter about that, because each had to pay forty dollars, including some who were not at the dance and many others who left before the trouble began or when it started.

Analysis:

This question calls for the articulation and application of norms for just punishment. Strictly understood, punishment is some loss or harm authoritatively imposed on a person in response to his or her wrongdoing. Punishment is wrongful unless it is intended to restore justice and is appropriate for that purpose. So, it never is just to punish a group for the wrongdoing of some of its members unless their wrongdoing constitutes a wrongful act of the group as such. If not all members have been proved guilty of complicity in a wrongful act, punishing the whole group to deter wrongdoing by its members is using a bad means to a good end. Misbehavior in a group should be dealt with not by punishment but by instruction, exhortation, sound rule making, careful investigation of infractions, and strict enforcement. Still, when a privilege extended to a group is abused by some unidentifiable members, the privilege may be withdrawn to safeguard the common good.

The reply could be along the following lines:

Punishment sometimes refers to rough handling or mistreatment totally unrelated to wrongdoing and often refers to various forms of discipline repugnant to the individual subjected to them—for example, chastising of a child or pet by inflicting slight pain or brief isolation. Strictly understood, however, punishment is some loss or harm authoritatively imposed on a person in response to his or her willful wrongdoing (see *LCL,* 891).

If punishment, strictly understood, is to be fair, it must be intended by the authority to promote the community's common good by restoring justice and must be suited to that purpose. When wrongs are done, wrongdoers incur a debt to society, and law-abiding people want them to pay the price of their wrongdoing. Sometimes anger about wrongs and hatred toward wrongdoers lead to demands for revenge. Acting on such motives, however, is always immoral, and so it can never restore the balance of justice. But that balance can be restored, not by taking revenge on wrongdoers, but by making them suffer what displeases them so as to restore balance with others who, in acting responsibly, have given up some degree of freedom to do as they please.[374]

Punishment may be used with the hope of reforming the wrongdoer and/or deterring others. Provided punishments are intended to restore justice and are suited to that end, these purposes also can rightly be intended. Neither, however, provides an adequate principle for just punishment. The reformation of wrongdoers need not involve inflicting any loss or harm, and may have little to do with what they have done, except that the wrongful behavior manifests their need for help. Treating a wrongdoer in such a way as to deter others will be unjust unless that treatment also is appropriate to restore the balance of justice.

374. See John Finnis, *Natural Law and Natural Rights* (Oxford: Oxford University Press, 1980), 262–64.

Strictly speaking, then, it can never be fair to punish an entire group for the wrongdoing of some of its members, unless those members' wrongdoing constitutes a wrongful act of the group as a whole. Yet sometimes common agency is wrongly attributed to a group, and all members are held responsible for acts that are neither acts of the group nor of each and every one of its members. Unfairly punishing a group's members who in no way share responsibility for wrongs done by other members perverts punishment and is counterproductive. By treating wrongdoers and law-abiding people alike, it increases the imbalance between them rather than overcoming it.

Someone might object that, while group punishment generally is unjust, in exceptional cases it can be just, since one purpose of punishment is deterrence, and sometimes only group punishment will deter. For example, on pleasant days when many windows are open, some of the men in a certain dorm harass women walking by outside by shouting obscene remarks. The women cannot identify the guilty parties and, despite exhortations by the dean of students, the men living in the dorm will not identify them. So, the objection goes on, the dean calls in the student identification cards of all the men residing on that side of the offending dorm, which means none of them can attend college events or get into the campus pub. The penalty works; the harassment ends and the cards are returned. My answer nevertheless is that, while deterrence often is among punishment's purposes, punishment may not be used for deterrence or anything else unless it is just in itself, that is, fair recompense for wrongdoing. Calling in the identification cards of a whole group of men to deter harassment by some is using an unjust penalty to prevent wrongdoing—a bad means to a good end.

Perhaps someone will respond: If other members of the group were not in solidarity with those shouting the obscenities, peer pressure would soon end the harassment; and if other members fail to identify the wrongdoers as they should, the whole group is justly punished on that basis. My answer is that, while some or even most other members of the group may be implicated in the wrongdoing by supporting it or failing to fulfill their duty to try to stop it, punishing this group as a whole cannot be justified unless each and every member's complicity is not merely plausibly supposed but proved. (Note, too, that group punishment often is not an effective deterrent and may even be counterproductive, since people's sense of being punished unjustly can provoke them to share in the misbehavior that deserves punishment.)

In cases of this sort, the proper approach is twofold: instruct the group about the wrongness of the behavior and everyone's responsibility to do what he or she can to stop it, and diligently enforce appropriate rules with adequate sanctions. Rather than calling in the identification cards of the whole group of men, the dean of students should have explained to them (and everyone on the campus) why the harassment is wrong and why anyone who sees the wrongness of shouting obscene remarks at women passing by should urge the guilty parties to stop and, if necessary, report them. If there was no adequate rule against this form of harassment, the dean at the same time should have promulgated a rule with a severe penalty, used appropriate means to identify at least some culprits, and punished them.

The case in which your predecessor "punished" the whole senior class by canceling their baccalaureate dinner dance is ambiguous. Perhaps he did intend the cancellation as punishment; if so, it was unjust. But he could have had, and perhaps did have, a different motivation: to prevent another disaster. According to your account, the class always had been unruly and special efforts already had been made to prevent trouble at its events. Such efforts having failed at the April Fools affair, it may well have been reasonable to judge canceling the baccalaureate dinner dance the necessary means to prevent more trouble, perhaps including additional serious injuries. In that case, the cancellation was fully justified—not as punishment, however, but as a necessary safety measure.

Your basketball coach's way of training players to avoid fouls is not ambiguous. The calisthenics he requires whenever a player makes a mistake are not punishment. Although they could be used as such, they are imposed, not for wrongdoing, but for mistakes. Moreover, since other coaches start practice sessions with calisthenics, the exercises are, not mere imposed suffering, but an appropriate part of the athletes' conditioning, and your coach surely is using them for this purpose. Unlike other coaches, he also is using them to develop teamwork. In games that count, each player's mistakes harm the whole team, and so every player must learn to avoid fouls. Individuals' mistakes in practice sessions need not trouble others, however, so the coach, rather than using the calisthenics as punishment, has another purpose in mind: to get the players into the habit of putting the team first by making individuals' mistakes the occasion for exercises which, though detested by all, would be an element of their training in any case.

Of course, this approach can be abused—for example, by making excessive and even harmful demands on people. Sometimes coaches, drill sergeants, and the like push people too far, perhaps even to a point where one suspects them of sadism. However, such excesses are possible even when the need to burden individuals for the success of a common effort is such that there is no question of group punishment. For example, when the band practices, the band master might require it to play a piece over and over until it is done flawlessly. This means skillful players must bear the burden of helping train those who make mistakes. When the band master says, "Let's play it again, and this time no mistakes!" nobody considers it punishment, though there may be audible groans. Still, if the practice session is extended so long that the band's members begin collapsing from hunger and fatigue, the band master has gone too far.

As you say, group punishment is not at issue when professors feel compelled to quiz a class because some of its members neglect to do assigned readings by way of preparation. In some cases, that step is analogous to the band master's requiring the group to play a piece over and over, for if the effectiveness of the class's meetings depends heavily on student participation, the common purpose will be impeded unless everyone is ready to contribute. In other cases, quizzing the whole class may be justified by the considerable benefit to those who need this motivation—and, to be realistic, even the best students do at times.

Of course, unreasonable demands sometimes are made in cases like this, too. To be fair, professors should not assign more work in preparation for each session of a course than they reasonably judge virtually every student can do passably without slighting any other responsibilities—not least, the responsibility to meet the legitimate requirements of other courses. Moreover, professors should be certain all assignments really contribute to the development of the course and are likely to be fruitful for most students. Then too, sometimes a professor finds that particular students receive little or no benefit from a burdensome requirement and can relieve them of it; in fairness the professor should do that.

How to bill students for damage caused by unidentifiable individuals in the residence halls is a perplexing problem. Your practice of including in the housing contract an explanation of how damage will be billed no doubt helps mitigate student resentment. But it does not ensure that the system is fair, since many students probably agree to pay the bills for damage only because they have no alternative to living on campus, and some may not realize what sorts of charges the housing contract will require them to pay. Nevertheless, assuming that some student or group of students sooner or later must cover the cost of all such damage, and provided students are free to choose the group among whom they will live, I do not think it necessarily unfair to assess charges as you do. For if a representative group of present and future students were asked to propose something fairer (and it might be worthwhile for you to convene such a group from time to time and put the question to them), I doubt they would find a more acceptable alternative.

Nevertheless, it seems to me that in fact the system may well be unfair, not because there is a more equitable way of allocating charges for damage, but because the college may be failing to do all it should to deal with the problem of damage. As you say, other students probably often know who the culprits are but are reluctant to tell on them. To remedy this situation, you should explain to the students that everyone suffers as a result of such damage, everyone would benefit by reducing its extent, and everyone can help do that by refraining from causing damage, taking responsibility for any damage he or she causes, admonishing others to do the same, and reporting those who selfishly refuse to cooperate.

The college also needs sound rules and diligent enforcement. Since the specifics must be appropriate to your situation, I offer the following only as a set of possible starting points.

When students do take responsibility for the damage they cause, it seems to me they should be billed only for the actual cost of repairs. When students fail to take responsibility and that is proven, they not only should be billed for the actual cost of repairs but punished severely—for example, required to perform the hours of work around the buildings and grounds that would earn at minimum wage a fine of one thousand dollars or ten times the cost of repairs, whichever is greater. Students deliberately and maliciously destroying either the college's or any member's property of significant value should be expelled, and their crime should be reported to the police and charges pressed. Campus security should be staffed by a sufficient number of adequately trained personnel to enforce these and other rules. Moreover, serious instances of property damage very often result from alcohol abuse, and the college may be negligent in enforcing reasonable rules in this matter; if so, a sound policy should be established and consistently enforced (see q. 163, above). If the college took steps such as these, property damage might well quickly dwindle to insignificance.

Finally, your predecessor plainly was unfair in recovering the cost of the damage resulting from the disastrous April Fools affair by billing every senior for an equal share of it, despite the fact that some members of the class were not at the dance, others already had left, and some left to avoid involvement in the melee. If he meant to punish the group, the charge patently was unfair, but even if he meant simply to recover the cost of the damages, it was unfair to impose the burden on the whole senior class, many of whose members plainly were not responsible for the damage, rather than treat it as current operating expense, which would have divided the cost among a far larger group. It would have been appropriate to conduct a vigorous investigation with a view to holding responsible those who were guilty, especially of beating up the security guards and seriously injuring one of them—offenses far more serious than property damage. But perhaps such an investigation was conducted without success.

In any case, the college owes restitution to the alumni who were unfairly charged forty dollars each for the damage on that occasion. Moreover, since what you say about alumni giving by members of that senior class indicates that your predecessor's handling of the affair was counterproductive, refunding the money with accrued interest and an apology very likely will be financially advantageous for the college in the long run.

169: May people whose government is grossly unjust evade income taxes?

My father has taught us to think about what is right and wrong. Up to now, after talking something over with him and thinking about it, I have been able to agree with him on things. But this time I can't agree with him, and I don't know what to do.

Dad has made a living for us by doing painting, repairs, and maintenance for homeowners and small businesses around town. I have been helping him Saturdays and vacations ever since I turned fourteen, and my younger brothers also began helping when they were old enough. Dad has not paid us for our work, but he always has seen to it that we had everything we needed and has given us many things we wanted. He also has been putting aside money to help us get a start in life.

I just graduated from St. Francis of Assisi High School, and I am not planning to go to college. I don't think I have a vocation to be a priest, but I want to live simply, as St. Francis and some other saints did. With Dad's help, I am going to find a place to live in a nearby town and try to make my living doing the kind of work he does.

When I begin earning money for myself, I don't think I should pay income taxes or support the government in any other way I can avoid. The Vietnam war was on when Dad got out of high school and, thinking it wrong, he went to jail for four years rather than be drafted. Today the U.S. is not involved in a war, but I think the government is so corrupt it would be just as wrong for me to pay taxes as it would have been for Dad to go to Vietnam.

Most people think the U.S. government is not so bad. But a political science course we had last year showed how great a country we could be but at the same time opened my eyes to a lot of things. The Supreme Court made abortion legal, and about a million and a half unborn babies are killed in this country every year, some at taxpayers' expense. A great deal of tax money has been and still is being spent for nuclear weapons meant to destroy an enemy society by wiping out whole cities, most of whose people are no threat to anybody. The public schools and state universities are supposed to be neutral about religion, but many of them undermine students' religious beliefs and teach them to live accordingly. People like my parents, who want a religious education for their children, get no public help, yet they have to pay taxes to support schools that won't serve their needs. A few years ago, the president had a hard time finding someone to be attorney general and filling other jobs, because he kept picking people who had cheated on their taxes and exploited illegal immigrants. Many public officials are caught cheating the people, and probably a lot more get away with it. And the U.S. uses its foreign aid to promote population control around the world.

I don't plan to tell the government I won't pay taxes. I never have had to file a tax return and I just won't start. Doing jobs for different people and getting paid for each job as I do it, I won't be employed by anybody. I will take only the work I can do by myself and won't hire anyone to help me. And I won't put money into anything paying interest.

I am not planning to spend everything I earn on myself. As Dad has done, I will keep track of what I spend for paint and other things, so I will know how much I am making. Then, like him, I will give ten percent of what I make to the Church. Each year I will work out what my federal and state income taxes would be; but instead of paying them, I will give at least that much to help some people who are being hurt by the government's corruption. For instance, some students have to drop out of St. Francis every year because their families can't afford the tuition, and I could give the tax money to the school to help one or more to stay.

Dad disagrees with me. Though he went to jail rather than go to Vietnam, he always has been very careful about paying taxes and thinks tax evasion is a sin. If you agree with him, I hope you can explain it, because to me it seems definitely wrong to support this country's corrupt government.

Analysis:

This question calls for application of the norm regarding tax evasion. The New Testament instructs Christians to pay taxes, and this moral instruction is still handed on by the Church's teaching. Though part of the money raised by taxation is used in doing evil, citizens generally may and should pay legally required taxes to support the good things even a bad government does. One might refuse to pay taxes as an act of civil disobedience, but that is not the questioner's plan. Under extreme conditions, some patriotic citizens could rightly withhold financial and other support from a bad government and try to serve the nation's common good by other means. But even then, lying would not be justified, and prolonged tax evasion is hardly likely to succeed without lying. Moreover, most citizens can rightly pay the taxes exacted by a bad government, in order to avoid punishment for not paying them.

The reply could be along the following lines:

Rome dominated the whole world of New Testament times, including Jesus' homeland. Devout Jews and Christians hardly considered Roman government good, for Rome not only oppressed and persecuted them but claimed for its empire and rulers a quasi-divine status that violated God's exclusive right to humankind's worship. Christians therefore looked forward to Rome's eventual destruction (see Rv 17–18). Nevertheless, the New Testament teaches Jesus' followers to pay legally required taxes.

The gospels record an exchange between Jesus and some people who confronted him with a question that seemed to create a dilemma: Should we pay taxes to the Roman emperor? A yes would offend his fellow Jews, a no, the Roman oppressors. Asking his challengers to produce the coin used to pay the tax, Jesus called their attention to the fact that it bore the image of the emperor and his inscription (which referred to him as "son of the divine Augustus"). By having and using the emperor's coin, these people implicitly acknowledged imperial authority, yet they were unwilling to believe in Jesus and acknowledge his divine authority. He therefore told them to give back to the emperor the things that are his (coins stamped with his image and an idolatrous claim) and to give God the things that are his (the obedience of faith, worship, and complete love: one's whole life and very self).[375]

Plainly, much more is conveyed by that exchange than that taxes should be paid even to a bad government. But if that were not true, what Jesus said would have been misleading. Moreover, St. Paul teaches that Christians should submit to rulers and pay taxes, because God gives rulers their authority so as to prevent and punish wrongdoing (see Rom 13.1–7; cf. 1 Pt 2.13–17). Handed down to us, this moral instruction remains part of the Church's teaching (see GS 30; *CCC*, 2238–40; *LCL*, 894–97).

You may find that teaching understandable if you reflect more deeply on your view that the government is so corrupt it would be as wrong for you to pay taxes as it would have been for your father to serve in Vietnam. True, the two are similar in one important respect—conscientious citizens are pressed by the law's threats of punishment to be involved in public acts they believe wrong. But participating in a war one believes wrong also differs in important ways from paying taxes to what one believes to be a bad government.

To begin with, though a war includes many small actions by individuals and groups, the whole war is one very large, complex action of the nation waging it. If a war is wrong, anyone actively and directly taking part in the fighting, or otherwise

---

375. See Mt 22.15–22, Mk 12.13–17, Lk 20.20–26; cf. Joseph A. Fitzmyer, S.J., *The Gospel According to Luke (X–XXIV): Introduction, Translation, and Notes,* Anchor Bible 28A Garden City, N.Y.: Doubleday, 1985), 1289–98.

trying to help win the war, becomes an accomplice in the bad action.[376] By contrast, a bad government is not a single action—indeed, not an action at all—but a social agent that does many different things. Though its bad acts do affect what it is, just as an individual's habitual and unrepented sins make him or her a bad person, even bad governments, like bad individuals, do many good things; and conscientious citizens can participate wholeheartedly in many actions (the good ones) of their bad government, just as conscientious individuals can participate wholeheartedly in many actions (the good ones) done by their bad relatives and associates.

This first difference points to another. Citizens who believe a war is wrong can avoid serving in it. Though likely to pay a price, as your father did, they can refuse to be accomplices in the evil. But unless they emigrate, citizens who think their government is corrupt cannot avoid being involved in political society and taking advantage of services it provides, such as protection against foreign and domestic threats. Even if one leaves one's homeland and goes to another country, one does not solve the problem, for some government is necessary and no government is perfect. Conscientious people cannot avoid being involved with one or another more or less bad government.

In the final analysis, however, a nation is not its government. A nation is a people living together in a region and sharing many common interests; a government is an organization needed by a nation to act for certain of its interests. Just as an individual may never deliberately commit any sin to achieve an ulterior end, however good, so not even to promote or protect its common interests may a nation ever fight a war that is wrong, insofar as that is one large bad action. But just as upright individuals can employ people who are sinners to achieve various goods, so a nation can and even must use its more or less bad government to protect and promote its common good (see *CCC*, 2242; *LCL*, 844–55).

Consequently, citizens can rightly pay required taxes to support the good things their nation does by means of government, even though the government uses some of the money to do bad things. In paying taxes, upright citizens intend to support the good things: many elements of national defense and law enforcement; regulation of prescription drugs, securities markets, interstate commerce; health care for the elderly, the disabled, and the poor; and so on. They do not intend to support the bad things, but simply accept misuses of their money they cannot prevent.

Of course, some people try to calculate what portion of government spending goes for various bad things, in order to withhold that percentage from their tax payment. But since one cannot designate the purposes for which one's taxes will be used, this strategy withholds some support not only from the misuses of public funds but from their good uses, to which support is due, while also still contributing to both the bad as well as the good. Bear in mind, too, that most people must accept the status of employees subject to tax withholding. Even if your plan for supporting yourself without attracting the attention of tax agents succeeds, few people who marry and have children could carry out such a plan and accept its financial constraints. And like any other evasion of taxes, not paying them to avoid support-

---

376. See *LCL*, 908–10; John Finnis, Joseph M. Boyle, Jr., and Germain Grisez, *Nuclear Deterrence, Morality and Realism* (Oxford: Oxford University Press, 1987), 342–64.

ing a bad government imposes an additional, unfair burden on citizens of modest means who cannot evade their taxes.

Another point, though incidental, is worth mention. When your father refused military service in the Vietnam war, he avoided fighting in a war he was convinced was unjust—something that would have been wrong in itself—and he openly defied the law and suffered the penalty. In that way he bore witness, unlike those who protested vehemently against the "unjust" war yet served when drafted so as not to go to jail. Though your plan to withhold taxes is conscientious rather than self-serving, carrying it out would not bear witness as your father's refusal to serve did. Quite the contrary. It would lead others who learned what you were doing and wished to evade taxes for selfish reasons to imagine themselves justified in doing so.

Of course, one might choose to withhold taxes openly and accept the consequences, precisely to bear witness, that is, as an act of civil disobedience (see *LCL,* 883–84). But that would hardly satisfy anyone sharing your view that it is wrong to pay taxes. Indeed, since open violation of tax laws invites tax agents to collect the amount due with interest and penalties, it is more appropriate for someone who thinks people should pay their taxes to practice civil disobedience by publicly refusing to pay.

One nevertheless can imagine extreme conditions under which citizens would be obliged to withhold taxes and other support from a government so deeply corrupt as to be no longer useful as a means of serving the nation's common good. In 1945, for example, Germans certainly had no obligation to support the Nazi government that faced imminent defeat, and citizens morally free and able to weaken that government and hasten its downfall by denying it their support should have recognized a patriotic duty to do so. Indeed, conscientious German citizens should have perceived such a duty even before 1945; and some did and fled the country, not only to save themselves but to serve their nation by opposing the Nazis.

Of course, patriotic citizens who continue to live under a government bad in various ways, but not as vulnerable and corrupt as the Nazi government, might at some point judge, rightly or wrongly but conscientiously, that they should no longer support their government by paying taxes. Being patriotic, they will do what they can to serve their nation's common good by means that do not involve the government. That appears to be the idea behind your plan to use what you otherwise would pay in taxes to help at least some of the people who are being hurt by the government's corruption.

Bad as the U.S. government is, however, it still serves the nation's authentic interests in many matters. Moreover, it is hardly likely to give way to anything less bad, because evils such as legalized abortion that have been read into the Constitution enjoy widespread support. You could join with others in trying to mitigate those evils through the political process. But what you have in mind is not a form of political action.

Besides, even if your plan were morally acceptable in other respects, you would sin if you did anything intrinsically evil in carrying it out. But lying is intrinsically evil, and you could hardly evade taxes year after year without sometimes lying.

By contrast, paying taxes need not be anything more than handing over one's money under duress, and that is not a sort of action wrong in itself. It need not be wrong to hand over money to very bad people likely to put it to very wicked uses. For example, one might give one's wallet to a robber—"Your money or your life!"—or pay ransom to a kidnapper, intending to forestall a threatened evil and foreseeing little likely benefit in resisting. Similarly, though your father could not serve in a war he considered unjust, he and other good people, anticipating little or no benefit from trying to evade taxes, could pay them even to a very bad government, intending only to avoid penalties that would harm themselves and their dependents.

One last thought. You say you wish to live simply, as some of the saints did. Even though the evangelical poverty of the saints imposed some burdens on others, it was justified as prophetic witness to important truths about the kingdom.[377] You also could bear powerful witness to the truth about the difference between worldly governments and God's reign. And by not having taxable income, you could avoid paying taxes without evading them. You might be able to do this in at least two ways.

One would be to limit the net income you earn each year to a sum that, with legitimate deductions and exemptions, would fall just below the minimum that is subject to income taxes. Could you subsist on so little income? Perhaps, if you gathered, begged, and produced for yourself—perhaps on a small subsistence farm—many of the necessities of life. Then too, you would qualify for various public programs to aid the poor, and you could justly take advantage of them provided you bore clear witness by your lifestyle against the government's wrongdoing and used a substantial part of your time and energy in serving the nation's common good—for example, by working to mitigate some of the injustices you rightly deplore.

Again, assuming you are right in thinking you do not have a vocation to be a priest, you might have a vocation to be a brother in some community—perhaps the Franciscans—that welcomes men called to religious life but not ordination. Life as a brother in a sound community would fulfill your wish to live simply. The sort of work you plan to do would make a welcome contribution to many communities. Finally, living in accord with your vow of poverty, you would have no personal income, and so, without violating the law, you would pay no income taxes.

170: May homeowners oppose rezoning to allow nearby lower-cost housing?

When we bought our home in the suburbs four years ago, the county's master plan for the area extending more than half a mile in every direction from our house required single-family homes on lots at least 75 by 160 feet. Most of the area has been developed accordingly. However, the plan was amended just after we moved in to allow a commercial strip a little over a third of a mile east of us, and the land

377. See LG 42–44, PC 13; John Paul II, *Vita consecrata*, 89–90, *AAS* 88 (1996) 465–6; *OR,* 3 Apr. 1996, xvii.

between that strip and the street that intersects ours, just five houses away, has remained undeveloped. Now that land's prospective developer is asking for a zoning variance to allow narrower blocks and much denser housing: six-unit sets of small town houses along the streets near us and solid rows of three-story apartment buildings along those ending at the commercial strip. The town houses would sell for about two-thirds the value of our house, and the apartments would rent with subsidies for low-income families.

If the rezoning is approved, the would-be developer would reap far more profit than under the present requirements; he claims the rezoning is necessary to allow a reasonable profit, since the development will require more grading than other parcels in the area. He has gained the support of several regional employers, who hope the availability of cheaper housing will attract applicants for lower paying jobs. They argue that their contribution to the local economy entitles them to the county's cooperation. The rezoning also has the well-financed backing of a local group called "The Affordable Housing Alliance," whose president, Aarona Zyx, also is the chair of our parish's justice and peace group. Mrs. Zyx and most of the others active in the AHA live in an enclave west of us, lying between a lake and a public park; it is fully developed with single-family homes worth three to six times as much as ours.

Just about everyone in our neighborhood civic association opposes the rezoning. The denser, lower-cost housing not only will result in a larger population, making the area more crowded and busier, but will create an economically poorer neighborhood, with all the usual problems. That will reduce our properties' value, because most buyers prefer a neighborhood without nearby lower-cost housing. The rezoning also will mean a tax increase. The new development will not enlarge the tax base enough to pay for the new schoolrooms and additional county services its residents will require.

I think these concerns are reasonable. My husband and I chose to live here to raise our children outside the troubled urban environment. We work hard and limit our other spending to meet our house payments, which go up when taxes increase. We relied on the county's master plan when we decided to buy, and I regard it as a promise that should be kept.

The AHA maintains that all new developments should help bring about neighborhoods with greater socioeconomic diversity, and Mrs. Zyx dismisses our concerns as selfishness. She argues that leaving people who cannot afford a single-family house living in a "ghetto of run-down housing" is unfair to them and divisive for the community. Apparently referring to our neighborhood, she says: "With homogeneous neighborhoods, diverse people, denied the opportunity to become good neighbors, go on fearing and hating one another." Developing the regional employers' view, she claims denying the rezoning would be unfair to those who would come to work and live here if there were affordable housing. Finally, she maintains that talk about the troubled urban environment and the problems of poorer neighborhoods is "nothing but a cryptic appeal to racial prejudice." Speaking as chair of the parish's justice and peace group, Mrs. Zyx also has said that the

AHA's view agrees with the gospel and Catholic social teaching, while our neighborhood civic association's position is in conflict with them.

What do you think? I realize I am not impartial, and I am open to correction. But I am not impressed with Mrs. Zyx's arguments and find her comments about racial prejudice annoying. By contrast with her solidly white neighborhood, ours is racially integrated, with over four percent African-Americans and nearly as many Asian-Americans, sprinkled fairly evenly among the whites, and all of us getting along very well together.

Analysis:

This question calls for the application of norms of social justice and for judgment by the Golden Rule. A reasonable judgment on the matter can only be made by considering all the facts and competing interests from the points of view of all those concerned, not least the people who would occupy the new housing. The community has a serious responsibility to help meet the need of less affluent families for affordable housing. God gave humankind the land, like other created goods, for everyone's use, and the poor deserve others' special consideration. Then too, everyone should seek to establish and build up communion among people of diverse gifts and potentialities. Moreover, Christians should be not only fair but merciful, and so, when other responsibilities permit, should subordinate their own legitimate interests to those of others. Still, these general norms do not clearly entail that the questioner and other members of the neighborhood civic association should support the proposed rezoning. Some compromise might well be fair.

The reply could be along the following lines:

I understand and sympathize with your concerns about the possible adverse effects of the proposed development on your family's interests. In view of those legitimate concerns, your readiness to entertain another, disinterested view of the problem is commendable. I hope my reflections will help you form your conscience in accord with your faith, as you plainly desire to do.

The moral issue on which proponents and opponents of the proposed rezoning disagree is whether proceeding with the planned development would be fair to all concerned. One cannot reasonably judge about that without considering all the facts and competing interests from the points of view of all the concerned parties.

Arguments on both sides involve questionable factual claims that should be examined critically and, if possible, made more precise. Additional information probably would establish or rebut some claims; others are more or less plausible. but hardly open to definitive proof or disproof.

The claim of the potential developer that the rezoning is necessary to allow a reasonable profit hardly deserves consideration if he gambled on rezoning in obtaining the land. His claim also can be tested by determining the prospective margin of profit likely to be realized in this way and comparing it with the margin realized by other developers in the area. The employers' claim that lower-cost housing is needed so that they can attract an adequate number of applicants for lower-paying jobs can be tested by investigating the availability of unemployed people who already live in the area or could commute from surrounding communities.

Your claim that the increased population will result in excessive crowding is vague. Exactly what burdens would be placed on present residents in their use of various facilities? The claim that the new, less affluent neighborhood will have "all the usual problems" of economically poorer neighborhoods also is vague and will be fallacious unless the comparison is with closely similar neighborhoods. Try to identify serious problems that regularly occur in new, suburban neighborhoods as comparable as possible in density and other respects with the one to be created by the proposed development. Evidence also is required that the proposed development will reduce the value of current residents' properties, and showing the probable extent and persistence of that loss. Similarly, the claim that your taxes will go up should be tested by analyzing the costs and revenues the development will generate, not only in the short term, but over an extended period. Finally, your claim that the county's master plan is a promise that should be kept is questionable. I doubt that the county gave assurances that it would neither amend the plan nor make exceptions. If not, in what ways and to what extent did its presentation of the plan warrant your reliance on its remaining unchanged?

Mrs. Zyx's assumption that denying the rezoning will leave people who cannot afford single-family homes dwelling in a "ghetto of run-down housing" likewise is vague. It requires evidence about the present housing of the people likely to move into the proposed development and alternatives currently available to them. The claim that diverse people living in separate, homogeneous neighborhoods "go on fearing and hating one another" and the accompanying assumption that the proposed development would reduce fear and hatred would deserve acceptance if they were applicable to your neighborhood and verified by your experience. But you indicate that your neighborhood is not entirely homogeneous and that residents get along well together. So, that claim and assumption need not be taken seriously without substantial evidence gathered by serious sociological studies and shown to be relevant to the present issue. Finally, her argument that talk about the "troubled urban environment" and the "problems of poorer neighborhoods" is "nothing but a cryptic appeal to racial prejudice" presupposes evidence that those speaking that way are appealing to racial prejudice rather than expressing sincere concerns, perhaps reasonable and perhaps not, about the likely behavior of less affluent people of whatever race.

The arguments of the potential developer, regional employers, and members of the neighborhood civic association are self-interested, but they could be sound. Even if unsound, however, they are not necessarily selfish; some or all of these parties could be sincere and fair-minded. If Mrs. Zyx dismisses the arguments of members of the civic association as mere selfishness, that response is ad hominem and not a sound argument. But your remarks about her type and place of residence also are ad hominem. However, she could have asked: Have you and your neighbors put yourselves in the place of the people who would occupy the new housing? And you might ask her whether she has put herself in your and your neighbors' place see *CMP*, 211–14; *LCL*, 282–84).

The county does have a serious responsibility to help meet less affluent families' needs, not least their need for decent, affordable housing. That responsibility might be fulfilled, at least in part, if all new developments were designed to create neighborhoods with greater socioeconomic diversity, as the AHA advocates. It is not clear, however, that socioeconomically homogeneous neighborhoods are inherently unfair to less affluent families or divisive to the community. People of different races probably live harmoniously together in your neighborhood partly because their socioeconomic similarity involves many common values and interests. Moreover, though segregation imposed on the basis of race is unjust and all discrimination on that basis should be regarded as suspect, not all separations among various groups of people need be unjust. Some are not imposed by unjust discrimination but are established by common agreement as mutually acceptable distancing to promote peace and allow similar people to associate agreeably.

Thus, while Mrs. Zyx plainly is trying to articulate a real requirement of justice, other arguments, more clearly grounded in the gospel and Catholic social teaching, can more forcefully show the community's responsibility with regard to the housing needs of less affluent families.

God created the whole subhuman world for human beings. He provides all material goods for everyone's use, so that all people can meet their genuine needs (see GS 69; *LCL,* 788–92). The poor, having great needs difficult or impossible for them to meet, deserve special consideration. The affluent and powerful owe the poor help to ensure that they receive their fair share of material goods (see *LCL,* 799–801). The need for decent housing is genuine and basic; the less affluent ought to have a fair share of desirable land to live on. So, while you and other members of your civic association have a legitimate interest in maintaining the value of your property and the quality of your area, you also must help less affluent people meet their need for housing.[378]

Moreover, as children of God called to heavenly fulfillment in the kingdom, all human beings share the same essential dignity. We are called to love others as Jesus has loved us. When asked, "Who is my neighbor?" Jesus answered with the story of the Good Samaritan. Its point is that we ought to make a neighbor of anyone in need, not limit our concern to someone we already recognize as a neighbor (see *LCL,* 308–9, 365–66). You and others in your area should be ready to welcome as neighbors at least some less affluent people who need decent housing, and you should be thinking about ways to help them become good neighbors, for their sakes and yours. If you succeed in building up good neighborliness among people differing more widely in their needs and gifts, the community as a whole and the lives of all its members will be enriched. The value of that achievement will not pass away; the good fruit of your effort will serve as material for the heavenly kingdom, where good neighbors will live together forever (see GS 38–39).

---

378. Used to evade this duty, exclusionary zoning is unjust; see William Tucker, *The Excluded Americans: Homelessness and Housing Policies* (Washington, D.C.: Regnery Gateway, 1990), 111–39; Constance Perin, *Everything in Its Place: Social Order and Land Use in America* (Princeton, N.J.: Princeton University Press, 1977), 163–207.

Therefore, having done your best to settle the factual questions on which the various claims you describe are based, bear in mind your grave responsibility toward your less affluent potential neighbors. Do not evade this responsibility by supposing that the low-cost housing, if not built in your neighborhood, will be built elsewhere. Others in circumstances similar to yours have similar reasons for being unenthusiastic about welcoming less affluent neighbors. So, put yourself in the place of less affluent families and ask whether the rezoning is appropriate. Moreover, Christians should not only be fair but merciful, and, other responsibilities permitting, should subordinate their legitimate interests to those of others (see *LCL*, 360–71). Unless you judge that your responsibility for your own family—especially for the well-being of your children—requires you to oppose the rezoning, be ready to give up some advantages of your neighborhood to make room for people who need affordable housing.

These norms do not show that you may or must take this or that position on the proposed rezoning. Perhaps you should advocate a compromise—for example, rezoning to permit the narrower blocks, but developed with single-family homes somewhat less costly than yours on the blocks near your home and the small, six-unit town houses near the commercial strip. While providing some housing more affordable than development according to the county's master plan would allow, a compromise like that surely would affect your neighborhood much less than the proposed development.

171: May undocumented workers be employed in violation of the law?

As the recently appointed interim principal of a Catholic school, I have inherited some undocumented immigrant employees who have been paid off the books for several years. My predecessors apparently had no problem with this arrangement.

On the one hand, I realize that employing undocumented immigrants involves technical violations of the law, though many generally law-abiding people seem to be doing it. On the other hand, the present situation seems mutually advantageous to both the workers and the school, since they probably could not get better jobs elsewhere and the school probably could not hire others to do the work so cheaply. Thus, terminating the arrangement would involve rather serious hardships for both parties to it.

I am wondering what I ought to do about this situation, and how grave my obligation is to do it.

Analysis:

This question calls for the explanation and application of norms regarding just wages and conformity to laws. Undocumented workers are willing to work for less not because their work is less valuable than that of other workers but because they need the work more. Employing them to save money unjustly deprives them of the money that is saved. Paying them off the books both violates presumably just laws and wrongly deprives society of tax revenue—things contrary to the common good—and deprives them of the benefit of having paid the taxes that were due on their earnings. Even if immigration laws are unjustly restrictive, employers who violate them are unfair to fellow citizens. Employing undocumented workers also is unjust to citizens and legal immigrants who could do the jobs. A Catholic school that engages in this practice gives bad example to its students, impedes its witness, and risks bad consequences for the Church. Therefore, the questioner should take steps to end the employment of the undocumented workers in a way fair to them.

The reply could be along the following lines:

Although you do not explicitly say the school's undocumented employees emigrated due to economic hardship in their home nation or nations, I shall assume that was the case. Employing such workers is unjust for several reasons.

Because undocumented workers have little power and are vulnerable in many ways, the employer can take advantage of the need that motivates them to accept wages, hours, and/or working conditions poorer than those that citizens and legal aliens would command. The fact that undocumented workers, constrained by their need, agree to the terms of their employment does not show that those terms are fair. You seem both to recognize that the school is taking advantage of these employees' need and to offer a typical excuse: "The present situation seems mutually advantageous to both the workers and the school, since they probably could not get better jobs elsewhere and the school probably could not hire others to do the work so cheaply." While that undoubtedly is true, it is equally true that the school has unjustly deprived these employees of every cent it has saved, since their illegal status and consequent need in no way lessens the value of their work by comparison with that of citizens and legal aliens. At best, what the latter are paid for the sorts of jobs for which undocumented workers compete probably does not exceed the minimum required for justice, and it may even fall short of it (see *LCL,* 765–67).

Paying undocumented workers off the books, moreover, violates the income tax and social security laws, and deprives the nation of revenues. These wrongs not only are contrary to the common good but unfair to the workers, who both incur liability for failure to pay income taxes and miss out on social security benefits. Finally, the fact that people employ undocumented workers holds out hope to other potential illegal immigrants, and so encourages them to try to enter the country.[379] Such attempts sometimes end tragically, and, if successful, add to the problem of illegal immigrants.

On the main issue—the moral acceptability of violating the immigration laws—you might argue that the United States' present immigration laws are much too restrictive. Since God provides the world and all its resources to meet the needs of all human beings, the argument would go, prosperous countries should admit

---

379. The U.S. Bishops' Committee on Migration, *One Family under God* (Washington, D.C.: U.S. Catholic Conference, 1995), 11: "We must face squarely the extent to which the presence of persons in illegal status in this country is directly related to our own willingness to use and dispose the labors of these people how, when, and where it suits us." This document as a whole provides a well-balanced treatment of the ethical aspects of immigration policy.

economic refugees, even at some sacrifice to their own living standards. For those living in comfort to refuse entry to the desperately poor is like people on a lifeboat refusing to take others aboard. Although refusing would be justified if picking up another survivor would sink the boat, people assured of their own survival cannot justly reject others in desperate need merely to maintain more pleasant conditions for themselves (see *CCC,* 2241; *LCL,* 862).

I am impressed by that argument, which points to a need for changes in the law.[380] Still, I do not see how it justifies employing undocumented workers in violation of existing law. Even if many economic refugees should be admitted to the United States, the country must have and enforce some laws limiting immigration, since otherwise it would be flooded with immigrants. Unrestricted immigration would have several bad results. Without adequate help to establish themselves, many immigrants would suffer grave deprivation; attempting to assist the flood of immigrants, governments at various levels and private organizations would exhaust their resources and/or worsen their deficits; and, competing with immigrants, poorer and less skilled citizens would suffer a deterioration in their already poor economic condition.

I am confident that, if your predecessors and others who employ undocumented workers considered what would happen if there were no immigration laws, they would agree that such laws are indispensable. But people who employ undocumented workers act as if they were exempt from the immigration laws. It is plainly unfair to fellow citizens to expect them to obey the laws while making an exemption in one's own favor—even if it also were in favor of the particular undocumented workers one has employed and come to know.

Consequently, even if many generally law-abiding people do employ undocumented workers, that does not show that the school is morally justified in doing so. The existing immigration laws are perhaps not entirely just, but the common good is better served by those laws than it would be by no laws, and in practice all laws should be presumed just and deserving of obedience unless the contrary can be shown.

Employing illegal aliens also is unfair to unemployed citizens and legal immigrants who could fill the same jobs.[381] Employers often rationalize by saying, "Nobody else wants the job"; but what they mean is that nobody but an illegal alien wants the job on the terms offered. Suppose the job were advertised repeatedly and the pay offered were increased by, say, ten percent each time the ad appeared. In that case, I am sure a citizen or legal alien would be found to fill any opening for morally acceptable work now performed by an illegal alien. If employers were truthful, they would say: "Nobody else will take the job unless I offer better wages, hours, and working conditions."

---

380. However, changes in U.S. law during the 1980s greatly expanded opportunities for legal immigration, and assimilating still more immigrants would pose greater challenges; see Elizabeth S. Rolph, *Immigration Policies: Legacy from the 1980s and Issues for the 1990s* (Santa Monica, Calif.: Rand, 1992).

381. See Philip L. Martin, *Illegal Immigration and the Colonization of the American Labor Market,* CIS paper 1 (Washington, D.C.: Center for Immigration Studies, 1986).

Someone will object: Granted, every job would be filled by a well-qualified citizen or legal alien if the terms were attractive enough, but those who employ illegal immigrants simply cannot afford to offer such terms for menial jobs. If that is the case, however, the employers should do without these services, just as many poor people must do without professional services they cannot afford. And if employers find it difficult or even impossible to do without the services currently provided by illegal immigrants, they should acknowledge the importance of those services, and stop regarding the jobs as menial.

For a Catholic school to employ undocumented workers gives the school's students a bad example of disrespect for law and risks grave damage to the Church. The students are hardly likely to remain ignorant of the unlawful practice, and if it is publicized in the wider community, the Church's reputation will suffer and legal penalties may be imposed. Moreover, every Catholic organization should give an example of good citizenship as well as justice toward the poor; if they do not, their wrongdoing is likely to provoke the antagonism of public officials, non-Catholic citizens, and, not least, poorer and less skilled citizens who suffer most from the competition of undocumented workers. This antagonism is likely to hamper the Church in carrying out her mission. A Catholic school administrator should avoid running such risks.

Therefore, my advice is that you discuss the school's employment of these undocumented workers with diocesan officials and/or your other superiors, with a view to terminating the practice promptly and in a way that is fair to the workers. Considering everything that is at stake, your obligation to do this is, in my judgment, a grave one.

Perhaps some way can be found for the school to employ these people legally, while rectifying the injustices done them by your predecessors. If not, they must be discharged. In doing so, however, you should make fair restitution to each of them for the low pay he or she has received, which also will soften the blow of losing their jobs. Moreover, the income tax and social security payments on their off-the-books wages must now be paid, together with all required interest and penalties.

You might argue that the school cannot afford all these payments. Duties in justice, however, should be accorded a very high priority; to meet them, you should reduce less urgent expenditures and, if necessary, borrow money. You also might argue that these undocumented workers and others like them will be worse off if you and other employers discharge them. But assuming you cannot find a way rightly to continue employing them, you must discharge them, even if that worsens their condition. Still, mercy also requires that those who have resources help people in need, and the Church has done a great deal to help needy migrants and refugees. Therefore, when you talk with diocesan officials, seek their help in finding some legitimate way to help meet these people's needs.

Of course, the school still will need the services that the undocumented workers have been performing. I suggest that you explain the situation to the parents and others who support the school, and enlist their help in solving the problem. They might be willing and able to contribute enough for you to continue employing the workers lawfully, if possible, or else replace them. The students and their parents also might be willing to contribute some of the services the school needs. A well-organized program of contributed service would not only reduce costs but build up the community. If those involved in the school invest more time and work in it, they will love it more, and in working together they also will grow in solidarity.

Does it follow that it never could be right to employ an undocumented worker? No. When someone in extreme need begs for help, the best response sometimes may be to give him or her a temporary job, thus providing immediate help and enhancing the needy person's self-respect, while one also perhaps looks for a more lasting way to help. According to current (January 1997) U.S. law, people need not ask for papers, report payments, or pay taxes on behalf of individuals they employ for casual domestic work in their private homes when three conditions are met: (1) the employment is on a sporadic, irregular or intermittent basis; (2) cash wages paid to *all* such employees total less than one thousand dollars during each calendar quarter; and (3) cash wages paid to *any one* such employee total less than one thousand dollars during any one year.[382] Under these conditions, therefore, an undocumented worker could be employed briefly without violating justice, provided one paid a just wage, supplied decent working conditions, and violated no other legal requirement unless it were reasonably judged to be inapplicable under the circumstances.

Nor is it difficult to imagine a case in which applying the law and deporting an illegal immigrant would be gravely unjust. In such as case, someone able to pay a just wage and provide suitable working conditions might have solid grounds for judging that the violation of relevant laws was justified. If such a person had no other responsibilities that made breaking the law too risky, he or she might then employ the alien as an undocumented worker without unfairness and perhaps even as a true work of mercy.

172: May an automobile supply store sell items often used illegally?

I have an auto supply store in Washington, D.C. Not all my customers are from the metropolitan area, and during tourist season even people from foreign countries sometimes make purchases. I also get some telephone and mail orders.

I do a brisk business in several brands of radar detectors and in a bypass of the pollution control equipment. These items often are used illegally, but they also have lawful uses. Some states outlaw radar detectors, but others permit them. And I've heard that pollution control equipment is not required by law in some foreign countries, while in this country mechanics trying to diagnose certain problems legitimately use the bypass to find out where the trouble is.

I would not stock these items if the law prohibited it. But no federal or D.C. law tells me not to sell them. However, various organizations campaign against

---

382. See United States Department of the Treasury, Internal Revenue Service, *Household Employer's Tax Guide for Wages Paid in 1996,* publication 926; United States Department of Justice, Immigration and Naturalization Service, *Handbook for Employers* (Nov. 1991).

radar detectors, and an environmental group that thinks the bypass should not be sold to the public has organized a boycott of stores that sell it. Apparently giving in to pressure, a large, regional, auto supply chain has announced it no longer will stock either item.

Since my wife and I have eight children to raise, I need every bit of profit. These items will sell even better now that the chain is discontinuing them. Even if I did stop selling such items, many others would keep on. I would like to go on selling them as long as the law allows it. Can you give me any support for thinking there is nothing wrong with that?

Analysis:

This question concerns cooperation in morally questionable activities. The morality of selling something often used unlawfully depends on both the morality of using the item and the seller's civic responsibility. Since radar detectors serve only to help in violating a law that should be obeyed, drivers should never use them. Since a pollution control bypass can serve a legitimate purpose, some people may permanently install it. Beyond complying with relevant laws, the owner of a business does not have a civic responsibility to refrain from supplying requested items often used unlawfully unless such self-regulation is likely to be effective in protecting or promoting the common good. These things presupposed, the norms regarding cooperation can be applied to answer the question. Promoting the use of radar detectors is excluded as formal cooperation in violating a law that should be obeyed, and even selling them to people who ask for them is, at best, morally questionable material cooperation. The questioner may promote the pollution control bypass only to people whose use of it is likely to be morally acceptable, but he may sell it to anyone who asks.

The reply could be along the following lines:

In my judgment, sound moral analysis provides no support for the view that selling radar detectors is permissible, but provides some limited support for selling the pollution control bypass, provided certain restrictions are observed.

I assume that you are right in saying no applicable law forbids or restricts the sale of the items in question. If that is not so, or if relevant new legislation is enacted, the law should be presumed just and almost certainly should be obeyed. Indeed, even if it were unjust, you almost certainly would be morally bound to conform to it in order to forestall the many bad effects of lawbreaking, including the risk of being punished (see *LCL*, 874–83).

Many legally permissible actions are morally wrong, and laws do not fully specify even the civic responsibilities of citizens. Thus, your question cannot be answered without first considering whether it can be morally right for anyone to use a radar detector or permanently install a pollution control bypass, and whether the common good calls for self-regulation in selling such items.

Radar detectors theoretically could have other uses, but in practice they are used to frustrate enforcement of speed limits. Drivers should accept the reasonable and common understanding of the intent of traffic laws, including speed limits, as a norm to be strictly observed (see *LCL*, 485–86, 876). Law enforcement officer generally cite only drivers who not only exceed the posted limits but clearly violate the norm flowing from the reasonable and common understanding of the law's intent. So, drivers who use radar detectors are seeking impunity for violating a legal norm they ought to observe. That intention is immoral.

Someone might concede that radar detectors usually are used to violate speed laws with impunity, but claim that some law-abiding drivers use them merely to know when they are being monitored so that they can make sure not accidentally to exceed the speed limit. Even if such drivers do not speed intentionally, however, they would not need radar detectors if they were strictly observing the law, rightly understood. That means not only intending not to speed but attending to speed limits, glancing regularly at the speedometer, and constantly maintaining the appropriate speed, rather than carelessly exceeding it now and then unless specially warned. Moreover, though a conscientious driver could intend to use a radar detector only to reduce the likelihood of being penalized for accidental speeding, using the device surely would be an occasion of sins of negligence regarding speed limits and probably would lead to sins of intentional speeding.

Again, some people argue that using a radar detector not only is lawful in some jurisdictions but can be morally justifiable. On many stretches of heavily traveled highways, they point out, most vehicles, including most large trucks, often go significantly over the posted limits, which are enforced only sporadically. Under these conditions, the argument goes, drivers abiding by the law often are followed too closely and passed dangerously, so that it is safer for them to move with the traffic stream, especially if they are driving small cars. Yet police using radar sometimes stop and ticket such drivers while neglecting speeding trucks. So, the argument concludes, reluctant speeders are entitled to use radar detectors so that they can drive as safely as possible without becoming targets of arbitrary law enforcement.

This argument's factual assumptions do not seem sound. On the one hand, at least when the traffic stream is not dense (and perhaps even when it is), observing the speed limit, as reasonably and commonly interpreted, is likely to be safer than speeding. On the other hand, police almost never stop drivers moving with a dense traffic stream in the less fast lane of a multilane highway or along a road with only one lane in each direction. Partly that is because, even if the traffic stream exceeds the posted speed limit, it may well be within the limit intended by legislators and enforced by traffic officers; partly it is because a dense traffic stream slows as soon as the police apply radar, since many deliberate, habitual speeders use detectors. So, in my judgment, someone reluctant to speed does not need a radar detector, and the money spent on such devices would probably suffice to pay the rare fines imposed on drivers proceeding as carefully as they can in a dense, fast-moving stream of traffic.

The pollution control bypass is a somewhat different matter. God has provided subhuman creation for the enjoyment and use of the entire human family, and the people of each generation owe it to one another and those of all future generations to preserve this gift (see *LCL*, 771–82). So, even where pollution control equipment is not required by law, people with the financial resources to help protect the environment should not use a bypass. But where the law permits, poor people who must use their vehicles to meet genuine needs and who cannot afford to use or repair pollution control equipment are morally justified in permanently installing a bypass. Where that is illegal, however, only poor people motivated by a need pressing and urgent enough to generate a conflicting duty can be morally justified in regarding the law as inapplicable to them and making an exception to it (see *LCL,* 878–79).

I now turn to your actual question. If the common good requires it, the law should prohibit or restrict selling radar detectors and pollution control bypasses. Where the law allows their sale, self-regulation by merchants might be their civic duty if it would serve the common good. As long as many merchants continue to sell these items, however, voluntary measures by a few will prevent hardly anyone from buying and using them. So, it would not serve the common good for you to abstain from selling these items to people determined to have them, and, therefore, your civic responsibility does not require you to do that.

Nevertheless, intending others' wrongdoing always is wrong. Normally the owners of businesses intend the use of products they sell. Plainly, anyone who encourages another to do what is wrong intends that he or she do it—or, at least, plan to do it—and the owner of a business certainly encourages people to use for their intended purposes any items whose purchase the business promotes, that is, anything it advertises, recommends, or displays to potential buyers. Therefore, owners of businesses certainly may not advertise, recommend, or even display anything with the intention of gaining sales volume that they are morally certain cannot be achieved without purchases for immoral use. If the use also is contrary to law, promoting its sale also encourages law breaking, and so violates the common good.

Owners of businesses sometimes handle morally questionable merchandise without promoting it; the items are never displayed but are brought out or ordered only when someone requests them. If not morally certain such items will be used immorally, they need not share the buyer's bad intention. Suppose they know such an item will be used immorally? Certainly, selling it involves intending its possession. But that need not involve intending its use, unless the seller either has chosen to do something to bring about that use or by means of that use achieves some end ulterior to that very sale. So, without intending the item's use, merchants could sell it to people who ask for it.

If sellers do not intend the immoral use of what they sell, they facilitate buyers' wrongdoing without necessarily sharing in their guilt. Still, doing something that facilitates others' wrongdoing often is sinful, and, in my judgment, owners of businesses should not stock or sell any merchandise customers could want only for some objectively immoral use. To do so may tempt an owner or employees to intend wrongdoing by promoting the items' use; it also will undercut the owner's witness to relevant moral truths, and it may be unfair to anyone who suffers injustice from the wrongdoing.

In the light of the preceding norms, promoting the purchase of radar detectors involves both intending speeding and violating civic responsibility. You may not advertise or display radar detectors, and neither you nor your employees may do anything else to encourage their use. In my judgment, moreover, you should not even stock them. That is likely to tempt you and/or your employees to encourage their use, and will make less credible the witness you should bear to drivers' responsibility to be careful and law abiding.

Since the pollution control bypass can have morally acceptable uses, it seems to me that you may stock and sell it to people who ask for it, without inquiring into their intentions. Often, proceeding in this way probably will contribute to buyers' wrongdoing, but that contribution, in my judgment, can be justified. The alternative would be to forgo handling an item for which there is a legitimate need. You also may encourage people who would rightly use this item to buy it. But I think you should not advertise it to the public at large or display it in your store, since you can be morally certain that will encourage many people to use it immorally and unlawfully.[383]

173: Must a person pay tax on past income unreported by an honest mistake?

For many years I ran my own business. Eight years ago I sold it, and have enjoyed a quite profitable second career as a management consultant to several companies. To maintain adequate health coverage and get certain other benefits, I have arranged to be on the payroll of at least one, rather than contracting with all of them for my services.

Recently I discovered that several years ago my accountant did not include in my tax return a substantial amount of income (about twenty-five thousand dollars); through no fault of mine, the W–2 form supplied by my employer did not include it, since the company's accounting department mistakenly classified it as a contract payment. I asked my accountant what to do, and he said there is no need to report that income now, because it was the employer's responsibility to include it with other compensation. He also said that, if the mistake was ever going to be caught, it certainly would have been caught by now. A second accountant also advises me against filing an amended return, saying that might well lead to my being unfairly treated by the government. I might be compelled to pay a large sum in interest and penalties, and my returns for past and future years might be subjected to close examination.

What do I do now? Must I file an amended return or, perhaps, make up for the underpayment in future years, for instance, by forgoing deductions allowed by law until the tax that would have been due has been paid? Or may I proceed as if I never noticed the mistake? That is what I would prefer because, while I realize that we should render to Caesar what is his, I would rather not pay our Caesar—the IRS—a dime more than I must.

---

383. The preceding analysis articulates the norms to be applied to other, more or less similar cases, not only by owners of a business like the questioner's, but by owners of other sorts of business, including those that sell books and magazines, rent videos, and so forth (see q. 83, above).

Analysis:

This question calls for application of the norm requiring payment of taxes. Unless the law provides otherwise, the questioner still owes the tax and should pay it. Even if the first accountant's risk assessment is accurate, his advice is not morally sound. Even if the prospective consequences of filing an amended return justified not doing so, the questioner could and should pay the full tax, together with the applicable interest, in another way. Still, people who faultlessly fail to pay taxes when due are not held to make payments beyond those required by law.

The reply could be along the following lines:

Many people regard taxes as a burdensome imposition whose justification, if any, is barely intelligible. On that view, overlooking taxable income is a fortunate mistake that hardly calls for rectification. However, material resources are necessary to protect and promote the common good, and loyal citizens should willingly contribute their fair share (see *LCL,* 894–97). Therefore, one ought to render to Caesar what one owes whether he can exact it or not.

Even granting your good faith in overlooking the tax due on the twenty-five thousand dollars, you still must pay the government whatever you owe. The tax laws provide that, if noticed within a certain number of years, even entirely honest mistakes involving no negligence are to be corrected when that will be to the government's advantage (and may be corrected if to the taxpayer's advantage). Of course, if the amount due were very small, one might judge uprightly that the cost to the government of processing an amended return, as well as the trouble to oneself in preparing and submitting it, justified not filing it. However, for the amount of tax undoubtedly involved in your case, just as you surely would file an amended return if you had overpaid your taxes, so you should be prepared to do the same to fulfill your civic duty. So, unless the period specified by law has expired, you would be violating your present obligation to pay taxes by proceeding as if you had not noticed the mistake.

Of course, even if the period specified by law has not expired, the accountant might be correct in saying that, if the error were ever going to be caught, it probably would have been caught by now; but in that case the advice that there is no need now to report the income reflects only a shrewd observation about likely consequences while ignoring truly prudent considerations about moral responsibility. Then too, if you are prosperous enough not to notice that so large an amount of taxable income was not taxed, you are hardly likely to suffer undue hardship if you now pay the additional tax including any appropriate interest and penalties.

Assuming that you should pay, how you ought to make the payment is a secondary question. The second accountant may well be exaggerating the chances of your being treated unfairly by the government if you file an amended return. But even if the second accountant's advice is sound, failing to file an amended return when appropriate to correct an underpayment of which one becomes aware violates the law, and it seems to me you would need a ground far more substantial than either accountant has offered to justify such a violation. If you nevertheless judge that you have a serious enough reason to make up for the underpayment in another way (for example, by forgoing allowable deductions in future years), you should be careful not to pay less than you owe (for example, by neglecting the interest and penalties that would be charged if you filed an amended return). The law is not unfair in specifying additional charges when taxes are not paid when due.

Does it follow that a person who by mistake has underpaid taxes never can be morally justified in not paying them? No. One can imagine a case in which the period set by law for correcting innocent mistakes has expired, and the mistake was entirely honest and in no way due to negligence—may indeed have been due to bad advice from the revenue service itself or from an expert whose guidance was reasonably accepted and followed. In such a case, a conscientious taxpayer has no legal duty to pay the tax and so can rest easy without paying it.

Finally, not violating the commandments is good, but, as Jesus told the rich young man, we are called to go beyond keeping the commandments.[384] Though, I do not blame you for wishing to give Caesar no more than is his, you also must give God what is his, and while what is Caesar's is limited, what is God's is not, for it includes what is Caesar's and all else too. So, having responded to the question you asked, I wish to call your attention to a prior question and make a suggestion.

Do you really need all the income you earn as a management consultant? Many owners of small businesses struggling to achieve or maintain profitability could benefit from the advice of a person with your expertise, but probably few could afford your fees. Consider spending at least part of your time helping struggling small businesses. You might offer your service without charge or, perhaps better, charge only a modest fee, contingent on future profits, if any. In any case, if you do not need all your income and yet choose not to forgo earning it, you cannot justify amassing ever increasing wealth. Rather, you should use your surplus income to help others, either by giving money to people in need or in some other way. Indeed, you would be wise to go further than justice requires in helping the poor, even to the point of impoverishing yourself, for in that way you would store up "an unfailing treasure in heaven, where no thief comes near and no moth destroys" (Lk 12.33).

174: May a man impoverish himself to get public funding for long-term care?

My father-in-law, Walter, is seventy-seven. He has been living for eight years with my wife and me, and our daughter, Melanie, now twenty. Devoting much of her time and energy to her grandfather, Melanie became his favorite.

Next month, she will be marrying a fine young man, a naval officer, and moving out of state, and Walter now needs more care than we will be able to give him here at home. So, he will have to go into a nursing home for long-term care, which will cost about a hundred dollars a day. If he pays for this with his income and savings, he will be impoverished in about four years, and then Medicaid will pay the

---

384. See John Paul II, *Veritatis splendor,* 16–21, *AAS* 85 (1993) 1146–50, *OR,* 6 Oct. 1993, iii–iv.

difference. If he had no savings, he would receive the same care, and Medicaid would pay from the start.

All Walter's savings are in a mutual fund currently worth around one hundred thousand dollars; since retirement, his only income has been his monthly social security payment, which he has contributed to our household, and a very small pension, which he has been using for pocket money. Yesterday, Walter told me what none of us had known—he made a will a few years ago in which he made Melanie his sole heir.

But though Walter wanted all his savings to go to Melanie, if he keeps them, the nursing home will get everything and she will get nothing. He is thinking of giving her his savings now, before making arrangements to enter the nursing home. He asked me whether I thought there would be anything wrong in that, and I really didn't know what to say. What do you think?

Analysis:

This question calls for application of the norms regarding obedience to laws. Federal law limits the extent to which the government pays for the care of people who voluntarily impoverish themselves, and one may not lie to circumvent that limitation. Arguments can be made both for and against the view that one may voluntarily impoverish oneself insofar as that can be done within the letter of the law. On the one hand, what the law permits can be presumed just; on the other hand, the spirit of a just law, which reflects the common good, can require more of conscientious citizens than the letter of the law does.

The reply could be along the following lines:

The purpose of Medicaid is to provide necessary care, not for everyone, but only for people too poor to afford it. Someone might argue that some provisions of the law establishing and regulating Medicaid are unfair, but, like other laws, this one should be presumed just unless the contrary is shown. Moreover, it seems to me that, at least as they apply to someone in Walter's situation, the legal provisions regulating Medicaid payments are in fact just.

You should check into the relevant legal provisions for yourself. But my understanding is that, if Walter gives his savings to Melanie, Medicaid will not pay for his care in a nursing home until thirty-six months have passed.[385] This rule plainly is meant to prevent what Walter is thinking of doing: voluntarily impoverishing himself by transferring his savings to Melanie, and so shifting the cost of his long-term care to taxpayers. Perhaps Walter is aware of the rule and hopes to circumvent it. But he can hardly do that without lying, which is morally excluded and, in a matter of such importance, surely would be grave matter.

Suppose he gives his savings to Melanie with the understanding that she will pay the cost of his care insofar as it exceeds his income until the thirty-six months are up and Medicaid kicks in. Assuming such an arrangement lawful,

---

385. This would be the effect of the law in force in January 1997, as I understand it, assuming Walter straightforwardly transferred his savings; if he used a trust, the waiting period would be sixty months.

would it be morally acceptable? There seem to me to be plausible arguments on both sides. I am not sure which is the sounder, but shall sketch both of them out for your consideration.

The argument that it would be morally acceptable is comparatively brief and simple.[386] Laws are to be presumed just not only when they establish requirements but also when they are permissive. Just as taxpayers may take advantage of the loopholes provided by tax law, so, one might conclude, people may arrange their affairs so as to minimize how much they must pay for long-term care before Medicaid kicks in.

However, at least in cases like Walter's, an argument also can be made for the contrary view, and the remainder of my response to your question articulates and defends this alternative without claiming that it is certainly or more probably the sounder.

Underlying the obligation to obey just laws is society's common good, and often it is clear that going beyond what is required by the letter of the law will serve the common good. In such cases, a citizen's moral responsibility can be to forgo taking advantage of what the law permits, and to act instead for the good it was meant to promote. Since welfare programs transfer some of the nation's always-limited wealth from the more affluent to the needier, people eligible for benefits from these programs should recognize that the amount budgeted must be limited and should be fairly shared with others who need help. That responsibility may be overlooked by those who try to obtain as much as the law allows from every program.

In making Melanie his sole heir, Walter wanted her eventually to have his savings, but he did not give them to her at that time. His reason obviously was that he might need the money for necessities in excess of his income. His long-term nursing home care is just such a necessity, and he will be able to cover its cost for about four years. Thus, it seems that his sole purpose in giving Melanie his savings before entering the nursing home would be to preserve part of them for her by shifting to taxpayers as much of the cost of his care as he can. Even if that is in accord with the letter of the law, it seems to violate its intent—to provide care for people who cannot afford it—and so seems to take unfair advantage of the thirty-six-month limit.

Still, if Walter owed someone ten or twenty thousand dollars, it would be right for him to use part of his savings to pay that debt before spending everything on his care in the nursing home. He might argue that he owes Melanie a debt of gratitude for what she has done over the years, and giving her his savings is his way of discharging it. He might bolster the argument by pointing out that, had he hired an outsider to do for him what the girl did gratuitously, he would have exhausted his savings years ago.

That argument would have some initial plausibility, since Walter no doubt does owe his granddaughter a debt of gratitude, and such a debt, while not legally binding, is a serious moral obligation. On this basis, he would have good reason to give Melanie a substantial gift, as a token of his appreciation, when

386. See qq. 97 and 169, above, for other discussions of the possible moral acceptability of impoverishing oneself.

he leaves the household. Might not that gift be the residue of his savings remaining at the end of thirty-six months?

Probably not. By contributing his social security income to the household, Walter has compensated the family as a whole for the expense of his living with them, and no doubt has used some of his pocket money for small gifts and treats for Melanie. Moreover, debts of gratitude can be paid in nonmonetary ways, such as words of thanks, signs of affection, and small acts of kindness, and Walter no doubt has been generous with these. Besides, he already has shown his gratitude by naming her his heir, and she will receive the residue of his savings if he dies before they are exhausted. Then too, surely not all the benefits deriving from this relationship have been on Walter's side. By goodheartedly devoting much time and energy during her adolescence to caring for her grandfather, Melanie has matured in character and acquired skills that will serve her well for the rest of her life.

Therefore, while he will be justified in giving Melanie a substantial gift on the occasion of his departure from the household and her marriage, the gift's value probably should not be determined by the limit of his legal obligation to use his own resources to pay for his care in the nursing home. Rather, he should judge conscientiously what he would give her if his income were adequate to meet his expenses without drawing down his savings, and should limit the value of his gift to that amount.

If Walter accepts this reasoning, he might well consider serving the common good by donating the portion of his savings not needed to pay for the first thirty-six months of care in the nursing home to a good cause that public programs do not support—for example, an organization defending the right to life. If he gives Melanie only a modest gift, he ought to explain to her the basis on which he formed his conscience in the matter. By doing so, he will both teach her a valuable moral lesson and more perfectly manifest his gratitude: "If my conscience did not forbid it, I would give you all my savings."

175: Should parents report to police a priest who sexually abused their son?

We live in a small city where Catholics are a minority, and our parish has only about a hundred families. We always have had only one priest; now he also must take care of another, smaller parish about twenty-five miles away. About two years ago our old pastor was moved and we were sent a much younger man, Father Jack, who had many new ideas and was enthusiastic. Everyone liked him.

Since we have five daughters, our only son, Frank, has been very close to me, often helping with chores. He has developed into a skillful painter and handyman. In June, Frank graduated from grade school, and being fourteen, big for his age, and ambitious, he wanted to go to work during the summer. We were pleased when Father Jack offered him a job—cutting the grass, gardening, and doing interior painting in the church and rectory.

At first, it seemed to go well. Frank talked a lot about his work and repeated things Father Jack had said. But after a few weeks, Frank became unusually quiet and seemed upset. When this went on for a couple of weeks, I took him fishing one Sunday afternoon and urged him to tell me what was bothering him. He did not want to talk about it, but finally he told me that one day Father Jack had begun by saying masturbation is wrong because it leaves a person lonely and ended by performing oral sex on him, and that they had been engaging in sexual acts together almost every day since.

Father Jack was away that evening, but the next morning I went to the rectory to confront him. At first he denied everything, but then he broke down and admitted that things were just as Frank had said. The priest told me he is a pedophile. Crying, he begged me not to tell anyone, and said he knew he needed help and would get it. I insisted I was going to see the bishop and called his office then and there. When I told the bishop's priest-secretary why I wanted an appointment, he asked to speak with Father Jack. As I handed him the phone I told him that if he denied what he had been doing I would go to the police, and he admitted everything to the other priest.

That afternoon, my wife and I drove to the city and saw the bishop. He was friendly and sympathetic, and angry with Father Jack. The priest would be removed from our parish at once, the bishop told us, and would be sent away for prolonged treatment. He urged us to look into counseling for Frank, spare no expense, and send along the bills. He also proposed that the diocese's lawyer meet with us, and we agreed.

When the lawyer came, he frankly told us that Frank and we had the right to sue both Father Jack and the diocese, and we would have a good chance of being awarded substantial damages. To settle the matter, he offered not only reimbursement for any counseling we chose and for Frank's pay for the rest of the summer, but an additional fifty thousand dollars. My wife and I would have been very reluctant to sue the Church, and so we gladly accepted and, with only some technical changes our own lawyer insisted on, signed a document releasing both the priest and the diocese of all civil liability. The check came a few days ago.

The diocese's lawyer made it clear that he and the bishop hoped we would not report the matter to the police but be merciful toward Father Jack, so that he would have a chance to be rehabilitated and the Church would be spared the scandal. We certainly do not want to hurt the Church, but Father Jack is not the Church, and my wife and I are troubled at the thought that this priest, who abused Frank, might be pronounced "cured" and assigned to some other parish. Our lawyer tells us we can go to the police without violating anything in the agreement we signed. Should we do it despite the bishop's wishes?

Analysis:

This question calls for the clarification of considerations bearing on a judgment that only the parents themselves can make. Ordinarily, Catholics should follow their bishops' policies in dealing with any problem within the Church, but in this case the presumption in favor of doing so is not decisive. In general, citizens should report crimes. But assuming Frank's parents have no legal duty to report Father Jack's crimes, they should do so only if they judge it their moral obligation despite its likely burdens and risks for their son. The bishop's promise to send Father Jack for prolonged treatment with hope for his rehabilitation suggests that he may be overlooking or ignoring the priest's evasion of responsibility. For several reasons, a priest who has engaged in sexual activity with a minor should not be returned to priestly ministry. In my judgment, apart from possible further harm to Frank, considerations against reporting Father Jack's crimes are not cogent.

The reply could be along the following lines:

Before addressing your question, let me offer a suggestion about your present care for Frank. Though you probably do not need any advice about how to look after your son, his whole life and salvation could be at stake if you acquiesce in the implausible view that the chief, or even the only, harm to a victim of sexual abuse is likely to be psychological.

Your son was a victim of sexual seduction. He was especially vulnerable inasmuch as he greatly trusted his seducer. Having suffered this betrayal of trust by a priest, Frank might eventually react, if he has not already, with a revulsion against priests in general, the Church, and even God. That could lead to despair and loss of faith. Be alert to signs of such trouble. Explain to Frank that Father Jack's misbehavior was the priest's personal fault. Help Frank understand that he still needs to share in the life of the Church by the ministry of priests, most of whom, despite human weaknesses, can be trusted to make Jesus' loving care available to everyone who has suffered and sinned.

Very likely, at the outset Father Jack's advances so confused Frank that he was incapable of either consenting to them or rejecting them. Still, he not only was seduced but cooperated for some weeks in sexual acts, even though this troubled him. Only God knows whether the conditions for mortal sin were met when he engaged in at least some of those acts. If you have not already done so, however, you should talk with Frank about his possible guilt. Since he probably feels far guiltier than he is, you will have to clarify for him how and to what extent the sexual activity was not his responsibility. At the same time, you must gently help him consider the possibility that, though being sinned against, he was led into sinning—unless you know that he already has examined his conscience in this matter and gone to confession if he found it necessary.[387]

If Frank has not obtained the pastoral care he needs, you should encourage him, when the time seems right, to talk with a priest he knows and trusts—perhaps your former pastor—or help him find a suitable adviser and confessor. Unfortunately, confessors' fidelity to Catholic moral teaching cannot be taken for granted today. If you must seek a suitable confessor for Frank, look for a priest entirely faithful to Catholic teaching as well as endowed with other appropriate traits of personality and character—perhaps a wise and gentle elderly priest who will provide sound guidance without arousing Frank's anxiety by reminding him of the priest who abused him.

---

387. Frank probably did not confess those sins to Father Jack and is hardly likely to do so now. But if he did, the absolution, being of a person not in danger of death by a partner in sin against the sixth commandment, was or would be invalid (see *CIC,* c. 977).

Not many fathers would have been as attentive as you were to the signs of abuse, and too few adolescents would have had enough trust in their parents to confide in them as Frank did in you. Your relationship with him plainly is excellent, and nothing you say suggests that he has serious psychological problems. Of course, he needs to be reassured that what he has suffered has not ruined him as a person, and that he can look forward to being a man like his father. Beyond that, it seems to me, he may well need little psychological help except what you and your wife will continue to provide. Moreover, as you may have known already or have discovered, it sometimes is hard to find a counselor who is entirely faithful to Catholic teaching, technically competent, and effective. My point is that if you have not already obtained psychological counseling for your son, you should be very careful about doing so; and if you have, you should watch for signs of trouble, as I expect you would do in any case.

In some jurisdictions, certain persons would have a legal duty to report Father Jack's behavior to the police. But the law seldom if ever obliges a minor victim's parents to take such a step. I shall assume it does not, and answer your question on that assumption.

Ordinarily, Catholics troubled by priests' activities or any other problem in the Church should deal with the matter in accord with the Church's own law and their bishops' policies. Thus, in view of your bishop's wishes that you not report Father Jack's behavior with your son to the police, it might seem clear that you should not. However, when a priest commits a serious crime, the problem it poses is not merely within the Church, as most people would acknowledge if the crime were homicide or kidnapping. Moreover, I believe that the real problems presented and revealed by the conduct of priests like Father Jack have hardly been acknowledged by bishops, including yours, and that thus far they have developed no adequate policy or procedure for dealing with those problems.[388] Moreover, you are concerned that the bishop's policy might result in Father Jack's being pronounced cured and reassigned to another parish, as many priests have been in similar situations. So, the usual presumption against acting contrary to one's bishop's policies and going to the public authorities about a problem within the Church cannot reasonably be considered decisive in this case. Therefore, I shall consider both the reasons for taking the unusual step of going to the police about this priest's misconduct despite your bishop's wishes, and the objections to and arguments against doing so.

In general, citizens have a moral obligation to report crimes (see *LCL*, 888–89). Failing to do so allows criminals to evade just punishment, whose infliction benefits society: first, by restoring the balance of justice that crime upsets; second, by restraining and even perhaps reforming the criminal; and third, by deterring the criminal and others from similar acts in the future. Then

388. Norbert J. Rigali, S.J., "Church Responses to Pedophilia," *Theological Studies,* 55 (1994): 124–39, reviews various episcopal policy statements and finds them wanting in two respects: (1) they assume that abusers are psychologically ill rather than morally at fault, thus oversimplifying the question of responsibility; (2) they confuse pedophilia (adults' or adolescents' sexual urges, arousal through fantasies, and sexual activity involving prepubescent children) with adults' sexual activity involving young people who have passed puberty.

too, the criminal may well have committed similar crimes previously, and some investigation is warranted to identify other victims, who may need help. Criminal investigations are an appropriate function of the police, but the police generally do not investigate until a crime is reported.

Still, the moral obligation to report crimes is not absolute. Because you bear special responsibility for your son's well-being, you should not go to the police unless he consents and you are confident it will not risk further, serious injury to him—for example, from embarrassing publicity or from the stress of giving evidence, especially if he were compelled to testify in open court and undergo hostile examination by Father Jack's defense counsel. Perhaps, however, the media and authorities in your city protect the privacy of juvenile victims of sex crimes, or perhaps you have good reason to believe Father Jack would plead guilty or that, for other reasons, reporting the crime will not result in undue stress for Frank. Your son may be willing to press the matter for the good of other young men; in that case, doing so might well help him come to terms with what he has suffered, rise above the injury, and, acting out of concern for others rather than personal animosity, help bring his abuser to justice.

You mention that the bishop hopes you will not report the matter but be merciful toward Father Jack so that he will have a chance to be "rehabilitated," which you take to mean pronounced cured and assigned to some other parish—an outcome whose desirability you and your wife question. The bishop certainly is right in encouraging mercy and he seems to be trying hard to handle properly the problem of clerical sexual abuse. Assuming your understanding of "rehabilitated" to be correct, however, I agree with you in questioning the value of such rehabilitation for both Father Jack and the Church.

With respect to Father Jack, while psychological compulsion may limit his moral responsibility and only God knows whether he sinned mortally, he told you he knew he needed help. Yet he hardly seems to have considered the possibility that he was at least gravely responsible for failing to get the help he needed to forestall not only violating chastity and his own priestly consecration but betraying Frank's trust and abusing his body. Moreover, by classifying himself as a pedophile and saying that he needs treatment, Father Jack suggested that he suffers from an unusual sexual psychopathology. Your son, however, is not a prepubescent child; he is a clean, fresh, young man, who would appeal to an unchaste, homosexual man, and Father Jack may well be nothing but that.[389] Whether he failed to seek the help he needs to deal with a compulsion or alleged the compulsion to hide the fact that he is simply an abusive homosexual, Father Jack was at best unconsciously evading the responsibility he ought to accept. Facing criminal charges might well lead this man to put aside his self-deception or

---

389. Philip Jenkins, *Pedophiles and Priests: Anatomy of a Contemporary Crisis* (New York: Oxford University Press, 1996), shows that the sad facts about the misbehavior of some priests have served as material for diverse constructions of the problem or crisis. Still, not all constructions are equally valid, and one suspects that some sexual abusers who are not pedophiles are so categorized by those who want to reproach the Church for clerics' misbehavior without condemning sodomy and other sexual activities outside chaste marriage.

dishonesty, examine himself, repent, and cooperate with whatever psychological or other help he needs.

With respect to the Church, the bishop's promise to send Father Jack away for prolonged treatment and his hope for his rehabilitation suggest that the bishop himself may be overlooking or ignoring the priest's evasion of responsibility. For *treatment* and *rehabilitation* suggest sickness rather than wrongdoing, and in this way make the sexual seducer as much a helpless victim as the person he seduces. Now, a bishop's failure to attend to evasion of responsibility by clerical sexual abusers is likely to harm the Church. It is likely to reassure abusers and potential abusers who are failing to get whatever help they might need to deal with their perverse inclination. It also is likely to elicit inappropriate sympathy for those abusers, forestall the severe measures against them required for the Church's good, and distract attention from the urgent question of who shares responsibility for abusers' wrongful behavior. Did fellow seminarians or priests know about Jack but ignore his "problem" or even cover up for him? Did Father Jack misbehave before, and did the bishop know it when he reassigned him to your small parish? Did Father Jack accept opinions dissenting from relevant Church teaching, apply them to others in pastoral practice, and, finally, apply them to himself?

The bishop plainly should ask and answer these and other relevant questions for himself, and should make or promote any reforms inquiry shows to be appropriate. Only accepting the humiliation of facing such questions and making whatever reforms are needed to go to the roots of clerical sexual abuse offer a prospect of freeing the Church from this burden. Moreover, your bishop and other bishops will never effectively deal with this problem unless they begin to work with equal vigor against the more widespread and more devastating spiritual corruption of the faithful and priests themselves by those working under the Church's authority who bring dissenting theological opinions into play in their professional activities.

Moreover, if criminal prosecution would prevent Father Jack from ever again functioning as a priest, that, in my view, not only does not argue against going to the police but even argues strongly for it. Beyond what I already have pointed out—that going to the police would press the issue of responsibility, with benefits for both Father Jack and the Church—it seems to me that neither this man nor any priest should again be allowed to function as a priest once he admits or it is solidly proved that he has engaged in sexual activity with a minor.[390] If or insofar as such misbehavior is the result of a psychological compulsion, it is doubtful that so serious a personality defect will be cured. If or insofar as the activity is sinful betrayal of the priestly office, it is neither loving toward the Church nor fair to potential victims once again to trust a man who did not shrink from betraying the trust the Church bestowed upon him and doing such great injuries both to her and to the person he victimized and/or led into sin.

But is the position I have outlined merciful? It may seem not, for God forgives any sin of anyone who repents, and Jesus enjoins us to be merciful as the Father is. So, if Father Jack and others like him repent and reform, should they not be restored

---

390. I am not dealing here with other cases of clerical sexual activity, which present somewhat different problems.

to some sort of pastoral ministry under conditions that will minimize the likelihood of a recurrence? No. Repentant clerical sexual offenders certainly should be forgiven. But only their victims and God can forgive them, and it does not follow that they should be allowed to function again as priests. Given all that is at stake, even a small risk of recurrence is too great. If Jack were a layman teaching in a high school, few parents of boys attending the school would doubt that his behavior warranted his permanent exclusion from teaching. The dignity of the priesthood demands that priests be held to at least as high a standard. For if a priest's consecration to act in the person of Christ makes it appropriate that he forgo even holy marriage and chaste marital intercourse, so that men unable or unwilling to promise this are not ordained in the Latin Church, that consecration makes it all the more appropriate that men unable or unwilling entirely to avoid sexual abuse of children not be permitted ever again to stand before the Church, acting in the person of Christ. Besides, just as very firm discipline is necessary to enforce the seal of confession (see *CIC,* c. 1388, §1), lest the faithful fear to entrust their most intimate secrets to priests, so very firm discipline is necessary to enforce the chastity of priests with minors, lest parents fear to entrust their children to priests in the privacy required for spiritual friendship and direction. Therefore, I repeat, the chance that criminal prosecution will prevent Father Jack from ever returning to pastoral ministry is no reason to forgo it.

Someone might say you implicitly promised Father Jack not to go to the police in warning him you would have him arrested if he did not admit his wrongdoing to the bishop's priest-secretary. But your threat did not logically imply a promise not to go to the police if he did admit it. Your threat simply was to report the wrong Father Jack already had done if he compounded that wrongdoing by trying to deceive the other priest about it, and that could not reasonably be taken to imply any assurance that, if he admitted what he had done, you would never go to the police about it.

Moreover, even if you did mean your threat to include such an assurance, the duty to keep promises is a matter of fairness, and sometimes a promise can be broken without any unfairness (*LCL,* 412–14). You made your threat in the heat of the moment as one private individual confronting another; citizens usually should report crimes and you have various good reasons, already explained, for reporting this one. Therefore, even if you meant to promise that you would not report Father Jack's behavior to the police, I think it would be fair for you to break that promise.

You mention possible "scandal" for the "Church." In a loose sense, *scandal* refers to bad publicity; in the strict sense, it refers to leading others into sin (see *CCC,* 2284–87; *LCL,* 232–39). Jesus warns: "If any of you put a stumbling block before one of these little ones who believe in me, it would be better for you if a great millstone were hung around your neck and you were thrown into the sea" (Mk 9.42; cf. Mt 18.6, Lk 17.1–2). Since clerical sexual abuse not only injures its victims as sexual abuse always does but poses a threat and obstacle to their and others' faith, the Church is injured far more by its scandalousness in this strict sense than she is by bad publicity about it.

Reporting Father Jack's behavior to the police probably will cause bad publicity. But since so many similar cases already have been reported, I do not think publicity about this particular case would cause much harm, though I am sure it would be embarrassing for the bishop and many priests of the diocese. Moreover, the bad publicity not only harms but benefits the Church. It motivates the bishops to try harder to prevent and limit the real scandal: priests leading children into sin. It also leads potential victims and/or their parents not to be overly trusting, in circumstances conducive to such abuse, and warns potential abusers to restrain themselves or, if they are suffering from a psychological compulsion, to tell their bishop as soon as they become aware of it, and in any case before they commit crimes.

Someone might argue that in accepting the settlement the diocese's lawyer offered, you undertook to refrain from going to the police about Father Jack. Insofar as the settlement covered not only the diocese's but Father Jack's liability, it may have been an inappropriate use of the Church's money. Even if that was a proper use of Church funds, however, it would have been improper for the diocese's lawyer to offer the settlement with the intention of dissuading you from reporting what Father Jack did, since that could well be your moral duty, both as a citizen and as a member of the Church. Rather, the offer of a settlement was appropriate only to compensate Frank and you for the damage that has resulted or might still result from Father Jack's misbehavior—damage for which he and the diocese were or might have been legally responsible. You, no doubt, were aware of and took into account the possibility that the damage included the transmission to Frank of HIV, which might eventually require health care costing far more than fifty thousand dollars.

Even if the settlement covered all the damage that monetary compensation can cover, it was, as the diocese's lawyer himself suggested, not more (and perhaps much less) than you might have been awarded had you sued. My point is not that you should have sued, for it would have been wrong for you to impose costs on your fellow Catholic laity, who ultimately bear the Church's financial burdens, beyond the amount you actually need or are likely eventually to need to deal with the consequences of what Father Jack did to your son. Unfortunately, however, no amount of money can make up for the intangible harm. Still, as I have argued, reporting to the police, though burdensome to Frank and you, is likely to counteract some of the evils involved in Father Jack's misbehavior and the conditions within the Church that contributed to it.

If you and Frank judge that you ought to report the matter to the police, I think you ought first to tell the bishop what you are planning to do and why. That not only will allow him to benefit from your thinking and do what he can to mitigate bad publicity but will manifest the respect and loyalty you should have toward him as your father in Christ. What if the bishop makes it clear he does not wish you to go to the police? If he gives you persuasive reasons for not doing so, then, of course, you will not. But in the absence of such reasons, his episcopal authority does not extend to forbidding you to report Father Jack's crimes, if you judge that to be your civic duty. So, you should not abide by his wishes in this matter against your son's and your own conscientious judgment.

176: May a lawyer serve clients whose cases seem hopeless?

My conscience as a lawyer sometimes is troubled when a client wants me to make an effort I consider pointless. It is not a question of being asked to do something illegal or immoral in itself; indeed, if the effort could succeed, the outcome generally would be entirely just. But knowing from precedents and/or experience that what a client wants to attempt is bound to fail, I am forced to choose between trying to do the impossible and refusing to comply—a refusal that might lead him or her to retain someone else, perhaps at considerable loss to me if the client is an important and continuing one.

For example, one of my most important clients, the owner of a manufacturing company here, has been the target of a campaign by the local newspaper. The editor is an environmental zealot. The factory is not an advertiser. The paper has been pressing my client to go well beyond what laws and regulations require in limiting the environmental impact of his operation. My client persuaded his employees and their union to take his side, and since the factory is a major employer, the campaign seemed to be going nowhere. But then the paper launched a series of editorials attacking my client's "character" by focusing on every embarrassing and question-able thing he has said and done since he was in kindergarten. While careful to avoid statements that would constitute libel according to settled law, the editor's tactic is contemptible and unfair, and my client wants to sue. Considering the facts of his case and the decisions in precedent cases that constitute the law of libel, I am convinced he will not win and have told him that. However, he wants his day in court so that, as he says, he can "put my side on the public record." I agree with him that the law should be on his side and can make the case that the court should develop the law in favor of my client. But I am as sure he will not prevail as one ever can be when it comes to what judges will do.

Another example. A client is being sued by his wife for divorce and custody of the children, three girls ranging in age from thirteen to six. The children now live with their mother. My client is willing to concede the divorce but wants to contest custody. I know this couple; they have been members of our parish for years. The woman took a feminist turn, declared herself a lesbian, and left the Church. My client is a fine father, a decent and hardworking man who remains a devout Catholic. There is no doubt in my mind that he should have custody of the girls. But, given the judge's preference for the mother in custody disputes and the precedent of a recent decision on homosexual parenting by our state court of appeals, there is equally no doubt that the wife will prevail. I estimate that attempting to get custody will cost at least ten thousand dollars, and I have told him I do not think we can win. But he feels he must try to protect the girls from their mother and give them a wholesome and Catholic upbringing.

Analysis:

This question calls for the derivation of norms. While serving clients, lawyers should make decisions, insofar as their other moral responsibilities permit, solely on the basis of each client's true and legitimate interests. It is usually wasteful, and so wrong, to press any civil case with no reasonable hope of success. Still, if these clients remain determined to attempt the impossible, they will obtain other counsel, so that the waste resulting from their futile efforts will not be prevented. Therefore, the questioner would not be morally required to withdraw.

The reply could be along the following lines:

Before considering the two cases you present, I wish to make a couple of preliminary points.

First, in presenting the problem, you express concern about the possibility that refusing to comply with an important client's wishes might result in considerable loss to you. I am sure it is virtually inevitable that you feel such concern; one naturally fears any serious, foreseen, possible harm to oneself. But it would be wrong to let that influence your judgments about how to handle a client's affairs. For the most part, pecuniary and other considerations can rightly be taken into account in deciding whether to accept a case or continue serving a client. But once the lawyer-client relationship is established and as long as it exists, you should firmly set aside such self-interested considerations. Then, so far as your other moral obligations permit, you should make all decisions about the client's affairs exclusively on the basis of the client's own true and legitimate interests. In serving those interests, you not only must zealously pursue clients' acceptable objectives but assiduously counsel them to shape their objectives by their legitimate self-interest. Fulfilling professional responsibilities in this way, of course, also serves your own profound and authentic self-interest, as loyal and unselfish service to others always does, by helping make you both a good person and a professional on whose integrity clients can rely.

Second, political society provides the system of civil law as a facility to assist its members in their efforts to obtain justice in their disputes with one another and, in some cases, with its own agencies and other parties. This facility has limited capacity, usually fully employed, so that, as you well know, cases seldom are heard without delay. Apart from some extraordinary reason for pressing a case that has no reasonable chance of success, doing so pointlessly employs some of civil law's limited capacity. Pointless employment of anything is waste, and waste of anything others rightly wish to use is unfair, because it impedes their appropriate use of it. In this matter, moreover, the waste is seriously unfair because it is likely to prevent others from protecting or obtaining important goods. Therefore, as a rule it is wrong to press any civil case with no reasonable chance of success.

The action for libel that the owner of the manufacturing company wishes to pursue against the local paper not only has, as you say, virtually no chance of success but is likely to be counterproductive. He wants to put his side on the public record, but few people are likely to have access to the actual record of court proceedings and not many of them are likely to consider it open-mindedly. Most people's impressions will be drawn from the media, including the hostile newspaper whose wrongdoing has provoked your client. At best, some television and radio reports will be fair to him. But the broadcast media are not likely to cover such a trial in depth and so their coverage, even if fair, probably will not help him much. When the trial ends and the newspaper prevails, the public is likely to mistake that outcome for an official declaration that its views of your client and his activities are sound and his positions are indefensible.

Since pressing the lawsuit will not be in your client's true and legitimate interests, you should do your best to get him to see this. It is not enough to tell him he will not win; tell him why he will lose and how the legal action will be wasteful and counterproductive. Then appeal to both his sense of civic responsibility and his legitimate self-interest to choose a different approach, offering more hope of solid benefits to himself and others for whom he is responsible, not least his business's suppliers, employees, and customers. Since his problem centers in public opinion about his business and his personal life, the alternative approach he needs probably will have to be planned and directed by someone skilled in public relations. If a suitable person in that field is employed by your client, I suggest you seek his permission to consult that person about the public relations aspects of the problem, and then work with him or her to sketch out the alternative approach. If the client does not employ an appropriate person, I suggest you seek his permission to consult one yourself.

Your other client's desire to obtain custody of his daughters, the eldest of whom is twelve, is reasonable in itself, and his purpose can be attained only by legal process. Therefore, you first should restudy the case and make every effort to discover a potentially effective legal strategy. (I admit, though, that the prospects are dim, especially since the children are living with their mother, and she can influence their perceptions of the situation and their attitudes toward their father.)

If you cannot think of a potentially successful strategy, I believe you should do your best to persuade your client not to contest custody. Point out to him that he can have no duty to attempt the impossible. Explain to him, too, that such a contest will compel the children to take sides and participate in their parents' struggle— something likely to harm both them and their relationship with at least one parent—probably himself. Suggest that he consider other ways of maintaining a paternal relationship with his daughters, despite his wife's gaining custody of them, and that he give thought to how best to use for this purpose his limited resources, including the ten thousand dollars that would be wasted in the custody battle. For instance, you might suggest that he consider giving up some income to spend more time with the children than he otherwise could and that he permit you to enter negotiations with his wife's lawyer with a view to obtaining generous visitation rights. Finally, without planting false hopes, hold out the possibility that he might have an opportunity to gain custody of the children at a later date, should their mother seriously neglect or abuse them, or, perhaps, lose interest in caring for them as they make demands on her and impede her pursuit of other interests.

Must you withdraw if either or both clients persist in pressing their hopeless cases? I do not think so. The clients might well obtain other counsel, so that your withdrawal probably would not prevent waste of civil law's limited capacity. This consideration is relevant because that waste, rather than anything about what you would do, provides the basic moral reason for not pressing these cases, and you will not be responsible for the waste if your clients insist on proceeding with or without your cooperation. Moreover, by continuing to serve them as best you can you can try to limit the waste and protect them from various harms they might suffer if their cases were handled by lawyers less familiar with them. In this respect, your situation is similar to that of a physician whose patients fail to exercise or watch their diets, continue smoking, drink to excess, and so on. Although they are abusing health care resources, the physician may continue caring for such patients.

Still, someone might argue that you must withdraw, on the ground that in these cases there is only a frivolous basis for the action. The American Bar Association's rule is: "A lawyer shall not bring or defend a proceeding, or assert or controvert an issue therein, unless there is a basis for doing so that is not frivolous, which includes a good faith argument for an extension, modification or reversal of existing law."[391]

The comment on the rule, however, makes it clear that an action is not frivolous simply because the lawyer believes the client's position will not prevail. It then adds: "The action is frivolous, however, if the client desires to have the action taken primarily for the purpose of harassing or maliciously injuring a person or if the lawyer is unable either to make a good faith argument on the merits of the action taken or to support the action taken by a good faith argument for an extension, modification or reversal of existing law."

In the libel case, your client wishes to benefit himself rather than harass or injure his opponent, and you say you can make a case that the court should develop the law to vindicate him. In the custody case, your client's objective also is legitimate, and you can present the case in favor of his being awarded custody of the children. It therefore seems to me that, while both cases are hopeless, there is a basis for each that is not merely frivolous in the rule's sense.

177: Must a lawyer seek an acquittal against a client's best interests?

I am a criminal defense lawyer and was retained by a man charged with assaulting and injuring a police officer. Working on the case, I noticed that the client seemed irrational and I became convinced that he was incapable of acting in his own interests. I obtained a ruling from the court that he was not competent to stand trial. The court committed him to a mental hospital, where he was forced to take medication. After a few months, his mental condition improved a great deal and he was certified competent for trial.

My client insists on pleading not guilty, because, he says, only an acquittal will keep his record clean. His story is that, though he may have been behaving strangely, he was not violating any law when the officer stopped him, said something about drugs, forced him to get down on all fours on the sidewalk, and began beating him about the head and shoulders. He claims that he fought back only in self-defense (he pulled one of the officer's legs so that he lost his balance, fell, and broke his wrist). I advised the client to plead not guilty by reason of insanity, but he refused and also refused to plead guilty to a lesser charge.

---

391. American Bar Association, *Model Rules of Professional Conduct* (1993), Rule 3.1.

At trial, he may be convicted. If so, in view of his previously clean record, he probably will be put on probation, under which he will be compelled to continue treatment and medication. But I now think we could win an acquittal, even without using an insanity defense, because the testimony of a witness—a sidewalk vendor mentioned in the police report—probably will help us more than it will help the prosecution. If acquitted, though, the client will walk out of the courthouse, cease medication, deteriorate mentally, become unable to care for himself, and perhaps become a serious danger to others.

The trial is scheduled, and professional ethics tells me I should try to win an acquittal. But is that really right? Whether or not my client is guilty, his conviction most probably would be in his own best interests and in the interests of society at large, while his acquittal would serve neither. I could withdraw, but that would only saddle someone else with the problem, because the public defender then would face the same dilemma. So, I am thinking of not calling the sidewalk vendor and not cross-examining him if the prosecution calls him.

Analysis:

This question calls for the application of the norms regarding promise breaking and fraud. While it can be reasonable to make an exception to most rules of professional ethics, the questioner's argument for not abiding by the client's objective and seeking his acquittal is unsound. If the questioner, rather than fulfilling the role of legal advocate for this client, presumes to act as arbitrator and promoter of his and society's best interests, he or she will betray and defraud the client. Moreover, in doing this, the questioner also would violate the duty of defense attorneys to play their role in seeking justice on the basis of truth through the process of criminal law.

The reply could be along the following lines:

Like the norms of any code of law, most norms of professional ethics include various exceptions and, even with those exceptions taken into account, are not absolutely binding. Sometimes the common good of the profession as a whole or of the larger society it serves requires a lawyer to make an exception to some norm of professional ethics, and occasionally such an exception might even be justified to prevent some great harm to the professional himself or herself, or to someone else. Still, there is a strong presumption in favor of conforming to the norms of professional ethics, and no exception is justified without cogent reasons. In the case described, the argument for making an exception to the rule that you should abide by your client's objective and try to win his acquittal seems to me extremely weak.[392]

To begin with, the argument for not seeking an acquittal is based partly on your judgment that a conviction most probably would be in your client's best interests, while an acquittal would not be. There are two sets of problems with that.

---

392. See American Bar Association, *Model Rules of Professional Conduct* (1993) Rule 1.2 (a).

First, how can you be so confident about the client's future behavior should he be acquitted? Even if you have been trained in psychology and sociology, experts' predictions frequently are mistaken in matters of this sort. Although you have some grounds for thinking that, if acquitted, your client would discontinue treatment and medication, he might decide to continue with them. Then too, even if it were certain that your client, left to himself, would "become unable to care for himself, and perhaps become a serious danger to others," the question would remain: Must he be left to himself? After an acquittal, you might try to maintain friendly communication with him, and, as a friend, you might be able to cooperate with one or more of his relatives or neighbors in persuading him to accept whatever help he needs.

Second, how can you be so confident conviction will benefit this client? His concern to keep his record clean is reasonable, for even if he were placed on probation, his status as a convicted criminal could be a serious burden to him. Then too, if compelled to accept continued treatment and medication while on probation, he might not cooperate fully, and so might be even less ready than now to live without supervision when the probation ended, as eventually it would. Furthermore, contrary to your expectations, if convicted he might be sentenced to prison, and conditions there might greatly harm him.

As a defense attorney you have undertaken to serve, not as the steward of society's best interests or even of your client's best interests in general, but as the advocate of his legitimate objective in a particular legal process. He claims he acted in self-defense, and he refuses to plead not guilty by reason of insanity. You have no way of knowing he is lying or mistaken; his psychological problems certainly should not be regarded as grounds for believing he did assault the officer. Indeed, you do not question his innocence. Legally, the state must prove him guilty beyond a reasonable doubt, and he is entitled to representation by a lawyer who will zealously protect his rights and win his acquittal unless the state really can overcome the presumption that he is innocent. Therefore, in failing to seek an acquittal, you would violate his right to present his case. In short, you would betray and defraud your client if you abandoned your role as his legal advocate and assumed a different one: that of arbitrator of his and society's best interests.

Furthermore, abandoning your role would injure the common good of the citizens of your state. To deal with crimes and allegations of crimes, they need a criminal process in which truth is brought to light and justice achieved through the conscientious cooperation of the various participants—jury, judge, prosecutor, witnesses, and defense counsel. To the extent that participants do not fulfill their assigned roles, they deprive their fellow citizens of the just process society needs. If in this case you were justified in doing less than your best, within the limits of relevant legal and moral norms, to win your client's acquittal, all lawyers in more or less similar cases would be justified in acting similarly on the basis of their personal judgments about what would be good for their clients and society at large. Clients would never know whether their lawyers were trying to serve their interests as they themselves understand them or were substituting their own judgments and choices. Society could not count on defense attorneys to fulfill their assigned role in the process of criminal law. Instead, the process would be undercut, as lawyers unilaterally decided what was best for their clients and society.

In view of these prospective consequences of doing the sort of thing you propose, you cannot soundly argue that you should omit questioning the sidewalk vendor so that your client will be convicted. That argument, like all consequentialist arguments, is plausible only if one focuses on a limited set of possible consequences and ignores others, some of them as likely to eventuate as those focused upon.

In sum, seek an acquittal. Since only God knows the future, you have no way of knowing that doing otherwise would be in your client's or society's best interests. Therefore, do your job, trust God to do his, and be confident that everything will turn out right—if not in this world, at least in the next.

178: Must prosecutors drop cases they believe they will not win?

I am one of several lawyers working as prosecutors in the office of the State's Attorney. While we all agree that a case should be dropped as soon as it becomes clear that there is little or no likelihood of winning a conviction, some of us think that a prosecutor may make an exception when that might bring about a better outcome, and I'd appreciate having your thoughts on the problem.

For example, I recently handled a case against a drug dealer and was confident of getting a conviction until, checking the evidence a few days before the trial date, I found that the drugs had vanished. I could have dropped the case at once, but I decided to go through with a scheduled meeting with the accused's counsel, Robert White. He plainly was unaware that the evidence was missing, and I said nothing about it. White offered to plead his client guilty to a reduced charge, and I agreed without arguing, though the bargain was so favorable to the accused that normally I would not have accepted it. One of my colleagues, Lisa Phan, took the position that what I had done was unethical. She cited a rule of legal ethics: "The prosecutor in a criminal case shall . . . make timely disclosure to the defense of all evidence or information known to the prosecutor that tends to negate the guilt of the accused or mitigates the offense."[393] I argued that I did not violate that rule or do anything wrong.

Currently, I am dealing with a different sort of case. A prominent businessman I'll call Baxter offered an exotic dancer a tip of one hundred dollars if she would have intercourse with him. She had performed at an office party and returned afterwards to pick up her wristwatch, which she had left in the restroom. She refused Baxter's proposition, but he would not take no for an answer. Within thirty minutes she filed a complaint of rape against him and checked in at a nearby hospital emergency room where the physical evidence was secured. Baxter stopped at a bar on the way home, and, with unusual efficiency, the police arrived there before he did. They were about to ask him to get into their squad car when a detective lieutenant arrived, told Baxter he would not be arrested if he could explain what

393. American Bar Association, *Model Rules of Professional Conduct* (1993), Rule 3.8 (d) "Special Responsibilities of a Prosecutor."

had happened, and questioned him. Baxter admitted having intercourse with the woman and, when asked about her demand that he leave her alone, merely offered the usual lame excuses: "She said 'Leave me alone,' but didn't mean it"; she is "just a whore" who was "asking for it"; and so forth.

That initial statement was taped and is definitely incriminating. Unfortunately, it also is of limited worth; it would not be admitted as a confession because the officers who arrived first had not read Baxter his rights, and the detective lieutenant, assuming they had, also neglected to do it. And, of course, when Baxter reached the police station, he called his lawyer and from then on insisted that, after he had intercourse with the woman with her full cooperation, she demanded a thousand dollars and threatened to go to the police, and he told her to go right ahead. The woman denies Baxter's accusation and has added to her initial report without changing it. She is a good student who works as a dancer for her college expenses. She says she is often propositioned and always refuses, and I believe her.

With the physical evidence and the victim's testimony, I can make a prima facie case. But investigation has failed to turn up any witness or other supporting evidence. In the end, a conviction will depend on her word, and I am virtually certain that at least one member of any jury I can get will not believe her, because Baxter is a respected member of this community with a previously unblemished record. His lawyers, of course, know this and refuse to plea bargain. Either I let this rapist walk away untouched or go to trial without any expectation of winning. I am inclined to the latter. The trial's trouble and embarrassment will be at least something of the punishment this man deserves and will serve as a deterrent to others. Phan, who disagreed with me about the other case, agrees with me about this one, but one of our male colleagues dismissed our view as feminist crusading and said it is wrong to take this case to trial.

Analysis:

The plea-bargaining case calls for the application of norms regarding truthfulness. The questioner perhaps deceptively indicated readiness to go to trial or, at least, fell short of appropriate candor in dealing with the defense attorney. The case of the businessman accused of rape calls for the derivation of a norm. Going to trial would abuse the legal process by using criminal proceedings as punishment and deterrence in the absence of conviction; and would impose unfairly on many of those affected, not least the victim of the crime. So, the prosecutor should not go to trial in this case. Still, under certain conditions a prosecutor may proceed with a case in which a conviction is quite unlikely.

The reply could be along the following lines:

In the first case, in which you accepted the plea of a drug dealer to a reduced charge, you may have assured Robert White, explicitly or implicitly, that you were ready for trial after you discovered the evidence was missing. If so, since in fact you could not proceed without the evidence necessary to make a case, you misled him, and the plea bargain was vitiated by that deception. Even if you did not give White any such assurance and his assumption that the incriminating evidence would be available was based only on your previous representation or that of someone else representing the state rather than, say, his client's own information, your silence, though not deceptive, was hardly candid. Arguably, such a lack of candor would have been unfair to White. More plausibly, in my judgment, it would at least have been a failure to meet proper standards of professional conduct, because prosecutors and defense counsel, though required to act as adversaries by the legal system, should cooperate in pursuing the system's overarching purpose: justice based on truth.

Still, I do not think what you did violated the rule requiring "timely disclosure to the defense of all evidence or information known to the prosecutor that tends to negate the guilt of the accused or mitigates the offense." While the information about the missing evidence would have been favorable to the accused, the rule simply was not relevant, since the fact that the drugs had vanished neither negated the accused's guilt nor mitigated his offense, but only rendered it impossible to prosecute the case. Indeed, the accused's acceptance of the plea bargain was an admission of his guilt at least in respect to the lesser offense.

In asking about this case, you take for granted the moral acceptability of plea bargaining as a method of settling criminal cases, but, as I am sure you know, some critics regard it as generally unfair in practice if not inherently unjust.[394] I do not think plea bargaining necessarily is unjust, and I do not know enough about how it is done in various places to judge whether it is generally unfair. It is not difficult, however, to see two respects in which it might easily involve serious abuses.

First, where there is significant but inconclusive evidence that someone has committed a serious crime (for example, a third offense of drug dealing), a prosecutor who thinks the accused more likely guilty than not may be tempted to try to induce a possibly innocent person to plead guilty to a minor charge (for example, unlawful possession) to avoid the risk of being convicted of the serious offense. This sometimes has the bad result that innocent people both lie and are wrongly convicted. To forestall this injustice, prosecutors should not bargain for a guilty plea to any serious crime unless certain beyond reasonable doubt that the accused really is guilty at least of the offense to which he or she will plead guilty.

Second, in cases in which both the prosecutor and the accused's counsel believe that the accused has committed a certain crime (for example, a third offense of drug dealing, conviction for which would result in a lengthy, mandatory prison term) both sides for the sake of convenience might be tempted to agree on a plea to an offense which the accused did not commit but which will result in a mutually acceptable penalty (say, selling drug paraphernalia, conviction for which will result in a brief term). Such an agreement would be seriously immoral, since it would be deliberate cooperation in abusing criminal process. Moreover, carrying out the agreement would involve lying and inducing the accused to lie in a grave matter—stating in a proceeding of public record that the accused is guilty of something other than any offense he or she committed.

---

394. See, e.g., David Lynch, "The Impropriety of Plea Agreements: A Tale of Two Counties," Law and Social Inquiry, 19 (1994): 115–33. Lynch describes several wrongs, including the two I shall discuss, that are sometimes, and perhaps often, involved in plea bargaining.

In the case of Baxter, the businessman accused of rape, I agree with your colleague who holds that it would be wrong to go to trial. Indeed, I believe there are at least two distinct though closely related reasons why it would be wrong.

First, if you go to trial without any expectation of winning, you will impose unfair burdens on many persons involved. Some other case more worthy of trial probably will be displaced; the time and work of the judge, the jury, and others will be wasted; witnesses will be inconvenienced. Among the witnesses, the alleged victim, even if she is eager to have Baxter tried, is likely to suffer most. She will be embarrassed and subjected to severe stress; and, if the outcome is as you expect, many people will mistakenly assume her allegations have been disproved and draw the conclusion that she lied.

Second, though the purposes of criminal process include punishment and deterrence, those goals can be achieved rightly only on the basis of a defendant's conviction. The requirement of conviction as the basis for punishment specifies the prosecutor's role in the criminal process. But your purpose in prosecuting Baxter would be to achieve those goals by the proceedings themselves without a conviction. You have no right to use the criminal process in that way—not even to bring about what you believe a better state of affairs. So, using the trial as Baxter's punishment and as deterrence to others would be abusing legal process and betraying your office.

In view of these reasons why it would be wrong to go to trial, I think that, if you reflect on your own motives and are honest with yourself, you will find that only your strong feelings are tempting you to do this. While you might rationalize the project as implementing your commitment to justice, it really would serve something akin to a thirst for revenge. But the Lord says: "Vengeance is mine, I will repay" (Rom 12.19). Instead of surrendering to the temptation to play God, you should hope he will do justice when he brings all humankind to judgment. And you should bear in mind that in due time you, too, will face that judgment.

Does this mean a prosecutor should never go to trial with a case in which a conviction is quite unlikely? No. A prosecutor may proceed provided two conditions are fulfilled: (1) he or she reasonably expects significant benefits for the common good that warrant the effort even though it is unlikely to succeed, and (2) he or she has no reasonable ground to doubt that, if a conviction were obtained, the admissible evidence would justify it. For example, a prosecutor might justifiably go to trial with a case against the leader of a criminal syndicate while expecting that jury tampering or intimidation of witnesses would lead to an acquittal. How would such a prosecution contribute to the common good? A conviction might be so great a public benefit that even a remote chance of it happening would warrant the effort. Moreover, going to trial might offer legitimate, secondary benefits, such as the opportunity to catch those using the expected, illicit tactics, or the arousing of public concern and official efforts to deal more effectively with the syndicate.

+   +   +

179: May a defense attorney impugn the testimony
of an honest witness?

I am employed as a staff lawyer at the public defender service. We handle only certain criminal cases in which the accused are unable to provide their own counsel. I have been assigned to defend a twenty-year-old punk, whom I'll call George. There is abundant evidence that he has robbed and beaten dozens of people, and now he is charged with murdering an elderly woman who died as the result of his abuse. The police report indicates that when arrested later the same night for another mugging, which was reported by a witness who identified him, George was high and very frightened. By morning he confessed to having robbed and beaten the woman, and signed a statement.

I was assigned George's case and immediately checked out his confession and how the investigation was conducted. The document gives me nothing to work with in defending him. I am not personally acquainted with the detective who obtained the confession, but I made inquiries and learned that he is one of the most careful and decent people on the force.

When I visited George in jail for the first time, I already was convinced that his only hope was to plead guilty to one or more lesser charges if the prosecutor would drop the murder charge. By then, however, George had regained his composure. He told me that he was "strung out" when he was interrogated, that the detective had taken advantage of him and mixed up different incidents, and that he is innocent of the elderly woman's death. Since then, he has consistently repudiated that part of his confession and refused to discuss a possible plea bargain on that charge.

George is now about to go to trial for the murder. Given the adversary system under which we operate, I must do everything possible to make some sort of case in this client's favor and to deflect or destroy the case against him. The only tactic with any hope of success is to impugn the testimony of the detective who obtained his confession. I must get the jury to believe that when George signed the document, he was an inexperienced, worn out, hungry, intimidated youth, who wanted nothing more than breakfast and a bed. (Since he has not been charged previously as an adult and the prosecutor cannot introduce George's long and telling juvenile record, I will be able to make the most of his youth.) In questioning the detective, I will have to come across to the jury as skeptical and critical of his inquisition of the suspect, hinting that only unfair tactics could have elicited so damning a statement. I will not encourage George to perjure himself, but I will put him on the stand in his own defense, and I expect he will lie convincingly. In my closing argument, I will portray him as the victim and the detective, careful and decent though he may be, as the villain.

I would have no hesitation about all this if this detective were like many I know or if George were a defendant for whom I felt some sympathy. As it is, I wonder whether the morality of my role as defense counsel should not give way to the morality of dealing with a decent fellow human being.

Analysis:

This question calls for the application of norms regarding truthfulness and for the derivation of norms for the work of a criminal defense lawyer. The questioner should provide this client with the most effective defense possible within the bounds of law and morality. The facts as recounted seem to support a reasonable opinion that the client is guilty of murder, but that opinion could be mistaken. The questioner, as defense counsel, should think the client might be telling the truth; on this basis, the questioner may elicit and use his testimony without intending to cooperate in perjury. The questioner may introduce the evidence favorable to the client and convey by appropriate behavior sympathy toward him and skepticism regarding the detective's account. But the questioner must avoid both lying and deception, and may not ask any question without a good faith basis. In summarizing the case for the defense, the questioner may assert only true propositions that would serve as reasons for finding the client not guilty, and may not make exaggerated claims about what the evidence and testimony imply.

The reply could be along the following lines:

George is entitled to a competent and earnest defense. Having been assigned his case, you must do everything possible to defend him—the possible here, of course, being limited by moral norms as much as by any other limiting condition. Thus, as you suggest, you may not encourage him to perjure himself. Likewise, in questioning the detective who obtained his confession, you may not set morality aside and proceed as though the end—gaining an acquittal—justified any means that might be effective.

Reading your statement of the case, many honest people unfamiliar with the adversary system and the professional responsibilities of lawyers are likely to think you cannot defend George without both lying and being unfair to the detective. In my judgment, however, you can defend your client without doing anything wrong, provided you clarify and rectify your own attitude and thinking about the case and your responsibilities.

It is only natural that some clients elicit your sympathy while others do not, and that some cases arouse your enthusiasm more than others. Likewise, when interviewing a person whose case you have been assigned, you cannot help making your own evaluation of the evidence and forming a favorable or unfavorable impression of the client. However, your concluding remark suggests that you are tempted to allow your personal feelings and judgments to influence how much of an effort you will make on George's behalf. It would be wrong to give in to that temptation. The justification for your work as counsel for the defense and the norms shaping that work are grounded, not in your personal feelings and judgments, but in the principle that anyone accused of a crime is to be presumed innocent and must be proven guilty, and in the belief, embodied in our system of criminal justice, that the accused needs a competent advocate to make the jury and/or judge aware of anything that might tend to show that convicting and punishing the accused are unwarranted. Therefore, firmly put aside your personal opinions and feelings, keep in mind George's right to be acquitted unless the state proves his guilt beyond reasonable doubt, and undertake your professional responsibilities as defense counsel with no more hesitation than if this were a client you liked and personally believed innocent.

The purpose of a trial, which you should cooperate in pursuing, is to reach a just verdict grounded in the truth. Even if George in fact is guilty, a guilty verdict will be just only if the admissible evidence supports it and relevant law is correctly applied. And the relevant law is both substantive and procedural, so that if there is any procedural fault in the authorities' handling of George's case, you should seek on that basis an order or verdict freeing him.

The facts of this case as you recount them do seem to support a reasonable opinion that George is guilty and has been lying in insisting he is innocent of the elderly woman's death. That opinion could be mistaken, however, since not even a reasonable and well-founded opinion is knowledge. The distinction may not matter much in some situations, but you must never lose sight of it in deliberating about your professional responsibilities toward any client or potential client. Somewhat as spouses have special reason to trust each other despite evidence of unfaithfulness that other people reasonably take as decisive, defense attorneys have special reason to give their clients the benefit of every possible doubt. Thus, you should suppose that George might be innocent, and you should not assume that his testimony in his own defense will be untruthful.

If George had admitted to you that he is guilty, you would have an entirely different problem. Then, if you put him on the stand, you would expect him either to tell the truth or to perjure himself. Telling the truth would do him no good, and, as his lawyer, you would not recommend it. Perjury would be seriously wrong, and so you could neither cooperate with it nor make use of it in defending him. Therefore, you probably would urge him to plead guilty, but at least not to testify. And if he insisted? You would be obliged to withdraw if you could do so without signaling his guilt. And if you could not withdraw? You would have to tell him that, though you would call him to the stand, he would have to tell his story without your guidance.[395]

However, if you explain to George that, supposing he is guilty, it would be both wrong and risky to perjure himself, and he continues to insist on his innocence, you should assume that he might be telling the truth. Given that assumption, you will be able to use his testimony in defending him. In calling him to testify, your intention should be: I wish my client to help himself by telling the truth that will tend to exonerate him. With this intention, you may and should proceed despite your opinion that he probably is guilty and will perjure himself, since as his advocate you have the duty, already explained, to give him the benefit of every possible doubt.

May you impugn the testimony of the detective who obtained the confession? You certainly may introduce the evidence that George was in an abnormal state of mind—according to the police report, both "high and very frightened"—and as whether that may not account for the confession. If George tells you he was

---

395. See American Bar Association, *Model Rules of Professional Conduct* (1993), Rule 3 with comment, "Perjury by a Criminal Defendant." In my judgment, the proposed alternative solutions are morally unacceptable.

mistreated in some respects, you may assume that he might be telling the truth and question the detective about those matters in such a way as to suggest the mistreatment occurred. You also may question the detective closely about each step of his investigation and dealings with George, with the expectation that he will affirm over and over that he perfectly fulfilled his responsibilities. Then, since it is reasonable to assume that no one is perfect, you may question his claim that he did everything perfectly.

To the best of your ability, by your tone of voice, facial expressions, and gestures you may convey sympathy toward your client and skepticism with regard to the detective's account. While this might seem deceptive, it need not be and can be justified. In the first place, it remains possible either that George is innocent or that his confession is not legitimate evidence against him. Your behavior should express and dramatize this possibility, and thus communicate it effectively to the jury and/or judge, so that they will give it whatever weight it deserves. Second, in acting as George's advocate, you are expected to set aside your personal feelings and opinions, and instead manifest an attitude as favorable as possible toward your client and as unfavorable as possible toward testimony and evidence tending to convict him. If you fail to do this, your behavior will suggest, falsely, that you concede that George should be convicted, whereas doing it will not constitute the assertion of anything at odds with the truth. Rather, it will suggest one or both of two truths: that you are in a position to give George the benefit of the doubt and that the prosecution's case may not suffice to ground a verdict against him—which could be true even if he did the deadly deed.

Nevertheless, to avoid lying, you must exercise great care and self-discipline in playing your part.

While your appropriate courtroom behavior need not assert anything false and while you make no straightforward assertions in questioning witnesses, as they generally do in answering questions, you often do make implicit assertions even in asking questions. For example, if you were to ask the detective whether he slapped George's face, the question would suggest he had done so and would implicitly assert that you had some ground for the suggestion. Without a good faith basis for asking the question, your implicit assertion would be false, and so you would be lying. Therefore, you may not suggest that the detective was guilty of any misconduct unless George alleges it or you have some other basis for supposing he was. Moreover, if you pursue any groundless line of questioning, you must expect either that its groundlessness will become evident or not. If it becomes evident, it will do your client no good and so is excluded; but if it does not become evident, it can be helpful only by being deceptive, and so will be dishonest.

In summarizing your case and offering your final argument, you will make assertions. Here, too, you are expected not to express your personal opinions and attitudes, but to put forward any sound argument and point to any facts helpful to your client. You could say something along the following lines: "Bear in mind that the defendant is only twenty years old, that he admittedly was caught committing another crime, and that he was high and very frightened. Bear in mind, too, that he knew the detective interrogating him was in control of the situation and had at his disposal all the resources of the police department. Then ask yourself: Am I really certain beyond all reasonable doubt that this statement, repudiated shortly after it was made and repeatedly since then, is trustworthy evidence?"

In doing your best, however, you may be tempted to make exaggerated claims about what the evidence and testimony imply. But that would be lying. Thus, you may not say, "The detective's testimony shows such and such," unless you really believe it does. Nor will it help to avoid the form of an assertion by putting the deceptive suggestion as a question: "Would not a reasonable person, hearing the detective's testimony, conclude such and such?" Unless you believe a reasonable person would draw the conclusion indicated, such a question remains a subtle form of lying.

In sum, you may call into question the testimony of a witness whom you believe to be decent and honest, provided you have a basis for doing so and avoid not only outright lying but deception. You must do your best to be an effective advocate for your client, but your role within the adversary system remains subordinate to your responsibility to cooperate in bringing about a just verdict grounded in truth.

180: May a lawyer select potential evidence for probable destruction?

I am an associate in a law firm, working under the direction of one of the partners, Ralph Klane, whose practice is almost entirely limited to labor union locals.[396] About eighteen months ago, the president of one of our clients retired, and the secretary of the local, whom I'll call Jikel, was elected to replace him. The former president was absolutely honest and extremely effective; union members revered him and employers respected him. Jikel would look bad by any standard, but compared with his predecessor, he is a disaster. Grievances of every sort get belated and inept handling, and managers at several companies are ignoring important contractual provisions with impunity. Some union members who have suffered as a result of Jikel's incompetence tried to force his ouster but failed. Three whose discharge probably should have been brought to arbitration, but whose cases he bungled in ways that now make that impossible, have threatened to file suit against him and the local, on the ground that contractual obligations toward them as union members were not fulfilled, resulting in financial damages to them through not being reinstated in their jobs.

In Mr. Klane's judgment—and I agree with him—the disgruntled union members have a case that is plausible but not good enough to prevail. We are confident that they will not be able to obtain competent counsel on a contingent-fee basis and they will not be able to afford to litigate the case to the end. The only real threat for Jikel and the local union concerns what might happen at discovery, when the plaintiffs' lawyers will want to examine every scrap of paper in the union's files that might be relevant.

396. A union local is a part of a larger union organized in a particular locality, comprised of the employees of either a single employer or several employers in that locality.

This morning, Klane and Jikel had a conference. I was not present. Afterward, Klane told me that, although the suit has not yet been filed, they decided we should make advance preparations. He directed me to go to the local union's office and scour the files, tagging (but not pulling or copying) all items of certain kinds, some to be tagged in one way, most in another way. Not understanding the directions, I began asking questions and eventually realized that the common feature of items of the kinds to be tagged in the first way is that they would be missed if not produced at discovery.

Carrying out this assignment will not be particularly difficult, but I am quite uncomfortable with it. Klane, of course, obtained Jikel's agreement to my going through his files and tagging them. I am confident Klane did not advise him to do anything about any of the tagged items, but I am sure Jikel will put two and two together, freely purge the files of embarrassing items that will not be missed, and even get rid of a few of the most sensitive items that will be missed. In effect, I will be selecting potential evidence for destruction. This skates along the edge of violating professional ethics, which forbids destroying or concealing a document or other material with potential evidentiary value, or counseling or assisting anyone else to do so.[397]

Up to now, I have got along well with Mr. Klane, but it is clear in this firm that associates must go along just to survive, and all the more so to make partner. I hope it will be all right for me to put aside my qualms of conscience and do the job.

Analysis:

This question calls for the confirmation and application as a moral norm of the rule of legal ethics that forbids destroying or concealing potential evidence. This rule is reasonable and important for achieving justice. All violations are gravely wrong and any deliberate violation by a lawyer raises a substantial question about his or her honesty and trustworthiness. Hence, the questioner must resist following instructions and if necessary refuse to follow them. Moreover, if Klane and/or other members of the firm persist in this project, the questioner should, in my judgment, report him and/or them for professional misconduct. Since doing that would be unusual and almost certainly would have consequences gravely detrimental to the questioner, the reasons requiring it must be stated clearly and the factors that impede self-regulation by the members of a profession must be explained.

The reply could be along the following lines:

Some rules governing activities of members of a profession bear on merely instrumental or otherwise secondary matters, while others bear on specific actions in respect to the good that those practicing the profession should serve. Bar Association rules regarding advertising fees and preventing the unauthorized practice of law are of the former sort. They govern important matters but do not shape a lawyer's participation in legal processes. A lawyer sometimes is justified in making exceptions to such rules, especially in their details, for the sake of

---

397. See American Bar Association, *Model Rules of Professional Conduct* (1993), Rule 3.4 (a).

superior and intrinsic values, particularly justice to be achieved through legal processes. By contrast, the rule you cite does bear on lawyers' specific role in legal processes. Therefore, assuming it reasonable, a lawyer is unlikely to be justified in making an exception to it.

But the rule forbidding destroying or concealing material with potential evidentiary value not only is reasonable; it is important. In times past, many societies tried cases by ordeal or personal combat, believing that God or fate would ensure a just outcome. But everyone eventually came to recognize that relying on fate is irrational, and faithful theists came to realize that God calls on human beings to cooperate in carrying out his wise and loving plan, so that relying on him requires that they not only seek good ends but use the means God provides, not least their intelligence, as fully as they can in pursuing them. So, nonbelievers and believers alike strove to develop sound norms for legal processes that were meant to reach just judgments (or settlements) by searching out the truth about people's relationships and other relevant facts. The processes work only if evidence is brought to light so that it can be considered. Necessarily, therefore, any violation of the rule about handling potential evidence is seriously wrong, since it makes unavailable part of the truth on which a just judgment (or a just settlement forestalling the trial) must be based. When one understands the purpose of this rule, one also sees why laws in some jurisdictions expressly prohibit suppressing evidence even when a suit has not yet been filed but is only anticipated.

Inasmuch as this rule bears on the essential activity of lawyers and is important, so that all violations are seriously wrong, any fully deliberate violation of it by a lawyer raises a substantial question about his or her honesty and trustworthiness. Thus, the situation you describe involves a challenge to your personal and professional character. Moreover, as you consider your responsibilities, you should put yourself in the place not only of the three union members who are threatening to sue but of other union members who are being badly served due to Jikel's shortcomings. Bear in mind how much is at stake for these people and how badly they and their families may be hurt if he is not held responsible.

I am sure your reading of the assignment you have been given is substantially correct. Mr. Klane has instructed you to tag certain items in the files of a client—Jikel and the local union of which he is president—in order to prepare for an anticipated lawsuit, in which the tagged items might have to be made available to the prospective plaintiffs. In itself, tagging relevant items could be prudent and entirely legitimate. However, tagging items in the manner Klane has specified—in different ways depending on whether or not plaintiffs' lawyers would realize they are missing—cannot be intended to serve any purpose except to signal which of the items can be disposed of safely. There would be no point to that unless Klane intended that the signal be used as a guide in purging the files. Hence, if you carry out Klane's instructions, both he and you will be deliberately preparing for someone to destroy or conceal documents or other material with potential evidentiary value. That not only "skates along the edge of violating professional ethics," as you put it, but clearly and directly violates the cited rule. Given the facts as you have described them, I can see no justification for you to make an exception to the rule

Therefore, you may not follow Klane's instructions. Contributing in this way to his incipient effort to forestall a just judgment or settlement would be seriously wrong even if you did not share his wrongful intention, as I assume you would not.

You might argue that in this case there is a justification for making an exception. You do not think the prospective plaintiffs can prevail, partly, it appears, because you think they will be unable to carry the litigation through to the end. But you may not act on the basis of that expectation. You do not know what evidence plaintiffs' lawyers will uncover or what sort of case they can build. If the evidence needed to build a powerful case is uncovered, plaintiffs' capacity to prevail might change. Their counsel might then agree to proceed on a contingent-fee basis; other disgruntled union members might help them; the evidence might force Jikel to resign and motivate those taking charge of the union local to offer a settlement; and so forth. Therefore, it would be unfair for you to make your prediction self-fulfilling by using it as an excuse to make preparations to purge the files.

What should you do? You might be tempted to try to evade the problem by purposely "misunderstanding" your instructions and tagging all the items of both sorts as you have been told to tag only those whose absence would be noticed. That would solve nothing, however, since Klane would be sure to find out what you had done, and you would be asked for an explanation. At that point, you would either have to lie, which would be wrong and probably ineffectual, or would have to own up to what you had done, which almost certainly would provoke Klane no less than if you simply refused to do as he has told you.

Therefore, rather than trying to evade the problem, talk with Klane at once. Tell him you are concerned about carrying out his instructions because, it seems to you, that would violate the rule about handling potential evidence. In this way, you will invite him to show you how doing it would be legitimate. However, I expect he will try to brush aside your objection by saying: "If you had more experience you would realize this is necessary to give Jikel the best possible defense" or "Nobody need ever know" or "Everyone stretches these rules a bit now and then."[398] In response, you should not only tell him why you think violating this particular rule is seriously wrong but point out that Jikel, incompetent as he is, can hardly be relied upon, and if he purges the files and it becomes known to plaintiffs' lawyers, the result could be disastrous—not only for him but for Klane and you. Suggest that Klane tell Jikel all items will be tagged in a single way and warn him not to attempt to purge his files.

And if he rejects your suggestion and refuses to amend your instructions? He might say nothing, and simply relieve you of the task and assign you to other work. If so, it seems to me, you will have fulfilled your responsibility. You have no

---

398. Klane might point out that Rule 3.4, entitled "Fairness to Opposing Party and Counsel," also specifies: "A lawyer shall not: . . . (e) in trial, allude to any matter that the lawyer does not reasonably believe is relevant . . ., or state a personal opinion as to the justness of a cause, the credibility of a witness, the culpability of a civil litigant or the guilt or innocence of an accused." But though these provisions (which, no doubt, often are violated) are included in the same numbered Rule, they in fact are logically distinct rules whose violation typically is far less likely to obstruct justice than is the violation of the rule against suppressing evidence.

authority to pursue the matter; you will not be cooperating in wrongdoing and will not even know for certain that the wrong is being done. Very likely, though, Klane will either insist that you carry out his instructions or tell you that someone else will do the job. Then you should appeal to the other manager or managers of the law firm to countermand his decision, if they can, or, if they cannot, to try to persuade him to change it. This appeal might succeed. If it does, it might benefit Klane by preventing him from violating an important ethical norm. It could even benefit you. Though your superiors might respond negatively, at least some of them are likely to respect you for your integrity and courage.

But, of course, the appeal also might fail. If so, or if you are threatened with dismissal, you should first warn Klane and then, if necessary, everyone in authority in the firm who supports him that, unless the project of getting rid of potential evidence is abandoned, you will report him and/or them for professional misconduct inasmuch as doing what is proposed would raise a substantial question about his and/or their honesty and trustworthiness.[399] If that warning is heeded, your days with the firm will be numbered, and you will have to pursue prospects elsewhere. If it is not heeded, you ought to carry out your threat and accept the consequences.

Merely questioning Klane's instructions already will involve some risk to your prospects with the firm, for, as you say, associates there must go along with their superiors even to survive, and all the more so to become partners. Why take that risk? For the sake of justice, which the legal profession is committed to serve; for the sake of the potential plaintiffs and, indeed, the other union members, who are likely to suffer due to the injustice; for the sake of the profession itself, which is corrupted by serious misconduct; for the sake of the client, whose true and legitimate interests will not be served by getting rid of potential evidence; and, not least, for your own sake. If you docilely followed these instructions, you would sacrifice your personal and professional integrity, prostitute yourself for job security and advancement, and risk your very soul. By doing what is right, you will reaffirm your commitment to justice, confirm your integrity, and preserve your hope of salvation.

Appealing Klane's decision to others managing the firm, if that becomes necessary, will involve an additional risk, but it will be required not only by the same set of values but by the good of the law firm itself. As an associate, you owe your loyalty to the firm more than to Klane. He happens to be your supervisor, but his misconduct will not be in the firm's true interest. Finally, the same set of values requires you to warn him and, if necessary, others managing the firm that you will report them for professional misconduct, and to carry out that threat if they do not heed it.

---

399. See American Bar Association, *Model Rules of Professional Conduct* (1993), Rule 8.3 (a). A lawyer's obligation under this rule to inform the appropriate authorities arises only when the violation of the Rules of Professional Conduct raises a substantial question as to the violating lawyer's honesty, trustworthiness, or fitness. Under Rule 8.4 (a), Klane already has committed an act of professional misconduct in attempting to induce the questioner to violate the Rules of Professional Conduct in an important matter.

Given the seriousness of what is at stake for you, I expect that you will ask others, such as your former law professors or fellow students, for advice. Almost certainly some, and perhaps most or even all, will say that you need not go so far as to threaten to report professional misconduct, much less carry out the threat, since such reports are rare indeed, while misconduct of various sorts is quite common. What I have advised you to do is seldom done. But that does not show that the advice is mistaken or asks too much of you. Rather, it points to a moral defect pervading all the professions and making their efforts at self-regulation weak and ineffective. The members of each professional community tend to overlook, tolerate, and even conceal one another's professional misconduct rather than admonish one another, report misconduct, and work together in enforcing sound norms of professional performance.

There are several reasons for this. First, practicing a profession focuses attention on the multitude of activities that are necessary means and distracts attention from the profession's overarching end. Justice is the end to which all lawyers should commit themselves on entering the legal profession; as officers of the court, they should prefer that good even to a client's interests incompatible with it. But if professional commitment weakens and justice becomes peripheral, legal practice easily becomes a game in which colleagues' rule breaking seems at worst foolishly risky. Second, anyone who attempts to enforce standards is vulnerable to one or another form of retaliation by wrongdoers and those with whom they have important common interests. Third, people in the same field share a common point of view, easily put themselves in one another's shoes, recognize their own deficiencies, and so are reluctant to judge others: There, but for the grace of God (or, perhaps, my good luck), go I. Fourth, and perhaps most important, comradeship motivates all professionals, more or less strongly, to be lax about colleagues' misconduct. Members of a professional community are comrades, sharing in the enterprise of the profession, with its common interests and challenges. This community is a genuine human value, and it engenders remarkably strong emotional bonds, which motivate members to protect one another, especially against threats perceived as coming from outside the group. To the morally immature, moreover, rules of conduct always seem to be extrinsic impositions; and, unfortunately, all of us are more or less morally immature. Thus, just as children detest tattletales, so professionals take a cool view of any colleague who informs on others' professional misconduct and are likely to make him or her a pariah.

Someone might argue that the custom of not reporting professional misconduct has nullified the rule requiring reporting and made it a dead letter. Customs often do modify rules, but a rule grounded, as this one is, in a moral obligation remains valid despite violations, no matter how frequent. Therefore, there can be a grave obligation to report professional misconduct in this case even though many, if not all, of your mentors and peers probably will advise against doing so.

There are many reasons why members of every professional community fail mutually to enforce standards of conduct, but none provides the slightest justification for laxity.

181: May lawyers lead clients to make possibly untruthful statements?

As a law student, I am confused by the rules about what a lawyer may and may not do when guiding a client in telling his or her story.

One of our professors proposed this case. During the winter, a growing number of people began using the block-long main corridor of a college as a shortcut from a metro station to a large office building. This extra traffic caused various costly problems, and so the administration persuaded the city council to enact an ordinance making it trespassing for anyone with no business with the college to cut through the corridor. Signs are duly posted, and the college temporarily hires extra guards to stop everyone who enters the building. A lawyer familiar with the situation, Mr. Lawry, is contacted by a woman, Ms. Doe, who tells him she was seriously injured in a bad fall in that corridor, and the college's liability insurance carrier is offering her a ridiculously small settlement. Lawry says: "Before you go any further, let me explain the legal situation to you. On the one hand, trespassers are not in a good position to recover damages for accidents on private property. On the other hand, people on the premises for business reasons, even just to get some information about an event at the college, have a far better chance of recovering. I guess you were in that corridor for some business reason, weren't you?"

Called on to comment, I said: "Surely a lawyer could not say that. It would be instructing the potential client to lie." But the professor pointed out that, provided Lawry did not know that Doe was not in the corridor for a business reason, he was not proposing what he knew or even believed to be false; rather than instructing her to lie, he was merely guiding her in telling her story to her own advantage.

After class, some of us had a lively discussion. I argued that what Lawry said would be practically the same thing as telling Doe to lie. One of my classmates suggested that Lawry could have accomplished his purpose without inviting Doe to lie by saying simply: "Trespassers are not in a good position to recover damages for accidents on private property, but people on the premises for business reasons have a far better chance of recovering. What you were doing in the corridor could be vital to your case. Can you recall exactly why you happened to be there?" That still seemed to me tantamount to suggesting that Doe lie.

But another clever classmate came up with a way of putting matters that seemed acceptable to all of us: "Trespassers are not in a good position to recover damages for accidents on private property, and the college has signs up in that corridor warning that people just using it as a shortcut are trespassing. If you were not there for some business reason, at least to get information about some event at the college or something of the sort, I doubt that you have a case."

Of course, there are many other situations in which a lawyer needs to guide a client in stating his or her case, and it would be interesting to know if there are any rules bearing on this matter.

+   +   +

Analysis:

This question calls for the derivation of a norm. Regardless of which of the three formulations the lawyer chooses, he either conditionally intends that the potential client lie in grave matter or unnecessarily tempts her to do so. If the client lies and thereby gains her objective, she is unlikely ever to repent. Leading another into such lying would be grave matter. It also is gravely wrong knowingly to subject another without good reason to significant temptation to commit a grave sin; and even unnecessarily risking leading someone to commit a grave sin that he or she is unlikely ever to repent is a most serious offense against love of neighbor. Therefore, lawyers should elicit their potential clients' and witnesses' full statements of facts before instructing them about the favorable and/or unfavorable legal implications of the facts.

The reply could be along the following lines:

Lawyers should help their clients use legal processes and other legitimate means to seek the benefits of just judgments or settlements based on the truth about their relationships with others and other relevant facts. Moreover, lying is wrong in itself, and lying under oath is always gravely wrong, since it adds the wrongness of irreverence toward God to lying's intrinsic wrongness. Therefore, it should be obvious that there is a general norm admitting of absolutely no exceptions: A lawyer may never instruct or induce anyone to lie, or assist or approve his or her doing so, and any of these wrongs is the more grave if the lying would be under oath.

Beyond that, it would be a mistake even to suppose that one always may guide a client or potential client to tell all the truth that would be to his or her advantage. Even when telling a truth would be to one's advantage, it sometimes may not be told because that would be unfairly disadvantageous to someone else. For instance, sometimes the duty to keep a secret requires that one suffer some harm or forgo some benefit.

It is an important part of a lawyer's responsibility to guide clients to tell the truths that are to their advantage when and as appropriate. Suppose Ms. Doe, in the example, was in fact in the corridor to pick up an admissions packet for a neighbor who was considering applying to the college, and you were retained to represent her. In preparing her to testify, it would be appropriate to tell her that the reason for her being in the corridor is important to her case and she should make it clear in her testimony. More generally, in advising clients a lawyer often has occasion to guide them in distinguishing between truths appropriate for them to tell and others that they have no obligation to tell and that, in their own interests, are better left unstated.

Your professor was right that, in the example proposed, Mr. Lawry is not quite instructing Ms. Doe to lie. However, he is inviting her to lie. Lawry's caution, "Before you go any further," clearly warns Doe against telling a story disadvantageous to her—that is, disadvantageous unless Lawry subsequently helps her pursue a settlement by lying. He tells her that having been in the corridor on business would support her claim for damages while having been there as a trespasser would not; in the context, that is an invitation to assert that she was there on business, whether that is true or not. Likewise, "I guess you were in that corridor for some business reason, weren't you?" puts in question form the proposition whose assertion, true or not, is recommended to Doe as advantageous. In guiding her in this way, Lawry does not unconditionally intend that she lie; after all, the assertion he suggests she make might be true. But he does conditionally intend that she lie, since he wishes her to make the advantageous statement—it will provide him with a case he is more likely to win—even if it happens to be false.

The first of the two reformulations suggested by your classmates was: "Trespassers are not in a good position to recover damages for accidents on private property, but people on the premises for business reasons have a far better chance of recovering. What you were doing in the corridor could be vital to your case. Can you recall exactly why you happened to be there?" This formulation does differ significantly from the one proposed in class, since a lawyer could use it without intending, even conditionally, that the potential client lie. However, since it was proposed as an alternative way of accomplishing "the same purpose," that immoral conditional intent would remain and the formulation's ambiguity would make no difference morally speaking. But even if it were used without any intention that the potential client lie, it would share the moral problem of the third formulation.

That third formulation, which seemed to your classmates and you entirely acceptable, was: "Trespassers are not in a good position to recover damages for accidents on private property, and the college has signs up in that corridor warning that people just using it as a shortcut are trespassing. If you were not there for some business reason, at least to get information about some event at the college or something of the sort, I doubt that you have a case." Though this surely could be said by a lawyer without conditionally intending that the potential client lie, it is hard to see why any conscientious lawyer would deliberately use even a formulation along these lines.

If the intent were to invite the potential client to lie, it would be as wrong to use this formula as the original one. But even without wrongful intent, it would be inappropriate for instructing a potential client, such as Ms. Doe, before hearing her story. Such an instruction is unnecessary at this stage and might well tempt the potential client to lie. Because of the sum at stake, the prospective lie would be grave matter. Now, even taking an unnecessary risk of leading someone into sin is a sin of scandal, and such a sin is grave if the sin to which it leads is grave. Therefore, even without wrongful intent, using the final formulation would be gravely wrong. Then too, the initial lie in telling the story might later lead to perjury, and a lawyer who unnecessarily risks encouraging perjury betrays his or her responsibility as an officer of the court, whose function is to achieve justice based on truth. Furthermore, if the desired outcome were obtained by means of the lie, the client would be unlikely ever to repent and make restitution. One can do nothing worse to anyone than lead him or her into a grave sin unlikely to be repented. Therefore, the wrong of using even the final formulation would be a most serious violation of love of neighbor.

This discussion can be summed up in a general norm which, though overlooked by codes of legal ethics, is more important than most norms they include: A lawyer should not in any way suggest or indicate to a potential client that the assertion or denial of any statement might be to his or her advantage until the individual, without guidance as to what might be advantageous, makes his or her own statement of the facts relevant to the case. Lawyers should follow an analogous norm in interviewing potentially helpful witnesses.

A criminal defense lawyer is especially likely to be tempted to violate these norms when clients or potential clients are accused of serious crimes. But the violation remains gravely wrong in itself. Moreover, the accused either is guilty or innocent. If guilty, these norms should not be set aside to save him or her from just punishment. If innocent, following the norms will help establish the truth, which is the natural ally of the innocent, while violating them will risk making him or her seem guilty.

Note, too, that lawyers who violate the norm in preparing the testimony of witnesses other than their own clients are vulnerable to exposure. The confidentiality of the lawyer-client relationship, which courts generally protect, does not hold here, so that a cross-examiner usually can require witnesses to answer questions about the involvement of lawyers other than their own counsel in preparing their testimony.

182: May a lawyer help a client violate the law?

The Immigration and Naturalization Service is threatening to deport an illegal immigrant. She will be given a court hearing to make her case for political asylum. However, though she fled her homeland after losing her job due to her political views and is likely to suffer further mistreatment if she is sent back, she probably will not win in court.

As a member of an organization dedicated to helping such persons, I am giving this woman free legal assistance. She is considering two unlawful possibilities: (1) improving her chances for asylum by overstating her role in the opposition to the regime in power in her homeland (thereby exaggerating the prospect that she will be imprisoned or worse if she returns there), or (2) participating honestly in the trial, but if, as we expect, unsuccessful in court evading deportation by going underground.

I firmly believe that this refugee and others like her ought to be given asylum and that deporting them is unjust. In my view, U.S. law does not make fair provision for such people, and the law's injustice is regularly made worse by the way it is applied. Yet my code of professional ethics tells me I may never knowingly use perjured testimony or assist or counsel a client to engage in any other conduct I know to be criminal or fraudulent.[400] If caught in a violation, I could be convicted of a crime and/or disbarred. Still, everyone admires and commends people—such as those who hid Jews from the Nazis—who violated laws and took personal risks to protect the innocent from injustice.

---

400. See American Bar Association, *Model Code of Professional Responsibility* (1986), DR 7–102 (A) (4) and (7); *Model Rules of Professional Conduct,* Rule 1.2 (d).

What should I do? Perhaps the possibilities should be distinguished, so that I should help this client do either (1) or (2) but not both. Or perhaps there are other possibilities; and if so, what might they be?

Analysis:

This question calls for applying norms regarding perjury and compliance with laws. The questioner should not advise or help any client to commit perjury. It might be morally permissible or even obligatory for a U.S. citizen to assist a refugee who was objectively justified in violating the immigration law or a lawful order to leave the country. But lawyers should provide an example of conformity to law and, if they practice law as part of their personal vocation, should avoid risking their professional status. Therefore, even if otherwise justified in helping a refugee violate the law, the questioner should minimize his or her complicity.

The reply could be along the following lines:

It is helpful to consider what the refugee herself should and should not do.

If in testifying she expressed her sincerely held but exaggerated view about the significance of her role in opposing the regime in power in her homeland, making the truthful overstatement would not be wrong. But you indicate that she contemplates deliberately exaggerating. Such overstatement would be wrong, for it would be lying and, indeed, lying under oath: perjury. Perjury not only is wrong as lying always is, but is more gravely wrong than other lying, because it dishonors God by calling him to witness the lie.[401] A good end cannot justify choosing as a means any act morally wrong in itself. Therefore, the refugee may not commit perjury, even as a means to avoid unjust deportation and its consequences, no matter how disastrous these might be.

Though defective in many ways, the government of the United States basically serves the common good, and its laws and legal procedures on the whole are just (see q. 169, above). Even forgetting its genocide, the Nazi regime was thoroughly corrupt; it greatly injured the German nation, issued and implemented many arbitrary edicts, and regularly used unjust methods to control people. What good people did under the Nazis is not necessarily a model for us. We Americans have good reason to presume the laws of our country to be just until the contrary is established, and, though a law requiring something wrong must not be obeyed, we often have good reason to comply with our country's laws even when convinced they are not just (see LCL, 880–81). By contrast, those subject to the power of the Nazi regime had good reason to presume that any edicts originating with it would be unjust and few reasons, other than concern about sanctions, for complying with orders they judged unjust.

Still, the worst people in this world are not totally corrupt and the best, except for Jesus and Mary, are not sinless; and no human government is totally unjust or perfectly just. In some respects, even under the Nazis, the rule of substantially just

---

401. Some courts permit an affirmation in place of an oath but still regard it as perjury to make a false statement under affirmation. Such statements, though not irreverent except as all sins are, remain an especially grave kind of lying.

law endured in Germany and deserved respect, and in some instances arbitrary impositions occur in our country and occasionally warrant noncompliance.

So, having honestly participated in a hearing, a refugee might be morally justified in illegally evading deportation and going underground, provided he or she has good reasons—for example, based on a reasonable fear of serious harm to himself or herself or on duties toward dependents.[402] Going underground, however, will be justified only if, all things considered, asylum is unjustly denied, that is, if the U.S. morally ought to grant it but does not. Thus, the client should consider everything, apply the Golden Rule, and ask herself: If I were a conscientious American citizen, would I consider it my country's duty to accept the burden of providing asylum for all refugees whose prospects if deported were as bad as, or worse than, mine truly are? She will be justified in ignoring a lawful order to leave the country only if she can honestly answer yes—that is, if she believes it certain or more probable than not that asylum should have been granted.

Moreover, since lying is excluded, she will not be justified in insincerely promising to comply with an order to leave the country (which, if the hearing results in that order, may be the only way for her to gain the freedom from custody necessary to evade deportation), or in fabricating and telling a cover story to conceal her illegal status from people she will have to deal with while residing illegally in the United States.

As for your responsibilities, you certainly should not advise or help any client to commit perjury. For a lawyer to advise or cooperate in perjury, no matter how good the end sought, is a great moral evil, for it adds to the evil of perjury itself a radical betrayal of the lawyer's role as an officer of the court and a servant of just legal process, which is vital to the common good of the whole society. Then too, as explained below, lawyers ordinarily should not advise or help clients engage in criminal conduct, even when the lawbreaking itself could be justified; a fortiori, they should never involve themselves in unjustifiable lawbreaking, such as perjury. Finally, even if perjury were a morally acceptable tactic, it would be risky. Lies often are unconvincing, and unconvincing liars seldom elicit the compassion of those they try to deceive. Therefore, advise your client not to commit perjury under any circumstances.

There is, however, a vast difference between perjury and presenting an effective, persuasive case. Help your client prepare her testimony, so that everything favorable to her case will appear as clearly and forcefully as possible.[403] Since there is no perjury in truthfully stating what one sincerely believes, help her present her honest opinion regarding all the difficulties she will face if repatriated, even if you consider her honest view overly pessimistic. And of course you may rightly advise her not to say anything more than she must to answer the questions put to her, since

---

402. Mark Gibney and Michael Stohl, "Human Rights and U.S. Refugee Policy," in *Open Borders? Closed Societies? The Ethical and Political Issues,* ed. Mark Gibney (New York: Greenwood Press, 1988), 151–83, show that the level of political terror in a country does not correlate well with favorable adjudications for people seeking asylum.

403. A guide for lawyers: Deborah E. Anker, *The Law of Asylum in the United States: A Guide to Administrative Practice and Case Law,* 2nd ed. (Washington, D.C.: American Immigration Law Foundation, 1991).

going further might harm her case, and neither morality nor law requires her to volunteer information that might be disadvantageous to her.

So much for the first possibility. What about advising or assisting your client in morally justified lawbreaking?

If the client is convinced she is doing the right thing, others could be justified in advising and helping her evade deportation—of course, after making their own conscientious judgment that, though unlawful, it is certainly morally permissible for them to help her or, at least, is more likely their moral obligation than not.

For lawyers, however, there usually are special considerations making it unreasonable, and therefore wrong, to advise or assist in anyone's lawbreaking, even if it is justified in itself. First, their example of conformity to law is especially important, and their involvement in any lawbreaking often provides bad example and leads others to violate the law unjustifiably. Second, they should practice their profession as part of their personal vocation: to help people obtain justice and protect them from various harms, to make a living for themselves and their families, and so on. If they practice law with such commitments, they have compelling reasons to avoid risking their professional status, and lawbreaking does that. For instance, if you were convicted of conspiracy to violate the immigration laws and disbarred for helping this particular refugee, you could not help other refugees in the future obtain the asylum to which they are legally entitled.

Therefore, in response to your client's inquiry about the possibility of evading deportation if asylum is not granted, tell her that is illegal and, as a lawyer, you cannot advise or help her violate the law. You may, of course, explain the likely consequences of going underground, even if doing so might encourage her to attempt it. Certainly, if you can think of any practical, lawful alternative that might solve her problem—such as seeking asylum in some third country—you should suggest it and, depending on your resources and her need, perhaps should assist her in pursuing it.

But suppose you can think of no such alternative, and you consider your client's prospects, if deported, so bad that, in your judgment, she is both morally justified in evading deportation and morally entitled to others' unlawful help. Might you then rightly judge that you should do something illegal to help her evade deportation? Perhaps. On the stated supposition, you would regard helping her not only as morally acceptable in itself but as the responsibility of anyone who could help and had no overriding reason not to. Still, if helping involved lying or doing anything else wrong in itself, it would be excluded.

But suppose one could help without wrongdoing? Even then, you would have overriding reasons to minimize your complicity, namely, to avoid, insofar as possible, two things: giving an example that might lead others to disrespect the law and risking your professional status. Some people are not only ready to help refugees whose deportation they judge would be unjust but also free of responsibilities that require them to avoid complicity in lawbreaking of this sort. As a member of an organization dedicated to helping refugees, you probably are acquainted with such people or know someone who would be likely to know them

If so, you could communicate anonymously with them, describe the refugee's desperate situation, and encourage them to help.

Note, though, that giving your client even such indirect help in breaking the law would violate the relevant provision, noted above, of your code of professional ethics. Like some violations of law itself, however, some violations of professional ethics are not morally wrong. If you were justified in helping your client violate the law, you also might well be justified in violating your code of professional ethics.

Someone might object that it would be hypocritical to try to avoid giving others bad example if one justifiably participates in violating the law and one's code of professional ethics. The objection begs the question. Hypocrisy is trying to appear virtuous when sinning, not trying to prevent the scandal that might result from a virtuous deed if it were done openly.

183: May a lawyer seek a court order believing it would be unjust?

A client, whom I'll call Jane, is plaintiff in a divorce action. She petitioned for custody of the children, child support according to the state guidelines, exclusive use of the family dwelling and its contents, and that her husband, Sam, be required to continue paying the mortgage payments. At the preliminary hearing, Sam disputed custody but we prevailed, and the court also ordered him to make all payments as we asked. At the time, he was well able to do that. However, a month later—almost six months ago now—his job was eliminated in a reorganization and he was forced to accept a demotion, which cut his salary by almost half and his take-home pay by more than a third. He then asked for a reduction in child support in accord with the guidelines; since the court would have granted it, I advised Jane to agree, and she did. While Sam has continued paying the child support, he now has fallen behind on the mortgage payments.

On my client's instructions, I discussed the situation with her husband's lawyer, and it became clear that Sam is not earning enough to subsist and also make the mortgage payments as well as pay child support. Lacking collateral and having missed payments on various accounts, he cannot borrow from a commercial lender. We therefore worked out an arrangement, to which Jane tentatively agreed—she would lend Sam half the mortgage payments, and he would repay the loan with interest from his share of the equity when the property is sold.

A few days ago, however, the judge who is handling the case sent a husband in a similar situation to jail for contempt. The local paper did a feature story on the case and also editorially criticized the judge for "reinstituting debtors' prison." Jane now wants me to ask the court to cite Sam for contempt. If he is threatened with jail, she believes his parents, though not prosperous, will draw on retirement savings to make the mortgage payments and keep him out of jail.

I am not sure that her expectations are realistic. But, knowing the judge, I expect that, if I carry out her instructions, he will accommodate her. In the circumstances, though, I do not think it would be just for the court to cite Sam for contempt. I could attempt to withdraw from representing this client, but since she wishes to proceed at once, she may not agree, and the judge might order me to continue representing her. If I do succeed in withdrawing, she probably will find someone else to represent her, and the outcome will be exactly the same. What do you think I should do?

Analysis:

This question calls for the derivation of norms. The questioner believes the contempt citation would be unjust. Though a lawyer should presume every client's cause just and should leave uncertainties about what is just to the court's judgment, the questioner may not intend that the court do something he or she is convinced it cannot justly do. The questioner should try to persuade the client to follow through on her tentative agreement and, if she will not, should try to withdraw from representing her. If ordered by the judge to continue representing this client, the questioner may not zealously represent her in the sense of intending to achieve her unjust objective, but may do those and only those things necessary to comply with the order.

The reply could be along the following lines:

In what follows I take for granted that the situation is just as you describe it. Sam simply cannot make all the payments he had been ordered to make. Jane regarded the resolution to which she tentatively agreed as fair. She now believes the judge will threaten to send Sam to jail for contempt. By seeking the contempt citation, she intends to pressure Sam's parents to make payments, by drawing on retirement savings, that the court could not order them to make.

For two reasons, I agree with your judgment that in these circumstances issuing the contempt citation would be unjust. First, the legitimate purpose of citing someone for civil contempt is to compel him or her to do what he or she has been ordered to do and could do but has refused to do. Thus, civil contempt always presupposes that the contumacious person has refused to do what he or she could do. But Sam simply cannot make all the payments he was ordered to make. He has a cogent defense for not making them, and any reasonable judge, rather than putting him in jail, would amend the prior order or require only that Sam do what he can to comply with it. This judge, however, may refuse to consider Sam's defense and arbitrarily order him jailed for failing to do the impossible. But since that order would be an abuse of judicial power, seeking it would be unfair. Second, Sam's parents presumably are not responsible for his failure to make the ordered payments. Moreover, not being prosperous, they have no duty to help their son and his wife, who, apparently, can make do without their help. So, if his parents make the payments as Jane anticipates, they will go beyond their duty solely in order to keep their son out of jail. Jane therefore intends the threat of jail to compel Sam's parents to do what they have no duty to do. That is tantamount to extortion and plainly is unfair. Therefore, seeking to obtain what Jane wants would be unjust. It also would be an abuse of legal process.

Someone might argue that seeking the contempt citation need not be unjust. Perhaps the judge has learned by experience that many defendants in such situations conceal assets or sources of income until pressed by the threat of jail.

However, jailing someone for failing to do the impossible surely is unjust; and so therefore is jailing a particular person in these circumstances, without evidence that this person is cheating and simply on the basis of the generalization that many people in such situations try to cheat. In threatening Sam with jail and intending to carry out the threat despite evidence about his inability to make the payments, the judge's intention would be to jail him even if that is unjust. And, in fact, on your statement of the case, Sam has no concealed assets or sources of income.

Of course, the judge might not accommodate your client. He might only threaten to put Sam in jail without intending to carry out that threat. But the threat then would be a lie, and a lie in a matter of this kind and importance surely would be gravely unjust. Furthermore, asking the judge to do something unjust would itself be unjust, even if you are not certain he will do it, since the intention in asking would be to effect the injustice, and the fact that an attempt to do something morally wrong may not succeed does not eliminate or even mitigate its wrongfulness.

Sam's parents may help him appeal the judge's decision, and, if appealed, it probably will be reversed. But it already is a serious injury to be subjected to an unjust order and compelled either to comply or appeal. Moreover, an appeal might not seem feasible to Sam without his parents' help, and the burden on them of helping would itself be unjust.

Someone might argue that you should accept and serve clients without using your personal moral standards to evaluate their objectives. On this view, you should leave the question of the justice of your clients' causes to their judgment and the court's. Certainly, in acting as an advocate you should presume your clients' desires to be just unless the facts and their own statements show the contrary, and you should not anticipate the court's judgment about any doubts you might have concerning the justice of your client's cause. But you are responsible for your own actions. You may not ignore evidence that tends to rebut the presumption in your clients' favor, and you may not intend that the court do something you are convinced it cannot justly do. Under certain conditions, as will be explained, you might continue acting for a client who is pursuing what you believe to be an unjust objective, without yourself intending to achieve it. Still, to represent a client who is seeking what you believe to be an unjust objective with the intention to achieve it would mean willing the injustice and thereby making yourself an unjust person. That would remain true, indeed, even if you were mistaken about the injustice of the client's objective.

What, then, should you do?

If you have not already done so, first try to persuade Jane to follow through on her tentative agreement to the arrangement previously worked out. Give the reasons why you think seeking the contempt citation would be unjust and explain why doing so might not be in her own best interests. If the judge threatens Sam with jail but, contrary to her expectations, his parents refuse to make the payments, at best she probably will gain nothing. If the judge does not carry out the threat, she probably will receive no more than Sam is now able to pay. If he is jailed, he will be entirely without income and unable to pay even what he has been paying. If he appeals and wins, resources will have been wasted in the litigation.

What if your best effort to reason with your client fails? Then, in my judgment, you should tell her that you cannot in good conscience seek the contempt citation and wish to withdraw from representing her. You say that, even if you succeed in withdrawing, she probably will find someone else to represent her, and the outcome will be exactly the same. Perhaps so. But unlike a case in which what a client wants is merely imprudent—for example, an action justly seeking an objective that the client almost certainly will not win—in this case the client's objective is unjust. You may continue to represent imprudent clients, who insist on pursuing objectives unreasonably, with an eye to mitigating the harm they will suffer and bring about (see q. 176. above). But no good end can justify intending injustice, and so you may not choose to continue representing a client whose objective you regard as unjust.

Moreover, you cannot be certain it will make no difference to the outcome if you withdraw. It will underscore all you have said in trying to reason with Jane, and so might lead her to reflect and change her mind. Also, she may not actually get someone else to represent her. However, even if she does and the outcome for her, Sam, and his parents is exactly the same as it would have been had you continued representing her, the outcome will be different for you. By refusing to cooperate with her unjust plan, you not only will avoid accepting any responsibility for the injustice she wishes to bring about but will bear clear witness to truth and justice.

Someone might point out that professional ethics does not require you to withdraw from the representation of a client merely because the client insists on a course of action you believe to be unjust.[404] In this matter, as in many others, however, moral responsibility requires more of a lawyer than the rules of professional ethics do. The latter no doubt are based on the assumption that every party to a case is entitled to zealous legal representation and that legal processes can be counted on to produce just outcomes. Since you should not share Jane's intention to obtain an unjust order, however, you cannot willingly serve her in this matter. But professional ethics does permit you to attempt to withdraw, inasmuch as you consider your client's objective repugnant.[405]

What if Jane does not consent to your withdrawal, the judge orders you to continue representing her, and you face severe consequences, perhaps even disbarment, if you refuse?[406] In that case, it seems to me, to avoid the consequences of refusing, you could do several things not wrong in themselves: draft and file the necessary papers, appear in court and present relevant evidence, and even say what you must in court. But you could not intend Jane's objective.

---

404. See American Bar Association, *Model Rules of Professional Conduct* (1993), Rule 1.16 (a).

405. See ibid., (b) (3).

406. It is unlikely—and in some jurisdictions unthinkable—that a judge would order a lawyer to continue representing a client despite the lawyer's sincere belief that doing so would contribute to an abuse of legal process. But the possibility cannot be ignored here because the judge perhaps has the authority to prevent the lawyer's withdrawal and, in any case, this judge does not seem to be inhibited by the limits of his or her authority.

Someone might object that, if you continue representing Jane, you must do so "zealously within the bounds of the law"[407] and so will not be able to avoid intending her objective. Certainly, in zealously representing clients, you intend to achieve their objectives. However, if you continue acting for Jane under the duress of a court order, you should not zealously represent her. You should do no more than you believe necessary to avoid the consequences of defying the judge. Your situation, it seems to me, would be analogous to that of a person being raped. Threatened with gun or knife, one can do various things necessary to bring about the rapist's objective—such as undressing and assuming a suitable posture—without choosing to engage in any sexual act, since all the behavior is directed to a different immediate purpose, namely, the avoidance of grievous injury to oneself.

Still, reluctant cooperation under duress with a morally unacceptable project can be morally wrong. Compliance can be an occasion of sin for the cooperator or others; it can prevent the cooperator from bearing appropriate witness; and it can be unfair to others injured by the wrong. But with appropriate precautions you could resist temptation and avoid sin, and your example in this case probably would not lead others to sin, as it might if, for example, you were complying with the orders of a despotic regime rather than of one bad judge. Your compliance would prevent you from bearing witness in this instance to truth and justice. But, considering what you have at stake and the rarity of this instance, I doubt that you have a strict duty to make the sacrifice required to bear witness. Of course, if you act under the judge's order for Jane and her unjust effort succeeds, you will be making some contribution to the injustice Sam and his parents will suffer. However, your contribution will be limited: by the duress, the greater contribution of others to the injustice, and the likelihood that someone else would have represented Jane had you defied the court. Moreover, you could fairly accept contributing to the injustice toward Sam and his parents provided you fairly compensated them—which, in my judgment, would not require making good their whole loss but some part proportionate to your comparatively small contribution to it.

Someone might reject the preceding solution and maintain that, even with the judge's order, you could not continue acting for Jane without intending her objective. Your situation, they might say, is not like that of someone being raped but of someone threatened with the loss of a well-paying job unless sexual favors are granted to the employer. A person who yields to such pressure does engage in sexual acts, however reluctantly, as means to an end, just as an ordinary prostitute does. I do not concede that your compliance under duress would be like prostitution; you could do what you must to avoid defying the court without sharing in Jane's action by intending her objective. Still, I agree that, if your compliance were like prostitution, you would be obliged to refuse to comply with the court's order. In refusing, of course, you would do what you rightly could to forestall or defend yourself against penalties. But you could not rightly will what you believe to be an injustice in order to evade the consequences, even if being disbarred were sure to be among them.

---

407. See American Bar Association, *Model Code of Professional Responsibility,* (1986), canon 7.

184: Should a lawyer insist that potentially lifesaving information be disclosed?

I am a lawyer working in the legal department of a relatively small automobile insurance company.

Yesterday afternoon the vice-president in charge of claims called me in and outlined the facts of a pending case. A policy holder was responsible for an accident in which the other driver, call him Herbert, suffered extensive and serious injuries. In line with standard company procedure in personal injury cases when our policy holder is clearly at fault, we promised to work out a fair settlement when Herbert's long-term condition became clear and meanwhile paid all his bills as they accumulated. After extensive rehabilitation, it appeared that he would suffer some permanent disability. He retained a lawyer who negotiated with our adjuster what seemed to be a reasonable settlement, assuming Herbert's condition was accurately described by the physicians who had been caring for him. Before approving, however, my superior in the law department (who now is away on vacation) required that our own physician verify his condition. Our doctor carried out a thorough thoracic examination. Unexpectedly, it revealed an aortal aneurysm—a possibly life-threatening condition.

If Herbert were our physician's patient, the doctor would immediately have put him back in the hospital for evaluation and care by specialists. Instead, the physician reported his condition to the adjuster, and they talked with the vice-president. The doctor's opinion is that it can never be proved that the aneurysm resulted from the accident but that it might have. The adjuster and the vice-president are convinced that, if we tell Herbert or his physicians what our doctor found, the previous settlement agreement will not be finalized and the eventual settlement will be far larger. The vice-president said that, while inclined to tell our physician to omit the evidence of the aneurysm from his written report and to tell the adjuster to consummate the tentative settlement, he wanted me to weigh the possible legal implications and report back to him before lunch today. I responded that we should have our physician tell Herbert's doctors about the problem at once, and, whatever the legal implications of not doing so, our moral obligation was obvious. The vice-president, calm and polite as usual, answered with a friendly smile: "Ms. Reed, please bear in mind that we do not employ you to give us medical or moral advice. I am asking you for your legal opinion, and I will appreciate having it, as I said, by noon tomorrow."

As a lawyer, I am constrained by confidentiality, so I cannot take the matter into my own hands and talk to Herbert's physicians. If the vice-president were a client rather than my employer, I would tell him to find himself another lawyer. As it is, I either must resign or follow orders and limit myself to giving technical legal advice, which, I am sorry to say, is likely only to confirm the vice-president in his inclination to withhold the potentially lifesaving information.

+ + +

Analysis:

This question calls for judgment by the Golden Rule and application of the norm regarding confidentiality. As a legal adviser, the questioner can warn the vice-president that failure to inform Herbert of the life-threatening condition could lead to a lawsuit against not only the company but the vice-president himself and others involved, and that the potential defendants cannot assume they will prevail in such litigation. The questioner should recommend that the vice-president promptly send Herbert a carefully worded warning to seek medical advice regarding the potentially life-threatening condition noted by the company's physician. If the vice-president rejects this recommendation and persists in the course of action to which he was initially inclined, applying the Golden Rule shows, in my judgment, that the questioner should take the steps necessary to ensure that Herbert receives the potentially lifesaving information.

The reply could be along the following lines:

The vice-president is asking you for legal advice about the course of action to which he is inclined: to direct the company's physician to omit from his report the evidence of the aneurysm and to direct the adjuster to consummate the tentative settlement. But you cannot draw out the legal implications without making some assumptions about future events that are not entirely predictable. When you say that, if you were to limit yourself to technical legal advice, that probably would only confirm the vice-president in his inclination to withhold the potentially lifesaving information, you must be assuming that it will remain a secret that your company had this information and withheld it, and thus that neither Herbert nor his estate will be able to seek redress for the risk to his life thus imposed on him.

Supposing that assumption to be operative, it seems to me you should be able to deal easily and briefly with the legal implications, since there will be none. But you should base most of your advice on the opposite assumption—that the secret will not be kept—since in that case not only the company but every individual involved may well suffer very serious consequences: not only directly, by losing a suit for damages, but indirectly, through losing good reputation and other things of great value.

All physicians should be committed to helping people preserve their lives and promote their good health. No matter who employs a physician to do an examination, he or she has a moral responsibility to inform the person whose life is at stake upon discovering a life-threatening condition. Hence, as you already told the vice-president, the company's physician should at once have told Herbert's doctors of the examination's unexpected finding, so that by now his condition would have been evaluated and appropriate care initiated.

Since your physician failed to fulfill this responsibility, the company's moral position is already compromised. The company will be grossly unfair to Herbert if it now takes advantage of that failure in order to consummate the tentative settlement. If this wrong resulted in his death or serious injury, it could provoke substantial legal claim against the company. However, the vice-president is assuming that the secret will be kept. But, as will become clear, that cannot be safely assumed.

Not as a medical or moral adviser, therefore, but as a legal adviser, you can tell the vice-president that, if he follows his inclination, the consequence might well be a lawsuit by Herbert or his survivors, and the company might well lose. You can recommend that he instead direct the company's physician at once to prepare his written report, including the evidence of the aneurysm, and that the adjuster deliver it to Herbert together with the settlement ready for signing and a covering letter along the following lines:

> We are pleased to be able to deliver the settlement previously agreed upon.
> Still, we are distressed that our physician's examination coincidentally turned up evidence of a serious medical problem of which your physicians may be unaware. We strongly urge you to ask them immediately to review the enclosed report.
> Assuming the problem was previously overlooked, we are gratified to be able to help by calling it to your attention.

The physician's report will warn Herbert, and such a covering letter might lead him to accept the previously negotiated settlement.

In presenting your recommendation, you can tell the vice-president that, by carrying it out promptly, he can protect the company from liability for withholding the vital information. You can explain, too, that, if he does not carry out your recommendation promptly, he will be risking serious harm both to the company and himself, for if the secret is exposed, he could be personally targeted by any lawsuit and undoubtedly would be held responsible by higher management. Finally, you can point out that he cannot count on the secret's being kept, since the physician, the adjuster, and other employees privy to the secret also might be vulnerable, and so would have a motive for revealing it.

If the vice-president accepts your recommendation and carries it out, your problem is solved. But if he does not? Consider your own true interests, not least your interest in being a Christian and an upright person, and, if that is not enough to make clear what you should do, put yourself in the place of the others involved and apply the Golden Rule. If your life were at stake, as Herbert's now is, you surely would expect a person in your place to make considerable personal sacrifices to provide you with potentially lifesaving information. Putting yourself in the place of others involved who will be hurt if the company's handling of the matter comes to light, would you not expect a conscientious person in your place to try to save them? Therefore, in my judgment, you should take the steps necessary to protect the real interests of everyone concerned.

You might begin by taking the matter to higher management, if you can do that without delay. If that is impossible or turns out to be ineffective, present the vice-president or higher management with an ultimatum: If my recommendation is not carried out, I will take the matter into my own hands and advise the company's physician that, for the good of the company, his own good, and for my sake too, he should at once supply Herbert's physicians with the information about the unexpected finding. No doubt you would be violating company policy and risking your job in doing this. However, as you should explain in presenting the ultimatum, your drastic action would be warranted. In refusing to be an accomplice in injustice and resisting it, you would be acting in the company's true interests, and your first duty as a lawyer employed by the company is to protect its interests, not simply do whatever management tells you, even when that is an injustice that risks great harm to the company.

If your first ultimatum is rejected and the company's physician also refuses to follow your advice, present a second ultimatum: If my original recommendation is not carried out, I will inform Herbert's lawyer about our physician's unexpected finding and make it clear that the information should be passed on at once to Herbert's physicians. If this second ultimatum is rejected or ignored, in my judgment you must carry it out.

The course of action I have suggested is complex, involving a series of steps, but you must proceed quickly. With Herbert's life at stake, think in terms of hours or, at most, a day or two. At every step, stress the urgency of the situation and make it clear that you will accept no delay.

What about lawyer-client confidentiality? If withholding the information about the life-threatening condition revealed by the company physician's examination would be criminal negligence likely to result in Herbert's death or substantial bodily harm, for you to reveal the information would be in accord with one of the exceptions stated in the confidentiality rule.[408] But even if this recognized exception does not apply, it seems to me your usual duty to preserve confidentiality is overridden by your personal responsibility toward Herbert. Withholding the information would be standing by while your client does Herbert the great injustice of seriously endangering his life for the sake of nothing more than avoiding the risk of a higher settlement.[409]

185: May a lawyer, seeking restitution for a client, threaten criminal charges?

One of my law firm's clients is a major computer software maker. The partner in whose section I currently work assigned me the task of getting the client's former vice-president for financial affairs to pay back funds he embezzled over a period of nearly three years. The company wants not only repayment in full but interest of twenty-three percent per year, based on its average rate of profit on investment during that time. Their argument is that, had the funds been available, they would have been used at least as effectively as the rest of the company's capital, and so fair restitution must include the lost profit. Moreover, they want repayment at once, not over an extended period. I consider the company's demands reasonable, and

408. See American Bar Association, *Model Rules of Professional Conduct* (1993), rule 1.6 (b) (1).

409. Considering Rule 1.6 as a whole, along with the official commentary and the corresponding material in *Model Code of Professional Responsibility* (1986), canon 4 and DR4–101, I think the requirement of confidentiality on the part of lawyers is more open to exceptions than might be supposed in view of considerations like those involved in the present situation.

the embezzler's lawyer says his client would meet them if he could. But he has convinced me that his client simply does not have sufficient assets of his own. He could repay promptly if his wife would agree to selling their jointly owned residence, but, unfortunately, she refuses to cooperate.

When I conferred with my superior, she said: "Tell the embezzler's counsel that our client is running out of patience and will report the matter to the police and press charges unless the property is on the market by the end of this month." I pointed out that at the first conference with our client I asked whether the matter had been reported to the police, and they said no; while they want their money, they do not want to press criminal charges against their former colleague. My superior replied: "I know the embezzler's wife well. She will not want to see her husband, the father of her children, in jail. Threatening criminal charges is sure to break the logjam."

I feel this tactic is dishonorable. But the rules of our professional ethics do not exclude it. How big an issue must I make of this?

Analysis:

No definite answer can be given to this question, partly because the information supplied is inadequate. But four problems can be sketched out to guide the questioner's further reflection. First, threatening criminal prosecution of the embezzler to motivate his wife to sell their house might be unfair to the wife, who was not a party to his crime. Second, because lying is always wrong and professional ethics forbids a lawyer in representing a client to make a false statement of material fact to a third party, the threat may not be made unless the client is prepared to carry it out. Third, it might not be in the client's best interests to carry out the threat. If not, the lawyer should not recommend doing so. Fourth, making the threat of criminal charges might be an abuse of criminal process to obtain restitution, which is a civil matter.

The reply could be along the following lines:

I see four problems with threatening to press criminal charges against the embezzler, but am not certain any of them is decisive, partly because some call for more information about the facts of the case than you have provided. But perhaps sketching out the problems I see will help your further reflection.

First, would it be fair to carry out this threat, inasmuch as it will be aimed at the embezzler's wife, who presumably did not participate in the crime? Perhaps and perhaps not; and on some assumptions about the circumstances, the fairness or unfairness will be clear, while on others it will not be. It surely would not be unfair if the embezzled funds were invested in the home, the objective is to compel the wife to make that part of the equity available for restitution, and her doing so would not leave the family homeless. But it would be unfair if the embezzled funds had been wasted in gambling, the couple had purchased the home with money the wife inherited from her parents, and making the equity available for restitution would leave the family homeless. But if the residence was purchased by the couple's cooperation over the years and only the embezzler's share of the equity will be needed for restitution, the fairness of compelling the wife to agree to sell is arguable

The argument against it is: She is not responsible for her husband's action and giving up her home would be a severe hardship. The argument for it is: The embezzler is a part owner, and at least his rightful share should be available to repay what he owes. Moreover, his wife and children stand to benefit from a resolution of his problem that would keep him out of jail and avoid a criminal record probably permanently damaging to his earning power.[410]

A second problem: Will the threat be a lie? Lying is always wrong (see *LCL*, 405–12). Moreover, in threatening that your client will report the matter to the police and press charges, assuming the client remains unwilling to press them, you would be knowingly making a false statement of material fact to a third party in representing the client—an act that would violate professional ethics.[411]

Someone might argue that you could solve this problem by bluffing—for example, saying that your client *could* report the matter and press charges. The possibility of doing so, after all, is real; calling attention to it would not assert anything, the argument would conclude, but only suggest that your client might proceed. I grant that in some contexts, such as warfare and certain games, a bluff does not involve an assertion, and so one can regard bluffing as legitimate in those contexts without admitting any exception to the exclusion of lying as always immoral. But despite their opposition, the parties to litigation, unlike warring enemies and people playing games, should cooperate in seeking justice on the basis of truth. Thus, litigation requires cooperation among officers of the court, each faithfully fulfilling the responsibilities of his or her proper role and communicating honestly with the others. Therefore, if a statement that your client could report the matter and press charges were intended to suggest that the client might proceed, it would be a false assertion unless the client, having been advised of the proposed threat, is willing to press charges in at least some possible circumstances. Moreover, being weaker, a threat that only kept open the possibility of criminal charges would be less likely to be effective.

Still, while a lying threat should be excluded, your client may feel that it would be morally acceptable in the circumstances. You can point out, however, that the same sympathy for a former colleague that may underlie the client's reluctance to press charges also should exclude using an insincere threat to manipulate him and coerce his wife. You can point out too that bluffs often have bad effects. They sometimes provoke unexpected and undesirable responses, often make it harder to arrive at a settlement later, and, if unsuccessful, tend to undermine the credibility

410. Someone might refer to q. 183, above, and object that, unless the embezzler's wife participated in his wrongdoing or directly profited from it, trying to compel her to help him repay would be inherently unfair. However, there are significant differences between the two cases. To begin with, in the other case, the husband's parents were related to the couple and their children as extended family, which is not the basis in our society for primary mutual economic responsibilities; in this case, the embezzler, his wife, and children are members of a nuclear family, which does ground such responsibilities. In the other case, too, the husband's parents had no reason to expect that making the payments would result in future benefits to themselves; in this case, the wife does have reason to hope that helping her husband repay what he owes will bring her and her children through present adversity and allow the family as a whole to enjoy a better future.

411. See American Bar Association, *Model Code of Professional Responsibility* (1986), DR -102, (A) (5); *Model Rules of Professional Conduct* (1993), Rule 4.1 (a).

of future threats. If the client is unconvinced but also remains unwilling to agree to carry out the threat of criminal prosecution, you should explain that professional ethics excludes making a false statement to a third party in representing a client, and recommend an alternative to lying: that the client not demand immediate repayment but instead offer to accept what the embezzler can repay now, together with a legally binding undertaking to pay the remainder over an extended period, with interest at a mutually agreeable rate.

A third problem: Would it be in your client's best interests to carry out the threat or would pressing criminal charges actually be self-defeating in relation to your client's objective of obtaining repayment? If the embezzler's wife resists the threat and your client presses charges, the result could well be that the embezzler will be less able to repay than if he is not prosecuted. If you judge that carrying out the threat would be counterproductive, do not recommend making it, since you could not recommend carrying it out and, as has been explained, a lying threat must be excluded.

The fourth problem: Would the threat of criminal charges to motivate the embezzler's wife be an abuse of criminal process to pursue a goal in a civil matter?

If the answer is yes—and a case can be made for saying it is—then making the threat would be an injustice, if not to the embezzler, at least to the public at large. Criminal processes should be directed toward justice as an aspect of the society's common good; civil processes are directed toward justice among contending parties. It seems to follow that the decision whether or not to press criminal charges should be made on the basis of the common good rather than of any party's particular interests. So, prima facie it seems that the threat you are considering would be an abuse of criminal process.[412] Perhaps that is why you feel this tactic is dishonorable.

Nevertheless, a case also can be made for the contrary view. Though clear in theory and in the legal system itself, the distinction between the ends primarily served by criminal and civil law—by the one, the common good of society as a whole; and by the other, the particular goods of those concerned—is not always so clear in practice. Some crimes—murder, for instance—are regularly reported and prosecuted without regard to the effects on private interests. Perhaps that also should be the case with embezzlement. In fact, however, probably most embezzlers who repay what they have taken are simply discharged and, perhaps, denied a favorable reference. Neither the police nor public prosecutors appear to take the initiative in such cases. Thus, with respect to crimes of this sort the public authorities apparently have concluded that the common good of society as a whole is sufficiently served even if the wronged party does not choose to press criminal charges. Insofar as the authorities have adopted that policy, it encourages wronged parties to use the threat of reporting embezzlement to the authorities as a means of obtaining restitution.

---

412. American Bar Association, *Model Code of Professional Responsibility* (1986), EC 7–2 DR 7–105A, forcefully takes this position; however, *Model Rules of Professional Conduct* (1983) does not deal with this matter. The norms of professional ethics in force where the question practices may or may not touch on it.

Perhaps your reflection—helped, I hope, by the preceding explanations—and/or your conference with the client will lead to a solution. Perhaps, though, you will conclude either that you cannot honestly make the threat or that, on other grounds, you cannot make it justly. If so, try to get your supervisor to understand why the threat should not be made; if she still insists, you must refuse. If making the threat would be making a false statement, point out that professional ethics precludes doing so. If the threat could be made honestly but not justly, however, explain your refusal as a personal matter of conscience, and ask to be excused from handling the matter. In either case, if your supervisor insists that you make the threat, appeal to the managing partner or partners. That will involve some risk to your job and your future prospects with the firm, but you must accept the risk, since the alternative would be to intend dishonesty and/or some other injustice. Saving your soul is far more important than keeping your job.

186: Must a lawyer admit how much a client is ready to concede?

The leading partner in the small firm where I have just started practicing law assigned me a case he deemed simple enough for a beginner. We have been retained by a home builder, one of whose projects went awry due to subsurface water resulting from the spring thaw. He should have foreseen the problem and provided drainage but failed to do so. As a result, shortly after the homes were occupied, sixteen were flooded on their finished and furnished lower levels. The builder belatedly corrected his mistake, but the owners, most of whose losses were not covered by insurance, have filed suit to recover for property damage, temporary loss of use of the space, and so on.

Even before the water receded, the builder asked the owners for lists of their losses; he checked out these claims, took photographs, and made his own estimate of each one's actual loss. When he retained us, he gave us these estimates and told us that, to settle these cases, he is ready to pay each owner an average of two thousand dollars more than the estimate. He hopes we will be able to persuade most plaintiffs to settle within that limit.

This morning I settled the first of these cases. The builder's estimate of the owner's actual loss was just over fifteen thousand dollars, and the owner's lawyer took me by surprise when he said: "I think that I could get my client to settle this case for about seventeen thousand dollars. Would your client be ready to pay that much?" While the offer signaled that the case could be settled for less, the honest answer, of course, would have been yes. But being acutely aware that I need to be right with the easy cases so as to settle them all, if possible, in accord with my instructions, I hesitated momentarily before answering: "That is on the high side."

For two reasons, that answer was not satisfactory. The first, of course, is that I lied, and I'd rather avoid lying if I can. But, in addition, my hesitation was noted, so that after much discussion I realized I could not do better and agreed to the settlement originally proposed. When I asked the partner who assigned me this matter for advice on dealing with this problem next time, he said: "Long experience has taught me that in cases of this sort it is best to ignore the other side's initial figure and to open by offering about two-thirds of your target figure. You should have been ready to shoot back: 'That's too much; something like eleven would be more like it.'"

What do you think of that strategy? If you think it, too, would be morally questionable, what alternative is there that is likely to be successful?

Analysis:

This question calls for applying the exceptionless norm that excludes lying. In the context of negotiation, one can make certain statements that would be untruthful in other contexts without lying. This is so because the language used in negotiating has a special meaning in this context. Still, given its special meaning, this language also can be used dishonestly, and that dishonesty should be avoided as should other lying in negotiating.

The reply could be along the following lines:

In my judgment, you could follow the advice of the partner who assigned you the case without violating legal ethics, which requires truthfulness in a lawyer's statements not only to clients and to other persons, but explains how this applies in negotiation: "Whether a particular statement should be regarded as one of fact can depend on the circumstances. Under generally accepted conventions in negotiation, certain types of statements ordinarily are not taken as statements of material fact. Estimates of price or value placed on the subject of a transaction and a party's intentions as to an acceptable settlement of a claim are in this category."[413] While an unsophisticated, honest person might regard this clarification as an instance of the evasive double talk it might seem to invite, I believe it is entirely consistent with the moral truth that lying always is wrong.

In every society, negotiation is a practice with various inherent assumptions and special norms. The comment's phrase, "generally accepted conventions in negotiation" refers to the assumptions and norms currently obtaining in this practice in the United States and, probably, most other English-speaking nations; these conventions are unlikely to change significantly in the near future. Experienced negotiators take them for granted and interpret one another's statements in their light. Hence, a negotiator's statements about price and value often do not mean what they seem to and would mean in other contexts.

However, in saying such statements "are not taken as statements of material fact," the ABA comment lacks precision and fails accurately to express the point its drafters plainly intended. While it is true that negotiators' statements have meanings other than those they would have in other contexts, such statements do assert something and are taken by the other party as factual. Thus, the statement you hesitated over but made, "That's on the high side," could have been made truthfully by an experienced negotiator, for he or she would have meant: "That's more than my client's instructions authorize me to accept at this stage of negotia-

413. American Bar Association, *Model Rules of Professional Conduct* (1993), Rule 4.1, Comment.

tions; he hopes to settle this claim for less than seventeen thousand dollars." Unfortunately, understanding your statement as you did, it was a lie, since, being unfamiliar with the conventions of negotiation, what you meant to assert was, in fact, false. Bearing those conventions in mind, however, next time you could say precisely the same thing without lying.

Similarly, had you responded to the other lawyer's question, "Would your client be ready to pay that much?" along the lines of the partner's advice by saying, "Something like eleven would be more like it," that would have asserted, not that your client was unready to pay seventeen thousand dollars, if necessary to settle the case, but that he was prepared to pay at least eleven thousand. This can be seen by considering how your partner in negotiation would have regarded different developments of your position as bargaining proceeded. If you later made it clear that your client preferred litigation to a settlement of eleven thousand dollars, the other lawyer would have objected that you were not bargaining "in good faith," in other words, that your initial statement of position had been untruthful and its implicit commitment insincere. But if the negotiation's outcome made it clear that your client was, indeed, prepared to pay fifteen thousand dollars, your counterpart would not have regarded your initial statement as in the least dishonest.

The explanation given here about the meaning of language in negotiations by no means justifies deception in that context. For example, it would be lying to try to bring about a quick settlement by hinting that your client might be forced into bankruptcy, if that is not true. Similarly, you would lie if you denied being authorized by your client to negotiate settlements in excess of his estimates or asserted that your instructions precluded a settlement that they in fact allowed you to make.[414]

Of course, not being an experienced negotiator, you might be uneasy in observing the usual conventions, and that nervousness might reduce your chances of serving your client's legitimate interests as effectively as possible. You might adopt an alternative approach that probably would work well and would avoid even seeming to distort the truth. Assuming there are no significant discrepancies between your client's estimate of each owner's actual loss and the owner's own estimate, you could begin each negotiating session by laying on the table your client's estimate of the owner's actual loss and the photographs he took to support it, then point out that your client already has shown that he wants to resolve the problems resulting from his mistake, and offer to settle the claim by paying in full for the actual damage. Having made an offer, based on evidence supplied by your client, you can demand comparable evidence for any added amount in an owner's claim of actual loss as well as proof that other grounds alleged, such as loss of use, involved real harm rather than brief, minor inconvenience. Naturally, you will

---

414. One can apply the preceding explanation of honesty in negotiation to other bargaining situations, such as buying and selling real estate, automobiles, and so forth (see qq. 144–46, above). There, too, lying within the negotiation—for example, saying one has received other offers when none has been made—is not only wrong in itself but unjust inasmuch as it is meant to take advantage of the other party.

challenge the other side's claims at every step, and so work toward a settlement that, on average, will not exceed the limit your client set.

A final point. The attitude you express by saying, "I'd rather avoid lying if I can," is not the worst possible one, but it is shared by many thoroughly dishonest people. Lying always is wrong. Usually, too, it serves manipulation, which is at odds with true community. While lying may seem unavoidable at times to people who have no hope, it should never be regarded as acceptable, especially by Christians, whose credibility is vital to the mission of sharing their faith with every neighbor (see Eph 4.17–25; cf. *LCL*, 405–12). Consequently, your attitude should be: I always can avoid lying and never will lie. To carry out this commitment, of course, you will need to cultivate reserve about confidential matters and learn how to tell the truth without unnecessarily jeopardizing your clients' and your own legitimate interests.

187: Should a lawyer help an unreasonable client disinherit her children?

I am a lawyer working alone; I limit my practice to estate, trust, and tax matters. One of my clients, a wealthy widow, called me to her home the other day to ask whether she could disinherit her two children by revoking the trusts she and her husband set up for them. When I said she could, she explained that she is angry with them and has told them she will disinherit them for opposing her when she told her physician in their presence to make sure she dies quickly when she no longer wishes to live. I asked her what she meant by that. She made it clear she wants the doctor to help her kill herself painlessly if and when she feels her life is not worth living. The children said this would be wrong and tried to get the doctor to say he would not help her. He did not argue, but my client is sure he is on her side and will do as she wishes.

The way the woman told me all this, as much as what she said, struck me as strange and out of character. Of course, I tried to talk her out of revoking the trusts. I said her children had a point and surely have her best interests in view. She told me to mind my own business and do the job or she would get another lawyer. I stopped arguing and agreed to prepare the necessary papers.

Now I am having second thoughts. If the children are disinherited, they will not be impoverished, since both make good livings and each received a small but substantial portion of their father's estate. The effect of revoking the trusts will be a far larger residue, to be divided among my client's nieces and nephews, whose financial condition is unknown to me. Consequently, I do not see anything inherently unjust in what she wishes to do, and if she seemed entirely rational and wanted to do it for other reasons—say, because her children were neglecting her—I would not hesitate. As it is, I wonder whether I should refuse. Of course, I can delay a few more days and try again to get her to change her mind, but I doubt that she will.

+ + +

Analysis:

This question concerns cooperation in an unreasonable act. The questioner should try to resolve his or her doubt about the client's legal competence. Unless she is not competent, the questioner, having agreed to do what she requested, should either do it or withdraw without delay. Materially cooperating with the client might be justifiable. But unless some responsibility requires the questioner to continue serving her, I believe he or she should refuse to cooperate, state the reasons for refusing, and try again to persuade the client to change her mind.

The reply could be along the following lines:

What you have agreed to do does not appear to be wrong in itself. Drawing up papers of the sort your client desires certainly is morally permissible. Moreover, disinheriting one's children is not necessarily unjust, and this client's children, having already been adequately provided for, apparently have no right to what they stand to lose. Still, if you proceeded, you would help to carry out an act that is objectively wrong inasmuch as it is unreasonable. Your client's children not only have a point. Their position is morally sound, while hers is objectively gravely wrong. Your statement of the problem does not mention other possible factors—such as the intentions of the children's father or a possible understanding between the parents—that could ground a claim by the children on at least part of what they stand to lose.

Several things might lead you to ask whether your client is legally competent. You say that what she did struck you as out of character and that she does not seem entirely rational. Those observations seem borne out by her unreasonable request for help in committing suicide, the fact that the request was made in her children's presence, her disproportionate anger over their opposition, and her shortness with you. If you judge that these things, or anything else you know about her, suggest she no longer is legally competent, I think you should try to resolve that question before proceeding. If you conclude she is not of sound mind, you should not cooperate with her in attempting to do something whose legal validity will be questionable. Rather, you should do what you can ("can" referring to moral acceptability as well as to other limits) to ensure that her existing disposition of her wealth will remain unchanged.

However, if you are not convinced that this client is legally incompetent, it seems to me that no moral consideration clearly precludes your cooperating with her. But should you?

Someone might say that, having agreed to do as your client wishes, you must prepare the papers rather than break your word. Plainly, however, you assume, and rightly, that neither your agreement to do as she asked nor your existing professional relationship with her binds you if there is a good reason for not carrying out her instructions. Nevertheless, since you agreed to prepare the papers and delay in deciding whether to do so is unnecessary, you should not delay in the hope of getting her to reconsider. Rather, you should decide what to do and do it promptly. Moreover, you are only likely to irritate this client unless you very soon either do as you agreed or tell her you have changed your mind.

If you needed the income from this client to meet your responsibility to support yourself and your family, that need might ground a moral obligation for you to carry out her wishes. But you do not mention such a need, and I assume you can afford to lose her business.

On reflection, you might become convinced of two things: (1) refusing to cooperate with her would only lead her to carry out her threat to get another lawyer; and (2) continuing your relationship with her would be in her true interests and in the best interests of others likely to be affected by the way her legal affairs will be handled. In that case, you might conclude that your commitment as a lawyer to serve clients to the best of your ability requires you to do as she wishes in this matter so as to preserve your relationship with her. However, if you consider these things carefully, you very likely will remain doubtful about them.

If neither your responsibility to support yourself and your family nor your responsibility toward your client requires that you maintain your relationship with her, I see no other moral consideration requiring you to cooperate with her. If there is none, I believe you should not prepare the papers as you agreed, but instead should do your best to persuade and encourage her to change her mind. Even if the children are not entitled to what they stand to lose, they will be wronged if they are disinherited for opposing their mother's suicidal desire. You should resist this wrong, not help bring it about. Besides, you should bear witness to the sacredness of human life and the truth about suicide, and refusing to cooperate with this client will do that, while cooperating with her, without a cogent reason for doing so, would suggest, at least to the children and perhaps to others, that you consider her plan morally acceptable. Last, not least, though you doubt that this client will change her mind, you should try for her sake to get her to do so, and you are more likely to succeed if, by refusing to cooperate, you show her how seriously you take the matter.

Your client's plan to end her life and/or her decision to disinherit her children might have consequences she has not considered—for example, her estate might be eaten up in costly litigation, in which you might be compelled to testify about how and why she revoked the trusts. Sketching out such possibilities to her might soften her resolution about one or both things. Then too, in directing her physician to end her life if and when she feels it no longer worth living, she may have incited him to commit a crime and may herself have violated the law. Explaining the legal significance of what she has done might put the matter in a different perspective for her. Finally, though, you should tell her that her desire to end her life when she chooses is suicidal, and that suicide is wrong, even if a person does not violate the law, or involve or injure other people. Even if your client is not a believer, in making this point you should explain that she can have no reasonable grounds for assuming that death will be an ultimate escape from suffering. Point out, too, the legal and moral right to refuse overly burdensome treatment and to request palliative care including the drugs required to control pain even if they incidentally shorten life.[41]

---

415. See John Paul II, *Evangelium vitae,* 65, *AAS* 87 (1995) 476, *OR,* 5 Apr. 1995, xiii; *LCL,* 53

If your best efforts at persuasion are fruitless and you judge that you should not carry out this client's instructions, you should not only say so but put your refusal and the reasons for it in writing. In that way, you not only will make your position clear to her but will have evidence that you have done so.

In billing, you should not, in my judgment, charge this woman for the time devoted to giving specifically psychological and/or moral counsel. Though providing such advice often is appropriate and sometimes morally obligatory, lawyers are neither especially able to give it nor retained for this purpose. They should recognize that such advice goes beyond the strictly professional service that calls for payment.

Finally, even if your attempt to get your client to change her mind fails and she gets another lawyer, you will have fulfilled your responsibilities to her and the others involved, and your witness to the truth about suicide may bear fruit you cannot now foresee and may never know.

188: Must a lawyer make restitution of a contingency fee paid by a lying client?

I am a lawyer who accepted a case on a contingent-fee basis—an arrangement by which a client pays no fee if he or she loses but pays a portion of the proceeds if he or she wins. The lawsuit was for an uninsured loss of personal property alleged to have occurred in a fire. My client was a woman who had been living in a carriage-house apartment that burned down due to the negligence of the owner, who lived nearby in the main house. There was no argument about his duty to reimburse my client for the property she lost; the issue was what her losses were.

She is a professional writer employed by a trade journal. In her spare time she had been working on a book, which she had almost finished. She said she had kept all her research materials and drafts in her apartment, and only backups of her computer disks at work. But her office at work had been burglarized shortly before the fire, and, she said, the backups were taken along with the computer and a good deal else. Working with her, I made the case that her loss was over fifty thousand dollars, negotiated a settlement for that amount, and last month received one-third of it as my fee—a good return for the twenty or so hours I devoted to the matter.

Today, however, by sheer coincidence a young man from Australia—a journalist spending a sabbatical here—asked me to draw up a contract with my former client to purchase all rights to her manuscript. This plainly is the book she had been working on. She gave it to him to look over two days after the fire, saying her employer was putting unreasonable obstacles in the way of her plan to publish it in the United States. Evidently, she had another copy or a set of backups, and her real loss in the fire was minimal. I declined to draw up the contract, on the ground that the other party to it had recently been my client.

Of course, when negotiating the settlement, I did not know my client's claim was fraudulent, but perhaps I should have realized that something was amiss. When she first came in, the story she told sounded a bit like fiction, because it was complete and entirely coherent, whereas truthful stories, particularly those of people who have suffered an unexpected loss, generally must be elicited bit by bit and are rarely entirely consistent on first telling. But she was a convincing liar—though, I must admit, her attractiveness and the prospect of the contingency fee probably dulled my usual skepticism.

Having been used as a tool of her fraud, I am trying to figure out my present moral obligations. Should I inform the party with whom I negotiated the settlement of the evidence of the fraud? If I do that, he surely will seek restitution, but, since she spends freely, I doubt he will get much back. Since I worked on the case in good faith, I do not believe he has any legal right to the fee she paid me. But what is my moral responsibility? Should I give part or all of it back to him?

Analysis:

The questioner first should tell the former client what he or she has learned and urge her to make just restitution. If she refuses, the problem stands as presented, and calls for applying the norms regarding confidentiality and restitution. Morally, the defrauded party should, in my judgment, be informed unless that would put the questioner at an unfair risk. If the former client makes full restitution, including the amount she paid as fee, the questioner may keep it. If not, he or she should, in my judgment, return at least part of the fee to the defrauded party. The amount to be returned can be determined only by applying the Golden Rule to all the relevant facts.

The reply could be along the following lines:

I assume that you have no legal duty to report your former client's fraud to the police. On that assumption, it seems to me that, before doing anything else, you should inform her of what you have learned and urge her to make restitution to the party she defrauded. In making the case for restitution, you probably should call to her attention the disciplinary rule of legal ethics, which I shall quote below, apparently requiring you to pass on the information you have received to the party she defrauded. Although she may not now have any of the money she received from the settlement, she could pay something each month and for this purpose also use the proceeds from her book. If she undertakes to make full restitution and you can verify that she is doing so, your problem is solved. But if your exhortation does not move her and you find no way to compel her to make restitution, you will be left with the problem as stated. The following is my response to it.

Setting to one side, for the moment, the canons and rules of professional ethics, I think you have a clear duty to inform the party with whom you negotiated the settlement that your client defrauded him. He has been wronged, and the information you easily could provide would help him obtain at least part of the restitution he deserves. Since your client used your honest efforts as an instrument of her wrongdoing, you have no moral duty to shield her by keeping secret the evidence of her fraud. Of course, it is important that lawyers usually guard their clients' confidences, so that people who need legal help will not be afraid to obtain it and will communicate freely with their lawyers about their problems, including any possible violations of law. But it would not undermine the public's necessary trust in lawyers to exclude from confidentiality evidence, such as you received, of a client's fraud obtained from independent sources after a case is over.

Still, some provisions of your profession's ethics seem to require you to keep secret the evidence you accidentally acquired. The American Bar Association's rule forbids a lawyer to reveal information relating to the representation of a client without his or her consent unless the lawyer reasonably believes that revealing it is necessary either (1) to prevent the client from committing a crime likely to result in someone's death or serious bodily harm, or (2) to protect the lawyer's own legitimate interests.[416] The explanatory comment on this rule makes it clear that it applies to all information relating to the representation of a client, regardless of how and when the lawyer acquires it. Now, while your client did something seriously immoral and unlawful, her crime did not involve killing or bodily injury and is past rather than prospective; and, while your work was instrumental to her wrongdoing, your legitimate interests do not at this time require you to reveal the evidence of her fraud. I say "at this time," because the situation could change—for example, if you eventually were charged with conspiring in her wrongful behavior.

At the same time, other provisions of professional ethics seem to require you to reveal your former client's fraud to the defrauded party. The ABA's *Model Code* states: "A lawyer who receives information clearly establishing that (1) His client has, in the course of the representation, perpetrated a fraud upon a person or tribunal shall promptly call upon his client to rectify the same, and if his client refuses or is unable to do so, he shall reveal the fraud to the affected person or tribunal, except when the information is protected as a privileged communication."[417] Since you learned of the fraud from a third party, you did not get the information from a privileged communication, and so, it seems, you ought to pass it on.

I do not know what rule would be considered applicable in this situation in the jurisdiction where your legal work unwittingly assisted this fraud. If the latter, you plainly should tell the defrauded party what you have learned unless your former client sets about to make restitution. If that would be considered a violation of the former rule, I think that in this application that confidentiality rule lacks moral force. And if you can safely circumvent it—for example, by communicating the evidence anonymously—it seems to me you should. If you cannot circumvent it, you might consider openly violating it.

In considering violating it, you also can rightly take into account the risk of harm to yourself. Having been innocently involved in the fraud, you need accept that risk only if the Golden Rule requires it—for example, if the risk to you is not great and you have a solid hope of significantly benefiting the defrauded party. But there is no such hope if you have good reason to doubt he will get much back, and in that case you need not accept the risk and can rightly keep the secret.

What, then, should you do about the contingency fee? It seems to me that, having earned it honestly, you may keep it if the client makes full restitution, including the

416. See American Bar Association, *Model Rules of Professional Conduct* (1993), Rule .6, "Confidentiality of Information".

417. American Bar Association, *Model Code of Professional Responsibility,* (1986), DR 7–102 (B).

amount you received as your fee, to the party she defrauded. But what if the defrauded party will not get full restitution unless you give him at least part of what you received? Put yourself in his place, and I think you will see that he is entitled to at least part of what you received as a result of the settlement.

The appropriate way for you to make any required restitution will depend on whether or not you can tell the defrauded party what you have learned. If you do tell him, you can offer at the same time to return at least part of your fee and try to reach a mutually satisfactory agreement on how much. But if you keep your client's secret, you must decide unilaterally how much you owe the defrauded party and choose a trustworthy intermediary to deliver the appropriate payment without revealing who is making it and why, except that it is "conscience money."

How much should you pay back? I cannot give you an exact answer; you must consider everything and apply the Golden Rule. That means considering, among other things, the possibility that, had you taken more care, the client might not have succeeded in her fraud, a possibility to which you allude by saying you perhaps "should have realized that something was amiss." Again, take into account that you received a substantial fee for relatively little work on a case that, but for the client's fraud, would have yielded a much smaller settlement and fee. If you paid tax on the income and will be unable to recover it, you may take that into account. Finally, if you are better off than the victim of the fraud, I think you should settle any doubts about what you owe him in his favor rather than yours.

189: May a lawyer handle matters that clients themselves could handle?

Having finished law school and passed the bar exams, I clerked for the judges in circuit court for a year. Last month I began working for this small firm—just three partners with me as an associate. Much of my time is spent sitting in on conferences between a client and one or another of the partners, going to court with them, and helping with their cases. But now and then someone not already a client calls or comes in with something the secretary considers simple enough for me to do on my own.

The person usually does need professional service, for example, to make a will or check out a contract; even when such legal instruments are simple, people can make mistakes with serious consequences. Occasionally, though, people come in with matters they could as well handle on their own. For instance, a young couple had gone to dinner to celebrate their engagement and put the $113.50 check on a charge card; the charge came through as $1,135.00; the restaurant said it was not their problem, and the young man was frantic because he did not know what to do I called the toll-free number on the statement and explained what had happened: the whole thing took a quarter hour, and we billed the young man thirty dollars Again, a recent widow had a number of questions about Social Security. I knew some of the answers and could have got the rest, but it soon became clear that all she needed to do was make an appointment at the local Social Security office. I did that and sent her off. We billed her fifty dollars.

Nothing in my training or in the code of legal ethics provides any guidance about such matters, but I wonder how fair it is to take this kind of business and bill people. The partners differ in how they handle these things. One day I saw the junior partner spend an hour with an elderly man whose checkbook he balanced. He billed the client $150. But I also saw the senior partner spend nearly half an hour talking with a young woman having trouble getting a travel agent to refund eight hundred dollars she had deposited for a tour that was canceled. I really admired the partner when he not only told her how to obtain the necessary forms and file in small claims court, but how to argue her case when it came up, then billed her nothing for all the advice.

Analysis:

This question calls for the derivation and application of a norm. People who come to law offices generally should not be charged for the time required to determine whether they need professional service and, if they do, to negotiate terms. Both the young man and the elderly woman should have been advised that they did not need a lawyer's service, or helped as they were, but without charge. Their bills should be canceled or payments refunded. Depending on the elderly client's competence, the junior partner may or may not have been justified in balancing his checkbook and billing him. The senior partner was more generous than necessary in advising the young woman.

The reply could be along the following lines:

When someone initially comes to a law office, the receptionist or lawyer should first determine whether the individual actually needs professional service. If so, the lawyer then should clarify the terms on which it will be provided. Normally, nobody should be billed for such a preliminary discussion. An exception would be warranted if someone began to present a complicated matter, so that even the preliminary discussion would require considerable time and/or research; in such a case, however, the lawyer should make it clear that continuing the preliminary discussion will result in charges, so that the inquirer will have an opportunity to negotiate the charges or terminate the discussion before incurring any. In any case, if the preliminary discussion makes it clear to the lawyer that the inquirer does not require professional legal service, the lawyer should point that out.

Neither the young man whose credit card billing was in error nor the widow who needed an appointment with the Social Security office required or received professional legal services. You either should have told the young man he could resolve the problem himself by calling the toll-free number and told the widow to call the Social Security office, or, to gain good will for the firm, should have done what you did, but without billing either party. Those bills ought to be canceled. If they have been paid, the payment should be refunded.

If at present you do not have authority to bill or not, as you think right, discuss the problem with the appropriate partner—if possible, with the senior partner you admire. I am confident a discussion will resolve the problem. But in the unlikely event that the firm will not allow you the discretion necessary to make judgments about billing, you should resign. While that might seem drastic, considering the amounts of money at stake, the issue would not be clients' money but the firm's unwillingness to let you make and act on conscientious judgments.

You also should consider bringing this problem about billing to the attention of relevant professional bodies and urging them to develop suitable norms regarding it.

The junior partner may or may not have been justified in billing for the hour he spent helping the elderly client balance his checkbook. The task probably could have been done by a relative or friend, or by a less costly bookkeeper. If, as one suspects, the client's ability to handle his affairs is impaired due to declining mental capacities, it was wrong to take advantage of him. However, a lawyer could appropriately spend an hour balancing someone's checkbook if that were an integral part of handling some more complex legal matter, such as settling a dispute with the Internal Revenue Service. Moreover, if the client is fully able to make decisions and knew he could get help balancing his checkbook more cheaply elsewhere, but is well able to pay and simply preferred having the junior partner do the work, I see no reason to fault the lawyer.

The young woman having trouble obtaining a refund of her deposit presented an interesting, borderline case. As soon as the senior partner understood her problem, he could rightly have told her she could file in small claims court without retaining a lawyer, and sent her on her way. Once he grasped the problem, he also would have been justified in telling her he could provide some legal advice and specifying the fee; and then, if she agreed, in billing her for the quarter hour or so he spent advising her how to argue her case in small claims court. The firm was more generous than it needed to be in that instance, perhaps because the young woman won the senior partner's sympathy. Indeed, depending on whether what he did conforms to the partners' mutual understanding about billing, in this instance he may have cheated the other partners out of their share of the relevant fee.

190: Should lawyers limit their earnings to a certain level?

As an idealistic college student, I was attracted to the legal profession because I felt it would provide an opportunity to obtain justice for vulnerable people. I went to one of the better law schools, graduated near the top of my class, did well on the bar exam, and went to work about eight years ago for a large firm in a major city. The job paid well and I received the maximum raises, so that I paid off my student loans and saved some money. However, I had to put in long hours and worked exclusively on contracts. I found this tiring and not enjoyable. Moreover, almost all the firm's clients were businesses or wealthy individuals, so that my work hardly was what I had imagined with youthful idealism when I decided to go into law.

Three years ago I married a classmate from law school, and we bought a house in a suburb about fifteen miles from my office. We started our family right away. My wife, who also had done well professionally, wanted me to be able to spend more time around home than I could if I stayed with the firm, given the long hours and the commuting, so two years ago I resigned from the firm and began my own practice. At the same time, my wife, not wishing to put our baby in day care, resigned her job with a law firm to share the practice with me, insofar as possible, doing the work at home. We are succeeding very well, much better in fact than I expected. The work is varied and sometimes challenging, and we enjoy what we do of it together.

Our income from the practice is growing steadily. Our fee schedule is about average in our area, and many of our clients have no trouble paying. But we know it is a real burden for some of them, and a residue of my youthful idealism still lingers. It would be interesting to have your thoughts on whether at some point we should limit our professional income by doing some pro bono work or should give away the excess, and, if we should, how to identify that point.

Analysis:

This question calls for the derivation of norms. Assuming the free market in legal services works to establish fair prices, the questioner and his wife may charge according to the average fee schedule for services to clients willing and able to pay. The couple can determine how much income they should earn by limiting their spending and saving to levels adequate to meet moderately their current and future genuine needs, which are the reasonable and appropriate means for fulfilling vocational responsibilities. When they begin to accumulate a surplus, they could donate their excess income to charity, but, in my judgment, it will be more appropriate for them to use their excess capacity to serve people who cannot afford needed legal services.

The reply could be along the following lines:

When the legal profession attracted you as an idealistic college student, you saw it as an opportunity to use your gifts and energy in serving others. That vision is not only consistent with organizing your life by the Christian principle of following Jesus but essential to doing so. You and your wife also seem to have had a sound basis and right attitudes in marrying and starting your family. Your asking about a possible responsibility to limit your professional income or give away part of it is another sign of your Christian sense of values. Therefore, I think you will understand and be able to accept the following response, which will show how you can use your vocational commitments to shape your financial affairs.

Some people argue that lawyers have organized and maintain a monopoly on the delivery of legal services, and that this monopoly, which resists the operation of market forces, enables them to extort unjust fees from clients. The monopoly, it is claimed, is particularly egregious in preventing trained nonprofessionals—so-called paralegals—from doing many sorts of work they could do as well as lawyers at far less cost. While there may be some truth to this view, in answering your question I shall assume its contrary: that, considering the character of the practice of law, the number of available practitioners, and the readiness of many lawyers to engage without charge in a preliminary discussion with a prospective client, there is in most places a rather free and effective market in legal services. As in other cases where there seems to be a free market, one also may begin with the presumption that the market in legal services usually works to establish fair prices (see q. 144, above). So, I see no moral problem in asking the average fee of those ready, willing, and able to pay. Indeed, you could be justified in charging them more than the average if your services are superior to those of other lawyers and so are more highly valued by prospective clients.

Of course, in some instances even the standard fee can be unfair, and you should settle for less—for example, if you take what seems a simple case, bad luck complicates it, the client never will be able to pay, and your withdrawal would spell disaster. Moreover, nobody is entitled to increase his or her income endlessly while amassing ever-growing wealth or spending ever more lavishly to satisfy fresh desires as they emerge. Plainly, that violates the moral norms that underlie property rights and Jesus' teachings about wealth (see *LCL,* 780–82, 789–92, 800–806, 811–14).

Thus, the primary question you and your wife must answer is: How much income do we need? To answer it, begin by reviewing all your activities and making sure everything you do contributes to carrying out your complete vocations as individuals and as a married couple—in other words, that your time, energy, money, and other resources are used for nothing but living out God's plan for your lives (see *LCL,* 113–29). Your vocational responsibilities as a whole determine your genuine needs, since you genuinely need all and only those things that are reasonable and suitable means to fulfilling those responsibilities. Thus, *genuine needs* refers to more than the conditions for bare survival and professional expenses; it embraces everything to be used in living a morally good life, and so includes such things as a good education for your children, decent recreation, and appropriate gifts to relatives and friends (see *LCL,* 801).

Even if you regulate the acquisition and use of wealth by the principle of genuine needs, however, it usually is possible to meet a genuine need more and less conveniently and pleasantly. Reflecting on other people's needs—especially those of the poorest of the poor—and applying the Golden Rule, any upright person will see the appropriateness of living simply, and a Christian, conscious of receiving all goods from God's merciful hands, will listen to Jesus' call to practice self-denial, when morally possible, for others' sakes (see *LCL,* 360–78). For instance, your family needs some recreation and entertainment, and this need could be met by taking a two-week vacation at a posh resort in the South Pacific. That vacation would be a pleasant experience, but it would cost, say, ten times as much as an alternative that would meet the need about as well, say, two weeks relaxing at the seashore or hiking in the mountains close to home, using moderately priced rather than luxurious facilities. Simplicity and self-denial indicate that one of the less costly alternatives is to be preferred.

Insurance and savings can be legitimate and necessary ways of providing against unacceptable risks and preparing to meet future responsibilities, such as your children's education and your own support when you can no longer work. But they also can be abused by wealthy people who try to provide for every eventuality, no matter how unlikely. Indeed, miserliness today often is masked as prudence—for example, insuring against losses that would not prevent one from fulfilling any responsibility and saving for retirement based on the most pessimistic assumptions about future economic trends. Even worse is proceeding as if accumulating wealth were an end in itself or using insurance contracts and investment vehicles as ways of gambling (see *LCL*, 789–92, 800–806, 815–17, 820). Therefore, consider carefully how much insurance and saving will be reasonable and limit them accordingly.

In sum, starting from a clear understanding of your vocational responsibilities and conscientiously identifying your genuine needs, you and your wife will limit both your spending and your saving, begin to accumulate a surplus, and so learn by experience how much income you need. You might consider donating the excess to charity; considered in itself, that would be commendable. Perhaps a chief executive officer successfully managing some large corporation can justly accept a salary of millions of dollars a year and use it rightly by living modestly while frequently helping less prosperous relatives, friends, and acquaintances, and generously contributing to worthy causes. But you have specific gifts and training for whose exercise many poor people have a great, unsatisfied need. By directly putting your gifts to work serving them, you not only will make appropriate use of your abilities for others' good but, at the same time, build up community between yourselves and those you serve.

So, to limit your income to the amount you need, it would, in my judgment, be appropriate for you to restrict your remunerated legal practice to the group of clients whose fair fees will provide you with income sufficient to meet your needs. That will free you to serve the pressing needs of some people who cannot pay for legal service. In thus fulfilling your original commitment to seek justice for the vulnerable, proceed as in making other vocational commitments. Match your gifts with opportunities for service by considering precisely what you can do, and the characteristics and urgency of others' needs. Since you have special experience with contracts, you might at first provide service especially in that area to clients, corporate or individual, who can show they need legal help but cannot afford it.

However, I do not think you should limit your pro bono service to deserving but poor clients who happen to come to you, since it may be easy for you to serve others even more deserving and poorer, perhaps by contributing a portion of your time to some legal aid society. That also would have the advantage of structuring your commitment, so that you would be more likely to fulfill it consistently. Eventually, when your children are raised and you have saved enough to retire, you might give up your established practice and begin a new one in a poor neighborhood, providing legal services at minimum cost—for instance, by organizing and overseeing a staff of paralegals and charging only enough to cover expenses.

191: May professionals bill two clients for the same time?

Like most lawyers and certain other professionals, I bill clients for all the time I actually spend on their affairs. This gives rise to various problems. Here are a couple to which I have not found satisfying solutions, though I have talked them over with a former teacher and some more experienced colleagues.

Clients normally are billed for time spent traveling on their business. Sometimes nothing else can be done for a client during that time, and I might say some prayers or work a crossword puzzle. But on occasion something can be done for another client, and I do it. May I bill both clients for that time?

Again, a client asked me to work on a problem new to me, which required many hours of research. Shortly after completing the work and billing the client—who was pleased with the result but distressed by its cost—something totally unexpected happened. A man I had never seen before came in and asked me to work on virtually the same problem. There was no conflict of interest, because helping him would in no way harm or even affect the first client, and the fact that I had worked on the problem for someone else in no way lessened the likely benefit of my services to the new client. I agreed, and he retained me at my usual hourly fee. With virtually no additional work at all I provided him with the result of my previous research.

May I bill the new client for two-thirds of the time I spent on the research needed to deal with this unusual problem, send half that payment to the regular client as a rebate, and keep half myself? If not, how about billing the new client for half the time I spent on the research and rebating that entire amount to the other client?

Analysis:

This question calls for the derivation and application of norms regarding billing. Professionals should seek only reasonable compensation for the whole of their practice, and generally this rules out billing two clients for the same time. Occasionally, however, a professional who cannot obtain such reasonable compensation except by billing two clients for the same time may bill both, though only if doing so is not unfair for some other reason. With regard to the second problem, having agreed with a client to provide services on an hourly basis, billing more hours than are actually spent serving that client would be fraudulent. So, the questioner may not bill the second client for any of the hours already billed to the first. However, if the questioner had proposed at the outset to bill the second client on a different basis, a fair agreement could have provided sufficient income to rebate part of the cost of the research to the first client.

The reply could be along the following lines:

Questions about double billing concern many professionals. Your examples point to an underlying problem. Billing a client for all the time spent on his or her business or case can be unfair. Professionals should seek only reasonable compensation—that is, compensation for the whole of their practice sufficient to meet moderately all their and their dependents' current and future genuine needs (see q. 190, above). For many professionals, the range of hourly rates usually charged by others for similar services and the time spent on a matter provide a good starting point for calculating fair fees, but other factors also must be taken into account, including any special characteristics either of the work done or of the two parties.

Though some professionals never bill clients for time spent traveling on their affairs or cases, doing so sometimes is justified. That is so only if the travel is appropriate for doing the client's business, not billing for it would leave one short of reasonable compensation for the whole of one's practice, and no other consideration that must be taken into account makes it unfair. Usually that condition, which justifies billing for travel time, is met because the time otherwise would not be productive and would go uncompensated, though it falls within the professional's normal working hours. But some professionals—for example, those just beginning their practice or spending much of their time in pro bono work—can obtain reasonable compensation for the whole of their practice only by billing for travel time even when it also is used on other productive work that is compensated by another client. Therefore, in your first example, unless billing both clients is necessary for you to obtain reasonable compensation for the whole of your practice and is not otherwise unfair, doing so would be unjustified and doing so merely to increase your income would be avaricious.

As for the second example, your client's distress at the cost of your service perhaps suggests that the fee was excessive. If so, you owe that client some restitution. Perhaps you failed to let the client know how much time you were spending or likely to spend. In that case, you may have violated the understanding on which you were retained.

Then too, in the early years of their practice, while gaining experience, professionals not only should charge lower than average rates, but sometimes should count part of the time spent on a client's behalf as used for improving their skills, and so not as billable to the client. Thus, if the problem that was new to you required a disproportionate number of hours of research due to your comparative inexperience, not all those hours should have been billed. Rather, you should have billed at your usual rate only as many hours as it would have taken you to earn the fee an average experienced practitioner would have earned by doing the same work in much less time, and you ought to refund the difference.

Even if your inexperience was not a factor in the time the research took and you in no way violated your understanding with the first client, so that the amount billed was justified, billing the second client for the same hours cannot be justified. Having undertaken to provide your services on an hourly basis, it would be fraudulent to bill the second client for more hours than actually spent on his or her business or case.

Of course, professionals who usually charge their clients by the hour may be justified at times in contracting on a different basis—for example, charging flat rates for services of certain kinds, charging an agreed amount for some particular service, or charging in proportion to the client's benefit from the service. Flat rates are especially appropriate for making simple, inexpensive, professional services available by advertising to people who otherwise would hesitate to take advantage of them, and also for spreading the costs of providing a service among its many users. Charging a special, negotiated fee for a particular service is especially appropriate for large jobs, especially difficult or repugnant ones, and those whose costs cannot otherwise be fairly distributed among clients. Charging in proportion to the benefit a client gains is especially appropriate in contingent-fee arrangements, which share the rewards of professional service with clients who otherwise could not afford to take the risks. In all such cases, however, the basis for every charge must justify it, and the method of billing must be stated clearly in advance and accepted by the client. In the second example, therefore, you need not have undertaken to provide service to the second client on an hourly basis. Rather, you could have explained the situation, offered the service at a higher price, and rebated at least part of the difference to the first client.

In suggesting the possibility that you solve some billing problems by charging a flat rate, negotiating a fee, or making a contingent-fee arrangement, I do not suggest these methods of billing are morally superior, since each method involves its own difficulties. What is morally required, rather, is that you seek only reasonable compensation for the whole of your practice, defraud nobody, and treat everybody fairly. When in doubt about how to bill, it is good to give clients the benefit of the doubt, bearing in mind that God keeps accurate accounts and will give everyone his or her due (see Rom 2.6–8, 2 Cor 5.10).

192: May a person serving on a jury compromise on a verdict?

I have been called for jury duty, and have been told I am likely to be selected to hear one or more criminal cases. Having talked with several friends who have served on juries, I am worried about the possibility that I will be on a sharply divided jury. I would not like being in that situation, and I am especially worried about three things that might come up.

One problem arises when the judge instructs the jury in such a way that it can find the defendant guilty or not guilty of diverse, more and less serious crimes. Suppose, for example, a man shoots and gravely wounds his wife and she seems at first to recover but then dies as the result of an infection that probably resulted from the wound. The jury might be instructed that, depending on its judgment regarding the facts, it could find the man either innocent or else guilty of murder or of assault with a deadly weapon. Suppose everyone on the jury agrees that the man shot his wife, but some think it was murder and others that it was assault with a deadly weapon; or suppose one or two jurors think he did not shoot his wife but the rest think he did and it was murder. May the jury compromise on assault with a deadly weapon in either or both of those cases?

Another problem comes up when two or more defendants accused of a crime such as robbery are on trial, charged with, say, not only robbery but assault, carrying concealed weapons, and so forth. Some jurors might wish to convict all the defendants on all the charges, while others might think one or more innocent on at least some charges. No doubt discussion sometimes leads people to change their minds so that a consensus is reached. But, if that does not happen, is it wrong to compromise to reach a verdict?

I have still another problem. What if the law and the facts seem to require a morally unacceptable verdict? For example, suppose someone peacefully demonstrating outside an abortion clinic technically violates the law. May a juror who believes the law wrong hold out for an acquittal?

Analysis:

This question calls for the derivation of norms for decision making by jurors. In view of their responsibilities, jurors seldom if ever are morally free to compromise. However, if the judge's instructions allowed jurors who believed a defendant guilty of a crime to vote truthfully to acquit him or her of it, jurors who believed all the conditions for both offenses were fulfilled could vote to acquit the defendant of the more serious crime to reach a verdict on the less serious one. However, jurors may never vote to convict any defendant of anything unless convinced beyond a reasonable doubt that he or she is guilty, and should not be a party to any compromise in which other jurors would vote for a conviction without that assurance of guilt. Finally, if convinced that the defendant violated the law but that the law is unjust, a juror ought to refuse to vote for either conviction or acquittal.

The reply could be along the following lines:

You are right to think ahead about your responsibilities as a juror, since the decisions of juries in criminal cases have a profound impact not only on defendants and their families but on society as a whole, including potential victims. The fundamental duty of jurors is to know and fulfill their specific responsibilities under the law. It is not to try, as some do, to bring about the result they happen to believe would be for the best—for example, convicting a defendant they think should be off the street or acquitting one whose punishment would be hard on his or her family.

You may be able to forestall or, at least, mitigate intractable disagreement with the other jurors by carefully fulfilling your responsibilities. So, before responding to your specific questions, I shall propose some norms for your jury duty.

When the jury is being selected to hear a particular case, you will be told something about it and asked various questions by the defense and prosecution lawyers and, perhaps, by the judge. Resist being influenced by the wish to be included in or excluded from the jury, and answer every question with complete honesty. If not confident you understand a question, ask to have it repeated and, if necessary, explained.

During the course of the trial, the judge probably will give the jury various instructions. Pay attention to those instructions and, again, ask that they be repeated and explained if necessary. Then, carefully follow the judge's instructions. If you observe other members of the jury disobeying, do not quarrel with them, since that is hardly likely to be effective and might well impede the cooperation that will be necessary to reach a verdict. However, if you think the infraction is likely to affect the outcome, tell the bailiff you wish to speak with the judge, and tell the judge what is happening. If you cannot do that before the verdict is about to be announced, at least then you should state that you believe the outcome was affected by one or more jurors' disregard of the judge's instructions.[418] This is not tattling; it is a strict duty.

As the trial proceeds, bear in mind that you ought to form your opinion on the basis of all the evidence and in conformity with the relevant law, regarding which the judge will instruct the jury only after both sides have presented their cases. Resist the tendency to form any firm opinion until the jury's deliberation is about to begin. The appearance, courtroom behavior, and irrelevant personality and

---

418. In some jurisdictions members of juries are held to such strict confidentiality regarding their communications with one another that they usually would be thought to violate their trust if they made public, or even reported to the judge, violations of his or her instructions. But such a duty surely cannot be absolute. A juror who observed a colleague threatening violence to induce another to change his or her position certainly would have a duty to make known this subversion of just process.

character traits of the defendant(s), witnesses, and lawyers are bound to affect your feelings. Take note of your favorable and unfavorable feelings, but do not let them distract you from the facts of the case and from the judge's instructions about the law, or otherwise unduly influence your judgment on the issue or issues the jury is to decide. In initially forming your opinion, bear in mind that you may have overlooked something or erred in your reasoning, and keep an open mind.

When the jury's deliberation begins, listen carefully to other jurors' views and the reasons they offer for them. If what they say seems to you inconsistent with the evidence or the judge's instructions, do not attribute bad motives to them. Also, avoid directly challenging them, for example, by saying they are wrong or have overlooked something or are guilty of faulty reasoning. Say you do not understand their view or cannot follow their argument, and ask for further explanation, or ask how they account for something you think they are overlooking. Similarly, if another juror manifests unreasonable grounds for a position you consider mistaken, rather than straightforwardly rejecting the grounds, express your puzzlement—for example, by saying you do not see how those considerations are relevant or are unconvinced that his or her underlying assumptions are sound. If one or more jurors seem so intent on a certain outcome that they are setting aside the responsibility to decide the case on the facts and the law, remind them of their basic duty and point out that the rule of law is safer than rule by individuals' judgments about what would be a good outcome.

In first stating your own view, propose it tentatively. For example: "Unless I am missing something, it seems to me . . .." If others disagree, ask them to point out what you have overlooked or where you have gone wrong in your reasoning, and listen carefully to what they say. If discussion makes it clear to you that your view is inadequate in some way, frankly tell the others that you are amending your view in that respect and what led to the change. If the jurors disagree about what was said in the courtroom or about the meaning and correct application of the judge's instructions, do not argue; suggest gently but, if necessary, repeatedly that the jury request the judge's help in resolving such issues.

If intractable disagreement with other jurors develops despite your effort to forestall it, remember that your responsibility is to decide the issue(s) on the basis of the law and the facts, in accord with the judge's instructions. Bear in mind particularly, that you should not vote to find a defendant guilty unless you believe the evidence establishes his or her guilt beyond reasonable doubt. To clarify the meaning of *reasonable doubt,* it will help to remember that this standard remains the same regardless of the seriousness of the crime of which a defendant is accused and its prospective punishment. If you are not sufficiently convinced of a defendant's guilt to vote for a conviction leading to a sentence of life in prison, you should not vote for a conviction that would lead to any lesser punishment.

I turn now to the first case you describe—members of a jury agree that a man shot his wife but disagree on whether his crime was murder or assault with a deadly weapon. May jurors who think the crime was murder agree to a verdict of assault with a deadly weapon? Yes. The jury will vote on each issue separately. Any juror convinced that the evidence verifies beyond reasonable doubt that what the defendant did fulfilled all the conditions for both offenses can and, with a possible exception I shall explain, should vote that he is guilty of both, and any member convinced that he is not guilty of murder can and should vote accordingly. The result will be that the jury will both return the verdict that the defendant is guilty of assault with a deadly weapon and report its inability to agree about whether the defendant is guilty of murder.

But what if some of the jurors who are convinced that the defendant is not guilty of murder say they will refuse to convict him even of assault with a deadly weapon unless all the jurors agree to acquit him of murder? In voting to acquit, a juror ordinarily thereby verbally or nonverbally takes the position that the evidence does not show beyond reasonable doubt that the defendant is guilty of the crime as the law, explained by the judge, defines it. Assuming that is the meaning of a vote to acquit, a juror who believed the defendant guilty of murder yet voted to acquit him would lie. And, since lying is always wrong, that would be wrong.

Suppose, however, the judge somehow makes it clear that jurors convinced that the defendant is guilty of murder are free to vote to acquit him if doing so is necessary to reach a verdict on the assault charge? I doubt the judge will do that. But if he or she does, a vote to acquit of murder no longer will have to express a position on the relationship between what the defendant did and relevant law; it can simply be a means to get other jurors to vote in accord with their conviction that the defendant is guilty of assault. Then, if a juror is convinced that the defendant is guilty of murder, that the common good requires his conviction, and that he probably will never be convicted of murder, he or she should vote to acquit him of it to reach the verdict that he is guilty of assault with a deadly weapon.

Compromise on such a verdict is altogether morally unacceptable in the second case, where most members of a jury think the man was guilty of murder but one or two think he was innocent. If you believe he did not shoot his wife, it will be wrong to agree that he was guilty of assault, even if you fear that he might be convicted of murder if retried. For if you are convinced that the defendant should be acquitted, compromising and agreeing to convict him would be both untruthful and a grave injustice to him. If you are in a small minority or entirely isolated, you might be tempted to give in, especially if you also happen to believe that the defendant probably was guilty, or if you have antagonistic feelings toward the defendant and his counsel, and/or are anxious to end the deliberation. But such temptations must be resisted.

Moreover, though you might be able to agree to a verdict of assault with a deadly weapon if you believed the defendant guilty of murder, you could not do that as a compromise with jurors who believed him entirely innocent. Since no juror should vote against his or her best judgment so as to find a defendant guilty on a particular count, offering such a compromise would be leading the other jurors to violate their consciences, and agreeing to the compromise, if others proposed it, would be condoning the violation of conscience. Therefore, you should not propose or support such a compromise, and you should resist any attempt by another or others to bully you or anyone else into accepting it.

In cases in which two or more defendants are on trial together, the jury surely will be instructed to deliberate and decide about each individually. Still, jurors might be tempted to disregard the instructions and trade votes to convict one or more defendants (on one or more counts) in exchange for the acquittal of one or more other defendants (on one or more counts). Confronted with any such proposal, you should reject it firmly and, instead, apply the previously explained norms to each defendant individually. In other words, never vote to find anyone guilty of anything whatsoever unless convinced the evidence warrants that verdict with respect to him or her.

Suppose you are convinced justice requires a verdict inconsistent with the law and the facts? Since the verdict you vote for should truthfully reflect your conclusion about the facts in light of the relevant law, it would be dishonest to vote for the opposite verdict, even if you believed the law unjust.[419] At the same time, putting yourself in the defendant's place, you surely would find it unfair to vote to convict him or her of violating a law you considered unjust. Therefore, in such a case, you would be obliged to refuse to vote for either verdict, explain why, and accept the consequences. Such a problem, however, probably would be obviated by the pretrial questioning. For example, before concluding it, the judge might ask whether anyone has any other reason that might disqualify him or her from serving on that jury. Any question like that would require you to state your position with regard to the questionable law, and the judge would exclude you from the jury.

193: Should those in authority seek consensus or make decisions unilaterally?

I am a high-ranking civil service employee in a department of the U.S. government. The managers above me are political appointees who come and go with changes in the administration and sometimes between times. In the years I've worked here, I've experienced different management styles, each with its own problems.

At one extreme is the autocratic style. The political appointees talk almost exclusively to one another and make the decisions, and we underlings are expected to implement them without arguing. This inevitably leads to many ill-informed decisions due to lack of experience, and often such decisions are virtually impossible to carry out and cause a great deal of frustration and foot dragging on the part of permanent employees, including me.

At the other extreme is the democratic style. The political appointees set up numerous committees and hold endless meetings in an effort to build consensus. This is time consuming, and, due to deep-rooted philosophical differences and the complexity of many of the issues, it seldom produces the desired consensus.

---

419. John Guinther, *The Jury in America* (New York: Facts on File Publications, 1988), 219–31, argues for the contrary position and cites several respected judges in support of it. But he fails to confront the ethical issue that so-called jury justice depends on jurors acting contrary to their undertaking to decide a case in accord with the facts and the law. Unless instructed otherwise, moreover, the judge's interpretation of the law is binding on jurors.

Instead, it almost always divides the permanent employees—and sometimes the political appointees themselves—into factions. The result sometimes is that nothing is done and problems remain unaddressed. Or else, to end the deadlock, decisions finally are made at the top level, and, while these are likely to be well-informed, the losers are frustrated.

We are now about to undergo yet another transition. Surprisingly, the person who has been nominated (and undoubtedly will be confirmed) as secretary of the department came by and asked everyone at my level to prepare a brief statement on the main challenges the department faces and what should be done to deal with them. I am going to seize the opportunity to address the overarching problem of management style. Of course, I already have my own thoughts on the matter, but I am seeking input from others as well.

Perhaps you will take this to be a problem in management technique rather than a moral question. However, I will be grateful for whatever you have to say from the moral point of view.

Analysis:

This query is both a technical problem and a difficult moral question: How should authority be exercised? The answer: Diverse styles are appropriate in diverse situations. More precisely, then, the question is: What style should the department's managers prefer in making decisions to guide the work of employees at the questioner's level and below? This question calls for the derivation of specific norms. Since authority should be exercised by those in the best position to make sound decisions, the managers should not usurp their subordinates' proper authority. In directing others' work, the managers should prefer a consultative style of decision making, by which all who will carry out the decision are encouraged to participate in deliberation; but, unless consensus spontaneously emerges, the managers alone should make the choice.

The reply could be along the following lines:

Situations that call for a decision and in which some of the proposed options are immoral involve considerations that would complicate discussion of your question. I shall consider only cases in which all the options under consideration are morally acceptable, so that employees could cooperate in good conscience with any decision the political appointees made.

The primary responsibility of those in authority is to make decisions that shape cooperation toward realizing the group's common purposes. Failure to proceed rightly in making decisions, as you point out, leads to bad decisions, undermines cooperation, and prevents the group from achieving its ends, with the further bad result that its most dedicated and conscientious members remain unfulfilled, become frustrated, and lose the motivation to do their work, so that they either resign or, as you put it, drag their feet. Therefore, your query—How should managers make decisions?—is both a problem in management technique and a difficult and important moral question. In responding to the moral question, I shall articulate some norms that I believe have wider validity in a way that will specify them to the situation you have described.

Plainly, diverse styles are appropriate in making diverse sorts of decisions. In emergencies, for instance, autocratic decision making can be indispensable; in matters that greatly affect employees' morale but have little other impact on their work's quality and productivity, decision making ought to be democratic. Moreover, competent managers often delegate their authority to others. But I assume you take for granted this variety of decision-making styles, and so I understand your question as more specific: How should your department's managers prefer to make decisions directing the work of employees at your level and below?[420] I shall cover the points I think you should make regarding that specific question.

The first point is that the political appointees, who are the top managers, need not make or even be involved in every decision in the department. Insofar as possible, they should focus their attention on a few matters: innovations and reforms in programs and policies affecting the work of the department as a whole or its major sections, internal conflicts not resolved at lower levels, and major external threats to the department's integrity or work. True, nothing in the department can be excluded from the purview of the political appointees, and they should intervene whenever necessary to correct serious abuses. Still, they normally should not attempt to micromanage by making day-to-day decisions directing routine activities, the inner workings of each office, or even the work of employees at your level in implementing established programs and policies.

The underlying principle of this distribution of decision making is that authority always should be exercised by those in the best position to make sound decisions. Carrying the principle through to its logical conclusion will mean that virtually everyone in the department will participate in authority, making some decisions that guide cooperation with at least one or a few other employees, since even workers at the lowest levels usually are in a better position to make certain decisions shaping moment-to-moment cooperation with their co-workers and superiors than are the latter themselves.

Turning to the decisions which the political appointees appropriately make, I come to a second point. Their preferred style of making decisions should be neither autocratic nor democratic but consultative. Decision making has two parts, which should be distinguished: (1) deliberation to discover and assess all available options and (2) the choice of one option to the exclusion of others. All who are able to contribute to (1)—deliberating—should be invited to share in it; that usually includes everyone who will be involved in carrying out the decision. Occasionally, well-conducted deliberation leads to consensus, a common preference for one option. Often, however, no consensus emerges, since two or more options are supported by weighty reasons, grounded in noncommensurable prospective advantages and disadvantages. As you remark, such issues often are complex and opposing positions sometimes reflect deep-rooted differences. In such cases, the individual or small group responsible for the cooperative effort as a whole must

420. The question does not concern how the managers as a group should make decisions, and so the response does not deal with that. In their case, however, a collegial process leading to consensus might well be appropriate. See Thomas A. Baylis, *Governing by Committee: Collegial Leadership in Advanced Societies* (Albany, N.Y.: State University of New York Press, 1989).

proceed to (2)—making a choice. The implications for consultative decision making of the distinction between deliberation and choice can be stated, although without literal accuracy, in terms of the two styles you distinguish: deliberation should be democratic, but when no consensus emerges choice must be autocratic.

The third point is that everyone should be free to suggest problems for consideration and those who will make the choices should consider every such suggestion, but they alone should initiate the deliberative process and regulate it. If others initiate deliberation, it will not involve the group as a whole; subgroups will pursue their own agendas, and time will be wasted discussing matters those in charge are not prepared to deal with. Those regulating deliberation should try to define the problem and seek the help of everyone involved in learning two things: the options for resolving it that are worth examining and the considerations for and against each option.

The fourth point is that, where it is appropriate for the political appointees to make a decision, they should make it clear to everyone that they mean to do so. If a consensus emerges, they of course should welcome it, but they should not expect universal agreement or waste time and effort seeking it. Head counting—that is, any form of consultative voting for and against options in order to determine a recommendation by those who do not have the choice to make—should be discouraged. It concedes the decision-making role to those whose responsibility should be limited to contributing to deliberation, and so confuses the two. Instead, the political appointees should ask for well-prepared briefs for and against each option. They also should direct that these briefs be studied and criticized by those who disagree with their contents and then rewritten in the light of all the criticisms received. In using these briefs, the political appointees should focus their attention—and make it clear to everyone that they are doing so—on the quality of the evidence and arguments, regardless of the numbers and status of the permanent employees supporting particular conclusions.

Someone might object that numbers and status can hardly be ignored, since the wholehearted support of those who will implement a policy is important to its success. While the support of subordinates who will implement decisions is necessary for their success, however, subordinates should support any legitimate decision, and those in authority should enlist their support without abdicating their own responsibility for making decisions. Of course, given pervasive habits of insubordination and other sinful social structures, leaders must take into consideration as a disadvantage any residual probability that subordinates' halfheartedness in implementing a decision will limit or negate its potential benefits. But that must not be confused with information about the subordinates' views on options. Many loyal and dedicated employees will carefully and energetically implement a decision for an option other than the one they preferred.

The fifth point is that in regulating deliberation the political appointees should review its results as they come in and regularly consider reformulating the problem, recasting the alternatives under consideration, widening the deliberative process, and so on. This is necessary to overcome the limitations of initial ignorance and take advantage of emerging data and insights. Moreover, only constant monitoring can lead to necessary procedural choices, such as to suspend deliberation by setting the problem aside for the time being or to terminate it with a definite decision and the beginning of its implementation.

The sixth point is that, when decisions are announced, the reasoning behind them almost always should be articulated, since, by clarifying the purpose in view, the reasons for a decision contribute to its accurate interpretation and provide the intrinsic reasons for implementing it. Oftentimes, the announcement of a decision also can enlist the support of those who favored some alternative by indicating, at least briefly, how the considerations supporting alternatives will be taken into account in other phases of policy making.

The final point is that this consultative process will work well only if everyone involved takes pains to communicate precisely and clearly but briefly. If those initiating and regulating the process fail to communicate carefully, other participants will not know what is expected of them and probably will develop false expectations about their roles in the process. If participants who try to offer their information and ideas are not clear and precise, or if they are verbose, their potential contribution will be, practically speaking, more or less unavailable to decision makers.

One can hope that, if this procedure is followed, the disadvantages of both the so-called autocratic and democratic styles will be avoided. The political appointees will talk with and hear from everyone with anything to contribute; their decisions will be well informed; and the reasons for them will be articulated as well as possible by those who favored the option selected, taking into account others' criticisms. While not everyone will agree with the final decision, implementing it will be possible and more likely to succeed. When consensus does not emerge spontaneously, time and effort will not be wasted seeking it. The clear awareness on all sides that certain choices will be made at the top level will incline employees at your level not to anticipate the outcome by taking an overly firm position. Excluding head counting and focusing on the quality of evidence and arguments for positions will discourage the formation of factions and instead promote more effective gathering of relevant data, more thorough analysis and criticism, and more willing acceptance of decisions. Finally, there will be less of something that undermines sound deliberation and is common to both the autocratic and the democratic styles—I mean the tendency of subordinates to tell superiors what they seem to want to hear.

Like other problems in interpersonal relationships, inadequacies in management styles such as you describe seldom are entirely the fault of those in authority. Subordinates' wrong attitudes and false expectations often impede sound decision making. Political appointees, for example, rightly take into account the considerations that motivated voters to favor their party, and the decisions they make based on such considerations should be respected by civil servants even if they personally favor the opposing party's policies. When a new administration must deal with various groups of uncooperative subordinates, distortions in the management process are inevitable. Therefore, while I have not focused on the duty of those at your level to obey the political appointees to whom you are subordinate, I suggest you reflect on that responsibility and also encourage your colleagues to examine their consciences regarding it.

194: Should a subordinate pretend to follow
an irrational directive?

I am a military officer, currently an instructor in an intensive training program. Our orders are that we are to deal with any problems that arise. Yet my fellow instructors and I have no discretion about the program's content and schedule, which are dictated in every detail by higher authority. We are to carry out the program on schedule, and at each stage we must grade personnel's performance by set standards. Since any military force must operate regardless of weather, we are forbidden to delay or cancel any exercise, no matter how bad the weather happens to be, unless carrying it out would involve unacceptable risks to the personnel.

This set of requirements sometimes creates real dilemmas. For instance, one wretched day, with sleet falling and visibility limited to a hundred yards, we were qualifying trainees for their ability to hit targets two hundred yards away. They could not see the targets, and we could not see whether they were hitting them. We had only two choices: fail and pass. Failing some trainees and passing others would have been arbitrary and unfair. Failing them all not only would have reflected badly on our work as trainers but subjected the trainees to additional work and demerits, which few if any of them deserved. We passed them all.

Some day the lives of these trainees and their buddies could depend on their being able to do what the program is supposed to train them to do. Therefore, I think it is wrong to qualify anyone unless we are sure the individual can perform according to the standard. Under the circumstances, though, what could we do except qualify all the personnel?

Analysis:

This question calls for applying the exceptionless norm excluding lying and for the derivation of norms for the action of subordinates who are given irrational orders. In grading, one makes a statement about the quality of a performance. Under the conditions described, the questioner had no basis for making any such statement, and grading any trainee was a lie. In situations such as that described, the order to test and grade regardless of conditions not only is unreasonable but irrational in the strict sense, inasmuch as it calls for something impossible. The order ought to be changed. If it is not and the situation described recurs, the questioner may not lie, and so must refuse to give grades, regardless of the consequences.

The reply could be along the following lines:

I agree with you that it is wrong to qualify anyone unless you are sure the individual can perform according to the standard. It follows that it was wrong to pass all the trainees, and you should not have done that. Nor should you have failed them all or passed some and failed others, not only for the reasons you give but for a more profound one, drawn from the very nature of grading.

To grade a performance is to make a claim about it, namely, that it either meets a standard (perhaps more or less perfectly) or does not. The statement of that claim subsequently will be used by the person graded and others in making decisions. When conditions make gauging performance impossible, giving any grade whatsoever is making a false statement, which will mislead those who rely on it. Under the conditions you describe, the trainees' ability to hit targets two hundred yards away could not be tested and graded. Thus, in giving a grade to each trainee, you deliberately made a false statement. No doubt, an ingrained habit of trying to comply with orders obscured the significance of what you did, but, perhaps without realizing it, you lied.

Someone might suggest you could have solved your problem and graded honestly by sending someone out to the targets to inspect them after each trainee attempted to hit them. Even if that was feasible, though, it would not have been a solution. Missing a target in those circumstances would tell nothing about a trainee's qualifications, and hitting it would be a matter of blind luck, so that grades of any kind still would have been false statements.

A military training program can reasonably include orders to do certain things that seem unreasonable, such as pointlessly trek from here to there and back again, because personnel must learn to obey orders that will seem equally pointless. But no program can reasonably include an order that is, strictly speaking, impossible to obey, since such an order is irrational and self-defeating. And the orders under which you are operating are irrational in commanding you to test and grade even when that is impossible. True, any military force must operate regardless of the weather, and so a realistic training program must not let bad weather interfere with exercises that train people for combat by simulating it, unless conducting the exercise would involve unacceptable risks to the personnel. But simulating combat is not what testing and grading do, since actual combat involves no testing and grading. Therefore, this element of the program must be recognized as requiring suitable weather conditions, and the orders under which you operate must be amended to eliminate the irrationality that currently vitiates them.

What should you do? Since it is lying to give any grade under impossible conditions, and lying is intrinsically wrong, you must not do it. Instead, acting together with your fellow instructors, if that is possible, but in any case without delay, call this problem to the attention of the higher authority responsible for the irrationality in the orders—going through the chain of command and using appropriate procedure, of course—and request that the necessary amendment be made. Very likely, there was no deliberate abuse of authority, but merely a failure in foresight, and a reasonable superior will correct the mistake.

However, if your request is rejected or not answered by the next time grading is required but impossible, you must resist your habit of complying with orders and refuse to grade. If that results in some sort of disciplinary measure, use available procedures to vindicate your position, with the hope that authority at some level will acknowledge and correct the irrationality of your orders. If worse comes to worst, you must be ready to suffer harm to your career or a formal disciplinary measure that might be imposed on you.

Someone might argue that the dilemma you describe is not so important that you would be morally required to refuse to obey orders and suffer the consequences. That argument is not sound. As has been explained, pretending to grade when grading is impossible is lying, and even venial sins of lying are great evils.[421] You do not have the option available to people whose actions, morally acceptable in themselves, contribute to another's wrongdoing in ways that can be justified when necessary to forestall gravely bad consequences. Besides, in this case lying is no small matter, since, as you point out, the trainees' ability to do the things for which you are qualifying them may someday determine whether they and others live or die.

Moreover, any organization, including a military force, is seriously harmed when irrational directives impede the cooperation essential for pursuing its purposes. Authentic obedience and loyalty require subordinates to call attention to such irrationality and, if necessary, resist it, rather than accommodate it by moral compromises allowing it to persist and even, perhaps, causing it to proliferate. In a situation of this sort, a Christian also ought to bear in mind that Jesus promised the kingdom to those who suffer for righteousness' sake (see Mt 5.10).[422]

195: May legislators follow public opinion against their own judgment?

I am thinking of running for the state legislature. But I am hesitant to do so because I foresee various moral problems, including one in particular. Officeholders generally are better qualified than the public—by training, experience, and access to relevant information—to judge what should be done. If I am elected, there will be times when my better judgment tells me to take one position on an issue while opinion polls show that the majority, even the overwhelming majority, of my constituents hold the opposite position. No one who hopes to be reelected can ignore public opinion. Under what conditions, if any, should a legislator make it the decisive factor in determining his or her position?

421. See John Henry Newman, *Apologia pro vita sua,* ed. Martin J. Svaglic (Oxford: Oxford University Press, 1967), 221.

422. This question focuses on a kind of problem that arises at times, though in somewhat different forms, in every organization, including the Church. Even the most conscientious superiors, those careful not to abuse their authority, have limited insight into the implications of their directives and limited foresight about conditions that can make executing them impossible. Subordinates ought, of course, to presume that their superiors' orders are to be obeyed, and should be prepared to obey orders that seem unreasonable, provided that is not morally excluded. Moreover, one must distinguish between cases in which obedience is impossible and those in which it is only difficult, calling for hard work and self-sacrifice; disobedience in cases of the latter sort must not be rationalized by calling the difficult "impossible." But when orders really are irrational, subordinates owe it to their organization, those it serves, their fellow members, and even their superiors to call attention to the irrationality and resist it, not accommodate and perpetuate it.

Analysis:

This question calls for the derivation of norms for the work of legislators. making decisions, Catholic legislators should not set aside faith and Chu teaching. If one knows one's vote will not affect the body's action, one can v with the prevailing group without intending what it does. Without intend wrongly, one can support adoption of the lesser or least evil of available mora evil options, intending thereby to prevent a more serious moral evil. Except in su a case, legislators may never support a proposal morally evil in itself or plai unjust. If a proposal is neither evil in itself nor plainly unjust, legislators may ta constituent opinion into account in judging what will better serve the comm good, all things considered. In a parliamentary system, legislators are expected follow their party's decision and generally may do so. But they never should supp a proposal they judge to be immoral in itself or plainly unjust.

The reply could be along the following lines:

As a basis for responding, I shall recall a number of points, though you no do are well aware of most of them.

In forming their consciences about the moral acceptability of proposed legis tion, Catholic members of a legislative body should look to their faith and Church's teaching, not set them aside. Since these are sources of truth about hun good, a legislator who neglected them would fail to fulfill his or her duty as a pul servant. The relevant truth taught by the Church also pertains to natural law anc will be accessible to people of good will who are not Catholics (see *CCC,* 195

Every freely chosen human act is either morally good or morally evil, a every political issue is a moral issue to the extent that society's common gc and justice toward individuals and groups are at stake. And though many of kinds of acts that are always wrong involve sexual activity outside marriage violate innocent human life, these are not the only issues about which mc compromise is impossible.

Some legislators, confronted with what they recognize as a moral issue, th that clearly stating their principled position early in the proceedings discharges tl moral responsibility and frees them to follow the party line or vote as see expedient. But legislators are morally responsible for everything they knowin and willingly do, not least for participating in the legislative body's specific a Thus, nothing else a legislator does can free him or her from moral responsibi for the votes cast—or not cast—on proposed legislation.

Because of the complexities of legislative procedure, affirmative or negat votes sometimes have a significance different from the one they might seen have. For instance, a measure's opponent might have to vote for it in order to eligible to move its reconsideration at a later session, when changed circumstan might make it possible to defeat it. In what follows, however, I set aside procedural complexity, and, for simplicity's sake, assume that a vote for a meas always expresses support for its adoption and implementation, while a vote aga always expresses opposition.

In voting, one generally contributes to a social choice, a joint decision of the group that is voting, and so either chooses what one votes for and intends that it be done or rejects what one votes against and intends that it not be done. However, if one knows on a particular occasion that one's vote will in no way affect the group's decision, voting for the proposal need not mean one intends it to be carried out and voting against need not mean one intends it not to be carried out. (Of course, like any other action, voting, to be morally good, requires more than an upright intention.)

In some cases, members of legislatures confront a limited set of alternatives, none of them morally acceptable, that they are powerless to improve. Then a legislator may rightly vote for the less (or least) immoral alternative. In doing so, he or she need not intend its adoption and implementation; rather, the upright legislator's intention will be to prevent greater immorality.

Having made these clarifications, I turn to your question.

Except in a case that falls under the last point above, if a proposal under consideration is immoral in itself or plainly unjust, legislators should never let their constituents' support for it persuade them to vote for it.

Suppose there were a proposal to solve the problem of homeless street people by gathering them up and killing them. That proposal would be immoral in itself. No matter how many of your constituents favored it, you would be obliged to vote against it. If you thought your vote might make a difference, it would be wrong to vote yes since you would be intending the killing. (In making a choice reluctantly, it is quite possible to intend an evil toward which one feels great repugnance.)

Suppose the proposal were to authorize local governments in your state to replace the real estate tax with a tax of a specified amount, say three dollars per day, on each individual occupying any residential unit in their jurisdictions. Surely you would judge that unjust, since it would tend further to impoverish the already poor by shifting to them the tax burden now borne by those more able to bear it; yet perhaps the majority of voters in your district would strongly support it. In such a case, it would be wrong to allow your constituents' opinion and the prospect of losing their support in a future election to motivate you to vote for the proposal, for that would betray the injustice's victims and undermine your witness to the truth and good at stake.

Even if you were sure your vote would not affect the body's decision, moreover, voting for a measure you considered immoral in itself or plainly unjust would be politically pointless unless you capitalized on it—for example, by claiming to share your constituents' prevailing view, which would be lying in grave matter. Since you will not be able to avoid explaining and defending how you voted on a controversial matter, if you consider a proposal immoral in itself or plainly unjust, you should do your best to persuade constituents who favor it to accept your position, vote according to your conscience, and try to retain or win the support of those who disagree with you by serving them well in legitimate ways.

Usually, of course, proposals under consideration are neither immoral in themselves nor plainly unjust. Instead they have real advantages and real disadvantages, so that legislators have good reasons for both supporting and opposing them. Both

possibilities are morally acceptable in such cases, and legislators must discern
how to vote. If your initial discernment pointed to a judgment at odds with the
opinion of the majority of your constituents, would you be justified in yielding
to their opinion? Perhaps. Their genuine collective discernment of what is best
for their community as a whole would more likely be sound than yours as an
individual. So, you would be justified if you thought your constituents were
sufficiently informed to be able to discern and believed their opinion was a
product, not merely of passions, but of genuine discernment—that is, discernment in view of the common good.

Someone will object that legislators should not be mere messengers, serving as
their constituents' agents and bound by their instructions, but guardians of the
common good, chosen by the people to deliberate and make decisions in accord
with their well-informed consciences; legislators who substitute constituents'
discernment for their own abdicate their proper responsibility. While granting the
stated view of the legislator's responsibility, I deny that yielding to informed
constituents' discernment need betray it. When discernment is appropriate and
constituents are in a position to discern, legislators have good reason for considering their constituents' prevailing opinion sound and forming their own consciences
accordingly. In such a case, refusing to act in accord with that opinion would mean
rejecting the best available index of the common good.

But what if you think your constituents' opinion is less a product of genuine
discernment than of passions? If your position on the matter certainly will not affect
the outcome, you need not resist your constituents' opinion. If your position may
or even certainly will affect the outcome, however, then, it seems to me, two kinds
of cases should be distinguished.

Sometimes you will confidently judge that, though one or more other options
are morally acceptable, a particular option definitely would be more conducive to
the common good. In such cases, you should not yield to a different opinion held
by your constituents unless, taking into account the political consequences of
resisting, you judge that doing so will serve the common good at least as well.
Suppose it seems clear to you that a proposal to increase and extend unemployment
benefits would better serve the common good than alternative approaches to
helping the unemployed, and suppose a pivotal bloc of voters opposed both that
proposal and euthanasia. If resisting their opinion on the unemployment measure
seemed likely to lead to your defeat at the next election by a proponent of
euthanasia, you might conclude that an alternative—say, a program to retrain and
relocate unemployed workers—together with remaining in office so as to oppose
euthanasia would be at least as conducive to the common good.

In other cases, though, your own judgment will not be so confident. You will
think a particular option more likely to serve the common good than others, but
you also will recognize that your judgment could be mistaken. In such cases, it
seems to me, you could rightly yield to your constituents' opinion. To some
indeterminable extent, it, too, will be the product of genuine discernment. And even
though it also is a product of passions, that is no less true of the opinions of every
other legislator's constituents. The democratic system has been constructed to

balance out such nonrational interests as much as possible, and, balanced out, public opinion is likely to be in line with the common good. For since many people are somewhat reasonable and civic-minded, and a few almost entirely so, the prospective benefits of alternative proposals are likely to shape informed public opinion as a whole toward the common good, while the system generally will operate to cancel out competing, nonrational interests.

In a parliamentary system, your responsibilities as a legislator would be somewhat different. In such a system, one's party matters more than it does in the United States. The party's campaign for election is more tightly organized, and during legislative sessions the leaders of each party can and sometimes do require their followers to vote as a bloc. In such a system, nobody should seek office as a member of a party that has a prospect of governing unless convinced that the common good will be better served with that party in power than with any alternative.

Of course, conscientious citizens with the gifts needed for service in parliament are likely to foresee that they will not be able to support every position of any party with a chance of governing. A member's differences with his or her party sometimes are consistent with conscientious service. Still, even those who think they could function within a major party without moral compromise sometimes should run as independents or join a party with no chance of governing. Though precluded from governing, such members of a parliament may be able to serve their constituents and the common good well by their committee work and their sometimes decisive votes on closely contested issues.

A parliamentary system is so constituted that members are elected and authorized to contribute to their leaders' deliberation and decisions, but have no right to resist when called on to support their party's common position. In most cases, this presents no moral problem. Reasonable parliamentary party leaders do not impose party discipline on members with conscientious objections. When a member's vote will not be decisive, the leadership hardly will discipline him or her for being absent. On some especially contentious issues, leaders openly allow members to vote as they believe right; on some others, the leadership often tolerates members' voting for reasons of conscience with the opposition.

If threatened with punishment by the party leadership, however, a member of parliament must vote according to conscience if the alternative is to cast a vote that could be decisive for something he or she considers immoral in itself or plainly unjust. In such a case, moreover, party discipline should be resisted, if possible, not only for the sake of justice in the matter at issue but for the party's good as well, since its true interest cannot lie in morally unacceptable legislation.

Your question and my reply focus on direct conflicts between a legislator's better judgment and constituents' opinion. Frequently, however, the conflict is indirect. A legislator's conscience and his or her constituents' wishes agree entirely in favoring some legislative proposal, but its passage requires votes that can be obtained only by voting for some other proposal about which the legislator has reservations. Confronted with such indirect conflicts, legislators' responsibilities are exactly the same as when the conflict is direct, and the norms already stated apply. If what is proposed is neither immoral in itself nor plainly unjust, legislators can rightly trade votes, provided they conscientiously judge that doing so serves the common good. But the temptation to rationalize may be great, not least because many legislators in such a situation wrongly violate their better judgment. That temptation must be resisted. Giving in not only betrays the common good but corrupts even legislators who, nevertheless, may remain ready to resist pressures to support a proposal they recognize as immoral in itself or plainly unjust.

196: Should the city council vote to supply needles to drug addicts?

I am a member of a city council. The head of the health department, Dr. Stevens, wants us to approve a program for supplying clean needles to people addicted to illegal drugs, as has been done in some other localities. The main objective of these programs is to slow the spread of AIDS and other diseases that, although less in the news, apparently cause even more damage. Stevens proposes to kill two birds with one stone, and also to keep the program's cost minimal, by putting it in the hands of volunteers, who will be trained by a local drug rehabilitation center at no cost to the city. These volunteers will talk with the addicts when exchanging needles and try to get them into rehabilitation, pointing out that in the long run addiction is as deadly as AIDS.

Public opinion and the council are divided. I am not sure whether to vote for or against. On the one hand, if the program works it will do some good at an insignificant cost—the needles themselves. On the other hand, it will put the city in the position of helping addicts get their fix.

Which consideration do you think is more important from a moral point of view? I probably also should ask whether you think there are others I am missing.

Analysis:

This question concerns cooperation in wrongdoing. Supplying addicts with clean needles is not wrong in itself; it is material, rather than formal, cooperation with their abuse of drugs. The morality of this material cooperation depends on rectitude of intention and acceptability of side effects. The intention—to limit the spread of disease and encourage addicts to accept treatment—is good. However, the availability of clean needles will make both initial and ongoing drug abuse more tempting. Moreover, in conducting a needle exchange program, the city will undermine the witness of the law against drug abuse by becoming an accomplice. Long-term benefits to individual addicts are uncertain. Alternatives should be considered—particularly better, more available, and better publicized treatment for addicts. If the common good calls for this alternative, a needle exchange program would not be fair to addicts.

The reply could be along the following lines:

I have argued elsewhere (see *LCL,* 534–40) that using a psychoactive substance is morally wrong unless one is motivated, not by mere emotion, but by a reason grounded in an intelligible good, such as health. Plainly, addicts' use of drugs never is motivated by such a reason. So, the proposed needle exchange program, in my judgment, would contribute to behavior that is not only unlawful but morally wrong, and, given its bad consequences, not least its harmfulness to addicts themselves, objectively gravely immoral—though the personal responsibility of addicts no doubt is limited by the compulsive character of their behavior.

While it does not follow that such drug use must be forbidden by law, existing laws forbidding it ought to be presumed just and binding. To be sure, arguments have been advanced for legalizing some or many currently illegal uses of drugs, but these arguments, at least with respect to drugs that are injected, have been answered cogently.[423] Moreover, even supposing some plan of limited and strictly regulated legalization were conceded to be preferable to prohibition, it would not follow that violating existing laws is morally acceptable, since acts violating these laws would be immoral even if the laws had never been enacted. Consequently, if the city adopts the needle exchange program, it will be contributing to behavior that is both gravely wrong and in violation of laws that should be presumed just and binding.

The immediate intention of the program and of the volunteers participating in it—that is, the object of their act—would be to collect used needles and distribute sterile ones. Neither those who supported the program nor the volunteers would have to intend that anyone actually use illegal drugs, and it is hardly likely they would intend that. So, adopting the program and carrying it out would not be wrong in itself. The ends in view would be to forestall the transmission of AIDS and other diseases, and to encourage addicts to enter treatment. These ulterior intentions are good.

Someone might object that at least those who set up the program would intend the unlawful use of drugs, since they would intend the program to slow the spread of AIDS, and this benefit would not be realized if the addicts did not use the clean needles to inject drugs. However, those responsible for the program could avoid intending the ongoing abuse of drugs and only accept it as a given. The situation is like others in which one may persuade someone determined to do a grave evil, which one cannot prevent, to do instead a less grave evil—for example, having fruitlessly tried to dissuade a suicidal man from jumping out a window above a crowded sidewalk, one might call his attention to a window overlooking a deserted alley and urge him at least to spare others.

Even so, doing something that helps another do wrong often is wrong. In this case, it is not likely that those helping drug addicts will be tempted to intend their wrongdoing. Indeed, it might be argued that the volunteers will be morally benefited by developing social virtues, inasmuch as they will unselfishly serve both drug addicts and the wider community. But the moral permissibility of accepting the projected program's side effects must be considered in reference to three things: scandal (leading others to do wrong), undercutting public witness to the truth about drug abuse, and fairness to the addicts and others.

---

423. For a case against legalization based on an extensive historical study: Jill Jonnes, *Hep-cats, Narcs, and Pipe Dreams: A History of America's Romance with Illegal Drugs* (New York: Scribner, 1996); summary of argument against legalization, 413–41.

Moreover, the proposed program's expected effects ought to be compared with the likely effects of available alternatives.

With clean needles easily available without cost, addicts can be generous in supplying them to people inexperienced in injecting drugs. So, some nonaddicts who otherwise would be unwilling to begin injecting drugs will be persuaded by a companion's offer of a clean needle to take that step. Indeed, since addicts are not registered, the possibility of picking up a discarded needle and exchanging it for a clean one will open the way for some young people to try injecting drugs for the first time. Thus, the easy availability of clean needles would remove one motive for people not yet addicted to steer clear of illicit drugs. Removing any motive to resist a temptation makes it more likely that weak-willed individuals will give in. So, the program may be counterproductive for some individuals by leading them into drug abuse.[424] Without morally compelling reasons for accepting this bad side effect, doing so will be scandal.

Besides, if members of the city council adopt the program Stevens proposes, they will be making the city an accomplice in the unlawful behavior of drug addicts. The volunteers, acting with the authorization of public officials, will be aware of the identity of illegal drug users, but rather than dealing with them as such, will help them in their ongoing unlawful behavior. This open cooperation of the city with the unlawful behavior of drug addicts will suggest that only the risks incidental to drug abuse are bad. Hence, the program will tend to undercut the law's effectiveness in teaching people, especially young people not yet addicted but tempted to abuse drugs, to avoid such self-destructive and socially harmful behavior. Then too, official complicity in addicts' law breaking will tend to make the law they violate seem arbitrary, and so will tend to undercut respect for that law and law in general. These bad effects are extremely serious, since law's effectiveness depends far more on forming the majority's practical reasoning and judgments than on forcing the unwilling minority to comply.[425]

Moreover, if the public authorities tolerate and even cooperate with drug abuse, in practice they will be legalizing it, at least under certain circumstances. But doing that would be an abuse of power by a city council, because the prohibitions of drug abuse were enacted by state and federal governments. Moreover, since the legal-

---

424. Panel on Needle Exchange and Bleach Distribution Programs, Commission on Behavioral and Social Sciences and Education, National Research Council and Institute of Medicine, *Preventing HIV Transmission: The Role of Sterile Needles and Bleach,* ed. Jacques Normand, David Vlahov, and Lincoln E. Moses (Washington, D.C.: National Academy Press, 1995), 199–200, notes these concerns but, after reviewing available research on existing programs, dismisses them (252), because of lack of evidence that the programs lead to increased drug use (though admitting that long-term effects are not yet known) and because: "The available scientific literature provides evidence *based on self-reports* that needle exchange programs do not increase the frequency of injection among program participants and do not increase the number of new initiates to injection drug use" (italics added).

425. Ibid., 105, notes that some are concerned about these potential bad effects and says "Ideological and moral concerns are not scientific, empirically based arguments; however, this in no way dilutes their importance." But the Panel quickly dismisses these concerns (105–6) and ignores them in its conclusions and recommendations (251–55).

ization will not be straightforward, it is likely to lead to confusion and uneven enforcement of relevant laws.

Whether exchanging needles would be fair to addicts themselves would depend on the program's benefits and harms to them, in comparison with possible alternatives. This consideration of prospective consequences might be helpful if accurate information were available—not only about immediate and easily observable consequences but about possible long-term bad effects. But I know of no solid evidence about the long-term results of needle exchange programs, and in the nature of the case it may be impossible to obtain. It is true that studies show a gradually decreasing proportion of returned needles contaminated with HIV.[426] Thus, the program Stevens proposes probably would reduce the rate at which addicts in the city are spreading AIDS, hepatitis, and other diseases, and perhaps would bring some addicts into treatment. However, it is unlikely that many drug addicts are so well organized and self-disciplined that they will regularly exchange dirty needles for clean ones or resist the urge to share a needle when they wish to inject drugs and happen to lack a clean one. Even the program's proposed message, that in the long run addiction itself is as deadly as AIDS, implies that addicts would receive limited benefits by being helped to avoid AIDS and other diseases if they persist in feeding a habit that eventually will kill them. Thus, the net prospective benefits of the program to individual addicts seem questionable.

Perhaps Stevens, considering things from the perspective of public health, is more interested in limiting the transmission of AIDS and other diseases from drug addicts to the population at large. However, the program will do that in the long run only if supplying clean needles to addicts will lessen the number of nonaddicts who otherwise would become infected. I doubt that there is much solid evidence on these matters.[427]

Public authorities should not resign themselves to the inevitability of vices such as drug abuse, regard those enslaved by them as hopeless cases, and seek only to limit further bad consequences. Rather, they should regard such a vice as a challenge to their creativity and look for constructive alternatives likely to help people live decent lives. One such alternative to Stevens's program might be to do what the city can to minimize the availability of drugs while training the city's welfare workers to deliver the message Stevens would have the volunteers deliver. But the welfare workers would come into contact with suspected addicts by helping them obtain food, medical care, and other necessities of life rather than by supplying clean needles. Volunteers could be trained to report drug dealers and help addicts willing to enter treatment deal with obstacles they might

426. See ibid., 251.
427. Ibid., having stated on the basis of evidence that needle exchange programs lower the proportion of contaminated needles in circulation, asserts as a "logical consequence": "The lower the fraction of needles in circulation that are contaminated, the lower the risk of new HIV infections." However, the Panel ignores the distinction between reducing the risk of transmitting the disease on each occasion of drug use and during a user's entire life, and so fails to consider the possibility that the programs may slow the rate of the epidemic while saving few if any lives in the long run.

encounter. Such a program probably would have many good effects and would be less likely to have bad ones.

Of course, this approach demands that good treatment for drug addiction be readily available, so that an addict can receive it without significant delay. Providing the needed treatment facilities may be very costly, but the common good seems to require this alternative, which would be beneficial in limiting the many bad social consequences of abuse. Then too, since addiction is as deadly as AIDS in the long run, a needle exchange program manifests little or no concern for addicts unless the city has good treatment available and promotes its use. Hence, offering clean needles instead of good treatment hardly would be fair to drug addicts.[428]

Since the likely consequences of the proposed program and a possible alternative do not provide a cogent reason to vote for the program, you should base your decision on the other moral considerations—the element of scandal and the undesirability of the city's complicity in unlawful behavior.

However, it does not follow that such a proposal could not be acceptable under other circumstances. Supplying addicts with clean needles would not be intrinsically wrong. Suppose it eventually became clear that such programs are quite beneficial and not very harmful? Might not the city then have adequate reason to become a reluctant accomplice in drug abuse? Perhaps. But in that case the laws would have to be modified so that, while selling drugs or possessing them in significant amounts would remain illegal, it would be lawful to buy and possess small amounts, and to use drugs in those situations in which the public authorities are involved.

197: When should law override parents' religious objections to health care?

I am a member of a committee of the state legislature that will deal soon with a problem I find puzzling. In this state, adult Jehovah's Witnesses, Christian Scientists, and others clearly have the legal right to follow their religious convictions in avoiding or refusing forms of health care that most people consider appropriate and even obligatory. This, I believe, is as it should be. The difficulty arises when such people, conscientiously following their beliefs, withhold care generally considered appropriate from their minor children or refuse such care on their behalf. In a recent case in another state, parents were prosecuted when, acting on their convictions as Christian Scientists, they did not obtain medical care for their critically ill child. My state's civil and criminal welfare statutes regarding child neglect and abuse include clauses exempting parents who choose prayer rather than medical care for their children. In recent years, nevertheless, several cases here have reached the courts, and, while the judges usually have overruled the parents and ordered

428. Ibid., 107 and 116–19, notes that many African-American leaders take this position but points out (119–20) that some support needle exchange programs, and takes the opposition into account only by saying (252): "Needle exchange programs *should be regarded* as a public health promotion and disease prevention strategy that fits within the broader harm reduction approach to public health" (italics added). Thus, on this issue the Panel offers a moral norm rather than looking for relevant evidence.

treatment, their decisions have been neither entirely consistent nor supported by cogent reasons. Legislation on the matter seems to be needed.

The problem is complex, with both procedural and substantive aspects. The procedural question concerns what mechanism to use in dealing with such cases, and I do not ask your advice about that. The substantive question is how far our law should go in respecting parental religious convictions in this matter.

It seems to me that various sorts of cases must be sorted out. Sometimes neither individual well-being nor public health urgently require providing health care, and I doubt that parental judgments should be questioned in such cases. Sometimes, however, care is more or less urgent to preserve life or treat serious disease or injury. Here some limits surely must be set on parental judgment, yet it seems at once necessary and virtually impossible to draw the lines.

Then too, it is not clear whether we should respect parental objections (our present law does not) to public health measures, like small pox vaccination.

Analysis:

This question calls for the derivation of norms for making law in this matter. The children of parents who object to a public health requirement on religious grounds should be exempted if, but only if, exempting them will not prevent the measure from achieving its good purpose. The state should neither (1) involve children in programs providing or promoting contraception or abortion without parental consent nor (2) require health care for children unless the parents objectively have a grave duty to seek or accept it. In the case of adolescent children whose parents refuse or omit health care on religious grounds, the law should take into account the difference between those children who agree with their parents and those who disagree. The law also should take into account whether the care is urgently necessary either to preserve life or to prevent serious and lasting impairment of functioning or bodily integrity. Parents who refuse or omit health care on religious grounds should continue to be exempted from criminal and civil liability, and should not be ordered to consent to care contrary to their conscience.

The reply could be along the following lines:

The last issue you raise, regarding public health measures, seems to me fairly simple and separable from the other questions, and so I shall reply first to it. In some cases, a public health measure requires only general, rather than absolutely universal, participation to achieve its purpose, so that the parents of children who object on religious grounds could be exempted easily enough. Small pox vaccination may be an example, but I leave that to experts; if it is, I believe religiously based parental objections to vaccination should be respected insofar as respecting them is consistent with the program's public health purpose. In other cases, such as the isolation of individuals afflicted with extremely contagious diseases, respecting parental objections would seriously impede an objectively reasonable public health measure. Then the parental objections should be overridden for the sake of the common good.

Turning to your other points, one must begin, as your question itself suggests, by limiting the field in which state intervention might be justified. At least two limitations seem to me necessary.

First, some public or publicly supported programs assume that adolescent children usually will engage in sexual intercourse. On this assumption they promote the use of condoms to impede sexually transmitted diseases (so-called safe sex), encourage the children to practice contraception, and/or offer them abortion services. Proponents argue that such programs are necessary either as public health measures or as health care for the children or both. However, complete abstinence from sexual intercourse is the only morally acceptable and fully effective way to deal with the problems these programs address. Moreover, neither contraception nor abortion services really are health care, since both interfere with normal reproductive functions and the latter destroys a new life. Therefore, parents rightly resist such programs, and children should not be involved without their parents' consent, much less against their objections, whether grounded in religious beliefs or not.[429]

Second, whenever parents do not objectively have a grave duty to seek or accept health care for their children, their forgoing it on religious grounds certainly should be respected. The state would violate religious liberty in overriding religiously principled parental objections to a health care measure when it would ignore the refusal or neglect of the same measure by parents who objected to it on other grounds or were simply lazy. Just as people in general often have acceptable reasons of various sorts for omitting or rejecting health care, even when others consider it appropriate, so parents can have various valid reasons to forgo care for their children. Its probable safety and effectiveness may be questionable; it may be painful or otherwise repugnant to the child; it may be costly or otherwise burdensome to the family. Then too, neglecting appropriate care for one's children's health, as for one's own, often falls short of being seriously irresponsible. Therefore, I think you first should define as clearly as possible the class of cases in which parents objectively have a grave duty to seek or accept health care for their children, so that you can limit public intervention to those cases and entirely exclude it in others.

I do not think it possible entirely to separate the substantive question—how far the state should respect parental religious convictions in relation to children's health care—from the procedural question about the mechanism to use in dealing with cases. However, I shall try to respond to your question without being more specific than necessary about procedural matters. Realizing that you will obtain expert testimony about them, I offer my thoughts on them only as tentative suggestions.

I agree with you in approving of current policy in your state according to which adult Jehovah's Witnesses, Christian Scientists, and others have the legal right to follow their religious convictions in avoiding or refusing forms of health care that most people consider appropriate and even obligatory. In accord with the principle

---

429. Analogously, assisted suicide and voluntary euthanasia should not be legally available to anyone and especially not to minors. But if they are made legally available to competent adults, it surely would be an additional wrong to make them available to minors without parental consent

underlying that policy, in cases of children nearing adulthood it would be wrong to ignore the difference between those who share their parents' religious convictions and those who do not. Indeed, as soon as children are able to judge what is at stake, make a free self-commitment, and carry it out, their religious convictions have the same moral value and claim to be respected as those of adults. While parental convictions no doubt influence children, their religious commitments are no less genuine or worthy of respect on that account, as virtually all who share a child's convictions acknowledge when the faithful child in a time of persecution lays down his or her life or makes lesser sacrifices.

Thus, legislation must set an age at which the child's views will be taken into account. Reasonable people will differ, but twelve seems to me a good choice. By then, most children seem to understand life and death, and seem able to make a personal religious commitment.

In drafting legislation, you will have to consider situations of at least four kinds.

(1) Emergency cases in which care is required to preserve life or to protect against serious and lasting impairment of functioning or bodily integrity, and the child either is younger than twelve or, if older, desires care the parents are refusing, or not seeking, on religious grounds. In such cases, the care should be given.

(2) All cases in which a child older than twelve refuses health care on religious grounds. In such cases, it seems to me, the child's position should be respected.

(3) Cases in which the care the parents are refusing or not seeking is not urgently required, and the child is younger than twelve. In such cases, it seems to me the presumption should favor the parents' position, but it should be open to rebuttal by evidence that the care is necessary to forestall lasting and serious impairment of functioning or bodily integrity.

(4) Cases in which the proposed care is not urgently required, and the child older than twelve desires it while the parents oppose it. In such cases, it seems to me the presumption should favor the child's position, but it should be open to rebuttal by evidence that the parents can reasonably refuse the care on nonreligious grounds.

If some private individual or entity, or some public entity or agent—such as the police or a social worker—believes parents are gravely failing in their duty to seek or accept some form of health care for a child, the first step, except in the most pressing emergencies, should be to call the parents' attention to the provisions of the law, reason with them, and listen to what they have to say. If discussion does not resolve the matter, health care providers may proceed in emergency situations, but otherwise neither they nor others who think a child needs care should override parental judgment. Rather, they should present the case to a judge, who should apply the law's provisions.

At times this approach would lead to overriding parents' religiously based objections. Nevertheless, I think your welfare statutes' existing exemption of such parents from civil and criminal liability for choosing prayer over medical care should be retained out of respect for religious liberty, since the exemption is compatible with appropriate state intervention. Thus, when adjudication leads to the judgment that health care should be given a child despite parental religious objections, the parents should not be held liable for forgoing or refusing care, or ordered to consent to it, since such holdings and orders would punish religiously committed parents for conforming to their beliefs or would attempt to compel them to violate their consciences. Instead, the court should take the matter out of the parents' hands by directly ordering that the care be given or appointing a guardian empowered to make the necessary decisions.

198: May a state legislator support casino gambling to get tax revenue?

I am a member of a state legislature. Proposals have been introduced at the last three sessions to legalize, license, and tax casino gambling—that is, gambling establishments operated as profit-making businesses. So far, no such proposal has made it out of committee, but this year it looks as though one will come to the floor and I will have to take a position.

The main argument for licensing casino gambling is the revenue we could gain by taxing the casinos' net receipts. A secondary benefit would likely be some increase in the tourism this state heavily depends on—and, even if it didn't increase, casino gambling would at least keep us competitive with states that already have it. Since average income here is not high, and would be considerably lower except for the people who move here to retire, most members wish to minimize the inevitable impact on our less affluent citizens. For that reason, casinos would be licensed only in the three counties with the largest retiree population and in major tourist centers, where the majority of the gamblers will be wealthy citizens and visitors who can well afford their losses—which will account for most of the casinos' profit and tax revenue

In past years, there has been some opposition to these proposals by people who oppose gambling as absolutely immoral. As a Catholic, I know I need not take that stand, but I do see various disadvantages and would like to adopt a position I can defend as reasonable.

Analysis:

This question concerns formal cooperation in scandal. People with good reasons for gambling need not risk much money; those who gamble significant amounts usually violate a duty to use their money in some other way. Seeking profit, casino operators intend this misuse of money, which is at least venially sinful. In doing so, they at least wrongly accept some patrons' mortally sinful gambling. So, casino operators scandalize many patrons—that is, lead them into sin, and legislators who support legalization of casino gambling to raise revenue and/or attract tourists formally cooperate in this scandal.

The reply could be along the following lines:

As the Catholic Church's teaching and practice make clear, gambling is not absolutely immoral, and in particular instances people can gamble innocently. Still the Church also teaches that several factors can make gambling seriously immoral (see *CCC*, 2413). Taking these factors into account, I believe you should oppose licensing casino gambling and think that you can make a cogent case against it.

An important part of that case will of course be to show the disadvantages of licensing that already concern you. Casinos operating as profit-making businesses inevitably bring with them undesirable secondary businesses and criminal elements, which exploit casino patrons and cater to their vices.[430] Excessive gambling at the casinos by some citizens also leads to an increase in crime and other social problems, such as suicide, family breakdown, and poverty. Moreover, at least some, and perhaps most, of the money spent on casino gambling would otherwise be spent on goods and services provided by other businesses in your state. Gambling by the state's residents surely will reduce their other spending, and, though some nonresidents who otherwise would not visit your state will come to gamble, the casinos will divert some money tourists would have spent at other establishments in your state.

The preceding outline of bad consequences must be filled in with detailed evidence, but I shall not try to gather it. Do your best to see to it that the committee does so.[431] Perhaps many members of the legislature already anticipate the problems, and their desire to prevent them at least partly explains past opposition and the current proposal's provisions limiting casino gambling to major tourist centers and three counties with large retiree populations. However, if the bad effects are not acknowledged, investigating the experience of other states that have licensed casinos will make clear what your state must expect.

My contribution to the case against legalizing and licensing casino gambling is to argue that any legislator who supports it to gain tax revenue and/or attract tourists intends—and so is morally responsible for—immoral gambling. Though some of your colleagues will not be moved by this argument, I think you and others who are conscientious will find it convincing, and your principled opposition to casino gambling might be sufficient to tip the balance against it.

When chosen for a good reason and engaged in virtuously, gambling can serve its purpose even if the amount risked is quite small (see *LCL,* 818–19). By contrast, people who gamble significant amounts of money often have no basic human good in view, and are motivated by mere emotion and the hope of getting something for nothing. Those who risk large amounts of money gambling almost always should use it for other purposes. Those who have only as much money as they need to meet their own genuine needs and those of their dependents should use it for that purpose; those affluent enough to have substantial surplus funds should use them to meet others' needs (see *LCL,* 780–82, 789–92, 800–806, 811–14).

---

430. See Craig A. Zendzian, *Who Pays? Casino Gambling, Hidden Interests, and Organized Crime* (New York: Harrow and Heston, 1993). Since the questioner is not asking about so-called "casino" nights sponsored and/or operated by churches and other nonprofit organizations, I do not consider here the moral questions they pose.

431. A good starting point: U.S. Congress, House of Representatives, *The National Impact of Casino Gambling Proliferation: Hearing before the Committee on Small Business,* 103d Congress, 2d sess., 21 Sept. 1994 (Serial No. 103–104). Especially useful are the prepared statements by Robert Goodman, director, The U.S. Gambling Study, Lemelson professor of Environmental Design, Hampshire College, and professor of regional planning, University of Massachusetts (56–70); Earl Grinols, professor of economics, University of Illinois (71–76); and John Warren Kindt, professor, University of Illinois (77–81).

Casino operators intend to maximize their profits and make every effort to exploit the weaknesses of potential patrons and motivate patrons to gamble large amounts. If all patrons gambled virtuously, the amounts gambled often would be so little that the operators hardly could achieve their end. Therefore, as a necessary means to the profits they seek, the operators intend at least venially sinful gambling, and in intending this they also foresee and at least accept any mortally sinful gambling that will occur. Intending that others sin venially, however, is itself wrong. No foreseen bad side effect of wrongdoing can be accepted rightly. So, casino operators cannot rightly accept any mortally sinful gambling. Therefore, they do a grave wrong of scandal, if not by intending that some of their patrons sin gravely, at least by intending that some sin venially and then wrongly accepting the more serious sins some will commit.

Since licensing casino gambling will lead to various problems for the state, the measure would have little or no support were it not for anticipated benefits. Though legislators might *vote for* a measure licensing casino gambling for other reasons, such as political pressures, those who *support* the legislation surely will intend that the state obtain the benefits that would come from taxes and/or tourists; they therefore will intend that the casinos have taxable receipts and attract tourists to gamble. Thus, anyone supporting a measure to license casino gambling shares the operators' intention to attract people to gamble and to collect the money they will lose. But as we have seen, in intending that, casino operators commit a grave wrong of scandal. Consequently, legislators who support licensing casino gambling also commit a grave wrong of scandal. In doing so, moreover, they corrupt the people rather than serve their true interests.

Some no doubt will argue that licensing casinos to obtain tax revenue is no different from taxing tobacco and alcoholic beverages, licensing establishments where alcohol is sold, and operating state liquor stores. They will point out that alcoholic beverages are widely abused and tobacco is deadly to many users and harmful to virtually all. Still, hardly anyone objects to the state's involvement with alcohol and tobacco. Therefore, they will conclude, nobody should object on moral grounds to licensing casino gambling.

If that argument were sound, it would not follow that the state should license casino gambling but that it should change its stance toward alcohol and tobacco. But the cases are not analogous, and the argument is unsound. Those who supported proposals to involve the state with alcohol and tobacco need not have intended to obtain tax revenue deriving from the abuse of these substances. Many people drink moderately, and the harmful effects of typical tobacco use became clear only in the 1960s. Faced with the fact that alcohol and tobacco were being sold and used, legislators may have intended to raise revenue from their legitimate use, while also trying to limit their abuse, partly by means of taxes and state liquor stores. By contrast, legislators support legalizing and licensing casino gambling not to limit it but precisely to obtain tax revenue and/or attract tourists.

Supporters also may argue that casinos should be legalized and licensed so that people of modest means will have a fair opportunity to enjoy this form of recreation, otherwise available only to those affluent enough to travel. But people of modest means generally ought to spend their limited funds on genuine necessities, including more economical forms of family recreation. And even if some of these can rightly gamble in casinos, the law need not facilitate their doing so. The state justly refuses to facilitate, and even inhibits, many good things when that serves the common good.

If the measure to legalize and license casino gambling nevertheless reaches the floor and seems likely to pass, I suggest you try to amend it so as to mitigate the evil. For example, you might seek to limit the hours of operation, forbid gambling on credit, severely restrict the availability of liquor, establish extremely heavy penalties for cheating by operators, and set limits to wagers that will impede the most grave excesses by gamblers.

You also might try to keep the casinos out of the three counties with large retiree populations. While many came from elsewhere, they are now among your state's citizens. As a legislator, you should be as concerned for them as for other citizens and try to safeguard their genuine interests and well-being. Though retirees usually do not have children to support and often have considerable savings, most will be unable to make up for significant losses by future earnings, so that excessive gambling is likely to do them irreparable harm.

Finally, if the legislation is certain to pass or actually passes, you might try to tie to it provisions channeling the revenue it raises into efforts to deal with the bad consequences of gambling and, if funds suffice, of other vices, such as the abuse of psychoactive substances, including alcohol and tobacco.

199: Should morality limit public funding of the arts?

I am a congressman representing a heavily blue-collar district. My constituents strongly support both traditional values and the interests of working people, including those with low incomes. Funding for the National Endowment for the Arts (NEA) is considered by one of the committees I serve on. Some of my constituents belong to an organization that opposes pornography and is demanding tighter regulations to exclude funding of morally offensive garbage posing as art. I agree with them as a matter of principle and, for once, see no political problem in pushing hard for what I think should be done.

As you certainly know, any restraints are sure to be condemned as a violation of free speech. In my view, freedom of speech is not at issue in this case. When the government pays the bill, the people are paying the bill, and most of them find much of this so-called art outrageous. There is no infringement on the free speech of these so-called artists by not buying their work. They are free to produce whatever they want, but the public is equally free to refuse to pay for it. Governments and the Church always have patronized the arts, but never paid artists to produce whatever they pleased. Rather, patrons always told artists what to produce, and setting some limits to NEA funding is far less restrictive than that, since it is merely a matter of telling those who want government money that there are a few things the public will not pay for.

I think I can tell the difference between what is pornographic and what is not. However, it is one thing to know what is pornographic, and another to draft legislation excluding it. How would you draw the line on projects that may be funded by the NEA?

Analysis:

Since pornography is constituted by intending something's use for an immoral purpose, purported objects of art are not easily identified as pornographic. However, this question implicitly calls for the articulation of legislative options that might serve the common good. Screening of applications by a representative panel probably would not be satisfactory or effective. Another possible approach would be to allow the NEA to subsidize only specified sorts of organizations in displaying or performing works created before a certain date. A third approach would be to abolish the NEA and limit government funding of the arts to instances in which art is used in educational programs or the government is a consumer of works of art—for example, in the construction and furnishing of public buildings and monuments.

The reply could be along the following lines:

Your question is not only difficult but perhaps even impossible to answer. Pornography is not simply a set of things, but an abuse of things, especially of the human body. An abuse is a use, and any use presupposes an intended purpose. That is why items created for legitimate purposes often can serve as pornography, and well-made items originally meant to be pornographic occasionally can serve a legitimate purpose. To identify something as pornographic is to see it as intended for an immoral use, namely, to arouse and/or satisfy illicit sexual desires. Those who wish to use something as pornography can pick out what they are looking for by its effect on themselves, but modest observers can identify pornography only by considering a set of clues in a particular context indicating the abusive intention of those involved. People who produce or display something they claim to be a work of art by that very fact deny that their intention is abusive. Thus, though it is easy to recognize instances of pornography offered for sale as such, those of the kind in which you are interested never will be so readily identifiable. Therefore, while there might be some way to define pornography so that you can draft legislation prohibiting its funding by the NEA, I do not know how to do that. Moreover, it is likely that some of the projects your constituents find highly repugnant are not pornographic but objectionable on other grounds—as blasphemous, sacrilegious, unpatriotic, or otherwise shocking.

Is there some other way to draw a line and deal with the problem?

One possible alternative would be to create a panel composed of a cross section of citizens to evaluate projects proposed for funding. Its work could supplement, rather than replace, the existing selection process. Like you, most people believe they can recognize pornography when they see it. The panel's mandate could be to screen all applications and reject those regarded as morally unacceptable by a certain proportion of panelists. Applications deemed acceptable by enough of them could then be evaluated by people more knowledgeable about the arts.

Even so, your constituents might not be satisfied with the result, while many proponents of funding probably would regard the screening as oppressive censorship. Moreover, the NEA funds proposed projects. So, though such a panel would prevent funding some things proposed, it would not be able to control what applicants do with the money they receive, and public funds still would pay for some things most panelists would have rejected.

The NEA grants that have provoked public outrage have been either to individuals, or for the display or performance of new or recent works, or both. A second alternative would be to specify the mission of the NEA so that it would no longer make such grants. Its sole mission would be to subsidize selected schools, museums, libraries, opera companies, orchestras, theater groups, dance troupes, and so on in displaying or performing works created before a certain date specified in the legislation. Other conditions for the eligibility of institutions and works also would be specified. By making the cut-off date remote enough—say, fifty years prior to the subsidized display or performance—the public would avoid subsidizing not only many mediocre works appealing only to passing tastes but the use of art to express partisan opinions on current political issues and to propagandize on behalf of various pressure groups: radical feminists, homosexual activists, and so on.

Another alternative would be to abolish the NEA.[432] As you pointed out, the U.S. government, like every government and the Church, necessarily funds the arts by paying artists for their work when it is required for some social purpose, such as a public building, monument, or celebration. In all such cases, the source of funding chooses the project and pays for it, and has every right to exclude not only pornography but anything that offends the sensibility of any significant segment of the sponsoring community. Even if Congress cannot control funding of the arts to keep public money from being used for projects morally repugnant to many citizens, it can radically limit such funding by restricting it to instances in which the public is the consumer of artists' works, exercising every consumer's right to specify what is to be purchased.

The U.S. and most state and local governments also fund the arts for use in education, again choosing some works and excluding others, as in all other cases in which the government is the consumer. If the NEA were abolished, at least part of its funding could be redirected to the states to expand their educational programs in the fine arts. Though not entirely free of problems, such programs are likely to be more responsive to local standards and interests.

Arguments for continuing the NEA should confront a single issue: For whom is the art the U.S. government subsidizes intended? The nation's common good is the only principle that can justify any appropriation. How does this subsidy promote this common good? Attempts to answer this question must not beg it by supposing that the satisfaction of every group's legitimate interests pertains to the nation's common good, which includes only the satisfaction of those legitimate interests that are both widely shared and best satisfied by cooperation at the national level (see *LCL*, 846–51).

432. For excerpts from a U.S. House of Representatives debate, see "Pros and Cons: 'Should the Congress Reauthorize the National Endowment for the Arts?'" *Congressional Digest*, 70:1 (Jan. 1991): 12–31.

If the nation's common good is recognized as the decisive principle and its limits are borne in mind, those who support funding the NEA face a dilemma. The projects it supports either do or do not contribute to the nation's common good by meeting the cultural needs of a substantial portion of the population. If they do, they will be popular enough to be profitable, and so will be promoted and distributed commercially, and will need no public subsidy. But if they do not meet the cultural needs of a substantial portion of the population, they are useful only to various minorities, many of whom are wealthy enough to subsidize such things. Since such projects contribute little or nothing to the nation's common good, they deserve no public subsidy beyond the matching grant they enjoy by virtue of the exemption from income taxation of donations to nonprofit educational and cultural organizations.

The proponent of funding will object that unless there is popular art that is not profitable, commercial interests will dominate the nation's taste. I concede. But such domination of taste by commercial interests is not prevented by public subsidies to artists whose work lacks wide appeal. In times past, popular art that was not commercial often was created by people using simple tools and inexpensive materials to make good and beautiful things, which they and their families used and enjoyed, or gave to others as presents. Popular taste now is dominated by commercial interests partly because most people are passive consumers.

Someone might point out that, in many instances in the past, governments and the Church went beyond purchasing art—such as buildings, monuments, and celebrations—for public or ecclesial purposes, and patronized artists for the arts' own sake. *For the arts' own sake* here, however, really means for the sake of those who desired the artists' works and enjoyed them, namely, the group controlling governmental or Church funds and the people who shared their tastes and opportunities to gratify them.

When emperors and princes, popes and bishops, used public or ecclesiastical resources in ways serving no properly public or ecclesial purpose, they abused their authority. Resources that should have been used to promote the common good of state or Church were diverted to the satisfaction of those in office and their friends. Therefore, the historical patronage of the arts by governments and the Church provides no sound model for funding the NEA. For the projects funded either served some public or ecclesial purpose—governmental buildings and civic monuments, cathedrals and monasteries—and so were unlike those funded by the NEA or, like those it funds, diverted communal resources to serve private cultural interests.

The proponent of subsidizing the arts might point out that many priceless works we still enjoy would never have been created if governments and the Church had not done more in subsidizing the arts than was necessary for public and ecclesial purposes. But some emperors and princes, popes and bishops also fathered illegitimate offspring who became outstanding people and even saints, and in neither case is what they did justified by its consequences. Then too, in neither case were the consequences always so good. Moreover, in both cases, even better consequences might well have followed had they not indulged themselves but devoted the money, energy, and time they abused to serving state or Church.

Some say that they advocate public funding of the arts, not to subsidize the tastes of the wealthy, but to relieve the ugliness of poverty-stricken inner cities by means of murals and community arts centers, which also would build up community. This argument is hardly cogent. Though the poorest of the poor surely enjoy a normal share of esthetic sensibility, they seldom are consulted about such programs. And very poor people rarely receive grants from these programs, even if these effect some cosmetic improvement in their depressing surroundings. Moreover, one suspects that attempts to deal with inner-city blight in this way are more appealing to suburbanites and artists than to typical residents of inner cities, who probably would prefer that the money be used for better schools and police protection, more regular garbage collection and street cleaning, repair of park and playground equipment, and so forth.

Some argue that subsidizing what initially appeals only to a few is necessary to foster a wide variety of creative initiatives that will elevate popular taste and tomorrow serve the multitude. Whether the funded work elevates anyone's taste is arguable, but even supposing it does, can this indirect contribution to the common good justify the subsidy? Moreover, while some creative efforts that initially appeal to few eventually serve the masses, most do not, and it is hardly possible to show that public funding of some portion of art work is necessary for future cultural development. There are other needs calling for public funding, and some, plainly more pressing than this—for example, better basic education for the very poor— will surely put it to fruitful uses. One cannot justify spending for a dim and uncertain result when there are many urgent and promising alternatives.[433]

Some argue that public funding is necessary because some people have great and rare gifts that, due to lack of a market, otherwise will be fruitless. That many people have great and unusual gifts of various sorts undoubtedly is true. But the common good of political society is limited. It is not the proper role of the U.S. government to pursue all human goods in every possible way, and therefore not its business to subsidize every gift that otherwise will be fruitless.

Some argue that subsidies to the arts are necessary to promote innovation and dialogue among diverse points of view, so that groups that want to use the fine arts to challenge the status quo and advocate their unpopular world views and lifestyles can have a forum. However, while the common good requires tolerating the expression of unpopular points of view, the very fact that most people do not share them suggests that the common good may not be served by supporting their expression. Even if it is, the government has no more business providing subsidies for such purposes than for spreading traditional forms of religion. Indeed, many unpopular world views and lifestyles are at odds with traditional theism, and subsidizing them while not subsidizing theism would give the former an unfair advantage. People who think the expression of an

433. See Harry Brighouse, "Neutrality, Publicity, and State Funding of the Arts," *Philosophy and Public Affairs,* 24 (1995): 47–56.

unpopular viewpoint desirable should subsidize it themselves just as religious believers should support their churches and missionary activities.[434]

200: Does everyone have a duty to try to stop abortions?

I am a woman, a nurse, and consider myself a feminist, but I accept the Church's teaching that abortion is always wrong. Indeed, if the Church did not teach that, I would have a hard time believing anything it does teach about practical matters. I also am convinced that abortion should no more be legal than killing you or me or anyone else. But the fact of the matter is that in this country abortion is legal and, at least for now, there does not seem much hope of making it illegal. We therefore need some clear guidelines on our duties regarding abortion.

I have friends who have done sidewalk counseling; one of them also has engaged in rescues.[435] For various reasons—one of which admittedly is coward-ice—up to now I have been unwilling to do either of those things. My friends think I am failing to do my duty. The one who has been involved in rescues argues that everyone has the same duty to try to stop abortions as to try to stop the killing of an already-born child, the only difference being that the Supreme Court's ukase has made abortion legal.

While I see the force of his argument, it seems to me to prove too much. Specifically, it seems to point to a duty to gun down abortionists—something a few people have done, but hardly anyone approves of, much less regards as a duty. Let me explain. My work as a visiting nurse sometimes takes me into rough neighbor-hoods at all hours. After one bad experience that I will not go into, I learned to use a handgun, got a gun and a license, and now carry the gun at all times in my shoulder bag. Suppose I am walking down the street and see a man brutally beating a small child with a baseball bat; I take out my gun and order him to stop; he shouts a threat at me, turns, and hits the child again. Surely, it would be right for me to shoot him, and, as I was taught to do, I would aim at the middle of his back to give myself the best chance of stopping him. If I killed him without using more bullets than necessary to stop him, I am sure nobody would object. But if everyone has the same duty to try to stop abortions as to try to stop the killing of an already-born child, then I have a duty to gun down abortionists.

While I would like to know what you think of the argument between my friend and me, I am more interested in the broader question: Does everyone have a duty to try to stop abortions?

+ + +

434. On the prevalence of politically motivated projects in the work funded by the NEA, see Joseph Epstein, "What to Do about the Arts," *Commentary,* 99:4 (Apr. 1995): 23–30; on the virtual impossibility of neutrality in governmental funding of the arts, see Brighouse, op. cit., 35–63.

435. The sidewalk counselor intercepts persons about to enter an abortion facility and attempts to dissuade them from having or participating in an abortion; the rescuer, though avoiding violence against persons, takes direct action to impede the performance of abortions—for example, by blocking the entrance of an abortion facility.

Analysis:

This question calls for applying norms regarding civic responsibility and the use of force to protect innocent people's lives. Everyone who recognizes the evils of abortion and its legalization should do something to oppose them. But since each individual has his or her unique personal vocation, each must discern what he or she ought to do. Prima facie, the justification of force to defend the innocent seems to extend to gunning down abortionists. Although arguments against doing so drawn from prospective bad consequences are not decisive, the action is unjustifiable insofar as, rather than being an effective means of protecting the lives of unborn persons, it is a revolutionary act that surely will not succeed.

The reply could be along the following lines:

Abortion and its legalization are great evils.[436] They differ in some ways from the mass murders carried out under Stalin, Hitler, and others, but also in some ways are comparable to those crimes and in other ways even worse: because of the greater numbers being killed, their total innocence and defenselessness, the essential role played by those primarily responsible for nurturing the victims, the widespread support of this slaughter by both rulers and people in so-called liberal democratic nations, and the complicity in the killings of so many religious leaders, educators, people trained in law, health care professionals, people in the mass media, and so on.

Everyone who recognizes the evils of abortion and its legalization should do something to oppose them. What that should be depends on an individual's unique opportunities and capacities. Opportunities—what can be done—are limited to what is morally acceptable as well as to what is possible in other respects; one's capacities are limited by one's other responsibilities. All of us should do what we can, that is, some of the morally acceptable things that are in our power and that we can do without neglecting duties that flow from other elements of personal vocation to which we already have committed ourselves or which, being inescapable, we have accepted as God's will. So, for instance, the contemplative nun and the bedridden man in a nursing home ought to work against abortion chiefly by praying for divine intervention or by writing letters of protest, not leaving the cloister or sickbed to participate in your friends' work at clinics.

Your friends' commitment to their effort is commendable, but they and others engaged in a particular sort of activity against abortion, its legalization, or any other injustice should not think or say that everyone should do the same. Whether or not you should take part in their efforts, they are wrong in pressuring you. Conscientiously examine your opportunities and capacities and discern what you should do about abortion. Though your appropriate contribution might partly coincide with theirs, it also might well be entirely different.

As for your friend's argument that everyone has the same duty to try to stop abortions as to try to stop the killing of an already-born child, your counterargument—that this would imply a duty on your part to gun down abortionists—

---

436. See John Paul II, *Evangelium vitae,* 58–63, *AAS* 87 (1995) 466–74, *OR,* 5 Apr. 1995, xi–xii; *LCL,* 488–505.

might not move him. He might accept that implication and urge you to put your gun and your skill in using it to good use. Of course, he might say it would be wrong to aim at the middle of the back of the brutal man in your example instead of aiming, say, at his shoulder, and, likewise, that it would be wrong for you to kill abortionists rather than choosing some less drastic way of stopping them—for example, cutting off their hands. However, that would not address the issue your argument raises, namely, whether you are soundly applying the principles that can justify using as much force as necessary to defend innocent life. Prima facie, it seems sound, for you could gun down an abortionist with precisely the same intention with which you would shoot the brutal man beating the child: not intending to kill or even injure him, but only to stop him and protect the victim.[437] Moreover, since in both cases those being stopped are engaging in objective injustices that should be stopped, in neither case would you be acting unfairly toward those you stopped, provided you used the minimally destructive means adequate to protect the victim.

Your friend could reply that, despite their common features, the two cases differ in other morally relevant respects. He might offer four arguments. First, that gunning down abortionists is hard to reconcile with the Christian gospel, which emphasizes loving even enemies and seeking the conversion of evildoers. A dead abortionist cannot repent; women prevented from obtaining the abortion they wanted are unlikely to be moved to repent by the abortionist's death; and many hearts, reacting self-righteously against the killing of an abortionist, are likely to be hardened with respect to the slaughter of the unborn. Second, he might say it clouds prolife witness by making it seem that even those who oppose abortion approve killing people when they think doing so would serve some good end. Third, he might say that the cases of shooting abortionists have proved it to be counterproductive. It provokes a strong, negative reaction from most people and countermeasures by public officials that impede every other form of prolife work, not least nonviolent direct action such as sidewalk counseling. Fourth, your friend could suggest with some plausibility that violence against abortionists serves as a bad example for many sorts of extremists, thus contributing to an increase in the lawlessness and unjustifiable violence already common in our society.

You can, of course, point out in reply that none of those considerations is decisive, since the gospel does not entirely forbid the use of force to defend the innocent (such as the child being beaten to death with the baseball bat), and although gunning down abortionists has some bad consequences, it also has various good side effects. For example, it bears witness to the truth that unborn babies are no different in human worth and personal dignity from people already born; it keeps alive the awareness that legalized abortion is morally equivalent to murder and not similar to other morally questionable practices and institutions tolerable in a

---

437. Of course, the questioner would expect that shooting the brutal man in the back would at least injure and might well kill him; but, assuming she did nothing more than necessary to stop him, she could do so intending only that, while accepting his injury or death as a side effect: see *CMP,* 233–36, 239–41; *LCL,* 468–69; cf. John Paul II, *Veritatis splendor,* 78, *AAS* 85 (1993) 1196, *OR,* 6 Oct. 1993, xii.

generally good and just society; and it serves as an example of unselfish courage in a society pervaded by self-indulgence and moral cowardice.

Your friend might reply in either of two ways. He could accept the conclusion and concede that under appropriate conditions, which probably seldom occur, it is morally right to use as much force as necessary to stop abortionists.

Or he could point out another difference between stopping the brutal man in your example and gunning down abortionists. The brutal man is an isolated wrongdoer whose violence is afforded no protection by society and its institutions. But abortionists are others' agents—they serve women who have decided to get rid of their unborn children—and both doing and having abortions are socially accepted, protected by law, and even, in some respects, supported by public policy. The fellow beating the small child with a baseball bat almost certainly will not be replaced if you shoot him. Thus, your effort very likely will achieve your good end of protecting the child. But if you gun down one or even many abortionists, the women who meant to use their services, and others who will decide to obtain abortions, certainly can—and almost all probably will—find someone else to kill their unborn babies. And while killing or maiming large numbers of abortionists might have a temporary deterrent effect on actual and potential abortionists, it probably would quickly provoke a well-organized public response. New governmental programs almost certainly would make doing abortions more lucrative and provide abortionists with special protections and privileges. Abortion probably would be at least as widely available as it is now, so that no fewer, and perhaps even more, unborn babies would be killed. Since our society already is deeply committed to the evils of abortion and its legalization, gunning down abortionists therefore would be pointless unless one went on to gun down the public officials who support abortion. But that would be starting a revolution with no prospect of success; and, like war generally, a revolution without a prospect of success is unjust to the nation, whose common good it injures rather than promotes. Therefore, your friend could conclude, gunning down abortionists is unjust, while nonviolent direct action—rescues, sidewalk counseling, picketing abortionists' homes—is just.

But should you participate? Perhaps. More likely, it seems to me, your unique capacities and opportunities call you to make your contribution in some other way—for example, working to persuade other nurses to resist pressures to participate in doing abortions and/or using your knowledge and professional contacts to help desperate women find a suitable alternative to abortion.

APPENDIXES

Appendix 1: Human acts and moral judgments

Moral judgments can refer to moral evaluations—made, as it were, from the outside—either of others' actions or of one's own past actions. Such evaluations often should be avoided; when called for, they should be subordinated to judgments that can guide prospective choices and actions, not least choices to repent one's sins and admonish others about their apparent sins (see *LCL,* 202–8, 216–39). This appendix considers moral judgments of another sort: those to be made from the inside, as it were, by people who are deliberating with a view to choosing, conscientious people who wish to find out what they should do and to do it. This perspective—that of the conscientious person deliberating—should be adopted by a moral adviser asked questions like those in this book. He or she should try to help each questioner reflect soundly and find the truth about what to do.

This appendix deals with several closely related topics: the genesis and structure of human acts, the principles of moral norms and their application to options considered in deliberation, the examination and improvement of emotional motives, and the process of discernment. These matters were treated in *The Way of the Lord Jesus,* volume one, *Christian Moral Principles* (especially in chapters two through ten), and in chapter five of volume two, *Living a Christian Life.* For the most part, I shall presuppose and merely summarize those earlier treatments. But I shall amend and add to my previous account of the Golden Rule, which requires putting oneself in others' places—for example: "What would I want other drivers to do if I were trying to merge into this traffic stream?" I shall explain how a conscientious person tries by this imaginative exercise and three other, somewhat similar ones to educate his or her feelings so that they will support rather than impede a reasonable judgment about what to choose and do.

My intention is to help readers recall or gather from the earlier volumes the elements provided there of accounts of the genesis of human acts and the making of moral judgments, and to see how those elements are complemented by additional considerations about the role of feelings in human actions and ways of bringing feelings into harmony with reason so as to constitute a more adequate account of human acts and moral judgments. I hope readers with a theoretical interest in these matters will find that the proposed responses to questions in this volume illuminate, by exemplifying, the elements of the treatment offered here and that it, in turn, will clarify the reasoning in the proposed responses.[438]

The genesis of human acts

The human acts on which moral judgments bear involve free choices and their execution. One can understand such acts by tracing their genesis, and one can better understand that genesis by comparing and contrasting it with the simpler genesis of the behavior of higher animals and small children. *Behavior* here refers, not to organic functions, reflexes, or random movements, but to the purposeful movements of an organism as a whole or its parts. Such movements presuppose the individual's awareness of inner states and/or environmental conditions, and are suited to facilitate survival and functioning. That adaptation is partly unlearned—"instinctive"—and partly due to past experience, memory, and imagination. But the genesis of behavior involves more than an awareness of existing conditions and the availability of a pattern for responding to them. It also involves a tendency—sometimes called "a motive" or "a drive"—to respond according to that pattern.

Because tendencies to respond sometimes make themselves felt by causing characteristic bodily changes, they also are called "feelings" or "emotions," words that aptly refer to experienced phenomena. Nevertheless, if behavior is flowing smoothly, tendencies to respond usually remain unconscious. So, I shall use *emotions* and *feelings* to refer to the tendencies themselves considered as principles of behavior that may or may not also make themselves felt.

Emotions or feelings can be divided into four general sorts: (1) to engage positively with something in the environment, (2) to engage destructively with something in the environment, (3) to avoid engagement with something in the environment, and (4) to avoid stimulation in general. As experienced emotions or feelings, these tendencies are: (1) desire, enjoyment; (2) hatred, anger; (3) disgust, fear; and (4) languor, quiescence. The fourth sort of tendency generally is overlooked because it leads to withdrawal from situations that arouse the other tendencies; yet the behavior involved in letting down and preparing to rest or sleep is a distinctive sort of purposeful movement requiring motivation no less than the others do.[439]

---

438. Given the purpose and limits of this appendix, it should be neither considered apart from the earlier treatments it presupposes nor mistaken for a summary version of the theory of natural law theologically articulated in chapters four through eight of *CMP*. For a summary, see the corresponding chapters of Germain Grisez and Russell Shaw, *Fulfillment in Christ: A Summary of Christian Moral Principles* (Notre Dame, Ind.: University of Notre Dame Press, 1991). Those wishing to understand and/or criticize the ethical theory insofar as it is the fruit of philosophical collaboration should focus on its articulation in two works: John Finnis, Joseph M. Boyle, Jr., and Germain Grisez, *Nuclear Deterrence, Morality and Realism* (Oxford: Oxford University Press, 1987), esp. chaps. 9–11; Germain Grisez, Joseph Boyle, and John Finnis, "Practical Principles, Moral Truth, and Ultimate Ends," *American Journal of Jurisprudence,* 32 (1987): 99–151.

439. The random movements of an animal or small child lacking motivation to do anything in particular do not constitute purposeful behavior; such movements may manifest the organism's readiness to adapt but are not themselves adaptive. The fourth sort of tendency is to desist from random movement and behave in ways adaptively shaped to meet the need or needs satisfied during rest and sleep.

A rabbit feels hungry, remembers a nearby garden, desires to eat the tender greens, and heads toward the garden; a two-year-old child feels hungry, remembers the cookie jar on the kitchen counter, wants to eat cookies, and begins trying to climb to the counter top. Both may achieve their goals and eat until satisfied—that is, until eating ceases to be enjoyable. Or the rabbit may see a dog, be frightened, and run back to its hole, still hungry but with its desire to eat overridden by fear; and the child may find cookies in the jar, eat one, feel tired, and curl up in the corner of the counter to sleep, still hungry but with the desire to eat overcome by languor.

Though their genesis is the same, however, animal behavior always is patterned solely by instinct and experience, while some instances of children's behavior soon manifest human intelligence. As infants learn to talk, they use language as a means of pursuing their goals, not least by putting their feelings into words. Before long, small children become manipulative: cajoling and threatening in order to get what they want. Moreover, they not only learn to use tools that are at hand but creatively solve problems. Still, as long as human behavior is determined by feelings and directed toward goals that are nothing more than imaginable states of affairs, intelligence plays only an instrumental role: Reason serves the passions. In this servile relationship, the goals of the master (passions) are not intelligible, and any intelligible goods the servant (reason) has in view are not ends in themselves but instrumental—for example, influence with those who can provide what one wants.

However, human reason is not limited to finding ways of attaining the goals of feelings that arise prior to and independent of the workings of intelligence itself. Children begin to play in a characteristically human way. They set objectives for themselves, strive to achieve them, and find not only emotional satisfaction but self-fulfillment in doing so. For example, having come to understand what it is to know, children go beyond asking questions out of spontaneous curiosity and start trying to figure things out. Beginning to appreciate familial bonds and friendship, children come to see the point in sharing what they have with others and in giving gifts.

Without emotional motivation to do something, nothing comes to mind as a possible action. So, an emotional motive and its goal remain necessary conditions for each such specifically human action. However, the genesis of human actions is more complex than that of behavior in which intelligence plays a merely instrumental role. Normal children of, say, six or seven begin to understand the goods that are aspects of the being and flourishing of persons, themselves and others—aspects to be pursued and/or safeguarded. While such goods can be viewed as means to one another, they are not essentially instrumental; being of themselves aspects of human fulfillment, they are basic goods.[440] Understanding basic goods and being aware of themselves, and of other humans as persons like

---

440. John Paul II, *Veritatis splendor*, 48 and 50, *AAS* 85 (1993) 1172–73, *OR*, 6 Oct. 1993, viii, calls such goods "chief" or "fundamental" rather than "basic"; what I say about such goods in *CMP* and shall say about them below is consistent with the encyclical's teaching about them—see, e.g., 13 (*AAS* 1144, *OR*, iii), 67 (*AAS* 1187, *OR*, x), 79 (*AAS* 1197, *OR*, xii).

themselves, people can look beyond the goals of feelings and generally can see the attainment of those goals as contributing to the fulfillment of persons. By acting for basic goods, they can seek to benefit both themselves and others as living wholes (see *CMP*, 115–20).

The more complex genesis of specifically human action involves an interplay between emotional motives and reasons for acting grounded in intelligible goods. Thus, though people need some emotional motivation if they are to eat at all and can eat simply on that basis, without a reason to eat and even despite a reason not to, a person's purpose in eating can include not only the goal of eating until satisfied but a reason: an anticipated benefit in terms of, say, health. With such an anticipated benefit in view, one can use imagination to elicit the desire for a goal—for instance, lessening the chances of having a heart attack—and eat something less appetizing than an available alternative and/or even limit eating despite the desire to eat more.

Insofar as basic goods are understood as possible reasons for acting and not acting, behavior that might be motivated by feelings not only can be overridden by other feelings—including the feelings aroused by a parent's "No, no"—but can be inhibited by a reason. This inhibiting of emotional motivation by reasons manifests another kind of motivation, that of the "will"—a person's capacity as a self-conscious subject to shape his or her life as a whole. Will is awakened by the understanding of basic goods, so that a person is alive to the various aspects of possible human fulfillment and can be concerned about or interested in basic goods insofar as possible actions might affect them (see *CMP*, 231–33). In normal adults, such rational concern generally is in play, at least in virtue of previous will acts; but if it is not, emotion determines adults' behavior as it does that of small children. Still, when one is interested in a basic good, the stronger emotion does not always prevail. Moreover, one generally can manipulate emotions by using imagination and focusing attention on one thing or another. Thus, as self-conscious subjects, people can determine themselves and act on reasons with a view to their own and/or others' fulfillment.

Such self-determination resolves indeterminacy between alternative possibilities: acting in this or that way, or, at least, acting or not acting. So, it occurs in and by choices. And since choices are self-determinations rather than determinations one undergoes—for instance, as a result of spontaneous feelings—one makes them with the awareness that one need not. Thus, though various conditions outside one's control must be satisfied for choice to be possible, the choice itself—to do this rather than that, to act rather than not—is not caused by any such condition. One freely makes one's choices.[441]

Like acts of intellectual knowing, choices are spiritual entities, not events or processes in the natural world, and they must be distinguished from the behavior that carries them out. Outward performances come and go. Choices remain as

---

441. The ability of human persons to make free choices is taken for granted in the Bible and solemnly defined by the Council of Trent; see *CMP*, 42–43. The reality of free choice also can be defended philosophically; see *CMP*, 45; Joseph M. Boyle, Jr., Germain Grisez, and Olaf Tollefsen, *Free Choice: A Self-Referential Argument* (Notre Dame: University of Notre Dame Press, 1976).

eterminations of oneself unless and until one makes an incompatible choice (see *MP,* 50–52). Some large choices bear on acts that can be carried out only by making and carrying out many smaller choices (see *CMP,* 54–55). Among these large choices are commitments—choices to cooperate with a particular person or group in pursuing a common good (see *CMP,* 236–38). The choice to accept Christian faith is a commitment that ought to organize a Christian's entire life.[442]

The basic goods: aspects of human fulfillment

Since no action or set of actions within one's power can ever fully safeguard or realize a basic good such as life and health, one chooses to act for an anticipated benefit, not with an expectation of definitively achieving or exhausting the good, but with a hope only of participating in it and/or contributing to its instantiation in others. So, particular acts or projects chosen for the sake of a basic good—for example, hygienic eating on a particular occasion or dieting to lose weight—instantiate that good somewhat as individuals of a natural kind instantiate a species. Still, as possible (and to some extent actual) aspects of real human persons' fulfillment, basic goods are more than mere logical entities; they can give meaning to individuals' lives and be common goods for whose sake people join in communities. Rather than either living routine and episodic lives by pursuing goals as regularly recurring but transient feelings dictate or else living lives planned to maximize the satisfaction of some set of wants, people can organize their lives by commitments to basic goods. And since these goods pertain to human fulfillment as such rather than to needs peculiar to individuals under given conditions, groups of people can organize a more or less extensive and open-ended common life by mutual commitments to one another bearing on the same good or set of goods.

Being aspects of the fulfillment of persons, the basic human goods correspond to the inherent complexities of human nature, as it is manifested both in individuals and in various forms of community. The following eight categories can be distinguished.[443]

(1) As *animate,* human persons are organic substances. Life itself, bodily integrity, health, and safety make up one category of basic good.

(2) As *rational,* human persons can know reality and appreciate beauty and whatever intensely engages their capacities to know and feel. Knowledge and aesthetic experience make up another category of basic good.

(3) As *simultaneously rational and animal,* human persons can transform the natural world by using realities, beginning with their own bodily selves, to express meanings and serve purposes. Such linguistic, cultural, and technical creativity can be realized in diverse degrees. Its realization for its own sake is another category of basic good: some degree of excellence in work and play.

442. See *CMP,* 393–97, 485–87, 690–93; *LCL,* 7–8; Grisez, Boyle, and Finnis, "Practical Principles, Moral Truth, and Ultimate Ends," 140–46. On faith as the basic commitment of Christian life—and therefore as the Christian fundamental option—also see John Paul II, *Veritatis splendor,* 65–67, *AAS* 85 (1993) 1184–87, *OR,* 6 Oct. 1993, x.

443. See *CMP,* 121–25, 135–39; *LCL,* 555–84. For a philosophical explanation and defense of the basic goods, see Grisez, Boyle, and Finnis, "Practical Principles, Moral Truth, and Ultimate Ends," 102–15.

The preceding categories of goods I call "substantive." Although the substantive goods provide reasons for acting, their instantiations, even when brought about in carrying out actions chosen to instantiate them, do not involve choices. Life knowledge, and skilled performance are basic goods just insofar as they can be understood as humanly fulfilling and, being so understood, can be chosen, cherished, enhanced, and handed on to others.

Another dimension of human persons is that they are *agents through deliberation and choice,* who can strive to avoid or overcome various forms of personal and interpersonal conflict—or, to put the matter positively, who can strive to foster harmony. So, certain forms of harmony are among the basic goods, and their instantiations include the choices by which one acts for them. So, I call them "reflexive" (or "existential") goods.

(4) Most obvious among the reflexive goods are various forms of harmony between and among individuals and groups of persons—living at peace with others justice, neighborliness, friendship.

(5) Within individuals and their personal lives, a similar good can be realized For feelings can conflict among themselves and also can be at odds with one's judgments and choices. The corresponding good is harmony opposed to such inner conflict—the inner peace of a morally mature and well-integrated person.

(6) One's choices also can conflict with one's judgments, and one's behavior can fail to express one's inner self. The corresponding good is harmony among one's judgments, choices, and performances—practical reasonableness and consistency between one's self and its expression.

(7) Then too, people experience tension with the very source and end of their reality—tension explained by faith as alienation from God due to sin. Attempts to overcome sin and gain peace with God are the concern of religion. Thus another category of reflexive good is the reconciliation and friendship with God that religion seeks.

(8) Finally, human persons are sexually differentiated and capable of a unique form of communion, marriage, which normally includes handing on, insofar as possible, not only bodily life but all the basic human goods. So, marriage including its fulfillment by parenthood, is another basic good. It is a reflexive good inasmuch as the self-giving of mutual consent is included in each of its instantiations. But unlike the other reflexive goods, the interpersonal communion of marriage also is a bodily good: unity in one flesh, which is actualized by sexual intercourse and further fulfilled by family life.

The structure of specifically human acts

In making a choice, one generally chooses to do something.[444] One's specifically human action is the unified whole: the choice and its execution. Before choosing, individuals deliberate about options they consider possible and interesting—I could do this or that—much as a deliberative body debates options proposed

---

444. If one can and should do something but chooses not to do it, one's adoption of the proposal also is a human act—a chosen omission (see *CMP,* 234)—but for simplicity's sake, shall not repeatedly mention omissions here.

members' motions. A choice to do something adopts a proposal just as a
oup's vote does, and in both cases carrying out what is decided completes the
tion (see *CMP,* 233–34).

Since the execution of the choice is proposed by the acting person (the
agent"), that state of affairs is the immediate goal ("proximate end") of his or
r choosing. The agent's purpose in adopting the proposal also is an end—the
od hoped for in making the choice (the agent's "end in view.")[445] In choosing
do the action, the agent determines himself or herself in respect to both that
d in view and the proximate end, and so can be said to intend them both. But
tend also can be contrasted with *choose* and used to refer exclusively to the
illing of ends in view. In that case, the execution of the choice will be thought
, not as the proximate end of choosing, but as a means of pursuing the end
e has in view.

As I said above, choices, like acts of intellectual knowing, are spiritual entities.
s intellectual knowing is reflexive—one knows oneself knowing—so also is
oosing. In choosing anything, not only does one realize that only one's choice
ill settle the indeterminacy, but one also chooses *to choose* what one chooses.
he choosing itself is intended—not, indeed, as a separate proximate end or
dditional end in view, but still as distinct from them, just as in knowing any truth,
e knows oneself as knower of the truth one knows.

Is the end in view really distinct from the proximate end of the choice?

Sometimes the reason for making a choice is a good instantiated in its very
ecution—for example, someone who plays golf as recreation and for exercise
t only desires to play and enjoys playing but hopes to benefit as a skillful
lfer and healthy person in and by the playing itself. In such cases, the agent's
d in view in making the choice coincides with the proximate end of making
, namely, its execution.

Sometimes, though, the reason for making a choice is a good instantiated in a
ate of affairs distinct from its execution but caused by it—for example, a father
ves his daughter medicine to clear up an infection. In such cases, the proximate
d of the choice (treating the infection) and the end in view (the girl's recovery
f health) do not coincide. Still, the father may be emotionally motivated not only
y anxiety about his daughter's health but by a paternal desire simply to care for
r. But sometimes when the agent's end in view does not coincide with the
roximate end of the choice, what the agent chooses to do has in itself no emotional
ppeal and is even strongly repugnant—for example, a woman very reluctantly
ooses abortion in order to avoid the burdens of pregnancy and of either raising
child or giving the baby up for adoption. Even in such cases, though, people's
oices have a self-determining character—that is, they determine the choosers,
t only in respect to the benefits hoped for (the ends in view) but in respect to
hat is done to carry out the choices (the proximate ends of the choices) (see
MP, 234–36; *LCL,* 468–69).

445. In many cases, agents have more than one end in view. So, here and in what follows, the
ngular should be understood as standing for both the singular and the plural—end in view or
ds in view, good or goods, and so on.

However, agents do not *do* everything that *results* from their actions. Whenever carrying out a choice involves outward behavior, that behavior has effects neither included in the agent's proposal nor in his or her end in view. For example, listening to recorded music may disturb neighbors; taking medication for an allergy may cause drowsiness; refusing to deny one's faith may lead to being killed. Sometimes such effects are not foreseen by the agent; but even if they are, they are not part of his or her action. Rather, they are side effects of the action. Since the foreseen side effects of carrying out a choice could be avoided by not making it, the agent freely accepts them in making the choice and permits them in carrying it out. So, agents bear some responsibility for their actions' side effects, and that responsibility is easily confused with their responsibility for choices they reluctantly make. However, since side effects are neither chosen nor intended as part of any end in view, agents do not determine themselves in respect to them as they do with respect to anything they choose, however reluctantly (see *CMP,* 239–41; *LCL,* 470–71).[446]

Sensory cognition and emotions, practical reason and will, are coprinciples of specifically human acts. Though agents usually do not become aware of emotional motivation, without it no conceivable course of action could be imagined as a real option and carried out (see *CMP,* 190). Moreover, many instantiations of each of the basic goods are emotionally appealing, and their emotional appeal complements the will's aliveness to the goods, which corresponds to practical intellect's grasp of them as aspects of human fulfillment to be pursued and safeguarded.

Still, reason and feelings often seem opposed. There are at least two explanations for that. First, when one has a reason for acting contrary to feelings and chooses to act on it, one may not notice the feelings that support doing so; thus one may forget that feelings conflict with one another and overlook the fact that reason and choice mediate conflicts that otherwise would be settled by the sheer force of the more powerful emotion. Second, when strong feelings press a person to act contrary to a reason for acting to which he or she is committed, the feelings allied with the commitment are taken for granted and not noticed, and emotion is experienced as an alien force threatening to overwhelm the self-conscious, self-determined subject and agent, so that the coprinciples of action seem radically opposed (see *CMP* 190–91; cf. Rom 7.14–25).

446. Even God foresees and accepts evils that he does not choose (see DS 1556/816; *S.t.,* 1 q. 22, a. 2, ad 2; q. 49, a. 2; 1–2, q. 79, aa. 2–4; *S.c.g.,* 1.96, 3.71). To deny this would be to deny at least one of three propositions, all of which pertain to faith: that God's will is perfectly holy, that his providence is all-embracing, and that some creatures have sinned with the result that evil is real. So, accepting bad side effects is compatible with good will. But choosing what is bad or having a bad end in view is not compatible with good will, because making a choice is self-determination with respect to everything included in the proposal adopted by that choice. Still, agents who wrongly accept side effects often have chosen previously to violate the good involved or in the course of deliberation have made a procedural choice to disregard the interests of the person or persons who will be adversely affected, and so have determined themselves wrongly. Thus, though the distinction between rightly accepting a bad side effect and choosing what would bring about the same state of affairs is morally crucial, there is little or no moral significance to the distinction between wrongly accepting a bad side effect and choosing what will bring about the same bad state of affairs.

asic goods and the first principle of morality

There are many inadequate and more or less mistaken accounts of moral inciples (see *CMP*, 97–113). An adequate account shows them to be the truths derlying sound moral judgments—judgments that direct people's choices and tions toward true human fulfillment. According to such an account, the starting int of all practical reflection is that the intelligibly good is to be done and rsued, and the bad is to be avoided (see *CMP*, 178–80). This first principle is nbodied in the understanding of each of the basic goods—such and such a sic human good (for instance, justice) is to be done and/or pursued, protected, omoted (see *CMP*, 180–83).

An account along these lines, grounding moral judgments in the goods that are pects of human fulfillment, is accepted by almost all contemporary Catholic oral theologians. But many of them have combined it with a theory called roportionalism," according to which sound moral judgments provide direction ward human fulfillment by identifying, from among the actions one could choose a given situation, the possibility that promises the best proportion of measurable nefits and harms for the people involved. Proportionalism is plausible, not least cause it seems obvious that settling for less than the best proportion between nefits and harms hardly would be reasonable. But despite its plausibility, pro- rtionalism is unworkable.[447]

One never can tell which prospective choice and action will bring about the best oportion of benefits to harms and contribute most to people's overall fulfillment. oral truth guides choices in a different way toward human fulfillment as a whole. elings often would lead one to focus exclusively on promoting one aspect or only me aspects of human fulfillment in one or only some people. And though the sic human goods are aspects of the fulfillment of every human individual and mmunity, reflection impeded by feelings can leave some persons out of account even treat them as if they were not persons, employ practical principles lectively, and ignore their unwelcome implications. One reasons rightly and is lly reasonable in choosing if, but only if, the judgment that shapes one's choice kes into account all the directiveness of all the principles of practical reasoning. ow, one who reasons rightly about what is to be done makes correct moral dgments. So, the first principle of morality can be formulated: *In voluntarily ting for human goods and avoiding what is opposed to them, one ought to choose d otherwise will those and only those possibilities whose willing is compatible th a will toward integral human fulfillment.*[448]

447. For criticism of proportionalism and defense of the moral absolutes it was meant to lace, see *CMP*, 141–71, the works cited there, and two more recent publications: John ul II, *Veritatis splendor*, 71–83, *AAS* 85 (1993) 1190–1200, *OR*, 6 Oct. 1993, xi–xiii; John nis, *Moral Absolutes: Tradition, Revision, and Truth* (Washington, D.C.: Catholic Univer- y of America Press, 1991).

448. See *CMP*, 178–84; cf. Grisez, Boyle, and Finnis, "Practical Principles, Moral Truth, d Ultimate Ends," 115–29. This formulation is closely related to the "norm of human tivity" articulated by Vatican II in GS 35 (see *CMP*, 183–84); it also spells out what Paul VI ant by saying that "human self-fulfillment may be said to sum up our obligations" (*Pop- rum progressio*, *AAS* 59 [1967] 263–65, *PE*, 275.16, with 275.13–15; see *CMP*, 184–85).

Integral human fulfillment refers to an ideal: a rich and ongoing sharing in a
the basic human goods by all individuals and limited communities in an entirel
harmonious community open to all human beings (see *CMP*, 186). While that idea
is a standard for good will, it is not a goal for human effort; without faith, on
cannot even know whether it can be realized. However, God promises to realiz
it as part of his heavenly kingdom (see *CMP*, 461–64). In the light of faith, then
integral human fulfillment is seen as part of the fulfillment of all things in Chri
(see *CMP*, 461–64, 814–16). And since one who consistently sought the kingdor
first of all would love as Jesus does and thereby fulfill the entire law, within th
context of the new covenant Jesus' new love commandment is also a way c
articulating the first principle of morality (see *CMP*, 603–6).

Modes of responsibility bearing on choices
unreasonable in themselves

Still, people wonder: What does love really require? The first principle c
morality is so general that by itself it provides no practical guidance. Moi
specific principles are required, with a clear bearing on the sorts of willir
involved in various kinds of actions. I call these more specific principle
"modes of responsibility," because they shape willing in view of the mor
responsibility inherent in it. Thus, modes of responsibility specify the fir
principle of morality by excluding as immoral the kinds of actions that involv
various ways of willing inconsistent with a will toward integral human fulfil
ment (see *CMP*, 189–92).

While the primary principle of morality articulates what is meant by *rig*
reason, the modes of responsibility exclude specific ways of acting unreasonabl
But one's concrete sentient self is part of one's whole self; so, one can right
satisfy the urgings of feelings when their particular goals are included within son
intelligible good, and that good, in turn, is chosen compatibly with integral huma
fulfillment. Still, one also can follow feelings against reason. Modes of respons
bility exclude the various ways in which that can happen.[449]

(1) While anger and hatred can motivate actions for which there are reasoi
(that is, actions that will promote intelligible goods or deal rightly with evi
contrary to them), hostile feelings often lead people to accept, or even to choos
the destruction, damaging, or impeding of an intelligible good—to act witho
hope of benefiting anyone and instead expecting, even hoping, to injure others c
perhaps, themselves. The willing involved in such destructive actions plainly
inconsistent with a will toward integral human fulfillment—with loving one
neighbor as oneself (see *CMP*, 215–16).

(2) One may have a reason to do something—the possible action would ser
some intelligible good in oneself or another, and one may even have committe
oneself to doing it. Yet one is deterred by languor and/or vague fears—me
feelings not allied with a reason, such as a real need for rest and recreation,

---

449. See *CMP*, 205–28. The first of the four modes mentioned here corresponds to the sevei
mode in *CMP*, the second here to the first and (in part) the fourth there, the third here to the thi
and (in part) the fourth there, and the fourth here to the eighth there.

real concern about some threat of harm. In such cases, the willing involved
▮ putting off or evading the possible action is incompatible with willing the
▮pect of human fulfillment that grounded the reason for doing the action, and
▮ one violates the first principle of morality (see *CMP,* 205–6, 210–11).

(3) People often experience desires or fears, have some reason for resisting
▮em, and have no reason for acting in accord with them—no hope that doing
▮ will benefit themselves or anyone else. Of course, in such situations, people
▮ten call the feeling "a reason" or rationalize that acting on the feeling will at
▮ast end the tension temptation is causing. However, the choice to give in is
▮compatible with willing the aspect of human fulfillment that grounded the
▮ason for resisting, and so, once more, against the first moral principle (see
MP, 208–11).

(4) However difficult it may be to put the preceding modes of responsibility into
▮actice, they are theoretically simple. In all of them the tension is between a reason
▮d its associated emotional motivation, on the one hand, and, on the other, feelings
▮ssociated from any reason. More complex, even theoretically, are kinds of cases
▮ which the tension is between options both of which involve reasons but only one
▮ which can be willed compatibly with the first principle of morality.

The starting point of all practical reasoning—good is to be done and pursued,
▮il is to be avoided—generally forestalls thoughts of choosing to destroy,
▮amage, or impede an instance of an intelligible good. But such thoughts arise not
▮ly when hostile feelings are in play—the kind of situation referred to in (1)
▮ove—but when destroying, damaging, or impeding an instance of an intelligible
▮od seems necessary as a means to prevent some other intelligible evil or to
▮hieve some intelligible good. In such situations, sometimes called "conflict
▮ses," does the first principle of morality call for a choice not to do the evil or a
▮oice to do it?

Though choosing not to do the evil would mean allowing the other evil to come
▮out or letting the prospective good remain unachieved, choosing to do the evil
▮ould be determining oneself against a basic good. And though allowing the other
▮il to come about or letting the prospective good go unachieved would not
▮spond to them as reasons for acting, neither would it negate them, whereas
▮etermining oneself against a basic good would negate its rational appeal. More-
▮ver, since intelligible goods are aspects of the being and flourishing of persons,
▮oosing not to do the evil would only mean accepting that some person or persons
▮ere injured or did not enjoy a benefit, while choosing to do the evil would mean
▮eliberately acting contrary to the good of some person or persons. Thus, consid-
▮ing conflict cases in general, anyone who accepts the preceding accounts of
▮man action and moral principles will see that the choice not to do the evil is
▮ accord with the first principle of morality while the choice to do it is
▮compatible with a will toward integral human fulfillment—with loving as
▮sus loves (see *CMP,* 216–22).

Of course, proportionalists argue that when someone has a proportionate reason
▮r choosing to do evil in a conflict situation, doing it is a mere piece of behavior
▮ithout moral significance of its own. The moral act, they say, cannot be defined

without including the end in view—for example, someone who chooses to kil
a terminally ill person to end his or her suffering will not, morally speaking, b
killing so much as ending suffering, provided the good of the person's no
suffering any longer outweighs his or her being dead before natural death woul
occur. But while the mercy killer's act as a whole is not as evil as the Mafi
hit-man's (who, of course, might say he is only earning his living), they ar
alike in choosing to end a human life and thereby determining themselve
against someone's good and that basic good itself.[450]

Moreover, this case exemplifies the previously mentioned unworkability c
proportionalism. Of course, one can imagine the states of affairs—living on an
suffering "like that" for, say, several more weeks, and being dead in a few minute:
with no more suffering—and one can compare the feelings this imagining evoke:
But one cannot measure and compare the intelligible goods at stake in the tw
options and rationally judge *in terms of the true fulfillment of the persons involve*
in the situation either that it will be better if the suffering person is killed now c
that it will be better if he or she dies later.[451] Proportionalists therefore focu
exclusively on concrete instances of human goods, omit from consideration th
aspect of their reality residing in people's choices and commitments (see *CM*
143–45), misconstrue the nature of morality, reducing it to effectiveness i
bringing about benefits and preventing harms (see *CMP,* 154–56), and, in despe:
ation, fall back on nonrational ways of making supposedly moral judgment
(see *CMP,* 159).

450. Not only those who dissent from exceptionless moral norms taught by the Church b:
some who try to defend them suppose that human acts basically are pieces of behavior that a:
specified by (are the kinds of acts they are due to) what they cause. John Paul II, *Veritar
splendor,* 78, *AAS* 85 (1993) 1196, *OR,* 6 Oct. 1993, xii, clearly and firmly rejects this mistake
view (his italics): *"The morality of the human act depends primarily and fundamentally on tl
'object' rationally chosen by the deliberate will,* as is borne out by the insightful analysis, sti
valid today, made by Saint Thomas (see *S.t.,* 1–2, q. 18, a. 6). In order to be able to grasp tl
object of an act which specifies that act morally, it is therefore necessary to place oneself :
the perspective of the acting person. The object of the act of willing is in fact a freely chose
kind of behavior. To the extent that it is in conformity with the order of reason, it is the cau:
of the goodness of the will; it perfects us morally, and disposes us to recognize our ultima
end in the perfect good, primordial love. By the object of a given moral act, then, one cann:
mean a process or an event of the merely physical order, to be assessed on the basis of its abili
to bring about a given state of affairs in the outside world. Rather, that object is the proxima
end of a deliberate decision which determines the act of willing on the part of the acting perso
Consequently, as the *Catechism of the Catholic Church* teaches, 'there are certain specif
kinds of behavior that are always wrong to choose, because choosing them involves a disord
of the will, that is, a moral evil' *(CCC,* 1761)."

451. Since proportionalists cannot show how to measure and compare benefits and harn
as their theory requires, they point out that goods and bads of various sorts often are measur:
and compared in other contexts. That of course is true, but the commensurability of vario:
sorts of goods and bads in various other contexts does not help proportionalists; see Finni
Boyle, and Grisez, *Nuclear Deterrence,* 261–66, and the detailed examination of conseque:
tialist arguments for and against the deterrent in the same work, 177–237, which illustrat:
well the arbitrariness and futility of such arguments.

Modes of responsibility and moral judgments

How are the preceding modes of responsibility related to moral judgments? Moral norms are applied in moral judgments—for example: "I could deny doing it; but that would be a lie, and lying is always wrong; so, I may not deny doing it" (see *CMP*, 254–63). Underlying specific moral norms are the modes of responsibility, which enable one to understand, criticize, and correctly apply sound moral norms one has learned and takes for granted, and even to develop new norms regarding new kinds of actions (see *LCL*, 266–68).

Ordinary language includes some names for kinds of actions described in ways that presuppose a moral judgment—for example, *cheating, doing one's duty*. An analysis in terms of the basic human goods and modes of responsibility can explain the presupposed moral judgments and make it possible to identify the specific actions about which they are accurately made. Ordinary language also includes many names for kinds of actions—for example, *sexual intercourse, writing a book*—described in ways that do not specify the sort of willing the actions involve or, at least, do not specify it sufficiently to make clear its bearing on basic human goods. Such kinds of actions cannot be characterized as morally good or bad; but of course they are never actually performed at this level of unspecified generality. Rather, in choosing to do them, people will in a definite way, and so engage in morally significant acts, which can be described and evaluated as such. Ordinary language includes only a few names for kinds of acts described in a way that sufficiently specifies the willing they involve and its bearing on basic human goods to bring them under a mode of responsibility. In such cases a moral norm, referring to the kind of acts without presupposing a moral judgment, can characterize them morally.

Each of the four modes of responsibility already considered characterizes the choices involved in various kinds of acts as incompatible with the first principle of morality—for example, "Do not repay evil with evil," "Never procrastinate," "Getting high is always wrong," and "One should never lie." Of course, in each case, the norm must be rightly understood. *Repaying evil with evil* does not mean causing injury incidentally to carrying out a choice to do some good, such as impose a just punishment, but choosing to injure out of hostile feelings. *Procrastinate* means choosing to postpone or delay needlessly—that is, without a reason grounded in an intelligible good. *Getting high* refers to a human act in which one chooses without a reason to satisfy desire despite the reasons for avoiding mind-altering substances. Without getting high in that sense, people sometimes use a mind-altering substance—for example, for pain relief or some other reason or wishing to be anesthetized. Lying is not merely uttering a false statement, as anyone can do by mistake or someone might do precisely in order to point out its falsity. *Lying* means intentionally asserting what one believes false. That involves a choice to present an outer self at odds with one's inner self, which always violates the good of consistency between inner and outer selves (see *LCL*, 405–12).

The mode of responsibility that excludes choosing to do evil for the sake of a good end is by no means the only one bearing on cases in which there is tension between options both of which involve reasons. Quite often, one has botl reasons and emotional motives for and against choosing to do something, bu the emotional motives for one option are not harmonious with the reason fo it. In such cases of mixed motives, the nonintegrated feelings, if not recog nized as such and discounted, may lead to a choice other than the one th agent otherwise would make on the basis of a reason and feelings integratec with it. For example, a man and a woman who must do some work togethe could do it either while other employees are around or after hours, and eacl also could do some other work by himself or herself at either time. There ar reasons favoring both options for scheduling the work together, but eroti feelings, which are not likely to help them get the work done, incline them t do it after hours. They need to recognize those feelings, set them aside, an choose between the options on the basis of the reasons in their favor and th feelings integrated with those reasons.[452]

Compared with the modes of responsibility I summarized previously, this one regarding mixed motives, usually directly enters into a conscientious person' reflection and very seldom is represented by a specific moral norm derived fron it. That is so because the unreasonableness of the willing that this mode exclude is not due to what is chosen or to the absence of a reason for the choice but only t the unintegrated emotional motive's possible effect on the choice—something tha very seldom will enter into the description of a kind of act for which ordinar language provides a name. Still, individuals, families, and other small group sometimes do identify kinds of acts likely to be wrongly chosen due to mixe motives and devise names for them. So, for instance, if the couple in the exampl work together after hours, associates might say with a wink that they are "toilin; overtime." But even if that expression were meant to refer to the work of couple thought to have mixed motives for working after hours, toiling overtime will no always be wrong; setting aside the erotic motivation, the couple may still think i best to work together after hours while taking due care to avoid romantic distrac tions. Thus, specific norms derived from this mode of responsibility will not b exceptionless; the same clarification of reasons and motives that grounds sucl norms can ground exceptions to them (see *CMP*, 256–59).

Affirmative responsibilities and side effects

The preceding modes of responsibility exclude making certain choices—and s acting—on the basis of emotional motives rather than reasons grounded in relevan

452. This mode of responsibility, regarding mixed motives, and its application are treated i *LCL*, 273–81, but there it is not called a mode of responsibility, and only the first thre examples—(a), (b), and (c) on 276–77 and 280–81—pertain to it; the other examples discusse there pertain to the Golden Rule and to other modes of responsibility that I shall articulate, below after dealing with the Golden Rule. Thus, the set of modes of responsibility treated in *CMF* 205–28, is incomplete. Moreover, the second is reducible to the fifth, and the sixth, I think, i reducible to two or more of the others. In *CMP* the modes of responsibility were distinguishe and articulated so that they would correspond to the Beatitudes (see *CMP*, 609–11, 627–59) though I remain convinced of the soundness of the other elements of the account in *CMP* of th relationship between Christian morality and natural law, I now see that the relationship betwee the modes of responsibility and the Beatitudes, while real, is more complex than I realized.

intelligible goods. But any good person—and not least a saint—not only avoids violating negative moral norms but uses his or her talents to do good, to do the truth in love. What is the source of the specific affirmative norms that shape those good actions? Good and holy actions in general are prescribed by the first principle of morality—choose possibilities whose willing is compatible with a will toward integral fulfillment, love God and neighbor. People ought to organize their lives by a coherent set of commitments, within an overarching religious commitment.[453] Having heard the gospel, one ought to make the commitment of faith (see *LCL*, 1–46), which entails the specific responsibilities of every Christian: praying, receiving the sacraments, and shaping one's life by a set of very general norms, expressed in the Beatitudes, which I call "modes of Christian response" (see *CMP*, 627–59). These in turn require that one accept and faithfully fulfill one's personal vocation, by making and carrying out a set of commitments that specify many affirmative responsibilities (see *LCL*, 113–29).

Conscientious Christians sometimes find it difficult to avoid acting on emotional motives rather than reasons, but they seldom find it intellectually difficult to answer the questions such temptations raise. That is not the case with affirmative responsibilities, where the questions that arise often concern the acceptability of bad side effects. In choosing to do something to fulfill a responsibility, one nearly always must accept at least the nonrealization of intelligible goods by not serving persons as one might if one chose a different option, and often one must accept some negative impact on an intelligible good and harm to a person. Fervent converts flee the world and go into the desert to fast and pray, leaving behind starving, sick, and unconverted people whom they otherwise could feed, care for, and evangelize. A man drives a taxi to support his large family and, as required by law, takes passengers to whatever destination they choose, including houses of prostitution and abortion clinics; thus, his work contributes to some passengers' wrongdoing. Those are bad side effects; it would be wrong to choose them as means or intend them as ends in view. Is it wrong to accept them?

Prudence and educating feelings

Ideally, one always would be able to answer that question by a prudent judgment, without the question becoming troubling.[454] But prudence presupposes experience and all the moral virtues (see *CMP*, 80–82, *LCL*, 246–48), and these are acquired by making and carrying out morally good choices. Even Jesus, despite his sinlessness, needed to mature morally (see Lk 2.51–52), and his character was not fully formed until he completed his passion (see Heb 5.7–10; *CMP*, 436). As we try to acquire virtues and the experience necessary for prudence, we are handicapped by the effects of original sin and our personal sins. We never become perfectly prudent.

---

453. See *CMP*, 393–97, 485–87, 690–93; *LCL*, 7–8; Grisez, Boyle, and Finnis, "Practical Principles, Moral Truth, and Ultimate Ends," 140–46.

454. See appendix 2, "Judging whether one's reason would be proportionate and proportionalism," for an explanation of how that prudent judgment would be made, and how the judgment that one has a proportionate reason for accepting side effects differs from a proportionalist "judgment" that one has a reason for choosing to destroy, damage, or impede a human good.

For the prudent person, moral insight would not begin only when reflective analysis becomes difficult, and moral judgment would forestall rather than forbid wrong choices (see *S.t*, 2–2, q. 47, a. 8; *CMP*, 80–82). Love fulfills the entire law; love *is* all that we *ought to be* (see 1 Cor 13). For us, even if in the state of grace, the gap between feelings, afflicted with concupiscence, and the love of God poured forth by the Spirit is manifest when we are tempted to get even with those who hurt us, to procrastinate, to drink to get high, to lie, to "toil overtime." Still, if we accept God's grace and are conscientious—that is, if we do our very best to find out what we should do and not do—then, with God's grace, we can choose uprightly, even if at times mistakenly, gradually gain moral insight, and so begin to become prudent (see *LCL*, 246–56). Therefore, difficult as reflective analysis may be—and inadequate as it is compared with perfect prudence—we must carry it out as well as we can whenever moral questions trouble us.

Moral reflection on accepting side effects obviously presupposes a choice in conformity with the preceding modes of responsibility. One cannot reasonably accept any bad side effects while choosing as one never should or choosing with mixed motives. However, accepting bad side effects often is morally questionable even when one's choice is good in itself—both what one is choosing and any end in view are consonant with every principle of practical reasoning—and all one's emotional motivation for making the choice is integrated with one's reason or reasons for making it. Questions about accepting side effects sometimes result from failing to pay attention to them and consider them carefully, so as to see precisely how they are bad and how bad they are. But even if one understands the intelligible good at stake and takes it as a reason against accepting some side effect, one may lack adequate emotional motivation to act on that reason. In that case, forgoing the choice so as to avoid the bad side effect will seem unrealistic, if not impossible.

Since emotional motivation pertains to sentient nature, it is fairly well proportioned to sentient goods and bads. But for the same reason, feelings are not naturally adequate to motivate us to act for intelligible goods and to avoid intelligible bads. This inadequacy is fourfold.

(1) Since an animal's behavior can serve only the individual itself and a few others—its mate, offspring, other members of its own group—emotional motivation does not naturally lead each individual to behavior that serves other members of its species, and it may lead it to behavior hostile to them. But my action can affect the human goods not only of me and mine but of anyone, and, unless there is a reason to treat people differently, the capacity everyone has to be humanly fulfilled is a reason to treat everyone alike.

(2) Since an animal's behavior can realize only sentient goods, emotional motivation does not naturally lead to behavior that contributes to flourishing that transcends the realization of such goods. But human action can contribute to human fulfillment not only in respect to survival and healthful functioning but in respect to the whole range of intelligible goods, including the reflexive goods that can make a person good in an unqualified sense (see *CMP*, 128–32).

(3) Since an animal's behavior can realize only imaginable goals and its imagination naturally is limited to a set of recurrent possibilities, emotional motiva-

ion does not naturally lead to behavior that realizes unfamiliar and entirely new goals. But human agents, individual and communal, can participate in and contribute to human fulfillment by trying different ways of acting and introducing new ones, revising and replacing existing methods and projects, and so on. And creativity often is required to overcome evil, to avoid accepting it, and to develop appealing alternatives to doing it.

(4) Since an animal's behavior can realize only transient goods, emotional motivation cannot naturally lead to behavior toward anything as lasting beyond this life. But human agents can act for goods that transcend time. Indeed, unless they do so, they will not be consistently reasonable—for example, faithful to commitments. "If the dead are not raised, 'Let us eat and drink, for tomorrow we die'" (1 Cor 15.32).

Even for animals, the initial, natural limits of emotional motivation are extended somewhat by experience and can be expanded greatly by training. Human emotional motivation, far more malleable than that of other animals, regularly transcends its initial, natural bounds. It often is drawn beyond those bounds by practical understanding of human goods, but when it is not, it may be drawn psychopathologically and perversely in respect even to sentient goods, as is shown by self-destructive behavior—for example, substance abuse. To play their part in a good human life, feelings obviously need to expand so that they can work in harmony with practical reason and motivate toward all the goals of the good acts that make up that good life. But even that is not enough. Feelings need to expand so that they can work in harmony with practical reason's recognition of the bad side effects of otherwise good options and can motivate, without nonrational limitations, against accepting them. This need to expand feelings can be articulated in four modes of responsibility corresponding to the four above-listed natural limitations on emotional motivation.

The Golden Rule

The first of those limitations—the focus of emotional motivation on the self and a few significant others—inclines people to prefer themselves and those to whom they are attached to all other people, even when there is no reason based on an intelligible good for doing so. Not only individuals but groups frequently act on this unreasonable inclination. Having done so and not repented, people develop rationalizations. Those others deserve to be treated differently because they are naturally inferior, or they pose a serious threat, or they are not persons in the whole sense." Habits and social structures—customary practices, laws, complex institutions—often embody such rationalizations. Those to whom such habits and social structures give an unreasonable advantage are likely to accept them uncritically as justifying the preference they enjoy and to invoke them in defending so-called rights.

But a will characterized by egoism and partiality plainly cannot be open to integral human fulfillment. So, many diverse cultures have recognized and formulated a mode of responsibility requiring that people be treated alike when there is no reason for treating them differently. Among philosophers, this moral requirement often is called "the principle of universalizability": If a rule is to be fair, it must omit proper names and apply equally to any and all persons who meet its intelligible conditions. No matter how the mode of responsibility is formulated, the key to its effectiveness in shaping sound moral norms and judgments is that the reasons or intelligible conditions that justify differences in treatment must be understood in terms of basic human goods, rather than in terms of something else, such as habits and structures embodying rationalization. So, my formulation expressly refers to feelings and intelligible goods: *One should not, in response to different feelings toward different persons, willingly proceed with a prefer-ence for anyone unless the preference is required by intelligible goods them-selves* (*CMP,* 211). A formulation along these lines can clarify the basis of specific moral norms of fairness, and explain why they sometimes admit of exceptions (see *CMP,* 256–57).

Nevertheless, the most famous formulation of this mode of responsibility does not refer to intelligible goods. It is the "Golden Rule" stated by Jesus in the Sermon on the Mount: "In everything do to others as you would have them do to you; for this is the law and the prophets" (Mt 7.12; cf. Lk 6.31). Compared with the universalizability principle and my own formulation, the Golden Rule offers one great advantage. It suggests a way of applying the principle: Put yourself in the other's place. The driver in a hurry, reluctant to make way for others, is instructed by the Golden Rule to ask: "What would I want other drivers to do if I were trying to merge into this traffic stream?" Even habits and structures of injustice can be criticized in this way (see *LCL,* 282–84).

Jesus clearly is assuming that those who will apply the Golden Rule love themselves—that is, seek genuine fulfillment in intelligible goods—and he takes for granted the goods that are reasons for acting or refraining from acting. The imaginative exercise of putting oneself in the other's place does not refer to those goods or even indirectly call attention to them. Plainly, the Golden Rule is not a law designed to catch people who are obdurate in injustice. Rather, it is a help for conscientious people who want to do what is right but for whom fairness is not yet second nature. Such people can share another's identity, as it were, by an exercise of imagination and, through that exercise, extend their feelings for themselves to embrace that other. This exercise not only helps them see what is right but affects their emotional motivation for the better, and thus inclines them to act fairly. Hence Christians who want to grow in the virtue of justice can do so by regularly using the Golden Rule in making moral judgments.

People who truly love themselves already are disposed toward virtue at least inasmuch as they are self-determined toward intelligible goods as aspects of their own fulfillment and that of those near and dear—they would not, for example, kill themselves or a family member. For such people, then, regularly applying the Golden Rule will bring to bear in all choices affecting others all the directiveness of practical reason's principles. Thus, with true self-love as their starting point, people grow not only in fairness but in love of neighbor (see *LCL,* 306–9). Moreover, for those whose self-love is transformed by the desire always to enjoy the benefit of Jesus' love, the practice of the Golden Rule means loving others as

Jesus loves them. That love is Christian mercy, which even prefers others' good to one's own whenever no other duty forbids that (see *LCL,* 310–17, 360–67).

When sound self-love cannot be taken for granted, however, one must not apply the Golden Rule without first making sure one would not have others choose as they should not or with mixed motives. Thus, someone who lies to spare another's feelings does not soundly argue: "If I were he (she), I would rather be lied to than told the truth." Moreover, one must remember that the Golden Rule bears on actions—"*Do* unto others"—not on states of affairs. Thus, though suffering people can rightly pray to die soon, someone who commits euthanasia does not soundly argue: "I would not wish to endure such suffering; so, the Golden Rule requires me to kill him (her)." Finally, in putting oneself in another's place when applying the Golden Rule, one should take along one's capacity to make sound moral judgments: all the truth one knows, one's moral responsibilities, one's ability to reason, and one's normal feelings with regard to the matters at issue.

Three other ways to expand feelings

The second natural limitation on emotional motivation is its focus on sentient goods. This limitation inclines people to prefer the aspects of human goods everyone naturally enjoys (even when there is no reason based in an intelligible good for that preference) to intellectual, moral, and cultural goods whose enjoyment presupposes various sorts of developed abilities—such as knowledge, moral virtue, and excellence in work and play. The inclination to prefer the aspects of goods everyone enjoys obviously leads to sensuality and materialism, but grossly unreasonable acts are excluded by prior modes of responsibility. However, commitments one is called to make or has made can make it reasonable to prefer to act for or protect an instance of good whose enjoyment presupposes a developed ability, and doing that can require that one forgo acting for a naturally enjoyable instance of good despite a reason—perhaps even one that otherwise would ground an obligation—to act for it.

As the mode of responsibility requiring impartiality among people is implemented by applying the Golden Rule, this one must be implemented by an analogous exercise of imagination. But whereas the Golden Rule expands feelings to embrace people with whom one does not naturally identify, the imaginative exercise needed here must educate feelings to respond to goods whose enjoyment presupposes developed abilities one lacks. Only those who have moral virtue—and the developed ability, if it is not itself a moral virtue—have the appropriate emotional motivation. So, the required exercise is to get to know such people and to share, at least imaginatively, in their excellent acts, so as to learn to feel as they do.

This exercise is not the only reason morally imperfect people should look to moral exemplars, but it does make such exemplars absolutely necessary. Morally exemplary people embody the prior modes of responsibility, including the Golden Rule, but those principles are intelligible in themselves. While such people sometimes provide a model for dealing with some very specific question, often our difficult moral questions do not seem to have been confronted by anyone whose example we can trust. Still, moral exemplars, and they alone, can teach us how to feel about instantiations of goods realizable only with developed abilities and in ways that contribute to human fulfillment as a whole only in the acts of morally upright people.

Jesus invites us to learn from him. We can do so by reading the Gospels as we do other stories, identifying with their hero, and imaginatively sharing in his acts. But the process will be far more effective if we do what we cannot do with fictional or many real heroes: enter into a personal relationship with Jesus and cooperate with him in carrying on his work (see *CMP,* 663–64). The Church also offers the saints as exemplars, and from among them we can select a few with whom we have suitable affinities and get to know them well.

Getting to know Jesus and the saints requires avoiding counterfeits and fictional accounts. Besides listening to the Gospels at Mass, we also should read each carefully as an account of Jesus' life. Commentaries and devotional works, even if sound, merit only secondary consideration. The writings of saints often are more helpful than things written about them, which always must be selected with great care.

Even so, Jesus cannot be a moral exemplar with respect to some elements of most peoples' personal vocations—marriage, work, and so on—nor are there adequate models even among the saints for some aspects of the vocations of most lay people. Nevertheless, deficient in virtue though we are, we can identify moral exemplars in our midst. They do not violate exceptionless moral norms; they treat others not only fairly but mercifully; and, if Catholics, they are devout. Associating with such a person greatly enhances one's feelings in regard to all the goods to which he or she is committed.

The third natural limitation on emotional motivation is its focus within a definite horizon on a set of goals to be achieved by using appropriate means. This limitation inclines people to persist in pursuing familiar goals in familiar ways and to be strongly attached to the ways and means, the projects and institutions that have served in fulfilling their commitments. The inclination can lead to pragmatic moral compromise, but doing evil to achieve good is excluded by a prior mode of responsibility. However, changes in one's gifts and the opportunities to use them in service can make it appropriate to give up familiar goals and the ways and means used to pursue them, to abandon projects, to end institutions or withdraw from them, and to seek new ways of fulfilling one's irrevocable commitments.

Our feelings need to be educated to engage fully with concrete things that implement our commitments, to disengage readily from those same things when they no longer do so, and to respond powerfully to the hazy images that beckon us to be creative—to envisage new goals, find new ways and means, undertake new projects, establish new institutions. For this, we need an imaginative exercise that will enable us to put into a larger but still concrete context the goals—and indeed, all the imaginable aspects—of everything good we have done, are doing and might yet do. If that inclusive, concrete context can be imagined as a goal corresponding to all the goods to which we are committed, passion for it not only will generate appropriate emotional motivation with respect to the various things that are or might become important to us but will end that motivation when it no longer is appropriate.

Morally serious nonbelievers recognize the problem and try to solve it in various ways. Some, for example, try to imagine how their lives will seem to them when they are about to die, or how they will be judged by "history." The Christian solution is to consider life as the set of good deeds that God prepared in advance for one to walk in, as one's unique part in his all-inclusive plan. One seeks the kingdom first, trusts providence, organizes life by the commitments of personal vocation, and constantly tries to carry them out. Meditating on heaven and hell stimulates one's feelings with regard to the all-inclusive context for all the things with which one is concerned in this life.[455]

Vatican II's teaching provides fresh material for that meditation, which now can be a more effective exercise than ever before. The Council teaches that those who obey the Lord while living their lives in this world prepare material for the heavenly kingdom, that this material includes all the good fruits of their human nature and effort, and that they will once more find these good fruits, unmarred by evil and completed, in the fullness of the kingdom (see GS 38–39). When we imagine the kingdom in this way, our passion for it is intensified by its richness in imaginable human goods, and that passion as it were infuses the materials for the kingdom with which we are and might be occupied in this life. Yet those materials may not include familiar goals and things to which we are attached, since they will be all, but only, what concerns us as we follow God's plan for our lives—no matter where it leads, no matter what it costs, no matter whether our obedient efforts to bring about concrete results succeed magnificently or fail dismally.

The fourth natural limitation on emotional motivation is its focus on the goods that can be realized in this life. This limitation inclines people to treat all goods as if transient and to regard difficult moral requirements as ideals. But nobody can be consistently reasonable unless he or she considers intelligible goods lasting and solidly real. Thus, our feelings must be educated to engage without wavering with certain concrete things that somehow embody changeless goodness. This calls for an imaginative exercise that sets those things apart and lifts them out of the flow of time.

The ancient sophists and modern utilitarians denied lasting reality and intelligible goods. Plato responded to the sophists by arguing for the immortality of the soul and the eternity of disembodied values. Nietzsche tried to answer the utilitarians by positing the regular, endless repetition of the entire history of the universe, including the precise details of each individual's life.

For Christians, this problem is closely related to the previous one. This visible world is passing away, but an invisible, permanent world already is coming to be. Risen in their own bodies, those who die in grace will live in that world, forever confirmed in holiness. Once again, Vatican II's teaching refines and develops the image of heaven. Yet the image of heaven's solid and unending reality probably is

---

455. Such meditation can be aided by sound theology of heaven and hell. An entirely sound and very helpful work: James T. O'Connor, *Land of the Living: A Theology of Last Things* (New York: Catholic Book Publishing Co., 1992).

less available to the sensibility of most Christians today than it was to that of those who participated with simple faith in liturgies celebrated in medieval cathedrals, joining with the angels and saints in thanking God while sunlight streamed through the stained glass and then receiving holy Communion with lively hope that this sharing in the one bread would be their foretaste of the banquet that will last forever.

Discerning between or among good options

Having carried reflective analysis as far as one can and done one's best to educate one's feelings, one sometimes confidently concludes that two or more options are morally acceptable though only one can be chosen. It is not yet clear which of these good deeds belongs to the life God has prepared for one to walk in (see Eph 2.10). Now, but only now, is the time for discernment (see *LCL*, 291).

Discernment returns to emotions, this time seeking to determine how well the possibilities otherwise judged good comport with the rest of one's individual personality. Even when fully integrated with reason, emotions do not simply echo it. They also resonate to the bodily, organic, and psychic dimensions of the personality; and these, insofar as they are integrated with faith, also are parts of one's better, Christian self. So, emotions which resonate to them pertain to grace, indicate God's will for one, and rightly tip the balance among possibilities otherwise judged good.

To discern is to compare two sets of feelings. One set is related to faith and integrated with it, and these Christian emotions are aroused by prayer, worship, spiritual reading, and so on. The other set includes those emotions bearing on the possibilities between which one must discern. These emotions are aroused by carefully and concretely considering as fully as possible what actually would be involved in the options under consideration. (It is assumed that the necessary investigating and information gathering already have been done.) Then one's Christian-faith emotions are compared with the sets of emotions related to each option—emotions reflecting not only the realities on which they bear but the reality of one's hidden self.

What is involved here is not some sort of objective measurement, but the effort to perceive an inward harmony. If the emotions related to one option plainly harmonize better with one's Christian-faith emotions, that can be considered the option which pleases one's Christian self, and one should choose as pleases this self.[456]

+ + +

---

456. This summary of the process of discernment is drawn from *LCL*, 292; see 291–93, including the footnotes, for a more adequate treatment of the matter.

Appendix 2: Formal and material cooperation in others' wrongdoing

Appendix 1 treats the genesis and structure of human acts, and the conditions for sound moral judgments. What has been said about those matters will be presupposed here. As in appendix 1, the analysis will be from the point of view of the agent—that is, the acting person—not that of an outside observer. The latter perspective can be appropriate for law; but the cooperation treated here must be distinguished from legally defined ways of being involved in another's action, such as being an accessory to a crime.

Formal and material cooperation were treated briefly in both previous volumes (see *CMP,* 300–303; *LCL,* 440–44), but the present, fuller treatment will not presuppose those earlier ones. It will include all their main points, add others, and amend some of their details.

Catholic moral theologians and documents of the magisterium use the expressions *formal cooperation* and *material cooperation* to refer to agents' involvement in others' objectively immoral actions. This technical use of *cooperation* may be confusing, because the word usually refers to working together for a common good. Rather than being morally questionable or wrong, it is good and often obligatory to do that; it both serves the common end in view and initiates or promotes community among the cooperators. But insofar as doing anything facilitates or contributes to another's wrongdoing, it cannot serve an authentic common good. If one is unjustifiably involved in another's wrongdoing, one is doing evil, and that cannot serve good or build up genuine community even with a wrongdoer; if one is justifiably involved in another's wrongdoing, community is prevented or damaged insofar as the other's bad will and one's good will are opposed, at least with respect to that matter. So, though I use *cooperation* in the technical sense both here and in the Analysis paragraphs of questions regarding involvement in others' wrongdoing, I avoid the term in proposed responses except when the questioner used it.

Accurately understanding cooperation and being able to analyze instances of it are important for moral advisers. Many difficult moral questions—not only in books of moral theology but in conscientious Christians' lives—concern cooperation. Many people, and even many moral advisers, wrongly assume that only formal cooperation is a serious problem. But the contribution made by one's otherwise good act to another's wrongdoing is a bad side effect, and accepting a bad side effect can be seriously wrong.

Some unreflective and/or unsophisticated people imagine problems regarding cooperation can (and perhaps should) be avoided by altogether avoiding cooperation. That, however, is virtually impossible and sometimes inconsistent with doing one's duty. Grocers materially cooperate with gluttonous eating, letter carriers with the use of pornography, and so on; and in many cases such people need their jobs to support themselves and their families. And though taxpayers materially cooperate with nuclear deterrence and other evils, paying taxes is morally obligatory (see *LCL,* 894–97; q. 169, above). Moreover, in

God's absolutely good act of sustaining the creatures he has chosen to create, he accepts as side effects all the wrongdoing and other evil in the universe (see *CCC*, 310–12); and Jesus teaches us to be like our heavenly Father, who sustains both sinners and upright people (see Mt 5.44–45). So, good people sometimes may and even should cooperate in others' wrongdoing, and cases involving cooperation require careful analysis and judgment.

I shall begin by explaining *formal cooperation* and *material cooperation,* dealing with what is proper to formal cooperation, and distinguishing it from cases in which a cooperator's act, though wrong in itself, is not formal cooperation. Accepting bad side effects always aggravates the wrongness of formal cooperation, and sometimes makes material cooperation wrong. So, I shall carefully examine the possible side effects of involvement in another's or others' wrongdoing, identify factors that should be taken into account in judging whether to accept them, and indicate how to make that judgment. Finally, I shall explain how my treatment of cooperation relates to that of other Catholic theologians and point out certain problems in an appendix to a document of the U.S. bishops.

What is meant by *formal cooperation* and *material cooperation*

In the technical language of moral theology, *cooperator* does not refer to everyone involved in another's wrongdoing. (1) Cooperation is distinguished from leading others into sin—which is what is meant by *scandal* in its strict, theological sense (see *LCL*, 232–39).[457] So, *cooperator* refers, not to someone who instigates another's wrongdoing, but to someone involved in wrongdoing initiated by another. (2) Formal cooperation usually is distinguished from the full involvement of two or more people in the same wrongful action—for example, a couple's joining in fornication or a gang's collaboration in robbing a bank.[458] So, *cooperator* is used to refer to someone involved in another's wrongdoing by an act more or less distinct from it. (3) Since cooperation is an action, *cooperator* is not used to refer to those thought of as only passively involved in wrongdoing—for example, citizens who avoid participating actively in an unjust war their country is fighting. (Still, omissions are actions, and one can wrongly cooperate by an omission.) (4) Problems about cooperation usually do not arise if the action is recognized as sinful even apart from the agent's involvement in another's wrongdoing. So, *cooperator* usually refers to someone whose act seems morally acceptable in itself—though, as will be explained, the formal cooperator's act, when accurately analyzed, turns out to be wrong, and often gravely so, in itself.

With these four restrictions in mind, one sees how questions regarding cooperation arise. Aware that what one might do would facilitate or contribute to some action or actions of another or others that one considers seriously wrong, one

---

457. I counted one kind of scandal as a type of formal cooperation (*LCL*, 440), but that was a mistake.

458. I counted such cases as formal cooperation (*CMP*, 301), and nothing important in what follows need be changed if one wishes to regard them as perspicuous instances of formal cooperation. But they plainly are not among the problematic cases that led theologians to make cooperation a subject of special study.

wonders whether that is a symptom of something seriously wrong with one's own prospective action.[459]

Using *cooperation* in this sense, one can draw a precise distinction between formal and material cooperation in another's wrongdoing. After considering previous attempts to define the two, St. Alphonsus Liguori put the matter this way:

> That [cooperation] is formal which concurs in the bad will of the other, and it cannot be without sin; that [cooperation] is material which concurs only in the bad action of the other, apart from the cooperator's intention.[460]

This way of distinguishing between formal and material cooperation was followed by virtually all subsequent manualists—that is, the authors of the moral theology textbooks used in all Catholic seminaries until around the time of Vatican II. It should be presupposed in interpreting teachings of the magisterium referring to cooperation. So, Alphonsus's succinct formula warrants the effort required to understand it as well as possible.

What, exactly, is meant by *formal* here? It refers to the form of the two acts that constitute the cooperation—that is, the elements of those acts that make them be the moral acts they are. Using *intending* in the broad sense, which includes both willing precisely what is chosen and willing the end in view, human acts are the moral acts they are primarily by virtue of the intending they involve. Thus, contributing to another's wrongdoing is formal cooperation if, and only if, the act by which one contributes agrees in bad intending with the wrongful act with which one cooperates.

Any other way of being involved is not involvement in another's wrongdoing precisely as wrongdoing. So, *material* in this context refers to that about a cooperator's act which involves him or her in a wrongdoer's act in such a way that the two acts share no bad intending in common. Whatever is badly willed by the wrongdoer is at most only an accepted side effect, foreseen but not intended, of the material cooperator's act.

Alphonsus's definitions make clear the fundamental moral difference between formal and material cooperation. Formal cooperation always is morally unacceptable, because, by definition, it involves bad intending. But intending is bad only if it is at odds with reason. So, formal cooperation involves intending at odds with reason, and any act by which one formally cooperates in wrongdoing is morally wrong in itself. By contrast, the material cooperator's act, if not wrong for some other reason, is wrong if, and only if, he or she should not accept the bad side effects of contributing to another's wrongdoing.

---

459. Any account of cooperation also applies to wrongdoing that certainly is not grave matter. However, people rarely if ever raise questions about such instances of cooperation, and treatments of cooperation usually do not explicitly discuss them. Questions also can of course be asked about what one already is doing or has done, and about other people's actions. These have been and must be discussed, but for simplicity's sake I deal with one's own prospective actions, which ought to be the main focus of ethical analysis.

460. St. Alphonsus Liguori, *Theologia moralis*, ed. L. Gaudé, 4 vols. (Rome: Ex Typographia Vaticana, 1905–12), 1:357 (lib. II, §63): "Sed melius cum aliis dicendum, illam esse *formalem*, quae concurrit ad malam voluntatem alterius, et nequit esse sine peccato; *materialem* vero illam, quae concurrit tantum ad malam actionem alterius, praeter intentionem cooperantis."

Alphonsus's definitions also make it clear that sometimes the moral act carried out by a certain outward behavior can be either formal or material cooperation, depending on what the cooperator intends. For example, two police officers, George and Jane, are assigned to prevent prolife workers from talking with women approaching an abortion clinic. George, who has invested money in the clinic and hopes it will maximize its profits, carries out the assignment so that the women coming to the clinic will get their abortions and not be dissuaded; Jane, a prolife feminist, carries out the assignment solely because she is afraid of losing her job if she refuses. George formally cooperates in abortion; Jane cooperates only materially.

The sharing in bad willing that constitutes formal cooperation

The intending involved in a human act often is complex. Choosing to do anything is intending, as a proximate end, the carrying out of the choice. But usually an agent also intends one or more ends distinct from that proximate end, and one end in view can be a means to another.

If the intending involved in a wrongdoer's act is complex and two or more of its elements are bad willing, does someone formally cooperate only by sharing all the elements of bad willing? No.

Angela, the boss of a criminal syndicate, wishes to burn down a rival gang's warehouse as an act of revenge. Tony, an employee of the rival gang, cooperates with her by providing information about the delivery date of some highly flammable goods. He has no interest in revenge but obtains perverse gratification from being present at large fires. So, Tony does not share all the bad willing that vitiates Angela's act—her end in view is revenge while his is perverse gratification. Still, his cooperation is formal, for he shares with Angela the bad intention of burning the warehouse.

Note that the shared element of bad will does not play the same role in the two agent's actions. Burning the warehouse is Angela's proximate end, her means to revenge. The proximate end of Tony's choice is providing the information; his intermediate end is Angela's arson, and that, in turn, is his means to perverse gratification, which is his ultimate end in view.

Formal cooperators also can intend in common only a bad end. Another gang's head, Sylvester, who shares Angela's desire for revenge against their common rival, does not care for her plan to burn the warehouse—the place is insured, and people in it are likely to escape the fire. His plan, to gun down the rival gang leader's aged mother, seems to Angela too risky. But to implement either plan, its proponent needs information the other has. So, Sylvester and Angela agree to disagree, exchange information, and proceed in their chosen ways to pursue the revenge they both desire. Though neither intends the other's chosen means, the shared bad end for which they supply each other with information makes their mutual help—his with her act of arson and hers with his act of murder—formal cooperation in wrongdoing.

People can formally cooperate, especially in some subtle fashion, in an action they abhor. Universal Appliance (UA) wishes to contract with Dependable Interim

Employees (DIE), a supplier of temporary workers. Christine manages DIE and wants the contract, but is told that workers of one of the kinds she must have available—"hostesses"—will be expected to provide sexual services, and she wants nothing to do with prostitution. The UA executive she is dealing with suggests a solution: DIE need only arrange with a reliable "escort" service to supply hostesses, and UA will contact the latter directly when a call girl is required. All DIE need do is act as a laundering go-between for the escort service's bills and UA's payments; the contract between UA and DIE will not even mention hostesses, and Christine never will be called on to supply one. Feeling that this solution will distance her sufficiently from the prostitution, Christine contracts with UA and makes the necessary arrangement with Cadillac Escorts. In doing this, however, she intends that Cadillac Escorts undertake and carry out its part of the arrangement—that is, meet UA's requirements for hostesses who will provide sexual services. So, she formally cooperates in prostitution. Of course, Christine does not intend the activities of the call girls in the same way some UA executives and their guests do. She disapproves; she finds them utterly repugnant. She intends them only as a means to obtain UA's contract and the legitimate business it will provide for DIE.

Without any overt involvement in wrongdoing, many people in positions of authority—including administrators of nonprofit organizations, managers of businesses, and public officials—sometimes formally cooperate with wrongdoing they personally deplore and perhaps even make serious efforts to prevent or end. Like Christine, they may do this by reluctantly using the wrongdoing as a way to obtain needed cooperation by others or as a means to protect goods for which they are responsible. People in authority also can be drawn into formal cooperation with morally unacceptable activities for whose execution they are given unwanted responsibility (see *LCL*, 441).

However, unless cooperative actions share at least some bad willing with the wrongdoing to which they contribute, even acts wrong in themselves that significantly contribute to others' wrongdoing constitute only material cooperation. For example, Cindy, not knowing that her employer, Dan, is homosexual, hopes to initiate an intimate relationship with him. She gets him to go hiking on a lovely afternoon in May, leads him to a swimming hole at an abandoned quarry, where they seem to be alone, and proposes that they skinny-dip. He refuses. She becomes angry and shoves him. He falls into the water, hits his head on a rock ledge, and is knocked out. Though Cindy is a good swimmer and is confident she could pull Dan out, she simply stands by and watches him drown. Though she tells no one what happened, the body is soon found. Traces of a scuffle the couple left at the swimming hole's edge, together with other circumstantial evidence, lead the authorities to suspect Dan's former companion, Jack, of homicide. Police question many people, including Cindy. Hoping Dan's death will be blamed on Jack, she supports the case against him by telling a completely fictitious but credible story about Dan's activities and confidences. Largely due to her testimony, Jack is indicted and put on trial for second degree murder. Teddy, a boy of thirteen, watches the television coverage of Cindy's testimony with considerable anguish. He was approaching the swimming hole just as Cindy and Dan arrived there, and had kept out of their sight but seen everything; however, because he was playing hooky and had been strictly forbidden by his parents ever to swim in the abandoned quarry, he has told no one. Police questioned every youngster in the area who was absent from school that day, but Teddy lied, saying he went to a shopping mall. The boy realizes he should tell what he knows but decides not to. Both Teddy's lying to the police and his decision to keep silent about what he knows are wrong. These bad acts significantly contribute to Cindy's effort to have her wrongdoing attributed to Jack. But Teddy does not choose or otherwise intend anything Cindy does, while she, not even knowing that he exists, in no way wills his acts. Thus, none of their bad willing coincides, and Teddy only materially cooperates with Cindy's wrongdoing.

The conditions for morally acceptable material cooperation

Immediately after distinguishing, as quoted above, between formal and material cooperation, St. Alphonsus goes on to state conditions under which material cooperation is morally acceptable. Since that statement should be read in its context, I quote both sentences:

> That [cooperation] is formal which concurs in the bad will of the other, and it cannot be without sin; that [cooperation] is material which concurs only in the bad action of the other, apart from the cooperator's intention. But the latter [material cooperation] is licit when the action is good or indifferent in itself; and when one has a reason for doing it that is both just and proportioned to the gravity of the other's sin and to the closeness of the assistance which is [thereby] given to the carrying out of that sin.[461]

The first condition for the moral acceptability of material cooperation is that the cooperator's act be "good or indifferent in itself"—that it not be evil independently of its constituting cooperation. The second condition is that the cooperator have in view as his or her end a reason that is "just"—that is, have a reason that is morally acceptable in itself. The third condition is that the morally acceptable end in view that is the cooperator's reason for acting be proportioned to two things: the gravity of the wrongdoing to which his or her action contributes and the proximity of that contribution to the wrongful deed—in other words, how closely the cooperator's outward behavior involves him or her in the outward behavior that carries out the wrongdoer's bad choice.

The first two conditions are clear and plainly necessary, and subsequent manualists followed Alphonsus in requiring them. They also followed him in requiring a proportionate reason for cooperating, but found it difficult to explain what a proportionate reason is and how it can be identified. Alphonsus's formula provides a starting point inadequate in four ways for investigating these questions.

First, the reason that must be proportionate, if material cooperation is to be morally acceptable, is the reason for doing the act, one of whose side effects is

---

461. Ibid., the second sentence is: "Haec autem est licita, quando per se actio est bona vel indifferens; et quando adest justa causa et proportionata ad gravitatem peccati alterius, et ad proximitatem concursus, qui praestatur ad peccati exsecutionem."

some contribution to another's wrongdoing.[462] To what must this reason be proportionate? According to Alphonsus, to two things: the gravity of the wrong-doing and how closely the cooperator's behavior involves him or her in the wrongdoer's behavior. However, the real question about the reason's proportionate-ness is whether one can reasonably prefer to do the act for that reason rather than forgo it so as not to contribute to the other's wrongdoing. To answer, the conscien-tious person wondering whether to choose to do what would constitute material cooperation must compare the reason for making the choice with the reasons for not making it. So, if material cooperation is to be morally acceptable, the reason for choosing to do the act that constitutes it must be proportionate to the reasons for not making that choice. *Some* of the latter reasons are grounded in the intelligible goods vitiated by the wrongdoing to which the act will contribute, and Alphonsus's formula rightly suggests that the reasons to forgo the act will be more or less strong partly in proportion to how grave the wrongdoing is and how closely the act will involve one in it. But it is *to the reasons for not doing the act* rather than to the gravity of the wrongdoing and how closely the act will involve one in it that one's reason for doing it must be proportionate if material cooperation is to be morally acceptable.

Second, only some of the reasons for not doing the act that constitutes material cooperation are grounded in the intelligible goods adversely affected by the wrongdoing to which the act will contribute. Almost never are the contributions material cooperation makes to the wrongdoing and its results the cooperation's only bad side effects, and sometimes, perhaps often, they are not its most serious ones. Further consequences always flow from knowingly doing what constitutes material cooperation in wrongdoing and accepting those basic bad side effects. In part, these secondary consequences are psychological effects on oneself and effects on one's future options; in part, they are effects on the wrongdoer and one's relationship with him or her; and in part, they are effects on third parties and one's relationships with them. Usually some of these further consequences are bad, and often one foresees and accepts them; if one does not foresee them, one may be morally responsible for failing to do so. Thus, Alphonsus's formula is inadequate insofar as it overlooks many possible reasons for forgoing acts that would constitute material cooperation—namely, all the reasons grounded in the intelligible goods that may be adversely affected by secondary bad consequences.[463]

462. A person who materially cooperates often has more than one end in view for doing the act that constitutes the cooperation. But, for simplicity's sake, I shall speak of the reason—in the singular—for doing the act. Thus, a proportionate reason may be grounded in a complex set of goods.

463. Alphonsus treats material cooperation in the treatise on charity; but, having distinguished between scandal and material cooperation, he overlooks its possible secondary bad consequences even on the wrongdoer. Alphonsus does consider (ibid.) the possibility that, out of charity toward the wrongdoer, one should withhold material cooperation to impede the wrongdoing *itself*, but he sets even this aside on the ground that forgoing a "just cause" for doing the act that constitutes material cooperation would be an instance of the grave inconvenience moralists thought sufficient to undercut duties of charity ("caritas non obligat cum gravi incommodo") that go beyond the

Third, when one is considering doing something that would constitute material cooperation in another's wrongdoing, how grave the wrongdoing is and how closely one's act will involve one in it are not the only factors that can affect the strength of reasons to forgo the act. Alphonsus himself briefly alludes to two others: the possibility that forgoing the act would prevent the wrongdoing and how much right one has to do the act.[464] But the magnitude of the various bad side effects, how likely they are to occur, and how much confidence the cooperator has in his or her own judgments also can affect the strength of the reasons to forgo an act that would constitute material cooperation.

The preceding inadequacies in Alphonsus's formula requiring a proportionate reason to justify material cooperation aggravate the problem posed by its fourth inadequacy, namely, its lack of guidance about how to judge whether the reason is proportionate. To be proportionate, the reason to do the act must be sufficiently strong that doing it is reasonable despite the more or less strong reasons to forgo it. But, having ascertained that a possible act is not wrong even apart from its constituting cooperation and that one's reason for choosing to do it would be morally acceptable, how does one compare the strength of that reason with the strength of the reasons, grounded in expected bad side effects, for forgoing it?

Nothing more need be said to remedy the first inadequacy. But the second calls for a fuller consideration of possible bad side effects of cooperation, which could ground reasons for forgoing acts that constitute material cooperation. Similarly, the third calls for a fuller consideration of factors that can affect the strength of the reasons to forgo an act that would constitute material cooperation. And the fourth calls for some consideration of the steps a conscientious person can take in trying to judge rightly whether the reason to do the act is proportionate—that is, strong enough to make it reasonable to prefer doing the act to forgoing it. I shall take up these three needed considerations in the order in which I have just stated them.

Note, though, that the first two of these considerations also are relevant to cases in which other factors morally exclude cooperation—cases in which it would be formal or in which the act that would constitute it would be wrong even apart from its constituting cooperation or, if morally acceptable, done with a bad end in view. Because those factors already constitute morally decisive reasons, theologians have paid little attention to the bad side effects of cooperating in such cases. But bad side effects ground additional reasons for avoiding cooperation that should be excluded on other grounds, and they often make it much worse than it otherwise would be. Thus, these additional reasons provide additional motives to resist temptations to cooperate wrongfully and to repent doing so, and attention to bad side effects also may be necessary for judging whether restitution is required and how much it should be. Moreover, sometimes reasons against cooperating grounded in bad side effects are perspicuous and persuasive for people who do not grasp the decisive reasons against it grounded in the act itself.

---

requirements of justice. (I maintain—*LCL*, 360–71—that mercy is the justice of the kingdom and its requirements are not morally optional, though obligations toward others can take precedence, since one cannot be merciful to some at others' expense.)

464. Ibid., 1:356 (lib. II, §59, 2° and 4°).

Various sorts of possible bad side effects of material cooperation

Actions often have bad side effects having nothing to do with cooperation. For example, a man's stressful job may contribute to his high blood pressure; and if carrying out some of his duties also constitutes material cooperation in wrongdoing, he surely ought to take into account not only the bad side effects of the cooperation but all the bad side effects of continuing to do the job in judging whether the reason for continuing is proportionate. For simplicity's sake, however, having made this point, I shall not mention it again.

The basic bad side effect of material cooperation is that one's action makes some unintended contribution to another's wrongdoing. That wrongdoing itself always has bad effects, and these often have further bad effects. The sorts of bad effects that flow directly from wrongdoing vary with different kinds and instances of wrongdoing. If one foresees the bad effects of wrongdoing in which one materially cooperates, one also accepts them insofar as one is aware that one's action contributes to them. Thus, one may accept irreverence toward God by materially cooperating in an act of sacrilege and one may accept injury to people by materially cooperating in injustices of various sorts. Since wrongly accepting another's irreverence would itself be irreverent and wrongly accepting another's injustice would itself be unfair to its victims, such bad effects and others flowing directly from the wrongdoing are not likely to be overlooked by conscientious people considering reasons against doing something that would constitute material cooperation.

Less obvious and more likely to be overlooked are possible consequences of one's own act that are bad or made worse precisely because it constitutes material cooperation in another's wrongdoing. In considering these secondary bad consequences, one should not focus exclusively on isolated acts. If material cooperation is ongoing or becomes a regular practice, it is likely to have more and graver such consequences than would an isolated act.

The secondary bad consequences of materially cooperating can flow from several things: (1) one's very accepting of the primary bad side effects of cooperating, (2) one's carrying out the act that constitutes material cooperation, and (3) the wrongdoer's and/or others' awareness and evaluation of the fact that one is materially cooperating.

(1) In materially cooperating, one's very accepting of the action's primary bad side effects—its contribution to another's wrongdoing and that wrongdoing's bad effects—can have bad effects on oneself. One's feelings can be adversely affected. Pedro, a large grocery chain's purchasing agent, buys produce from growers who mistreat their migrant workers. Merely doing his job, Pedro makes his purchasing decisions solely on the basis of quality and price; he does not intend, but only accepts, the contribution that buying from these growers makes to their injustice and its many bad effects on the workers and their families. Still, accepting these primary bad side effects of doing his job affects his feelings, so that the injustice seems to him less important and less repugnant than it otherwise would. Moreover, his disposition toward the migrant workers may be affected in a way that will impede good relationships with them. Suppose members of his extended family

are among the exploited workers. If his material cooperation is not morally acceptable, it is a betrayal. But even if what Pedro is doing is justified, his willingness to do his job and accept its contribution to the growers' injustice hardly disposes him toward solidarity with his exploited relatives.

(2) The preceding sorts of bad effects can be intensified by carrying out an act that constitutes material cooperation. Moreover, actually materially cooperating, especially by an ongoing activity or regular practice, has additional bad effects. Performance, especially repeated performance, tends to become habitual; interaction with wrongdoers tends to generate psychological bonds and interdependence. Thus, cooperation often leads to opportunities and temptations to engage in further cooperation. Even if the initial cooperation otherwise is morally acceptable material cooperation, the further cooperation may be formal or, though still material, morally unacceptable. In this way, material cooperation often is an occasion of grave sin.

Helen accepts a job doing secretarial work at an export-import company, initially simply taking dictation and typing letters. She learns and overhears enough to know that the letters sometimes include lies, but she types them carefully, corrects mistakes in grammar, and so on. Considered in itself, such secretarial work may be morally acceptable material cooperation in lying. But Helen's desire to keep her job and get ahead may lead her to suggest an occasional amendment to make a letter more effective, and if that means to make a lie more credible, she begins formally cooperating with the lying. Or, having manifested her talents, she may be assigned to draft deceptive letters, so that she must intend to lie. But even if no temptation to cooperate formally arises, Helen may discover that her employer is one of the "legitimate" enterprises of a criminal syndicate, and that the lies in the letters she types are essential to a way of doing business that is marginally lawful and grossly immoral. Knowing more now about the seriousness of the wrongdoing and its bad consequences, she might well no longer have a proportionate reason to be involved; if not, the secretarial work she has been doing from the start is now wrongful material cooperation. But if Helen likes her job, is doing well in it, and has received some pay raises, she may find it hard to quit.

(3) The wrongdoer and others who observe someone doing something that constitutes material cooperation in wrongdoing often know or assume that the cooperator knows how his or her action is contributing to the wrongdoing and its bad effects. Given this knowledge or supposition, they often take the cooperator's willingness to cooperate as significant, evaluate that willingness, and draw practical conclusions. Consequently, what a material cooperator is doing can: (3.1) have bad moral effects on the wrongdoer, (3.2) scandalize third parties, (3.3) lead to disharmony between the cooperator and the victims of the wrongdoing, (3.4) impede the cooperator from offering credible witness against the wrongdoing, and/or (3.5) impede the cooperator from carrying out his or her vocation in other respects.

(3.1) Since cooperation in another's wrongdoing is distinct from scandal—that is, leading another into sin—one might suppose that material cooperation cannot have bad moral effects on the wrongdoer. But cooperation by "good" people reassures sinners and encourages them to be obdurate. Moreover, material cooperation contributes, sometimes decisively, to the wrongdoing's success, and success in wrongdoing also encourages obduracy and impedes repentance. Of course, some wrongdoers lack sufficient reflection or even sincerely think what they are doing is good; they are not serious sinners. Yet even if they are not guilty of grave sin, their state of mind is bad. It falls short of moral truth and is morally vulnerable. Even for masters who thought slavery justifiable, owning slaves was an occasion of various sins, not least the sin of resisting the truth about slavery, if and when the light dawned, and then knowingly persisting in the injustice.

(3.2) Third parties can be scandalized by someone's material cooperation. This can happen in various ways. Sometimes the fact that "good" people are involved makes wrongdoing seem not so wrong and provides material for rationalization and self-deception by people tempted to undertake the same sort of wrong. Perhaps more often the material cooperation of "good" people leads others to cooperate formally or wrongly, even if only materially. Thus, if medical residents, compelled to choose between giving up their careers and materially cooperating in morally unacceptable procedures, give in to the pressure, their example may lead other health care personnel, who could resist without great sacrifice, to cooperate materially when they should not. This bad effect might suffice to require the residents to forgo what otherwise would be morally acceptable material cooperation.

(3.3) Victims of wrongdoing often perceive at least certain sorts of material cooperators as participants in the injustice they suffer. Such a perception can lead to serious tension between victims of wrongdoing and material cooperators in it, and this tension can damage or impede the relevant community—ecclesial communion, neighborliness, friendship, familial communion. Thus, the likelihood or significant risk that involvement in an injustice will cause disharmony with its victims is an evil grounding a reason to forgo what would constitute material cooperation. Even if the cooperation otherwise would be morally acceptable, this reason could be decisive. Pedro, in an earlier example, has relatives among the migrant workers exploited by growers from whom he purchases large quantities of produce. Even if his material cooperation otherwise would be morally acceptable, family harmony might well require him to forgo it by giving up his job.

(3.4) Materially cooperating in wrongdoing often is incompatible with bearing witness against it. The secretary who prepares letters containing lies probably will lose her job if she makes it known that her employer lies to correspondents or points out to those who draft the letters that what they are doing is wrong. Even if one is free to bear witness against the wrongdoing in which one materially cooperates, one's involvement may detract from the credibility of the witness, since that depends on the clear correspondence between words and deeds. If Pedro sets out to campaign against the exploitation of migrant workers, he may find that nobody will take him seriously as long as he continues doing business with the growers who exploit them.

(3.5) People should shape their lives in accord with their personal vocations by making and carrying out various commitments (see *CMP*, 559–62, 663–64, 690–95; *LCL*, 113–29). Commitments bear on specific intelligible goods and generate responsibilities toward a particular person or group with whom and in whom the goods are to be realized. Material cooperation in the wrongdoing of persons and groups often impedes carrying out responsibilities flowing from vocational commitments. Tim has been drinking too much, mistreating his wife, Wendy, and neglecting their children; she of course wants him to stop drinking, but at the same time she facilitates his growing dependence on alcohol by materially cooperating: fulfilling some of his responsibilities for him, making excuses and covering up for him, and so forth. Under some conditions, Wendy's material cooperation may be justified, at least as a temporary measure. While she engages in it, however, she will be unable to work effectively with Tim to overcome their marital problems and raise their children. Similarly, the president of a Catholic college who cooperates materially with various other administrators and faculty members in actions that tend to secularize the institution undercuts his or her own ability to work with all members of the college community for their common good as a Catholic college. Ideally, all wrongdoers and material cooperators in their wrongdoing should be working together in some sort of authentic community for common goods. But material cooperation always not only accepts a bad situation but makes it workable—and so, usually, more likely to endure and harder to overcome.

Factors that can affect the strength of reasons against cooperating materially

Because interpersonal relationships involve moral responsibilities, anyone reflecting on the possible moral acceptability of material cooperation should consider any relationship he or she has with the wrongdoer and others who may be adversely affected. The responsibilities flowing from vocational commitments not only can ground a reason against cooperating materially, as has been explained, but can affect the strength of other reasons against doing so. For instance, if one has a special responsibility to set a good example for those who might be scandalized by an action constituting material cooperation, one has a stronger reason to forgo it. By the same token, if something must be done to fulfill a responsibility flowing from a vocational commitment, there is a stronger reason to accept bad side effects in doing it than if one could forgo the activity without slighting any such responsibility. For example, if a sixty-year-old man cannot support his family unless he keeps a job that involves materially cooperating with subtly fraudulent practices of his employer, he has a stronger reason for keeping the job than he would if he could afford to take early retirement.

The preceding example points to another significant factor: whether there is a feasible and morally acceptable alternative way to pursue one's good purpose. For example, a computer programmer whose work involves material cooperation in fraud has less reason to keep that job if he or she can easily get a satisfactory position with some morally unproblematic enterprise.

Another factor to consider is the effect forgoing the action that constitutes material cooperation would have on the wrongdoing. If forgoing the action certainly or probably would prevent the wrongdoing or impede it and greatly mitigate its bad effects, there is a stronger reason to forgo the action than if forgoing the action probably would have little or no effect on the wrongdoing.[465]

Alphonsus's formula for proportionate reason takes into account that the more grave would be the wrong with which one would materially cooperate, the stronger must be the case to justify doing so. But all the bad effects of cooperating that ground reasons against doing so also can vary in magnitude—can be more or less—in diverse ways, and not all their differences in magnitude correspond to differences in gravity among various sorts of wrongdoing. For instance, the number of victims of a sin of injustice and the gravity of the sin usually are independent variables. So, the magnitude of the prospective bad effects of material cooperation also must be taken into account.

In appraising the magnitude of bad effects, one must reduce those with respect to instrumental goods (such as property) to basic human goods (such as life, health, and bodily integrity) for whose pursuit instrumental goods are means. For instance, the loss of fifty dollars is almost sure to be more detrimental to a poor person than the loss of five thousand to a billionaire.

Whenever a bad effect will be detrimental to more than one person, the greater the number of those who will be adversely affected, the stronger is the reason against cooperating and accepting the bad side effect.

In considering bad effects on substantive goods, one must take several different measures of magnitude into account. How extensive is the damage? A person is damaged more extensively by losing his or her life than by losing a leg, more extensively by losing a leg than by losing a toe. How lasting is it? Loss of a leg is more damaging than a broken leg that will heal. How greatly will the damage disrupt the person's life? For many people, loss of an arm is more disruptive than loss of a leg.

In considering bad effects on reflexive goods, one must use other appropriate measures of magnitude. In regard to adverse effects on the cooperator's feelings and dispositions, the extent of injury depends on the likely seriousness of their negative effect on his or her subsequent actions. In regard to moral detriment to the wrongdoer, occasions of sin for the cooperator, and scandal to third parties, the extent of injury to the person adversely affected depends on whether the sin is or would be venial or mortal, less or more grave, more or less likely to be repented. In regard to tensions with victims of wrongdoing, the bad effect can be a more or less serious impediment to a good relationship that should be more or less central to the lives of those involved. In regard to impairment of the cooperator's witness and other obstacles to fulfilling his or her vocation, the bad effects can be a more or less serious detriment to serving goods whose service is more or less central to a person's vocation.

Finally, in considering factors that can affect the strength of reasons against cooperating materially, one presupposes various judgments. Sometimes, the judgments presupposed are confident—sure beyond reasonable doubt. But if not, one should judge how confident one can be in these judgments, and take that assessment

---

465. Many manualists recognized the significance of cooperation without which the wrongdoer could not proceed, and called such cooperation "necessary."

into account. Thus, in considering possible bad effects of cooperating, one may need to ask oneself several questions. Am I sure the prospective effect is bad, or confident it is more likely bad than good, or only unsure it is good? Am I sure the bad effect will occur, or is it more likely to occur than not, or is it only a risk, and, if so, how great a risk? Questions about the occurrence of a bad effect, especially one that depends on others' awareness and assessment of the cooperation, often cannot be answered without asking further questions: Am I sure others will pay attention to my material cooperation, regard it as significant, and draw practical conclusions from it; or are others only more likely to do those things than not; or is their doing them only a risk, and if so, how great a risk? Moreover, in considering factors that can affect the strength of the reasons for and against cooperating, one often must make analogous judgments—for example: How likely is it that the wrongdoing will be prevented if I do not cooperate? How confident can I be that those adversely affected will be few? Greater certitude about whatever tells against the moral acceptability of cooperating, and less certitude about whatever tells for it, strengthen the case against cooperating. Conversely, greater certitude about whatever tells for the moral acceptability of cooperating, and less certitude about whatever tells against it, strengthen the case for cooperating.

Judging whether one's reason would be proportionate and proportionalism

As has been explained, one's reason for doing an act that would constitute material cooperation in wrongdoing must be proportionate to the reasons for not doing it, which are grounded in the intelligible evils that would be instantiated in the various anticipated bad side effects of cooperating. But how can one judge whether one's reason would be proportionate—that is, sufficiently strong that doing the act would be reasonable despite the more or less strong reasons to forgo it?

A proportionalist might say a reason is proportionate if the goods the agent expects to realize in and by doing the action are commensurate with the expected bad side effects. In trying to supply theological support for proportionalism, proponents call ends that, on their view, justify exception making "proportionate reasons," profess that they are merely extending the role played by proportionate reason in the traditional principles regarding material cooperation and double effect, and assume that the traditional criteria of proportionate reason establish the practicability of using so-called proportionate reasons to justify making exceptions to the disputed moral norms.[466]

However, proportionalism requires a way of identifying a proportionate reason that plainly cannot be followed in judging the acceptability of material cooperation and of bad side effects in general. The proportionalists' claim assumes that the intelligible goods at stake in the available options can be measured and compared, and that, on this basis, one sometimes can rationally judge that the choice to make the exception—to practice contraception, lie, engage in adultery or sodomy, abort a baby—is justified by the prospect that the action will result in a better (or less

---

466. See, e.g., Richard A. McCormick, S.J., *Notes on Moral Theology: 1981 through 1984* (Lanham, Md.: University Press of America, 1984), 63–71.

bad) outcome, in terms of the true fulfillment of the persons involved in the situation, than carrying out any alternative one might choose.[467] But simply thinking through the check lists of the two preceding sections—indicating the complex information that must be taken into account in judging proportionate-ness—should make clear the impossibility of measuring and comparing the intel-ligible goods and bads so as to use the results as premises for a rational judgment that one's reason for cooperating would, or would not, be proportionate.

If someone remains unconvinced that the undertaking would be hopeless, he or she should try to carry out such an analysis. Since the proportion of goods to bads could be determined only by comparing measurements, and since measurements can be compared only if made by a common standard, the first step would be to find a single standard by which to measure all the intelligible goods and bads at stake. But in considering any two or more options available for choice, one has no single standard for measuring different prospective instantiations and privations of even the same sort of good. Moreover, this is inevitably so. The prospective instantiations of intelligible goods and bads are benefits and detriments to the true fulfillment of the persons involved, and the true fulfillment (or its opposite) of persons is not a sensible or imaginable state of affairs—not a set of concrete entities whose values and disvalues can be measured and commensurated.

Experience in thinking through problems of material cooperation points to the only practicable alternative to this impossible procedure. Sometimes, care-fully taking note of the diverse reasons for and against doing the act that would constitute material cooperation and the many factors that affect the strength of those diverse reasons, one clearly sees that one of the two sets of reasons, considered as a whole, constitutes a stronger argument than the other. But if one cannot measure and compare the goods at stake, how does one make the judgment about the comparative strength of the arguments for and against doing an act that would constitute material cooperation? Ideally, it would be the work of prudence, appraising the two arguments by the only relevant principle that includes all their grounds: the first principle of morality. By this appraisal, the judgment compares doing the action and forgoing it with the end of all morally good actions—what St. Thomas calls "the whole of living-in-a-good-way" or "the common end of the whole of human life,"[468] and what I call "integral human fulfillment." Since that ideal comprises the directiveness of all the principles of practical reason working together in concert, the prudent judgment about the comparative strength of the two arguments applies the principles of practical reason to the particular case.[469]

---

467. See, ibid., 166–71; note McCormick's explicit admission (169) that a *calculus* is required: ". . . a balancing or calculus is called for in the analytic process only when elements of an action are considered abstractly, before giving them a moral definition. For example, if no calculus were required, every killing would be a murder."

468. *S.t.*, 2–2, q. 47, a. 2, ad 1: "totum bene vivere"; a. 13, c.: "communis finis totius humanae vitae." Also see *S.t.*, 1–2, q. 21, a. 2, ad 2, where Thomas contrasts the moral virtue of prudence with technical skill in achieving a sensible or imaginable state of affairs; the former is concerned with the common end of human life, while the latter is concerned with a *finem particularem.*

469. See *S.t.*, 2–2, q. 47, a. 6, c. and ad 3.

This applying of the principles is not reasoning deductively from them to the particular case; rather, it is recognizing that either the argument for doing the action or the argument against doing it more adequately embodies or employs of the principles. The arguments for and against doing an act that would constitute material cooperation—and, in general, for and against accepting side effects—are instances of a kind of reasoning logicians call "inductive." Though this kind of inductive reasoning differs from its theoretical kinds, including generalization and argument for a hypothesis, it is more like the latter than the former. However, an argument for moral acceptability presupposes the first principle of morality and evaluates possible actions, while an argument for a hypothesis presupposes the data to be explained and attempts to grasp their principle.[470]

From the judgment about the comparative strength of the two arguments—the judgment that one's reason is proportionate or that it is not—another follows: either that the act is to be done or that it is not to be done, as the case may be. Since this judgment is not theoretical but practical, its truth depends on its conformity, not to some pre-existing state of affairs, but to what St. Thomas calls "right appetite"[471]—an upright will and feelings integrated with it. Thus, prudence presupposes the moral virtues, which rectify the will and feelings.[472] Moreover, the judgment of a perfectly prudent person would not only indicate that the act *should be* done (or not) but efficaciously direct *that it be* done (or not).[473]

How the conscientious person can approximate prudence

Especially in this section, I shall assume that the reader already is familiar with appendix 1.

Christians who have not relinquished the grace that justifies (see DS 1528–30/799–800) enjoy an advantage in the pursuit of virtue. Love of God and neighbor adapts the will to the divine-human communion of the heavenly kingdom, which includes integral human fulfillment (see *CMP,* 578–86, 599–603, 814–22; *LCL,* 132–33); hope proposes the kingdom as the ultimate end to be intended in every choice (see *LCL,* 80–87); and the fundamental option of faith, together with the upright commitments of personal vocation that implement it, provide the core of the moral virtues (see *CMP,* 192–94, 393–96; *LCL,* 7–8). Yet even when we see more or less clearly that material cooperation would be (or is) wrong, we

470. Unable to show how to carry out the measuring and comparing their theory requires, some proportionalists have suggested that they never meant *greater good* and *lesser evil* to be taken literally, and assert that what they had in mind would not require any calculus. So, they say that a proportionalist judgment justifying an exception to a disputed moral norm also can be made by a prudent appraisal of the comparative strength of the arguments for and against the exception—see, for example, Richard A. McCormick, S.J., "Notes on Moral Theology: 1985," *Theological Studies,* 47 (1986): 87–88. But in making this move, proportionalists must either maintain their principle—maximizing concrete goods and minimizing evils—or give it up. If they keep it, judging that the argument for an exception is stronger than the argument against it still will require the impossible measuring and comparing of goods and bads. But if they give up their principle, they have no plausible argument for making exceptions to the norms that protect basic human goods.

471. See *S.t.,* 1–2, q. 57, a. 5, ad 3.

472. St. Thomas, *S.t.,* 2–2, q. 47, a. 13, ad 2.

473. See *S.t.,* 2–2, q. 47, a. 8; a. 13, c.

sometimes are tempted to do (or continue doing) what constitutes it. And sometimes in difficult cases after considering all the relevant information as well as we can, we remain uncertain whether material cooperation would be morally acceptable. Moreover, these symptoms of the imperfection of prudence, and so of the presupposed moral virtues as well, call into question even our confident judgments. Therefore, in making judgments, we need all the help we can get from reflective analysis, to ensure a sound foundation, and from exercises of imagination—to expand feelings to correspond to practical reason and good will.

Reflection should begin, of course, by making sure that formal cooperation is not in question and that the first two requirements for acceptable material cooperation are met—the action constituting it would be morally acceptable in itself and one's end or ends in view in choosing it would be intelligible goods. If these fundamental conditions are not satisfied, there can be no proportionate reason for cooperating—either the act would be wrong in itself or one would lack a morally acceptable reason for doing it. At this initial stage of reflection, exceptionless moral norms and the modes of responsibility that can generate them come into play. If they do not exclude the prospective action, one does have a reason for doing it, and it is meaningful to ask about its proportionateness.

But exceptionless moral norms also contribute more subtly to the reflection. If one were willing to do what they forbid, one's will and the feelings integrated with it would be disposed more or less unreasonably toward relevant intelligible goods and the persons or groups of persons who might be benefited or harmed in respect to them. For example, people who regularly tell lies, even if only in light matter for the sake of convenience, or who often act spitefully, can hardly expect to make a sound appraisal of the proportionateness of reasons for materially cooperating in wrongdoing when any of the reasons against doing so touch on goods or people toward whom their hearts are ill disposed. Among other things, lying violates integrity and truth, and spitefulness violates harmony with others and mercy; and a will and feelings even slightly warped by habits of these sorts are likely to obscure or distort some of the information on which the judgment about proportionateness bears. So, to judge rightly about the moral acceptability of material cooperation—and, for that matter, about anything not settled by the hard-edged norms prescribing strict duties and forbidding kinds of acts that are always wrong—a conscientious Christian must repent and firmly intend to avoid not only mortal sins but deliberate venial ones. Therefore, when starting the process of reflection that prepares for such a judgment, one needs not only to make sure that the act contemplated is morally acceptable in itself but to examine one's conscience, repent sins, and make a firm purpose of amendment in respect to all of them, so that one can say to oneself, honestly and confidently: "If this act were not morally acceptable in itself—even if it were only, say, a 'harmless' lie or a petty act of spite—there would be no question of accepting its bad side effects, since I simply would not do it."

The next step in reflection is to develop the arguments for and against doing the action that would constitute material cooperation. One must consider the reason for doing the action and all its bad side effects, which ground the reasons for forgoing it, as well as the many factors that might affect the strength of the reasons.

While doing this, one also should try to think of an acceptable alternative way of serving one's good purpose. But even if one finds none, gathering the relevant information and considering the case for doing the act and the case against may clarify the question and settle it.

If not, one should go on to look for mixed motives—that is, emotional motives not integrated with reasons. A woman wonders if she must give up a job that involves materially cooperating in her employer's serious and constant wrong-doing in his personal life. She needs a job to support herself and her aged mother, but she also is attached to her present job because she enjoys congenial relationships with two fellow employees, whose jobs do not involve them in the wrong-doing. Becoming aware of this emotional motive, she asks herself whether those relationships constitute a reason for keeping the job and concludes that they do not. On the one hand, the three already regularly spend time together apart from work, and their friendship can continue even if she goes to work elsewhere; on the other hand, she gets on well with most people and generally has no trouble making new friends. Having clarified the matter, she sees that she should look for a new job.

Mixed motives also can affect reasons against materially cooperating. A conscientious young man goes to work as a letter carrier. Though he dislikes handling pornographic magazines, he has no qualms about delivering those edited for heterosexual men. But he wonders whether he may deliver those for homosexuals. Considering the reasons against, he finds that they tell as strongly against delivering anything he recognizes as pornography, and he also realizes that he has a far stronger antipathy toward sodomy than toward fornication or even adultery. Having clarified the problem, he sees its solution. He may deliver the indecent magazines if the postal service's rules require it, and if the rules are not clear, he may follow the judgment of his superiors.

But suppose that self-examination uncovers no mixed motives or that clarifying those motives one finds leaves the moral acceptability of material cooperation unclear? Then one should focus on the different ways in which one's material cooperation would adversely affect various persons or groups—or, at least, prevent one from benefiting them as one might. Considering separately each such person or group affected in a distinctive way, one should then apply the Golden Rule. Doing that, of course, presupposes that one rightly loves oneself and would not wish anyone to do anything adversely affecting oneself in respect to any intelligible good. Moreover, in applying the Golden Rule, one must bear in mind that, having been freed from evil and enriched with many goods by God's mercy in Jesus, one never should be willing to relinquish these blessings, and so always must be ready to share them with others, not least with the wrongdoer and any third party who will be worse off morally and spiritually if one cooperates rather than forgoes the act that would constitute material cooperation.

In many difficult cases of material cooperation, careful application of the Golden Rule will result in a clear judgment. If not, one can go on to the imaginative exercises that implement the other three modes of responsibility—the modes that articulate the normativity of the basic goods when emotional motivation falls short in respect to some of them or some of their aspects as intelligible goods, in respect to some of their instances, or in respect to the solid and enduring reality of intelligible human goods.

Occasionally, none of this helps: neither the most conscientious reflective analyses, including careful clarification of possible mixed motives, nor the application of the Golden Rule and the other imaginative exercises to educate feelings results in a confident judgment. The moral acceptability of material cooperation remains unclear. Should one then regard one's reason for cooperating as proportionate? Yes and no. In rare cases the arguments for and against may be so well balanced that the perfectly prudent person would find them equally strong, so that either course would be morally acceptable. Of course, aware that one's prudence is imperfect, one knows that the lack of a clear result may be due to one's imperfection. But being unable to do better, one must proceed as if one were perfectly prudent. Therefore, one may proceed on the assumption that the arguments for doing and forgoing the act are equally strong.

In that case, one should discern. Assuming that one has already gathered the necessary information and aroused one's feelings related to faith and relevant commitments of personal vocation, this discernment will not be difficult. At this final moment, though not a moment before, the conscientious person rightly sees the indication of God's plan and will in what his or her better, Christian self feels comfortable with.

How the preceding account of cooperation is related to other theological views

The preceding account is rooted in the common, Catholic theological tradition insofar as it distinguishes formal from material cooperation precisely as Alphonsus did and maintains, with him, both that formal cooperation in wrongdoing can never be morally acceptable and that material cooperation is acceptable only if three conditions are met: the act that constitutes it is morally acceptable in itself, one's reason for doing that act is morally acceptable, and that reason is proportionate. But the preceding account goes beyond Alphonsus and the common theological tradition in explaining more precisely what a proportionate reason is and in providing an account of how to identify such reasons.

Some of the manualists who followed Alphonsus already developed his brief indications about proportionate reason by calling attention both to additional bad side effects that can ground reasons against cooperating and to additional factors that can affect the strength of those reasons. And some also recognized that the problem of judging whether material cooperation is acceptable is part of the general problem of judging whether bad side effects are acceptable. The present appendix takes up those lines of development and advances them. Together with the preceding appendix, it also provides two things that the manualists lacked and some of them plainly wished they had: an analysis of the structure of human acts that facilitates distinguishing in practice between formal and material cooperation, and an account of moral judgment that provides guidance for judging whether one's reason for doing what would constitute material cooperation—or, more generally,

for accepting the prospective bad side effects of any action—is proportionate
to the reasons against.

The account of material cooperation offered here departs from Alphonsus and
the manualists who followed him mainly in regard to the moral significance of
proximity—that is, of how closely the cooperator's outward behavior involves him
or her in the wrongdoer's outward behavior carrying out his or her bad choice.
Making closeness of involvement a central criterion for judging the proportionate-
ness of one's reason to cooperate, the manualists distinguished immediate from
mediate cooperation, and subdivided mediate cooperation into proximate and
remote. *Immediate cooperation* referred to behavior that constituted part of the very
execution of another's bad choice; *proximate cooperation* and *remote cooperation*
referred to behavior separate from the bad choice's execution that contributed more
or less directly to it. Some manualists denied that immediate cooperation can be
only material and argued it necessarily is formal; many held that immediate
material cooperation either always is wrong or is wrong unless only an instrumental
good, rather than a basic human good, is at stake—as when bank employees
threatened by armed robbers, cooperate by opening the bank's vault, putting the
cash in bags, and so on. The manualists did not agree on precise criteria to
distinguish between proximate and remote cooperation; similarly, they reached
little or no consensus about the rules some of them proposed about the acceptability
of kinds of material cooperation specified in terms of the distinctions regarding
closeness of involvement.

By contrast, the present account does not treat the closeness of a material
cooperator's involvement as morally significant *of itself*. The difference is not as
great as it might seem, because closeness of involvement correlates more or less
well with many of the factors affecting the strength of reasons not to cooperate. For
example, involvement in others' wrongdoing usually is more likely to impede a
cooperator's witness, be an occasion of sin to him or her, have bad moral effects
on the wrongdoer, and scandalize others if it is immediate material cooperation
than if it is mediate, and, when mediate, if it is proximate than if it is remote. Still,
closeness of involvement is morally insignificant unless correlated with some
factor that affects the strength of a reason not to cooperate. For example, the
secretary who types letters including lies immediately cooperates with wrongdoing
in which goods of the person—integrity and truth—are at stake. Again, part of the
grave injustice of the suffering and death imposed on Jesus was parading him
as a criminal to Calvary, and he cooperated in that injustice by carrying his
cross—immediate material cooperation in a grave injustice, with no merely
instrumental good at stake.

The treatments of cooperation by some of the manualists included another
confusion worth mentioning. In trying to identify those held to restitution, some
medieval authors list nine specific ways of having something to do with another's
injustice: commanding it, counseling it, consenting to it, inciting it by flattery or
challenge, aiding it in some way, participating in it and/or its fruits, being silent
about it beforehand, not preventing it, not reporting it. Some of these could be
ways of cooperating, either formally or materially, but others—commanding and

counseling—are ways of giving scandal. Moreover, when St. Thomas deals with these ways in his discussion of restitution, he does not call them "modes of cooperating."[474] In his treatise on charity, Alphonsus first treats scandal, then deals with formal and material cooperation without mentioning the nine ways.[475] But in dealing with restitution, he lists them and uses the word *cooperation* in referring to them.[476] Some subsequent manualists included the nine ways in their treatments of formal and material cooperation, and referred to them as nine "modes of cooperation"; that tended to confuse formal cooperation with scandal and to obscure the reality of formal cooperation in cases where scandal plainly is impossible.[477]

In recent years, many people have noted that, especially in a pluralistic society, much of what one takes to be wrong is done by people who may be in good faith, and that the consciences of wrongdoers in good faith deserve respect. From these true premises, various theologians who dissent more or less radically from Catholic moral teaching have argued that the received, common theology of cooperation should be modified to remove certain kinds of acts from the category of formal cooperation and allow them.

In developing their arguments, these theologians sometimes invoked Vatican II's teaching on religious liberty and/or some theological theory of toleration or compromise; sometimes, too, assuming relevant norms to be either false or questionable, they said or implied that presumed wrongdoers may well be, or simply often are, not only in good faith but objectively correct in their judgments. In any case, such arguments focused on two things—the human dignity and rights of presumed wrongdoers and the importance of treating them justly and/or mercifully—and concluded that the other party's presumably good-faith judgment about his or her action can justify cooperation that otherwise would be wrong.

For example, with his characteristic straightforwardness, Charles Curran stated the general thesis: "There can be no formal cooperation when the individual

---

474. See *In Sent.,* 4, d. 15, q. 1, a. 5, qu'la 3; *S.t.,* 2–2, q. 62, a. 7.

475. St. Alphonsus Liguori, op. cit., 1:336–65 (lib. II, §§43–80).

476. Ibid., 2:58–70 (lib. III, §§557–78).

477. Roger Roy, C.Ss.R., "La coopération selon saint Alphonse de Liguori," *Studia Moralia,* 5 (1968): 403–4, explains the distinction in Alphonsus between scandal and cooperation, but later 425–26) says that Alphonsus does not regard cooperation as formal unless the cooperator not only concurs in the wrongdoer's bad intending but positively influences it—somehow incites or encourages the bad will. However, Alphonsus does not include that condition in his definition of formal cooperation. Crucial to Roy's argument is the passage he cites in his n. 112 from Alphonsus' treatment of restitution: "Nec verum est, quod formaliter tunc concurris ad peccatum uris: nam hoc esset, si positive tu influeres in ejus malam voluntatem" (op. cit., 2:67 [lib. III, §571, 2198]). But Roy overlooks the fact that Alphonsus, having distinguished two aspects of the act of theft, is focusing on sin precisely as such. One does not formally concur in the thief's *sin* s such unless one intends that the thief sin, and that would involve scandal—doing something to ring about the sin. Yet one can formally cooperate in a thief's *act* without doing anything to bring bout the bad will it involves; one formally cooperates in theft by doing anything that involves atending that someone already determined to steal carry out the plan successfully—for example, hoose to provide a tool needed to do the theft in exchange for a share in the proceeds.

involved [the presumed wrongdoer] does not have a bad will."[478] Applying this to the case of a "doctor who believes in his own conscience that sterilization is wrong when done for contraceptive purposes but has a patient who believes it is morally and medically good," he at once concluded that "the doctor can do such an operation without cooperating with the bad will of the patient because the patient has no bad will in this case" and then drew the further conclusion: "Without unduly sacrificing his own conscientious principles, the doctor could argue that in this case he is providing the service for which this individual person has a right even though he himself disagrees with the operation from a moral perspective."[479] This view, Curran quickly added, did not entail that cooperation would be *required* of the doctor or justified in every kind of case;[480] acts that violate public order or injure innocent third parties (such as abortion), he held, might cause "disproportionate harm to another person or society."[481]

In fact, actually doing the sterilization, the physician in Curran's example would be not merely a cooperator in the action but a, or even the, principal agent. Curran's conclusion could be correct only if one could rightly choose to act contrary to one's own conscience. But the same thing also is true of formal cooperators, such as hospital administrators who, among other things, must see to it that sterilization procedures are carried out "properly"—that is, with competent techniques to ensure that patients who undergo them will not get pregnant again.[482] Administrators might prefer that no sterilization be done in their hospitals, but they cannot commit themselves to ensuring that a sterilization be done properly without intending that sterility be achieved, and they cannot intend, without choosing contrary to conscience, that any sterilization be done while believing no sterilization ought to be done.

Considering in general the kind of view exemplified in Curran's case, one sees its fundamental flaw. Religious liberty and toleration primarily are a matter of accepting others' acts, but formal cooperation primarily is a matter of one's own intentions. Therefore, it raises quite different moral problems. All moral agents are responsible for their own acts, and formal cooperation is absolutely excluded because it involves bad intending *by the cooperator.* The principal agent's bad intending may be more obvious, but once analysis makes it clear that any of one's own intending would be bad, one cannot rightly choose to act with such a will.

Moreover, another's possible good faith is one thing; whether his or her act includes bad intending is another. For example, a physician who agrees to do an abortion for three hundred dollars, takes the money, and carries out the procedure as agreed plainly intends both to abort a baby and to obtain three hundred dollars; but only God knows whether this physician sins and, if so,

478. Charles E. Curran, "Cooperation: Toward a Revision of the Concept and Its Application," *Linacre Quarterly,* 41:3 (Aug. 1974): 160.

479. Ibid., 161.

480. Ibid., 161–62.

481. Ibid., 162.

482. Curran's main objective in his article appears to have been to defend the cooperation of administrators who were authorizing sterilizations in their hospitals (see ibid., 162–64).

precisely what the sin is. To be in good faith, a person must have done his or her duty in trying to find out what choice would be right, judged that an action of a certain kind with a certain end in view may be chosen or is to be chosen, and chosen in according with that judgment. But such a person's judgment—which is his or her conscience—can be mistaken. If it is, some or all of his or her intending will be bad. While others' judgments of conscience never are directly accessible, the intentions that shape their actions, though sometimes hidden or obscure, often are obvious—as the physician's are in the example—from the intrinsic connection between their evident deeds and entirely credible words. Therefore, though the common teaching of the manualists on cooperation presupposed that one can recognize others' wrongdoing by identifying their bad intentions, it did not assume that one can know anyone to be in bad faith.

Though nothing can justify formal cooperation in wrongdoing, the views I have been criticizing do call attention to truths to be taken into account in judging whether one's reason to cooperate materially is proportionate. However, bearing in mind that the consciences of people in good faith deserve respect and that the wrongdoer may be in good faith will sometimes tell against the judgment that one's reason for cooperating would be proportionate. Just as ultimately judging others and morally condemning them require insight human persons lack, so do ultimately judging others and morally acquitting them. Wrongdoers really in good faith often will be ready to correct their mistaken consciences, and they and others will benefit greatly by their doing so. Wrongdoers not really in good faith also may be morally injured, rather than benefited, by others' cooperation. Therefore, in either case, forgoing the act that would constitute material cooperation with objective wrongdoing can be not only compatible with respect for the dignity of another's conscience but, precisely, an exercise of such respect.

An appendix on cooperation in a document of the U.S. bishops

At their general meeting in November 1994, the full body of Catholic bishops of the United States approved a revised and expanded text of their *Ethical and Religious Directives (ERDs)*, a document summarizing much of the Church's moral teaching regarding health care.[483] The last of the document's six parts, which concerns acts by which Catholic health care institutions and providers form new partnerships with other health care institutions and providers, includes an introduction and four directives.[484] Toward the end of the introduction, the bishops observe that "potential dangers require that new partnerships undergo systematic and objective moral analysis." They state that the four directives are meant to help institutionally based Catholic health care services in this analysis, and that they have established an ad hoc committee for the same end. They then call attention to "An appendix at the end of the Directives [which] offers a clarification of the terms relative to the principles governing

---

483. National Conference of Catholic Bishops, *Ethical and Religious Directives for Catholic Health Care Services* (Washington, D.C.: United States Catholic Conference, 1995).
484. Ibid., 25–27.

cooperation and their application to concrete situations."[485] The appendix is brief, a single page. Its title is: "The Principles Governing Cooperation." The text:

> The principles governing cooperation differentiate the action of the wrongdoer from the action of the cooperator through two major distinctions. The first is between formal and material cooperation. If the cooperator intends the object of the wrongdoer's activity, then the cooperation is formal and, therefore, morally wrong. Since intention is not simply an explicit act of the will, formal cooperation can also be implicit. Implicit formal cooperation is attributed when, even though the cooperator denies intending the wrongdoer's object, no other explanation can distinguish the cooperator's object from the wrongdoer's object. If the cooperator does not intend the object of the wrongdoer's activity, the cooperation is material and can be morally licit.
>
> The second distinction deals with the object of the action and is expressed by immediate and mediate material cooperation. Material cooperation is immediate when the object of the cooperator is the same as the object of the wrongdoer. Immediate material cooperation is wrong, except in some instances of duress. The matter of duress distinguishes immediate material cooperation from implicit formal cooperation. But immediate material cooperation—without duress—is equivalent to implicit formal cooperation and, therefore, is morally wrong. When the object of the cooperator's action remains distinguishable from that of the wrongdoer's, material cooperation is mediate and can be morally licit.
>
> Moral theologians recommend two other considerations for the proper evaluation of material cooperation. First, the object of material cooperation should be as distant as possible from the wrongdoer's act. Second, any act of material cooperation requires a proportionately grave reason.
>
> Prudence guides those involved in cooperation to estimate questions of intention, duress, distance, necessity, and gravity. In making a judgment about cooperation, it is essential that the possibility of scandal should be eliminated. Appropriate consideration should also be given to the Church's prophetic responsibility.[486]

This treatment of cooperation seems to me unsatisfactory in several respects.

One reasonably assumes that *object* is used with the same meaning throughout. But what meaning? There are two possibilities. (1) "Object of the wrongdoer's activity" in the first paragraph might mean what John Paul II means by "object of an act which specifies the act morally," namely, "the proximate end of a deliberate decision."[487] But if that is its meaning, the appendix's definition of formal cooperation, though narrower than Alphonsus's, would follow him in defining it by agreement in bad willing—one formally cooperates only in somehow intending precisely what is the proximate end of the wrongdoer's deliberate decision. If *object* has that meaning in the phrases "object of the cooperator" and "object of the wrongdoer" in the appendix's second paragraph, however, it is defining immediate material cooperation by agreement in the proximate end of a deliberate decision—which by definition constitutes formal cooperation. (2) *Object* in the second paragraph might refer to the behavior that carries out a choice. If that is its meaning,

485. Ibid., 26.
486. Ibid., 29.
487. John Paul II, *Veritatis splendor,* 78, *AAS* 85 (1993) 1196, *OR,* 6 Oct. 1993, xii.

the appendix follows the manualists who defined immediate material cooperation by its contribution (without any bad intending) to the carrying out of the wrong-doer's bad intention. But if *object* has that meaning in "object of the wrongdoer's activity" in the first paragraph, one could formally cooperate without any agreement in bad willing—for example, the secretary who types letters containing lies would be formally cooperating in lying, and Jesus in carrying his cross would have been formally cooperating in the wrong done him.

In the first paragraph, the sentence concerning implicit cooperation is written from the perspective of an outside observer rather than of the acting person. I do not know what could be meant by *explicit* and *implicit,* used in reference to acts of the will. Since acting persons consciously intend both the objects of their acts—that is, the proximate ends of their choices—and their ends in view in making their choices, they are aware of all their own intending, though they may not reflexively focus on it, may not keep it in mind once a choice has been made, may not talk about it, and, if they do, may not speak accurately or truthfully about it. Used in reference to an intention underlying someone else's activity, *implicit* apparently refers to the status of an intention denied by the cooperator but inferred from the situation and his or her outward behavior.

No matter what the appendix's key terms mean, however, they must be used in the same sense in two of the first paragraph's statements: "If the cooperator intends the object of the wrongdoer's activity, then the cooperation is formal," and: "If the cooperator does not intend the object of the wrongdoer's activity, the cooperation is material." Assuming no cooperator can both intend and not intend the object of the wrongdoer's activity, it follows that no cooperation can be both formal and material. In the second paragraph, however, the statement that "immediate material cooperation—without duress—is equivalent to implicit formal cooperation" implies that some cooperation is both material and formal. Thus, the appendix's confusions lead to self-contradiction.[488]

The appendix's third and fourth paragraphs deal with the conditions for morally acceptable material cooperation and the judgment about acceptability. In my opinion, the indications regarding conditions are inadequate; many sorts of bad side effects and relevant factors are overlooked. The final sentence, referring to the Church's prophetic responsibility, points only weakly and obliquely to the duty of

---

488. Taken by itself, the second paragraph's statement, "Immediate material cooperation is wrong, except in some instances of duress," is coherent and, as I explained earlier, was the view of some manualists, while others regarded all immediate cooperation as formal. However, neither group identified immediate material cooperation with implicit formal cooperation. For example, John A. McHugh, O.P., and Charles J. Callan, O.P., *Moral Theology: A Complete Course,* rev. Edward P. Farrell, O.P., vol. 1 (New York: Joseph F. Wagner, 1958), begin by too narrowly defining *formal cooperation* in terms of intending *the sin* of the other party (§1508) and then, to broaden the category, introduce the concept of *implicit formal coopera-tion,* which they define in terms of intending the bad end of the wrongdoer's external act (§1511) and/or cooperating by an act evil in itself (§1517). But McHugh and Callan nowhere say or imply that immediate material cooperation constituted by an act that is morally acceptable in itself is equivalent to implicit formal cooperation; in fact, they give several examples (in §§1521–23) of cases they regard as immediate material cooperation that they consider morally acceptable, and some of these cases involve no duress.

Catholic individuals and institutions to bear witness to relevant moral truths and to fulfill other aspects of their personal vocations and communal missions. The last paragraph's first sentence, concerning prudence, suggests that all the matters listed are subject to estimation—that is, approximation or rough calculation—whereas exercising prudence requires careful gathering of information, accurate analysis, and rational, though not always deductive, judgment.

The moral significance of various sorts of pressure

The suggestion in the appendix's second paragraph that duress sometimes can justify material cooperation also calls for clarification.

Duress is used in a narrow sense, generally in legal contexts, to signify physical compulsion or restraint, or a credible threat adequate to motivate a person of ordinary good character, by which someone is *unlawfully* caused or motivated to do or forgo some act. In this narrow sense, the bank employees threatened by armed robbers cooperate under duress in making the bank's money available. From the moral point of view, the significance of such duress is that it constitutes a reason for acting that ordinarily is not given, and so can be a circumstance in which outward behavior that usually carries out a morally bad choice instead carries out a good one. Thus, absent either duress or some bad intention, the employees would not turn over the bank's money to anyone not entitled to it; but under duress, their opening the safe, putting the money into bags, and so on carry out choices, not to defraud the bank or do any other wrong, but simply to behave outwardly as the robbers demand in order to—a good intention—avoid being hurt or killed.

Of course, *duress* often is used less strictly to refer to various sorts of pressures leading people to act differently than they otherwise would. The significance of such duress varies greatly from the moral point of view.

In some cases, individuals or groups under great pressure panic or erupt, and are paralyzed or behave irrationally without deliberation and choice; they have no moral responsibility for what they do or fail to do under that duress, though they may be responsible for being in the situation or for being unprepared for it. In some cases, persons and groups choose under some pressure to do what otherwise would be unreasonable because it is contrary to their own legitimate interests—for instance, to yield some good to which they are entitled in order to forestall greater losses. They do no wrong if, under that duress, they choose reasonably what they otherwise would reject. In some cases, persons and groups choose under some pressure to do something with bad side effects that they otherwise would not accept. They do no wrong if the duress grounds a sound and decisive reason for accepting those side effects. But in some cases, individuals, families, nations, businesses, and other organizations choose under pressure as they should not. Either they yield to the pressure and accept bad side effects without a proportionate reason for doing so or they choose under pressure to do something evil in itself—for example, commit perjury, abort an unwanted baby, torture prisoners, cheat customers, arrange for others to provide morally unacceptable services they do not wish to provide. Those who do such things under duress do the wrong they choose to do;

but their guilt in doing it may be mitigated, and if they avoid self-deception and rationalization, that guilt might well give way to the grace of repentance.

In general, transient episodes of unusual pressure are likely to occasion either an upright choice of behavior that otherwise would be wrongly chosen (if chosen at all), or behavior without choice, or a choice with mitigated guilt that may be repented. Permanent conditions and ongoing processes that exert constant pressure are more likely to occasion choices either to make the sacrifices necessary to escape the pressure or to achieve a modus vivendi with it. If those choices are bad, the ongoing pressure and structured accommodation with it are likely to impede repentance. Thomas More and John Fisher resisted duress; had they practiced self-deception and rationalized giving in to King Henry's pressure, they probably would have lived well as his good servants and died unrepentant.

INDEXES

Unlike those in volume one, all references in these indexes *are* to the book's pages. The indexed material may appear either in the text, or in one or more of the footnotes, or both.

There are five indexes. Four are to (1) Sacred Scripture, (2) the Vatican II documents, (3) the *Catechism of the Catholic Church*, and (4) the Code of Canon Law. The fifth index is a list of names and subjects, which includes all authors quoted or mentioned in the book and a guide to locating treatments of topics. Some items indexed separately in volume two are indexed here in the names and subjects index: the teachings of the Church gathered in the handbook edited by Denzinger and Schönmetzer under *Church teachings (Denzinger and Schönmetzer)*, the documents of popes and the Holy See under the name of the pope or curial office, and the works of St. Thomas under *Thomas Aquinas, St.*

These indexes have been designed primarily for recapturing information after one has become familiar with the book. Readers wishing to explore a subject may find helpful the Contents and the cross references in the text to other questions. The Preface and User's Guide contains important advice about using the book. It also should be borne in mind that a complete question is the smallest unit in which one can expect to find everything needed for an accurate understanding of any of its parts, and that the Analysis paragraph is not to be taken as a summary, much less as an adequate reply to the question.

Subject entries represent concepts rather than words; the words in the index may not appear on the pages listed. Also, in most cases, only some of the pages on which a topic is mentioned are listed in the names and subjects index. The places indexed are those that are especially noteworthy.

Readers familiar with volume one may wonder why they do not find here a list of key words. It is assumed that studious readers will be familiar with volumes one and two, and necessary explanations of technical vocabulary pertaining to a question's subject matter are provided as needed. It remains true that readers may find it helpful to have at hand a good dictionary.

1: Sacred Scripture

2: The Second Vatican Council

Apostolicam actuositatem
5–8: 520, 703
5–7: 393
7–8: 567
16–17: 567

Ad gentes
7: 2

Dignitatis humanae
1: 6
2: 2, 6, 309
11: 81

Dei verbum
8: 51
11: 25

Gaudium et spes
18: 10
28: 619, 628, 715
30: 727
35: 857
38–39: 42, 98, 336,
    369, 441, 658, 696,
    734, 869
50: 146, 301
67: 711
69: 452, 594, 734

Lumen gentium
12: 107
14: 2
37: 649
42–44: 730
43–44: 31
48: 23–24

Perfectae caritatis
12–14: 31
13: 730

Presbyterorum ordinis
16: 30

Sacrosanctum concilium
21: 52
22: 53
47: 54

Unitatis redintegratio
2–3: 2
3–4: 170
11: 7
13–23: 2
13–18: 2
14–18: 2

+ + +

3: The Catechism of the Catholic Church

+   +   +

4: The Code of Canon Law

+ + +

5: Names and Subjects